Chapter 1

Disorders of Learning and Behavior

W9-AFG-371

OVERVIEW

This chapter addresses general concepts related to learning and covers currently defined clusters of behavior and their related causation. Constructs such as mildly handicapped, learning disabilities, attention deficit disorder, dyslexia, and developmental language disorders are discussed. It is intended that the reader will gain a perspective or an overview regarding why students do not achieve according to expectation or have problems in school. The material covered receives further elaboration in other chapters in the book.

STUDENTS AT RISK

In a national study of at-risk students completed by Phi Delta Kappa (PDK) International, a professional education association, *at risk* was defined as students who are likely to fail in either school or life (Frymier, 1988). In most classrooms there are students who do not achieve at the same level as the majority of their classmates; many of these children exhibit social-emotional problems. Difficulties emerge when they do not have the necessary skills to perform a specific task and lack the motivation or maturity to persist in the face of obstacles or discouragement. Persistent failure, in most cases, results in a continuing state of frustration. Daily school tasks become laborious and the students at risk refrain from maintaining a level of achievement that leads to automatic, efficient learning.

Most school systems today use categorical labels (e.g., deaf, hearing impaired, blind, visually impaired, mentally handicapped, learning disabled, physically handicapped, speech impaired, and gifted) for students who have special needs and are eligible for special education services. Others assign special needs students to generic classes designed for mildly, moderately, or severely handicapped. Johnson (1988) cautions that the learning disabled should be differentiated from other underachievers and that mild, moderate, and severe conditions should be observed in all types of handicapping conditions. She further states that subtypes of different groups of learning handicapped populations should not be made synonymous. Subtypes of learning disabilites, she suggests, are not the same as subtypes in reading.

Students with learning problems may also be found in other types of special school programs such as classes for compensatory education, bilingual programs for speakers of languages other than English, remedial reading classes, early intervention programs such as Head Start, and dropout prevention programs. There are still a number of students who are underserved, who, although exhibiting learning problems, are not identified as special needs learners. They are often classified as underachievers. Many of these students need special assistance beyond remedial help.

CONTRIBUTING FACTORS

Some of the reasons that contribute to at-risk behavior are discussed in the following sections under the categories of biological, cognitive, social-emotional, home, economic and cultural, and instructional factors. These categories listed are not mutually exclusive and independent as reasons for failure. The authors recognize that there may be considerable overlap among the categories but have chosen to deal with the rationale for failure in this way for ease of understanding.

Biological Factors

· Genetic predisposition to certain types of disorders
· Fetal exposure to nicotine, alcohol, drugs, toxic agents, and/or improper diet
· Fetal or postnatal stroke or trauma
· Birth complications or low birth weight
· Infection such as encephalitis or meningitis
· Damage during childhood caused by exposure to heavy metals such as lead, mercury, and other chemicals
· Chronic medical problems resulting in loss of time in school; use of medication with side effects
· Central nervous system dysfunction resulting from a variety of causes manifested in disorders of perception, memory, attention, hyperactivity, and motor problems

DISCUSSION

The Importance of Genes
Genes may dispose an individual to weak resistance to infection or predispose a child to a different arrangement of the nervous system. Vulnerability to hormonal, heavy metal, and other damage to the developing nervous system is interdependent with genetics. The area of genetic research has gained important new information through enzyme studies, the study of the structure and function of deoxyribonucleic acid (DNA), and cellular photomicrography (Cegelka & Prehm, 1982). Recently, new single gene and chromosome syndromes have been identified. There is reason to suspect a possible genetic or sex-linked basis for learning disabilities due to the fact that four times as many boys as girls exhibit learning problems, and there is a tendency for severe reading disorders to recur in some families. Knowledge about how genes influence health and learning is also important in terms of prevention.

Fragile-x Syndrome (fra [x]), a recently identified chromosomal aberration that runs in certain families, has been found to be associated with mental retardation and learning disabilities (Berdine & Blackhurst, 1985; Turner & Opitz, 1980; Bishop, 1982). The syndrome affects the X-Chromosome and is typically exhibited in males, although females can be affected. The reason is that males carry one X-Chromosome (xy) and females have two (xx). Next to Down's Syndrome, it is the second leading cause of mental retardation that can be traced to a genetic aberration. Fragile-x Syndrome has in some cases been diagnosed as autism (Brown, Sherbenou, & Dollar, 1982).

Maternal Ingestion of Alcohol and Drugs
Evidence shows that 15 percent of pregnant women (ages 15–44) are substance abusers. Approximately 34 million women consume alcoholic beverages, and more than 18 million are cigarette smokers. Over 6 million women are users of illicit drugs; of this, 44 percent have used marijuana and 14 percent have used cocaine at least once (National Institute on Drug Abuse 1989).

A 1988 survey of 36 hospitals across the United States, representing approximately 155,000 pregnancies annually, found that on an average 11 percent of pregnant women used heroin, methadone, amphetamines, PCP, marijuana, and, most commonly, cocaine. The study, conducted by the National Association of Perinatal Addiction Research and Education, indicated that approximately 375,000 infants each year may be affected by their mothers' drug use (National Institute on Drug Abuse, 1989).

More women today than ever before abuse drugs during pregnancy, endangering the well-being and lives of their children as well as themselves. Educators must face the prospect that the children resulting from these pregnancies are coming to school with a variety of complications related to behavior and learning. Already in our schools is the advance guard of what will surely swell into an epidemic in a few short years: the "drug babies." The question for today is, What preparation are we making? "We are facing the emerging of what some are now calling a 'bio-under-class' " (Greer, 1990, p. 382). Scientists are beginning to explore how these drugs affect children in terms of physical coordination, language, and emotional development.

> Among young children who survive such infancies, the symptoms now turning up in the classroom go well beyond 'post-drug impairment syndrome,' which are bad enough: poor abstract reasoning and memory, poor judgment, inability to concentrate, inability to deal with stress, frequent tantrums, a wide variety of behavior disorders, and violent acting out (Greer, 1990, p. 383).

COCAINE. Physicians report that pregnant women who use cocaine produce a hostile environment for the developing fetus, by way of poor circulation. Cocaine has been shown to cross the placenta rapidly. It accumulates and maintains a longer half-life in the fetus (than in the mother) due to the fact that the enzymes required to break it down are not fully developed.

Recent studies have indicated that regular cocaine use in mothers prenatally is related to intrauterine growth and development (Chasnoff et al., 1989; Zuckerman et al., 1989; Smith & Deitch, 1987). Use of cocaine throughout pregnancy was found to have a significant effect on children's birth weight and length. Head circumference is often smaller in infants exposed to narcotics, when compared with normal infants. These problems are thought to be a result of intermittent diminution of placental blood flow that is caused by maternal cocaine use (Woods, Plessinger, & Clark, 1987). It is hypothesized that cocaine may also act on fetal brain transmitters in the first trimester, affecting the newborn infant in subtle ways (Barlow, 1982).

Cocaine use has been shown to increase the risk of hemorrhage and premature delivery. Crack-using mothers are giving birth to addicted babies who are having strokes and seizures and suffering from withdrawal. Other potential risks to children exposed to drugs in utero include fetal hyperactivity, malformed genitals, missing bowels, and subtle long-term deficits in mental or neurological functioning. Pregnant women injecting cocaine carry the added risk of contracting Acquired Immune Deficiency Syndrome (AIDS) if the user shares a hypodermic needle with a person already injected with HIV, the AIDS virus.

MARIJUANA AND SMOKING. Researchers agree that the impact of marijuana use in the pregnant female and its effect on the fetus is dose-dependent. The more it is used, the worse it is for both mother and child, especially with the high potency variety of marijuana that is available today (Zuckerman et al., 1989). An adverse effect that has been linked to marijuana includes impaired estrogen production in the placenta. This can retard placental development. It is reported that even a single episode of marijuana use can lead to prolonged exposure of the drug to the fetus. Like cigarettes, marijuana smoking may also impair the amount of oxygen available to the fetus. This is further complicated by a tendency of marijuana to increase the heart rate and blood pressure of the mother, resulting in a reduction in placental blood flow to the fetus. This can also result in prematurity and difficult labor (short or long). Marijuana also can lead to fetal growth retardation, and frequently infants are born addicted.

ALCOHOL. Reported effects of maternal alcohol intake are varied. One of the more common effects of maternal alcohol abuse is fetal alcohol syndrome (FAS) in the child. In order to be diagnosed as having fetal alcohol syndrome, a child must exhibit at least one feature in each of the following three areas: growth, central nervous system function, and craniofacial appearance (Clarren, Bowden, & Astley, 1985).

1. *Growth:* The child exhibits prenatal or postnatal growth retardation in weight, length of head, or head circumference, or any combination of these three resulting from a diminished number of cells.
2. *Central Nervous System:* The child exhibits neurologic abnormality, delay in development, or intellectual impairment.
3. *Craniofacial Appearance:* The child appears microcephalic, exhibits microphthalmia, or short palpebral fissures or both; poorly developed philtrum, thin upper lip, and flattening of the maxillary area. There are many other associated physical problems such as strabismus, myopia, posterior rotation of the ears, cleft lip or palate, and cardiac anomalies.

The most devastating effect associated with FAS is the degree of mental retardation observed in these children. The average IQ of a child affected by alcohol is between 65 and 70. Few of these affected children have IQ scores within the normal range. Behavioral problems are also characteristic of these children, the most common being hyperactivity and distractibility. Many exhibit conduct disorders and other types of emotional problems. In almost every situation, heavy drinking was associated with an increased incidence of congenital anomalies (Clarren, Sterling, & Smith,

1978). Many more children may also be suffering from milder FAS, known as fetal alcohol effect (FAE).

Possible alcohol effects have also been noted in children of mothers who consumed only one to two ounces of alcohol daily during pregnancy (Streissguth et al., 1984). No safe levels of alcohol intake during pregnancy have been found. The stage of maternal alcoholism and the degree of alcohol dependence can be as important as the amount of alcohol consumed by the maternal drinker. Binge drinkers are especially at risk of producing an FAS child.

In a recent study (Frezza et al., 1990) women were found to be more susceptible than men to intoxication and liver disease from alcohol. It appears that the stomach enzymes of women do not oxidize alcohol as well as the stomach enzymes of men. This allows more of the toxic ethanol to reach the blood stream and liver.

Other Toxic Substances
Environmental hazards include *pathogens,* which are disease-causing agents; *teratogens,* which are toxic agents that can cause fetal malformations; and *carcinogens,* which are cancer-causing agents. Peripheral and central nervous system insult can occur in the developing fetus from a variety of toxicants, including organic tin compounds, thallium, mercury, manganese, lead, and arsenic (Bonnet, 1988).

Lead readily crosses the placental barrier at early gestation. Lead poisoning can result in high levels of toxicity and central nervous system dysfunction. Exposure to lead in the environment of young children or during prenatal development can affect the nervous system.

> About 10% to 12% of women of childbearing age in major metropolitan areas of the United States are exposed to sufficient lead to have blood levels of 10 ug/dl or higher. Sources of lead include drinking water, lead paint chips, ambient air, lead in dust and soil, and lead in food and beverages. (Bonnett, 1989, p. 15)

Areas of heavy and high incidence of automobile exhaust concentration are also a hazard in terms of lead toxicity (Bellinger et al., 1987; Beningus et al., 1981). Other hazards include pottery with lead-based glazes and ingestion of lead-based paint by very young children, which leads to central nervous system injury.

Whereas lead affects social behavior and myelinization of the neurons in the brain, mercury poisoning is known to affect cerebellar development. Sources of mercury poisoning include agricultural pesticides and residue from mining, pulp, and other industries.

Serious cases can cause mental retardation, tremors, paralysis, and speech defects. Nitrite poisoning is a concern to areas where contaminated water is used to prepare milk formula. Cadmium toxicity affects the brain and can cause brain damage. Transgenerational effects can also result that may reach two or more generations from the affected individual with respect to nutrition, hormones, or the toxic effects of drugs (Bonnet, 1989; Campbell & Perkins, 1988).

Hormones and the immune system are other reasons that may have triggered brain changes leading to a deficiency. A disruption in the cells can be caused by exposure to the fetus during the first trimester to the sex steroid testosterone, which may affect nerve cell migration. It is hypothesized that one of the causes of dyslexia is exposure of the brain of a fetus to the sex hormone testosterone, which produces abnormalities in the development of the left hemisphere as early as three months into gestation. Male fetal testes produce testosterone during intrauterine life, whereas the female gets the testosterone from the maternal placenta. An important factor in fetal damage is maternal circulating antibodies that reach the central nervous system and attack the neurons or blood vessels of the transplacental passage, causing neuronal dysfunctions (Galaburda, 1988; Geschwind & Behan, 1982).

Infections and Diseases
A number of infectious diseases can result in damage to the fetus during prenatal development. They include the following:

- Toxoplasmosis is contracted by handling infected or raw meat or the feces of small animals such as cats, who transmit this infection to the pregnant female. The disease is caused by an intracellular protozoan (Toxoplasma gondii). The child can be born with visual defects, brain damage, microcephaly, hydrocephalus, and convulsions.
- Congenital Cytomegalovirus Infection is contracted by the mother and can result in neurological damage to the fetus as well as deafness, blindness, seizures, cerebral palsy, microcephaly, or mental retardation in the newborn.
- Rubella, German measles, if contracted during the first trimester of pregnancy, can cause a variety of neurological insults to the fetus. Transplacental infection of the fetus produces deafness, cardiac anomalies and circulatory dysfunction, glaucoma, microcephaly, and mental retardation.
- Congenital Syphilis, resulting from transplacental infection from the mother, can affect every organ of the fetus that has been exposed. It can cause premature birth, stillbirths, epilepsy, visual defects, deafness,

cerebral palsy, hydrocephalus, and mental retardation.

- Genital Herpes is another infectious disease that can be fatal or cause severe visual, auditory, or neurological problems in the fetus. It is acquired as the baby passes through the birth canal.
- Encephalitis, inflammation of the brain, or Neonatal Meningitis, an inflammation of the brain lining or membrane, can result in hydrocephalus, neurological disabilities, hearing defects, seizures, and mental retardation.
- Gestational and obstetric disorders can result in undernutrition, and prematurity, and hemolytic disease or destruction of the red blood cells.
- RH Factor Incompatibility, where the mother is RH negative and the fetus is RH positive, can result in severe problems when the immune response system in the mother is triggered, causing the production of antibodies by the maternal spleen. This can result in damage to the fetus such as cerebral palsy, deafness, perceptual problems, hyperactivity, delayed speech, or learning disabilities. Women at risk often come from the poverty level of our society and may not be exposed to good medical supervision, which could intervene appropriately in this area of concern.
- Otitis Media (OM) is an inflammation of the middle ear that increases the risk of hearing impairment with concomitant problems in language and learning.

Radiation
Radiation can affect the fetus through maternal pelvic irradiation. Congenital malformations may be due to manmade as well as natural radiation. Damage occurs mainly during the first trimester of pregnancy when radiation can alter the function of an organ, causing it to produce cells that result in deformities. Prenatal radiation can cause spina bifida, cleft palate, hydrocephalus, and microcephaly.

Hypoxia and Anoxia
Neurological impairment can result from hypoxia (limited oxygen to the tissues) or anoxia (total lack of oxygen) during the birth process or soon after. It can occur in the fetus where the placental blood supply may be blocked.

Low Birth Weight
Maternal undernutrition during pregnancy affects the nutrition of the placenta. This is of special concern for the mothers from lower socioeconomic classes where poor nutrition may be a factor that predisposes low birth weight. Heavy cigarette smoking is another critical factor. Low birth weight, especially in preterm babies, has long been thought to be related to maturational lag and is a marker for the identification of children who might exhibit developmental learning difficulties in their early school years. Some problems are related to overall intelligence and to motor development (Cohen, 1983). Prematurity is a serious health problem when the birth weight is below 5½ pounds. As advances in medicine increase the survival rate of these babies, schools will have to provide intervention programs for preschool and primary-age children who are at risk for normal development.

Cognitive Factors

- Lack of knowledge of basic skills at an automatic level of understanding
- Severe language disorders resulting in problems with comprehension and meaning
- Problems with attention
- Poor reflective thinking skills
- Inability to generalize newly acquired learning in different contexts and settings
- Ineffective use of study strategies and poor problem-solving skills

DISCUSSION

Knowledge Acquisition
Learning disabled students have difficulty with accessing and coordinating a number of mental activities. This includes planning, checking, monitoring, revising, evaluating, and testing during the process of learning and problem solving (Duffy et al., 1986). They have problems with organizing and coordinating information, which involves higher-order processes known as executive functions. Students have difficulty with self-evaluation, predicting outcomes, organizing strategies for use in specific situations, and reflective thinking. How to use automatized subprocesses is also a problem area (McLoone et al., 1986).

Lack of success in the classroom for many learning disabled students is due to their inability to shift from one strategy to another, to abandon inappropriate strategies, to process information with one strategy and then select another, or even to consider several processing approaches in rapid order (Swanson, 1987). For example, children with learning disabilities are deficient, slow, or inaccurate in spelling and reading when phonetic encoding skills are not automatized to the extent that they are available for complex processing.

Attention
Attention can be another problem area. This involves the conscious focus of thoughts on an object or event.

It also involves the selection of information and an intensity of effort, or how much energy the learner has to use to retrieve information or to stay on task. Selection is important to the process of ignoring or screening out things that could interfere with the task to be accomplished. For example, thinking about the individual notes or keys on the piano can inhibit good performance. Selection in attention also helps maintain the automatic processes. The process of selection is both at the automatic level and under voluntary control in terms of degree and intensity. What interferes with "normal" attention processes is of importance in teaching. Simple automatic acts such as walking, running, and chewing gum can be accomplished with little thought and require little mental energy, but more complex tasks such as mathematics operations require a great deal of mental energy.

Language

Language is the essence of learning. Success in school is determined to a large extent by how well students effectively use all aspects of language. There are many children, mostly males, who fail to develop language normally. Some students are classified as having speech or production problems, whereas others are classified as having specific types of language disorders such as receptive (understanding), expressive (speaking and writing), or inner (thinking) language problems. A more severe language impairment is aphasia, where individuals lose (partially or completely) their ability to speak, even though they know what they want to say.

Social-Emotional Factors

· Feelings of helplessness, lack of self-worth, and perceived external locus of control (outside forces) resulting in lowered expectation of future success and avoidance of the task
· Inability to "keep up" with the other students and lack of incentive or intrinsic motivation to "try" when falling behind
· Negative beliefs and lowered expectations about performance in school, grades, and norm-referenced tests
· Negative labels used by teachers who attribute failure to lack of ability
· Sensitive-withdrawn behavior that inhibits requests by the student for assistance in learning
· Inability to understand nonverbal cues and adjust behavior accordingly
· Lack of social skills that are essential to developing personal relationships for acceptance by authority figures and peers

· Inadequate relationships with siblings, peers, and meaningful adults
· Aggressive-acting-out behavior that often leads to time away from academic tasks and ostracism by peers and adults
· Inconsistent patterns of school attendance and achievement because of drug- and alcohol-related problems

DISCUSSION

Social Skills and Personal Relationships

A number of studies have indicated that learning disabled children are lower in status in the opinion of their peers than their nonlearning disabled agemates (Gresham & Elliott, 1989; LaGreca, 1981). Children with learning disabilities are reported as consistently having more problems in social situations than nonlearning disabled children as rated by teachers (Gresham & Reschly, 1986). Related issues that need to be examined in terms of social acceptance include the kinds of social difficulties observed and the characteristics of students who have greater difficulty with peers and with teachers. A study by Rourke (1987) suggests that although some learning disabled students do suffer from social-emotional disturbances, most do not. Poor peer relationships are a sign of serious problems of adjustment (Parker & Asher, 1987).

Overall, self-monitoring of social skills is poor and failure in general is viewed as insurmountable. Illness is often feigned as a means of avoiding academic work, participating in social interaction, or staying out of school. A history of poor school attendance is not unusual. In severe cases, students have been known to acquire a fear of the dark, experience bedwetting, and develop ulcers and other types of physical problems.

Aggressive Behavior

Students who have been rejected by their peers because of aggression tend to have other problems that affect their performance in school (French & Waas, 1985). Aggressive-acting-out students are sometimes destructive and may even hurt themselves or others. It is not unusual to hear similar complaints about them from students, teachers, administrators, support personnel, and even the parents themselves. Students who have this type of behavior problem have been described as children who are "hurting" emotionally. They appear to be in a constant state of conflict. Acting-out, aggressive students often come from hostile home situations. Parents may be rejecting or apathetic and do not provide adequate role models, which could result in ineffective socialization of the child. Students from these environments may not have learned to establish or develop trusting relationships, which can also result in unsocialized behavior. Others have been described as exhibiting learned helplessness, attributing failure to external factors beyond their control.

Motivation

Students' beliefs about their capabilities to exercise control over events in their lives are basic to how they operate in terms of motivation. Learning disabled students are more likely to attribute their failures to insufficient ability as opposed to insufficient effort (Licht, 1983). They also generally perceive their competence as significantly lower than nondisabled learners (Harter, 1985).

The perceived importance of a task has a great deal to do with an individual's motivation to respond to a task or to the analysis of a task. The teacher should always explain the purpose of a task to the student. The task, in a sense, determines the amount of mental effort to be expended. Easier tasks require less mental effort than more complex or difficult tasks.

Home Factors

- A lowered educational level of significant adults or a lifestyle at home where there is low expectation for achievement with few rewards for performance in school or goals for potential careers
- A home environment that is not conducive to good study habits, completing homework assignments, or enriching educational experiences
- Poverty and/or reduced family income influencing the quality of home life, security, and diet
- Poor language models that may not promote correct usage or the expansion of vocabulary
- Lack of daily interaction and conversation promoting education and discussion regarding ongoing educational activities
- A home that does not stress a continual work ethic
- An abusive home environment

DISCUSSION

Adults in the home environment have a profound influence on the physical, cognitive, and social development of children. Parents, guardians, and others are the role models for children and provide encouragement, intellectual stimulation, and a climate that fosters emotional well-being. Emotions, attitudes, motivation, and self-esteem emanate from family support.

Child Abuse

Unfortunately, many children come from dysfunctional home environments. The maltreatment of children is one of the serious concerns of present-day society. The cause and treatment of child abuse, heretofore a social pariah that was unapproachable in the schools, is now a central issue for all educators. It is unclear if incidences of child abuse are actually increasing or if we are becoming more aware of what has always been a prevalent and pervasive problem in our society. The cases reported represent only a fraction of the actual number (Parke & Collmer, 1975). Cases go unreported because of possible repercussions and because local abuse laws are interpreted differently (Fraser, 1979; Gelles, 1982). Characteristic of the problem is physical or mental injury and sexual molestation caused by another human, rather than by accident.

Parents are considered the main perpetrators of the problem (Zirpoli, 1986). Most early theories centered on the concept of a personality disorder on the part of the parent for the neglect or abuse of the child. Kempe and colleagues (1962) talked about the battered child syndrome that resulted from parental pathology, whereas the environment was of secondary importance. Early theorists postulated maltreatment that resulted from emotional disorders. Later researchers (Steele, 1976) suggest that pathology in parents could account only for about 10 percent of the problem.

Most recently an ecological concept of child abuse is receiving support (Howze-Brown, 1988). This multifactor approach involves understanding the individuals, the familial aspects, as well as the social and cultural factors that play a role in creating an environment in which child abuse occurs. Individual factors include characteristics of the child, parents, and other primary persons and their unique life experiences. What they bring to the situation is an important concern. Familial factors include the structure and function of the family and its milieu. This may include family violence, single-parent families, discipline in the home, and roles of family members. Social areas of concern deal with formal and informal relationships and include unemployment, housing, and overall quality of life.

The cultural aspects of the ecological theory deal with values and beliefs concerning violence, punishment, husband-wife relationships, the role of the father in the home, sexism, and attitudes toward others (racism). The focus in treatment is on all of these critical factors and takes into account a variety of interacting variables that precipitate and reinforce the continuance of neglect and abuse (Vondra & Toth, 1989; Hamilton, 1989; Pardeck, 1989).

Sexual Abuse

Schechter and Roberge (1976) define sexual abuse as "the involvement of dependent, developmentally immature children and adolescents in sexual activities which they do not fully comprehend, are unable to give informed consent to and that violate the social taboos of family roles" (p. 64).

Recent events and research suggests that there is a high incidence of sexual abuse in our nation, most of which goes unreported. In a random sample of adult women in San Francisco 12 percent reported at least one episode of intrafamilial sexual abuse before the age of 14 (Russell, 1983). In the same study, 28 percent reported intrafamilial, as well as extrafamilial, sexual abuse before the age of 14.

Economic and Cultural Factors

- Lowered expectation for success based on stereotyping of students because of socioeconomic level, race, or cultural heritage
- Inappropriate placement for services due to failure of due process procedures, or culturally biased assessment tools
- Cultural antipathy to labeling students for special services
- Language difficulties and linguistic awareness problems of speakers of languages other than English
- Lack of coordination and poor communication between the home and the school
- Lack of community support for educational programs and school needs

DISCUSSION

Our society is becoming more multicultural and multiethnic with concomitant concerns about socioeconomic influences as changes occur. As new immigrants join established communities, factors of culture, language, and economic security become evident as school concerns. Factors associated with poverty, for example, increase the risk of school failure. Economic and social deprivation affect parental attitudes, family goals, resources, and involvement with school concerns. Nutritional deficiencies cause illness, low energy levels, and absenteeism. This leads to gaps in learning and potential dropouts. Literacy is an overriding concern for successful inclusion in society.

Many educators and parents feel that the labels and test bias that are attributed to special education placement are undesirable even with the availability of special services (Reschley, 1988a). There is also a questioning of the entire role of IQ testing in diagnosis and classification.

Instructional Factors

- Inability to adjust to school because of continued teacher ineffectiveness
- Faulty learning because of lack of readiness or maturity
- Prolonged failure because the student does not receive intervention, remediation, and reevaluation in a timely manner
- Uneven learning with noticeable gaps in acquisition of content due to frequent absences from the classroom (e.g., expulsions, time-out, illnesses, truancy, drug or alcohol problems, compensatory or special education resource room "pull-out" programs)
- Inability of the teacher to motivate the student sufficiently to maintain interest in classroom activities, causing apathy, boredom, and inconsistent completion of assignments
- Lack of effective classroom management strategies by the instructor, resulting in loss of time on task and disruption of student programs
- Instructors not providing enough practice to bring students to a level of accuracy or automaticity
- Lack of feedback from the instructor to the student, resulting in perpetuation of errors and lack of growth
- Failure to provide for sufficient individual student-teacher interaction needed to maintain motivation and personal commitment
- An overemphasis by the instructor on independent activities instead of teacher-directed instruction
- Teaching students new material without awareness of the students' prior knowledge
- Insufficient time spent on comprehension, problem solving, higher-order thinking skills, and strategic learning, enabling the student to generalize and synthesize facts and concepts

DISCUSSION

Effective schools have an orderly, healthy climate where achievement is expected. Students' learning difficulties can be compounded by teachers whose classrooms do not reflect a good social-emotional climate. Students tend to react negatively to boredom, failure, and peer disapproval. The student who is under constant stress to keep up with the others may expend a great deal of unnecessary energy. Students who require structure and organization in their lives may not adjust to a poorly organized classroom. Traditional modes of discipline may not work for students who have experienced a long history of failure. A more comprehensive and precise analysis of behavior is needed in cases where students do not respond to everyday classroom procedures.

Large classes limit the time teachers can spend with each learner. This inhibits the amount and type of feedback that students with learning problems receive. When opportunities for reinforcement of new learning are limited or curtailed, students with learning difficulties suffer.

Inadequate or inappropriate initial teaching is a critical factor in accentuating the problems that already exist in learning disabled children. Many of these students fail to "catch up," and the gap between them and their agemates becomes too great to overcome as well as emotionally debilitating.

Scheduling is another important factor in terms of when students receive academic instruction. The time of day can be important for some learners. In some cases the previous activity must be considered, such as having a reading lesson right after physical education might not be advisable.

Researchers Kavale and Forness (1986) have combined knowledge of the normal teaching-learning process with factors operating in students labeled as learning disabled and offer a description of how some students disassociate themselves from academic learning. Disassociated behavior appears to accompany interactions that result in unsatisfactory instructional activities, which in turn results in reduction in attention and time actually engaged on task. The student exhibits a lack of attention to the kinds of cues that enable the development of effective learning strategies.

A major contributor to failure, in terms of academic tasks, is the extended Academic Learning Time (ALT) needed for problem learners to accomplish tasks. At its core, ALT refers to student time on task when that task is directly "related to the outcome measure being used (often an achievement test), (and) during which a student experiences a high success rate" (Berliner, 1984, p. 60). Those students who are slow to respond, but are required to master segments of material in lengths of time designed for nonproblem learners, sometimes disassociate themselves from the task. Therefore, time becomes a critical variable in learning.

The discrepancy between time actually spent on task and the time needed to learn the task is an important indicator in learning problems. It follows that those who need more time learn less in a given period of time (as set for normal learners, for example). At some point the time differential becomes so great that the student literally "gives up" or disassociates himself or herself from the activity.

Several specific categories of at-risk students have emerged in the past two decades. Although not mutually exclusive, they provide a structure by which

parents and educators can view children with respect to better understanding the nature of the problem as well as to providing an appropriate educational environment.

THE LEARNING DISABLED STUDENT

A significant portion of the school-age population exhibits learning disabilities (LD) severe enough to require special attention. The disorder is prevalent in about 4 percent of all school-age children nationally and represents more than 40 percent of students receiving special education services (Keogh, 1987). The prevalence of learning disabilities varies across the country and within states, from 26 to 64 percent of the handicapped population (McKinney, 1987). Some contend that an EMR (educable mentally retarded) for LD shift has occurred for some minority groups in some states (Ortiz & Yates, 1983).

Learning disabled students are viewed as having a complex array of symptoms in terms of types as well as combinations of problems. LD manifests its debilitating effects in subtle ways, such as in a student's attention to tasks, or in more complex ways, such as those dealing with social behavior and with severe disability in learning academic subjects (for example, reading or mathematics).

The field of learning disabilities does not have a clear theoretical basis from which to guide the identification of students and to establish policies and educational practices. Heterogeneity of the population makes it difficult to develop a comprehensive definition. There is a lack of consensus regarding specific classifications within the category and there is little agreement as to a single definition of learning disabilities. Since the early 1960s, the term *specific learning disabilities* has connoted a broad range of disorders having no one specific cause.

Earlier, the concept of "development imbalances" was proposed by Gallagher (1966). This was later characterized by uneven patterns of abilities in learning disordered students whose profile of uneven abilities (high and low) is supposed to distinguish between learning disabilities and mental retardation (Hallahan & Kauffman, 1976).

The definition of mental retardation by the American Association of Mental Deficiency (AAMD) is as follows: "Mental retardation refers to significantly subaverage general intellectual functioning resulting in or associated with impairments in adaptive behavior and manifested during the developmental period" (Grossman, 1983, p. 1). The primary difference between this definition and the one offered in learning disabilities is the emphasis placed on intellectual subnormality in combination with low adaptive behavior (Kirk & Gallagher, 1986).

Mentally retarded students appear to exhibit a "flat" pattern of test results. They are consistently low in subtests on an intelligence scale, as compared to a learning disabled student, who would have a great deal of scatter with highs in some subtests (in the normal range or higher) and lows in others. Tests of intelligence, such as the Wechsler Intelligence Scale, for example, have been indexed to learning and behavioral classifications by a wide group of researchers (Bannatyne, 1974; Bush & Waugh, 1976; Keogh & Hall, 1974; Vance & Singer, 1979). Factor-analytic studies, with respect to subtest recategorization and scatter analysis, still show little evidence of a stereotypical pattern that could clearly define learning disabilities (Kavale & Forness, 1984).

Definitions of Learning Disabilities

In 1967, the National Advisory Committee on Handicapped Children submitted a definition of learning disabilities in its report to Congress. This slightly modified definition was incorporated in the Education for All Handicapped Children Act of 1975 (Public Law 94–142). The definition reads as follows:

Specific learning disability means a disorder in one or more of the basic psychological processes involved in understanding or in using language, spoken or written, which may manifest itself in an imperfect ability to listen, think, speak, read, write, spell, or to do mathematical calculations. The term includes such conditions as perceptual aphasia. The term does not include children who have learning problems which are primarily the result of visual, hearing, or motor handicaps, or mental retardation, or emotional disturbance, or of environmental, cultural, or economic disadvantage. (U.S. Office of Education, 1977, p. 65983).

When the legislation became effective in 1977, the United States Office of Education specified the operational rules for identifying students eligible for services under the category of specific learning disabilities. Within the regulations, the concept of a severe discrepancy between a learner's achievement and potential for learning was included.

The National Joint Committee for Learning Disabilities (NJCLD) proposed a revised definition in 1981. The definition reads:

Learning disabilities is a generic term that refers to a heterogeneous group of disorders manifested by significant difficulties in the acquisition and use of listening, speaking, reading, writing, reasoning, or mathematical abilities. These disorders are intrinsic to the individual and presumed to be due to central nervous system dysfunction. Even though a learning disability may occur concomitantly with other handicapping conditions (e.g., cultural differences, insufficient/inappropriate instruction, psychogenic factors), it is not the direct result of those conditions or influences (Hammill, et al., 1981, p. 336).

The NJCLD was comprised of representatives from the American Speech-Language-Hearing Association (ASHA), the Association for Children and Adults with Learning Disabilities (ACLD), the Council for Learning Disabilities (CLD), the Division for Children with Communication Disorders (DCCD), the International Reading Association (IRA), and the Orton Dyslexia Society.

Five of the six groups accepted the definition. The ACLD board disapproved and presented the following definition:

- Specific Learning Disabilities is a chronic condition of presumed neurological origin which selectively interferes with the development, integration, and/or demonstration of verbal and/or nonverbal abilities.
- Specific Learning Disabilities exists as a distinct handicapping condition in the presence of average to superior intelligence, adequate sensory motor systems, and adequate learning opportunities. The condition varies in its manifestations and in degree of severity.
- Throughout life the condition can affect self-esteem, education, vocation, socialization, and/or daily living activities. (*Special Education Today,* 1985, p. 1)

Another modification of the revised (1981) definition has been proposed by the federal Interagency Committee on Learning Disabilities (ICLD). The ICLD formed as a result of the Health Research Extension Act of 1985 (P.L. 99–158) and was mandated by Congress to determine the status of this category. Due to the work of this committee in 1987, the revised definition was formulated and submitted to Congress:

Learning disabilities is a generic term that refers to a heterogeneous group of disorders manifested by significant difficulties in the acquisition and use of listening, speaking, reading, writing, reasoning, or mathematical abilities, or of social skills. These disorders are intrinsic to the individual and presumed to be due to central nervous system dysfunction. Even though a learning disability may occur concomitantly with other handicapping conditions (e.g., sensory impairment, mental retardation, social and emotional disturbance), with socioenvironmental influences (e.g., cultural differences, insufficient or inappropriate instruction, psychogenic factors), and especially with attention deficit disorder, all of which may cause learning problems, a learning disability is not the direct result of those conditions or influences. (ICLD, 1987)

A notable addition to the definition was evidence of social skills deficits as a primary learning disability. This was significant for the following reasons:

1. It established social relationships within the area of learning disabilities as a separate classification.
2. It gave social skills credence as a topic for research and study.
3. It established the area as a major topic for funding.
4. It gave social skills deficits equal status with language skills and academic difficulties. (Gresham & Elliott, 1989)

The position taken by the ICLD is that social skills is a primary cause of deficits, as is the case for academic problems, and by definition it is implied that it should be viewed as resulting from central nervous system (CNS) dysfunction (Hazel & Schumaker, 1987). There are serious doubts expressed about this conclusion because learning disability and mildly mentally retarded and behavioral disordered students appear to exhibit the same kinds of social skills (Reschly & Gresham, 1988; Gresham & Elliott, 1989).

When viewed as a secondary cause of problems associated with academic difficulties, deficits in the social skills area can be seen as being a side effect to other kinds of problems. There appears to be a correlation between academic achievement and social skills functioning and also with peer acceptance (Bursuck & Asher, 1986). But this does not prove cause-effect relationships. It has yet to be definitively proven that remediation of academic deficits results in an improvement in social skills. There is also the fact that many students with social skills problems do not exhibit academic problems. The main problem in the

issue of primacy of social skills in learning disabilities is the paucity of adequate assessment instruments in the area of social skills measurement. The ICLD definition does cause educators to focus on social skills as a major area for remediation. Many feel this is reason enough to target this aspect of behavior.

Social skills are defined as cognitive functions and specific behaviors that are manifested in human interaction. These behaviors include verbal interaction and nonverbal responses that are overt in nature. These responses are essentially learned and deemed appropriate or inappropriate based on the standards of a particular culture. Studies have indicated that students with learning disabilities as a group are less well liked by their peers and more likely to be rejected than their nonhandicapped agemates (Gresham, 1982, 1983a). Two hypotheses have been set forth regarding poor social skills development in learning disabled students:

1. Neurological dysfunction is responsible for poor social skill development.
2. Academic failure, isolation, and rejection by others are also listed as causes.

The Interagency Committee has proposed that this definition be used in studies of prevalence of learning disabilities, research, diagnosis, administrative actions, and the formulation of legislation.

The federal definition in P.L. 94–142 has been adopted by most states and has the legal status under which federal programs are administered and eligibility is determined. NJCLD proposed changes reflected the following concerns with the federal definitions:

1. Terms such as *minimal brain dysfunction* were obsolete and disfavored by many professionals.
2. By using the word *children,* the concerns for adolescents and adults would not receive adequate emphasis.
3. "Basic psychological processes" has promulgated a debate over the definition of curriculum-direct instruction of academic subjects (e.g., reading, writing, etc.) or training of abilities (e.g., memory, perception, etc.). This debate has overshadowed the intent of the phrase that the learning disability is intrinsic to the individual (Hammill et al., 1988).
4. Spelling should more appropriately be subsumed under written expression rather than listed as a separate area.
5. The exclusionary provision that the learning disability does not occur concomitantly with other handicapping conditions (e.g., deaf, blind, etc.) or as a result of environmental, cultural, or economic dis-

advantage does not realistically reflect the population of students requiring special education services. Learning disabilities is not solely an Anglo-American, middle-class disorder.

6. Learning disabled students are more heterogeneous than homogeneous.

The ACLD definition stresses the neurological origin of learning disabilities and includes nonverbal and nonacademic abilities of the learner. Social skills, central nervous system dysfunction, socioenvironmental factors, and attention deficit disorder are highlighted by the Interagency definition.

Similar concepts are implied in most of the definitions:

1. Central nervous system dysfunction or neurological dysfunction is evidenced by the learner. A main assumption is that school failure is caused by neurological dysfunction aggravated by environmental variables (Kavale & Forness, 1985).

2. The learner may have a combination of disorders in acquiring, using, or understanding how to listen, think, speak, or reason, and further have difficulties in certain subject areas (e.g., reading, written expression, mathematics).

3. Earlier definitions specifically excluded children whose learning problems were primarily the result of other handicapping conditions (e.g., visual, hearing, motor handicaps, mental retardation, or emotional disturbance) or of environmental, cultural, or economic factors. Later definitions reflect the practicality of diagnosing students and address the fact that learning disabilities can occur concomitantly with other handicaps, economic disadvantage, and in bilingual students. The availability of funding probably will continue to influence exclusion. New definitions will periodically be presented to reflect changes in terminology, breakthroughs in science and research, and sociopolitical regroupings of students within the schools. This will impact eligibility, prevalence, and service delivery.

Characteristics of Learning Disabled Students

Students with learning disabilities may exhibit a broad range of characteristics on a continuum from mild to severe. Characteristics may be noted in the following areas:

Difficulties in Academic Subjects: Reading problems can involve acquisition of skills, decoding, fluency, and/or comprehension. Mathematics disabilities may also involve reading as well as operations, abstract symbolic thinking, concepts, and problem solving. Written language problems occur in spelling, handwriting, and the process of written expression. Deficiencies in study skills become more noticeable as the student reaches higher grade levels.

Developmental Language Disorders: Difficulties in language include such areas as oral expression, listening comprehension, and overall verbal facility with grammar.

Disorders in the Learning Process: Problems with cognition may involve perception, memory use and retrieval, and thinking.

Attention Problems: Difficulty with selective attention, attention span, and sustained attention may be evident.

Motor Difficulties: Students may exhibit a general awkwardness, poor handwriting, or problems with fine motor tasks.

Hyperactivity: Excessive movement may be noted.

Social-Emotional Problems: This is often manifested in social perception disorders, learned helplessness, and social interactions with others.

McCarthy (1988) suggests that a constellation of symptoms is important for identification in that it goes beyond the limited focus of the discrepancy formula that emphasizes the discrepancy between academic achievement and cognitive ability.

Causes of Learning Disabilities

The observation of multifaceted symptom clusters enables professionals to infer certain types of brain dysfunction. This includes a delay in the development of the neural system or damage to the circuitry to certain areas of the brain, such as the cortex or the subcortex. Many of the observed behaviors of students can be described as scattered. The following is a brief list of possible physiological causes of compromise to the central nervous system in the developing fetus and young child:

1. Interference during critical stages of fetal development of the nervous system and of the neural apparatus occurring during cellular differentiation and maturation (Boer, et al., 1988)

2. Genetic factors that predispose the fetus to certain types of disorders, including variations in the central nervous system

3. Factors related to maternal behavior that affect the fetus in utero such as antibodies (blood incompatibility), ingestion of heavy metals, poisons, drugs, and alcohol during critical periods

4. Fetal trauma to the developing organism
5. Fetus affected by thyroid hormone or by testosterone (McCarthy, 1988); thyroxine can have a strong negative effect on cerebellar development early in gestation
6. Irregularities in the amount of available neurotransmitters such as acetylcholine to the brain (Rosengarten, Freidman, & Friedhoff, 1983)
7. Birth trauma resulting in prenatal anoxia, hypoxia, or ischemia to the central nervous system
8. Compressed head of the fetus at birth resulting in hemorrhage
9. Damage during childhood caused by physical, chemical, or metabolic trauma
10. Infections to the young child, such as those due to encephalitis or meningitis
11. Problems resulting from galactycemia and other metabolic disorders that cause toxic levels of ammonia to rise in the brain in young children
12. Disorders due to exposure to heavy metals such as lead and mercury

From a medical perspective, steps can be taken to limit the effects of the problem. Prevention systems need to be put into place. This includes improving prenatal care, especially among the poor, and emphasizing areas dealing with the toxic effects of drugs (Rakic, 1988a). Other causes of learning disabilities are discussed in Chapter 4.

IQ-Achievement Classification

Exact psychological processes that define the condition of learning disability in children are not as yet identified, nor is the way these processes are measured uniformly agreed upon. These "topical markers" (Keogh et al., 1982) need to be identified in order to establish a classification system. Inadequate psychometric assessment tools and the absence of an established etiological classification system has led to a reliance on the IQ-achievement discrepancy for determining eligibility of services. To operationalize the definitions, many school systems use formulas to determine the severity of the gap between a student's potential (IQ) and what he or she has learned (achievement). Although the currently used definitions do not refer to the gap per se, the rules and regulations issued by the states permit use of the concept to specify cutoffs for service eligibility or to delimit subgroups.

Available methods for calculating discrepancy scores present methodological problems in terms of delineating subgroups or categories. Different methods seem to identify different children as well as different numbers of children at different levels of ability (Alberg, 1986). Fairness of IQ measures for all cultures and socioeconomic groups in our society has to be considered. Severity of the gap has not been uniformly defined. How many years of discrepancy at what grade level really is a cause for concern? Do discrepancy scores actually indicate the presence of learning disabilities? Most definitions of learning disability do not include the concept of ability-achievement discrepancy. Because students exhibiting learning disabilities are defined as having specific rather than general deficits, they display poor achievement regardless of average or above-average ability. Students can display symptoms associated with learning disabilities and still not show a significant discrepancy between potential and achievement. IQ-achievement discrepancies can result from motivational or emotional factors, as well as from poor teaching. Therefore, discrepancy criteria, as a means of subgrouping, does not as yet meet the need for an accurate and consistent subsystem. The specific formulas and evaluation devices currently in use are discussed in detail in Chapters 5 and 6.

It is obvious from reading the definitions that a perfect or single comprehensive definition has not been written that encompasses the heterogeneity of the learning disabled population. The many professional organizations, advocacy groups, researchers, and educators have not as yet reached consensus. Some feel that multiple definitions may be needed—one for theoretical consideration and another to specify operational criteria for identification of the students. Current literature suggests that learning disabilities are manifested in multiple syndromes, subsets, and subgroups.

A definition, however, gives us a basis for determining the parameters of our diagnosis and guides us toward identifying appropriate learners for appropriate placements. Beyond academic achievement, there are many behaviors to be observed. The absence of these behaviors may be as important as their presence for helping us to feel confident about our prescriptive programs.

Subtypes of Specific Learning Disabilities

McKinney (1988) has done a comprehensive review of this emerging area of research to determine whether empirically discrete subtypes of learning disabled students can be identified. He states that "subtyping of learning disabilities is an attempt to divide heterogeneous groups of children into more homogeneous subgroups of children, subgroups that reflect different patterns of specific disabilities" (p. 255). Most of the research reflects three major approaches to classifying students: clinical-inferential subtypes, empirically derived subtypes, and rationally defined subtypes.

CLINICAL-INFERENTIAL CLASSIFICATION

In the early 1960s, learning disabled students were often described by what they were not. They were not mentally retarded or emotionally disturbed. Early hypotheses speculated that subtle neurological factors were causing ability deficits and uneven patterns of development. The uneven ability profile concept was used to distinguish between learning disability and mental retardation.

Children were grouped according to their pattern of abilities and deficits on diagnostic tests (Bannatyne, 1971; Boder, 1973; Myklebust, 1971). Clinical interpretation of the Wechsler Intelligence Scales (WISC) grouped the subtests into categories, and learning disabilities were determined by a pattern such as Bannatyne's categories: verbal conceptual (similarities, vocabulary, comprehension), spatial (picture completion, block design, object assembly), sequential (arithmetic, digit span, coding), and acquired knowledge (information, arithmetic, vocabulary). Kavale and Forness (1984) analyzed 94 studies of the WISC scatter analysis and concluded that there was little evidence for a pattern approach to learning disabilities subtypes. Boder (1973) reported the identification of three subtypes of language disability: dysphonetic (67 percent) whole word readers with nonphonetic spelling errors, dyseidetic (10 percent) "word-blind" with laborious phonetic attempts at words, and alexics (23 percent) mixed. Johnson and Myklebust (1967) proposed auditory and visual subtypes of reading disorders and later added a combination of mixed auditory and visual deficits.

Clinical-inferential studies have had limitations, including the selection of the clinical samples and the theoretical orientation of the investigator. Many of the early samples did not represent the sociodemographics of today's school population. The reliability and validity of the measures used in the earlier subtype efforts have also been questioned. The clinical-inferential attempts at more discrete subgroups have resulted in establishing goals for more careful research.

EMPIRICAL CLASSIFICATION

The empirical classification method uses multivariate statistical classification techniques to subdivide learning disabled students based on their patterns of performance across a set of measures. Techniques such as cluster analysis are designed to be descriptive and

depend on the good judgment of the investigator in determining how the students in a given subtype are alike. In cluster analysis, the students are given a group of tests and they are then clustered or matched into subgroups according to similarity of performance patterns on selected variables (Senf, 1986).

RATIONALLY DEFINED CLASSIFICATION

Another approach to subtyping is to select a subgroup of students with one common characteristic. Torgesen (1982) and colleagues have done research on short-term memory disorders. They have identified a subgroup unaffected by incentives. Torgesen states that children with one common characteristic under study are likely to vary greatly in other characteristics.

Intervention Based on Subtypes

The practical value of subtype classification will, in the final analysis, be determined by how students with specific subtypes of learning disabilities respond to different instructional procedures. There is little supportive research in this area because the field of study is new. Using 30 students from the original six subtypes in one of the Northwestern Studies, Lyon (1983) found that there is support for teaching practices and methods that take advantage of the child's strengths as determined by subtype characteristics, as opposed to those that attempt to strengthen their weaknesses.

It seems logical that the learning disabled population of students may be composed of a number of distinct homogeneous subtypes. Senf (1986) cautions that the population from which the subgroups are derived has to be specified or it will be difficult to integrate findings across the studies into a broader context. The examination of a subgroup that is not large enough or representative of the population may be of dubious value and misuse of classification could occur. He further states that researchers need a working theory from which to predict behavior distinctive to each subgroup.

ATTENTION DEFICIT DISORDER

Previous discussions centered around the learning disabled who are primarily referred to special education because they are failing in academic subjects in school. There is another group of students who may or may not fit the criteria for learning disabilities, but may be at high risk for social and academic problems. There is a high correlation between the severity and intensity of these students' outgoing behaviors (attention and activity) and their referral to special education, especially if they display high levels of aggression. One subgroup of these students may be inattentive, impulsive, hyperactive, overreactive, or aggressive, whereas another group may not show the hyperactivity but are still inattentive, impulsive, anxious, and even more socially withdrawn. Their attention deficits have evolved into a category called attention deficit disorder (ADD). (Many of the terms used here are defined in the Glossary, and are elaborated on in Chapters 4, 5, and 6.)

Overview of ADD

Since the late nineteenth century, members of the medical community and others have been interested in the symptoms occurring as sequelae from brain injury. Behavioral manifestations of inattention, hyperactivity, and impulse control were first noted after an infection or insult to the brain. Later observations centered on individuals without known causes who showed similar behavior. An underlying assumption was made that there was a neurological dysfunction intrinsic to all of these individuals causing learning problems (Orton, 1937; Goldstein, 1936).

Strauss and colleagues (Werner & Strauss, 1941; Strauss & Lehtinen, 1947) studied brain injured children. They classified institutionalized, mentally retarded children into two groups: exogenous (neurologic evidence of brain damage) and endogenous (cultural-familial mental retardation). Strauss and Kephart (1955) began to look at the excessive behavioral characteristics of hyperactivity, impulsivity, perseveration, and distractibility in children with normal intelligence who had learning problems. Since a history of insult to the brain was hard to pinpoint in most of these children, the term *minimal brain damage* was used.

Laufer and Denhoff (1957) wrote about a hyperkinetic behavior disorder in the pediatric literature. This was transformed into minimal brain dysfunction (MBD) by Clements and Peters (1962). A cluster of signs or abnormalities noted on neurologic examination or electroencephalogram (EEG) was used to detect hyperkinesis, impulsivity, and learning and attention disorders.

The concepts of MBD and hyperkinetic reaction of childhood have lost favor because research has failed to establish their diagnostic validity (Ostrom & Jenson, 1988). The scientific community has had difficulty establishing diagnostic criteria for learning disabilities and classifying childhood neurobehavioral disorders.

The search for the validation of a classification system and a syndrome definition has lead to attention deficit disorder (ADD) as an entity.

Definition of ADD

In 1968, the American Psychiatric Association (APA) published the *Diagnostic and Statistical Manual of Mental Disorders,* DSM II. In this manual, activity problems in children were called a hyperkinetic reaction of childhood. A significant advance was made in 1980 in the third edition (DSM III) when the category of attention deficit disorder (ADD) was established. The earlier category was replaced and the emphasis shifted from activity to attention as the major symptom of the disorder because "attentional difficulties are prominent and virtually always present . . ." (p. 41).

DSM III differentiated between ADD with hyperactivity (ADDH) and ADD without hyperactivity (ADD no H). The latest revision, DSM III-R, dropping this classification, now defines the three main characteristics of attention deficit hyperactivity disorder (ADHD) as "developmentally inappropriate degrees of inattention, impulsiveness, and hyperactivity" (American Psychiatric Association, 1987, p. 50). In DSM III-R, the APA established a diagnostic category of undifferentiated attention deficit disorder corresponding to the previous ADD without hyperactivity (Ostrom & Jenson, 1988). At the present time, consensus has not been reached by all professionals on this definition.

The DSM III, used by professionals to diagnose ADD, currently reflects the consensus of clinicians and their experience rather than hard criteria. There is a great need for studies on diverse groups of children divided into homogenous subgroups, and studies done by the various professionals who treat ADD with hyperactivity.

Shaywitz and Shaywitz (1988) ask the key questions regarding syndrome validity as it applies to ADD: Can a group of children who have difficulties with concentration, impulsivity, and excess activity be "reliably and meaningfully differentiated from children who have other symptoms that make up what is termed the external dimension of behavioral disorders? Does ADD as defined by DSM III represent a valid classification category?" (p. 381). They propose that the term *ADD* be used to describe only those individuals who satisfy the diagnostic criteria. For students exhibiting the criteria plus other features (e.g., mental retardation, conduct disorder, etc.), they propose the term *ADD-plus (ADD-P)*. There is a controversy over the distinctiveness of hyperactivity from such conduct disorders as aggression, lying, stealing, cheating, and so on.

DSM III-R suggests that ADHD "may occur in as many as 3 percent of children" (pp. 50–51). Shaywitz and Shaywitz (1988) feel that the figure of 3 percent is too stringent and that the ADD prevalence is closer to 20 percent of the school-age population. ADD is more common in boys, with a ratio of at least 2:1 over girls.

Educators and other professionals need to formulate their own opinions about ADD as they critically examine current findings in the literature and attempt to describe the neurobehavioral characteristics of children. Subjectivity and good judgment are inherent in many diagnostic decisions and can affect the outcomes of classification and eligibility for inclusion in a category. Although DSM III-R provides a category of ADD and symptoms, educators must seek the most reliable operational criteria to determine whether children have the disorder.

Current literature recommends that to assess elementary-age students who may have a high probability for attentional problems, teachers, psychologists, and parents use standardized rating scales or checklists in multiple settings (e.g., the classroom, in recess, at home, etc.). A multifaceted approach looks at a number of factors: academic, emotional, social, physical, developmental, situational, and, where feasible, direct measures of attention and activity level using more clinical procedures (Ostrom & Jenson, 1988). For older students, an analysis of peer acceptance can give information about social skills and group assessment. Older students may have less movement, but they may exhibit similar academic and behavioral characteristics with more sadness and depression present.

Problem of Attention

"Attention is a complex and ambiguous concept with many definitions and a vast and diversified research literature" (Ostrom & Jenson, 1988, p. 254). By definition, ADD is a generalized attentional disorder that is not evidenced by consistency in all tasks and situations. It is unpredictable and inconsistent in a variety of situations, and it has to be inferred from an individual's response to stimuli.

Attention relates to the individual's "ability to deal with increasing amounts of information" (Stankov, 1983, p. 471). Gibson and Rader (1979) define good attention as selective perception of information that has optimal use and relation to the goal or the task at hand. Posner and Boies (1971) feel that three major

component processes should be included in studies of attention: (1) alertness, (2) selectivity, and (3) processing selectivity.

Subtypes

Two subtypes were differentiated in DSM III: attention deficits with hyperactivity (ADDH) and without (ADD no H). ADDH students are inattentive, impulsive, and hyperactive. Boys are often more nervous, overactive, unpopular, self-destructive, and aggressive than girls. Boys' problems are usually noticed, but girls who are likewise affected, but who are less disruptive in class, may go undiagnosed. ADDH students as a group are more rejected by their peers. They have low self-esteem and are likely to be behind in reading and mathematics. Hyperactivity with aggression are precursors for poorer outcomes in adolescence. ADD no H students are also high risk for academic and social problems. They are inattentive and impulsive and have poorer school performance. These pupils are less happy, rejected by peers, and more concerned about physical appearance. Some are less proficient in sports and are shy and withdrawn.

Rosenthal and Allen (1980) state that ADHD children are susceptible to distraction when the stimulation comes from the task itself, in contrast to distractors that occur externally. Distracting stimuli not only involve sustaining and organizing attention but they appear to be related to a disinclination to invest attention and effort (Douglas & Peters, 1979).

Other problem areas include vigilance and impulse control. Tarnowski, Prinz, and Nay (1986) found that the ADHD group displayed recall problems when required to do more than one task, suggesting susceptibility to intratask distractors.

A recent study indicated that ADD children appear to have substantially more problems with impulsivity, attention span, and overactivity than LD and normal children. Children with ADD also seem to have more problems with foresight and planning than normal children (Kuehne, Kehle, & McMahon, 1987).

Children in one study exhibited less cardiac deceleration in response to certain stimuli, and had slower reaction times. Vigilance and discrimination learning were also poor and they were found to be more field dependent and impulsive than normal children (Rosenthal & Allen, 1978).

All children have some problems in behavior, but what separates abnormal from normal behavior may be "quantitative deviations in frequency and severity" (Edelbrock, 1986, p. 36).

Causes

The precise causes of attention deficit disorder remain essentially undetermined. One reason is b cause of the difficulty of acquiring accurate prenat histories and early histories of children. There is as yet only symptomatic treatment. New research approaches must be developed to determine the mechanisms responsible for the deficits observed in afflicted children.

A cognitive and neuropsychological analysis (Ackerman et al., 1986) shows these students as primarily having difficulty with sustained attention. This is attributed to frontal lobe and limbic brain dysfunction. (See brain illustrations, Figures 3–1 and 3–2 in Chapter 3.) Children with reading disabilities, on the other hand, are thought to have problems in selective attention, which is attributable to temporal lobe dysfunction. Although the attentional problems of children with reading disabilities may be similar in some respects to those of children with ADD, in children with reading disabilities, these difficulties will become evident only in situations that require reading and that stress their already impaired information processing (selective attention) capabilities (Ackerman, Dykman, & Peters, 1977). Evidence now exists linking frontal lobe dysfunction to children with ADD with hyperactivity (Lou, Henriksen, & Bruhn, 1984).

Such behavior could be caused not only by distractibility or basic problems in sustaining attention but by failure of the task's difficulty or interest levels to match the child's chronological age, mental age, or cultural background. Lack of motivation or inadequate reinforcements that relate to the task itself may also be contributing factors (Shaffer & Schonfeld, 1984).

There are a number of types of attention disorders that may be related to several mechanisms. Tourette syndrome is a disorder in which "there are repeated interruptions of ongoing behavior and thought by intrusive thoughts or by discontinuities in attention sequence while the individual is tracking an event. This results in missing elements in the experiential sequence of events unfolding in the environment" (Bonnet, 1989, p. 15). Tourette syndrome first shows up in childhood and affects four times as many boys as girls. This disorder also produces unusual, purposeless, repeated movements called tics. Some affected children also suffer from hyperactivity, poor attention span, and emotional difficulties. Drug treatment, when necessary, improves the condition for most cases. The syndrome causes an interruption in the sequence of events with accompanying attention deficits. This can affect the intake of information provided from the environment that is important to normal learning.

va

F

atter

a bas

ADD w

gested

deficits t

lieve that

dependent

It is poss.. e that children with mild learning disabilities in language, for example, may perform adequately in reading, if they have good attentional skills. However, with the additional problem of an attention deficit, a reading disability could occur. This reading problem could be relatively mild. The cognitive deficits associated with the reading problem could be difficult to diagnose. Conversely, it is likely that a severe problem in the cognitive areas that are vital to reading, along with attentional difficulties, could produce reading disabilities (Felton & Wood, 1989).

ADD and Learning Disabilities

An attention deficit disorder with or without hyperactivity is not the same as having a learning disability. That is, there are children with poor attention and control whose academic performance is within normal range. What is below expectancy is the behavior exhibited while learning (Duane, 1988).

Children with attention deficit disorder have constitutional impairments in attentional mechanisms, and their learning problems are secondary; on the other hand, children with learning disabilities have basic processing problems, and their failure experiences in school leads to frustration and secondary attentional problems (Rosenthal & Allen, 1980). Learning disabled children have deficits of attention primarily in the area of selectivity or distractibility, which is not necessarily true for hyperactive children. LD students appear to have a predisposition toward one or more specific learning disorders that leads to increased

...g tasks ...arning disabled ...udents tend to show ...(generalized) deficits in ...ki contends it is not useful to ...attentional disorder. It is more ...k of specific deficits that are associ- ...ific tasks or situations that bring about ...attention.

...owski, Prinz, and Nay (1986) found that deficits ...sustained attention, as measured with the Continuous Performance Test (CPT), were present in ADHD children both with and without learning disabilities, but were not present in learning disabled children without ADHD.

Labels such as *hyperactivity* or *attention deficit disorder* rely to a large extent on the tolerance level and accuracy of observation of teachers. A clear understanding of such constructs is important to the direct objective identification of problems of attention and its relationship to academics and school performance in general.

DYSLEXIA

Educators are familiar with common observable signs and types of reading disorders and the standard assessment procedures used to identify most classroom reading difficulties. Chapter 6 covers this area in depth. As noted in previous sections, students with learning disabilities are not a homogeneous population with regard to reading disorders. Some learning disabled students have intact reading skills, whereas other students have unique combinations of mild to moderate reading problems (e.g., decoding, comprehension, fluency, etc.). However, there is one group of students who seem to have extreme difficulty recognizing letters and words and interpreting what is seen. After these students are referred for evaluation, the educators participating in a followup conference may see either the term *severe reading disorder* or the term *dyslexia* written on the student's evaluation report.

Overview of Dyslexia

It is important to know what psychologists and diagnosticians mean by the term *dyslexia* and to be familiar with some of the current research on dyslexic students being conducted by various disciplines. Even though dyslexia is not a frequently used term, educators need to be aware of developments in the area of neurodevelopmental factors associated with dyslexia.

Almost ten times more males than females have dyslexia. Gaddes (1980) and Hynd, Cohen, and Obrzut (1983) estimate that approximately 5 percent of the population, or nearly eleven million children and adults, have severe reading disabilities.

In 1900, Hinshelwood coined the phrase "congenital word blindness." Later, Orton (1925) suggested a construct associated with twisted symbols or "strephosymbolia." The enigma is that dyslexics fail to learn despite having normal intelligence and intact sensory functions. As a group, they have had adequate opportunity, do not lack socioeconomic advantage, and do not suffer from severe emotional problems or comprehensive neurological impairments.

Definition of Dyslexia

Dyslexia is defined as "a rare but definable and diagnosable form of primary reading retardation with some form of central nervous system dysfunction. It is not attributable to environmental causes or other handicapping conditions" (Harris & Hodges, 1981, p. 95). The proximal effect of the disorder is the inability to decode the written word. *Developmental dyslexia* is used to describe the presence of the disorder from early development, whereas *acquired dyslexia* refers to a known injury that has occurred during later development.

Gough and Tunmer (1986) suggest that there are three forms of dyslexia:

1. A decoding disability, which is called *dyslexia*
2. A comprehension disability, which is called *hyperlexia*
3. Both a decoding and a comprehension problem

Denckla (1978a) labels students with dyslexia and no other disorder as "pure" dyslexia and those with other additional problems as "dyslexia plus."

Characteristics

Dyslexic individuals manifest the following symptoms:

1. Dyslexic readers appear to be seriously deficient in decoding skills (Firth, 1972; Vellutino, 1979).
2. They tend to be slower and less accurate in naming letters, words, objects, colors, and numerals when compared to normal readers.
3. They perform poorly on tests of linguistic skills associated with the brain's left hemisphere (read-

ing, writing, and spelling). Stuttering may be present and speech is sometimes delayed.

4. Some students exhibit ambidexterity.

5. Dyslexic persons read outside the foveal field (central fovea of the retina), and generally there are different learned strategies for task-directed vision. Developmental dyslexia, for example, can involve alterations in retinal, occipitotemporal, and occipitoparietal distribution of visual information processing. (See brain illustrations, Figures 3–1 and 3–2 in Chapter 3.)

Subtypes

A behavioral-psychometric approach is one way of viewing subtypes. The level and performance of normally achieving readers and those with severe reading problems are determined and compared using standardized psychometric or behavioral measures. Boder (1973), who had done extensive work in distinguishing between good and poor spellers, has developed a classification system for dyslexics. Her method distinguishes between normal readers and three types of dyslexics, based on the students' abilities to handle reading and spelling of phonetic and nonphonetic known sight words. All three types of dyslexics were unable to spell 50 percent of their sight vocabulary at reading level.

Dyslexics who are dysphonetic (67 percent) as a group lack word analysis skills and tend to read entirely through visual recognition of whole words in their limited sight vocabulary. Their reading is more global than analytical. Their spelling errors are nonphonetic, often accompanied by bizarre errors, and may include various types of word substitutions. Dyseidetics (10 percent), conversely, laboriously sound out each word phonetically with little recognition that these words have been seen before. Alexics (23 percent), or mixed, have low reading skills and display the nonphonetic errors of the dysphonetic group. In terms of overall reading achievement, the latter group is the most severely impaired.

Causes

Since dyslexic readers do poorly on semantic-linguistic tasks or on perceptual or cognitive variables important to reading, it is inferred that these deficits are related to deficient neurological substrata (Gaddes, 1981; Taylor & Fletcher, 1983). The causes are not fully known, but it is felt that subtle brain abnormalities rather than gross pathology is involved, caused by a complex system of interacting factors.

Galaburda and associates (1987) have recently found that a dyslexic brain has an abnormally large right hemisphere. This cellular difference probably takes place in the second trimester of pregnancy, when the outer cortex (which governs thought, language, and other higher functions) is formed. It is speculated that it might be caused by subtle injury to the fetal brain, such as a small stroke, virus, maternal stress, or variation in testosterone, all of which alter the way the brain takes shape.

Galaburda and colleagues (1985) concluded that in a dyslexic brain, the right side has too many brain cells, suggesting that something has interfered with the normal pruning process. Postmortem studies of normal and dyslexic individuals indicated that the left hemisphere of normal brains were larger and more developed. Certain areas of the right hemisphere of dyslexics were more developed and contained a greater number of cells than normals. The central nervous system of the dyslexic appears to be reordered or rewired around misplaced nerve cells with a concomitant major increase in the total number of nerve cells. That is, the right hemisphere has more nerve cells than the more common left hemisphere.

It is suggested that with too many cells, the right side will have taken up the lion's share of the connections. The left side of the brain, which becomes differentiated, or comes along approximately ten days later, finds that there is no place to connect, and the result is a reorganized brain. This is a subtle kind of brain pathology in which the underpruned right side of the brain may have taken up all or most of the connective sites, and the left side of the brain is essentially closed out.

Postmortem examination of the brain of dyslexic persons has disclosed a deficiency in the language areas of the brain. As Duffy, Denckla, and Sandini (1980) stated, "The regions that we have shown to differ electrophysiologically between the brains of dyslexics and normal boys appear to be among the regions normally involved in speech and reading. Thus, dyslexia-pure may represent dysfunction within a complex and widely distributed system, not a discrete brain lesion" (p. 417).

Focal disorganization of the cells was found in the language cortex of the left hemisphere. The left greater than right, asymmetric nervous system is thought to exist in about 65 percent of the general population. In studies by Galaburda and colleagues (1985), small microscopic lesions were found that can affect the "wiring diagram" of the brain and cause widespread changes as indicated by computer assisted electroencephalograms (EEG). Clumps of immature nerve cells that cause damage to the brain's surface (ectopias) are irregularly arranged farther apart than layered nerve cells (dysplasias), and form tiny enfoldings inside the brain called micropolygyria, where there should be none. These changes could occur between the 18th and 24th weeks of gestation. It is postulated that a broad range of behaviors involved in information processing might be affected.

Weintraub and Mesulam (1983) studied individuals with average intelligence who exhibited signs of right hemisphere learning disabilities. The individuals in this study also exhibited emotional and interpersonal difficulties, shyness, visuospatial disturbances, and inadequate paralinguistic communicative abilities. Other symptoms observed included avoidance of eye contact, and reduced use of gestures and body-facial responses that generally accompany normal speech. Chronic depression and extreme shyness were also two frequently reported symptoms. They were described as loners who dislike one-to-one interactions. In academic areas a very high incidence of persistent problems with arithmetic and spelling was reported.

Problems with the basic levels of arithmetic were serious, but some of these individuals could deal with abstract mathematics and calculus. Introversion, social perception problems, emotional difficulties, inability to display affect, and impairments in visuospatial representation seem to run in their families.

Lateral Dominance and Dyslexia

The importance of establishing lateral dominance, which is the tendency to use the right or left side of the body as a preference, such as favoring one hand, eye, foot, or ear over another, was postulated by Samuel Orton (1925). He suggested that reading difficulty (dyslexia) is a result of incomplete cerebral lateralization due to a lesion in the dominant hemisphere. This affected the visual presentation of symbols and altered meanings. Orton felt that the lead or control of reading, speech, and writing originated in one hemisphere. He generalized this theory because of the study of unilateral hemisphere damage to adult alexics, aphasics, or those exhibiting agraphia. Students are often described as having right, left, or mixed laterality (mixing right and left functions). In reviewing the research, Kinsbourne (1986a) concluded that diagnostically there is doubtful significance to mixed laterality as a factor in dyslexia.

It should be noted that study of adult aphasic cases and animals are the main source of information by which inferences are drawn to school-age children. There is also a paucity of replicable research to support important findings (Hynd & Semrud-Clikeman,

1989). However, many scientists believe that neural substrate abnormalities are associated with developmental dyslexia.

The study of neurobiology of neural substrates and associated developmental dyslexia, in the long run, offers the potential for a greater understanding of the problem and opportunity for subsequent programming for students suffering from brain-related language disabilities.

DEVELOPMENTAL LANGUAGE DISORDERS

Mainly, what sets us apart as humans from other species is a complex communication function called language. Our thoughts are transmitted as we listen, comprehend, speak, read, write, and use gestures or body language. This requires the integration of many elements, including sensory, attention, perception, motor, cognition, and linguistic functions. We use language to convey our thoughts and express feelings and to request information from others.

We do not have a unitary theory about how language is acquired. Information about currently accepted theories will be presented in Chapter 2. To better understand language in learners, observed behaviors are classified under three types of language: receptive language, expressive language, and inner language.

Observable Behaviors

RECEPTIVE LANGUAGE
Receptive language enables the student to comprehend speech and to relate words and speech to meaning. It is the basis of understanding in the communication process. Students with receptive language disorders may experience the following:

1. They may have problems deriving meaning from words or abstract concepts.
2. They may have difficulty in relating the spoken or written word with the appropriate unit of experience.
3. They may be frustrated by conversation.
4. They may not be able to carry out a series of directions even though they do not have memory problems.
5. They have difficulty with figurative language. For example, the students may not understand such statements as "He was chewed out" or "She has had it."

6. They may not be able to associate the /m/ sound in *mother* with the /m/ sound in *man,* causing difficulty in learning phonics. Students may not transfer the sound of m in one word to the sound of m in another word (may be memory).
7. They may not be able to associate a word they can read with the appropriate unit of experience. These students are sometimes referred to as word callers. They can read but do not understand.
8. They may have difficulty with verbal or written language and arithmetic in that they may not be able to associate words or numerals that they see with meaning.

EXPRESSIVE LANGUAGE

Expressive language is the act of producing and using words to describe, show action, or characterize a message that conveys an intended meaning. Students with expressive language disorders may experience the following:

1. They are unable to express manually the function of an object even though, when asked, they may be able to identify it from among other objects. For example, the students may be able to identify a hammer from among other objects, but not be able to show what to do with it manually.
2. They may exhibit poor speech patterns and be unable to say words.
3. They may have difficulty in retrieving the motor act of speech even if they have a model or can comprehend or recall the act.
4. They will have difficulty imitating words, regardless of whom they are attempting to model.
5. They may exhibit difficulty in recalling or retrieving words for use in speaking.
6. They may not be able to express themselves in a complete sentence.
7. They may use gestures and vocalization to make wants known.
8. They can sometimes retrieve words when seeing or feeling the concrete object.
9. They can generally read better silently than orally.
10. They may have nonfluent speech that includes hesitations like stuttering.
11. They may not be able to sequence their thoughts or ideas.
12. They may use word substitutions such as *whatchamacallit, thingamajig,* or *gizmo.*
13. They have problems with the smooth and natural flow of the English language. They cannot structure thoughts into grammatically correct verbal units or sentences.
14. They may understand what they say but answer in single words or phrases with inadequate language structure.
15. They may have poor syntax (e.g., they may omit words, distort the order of words, or use poor tense).
16. They may recognize correct sentence structure but not be able to reproduce a meaningful sequence themselves.
17. They may use telegraphic speech (e.g., mom-dad-me-go) in attempting to formulate a sentence.
18. They may write the way they speak.
19. They may not be deficient in understanding quantitative relationships and may do well in computation as long as it is written and not oral.

INNER LANGUAGE

Inner language is the language with which one thinks. It serves to integrate experiences with a native spoken language. Inner language can also be thought of as inner speech. Inner speech, in this sense, relates to thinking; outer, or external, speech provides for communication between people. Students with inner language conflicts may experience the following:

1. They may incorporate a language other than standard English as their native language, and cannot, or will not, integrate standard English as a functional language. The other language can be sign language, a foreign language, or a dialect.
2. They may think or solve problems in their native language even though they can speak fluent standard English.
3. They may have internalized the phonetic, or sound, system of a foreign language and have difficulty in learning the English phoneme-grapheme system.

Characteristics

Developmental language disability is characterized by the failure of normal language function in the absence of such factors as deafness, mental deficiency, motor disability, or severe personality disorder. This failure can be exhibited in the child as a disability in expression with normal receptive (understanding) abilities or as a disability in both the receptive and expressive areas of language. There are children who also have concomitant speech articulation problems that accompany a developmental language disorder. Conversely, not all children with articulation problems exhibit delayed language development. The disability is specific to language in most cases and is developmental or congenital as opposed to acquired.

Causes

Etiologies involved in developmental language impairment focus on intrinsic factors such as a neurological basis and include genetic, metabolic, and hormonal causes. Disorders can also result from extrinsic insults, including trauma, infections, or exposure to toxic substances such as chemicals and metals that affect the growth of the fetus in utero.

Tallal (1988) concludes that:

> Developmental language impairment, with concomitant temporal auditory processing, motor, and memory deficits, appears to be consistent with a pattern of innate or progressive dysfunction of the left temporal association cortex, which may be due to the presence of a functional deficit within the left hemisphere, to an abnormal state of cerebral asymmetry, or to disordered interhemispheric integration. (p. 236)

Geschwind (1979) suggests that the child may have a genetic predisposition to a left temporal lobe that is less than normal. Neurological abnormality may also occur because of a variety of intrinsic or extrinsic factors that interfere with such brain activity as cell migration in the brain or normal development of myelinization (Musiek, Geurkink, & Kietel, 1982). The timing of the neural insult may be crucial in knowing what type of language impairment will occur.

Research on genetic causation is inconclusive. Because of the 2 or 3:1 male to female ratio for language impairment, scientists are researching for a chromosomal abnormality. Melnick, Michals, and Matalon (1981) report that children treated for inborn errors of metabolism have a high occurrence of disorders of language.

Damage to the fetus resulting from abnormal hormone secretions may be genetic or as a result of the mother's use of drugs or from severe stress of the mother. A variety of toxins in the environment may harm children at prenatal, perinatal, and postnatal stages of development. The research is not conclusive on the impact of such contaminants as tobacco smoke, pesticides, dioxin derivatives, and so on; however, the consequences of lead poisoning and excessive alcohol consumption have been shown. Impairments of learning and a variety of disabilities are noted in children of mothers who consumed excessive alcohol during pregnancy.

Infections may cause problems associated with language impairment. Prenatal infections such as syphilis, toxoplasmosis, rubella, herpes simplex, and so on result in children born with multiple handicaps, including mental retardation, seizures, cerebral palsy, learning disabilities, and hearing loss (Sever, 1986). A postnatal ear infection (otitis media) or inflammation of the middle ear causes some children to be at an increased risk for hearing impairment and to result in possible learning and language disorders (Levinton, 1980). Otitis media is not a direct predictor of developmental language deficits, but those involved in a study analysis of a child should seek this information as part of a case study.

Language Components

To understand the linguistic differences between normal and affected children, it is helpful to understand the various systems of language and how these systems are interrelated. Too often in schools the language areas are considered in isolation (e.g., reading, writing, spelling, etc.). Throughout this book the reader will be constantly reminded how language influences all areas of learning including mathematics. Relationships will be noted between oral and written communication and between the processes we have previously discussed (e.g., listening and reading [receptive processes] and speaking and writing [expressive processes]).

The components of language are studied by linguists. They study the units, nature, and development of human speech. There are four major hierarchical components of language: phonology, morphology, syntax, and semantics. Pragmatics is also often included in the list. Bloom and Lahey (1978) grouped the components into three sections: form (phonology, morphology, and syntax), content (semantics), and use (pragmatics).

PHONOLOGY

Phonology is the study of speech sounds of a language. Phonemes are the smallest units of specific speech sounds that form words. Alone they have no meaning but in combination they contribute to how meaning can be changed. A *b* in isolation has no meaning, but if *hat* is changed to *bat,* the *b* is significant. In English we have approximately 45 phonemes, mostly vowels and consonants. In reading, the phonemes are matched to written graphemes. Phonics is the method of teaching reading where letter-sound correspondence is taught to students.

Phonology describes how individuals gain comprehension of the production of speech sounds. Some feel that older language impaired students have the same phonological processes as the grammars of younger normal children. Therefore, there is a delay in their phonological acquisition and their brain maturation (Tallal, 1988). Others feel that there is a chronic deviance in brain function (Rapin & Allen, 1988).

Problems commonly associated with phonology production are auditory discrimination and speech articulation problems that happen when the student cannot produce the phonemes appropriately. Phonemic segmentation problems occur during sound blending in reading.

MORPHOLOGY
Morphology is the study of the smallest meaningful units of speech in a language. Morphemes can stand alone, such as the root word *dog*. Morphemes can also be smaller combinations of sounds that contribute meaning to words and are often attached to change the meaning (e.g., *dogs*). These allomorphs consist of affixes such as prefixes *(un, re)*, suffixes *(tion)*, verb tense forms *(ed, ing)*, plurals *(s)*, shifts from adjective to adverbs *(ly)*, and so on.

To test language impaired children on the use of morphemes, check their understanding of the meaning of words with morphemes (reception) and their correct usage of vocabulary (expression).

SYNTAX
Syntax involves how words are arranged in a given order to make meaningful, grammatical phrases and sentences. In grammar we string together categories of words (e.g., nouns, adverbs, conjunctions) to denote the meaning we intended to impart. Language impaired students produce strings of words or ill-formed sentences that lack syntactic structure.

SEMANTICS
Semantics refers to the ability to get meaning from words and sentences. To understand the abstract basis or deep structure of language, students need to know multiple definitions of words, synonyms, antonyms, the relationship among ideas, figurative language, classifications, and associations.

PRAGMATICS
Although pragmatics may not be considered a system of grammar, it does involve the use of language in social situations. Language impaired students may have difficulty in conversation with agemates and adults. They often have difficulty with the following aspects of verbal behavior:

1. Asking questions in conversation
2. Smiling and using appropriate eye contact while talking
3. Fully and accurately communicating information
4. Negotiating
5. Making requests and asking for clarification
6. Remaining on topic
7. Regulating conversation to give feedback and/or listen

This superficial understanding of how to use different types of language depending on the listener can lead to misunderstanding and social rejection.

The previous pages of information illustrate the fact that learning impairment can be a complex phenomenon with many and varied reasons why students at risk have difficulties at home and in school. Educators are continually seeking new information that will lead to a greater understanding of the variability that is seen among learners.

Definitions and causations of learning disabilities and related disorders are discussed next in Chapter 2, with an analysis of currently accepted learning theories.

Chapter 2

Theoretical Foundations

OVERVIEW

This chapter provides an overview of theories of learning that are being applied in most school systems today. The discussions elaborate upon each of these theories and suggest how they can be used as a basis for educational programming.

Learning theories are important because they provide a means of explaining and understanding student performance. They help us understand how students learn and why they behave as they do. Theoretical foundations form the basis for making decisions about how to teach and how to conduct an effective learning environment. Otherwise we are controlled entirely by trial and error. Theories give us a trail to follow that has been previously traveled by others with stories of success. This is motivating and energizing to educators who also want to experience the good feelings that go along with having successful experiences with students.

Theories have to make sense, be logical, offer a rationale, and be continually tested. No one theory can as yet be applied to all learners, therefore, we use the concepts of different theories as required by different situations. The two main theoretical approaches to learning are behavioral and cognitive. Within these main areas there exists a variety of subtheories that are explained in detail.

Behavioral theory and one particular form of it, operant learning, is discussed first because it can be applied to learners exhibiting learning disorders as well as those who do not. The concepts inherent in behavior modification are envisioned as just plain good classroom management. The cognitive-developmental theories that follow tend to focus mainly on their application to problems in learning.

The educator will identify aspects of the various theories and how they relate to previous experiences he or she has had both inside and outside of the classroom. Many aspects of the theories discussed will be incorporated into the reader's knowledge base and create a greater understanding of how to apply various techniques to teaching students. Other areas in the book will also reflect the main concepts espoused in these theories. The outcome or goal in theory application is to assimilate the bits and pieces learned into a framework that instills confidence in approaching problems and in seeking solutions.

INTRODUCTION

Processes and mechanisms that comprise children's learning have become a prime focus for different groups of professionals, all of whom approach the subject with a preconceived conceptual model and methodology depending on their training and orientation.

Behaviorists tend to emphasize observable behaviors and how the environment influences behavior. Behavioral approaches to social-emotional maladjustment, such as operant learning and behavior modification, focus on observable behavior. The mode of treatment is to use a combination of techniques that will decrease the frequency of undesirable behavior(s) and strengthen desirable behavior(s). Student problems are defined in terms of appropriate behavior, target behavior, or treatment goals rather than by labels or constructs.

With respect to teaching students with learning problems, there is a trend toward more cognitive-type interventions, both in treatment and in classroom situations (Kendall & Hollon, 1979). Cognitive behavior modification (CBM) has been successfully employed in teaching academic skills to students exhibiting learning difficulties (Meichenbaum & Goodman, 1971). Basically, the principles involve teaching learners how to think and that observable behavior can be changed. Verbal mediation is used as a primary tool within the context of self-mediated cognitive strategies; that is, students are taught to monitor their own behavior through verbal feedback.

Professionals who account for behavior in terms of processes that are internal to the individual are generally cognitive theorists. The basis of behavior is therefore explained as a function of internal structures. The act of knowing is called *cognition,* and how information is processed is deemed important. Also of concern is how information is transferred (at both the conscious and the automatic levels) and how information is stored (memory). How a person selects and uses information as well as the strategies used in making decisions are of more concern than the anatomy and chemistry of information storage and retrieval.

Educators favoring cognitively oriented approaches to diagnosis, for example, will investigate problem areas associated with how the student processes information, makes decisions, and attends to tasks.

Both cognitively and behaviorally oriented educators have common areas of concern about the individual and the environment. The main difference between the two approaches is on areas of emphasis and on procedures used to assess and monitor behavior. Teachers need to extrapolate selectively from all theories the ideas and techniques that work for them to be effective with classroom instruction and to control behavior.

OPERANT LEARNING THEORY

Behavior modification, as an applied behavior learning concept, is based on operant conditioning or operant learning theory. Operant theorists believe that if inappropriate behavior is learned then appropriate behavior can also be learned. The basic, underlying principle of reinforcing desirable behavior and reducing or extinguishing undesirable behavior is also fundamental to this theory.

Skinner (1938) proposed a theory in which behavioral principles are descriptions of the relationship between an individual's behavior (response–r) and events from the environment that impinge upon that individual (stimulus–s). The theory proposes that environmental stimuli exert control over our responses and such factors as mood, feelings, or mind are mainly irrelevant unless there is some way to measure them. We differentiate stimuli according to their function, with respect to how they exert control, and the way in which they precede a response.

Some stimuli act as cues and limit certain behaviors. These cues are called discriminative stimuli. They tell us that if we respond in a certain way to them, reinforcement will likely follow:

> A reinforcer is any event that increases the strength of the behavior it follows. The only way to determine whether or not a given consequence is a reinforcer is to observe its effects on the behavior it follows. . . . Reinforcement must immediately follow the desired behavior in order to have maximum effect. (Hall, 1975, p. 2).

Operant or stimulus response theory proposes that we must focus our attention on how individuals respond to stimuli that follow responses (i.e., The teacher gives homework—John doesn't complete the homework— What does the teacher do?)

Emphasis is placed on strengthening or increasing behaviors that are desirable, and weakening or reducing behaviors that are undesirable. Consequences of acts and their effects on behavior are what is important. Desired learner outcomes are modified to a great extent based on the following:

1. Stimuli that are reinforcing
2. Stimuli that are punishing
3. Stimuli that neither punish nor reinforce

Punishment refers to the procedure of following a behavior by a consequence which decreases its future strength or probability. Thus, any event which decreases the strength of a behavior that it follows is called a punisher. (Hall, 1975, p. 2)

It is important to understand how to manipulate stimuli and how to shape behavior through the differential reinforcement of successive approximations to specific target behaviors (Becker, Engelmann, & Thomas, 1975). Teachers who want to be more exact in their response to students' needs integrate operant theory with task analysis. They can plan for the presentation of situational cues in order to elicit the responses necessary for learning to take place. Appropriate consequences for each learner must be identified, as all students do not respond to the same stimuli. The effects of consequences can take several forms according to MacMillan:

1. Strengthen the response it follows, because it is a pleasant or desired stimulus; this stimulus is said to be a positive reinforcer.
2. Lead to the termination of a noxious stimulus, and hence serve to strengthen the response it follows; this stimulus is said to be a negative reinforcer.
3. Lead to the presentation of a noxious stimulus, which serves to weaken the response it follows; this stimulus is a form of punishment.
4. Lead to the withdrawal of a desired stimulus, which serves to weaken the response it follows, this stimulus is another form of punishment. (1982, p. 394)

In general, we are concerned with antecedent stimuli, responses that follow, and the consequences that follow the responses. Contingencies that interrelate these three factors are the conditions under which consequences are presented. Contingencies such as what stimuli will be presented, which are the desirable outcomes, and when and what type of rewards or consequences will be given are planned and con-

trolled by the teacher. Both antecedent stimuli and consequences can be manipulated to modify behavior. Elements that precede and elements that follow a specific response are both important and need to be considered in terms of modifying behavior.

Extinction is the process of removing or withdrawing reinforcement until behavior returns to a lower level; in other words, if reinforcement is withdrawn, behavior will decrease in rate. Students who raise their hands all of the time will soon stop if the teacher ignores them.

Implications for Teaching

In setting up a classroom, minimum standards of behavior need to be established and ways to achieve closer approximations to goals should be identified along with a variety of appropriate reinforcers. Instructors need to identify students' likes in terms of activities. Even small improvements need to be rewarded. A continuous and immediate reward system should be established so students will associate the appropriate required behavior with the specific reinforcer.

It is also important to do the following:

1. Identify and define the target behavior(s).
2. Obtain a baseline of data regarding the behavior(s) observed.
3. Observe and note what is maintaining the behavior(s).
4. Remove or change the reinforcing consequences.
5. Record the behavior over a period of time.
6. Determine if the behavior increases or decreases according to expectation.

There are many behaviors that teachers want students to exhibit in academic as well as in social relationships. There are also various behaviors that students bring to school that interfere with learning and their relationships with teachers and peers.

Further elaboration of operant learning theory is discussed in Chapter 4.

COGNITIVE LEARNING THEORIES

Cognition has been defined as "the combined act of perceiving, attending, thinking, remembering, and knowing" (Hresko & Reid, 1988). An individual processes information from the environment mainly in a selective fashion. This input of stimuli is processed based on previous learning. The extent of meaningfulness and relevance that is extrapolated is based on the unique integrity of the nervous system and the organizational abilites of the individual.

A main goal in employing cognitive theories is to identify maladaptive cognitions of students and determine causes as well as precipitating factors that sustain their cognitive processes. Cognitive learning theory, in general, advocates that along with achievement, cognitive processes need to be assessed and deficits determined before appropriate intervention can be instituted.

There are several cognitive learning theories of importance, all of which have common elements as well as some unique characteristics in terms of how students learn and how to address individual needs. These theories include cognitive behavior modification (CBM), information processing, theories related to memory, schema theory, and social cognitive theory.

COGNITIVE BEHAVIOR MODIFICATION (CBM)

The main premise behind cognitive behavior modification (CBM) is that learning disabled students, regardless of etiology, can behave appropriately if given proper instruction (Torgesen & Wong, 1986). CBM is a cognitive behavioral approach that can be applied to instruction and to social interaction. It emphasizes self-instruction, self-monitoring, and self-evaluation techniques.

Meichenbaum (1980), as a proponent of CBM, places great emphasis on verbal development and verbal interaction and how verbal behavior influences cognitive development. He further suggests that the social and academic attributes of learning disabled students can be enhanced through an environment in which:

1. Adults model behavior (a task).
2. Students perform the same task under adult direction.
3. Students perform the same task with overt self-instruction (verbalization).
4. Students perform the same task with faded overt self-instruction (whispering).
5. Students perform the same task using nonverbal or covert self-instruction.

Some of the principles of CBM originate from Soviet research and the theory of the "zone of proximal development" proposed by Lev Semenovich Vygotsky, a Soviet linguist and psychologist (Belmont & Freeseman, 1988). This theory examines the discrepancy between what a learner is capable of doing and his or her actual level of development. Much of the findings of research regarding children's deliberate learning strategies are based on the premises and key ideas of zone theory.

THEORY OF ZONE OF PROXIMAL DEVELOPMENT
Vygotsky suggested that thinking, as an activity, is developed and maintained by interpersonal experience. An important element of this process is the social influence of the teacher. The responsibility of the instructor is to facilitate the passing on of learning or thinking skills to students. This process of "transfer of responsibility" for learning is tantamount to reaching a goal for the student (Rogoff & Gardner, 1984).

Vygotsky stated that human learning occurs with a transfer of responsibility from the teacher to the learner. This process involves, first, the analysis of the task; second, the breakdown of the child's behavior when approaching the task; and finally, the sequencing of hints, cues, explanations, and demonstrations appropriate to the learner's aptitude and understanding. Effective teaching is recognized or determined by both the procedures used in the process and the effects gained through interpersonal relationships. Vygotsky postulated that the arena of activity that surrounds this transfer is the "zone of proximal development" (ZPD). The lowest level or strata of problem solving is when the child works by himself or herself, and the upper limit or strata where additional responsibility for learning is required is where the child elects to accept assistance from another individual (e.g., the teacher, instructor, or parent).

A learner who does not remember to use a strategy without a reminder is said to be at the upper limits of his or her zone. The learner who maintains the strategy, but who cannot generalize it to other situations, is said to be at mid-zone. Those who can both maintain and generalize a strategy are said to be at the low end of the zone (requiring little or no assistance) and may be in a position to use the strategy spontaneously in appropriate situations (Saxe, Guberman & Gearhart, 1987; Palincsar & Brown, 1984).

It has been suggested that learning disabled students have "zone widths" at least as large as normal learners and wider than mentally retarded learners (Day, 1983). Learning disabled students, however, need more prompts to learn the criterion rule than do normal learners, but they are equally proficient on near-transfer tasks (Day & Hall, 1987). The problem for learning disabled students seems to be in the area of metacognitive deficits with concomitant lack of strategy behavior. Learning disabled children also appear to have problems with responding appropriately and with motivation.

The concept of "zone" resembles the concept of "readiness" to many educators. It also appears like behavior shaping in operant theory. Zone of proximal development is different from readiness in that it is designed to determine in a practical manner where instruction can be initiated and enhanced with the support of the teacher. The teacher begins teaching toward the upper limits of the ZPD by working closely with the student and directing the entire process by guiding the learner, giving appropriate practice, cues, and demonstrations. Gradually, the teacher reduces the support until the student has incorporated, stabilized, and internalized the skill. The student's new level of performance then becomes the foundation or basis for a new, higher-level content or skill.

DYNAMIC ASSESSMENT

The zone of proximal development (ZPD) is actually a measure of learning potential, the parameters of which are set by the lower limits of independent work and the higher limits of different levels of assistance. Dynamic assessment is a key concept in zone theory. Dynamic assessment is intended for use with individuals for whom psychometrically based standarized tests miss important qualitative and diagnostic dimensions. This includes more refined discrimination between "retarded" and "disadvantaged" performance, findings on the modifiability of the learner, and procedures and hypotheses for remediation.

Many educators have asked what would happen, for example, if the tester assisted the learner during the administration of an IQ test, helping him or her to think about different ways to complete the required tasks. Results of this kind of administration might be quite different from the static manner in which these tests are presently administered. ZPD assessment is different from standard IQ assessment and from traditional psychometric assessment in general. An examiner must be very skilled with the materials and procedures of static tests, but must also be familiar with diagnostic teaching with its inherent flexibility.

In using Vygotskian logic, a major objective is to find out how far a learner can go without assistance, such as how to use a concept, a skill, or a way of thinking in attempting to achieve a specific goal. Then the instructor should ascertain how the learner can achieve with assistance. The upper limits are important to help us determine the appropriateness of the materials, content, or the goals that were set.

An assistance approach or collaboration between teacher and learner involves giving the student cues and hints, and demonstrating or modeling how a task can be accomplished. The more the learner gets in-volved verbally with the teacher in the process, the higher the ZPD is said to be.

Reuven Feuerstein (1980) is another proponent of dynamic assessment. He has a program that is very much like the Vygotskian approach to activating student learning potential. His approach is based on the ideas established in the zone of proximal development (Kamphus & Reynold, 1987). Feuerstein advocates a process where the student and instructor are both actively involved, as in his Feuerstein Instrumental Enrichment (FIE) program that facilitates cognitive mobility. Feuerstein's Learning Potential Assessment Device (LPAD) is an example of a dynamic assessment system.

Dynamic assessment generally follows a test-intervene-retest (in Feuerstein's case, intervene-mediate) model. The tests/retests used, with the interventions interceding between these, vary considerably with different clinicians/researchers.

The LPAD represents a dramatic departure from the traditional norm-referenced testing. Elements of the test relate to a process-deficit model to the extent that it attempts to identify basic learning processes. The degree of learner modifiability is emphasized, not the static abilities of the student. The examiner also functions as a teacher and the testee becomes a student in the test situation, which is a unique approach and a change from traditional testing. The approach also gives consideration to sociocultural factors and different learning styles. The LPAD is also designed to measure improvement that is an outcome of teaching. The assessment looks at the following:

1. How difficult is it to teach the student basic concepts?
2. Does the student grasp the meaning of basic tasks (pretest)?
3. Can the learner apply new learning to a progression of difficult tasks related to the new learning (generalization)?
4. How does the student learn best (concrete level, pictures, verbal explanation, etc.)?
5. Can the student utilize different learning strategies?

Feuerstein has developed instrumental enrichment procedures that could be used to complement the assessment. These procedures describe psychoeducational strategies. The learner develops problem-solving strategies useful for gathering data (input), processing data (elaboration), and reporting results (output). The idea is to effect the student's cognitive behavior, social interaction responses, and adaptive behavior through a process of instrumental enrichment (Feuerstein, 1980).

In Feuerstein's program the students are taught through lessons and verbal exchange to organize information (input), arrive at certain solutions (elaborate), and then to express a desired response either orally or in written form (output).

A simplified illustration of his process is as follows:

Input Level	Elaboration Level	Output Level
Search strategies Information gathering Precision and accuracy	Definition of problem Planning strategies Use of cues Inductive and deductive reasoning Hypothetical thinking	Reflective responses Impulse control Control of egocentric communication

IMPLICATIONS FOR TEACHING

Cognitive behavior modification, which includes elements of Zone Theory, has important applications to teaching and learning. It takes a balance of responsibility in a self-adjusting, reciprocal relationship between teacher and student to achieve success. The labor of learning is continuously negotiated to increase the learner's share of the burden of attaining a specific goal. It is important to determine goal-relevant strategies and complete the task analysis that leads to appropriate use of strategies (Saxe, Guberman, & Gearhart, 1987). What opportunities can be enlisted during the day to teach the target skill by using appropriate hints, cues, and demonstrations? The teacher must adjust the quality of his or her assistance during the problem solution period in direct response to the student's pattern of success and failure.

Attribution research gave researchers a clue as to the importance of student feelings, perceptions, and attitudes about their own performance. Current thinking (Palincsar & Brown, 1987) is that the teacher should assume a major role as expert (Berliner, 1986) at first, but then gradually shift the responsibility to the student (Vygotsky, 1978; Wertsch, 1979). It appears that learners progress from external control by adults to internal control by themselves. The process of shifting this control is both the art and science of teaching. A recurrent theme is the "quality" of interactions between the teacher and the student. It appears that a balance must be attained between the use of behavioral and metacognitive techniques in academic as well as classroom management.

The students are active participants, use overt verbalization, use a series of distinct steps, model the target behavior, and learn to plan and reflect before giving a response. One of the most important variables in the process is continuous feedback.

METACOGNITION AND LEARNING

Metacognition relates to an individual's awareness of how he or she uses systematic and efficient strategies for learning. Some students exhibiting learning problems may become more efficient learners if they are taught specific types of learning strategies. The supposition is that self-awareness of how one thinks is a developmental ability which can be improved by training in metacognitive skills or, more precisely, the use of appropriate strategies in learning. Cognitive behavior modification and metacognition have a common base, which is, to the greatest extent possible, learners should function as their own teachers.

Brown (1978) uses the phrase "knowing about knowing"; the individual's awareness of his or her own cognitive processes and the way these processes operate. It has been called a "self-communication or internal dialogue that one engages in before, during, and after the performance of a task." Brown, Campione, and Murphy (1977) state that metacognitive development refers to

the ability to stop and think before attempting a problem, to ask questions of oneself and others, to determine if one recognizes the problem, to check solutions against reality by asking not "is it right" but is it reasonable, to monitor attempts to learn to see if they are working or worth the effort. (p. 3)

Garofalo and Lester (1985) discuss two separate but related aspects of metacognition: (1) knowledge and beliefs about cognitive phenomena, and (2) control and regulation of cognitive actions. They use Flavell's (1976) definition:

"Metacognition" refers to one's knowledge concerning one's own cognitive processes and products or anything related to them, e.g., the learning-relevant properties of information or data. . . . Metacognition refers, among other things, to the active monitoring and consequent regulation and orchestration of these processes in relation to the cognitive objects on which they bear, usually in the service of some concrete goal or objective. (p. 232)

They distingush cognition from metacognition by stating that cognition is involved in doing and metacognition is involved in choosing and planning what to do and monitoring what is being done.

Metacognition involves many correlates, including areas of personality development such as achievement needs, failure avoidance, locus of control, level of aspiration, and learned helplessness. Brown attributes importance to the role of metacognition in role-taking, social-cognition, and the overall processes of communication.

Metacognition and Learning Disabled Students
Problems with metacognition have been inferred to be the reason why some students cannot apply known skills to new situations (Borkowsi & Cavanaugh, 1979; Schneider, 1986). Poor readers, impulsive learners, and learning disabled students have been found to have similar metacognitive deficits (Douglas, 1983). Some learning disabled students perform poorly in academic tasks because they lack an ability or an inclination to spontaneously employ efficient and organized strategies (Torgesen, 1977). Metacognition, as stated earlier, can be defined as an individual's awareness of his or her systematic use of efficient strategies for learning. It is felt that learning disabled students can learn to use efficient strategies. The underlying concept is that an individual's self-awareness of how he or she thinks is a developmental ability which can be improved by training in meta-cognitive skills. This will aid the student in using appropriate strategies for learning specific tasks.

Many teachers have reported their observations concerning the poor study habits and disorganized work of their learning disabled students. Hallahan and associates, in their research on selective attention (1983), support the hypothesis that learning disabled students exhibit deficiencies in their use of task-appropriate strategies. Their research has indicated that learning disabled students are not as quick to develop efficient response or encoding strategies such as labeling and verbal rehearsal. Hallahan, Kauffman, and Ball (1973) have shown that selective attention and performance could be significantly improved after students are instructed to use a verbal rehearsal strategy on a serial recall task.

Students' beliefs about their abilities can affect school achievement or performance in general. They need to feel their difficulties can be overcome so they will believe they can succeed. Students who feel they cannot control their difficulties (improve) tend to display maladaptive behavior such as poor problem solving strategies and poor affective reactions to achievement situations. Teaching children that their failures are due to lack of effort on their part seems to increase persistence and improve performance when presented with difficulties.

Metacognitive Activities
The results of the various studies in the area of metacognition suggest the following applications. The student should:

.1 Clairfy verbally the purpose of doing an assigned task, including the demands of the task that are explicit as well as implicit.
2. Identify verbally the important aspects of an assignment, whether it be a paragraph to be read or written or a verbal statement summarizing an occurrence or event.
3. Focus his or her attention on the relevant and cogent and concentrate on what is important and not trivial. Verbal feedback or rehearsing is important here.
4. Monitor his or her own reading for comprehension by "chunking"' for example, dividing reading assignments into smaller segments. Visual clues such as pencil marks can be made to separate the segments.
5. Review orally and self-question (self-interrogation) material to be learned.
6. Practice recovering from distractors or disruptive influences.
7. Practice techniques for efficient thinking (Brown, 1978; Flavell, 1978) across subjects and in different settings, such as:
    Problem identification
        . . . What is the problem?
        . . . How difficult is the problem?
        . . . Is it a problem I can solve?
    Predicting outcomes
        . . . What/who will be affected by the outcomes?
        . . . What will happen if I use this strategy?
    Checking/Verifying
        . . . Is the information valid?
        . . . How can I check what is stated or what I have done?
    Monitoring activities
        . . . How successful is the strategy?
        . . . Where did it break down?
        . . . What alternatives do I have?
        . . . Checking outcomes against different criteria.
8. Practice finding his or her own errors (self-correction).
9. Brainstorm about the best way to do something. Methods to achieve the above include:

VISUAL IMAGERY. Students need to mentally imagine in their "mind's eye" what the material they are studying is saying. They can close their eyes and try to visualize what is happening.

SELF-INTERROGATION. The student is trained to think didactically; questioning assumptions through self-interrogation (self-questioning).

SELF-INSTRUCTION. Using verbal mediators such as "talking to oneself" or "thinking out loud," the student learns to comprehend the task, produce mediators, and use the mediators to arrive at solutions. The primary outcome is reflective thinking and the reduction or inhibition of impulsive responses.

Examples of a self-instructional strategy (Meichenbaum, 1977):

1. What is the task, or what do I have to do?

Example:
I have to remember the names of all the players.

2. Respond to the question and develop a rehearsal strategy.

Example:
If I remember the first letter in each name it might help.

3. Next, I have to figure out the best way to remember this mnemonic or rehearsal strategy.

Example:
"First there is P for Peters, then J for Johns, that's PJ. Keep going. R for Rush, K for Kant, that's easy. PJ and RK, PJRK, Peters, Johns, Rush, and Kant. That was easy."

4. Self-reinforcement is the last step.

Example:
"I got it right! I'm doing great!"
or
"I got it wrong, where did I have trouble?"

The important thing to remember is that self-instruction

1. Helps the student problem solve
2. Provides feedback about the rehearsal strategy
3. Involves imitation or modeling
4. Helps the student guide his or her own behavior through oral or silent verbal feedback
5. Helps each student develop his or her own style and individual language used in the process

The metacognitive process of self-instruction operates in a multitude of tasks and in various settings.

MODELING. The student learns by watching others do it correctly. Modeling tends to decrease impulsive behavior and promotes reflective thinking. The student can even learn how to model thinking behavior.

Classroom Activities

Metacognitive training can be beneficial for many students, especially those with learning disabilities. A variety of metacognitive techniques are available for addressing academic and social problems. These techniques can be woven into teaching activities.

1. Present students with a variety of tasks and ask them to "plan to produce a plan."
2. Ask students the details of how they will go about doing an assignment.
3. Emphasize the process rather than the product of an assignment. The answer in arithmetic may not be as important as how the student arrived at the solution.
4. Develop alternative solutions to solving problems with students.
5. Provide means-end and cause-effect situations for discussion.
6. Differentiate among facts, ideas, choices, solutions, and information.
7. Go through different types of decision making processes.
8. Use modeling procedures.
9. Use behavioral rehearsal and role-playing techniques.
10. Encourage reflective thinking before responses as opposed to impulsive reactions.
11. Train in the skills that are related to the ultimate goal and use academically relevant material.
12. Teach the students how to estimate or predict task difficulty.
13. Encourage self-interrogation, self-test, or monitoring strategies for learning or retaining information.
14. Help the student learn to adjust the strategy to what the task requires.
15. Teach the students how to use explicit as well as implicit information (what is there and what is not there).
16. Practice the use of feedback—what will happen if?

A highly trained teacher is one who monitors and mediates the whole process. The teacher is the key to the kinds of interactions that occur and needs to be aware of the cognitive deficiencies in students, which could include (Messerer, Hunt, Meyers, & Lerner, 1984):

1. Lack of precision
2. Poor organization strategies
3. Difficulty in perceiving and extracting relevant information
4. Difficulty forming hypotheses (what if?)
5. Imprecise language

6. Trouble coordinating perception with memory
7. Discrimination difficulties
8. Lack of strategies to check correctiveness of a solution

Students need activities that will help with:

1. Concentration (relaxation, reduced stimuli, biofeedback)
2. Organization of thinking (extraction, priority, strategies)
3. Systemization (sequencing, reasoning, application to problem solving)
4. Reflective thinking (impulse control)

Generalization of Skills
Teach skills that can be generalized; or, more precisely, teach generalized thinking skills that can be applied to a variety of situations. Students need to know how to think as well as what to think.

Teachers must do the following:

1. Help the student understand the task to be learned.
2. Demonstrate or tutor the student in the processes or strategies required to master the task.
3. Present a similar task to see if the student can transfer the strategy to new situations.
4. Note where the student fails if the transfer does not occur.
5. Interpret why and how the failure occurred to the learner.
6. Continue to practice the strategy with the student until transfer occurs.
7. Try a different strategy or reexamine the efficiency of the learning cues if transfer does not occur.
8. Identify other strategies and demonstrate how they are used in different situations.
9. Train the student in the use of several strategies and practice these in a variety of situations.
10. Let the student analyze the task and generate his or her own strategy through self-instructional procedures.
11. Learn the student's skill repertoire and build on it. Reward the student for good work. (How many ways does a particular student respond to different situations; e.g., what does he or she do when presented with _____ ?)

The main concept in applying any theory to the classroom is to discern how it can be used to help learners realize their learning potential.

METAMEMORY
A good deal of research in metacognitive development has been conducted on metamemory (Miller & Bigi, 1976). Metamemory has been defined by Flavell and Wellman (1976) as an individual's knowledge of anything germane to information storage and retrieval. This includes an individual's knowledge about memory tasks and memory strategies. For example, young children (ages 5–6) know that the more items you have to remember the harder it is to learn. Children can learn memory techniques that will help them remember more things over a longer period of time. An individual's ability to remember is particularly determined by his or her knowledge of what strategy or thought processes can be used in particular situations that will be useful in retaining the desired information. The student develops a sense of:

1. Knowing which situation requires the use of memory
2. Knowing when and how to prepare for a memory task
3. Knowing precisely when to retrieve information
4. Knowing how to scan material before deciding on answers
5. Knowing how to plan to use a plan

In the area of metamemory, researchers found that metamemory correlated with strategic behaviors on tests of strategy transfer.

Metamemory and metacognitive theory have important applications in formal instructional settings. The problem is that many students tend to exhibit failure in the area of strategy generalization, especially younger children who are taught new strategies. The use of strategies in nonlearning disabled students has been found to be voluntary, effortless, and automatic. Memory strategies are skills that can be taught and students can practice them out loud. They can provide the teacher with some idea of how learning is progressing. Seeing strategies used and charting the progress made can be satisfying to both the teacher and the learner.

METAREADING
Metareading research has been carried out in three main areas: the student's awareness of the features and function of reading, his or her ability to monitor comprehension, and how to apply strategies appropriately (Brown, 1981).

Poor readers were found to exhibit:

1. Less awareness of the communicative/informative function of reading
2. An overemphasis on decoding
3. Less use of appropriate strategies for processing

4 Less awareness of their own comprehension level (Short & Ryan, 1984)

Trainable task-appropriate strategies that can be applied to the monitoring of comprehension can be accomplished by summarizing, self-directed questioning, clarifying, and predicting. There is evidence, for example, that poor readers are deficient in the use of these strategies and they could become useful skills to these learners if taught within the context of reciprocal teaching. This is an example of a socioinstructional approach (Palincsar & Brown, 1984).

Critical questions to be answered include:

1. Has the student improved on the training task?
2. Has the student improved in the use of trained strategies?
3. Can the student work independently with assigned materials?
4. Is the training effect being generalized to new situations across settings in academic subjects?
5. Is the training strategy being generalized to new and different tasks in academic subjects?

The research on metacognitive learning gives us some insight into the problem and a rationale for inferring that dysfunctional learning styles may result from a lack of understanding of the interrelation between the required task, the strategies used to complete the task, and the outcome or observed behavior.

Learning-Strategies Instruction

Strategy research has been shown to have considerable application to classroom teaching and control of classroom behavior (Belmont & Freeseman, 1988). It also has relevance to socioinstuctional approaches to classroom organization (Scarr, 1979).

Recently, methods of observing, manipulating, and directly teaching the use of deliberate learning strategies to children has received a great deal of attention. Flavell (1979) used the term "cognitive enterprise" to describe how learners use self-aware, goal-oriented strategies for problem solving, planning, and approaching new learning. Rather than being passive learners, Flavell illustrates how most children use their child-centered, internal cognitive experiences to respond boldly to new knowledge in individualized ways.

Much of the current research focuses on strategy instruction as it pertains to social development, especially to the fostering of student learning. The act of

learning in learners has been described as a goal-directed strategic activity that operates and develops within a complex social system (Bronfenbrenner, 1979; Gelman, 1979).

Early studies indicated that students who spontaneously engage in active memorization exhibit better recall on memory tests than their agemates who do not "actively" participate in memory tasks. Also, younger children tend to approach the task by verbalizing out loud or using speech, whereas older students tend to "think it out" in their heads (Flavell, Beach, & Chinsky, 1966).

Young children who do not spontaneously engage in memory activity can be taught to use an appropriate strategy such as associative imagery or rehearsal. Learners who are taught strategies and use them appropriately exhibit higher performance levels in academic tasks than others who do not receive this instruction (Palincsar & Brown, 1984).

Older students fail in the performance of many tasks when they are told not to use their own usual techniques to remember things and to just try to learn in a passive manner much like younger children. The link between active learning strategies and improved performance has received a great deal of attention and support (Meacham, 1977). Attention and motivation enter into the learning process. Data from research suggests that learning disabled students or inferior learners do benefit from the use of strategies. Strategy instruction and the inferences made about strategy use is centered around the concept of metamemory, which is an individual's knowledge about strategies and the self-awareness and other personal qualities necessary to apply them (Forrest-Pressley, MacKinnon, & Waller, 1985).

A learning strategies approach is an intervention alternative mainly for adolescents exhibiting learning problems (Deshler & Schumaker, 1986). The focus is on how to learn rather than on the teaching of specific curriculum content. Students are taught to rely more on independent activity. They learn techniques and rules that enable them to solve problems and complete tasks with a minimum of instructional intervention from teachers. These metacognitive techniques include strategies

· For summarizing and memorizing information
· For developing good visual imagery skills
· That emphasize paraphrasing and self-questioning for reading and in the content areas
· For interpreting visual aids, enabling the student to interpret charts, tables, diagrams, and pictures.

In addition, a multipass strategy (Schumaker, Deshler, Alley, & Denton, 1982) is taught for extrapolating information from textbooks by passing over (surveying) a chapter three times to acquire critical information. Listening and note-taking strategies are good for abstracting key words and for using organizational cues to facilitate memory processes. Strategies dealing with using mnemonic devices (Robbins, 1982) and paired associates have been shown to be useful.

Strategies for written expression and the demonstration of competencies are also important. They help the student write in an integrated and cohesive fashion. Other strategies aid the student in detecting and correcting errors and in how to take tests.

Instruction in learning strategies requires an understanding of the curriculum demands that resulted in the student's failure in the first place; such as reading, writing, and note-taking. This information must be matched with a task-specific strategy. The student learns to use the strategy automatically, therefore practice and motivation are key ingredients. The student must first be assessed in terms of how he or she approaches and performs the task. Then he or she analyzes the results of the performance with the teacher. After the analysis, the student is introduced to the new strategy. First, the strategy is modeled for the student by the teacher who verbalizes the whole process aloud. The student then demonstrates the new strategy. Later, the student rehearses the strategy aloud. After practicing the new strategy in a variety of ways and settings with various degrees of difficulty, the student practices the skill to a mastery criterion. The student gets continual reinforcement and corrective feedback throughout the process.

The goal is that the student be able to generalize a strategy to all learning situations or environments. This requires practice in different settings. According to Deshler and Schumaker (1986), adolescent students (grades 7–12) "seem to benefit most if they master three to four strategies per year."

The teacher needs to determine which students can benefit from learning these strategies and the long-term effects in terms of academic success. Finally, the teacher must be able to correlate the teaching of learning strategies with good teaching practices for optimal success.

ADDITIONAL SUGGESTIONS FOR TEACHING LEARNING STRATEGIES

· Pay careful attention to the time allotted to learning tasks.
· Determine the learner's optimal time needed to learn specific tasks.
· Reduce the heavy demands that are made on reading and writing on assignments and tests.

· Use more small group instruction.
· Provide more individualized instruction.
· Focus on accommodating students in the regular classes so they will attend and get passing grades.
· Make courses interesting and relevant.
· Plan instruction that is motivating, personalized, and meaningful.
· Base grades on achievement and merit.
· Encourage a high percentage of attendance by striving for a higher rate of success in academic subjects.

The main premise of strategy learning is that students can develop executive skills that they can use to monitor their own performance. These regulatory and monitoring skills become part of their knowledge base.

A learning strategies approach has many advantages:

1. It is immediately task-relevant.
2. It offers a direct intervention such as teacher-directed drills of specific procedures needed.
3. It offers dyadic instruction that emphasizes the interaction between the teacher and the student. This is important when considering the learner's strengths and weaknesses with regard to the strategies that are taught. This includes strategies that are used for math problem solving in test taking or strategies where rules are not enough. The teacher-student interaction must be considered where the teacher knows the students' learning patterns.

Learning disabled students can be taught to:

1. Organize things according to common categories such as sports, work, play.
2. Rehearse category lists or components.
3. Use retrieval cues based on characteristics of items or components of a category, as for a test for example (Cooney & Swanson, 1987).

The concept of access is important to the strategy approach. It means that the information necessary to complete a task resides within the child and the student must learn how to access this information in a flexible manner. This is accomplished at the conscious level when the student describes and discusses ways to access information while simultaneously coordinating a number of mental activities. These activities are part of the executive function and they help the learner decide on the appropriate strategies to use for specific tasks.

IMPLICATIONS FOR THE CLASSROOM

The teacher becomes the model or interrogator and guides the learner's strategic thinking by setting up an appropriate sequence of activities. The learner's self-regulating controls begin to operate, and the teacher's level of participation diminishes, as in the concept of "zone theory." Basically there is a continuum where the student moves through a metacognitive phase where the instructor consciously directs, motivates, and elicits learning strategies to a more automatic and less directed form of processing information. The advantages include the following (Swanson, 1989):

1. The emphasis is placed on what can be changed.
2. Students consciously respond to direction-rule creation and rule following.
3. Environmental factors are included that affect students differently.
4. Students are actively involved in the process.
5. It lends itself to the development of materials for the instructional process.

Factors involved in a strategy program include the demonstration of the processes used to complete a given task such as writing a letter. This includes planning the letter, discussing the plan, and outlining the steps. It is important to have a complete model of a strategy that can be used to complete a task. A good strategy user should (Pressley et al., 1989):

1. Have more than one strategy to use for a given task.
2. Be able to order several strategies to complete a complicated task.
3. Use metacognitive factors to monitor performance.
4. Understand the value of the strategy in the way it is used for solving problems.
5. Have the basic knowledge with which to solve the problem.
6. Have some method of evaluating the results.

One example is rehearsal, which, as a strategy, is a controlled process and a technique that helps in maintaining information in memory. Rehearsing a mnemonic system can increase memory performance. It involves associating what is to be remembered with what is already known and can be useful in teaching the learner to improve his or her memory.

Reading strategies are also useful because they may not be associated with classroom activity. Learning how to select and use strategies can regulate the quality of the learner's performance. Students learn skills that enhance learning, and the strategies are designed to fit the personal learning style of each student. According to Paris and Oka (1989), effective strategy instruction includes:

1. Emphasis on both process and context
2. How to use a particular strategy
3. Knowing when to use strategies and seeing their usefulness
4. Including teacher-student verbalization about the use of strategies
5. Setting meaningful goals
6. Emphasizing the kind of teaching that leads to generalization

Strategy instruction should be combined with direct instruction in teaching students how to analyze tasks, how to respond to the requirements of tasks, how to monitor their personal responses, and, finally, how to develop a belief about the use of strategies (Borkowski et al., 1989).

Stated another way, unless the student understands a number of strategies, and how to control and implement them along with how to gain recognition of the importance of effort in producing a successful performance, minimal results can be expected. The key words and phrases in strategy instruction are *elaborating, skimming, imagining, paraphrasing, drawing conclusions, mnemonics, prioritizing, reviewing, accessing prior knowledge, identifying,* and *recognizing cogent features.*

Other factors in teaching strategies to consider include:

1. Do not rely on one or two "quick fix" simple strategies alone.
2. Focus on a skill area.
3. Teach a few strategies well rather than just reviewing a whole series of them rapidly.
4. Get students involved in the process and to generalize what they have learned.
5. Give students feedback.
6. Weave strategies into the curriculum.
7. Determine why a strategy was successful or not.

In terms of strategy intervention, an instructional goal should be to improve the student's executive function or monitoring skills for a smoother coordination of information processing and selection of strategies for particular tasks.

Strategies must be related to student abilities. A match must be made between learner characteristics and specific strategies (Levin, 1986). The learner's processing strength and cognitive capacity are important variables in strategy instruction. Recall appears to be related to cognitive effort (Swanson, 1984b).

Learning disabled students exhibit inferiority in how much information they can recall or retain in semantic memory, as well as how they assess it (Swanson, 1986). Also, some LD students have problems with strategy transformation, which is the inability to rely on memory retrieval processes or to solve problems or reduce information to a rule or function while visualizing relationships. Many cannot combine several strategies or replace a complex strategy with a simpler one (Swanson & Rhine, 1985).

The learner becomes the focal point, not the teacher or the materials. The student is provided with experiences or instruction in a variety of ways in which he or she can "construct meaning." This can be accomplished through reading, imitating models, or discussing issues that lead to making inferences, seeing relationships, drawing conclusions, and using one's imagination.

An important goal for teachers is to help learning disabled students to become better processors of information. The teacher needs to understand that good academic performance requires that the student interpret by using several kinds of mental abilities and that learning disabled students could have problems in any combination of these abilities.

It is also important to understand that "positive effort-related attributions and their concomitant motivational properties increase the likelihood of successful strategy-based performance, given prerequisite specific strategy knowledge." (Groteluschen, Borkowski, & Hale, 1990, p. 98).

It appears that as learners succeed, they reinforce more positive beliefs about their own capabilities and experience improvements in their executive processes. This entire process, it is suggested, leads to an overall improvement in strategy skills acquisition.

INFORMATION PROCESSING THEORY

Information processing theory is a combination of information theory and computer technology (Loftus & Loftus, 1976). The information processing approach to learning is viewed as the study of how sensory input is transformed, reduced, elaborated, stored, retrieved, and used (Newell, 1980; Neisser, 1976). Three components are identified:

1. A structural component like a computer that defines and delineates how information can be processed (e.g., sensory storage, short-term memory, long-term memory)
2. A control or strategy component like the software of a computer system
3. An executive process that oversees and monitors learner behavior (strategies)

The essence of this theory is to understand how learners select, extract, maintain, and utilize informa-

tion available from the environment (Hresko & Reid, 1988). The main premise is that individuals involved in learning bring to tasks that which is required for successful processing. Learning requires the integration of processes called sensation, perception, attention, and memory. These processes are controlled by a higher-order mental process called the "executive function" (Anderson, 1975) or "central control function" (Blumenthal, 1977). Executive processes such as planning, monitoring, and evaluating operate when individuals are required to match a particular strategy with a given task (Butterfield & Belmont, 1977). The learner is required to coordinate several kinds of cognitive abilities simultaneously.

Cognitive psychologists now better understand how learners think, use their reasoning abilities, and how learning occurs in general. Several important concepts are involved in information processing:

1. *Attention* is a prerequisite to effective information processing (Gagne, 1985). In order for attention to occur, the student must be motivated and the classroom environment conducive to learning. Things that affect attention are novelty in presentation, verbal behavior with movement and gestures, varied inflection, chalkboard writing, visual aids and other cues, as well as continuous questioning. Factors such as noise, lighting, temperature, and comfort should also be considered (Slate & Charlesworth, 1989).

2. *Active learning* is a key concept where learner involvement is considered crucial to success. Student participation can be increased by reduced talking by teachers and encouraging discussions, group interactions, and individual activities. Another good approach is to ask questions that go beyond recall of facts. All assignments should be graded, returned, and discussed with students. Students should be "cued" when watching films or videotapes to increase their attention to important concepts.

3. *Meaningfulness* of information is important so that the learner will be able to generalize the new learning or rules to new situations. Learners need to see the relationship between facts, principles, and concepts, and associate these relationships with new information. This is accomplished by showing students how to relate new information to information already learned. Use of outlines, charts, diagrams, and demonstrations is beneficial. Students can also paraphrase information to show meaningful understanding and practical application of illustrated material.

4. *Organized information* is more easily understood than fragmented information. Information stored in long-term memory can more easily be retrieved if new information is organized for voluntary, active processing. New material should be presented slowly and in a clear organized fashion (Biehler & Snowman, 1986). Students should be able to see how information interrelates. It helps to use outlines and objectives so the purpose of the lesson will be understood. Students should be told what will happen and then receive a summarization after the experience. Skills involved with notetaking, mapping, and/or networking are taught to help the learner see schemas or relationships. Students have to practice organizing information.

5. *Advance organizers* are very useful in teaching organization and structure. Lists of concepts or headings are examples of advance organizers. Advance organizers can be written or oral; both provide concrete ways of fostering learning.

6. *Memory aids* can be helpful, such as using the peg word rhyme system or the key word method. In the peg word rhyme technique, students are asked to form visual associations between target words and rhyming words (e.g., *five-alive, six-fix, seven-heaven,* etc.). In the key word strategy, students are asked to associate the word to be learned with another word that is important to the student. These techniques provide a structure for organizing information. Mnemonics is another technique for linking unrelated bits of information or material and language. All of these are cues to remembering. Using visual imagery is an excellent memory aid for disabled learners (Higbee, 1977). Students should develop visual images for ideas or concepts.

7. *Overlearning* information is an important concept in teaching. It is important to review material previously presented prior to introducing new information. Overlearning can be accomplished by repetition using different approaches, and drill and redundancy in learning. Lessons should begin by asking short questions about the previous lesson. Daily and periodic review is essential, as well as the review of tests.

Information processing in the learning disabled will be affected by the student's motivational pattern, such as attribution styles and the student's previous history of success and failure in school and at home (Humphreys & Revelle, 1984).

Information processing models, in general, "adopt the idea that 'expert support' is provided by the teacher during the early stages of learning but is faded as instruction proceeds and as the student becomes successful and assumes the primary responsibility for learning" (Lenz, Bulgren, & Hudson, 1990, p. 125).

Implications for Teaching

In applying the concepts of information process theory, it is important to remember the following:

1. Students must receive feedback and be aware of progress in a manner that will result in improved learning.
2. Students need to access prior knowledge and integrate this knowledge with new learning through associative activities.
3. Instructors must have a knowledge of the communication skills of the learners as well as their present ability levels with information processing.
4. It is imperative to gain the students' attention and to provide an environment that is beckoning and receptive.
5. Learners must understand the "why" and "what" of what is being taught as well as where this information will enhance their overall knowledge base in terms of content and function.
6. Instructors are encouraged to lead the students through the process of learning, using a stepladder approach and continuous verbal interaction and support.
7. Teachers are requested to mix adult-led learning with peer modeling and assistance, moving back and forth as appropriate. The ultimate goal is to provide more opportunities for learning to occur within the social context of the peer environment.
8. Instructors must integrate the various aspects of knowledge (strategic, semantic, and procedural) throughout all aspects of content area instruction.

Teachers play a key role in setting the stage for how instruction is carried out and monitored as well as anticipating the roles of different players (i.e., the student, his or her peers, and important or significant others). Generally, the reciprocal teaching model seems to be the most appropriate instructional strategy. By guiding the student through the process of strategy acquisition and use, the learner becomes accustomed to being aware that learning is about to occur, that willingness to participate is essential, that new information is important, and that prior knowledge will be needed. The learner gets into the habit of verbally elaborating concepts, differentiating between ideas and things, formulating appropriate associations and conclusions, and separating out the important and relevant concepts to be learned. The problem-solving mode of learning becomes the pattern for orienting the students and guiding them to gain new understandings and for motivating them to proceed further in acquiring skills and in applying new knowledge to different tasks.

Automaticity

Processing that requires little mental effort is called automatic. Learners, as a group, have limited capacity in certain aspects of memory to the extent that it is difficult to do arithmetic without paper and pencil or to remember more than four or five names of people at an initial introduction. The process used to select desired information from our memory gives us a clue as to how we learn and the effects of practice. The more automatic our mental processes are, the less mental effort we need to exert. Consider learning disabled students who are dysfunctional in good information processing and the additional energy they may need to expend (compared to agemates) in solving problems where their problem-solving processes are not as automatic.

Such cognitive processes as reading and arithmetic should become automatic with practice (Mayer, 1987). Meaningful repetition seems to lead to automaticity, allowing the short-term memory function to focus on other aspects of the content to be learned. Students may also need more time on task for automatic behavior to occur.

Automaticity also represents the speed at which students can access information from long-term or short-term memory and respond accordingly or appropriately. Descriptors such as *preattentive* and *involuntary processing,* precipitated by stimulus events, are used to describe this phenomenon (Neisser, 1988).

Another characterization of automaticity involves rapid, involuntary parallel processing, as opposed to slow, sequential, and subject-controlled processing (Schneider & Shiffrin, 1977). Automaticity in every application is affected by practice and experience. Automaticity occurs when there is little if any thought given to responding to the requirements of a task.

Automatic information processing is not under the conscious direction of the learner, whereas information processing involves a controlled effort and conscious attention. Automatization appears to be mainly at the preconscious level. Due to deficits in automatic learning, students must learn to allocate attention and exert a conscious effort to attend to tasks and parts of tasks. Sternberg and Wagner (1982) have offered five possible reasons for slow automatization of learning disabled students:

1. Unable or unwilling to construct or operate on specific forms of mental representations.
2. Unable or unwilling to receive information and organize same into higher-order units to be used for storage or greater amounts of information
3. Distaste for certain tasks (e.g., reading, mathematics)
4. Poor motivation
5. Neuropsychological deficits

An assessment of the learning disabled student's performance should include both experiential (automatized behavior) as well as contextual (adaptive behavior) measurements.

Executive Function

The executive function phase of learning tells how the processing of information begins or how the learner uses a strategy to select appropriate strategies for learning a task. Students must select and reject the best from among several appropriate strategies and also select and reject strategies based on their suitability for specific tasks. Several steps are involved:

1. Prioritization of strategies is the first step. This is based on the prescribed task and the student's preference.
2. Next is to make the kinds of decisions that have to be made at specific points in implementing a strategy.
3. A third level executive function involves decisions related to any unsolved processing stage.

Executive function is viewed by some as one variable among an interactive set of constructs that includes skills, knowledge, and motivation (Kurtz & Borkowski, 1985). Students may have problems with executive function in one domain (reading, for example) and not have difficulties in another domain (such as math or science).

Metacomponents are defined as "higher order executive processes that are used to plan, monitor and evaluate one's task performance" (Kolligian & Sternberg, 1987). The following are metacomponents of the executive function listed by Kolligian and Sternberg:

1. Analysis of the nature of the task
2. Lower order processes that are selected to accomplish the task

3. Strategies that are selected which combine the lower-order processes
4. Mental selection on which the lower processes act
5. Mental resources that are used in task performance
6. Task performance monitoring
7. Task performance evaluation

Metacomponents are described as the "central sources of individual difference in general intelligence" (Sternberg, 1980). The executive function pertains to the "how" of strategic behavior, whereas metacognition refers to the "knowing" about strategic behavior (Swanson, 1988b).

Swanson (1988b) reports a list of implications for teaching and includes probing questions that can be used to assess stages:

1. Can you tell me what your choices are?
2. What steps are you going to follow?
3. If that works, what will you do next?
4. If your overall plan fails, what alternative do you have?
5. Where would you search for the answer if your first suggestion is incorrect?
6. If your answer is correct, what else may be a correct approach or answer?
7. On the outcome of the step you mentioned, what will be carried out simultaneously (at the same time)? Next? Last?

The focus of the executive function is to detail the student's coordination, direction, and organization of search strategies and problem-solving routines.

Some researchers feel that instruction should focus on improving learning disability students' metacognitive knowledge about learning as a way of developing or strengthening executive control skills. This cannot be accomplished quickly. It may be easier for a student to learn a strategy such as taking notes, marking a paper for memory purposes, or making a decision as to which strategy to use. Executive function requires the combining of prior knowledge, which is not something that can easily be trained.

Correlates of an Information Processing System

EXPLANATION OF DESIGN OF CORRELATES OF AN INFORMATION PROCESSING SYSTEM

It is important to understand the relationships between the various aspects of learning so that educators will be better able to communicate with each other, with parents, and with students their concerns about student progress. The terminology used in the ensuing discussion and related paradigm (Figure 2–1) is designed to describe behavior and to help educators make some judgments about how this behavior is interrelated and comprises the entities that we commonly refer to as language (i.e., reading, writing, spelling, mathematics) and other subject level areas. A good understanding of the subareas is important in terms of explaining certain characteristics of learners and in looking for possible causation for unacceptable performance. No implication is inferred regarding exact cause-effect relationships; however, there is a history of many years of work in which the principles inherent in this theoretical framework were used as a basis for programming with thousands of learners.

This orientation does not preclude accepting or rejecting the plethora of research that has still left us unsure as to the exact nature of learning, how it occurs, and the relative value of the various intervention systems. The language that describes behavior still stands on its own merits as a means of communicating our concerns.

Figure 2–1 depicts the learning design and the important parameters that pertain to the learning patterns of students. It provides the teacher with a framework within which to identify strengths and weaknesses in the learning processes. After identifying these learning and behavior correlates as they pertain to particular students, the teacher can develop specific educational strategies for each learner.

VERBAL LEARNING SYSTEMS

Most of what occurs in school can be termed *verbal learning.* By this we mean speech, reading, writing, spelling, and arithmetic. We are concerned in verbal learning with the student's ability to deal with symbols at different levels.

Sensation

Sensory aspects of learning involve both verbal and nonverbal learning systems. The teacher must determine early in the school year whether the learners are able to see and hear (acuity). This can be done through tests of auditory and visual acuity or by merely lining the students up at the back of the room and asking them to respond to their names (auditory) or to symbols on the chalkboard in the teacher's everyday writing (visual). The student who cannot respond appropriately should be referred for further evaluation. Ocular motor disorders and other disorders of vision may also affect learning.

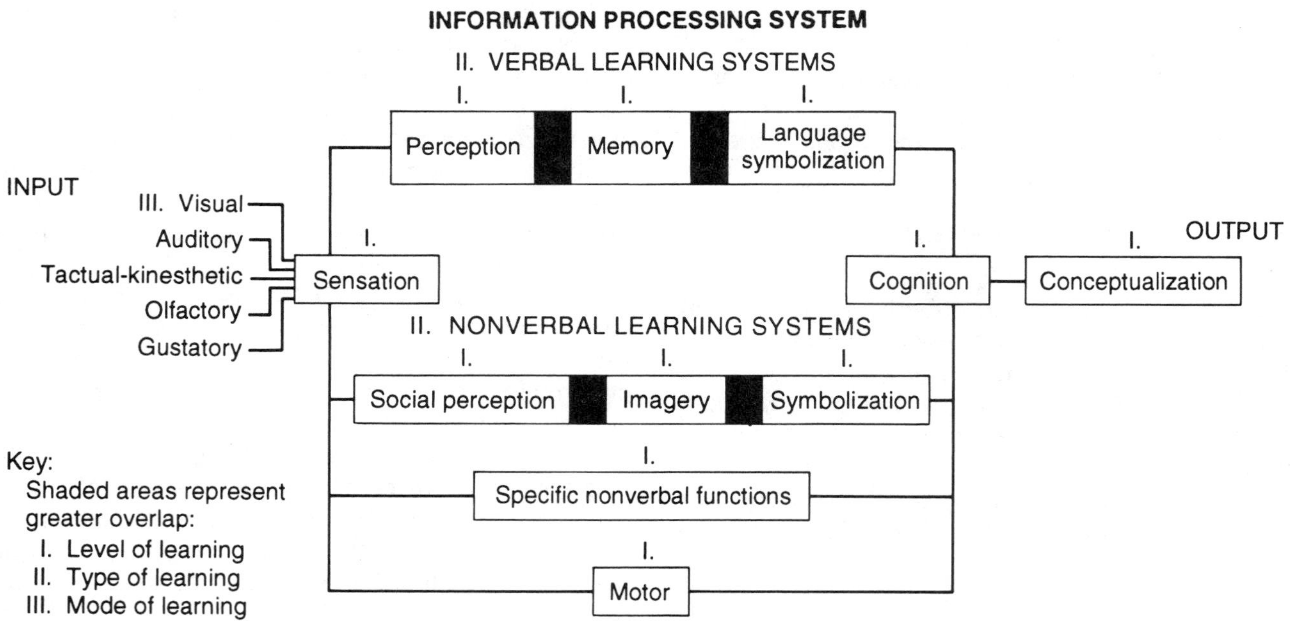

INFORMATION PROCESSING SYSTEM

II. VERBAL LEARNING SYSTEMS

I.   I.   I.

| Perception | Memory | Language symbolization |

INPUT

III. Visual
Auditory
Tactual-kinesthetic — Sensation
Olfactory
Gustatory

I. Sensation

II. NONVERBAL LEARNING SYSTEMS

I.   I.   I.

| Social perception | Imagery | Symbolization |

I.
Specific nonverbal functions

I.
Motor

I. Cognition

I. OUTPUT
Conceptualization

Key:
Shaded areas represent greater overlap:
I. Level of learning
II. Type of learning
III. Mode of learning

Figure 2–1   Design of Correlates of an Information Processing System

The tactual (touch), olfactory (smell), and gustatory (taste) modalities can also be used in teaching. The teacher should determine whether or not the students can acquire accurate information through haptic processes. This can be done by experimenting with the students' ability to identify different textures sight unseen. Students should be able to describe familiar objects just by touching them and be able to ascertain whether their textures are different or similar.

Sometimes the most obvious problem is overlooked in our attempt to seek complex reasons for learning failure. Sensation is the most primitive level of learning, and the possibility of sensory dysfunction should be considered in all cases where learners react atypically to auditory or visual stimuli.

AUDITORY ACUITY. Students with an auditory acuity problem may exhibit any or all of the following:

1. They may be restless and exhibit poor behavior, often disturbing other students in their attempt to get the information they missed.
2. They may have difficulty in following directions and ask for repetitions from the teacher and others. (Check auditory memory.)
3. They may miss a great deal if the teacher speaks while facing the chalkboard, or if they sit in the back of the room.

It is important to note that even a minor uncorrected hearing loss may be a problem if the student is seated too far away from the teacher or if the student's better ear is facing the wall. If the teacher will line up all the students at the back of the room at the beginning of the school year and call their names in his or her usual voice, the teacher will quickly identify those who cannot hear from the rear of the room. Further evaluation and referral may save a student from a great deal of frustration. Some students may have hearing aids but refuse to wear them for cosmetic reasons.

VISUAL ACUITY. There are a number of visual disabilities a teacher should be aware of in attempting to teach a problem learner.

1. The student may exhibit difficulty with near- or far-point vision.
2. Suppression of vision may occur if the "bad eye" interferes with the "good eye," causing the student to see a double image. (Check unusual head tilt in reading.)
3. Convergence difficulties may result from muscle imbalance in that the student cannot focus on a given task for a period of time.
4. Scanning or ocular pursuit problems may interfere with visual tracking and reading.
5. The following signs also need special attention: blinking; crossed eyes; unusual head tilt; tearing, redness, or inflammation of the eye; and fatigue.

Perception

In viewing perception, we are leaving the realm of the senses alone and entering into processes that involve other brain functions. The area of perception includes the following subcategories:

1. *Discrimination:* Seeing or hearing likenesses and differences in sounds and symbols.
2. *Object Recognition:* The ability to view objects, geometric shapes, letters, numerals, and words and recognize the nature of these visual stimuli with a high degree of constancy.
3. *Figure-Ground:* The ability to separate what one wishes to attend to visually or auditorily from the surrounding environment.
4. *Localization and Attention:* The ability to locate and attend to stimuli in one's environment.
5. *Closure:* The ability to recognize objects even when parts of the objects are missing, to synthesize sounds (auditory) and symbols (visual), or go from the parts to the whole. (In reading, this can be called blending.)

AUDITORY DISCRIMINATION. Students with problems in auditory discrimination may be unable to hear fine differences between letter sounds. They may be unable to differentiate the following:

1. Sounds such as *f–v, p–b, t–d.*
2. Vowels or consonants in spelling. Students may omit these in words. For example, they may spell *varnish* as *vrnsh.* (Check visual memory.)
3. Similarities in sounds within a word. For example, students may not be able to discriminate that the *and* in *hand* and *sand* are the same sounds.
4. Similar beginning or ending sounds in words, such as *man–mat* or *pant–rat.*
5. Short vowel sounds, such as the *i* in the word *bit* or the *e* in the word *bet.*
6. The second consonant in consonant clusters, such as the *l* in *fl* or the *t* in *st.*
7. The quiet consonant. Students may drop it in blends and in spelling words. For example, they may read *rust* as *rut.*

VISUAL DISCRIMINATION. The student with problems in visual discrimination may be unable to distinguish fine differences between letters such as *n* and *h* and *e* and *o*. Therefore, they fail to note details of words such as *snip* and *ship* or *red* and *rod*. Some students with this difficulty may not be able to match letters accurately. Of course, some students make visual discrimination errors because they "look too quickly"; they do not have actual visual discrimination problems.

OBJECT RECOGNITION. Students with difficulties in recognizing an object cannot efficiently integrate visual stimuli into a uniform whole. Their attention is drawn to the parts rather than to the entire configuration. This condition is known as *central blindness.*

AUDITORY FIGURE-GROUND. Students with auditory figure-ground difficulties may exhibit forced attention to noises or sounds in their environment. They may attend to irrelevant sounds and may not be able to concentrate on the task at hand or to the speech of others. It has been said that "They hear too well." For example, the student may hear the police siren or fire engines long before anyone else does. One student stated that he could not concentrate on what the teacher was saying with the other students sharpening pencils and shuffling their feet. Appropriate seating and a reduced auditory stimulus environment should be considered in setting up a program for these students.

VISUAL FIGURE-GROUND. Students who cannot distinguish an object from the general irrelevant stimuli in the background and find it difficult to hold an image while scanning the total pattern may have a visual figure-ground disability. Often teachers complain that these students appear to have difficulty completing their work. The learners may lose their place in the book easily or skip sections of a test. The students may not complete material presented on a crowded paper. Therefore, teachers should avoid using books or workbooks that have a lot on a page, with small print and very few "white spaces" in which students may write. Material that is too colorful or distracting should also be avoided.

AUDITORY LOCALIZATION AND ATTENTION. A student with problems in auditory localization and attention may have difficulty in locating the source and direction of the sound. Some teachers sometimes give instructions from behind students. In order to attend, the student with a localization problem must first locate the source of sound. Attention may be affected by excessive auditory or visual stimuli in the environment. Anxiety will also affect attention.

AUDITORY CLOSURE (BLENDING). Sometimes a student may be unable to break a word into syllables or individual sounds and blend them back into a word. An example of this type of problem with synthesis is the inability to form *cat* from *c a t.*

VISUAL CLOSURE. A student may not be able to retain a visual image of a whole word. If given the word in parts as in a puzzle, he or she may be unable to put it together again correctly. This disability becomes a problem when teachers attempt to teach blending using letters printed in the center of cards, like this:

[a] [n] instead of using letters printed at the edges of the cards, like this: [a][n]

Memory

Learners are required to remember that which they have heard, seen, or felt. It also involves retaining auditory, visual, and tactual stimuli in sequence. Memory entails both long-term and short-term processes. Other aspects of memory that are also a part of language association are auditory language symbol association and visual language symbol association. The former is the ability to relate a sound to a sound (for example, generalizing the sound of *m* in *man* to be the same as the sound of *m* in *map*), and the latter is the ability to integrate sounds to symbols (such as relating the sound *m* to the symbol *m*).

AUDITORY MEMORY. Some students may have difficulty with rhyming word sounds. They may be unable to hear one word and think of another word with the same ending. For example, given the word *mouse,* they cannot respond with a word like *house.* This difficulty may display itself in the inability to associate a letter with its sound, or auditory referent. Watching a student to see if he or she can associate the sound *m* with the symbol *m,* for instance, also may reveal an auditory language association problem. This inability may be evident in bizarre spelling patterns, such as writing letters randomly for words or writing just one word for everything (say, *cat* for each word given on a spelling test). Technically, this condition is referred to as an inability to form phoneme-grapheme relationships.

A student may have problems in drawing auditory to visual relationships. One way of testing for this disability is to see if, given the sounds *tap-tap-tap,* the student can draw the right amount of corresponding dots, . . . , or the numeral 3. In this case, it is also important to check auditory language association.

Some students may have difficulty remembering the sounds of letters given orally. They may be unable to remember the sequence of sounds in a word.

VISUAL MEMORY. Students may be able to remember the letters of a word, but not the visual sequence, so that a simple word can be misspelled, sometimes several different ways on the same paper. For example, the student may write the word *not* as *ont* or *ton* *(a variable response),* or he or she may spell it *ont* consistently *(a fixed response).* It appears easier to remediate a variable response than a fixed response whereby the student has stabilized an incorrect pattern. Even though students may know a word in one context, when it is presented in a new situation, they think they have never seen it before. Some students

exhibit reversals in reading and writing, such as confusing *b* and *d* and *was* for *saw.* Inversions such as *m* for *w* can be observed when *me* and *we* are taught together. When writing, students may either forget to punctuate or make odd punctuation marks. For example, they may write $ for ? or write ¿ for ?. Sometimes when writing, students may not remember some lower case letters and substitute capital letters in the middle of a word. In all cases of reversals, however, it is a good idea to check visual discrimination as another possible causative factor. The physiological basis for memory is discussed in Chapter 3.

There are different levels of memory to include:

1. Recall—without the referent present.
2. Recognition—with the referent present.

Imagery is important to the whole process of memory and thinking (cognitive processes). The teacher can generate images or mental pictures as a vital tool of instruction. Images are also important for problem solving in mathematics.

Language Symbolization

In the area of language, we are concerned with whether or not individuals can apply meaning to words based on their experiences. Are they just word callers? Can they express themselves meaningfully and sequentially? Does a student have a speech impediment, such as an articulation defect or a stuttering pattern?

RECEPTIVE LANGUAGE. Good receptive ability enables students to relate speech and words to meaning; they not only can hear and see words but also can understand them. Students with receptive problems may not be able to relate spoken or written words to the appropriate unit of experience. For example, a student might have difficulty in relating the word *bridge* to the concrete object. Students may be frustrated in conversation and not be able to "decode" input coming in visually and auditorily at a normal rate. The more specific problem areas under language receptivity are the following:

1. *Visual Language Classification:* Students with difficulty in this area often cannot understand difference and sameness by category classification of objects presented visually. For example, when a student is shown a picture of a car and asked whether it belongs with a picture of a pen, knife, hat, or truck, he or she cannot discern the correct classification. In this case, it is vehicles or transportation; therefore, car belongs with truck.
2. *Visual Language Association:* Students with difficulty in this area are unable to understand non-

categorical relationships between objects or pictures of objects presented to them visually. For example, when a student is shown a picture of a dog and asked whether it belongs with a picture of a bone, car, hat, or crayon, he or she cannot discern the correct association. In this case, dog is associated with bone.

3. *Visual Language Symbol Association:* Students with difficulties in this area are unable to deal with symbols used in the process of decoding that includes relating letters to words to ideas. They may be able to deal with relationships at the object and picture level, but when ideas or concepts are translated into words they have difficulty.

4. *Auditory Language Classification:* Students with problems in this area often cannot understand difference and sameness by category classification of objects presented orally. For example, when a student is asked whether a boy belongs with a lamp, dress, man, or door, he or she cannot discern the correct association of boy with man.

5. *Auditory Language Association:* Students who exhibit difficulty in this area are unable to understand noncategorical relationships between words presented orally. For example, when a student is asked whether an oar belongs with a door, sky, lamp, or boat, he or she cannot discern the correct association of oar with boat.

EXPRESSIVE LANGUAGE.   Learners should be able to use words that describe, show action, or characterize. But students with expressive disorders cannot do that. Their difficulties may be motor or verbal. In speech, their verbal expressions may be unclear, unintelligible, and nonsequential, involving a great deal of gesturing and pantomiming. Students may have difficulty retrieving words or performing the motor act of speech. In writing, the students may exhibit difficulty in expressing ideas in a logical sequence. Some students have difficulty with writing simple sentences; others cannot summarize by writing the content of material presented to them.

Motor Language Expression.   Motor language expression includes the following subcategories:

1. *Manual Language Expression:* Students with difficulty in manual expression may be unable to discern the function of an object even though, when asked, they may be able to identify it from among other objects. For example, a student may be able to identify a spoon from among other objects but be unable to show you what to do with it manually.

2. *Speech (Oral Production):* Students may exhibit poor speech patterns. They may have difficulties articulating; omit initial, medial, or final sounds; substitute (*wabbit* for *rabbit*); distort (lisp, sloppy *s*, or hissing); or add sounds to words (*sumber* for *summer*).

3. *Written expression (Visual Language Graphic Association):* Students exhibiting a disorder in this area of encoding have problems with writing words to express ideas or concepts. Some cannot write a sentence that indicates a complete thought or write a paragraph on a theme. Others cannot write definitions of words or record in a meaningful sequence an event or real-life experience.

Verbal Language Expression.   Students exhibiting a disorder in this area may be able to identify a pencil from among other objects presented visually and may be able to show you what can be done with it, but they are unable to talk about it in a meaningul way or describe its function. They may be unable to retrieve words for speaking. Verbal expression disorders also include syntax and formulation problems, which are characterized by difficulty with the smooth and natural flow of the English language. The students may be unable to structure their thoughts into grammatically correct verbal units or sentences. A contributing factor to poor syntax utilization and to poor listening skills in kindergarten children may be auditory discrimination deficiencies (e.g., discriminating among sounds). (Marquardt & Saxman, 1972.)

Inner-Language.   Inner-language is the language with which one thinks. It serves to integrate experiences with a native spoken language. Inner-language can also be thought of as *inner-speech.* Inner-speech, in this sense, relates to thinking: outer, or external, speech provides for communication between people.

Students who read well may not be able to understand the meaning of what they read. They may have difficulty transforming experiences into symbols. If English is their second language, they may think in their native tongue. Difficulty may arise in their trying to take an examination in English while thinking out the problems in Spanish, for example. Inner-language conflict may result from the unwillingness of a student to give up his or her native language or dialect for Standard English.

NONVERBAL LEARNING SYSTEMS
Social Perception (Cognitive-Social)
Some students have difficulty in gleaning meaning from gestures and expressions or from what others think are easily discernible cause-effect relationships. They are unable to understand the significance of the

behavior of others and, in some cases, appear to be emotionally disturbed or exhibit strange behavior patterns.

Imagery

Imagery in this sense refers to an ability to recall places or events that do not involve symbols, such as how something looks or sounds as part of an experience. Students with difficulty in this area may not be able to describe their visit to the circus or the way their room looks.

Symbolization

Nonverbal symbolic language refers to deriving meaning from symbols or symbolic representations other than words. Students with difficulty in this area have problems assigning meaning to such nonverbal, abstract subjects as art, religion, music, holidays, or patriotism. There is a language of art and music from which the individual cannot derive meaning. It appears that this disorder is sometimes accompanied by problems in the spatial area, such as having difficulty in understanding measurement and exhibiting a poor sense of direction.

Specific Nonverbal Functions

Nonverbal aspects of learning that have been recognized as important to verbal learning are *body image, spatial-temporal orientation, laterality,* and *directionality (left-right orientation).* Spatial readiness has been considered by many to be one of the prerequisites for many of the academic functions that are called reading, writing, and arithmetic. A good body image enables the students to relate themselves to their environment. Adequate *spatial-temporal* orientation appears to be important to arithmetical operations and in learning to tell time.

BODY IMAGE. Learners with poor body image often indicate this in their human figure drawings. They tend to draw distorted or asymmetrical figures, for example, feet coming out of the head or facial features in the wrong places. This may be due to the students' unfamiliarity with the locations of different parts of the body. The students may not be able to organize themselves physically for a task and may exhibit concomitant difficulties with spatial concepts.

SPATIAL-TEMPORAL ORIENTATION. The student with spatial-temporal difficulties may not understand such concepts as *before, after, left,* and *right* or even simple words such as *in* and *out.* Sometimes reversals of letters and numerals are evident, along with difficulties in doing arithmetical operations beyond rote memory.

Students may exhibit poor alignment of numerals and inadequate spacing in writing. Watch for the student whose number alignment is erratic on such activities as numbering for a spelling test. Students may have difficulty in understanding measurements, maps, and graphs; they may have a poor sense of direction. Learning how to tell time is often a problem for learners with spatial-temporal difficulties.

LATERALITY AND DIRECTIONALITY. Laterality, or sidedness, that is not established, may be evident in students who cannot relate themselves physically to an object in space. They may not be able to tell how far or how near something is in relation to themselves. Directionality also pertains to making spatial judgments about object-to-object relationships in space. Directionality problems are manifested by poor left-right orientation.

Motor

Teachers have become more aware recently of the importance of gross motor and fine motor efficiency for handwriting as well as for many other motor activities that are required in school. It is also apparent that the clumsy or awkward children often become socially unacceptable to their parents, their teachers, and their peers.

GROSS MOTOR. The students may exhibit poor coordination, clumsiness, and general difficulty with large-muscle activities required in sports.

1. *Balance and Coordination:* Students with balance and coordination problems have difficulty in using both sides of the body simultaneously, individually, or alternately. Poor coordination may affect self-concept, as well as inhibit participation in motor activities.
2. *Body Rhythm:* Students with body-rhythm difficulty may not be able to perform body rhythms to music or use band instruments effectively. They may have a dysrhythmic walk, which often accompanies coordination difficulties.

FINE MOTOR (EYE-HAND COORDINATION). The student may not be able to coordinate eye and hand movements to achieve a specific task. Handwriting, as well as other activities that involve fine movement (e.g., sorting, buttoning, doing puzzles, sewing), may be poor.

FINE MOTOR (FINGER STRENGTH). The student may lack the finger strength required to grasp a pencil or to hold an object. However, this may be maturational in young children.

Cognition

Cognition is the mental process or combined acts of knowing, as through awareness, perception, thought comprehension, reasoning judgment, and retention. These mental processes are controlled by higher-order central control processes known as executive functions.

Conceptualization

Conceptualization involves the formation of concepts. It explains how a student thinks and uses judgment. It is dependent on the integrity of all the previously mentioned levels of learning, such as sensation, perception, memory, and cognition. Conceptualization is the highest level of thinking and learning.

THEORIES RELATED TO MEMORY

It is now recognized that learning and memory take many forms, are controlled by different areas of the brain, and may even have different chemistries. Measurement of different brain functions has been a major step toward defining a problem or dysfunction, especially with regard to determining whether damage is diffuse or limited. Neurodiagnostic studies hold promise for providing procedures for studying brain behavior relationships.

Short-Term/Working Memory

Short-term memory or working memory is a combination of storing and processing information. New information is temporarily stored, whereas information that has been previously processed and is in long-term storage is activated and manipulated (Baddeley, 1981; Swanson, et al., 1990). Baddeley (1985) and colleagues list three systems of working memory: the central executive system, which selects and operates processes such as information organization and long-term memory retrieval; the articulatory loop, which is used for storage and verbal memory; and the visuospatial "scratch pad," which specializes in spatial memory and imagery. When the storage capacity in the peripheral systems (articulatory loop and visual-spatial scratch pad) is exceeded, some central executive capacity must be used for storage. When that happens, less processing can occur. The capacity for storage in working memory is small—approximately seven digits, for example, for the average person (Miller, 1956; Bos & Vaughn, 1988).

Swanson, Cochran, and Ewers (1990) feel that working memory processes underlie individual differences in learning ability. Their findings suggest that the memory problems of learning disabled students are related more to central processing ability instead of memory span, visuospatial abilities, or short-term recall. Individual differences in memory performance depend on how much demand is placed on the central processing system and the capacity of the peripheral systems.

It appears that rapid forgetting occurs over seconds and retention improves with the number of reinforcements (Adams & Dijkstra, 1966). This helps to explain why tracing appears to help in writing, spelling, and reading for some dyslexic children (Fernald, 1943). Metacognitive strategies such as rehearsal, visual imagery, and mnemonics also aid in retaining the material stored in working memory.

Forgetting is partially explained by interference theory (Adams, 1967). It is suggested that spontaneous trace decay is another reason for forgetting. Insofar as short-term or working memory is concerned, recognition is a far superior form of retention than recall, and can be used effectively in teaching. When initially presenting a concept, the teacher can request a recognition response first and then strive for recall responses. This is helpful in word recognition tasks and in spelling. Frostig (1966) emphasized the need for repetition and overlearning in regard to short-term memory, using many trials until the motor act can be reproduced perfectly.

The main problem for learning disabled children is to remember which graphemes are associated with which phonemes, considering that the orthography of the English language is so irregular.

Skill in grapheme-phoneme conversion is important for word recognition. As students read, they must hold the sequence of words in short-term memory, as comprehension processes integrate the words into a meaningful conceptual structure, which is then stored in long-term memory (Stanovich, 1986).

The phonetic code may be the most stable short-term memory code (Baddeley, 1966). Short-term memory may be related to reading comprehension ability in terms of how a student develops a stable phonological code (the sounds of our language). The inability to comprehend text can be traced to short-term memory deficits in some students, suggesting a causal connection between these deficits and reading ability. Memory deficits displayed by poor readers are explained in two ways (Torgesen & Wong, 1986):

1. The deficit exists in the formation and maintenance of phonological codes in short-term memory.

2. There is failure to employ effective memorization strategies such as elaboration and imagery (Bauer, 1977).

Poor readers are also less likely to use verbal rehearsal strategies (Torgesen & Goldman, 1977). Learning disabled readers exhibit poor performance on memory tasks that require the use of several different strategies and control processes (Foster & Gavelek, 1983). Short-term memory problems can affect more than the holding of information. They can also affect the entire process of cognitive planning, study strategies, and the understanding of more complex text-level information.

Attentiveness is also an important factor in working or short-term memory, as many learning disabled students are unable to attend to the task at hand. Although some learning disabled readers do as well as agemates who do not have reading problems in nonlinguistic areas, there is evidence that short-term memory deficits can affect the learning of all types of material related to linguistic tasks, and, as such, is a cause of early reading failure.

Semantic Memory

Semantic memory enables us to determine how concepts relate to each other and how to organize knowledge so we can retrieve same or add same to new information for long-term memory purposes (Bos & Vaughn, 1988). Some researchers believe that semantic memory is comprised of retrieval strategies, verbal knowledge, and reconstruction processes (Swanson, 1988). Reconstruction processes involve associative thoughts, recoding of information, or the ability to reorganize, reconstruct, or transform information.

Semantic memory is facilitated by how the student uses verbal knowledge that is stored in his or her memory. This includes how concepts and ideas can be expressed verbally by the learner. Semantic memory helps the child remember the gist or sense of a situation or experience by being able to recall critical information. This includes both declarative or verbal knowledge and verbal strategies such as clustering of information by categories or classifying information using words to represent thought processes.

Motor Memory

All animals have a repertoire of motor behavior that ranges from innate motor responses to volitional motor tasks such as handwriting. Once motor responses are learned, they are retained at a very high level of retention or stability (Adams, 1967). Possible reasons for the retention of motor memory habits are overlearning, lack of interference, and memory traces that are strong and resistant (Adams, 1967).

Automatic motor responses include those that deal with eye movements, speech articulation, and the many built-in automatic muscular activities such as heartbeat and breathing.

Autobiographical Memory

Another type of memory discussed in the literature is autobiographical. This is memory that is part of an individual's own life experiences. An alternative term suggested for autobiographical memory is *ecological memory*, which infers a biological-evolutionary approach to memory. Another term used to describe this phenomenon is *everyday memory* (Banaji & Crowder, 1989). This is how a person remembers sources of information, arguments, or material relevant to the individual's thought processes.

SCHEMA THEORY

According to schema theory, the information stored in the brain is clustered in a pattern of organized structures called schema (S) or schemata (PL). These cognitive structures of prior knowledge are also standardized mental pictures of experiences. They include an organized way for incoming information to be acquired, organized, and retrieved in working memory. Therefore, schema theory is similar to information processing theory. Both emphasize how information is structured in memory and how it can be retrieved and used to enable us to blend incoming information from new experiences with previous events.

Our schemas facilitate higher-order thinking skills, such as making inferences by permitting us to bring meaning to our experiences. We can understand new ideas and concepts as they unfold in the events of everyday life, as well as through the content of what we read.

An example would be the clues that an individual gets from reading a story and how the clues suggest certain interpretations of that story. As a reader reads the story, the interpretations become clearer and clearer until he or she feels that the correct interpretation was made and that the interpretation is consistent with the clues provided.

A student reading a story about baseball player Babe Ruth uses several schemas as he or she reads—schemas for the game of baseball, for the stadium, for travel to and from the stadium. As far as schema dealing with the stadium is concerned, the student may include personal experiences, such as walking into the stadium and buying hot dogs, sodas, popcorn, and also relate the experience to going to different stadiums. The student reads the story and interprets it by using existing schemas. He or she also continually integrates the unfolding of a story with prior experiences, adding new ideas and concepts to the existing schema. Schemas are thought to be able to interlock to form more complex schemas. Students coordinate, reorganize, and combine schemas. Schemas can also be differentiated and then later recombined by learners.

Implications for Teaching

The more the students can integrate background or prior experience (schema) with the text to be learned, the easier will be the understanding and mastery of content. Schema theory suggests that the integration of new learning into existing schemas is at the crux of comprehension. In reading, an example would be schemas involving semantic learning, syntactic relationships, and the rules dealing with the recognition and phonetic formulation of words. The brain organizes and retrieves this information as it interprets input from new information, such as the reading of a story. Students with reading problems should be instructed in how to anticipate events in a story by using existing schemata to predict the outcome of events or the reactions of the characters (Smith, 1983).

It is important to understand how a student's schemata relate to the story or the text. The arrangement of the words and ideas and how they are presented makes a difference in how the learner applies existing schemas in terms of understanding the text. Therefore, text structure, story structure, and grammar are an integral part to the development of new schemata.

The understanding of a story schemata can be taught. A story has a setting, a beginning, an action and a reaction, an attempt to achieve a goal, an outcome, and an ending (Whaley, 1981). Another schema for stories includes a setting, theme, plot, and resolution (Bower as reported by Guthrie, 1977).

A schema can also involve a chronological pattern, which includes the sequence of events, the actions of the main character, and the events surrounding the story. There is also schema for the structure of stories or how they are written, such as title, subsections under the title (chapters), subtopics under each chapter, and details under each subtopic. A student needs to understand what subarea schema of a story need to be understood before the overall schema of the story can be comprehended (Catterson, 1979).

Science and social studies materials contain many new terms and concepts that require interpretation before the information can be incorporated into existing schemas. Inadequate prior experiences, which often occurs in students with limited backgrounds, can have a great influence on student comprehension (Alexander & Heathington, 1988). These students can profit from a program that emphasizes expanding vocabulary in order to increase the number of words around a concept. They need to discuss relevant terms and concepts prior, at times during, and after reading a science or social studies chapter to see how their schemata relates to the material to be learned. The more opportunities for new information to be presented or rehearsed, the more likely it is to be incorporated into existing schemas.

SOCIAL COGNITIVE THEORY

Teachers have long recognized that students who exhibit learning difficulties have attitudinal or motivational problems that interfere with their classwork. These students have a tendency to become less involved in their schoolwork and to exhibit high rates of off-task behavior, poor concentration, and lack of persistence when they are presented with difficult tasks. Reasons for this type of behavior have been postulated to be related to failure in early school years, followed by feelings of inadequacy, leading to self-doubts, and finally resulting in a diminished achievement effort. The development of "helplessness" belief occurs over a long period of time in many situations and across a variety of tasks. It is widely accepted that students' beliefs about their abilities can affect their achievement efforts and accomplishments (Andrews & Debus, 1978; Fowler & Peterson, 1981). Another important factor is that this belief system can result in a sequence of maladjustive achievement behaviors, such as a lower expectation of future success in testing, academics, social interactions, and a host of other life situations (Kistner & Licht, 1983).

The study of how individuals exercise control over their own thought patterns, motivation, and actions is central to social cognitive theory. Self-related processes and self-generated activities are thought to be integral to causal processes. Students do affect change in themselves and their situations, and there are identifiable mechanisms through which these changes are affected.

Bandura (1986) points out that learners are not totally autonomous nor simply mechanical respondents to environmental factors, but are influenced by interacting determinants where self-generated activity is a contributing factor. There are studies that have shown a positive correlation or association between achievement and externality (Blount et al., 1987). Research data indicated that academic failure is partially a result of children's externality and related affective problems (Tarnowski & Nay, 1989).

Using self-report questionnaires on students, a study by Saracoglu and associates (1989) found that students with learning disabilities reported significantly lower self-esteem, and fewer academic adjustments and personal-emotional adjustments than their nonlearning disabled peers. It is suggested that for many individuals with learning disabilities, low self-esteem and emotional problems continue into adulthood (Buchanan & Wolf, 1986). There are several key factors involved in social cognitive theory that apply to learning-problem students. They are:

1. *Locus of Control:* Internal locus of control refers to factors that the individual has the power to change, such as effort and attitude. External locus of control, which is highlighted as a prevalent factor in learning-problem students, is related to ability, intelligence, luck, and difficulty of task.
2. *Learned Helplessness:* This is the negative reaction some students display in failure situations, such as overreacting to negative feedback, lower expectation of future success, lowering performance levels, and lack of perceived independence. The reaction to failure is the most cogent aspect of the problem. This includes negative affect, avoidance of task, and stated lack of ability: "I'm stupid" or "I'm not smart like the other kids."
3. *Attribution Theory:* Students with learning problems tend to attribute or associate success or failure to external locus of control rather than internal locus of control (Pearl, Bryan, & Donahue, 1980). The teacher has to be concerned with the degree to which the individual can control outcomes and consider factors that vitiate the individual's ability to problem solve in academics as well as in the social areas. The student may have good reasons for how he or she feels about external attributions.
4. *Self-Efficacy:* Self-efficacy (one's feelings about personal competence) and learned helplessness are closely related constructs. It is suggested (Bandura, 1986) that intervention or educational procedures can serve as a way for teachers to help students create strength and maintain expectation

of personal competence. This relates to a person's belief that he or she can perform the behaviors required to produce a certain outcome. A person can believe that a certain behavior will produce a certain outcome but not believe that he or she can produce the behavior necessary to achieve the outcome.

Some learning disabled children have a low sense of efficacy in that they have no basis or history of success in the regular classroom. Many of these students exhibit behaviors such as withdrawal or aggression. Students with low self-efficacy tend to avoid settings in which they feel they cannot successfully cope.

Learning disabled students' beliefs about their capabilities to exercise control over events in their lives is basic to how they operate in terms of motivational, cognitive, and effectual processes. Student thinking is effected by self-efficacy beliefs. This could be self-aiding or self-defeating, depending on the learner's self-appraisal or capabilities.

Cognitive functioning is affected by self-efficacy belief through the influence of motivational and information processing operations. For example, the stronger the learners' belief in their memory capacity, the more effective they are in processing memory tasks. This in turn helps to improve their overall memory performance (Berry, 1987).

It takes a strong sense of efficacy to stay on task in the face of failure. The student who has a strong belief in his or her problem-solving capabilities remains highly efficient and can perform in complex decision-making situations. Those who experience self-doubt behave in an erratic manner in terms of analytical thinking (Bandura & Wood, 1989). The quality of analytical thinking affects the student's performance. The low self-efficacy student visualizes incidents of low success and focuses on how many things can go wrong (Feltz & Landers, 1983; Bandura, 1988a).

Motivation

Most human behavior is purposeful and therefore is directed and controlled by forethought. Learners anticipate the consequences of a certain action, so they set goals and plan courses of action in order to produce the desired outcomes. Psychosocial functioning is regulated by the interaction of self-produced feelings and influences of the environment. Motivation plays a key role in the process. Cognitive motivation or goal orientation is controlled by three variables:

1. How learners perceive the effectiveness of their self-evaluation

2. How learners perceive their self-efficacy for goal attainment
3. How they affect an ongoing readjustment of their own internal standards

Students seek satisfaction from successfully achieving valued goals. The goal is to help them recognize that goals are subject to change and not cast in stone. Goal achievement satisfaction depends on the progress being made. Students must feel they can lower goals, maintain goals, or even raise them if they have been set too low. This is part of the readjustment of internal standards.

Bandura states:

Properties of a self-motivational control system must include (a) predictive anticipatory control of effort, (b) affective self-evaluative reactions to one's performances rooted in a value system, (c) self-appraisal of personal efficacy for goal attainment, and (d) self-reflective metacognitive activity concerning the adequacy of one's efficacy appraisals and the suitability of one's standard setting. Evaluation of perceived self-efficacy relative to task demands indicates whether the standards being pursued are within attainable bounds or are unrealistically beyond one's reach. (1989, p. 1180)

Another way the anticipatory mechanism operates is through the individual ability to envision likely outcomes. Outcome expectancy is also affected by self-belief of efficacy (Lent & Hackett, 1987). Many individuals will not pursue outcomes that they feel will not result in success.

Motivation as well as complex patterns of behavior are influenced by feedback. Conceptions are formed by observational learning. Foresight guides appropriate behavior and the internal corrections necessary for behavioral proficiency. Foresight develops in the learner through a continuous cognitive synthesis of preexisting knowledge, along with internal adjustments and guided instruction. Forethought guides the selection of actions, and the results of those actions (feedback) determines the new chosen course. When an action becomes routine, the learner's cognitive processes begin to rely on automatic behavior, and he or she becomes partially disengaged. This allows for cognitive processes to be used for higher order activity.

Reciprocal causation, which is a way of looking at cause-effect relationships, is based on the notion that individuals partly determine the nature of their environment and are at the same time influenced by it. In-dividuals have the capacity to manipulate symbols and think reflectively, generating new ideas and new actions that can go beyond past experiences. They can influence their motivation and actions by learning the tools of self-regulation and self-influence.

Motivation is affected by a self-efficacy belief, which determines the amount of effort that will be expended and how long the learner will stay with the task. The stronger the belief, the greater the effort (Bandura, 1988a). Self-doubt results in a lack of effort and the settling for mediocre solutions (Cervone & Peake, 1986). Success in the classroom requires an optimistic sense of personal efficacy. Failure, setback, and frustration are impediments to perseverance and result in self-doubt. The speed of recovery is very important where self-doubt is concerned. A quick recovery eventually leads back to self-assurance as the learner experiences new successes and encouragement. Selling only one painting did not stop Vincent Van Gogh from continuing his art.

Many believe that misjudgment can also produce dysfunction. Many learning disabled students miscalculate and misjudge their capabilities.

Motivation orientation has had a significant effect on learner performance (Haywood & Switzky, 1986b). In past years emphasis has been placed on extrinsic motivation, such as using a token reward or other type of incentive systems. Educators need to attend to the intrinsic aspects of the learner's self-system as well, and match instructional approaches with motivational characteristics. Motivational orientation is a learned trait and is based on task-intrinsic factors.

Extrinsic and Intrinsic Motivation

Individuals who depend only on the environment to provide comfort, security, and satisfaction are said to be task-extrinsically motivated. Overall, stability appears to depend on a balance of task-intrinsic and task-extrinsic factors. Attribution theory suggests that the level of performance that an individual perceives as possible is based on how causation is viewed. Is the causation a result of the student's abilities or effort or is it the effect or outside forces such as luck or chance? Students need to develop feelings of control and competence so they can deal with both success and failure.

Learners with mild handicaps (learning disabilities, educable mentally handicapped, or behaviorally disordered) who experience continuous failure and unhappiness in social situations often develop an extrinsic motivation orientation (Deci & Chandler, 1986; Deci & Ryan, 1985).

Motivation that is intrinsically self-directed is a good approach for education in general. This means that students learn out of curiosity, being challenged, and the idea that gaining competence leads to self-satisfaction and more self-determination (Haywood & Switzky, 1986a). Intrinsic motivation is a key factor in the integration of new material into the cognitive schema. Students like to view themselves as not being totally controlled by outside forces but as individuals who can also initiate behavior (Deci & Chandler, 1986). Intrinsically motivated behavior does not depend primarily on external rewards to be sustained.

Intrinsic pleasure, as a rule, leads to increased motivation and mastery behavior. Two main systems are involved:

1. A system of self-rewards (how you reward yourself)
2. A standard or way to master or achieve goals that also enables the student to depend less on outside rewards or social reinforcing for motivation

In learning disabled students, dependency behavior is often reinforced by well-meaning peers and adults. There are some adults who actively disapprove of independent mastery attempts of children who are their responsibility. Many of these learners fail to develop critical systems for internal decision making (Harter, 1978).

Personality and motivational characteristics of learners dictate how they compensate for problems, resulting in either a boost in learning or, on the negative side, greater intensification of learning deficits (Haywood & Switzky, 1986b). Switzky and Schultz (1988) believe that the facilitation of learning through motivation that is intrinsic and free from the teacher's control and practices (extrinsic control) should be the main goal of education.

Over a long period of time, classrooms that focus on learning that is reinforced primarily with external controlled feedback may inhibit student creativity. An intrinsic orientation must be incorporated into the learning environment, where teachers move beyond rewards and punishments, and focus on learning and involvement as incentive for continued participation.

The teacher should model task-intrinsic behavior and motivation through the use of a mediational teaching style (Feuerstein, 1980). The teacher using a mediational approach tries to elicit active learning through participation and encourages the learner to think while providing information and encouraging feedback. Asking the student "Why did you answer that way?" or "Is there another way to solve that problem?" are examples of mediational teaching that enhances cognitive processes and the use of strategies.

Stress and Depression

Stress and depression are also associated with an individual's self-belief system. Thinking processes are affected, as well as the ability to cope with aversive situations in the environment. Learners need to feel able to exercise control over threatening situations, or the environment will be perceived as full of danger and hazards resulting in an impaired level of functioning (Bandura, 1988b; Lazarus & Folkman, 1984).

Effective coping skills operate as a cognitive mediator, reducing the learner's internal distress and physiological arousal. Individuals base their actions on how they perceive their own coping efficacy in risk-taking situations. Perceived self-inefficiency that results in feelings of low self-worth can also result in periods of depression (Cutrona & Troutman, 1986; Holahan & Holahan, 1987a).

Implications for Teaching

Learning disabled students can learn to exert some influence over their lives by being encouraged to select and control various aspects of their environment and even to construct environments. This is accomplished slowly at first, with increased control released to the learner as appropriate. The learner creates a beneficial environment and then exercises control over it, thus increasing self-efficacy beliefs. Social competencies and interests are developed, as part of everyday life in school. The power of self-efficacy belief is also developed through a selective process in career decision making and in career development. The more self-effective the learner becomes, the wider the range of career options that are considered appropriate and the better is the overall educational preparation (Hasazi, Gordon, & Roe, 1985).

Selective or choice types of behavior must be encouraged to increase learner interest levels and the desire for increased competencies. Just "saying it" is not good enough. Self-efficacy beliefs must be internalized through experiences that include accurate information and purposeful, meaningful, and successful activities. Negative experiences can reinstate a low self-belief in one's capabilities (Kent & Gibbons, 1987). Therefore, the learner must develop a resilient self-efficacy structure. This comes through encouragement, persistence, and the mastering of continuously more difficult tasks. The importance of the development of resiliency in learners cannot be overstated. It is a prime factor in helping individuals deal with stress, failure, and a host of other disappointments in life. Setbacks can serve a useful purpose in learning about what sustained effort means. The learner must learn to rebound from difficulties or failures.

MATURATIONAL THEORY

As a species, humans generally tend to develop uniformly within the species for males and females and within a "reasonable" amount of variation in terms of time, normal growth, and performance. What is sometimes thought of as a learning disability may in fact be a maturational lag in certain neurological processes.

The term *maturational lag* has been used for many years. Among the first to put forth this theory was Bender (1963). She listed symptoms of maturational lag as weak cerebral dominance or lack of dominance of one side of the brain over the other, immature electroencephalogram records of brain imagery, and delayed speech and motor behavior. The pattern of maturational development is also slower for "preemies" (premature births) than for normal developing children. DeHirsch, Jansky, and Langford (1966) worked with premature children and found that, as a group, they tended to lag in several areas, which included reading skill acquisition. Problems were exhibited in language comprehension, verbal expression, word identification, vocabulary, sentence elaboration, and speech patterns (articulation defects).

Bannatyne (1971) stated that "it is important to realize that neurological dysfunction resulting from brain impairment or biochemical imbalance or some genetic abnormality, can also be associated with maturation lag" (pp. 395–396).

Sex differences in maturation have been reported by Maccoby (1966) and Schiffman (1965). Girls develop many verbal functions earlier than boys. Males tend to mature at a slower rate than females (Bayley & Jones, 1955). Studies of a wide range of learning and behavior disorders include a significantly higher proportion of males than females (Bayley & Jones, 1955). Since maturation lag is primarily genetically determined, it is suggested that many genetic dyslexic children have a maturational lag (Bannatyne, 1971).

The concept of readiness is central when we address the needs of children who exhibit maturational lag. Students who suffer from maturational lag tend to have their main difficulties in the first three years of schooling (K–2). The educational system must make provisions for such "high-risk" learners so they can be taught in a continuous fashion at their own rate of learning. The rate of learning and the material needed for this slower rate, as well as the overall class environment, are different for these students. Many of these children fall behind, never catch up, and become the "dropouts" of the future. Most are intelligent and creative, and it should not be assumed that they are mentally slow or incapable of learning.

Most schools require that certain plateaus in academic areas be achieved in a prescribed period of time for each grade level. This means that young learners must be "ready" to learn that which is taught, when it is taught. Students with maturational lag simply may not be ready to fit into a particular time schedule as established by curriculum guides, teachers, authors, book companies, or individuals responsible for setting standards for grade-level academic performance. Kirk (1967) indicated that students tend to perform in tasks that they feel comfortable with and enjoy, and tend to reject or not participate in tasks that are felt too frustrating and uncomfortable. Teachers must be willing to work with children, anticipating and dealing with their frustrations and not avoid them.

Piaget's Cognitive Developmental Theory

Piaget placed great importance on mental development as a natural, interactive experience between the child and the environment. He felt that growth was a self-directed process. The teacher needed to use a cognitive developmental approach to learning, guiding the learner and providing opportunities for the learner to experience, gain insights, and discover principles.

Cognitive growth occurs in a series of invariant and interdependent stages, depending on the maturational level of the learner. Only certain tasks can be mastered at each stage. As a child grows and experiences more (matures), his or her ability to think in terms of quality, depth, and breadth of understanding increases.

Piaget gives us stages in which learning takes place and delineates them by using a schematic interpretation of these stages of development as a guide. Growth unfolds in a sequence or in stages. Each stage is folded into the next and is also a prelude to the one that follows. Students vary in the rate with which they go through these stages. This is due to both reasons of heredity and environment. Students learn to adapt to their environment through experiences. Intelligence is viewed as an adaptive process where the child adapts to each new situation while at the same time the environment is being modified by the child (Flavell, 1963).

MAIN CONCEPTS IN PIAGET'S THEORY

There are three main concepts in Piaget's theory: assimilation, accommodation, and equilibrium. *Assimilation* has to do with how the child perceives the environment in terms of how it fits into existing systems. The child interprets new or novel experiences in the light of previous learning.

Accommodation pertains to the process of adaptation of existing psychological structures to the new reality or experiences. Only a certain amount of information can be assimilated in a given period of time. Cognitive or mental structures are continually being modified to accommodate new experiences.

Intelligence is therefore a function of both assimilation and accommodation. Assimilation and accommodation force the learner to develop new cognitive structures in order to account for new learning.

Equilibrium comes into play when new experiences and challenges constantly interfere with the mental homeostasis or balance of the learner. Equilibrium is the mental process of putting the assimilation and accommodation of experiences into a state of balance. For example, in assimilation, a student learns new concepts in science, such as why the sky does not fall or why the sun moves from one place to another. He or she fits this into existing cognitive structure.

Behavior or schema are viewed as mental structures used by the individual as a basis for interpreting new information. The more new information is presented or rehearsed, the more it is liable to be incorporated into existing schemas. Schemas are thought to be able to interlock to form more complex schemas. The learner coordinates visual and auditory schemas, as well as reorganizing schemas and combining schemas. Schemas can also be differentiated and then later recombined by the learners. Students will develop schema if presented with objects that allow them to learn.

Piaget (1952) felt that the child will learn to ignore distraction when he or she understands how it hinders or gets in the way of problem solving. This self-awareness of reasoning processes seems to result in more effective learning. Piaget has given us important insights into children's social and academic development (Pullis & Smith, 1981).

MATURATIONAL STAGES

Sensorimotor Stage (0–2 years of age):

1. The child learns through senses and movement interacting with physical environment.

2. The child is introduced to space, time, where things fit, what exists and is stable, and what can be destroyed.
3. Education focuses on early sensory motor learning (perceptual-motor activity).

Preoperational Stage (2–7 years of age):

1. The child learns to make intuitive judgments and think with symbols.
2. Language is used for communication and to represent the universe.
3. Perception is developed as an important aspect of thinking.
4. Children attribute only one function to an object (e.g., father is a father; he cannot also be a doctor).
5. Ideas about conservation are immature (i.e., show the child two identical objects, change the shape of one and the tendency is to think the weight of the one changed is different from the matching object). Concept-weight does not change because the shape of an object is altered.

Concrete Operational Stage (7–11 years of age)

1. The child can interpret new relationships, perceive the consequences of acts, and logically formulate the concept of groups.
2. Thinking is more organized and systematic as new concrete experiences are incorporated into cognitive schema.
3. The child can understand the concept of threeness, for example, or what has three without counting or touching.

Formal Operations (11 years of age and over)

1. This stage generally begins at about age 11 for most children and is a giant leap in terms of thought processes.
2. Shifts occur from thinking that is directed by observation to thinking that directs observation.
3. The learner can handle abstract concepts or theories without the necessity for concreteness.
4. Problem solving and dealing with logical relationships becomes generalized.
5. Children learn to classify, associate, and manipulate ideas. What will happen if? or If I reverse the process, what will happen?

Implications for Teaching

Piaget views the stages of maturation as sequential and hierarchical, and each transition involves maturation and opportunities to learn. Schools cannot "go too fast" or introduce information that is inappropriate to the stages of child development. Children may only be memorizing information without fully understanding the main ideas or concepts that are taught. Students are prepared to learn if the material is presented to them as challenging, and there is little need for extrinsic rewards if the information is appropriate to the age level.

Learning occurs as an integral part of a social experience. Interaction with peers is a part of that social process and enables learners to compare ideas and identify differences and similarities. Feedback is very important to developing concepts and to increasing reasoning abilities.

Content should be taught according to stages of development and not just by levels with experiences tied directly to concepts. Readiness becomes a key concept, and knowing when a child is ready to learn is the responsibility of the school.

THEORIES OF LANGUAGE ACQUISITION

Currently several main theories of language acquisition are being expressed: (1) behavioristic (environmentalist): (2) nativistic; (3) interactionistic; (4) psycholinguistic; and (5) cognitive.

Behavioristic (Environmentalist) Theory

The premise in this theory is that children are born without prior knowledge in the area of language, but, through the principles of operant conditioning and by responding to the natural environment, spoken language is acquired. Processes of modeling and reinforcement have a great influence on shaping behavior and on the production and use of speech. Word meaning, or the understanding of words, is improved through differential reinforcement. Syntactic skills are developed by learning and responding to appropriate input, depending on the model and environmental circumstances.

As suggested by B. F. Skinner (1959), a child's language is shaped by others through selective reinforcement of vocalization and the imitating of the speech of primary adults. The child is cuddled and reinforced for approximations of the speech sounds and words desired, and for reproducing them spontaneously and appropriately. Imitation and practice are the key elements in the process. The child associates "Daddy" with Daddy only when the word is paired with the physical presence or things that are associated with Daddy himself.

The behavioral approach to intervention is direct and systematic (Hallahan et al., 1983). A child's language profile is analyzed and the deficient skills requiring intervention are paired with activities designed to improve those skills. The learner is appropriately reinforced for accurate performance, and the instructor becomes the primary model. Praise is commonly used along with continuous practice in a variety of situations. The child is taught correct usage directly as opposed to a discovery type instructional process.

Nativistic Theory

The greatest proponents of this position are Chomsky and Halle (1968). The premise in this position is that children have innate capacity or native ability to generate and deduce constructs of grammar, which enables them to generate a theory of grammar and to understand and produce an infinite number of sentences. Language abilities are believed to be mainly genetically transmitted, and humans are thought to be "prewired" for language development (Mercer & Mercer, 1985). Nativists believe that thought comes before speech and base this notion on the fact that infants can understand complex language long before they speak. Also, children express complex thoughts by using simple utterances. Their imitative behavior is a combination of actual imitation and individualistic interpretation of language rules. They create their own combinations of words. Nativists usually stress both the importance of the environment, as well as the importance of innate abilities on the language behavior of the child.

Language development occurs through the process of maturation, and the environment also plays an important role in that process (Lenneberg, 1967). Parents provide the growing child with the words while the child provides the cognitive processes necessary for language development. According to McNeill (1970), different configurations of words can represent similar ideas, suggesting an underlying structure to language and children have the innate ability to understand that two sentences can have the same "deep structures" according to nativists. Intervention involves providing opportunities for the children to discover the relationship between the structure of their sentences and the universal aspects of the deep structure or abstract level.

The adult, rather than initiate instruction, responds to how the child uses language. A technique called *expansion* is used where the adult responds and expands in an interpretive manner to what the child says. The child may say, "Daddy, come," and the adult may respond with, "Yes, Daddy is coming." It is expected that the child will learn the grammatically correct form through this type of interaction.

Interactionist Theory

Piaget contributed greatly to our understanding of children's thinking and to the doctrine of readiness (Flavell, 1963; Piaget, 1962). According to Piaget, a child's learning is constrained by his or her current stage of cognitive development. Through spontaneous development, the child initiates and interacts with reality transforming it on the basis of his or her conceptual stage of development. Language is acquired as children assimilate the language of the environment and modify it to accommodate their own knowledge of the environment and the way they think about it. Reasoning is directly related to how language is assimilated, and with maturity, children develop more complex thought patterns. Therefore, thought is a prerequisite to developing meaningful language (Flavell, 1977). Once language is acquired, children use it to expand their thoughts, so thought precedes speech. As speech improves, it enhances thought. A leader in this movement is Myklebust (with Bannochie & Killen, 1971), who proposed that as the child interacts with the environment, he or she will develop meaning. Words without meaning are not words.

Piaget's theory of readiness suggests that a child's cognitive development (for educational purposes) should be accurately assessed before the instructor determines what should be taught (Flavell, 1963). The rate at which new concepts are introduced is important. Teachers cannot rush students into transitioning into the next stage of cognitive growth because instruction cannot accelerate learning if the students are not at the appropriate stage, according to Piaget's concept of spontaneous development. This is related to the concept of readiness or self-discovery learning of basic concepts and should supercede direct instruction. The overall premise is that cognitive modifiability cannot be influenced by classroom practice if the learner is not at the receptive stage of learning.

These views have been challenged (Brainerd, 1978). Reuven Feuerstein's Instrumental Enrichment is an example of an attempt to accelerate cognitive development. Feuerstein's approach has focused on handicapped students, many of whom are severely mentally retarded. The treatment approach in this program emphasizes teaching natural language, as opposed to drills or structured activities. Activities are centered around play where the teacher models the intent of the child's message. Spontaneous talking is used during the teaching of phonemes, morphemes, syntax, semantics, language rhythm, and intonation (Berry, 1980).

Receptive and expressive language are inextricably related. If the child does not understand what the other person has said, he or she cannot respond in a meaningful manner. Often expressive disorders are accompanied by a weakness in the receptive area. An expressive disorder accompanies a paucity of conversation with its accompanying natural interaction, and often results in impaired comprehension (Denckla, 1977).

Psycholinguistic Theory

This theory is based to a large extent on the biological and genetic foundations of language proposed by Chomsky (1965) (Lenneberg, 1967). The underlying idea is that children are innately prepared to learn and use language. Psycholinguistic approaches (Kirk, McCarthy, & Kirk, 1968a) were based on the assumption that language abilities or processes could be differentiated, and that clusters of skills could be assessed and trained using educational programs. Psycholinguists believe that children learning a language do not merely incorporate a set of sentences into their cognitive repertoire, but instead they internalize the language system as a totality, and out of this comes the expression of language. In order to understand the breakdown in the process, a thorough analysis of language expression and production is necessary. Learning a language is an unfolding process and requires appropriate nurturance under optimal environmental circumstances. The child, as in the nativistic approach, needs a stimulating environment that encourages good language usage.

Cognitive Theory

Cognitive theory is most closely associated with nativistic theory. Some refer to a cognitive-psycholinguistic approach (Hallahan et al., 1983), which is a combination of psychology and linguistics. This position is not in accord with the behaviorists, and the intervention approach proposed is basically conversational interaction with adherence to the precepts involved in the process of expansion (previously discussed under Nativistic Theory). The instructor reads stories, asks questions, and uses the students' responses as a basis for eliciting improved grammatical versions of previous responses to the original questions. Self-correction is encouraged along with the development of good listening skills. Corrective programs are designed to help children develop skills in processing and interpreting language (Hallahan et al., 1983).

Cognitive theorists purport that by incorporating new experiences into existing schema (assimilation), the child strengthens his or her knowledge base and thus enhances the cognitive structure. Therefore, the child needs active experiences that build meaning. This requires the teacher to provide interactions that involve the child, the language, and the environment (Bloom & Lahey, 1978).

Within the construct of cognitive theory it is important to first understand the nature of the language problem. It is also necessary to delineate the underlying factors that describe how the problem is manifested. Two main areas of diagnosis are emphasized:

1. Compare the development of language impaired children with those who are not language impaired. A psycholinguistic approach can be used to differentiate among students with or without problems.
2. Examine the integrity and interrelationships between the sensory, perceptual, motor, and cognitive mechanisms that are thought to be prerequisites to normal language acquisition. This can be accomplished by using a neuropsychological approach.

Chapter 3 deals with the brain and learning, and delineates anatomical as well as physiological areas of concern.

Chapter 3

Neurobiology of Learning

CHAPTER OUTLINE

Overview
Brain Anatomy and Physiology
Neurotransmission
Memory and the Brain
Factors Affecting the Brain
Brain-Related Research

OVERVIEW

This chapter reviews learning from a physiological perspective. It includes a discussion of the brain and its relationship to learning. This perspective will give the educator a basic understanding of how problems in learning can originate with damage or insult to the brain.

BRAIN ANATOMY AND PHYSIOLOGY

The brain orchestrates behavior, movement, feeling, sensing, and automatic functions like breathing and heartbeat. The different regions of the brain are intimately interconnected. The processing of information generally involves the activation of several regions. An insult to one area of the brain may impair the performance of other areas of the brain.

The central nervous and peripheral systems consist of the brain and spinal cord. Among the functions of the central nervous system are:

1. Control over our automatic functions such as breathing and heart rate, digestion, blood pressure, and release of certain hormones

2. Evaluation of sensation, which is the accumulation of information from the environment
3. Control of voluntary functions such as moving our muscles
4. Control of the seat of cognition that we associate with language and thought
5. Control of the center of spirituality that causes humans to have beliefs, even in things that cannot be fully understood

The peripheral nervous system is comprised of the cranial and peripheral nerves. The peripheral nervous system has two main components: an afferent system that conducts information to the central nervous system and an efferent system of neurons that conducts information away from the central nervous system.

Cerebral Hemispheres

The largest part of the brain is the cerebrum. It has a cortex of gray matter and a core of white matter that contains gray matter regions (nuclei). The cerebrum is separated into almost identical halves called the right and left cerebral hemispheres. The two hemispheres

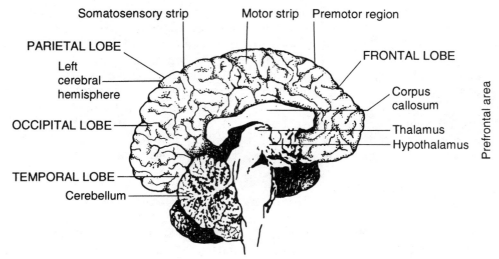

Figure 3-1 Brain—Side View

are connected by an arched mass of white matter called the corpus callosum. (See Figures 3-1 and 3-2.)

Functions of the one side of the body generally are controlled by the opposite hemisphere. Language, however, is controlled by the left hemisphere. It has long been thought that hemispheric specialization is related to the development of different skills and two different types of processing: linguistic processing and visual-spatial processing.

The left hemisphere in most individuals is specialized for sequential linguistic, analytic processing. The right hemisphere is associated with thinking processes. The left hemisphere also deals with control or "will." Damage to the right hemisphere is associated with difficulty in performing visual-spatial tasks. Students with this type of damage may not be able to recognize faces or reproduce geometric forms or designs.

Cortical Lobes

Each hemisphere is divided into four cortical lobes that control specific mental and body functions. They are the frontal, parietal, temporal, and occipital lobes.

Voluntary movements are controlled by the frontal lobe. This includes fine-motor functions involved in speaking and writing, and gross movements necessary for walking. The frontal lobe also contains regions necessary for association, making plans, establishing one's identity, and regulating complex emotions and intellectual tasks that represent the behavior of human beings. Without the frontal lobe, an individual could

not plan a meeting or decide to protect his or her home when a storm threatens.

The temporal lobe is associated with memory for a sequence of events. Students with damage to this area may have difficulty remembering who lived first— Abraham Lincoln or Thomas Jefferson. Many who suffer damage to this area can remember the events themselves, but cannot order the sequence and relate them to other events.

The temporal lobe is not only involved in memory but it also is involved with strong emotions. Memories of the first home run are stored there, as well as feelings of jealousy and hate. The temporal lobe contains an auditory cortical area and a region critical for memory called the hippocampus. Damage to the hip-

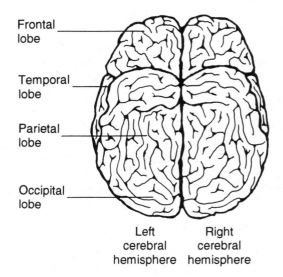

Figure 3-2 Brain—Top View

pocampus can cause one to forget information that is very recent or even momentarily presented. Recalling songs learned as a child is a function of the brain's hippocampus. It is also essential to long-term memory, such as remembering the combination to a safe or a long list of addresses, and critical to learning in general.

The parietal lobe receives mainly somatosensory input and is involved in orienting the body in space. The occipital lobe is the screen on which visual images are displayed.

The cerebellum, located beneath the occipital lobe, among other things controls coordination and posture. The brain stem and spinal cord influence such automatic functions as heart rate, respiration, and blood pressure. The brain stem and spinal cord are the sites of communication between the central nervous system and muscles and sense organs.

There are several clinical syndromes associated with the cerebellum and the basal ganglia. Basal ganglia, which lie deep in the cerebral hemispheres and in the upper brain stem, are involved in motor coordination. Cerebellar disorders are associated with awkwardness of intentional movements. Problems associated with basal ganglia involve meaningless, unintentional movements that occur unexpectedly. Cerebellar disorders include ataxia, which is manifested in awkwardness of posture, problems with gait, poor coordination, tremor, and nystagmus (involuntary, rapid eye movements). Basal ganglia disorders include Parkinsonism, chorea (sudden jerky movements), athetosis (snake-like movements), and a disorder evidenced by sudden flail-like movements of one arm called Hemiballismus (Goldberg, 1988). The brain can also be viewed by sections.

THE FOREBRAIN
The forebrain is the largest area of the brain and contains the two hemispheres, each of which contain a hypothalamus, which helps regulate vital body functions such as temperature and blood pressure. Drives like the "fight or flight" reaction and sexual desire are also seated in the hypothalamus. The cerebral cortex, or outer layer of the cerebrum, is a major part of the forebrain. It functions like a command center and contains more nerve cells than any other structure. The cortex receives information from the various sense organs and integrates this information with memories of past experiences. It also coordinates motor responses. The cortex is bunched up in folds and fits within the skull. The folds of the surface of the brain give the impression of a walnut covered with blood vessels. The motor strip is responsible for voluntary movements. The somatosensory strip receives differ-

ent sensations such as heat, pain, and touch. The auditory cortex receives and integrates sounds. Broca's area coordinates many complex movements that are needed for speech. Another area affecting language is Wernicke's area, which lies near the auditory cortex. Damage to this region often results in problems with the comprehension of spoken words. Learners can produce words, but what they say is not meaningful. In reading, they are called "word callers." Difficulty is also observed in labeling or naming objects.

THE MIDBRAIN
The midbrain functions as a relay station for information about sound and sight, and for most of the other messages coming into or out of the forebrain. There are specialized nerve cells in the midbrain that play an important role in regulating movement.

THE HINDBRAIN
The hindbrain controls breathing and heartbeat. The cerebellum is a part of the hindbrain that helps coordinate movement, such as running, walking, or climbing steps without falling over. It is also involved in intricate movements like threading needles, painting with a fine brush, or tying knots. The hindbrain contains nerve tracts that pass between the spinal cord and higher centers such as the reticular formation. The reticular formation is important to the coordination of sensory motor functions and arousal.

It is, simply, any area of grey matter that is unlabeled in diagrams. As more becomes known about it, more labels will appear and its size will diminish. It has important motor and sensory functions, including those relating to the automatic nervous system (e.g., centers in the medulla controlling heart rate and blood pressure). Multisynaptic pathways through the reticular formation, from hypothalamus to spinal cord, convey sympathetic information.

Recently, endogenous chemicals with opiate-like activity (endorphins) and their receptors have been found in various areas of the reticular formation (e.g., the grey matter surrounding the aqueduct, and cells along the midline of the brain stem). The implication of the system in the relief of pain is currently a topic of great interest (Goldberg, 1988, p. 66).

Damage to the reticular activating system can also result in impairment of attention, wakefulness, and consciousness of environmental stimuli. The levels of various states of consciousness, such as total alert ness to deep sleep, are influenced by activity in the reticular formation. This system is also sensitive to the influence of substances such as drugs.

THE INNER BRAIN

The inner brain lies deep within the forebrain and contains the structures that direct highly developed mental, emotional, and motor abilities. The hypothalamus is involved with many important functions such as waking, hunger, and the flow of adrenalin needed for an important meeting, for example. The hypothalamus, which is the size of a fingernail, is also the brain's emotional center. It is associated with the hormones that make an individual feel happy, angry, or depressed.

The thalamus is a sensory relay and integrative center that connects with many areas of the brain such as the hypothalamus, cerebral cortex, basal ganglia, and the brain system.

THE SPINAL CORD

The spinal cord descends from the brain, inside the backbone. Nerves connect the brain and spinal cord with the sensory organs, muscles, and skin, and all the organs of the body. If the bones of the back were removed to display the spinal cord, the nerves coming out underneath each rib and going out into the arms and legs could be seen. The roots can be seen below the spinal cord. Nerves from both the brain and spinal cord go out to the sensory organs, the muscles, the skin, and to all other organs of the body.

Underneath the membrane that covers and protects the brain is a layer of clear cerebrospinal fluid. Beneath that fluid is the brain. The cerebrospinal fluid, which flows over the brain, also circulates down the spinal cord. This fluid can be withdrawn from below the spinal cord through a procedure called a spinal tap or lumbar puncture. Examination of this fluid sometimes assists in diagnosing certain pathologies.

Brain Cells

Nerve cells or neurons (see Figure 3–3) control all the complex functions of the brain such as memory, emotions, sensation, or motion. The gray matter of the brain is made up of mainly cells and their axons. The white matter contains axons that are covered by a fatty substance called myelin. Many nerve fibers are insulated with myelin, which makes them appear white and which provide faster conduction of nerve impulses. A nerve is a collection of nerve cell fibers. The majority of nerve cells (neurons) are located in the gray matter of the brain. Neurons are the basic units of communication in the body, and the intricate structure

of these cells facilitates their communication with one another. Neurons collectively sense environmental changes, swiftly integrate sensory inputs, then activate effectors (such as muscles and glands) that can carry out coordinated responses (Starr & Taggart, 1987). Information flow throughout the body depends on how the neurons are organized into interconnecting circuits. The brain also contains glial cells. These are supporting cells that regenerate. The membranes of these cells contact the axons in order for transmission to occur faster.

There are three parts to a nerve cell: the cell body, the axon, and the dendrites. The cell body contains the nucleus where the genes or the units of heredity are located. The machinery for making proteins and producing energy to power nerve cell activity is also held within the cell body. Dendrites are complex processes that branch out from the cell body to increase the area of reception from other neurons. Messages then pass through the nerve cell body and down the single long axon to another nerve cell, a muscle, or an organ. These messages, or nerve impulses, are transmitted at each level across a gap called synapse to affect the next cell or membrane. This is accomplished by release of chemical substances called neurotransmitters (e.g., acetylcholine at the neuromuscular junction).

Synapses are spaces between nerve cells and are the places where neurotransmitters are released. Synapses are a crucial part of our nervous system. The branch of the nerve cell body is surrounded by a membrane, and junctions coming from other nerve cells, via their fibers, make synapsis with this nerve cell body.

Synaptic integration is the moment-by-moment combining of excitatory and inhibitory neurotransmitters acting on adjacent parts of a neuron. When something interferes with synaptic functioning, the consequences can be very serious. For instance, lack of inhibitory control of neurons in muscles can result in spasticity of the muscles.

Some nerves carry information toward the brain. The stimulation of our sense of smell is a good example. Chemicals from a hamburger will excite the specialized endings of nerve fibers located in the membrane lining the nose. Impulses are carried to the brain and we experience the sense of smell.

We control impulses that originate from the brain to produce an effect or action. An example of this process is movement. Impulses traveling along nerve fibers to muscles in our limbs enable us to move. The direction, strength, and the coordination of movements are controlled by these impulses. The brain does things that we are aware of and also things that

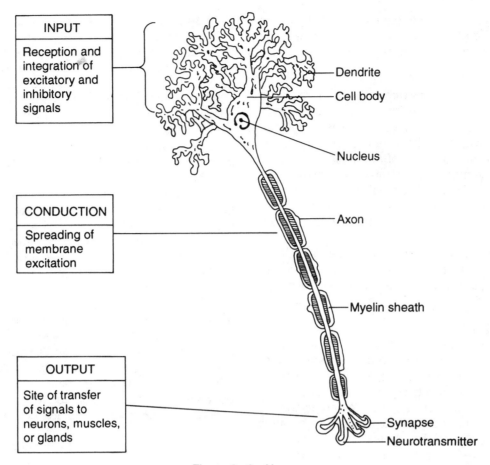

INPUT

Reception and integration of excitatory and inhibitory signals

Dendrite

Cell body

Nucleus

CONDUCTION

Spreading of membrane excitation

Axon

Myelin sheath

OUTPUT

Site of transfer of signals to neurons, muscles, or glands

Synapse

Neurotransmitter

Figure 3–3   Neuron

we do not consciously control, such as heart beat or breathing. The brain is also the cognitive center of the body. It is the center of ideas, feelings, and memory.

NEUROTRANSMISSION

The simplest organizational unit of a nerve cell action is called the reflex arc. If you accidentally stub your toe on a step, nerve fiber endings in your toe transmit impulses through the nerve to the spinal cord where impulses are immediately relayed to another neuron and the flexor muscle in your leg, causing the foot to withdraw. Innervation of the motor neurons is called a reflex arc because it was done without thought. Simultaneous impulses also travel to the brain and give the sensation of pain, which is a part of the process that is consciously perceived.

Nerve cells communicate with each other through an electrochemical process called neurotransmission. An electrical message from the brain travels down the length of the nerve cell axon and stimulates release of

chemical neurotransmitters from tiny vesicles at the axon ends. This chemical produces an effect on the contacted cell membrane, allowing it to transmit an impulse or to block an impulse. Neurotransmitters cross the synapse and attach onto receptors on the dendrites or other parts of an adjacent nerve cell. The interaction of neurotransmitters and receptors generates a second electrical message. The new message is transmitted along other nerve cells until it reaches its target. The brain's orders are carried out in this way.

Not all receiving nerve cells "fire" after neurotransmitters find receptors. One nerve cell may have thousands of receptors capable of receiving conflicting neurotransmitter messages from hundreds of other nerve cells. An excitatory neurotransmitter may tell the receiving nerve to fire, whereas an inhibitory neurotransmitter may change the command to fire. The particular mix of excitatory and inhibitory neurotransmitters determines whether firing takes place and whether messages are relayed or stopped. This is dependent on the particular mix of excitatory and inhibitory neurotransmitters.

Neurotransmitter Effects

Acetylcholine is an example of an excitatory neurotransmitter. It can affect contraction of the heart, blood vessels, and intestine, and it stimulates glands to secrete. Lack of acetylcholine has been linked to muscle weakness and memory loss.

Serotonin is an inhibitory neurotransmitter. It constricts blood vessels and brings on sleep. It is also involved in temperature regulation. Dopamine is another inhibitory neurotransmitter. It dilates blood vessels and influences behavior and control of complex movements. Tremors and muscular rigidity can result from loss of dopamine. Abnormally increased body movement can also result from excess dopamine.

Ten years ago only a few neurotransmitters were identified as the chemical message carriers between nerve cells that allow the brain to do its work. Now, through improved techniques, science has identified many more substances involved with neurotransmission and have also determined some of their functions.

There is a chemistry of memory and learning that involves understanding (encoding). This chemistry, which is vital to how information is stored and processed, is also affected by different enzymes. The enzyme calpar, for example, is thought to be involved in certain neuropathological conditions. Calcium also plays an important role in memory. Disorders of calcium regulation can affect the plasticity of the synaptic connections and in turn affect learning. Data of this nature will aid in the diagnosis and intervention of brain-related causes of learning disabilities in the future.

MEMORY AND THE BRAIN

Memory is a critical factor in the process of learning for all individuals. Memory problems exhibited by learning disabled children reflect problems with storage and retrieval. Memory also refers to an ability to recall places or events that do not even involve symbols, such as how something looks or sounds as part of an experience. Students with difficulty in this area may not be able to describe their visit to the circus, their neighborhood, or the way their room looks.

The understanding of the machinery in the brain that processes memory, mainly the recall of facts and experiences, is important when there is a disruption due to disease, pathology, or by reason of genetic heritage. A key question is, What is learning in terms of memory? Another question is, How are learning and memory neurologically related? It is difficult to analyze memory formation or functions, but recent research has given us a greater understanding of how learning occurs.

Memory trace is a hypothetical construct that suggests how the neural representation of bits of information are organized. Conscious experience entails thinking about things or recalling objects or events in the past. It also involves comparing previous learning or experience with new learning or experiences. Rational connections are then made that are based on how the individual perceives possible relationships. This is accomplished by making comparisons. Conscious experience involves a capacity for memory and the ability of the individual to store and retrieve information.

There are at least two stages involved in the formation of memory trace (Starr & Taggart, 1987). One is short term and lasts for seconds or minutes. Long-term memory or storage is where information is put into more complex neural representation and is more permanent in terms of how long it lasts. Short-term memory involves a brief period of neural excitation; long-term memory depends on chemical or structural changes in the brain (Wood, 1983).

The brain and spinal cord, as integrating centers for long-term memory, contain interneurons that integrate information coming in from sensory lines. These interneurons in turn influence other neurons. Information from the integrating centers is relayed away from the central nervous system to the muscles and glands by motor neurons. When the signals carried by motor neurons change the activity of an effector cell, for example, a response to the change is initiated.

Neurologically speaking, "learning can be broadly defined as a lasting change in behavior, resulting from prior experiences" (Cotman & Lynch, 1988, p. 1). It involves two types of memory—one for skills and procedures associated with the cerebellum, and one for facts, called declarative memory, that is associated with the medial-temporal lobe.

Procedural, Skill, or Rule Memory

This type of memory includes playing an instrument, driving a car, or linguistic syntax such as the construction of sentences. Procedural memory is stored in the cerebellum. Thompson (1986) discusses skill learning that is stored in the cerebellum. The cerebellum is generally important to skill coordination, which will be defective with cerebellar injury. Procedural memory is not affected by hippocampus and amygdala damage. Procedural memory encompasses skill or rule memory that is developed by continuous practice or conditioning. Skills that could be affected by insult to the cerebellum are riding a bicycle, typing, driving a car, solving puzzles, or using linguistic syntax, which is the grammatic structure of language.

Factual or Declarative Memory

This involves memory of dates, faces, places, individuals, and the semantic aspects of languages such as understanding and meaning. Factual or declarative memory can be affected by insult to certain areas of the brain.

Factual memory has two subcategories:

1. Simple factual memory, such as memory of what your house looks like, which is acquired rapidly and stored in a system with a tremendous capacity
2. Episodic memory, such as memory of experiences at a football game or a class reunion

The brain changes sensory information into declarative (factual) memories. Damage to the hippocampus, which is located deep in the brain, roughly between the ears, and/or the amygdala, which is located in the temporal lobe, can affect this type of memory. It appears that the cortical systems, the hippocampus, and the cerebral cortex are all related to declarative storage or memories that deal with facts.

There are also qualitative distinctions that the brain makes between simple experiences, such as visiting an art exhibit (simple factual), and more emotional experiences, such as going to your sister's wedding (episodic). Studies have shown that pathology can selectively affect different aspects of memory. In explaining behavior, it is important to be aware of the different forms and sensitivities of memory. The two systems of memory are interconnected and operate as a unitary complex system (Cotman & Lynch, 1988).

Physiology of Memory

Memory can be described as having three main physiological components. The first level, or the basic element of memory, is the synapse of the neurons where actual decoding of stimuli occurs as well as the mechanism for dealing with understanding and meaning. The next or second level in the process involves clusters of brain cells, called regions, that are responsible for storage, retrieval, and the processing of simple factual memory or episodic memory. The third level of memory can be viewed as having circuits that contain the complex learning that comprises both of the other two lower levels of cell structures (synapsis and regions).

Bear (1987) discusses widely dispersed areas of neural development that comprise a neural circuit. These circuits may be disturbed throughout their development to the extent that damage causes developmental delay and learning disabilities, as well as other neurobiological disorders arising early in development.

Some events that trigger responses in the brain are not learned, such as the individual's reaction to cold. Certain patterns of activity are needed to bring forth specific memories. Certain chemical processes are triggered by specific events, and these produce long-lasting changes in the synapsis (neural connections). The chemistry of memory, or the chemistry that would promote or improve memory, is not clearly defined. It is known that neurons are comprised of proteins and lipids that are continuously broken down and replaced as part of the long-term memory process. It is now known that the adult brain can grow new synapsis after an injury.

Scientists recently learned that even though brain cells cannot divide and replicate, many of the active undamaged cells even in the elderly brain can grow more dendrites and axons, enhancing intercommunication. The degree of the compensatory mechanism of plasticity probably accounts in part for how much maintenance of normal intellectual functioning and brain metabolism exists as individuals grow older.

In humans, encoding is thought to be accomplished in the cortex. The cortex and subcortical regions appear to be the site of memory storage. The most important part of the visual memory neural system is the hippocampus and the amygdala. Combined with other structures, they make up the limbic system. The hippocampus plays an important role in the formulation of new factual memories. It is involved in the transfer of information back and forth between the two hemispheres of the brain, and also functions as a secondary temporary storage hold. The hippocampus is of interest for its role in short-term or working memory. It is thought to act as a buffer, similar to a buffer of a computer, by receiving and holding new information a short while before sending it on for storage as long-term memory in other parts of the brain. When the hippocampus is damaged. short-term memory is impaired, a finding borne out of studies of human amnesiacs and by cognitive tests on monkeys. In studying primates (monkeys), Mishkin (1978) and Mishkin, Malamut, and Bachevalier (1984) found that losing the function of the hippocampus causes them to forget how two objects related to each other spatially. In humans, an example of this problem would be an individual who might remember five friends' faces, but not be able to tell how they relate spatially in terms of where they live compared to each other. New learning can take place but is lost in a short period of time.

The hippocampus is one of the sites in the brain susceptible to damage from stroke, head trauma, and various diseases such as cancer or injuries. The amygdala is responsible for both storing information as well as the emotional characteristics of stored information. Damage here, it is thought, results in problems associated with socially acceptable behavior, or with how an individual feels about his or her place or status in the family. An individual may remember the family but not have feelings about how he or she is perceived emotionally by family members. The amygdala is also required for integrating visual and tactile kinesthetic memories. Studies indicate that each of the five senses has neural connections leading to the amygdala.

Researchers are trying to determine how damage to the memory-related structures relates to learning disabilities by studying patients who have had brain injury with concomitant memory deficits. An important area of study is the relationship between synaptic processes and the different cell organizations when learning occurs and memory patterns are formed.

Both memory and emotion are associated with the limbic system. The limbic system is made up of subcortical structures such as the hypothalamus, the hippocampus, and the amygdala. It appears that the memory function of the limbic system is influenced by the power of the emotional overlay associated with particular experiences. Mood, emotion, and motivation associated with the limbic system appears to exert an important influence on memory. Material learned under conditions of sadness or happiness, for example, seem to be easier to recall and are remembered in more depth (Mishkin, Malamut, & Bachevalier, 1984).

There are several unanswered areas of concern dealing with memory. First, there is a need to identify the precise physiological variables that are a part of the mechanisms of memory as it is presently understood. Another area of study is the effect of such disturbances as drugs, injury, or anoxia (lack of oxygen) on the various elements and levels of memory.

FACTORS AFFECTING THE BRAIN

Factors that affect the brain often result in lesions to specific areas involving sensory and motor functions. Agnosias are disabilities that involve complex cerebral lesions. Insults that result in complex motor disabilities are called apraxias. It is often difficult to distinguish between agnosias and apraxias. When language function is impaired due to lesions, the disabilities are termed *aphasias*. Aphasias can be tied to motor dysfunction (lesions), such as writing, and speech or receptive problems, as in reading or listening. For aphasia to occur, the lesions must be located in the dominant hemisphere, which is the left hemisphere in right-handed individuals and also in many left-handed people (Goldberg, 1988).

Factors affecting the brain are many and varied and include the effects of early and/or persistent child abuse; damage resulting from toxic substances such as drugs, alcohol, and certain minerals; early deprivation; poor nutrition; and oxygen starvation. These can act in the prenatal, perinatal, or postnatal stages of life.

Prenatal causes of brain damage can result from RH factor incompatibility, overexposure to x-rays, cigarette smoking, medications toxic to the fetus, bleeding, and prematurity (Knobloch & Pasamanick, 1974).

Perinatal factors include difficult delivery, oxygen starvation at the time of delivery, prolonged labor, premature separation of the placenta, intracranial hemorrhages, and drugs (Colletti, 1979).

Postnatal damage can occur from trauma to the head, strokes, infections, such as encephalitis and meningitis, and tumors.

Injury to the developing brain, or spontaneously arising neuroanatomical abnormalities during late gestation (16–24 weeks), can result in developmental dyslexia (Galaburda et al., 1985). Damage to the nervous system can impact individuals in different ways, depending on the age at which the injury was sustained. Older individuals tend to suffer greater debilitations than children.

The fact that the brain can repair itself and neurons can engage in new growth has important implications for recovery of functions. Damage to one area during the developmental stages can result in new circuits being formed by undamaged residual neurons. New connections can grow and replace old and damaged connections. Major damage, however, can affect even the development of new pathways, especially during the critical periods of early development, and still result in abnormal circuits. This can also be true in areas affecting attitudes, emotion, and goal direction.

Individuals who experience brain injury may exhibit one or more of the following:

Poor memory	Perseverative behavior
Impulsiveness	Poor judgment
Poor or low attention	Easily fatigued
Lack of concentration	Impaired judgment
Dependence on	Inability to generalize
concreteness	Catastrophic reactions

Slow to respond	Clumsiness/poor motor
Problems with language	control
Inconsistent behavior	Restlessness
Slow information	Slow motor development
processing	in childhood
Inflexibility—fear	Poor generalizability
of change	Poor automatization
Problem with staying	learning
on task	

The migration and connection of neurons are influenced by genetic factors as well as epigenetic factors, which are environmental influences in the uterus. This includes hormones, body chemicals, diet, toxins, infections, and all the other elements that might be transmitted from the mother to the fetus. Testosterone, for instance, is known to alter the way the brain takes shape. Progesterone, estrogen, and the adrenal steroids are also thought to play a role in the developing infant brain.

Competency in learning depends on the integrity and effective operation of the neural circuits. These store information and transfer it in a form that can be retrieved. The system undergoes continual molecular changes as new synapses are formed. One theory that relates to memory is based on insult to the network of cortical and subcortical structures that facilitate the process of understanding (encoding). Using the network concept as a frame of reference, it is possible to formulate certain hypotheses about possible causes of learning disabilities.

Neurophysiologists have been collecting data on the various brain states such as arousal and attention. It is well documented that disturbances in certain areas of the brain can result in poor attention. Hyperactive children are thought by some scientists to have disturbed arousal mechanisms. Arousal is the sense of awareness and selective screening of stimuli such as hearing your telephone ring but not paying attention to it. Other physiological elements related to arousal disorders include endocrine and hormonal problems and their effects on the strength of trace memory. Hippocampal rhythm or activity in the brain may be affected by problems associated with cholinergic neurons or cells in the forebrain, and disturbance in this system could affect the learning process.

Learning requires more than just awareness and a focus of attention. It also involves motivation. Study of brain dysfunction will invariably lead to new treatment strategies that have great importance for the education of learning-impaired students. The future holds important answers in terms of prevention and correction of brain-related disorders.

BRAIN-RELATED RESEARCH

Researchers are only beginning to document how the brain develops and operates, but they know that between the twentieth week of gestation and the end of the first year of life, millions of neurons are migrating and interconnecting with each other to create the final shape of the individual brain.

Important research in neuroanatomy and neurophysiology has focused on the effects of various anomalies of brain structure on learning. Brain-related learning dysfunction has been determined by many to be an important study area that may provide answers to long-term concerns about student performance in school (Mishkin, Malamut, & Bachevalier, 1984; Grossberg & Stone, 1986; Merjanian et al., 1986; Staubli, Roman, & Lynch, 1985). Currently, there is evidence that some students who exhibit school failure do have central nervous system dysfunction.

Animal Research

A better understanding of the anatomy of memory formation has been achieved through primate studies of the hippocampal formation and the amygdala. Insult was introduced and a deficit was produced in the animal's ability to recall which of two objects was previously presented (Murray & Mishkin, 1984; Zola-Morgan, Squire, & Mishkin, 1982).

Structural changes have also been observed in rats as a result of manipulating their environment. Rats raised in an "enriched" environment showed an increase in the number of synapses per neuron (Turner & Greenough, 1983). Greenough, Larson, and Withers (1985) demonstrated the effects of motor training on rats' preferred paw. After 16 days of training to use the nonpreferred paw, branching of the dendrite structure of the synapse was found to be greater on the side opposite the preferred paw.

Memory studies with rats suggest that memory deficits in rats that have had hippocampal damage resembles the type of rapid forgetting described in individuals who have also experienced hippocampal and temporal lobe damage (Staubli, Roman, & Lynch, 1985; Staubli et al., 1986). Studies of this nature are proving useful in terms of associating brain research with animals and studies of humans suffering brain insult.

Human Research

Several different types of professionals are interested in the neurobiology of the brain and its relationship to learning. Neuropsychologists combine psychology and neurology to study perceptual, cognitive, and motor deficits in relation to brain structure and function. Neurobiologists deal more with the physiology and chemistry of the brain in order to understand better the relationships between structure, function, and behavior. Educators who work with the students who manifest cerebral dysfunction need to understand the nature of these disorders and the implications for learning.

Lessened ability to learn new skills and to function independently in adult life may result from many kinds of insults to the developing brain. Studies of adults and children enable us to understand the relationship between cognitive dysfunction and learning at different stages of development. Neuropsychological studies of humans suffering from brain injury have demonstrated that specific structures in the brain, such as the hippocampal formation can be tied to certain memory formations (Zola-Morgan, Squire, & Amaral, 1986).

Neuropsychologists have studied individuals in whom the fibers that connect the two cerebral hemispheres were severed. This split brain research indicated that after the surgery separating the two cerebral hemispheres, it was possible to isolate the function of each hemisphere. They were able to present information to either hemisphere alone without intrahemispheric communication (Sperry, 1968).

Galaburda and colleagues (1985) reported that the brains of several deceased dyslexic individuals indicated a disorganization of the cell structure in the language cortex. McBride and Kemper (1982) reported that damage to certain cortical areas as described in dyslexic learners appear to reflect injury during the late gestation period of the developing brain of the fetus.

Research dealing with humans has expanded our knowledge base in areas dealing with the brain and different types of learning such as sensitization, habitualization, and classical conditioning. We now understand how specific biochemical mechanisms, such as memory, can be identified and how physiological activity can affect changes in neural synapses, and that there are defined networks of cells related to specific learning. Learning occurs throughout life. Early learning affects later learning, and insult during the developmental stages has different effects on the neural pathways as growth proceeds (Galaburda et al., 1985). Early environment and experience is thought to affect each sensory system with its associated circuits. The concept of plasticity of nerves is important in that the younger child appears to have a more plastic system than the older individual. Critical periods are therefore present for the various types of learning.

Brain research suggests that sequential and linguistic tasks are related to left-brain function, and simultaneous and visual-spatial tasks are related to right-brain functions (Wood, 1983). Tasks related to reading, arithmetic, and spelling are determined to be left-brain functions. Activities involving art, intuitive thinking, and spatial thinking are determined to be right-brain tasks. It is important to understand that learning involves sequences of cellular events, and that a disturbance of any sequence in these events could affect the acquisition and storage of new information.

Chapter 4

Behavior Management

OVERVIEW

The behavioral-cognitive approach to teaching can be utilized by educators with a modicum of training in any educational setting. Teachers are concerned with behaviors that disrupt school activities and that inhibit learning. They are also concerned with instructional tactics or strategies that will enhance learning.

Often students exhibit certain clusters of behavior that can be called symptoms or indicators of certain types of problems. Clustering of behavior suggests the following classifications:

1. Aggressive (Acting Out/Passive)
2. Sensitive-Withdrawn
3. Immature-Dependent
4. Psychotic-Neurotic
5. Delinquent-Unorthodox
6. Social Disorders (Cognitive-Social Skills and Adaptive Behavior)
7. Attention Deficit Disorders (hyperactivity, inattention, impulsivity)
8. Control Factors (distractibility, perseveration, disinhibition)
9. Motivational Factors

These classifications are not mutually exclusive and sometimes overlap in particular individuals.

It is important to note that any of these behaviors can appear at one time or another in any individual. Our concern here is for the student who consistently exhibits patterns of behavior that interfere with learning in school. In viewing behavior, a great deal depends upon the frustration level and coping ability of the teacher. What is construed as problem behavior is, to a large extent, dependent upon the "eyes of the beholder." Terms such as *emotional disturbance* and *behavior problem* have different meanings to different people. Therefore, each case must be considered on its own merits, with consideration given to the attitudes and feelings of the teacher, the observable behaviors of the student, the environment in which all of this is taking place (which includes school, home, and community), and the dynamic interactions that occur among all of these factors. This type of ecological assessment provides a more comprehensive picture of the context in which specific behaviors occur.

There are often many reasons for behavior that are not easy to pinpoint. The teacher's responsibility is to probe, accepting relevant information and rejecting gossip and generalizations to particular students or groups. Sometimes students react differently away from school. It is axiomatic that attitude has a profound effect on behavior and that an individual's perception of a situation can alter the individual's subsequent behavior. It is reasonable to expect that an individual's early social interactions can affect later behavior, in terms of developing generalized expectancies or cognitive sets that mediate these human interactions. The young child in a reading group who suffers embarrassment and humiliation by the teacher and peers, no matter how well-intentioned, may suffer anxiety later in similar situations. These are gray areas of behavior that are difficult to categorize and the parameters indicated in this chapter serve as guidelines for looking at different types of behavior.

CLASSIFICATIONS

The following descriptions of behavior can be used easily by the teacher to describe students who fall more into one category than into another and to focus on target behaviors to be modified. Procedures for dealing with these behaviors are included. If teachers use categorical labels in discussing students or in writing reports, they should define quite specifically what these labels or constructs mean and imply.

Aggressive (Acting Out/Passive)

Behavior which could be described as aggressive can either be acting out or passive and can be an effect of many factors. Acting-out behavior is particularly disturbing to the teacher because it tends to disrupt classroom activities and interferes with the teacher's ability to instruct. Acting-out students are usually a problem to their peers as well as to the teacher and are easily identified. Passive-aggressive students are resistant to school activities and appear unmotivated. These students do not exhibit the anger of the acting-out learners, but the rebellion and hostility are present nonetheless.

OBSERVABLE BEHAVIOR: AGGRESSIVE (ACTING OUT/PASSIVE)
The student

1. Disrupts other students by moving about excessively and by being annoying
2. Is disrespectful or discourteous to peers or adults
3. Behaves in a complusive manner
4. Is negative and does not do what is required of him or her
5. Is rough or noisy

6. Exhibits long periods of unhappiness
7. Is destructive to his or her own belongings
8. Does not complete assignments as requested
9. Indicates poor or bad feelings about school
10. Uses profanity excessively
11. Will not sit or stand still according to command
12. Will not stay with or complete a learning task within a normal time limit
13. Will not obey commands from authority figures
14. Is uncooperative in group learning or recreation activities
15. Fights with others without provocation
16. Is hot-tempered and flares up easily
17. Is undependable
18. Destroys the belongings of others
19. Behaves like a clown
20. Tests to extreme limits
21. May be diagnosed as hyperactive

DISCUSSION: AGGRESSIVE (ACTING OUT)
French (1986) found that among students rejected in school, those who manifest aggression make up a distinct group and have problems with self-control, conduct disorders, and withdrawal. These students who are rejected by their peers need special attention and should be identified early so that appropriate interventions can be instituted (Coie, 1985).

Sociometric devices, such as peer sociometric scales, are one method of identifying socially rejected learners. Teacher ratings and naturalistic observation are other methods of assessing students' school role functioning. These devices along with student interviews may help determine the levels of aggression and the precipitating factors. Although intervention for social skills deficits tends to focus on building appropriate social behavior, intervention designed to modify aggression has traditionally targeted directly on the behavior to be changed.

It appears that a combination of treatment methods may be necessary for some students, which includes self-monitoring and dealing directly with the underdeveloped aspects of appropriate behavior (Ladd, 1985). Research suggests that aggressive behavior tends to decline with age (Hartup, 1974).

Some learners have a desperate desire for attention and require a great deal of "eye contact." Most teachers do not have the time to give individual attention to learners with this problem and may find that the students will do almost anything to get the teacher's attention or to engage in conversation. Attention-getting behaviors may take a negative form and the students may disturb other learners by making strange noises, breaking things, interrupting the teacher, and doing a myriad of other noxious things.

The inability to control aggressive impulses is one indicator among many of social immaturity in older students. Sometimes it appears to be an impossible task to try to control aggressive students who meet life situations with a frontal attack, often frightening parents, teachers, and peers with their bold actions and feelings of power. The teacher's initial impulse often is to strike back, to punish, and to get revenge. This in many cases reinforces the behavior rather than diminishes it. Aggressive-acting-out students can often be found in the halls—sent there by the teacher—or in the principal's office. Teachers and parents may feel guilty about having punished these students. These are normal feelings, but care should be taken so the student will not perceive them.

Some parents condone or even admire and reward aggressive behavior. However, the school cannot let aggressiveness go beyond generally accepted normal limits. The students who disrupt learning, upset their classmates, and keep teachers in a state of anger and anxiety may require additional specialized attention, and this should be considered before expulsion from school is decided upon.

Aggression has many underlying causes, a few of which include:

1. A concomitant to failure in learning
2. An organic brain dysfunction
3. A reaction to treatment at home
4. A symptom of repressed hostilities
5. A reaction to unmet needs

Other factors that relate to aggressive behavior include the following:

1. *Boredom:* The learners may become bored with school because they are not learning and cannot cope with the instructional program and the materials which may be beyond their grasp.
2. *The Phenomenon of Natural Movement:* Children must move around, wrestle, or otherwise engage in body contact with each other as part of the natural developmental growth process. The "anxious" teacher who makes a "mountain out of a molehill" in these situations may create problems where none exist.
3. *Coping Behavior (Panic and Anxiety):* Panic-coping is probably one of the most critical areas of concern in students who exhibit a learning disability. Pressure from parents, teachers, and peers can result in a continual state of frustration with accompanying anxiety. This anxiety can become specifically associated with a particular learning task such as reading, writing, or arithmetic. The students who fail in reading and at the same time receive a great deal of pressure to learn to read may become anxious and tense when asked to read from a book. They may even generalize this anxiety to all books. Perhaps students who are "book anxious" need to be taught to read away from books completely. They should be given a book only when they can achieve 100 percent success in terms of the reading vocabulary of that particular volume or section of a volume. The student must develop good coping behavior patterns in order to deal with continuous frustration in academic areas.

DISCUSSION: AGGRESSIVE (PASSIVE)
Passive-aggressive learners may not appear to care, but there is usually an inner conflict where they are torn between simultaneous feelings of love and hate for parents and/or teachers. Parents who apply pressure beyond ordinary limits sometimes foster passive-aggressive behavior in their children. These students may have an unconscious desire to fail in school and to hurt themselves through poor academic achievement. This may be one way of "getting back" at parents who have been very demanding.

Passivity can seriously interfere with learning. Passive students who exhibit shy, fearful, and unobtrusive behavior may be overlooked by the teacher. Their way of dealing with a poor sense of self and a lowered ego is to withdraw. When asked to perform tasks that result in failure, the passive learner often develops a sense of helplessness and exhibits confused and disorganized behavior.

The coping mechanism most frequently used when faced with stress or unpleasant tasks is passive resistance and avoidance. Along with an overdependence on adults, there is a tendency to avoid eye contact, to become uncomfortable when complimented, and to desist from asking questions.

TREATMENT CONSIDERATIONS: AGGRESSIVE (ACTING OUT)
Following are some general suggestions to keep in mind when working with aggressive-acting-out students.

1. In general, these students do not respond satisfactorily to the following:
   a. reasoning
   b. physical punishment
   c. excessive isolation
   d. withdrawal of privileges
   e. withdrawal of social reinforcement
   f. verbal and social rewards

2. The best treatment for aggressive-acting-out students is, if possible, to anticipate the episode and remove the students from the situation for a short time, while directing them into another activity.
3. A "cooling-off" period is important. This means giving the students an opportunity to be off by themselves so they will have time to think about the situation and the ensuing results.
4. After a particular episode, place the student in a time-out room or corner. This should be an isolating, nonrewarding experience—not a reinforcement for aggression.
5. Aggressive students particularly need structure in their lives and boundaries delineated for them in terms of their behavior. They need to know just how far they can go. Therefore, limits must have a purpose and not just become a set of rules. Limits should be few at first, slowly increased, and verbalized to the learner in a simplified manner.
6. Organize the school day so that, through the planned unfolding of school activities, the students will have satisfied many of their unmet needs (e.g., need for approval, need for recognition, need for acceptance).
7. The teacher must be specific in giving directions. "Stop playing," or "Do your work," or "No talking," is not specific enough for the aggressive learner.
8. Since many of these students have a low frustration tolerance, allow them more time than ususal for shifting from one activity to another.
9. Avoid frustrating the learners by having them do things that can be accomplished with at least some success.
10. Use self-checking materials and involve the students in projects so they will not become bored and get into trouble.
11. Provide stimulating and physically active, tension-releasing activities.
12. Students exhibiting hostility and aggression (active or passive) should have opportunities to displace this behavior through activities such as running (jogging), contact sports, arts and crafts, manual arts, using a punching bag, or gardening. Agriculture is an excellent vehicle for displacing aggression.
13. Introduce novel or attention-getting activities into the program.
14. Aggressive behavior may be a concomitant to hyperactivity. In this case the student should be permitted to leave his or her seat or engage in some other activity for a brief period of time to prevent aggressive episodes.
15. Utilize techniques which will help the student to delay or postpone gratification.
16. Utilize the Premack principle and pair a low probability behavior (e.g., sitting in a seat) with a high probability behavior (e.g., sitting in a favorite chair). The former should be strengthened.
17. In extreme cases, the length of the school day may need to be shortened. The student will only attend part of the day, to be increased accordingly.
18. Verbally aggressive students who ridicule others may require the following:
    a. separation from the group along with teacher-student discussion about the student's actions
    b. reward for not verbally disturbing the class
19. Look at antecedent behavior when fighting occurs in the classroom. Was the incident provoked by a student who has a pattern of fighting or by an accident-prone student with poor motor control?

TREATMENT CONSIDERATIONS: AGGRESSIVE (PASSIVE)

Following are some general suggestions to keep in mind when working with passive-aggressive students.

1. For the passive-aggressive student, it is important that the teacher not "nag." The teacher should insist that the learner carry out short directions or assignments and get him or her started.
2. Several other approaches can be used.
    a. The child should be encouraged to express himself or herself verbally as he or she works. This will allow for feedback of the child's thought processes and feelings.
    b. Strategies that include paraphrasing, questioning, and predicting will engage the learner in verbal discourse.
    c. Utilizing advance organizers, such as cards, charts, and other visuals, are helpful.
    d. Provide the student with visual evidence of success by graphing work or through other record-keeping systems.
    e. Help the learner to make judgments and feel comfortable with making mistakes through a "celebration" of errors, followed by an analysis of reasoning in solving problems.

Sensitive-Withdrawn

Students who can be described as fitting into the sensitive-withdrawn category may exhibit anxious or even depressed behavior. These students are generally shy, self-conscious and prefer not to be the "center of attention." They simply prefer not to call attention to themselves. The following are examples of some of the observable behaviors under this category.

OBSERVABLE BEHAVIOR: SENSITIVE-WITHDRAWN
The student

1. Exhibits feelings of insecurity
2. Becomes unhappy or cries easily
3. Likes to be left alone and withdraws from others
4. Becomes frustrated in everyday situations
5. Overreacts to the negative statements or behavior of others
6. Is anxious or fearful for no apparent reason
7. Does not participate in recreation or play activities with others
8. Is easily embarrassed or behaves in a self-conscious manner
9. Exhibits feelings of poor self-worth
10. Is shy in social situations
11. Is unable to be at ease and enjoy himself or herself with others
12. Exhibits little self-confidence

DISCUSSION: SENSITIVE-WITHDRAWN

In contrast to the aggressive-acting-out students, the markedly sensitive, withdrawn students avoid situations that will place them in conflict. They are of concern to teachers who may perceive them as unhappy and unable to develop because of poor social interaction habits or class participation. Their behavior is generally not considered "bad" or punishable, but is disconcerting to parents and teachers who reward and are in turn rewarded by positive social interaction. Teachers as a group are less sensitized to these types of students and, except for extreme cases, complain little about them. Some teachers, on the other hand, equate sensitive, withdrawn behavior with being "well behaved" and describe the student as "quiet" and "well-mannered."

Generally, treatment for this type of student is focused on gradual desensitization, and strategies are employed to include the student in daily activities of school life. Some students are quiet and pretend to "play the game." They seem to be occupied with the required task. The student who is holding a book may be doing just that and nothing else. Therefore, in defining and charting task-related behavior, it is important to be certain that it is purposeful—rather than nonpurposeful—task-related behavior that is observed. Withdrawn students may have more problems to overcome than those who are acting out. The acting-out learners are still, in most cases, fighting to survive, while the withdrawn learners may have already given up hope. It will take the combined effort of the school, the home, and the community in dealing with the total learner to facilitate any real changes in the behavior of these students.

TREATMENT CONSIDERATIONS: SENSITIVE-WITHDRAWN

The following are some general suggestions to keep in mind when working with sensitive-withdrawn students.

1. Condition the students to variable input (praise or punishment) slowly.
2. Involve the students in small group activities with one or two other students in the class.
3. Understand that these students may retreat for long periods from perceived negative interactions.
4. Be cognizant that these students may prefer familiar situations perceived to be "safe."
5. Give short assignments with built-in opportunities for free time and personal interaction.
6. In teaching situations, remember that these students do not want to be "singled out" and do not respond to forced participation.
7. Seat the students in an area that will present them with fewer opportunities for withdrawal and isolation.
8. Refrain from any intimidation or coercive tactics. These students are easily intimidated and respond negatively to coercion.
9. Do not rush the students. Give them an opportunity to respond at their own rate.
10. Avoid criticizing or reproaching the students in public.
11. Elicit appropriate behavior through the utilization of modeling techniques.
12. Strive for successive approximations to desired behavior.
13. Remember that the primary target behavior is to increase participation.
14. Provide opportunities for the students to express themselves in different ways (i.e., art, music, writing).
15. Do not back the students up against the wall so they may have to "lose face."
16. Reinforce the students consistently for even simple tasks at first, particularly individual efforts that are nonsolicited.
17. Avoid setting qualifications for participation that cannot be met by the sensitive-withdrawn students.
18. Use alternative methods to encourage verbal communication. Some students will not readily talk to parents, teachers, or peers, but may talk over telephones or walkie-talkies.
19. If the withdrawn students appear to daydream excessively, provide structured interruptions (eye contact, touch, etc.) and rewards for completing assignments on time (use good judgment).

20. Some shy students are also perfectionists and may require private discussions with the teacher concerning realistic expectations in the classroom.

Immature-Dependent

Immature-dependent students often exhibit behavior inappropriate for their chronological age. These students require a great deal of patience and many opportunities to learn particular tasks in different situations before appropriate social behavior can be stabilized. The following are some of the observable behaviors for these students.

OBSERVABLE BEHAVIOR: IMMATURE-DEPENDENT
The student

1. Requires constant direction and relies a great deal on others
2. Prefers to play or interact with younger people
3. Appears inactive or apathetic at inappropriate times
4. Needs a great deal of support and "stroking" from others
5. Has difficulty making decisions
6. Does not attend to activities that require a degree of concentration
7. Is easily influenced by others
8. Exhibits passive behavior
9. Appears absentminded or lost in thought to excess
10. Demands an unusual amount of attention
11. Continually complains of physical pains such as stomachaches and headaches

DISCUSSION: IMMATURE-DEPENDENT
Teachers sometimes lose patience with these children because they are so demanding of time and dependent upon them for every little thing. Some students cry easily, or exhibit other immature behaviors. Some are continually complaining to the teacher about students who are picking on them, or they are observed constantly bickering with other students. Many tend to socialize with younger children and have difficulty getting along with their peers. They have problems with independent activities and require constant reassurance. Some students may cheat and/or lie to cover up their feelings. This is essentially a parent-child problem in terms of overdependence that transfers to the school. The concept to keep in mind in working with these students is independent functioning. All school activities should be geared to accomplish this by gradual increments to insure success. The students must learn to trust themselves and depend on their own judgment rather than only on the judgment of others. The teacher can insure success by calling on the students when they are sure the students know the right answers to the questions asked. Parents tend to control or direct the students' lives, permitting little opportunity for independent action or for "growing up." This classification or category of behavior is difficult to define.

TREATMENT CONSIDERATIONS: IMMATURE-DEPENDENT
These students need specific opportunities to learn socially acceptable behavior. The following are some general suggestions to keep in mind when working with immature-dependent students.

1. Provide a structured environment that will initially require monitoring and supervision.
2. Begin with simple or elementary activities or small assignments that will require the student to make decisions such as selecting between two choices and then gradually moving to more choices and longer assignments.
3. Provide many trials in different situations for learning acceptable social behavior.
4. Carefully consider rewards for independent activity and acceptable social behavior as part of the total treatment program.
5. Use both scheduled and spontaneous times for teacher-student or other adult-student private discussions about feelings. The adult can share expressions of concern, "I know how you feel . . ." These times can be used to plan for and encourage self-activated and more independent behavior.
6. Include the students in activities that provide a creative expression of feelings (e.g., drama, art, music, crafts, writing).
7. Plan small groups where the students can work with peers and on occasion model another student's leadership.
8. Use structured group activities that involve a small group of students working on a carefully planned class project.
9. Involve the students in competitive games where they have a good chance for success.
10. Include the immature-dependent students in the assignment of responsibilities in the classroom (e.g., caring for material, animals or plants, delivering messages, etc.).
11. Encourage participation in hobby clubs or special interest groups.

12. Discuss with parents or guardians activities that will increase the students' freedom to successfully perform independent tasks (e.g., going to sports events with friends, visiting other homes).
13. Gradually allow the students to confront disagreement with friends at school or at home. Avoid interceding for the students and interfering with situations in which they can begin to solve their own problems.

Psychotic-Neurotic

Services for students exhibiting behavior that is clearly psychotic or symptomatic of severe neuroses are limited in terms of public school programming. This category is not to be confused with those students who exhibit episodes of aberrant behavior but who for the most part function quite effectively in educational situations. It is the student who consistently manifests deep-seated, bizarre, aberrant, or fearful behavior that we are concerned about in terms of classroom management. The following are examples of behavior that fall into the category of being psychotic-neurotic in nature.

OBSERVABLE BEHAVIOR: PSYCHOTIC-NEUROTIC
The student

1. Exhibits inappropriate affect, such as laughing or crying at the wrong time
2. Exhibits unintelligible or strange speech patterns
3. Is not reality-oriented in mannerisms or speech
4. Tells lies excessively and tends to exaggerate greatly
5. Enjoys inflicting pain on self
6. Feels that people want to physically hurt him or her
7. Exhibits long periods of silence and almost complete withdrawal
8. Behaves in a bizarre manner
9. Exhibits compulsive behavior, such as excessive hand washing
10. Appears extremely nervous
11. Enjoys inflicting pain on others
12. Thinks everyone is talking about, and plotting against, him or her
13. Is fearful much of the time
14. Exhibits long periods of silence and withdrawal followed by extreme activity and excessive verbal behavior
15. Is extremely fearful about going to school
16. Has unreasonable fear of animals, heights, water, open places, etc.
17. Has severe feelings of inferiority

DISCUSSION: PSYCHOTIC-NEUROTIC
The kinds of problems that are dealt with in this section are serious to the extent that they affect the emotional lives of all the students. These students, as a group, do not benefit significantly from school activities. Many of these students experience uncontrolled anxiety that is devastating and debilitating. This calls for comprehensive support and crisis approaches that will reduce the suffering. Teachers working with specialists and parents need to use techniques that will reduce anxiety. Generally, medical cooperation and supervision is part of the treatment program, and medication may be part of the overall treatment schedule.

Students who exhibit unreasonable fears may not be reality oriented. Bizarre behavior is not readily accepted by peers or teachers. Children who are severely disorganized, autistic, schizophrenic, or school phobic, for example, require specialized services in most cases. These services may be supplied by a total community service system which includes mental health, special instructional programs, and related support services. Schools that do serve these youngsters through special programs require specialized or highly trained personnel. For many severely emotionally disturbed children, the process of treatment is long and the projected outcomes in terms of positive results are more limited than for the other categories discussed. Disagreement exists as to the specific nature or causes of particular types of disorders such as autism, for example. In dealing with autism we have to rule out such factors as deafness and retardation. Some of these students will require lifelong institutionalization or supervision. Many small or rural communities have had to combine resources in order to be able to provide services for these students.

TREATMENT CONSIDERATIONS: PSYCHOTIC-NEUROTIC
The following are some general suggestions to keep in mind when planning services for psychotic-neurotic students.

1. It is difficult to provide treatment for many disturbed students in regular school settings.
2. There are deep underlying causes for bizarre or aberrant behavior that require professional attention.
3. Some of these students will need trained teachers and require long-term treatment.
4. Utilize a community-based mental health approach where available.

5. Some of these students may be able to function in academic settings within a limited school day.
6. Reinforce any successful school or home activity.
7. Teachers must recognize their professional limitations and not go beyond them in attempting specific treatments.
8. For *school phobic* students, the following considerations are suggested:
   a. At first, allow the parent or a friend to attend school with the student for a limited school day (one-half hour, one hour, one and one-half hours). This is a process of desensitization.
   b. Alternate people who come to school with the student (i.e., father, grandmother, aunt, friend).
   c. If necessary, allow the student to telephone home during the school day.
   d. Permit the student to bring to school objects to which he or she is particularly attached.
   e. Set up a schedule of reinforcement that includes other individuals in the school (i.e., school nurse, secretary, bus driver, cafeteria worker).
   f. Do not single out the student in an embarrassing manner.
   g. Use a variety of reinforcements on a continous basis at first and reward the student for coming to school regularly.
   h. Provide the student with individual as well as group tasks that will gain approval from classmates.
   i. Include the student in high interest and stimulating activities (i.e., television, movies, trips).
   j. Seat the student close to the teacher.
   k. Let the student know that he or she was missed when absent from school.
   l. Speak to the student's parents or guardian on the telephone when the student is at home, and praise the student's efforts.
   m. Set up a schedule at home and in school and stick to it.
9. For *general fearfulness,* consider the following:
   a. Discuss the causes and nature of things that frighten the student.
   b. Do not force participation. Allow the student to set up his or her own goals each day.
   c. The student can act out a fearful situation through role playing.
   d. Avoid reminding the student of his or her fears. The idea is to reduce anxiety.
   e. If the student is afraid of written tests, permit him or her to take oral tests.

   f. Condition the student to animals (for example, a hamster) by successive approximation; the learner can stay in the same room, stand near the animal or touch it when held by the teacher, and finally hold and stroke it.
10. *Depressed students* need the following considerations:
    a. Establish a warm student-teacher relationship. Expect to be tested and possibly rejected.
    b. Insure success and inspire confidence in the student by freely praising him or her for successful efforts.
    c. A busy student will have less time to become depressed.
    d. Avoid timed tests or long drawn out assignments for depressed students.
    e. Medication may be needed for depression and other emotional disorders under strict medical supervision.
11. For *violent behavior,* consider the following:
    a. The student should be separated from another student or from the group immediately.
    b. If a student displays weapons and exhibits homicidal tendencies, school officials must attempt to remove the weapons. Parents and/or other authorities must be included in a staff meeting of the professionals who can provide immediate help in determining the cause of the behavior.
    c. A student who shows excessive brutality and sadistic behavior should be referred by the classroom teacher to the personnel in the schools or community agencies that can provide diagnosis and treatment. Lines of communication, support, and follow-up to the classroom teacher should be established prior to the student's return to the classroom.
    d. Students who inflict pain upon themselves will require specialized care and may need a variety of techniques including operant conditioning and individual counseling.
    e. The student who makes comments about suicide should not be ignored. Prevention will require supervision and immediate attention by trained personnel.

Delinquent-Unorthodox

Delinquent-unorthodox students come from environments that foster the development of gangs and a gang philosophy of life leading to delinquency.

These students for the most part do not exhibit disturbed social relationships. The behavior exhibited is quite realistic when considered within the circumstances or context of the local environment and the life-space of the individual. Unlike the other categories of behavior, the delinquent students may be quite well adjusted within the framework of their own peer group. There are many reasons for delinquent/criminal behavior. Some of the more-often-quoted causes of criminal behavior are (Fagen & Long, 1976):

1. Larger unskilled labor force—out of work
2. Overly strict, lax, or erratic parent-rearing practices
3. Overuse of television (i.e., murder and violence)
4. Lowering of morals, standards, and values
5. Inefficient law enforcement
6. Lack of effective adjudication—courts
7. Inadequate rehabilitation programs
8. Lack of national, state, and local commitment to teach students to cope with frustration and the demands of society, home, and school

OBSERVABLE BEHAVIOR: DELINQUENT-UNORTHODOX
The student

1. Exhibits variable habits of sleeping
2. Exhibits excessive loyalty to peers
3. Rejects figures representing authority
4. Is a member of a gang
5. Adheres to the gang's code of ethics and morality
6. Exhibits unorthodox social behavior
7. Steals in collaboration with others
8. Is often truant from school
9. Seeks the company of other delinquents
10. Does not express remorse for delinquent behavior

DISCUSSION: DELINQUENT-UNORTHODOX
Efforts have been made to show that school failure can be tied to delinquent behavior (Coleman, 1976). Mauser (1978) suggests that there may be a link between juvenile delinquency and learning disabilities. This is because, in general, there appears to be striking similarities in the educational needs, attitudes, and self-concepts of learning disabled students and those of students classified as juvenile delinquent. The AIR (American Institute for Research) Report (Murray, 1976) concludes that a broad pattern of learning handicaps, including learning disabilities, may exist among delinquents. Berman and Siegal (1976), after two studies, concluded that there is support for the link between learning disabilities and juvenile delinquency. While there is a no significant difference between learning disabled and others as to the incidence of delinquency, a larger portion of learning disabled juvenile delinquents are adjudicated than are normals. This is thought to be more a function of

differentiated treatment, in which the courts are influenced by the poor academic records of the learning disabled and their histories of academic failure.

The overriding concept in gang-related delinquent-unorthodox behavior is peer orientation and peer loyalty. Authority is something to oppose and schooling is not valued. As a group these students are more truant and tend to drop out of school at an earlier age than the average student. Security and recognition is sought from within the gang. Each member of the gang is under tremendous pressure from the group to conform to its own set of rules and regulations.This group loyalty is very difficult for the school to deal with, as a change in the behavior of the entire group is usually required before individuals within the group will respond to a more conformative style of life. These students are annoyed with problem situations which constrict or confine them. They are much less concerned about standard rules of right or wrong in terms of infractions which may result in guilt or remorse. It is difficult to orient the group away from delinquent behavior. In attempting to change the behavior of one individual we are in a sense asking him or her to "join us" and give up the gang. Without changing the environment, this is an extremely difficult task. It is also important to understand that we are dealing with varying degrees of "gangness," different types of behavior, and various degrees of affiliation.

Individual students may feel the need to engage in a personal battle with adults, whether they be parents, teachers, or others who represent authority figures. Many experienced teachers have learned that it is almost axiomatic that students will test limits in terms of interpersonal relationships. Sometimes opportunities for testing limits in different situations are not readily available in the home or community. In many instances where they are available in the students' out-of-school life, individuals who are important to them may not be consistent in the way they permit or react to testing. Students are generally uncomfortable with ambiguity or inconsistency and will force the teacher to deal or not to deal with different kinds of behaviors. It is the way the teacher deals with testing behaviors both initially and continually that makes the difference in many cases between the establishment of rapport or constant discontent in the classroom.

Today, teachers are more aware of peer group loyalities than in previous years. This may be due to the effects of the media, such as television shows depicting "gang" life, and of recent changes in our society in the behavior of young people. Peer group loyalty is especially cogent with respect to youth group activity to achieve change in our society. This loyalty goes beyond the "I'll show you I'm brave and not chicken" kind of loyalty that commonly exists in gang psychology—and which, to some extent, has always existed as a developmental phenomenon in the growth process of most young people. Today, this posture or attitude is being observed more and more in children in the elementary schools.

In many situations, teachers misunderstand this form of exhibiting group loyalites as being hostility directed toward the teacher personally; some teachers have become fearful of students. In some instances, hostility truly is directed toward the teacher; however, if it is treated as hostility and returned in kind, it can result in unfortunate and unhappy situations for all involved.

TREATMENT CONSIDERATIONS: DELINQUENT-UNORTHODOX

The principal need is for programs that focus on prevention that begins early (kindergarten) and continues throughout the grades. The second area is the training of teachers who will become aware of the problems and know how to deal with them within the confines of the regular class. This involves support, provisions for training, and problem-solving opportunities as shared responsibility between regular and special educators.

Assembling a cadre of resource individuals (counselors, psychologists, court workers, social workers, etc.) is necessary for input in gathering or developing the curriculum materials necessary to have a good school-based program. An assessment program that provides a framework for what areas need to be emphasized (e.g., cognitive, emotional, social, etc.) is vital. Another important area is curriculum application that instructs in academics and also inculcates a systematic understanding of the value of self-control. The student must learn to control his or her own behavior (e.g., when to put on the stops, when to postpone, when to assert one's feelings and position, etc.). Directing personal behavior implies the attainment of flexibility, which is so difficult for learning disabled adolescents.

The following are some general suggestions to keep in mind when working with delinquent-unorthodox students.

1. These students are primarily peer oriented.
2. They do not respond to an authoritative approach to changing their behavior.
3. These students generally exhibit behavior extremely inappropriate to school settings.
4. Their parents may be negligent and not provide enough socialization.
5. Street ideas override home or social values.
6. The behavior of most of these students tends to be resolved as they get older.
7. The school and community must channel these students' energies to socially acceptable activities.
   a. Develop a project to build a team clubhouse under supervision.
   b. Groups of students can repaint different areas within the school.
   c. A group of students can plant a vegetable and/or flower garden.
   d. Students can earn money for cleaning-up activities.
   e. Encourage the courts to force youthful offenders to repair damaged property.
8. Reinforce participation in the desired value system through involvement in school decision-making activities.
9. Insure success in school tasks.
10. Do not negate the power and loyalty of the group; focus attention on modifying the behavior of the group if possible.
11. Visit the home and discuss problems with the parents and the student.
12. Send a registered letter to parents if the student is consistently truant.
13. Competitive sports is one of the best ways of redirecting the delinquent student.
14. Counsel privately with the student assuring him or her that the discussions will be highly confidential.
15. A job after school may keep a delinquent student from getting into trouble.
16. For some students, a work/school program should be considered.
17. Provide opportunities for after school informal interactions or rap sessions.
18. Avoid using threats. They result in the opposite behavior more often than the desired behavior.
19. Sometimes it is best to ignore some behavior instead of constantly being in conflict with the student.
20. Avoid open confrontation and show honest interest. Most importantly, be patient. It took years for the student's problem to develop and it will not disappear in a few weeks.
21. In serious situations, a gang leader may have to be separated from his or her followers. He or she should, however, be reinforced for on-task and appropriate behavior.
22. In terms of prevention, counseling and supervision appear to be key concepts.
23. Attention must be given to academic success and recognition of self-worth. This includes providing training in self-direction.

24. The school can set up an "Intervention Center" where diagnosis, treatment, and monitoring of potential or habitual delinquents can occur.

CRIMINAL BEHAVIOR

Educators have long been concerned about the relationship between learning disabilities and criminal behavior. Studies have indicated that a significant percentage of adjudicated youth and adults are also learning disabled (Brier, 1989). Linkage between learning defects and criminal behavior are explained on the basis of susceptibility, school failure, and differentiated treatment. The question is whether or not having a learning disability is the primary cause of delinquent behavior. The majority of learning disabled students do not become delinquent (Porter & Rourke, 1983). One recent study suggested that "multifactor explanations" are needed (Brier, 1989). It appears that a substantial number of children who are diagnosed as learning disabled and who also have disorders of attention and impulse control may be predisposed to or at risk for delinquent behavior, or at least the increased likelihood of exhibiting noncompliant, aggressive, and antisocial behavior (Ackerman, Dykman, & Peters, 1977; Flicek & Landau, 1985; Loeber & Stouthamer-Loeber, 1987).

In one longitudinal study (childhood to adulthood), 50 percent of the individuals followed who had attention deficit disorders with hyperactivity (ADDH) became delinquent and drug abusing (Gittelman-Klein, 1987). ADDH with aggressivity may increase the likelihood of delinquency (Satterfield, Hoppe, & Schell, 1982). Those who exhibit language deficits in conceptualization, comprehension, and judgment are also thought to be more susceptible to becoming delinquent (Blalock, 1987; Lutey, 1977).

The majority of offenders seem to have weak verbal skills and low conceptual and reasoning skills while displaying adequate motor skills. As a group, they tend to exhibit low language skills (Quay, 1987; Hubble & Groff, 1981; Wilson & Hernnstein, 1985). The conclusion is that language deficits play an important role in delinquency.

School failure with accompanying frustration, rejection, negative self-image, and proneness to dropping out are said to be another logical cause of delinquent behavior (Amster & Lazurus, 1984; Murphy, 1986).

Some theorists point out that educational failure and conduct disorders emanate from a common cause, which in the young person is manifested by an active, aggressive, oppositional temperament (Wilson & Hernnstein, 1985). These types of children antagonize others, exhibit poor attention, and pay little attention to rules. Social rejection by peers of learning disabled children who are being ignored or ostracized, and receiving negative comments, are also considered to be important factors (LaGreca, 1981). Another factor that appears to be a critical variable in learning disabled students is a strong desire to achieve and an inability to do so (Elliot, Huzinga, & Ageton, 1985). School failure is viewed as a primary contributing factor as is dropping out of school. Both are considered high-risk factors in causing delinquent behavior.

Dunivant (1982) found that learning disabled youth were 200 percent more likely to be arrested for committing an offense and they had a high probability of being adjudicated as a delinquent. It appears that learning disabled students are treated differently from nondisabled offenders by the legal system. Some authorities feel that learning disabled students lack the strategies necessary to avoid problems within the judicial system, which include the process that occurs from getting caught to getting out. The negative behavior observed in these individuals includes poor eye contact (very little) with authority figures, poor verbal interaction, abusive behavior characteristics, and extraneous or annoying body movements (Dunivant, 1982; LaGreca, 1981).

Several predisposing factors are suggested that lead youngsters toward delinquency: low intelligence, psychopathology in the parent, and problems with management of behavior at home (Wilson & Hernnstein, 1985). Criminal behavior and alcoholism in the father also appears to be a strong predictor of delinquency (Rutter & Giller, 1984). Children tend to follow their parents' antisocial behavior. The parent dropping out of high school is another predictor (Robins, 1978).

Harsh or lax punishment, and neglectful, erratic, or inconsistent treatment by parents have been found to be other predictors of juvenile delinquency (Kazden, 1987; Snyder & Patterson, 1987). Most of the offenders come from families that express little encouragement and affection and do not involve children in problem solving or family discussions. Parents in these families are often critical, demanding, and insensitive, with inappropriate expectations. The parents or guardians are unable to establish rules that will be followed (Chapman & Boersma, 1979; Reid & Hresko, 1981).

DROPOUTS

When school becomes frustrating, given there are no family hardship reasons or illness to be concerned about, some learning disabled adolescents will opt to stay out. If the curriculum alternatives and support system are not there, students often drop out. General reasons for dropping out include:

1. Home environment that places little value on learning and continued education
2. Real or perceived prejudice against minorities
3. Lack of interest by the student; unmotivated or just plain bored with the curriculum
4. Poor overall school adjustment
5. History of grade failure
6. Poor reading ability and overall deficits in the language skills
7. Getting a job; making money
8. Not belonging to anything in school or not participating in school events (i.e., clubs, sports, etc.)
9. Friends who dropped out
10. Truancy; staying out of school and getting away with it

A review of the histories of many dropouts reveals several consistent patterns of behavior, such as truancy, fighting, disrespect to teachers, constantly breaking school rules, and overall disruptive behavior. Occasionally the "nice quiet student" drops out because of problems at home, but on the whole, problems in school begin to forecast the future for the majority of the dropouts.

About 25 percent of U.S. students drop out of school prior to graduation, compared to a graduation rate of 93 percent for Japan (School Dropouts, 1986). Students with handicaps drop out of school at an even higher rate (Wolman, Bruinicks, & Thurlow, 1989). Two major areas of concern are identified: dropouts among the general population, and dropouts in special education as a whole.

Dropouts among the General Population
Dropping out of school and high unemployment rates appear to go together (Rumberger, 1987; Grossnickle, 1986; Pallas, 1987). The dropout effect on society extends far beyond concerns over unemployment. It includes the concomitant increases in delinquency, overall crime rate, and use of illegal substances. The fact that there is a related strain on tax revenues and an increase in community social problems cannot be overlooked (Clark, 1987; Stengel, 1988).

Two issues are most cogent in comparing dropout rates. The first is related to how a dropout is defined, such as how long a student stays out of school before he or she is identified as a dropout. This includes different types of students such as those in special education or General Education Development (GED) programs, or those who return after being out for a long period of time. All are part of the problem of definition (Pallas, 1987; Rumberger, 1987).

The formula used to calculate dropout rates is the other main issue and reflects different approaches such as how cross-sectional or longitudinal data are used. A cross-sectional approach might try to assess the number of students who drop out in a given year by dividing the number of dropouts by the total enrollment (Doss & Sailor, 1987; Hammack, 1986; Morrow, 1986). The longitudinal approach answers questions related to the percentage of students entering school, say at x level, who do or do not complete school (graduate), after y number of years. In this case, dropout number x is divided by the number of students originally identified.

Dropouts in Special Education
The droput rates, characteristics, and results of special needs students leaving school were presented in the Tenth Annual Report to Congress by the United States Department of Education in 1988. It was estimated at that time that 26 percent of handicapped students (all categories and levels) dropped out of school during the year 1985–86. This figure is deemed a low estimate by some experts. Some studies show that students with handicaps drop out of school at a higher rate than nonhandicapped students (Stephenson, 1985). This appears to hold true for students who attend mainly special education classes, as well as for those who are mainstreamed (Wolman, Bruinicks, & Thurlow, 1989).

Most of the special needs students who drop out of school, estimated at 29 percent, are those with emotional disturbance, followed by those with mental retardation and learning disabilities (United States Department of Education, 1987).

Special education students who drop out of school tend to do so for reasons mainly involving negative attitudes toward school, low participation in school activities, poor attendance, disruptive behavior, low achievement, repetition of grades, or a combination of these factors.

What happens to students in special education who drop out of school? Students with mild handicaps who drop out of school do not do as well job-wise (lower employment rate) as those who stay to graduation. There is high variability in employment rates within groups, especially among the learning disabled. This is said to be partially related to where the students live (urban vs. rural settings) and to differences in employment rates by state. Also, many of the same characteristics that define a student for special education also define that student as being dropout-prone such as academic problems, grade repetition, being older than classmates, having an external locus of control, and so on. As previously indicated, students with emotional deficits are more at risk to drop out than any other handicapping category (Bruininks et al.,

1988; Edgar, 1987; U.S. Department of Education, 1987).

It is evident that a high proportion of students, handicapped and otherwise, are dropping out of school. Both groups find it difficult to adapt to the way schools are presently set up. Early identification and preventive measures seem to be one answer. An evaluation of viable alternatives to identify those that work with older students is another.

Dropout Characteristics—General Population
Dropout self-reports of why students leave school is a primary means of determining reasons for leaving. It is difficult to formulate final judgments regarding cause-effect relationships because of too many intervening variables. Sometimes the student really doesn't know why he or she is leaving school. Causative factors tend to cluster around two main areas: characteristics of students and school-related causes that encompass how the school is organized and managed.

Student-Related Factors
Wolman, Bruinicks, and Thurlow (1989) have identified several categories of student-related factors. These include factors related to demography, social and family concerns, personality, early transition to adulthood, deviant behavior, and factors involving in-school life. Studies suggest that minorities drop out of school at a greater rate than nonminorities. (California Dropouts, 1986; Ekstrom et al., 1986; Rumberger, 1987). Males tend to drop out more frequently than females (Stephenson, 1985), and students from urban areas drop out at a greater rate than students who live in rural or suburban areas (Pallas, 1987).

Reasons for dropping out that are social and family related include coming from a single-parent home or a home where education is not valued and there is little motivation engendered to stay in school. That includes little extension of learning at home and few if any learning aids such as books and educational games (Ekstrom et al., 1986).

According to Hess (1987), Hess and Lauber (1985), Pallas (1987), Rumberger (1983), and Howell and Freese (1982), some of the student related-factors include:

1. Low self-esteem
2. External locus of control
3. Inadequate feelings of efficacy
4. Pregnancy
5. Early marriage
6. Preferring work over school (having a job)
7. Low grades and academic achievement
8. Reading deficiencies

9. Low intellectual development
10. Retention in the early grades
11. Behavior problems
12. Low priority placed on education
13. Low vocational aspirations

The overall school structure and its perceived place within the local community are part of the school-related factors. Schools that are overcrowded, have a student body that is perceived as being mainly underachievers, and where there is low student and staff morale and a history of low standarized test results appear to have more dropouts (Hess, 1987; Fine, 1986).

Other characteristics include overall poor attendance, poor administrative leadership, inadequate levels of instruction, and a low level of classroom discipline. Trying to raise standards rapidly without adequate preparation time can be another reason for students leaving school (School Dropouts, 1986).

School Retention and Reentry Programs
Retention programs appear to focus on prevention, whereas reentry programs try to attract students back to school and keep them there until they graduate. Reentry programs appear to emphasize or attract students to better employment opportunities. The majority of prevention programs focus on the needs of high-risk students and implementing early intervention during the early grades (Hahn, 1987; Hamilton, 1986; Orr, 1987; Clark, 1987; Barr & Knowles, 1986).

According to Clark (1987), Hahn (1987), Orr (1987), and California Dropouts (1986), other strategies for keeping students in school include:

1. Improving vocational education programs
2. Providing more personalized counseling
3. Installing special programs designed to improve self-education and self-esteem
4. Providing a supportive peer group and establishing an ombudsman concept
5. Increasing the involvement of families (home)
6. Allowing pregnant girls to stay in school
7. Working with community agencies
8. Providing better social services, including health care
9. Working with the business community
10. Providing good work experience and on-the-job training
11. Combining or relating work to academic instruction
12. Implementing a good job skills and job-related skills program

What Can the School Do?

There are several critical areas that can be developed:

1. Personal attention is needed. This can be accomplished by developing a "buddy system," where students are paired voluntarily and meet on a regular basis on school time to share problems and successes. An older, well-adjusted student paired with a younger student (potential dropout) is a good idea. The ombudsman approach also has merit where a teacher, or any adult in school for that matter, takes responsibility to see that a student attends school and helps with the various problems that arise on a day-to-day basis. Access to a "strong shoulder" is an important thing to a frustrated, unhappy student.

2. Add something to the curriculum or revise the instructional procedures. Is reading or a particular academic subject a problem? For example, tutors should be available on a voluntary basis to help students.

3. Develop *strong* attendance rules; unless the reasons are outstanding, there is no excuse for staying out of school. The school can even go so far as having someone (volunteer) get the student to school in the morning by going to the home. Truancy is a principal cause of failure in academics. If they are not there, you cannot teach them anything. The parents must be held responsible by the school and the courts for their children attending school. The authorities must also get these youngsters off the street and into the schools. This requires a no-nonsense, coordinated effort. This is one of the ways we can have an impact on community crime. The courts, child welfare agencies, and clinics have to be in close contact with the schools. Laxity will cause the system to break down. The student in school is a captive audience, and we can deal with the failure in academics or personal problems.

4. Find ways for students to earn some money through part-time employment by enlisting the aid of local businesspersons and the community at large. This is a community problem. Some of these young people lack the personal spending money they need and stay out of school to get a job that is usually poor paying.

5. Adolescents on the streets who do not work are apt to get into trouble. After seeing all the movies in the neighborhood, being disillusioned with the realities of trying to get a job without finishing school, and being unsupervised, the probability of criminal activity always looms large. There is no substitute for an open door; i.e., access to

the principal, assistant principals, counselors, approachable teachers, school staff—anyone the student feels comfortable with. So many schools are "closed," "rigid," or "formal." The staff needs to present an openness and a willingness to be "put out" by taking on the responsibility for sharing a student's concerns. Homeroom counseling before or after class has been shown to be helpful in certain situations; and, finally, a telephone call to the home can go a long way toward letting the student know that someone cares.

CHILD ABUSE

The focus in treatment of dysfunctional families with child abuse is on all of the critical factors involved, and takes into account a variety of interacting variables that precipitate and reinforce the continuance of neglect and abuse (Vondra & Toth, 1989; Hamilton, 1989; Pardeck, 1989). The traditional treatment mode of individual counseling is not recommended within this approach.

Programs that offer group-parent education and self-help, such as Parent Anonymous, are recommended. Clients have shown that long-term treatment can effect a positive change in behavior (Kadushin & Martin, 1988). Much is still unknown about effective treatment in this area, but according to Powers, Jaklitsch, and Eckenrode (1989), depression, low self-esteem, lack of school success, and criminal behavior are reasons that are connected with abusive treatment among troubled youth.

A suggested strategy for intervention (Schmitt & Beezley, 1976) includes:

1. A diagnostic assessment of the student and the family
2. A team approach to planning and treatment
3. The use of alternative treatment approaches when necessary
4. Continuous assessment of the entire process

Psychodiagnostic treatment approaches can be integrated within the strategies listed above. Defining the role of the family in maltreatment, however, is the key to finding solutions. The concept of "transaction" is used within this sytem. This is the determination of how the behavior of family members is shaped and molded by other family members (Sameroff, 1975). Through the use of "transaction," the participants gain insight into why maltreatment occurs. The parent and the child become partners in the process of discovering the realities that exist in their lives (Pardeck, 1988). Family therapy in general is the dominant approach and it is reported to be an effective treatment mode.

Some 60 percent of abusive parents were themselves abused children. Mothers are more likely than fathers to inflict serious injury, whereas males in general appear to be more abusive (Johnson & Showers, 1985).

Abusiveness in families has been traced in part to a stressful life (Starr, 1982). Other factors in abuse include unwanted pregnancy, having unrealistic expectations of children, thinking of children as adults, and emotional insecurity. Many parents who abuse children experience a sense of failure and social isolation (Garbarino, 1982).

Reasons for Child Abuse

Probably the most cogent or significant factor in child abuse is the idea that parents are willing to inflict physical punishment on children for perceived misbehavior (Zigler, 1979). The tendency is for abusive parents to use less positive reinforcement (Burgess & Richardson, 1984).

The typically abused child is a male under four years of age who has been abused for about three years (Johnson & Showers, 1985). Children who were abused have been described as "being messy," "crying a lot," and having "poor sleep" habits. Many have difficulty with toilet training (Nesbit & Karagianis, 1982) and/or are bed wetters. The need on the part of the children for extra attention and additional care is seen as two of the prime reasons for abuse.

Child Abuse and Handicapped Students

Children born prematurely, many of whom are handicapped, represent a significant group of the abused population (Fontana, 1971). It has been argued that child abuse is a significant cause of mental retardation (Brandwein, 1973).

Children with behavior disorders are in a special position because of the nature of their disability and are likely to be abused (Stringer & LaGreca, 1985). Children who were aggressive and disruptive in school were also found to be abused (Bousha & Twentyman, 1984; Lorber, Felton, & Reid, 1984). Being handicapped appears to be a long-term risk factor, especially where there are other long-term family causes (Glaser & Bentovim, 1979).

SUICIDE AND DEPRESSION

Suicide is one of the top three causes of death for individuals under 24 years of age (Peck, Farberow, & Litman, 1985). The United States reports approximately 6,000 adolescent deaths each year, and suicide is on the upswing at an alarming rate.

Recent studies have suggested that there is an underlying neurological and endocrine basis for suicide (Mann et al., 1986). There is also a likelihood that depression may accompany certain types of brain injury (Cullum & Bigler, 1988). Levels of anxiety and depression appear to increase with damage to the right frontal region of the brain (Grafman et al., 1986). Depression is also thought to be caused by left hemisphere damage (Heilman, Watson, & Bowers, 1983).

Rourke (1987) formulated a nonverbal subtype of learning disability (NLD) with predisposing suicidal tendencies, which also has several unique features that include computational problems in arithmetic, and social, adaptive, and cognitive difficulties. The Nonverbal Learning Disorder (NLD) syndrome may predispose an individual to a higher suicidal potential. These persons have a tendency to become depressed under stress because of the inability to cope, lack of insight, and being unable to respond to novel situations in a normal manner.

This classification is based on several characteristics not all of which may be found in any single case. Many of these students indicate overlap within shared characteristics. These learners are thought to be more suicidal because of a tendency toward psychopathology due to a biochemical abnormality present in the central nervous system.

Since depression is closely linked or a precursor to suicide, it is important to recognize symptoms of depression in students. These include:

1. Low academic achievement
2. Problems with peers
3. Conduct disorders
4. Suicide attempts in severe cases (National Institute of Mental Health, 1985; Poznanski, 1982).

In one study, Worchel, Nolan, and Wilson (1987) found evidence of cases of depression for girls aged 6–14 years, but not for girls in the tenth or eleventh grades (ages 15–17). It appears that younger girls may be experiencing more depression than younger boys. One rationale for this finding is that boys act out their problems more than girls (Edelbrock, 1984). Girls, it seems, relate more than boys to such things as feeling sad, being alone, and feeling tired. Girls also appear to be more worried about doing the wrong thing, not being liked, or thinking that bad things are about to happen. Boys appear to worry more about fighting or being pushed too hard to do things.

Social Disorders (Cognitive-Social Skills and Adaptive Behavior)

There is a group of students who have difficulty interpreting the social environment and dealing with social situations. Some of these students, even those who show high levels of intelligence, cannot formulate acceptable sound judgments. Their behavior is often perceived by peers and adults to be inappropriate and strange.

Students with learning difficulties seem to have problems in three cognitive-social skill areas (Schumaker & Hazel, 1984):

1. *Selection of Socially Acceptable Behavior:* This entails going beyond understanding what is acceptable behavior to choosing the kinds of social behavior that an individual actually plans to use. Students with learning problems seem to have more problems than their agemates in the sense of choosing less socially acceptable behaviors. This propensity to choose antisocial behavior when pressured may be a link to juvenile delinquency (Bryan, Werner, & Pearl, 1982). Another factor is the relationship between socially acceptable behavior and popularity.

2. *Discrimination of Social Cues:* These students, even those who show high levels of intelligence, cannot formulate acceptable sound judgments. They are unable to interpret cues like facial expressions, motor actions (body language), and voice tone (Gerber & Zinkgraf, 1982; Pearl & Cosden, 1982).

3. *Role-Taking Skills:* Role-taking skills have been defined as the ability to "understand and take into account the thoughts (cognitive role-taking) and feelings (affective role-taking) of another individual as distinct from one's own" (Bruck & Hebert, 1982, p. 353). Some researchers believe that learning-problem students as a group tend to do poorer in this area (Horowitz, 1981).

The following are some of the observable behaviors under this category.

OBSERVABLE BEHAVIOR: SOCIAL DISORDERS (COGNITIVE-SOCIAL SKILLS AND ADAPTIVE BEHAVIOR)

The student

1. Misinterprets what he or she sees and gives the wrong response
2. Has difficulty with projective tests, such as the Thematic Apperception Test or Rorschach Test
3. May be able to perceive individual objects, but fails to comprehend the meaning of their relationships
4. May not derive meaning from gestures or expressions of others
5. May not be able to size up a situation (e.g., he or she may require constant interpretation while watching a TV show, watching a film, or listening to a story)
6. Literally does not know enough to come in out of the rain
7. Is directed at home and rarely has opportunities to make up his or her own mind
8. Reacts inappropriately to situations, criticisms, and guidance from others
9. Has difficulty in understanding the subtleties in humor
10. Has difficulty in understanding figurative speech
11. Attends to the minor details instead of the major details in completing a task
12. Misreads emotions, moods, and attitudes of people
13. Misunderstands motives (why people do what they do)
14. Fails to associate an incident with its implications for people and society
15. Consistently says the inappropriate thing at the inappropriate time
16. Does not understand facial expressions
17. Has difficulty in pretending or anticipating the outcomes in stories

DISCUSSION: SOCIAL DISORDERS (COGNITIVE-SOCIAL SKILLS AND ADAPTIVE BEHAVIOR)

Teachers in both regular and special class settings need to structure their classrooms and style of teaching in such a manner as to provide for opportunities for beneficial social behavior. Mainstreamed mildly handicapped children are often poorly accepted, neglected, or socially rejected by their nonhandicapped peers (Gresham, 1982b). These students are reported to have low academic self-concepts and expect to fail in school (Hiebert, Wong, & Hunter, 1982). Teachers and parents see them as low academic performers, exhibiting more socially unacceptable behavior than their normal-achieving peers. Educators often fail to emphasize the importance of social skill instruction in mainstreamed children (Cartledge & Milburn, 1978; Gresham, 1983). Teachers sometimes feel that social skills training takes up too much time and that they lack the training or interest to undertake such a responsibility.

Learning disabled students were found to have problems in accepting criticism, giving criticism, and giving positive feedback (Schumaker, Hazel, Sherman, & Sheldon, 1982). They are more likely to be ignored and to receive punishing statements (Bryan, 1974). Remedial teachers need to work on building positive feelings in these students.

Social skills training should be built on an instructional model that promotes self-efficacy through participant modeling of behavior, behavior rehearsal techniques, direct reinforcement, and peer initiation strategies. Opportunities for successful performance should be emphasized in the regular classroom where appropriate social behavior can be demonstrated. The teacher needs to reinforce positive social interactions in a variety of ways.

Studies suggested that children who were deemed popular gave and received more positive reinforcement than those identified as unpopular (Gottman, Gonso, & Rasmussen, 1975; Masters & Furman, 1981). Positive reinforcement is defined as social skills that involve praise, agreement, affection, warm greetings, and sharing. Positive initial or entry behavior is one reason given for the success of popular students.

Some students gain entry into the group by using low-risk tactics such as "hanging" around the group waiting for an invitation to participate, as opposed to low-risk tactics such as asking questions and making remarks about the group (Dodge et al., 1983). High-risk behavior is more frequently used by popular students. Popular students display more pro-social behavior such as making good suggestions, showing approval, being supportive, and being affectionate (Dodge, 1983).

After the identification of the social skills that are desirable, the next step is to determine how they can be taught. One approach is through direct instruction, discussion, modeling, and rehearsal of the desired skills. The other approach involves social cognitive problem solving and cognitive problem solving (Michelson & Mannarino, 1986).

The American Association on Mental Deficiency (AAMD) defines adaptive behavior as "the effectiveness or degree with which individuals meet the standard of personal independence and social responsibility expected for age and cultural groups" (Grossman, 1983, p. 1).

The concept of deficits in adaptive behavior is an important consideration when viewing an individual within the context of the environment and its prevailing social structures. This is true for all students who have deficits in behavior or learning and who are diagnosed as mentally retarded, learning disabled, or emotionally disturbed (Harrison, 1989).

Adaptive behavior is a prime assessment consideration in the identification and diagnosis of students for special education placement. Another reason for assessing adaptive behavior is to plan a treatment-educational intervention program (Witt & Martens, 1984).

Adaptive behavior training is a vehicle for achieving effective mainstreaming of mildly handicapped stu-

dents in regular education programs. Adaptive behavior can be rated by parents, teachers, or others who have had the opportunity to observe the learner over an extended period of time and can make accurate judgments using adaptive rating skills.

It is evident that there will be much variation within groups or categories in the area of adaptive behavior. Even gifted students may have adaptive behavior ratings that are below their expected levels based on measurements of intelligence.

There are many distinctions between adaptive behavior and intelligence. Some feel that both may be a part of the same general construct (Harrison & Pottebaum, 1987); others think they are separate constructs (Mercer, 1979; Coulter, 1980).

Adaptive behavior is associated with everyday behavior, whereas intelligence is viewed as conceptualization or how an individual uses his or her thought processes. Adaptive behavior can be modified or changed with training, whereas intelligence is viewed as a relatively stable phenomenon.

Both have similar definitions and similarities in their presumed causes. Both have been defined as the ability to cope with one's environment (Nihira et al., 1974). Some children display adequate adaptive behavior but do not do well on tests of intelligence. Some reasons are as follows:

1. Adaptive behavior relates to an individual's everyday behavior, while intelligence relates to thought processes or how an individual thinks mainly in social situations.
2. Adaptive behavior emphasizes common or typical behavior, while intelligence deals with the full range of performance on essentially achievement tasks.
3. Adaptive behavior is essentially nonacademic and nonabstract, while intelligence focuses on the abstract and academic learning. (Meyers, Nihira, & Zetlin, 1979).

Adaptive behavior and intellectual ability are essentially separate but there are some relationships. A modest positive correlation between adaptive behavior and intelligence suggests that both types of measurements should be included in the assessment of students' mental abilities. A causal relationship between the two needs has yet to be proven (Harrison & Pottebaum, 1987).

There are a number of social overt behaviors that could be identified for training programs in terms of the need for modification of behavior. There are students who exhibit deficits in certain areas of nonverbal as well as verbal behavior. This, on the average, includes problems associated with

Asking questions in conversation
Using complex statements
Making fewer conversational and self-disclosing
    statements
Smiling while talking
Hand illustration while talking
Giving and accepting criticism
Resisting peer pressure
Forward body lean in conversation
Fully and accurately communicating information
Making rejection statements
Disagreeing and arguing less with people
Negotiating
Making requests
Making positive statements

In another sense, many of these students have difficulty making and keeping friends and endure more social rejection than do their agemates, even though they may try hard to be accepted.

It has been noted that students with difficulties in this area tend also to have problems in perceptual-motor tasks and to exhibit poor self-image and immature concepts of body image. Teachers report that these students are not emotionally disturbed but lack emotional depth. They appear to have a superficial understanding of the meaning of social situations. Characteristically, this kind of problem in social relationships will affect the learner in every aspect of daily life. It can occur with or without problems in other areas of learning.

TREATMENT CONSIDERATIONS: SOCIAL DISORDERS (COGNITIVE-SOCIAL SKILLS AND ADAPTIVE BEHAVIOR)

Social skills deficiencies require that training in these areas becomes part of the school curriculum. This includes activities designed to provide for the integration of social skills into both school and out-of-school life. The idea is to reduce these feelings of social inadequacy and increase chances for successful interpersonal interactions. Students should not be rewarded for inappropriate behavior.

Students are taught how to think through and determine ways to deal with social problems (Spivack & Shure, 1982). The main skills in problem solving are:

1. How to be aware of problems
2. How to think about possible solutions
3. How to determine the what if of proposed solutions
4. How to determine possible overall consequences of actions
5. How to see the relationship between one's behavior and the feelings and reactions of others

It is felt that training in these areas can result in better social adjustment.

Instruction should use the following areas as vehicles for teaching social skills:

1. Analyzing of examples of interpersonal difficulties
2. Being able to verbalize feelings
3. Identifying overall goals for different types of situations
4. Using cognitive strategies, modeling, role playing and appropriate feedback that addresses the cognitive and emotional aspects of social interaction. (Weissberg, 1985).

Behavior rehearsal and roleplay are recommended for social skills training along with discussions of skills dealing with modeling and feedback. Direct instruction supplemented by media presentation should provide the learner with an understanding of the skills that are important. This should be followed by practice and accompanied by a reward system.

Students who receive training in interpersonal cognitive problem solving seem better able to come up with solutions and anticipate the consequences of behavior of others than those who do not (Gesten et al., 1982; Sarason & Sarason, 1981). Children receiving this training were found to be better adjusted and more socially competent (Weissberg et al., 1981). In the Weissberg study, students learned to identify upset feelings associated with certain situations and to try other solutions to solving problems when the initial attempt failed.

Other researchers (Elias, 1983) used videotapes successfully that modeled problem-solving techniques and included discussion, clarification, and reinforcements for exhibiting appropriate behavior.

Students appear to benefit from being coached on specific social skills and given the opportunity to role-play these skills followed by discussion. Another method involved training in conversational skills, which resulted in improved social interaction (Bierman & Furman, 1984).

Another aspect of social skills training involves peer group training to deal with social perception biases. Skill training sessions are important for peer helpers so they can avoid the kinds of behavior that reinforce antisocial behavior in the students with problems with whom they are interacting. Peers used properly can be effective change agents in shaping the behavior of students with problems (Kalfus, 1984). Social skills training for peers can be designed to remediate social skills problems in students with behavior disorders, especially in mainstream settings (Hollinger, 1987). Roleplay is one suggested device enabling students to understand how difficult behavior evokes different kinds of responses.

The following additional suggestions should be considered when planning activities for the learner with social perception problems:

1. The teacher can train the student through the interpretation of good pictures or photographs. He or she should be careful not to overstimulate the learner with too much input and should begin with simple pictures.
2. The teacher should show the student action pictures.
3. The teacher can train the student with sequence pictures or comic strips, record the student's responses, and lead him or her through by asking questions.
4. The teacher can build in good social perception through language experience utilizing the science curriculum and by helping the student understand cause-effect relationships.
5. The teacher should talk the learner through situations. Sometimes the student will not profit from modeling (imitation) alone and will need an explanation of what he or she is doing.
6. Often the learner has good verbal ability, but cannot explain the significance of the action or sequence of actions in pictures. Use cartoons without the captions to elicit responses about the actions and the humor in the pictures.
7. Lead the student through and explain classroom or playground games especially those that involve gestures or verbal cues that appear to confound the learner.
8. Show the learner realistic pictures or photographs of children and adults who are expressing a particular feeling or emotion (e.g., anger, happiness, fear, sorrow). Have the student identify the feeling and then try to explain what led up to the feeling in the picture. Have the learner imitate the same feeling in a mirror. Finally, show the learner pictures in which more than one person is displaying emotions and ask the learner to discuss the significance of the scenes.
9. Use pictures of famous paintings and ask the student to explain what is happening, what happened before, what will happen next, or where the action may occur.
10. What will happen if? types of games are useful.
11. Students can be rewarded for smiling, sharing, positive physical contact, and verbal com-

plementing. This can be taught through direct instruction, modeling, and social praise.
12. Cognitive problem-solving interventions using self-instruction strategies can be utilized (Kneedler, 1980).
13. Behavioral role-playing has been found to be useful. Students showed improvement in novel role-playing situations (Schumaker & Ellis, 1982).
14. The instructor needs to enhance and maintain motivation for solving interpersonal problems (Adelman & Taylor, 1979) through:
    a. reinforcing positive perceptions and diminishing negative perceptions
    b. responding positively to intrinsic justifications
    c. working with students on how to implement realistic methods for change
    d. giving the student feedback

Attention Deficit Disorders

The American Psychiatric Association in 1980 changed its terminology regarding the construct of Minimal Cerebral Dysfunction. This was due to difficulty with the verification of this diagnosis through standardized external assessment. Instead of Minimal Brain Dysfunction, the new terminology was Attention Deficit Disorder (ADD). In 1987, the American Psychiatric Association revised the diagnostic criteria for the condition that is now identified as Attention-Deficit Hyperactivity Disorder (ADHD):

A. A disturbance of at least six months during which at least eight of the following are present:

(1) often fidgets with hands or feet or squirms in seat (in adolescents, may be limited to subjective feelings of restlessness)

(2) has difficulty remaining seated when required to do so

(3) is easily distracted by extraneous stimuli

(4) has difficulty awaiting turn in games or group situations

(5) often blurts out answers to questions before they have been completed

(6) has difficulty following through on instructions from others (not due to oppositional behavior or failure of comprehension), e.g., fails to finish chores

(7) has difficulty sustaining attention in tasks or play activities

(8) often shifts from one uncompleted activity to another

(9) has difficulty playing quietly

(10) often talks excessively

(11) often interrupts or intrudes on others, e.g., butts into other children's games

(12) often does not seem to listen to what is being said to him or her

(13) often loses things necessary for tasks or activities at school or at home (e.g., toys, pencils, books, assignments)

(14) often emerges in physically dangerous activities without considering possible consequences (not for the purpose of thrill-seeking), e.g., runs into street without looking

B. Onset before the age of seven.

C. Does not meet the criteria for a Pervasive Developmental Disorder

Criteria for Severity of Attention-Deficit Hyperactivity Disorder:

Mild: Few, if any, symptoms in excess of those required to make the diagnosis and only minimal or no impairment in school and social functioning.

Moderate: Symptoms or functional impairment intermediate between "mild" and "severe."

Severe: Many symptoms in excess of those required to make the diagnosis and significant and pervasive impairment in functioning at home and school and with peers. (pp. 52–53)*

An attention-deficit disorder that exists without hyperactivity is referred to as Undifferentiated Attention-Deficit Disorder:

This is a residual category for disturbances in which the predominant feature is the persistence of developmentally inappropriate and marked inattention that is not a symptom of another disorder, such as Mental Retardation or Attention-Deficit Hyperacitivity Disorder, or a disorganized and chaotic environment. . . . Research is necessary to determine if this is a valid diagnostic category and, if so, how it should be defined. (p. 95)

*From the *Diagnostic and Statistical Manual of Mental Disorders* (3d ed., revised) by the American Psychiatric Association, 1987, Washington, D.C.: Author. Reprinted by permission.

HYPERACTIVITY

Students who are constantly on the move and who have been described as hyperactive or hyperkinetic may exhibit a short attention span. They continually shift around in their seats, tap their feet, and play with things, creating a disturbance in the classroom. The learners appear to lack the inner control seen in other students.

The underarousal theory of hyperactivity (Zentall, 1975; Zentall & Zentall, 1976) postulates that hyperactive students are more readily underaroused with tasks involving minimum stimulation. They increase verbal and nonverbal activity in low-stimulation tasks or environments as a way of maintaining a sense of balance. This is a form of coping mechanism to deal with different levels of stimulus input.

In terms of listening tasks, hyperactive children were found to be more verbally and nonverbally active than controls during transitions between tasks and during the performance of tasks when

1. They had to assimilate information given to them verbally
2. They had to match verbal information given with visually presented information
3. There was a delay that required them to get additional information (Zentall, 1975)

Observable Behavior: Hyperactivity
The student

1. Is constantly moving (running, fidgeting, climbing, etc.)
2. Cannot control his or her movement and is unaware that it is occurring
3. May fatigue earlier in the school day because of the hyperactivity
4. May also be distractible. Both behavioral manifestations often go together
5. Has excessive movements even though he or she may be engrossed in a particular activity
6. Exhibits increased or excessive verbal activity
7. Disturbs other students with excessive movement or verbal behavior
8. Does not exhibit appropriate social behavior
9. Does not attend to situational clues

Discussion: Hyperactivity
Hyperactive children with learning problems are noted to have disturbances in peer relations (Pelham & Milich, 1984). This includes fights, interrupting other children, and in general experiencing peer rejection.

The results of studies (Pelham, 1981) suggest that both aggressive and nonaggressive hyperactive children are disliked by their agemates, albeit for different reasons, such as the impact and frequency of the behavior. Cognitive deficits in attention, impulse control, and arousal modulation are detrimental to the development of appropriate and efficient attentive and metacognitive skills. Hyperactive students, through lack of attention,

1. Fail to attend to situational clues, thereby affecting their awareness ability
2. Will not be as "connected" in discourse, therefore vitiating the development of friendships
3. Fail to demonstrate appropriate social behavior
4. Fail to master basic cognitive information, such as how to "size up" a situation

Hyperactivity, or hyperkinetic activity, is one of the characteristics of brain-injured students. This does not imply that all hyperactive students are brain injured. Some students exhibit hyperactivity due to learning that occurs in situations that are noisy and over-stimulating. The learners who have random movements are a problem in the classroom because they tend to take the other students off task. It is important for the instructor to get some indication of how long the students can stay on task. This can be charted. (See Form 4-1; also see Form 4-4, later in this chapter.)

Hyperactive students do not always have the same pattern of behavior. Some move more than others, some make distracting noises. Some students are very verbal and bright and are liked by their peers. Others are unhappy and aggressive and are perceived in a more negative way. These students do not move about to gain the teacher's attention. Often they are unaware of the disturbing behavior. In young students some movement should be anticipated and considered normal. It is the atypical movement that should be noted; how much and when it occurs. Unfortunately, hyperactive students often are punished and isolated for their restless behavior and consequently are not in class enough to successfully learn or complete assignments.

These students require an overall reduced stimulus environment and a patient, structured teacher. Hyperactivity and/or distractible behavior can be modified by a highly supervised and well-managed program, which could include a drug regimen and student self-monitored activities. Drugs are another alternative and must be highly controlled and monitored under strict supervision.

Treatment Considerations: Hyperactivity

1. Keep manipulative material away from the learner, unless he or she is using the material for a specific activity.
2. The student should be given structured, high-attention tasks or activities (e.g., using a tape recorder).
3. Have the learner exercise or move about between activities. At specified times give the entire class a "visiting" break and encourage them to walk around, quietly talk to friends, sharpen pencils, and so on.
4. Always follow a high-stimulus activity such as music or physical education with a low-stimulus activity (e.g., resting head on desk, playing a quiet game).
5. Allow the learner to rock in a rocking chair.
6. The young hyperactive student may work better on a carpet or in some other "low" environment than at a desk.
7. High-stimulus clothing or jewelry on the instructor may interfere with the attention of the student.
8. The student could fold his or her hands or put them in pockets when quiet attention is required.
9. The teacher can cue the learner with a touch on the hand or shoulder or some other specified signal.
10. Put color or attracting devices into the learning materials instead of on too many bulletin boards.
11. Push the student to longer periods of attending and on-task behavior. Use Forms 4-2 and 4-3 to establish a baseline of time on task.
12. Reward on-task behavior with a system (e.g., stars, use of a favorite game, private time with the teacher).
13. Use contracts to specify desired behavior.
14. Through example, and sometimes by discussing the problem directly with the class, teach the learner's peers how to ignore the active behavior.
15. Encourage the learner to participate in outside clubs or activities where the active behavior can be channeled into pleasant activities.
16. Plan alternative activities that will permit physical involvement during a lesson.
17. Avoid verbal attacks or commands in front of other students when the learner exhibits hyperactive behavior.
18. Psychostimulant medication may be needed for some students.
19. Social skills training may be helpful (see page 80).
20. Operant behavioral intervention can be utilized alone or along with a drug regimen.

AMERICAN PSYCHIATRIC ASSOCIATION
DIAGNOSTIC CRITERIA FOR ATTENTION-DEFICIT HYPERACTIVITY DISORDER (ADHD)

NAME _____   EXAMINER _____

AGE _____   DATE _____

GRADE _____

	Date All Entries		
	1	2	3

A. A disturbance of at least six months during which at least eight of the following are present:

   (1) often fidgets with hands or feet or squirms in seat (in adolescents, may be limited to subjective feelings of restlessness)

   (2) has difficulty remaining seated when required to do so

   (3) is easily distracted by extraneous stimuli

   (4) has difficulty awaiting turn in games or group situations

   (5) often blurts out answers to questions before they have been completed

   (6) has difficulty following through on instructions from others (not due to oppositional behavior or failure of comprehension), e.g., fails to finish chores

   (7) has difficulty sustaining attention in tasks or play activities

   (8) often shifts from one uncompleted activity to another

   (9) has difficulty playing quietly

   (10) often talks excessively

   (11) often interrupts or intrudes on others, e.g., butts into other children's games

   (12) often does not seem to listen to what is being said to him or her

   (13) often loses things necessary for tasks or activities at school or at home (e.g., toys, pencils, books, assignments)

   (14) often engages in physically dangerous activities without considering possible consequences (not for the purpose of thrill-seeking), e.g., runs into street without looking

B. Onset before the age of seven.
C. Does not meet the criteria for a Pervasive Developmental Disorders.

Comments

Form 4-2

NAME: ____________________ Beginning Date ____________________

AGE: ____________________ Ending Date ____________________

MANN STUDENT OBSERVATION WORKSHEET

On/Off Task and Target Behaviors

Teacher: ____________________ Grade: __________

Observer One: ____________________ Observer Two: ____________________

CHECK ONE: ☐ On Off Task

☐ Target Behavior

Behavior Desired:

____

____

Obs. Nbr.	Day & Date	Observ. Time	Nbr. of Beh.	Time OFF Task	Time ON Task	BEHAVIOR OBSERVED: Bothers Teacher	Bothers Student	Talking	Playing	Bathr./Drink	Aggres./Fights	Out of Seat	Daydream/Sleep	Walk – Run	Does Other Work	Other:	COMMENTS – TREATMENT

NOTE: Draw a dark line to indicate end of period.

(continued)

NAME: _____   Beginning Date _____

AGE: _____   Ending Date _____

MANN STUDENT OBSERVATION WORKSHEET (Continued)

OBSERVER: _____

Obs. Nbr.	Day & Date	Observ. Time	Nbr. of Beh.	Time OFF Task	Time ON Task	Bothers Teacher	Bothers Student	Talking	Playing	Bathr./Drink	Aggres./Fights	Out of Seat	Daydream/Sleep	Walk – Run	Does Other Work	Other:	COMMENTS – TREATMENT

NOTE: Draw a dark line to indicate end of period.

Form 4-3

NAME: _____

AGE: _____

Beginning Date _____

Ending Date _____

MANN STUDENT GRAPHING WORKSHEET
On/Off Task and Target Behaviors

Teacher: _____

Grade: _____

Observer One: _____

Observer Two: _____

CHECK ONE: ☐ On/Off Task ☐ Target Behavior

Behavior Desired:

_____

_____

Period:	BEHAVIOR OBSERVED										
	Bothers Teacher	Bothers Student	Talking	Playing	Bathr./Drink	Aggres./Fights	Out of Seat	Daydream/Sleep	Walk – Run	Does Other Work	Other:
	CODE SYMBOL										
	a	b	c	d	e	f	g	h	i	j	k

Frequency: _____

Time: _____

Frequency: _____

Time: _____

21. Self-monitoring types of activities are found to be useful where the student is required to respond to a cue tone and is rewarded for on-task behavior.

INATTENTION

Inattention and hyperactivity often go together. There are, however, students who do exhibit attention deficits without hyperactive behavior. Academic underachievement and inattention also seem to go together as characteristics of learning-problem students. It is assumed that attention for the most part is under the individual's control. It is logical and reasonable to believe that a student's understanding or awareness of attention as a construct should affect how it is manifested or applied. As in "metacognition," described as a learner's awareness of his or her own cognitive capacity, meta-attention likewise concerns the degree to which a student's attentional behavior reflects his or her understanding or awareness of the processes of attention. The important factor to consider is selective attention; that is, to attend to what is relevant while screening out that which is irrelevant.

In one study (Loper et al., 1982) older students were found to be more impressed with interest level or concentration (internal rewards) as an incentive to attention, while younger students were more impressed with external rewards such as promise of material things.

Observable Behavior: Inattention
The student

1. Does not approach academic tasks in an efficient manner (lacks problem-solving techniques)
2. Exhibits passivity and dependence in learning (learned helplessness)
3. Is often impulsive and poorly directed in his or her behavior
4. May not exhibit reflective thought patterns
5. May display attention that is "forced" or directed to other things rather than the task
6. Shows a lack of insightful thinking during academic assignments
7. Does not use verbal mediation in solving problems; i.e., talking oneself through a problem
8. Often exhibits impulsive behavior in responding to school and academic tasks
9. Tends to blame himself or herself for failure as a lack of ability rather than as a lack of effort
10. Exhibits poor sustained attention
11. In terms of a memory bank, is said to have poor image storage
12. May be deficient in search strategies; i.e., what has to be done to solve a problem
13. Is unable to adapt or generalize search strategies from one situation to another
14. Has limited memory bank schemata for problem solving

Discussion: Inattention
In the past, students with attention problems were treated with drugs, placed in stimulus-free environments, placed in a behavior modification program, or any combination of the three. All of these approaches have their place, and have resulted in some successes, but none were found to be overwhelmingly effective.

In recent years, Cognitive Behavior Modification (CBM), or self-monitoring, has been used with very encouraging results. This technique actually involves the student physically in the treatment process. The student is required to monitor his or her on-task behavior. Research (Hallahan & Sapona, 1983) suggests that self-monitoring of attention during academic work leads to increases in academic proficiency and in many cases increases in academic work.

A cue tone procedure has been shown to be helpful; i.e., student hears a tone which rings intermittently and asks himself or herself if he or she is on task. He or she then records his or her responses appropriately.

In general, self-monitoring of attention in inattentive learning-disabled children does increase attention and academic productivity in tasks for which they already have skills (Hallahan, 1983). This form of cognitive behavior modification is designed to

1. Change overt behavior
2. Modify an individual's cognitive operations toward goal achievement, which can be determined by changes in overt behavior in new situations

Treatment Considerations: Inattention
1. Cognitive Behavior Modification (CBM) techniques are suggested as an instructional strategy which includes the student in the process. The student
   a. self-monitors his or her behavior (on or off task), using a cue tone or some other intermittent attention-getting device
   b. develops strategies for attacking academic problems from alternatives
   c. comes to believe in his or her own abilities (deals with learned helplessness) and self-rewards successes
   d. produces appropriate strategies spontaneously with practice
2. CBM techniques are easiest to implement during seatwork.

3. The CBM system works best when students are working on tasks for which they already have the skills.
4. The student needs to feel he or she is a co-partner in the learning process.
5. The recording of academic responses or attention to task after using a cue tone or other attention-directing device is useful for increasing academic productivity.
6. Parents and significant others interacting with the student may influence what he or she attends to and in shaping thought processes and strategies. They can call attention to on-task, goal-directed behavior.
7. Teach the students to become aware of how they are learning and how to communicate their goals.
8. Teach the student to detect problems in learning and communication. Use role-playing or "replay" games, for example.
9. Use the following teaching strategies (Brown, 1979):
   a. Clarify the purpose of the activity.
   b. Identify important aspects of the task.
   c. Focus attention on key elements; e.g., words, ideas, concepts, and concentration on major areas.
   d. Monitor the process (student self-monitors).
   e. Review and self-question.
   f. Correct strategies and failures.
   g. Screen out disruptions and distractions.
10. The instructional sequence for the above is
    a. teacher models behavior by verbalizing aloud
    b. student imitates behavior by verbalizing aloud
    c. student imitates behavior (silently or uses internal speech)
    d. student generalizes the behavior to other problems, other subjects, across settings
11. The basic skills needed to produce results in improved thinking are:
    a. predicting (What will happen if?)
    b. planning (How can this be done?)
    c. monitoring (How am I doing? and Where am I going?)
    d. checking (Does this check with other things?)
12. Reflective thinking, interpretation, and information-giving can be modeled for student imitation (cognitive modeling).

IMPULSIVITY

Impulsive behavior has been identified as common among students with learning problems. Impulsive learners lack self-control and react too quickly. They make too many errors and appear to be less reflective than their peers. The teacher must determine the type of intervention that will produce impulse control in the student. Lack of self-control is the most common problem in those who exhibit impulsive behavior patterns.

We often see students exhibit acting out behavior, aggression, and absence of control in the classroom. This type of behavior invariably results in poor interpersonal relationships, lack of completion of classroom assignments, and poor general problem-solving ability. Affected students have a tendency to respond first without delaying or thinking about the possible alternatives. The impulsive response is fast and often inaccurate. The following behavior is exhibited by these students.

Observable Behavior: Impulsivity
The student

1. Quickly responds to questions before thinking out his or her answers
2. Is excessively talkative
3. Rushes into an activity before the instructor has completed the directions
4. Is impatient with repeated tasks and does not like to review old learning
5. Avoids anxiety-producing situations and is unreflective in resolving problems
6. Cannot monitor his or her own behavior
7. Does not inhibit his or her own response
8. May not understand the problem or task and, therefore, cannot produce the mediators or correct strategies
9. May know the strategies but cannot produce them spontaneously or appropriately
10. May not use appropriate cognitive strategies to guide or regulate his or her behavior

Discussion: Impulsivity
If possible, the teacher should carefully chart the impulsivity of the learner and establish a baseline of behavior. Is there a pattern in the occurrence of his or her actions? The instructor should try to be as objective as possible in dealing with an impulsive student. Since the behavior may easily distract the teacher and other students, confrontations can occur. The instructor must be organized and anticipate the student's behavior. The instructor particularly serves as a role model for this category of students.

The objective in the training of nonimpulsive behavior is to establish self-control through

1. Developing a capability to inhibit responses, such as reflective evaluation of response alternatives
2. Increasing the child's repertoire of cognitive problem-solving abilities so he or she can select an appropriate task from several possibilities

3. Using a systematic approach to dealing with the problem, which includes
   Student learns to monitor himself or herself.
   Student learns to evaluate his or her behavior.
   Student learns to reward himself or herself.

The student is placed in the position of feeling he or she can achieve change and control the situation by basing decisions on more information in a systematic fashion.

Teachers can apply treatment procedures based on the principles of self-instructional training (Meichenbaum, 1977) and on those of modeling (Bandura, 1977) and response-cost contingent on errors during the training tasks. Psycho-educational tasks, such as sequence of objects or ideas, can be used with appropriate training material. The teacher and the student work together using verbal instructions.

The following cognitive training task is modeled after Meichenbaum's approach and involves verbal self-instructional procedures. The student is taught through a modeling process with the instructor to ask the following questions (aloud, then silently).

1. What do they want to do? (relevancy)
2. How can it be done? (alternatives)
3. What's coming up? (looking ahead)
4. If I miss it, that's ok. I'll just try something else. (self-evaluation)
5. If I get it right, then hurrah for me. (self-reward)

This is accomplished through the following modeling sequence:

1. Teacher models task and talks out loud while the student observes.
2. The student does the task, talking it through out loud (later whispering, then silently).
3. The teacher does the task, acting out the process with thinking-type behavior (say *hmm,* close eyes, draw a model, look reflective, look up, etc.)
4. The student imitates the teacher's behavior.

The idea is to focus on step-by-step verbalization that will help the student perform the desired task.

Treatment Considerations: Impulsivity
1. Set rules and limits for classroom activities.
2. Organize schedule, and/or state the steps the learner must take in making a transition from one activity to another.
3. Reward the student for self-monitoring the completion of assignments. If possible give immediate feedback to carefully completed tasks.
4. If the student has more than one teacher, then all must attempt to coordinate steps in the completion of material.

5. The talkative student will need outlets for his or her behavior (e.g., reading into a tape recorder, telling stories to younger students, a chance to visit with other students during the day).
6. Refuse to accept wild guesses. Ask the student to verbally explain what he or she did and why.
7. Disguise review activities. The student has to see the value and quality of each lesson.
8. Avoid anger and derogatory remarks about the student's work. Keep folders of baseline work (e.g., samples of best handwriting) and ask the learner to compare his or her "sloppy" work with the "best" and then discuss a solution to the problem.
9. Provide short assignments with short, simple directions.
10. If the learner rushes through assignments, discuss the pacing and time restraints of a task.
11. Assign the learner to work with classmates as a peer tutor, with the responsibility of helping them check their work.
12. Discuss different solutions to problems to aid the student in seeing choices before he or she takes impulsive action.
13. Teach the student how to plan homework, to handle multiple assignments, and to effectively study independently.
14. Explain to the student how to handle frustration and errors. He or she needs to know that everyone makes errors, stops to evaluate what happened, and then proceeds to a better solution. The impulsive student needs to actually work through activities or problems that require reflective behavior.
15. The teacher can use cue cards. Make a set of 5″ × 7″ cue cards with the words

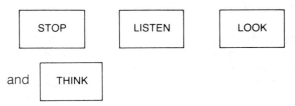

or others as necessary to help the student with self-instructional training.
16. The use of combined self-instruction and response-cost training (see page 105) produced the best results in reducing impulsive responding in young children (Nelson, 1976).

Control Factors

Factors that affect self-control are those behaviors that originate from within the student and/or are precipitated by stimuli in the environment. These factors cause the student to exhibit atypical behavior or behavior that hinders him or her in terms of school adjustment and the acquisition of new concepts.

DISTRACTIBILITY

Distractibility can accompany deficits in the sensory, perceptual, memory, or language levels of learning or be related to emotional problems. The distractible learners exhibit intermittent attention. Further observations include the following:

Observable Behavior: Distractibility
The student

1. Exhibits "forced attention" to extraneous stimuli within the environment and cannot attend to the task
2. May respond to the teacher next door, following that teacher's directions
3. May be distracted by visual or auditory stimuli or both
4. Is unable to focus his or her attention selectively

Discussion: Distractibility
The distractible learners have difficulty attending to tasks for the same lengths of time that their peers do. They attend to irrelevant auditory and/or visual stimuli (e.g., hall or playground noises, air conditioners, moving mobiles, crowded colorful bulletin boards, flickering lighting) and are easily attracted away from designated tasks. The rate, amount, sequence, and optimal teaching moment for teaching should be considered. These learners fatigue easily; therefore, the types of classroom activities should be carefully scheduled. The learners may not listen attentively to a story after another auditory input lesson (e.g., listening to a lecture followed by a skill tape cassette). Additional factors that relate to distractibility include the motivation of the learner, the encouragement or incentives used to gain and keep the attention of the student, and the interest value of the task presented. The distractible student may also exhibit difficulties with vigilance (the ability to maintain concentration on a task). These less attentive learners are more apt to respond to extraneous stimuli than to the task required.

Treatment Considerations: Distractibility
1. The teacher should reduce the input or stimulus in the room.
2. Provide a place to "escape" from distraction. Study or learning cubicles or a big carton with little windows can be utilized to aid the student to stay on task. Many students should be encour-aged to use the areas for independent activities. These areas must not be used for punishment too.
3. Put the distraction (color, etc.) into the material rather than on the walls.
4. The teacher should condition the learner by building in distraction (materials, bulletin board, etc.) a little at a time.
5. Involving the student in a motor act often reduces distraction. Manipulative materials such as clay, sand, wooden letters, felt letters, and finger paints are good.
6. Seat the student directly in front of the instructor.
7. Sometimes earplugs will help the student to concentrate on a specific task such as reading or taking a test.
8. Separate the learner from the group and require him or her to do brief tasks that will be successful.
9. The student should complete a task and return the learning material immediately to its designated place.
10. To aid the student in completing all of the sections on a page, allow him or her to use a piece of paper to mask out one section at a time. A tachistoscopic device can be made by cutting a window in a piece of cardboard.
11. Material or activities should be presented to the learner in small units and evaluated as soon as possible after completion.
12. Utilize concrete material that will heighten the student's attention to the task.
13. Avoid giving the student vague assignments that involve dealing with a great deal of materials simultaneously.
14. The student should be able to envision both the beginning and the end of an activity.
15. Reduce verbal instructions as much as possible.
16. Such media forms as overhead projectors are useful in focusing the students' attention.

PERSEVERATION

Once perseverating learners attend to a task they do not easily stop and transfer their attention to a different task. Since they have difficulty attending to differences, they tend to keep going with the first activity. The following behaviors may be noted in learners in this category.

Observable Behavior: Perseveration
The student

1. May say a word over and over
2. Cannot shift from one activity to another
3. Tends to repeat the previous response on tests or in classwork

4. May add all the problems in arithmetic, for example, even though he or she can easily see that half of them are subtraction

Discussion: Perseveration

Students who perseverate at first require monitoring of changes in tasks. Develop a system that will permit them gradually to divide a task into segments, note where changes occur, and make a transition smoothly into each section. Use short activities (i.e., addition, subtraction, multiplication problems) at the individual learner's level, so that the learner can attend to starting tasks, switching them, and then checking them. Everyone working with the students should be aware of the behavior and should be consistent in providing similar activities that will ensure success at the task as well as the development of self-monitoring.

Treatment Considerations: Perseveration

1. The student must learn to listen, wait, and then respond correctly.
2. Perseveration can be broken in many cases with a motor act. For example:

   John draws this: ○ .
   The teacher says, "John, give me your eraser." (motor act)
   "Now John, draw this: ▢ ."

3. Another technique is to go to something else and then come back to the next task.
4. Red lines as a key to a change in directions or process are helpful for the student with this difficulty.
5. Warn the student that a change in activity is coming up.
6. "Simon says" or "Follow the leader" type of games can help the student to learn to shift behavior.
7. Physically move the student from the present task to the new activity.

DISINHIBITION

Learners exhibiting disinhibited behavior appear to have difficulty in shifting easily from topic to topic in conversation. They often give unusual responses to questions or have a jumbled sequence of thoughts. Past experiences are retrieved and inappropriately added to the train of thought.

Observable Behavior: Disinhibition

The student

1. Gets carried away by his or her own thoughts
2. Gives inappropriate responses that are unrelated to the question asked

3. Cannot put on his or her "braking mechanisms," or control himself or herself

Discussion: Disinhibition

These students need specific considerations in activities requiring the initiation and completion of an activity as well as verbal language expression. Instructions must be in detail, properly sequenced, and, in some cases, recorded by the student. To prevent the learner from making wild guesses and rushing through assignments, the teacher and learner should plan together how much time will be required for the task. The development of a success mode of behavior will depend on the length of the assignment and the student's ability to stay on task.

Treatment Considerations: Disinhibition

1. The teacher can help the student stay on the task or idea by touching him or her or by using such "breaking words" as "no" or "wait."
2. Give the student something to do with his or her hands (manipulatives).
3. The teacher should be calm and not appear irritated when giving directions.
4. Reward on-task behavior, and do not reward inappropriate behavior.
5. The instructor can plan specific steps with the learner to accomplish a particular activity.
6. Behavior modification techniques are found to be very helpful with disinhibited learners.
7. Do not accept a wild guess. Ask the student to rethink his or her response and come up with a better answer.
8. Purposeful activity that is verbally explained while being accomplished is a helpful technique to counteract disinhibition (e.g., John does simple tasks and explains what he is doing as he does it).
9. Plan small discussions that will train verbal interactions. Lead the student and help him or her focus thoughts through responses to questions.
10. Provide objects or pictures to help the student stay on the topic.
11. If the student's unusual responses appear to be interpreted by classmates and others as bad manners, use social situations to channel participation. Play "what will happen if" types of games to discuss manners, and appropriate verbal responses.
12. If the student confuses fantasy with reality when he or she responds, channel the creativity into projects that will have a theme or focus but will be enjoyable to the student. Puppet plays, roleplaying of book characters or historical figures, interviews, and similar activities can be used.

Motivational Factors

Teachers have long recognized that students exhibiting learning difficulties have attitudinal or motivational problems that interfere with their classwork. These students have a tendency to become less involved in their schoolwork and to exhibit high rates of off-task behavior, poor concentration, and lack of persistence when they are presented with difficult tasks. Reasons for this type of behavior have been postulated to be related to failure in early school years, followed by feelings of inadequacy, leading to self-doubts and finally resulting in a diminished achievement effort. The development of "helpless" beliefs occur over a long period of time in many situations and across a variety of tasks. It is widely accepted that students' beliefs about their abilities can affect their achievement efforts and accomplishments (Andrews & Debus, 1978; Fowler & Peterson, 1981). Another important factor is that this belief system can result in a sequence of maladjustive achievement behaviors such as lower expectation of future success in testing, academics, social interactions, and a host of other life situations (Kistner & Licht, 1983).

OBSERVABLE BEHAVIOR: MOTIVATIONAL FACTORS
The student

1. Feels unable to overcome difficulties
2. Does not take credit for success and attributes same to external factors such as luck rather than internal factors such as self-effort or ability (Boersma & Chapman, 1981)
3. Exhibits a type of learned helplessness (Seligman, Maier, & Geer, 1968)
4. Gives up easily and refuses to continue a task

DISCUSSION: MOTIVATIONAL FACTORS
Motivation needs to be considered as either a prime or concomitant factor in dealing with all students who exhibit learning difficulties. Many students feel helpless and powerless with respect to directing or being part of the directing of their educational progress. They find the external environment or locus completely controls their lives. Students who exhibit failure may internalize a negative self-image and a failure-avoidance mode of behavior. They avoid risks and unhappy responses of their parents and teachers, which affects their motivation and hence their performance. Motivation is greatly influenced by how an individual feels about his or her own personal confidence. Some students have even learned to attribute all or most of their school behavior to "others" and seek every opportunity to blame someone else for their lack of motivation and performance. These students need opportunities to experience their own successes in terms of how much control they have had in the process. This internal sense of participation and accomplishment will affect motivation and develop a higher sense of self-efficacy.

TREATMENT CONSIDERATIONS: MOTIVATIONAL FACTORS

1. Expose the student to "intermittent failure," such as giving him or her more work than usual that can be completed in a given period of time.
2. Help the student recognize that his or her failure to complete the task is due to insufficient effort or wasting of time. Show the student that increased effort can result in improved performance.
3. Use an attribution retraining approach by having students verbalize the appropriate effort attributions. "This didn't work because I . . ." (verbalize the ineffective task strategy).
4. Increase the motivational value of academic work by working toward a goal that is highly valued.
5. Increase self-instructional strategies to understanding the task by perceiving and labeling what is important, classifying the information, defining the problem and selecting a correct response from alternatives.
6. Other attributes include: control of impulse responses, attending to relevant cues, selecting the correct goal, dealing with frustration, and reinforcing self-control (Meichenbaum & Goodman, 1971).
7. Teacher feedback regarding student's attributional processes is deemed a vital factor. Techniques that convey differential strategies, foster self-control, and increase motivation are vital to establishing personal control.
8. Decrease dependency by reducing "overzealous" praise. Place the student in an active role.
9. Teach problem-solving strategies.
10. Self-efficacy may be promoted by teaching social skills. This includes participant modeling of behavior, rehearsal (practice), direct reinforcement techniques, and peer imitation strategies.

Learning disabled adolescents have been shown, in a study by Silverman and Zigmond (1983), as not seeing themselves as incompetent or as even having poor self-concepts. It is possible that these students have found ways outside of school of neutralizing the debilitating effects of underachievement and poor competence in academic subjects. The question to ask is, why do these individuals have adequate self-concepts? It may be that school success is only one part of life for today's students and that the peer culture values things outside of school as well as academic success in school.

PHARMACOLOGY, LEARNING, AND BEHAVIOR

Pharmacology and its effects on learning and behavior are discussed from several points of view, including medication effects on learning and/or attention impaired children, and substance abuse and school-age children.

Medication Effects on Learning and Behavior

The question of the long-term and short-term effects of psychostimulant drugs (e.g., ritalin, dexidrine, cylert, etc.) on learning and hyperactivity of children has not been resolved in terms of usefulness. Generally, stimulants are thought to have little or no long-term effect on ADD or LD children in terms of academic performance (O'Leary, 1980; Werry, 1981). Some short-term effects on productivity and academic tasks have been reported for ADD and LD children. This involves aspects of behavior and information processing related to learning such as memory, or activity level and elements of learning that include academic subjects such as reading, writing, and arithmetic.

Nothing conclusive can be stated about stimulants and memory. Sometimes memory improves and sometimes it does not with stimulants. Methylphenidate (MPH) has been shown to increase children's performance on short-term memory tasks (Sprague & Sleator, 1977). Ritalin, dexidrine, and cylert are the medications of choice for children exhibiting attention deficits (Levine, 1987). Although the duration of action of ritalin and dexidrine are from three to five hours, with an effective onset time of approximately 30 minutes, cylert taken in one daily dose has a longer effect. However, it takes three weeks for cylert to become effective. Individual student metabolism is an important factor in prescribing these drugs.

Effective teaching time must be planned around ritalin because of the short-term duration of its effects, or a repeat of the drug must be taken. Side effects of ritalin include poor appetite and insomnia. It should be noted that tolerance levels change. Effects on growth have not been demonstrated thus far (Gross, 1976), but it is presently thought that long-term negative effects are negligible (Levine, 1987).

MEDICATION AND HYPERACTIVITY
Forness and Kavale (1988) report that stimulant drugs can control hyperactivity in school-age children. In administering drugs, care has to be taken in monitoring them so the students' quality of academic performance, motivation, concentration, and mood are not adversely affected. Teachers also need to look for changes in fine and gross motor performance, as well as overall motor coordination.

Drugs that control attention and hyperactivity can help to improve academic performance in some students and reduce noxious behaviors if properly administered. A drug regime is not to be construed as the main component in any management program. Stimulants should play a supportive role to a good behavior management program, and be discontinued when no longer necessary. Care must be taken in administering dextroamphetamines and methylphenidate to the extent that the child's appetite is not unduly suppressed to the extent that there is serious weight loss, and in some cases anorexia (*Nutrition Reviews,* 1973). In cases of students taking ritalin, appetite suppression, facial tics, and insomnia are significant side effects. Taking ritalin in the late afternoon or evening may cause insomnia in some children. Teachers and parents should also look for signs of Tourette Syndrome in children on drug regiment.

MEDICATION AND ATTENTION
Ritalin is used to help youngsters focus their attention better, exhibit "tolerable" classroom behavior, and improve academic performance. Attention or vigilance has been shown to improve in ADD and LD children on tasks related to response rate over time (Pelham, 1981). Some researchers report that control of deviant behavior seems to improve (Aman & Werry, 1982). The research does not support the idea that drugs improve selective attention, which is described as the degree to which performance breaks down in the presence of distracting factors (Pelham & Bender, 1984; Harvey, Weintraub, & Neale, 1984).

MEDICATION AND ACADEMIC PERFORMANCE
Stimulants do not appear to affect performance on such academic skills as reading achievement, and are not recommended for reading disorders in general (Aman, 1978). Stimulant drugs have proven helpful in improving handwriting and overall retention (Rapport, Murphy, & Bailey, 1982; Yellin, Hopwood, & Greenberg, 1982; Rie & Rie, 1977; Ackerman & Dykman, 1982).

Caution is suggested in forming generalizations because factors such as motivation and attentiveness may have played an important role in the results of many of these studies. Drugs are also reported to be helpful in improving impulse control and sustained attention, as well as beneficial to increasing inhibitory behavior over impulses. It is hypothesized that an increase in concentration should have a concomitant effect on academic subjects (Douglas, 1983; Conners & Werry, 1979). In general, the amount of time children spend on academic tasks seems to be an excellent predictor of school achievement (Berliner & Rosenshine, 1977), and stimulants seem to affect time on tasks.

Substance Abuse and School-Age Children

It is estimated that between 20 to 30 percent of our total population misuse psychoactive drugs to the extent of being at risk of serious dysfunction. Substance abuse is significantly related to serious crime, not only from the activity surrounding the sale of illegal substances but also from the behavior of individuals who have become users.

Drug use among children is much more prevalent than parents expect. Educators who are aware of the problems in their schools admit that denial exists at all levels within the school system, in the home, and with various segments of the community. It is important to note the following facts:

1. Drugs are not confined to any one population, group, or economic level.
2. Drugs affect the middle and elementary schools, as well as the high schools.
3. There is no such thing as safe and responsible use of an illegal substance.

Illegal substances are being trafficked within the school and adjacent environment. Many teenagers buy their drugs at school. Many 12- and 13-year-olds not only use drugs but also traffic in illegal substances.

TYPES OF DRUGS USED
Alcohol
Alcohol is the drug most commonly used by children. Approximately 30 percent of boys and 22 percent of girls classify themselves as "drinkers" by the age of 13. Alcohol is a depressant. It is easy to obtain, and children see their parents and other adults using alcohol and imitate their behavior.

Marijuana
Marijuana is second in usage to alcohol. The active ingredient THC causes a "high" when it is smoked or eaten. It provides the student with a short-lived sense of well-being and a state of relaxation. High-potency marijuana is addictive.

Cocaine
Cocaine is a stimulant and most often snorted by the user. It can also be injected into the bloodstream. Crack, a crystallized form of cocaine, is smoked. Crack is found to have a short "effect time" of between 3 and 4 minutes; a new designer drug on the streets, "ice," which is a methamphetamine derivative, has been known to maintain its effects or "high" for as long as 6 to 8 hours. Narcotics such as heroin and cocaine can affect children's sensory feelings, making them less conscious of pain and reducing their desire for food. Drugs such as cocaine are very physically addictive; withdrawal from even short-term use can cause violent reactions.

Depressants
Depressants are produced in laboratories and include barbiturates, tranquilizers, and methaqualone. Alcohol also acts as a depressant. After a short "high," there are a great deal of undesirable effects with all depressants, the worst of which is addiction. Barbiturates and tranquilizers, which are prescribed by doctors to relieve pain, can be highly addictive if used over a prolonged period of time.

Hallucinogens and Inhalants
Drugs such as LSD cause an hallucinogenic experience or a "trip" that can last minutes or hours, depending on the strength of the drug taken. The reaction can be positive or it can produce mentally debilitating effects, including recurrences, without warning, days, weeks, or even months after the drug was last used.

Inhalants are substances such as nail polish remover, gasoline, paints, aerosols, typewriter correction fluid, freon, airplane glue, adhesives, nitrous oxide, solvents, etc., that when inhaled produce an intoxicating state. The user feels sleepy, drunk, and sometimes confused, anxious, or overactive. Speech is affected and suffocation can be a result of keeping a bag over the head for a long period of time. Overall effects include brain damage, severe cardiac problems, and, in many cases, death. Inhalants are popular because they are easy to get, they look innocuous to parents and teachers, and they deliver a "high" faster than alcohol. Symptoms include drunkenness, dizziness, exhilaration and euphoria, salivation, nausea and vomiting, disorientation, lessening of response to pain, hallucinations, and unconsciousness (U.S. Department of Education, 1987; William Gladden Foundation, 1987).

SYMPTOMS OF DRUG DEPENDENCE

There are many symptoms of drug dependence that the teacher can observe. The student:

1. Cannot concentrate in school and school work deteriorates
2. Reduces participation in school group social activities
3. Has a daily preoccupation with drugs
4. Exhibits loss of weight, problems with memory, and low self-image
5. Confuses what is normal behavior with what is abnormal behavior in school
6. Is frequently drowsy or falls asleep in class
7. Frequently uses eye drops or breath mints
8. May exhibit increased absenteeism from school (National Council of Juvenile and Family Court Judges, 1988)

SCHOOL-BASED PROGRAMS

School-based programs can be divided into three basic approaches:

1. The school can focus on increasing student knowledge and changing attitudes.
2. Curriculum can be modified to include the teaching of values and decision-making tools.
3. The entire school can embark on a program of helping students to develop social competency skills. (U.S. Department of Health and Human Resources, 1989)

Many types of programs have been implemented with varying degrees of success. Programs delivered by peers and parents, working with teachers, were found to have more positive outcomes than others (Schaps, et al., 1980). Students exposed to a "facts curriculum" have been reported to have a lower alcohol consumption rate—the results were sustained at a six-month followup. The effective use of peer leaders has also been considered an appropriate strategy in prevention with young people (Rootman, 1985; Botvin et al., 1984).

The goal of both prevention and intervention is to reduce the incidence of problems related to substance abuse. Programs are often geared to those who consume alcohol or drugs either heavily or frequently. Although it is important to help these individuals to receive early treatment and to modify their behavior, there is a large population of students who are experimenting, and who need particular measures of prevention and intervention in order to avoid more permanent risks to their health and school performance.

In order to provide services to students who are impaired due to substance abuse, the school will need to do the following:

1. Form a community infrastructure of social agencies, schools, treatment programs, churches, and other related systems for purposes of helping establish policies and procedures for addressing maternal use of alcohol and drugs and the after effects in terms of children's needs.
2. Communities need to determine the nature and extent of the problem, which is to be used as a basis for community education, programming and training.
3. Schools need to gear up assessment and placement teams and provide teacher education in this area.
4. Student information activities need to be enhanced and extended to this area.
5. Appropriate changes in instruction and curriculum need to be implemented.
6. Regular and special education teachers will need to work very closely in providing education services to the students who were born with alcohol or drug-related defects.
7. Teacher education programs must prepare professionals to deal with these children at various levels (Greer, 1990).

Along with the suggestions offered in each of the problem areas discussed, the teacher will need to consider implementing a comprehensive behavior management program.

BEHAVIOR MANAGEMENT

A behavioral approach to management has certain characteristics which include not only an orientation to observation but a system of consequences for behavior. It rewards appropriate behavior and does not reward or punish inappropriate behavior. It initially focuses on extrinsic rewards but soon shifts to intrinsic motivation, emphasizing self-safisfaction as a primary motivator.

Certain elements stand out and include (Lieberman, 1982):

1. The behavior must be specific, describable, and observable, if possible.
2. Baseline information must be collected under replicable circumstances.

3. Positive as well as negative consequences of behavior must be determined.
4. Short-term consequences are provided.
5. Praise is used appropriately.
6. All procedures must be accessible to determine possible reasons for failure.

Caveats:

1. The student may not wish to participate.
2. The system may be reduced to extortion on the part of the student.
3. Different rewards mean different things to different people.
4. Teachers and parents are not always consistent in their responses.
5. Too much is often expected.
6. All systems contain errors.

In viewing the whole concept of behavior management, the following general considerations are important.

1. The teacher should be primarily concerned with reinforcing good behavior. The teacher should be careful not to emphasize bad behavior by trying too hard to discourage it. The idea is to reward the student for the way he or she handles himself or herself or deals with problems that come before or precipitate negative behavior. For example, rather than rewarding not fighting, the teacher rewards doing math or science, etc.
2. In reality, when we reward a student for not doing something bad, we are, in effect, reinforcing a subtle form of extortion. To reward a student for doing something that we want him or her to do (arithmetic) which replaces a negative or target behavior (fighting) that we don't want him or her to do, is really good business and is considered a form of free enterprise.
3. It is important that we think about getting out of the business of "paying off" for nonbehavior. The payoff sometimes leads to continued and greater payoffs. For example, one student stopping another student in a school hallway says, "You know, kids in this school are being beaten up on the way to school. For one dollar a week I can give you protection and guarantee that you will not be beaten up" (paying off for nonbehavior). After three weeks of payoffs, when the students meet again, the protector says, "Have you noticed how two of your friends got beaten up last week? They didn't have any protection. Since my expenses have gone up, I'm going to need two dollars a week from you" (continued and greater payoff).

4. It is important to recognize that "normal" is a relative term. Behavior management involves attending to different dimensions of behavior simultaneously.

Specific Considerations in Behavior Management

1. Intracategory: Are we observing clusters of behavior which seem to fall into a particular category?
2. Intercategory: How much overlap in terms of observable behavior is there among the different categories of behavior?
3. Is the behavior occasional, what is the duration, and how severe is the episode?
4. Is the behavior chronic and what is the severity?
5. Can the teacher deal with the behavior within his or her present knowledge base and situation?
6. What are the resources available to help the teacher to improve the situation or to reduce the problem to a level where it can be dealt with effectively within the classroom by the teacher alone?
7. What alternatives are available that will enable the teacher to be able to deal with the problem behavior more effectively?

The underlying assumption in any behavior management program is that the individual imposing the treatment is also willing to change and to accept new ideas. This is not always the case. Many educators are accustomed to dealing with problem behavior in "their own way" and are chary of trying alternative approaches. Some educators resort to physical punishment as a means of modifying behavior or of controlling students. It is said that education is presently the only profession that has the "legal" right to beat its clients into submission. The concept of power or control must be considered when we ask "To what purpose do we use what kinds of behavior management techniques?" "Do the students control us or do we control the students?" is a frequent question. What constitutes a loss of control? Does yelling and striking a student with a paddle constitute a loss of control? What about the whole matter of motive in dealing with behavior? Should we consider what motivates a student to behave as he or she does—or are we, as teachers, going to lash out at anything that disturbs us or that interferes with our perceived needs and goals?

Behavior Modification

Behavior modification as an applied behavior learning theory is based on the idea of operant conditioning or operant learning and the belief that if behavior is learned, it can also be unlearned, and if inappropriate behavior is learned, then appropriate behavior can also be learned. The basic, underlying principle of rewarding desirable behavior and reducing or extinguishing undesirable behavior is fundamental to this theory. It involves a process by which behavior is observed and appropriate techniques to modify this behavior are imposed. It is generally felt that it is easier to deal with specific target behavior than it is to try to restructure a student's total personality. Difficulty with a straight behavior modification approach tends to occur when behaviors of different types appear in the same student or when different types of reinforcers are found to be unsuccessful. Time, self-discipline, and attention to detail on the part of the observer are important factors in behavior modification. Some teachers have difficulty dealing with these factors and, therefore, avoid behavior modification techniques. A behavior modification approach if appropriately utilized, however, can be successfully implemented in school settings.

ANALYSIS OF CONTINGENCY MANAGEMENT

The observer must be aware of the following aspects of student-teacher interaction.

1. Examine or observe the event (what happened?): Teacher says, "Class, may I have your attention?"
2. Analyze the action of the participant (who responded in what way?): The students stop talking and attend to the teacher.
3. Interpret the outcomes (what happened?): The teacher says, "That is good."

EVENT → ACTIONS → OUTCOMES

ACHIEVING DESIRED BEHAVIOR

Reinforcement

A stimulus that results in an increase or strengthening of the behavior it immediately follows is called a reinforcer. Praise or material rewards that result in desired behavior are reinforcers. Whether or not a particular stimulus is a reinforcer must be determined by observing its effects on the behavior it follows. In order to have maximum effect, the reinforcement must immediately follow the desired behavior. The immediacy of the reinforcement that follows the target behavior relates to how effective the reinforcement will be. Chastising a student two hours after a particular event is not as effective as doing it immediately after the episode. Complimenting or giving praise operates the same way. Reinforcement must be contingent on the target behavior. If you want the behavior to occur before you give a reward, then you are establishing a contingency. A reward for one student may have the

opposite effect on another. The teacher saying, "Good work, Susan," may encourage Susan to stay on task. Saying "Good work" to John may, in effect, slow down or stop his efforts. Reinforcers, therefore, must be tested for individual children.

PRIMARY REINFORCERS. Things such as food, drink, warmth, and sexual stimulation that satisfy biological needs or needs that sustain life are called primary reinforcers. They do not depend on previous conditioning for reinforcing value.

SECONDARY REINFORCERS. Things like praise, toys, money and that are not directly related to biological needs, are called secondary or conditioned reinforcers. Where primary reinforcers are paired with secondary reinforcers—such as giving praise with food—or when secondary reinforcers become desirable in and of themselves—such as praise alone—they can have strong reinforcing power in terms of modifying behavior. Some secondary reinforcers such as toys may be unimportant to some children and, therefore, have little or no reinforcing power. When a mother's touch is paired with food or drink the mother's touch can become a strong secondary reinforcer. Teachers usually use secondary reinforcers in school settings. Words, touch, body movement, or posture can have great reinforcing properties. There are always exceptions to the rule in that some students shun praise and others do not respond to competitive situations. Some reinforcers such as praise, touch, or eye contact have a generalized effect on a wide range of behaviors.

TYPES OF REINFORCEMENT. There are two types of reinforcement: positive and negative. Both can increase or strengthen behaviors that follow. Neither should be confused with the concept of punishment.

Positive reinforcers include anything that is desired or needed by the student. Positive reinforcers tend to strengthen the response that has just occurred, making it likely that the response will recur. For example, William, working intently, gives the teacher his math paper and the teacher says, "Good work." That is a positive reinforcer. To be effective the positive reinforcer must follow immediately after the target behavior is achieved. Getting something good to eat contingent on desired behavior, is positive reinforcement because it tends to strengthen the response that follows. Teachers, too often, believe that behaving correctly is only what students are expected to do. They simply ignore good behavior. It is suggested that to encourage children to continue behaving well, we need to positively reinforce their good behavior and not just wait for them to misbehave. Students have been heard to say about certain teachers that it is extremely difficult to "Get a nice word out of him or her" or that "He or she is grouchy."

A *negative reinforcer* includes anything unpleasant or not desired by the student. Negative reinforcement involves taking away something noxious contingent upon the desired behavior. Negative reinforcers weaken the response that immediately precedes the onset of the negative reinforcer. This can occur in different ways.

1. Negative reinforcement strengthens the response that takes away the negative reinforcer.
2. Negative reinforcement also suppresses the behavior that brought on the negative reinforcer. For example, a student is reinforced for giving a response. By doing this he or she avoids punishment such as the case in which a teacher constantly yelled to keep the class quiet. The students responded by working quietly. Another case was the mother who nagged for better grades which motivated her child to get better grades. However, keeping quiet as in the first case or getting better grades in the second case may have reduced the yelling and nagging (punishment), but at the same time it tended to reinforce the behavior (yelling and nagging) of the person who is doing the punishing.

It is important to remember that negative reinforcement is a double-edged sword. We have many well-meaning, yelling teachers and nagging mothers who, while achieveing their goals, become disliked by the children in the process.

Another consideration is the fact that while negative reinforcement results in an increase in the behavior that it follows, it is not to be confused with punishment. It is probably better to think of both positive and negative reinforcement as ways of modifying behavior and not worry too much about whether a particular response is negative or positive. Just think about the behavior that is occurring and the responses or consequences that are permitting it to continue.

REINFORCEMENT SCHEDULES. The four types of reinforcement schedules that are generally utilized include fixed ratio, variable ratio, fixed interval, and variable interval.

	Fixed	Variable
Ratio	Fixed Ratio	Variable Ratio
Interval	Fixed Interval	Variable Interval

Fixed Ratio: In this case reinforcement would occur after a specific number of responses. For example, after every three responses the student would be reinforced.

Variable Ratio: Reinforcement in these situations would occur after a varying number of responses. For example, the student would be rewarded after one response, then after five responses, and then after three responses, with the number of responses between reinforcers averaging three.

Fixed Interval: This involves reinforcement after a specific interval of time. For example, the student would be reinforced after a ten-second delay.

Variable Interval: This involves reinforcement after different intervals of time. For example, the student would be reinforced after ten seconds, then after fifteen seconds, and then after five seconds, with the intervals averaging ten seconds.

It has been found that variable schedules of reinforcement produce more results than fixed ratios. It can be concluded that variable ratio reinforcement should produce the greatest response rate while the fixed interval would produce the least response rate.

APPLICATIONS TO TEACHING. Reinforcers strengthen behavior and can be used to develop new skills. The following are some concepts to be considered.

1. Of all the reinforcers that are available to me, which will work with a particualr child? Someone once said that "every student has his price." The reinforcer that works may be highly individualized.
2. How can I test for the most appropriate reinforcer? Observation of students at play and work are effective, or the teacher can talk to the student and probe for his likes and dislikes.
3. Does the same reinforcer function effectively at different times and in different situations? Ice cream, for example, may not be reinforcing in the winter for some students.
4. Secondary reinforcers work better if paired with food; for example, saying, "Good job, John" as he is given a bit of food and a pat on the back.
5. When can I take away the food and the pat and just rely on praise?
6. Tokens and food are good to start with, particularly when working with nonverbal children exhibiting a slow rate of development. Some of the more commonly used reinforcers include:

a. A "time" or "clock stamp" can be used with a time clock. The teacher stamps small pieces of paper with the clock stamp and the number of minutes of on-task behavior is marked as indicated by the time clock that is left on the student's desk. The teacher then will write in the minute and hour hands that will indicate the amount of time that the student has worked at a particular task. This is later tallied and "time" is exchanged for tangible rewards.

b. Token reinforcement, later to be exchanged for tangible rewards.

c. Different colored stars to be later exchanged for toys, school supplies, or opportunities to play in a pleasant setting.

7. Reinforce the student only when he or she performs the desired behavior. Do not reinforce him or her randomly. In some cases you may want to reinforce successive approximations. For example, John could be reinforced for taking out his paper and pencil first, although the terminal behavior is to complete arithmetic problems copied from the chalkboard.

8. Do not reinforce any inappropriate behavior such as aggression or continually getting out of the seat.

9. Reinforce *immediately* after the desired behavior is completed.

10. Reinforce the student frequently and in small amounts, especially when you are teaching a new concept. Tokens or stars are small and can be given frequently in the lesson without losing their reinforcement value.

11. The Premack Principle can also be utilized in modifying behavior. For example, follow a low probability behavior such as taking out the garbage with a high probability behavior such as watching the T.V. or eating a favorite food. The latter (T.V. or food) should strengthen the former (taking out the garbage). Another example would be saying to students, "As soon as we put away the materials, we can have our snack, etc." The snack, in this case, may reinforce the putting away of materials.

Shaping

Sometimes students who are severe stutterers will not read aloud or answer questions orally in the classroom. In some cases they do not speak at all. How can we achieve the target behavior of attaining a modicum of verbal participation in classroom activities? *Modicum* is relative and must be defined specifically for each individual student. Shaping, in this case, means to reinforce successful approximations to the final target behavior by taking the student closer and closer to what we want, utilizing as a vehicle less threatening or nonthreatening situations. This may take a long time and require many interim steps. For the stuttering student the following is suggested:

1. Indicate privately to the student that you understand his or her problem and that while you will not force him or her to speak out loud (thereby relieving some of the student's anxiety), you are at the same time going to help him or her work through the problem.

2. We can then determine, with the student, situations in which he or she feels comfortable when speaking.

3. Through further approximations, in one-to-one interactions, determine with the student situations in which he or she will speak by choice. These situations should resemble general classroom activities. This could involve his or her speaking freely or responding to questions in a small group of two at first, then three, four, etc.

4. Finally, through reinforcing successive approximations, achieve the target behavior of class oral participation and continue intermittent reinforcements.

Modeling (Imitation)

Many educators believe that desirable as well as undesirable behavior patterns exhibited by students are a result of modeling after those of others. This occurs in different environments involving social interaction with people who constantly demonstrate certain behaviors. Kindness, patience, loudness, and punitive behavior, for example, are considered learned for the most part. Teachers need to be aware of their potential impact on students' behaviors in terms of their own modeling potential. Especially in the early grades, if the teacher is calm and warm, the students are likely to model or imitate these patterns of behavior. In utilizing modeling in modifying behavior, especially with the sensitive-withdrawn child, it is suggested that the teacher model desirable behavior with another student; i.e., reward another student for exhibiting the desirable behavior and then reward the target student for imitating the same behavior.

Imitation is an important skill to learn and a powerful tool in teaching new behaviors. The whole concept of imitation must be taught deliberately to those in whom it is not present, that is, in students who are unable to imitate. The teacher must present models that can be easily imitated and then praise the correct imitation or successive approximation to imitating the target behavior.

Prompting and Fading
Some students need to be shown or prompted to enable them to accomplish a particular task. The teacher may hold a student's hand and actually move it through the proper sequence in writing a manuscript "a" on the chalkboard, for example. The gradual lessening of direction and pressure from the teacher's hand will allow the student to take control. The teacher should slowly remove his or her hand as the student takes full control of the movement. This is one form of fading. Fading is the gradual withdrawal of support after the student has mastered each step or aspect of a specific event. This helps the student to achieve success and encourages further attempts at more difficult tasks. An example of prompting is when arrows are placed near a letter with a red dot ($\downarrow$M), enabling the student to know where to start and in which direction to proceed when writing the letter M

Generalization
Individuals are constantly reacting to new situations in a manner that is congruent with the way they responded to similar situations in the past. This is especially true if a particular set of behaviors was reinforced in the past. The greater the similarity between situations, the more generalized the response. Learning to ride a bicycle on one type of bicycle will enable the individual to ride other types of bicycles. The bicycle riding response will generalize itself to all bicycles. In terms of response generalization, it appears that in certain situations students will exhibit a generalized response to stress or happiness. An example would be the learner who, when happy, starts out by laughing but then makes funny noises and begins to jump up and down in his or her seat. The same response seems to occur each time.

Generalization is an important part of behavior management. We want behavior learned in the classroom to be generalized at home and to all social situations. Good manners at the table is an example of this phenomenon. Good behavior in the classroom should be generalized in the playground.

Deprivation and Satiation
Deprivation relates to the length of time since a reinforcer has been available to an individual. A game is more likely to be reinforcing after concentrated work such as reading or writing than immediately after a physical education class. An example of satiation is the situation in which a student is given too much of a particular reinforcement at one time and the value of the reinforcer is lost. Too much praise may make praise ineffective as a reinforcer. The teacher should vary reinforcers and learn to use generalized reinforcers, such as eye contact, effectively to control behavior. Continuous reinforcement, where every response is rewarded, is effective in acquiring good behavior. Intermittent reinforcement, however, is most effective in maintaining the desired behavior after it has been established.

WEAKENING BEHAVIOR OR PERFORMANCE
Punishment
Punishment can be verbal or physical and is used by many educators to decrease undesirable behavior. However, in particular students, it can result in an increase in more aberrant or more severe behavior. It also may not necessarily result in improved behavior. The student who is "paddled" may physically abuse or hurt another child or "get even" with the teacher through active or passive aggression. Punishment, for the most part, presents a moral and ethical issue, depending on the situation in which it is utilized. In certain critical or severe situations punishment may be necessary, particularly when injury or health may be at stake. For example, immediate punishment may be in order for the child who takes pills from the medicine cabinet and eats them or for the child who runs out in the middle of the street in front of cars. The following are considerations to keep in mind:

1. The child should understand in advance what he or she will be punished for.
2. Punish a child immediately after the behavior occurs, preferably, or while it is occurring, if possible.
3. Punishment should be consistent and accomplished with some objectivity.
4. Punishment should only be used in severe or critical situations where a quick change in behavior is necessary.
5. Continue to reinforce appropriate behavior. For example, praise a child for not going to the medicine cabinet without permission.
6. Use of punishment may lead not only to more aggressive behavior by the child, but also may result in the individual doing the punishing becoming accustomed to using physical punishment as a means of modifying behavior.

Overcorrection
Overcorrection as a technique for decreasing target behavior involves extending the treatment beyond the

correction of a specific act. For example, the student who throws paper on the playground may be required to clean up the whole playground and perhaps sweep the halls. The following are important considerations:

1. The student must understand what behavior is being punished. In this case it is throwing paper on the playground.
2. The overcorrection procedure must be directly related to the undesirable behavior. Having him or her sweep up the halls may be too far away from throwing paper on the playground.
3. The overcorrection should require longer periods of time than the behavior being corrected.

The idea of work should never be construed as punishment.

Time-Out

Time-out is a form of negative reinforcement in which the opportunity for reinforcement is removed for a given time. The time is contingent upon a particular response from the student. For example, the teacher could isolate the student every time he or she does something that is undesirable. Seating the student in a corner by himself or herself and not allowing anyone to talk to him or her is not a new concept in modifying student behavior. There are several important steps, however, to follow for maximum effect.

1. The student should know the rules regarding what behaviors will result in "time-out."
2. How long the student will have to be in a time-out situation should be clearly specified. (Probably not more than 5 minutes in most situations).
3. Be consistent and use the time-out every time the undesirable behavior occurs.
4. Time-out areas should be supervised and the student should know the effects of getting out early without permission.
5. The activity should be carried out in an objective manner.
6. Time-out should be repeated if the student "fools around" or fails to do what is required.
7. At the end of the time-out continue to reinforce appropriate behavior immediately.

Response Cost

Response cost is a form of treatment where the student is penalized in some manner for undesirable behavior. Examples of response cost are fines, losing one's license, or having to give up something that is valued. The following are factors that should be considered.

1. The response cost must be specified. The fine, or whatever it is the student has to give up, should be reasonable. Taking away six months of television for not doing homework for one night is not reasonable.
2. Time-out and overcorrection have been used successfully in educational settings. However, it is important to recognize that they are forms of punishment.

CONTROLLING THE FREQUENCY OF BEHAVIOR

For years students exhibiting a broad range of behavior problems—from outward aggression to withdrawal—have received various kinds of responses from parents and teachers. These include:

Physical punishment
Threat of loss of privileges
Verbal abuse
Isolation or removal
Appeal to better instincts

For most students, one, or any combination of these responses to noxious behavior, has been deemed effective on occasion; but, for the most part, none of these "treatments" has really proven to be an overwhelming success. One reason is the obvious emotional involvement of the individual giving the punishment. There is a tendency for teachers, for example, to take the student's behavior as a personal affront and to deal with the student on an immediate basis, not thinking about how to deal with the student's recurring problem behavior within a systematic process.

It is suggested that, in dealing with noxious or undesirable behavior, the teacher should become aware of and deal with the frequency of behavior first, the ultimate goal being to decrease excessive behavior and increase diminished behavior so that the classroom can become tolerable for everyone. Several cogent factors emerge:

1. Certain kinds of behavior related to conduct need to be reduced (Quay, 1979). They are purely and simply "excessive." In general, aggressive types of behavior involving negative student-to-student interactions and student-teacher conflicts can be tolerated if they occur occasionally and if the precipitating cause is identified and there is reasonable understanding of why the behavior occurs. The reality of life is that certain types of individuals have difficulty getting along with other types of individuals. It is only when the behavior becomes excessive—to the extent that it interferes with ongoing school activities, causes disruptions, and extends beyond the frustration tolerance of the teacher—that crisis situations occur.

2. Another type of behavior can be termed "diminished" to the extent that the student does not exhibit enough of a desired behavior. That is the case with the withdrawn student who does not interact enough with others or rarely participates in class discussions or activities. In this situation the desired behavior needs to be increased. This may sound like an oversimplification, but the point to be stressed is that the mind-set of the teacher is important in terms of how to approach this problem. In this case the mind-set is that behavior needs to be increased. The steps that follow can be implemented in almost any type of environment. It involves the following:

a. Establish a baseline of information (data) regarding the frequency of behavior under concern.

b. Collect additional data over a period of a week or more as necessary regarding the pattern of this behavior.

c. Discuss the findings with the student and together decide on the kinds of actions that need to be taken to either reduce or increase the behavior as the case may be.

d. Be sure to provide opportunities during the school day for the behavior to be modified, e.g., good behavior rewarded.

e. The student should have the opportunity during the modification process to verbalize the amelioration plan or the self-mediation necessary for the desired effect.

f. Intermittent reinforcement should continue after the desired effects have been sustained. It would be very helpful to know what motivates the student and the kind of reward system that will prove successful.

The approach recommended combines a traditional behavioral orientation and one that entails cognitive restructuring. The whole idea is to control the frequency of behavior.

CONTRACTING

Contracting is another reinforcing and motivating technique that can be used in a classroom to achieve desired learner outcomes. A negotiated contract becomes a tangible exhibit of an agreement between the teacher and the student and involves an exchange process. The written contract should always be negotiated and contain conditions of exchange so the student understands that if he or she completes a preset task, with or without conditions, something will be given in return. The contract form itself is not intended to become the reward, even if reinforcers such as stars or written praise are visible on the completed contract.

A qualifying criterion for success must be discussed and also agreed upon if it is to be listed on the contract; for example, the task may be completing 25 subtraction problems. A qualifying condition could be that the 25 subtraction problems need to all be correct. The contract can also include time parameters for completion.

Interim Review of Contracts

Opportunities for an interim review should be explained to the student. The student should understand what is required for the contract to be fulfilled, and it is a good idea to restate all of the conditions to ensure understanding. It is suggested that both the teacher and the student get a copy of the contract and that the original be filed in a "special place." The instructor can also set up a contract system that rewards the student intermittently for successful completion of parts of the task or for approximating the task. The intermittent reward system should be discussed with the student. This type of reinforcement is motivational to students who may see the entire task as overwhelming. Small, frequent reinforcement has been found to be very helpful.

Rewards

The reward for successful completion of a task should be given as soon as possible or given according to the desires of the student, if it fits into the student's daily school schedule. Care should be taken to write contracts that are clear and achievable and that the reward is realistic and can be accomplished. Do not deviate from the contract or substitute one reward for another, as the student may perceive variations as dishonesty. The student can be rewarded in a variety of ways, including the following:

1. Time out for satisfying experiences
2. Tangible rewards such as toys, games, colored pencils, key chains, or even certificates
3. Food
4. Recreation time or special activities
5. Special visitation time (principal, teacher, other)
6. Special outside-of-school events (sports, bazaars, plays, etc.)
7. Tokens that can be traded for a variety of things
8. Time with special machines (computers, typewriters, VCR, etc.)
9. Running special errands
10. Parties
11. Work in the library or office

12. Listening to music, stories
13. Getting a new book
14. Being class leader for the day
15. Being allowed to go first in classroom activities

The contract should be written in the presence of the student with his or her approval of the wording and conditions. Students can also write their own contracts, including conditions that can be negotiated with and approved by the teacher. Students need to be encouraged continually and reminded about how close they are to completing a contract. Completion of a contract is indeed a special event that deserves celebration and a note home to the parents.

OBSERVING AND CHARTING BEHAVIOR

Students exhibiting learning disabilities in the elementary school seem to exhibit a "relatively stable pattern of classroom behavior" (McKinney & Feagans, 1983). These patterns of behavior distingush them from their average-achieving agemates and appear to be an important factor in terms of failure in school. As far as assessment and instruction are concerned, such factors as on-task behavior and adaptive behavior are rarely part of evaluation and programming for the students. Behavioral measurement is not commonly used in either regular education or special education programming. Task-oriented and independent behavior are deemed essential for success in academic as well as social areas of learning. Therefore, the techniques of applied behavioral analysis that consider these factors are deemed both appropriate and useful for classroom purposes.

Observing and charting behavior have effects both on those observing and on the student whose behavior is being analyzed. These are:

1. Through counting the behavior under concern, the observer may find that it may not be happening as often as was believed.
2. It may be observed that the behavior occurs only at a certain time during the day or is precipitated by a particular situation. The observer may gain an understanding of why the behavior occurs.
3. The student may modify his or her own behavior merely by virtue of the fact that he or she now observes that someone is watching him or her and then writing things down (counting).
4. The student may relate a particular behavior with someone counting or charting, and this kind of association may result in a change in behavior.

Observation and accurate recording of events or behaviors will give the teacher an idea of how often a particular behavior occurs. This can be accomplished easily by using a checklist. The teacher may want to note the amount of off-task or on-task activity that is occurring for a particular student. The frequency of the behavior can be charted to show how the student is performing over a period of time. It can then be determined if there is improvement, no change, or a decline in performance in terms of the student's behavior. The following are important in charting behavior:

1. Establish a baseline for particular behaviors by determining the current level of performance.
2. Estimate the time or duration of a particular behavior as well as how many times it occurs within a given period. For example, John may get off-task during a 30-minute reading period an average of five times for a given five-day period. He stays off-task an average of three minutes each time before going back to work.
3. Wherever possible have another observer check out and verify the results or count. Material needed will include a pencil, copies of the forms, and a stopwatch, regular watch, or clock. The Mann Student Observation Worksheet (Form 4-1) and the Graphing Worksheet (Form 4-2) can be utilized in observing and charting behavior.
4. The sequence involves pinpointing behavior, recording behavior, and then controlling the consequences or alternatives. It is suggested that the teacher discuss the findings of a particular behavior over a given period of time with the student. The teacher should attempt to arrive at an agreement with the student that this is an area of concern that needs to be improved.
5. If behavior is charted over a period of time, the teacher should discuss the progress or lack of it with the student. Reinforcement of improved or desirable behavior that has been charted should be accomplished on a continuous basis even after the undesirable behavior is no longer a problem. The teacher should continue to reinforce the desired behavior.

Determining the Effectiveness of Treatment

The teacher needs to know if the intervention or treatment program has modified the behavior of the learner (in accordance with expectations). A logical method of determining this is to stop the treatment or return to a baseline mode and see if the desired behavior is maintained. The basic design for implementing a behavior modification program is shown in Figure 4–1.

There are situations, such as in severe cases of aberrant behavior that is self-injurious or injurious to others, in which the teacher may not want to discontinue the treatment and return to a baseline mode. An alternate approach to using the basic ABA design is to chart the student's progress with his or her participation. (See Figure 4–2.)

1. The student notes that he or she is exhibiting the target behavior (talking out of turn) an average of five times during a science period each day for five days.
2. The student then specifies his or her own projected treatment plan that includes specifying the maximum number of times he or she will exhibit the target behavior for a five-day interval (treatment period).

   Example: Student, "I will try to talk out of turn (target behavior) less than five times each day." Using the baseline data as a guideline, the student states, "I will not talk out of turn more than four times on Monday, three times on Tuesday, three times on Wednesday, two times on Thursday, and one time on Friday." The teacher observes the student's behavior and records the incident accordingly.

3. During the treatment period, the student and teacher chart the student's actual behavior (talking out of turn).
4. The process of charting enables the student to monitor his or her own behavior.
5. This approach lends itself very well to "contracting," where the student agrees in a written document to adhere to a schedule of behavior as outlined in a simple agreement contract.

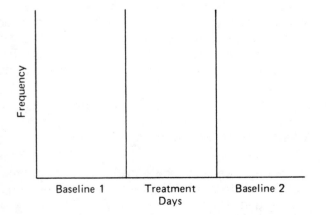

Figure 4-1 Design for Implementing Behavior Modification Program

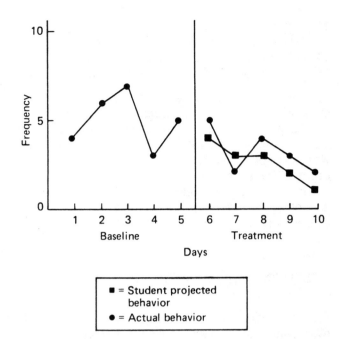

Figure 4-2 Chart of Student's Behavior

6. After the treatment period, the student and the teacher review the results. The student indicates how the treatment period compares with the baseline period and then formulates new goals for the next period.

The students soon learn that they can control their own world. This technique is particularly appropriate for immature-dependent students who may discover that they can do a great deal to control their own destiny.

Multiple Baseline

Another alternative method for determining whether or not a particular treatment is effective is to examine antecedent behavior in several children simultaneously, establish a continuum of baselines, and apply a treatment program. Then comparisons will indicate whether or not the treatment has been effective. This approach is designed to determine the effectiveness of a particular reinforcer in a particular individual and often is difficult to interpret. (See Figure 4–3.)

1. The observer charts the concurrent baseline behavior of three students (five days).
2. After the first five days, treatment is applied to student 1 and baseline is continued for students 2 and 3.
3. At the end of the second week, student 2 receives the treatment along with student 1 as the observer continues to collect baseline data on student 3.

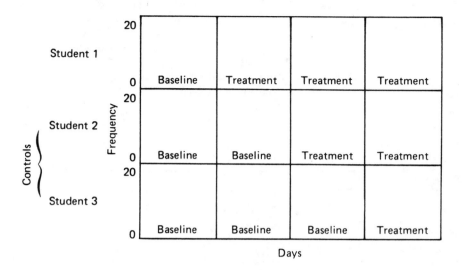

Figure 4-3 Multiple-Baseline Treatment

4. The third week student 3 receives the same treatment as 1 and 2.
5. After the fourth week comparisons are made between baselines and treatments for all three (1, 2 and 3) to determine the following:
   a. Did all three students improve while receiving the same treatment for a five-day treatment period?
   b. Was there no improvement in the behavior of any of the students using the same treatment?
   c. Was there a great deal of variability in treatment effects when comparisons are made of the three students?
   d. Was the treatment detrimental to the three students, causing a negative reaction?

Another approach to determining treatment effectiveness is to examine the generalization of treatment in one situation to other situations, as shown in Figure 4–4.

The Mann Student Observation Worksheet

The Mann Student Observation Worksheet is but one of many techniques available to teachers for the charting of observable data. The Observation Worksheet can be put on a clipboard for easy management. Following is a step-by-step analysis of how the Worksheet can be completed. The sample form (Form 4-2) and Figures 4–5 and 4–6 (the case study of a particular student's observation and treatment program) should be referred to while reviewing this section.

1. *Name:* Student's name.
2. *Age:* The age can be listed by birthdate and number.

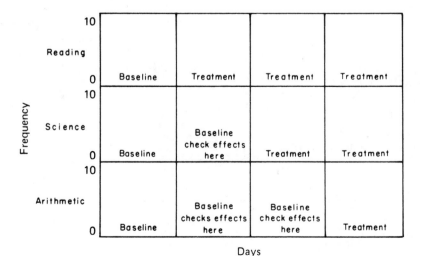

Figure 4-4 Behavior Generalization

NAME: *Lisa Smith* Beginning Date *10-3-78*

AGE: *7-4-70 (8)* Ending Date *10-28-78*

EXAMPLE A
MANN STUDENT OBSERVATION WORKSHEET
On/Off Task and Target Behaviors

Teacher: *Mrs. L. Brown* Grade: *3*

Observer One: *Mrs. L. Brown* Observer Two: _____

CHECK ONE: ☒ On Off Task
            ☐ Target Behavior

Behavior Desired:

stay on task during reading period

Obs. Nbr.	Day & Date	Observ. Time	Nbr. of Beh.	Time OFF Task	Time ON Task	Bothers Teacher	Bothers Student	Talking	Playing	Bath./Drink	Aggres./Fights	Out of Seat	Daydream/Sleep	Walk – Run	Does Other Work	Other
1	M. 10/3	9:30-10:30	50	10		✓	✓	✓				✓		✓		
2	T. 10/4	" - "	55	5		✓	✓	✓				✓		✓		
3	W. 10/5	" - "	40	20			✓					✓				
4	TH. 10/6	" - "	50	10		✓	✓	✓				✓		✓		
5	F. 10/7	" - "	50	10		✓	✓					✓		✓		
5	5 Days	5 Hours	245	55		4	5	3				5		4		

End period 1-baseline

Begin Period 2-continuous reinforcement

Obs. Nbr.	Day & Date	Observ. Time	Nbr. of Beh.	Time OFF Task	Time ON Task	Bothers Teacher	Bothers Student	Talking	Playing	Bath./Drink	Aggres./Fights	Out of Seat	Daydream/Sleep	Walk – Run	Does Other Work	Other
6	M. 10/10	9:30-10:30	35	25		✓	✓					✓		✓		
7	T. 10/11	" - "	20	40								✓				
8	W. 10/12	" - "	25	35			✓							✓		
9	TH. 10/13	" - "	30	30		✓	✓					✓		✓		
10	F. 10/14	" - "	20	40								✓				
5	5 Days	5 Hours	130	170		2	3					4		3		

End period 2- continuous reinforcement

Begin period 3- variable reinforcement

COMMENTS – TREATMENT

P1- off task; 245 minutes
On task; 55 minutes
Problem areas
Talking
Out of Seat
Bothers Students
Walk- Run
Playing
Treatment plan for
P2 (5 days)
continuous token
reinforcement (colored
discs) to be exchanged
for school supplies
for on task behavior
i.e., group participation
silent reading and
other independent
activities

P2 - off task; 130 minutes
On task; 170 minutes
Problem Areas
Talking - decreased
Out of Seat - decreased
Bothers students - decreased
Walk-run - decreased
Playing - decreased

Treatment Plan for P3 (5 days)
begin variable
reinforcement (continue
to use colored discs)
and - add praise,
smiles, etc. to reinforce
on task behavior
of reading, participation
and other independent
activities

NOTE: Draw a dark line to indicate end of period.

Figure 4-5

NAME: Lisa Smith

AGE: 7-4-70 (8)

Beginning Date 10-3-78

Ending Date 10-28-78

EXAMPLE A
MANN STUDENT OBSERVATION WORKSHEET (Continued)

OBSERVER: Mrs. L. Brown

Obs. Nbr.	Day & Date	Observ. Time	Nbr. of Beh.	Time OFF Task	Time ON Task	Bothers Teacher	Bothers Student	Talking	Playing	Bathr./Drink	Aggres./Fights	Out of Seat	Daydream/ Sleep	Walk – Run	Does Other Work	Other:	COMMENTS – TREATMENT
11	M.10/17	9:30-10:30		35	25			✓				✓					P.3- off task; 140 minutes On task; 160 minutes Problem Areas Talking Out of Seat Bothers Students-eliminated Walk-run-decreased Playing-eliminated Treatment plan for P-4 (5 days) establish a new baseline; reinforce with praise, smiles and remove token reinforcement.
12	T. 10/18	" - "		30	30			✓									
13	W.10/19	" - "		20	40							✓					
14	TH. 10/20	" - "		25	35							✓		✓			
15	F. 10/21	" - "		30	30			✓				✓					
5	5 Days	5 Hours		140	160			3				4		1			

End period 3-variable reinforcement

Begin period 4-new baseline

Obs. Nbr.																	
16	M. 10/24	9:30-10:30		20	40							✓					P.4- off task; 135 minutes On task; 165 minutes Problem Areas Talking Out of Seat Bothers students-eliminated Walk-run-eliminated Playing- eliminated Continue social reinforcement, i.e. praise, smile, touch, etc.
17	T. 10/25	" - "		35	25			✓				✓					
18	W. 10/26	" - "		30	30			✓				✓					
19	TH. 10/27	" - "		35	25			✓									
20	F. 10/28	" - "		15	45												
5	5 Days	5 Hours		135	165			3				3					

End period 4 - new baseline

Continue social reinforcement

NOTE: Draw a dark line to indicate end of period.

Figure 4-5 (continued)

NAME: *Lisa Smith*

AGE: *7-4-70 (8)*

Beginning Date *11-1-78*

Ending Date *11-25-78*

EXAMPLE B
MANN STUDENT OBSERVATION WORKSHEET
On/Off Task and Target Behaviors

Teacher: *Mrs. L. Brown*

Observer One: *Mrs. L. Brown*

CHECK ONE: ☐ On/Off Task
           ☒ Target Behavior

Grade: *3*

Observer Two: _____

Behavior Desired:

Increase staying in seat during reading period

Obs. Nbr.	Day & Date	Observ. Time	Nbr. of Beh.	Time OFF Task	Time ON Task	Bothers Teacher	Bothers Student	Talking	Playing	Bathr./Drink	Aggres./Fights	Out of Seat	Daydream/Sleep	Walk – Run	Does Other Work	Other:
1	M. 11/1	9:30-10:30	20													
2	T. 11/2	" - "	18													
3	W. 11/3	" - "	22													
4	TH. 11/4	" - "	26													
5	F. 11/5	" - "	27													
5	5 Days	5 Hours	113													

end period 1 - baseline data

begin period 2 - continuous reinforcement

6	M. 11/8	9:30-10:30	12													
7	T. 11/9	" - "	10													
8	W. 11/10	" - "	4													
9	TH. 11/11	" - "	6													
10	F. 11/12	" - "	6													
5	5 Days	5 Hours	36													

end period 2 - continuous reinforcement

begin period 3 - variable reinforcement

COMMENTS - TREATMENT

P1- Out of seat 113 times Treatment plan for P2 (5 days) continuous token reinforcement (colored discs) to be exchanged for staying in seat and doing on task activities i.e, group participation, silent reading and other independent activities.

P2 - Out of seat 36 times Treatment plan for P3 (5 days) begin variable reinforcement (continue to use colored discs) and add praise, smiles, etc. to reinforce staying in seat doing on task activity, such as reading, participation and other independent activities.

NOTE: Draw a dark line to indicate end of period.

Figure 4-6

NAME: *Lisa Smith*

AGE: *7-4-70 (8)*

Beginning Date *11-1-78*

Ending Date *11-25-78*

EXAMPLE B
MANN STUDENT OBSERVATION WORKSHEET (Continued)

OBSERVER: *Mrs. L. Brown*

Obs. Nbr.	Day & Date	Observ. Time	Nbr. of Beh.	Time OFF Task	Time ON Task	Bothers Teacher	Bothers Student	Talking	Playing	Bathr./Drink	Aggres./Fights	Out of Seat	Daydream/Sleep	Walk – Run	Does Other Work	Other:
11	M. 11/15	9:30-10:30	8													
12	T. 11/16	" – "	7													
13	W. 11/17	" – "	5													
14	TH. 11/18	" – "	8													
15	F. 11/19	" – "	3													
5	5 Days	5 Hours	31													

End of period 3 - variable reinforcement

Begin period 4 - new baseline

16	M. 11/21	9:30-10:30	6													
17	T. 11/22	" – "	9													
18	W. 11/23	" – "	7													
19	TH. 11/24	" – "	4													
20	F. 11/25	" – "	7													
5	5 Days	5 Hours	33													

End period 4 - new baseline

COMMENTS – TREATMENT

P.3- Out of seat 31 times treatment plan for P.4 (5 days) Establish a new baseline; reinforce staying in seat with praise, smile and touch and remove token reinforcement.

P.4- Out of seat 33 times continue social reinforcement, i.e, praise, smile, touch, etc.

NOTE: Draw a dark line to indicate end of period.

Figure 4-6 (continued)

3. *Beginning Date—Ending Date:* The beginning date is the first day of observation and the ending date is the last day of observation.
4. *Teacher:* Teacher's name.
5. *Grade:* Student's present grade level.
6. *Observer 1—Observer 2:* The observer can be the teacher or any other person. If possible, it is good to have two individuals observing a student's behavior to see how they correlate for reliability.
7. *Check One: On/Off Task* or *Target Behavior:* The observer must decide whether he or she wants to focus on *On/Off Task* behavior and delineate the frequency of specific behaviors observed or to just focus in on one specific *Target Behavior. Check On/Off Task* when there are any behaviors that interfere with on-task activity. If *On/Off Task* is checked, it indicates that the observer desires to identify the behavior which is interfering with on-task behavior. Regardless of which area is checked, the observer must indicate under the *Behavior Desired* section the task involved and the target behavior.
8. *Obs. Nbr. (Observation Number):* 1 = first obs.; 2 = second obs.; 3= third obs., etc. The number of observations will depend upon the frequency of the behavior. Low frequency behaviors will require longer periods of observation.
9. *Day and Date:* The day and date for each observation or group of observations is indicated.
10. *Observation Time:* Two time periods are recorded; the time the observation period begins and the time it ends.
11. *Nbr. of Beh. (Number of Behaviors):* If *On/Off Task* is checked, skip 11 and go to 12. See Example A. If *Target Behavior* is checked, it indicates that the observer will be counting the incidence of a particular behavior and marking the frequency of the behavior in the *Nbr. of Beh.* column. In this example the *Time Off-Task* and *Time On-Task* columns and the *Behavior Observed* sections would not be used. (See Example B).
12. *Time Off-Task* and *Time On-Task:* When the observer checks *On/Off Task* behavior, he or she would skip the *Nbr. of Beh.* column and complete the columns for *Time Off-Task* and *Time On-Task,* and the *Behavior Observed* section. The *Time On-Task* and *Time Off-Task* behavior can be monitored in the following manner:
    a. Use a stopwatch for exact timing or a wall clock or a wristwatch and record the interval of observation.
    b. The observer can time either *Time Off-Task* or *Time On-Task*. It is not necessary to observe for both. Record either *Time Off-Task* or *Time On-Task* and subtract from total time for other record.
    c. A trained aide, student teacher, or volunteer can also be an observer.
13. *Behavior Observed:* Observation of behavior requires a simple yes ($\sqrt{}$) or no (blank) response. Some observers prefer to use a yes (+) and no (−) type of notation. The observer is asked to judge which of the behaviors from this section are deemed to be problem areas. These problem areas can at some later time also be treated as *Target Behaviors.* Example B is an example of charting a *Target Behavior.* The important considerations to keep in mind are (1) to determine how much time the student is on or off task and (2) to pinpoint with reasonable accuracy the type of specific behavior the student exhibits when he or she is off task. Following are some definitions of *Behavior Observed:*
    a. Bothers Teacher
       The student who exhibits *excessive* direct contact with the teacher, verbally or otherwise. An example would be the student who continually leaves his or her seat to ask the teacher questions and/or often disturbs the teacher when he or she is working with other students.
    b. Bothers Students
       The student who continually annoys others with excessive verbal behavior or physical contact to the extent that it is obviously a nuisance type of attention-getting behavior.
    c. Talking
       Constant talking by the student to others in the class as well as talking out inappropriately in class.
    d. Playing
       The student may be involved in any kind of play, exhibiting verbally or through actions that he or she is attending to toys, games, "fooling around" and other self-entertaining activity.
    e. Bathr. (Bathroom)-Drink
       This is interpreted as the student who does not have a physical problem but nevertheless goes to the bathroom and/or water fountain to excess.
    f. Aggres. (Aggressive)-Fights
       This refers to the hostile, angry student who may be fighting—not just playing in a manner that looks like fighting. The student may strike another individual, or break and throw things in anger.

g. Out of Seat

The learner is of concern because he or she is out of the seat constantly but not necesarily walking or running around the room. This student is off-task, and prefers to stand by his or her desk, sit on the floor, or do other things in other than the designated work area, i.e., at desk, table, etc.

h. Daydream-Sleep

This student may appear withdrawn and is, in fact, not attending to the task required by the teacher. He or she does not respond to questions or participate in class activities, appearing to be preoccupied with his or her own thoughts. Sleep refers to the student who is actually sleeping and not just resting his or her head for a few minutes. Check for physiological problems or lack of sleep at home.

i. Walk-Run

This involves *excessive* walking or running around the room and not just going to or coming from a work activity.

j. Does Other Work

The student who is involved in doing some other kind of school work, such as arithmetic during the reading period, and does not stay on the required task.

k. Other

The behavior should be specified in the allotted space and clarified in the *Comments-Treatment* section. It refers to any other behavior that is observed and deemed to be a problem to the extent that it interferes with or replaces on-task activity.

14. *Comments-Treatment:* In this section the observer would indicate the period of observation (P), i.e., $P_1 = 5$ days of observation, etc., and the following information:

a. A summary of the *On-Task* and *Off-Task* time, a delineation of the *Behavior Observed,* and the treatment plan for the next period. If the observer has checked the box next to *Target Behavior,* then the incidence or frequency of the *Target Behavior* would be stated along with the treatment plan for the next period. (See Figures 4–5 and 4–6.)

15. *Dark Line Across:* A dark line across allows for and indicates the following:

a. The end of a period and kind of data observed and indicated, i.e., baseline, treatment, etc.

b. The totals for each of the columns in the observation areas for a particular period.

c. The beginning of a new period and the kind of data that was observed and indicated for the new period.

The Mann Student Graphing Worksheet

After completion of the *Mann Student Observation Worksheet,* the data can then be recorded (graphed) on the *Mann Student Graphing Worksheet.* See Form 4-3, Case Study Example A (Figure 4–7), and Case Study Example B (Figure 4–8).

The *Mann Student Graphing Worksheet* should be thoroughly reviewed along with the information provided in this section.

The *Mann Student Graphing Worksheet* and the *Mann Student Observation Worksheet* can be utilized in the following manner:

1. To provide a graphic illustration of a student's observed behavior, treatment plan, and outcomes
2. To describe a student's behavior when talking with parents, principals, or other appropriate individuals
3. To describe the ecological context of behavior

The following is an analysis of the *Mann Student Graphing Worksheet.*

1. The heading is the same as found in the *Mann Student Observation Worksheet.*
2. *Behavior Observed:* The observer transfers the *Behavior Observed* from the *Observation Worksheet* to the *Graphing Worksheet.*
3. The *Behavior Observed* section contains a coded symbol (letter) for each of the behaviors. This section contains a compilation of all of the cogent *Off-Task* behaviors.
4. The dark line separates the periods.
5. The graphs can indicate the following:
a. One graph illustrates the frequencies of behavior for a particular interval of time.
B.L. 1 (Baseline 1)
C.R. (Continuous Reinforcement)
V.R. (Variable Reinforcement)
B.L. 2 (Baseline 2)
b. The other graph can represent the plotting of the *Time On-Task* for a specified period of time.

The Behavior Observation Form

The Behavior Observation Form (Form 4-4) provides an excellent and easy way to record information re-

NAME: *Lisa Smith*

AGE: *7-4-70 (8)*

Beginning Date *10-3-78*

Ending Date *10-28-78*

EXAMPLE A
MANN STUDENT GRAPHING WORKSHEET
On/Off Task and Target Behaviors

Teacher: *Mrs. L. Brown*

Grade: *3*

Observer One: *Mrs. L. Brown*

Observer Two: _____

CHECK ONE: ☒ On/Off Task ☐ Target Behavior

Behavior Desired:

stay on task during
reading period

Period:	BEHAVIOR OBSERVED											Other:
	Bothers Teacher	Bothers Student	Talking	Playing	Bathr. Drink	Aggres. Fights	Out of Seat	Daydream Sleep	Walk – Run	Does Other Work		
	a	b	c	d	e	f	g	h	i	j	k	
	CODE SYMBOL											
P₁ 1		✓	✓	✓			✓		✓			
2		✓	✓	✓			✓		✓			
3			✓				✓					
4		✓	✓	✓			✓		✓			
5		✓	✓				✓		✓			
P₂ 6		✓	✓				✓		✓			
7							✓					
8			✓				✓		✓			
9		✓	✓	✓			✓		✓			
10							✓					
P₃ 11			✓				✓					
12			✓									
13							✓					
14							✓					
15			✓				✓					
P₄ 16							✓					
17							✓					
18			✓				✓					
19			✓				✓					
20												
total		6	13	4			16		7			

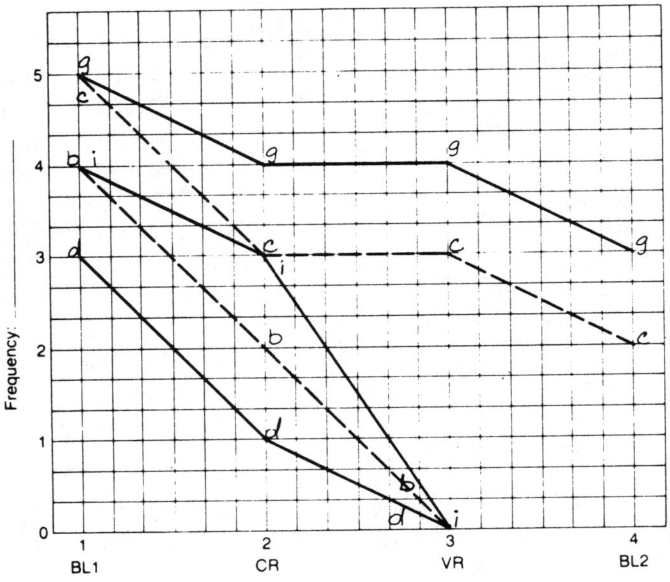

Time: *Period (5 Days)*

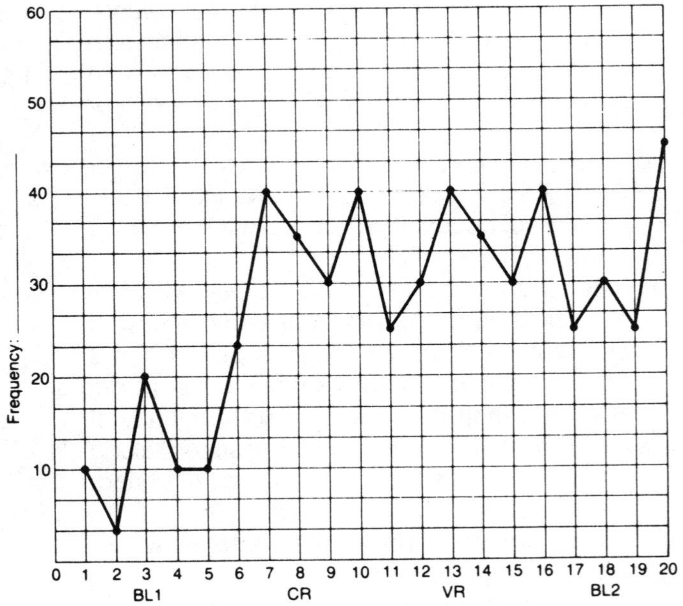

Time: *Day (On Task)*

Figure 4-7

NAME: _Lisa Smith_

AGE: _7-4-70 (8)_

Beginning Date _10-3-78_

Ending Date _10-28-78_

EXAMPLE B
MANN STUDENT GRAPHING WORKSHEET
On/Off Task and Target Behaviors

Teacher: _Mrs. L. Brown_

Grade: _3_

Observer One: _____

Observer Two: _____

CHECK ONE: ☐ On/Off Task ☒ Target Behavior

Behavior Desired:

Increase staying in seat
during reading period)

Day	Period	Bothers Teacher (a)	Bothers Student (b)	Talking (c)	Playing (d)	Bathr. Drink (e)	Aggres Fights (f)	Out of Seat (g)	Daydream Sleep (h)	Walk – Run (i)	Does Other Work (j)	Other: (k)
P1	1											20
	2											18
	3											22
	4											26
	5											27
P2	6											13
	7											10
	8											4
	9											6
	10											6
P3	11											8
	12											7
	13											5
	14											8
	15											3
P4	16											6
	17											9
	18											7
	19											4
	20											7

BEHAVIOR OBSERVED

CODE SYMBOL

Frequency: _____

Time: _____

Frequency: Target Behavior - Out of Seat

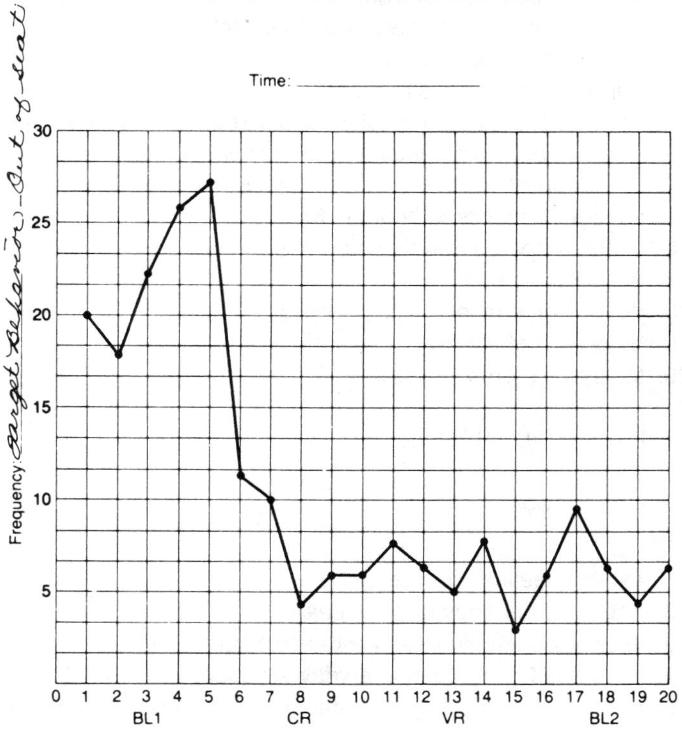

Time: _Day_

Figure 4-8

MANN-SUITER-McCLUNG BEHAVIOR OBSERVATION FORM

NAME _____   EXAMINER _____

AGE _____   DATE _____

GRADE _____

Date All Entries

GOALS AND OBJECTIVES	Present Level	Short-Term	Long-Term
BEHAVIORAL-COGNITIVE FACTORS			

AGGRESSIVE (ACTING OUT/PASSIVE)

Target Behavior
The student

1. disrupts other children by moving about excessively and by being annoying.
2. is disrespectful or not courteous to peers or adults.
3. behaves in a compulsive manner.
4. is negative and does not do what is required of him or her.
5. is rough or noisy.
6. exhibits long periods of unhappiness.
7. is destructive to his or her own belongings.
8. does not complete assignments as requested.
9. indicates poor or bad feelings about school.
10. uses profanity excessively.
11. will not sit or stand still according to command.
12. will not stay with or complete a learning task within a normal time limit.
13. will not obey commands from authority figures.
14. is uncooperative in group learning or play activities.
15. fights with others without provocation.
16. is hot-tempered and flares up easily.
17. is undependable.
18. destroys the belongings of others.
19. behaves like a clown.
20. tests to extreme limits.

SENSITIVE-WITHDRAWN

Target Behavior
The student

1. exhibits feelings of insecurity.
2. becomes unhappy or cries easily.
3. likes to be left alone and withdraws from others.
4. becomes frustrated in everyday situations.
5. overreacts to the negative statements or behavior of others.
6. is anxious or fearful for no apparent reason.
7. does not participate in recreation or play activities with others.
8. is easily embarrassed or behaves in a self-conscious manner.
9. exhibits feelings of poor self-worth.

(continued)

NAME _____   EXAMINER _____

AGE _____   DATE _____

GRADE _____

Date All Entries

GOALS AND OBJECTIVES	Present Level	Short-Term	Long-Term
10. is shy in social situations.			
11. is unable to be at ease and enjoy himself or herself with others.			
12. exhibits little self-confidence.			

IMMATURE-DEPENDENT

Target Behavior
The student

1. requires constant direction and relies a great deal or others.
2. prefers to play or interact with younger people.
3. appears inactive or apathetic at inappropriate times.
4. needs a great deal of support and "stroking" from others.
5. has difficulty making decisions.
6. does not attend to activities that require a degree of concentration.
7. is easily influenced by others.
8. exhibits passive behavior.
9. appears absentminded or lost in thought to excess.
10. demands an unusual amount of attention.
11. continually complains of physical pains such as stomachaches and headaches.

PSYCHOTIC-NEUROTIC

Target Behavior
The student

1. exhibits inappropriate affect, such as laughing or crying at the wrong time.
2. exhibits unintelligible or strange speech patterns.
3. is not reality-oriented in mannerisms or speech.
4. tells lies excessively and tends to exaggerate greatly.
5. enjoys inflicting pain on self.
6. feels that people want to physically hurt him or her.
7. exhibits long periods of silence and almost complete withdrawal.
8. behaves in a bizarre manner.
9. exhibits compulsive behavior, such as excessive hand washing.
10. appears extremely nervous.
11. enjoys inflicting pain on others.
12. thinks everyone is talking about, and plotting against, him or her.
13. is fearful much of the time.
14. exhibits long periods of silence and withdrawal followed by extreme activity and excessive verbal behavior.
15. is extremely fearful about going to school.
16. has unreasonable fear of animals, heights, water, open places, etc.
17. has severe feeling of inferiority.

(continued)

NAME _____   EXAMINER _____

AGE _____   DATE _____

GRADE _____

Date All Entries

GOALS AND OBJECTIVES	Present Level	Short-Term	Long-Term

DELINQUENT-UNORTHODOX

Target Behavior
The student

1. exhibits variable habits of sleeping.
2. exhibits excessive loyalty to peers.
3. rejects figures representing authority.
4. is a member of a gang.
5. adheres to the gang's code of ethics and morality.
6. exhibits unorthodox social behavior.
7. steals in collaboration with others.
8. is often truant from school.
9. seeks the company of other delinquents.
10. does not express remorse for delinquent behavior.

SOCIAL PERCEPTION DISORDERS (Cognitive-Social Skills)

Target Behavior
The student

1. misinterprets what he or she sees and gives the wrong response.
2. has difficulty with projective tests such as the Thematic Apperception Test.
3. may be able to perceive individual objects, but fails to comprehend the meaning of their relationships.
4. may not derive meaning from gestures or expressions of others.
5. may not be able to size up a situation. For example, he or she may require constant interpretation while watching a TV show, watching a film, or listening to a story.
6. literally does not know enough to come in out of the rain.
7. is directed at home and rarely has opportunities to make up his or her own mind.
8. reacts inappropriately to situations, criticisms, and guidance from others.
9. has difficulty in understanding the subtleties in humor.
10. has difficulty in understanding figurative speech.
11. attends to the minor details instead of the major details in completing a task.
12. misreads emotions, moods, and attitudes of people.
13. misunderstands motives (why people do what they do).
14. fails to associate an incident with its implications for people and society.
15. consistently says the inappropriate thing at the inappropriate time.
16. does not understand facial expressions.
17. has difficulty in pretending or anticipating the outcomes in stories.

(continued)

NAME _____   EXAMINER _____

AGE _____   DATE _____

GRADE _____

	Date All Entries		
GOALS AND OBJECTIVES	*Present Level*	*Short-Term*	*Long-Term*

ATTENTION DEFICIT DISORDERS

HYPERACTIVITY

Target Behavior
The student

1. is constantly moving.
2. cannot control his or her movement and is unaware that it is occurring.
3. may fatigue earlier in the school day because of the hyperactivity.
4. may also be distractible. Both behavioral manifestations often go together.
5. has excessive movements even though he or she may be engrossed in a particular activity.
6. exhibits inappropriate social behavior.
7. fails to attend to situational clues.
8. exhibits increased or excessive verbal activity.
9. disturbs other students.

INATTENTION

Target Behavior
The student

1. lacks problem-solving techniques.
2. exhibits passivity and dependence in learning (learned helplessness).
3. does not use reflective behavior in learning.
4. exhibits impulsive behavior in social and academic situations.
5. exhibits poor search strategies.

(continued)

NAME _____ EXAMINER _____

AGE _____ DATE _____

GRADE _____

	Date All Entries		
GOALS AND OBJECTIVES	*Present Level*	*Short-Term*	*Long-Term*

6. exhibits poor sustained attention.
7. lacks insightful thinking.
8. exhibits memory problems.
9. tends to blame himself/herself for failure (stupidity).

IMPULSIVITY

Target Behavior
The student

1. quickly responds to questions before thinking out his or her answers.
2. is excessively talkative.
3. rushes into an activity before the instructor has completed the directions.
4. is impatient with repeated tasks and does not like to review old learning.
5. avoids anxiety and is unreflective in resolving problems.
6. cannot monitor his/her own behavior.
7. does not inhibit his/her own responses.
8. does not use appropriate cognitive strategies.
9. has difficulty understanding easy tasks.
10. exhibits poor reflective thinking.

DISTRACTIBILITY

Target Behavior
The student

1. exhibits "forced attention" to extraneous stimuli within the environment and cannot attend to the task.
2. may respond to the teacher next door, following the teacher's directions.
3. may be distracted by visual or auditory stimuli or both.
4. is unable to focus his or her attention selectively.

(continued)

NAME _____ EXAMINER _____

AGE _____ DATE _____

GRADE _____

| | Date All Entries | | |
GOALS AND OBJECTIVES	Present Level	Short-Term	Long-Term

PERSEVERATION

Target Behavior
The student

1. may say a word over and over.
2. cannot shift from one activity to another.
3. tends to repeat the previous response on tests.
4. may add all the problems in arithmetic, even though he or she can easily see that half of them are subtraction.

DISINHIBITION

Target Behavior
The student

1. gets carried away by his or her own thoughts.
2. gives inappropriate responses that are unrelated to the question asked.

COGNITIVE-MOTIVATIONAL FACTORS

LEARNED HELPLESSNESS

Target Behavior
The student

1. overreacts to negative feedback from teachers.
2. has lowered expectation of future success.
3. lowers performance levels after experiencing failure.
4. lacks perceived independence in school tasks.
5. displays negative affect in attempting even easy tasks.
6. avoids tasks that appear difficult.
7. verbalizes lack of ability (e.g., "I'm stupid.").

(continued)

NAME _____ EXAMINER _____

AGE _____ DATE _____

GRADE _____

Date All Entries

GOALS AND OBJECTIVES	Present Level	Short-Term	Long-Term

ATTRIBUTION

Target Behavior
The student

1. attributes success in academics to luck.
2. attributes failure to lack of ability or intelligence.
3. feels others cause him/her to fail in school.
4. feels there is no sense in trying.
5. continually says, "It's not my fault."

LOCUS OF CONTROL

Target Behavior
The student

1. does not feel he/she has the power to change his/her effort.
2. does not recognize the ability to change his/her own attitudes.
3. feels controlled by good or bad luck.
4. feels that his/her learning problem is related to poor ability or not being "smart."
5. feels that the difficulty of a task rather than effort controls success.

SELF-EFFICACY

Target Behavior
The student

1. knows how to produce a certain outcome, but feels that he/she cannot produce the necessary behavior.
2. does not feel he/she can ever be successful in school.
3. withdraws from classwork or testing after experiencing a failure.
4. will not participate in settings in which he/she cannot be in control.
5. displays a failure attitude before even attempting a task.

(continued)

NAME _____   EXAMINER _____

AGE _____   DATE _____

GRADE _____

	Date All Entries		
GOALS AND OBJECTIVES	*Present Level*	*Short-Term*	*Long-Term*

METACOGNITIVE ABILITIES

Target Behavior
The student

1. is unable to plan for the solution of a problem or academic task.
2. is unable to determine if a task requires the use of memory.
3. is unable to prepare for a memory task.
4. is unable to determine ways to retrieve information.
5. is unable to scan material for answers.
6. is unable to clarify the purpose for doing a task.
7. is unable to cull out or attend to relevant information.
8. is unable to predict outcomes.
9. is unable to summarize an occurrence.
10. is unable to verify information or check correctness.
11. is unable to self-monitor the learning of a task.
12. is unable to self-correct his or her own errors.
13. is unable to remember how to use mnemonic devices.
14. is unable to use visual imagery techniques.
15. is unable to self-question assumptions.
16. is unable to imitate the modeling of an instructor.
17. is unable to deal with distracting information.
18. is unable to think out loud.
19. is unable to differentiate between facts and ideas.
20. is unable to role play in even well-defined situations.
21. is unable to estimate the difficulty of a task.
22. is unable to systematize the solution to a problem.
23. is unable to concentrate on a given task.
24. is unable to use precise language in problem solving.
25. is unable to formulate a what-if hypothesis.
26. is unable to paraphrase material.
27. is unable to find cue words in arriving at solutions.
28. is unable to use good reasoning or common sense in solving problems.
29. is unable to listen and interpret information.
30. is unable to take notes on information presented orally.
31. is unable to take notes from written material.

COMMENTS

lated to the behavioral-cognitive areas of concern. It can be used to pinpoint specific behaviors as well as provide a continuous record of a student's progress. There is no scoring system associated with this checklist; however, clustering of different types of behaviors can provide a basis for more in-depth testing. Possible problem areas can be quickly identified, and the teacher can immediately deal with certain targeted behaviors.

APPLICATIONS

1. As a general checklist for behaviors. The modification of desired behaviors can then become a part of the student's academic program.
2. As a reference for additional testing, to determine the present level of functioning and to set goals and objectives for program planning.
3. As a basis for establishing behavioral-cognitive goals and objectives for Individual Educational Planning.
4. As a basis for coding or organizing behavioral-cognitive materials by specific content areas.

5. Teachers using this form can develop a continuous progress profile to indicate progress to administrators, parents, and others.

HOW TO USE

The behaviors indicated under behavioral-cognitive factors are listed as negative statements. They are, therefore, to be envisioned as target behaviors and treated in the following manner under the basic headings "Present Level," "Short Term," and "Long Term."

1. Under "Present Level" they are noted (dated) as target behaviors that have been identified in the learner and must be addressed; i.e., programmed for specifically as part of the student's education plan.
2. And, as appropriate, listed under "Short Term" or "Long Term" goals.

Activities for each of these behavioral-cognitive areas can be found in this Handbook as well as in other sources. The Behavior Observation Form can become the basis for the curriculum program.

Chapter 5

Assessment: Rationale and Management

OVERVIEW

Educators today are taking a more ecological view of student performance. Achievement is viewed as a function of student development and aptitude, the skills and attitude of the teacher, and the environments that impinge on the learner, such as the classroom and the home. The dilemma lies in determining which of these factors are strong and which ones are inhibiting the learner's success in academic subjects and social interactions. It is important to understand the relationships that exist among the following:

The arrows reflect dynamic-interacting relationships among all three factors to be considered.

1. Should we focus our attention on changing or modifying the behavior of the student(s)?
2. Should we concentrate on changing or modifying the behavior of the teacher(s)?
3. Should we spend our energies on changing or modifying the environment(s) (program, classroom, curriculum materials, class size, home, etc.)?
4. Should we use a combination of 1, 2, and 3?
5. Should we provide no change at all?

By carefully examining the interactions among the components, one can gain insights as to causation and better predict future outcomes. Determining which areas need to receive the appropriate amount of emphasis is a function of assessment and diagnostic-prescriptive teaching. The ongoing gathering of information in many environments using appropriate measures leads to better instruction and improved student learning.

Because of the increasing number of students referred to special education and the diversity of problems exhibited by this population, school personnel are examining the diagnostic process by which students are evaluated and placed in programs. The focus in assessment is shifting from primarily a student-assessment model relying on traditional formal evaluation to a school-based consultative model involving collaboration and input from all individuals concerned with a student's environments (Bush et al., 1989). Student study teams, faculty interaction sessions, and consultation are resulting in faster evaluations and more followup consultation.

This chapter has descriptions of consultation approaches along with ideas for school-based management of assessment that will provide suggestions as to how to structure a school for effective and efficient evaluation. It is important to develop a system or a framework for identifying students' learning characteristics. This will save time and energy so often expended in just jumping from one test to another. Teachers who acquire diagnostic skills and are able to consult with support personnel will have fewer referrals to special education.

Consultative services that emphasize problem solving and are solution oriented appear to fit the organizational plan outlined in Levels I and II of the School-Based Organization and Management Design for Continuum of Educational Services found in this chapter. This type of service focuses on both academic and social behavior of students within the ecology of the home, school, and community. In this process, school support staff with administrative involvement work with parents, other school personnel, students, and outside agencies or professionals within the subsystems outlined in Level I, General Program Assessment Procedures, or Level II, Intervention Team Assessment Procedures. Student study teams or intervention teams (Level II) are made up of the regular education teacher, special education teacher, school psychologist, other specialists such as reading or counseling, and an administrator. Level III, Special Education Assessment Procedures, includes special education procedures of referral, evaluation, procedural safeguards, placement, and monitoring of pupil progress.

Other aspects of assessment covered in this chapter include the rationale behind different types of assessment, levels of assessment, and an array of

procedures. Also discussed are related and integral factors to assessment, such as the learner's social and cultural milieu. Chapter 6 follows with specific assessment instruments and forms for recording information.

SCHOOL MANAGEMENT OF STUDENT ASSESSMENT

Effective organization and management of assessment procedures can provide the structure by which educational goals and objectives are effectively realized. Organization and management systems must be in place and functioning as the basis or foundation for any collaborative relationships that are developed among educators. Good organization and management of assessment procedures also provide the framework by which all students have access to the system or, more precisely, to a continuum of educational services based on their individual needs. The concept of school-based management and educational programming is of paramount concern. This is particularly valid as schools plan for the provision of a full-service design not only for students who represent diverse cultural backgrounds, but also for those who, because of the variability they exhibit in learning, require precise teaching approaches and an accommodating learning environment. In particular, there is a need to consider existing practices and address critical needs and concerns in how services are delivered to students with learning problems in regular classrooms.

Planning an Assessment Program

Most effective planning for assessment procedures is accomplished as early in the school year as possible, preferably during the preplanning days. If at all possible, initial planning should begin in the spring for the fall of the next school year. Planning should be a total school process in which educators, by sharing information with each other about students and by writing cogent information into records, prepare for appropriate educational strategies, especially for *high-risk* students.

Planning an evaluation system can be simple or very complex and time-consuming, depending on the orientation of the staff and the resources available. Most classroom teachers are mainly concerned about the educational needs of the students assigned to them. A total-school approach to planning assessment procedures is broader in scope because it is

PART A GENERAL DESIGN

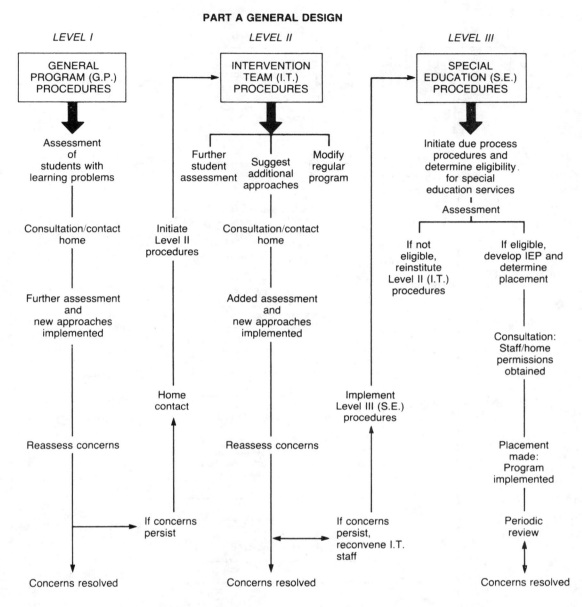

Figure 5-1   School-Based Organization and Management Design for Continuum of Education Services

important to identify all high-risk students in all class-rooms in order to make early and appropriate decisions about how to utilize the myriad of services available within the school. This type of planning involves a sharing of responsibility, or team approach, to maximize the development of a comprehensive, or full-service, program for each student. Students with learning and behavioral difficulties will especially benefit from this orientation. A full-service model by definition involves more than one person in the process of assessment and program planning. Those involved could include administrators, support staff such as resource people, psychologists, teachers, parapro-

fessionals, and parents. Together, they decide where, how, and by whom a student can best be served within existing alternative environments. There should be an openness among educators in the school that will make it easy for a teacher to ask for assistance.

Design for Continuum of Educational Services

After reviewing and analyzing a variety of school systems, common elements were examined within a School-Based Continuum of Service Design. This design (Figure 5-1) was developed as a frame of reference by which observed assessment practices and

129

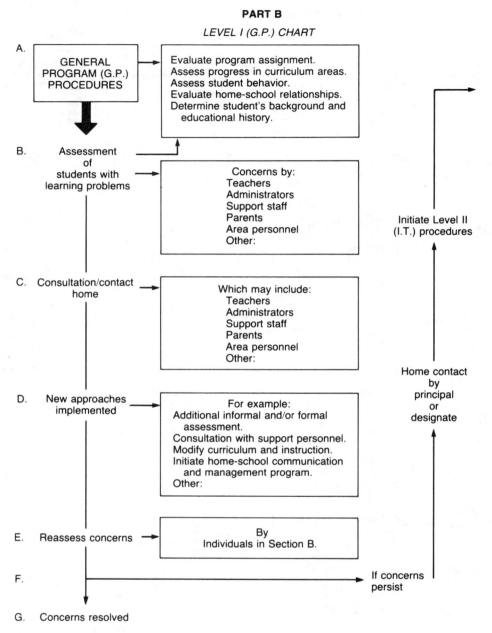

PART B

LEVEL I (G.P.) CHART

A. **GENERAL PROGRAM (G.P.) PROCEDURES** → Evaluate program assignment.
Assess progress in curriculum areas.
Assess student behavior.
Evaluate home-school relationships.
Determine student's background and educational history.

B. Assessment of students with learning problems → Concerns by:
Teachers
Administrators
Support staff
Parents
Area personnel
Other:

C. Consultation/contact home → Which may include:
Teachers
Administrators
Support staff
Parents
Area personnel
Other:

D. New approaches implemented → For example:
Additional informal and/or formal assessment.
Consultation with support personnel.
Modify curriculum and instruction.
Initiate home-school communication and management program.
Other:

E. Reassess concerns → By Individuals in Section B.

F. If concerns persist

G. Concerns resolved

Initiate Level II (I.T.) procedures

Home contact by principal or designate

Figure 5-1 (continued)

procedures can be clearly delineated. A school-based design for management and organization provides a basis for determining possibilities within educational programming for students to derive optimum benefits. The underlying assumption is that any educational management system, in order to be effective, must begin with the premise that the organization will revolve around the need to respond to students in schools and that all activities planned should emanate from that premise. The parameters indicated in the paradigm can serve as a basis for evaluating various components of existing assessment systems and as a management and organization tool for planning new programs.

Three primary educational service components emerge in most school systems, as indicated in Figure 5-1.

LEVEL I   General Program Assessment (G.P.) Procedures
LEVEL II Intervention Team Assessment (I.T.) Procedures
LEVEL III Special Education Assessment (S.E.) Procedures

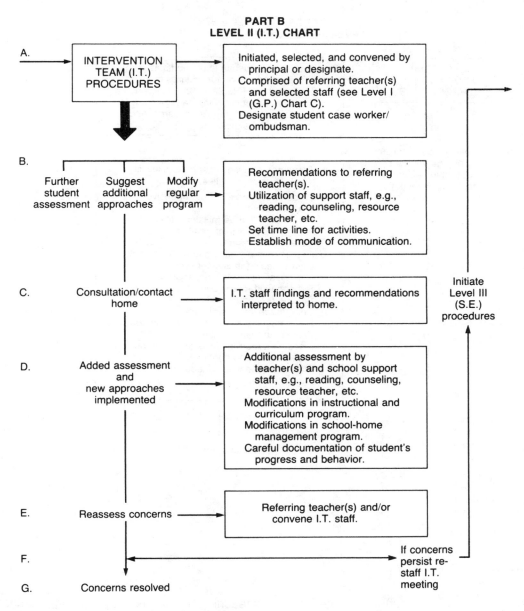

Figure 5-1 (continued)

All of the schools observed have at least two of the procedural systems (LEVEL I and LEVEL III). Some schools have all three procedural systems (LEVEL I, LEVEL II, and LEVEL III). Figure 5-1 is divided into two parts. Part A illustrates all three levels (I, II, and III) and how they interrelate with each other. Part B represents each level independently and shows the intrarelationships of the three levels.

LEVEL I: GENERAL PROGRAM ASSESSMENT (G.P.) PROCEDURES

Within the area of general program assessment procedures, teachers are involved in providing a system by which students with learning problems receive educational services through the auspices of the general education program. The LEVEL I assessment procedures are general school processes that teachers implement day to day in trying to educate students. Diagnosis at this level should be done early in the school year. Every teacher should be responsible for identifying students' basic skill levels. This should be accomplished for all students, but especially for those exhibiting developmental lags or learning problems. In this way the extent of variability will be identified early. The range will be from those who are below expected performance to those who are far above expected performance for each grade level. Early assessment is particularly important for students in the

131

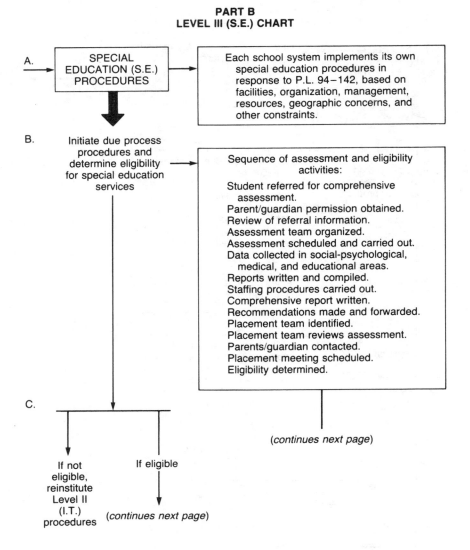

PART B
LEVEL III (S.E.) CHART

A. SPECIAL EDUCATION (S.E.) PROCEDURES

Each school system implements its own special education procedures in response to P.L. 94–142, based on facilities, organization, management, resources, geographic concerns, and other constraints.

B. Initiate due process procedures and determine eligibility for special education services

Sequence of assessment and eligibility activities:

Student referred for comprehensive assessment.
Parent/guardian permission obtained.
Review of referral information.
Assessment team organized.
Assessment scheduled and carried out.
Data collected in social-psychological, medical, and educational areas.
Reports written and compiled.
Staffing procedures carried out.
Comprehensive report written.
Recommendations made and forwarded.
Placement team identified.
Placement team reviews assessment.
Parents/guardian contacted.
Placement meeting scheduled.
Eligibility determined.

(continues next page)

C.

If not eligible, reinstitute Level II (I.T.) procedures

If eligible

(continues next page)

Figure 5-1 (continued)

primary grades (K–3), so that younger learners will not experience continued debilitating failure. The teacher should correlate assessment information with curriculum and instructional objectives in the basic skill areas for each student. In this way, grouping will be flexible to the extent that students who are developing at different rates can progress as fast as new learning is mastered (individualized instruction).

In cases where more diagnostic information is needed, teachers should implement an analysis of learner performance in the particular skill areas of concern. This includes further observation or assessment through teaching. Case studies on particular students can be prepared. Teachers should find out present levels of functioning prior to formalized instruction. This provides for more precise approaches to teaching and for more appropriate curriculum modification. Prevention and intervention should emerge as primary orientations as opposed to remediation. The concept of remediation implies "trying to catch up"; while prevention and intervention are associated with beginning with the present level of functioning and proceeding in accordance with the learning rate of the student to reduce constant failure.

Students within this level of service are viewed as having learning problems because they exhibit a discrepancy in performance in academic areas between themselves and their peers. Some exhibit maladaptive behavior that interferes with learning. The teachers of these students, either alone or with the aid of administrators and support staff, attempt to do the following:

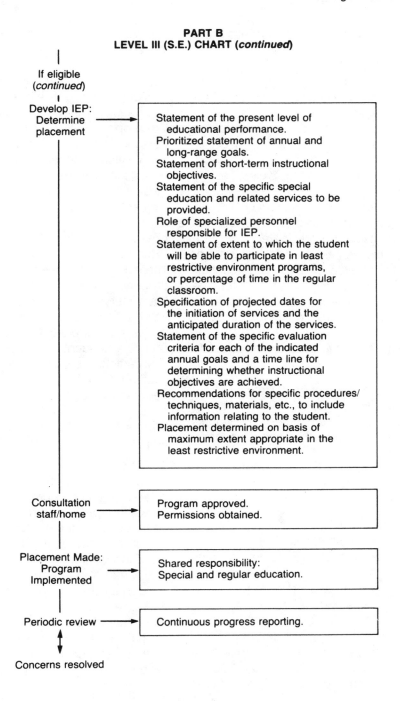

PART B
LEVEL III (S.E.) CHART (*continued*)

If eligible
(*continued*)

Develop IEP:
Determine
placement
→
Statement of the present level of
  educational performance.
Prioritized statement of annual and
  long-range goals.
Statement of short-term instructional
  objectives.
Statement of the specific special
  education and related services to be
  provided.
Role of specialized personnel
  responsible for IEP.
Statement of extent to which the student
  will be able to participate in least
  restrictive environment programs,
  or percentage of time in the regular
  classroom.
Specification of projected dates for
  the initiation of services and the
  anticipated duration of the services.
Statement of the specific evaluation
  criteria for each of the indicated
  annual goals and a time line for
  determining whether instructional
  objectives are achieved.
Recommendations for specific procedures/
  techniques, materials, etc., to include
  information relating to the student.
Placement determined on basis of
  maximum extent appropriate in the
  least restrictive environment.

Consultation
staff/home
→
Program approved.
Permissions obtained.

Placement Made:
Program
Implemented
→
Shared responsibility:
Special and regular education.

Periodic review → Continuous progress reporting.

Concerns resolved

Figure 5-1 (continued)

1. Reevaluate the student's program assignment.
2. Assess the student's progress in curriculum areas (usually using norm-referenced types of evaluations).
3. Assess the student's behavior patterns.
4. Evaluate home-school relationships.
5. Review the student's background and educational history.

If it is apparent that a student is not adjusting to the classroom environment and is not learning, the teacher can try the following:

1. Try a variety of direct teaching activities that will involve the student and permit more direct observation of how the student performs. Give as much feedback as possible.

2. After teaching and testing, note the student's progress.

3. If the progress is still not acceptable, modify instruction by varying the rate, amount, and sequence of instruction. Look for optimal times for instruction when the student is learning.

4. Modify the complexity of the tasks. Refer to the classroom accommodations mentioned in Chapter 7.

5. Analyze classroom procedures (e.g., rules, seating arrangement, etc.).

6. Explore the appropriateness of materials.

7. Determine the student's involvement in classroom activities and motivation to participate.

8. Use non-biased assessment for the culturally or linguistically different student by using teacher-made and criterion-referenced tests that determine the level and quality of an individual's performance in relation to specific instructional objectives or criteria.

9. Involve the parents and give them opportunities to provide successful experiences at home.

There is generally some form of consultation or contact with the home (parents or guardians) made by the responding teacher and sometimes individuals representing administration or other school support staff.

Usually out of this process emerge suggestions for "new" approaches for helping the student, which could include:

1. Additional informal and/or formal assessment.

2. Further consultation with school support personnel (e.g., reading, counseling, etc.). In some programs the special education person also functions in the role of consultant. This is an important role since Public Law 94–142 (The Education for All Handicapped Children Act of 1975) mandates that regular and special educators work together and accept shared responsibility for students with special needs.

3. Modification of the curriculum and instructional program.

4. Initiation of a home-school management program.

5. Change in academic placement.

After a "reasonable" amount of time has elapsed, there should be a reassessment of previous concerns. It is expected that the concerns would have been resolved. If the problems persist, other procedures are initiated. In most cases, from this kind of basic frame of reference (LEVEL I procedures), students are often referred directly for Special Education procedures (LEVEL III). Referral and placement may result from

one teacher's inability to cope with the student's learning style, conduct, or both in the regular classroom setting. There is a question as to how many well-behaved students, who in fact need special education services, never get referred. As a response to these general classroom dilemmas, some schools have provided opportunities for problem students and school personnel to be involved in some type of LEVEL II intervention procedures prior to referral for special education services. Although there will be variations in these procedures from school to school, the basic elements should be similar.

LEVEL II: INTERVENTION TEAM ASSESSMENT (I.T.) PROCEDURES

These kinds of procedures involve additional groups of individuals who in this role can be described as team intervention oriented. These procedures are activated when events indicate that LEVEL I kinds of activities are not effective in providing for the needs of particular students. A very important dual role within this particular process is that of both prevention and intervention before LEVEL III or special education procedures are initiated.

Level II-types of programs include procedures that bridge the gap between LEVEL I and LEVEL III. Examples of LEVEL II kinds of intervention include:

1. Programs for "high-risk" children or "early identification" in elementary schools as a prevention-intervention procedure.

2. Reentry programs in senior high schools that function prior to the implementation of special education procedures for delinquent youth.

3. "School Intervention Teams" and "Pupil Service Teams" that attempt to resolve student problems as part of LEVEL II-type intervention procedures.

4. Procedures to identify gifted and talented students so that programs can be developed that address their needs. This is an important area since many of these students do not receive special education services.

After other interventions have been tried and the student's progress remains below his or her potential, or a behavior problem persists, the teacher may need assistance from others in the school. The aid can come from special education teachers, resource teachers, reading teachers, and psychologists. However, in many schools the most immediate help will come from a LEVEL II intervention team comprised of classroom teachers and other professionals. The committees or teams are called by a variety of terms including grade level committees, referral teams, guidance groups, teacher support teams, etc. In most cases programs are initiated, participants selected, and meetings convened by the principal of the school or a designate.

Chalfant, Pysh, and Moultrie (1979) stress that Teacher Assisted Teams are not the same as multi-disciplinary teams comprised of specialists. The teams are peer problem-solving committees of classroom teachers who can deal with day-to-day problems in a school. The composition of a team can vary in size and may or may not include special teachers. A team of three elected teachers plus the referring teacher and a parent is a workable unit. By rotating one teacher per semester, more teachers can participate.

In LEVEL II the diagnostic skills acquired by a teacher should include emphasis on team skills. These team skills are important and vital to developing collaborative efforts. Diagnostic programs at this level function as a collaborative effort by a total school staff as compared to the single classroom orientation for LEVEL I General Program Assessment Procedures. The individuals selected need to be able to offer a variety of alternatives in the areas of diagnosis-student assessment, curriculum-instruction, educational management, and behavior management. The team members need to be able to function as a unit, to remain on task, to communicate well, and to be able to arrive at solutions or recommendations in a limited amount of time. The group leader needs an understanding of group process skills and how to facilitate the work of the group in an organized fashion. Chalfant recommends that participants role play and practice first setting guidelines for group decision-making.

Meetings are held on either a formal or an informal basis. Strategies are developed that include the consideration of "time" as a critical variable. Of particular concern is the time necessary for people to come together. Some programs respond to this concern by developing a special form that is circulated for effective communication. The teachers and administrators write on the circulated form particular problem areas and indicate which staff members need to meet together to resolve specific concerns. It has been found that the entire team does not have to get together on a once-a-week formal routine.

All team members should read the information on the referral form or summaries of observations prior to the meeting. Brief agendas or simple checklists can help a team stay on task. Everyone has to come prepared. The referring teacher has to explain the problem, state what has been tried to solve the problem, and provide samples of the student's testing and classroom work.

Group meetings can be set up to review the information accumulated on students who exhibit particular difficulties for purposes of making recommendations about the next steps. The "teams," which can include teachers, administrators, support personnel, and parents, direct their attention to the following questions:

1. How can high-risk students at any grade level who need additional or expanded services be identified according to a prearranged schedule?
2. Who will participate in the process of identification, screening, diagnosis, programming, and follow-up for these students?
3. How will due-process procedures be followed in applicable cases?
4. How will the parents or guardians be involved initially, and to what extent will they be consulted in accordance with a prescribed schedule?
5. Are the individuals who are responsible for a program for a particular student willing and able to accept this responsibility?
6. Are staff development opportunities available on an ongoing basis so that teachers needing additional skills can become competent to deal with the different learning styles of their students?
7. Is attention being given to the special needs of students including areas of curriculum programming and educational management as well as diagnostic procedures?
8. Are programs designed that will set students apart because of learning and behavior difficulties, or will the orientation be toward serving students in as "normal" an environment as possible?
9. Before a student is referred to special education, will the appropriate support personnel be given the opportunity for input?
10. Will a student be told that a problem exists, and will the student be helped to understand what is happening? Will the student be given an opportunity to be part of the whole process of determining his or her educational program?
11. Will the data or information related to the student be protected by confidentiality?
12. How will it be determined that the program designed for a particular student is being carried out in an individualized manner, not just a report written to satisfy the requirement that a prescription be prepared?
13. What does each teacher do as a part of his or her ongoing educational activities to keep track of student progress?
14. What kinds of support services are available (e.g., reading, counseling, special education, psy-

chologist, etc.) that can be utilized for diagnostic purposes?

Not all problems lend themselves to quick answers. If family problems, medical concerns, or problems that require additional expertise are discussed, a follow-up meeting should be scheduled with other professionals.

Teacher support teams can be used to

1. Clarify the nature of the problem
2. Generate instructional alternatives
3. Monitor the implementation of recommendations
4. Refer students for additional evaluation

One advantage of this type of intervention (LEVEL II) is more specific and in-depth recommendations from a variety of individuals. New approaches and other suggestions are provided to the teachers responsible for the education of these students prior to special education referral. The value of this type of assistance cannot be overstated. Some of the recommendations that may result from LEVEL II intervention include:

1. Suggestions for additional criterion-referenced assessment, such as the use of observational devices by teachers and school support staff (e.g., reading, counseling, resource teachers, etc.).
2. Suggestions in areas involving educational management.
3. Precise ways to modify the instructional and curriculum program.
4. Additional behavior management techniques.
5. Suggestions for ways to improve the school-home management program.
6. Careful documentation of the student's progress and behavior.
7. Assignment of designated case workers and/or ombudsmen. These case workers are not necessarily the student's teacher, but individuals who can contact the student regularly to help with particular problems.

In most instances, only after responses to LEVEL II kinds of procedures are found to be ineffective are special education procedures implemented. LEVEL II kinds of procedures provide a means by which schools can begin to reduce unnecessary referrals for special education services. These procedures also represent a system by which students who are referred for special education placement, and found to be ineligible, can again receive intervention kinds of programs as an alternative to going directly to LEVEL I General Program Assessment Procedures. Without LEVEL II, students would, for the most part, remain with the same teacher and receive the same kind of program that resulted in their being referred to special education in the first place.

As school and home become involved in providing for the needs of students through a continuum of services procedures, there tends to be a greater degree of trust established. People have more opportunities to communicate with each other and to work together in trying to resolve particular problems prior to the formalized meetings which are a part of special education procedures.

It was observed that LEVEL II intervention-types of procedures provide an opportunity for special educators, general educators, and support personnel to interact together as part of a total school effort in dealing with persistent problems. Referral to special education is more of a group decision through LEVEL II procedures than through LEVEL I procedures and has the potential for establishing more effective communication in cases where special education procedures need to be implemented.

LEVEL III: SPECIAL EDUCATION ASSESSMENT (S.E.) PROCEDURES

Since it is mandated that general educators become more involved in the process of identification, placement, and programming for students with special needs in their classrooms, provisions must be made for helping teachers to play a more participatory role in this process. Administrators are finding that the process involved in developing an individualized educational program (IEP) can become the focus for formulating judgments about many aspects of compliance with the law. IEP development for the most part is a management system. Procedures generally follow as a condition of the major legislative requirement which specifies adequate assessment, placement in least restrictive environments, parental involvement, and procedural safeguard concerns. Student assessment at this level is very precise and usually multidisciplinary, e.g., psychologists, therapists, teachers, diagnosticians, and so on.

LEVEL III Special Education Assessment (S.E.) Procedures are generally prescribed by school systems in keeping with regulations that are, for the most part, monitored by state agencies through a system of compliance officers. They all contain basically the same ingredients. The following is a sequence of assessment and eligibility activities that represent most LEVEL III-types of procedures:

1. Initiation of due process procedures and determination of eligibility
   a. Student referred for comprehensive assessment

b. Parent/guardian permission obtained
c. Review of referral information
d. Organize assessment team
e. Schedule and carry out assessment
f. Collect data in social, psychological, medical, and educational areas
g. Write and compile reports
h. Carry out staffing procedures
i. Write comprehensive report
j. Make and forward recommendations
k. Identify placement team
l. Review assessment by placement team
m. Contact parents/guardians
n. Schedule placement meeting
o. Determine eligibility

Out of this sequence of activities comes the development of the Individualized Educational Program (IEP) and the determination of placement.

2. Development of IEP and determination of placement
   a. Statement of the present level of educational performance
   b. Prioritized statement of annual and long-range goals
   c. Statement of short-term instructional objectives
   d. Statement of the specific special education and related services to be provided.
   e. Role of specialized personnel responsible for IEP
   f. Statement of extent to which the student will be able to participate in least-restrictive environment programs, or percentage of time in the regular classroom
   g. Specification of projected dates for the initiation of services and the anticipated duration of the services
   h. Statement of the specific evaluation criteria for each of the indicted annual goals and a time line for determining whether instructional objectives are achieved
   i. Recommendations for specific procedures, techniques, materials, etc., to include information relating to the learning characteristics of the student
   j. Placement determined on basis of maximum extent appropriate in the least-restrictive environment
   k. Program approved
   l. Permissions obtained
3. Shared responsibility for program implementation: special and regular education
4. Continuous progress reporting and periodic review
   a. Review programs and services
   b. Modify long- and short-term goals

c. Reformulate specific procedures, techniques, materials, etc., and additional services deemed appropriate

The primary outcome of any assessment program at this level should be the identification of those who need specialized services as well as those who do not need such services. The key concept is to set up an assessment system that incorporates the least amount of error in the identification process and that makes optimal use of the element of time. Present systems of referral and student assessment should be reviewed to determine whether or not students who in fact need special services are getting them. This requires a description of personnel roles, procedures, and the evaluation process. Time, on the other hand, is another critical factor. Negative effects can accrue from too little or too much time taken for such things as referral and diagnosis. Time can be a vitiating factor where there is poor communication between professionals.

The transition from special education programs back to a mainstream classroom is a critical aspect of the IEP. If this step is neglected, a student may remain too long in a program. If the transition is not smooth, the student may again face failure. The participants on an IEP team need to know the following:

1. Can the regular classroom accommodate the student without major changes?
2. Can the student cope with the curriculum requirements or the behavioral demands?
3. Has the student met the goals?

INDIVIDUALIZED EDUCATIONAL PROGRAM

The Education for All Handicapped Children Act of 1975 (P.L. 94–142), provides guidelines for students who will be receiving special education services through local and state agencies. These regulations directly involve the students and their parents or guardians. The students' teachers (regular teachers and specialists or resource personnel) will become involved in the development and implementation of an Individualized Educational Program (IEP) for each student receiving special help. P.L. 94–142 defines an IEP as: " . . . a written statement . . . developed in any meeting by a representative of the Local Education Agency who shall be qualified to provide, or supervise the provision of . . . instruction . . ., the teacher, the parent or guardian . . . and when appropriate [the] child . . ." (Sec. 602[19]).

Components of an Individualized Educational Program (IEP)

Components of an Individualized Education Program (IEP) include the following:

1. A statement of the present level of educational performance
2. A prioritized statement of annual and long-range goals
3. A statement of short-term instructional objectives
4. A statement of the specific special education and related services to be provided
5. Specification of the role of specified personnel responsible for IEP
6. A statement of the extent to which the student will be able to participate in least restrictive environment programs or the percentage of time in the regular classroom
7. Specification of the projected dates for the initiation of services and the anticipated duration of the services
8. Statement of the specific evaluation criteria for each of the indicated annual goals and a time line for determining whether instructional objectives are achieved
9. Recommendations for specific procedures/ techniques, materials, etc., to include information relating to the learning characteristics of the student

Statement of the Present Level of Educational Performance

Although principals may not choose to sit in on all the mandatory conferences required in the process that will ultimately lead to individualizing a program for a student, they have major responsibilities in the entire process. First, a principal's attitude concerning students with special needs will influence all the personnel within a school. A positive feeling of advocacy by the principal for the access of handicapped students to education within the system may greatly aid in the development of support by all school personnel (secretaries, cafeteria workers, volunteers, teachers, bus drivers, etc.). The principal can facilitate the shared responsibility among staff that must occur for special services to be meaningful. Before the first meeting concerning a student, the principal, in cooperation with teachers and local school agency officials, should review the guidelines for an IEP. In many school districts, these guidelines are printed in a booklet for all schools to use. The principal or a designate must review with the faculty the due process procedures for the student; the confidentiality of all

reports, meetings, or other communication concerning a student; the organizational plan for scheduling meetings with the members of the IEP team; and the forms that are required at various stages of developing an IEP. Since the principal is ultimately responsible with the teachers for the success of the student, the procedure for reviewing the plans for special needs students should be established. The principal must monitor to some degree the overall accountability of the program; therefore, lines of communication should be specified when the IEP process commences.

The types of teachers involved in the process of reevaluating either a student who is already receiving special services or a child who has been referred for special help will probably vary with the type of handicap or services required. All of these professionals should understand their roles in the evaluation process. The regular teacher can provide observational data by using checklists such as the Mann-Suiter-McClung Developmental Checklist and information on academic performance by using the Mann-Suiter Spelling, Reading, Writing, Written Language, and Arithmetic Screens. The Developmental Skills Worksheets in each chapter would also help the regular teacher to prepare to give input to other professionals and parents at an IEP conference. Diagnosticians, special education teachers, and psychologists will provide the data from more comprehensive tests that will establish such areas a cognitive functioning, academic performance, and adaptive behavior.

Those who are involved in the evaluation process must particularly be aware of the following:

1. Have all the due process procedures involving the parents or guardians been completed prior to an evaluation of the student?
2. Are all the required forms signed and on file?
3. Have the tests been carefully selected based on their validity?
4. Are the tests nondiscriminatory with regard to race or culture?
5. Is more than one type of test procedure being used?
6. Which tests are norm referenced and which ones are criterion referenced?
7. What kinds of observation, screening, or testing will each teacher or evaluator be using and is there a basic understanding of what the student will be required to do?
8. Who will inform the parents or guardians and the student about the evaluation process?
9. Will it be necessary to administer the test in the student's native language or another mode of communication?

During the IEP conference, the present level of educational performance of the student must be clearly stated in language that the parents or guardians can comprehend.

Prioritized Statement of Annual and Long-Range Goals

Annual goals are statements reflecting a reasonable expectation of what the learner can achieve during the year. Team members must determine the reality of the goals; defend their appropriateness with regard to grade level promotion, graduation, potential after-graduation employment, and other administrative rules or policies; and be prepared to mediate concerns of the parents or guardians and the instructional staff if the goals are unmet within a specified time.

Statement of Short-Term Instructional Objectives

Administrators need to monitor the quality of the written instructional objectives and if necessary plan with their staffs the type of staff development meetings that will facilitate a meaningful and manageable process. Principals must work carefully with their staffs to improve the paperwork load or time constraints that may inhibit the process.

The teachers must join in a collaborative effort to write the types of statements that can be measured and observed and are written in a language that everyone involved in the process can understand, including the student. The teachers should examine the scope and sequences of subject matter skills as well as such development skills lists as those included within this book. The short-range goals must be attainable within a framework that permits modification once the process of instruction begins. Since parents and in some cases the student will attend IEP conferences, the teachers should be prepared to state the goals in terms of what the student knows and how the short-term goals in an IEP will build on those strengths.

Statement of the Specific Special Education and Related Services to Be Provided

Principals have to know what services will be provided by the school and what additional services may be secured from the community. They must mediate or know from whom to seek information if unrealistic services are either recommended by the committee or demanded by the parent. They or their designates must be knowledgeable about such services as transportation, mechanical devices, and services by ancillary teaching personnel (e.g., speech and therapy).

Regular and special education teachers must also be knowledgeable about what services are available within the system. The teachers must also consider how the service will blend into the students' ongoing programs and the long- and short-term goals. The committee members must avoid too many unrelated services that fragment the children to such a degree that the goals of their programs cannot be attained. If some of the support services to the regular teacher are not specifically funded, then the committee should examine the reliability and quality of such assistance as parent volunteers or peer tutors.

Role of Specified Personnel Responsible for IEP

A system of communication for staff members and parents should be set up that will permit accessibility when unforseen episodes or breakdowns in the collaborative effort occur. Principals have to have a clear understanding of the roles of their staff, especially such personnel as resource teachers who may perform a variety of tasks in many settings. A principal has to know the staff's strengths and weaknesses and must be prepared for conflict and know the steps to mediate and resolve adversarial relationships. Encouragement and praise of staff, as well as solicitation of alternatives for improving the implementation of an IEP within a school, all add to good morale and more commitment from everyone to continue the extra effort that may be required in meeting the needs of the students.

Both regular and special teachers have to know how their work can aid students. Many organizational problems prevent a maximum use of their efforts. The following issues should be resolved in the role delineation of regular and special teachers:

1. When can they meet for ongoing evaluation? If they can't meet often because of conflicting schedules, then some other type of written communication should be planned.
2. Which teacher will communicate with the parents?
3. If the student's behavior deteriorates, what help is available and when?
4. How can schedule conflicts be avoided?
5. If the IEP has been written primarily by one teacher, can the other teachers succesfully carry out their part of the long- and short-range goals?
6. What grading system will be used for the student? If the report card for the student with special needs is atypical, who informs the child and the parents?

Statement of Extent to Which the Student Will Be Able to Participate in Least-Restrictive-Environment Programs, or Percentage of Time in the Regular Classroom

Every school should participate in an orientation session concerning services for handicapped children, what is required to receive such services, and what such terms as *least restrictive environment* mean. Working definitions will greatly aid the faculty in the planning process. For example: Least restrictive environment is the place where handicapped students receive special services while, to the greatest extent appropriate, their education with nonhandicapped students is maximized. The staff has to do a needs assessment of what has to be changed to provide an environment that is in compliance with the law and that facilitates access and mobility within the school. The following should be considered:

1. Have physical barriers been removed (e.g., benches, plants, etc., in the hallways)?
2. Do all the students have access to classrooms, bathrooms, lunchroom, library, etc.? For example, can a wheelchair roll under the lunch tables or science lab tables?
3. Are signs that promote labeling removed (e.g., special class for retarded children)?
4. Are special classes placed throughout the school or are they all placed in one wing?
5. Have safety features in the school been accounted for? What happens during fire drills when a student is enroute from one teacher to another?
6. Does the entire staff understand special medical problems (e.g., seizures)?

The principal usually sets the example for labels within a school. Such words as "those children" are often picked up and repeated by secretaries or other building personnel.

Teachers are usually most concerned about the following:

1. Which subjects will be missed if a student goes to a special class, and how can that subject be made up?
2. How much extra time will the special needs child require?
3. What happens when other children ridicule a child?
4. How can a child receiving special services make the transition from room to room?
5. Who will do the grading when several teachers teach parts of the same subject (e.g., reading)?
6. How can information be coordinated to benefit the student (e.g., ongoing evaluation, improvement

or failure in achievement, reporting to the parents)?
7. Will the time required to provide an individualized plan be excessive?
8. Where will the resource teacher best work with the student—in the regular classroom with the regular teacher or in a separate room?
9. What should the regular and special teachers know about each other's available resources?

Specification of Projected Dates for the Initiation of Services and the Anticipated Duration of the Services

Everyone should keep good records and document the progress of the services. If it is evident that services will be either terminated or extended, the information leading to the decisions should not be a shock to the children or their parents.

Statement of the Specific Evaluation Criteria for Each of the Indicated Annual Goals and a Time Line for Determining Whether Instructional Objectives Are Achieved

Ongoing evaluations, which may include reports, conferences, and other communication completed on schedule, should facilitate continuity and improved services. Principals must allow teachers (regular and special) to admit failure or to ask for help if the student is not making the progress the committee anticipated. It is difficult to defend extended failure when intervening steps have not been used.

Teachers need to know how to evaluate goals and set up a continuous evaluation system. They must develop an informal system of daily or weekly spotchecking of progress, as well as methods of determining mastery of skills.

Recommendations for Specific Procedures/ Techniques, Materials, etc., to Include Information Relating to the Learning Characteristics of the Student

As the financial broker of available resources, the principal often has to determine if the material required by the teachers fits the existing budget categories. If a teacher needs materials that are atypical, then the principal must have a good understanding of additional sources of revenue (e.g., parents, clubs). The administrator has to have not only a knowledge of the appropriateness of educational materials, but also a management system for the materials in a building.

How to effectively distribute, get multiple usage, modify, code, store, and avoid duplication are all important in cost-effective management.

Teachers are also concerned about the availability and classroom management of materials. A vital part of an IEP is how the student will acquire the prescribed skills and how much will be individualized. With class size, grouping, and time all impinging on individualization, the teachers need materials that can be made as student directed as possible. If teachers must share materials or the student has to use materials in a centrally located library, then the materials have to be coded and scheduled.

When teaching techniques or curriculum materials are atypical, then the instructor has to know how to make the transition from a supplementary to a major program. If the material is a game, then the students have to know why they are using it and perhaps what subject it applies to.

SCREENING

One of the first steps in the assessment process is to plan a system of screening to find out which students may have learning problems or special needs. Screening, as a part of ongoing classroom activities, can easily be done through the use of observational checklists, interviews, and informal evaluation devices, such as the inventories in Chapter 6.

A system of screening or informal evaluation can be established in any learning situation and for any grade level. To be worthwhile, screening should provide a basis for initial teaching strategies and further evaluation. Accomplished as a part of everyday school activities, screening can provide the teacher with important input needed for total educational programming. Screening for potential school failures will provide initial information on all students, not only those exhibiting obvious learning and behavior difficulties.

All records of students, especially those of students who are exhibiting school failure, should be reviewed in the spring of the year by the teachers who will be getting the students in the fall of the next year. Special attention should be given to how the students were taught and what kinds of material were used in the process, as well as to the vocabulary used to describe their behavior. Initial screening provides a backup system for the teacher to make comparisons between what is observed in the classroom and what is indicated through more formalized evaluation. In this way the teacher can accept or reject data, depending on whether they correlate or do not correlate with observed behavior.

Observation

Teachers can gain useful information about students during interactions with peers and during performance on classroom assignments and evaluation procedures. The observer should be able to answer the following questions:

1. How much did the student accomplish in each subarea of the test before time was called? Was the student successful as far as he or she went?
2. Did the student just put down written responses without any rationale for what he or she did?
3. Did the student understand the directions and was he or she able to cope with the number of directions?
4. How successful was the student in terms of the amount of work completed?
5. Was the student observed to be "a slow worker"?
6. Was the student allowed to complete the test so that the individual evaluating the student could determine how much the learner could complete correctly if time was not a factor?
7. Was there a great deal of guessing?
8. Did the observer indicate any circumstances that would prevent the student from doing optimal work, such as anxiety, poor motivation, or illness?
9. Were there any cultural (language-bilingual) or ethnic-related concerns that should be considered?
10. How did the student arrive at the observed response even though the response itself may be deemed incorrect?
11. How does the student feel about his or her performance?
12. What are the pressures impinging upon the student (i.e., home, teachers, peers, special groups, etc.)?
13. Is the observation focusing on the weaknesses of the student, or is understanding the strengths of the learner considered to be just as important for educational programming?
14. What reasons are suggested for present levels of performance in terms of history and observed behavior?
15. Are the eyes and ears of other individuals in the school—including secretaries, custodians, aides, paraprofessionals, and volunteers—used for additional diagnostic information?

Information—Case History

Along with observation, it is important to develop a system for acquiring the previous history of a student's performance. This can be accomplished by reviewing records and interviewing parents (guardians) and previous teachers, as well as interviewing the student.

There are numerous forms in this book that will assist the reader in recording data during interviews. Refer to the Behavior Observation Form in Chapter 4, the Mann-Suiter-McClung Developmental Checklists in Chapter 6, and the Mann-Suiter-McClung Parent Conference Guide in Chapter 7.

The following questions can be used to gain case history information:

1. What is the history of early development (e.g., prenatal and birth conditions, age when student first sat, crawled, walked, talked in sentences, was toilet trained, etc.)? Is there a history of infections, delay in motor or language development, or problems with sleeping or feeding?

2. Is the student new to the community and has he or she been moved about to a great extent?

3. Has the student been excessively absent? What is the attendance record?

4. What have others (teachers, peers, administrators, other school workers, etc.) said about the student? What kind of words have been used to describe the student?

5. Who were the teachers who were successful with the student, and what did they do to provide for successful experiences?

6. How was the student initially taught, and what were the results? Has the student been continually taught in essentially the same manner, using the same basic approach in reading, for example? What methods of teaching were used with the student? Have there been any recent drastic changes in methods or techniques of instruction?

7. Has the student ever experienced any serious medical problems? Has the student had any serious physical injury or disease?

8. Has the student indicated any severe emotional problems or maladaptive behavior (e.g., depression, aggression, etc.)? Has the student ever had any serious emotional upheaval or traumatic experience?

9. When was the last time the student's vision or hearing was checked? What is the current condition of eyesight and hearing?

10. When was the last time the student had a comprehensive evaluation? By whom was this accomplished? What did the results indicate and what action was taken as a result of this procedure? Was the action effective in promoting learning and good adjustment?

FORMAL TESTING

After screening, some students may require more in-depth testing. Formal tests are instruments that have been used with large groups of students. They can be criterion-referenced tests or norm-referenced tests. Criterion-referenced measurement is a method of determining the level and quality of an individual's performance in relation to specific instructional objectives or criteria. Criterion-referenced tests measure mastery of specific skills and describe performance. The student's test results are compared against a specific criterion, not other students. Norm-referenced measurement compares an individual's performance with the performance norms of the population on which a particular measuring instrument was standardized.

Formal tests usually have a manual that outlines administration procedures, scoring, and interpretation. Information is provided about the test's validity (how well it measures what it purports to measure) and reliability or internal consistency, which is the extent to which the test can dependably be repeated.

The individuals responsible for formal assessment must clearly understand why they are doing what they are doing. They must determine whether or not they are in fact assessing the skills that are critical to success in the academic areas under concern. Testing for labeling is not quite the same as testing for curriculum programming. Tests should be appropriate to the student populaion in terms of age, sociocultural background, native language, experiences, and specific problem areas of concern. Whenever possible, students should be tested in their primary language. Individuals responsible for formal testing must provide a basic interpretation of the results to the parents or guardians in their native language whenever possible, indicating how this information will be used.

Lists of commercial formal tests are provided in Chapter 6 at the end of each section of inventories.

Minimum Competency Testing

Over 40 states have enacted legislation calling for some form of minimum competency testing prior to graduation from high school. Many school systems are striving for educational excellence and minimum standards of achievement. This has led to educational change most notably in the area of minimum competency testing. The desire for accountability in public education has caught the marginally achieving student in a bind. Students who are transitioned to regular education must perform in a manner expected of

their nonhandicapped agemates. Still essentially under special education auspices, many students face
the prospect of failing high school graduation standards. Both minority and nonminority learning handicapped students are facing the same dilemma.

There are three main policy options with regard to
minimum competency tests (MCTs):

1. Handicapped students should be required to pass
   the standard MCT prerequisite to receiving a diploma. This has been adopted in some states and
   requires that procedural and due process rules are
   not violated, and also that handicapped students
   are given adequate notice so they can prepare for
   the test by reviewing the material that the test will
   cover.
2. Handicapped students should be exempt from taking the statewide MCT and granted a regular high
   school diploma based on successful completion of
   their Individual Educational Program (IEP) requirements. This concept has been adopted in 21
   states, but in several states the students are given
   a special diploma or certificate of completion.
3. Differential competency standards should be developed for handicapped students. Florida is one
   state that uses minimum competency standards for
   the various categories of handicapping conditions
   (Grise, 1986). These standards are called *special
   competency tests* (SCTs). The mildly handicapped
   are encouraged to take the regular MCTs so they
   can receive a "regular diploma." Students who
   pass the SCTs receive a "special diploma."

ROLE OF PARENTS IN ASSESSMENT

Parents of potential school failures can play a role in
assessment by providing the teacher with information
about the student's life at home. This information will
enable the teacher to verify or negate different
aspects of the student's behavior in school. Educators
must ask the right questions of parents. The following
will provide important information.

1. How did the student's early development compare
   to that of other children in the family?
2. Were there any early signs of delayed or inadequate development such as speech, language,
   or motor development? Did the child exhibit any
   early inappropriate behavior before coming to
   school? What did the parents do about any special
   problems or disorders in the child's life?
3. How do the parents discipline the student? This is
   especially important, since some parents resort to
   excessive physical punishment in order to modify
   behavior.

4. Do the parents view the learner as different from
   other children? How?
5. What kind of stimulation is provided the child at
   home? Is the student left alone for long periods of
   time? Who is with the child at home, and what kind
   of language interaction does he or she receive from
   adults and peers?
6. How do the parents feel about the school and what
   the school is trying to do for their child? Is there an
   adversarial relationship between the home and the
   school?
7. How does the student spend his or her leisure
   time?
8. What are the things he or she likes to do at home?
9. Have you noticed any unusual recent changes in
   behavior such as eating or sleeping habits, irritabil-
   ity, prolonged depression, apathy, and so on.

CURRICULUM-BASED ASSESSMENT (CBA)

Curriculum-based assessment (CBA) involves the
continuous evaluation of instructional needs by
measuring student performance within a specific area
of content (Tucker, 1987). CBA is a generic term that
encompasses a variety of practices and includes tests
that are devised by teachers using materials in the
curriculum and administered to students as a part of
classroom activity to determine mastery of specific
content.

Short tests can be developed that tie directly into
curriculum goals for a particular grade level or subject
area. These short tests or screens can be designed to
be completed within a preset time frame. For example,
a sample could be taken from a story of 100 running
words and read aloud within a time frame of one
minute. Performance is measured by calculating the
rate of correct words read aloud per minute. The same
system can be applied to arithmetic (for example, the
number of addition math problems completed in a
minute) or in writing (such as the number of words
written correctly and legibly within one minute). One
minute is the usual standard, but this is flexible (Marston, Tindal, & Deno, 1984). Some educators refer to
these short tests as *probes* (Bursuck & Lessen, 1987).

After scoring, the results can be used to modify the
program up or down. The student rate of performance
can be compared to peers and graphed accordingly.
The student should improve as the year progresses. A
rank order of student progress can be prepared, for
example, in skill areas including handwriting (manuscript and cursive), spelling, oral reading, math computation, and math numeration.

The following is an example of curriculum-based
assessment using spelling. Students are required to

master responsibility for 50 spelling words over a period of weeks. The assessment procedure would involve:

1. Randomly selecting 20 words from a list of 50 the student is required to master
2. Dictating the words that should be written on lined paper
3. Introducing a word every seven seconds
4. Testing for two minutes or until 20 words have been dictated, whichever occurs first
5. Scoring that is based on the number of words spelled correctly per minute

Spelling performance would be measured at least twice weekly and the students' scores graphed. The rate of actual student progress is plotted and compared to a line representing the desired or projected rate of progress. If the actual rate is decidedly lower than the desired rate of progress, the instructional program is modified accordingly. If the opposite is true, the teacher may want to accelerate the number of words to be learned. The teacher can identify the approaches that work and do not work for a student. Sometimes, a slower rate is all that needs to be changed for the learner.

CBA encompasses several main concepts, including the need to utilize more specific goals in teaching, establish more complete educational goals, and determine if the instructional program is working or if it needs to be changed. By keeping a continuous data base, teachers can make instructional modifications in students' progress when it is needed (Fuchs, Fuchs, & Stecker, 1989).

Fuchs and Fuchs (1984) indicate that teachers prefer unsystematic and intuitive impressions of a student's performance over hard and fast objective measurement. Many feel that the learner knows more than what is shown on achievement tests. The impressions of a student's progress often dictate feelings about how instructionally appropriate a program is. Even though informal or unsystematic evaluation has the tendency to overrate students, it is preferred by many teachers over objective measurements. More systematic observation and frequent measurement, such as that provided by curriculum-based assessment, could enhance teacher judgement (Fuchs & Fuchs, 1986).

Other types of curriculum-based assessment include standardized tests when the testing material has been drawn from specific content, such as in reading, math, spelling, or written expression, in which precise directions for administration and scoring are provided (Deno, 1986; Deno & Fuchs, 1987). Certain standardized measurements of global achievement can be applied to classroom content by using the same rules that are applied to other CBA procedures. Formal tests need not be excluded because they can be used for a variety of purposes in areas that deal with measuring mastery of content (Germann & Tindal, 1985). Tests can also be used for norm-referenced screening and referral (Shinn, Tindal, & Stein, 1988). Formal tests can be used to assess school programs and to establish instructional plans that are designed to enhance student achievements.

Curriculum-based assessment is an alternative to traditional testing. CBA is designed to measure the level of student achievement in relation to an expected curricular outcome (Tucker, 1985). In terms of application, the responsibility for establishing the parameters for assessment in a school setting can be shared between special education teachers and regular teachers. Several areas need clarification and agreement in the shared responsibility arrangement:

1. Assessment of academic and other task-related skills may not be appropriate for the measurement parameters of commercial testing devices (Deno & Fuchs, 1987). The test does not measure what the student knows.
2. The regular educator is the primary source of information and the first line of screening, assessment, and the instruction of appropriate skills (Ysseldyke, 1983).
3. A student's academic performance and social behavior can be compared to other students at a particular grade or within age-relevant parameters (Shinn & Marston, 1985), but this comparison may provide erroneous information for critical decisions because of social and cultural differences. Social-cultural validation, therefore, becomes very important.
4. Student assessment should be linked to the instructional program, therefore classroom-based assessment should be geared to making educational judgments (Marston, Tindal, & Deno, 1984).
5. Assessment should be a team project with a common focus and a common language designed to achieve a more effective interaction between professionals.
6. Assessment should be based on examining academic behavior relative to other task-related behavior within the context of the classroom, not in isolation of the environment that is the center of activity.

The overall approach is viewed as a part of overall assessment and as a supplement to traditional testing, and not as a replacement for standardized tests presently in use. The specification of goals is critical to curriculum-based assessment (Fuchs, Fuchs & Stecker, 1989). It helps to define the curriculum-based assessment process goals that establish:

1. The condition of the measurement process and the material that will be used
2. The behavior that will be measured
3. The criteria for judging mastery
4. The connection between goals and measurement

Examples of curriculum-based measures are inventories, error analysis, and sequentially arranged curriculum objectives (see Chapter 6).

DYNAMIC ASSESSMENT

The aim of this type of assessment is to combine the examination of a student's readiness to learn with instruction in cognitive content and cognitive skill areas (Lidz, 1987). This involves a test-train-test cycle with variation in the target skills and the content areas of learning. One of the main outcomes is to analyze how deficiencies in learning performance relate to the present competencies and readiness levels of the learner so that new competencies can be specified. The student is provided with immediate feedback on how to improve performance.

Dynamic assessment is also designed to determine how much help a student will require to facilitate learning. The goal is to achieve as much self-regulated, problem-solving behavior as possible. The student develops an internalized model of how to perform a task. Hints and cues that are effective help the learner to improve problem-solving performance by extending, modifying, or replacing existing problem-solving strategies (Duran, 1989). The important thing is to identify the kinds of hints or clues that promote new learning in specific students.

The preordered hint and clue approach does result in statistically significant improvements in criterion problem-solving tasks (Campione & Brown, 1987; Bransford et al., 1988). Teaching that allows the instructor to assist the learner early during the course of learning can be a part of effective instruction. The learner establishes a baseline through independent effort and then information is gleaned from how the learner performs with various levels of asistance, aiding the learners to gain new competencies (Tharp & Gallimore, 1988). The same Vygotskian principles can be applied to testing. What effect would clues or useful hints have on learner performance? Some students will eventually learn to self-generate clues and hints and perform at an automatic level.

Assessment, to be effective, should assist the teacher in everyday instruction. Dynamic assessment is an assisted performance tool that provides the teacher with knowledge about how to organize and manage a program of instruction.

ASSESSING YOUNG CHILDREN

A developmental approach to assessment considers the various aspects of cognitive-developmental learning that are important to success in formal academics. Many young children bring to school developmental delays in one or more areas considered necessary for success in academics. Skills in the gross and fine motor areas, social-emotional development, language, and cognitive areas must be assessed so that teachers will know where to begin to teach. Some behavior problems may be functional and others maladaptive. Appropriate assessment should reveal the learner's mode of learning and suggest avenues of instruction. One suggested approach to assessment in young children is to design a structured assessment program, one in which behaviors are identified that are directly related to desired learner outcomes. There are advantages to early identification:

1. It is sometimes difficult to distinguish between developmental-maturational lag and learning handicapped deficits (which have more long-lasting effect). The difference is in the rate of development. Is the child really at risk or does he or she simply need more time to mature?
2. There is a possible detrimental effect associated with labeling. Does labeling outweigh the need to identify the child so he or she can receive services? The role of the school is to provide services without the label if possible. The category "high risk" or "early intervention" appears to be appropriate for young learners with problems.

Early screening should be followed if necessary by measuring intelligence, social-emotional behavior, and motor and preacademic behavior, which includes language development. Preacademic areas of assessment appear to reflect more accurately the high-risk category of students (Magliocca et al., 1977). Preacademic skills include personal knowledge of family, address, telephone number, colors, letter sounds, and letter names. The student is asked to recognize and names, shapes, and parts of the body, and exhibit certain motor abilities. Many of these skills can be assessed by using simple checklists (see Chapter 6). Predictive assessment devices should be administered during the spring of the kindergarten year, affording the teacher observation time to make important decisions for first-grade placement.

Teacher perception of behavior was found to be a good predictor of school problems in young children (Keogh & Becker, 1973; Glazzard, 1977). Teachers who are able to use preacademic checklists that are related to academic criterion performance have an impressive identification rate.

LANGUAGE ASSESSMENT

Does the language used by the student draw more attention than the message that it is intended to convey? If the answer is yes, then further study of assessment is indicated. The teacher, as a constant observer of children's language, is in an optimal position to observe irregularities in a child's language performance when compared to other students. Language assessment is concerned with linguistic abilities, whereas speech evaluation looks at voice and articulation.

Oral language problems can be observed and the following should be noted:

1. How does the child use language functionally in everyday classroom activity, at play, and in interaction with other students?
2. Has a sample of the student's spontaneous speech been recorded and evaluated according to a set of criteria?
3. Does the student exhibit delayed speech?
4. Does he or she use little language or use an unusual word order?
5. Does the learner speak in one- or two-word phrases or sentences?
6. Is the parent concerned about the student's use of language?

The severity of a child's language problem needs to be determined in order to provide for appropriate intervention. Teachers not experienced in language assessment need to refer students to professionals, such as speech and language therapists who are specially trained in this area. All assessment of language must consider the child's dialect and cultural background. Continuous assessment is also needed to determine the efficiency of the intervention and, if individual therapy is used, when and if it should be terminated.

ASSESSMENT OF LIMITED ENGLISH PROFICIENT (LEP) STUDENTS

A number of students with Limited English Proficiency also exhibit learning and/or behavioral disorders. The Education for All Handicapped Children Act (P.L. 94–142) guarantees a culturally unbiased valid assessment.

Several important factors need to be considered in assessment:

1. First- and second-language screening for capability and proficiency must be accomplished to determine the need for language-related services.
2. The assessment must be multidimensional, using more than one instrument and procedure where results can be cross-validated.
3. Tests are to be used to assess the learner's linguistic skills, as well as academic and social-emotional aspects of behavior.
4. Test instruments must possess reliability and validity in terms of the populations tested. This includes using trained bilingual testers, local norms, translations when appropriate, structured interviews, and so on.
5. Both social and communicative language proficiency should be measured. For LEP students, language proficiency will be enhanced through the use of the language of greatest facility (Ochoa, Pacheco, & Omark, 1988).
6. LEP students being considered for special education placement should be tested in both English and in the primary language. This is true for vocabulary, verbal expression, reading, writing, and math. Several factors affect the rate of second-language development, according to Krashen (1981). These include age, instructional method, attitude, and aptitude.
7. It is important to look beyond language differences and assess cognitive functioning and critical thinking.
8. Instructional goals must be based on and deal with deficits in both the primary and secondary language. This is accomplished through the IEP if the child is being assessed for special education services.
9. Exit criteria should be the same as those used in traditional bilingual programs to ensure fair and equitable treatment (Baca & Bransford, 1982).
10. Competent and licensed staff should be working with these students. This includes appropriate bilingual personnel as needed for diagnosis and educational programming, and requires appropriate teacher preparation programs.

LEP students with learning disabilities require careful study and diagnosis prior to making decisions about placement, in order to account for primary language abilities, other deficits, and cultural variables in terms of content and human interaction.

Language Disorder or Language Difference

Differentiating between language disorder and language difference is an important and sometimes difficult task in assessment. Studies suggest that if a language disorder is manifested in the primary language it should also be reflected in the second language (Ambert, 1986; Langdon, 1983; Linares-Orama, 1977).

It is important to assess LEP students in both English and the home language. Before a language disorder is applied to a learner, implying the presence of learning disabilities, several factors need to be considered:

1. How long has the learner lived in the country? Children of migrating families (back and forth) display more difficulties in the Spanish language (Langdon, 1983).
2. Poor attendance is a major factor. It takes two years to gain basic communication skills in English. Five to seven years of English in school may be necessary for academic success or for de-contextualized English language usage (Cummins, 1984). Low attendance is a contributory factor to extending the time limits for English language competency.
3. The type of school programs the learner has attended is a consideration. What language was used in the instructional program? Cummins (1984, p. 223) points out: "A learning disability in many students is pedagogically induced rather than a reflection of some intrinsic processes."
4. How language is used in the culture is another consideration. It may be culturally inappropriate, for example, to ask questions or to retell a story or even to extend a great deal of verbal output in some cultures. Verbal behavior, in a sense, is withheld.
5. What is the language experience or linguistic background of the student as compared to peers? The child may not be able to express himself or herself because of the way he or she is treated in the family. Also, do the parents see the child's language as a problem?
6. Additional factors, such as the learner's health, slow rate of development, mental retardation, emotional handicaps, or sensory problems, must also be considered.

There are limitations to testing LEP students with or without learning disabilities. They are:

1. Validity and reliability are affected by student lack of language proficiency, lack of familiarity with test content, lack of understanding, sensitivity by examiner of the student's culture, and the student's unfamiliarity with how to take tests. The learner in effect has to pass a literacy test with every test he or she takes.
2. Tests of achievement and aptitude do not, as a rule, give the teacher prescriptive information or ideas about instructional approaches. Even the directions are foreign to some LEP students and have to be taught separately.

Communicative competence is now being used as a synonym for *language proficiency* by sociologists and ethnographers (Duran, 1989). Paper and pencil tests are very different from the natural communicative activities of LEP children (Duran, 1988). It is important to determine how an LEP student interacts with teachers in using language, in the classroom, and in everyday activities. Testing, therefore, is not the best way of establishing a communicative competency by its very nature (e.g., unnatural, structured, unfamiliar, controlled, and requires a good working knowledge of a foreign language). Some children can even teach a task to another student, but cannot respond to the teacher's questions about the task (Carrasco, Vera, & Cazden, 1981).

Assessing Migrant Students

Mildly handicapped migrant students who are part of the "stream" require special attention (Baca & Harris, 1988). Several important factors need to be considered (Salend, Michael, & Taylor, 1984):

1. Teachers need to be aware of the problem in its totality. It is also a family problem.
2. Educators need to share information about these students (special educators and migrant educators).
3. Educators need to be continually communicating about the educational needs of these students as they move around.

Migrant children have to deal with the harsh realities of life, namely, poor nutrition, hard work in the fields, constant mobility, poor school attendance, and fear, if they are illegal entries.

The same testing and cultural interventions that apply to nonmigrant groups apply to migrants, except that frequent changes in school can result in being separated from peers, and the good influences that could occur through continued relationships. It is recommended that:

1. Migrant students verbalize their experiences and talk about places they have lived.

2. They should trace these movements on a map.
3. They should write to nonmigrant friends as they move around.
4. Migrant children and others talk about how important their work is for the economy.
5. Parents of migrant children come to school and be encouraged to participate in home-school learning programs.
6. Educators who understand migrant culture be a part of the education program.
7. Educators set up communications with those who provide for migrant services in the community.
8. The Migrant Student Record Transfer System (MSRTS) be utilized as a computerized bank nationwide for tracking migrant families. Interstate cooperation is very important if special problems are to have any real meaning. Section 143 of Public Law 95–561 promotes interstate cooperation. The Portable Assisted Study Sequence (PASS) program is a good example of helping migrant students get high school diplomas.
9. Help be given to migrant families to obtain relevant documents such as birth certificates, immunization papers, as well as medical documents and histories of special problems in children.
10. Families be given lists of the names, addresses, and phone numbers of people and places that are serving their mildly handicapped child.

SOCIAL SKILLS ASSESSMENT

There is promising evidence for the effectiveness of social skills training, but limitations are noted due to the inadequate availability of assessment devices that measure outcomes (Hughes & Sullivan, 1988). There are some recently reported positive developments regarding the use of rating scales that assess teachers, parents, and self-reports of behavior. These scales better enable researchers to define deficits with respect to norms regarding the whole population in general.

Studies indicate that learning disabled children, as a group, are less accepted by their agemates and exhibit social behavior that is less accepted than nonhandicapped students in many areas of interpersonal relationships (Gresham, 1988). It is reasonable that educators should plan for dealing with social deficiencies as integral to the total program. It is important to differentiate between whether a student has a deficit in a specific social skill area (the behavior is not in his or her repertoire) or if the behavior exists within the student's response repertoire but he or she opts not to exhibit it in school-related social situations.

Good observations, including using roleplaying techniques, should help differentiate between these two factors. If it is the latter, the problem is then to determine the antecedents in the classroom or home that mitigate against the learner exhibiting the behavior.

Social competence, as a basic aspect of human behavior and as an integral dimension to intelligence, has been conceptualized by Gresham (1986a) as having three subdomains: adaptive behavior, social skills, and peer acceptance.

Adaptive behavior is a multidimensional construct and, for educational purposes, involves the understanding of the necessary cognitive competencies, the social context in which these competencies are exhibited and viewed by others, and the method by which they are measured. The characteristics of the respondent are central to viewing the entire construct. Differences in adaptive behavior to a great extent determine the kind of measures that are used (Gresham & Reschly, 1987), which in turn leads to or determines the classification and placement of the students (Gresham, 1986b; Hops & Greenwood, 1981).

Social competence involves exhibiting behaviors that maximize and reinforce social interaction, while decreasing the probability of punishment or other kinds of negative results. Peer acceptance is one of the outcomes of appropriate social behavior. If adaptive behavior and social skills are adequate, peer acceptance should be forthcoming.

There is a growing interest in social skills training with the expectation that intervention will lead to: (1) an increase in the student's academic performance, (2) improvement in the use of skills that are taught in the training program, and (3) improved peer acceptance and improved ratings of adjustment by teachers and others. The important overall question is, "Does social skills training predict important current or future outcomes?" (Gresham, 1983a). Further, is the child able to generalize the skills taught to everyday interactions with people in different social situations?

Along with academic performance, other methods of assessing effects of training include using observation checklists in natural settings, roleplaying or analogue assessment, self-report measures, or asking the student to solve problem situations involving social decisions. Peer nominations or ratings and teacher ratings of social competence are also commonly used.

Social Skills Assessment Approaches

Studies of sociometric assessment have consistently shown that learning disabled students are more poorly accepted and more often rejected than their nonhand-icapped agemates (Gresham, 1988). In the area of social skills assessment, it is easier to get general information about a student than it is to get a precise picture of specific clusters of behavior. For the most part, teachers can readily elaborate on a student's behavior by using incidents in the classroom or observations during play or at lunch, which are useful in identifying the problem. In and of themselves, these observations are not enough to label a student or even to specify a particular type of deficit. Before educators initiate a program designed to teach students how to maintain eye contact, improve body posture, or in-crease question making, it is important to know whether the students are deficient in these behaviors to begin with or if these behaviors are in fact really important to achieving improved peer acceptance (Maag, 1989).

It is concluded that more than one assessment pro-cedure is needed for a definitive diagnosis (Gresham & Elliott, 1989). There are many opportunities to observe a student in social situations in school: during play, academics, lunch, recess, coming and going from home to school, and vice versa.

Several questions need to be answered:

1. Does the student exhibit the behavior consistently in different school social situations?
2. Does the student exhibit the behavior at home?
3. Who is upset by the behavior? Is the student upset by any aspect of his or her interaction with peers, adults, etc.?
4. Who would be in a position to observe the student and can they be trained to observe and document appropriately?
5. Once the target behavior(s) is (are) identified, will the teacher know what to do?

The observation of the student's behavior should be functional to the extent that the antecedents (what led to the behavior), the sequence (what happened), and the consequences (what were the results) are all documented.

RATINGS BY TEACHERS AND PEERS

Teacher and peer ratings of behavior are one of the most frequently used ways of getting data. Teachers use behavior problem checklists (Quay & Peterson, 1975; Walker, 1980) and other teacher-related scales (Matson, Rotatori, & Helsel, 1983). It is recommended that these types of scales be used along with naturalistic observation.

Peer rating or sociometric assessment is different because all the students in a class are asked to rate each other by using a Likert-type scale. This involves criteria such as identifying best friends, individuals you like to play with or do homework with, and so on. The main factors measured include likability, friendli-ness, and popularity. Peer assessment is another type of evaluation. It differs from peer rating to the extent that students are asked to rate peers on various be-havioral characteristics instead of with whom they pre-fer to play or work.

NATURALISTIC OBSERVATION

Naturalistic observation involves defining behavior and recording the frequency and situation of occur-rence after observing these behaviors in the natural setting. These data are then analyzed for ecologically (within the entire environment) appropriate evaluation of a learner's social skills (Elliott, Gresham, & Heffer, 1987; Feindler & Ecton, 1986).

Target behaviors are observed, using a pre-designed observation and recording system. The observations can be accomplished on a continuous basis focusing on antecedents, sequences, and con-sequences of behavior. Such questions as what main-tains the behavior or what prevents appropriate be-havior from being exhibited are often answered.

ROLEPLAYING ASSESSMENT

Roleplay or analogue assessment can be used as a supplement or instead of naturalistic observation. Stu-dents are asked to respond to preestablished or "staged" circumstances, and their performance or re-sponses are recorded (Beck et al., 1982; McCloskey & Quay, 1987). Behavior categories, such as disruptive, incoherent, and information requesting, are used to assess the student's behavior during the roleplaying situation. Roleplay is useful because teachers do not have to wait for behaviors to occur, such as those observed in naturalistic observation.

TASK ANALYSIS

In task anaylsis the learner is required to complete a task in which subcomponents, requiring certain skills that the learner may be deficient in, are identified for future programming (instruction). Failure to complete the overall task, even with successful completion of the subtasks, suggests that the student has a lack of strategies for using or coordinating all of the subtasks in order to complete the overall task (Gagne, 1985; Howell & Moorehead, 1987).

Some authors suggest that the analysis of tasks should focus on the kinds of strategies needed for different types of behavior rather than on just one behavior (Scandura, 1982; Rathjen, 1984).

MEASURES OF SOCIAL-COGNITIVE PROBLEM SOLVING

In this approach students use their problem-solving skills to indicate their competency in problematic social interactive situations. The student may be asked to read a story and answer questions, or complete a matching task that presents a conflicting, hostile, or ambiguous situation (Hughes, 1988).

INTERVIEWING

The student is asked direct questions about what strategies he or she would use in specific situations (Howell & Moorehead, 1987). Imagery or recall is used where students are asked to imagine or relive an experience (Meichenbaum, 1985). Interviewing that focuses on problem solving, making friends, dealing with conflict, and peer interaction can also be very useful (Hughes & Hall, 1987).

SELF-MONITORING

This technique helps to identify and continuously evaluate how students use social skills strategies. One method is to ask the students to keep a daily diary where they record their thoughts and experiences and how they responded to different situations (Maag & Meinhold, 1985). Other types of measurements in the area include multiple-choice tests (Reardon et al., 1979; Michelson & Wood, 1980; Matson, Esveldt-Dawson, & Kazdin, 1983).

Reciprocal Kinds of Assessment

All data should be viewed within the context of the environment in which it occurs (Strain & Odom, 1986). This involves a type of social reciprocity where individuals exhibit the ability to engage in interactions that are mutually reinforcing (Strain & Shores, 1977).

Factors of reciprocal relationships, such as cultural relativeness, age of respondents, and other external differences, should be considered (Kendall, 1985). Student behavior should be viewed within the configuration of environmental antecedents and consequences. Student attitude toward participation is another factor that may be due to how the environment affects the student. Reciprocity involves student behavior, cognition, and the environment, and how each component interacts with the other. Both individual specific and contextual factors can be identified that affect learner social competence (Strain, Odom, & McConnell, 1984). Just because a student exhibits "new" behavior does not mean that he or she will be immediately accepted and perceived in a different manner by peers.

Implications for Teaching

Determining student-specific deficits is a process that begins with general or global descriptions of behavior and situations to more specific kinds of information. Training is based on responding to the specific behaviors needed in an attempt to generalize these behaviors to all social situations. Appropriate target behaviors that are related to student sociometric status must be identified in order to attain social validity. The concept of social validity (Maag, 1989) means that the teacher must determine if changes in the student's behavior in actuality is having an overall positive effect on the student's life (Wolf, 1978).

Often, lack of improvement in sociometric evaluation by peers is due to trying to overcome a bad reputation and this may take time. Peer acceptance may not come easy in some situations. The student needs the teacher's support to understand this phenomenon. Sometimes the behavior of a student is so subtle that tests do not pick it up. The teacher must be a good observer to pick up these subtleties. The method found most effective in identifying problem behavior in the social skills area deals with identifying target behaviors, classifying them, and selecting those behaviors deemed most critical for change. In all of these we apply a multidimensional method of assessment and view all available information from a reciprocal assessment perspective.

ASSESSMENT AND LEARNING DISABILITIES

Most definitions of learning disabilities contain references to school failure, deficiencies in the basic psychological processes, and poor learning due to a variety of reasons, along with some inference or statement regarding underlying neurological causes. Much of the research has focused on single abilities, such as memory, and fails to explain the heterogeneity of the category and the broad range of problems exhibited by the students (Kavale & Forness, 1985; McKinney, 1987). For example, there are a number of students who exhibit significant learning deficits but do not quite fit current definitions. Students who experience environmental deprivation or who exhibit other handicaps are generally excluded from programs. Is it proper to say that these students will not benefit from learning disability-type programs?

A great deal of latitude is given to school districts with respect to special education placement. Students exhibiting socially or emotionally based learning problems often get into special education classes. It is important to separate those students who can benefit primarily from a good tutoring and a remedial program from those who need comprehensive special education services.

Not the least of the concerns is the fact that special education learning disability programs are very expensive when compared to a good remedial approach. When Public Law 94–142 was established, the projected learning disabilities population was set at 2 percent of the school population. In 1987, the proportion of learning disabled students deemed eligible for services ran as high as 4 percent of all school children nationally (Keogh, 1987). At the same time, the mentally retarded population has declined. The trend is clear, and educators are concerned about eligibility requirements. One obvious conclusion is that slow learners and underachievers are also being classified as learning disabled. Some educators say, as long as students get served, why the fuss? Others respond by saying that it confounds the research and that misclassification is counterproductive to the presently established system. Still others are saying that we need to reexamine the system and formulate new patterns of service that do not require precise definitions (Reynolds, 1988).

IQ/Achievement and Discrepancy

The validity of new identification procedures based on the concept of IQ/achievement discrepancy has received a great deal of attention in recent years (McKinney, 1987). Experts lack agreement as to the variables called "major markers" that are the key identification factors in learning disabilities. Our present behavioral measurements lack the preciseness necessary for total accuracy in assessing these variables. However, the IQ/achievement discrepancy criteria have been adopted by many states with specified types of measurements listed for calculating learner discrepancy profiles.

Cutoffs for eligibility and placement have become more stringent because of the large increase in the number of learning disabled students identified by the various methods. The dilemma in the process is the determination of the best way to quantify discrepancy. Actual performance is not as much of a problem as determining expected performance. Expected performance is usually based on age, grade, or intellectual potential. Expected performance is defined differently from state to state, resulting in the variability in the number and types of children served.

Four basic or common methods of computing discrepancy have been utilized:

1. Deviation from the grade level that compares achievement scores in grade equivalents to the student's grade placement. Two methods are currently used to compute the discrepancy:
   a. A constant level of deviation is used across the grades such as achievement one or two years below grade level placement. The problem is that two years below grade level 10 is not as devastating as two years below grade level 3.
   b. The second method, which is often combined with an IQ cutoff, uses a graduated deviation approach with increases as grade placement increases. For example, 1 year for grades 1–3; 1.5 years for grades 4–6; 2 years for grades 7–9; and 2.5 years for grades 10–12 (Lerner, 1989). The tendency in this method is to over-identify individuals who are diagnosed as slow learners or borderline mentally retarded (IQs between 70 and 90). Students with above-average intelligence are less likely to be identified in this process.

2. An expectancy formula, which is derived from utilizing the student's age, number of years in school, and mental age (MA) in a ratio equation, is used to arrive at an educational quotient or an expected grade performance. Sinclair and Alexson (1986) mention a number of formulas currently in use. In the following examples, the student is 10 years old with an IQ of 90. The Mental Age (MA) was determined by multiplying performance IQ × CA/100.

   a. Bond and Tinker (1973)

   $$\frac{YIS \times IQ}{100} + 1.0$$

   For example: $\frac{4 \times 90}{100} + 1.0 = 4.6$

   b. Harris (1975)

   $$\frac{2MA + CA}{3} - 5.2$$

   For example: $\frac{2(9) + 10}{3} - 5.2 = 4.1$

Where:

CA = Chronological Age
YIS = Years in School
IQ = Intelligence Quotient
MA = Mental Age

3. The most frequently used procedure is Erickson's z-score model (Erickson, 1975), which converts achievement and IQ scores into standard scores with the same mean and the same standard deviation (SD). This score allows for the comparison of scores across tests, subtests, age, and grade levels and circumvents many of the statistical criticisms leveled at age/grade expectancy formulas. (z-score = z-score reading, GMRG = Group Main Reading Grade, SD = Standard Deviation)

$$\frac{\text{z-score R} - \text{GMRG}}{\text{SD of Scores (13.57)}} \ (89.71)$$

In the standard score comparison formula, the student's aptitude and achievement scores are simply subtracted and the resulting discrepancy is compared to a chosen numerical standard of significance. Individual states have their own cutoff point.

The standard score method involves converting achievement scores to the same standard score units in IQ tests and subtracting the two measures. An example is $M = 100$, $SD = 15$. The problem is that IQ and achievement scores may be correlated. This would produce discrepancy scores that are biased by a statistical effect called regression toward the mean. This means that there is a tendency for extreme scores (high or low) on one test to be less extreme on a correlated measure and puts the reliability of the measurement of discrepancy in doubt. The amount of significant difference for students at the low or high IQ levels would be different, as compred with students with average IQ. Some states use a 15-point cutoff for defining a "severe discrepancy" for all age groups. Other states vary in cutoff numbers. The extent to which this makes a difference in terms of numbers of students identified is still not known.

4. The fourth method for quantifying discrepancy is to use a regression equation to predict academic performance from student IQ scores. The discrepancy, therefore, would be defined as the difference between predicted achievement and measured achievement. This method is considered to be the most sound statistically for measuring underachievement, although it does require additional costs.

Many of the tests used in assessment of learning disabilities do not meet acceptable psychometric standards, or the correlations that are necessary between the measures lack adequate investigation (Salvia & Ysseldyke, 1985). Both the grade-level deviation and the expectancy formula approaches have been shown to have serious limitations (Cone & Wilson, 1981; Forness, Sinclair, & Guthrie, 1983).

Many states have adopted the standard score method. The standard score method appears to be easier to use and implement in terms of practicality and cost.

Limitations

One problem with the standard score approach is the fact that many older students who qualified in the early grades could be declassified when reevaluated because of statistical flaws in the system. To account for this, school systems use a combination of criteria and not a sole-source instrument for eligibility. Decision making for placement is often based on combining tests with other considerations, such as recommendations, space availability, what is best for the student, and the sociopolitical realities of the particular system. A good identification system should do the following:

1. Reduce the pool of students who might be eligible
2. Declassify others who were labeled inappropriately under previous criteria
3. Produce changes in the characteristics of the children served

Most school systems do not want to deny services to children who would have qualified for programs under former criteria.

The IQ/achievement discrepancy cannot be said to be relevant or specific to learning disabled children only. It is only one measure of underachievement, and it does not tell us why the student has failed or is failing in school. Also, it is not as valid with gifted learning disabled students or with children who exhibit borderline intelligence. There is still a tendency to overidentify, based on how the calculations are done.

Discrepancy should not be calculated on a single criteria, but on many different academic problems, as well as a display of characteristics that have been continually associated with learning disabilities such as attention disorders, social inadequacies, or language deficits.

Most states require additional procedures to determine "genuine" learning disability, especially with bright students. Uniform practices among states are not envisioned for the near future because of the use of different cutoffs and different formulas. Another questionable area deals with the prognosis of long-term academic outcomes. More stringent discrepancy criteria may not tell us who can be best served by learning disability programs.

Overall, the IQ/achievement discrepancy approach offers an objective approach to identification that will solve some important problems for schools. This does not imply that the most effective forms of service will be provided. The identification of coexisting problems is important in defining a student. It is necessary to get as much reliable data as possible under optimal and sometimes not so optimal conditions. This is important prior to the labeling process so that we will avoid misidentification and misplacement of students. The power of sociopolitical realities and numbers of students presently qualified for limited spaces cannot be underestimated in the total picture of the labeling process.

Finally, the important outcome of the diagnostic profile is a workable and effective treatment strategy. Although the etiology provides us with a basis for understanding the problem, it is the good work of the educator in programming for the variability exhibited by these learners that is really the key factor in the education process.

CONTINUOUS PROGRESS EVALUATION

Continuous progress for each learner is based on his or her rate of learning. The teacher needs to formulate some realistic expectations based on each student's previous learning. Continuous progress assessment from week to week can include changes in such factors as school attendance, time on-task, ability to work in groups or independently, and attitude toward peers and teachers.

After establishing a rate of learning for a subject level, such as the number of new reading sight words learned over a two-week period, or the number of words the student learned to define over two weeks, or the number of stories the student read over two weeks, or the number of new math concepts learned over two weeks, the teacher can establish a baseline of learning. It is relatively easy then to make comparisons based on projected objectives. It is important to get baseline data for continuous comparison. The following are additional considerations in the area of continuous-progress evaluation:

1. The perceptive teacher is constantly evaluating, accepting, and rejecting, and at the same time reprogramming in keeping with the student's needs at a particular time.

2. The teacher who uses a continuous progress mode can differentiate when a student is taking a day off to daydream from when he or she is frustrated by the work or is emotionally upset. The perceptive teacher knows when to be there ahead of time and how to get the student back into academic activity.

3. Good observation must become a habit. Teachers need to be looking and listening all the time. The "well-behaved" student with learning problems often loses out and may be ignored.

4. One-time testing often gives spurious results, but continuous evaluation allows a teacher to look at students at different times in different ways while they are doing similar or the same activities.

5. By keeping a daily or weekly anecdotal record, or log, for students exhibiting problems, the instructor can constantly document students' performances.

6. All testing does not have to be standardized. When an auspicious time occurs, use a checklist or a quick informal test based on the material to be learned.

7. Teachers are encouraged to train others to observe for them as a part of the continuous evaluation of students. Paraprofessionals, volunteers, tutors, and the students themselves can be taught methods of charting progress.

8. The teacher can ask the students to evaluate their own feelings about their progress in academics, social adjustment, or their goals. Is there a discrepancy between the teacher's evaluation and the students' evaluation? Some students may not see the important progress they have made.

9. One problem for a team of teachers involved in tracking the continuous progress of a student is finding time during the school day to get together to share records, classwork, testing, etc., and to discuss the student's progress. Early in the year, the school staff should establish a procedure by which volunteers, aides, or others can be used to free the teachers for urgent consultations. For less urgent cases, the teachers can share information by exchanging folders, clipboards, or using daily summary sheets of progress.

Further discussion of the classroom management of continuous evaluation and sample forms will be found in Chapter 7.

Chapter 6

Assessment Devices and Procedures

CHAPTER OUTLINE

OVERVIEW

This chapter includes checklists, screening and assessment devices, sources of additional testing instruments, and some general procedures for assessing students that can be administered by teachers.

Most authorities agree that teachers can predict with a fair degree of accuracy those students who will have learning problems in future grades. A great deal depends on good observation. The materials in this chapter will enable teachers to identify potentially "at-risk" students. Early intervention is an important step in designing programs for these students.

MANN-SUITER-McCLUNG DEVELOPMENTAL CHECKLISTS

The Mann-Suiter-McClung Development Checklists (Form A, Ages 4–6; Form B, Age 6 and Over) are screening devices that can be used to determine the presence or absence of prerequisite critical language skills for subject level learning in students. The checklists can be used in a variety of settings by anyone involved in the diagnostic-prescriptive process. Trained paraprofessionals, aides, parents, or volunteers can give the checklists. They can be used as a checklist only or as an ongoing evaluation of the student's progress. For ongoing evaluation, the examiner records the date on the list when it appears that the student has mastered or shown improvement in the task under concern. Directions and items can be modified for any school in accordance with local norms or language. (See Forms 6–1 and 6–2.)

Suggestions for Observation Using the Checklists

It should be noted that items checked yes indicate difficulties in an area. Items checked no indicate no problem for the particular item. For younger children, use good judgment. Only check items yes for them if the behavior appears to be excessive for their age group (speech is a good example).

Suggestions for using the checklists for one student or a group of students include the following:

1. Administer one section of the checklist at a time. During a segment of time (e.g., several days or a week), observe the particular students and check only one area, such as auditory. Place one or more copies of the auditory section on a clipboard and carry it from place to place. Also attach a list of all of the names of the students in a class or group. As you check a particular area for a few students, generally notice the behavior of all of the students. Star the names of those that may need more in-depth observation. Add additional sections as needed.
2. Observe one student or a few students and complete an entire checklist.
3. Have other people aid in checking selected items. The following support personnel, in addition to volunteers, parents, tutors, and aides, may assist in parts of the checklist:
   a. Auditory—speech and language teachers, music teachers, nurse
   b. Visual—nurse
   c. Motor—physical education teacher
   d. Speech—speech teacher
   e. Language—speech teacher, reading teacher
   f. Behavioral-cognitive factors—counselors, psychologists
4. Counselors or social workers who make home visits can use selected items on the checklist when interviewing the parents or guardians.
5. Use the checklist during parent-teacher conferences to gain input from the parents. Parts of the checklist can be sent home prior to the conference. The checklist will provide indications of both strengths and weaknesses that should be discussed. As an interpreter of data to parents,

consider the language used in describing learning problems.
6. Use the checklist before a group discussion or school staff meeting concerning a student with learning or behavior problems. The specific items of a checklist will provide those discussing a student's problems with professional and accurate information to begin to seek a solution.
7. A checklist may give insight into areas of the curriculum that are being neglected. By quickly perusing the checklist, you may find areas where either diagnostic or curriculum materials are needed.
8. Many teachers direct interns or student teachers for their clinical or classroom teaching experiences. A checklist provides the beginning teacher with parameters of what to look for in students. This information will aid the student teacher in documenting observational experiences.
9. Use the checklist to discuss strengths and weaknesses with the student. It may not be necessary to actually show the student the checklist, but it will help you to remember to enumerate what the student can do. The self-concept of the student is especially important if he or she perceives that people are looking at areas that may be very sensitive and personal.
10. Use the checklist as a guide to additional screening and more formal testing. Time is a critical concern for most classroom teachers. Careful observation should help the teacher focus in on the critical next areas to be evaluated.
11. Under *Other,* list items that are specific to a particular classroom.

Performance Implications

1. Look for clusters of behavior within an area. This will provide a basis for additional screening of certain areas.
2. Focus on what is relevant. Some students may exhibit an overall immaturity, lack of readiness, or slower-than-normal rate of development. By being aware of certain critical areas it will be easier to provide an individualized educational program for the learner.
3. Match the checked items on the checklist to achievement testing and look for consistent or inconsistent patterns.
4. Wherever multiple causations are listed in parentheses after an item and you have doubts about

MANN-SUITER-McCLUNG DEVELOPMENTAL CHECKLIST—REVISED (FORM A)

EXAMINER _____ DATE _____

NAME _____ ADDRESS _____

DATE OF BIRTH _____ SEX _____ RACE _____ PHONE _____

SCHOOL _____ TEACHER _____ GRADE _____

NUMBER IN FAMILY _____ POSITION IN FAMILY _____ GLASSES _____ HEARING AID _____

BILINGUAL _____ NATIVE LANGUAGE _____ NURSERY _____

PERTINENT FACTS KNOWN IN PRE-SCHOOL HISTORY _____

_____

_____

Ages 4–6

AUDITORY (SENSORY, PERCEPTION, MEMORY)	YES	NO
1. The child's voice is excessively loud.	——	——
(hearing) excessively soft.	——	——
monotone.	——	——
2. The child fails to tell when sounds are the same or different (discrimination).	——	——
3. The child fails to follow three directions (memory-sequence)	——	——
4. The child fails to follow the rhythm in band playing activities (memory-sequence)	——	——
5. The child is unable to identify most of the letter names (visual-auditory associative memory)	——	——
6. The child is unable to identify rhyming words (discrimination)	——	——
7. Other _____		
_____	——	——

VISUAL (SENSORY, PERCEPTION, MEMORY)

	YES	NO
8. Squinting, redness, or watering of the eyes is present (ocular-motor).	——	——
9. The child's eyes appear to be crossed (ocular-motor).	——	——
10. The child works close to the paper or desk (acuity/ocular-motor).	——	——
11. The child is unable to tell when objects are different or the same (discrimination).	——	——
12. The child is unable to match shapes or forms (discrimination).	——	——
13. The child is unable to do simple puzzles (discrimination/closure).	——	——
14. The child is unable to sort objects by color (discrimination/motor or color vision disorder).	——	——
15. The child is unable to sort objects by size (discrimination/motor).	——	——
16. The child is unable to sort objects by shape (discrimination/motor).	——	——
17. The child is unable to match letters, numerals, and simple words (discrimination).	——	——
18. The child fails to find objects or pictures of objects hidden amongst irrelevant background (figure-ground).	——	——
19. The child has difficulty in completing work presented on a crowded page (figure-ground).	——	——
20. The child is unable to identify missing parts in pictures of familiar objects (closure).	——	——
21. Other _____		
_____	——	——

(continued)

MOTOR (GROSS, FINE, BODY IMAGE, LATERALITY, SPATIAL-TEMPORAL)

		YES	NO
22. The child fails to do the following:			
(gross motor) run _____		____	____
jump _____		____	____
hop _____		____	____
skip _____		____	____
23. The child is unable to throw a ball. (gross motor)		____	____
24. The child falls often. (balance/coordination)		____	____
25. The child excessively drops things (e.g., pencil, eraser). (fine motor)		____	____
26. The child is unable to string beads. (fine motor/visual)		____	____
27. The child is unable to hold a pencil or crayon properly. (fine motor)		____	____
28. The child fails to color within boundaries. (fine motor)		____	____
29. The child fails to cut. (fine motor)		____	____
30. The child fails to tie shoes and button buttons, etc. (fine motor)		____	____
31. The child fails to use one hand consistently. (handedness)		____	____
32. The child is unable to copy a circle. (fine motor/visual)		____	____
33. The child is unable to copy a square. (fine motor/visual)		____	____
34. The child is unable to print his or her name. (fine motor)		____	____
35. The child is unable to locate and name the different parts of his or her body. (body image)		____	____
36. The child is always stepping on someone's feet. (spatial)		____	____
37. The child is unable to estimate larger or smaller. (spatial)		____	____
38. The child tries to stuff big things into little places. (spatial)		____	____
39. Other _____			
_____		____	____

SPEECH

Articulation

40. The student distorts sounds or words (e.g., *shing/sing*).   ____ ____
41. The student omits sounds (e.g., *hep/help.*).   ____ ____
42. The student substitutes one sound for another (e.g., *wead/read*).   ____ ____
43. The student uses immature speech patterns (baby talk).   ____ ____
44. The student exhibits sloppy speech.   ____ ____
45. The student protrudes his or her tongue for *s* and *z* sounds.   ____ ____

Voice

46. The student's voice is weak or soft and can hardly be heard. (volume/check hearing) ____ ____
47. The student speaks excessively loud. (volume/check hearing)   ____ ____
48. The student's voice is husky, hoarse, nasal, breathy, or guttural. (quality)   ____ ____
49. The student speaks in a monotonous voice.   ____ ____

Fluency

50. The student repeats syllables, words, and phrases.   ____ ____
51. The student's speech is irregular, exhibiting sudden starts or stops.   ____ ____
52. The student talks too fast and therefore is difficult to understand.   ____ ____
53. The student finds it difficult to get the words out. (looks like stuttering)   ____ ____

Other Problems

54. The student stutters or stammers, which includes repetition of syllables or words, repetition
    and prolongation of sounds, and spasms and distortions of the face and organs of speech. ____ ____

(continued)

	YES	NO
55. The student exhibits cleft palate speech. (nasal quality)	——	——
56. The student exhibits cerebral palsied speech (slow, labored, and spasmodic).	——	——
57. The student avoids speaking in classroom activities.	——	——
58. The student avoids speaking to peers.	——	——
59. The student's speech deteriorates under stress.	——	——
60. Other _____	——	——

LANGUAGE (RECEPTION, EXPRESSION)

61. The child consistently fails to understand directions. (reception)	——	——
62. The child is unable to associate common objects, such as a dog with a bone. (reception)	——	——
63. The child becomes confused by conversation. (reception)	——	——
64. The child is unable to classify objects by category, such as dogs, cats, vehicles. (reception)	——	——
65. The child fails to understand the language of space (e.g., *over, under, between, less*) and time (e.g., *early, late, soon, after*). (reception/spatial-temporal)	——	——
66. The child talks in disconnected phrases. (expression)	——	——
67. The child communicates with gestures and sounds. (expression)	——	——
68. The child speaks in single words or short phrases only. (expression)	——	——
69. The child fails to name familiar objects. (reception/expression)	——	——
70. The child is unable to state full name, age, home address. (reception/expression)	——	——
71. Other _____	——	——

BEHAVIORAL-COGNITIVE

Aggressive (Acting Out/Passive)

72. The student is overtly or passively negative and does not do what is required of him/her.	——	——
73. The student is irritable and unhappy.	——	——
74. The student is destructive of his/her own belongings.	——	——
75. The student is destructive of other people's property.	——	——
76. The student is hot-tempered and flares up easily.	——	——
77. The student is disruptive (moves about excessively and bothers other children).	——	——
78. The student's behavior provokes unkind attitudes and expressions from others.	——	——
79. The student is poorly motivated and appears not to care about school.	——	——

Sensitive-Withdrawn

80. The student exhibits feelings of insecurity.	——	——
81. The student becomes unhappy or cries easily.	——	——
82. The student likes to be left alone and withdraws from others.	——	——
83. The student is shy in social situations.	——	——
84. The student exhibits little self-confidence.	——	——

Immature-Dependent

85. The student requires constant direction and relies a great deal on others.	——	——
86. The student prefers to play or interact with younger individuals.	——	——
87. The student does not attend to activities that require a degree of concentration.	——	——
88. The student is easily influenced by others.	——	——
89. The student appears to be absentminded or lost in thought to excess.	——	——

(continued)

	YES	NO

Psychotic-Neurotic

90. The student enjoys inflicting physical pain on self and/or others. ____ ____
91. The student feels that people want to physically hurt him/her. ____ ____
92. The student exhibits compulsive behavior, such as excessive hand washing or door opening. ____ ____
93. The student appears to be extremely nervous. ____ ____
94. The student thinks that everyone is talking about and plotting against him/her. ____ ____
95. The student exhibits *unusual* fears (e.g., water, heights, dirt, taking tests). ____ ____

Delinquent-Unorthodox

96. The student rejects figures representing authority. ____ ____
97. The student adheres to a gang's code of ethics and morality. ____ ____
98. The student is often truant from school. ____ ____
99. The student seeks the company of other delinquents. ____ ____
100. The student does not express remorse for delinquent behavior. ____ ____
101. Other _____

_____ ____ ____

Social Perception (Cognitive-Social Skills)

102. The student reacts inappropriately to situations, criticisms, and guidance from others. ____ ____
103. The student fails to get meaning from gestures and expressions of others. ____ ____
104. The student loses the essence of the event in the plot of stories read to him/her, films, stories on television, etc. ____ ____
105. The student misunderstands motives (why people do what they do). ____ ____
106. The student fails to associate an incident with its implications. ____ ____
107. The student consistently says the inappropriate thing at the inappropriate time. ____ ____
108. Other _____

_____ ____ ____

Hyperactivity (Attention Deficit)

109. The student exhibits excessive movement and verbal behavior. ____ ____
110. The student cannot control his/her movements. ____ ____
111. The learner is overactive and constantly out of seat. ____ ____
112. The learner exhibits inappropriate social behavior. ____ ____

Inattention (Attention Deficit)

113. The student does not use reflective behavior in learning. ____ ____
114. The child responds too quickly and often inappropriately. ____ ____
115. The learner exhibits poor sustained attention. ____ ____
116. The student seems to lack insightful thinking. ____ ____

Impulsivity (Attention Deficit)

117. The learner is impulsive and unpredictable in his/her actions. ____ ____
118. The learner responds too quickly and is more often wrong than not in his/her response. ____ ____
119. The student is not reflective in his/her approach to problems. ____ ____
120 The learner does not or cannot monitor his/her own behavior. ____ ____
121. The student seems to rush into activities before thinking out what is required. ____ ____

(continued)

Distractibility (Attention Deficit)   YES   NO
122. The learner is very active and easily overstimulated. (distractible)   ——   ——
123. The learner is unable to stay in his/her seat for a reasonable period of time. (distractible)   ——   ——

Perseveration and Disinhibition
124. The student has to do things one more time or report a previous act that is no longer
     appropriate. (perseveration)   ——   ——
125. The student is easily carried away by his/her own thoughts, giving inappropriate answers
     to questions. (disinhibition)   ——   ——
126. Other _____
     _____   ——   ——

Cognitive-Motivational (Learned Helplessness, Attribution, Locus of Control, and Self-Efficacy)
127. The student does not react normally to criticism (learned helplessness)   ——   ——
128. The learner has a low expectation for future success. (learned helplessness)   ——   ——
129. The student seems negative and just does not try. (learned helplessness)   ——   ——
130. The student feels he/she is stupid and has bad luck. (attribution)   ——   ——
131. The student gives up before trying. (attribution)   ——   ——
132. The learner blames others for his/her failure. (attribution)   ——   ——
133. The learner feels he/she cannot control his/her environment. (locus of control)   ——   ——
134. The student feels he/she is controlled by good or bad luck. (locus of control)   ——   ——
135. The learner blames the work for his/her problems, not his/her effort. (locus of control) ——   ——
136. The student retreats from classwork and wastes a lot of time. (self-efficacy)   ——   ——
137. The learner knows what to do but says he/she cannot do it. (self-efficacy)   ——   ——
138. The student has a failure attitude. (self-efficacy)   ——   ——
139. Other _____
     _____   ——   ——

MANN-SUITER-McCLUNG DEVELOPMENTAL CHECKLIST—REVISED (FORM B)

EXAMINER _____ DATE _____

NAME _____ ADDRESS _____

DATE OF BIRTH _____ SEX _____ RACE _____ PHONE _____

SCHOOL _____ TEACHER _____ GRADE _____

NUMBER IN FAMILY _____ POSITION IN FAMILY _____ GLASSES _____ HEARING AID _____

BILINGUAL _____ NATIVE LANGUAGE _____ NURSERY _____

PERTINENT FACTS KNOWN IN PRE-SCHOOL HISTORY _____

_____

_____

Age 6 and Over

AUDITORY (SENSORY, PERCEPTION, MEMORY)   YES   NO

1. The child's voice is excessively loud.   ____   ____
   (hearing)   excessively soft.   ____   ____
                          monotone.   ____   ____
2. The child consistently asks to have words or directions repeated (hearing/memory).   ____   ____
3. The child fails to tell when sounds are the same or different (discrimination).   ____   ____
4. The child is unable to pay attention to speech or other activities when there is noise in the room or in the background (attention).   ____   ____
5. The child fails to follow three directions (memory-sequence).   ____   ____
6. The child fails to transfer sounds, for example, understanding that the sound *m* in the word *man* is the same as the sound *m* in the word *mop* (auditory-auditory association).   ____   ____
7. The child is unable to identify most of the letter sounds (visual-auditory associative memory).   ____   ____
8. The child is unable to identify most of the letter names (visual-auditory associative memory).   ____   ____
9. The student is unable to distinguish between similar sounding letters *(d/t, p/b)* (hearing/discrimination).   ____   ____
10. The student fails to blend letter sounds into words (e.g., *c—a—t*) (closure/blending).   ____   ____
11. The student fails to state the days of the week in sequence (memory-sequence).   ____   ____
12. The student fails to state the months of the year in sequence (memory-sequence).   ____   ____
13. The student fails to repeat word sentences in the correct sequence (memory-sequence).   ____   ____
14. Other _____

_____

VISUAL (SENSORY, PERCEPTION, MEMORY)

15. Squinting, redness, or watering of the eyes is present. (ocular-motor)   ____   ____
16. The child's eyes appear to be crossed. (ocular-motor)   ____   ____
17. The child works close to the paper or desk. (acuity/ocular-motor)   ____   ____
18. The child is unable to do simple puzzles. (discrimination/closure)   ____   ____
19. The child is unable to match letters, numerals, and simple words. (discrimination)   ____   ____
20. The child has difficulty in completing work presented on a crowded page. (figure-ground)   ____   ____

(continued)

	YES	NO

21. Other _____ ____ ____

22. The student fails to keep his or her place on a page when reading material at the independent level. (figure-ground) ____ ____
23. The student is unable to copy from the chalkboard without excessive eye movements going from the chalkboard to the paper. (memory-vision) ____ ____
24. Other _____ ____ ____

MOTOR (GROSS, FINE, BODY IMAGE, LATERALITY, SPATIAL-TEMPORAL)

25. The child fails to do the following:
   (gross motor) run _____ ____ ____
   jump _____ ____ ____
   hop _____ ____ ____
   skip _____ ____ ____
26. The child is unable to throw a ball. (gross motor) ____ ____
27. The child excessively drops things (e.g., pencil, eraser). (fine motor) ____ ____
28. The child is unable to hold a pencil or crayon properly. (fine motor) ____ ____
29. The child fails to color within boundaries. (fine motor) ____ ____
30. The child fails to cut on the line. (fine motor) ____ ____
31. The child fails to tie shoes and button buttons, etc. (fine motor) ____ ____
32. The child fails to use one hand consistently. (handedness) ____ ____
33. The child is unable to copy a circle. (fine motor/visual) ____ ____
34. The child is unable to copy a square. (fine motor/visual) ____ ____
35. Other _____ ____ ____

36. The student is unable to catch a ball. (gross motor) ____ ____
37. The student fails to jump rope in a coordinated manner. (balance/coordination) ____ ____
38. The student is unable to identify left and right sides of the body. (laterality) ____ ____
39. The student fails to perform exercises and sports activities appropriate to his or her age group in a coordinated manner. (motor) ____ ____
40. The student is unable to draw a human figure with the body parts in proper position and correct relationship.(body image) ____ ____
41. The student is unable to tell time. (spatial-temporal) ____ ____
42. The student is unable to copy a diamond. (fine motor/visual) ____ ____
43. The student is unable to write letters, numerals, and words legibly. (fine motor/spatial) ____ ____
44. Other _____ ____ ____

SPEECH

Articulation
45. The student distorts sounds or words (e.g., *shing/sing*). ____ ____
46. The student omits sounds (e.g., *hep/help*). ____ ____
47. The student substitutes one sound for another (e.g., *wead/read*). ____ ____
48. The student uses immature speech patterns (baby talk). ____ ____

(continued)

	YES	NO
49. The student exhibits sloppy speech.	___	___
50. The student protrudes his or her tongue for *s* and *z* sounds.	___	___

Voice

51. The student's voice is weak or soft and can hardly be heard (volume/check hearing)	___	___
52. The student speaks excessively loud. (volume/check hearing)	___	___
53. The student's voice is husky, hoarse, nasal, breathy, or guttural. (quality)	___	___
54. The student speaks in a monotonous voice.	___	___

Fluency

55. The student repeats syllables, words, and phrases.	___	___
56. The student's speech is irregular, exhibiting sudden starts or stops.	___	___
57. The student talks too fast and therefore is difficult to understand.	___	___
58. The student finds it difficult to get the words out. (looks like stuttering)	___	___

Other Problems

59. The student stutters or stammers, which includes repetition of syllables of words, repetition and prolongation of sounds, and spasms and distortions of the face and organs of speech.	___	___
60. The student exhibits cleft palate speech. (nasal quality)	___	___
61. The student exhibits cerebral palsied speech (slow, labored, and spasmodic).	___	___
62. The student avoids speaking in classroom activities.	___	___
63. The student avoids speaking to peers.	___	___
64. The student's speech deteriorates under stress.	___	___
65. Other _____	___	___

LANGUAGE (RECEPTION, EXPRESSION)

66. The child consistently fails to understand directions. (reception)	___	___
67. The child becomes confused by conversation. (reception)	___	___
68. The child fails to understand the language of space (e.g., *over, under, between, less*) and time (e.g., *early, late, soon, after*). (reception/spatial-temporal)	___	___
69. The child talks in disconnected phrases. (expression)	___	___
70. The child communicates with gestures and sounds. (expression)	___	___
71. The child speaks in single words or short phrases only. (expression)	___	___
72. The child fails to name familiar objects. (reception/expression)	___	___
73. The child is unable to state his/her full name, age, and home address. (reception/expression)	___	___
74. Other _____	___	___
75. The student fails to recognize multiple meanings of words (e.g., *sail, sale*). (reception)	___	___
76. The student fails to interpret cause-effect situations or relationships. (reception)	___	___
77. The student uses words like *watchamacallit* or has strange words for common things with his/her experience. (expression)	___	___
78. The student fails to express himself/herself verbally in a meaningful manner. (reception/expression)	___	___
79. The student fails to express himself/herself in written communication in a meaningful manner. (reception/expression)	___	___

(continued)

	YES	NO

80. The student is unable to relate facts and a sequence of events about a past experience. (reception/expression) _____ _____
81. The student is unable to read a paragraph or story at the independent level and orally paraphrase it. (reception/expression) _____ _____
82. Other _____

_____ _____ _____

BEHAVIORAL-COGNITIVE

Aggressive (Acting Out/Passive)
83. The student is overtly or passively negative and does not do what is required of him/her. _____ _____
84. The student is irritable and unhappy. _____ _____
85. The student is destructive of his/her own belongings. _____ _____
86. The student is destructive of other people's property. _____ _____
87. The student is hot-tempered and flares up easily. _____ _____
88. The student is disruptive (moves about excessively and bothers other children). _____ _____
89. The student's behavior provokes unkind attitudes and expressions from others. _____ _____
90. The student is poorly motivated and appears not to care about school. _____ _____

Sensitive-Withdrawn
91. The student exhibits feelings of insecurity. _____ _____
92. The student becomes unhappy or cries easily. _____ _____
93. The student likes to be left alone and withdraws from others. _____ _____
94. The student is shy in social situations. _____ _____
95. The student exhibits little self-confidence. _____ _____

Immature-Dependent
96. The student requires constant direction and relies a great deal on others. _____ _____
97. The student prefers to play or interact with younger individuals. _____ _____
98. The student does not attend to activities that require a degree of concentration. _____ _____
99. The student is easily influenced by others. _____ _____
100. The student appears to be absentminded or lost in thought to excess. _____ _____

Psychotic-Neurotic
101. The student enjoys inflicting physical pain on self and/or others. _____ _____
102. The student feels that people want to physically hurt him/her. _____ _____
103. The student exhibits compulsive behavior, such as excessive hand washing or door opening. _____ _____
104. The student appears to be extremely nervous. _____ _____
105. The student thinks that everyone is talking about and plotting against him/her. _____ _____
106. The student exhibits *unusual* fears (e.g., water, heights, dirt, taking tests). _____ _____

Delinquent-Unorthodox
107. The student rejects figures representing authority. _____ _____
108. The student adheres to a gang's code of ethics and morality. _____ _____
109. The student is often truant from school. _____ _____
110. The student seeks the company of other delinquents.
111. The student does not express remorse for delinquent behavior.
112. Other _____

_____ _____ _____

(continued)

Social Perception (Cognitive-Social Skills)   YES   NO
113. The student reacts inappropriately to situations, criticisms, and guidance from others.   _____ _____
114. The student fails to get meaning from gestures and expressions of others.   _____ _____
115. The student loses the essence of the event in the plot of stories read to him/her, films,
     stories on television, etc.   _____ _____
116. The student misunderstands motives (why people do what they do).   _____ _____
117. The student fails to associate an incident with its implications.   _____ _____
118. The student consistently says the inappropriate thing at the inappropriate time.   _____ _____
119. Other _____
     _____   _____ _____

Hyperactivity (Attention Deficit)
120. The student exhibits excessive movement and verbal behavior.   _____ _____
121. The student cannot control his/her movements.   _____ _____
122. The learner is overactive and constantly out of seat.   _____ _____
123. The learner exhibits inappropriate social behavior.   _____ _____

Inattention (Attention Deficit)
124. The student does not use reflective behavior in learning.   _____ _____
125. The child responds too quickly and often inappropriately.   _____ _____
126. The learner exhibits poor sustained attention.   _____ _____
127. The student seems to lack insightful thinking.   _____ _____

Impulsivity (Attention Deficit)
128. The learner is impulsive and unpredictable in his/her actions.   _____ _____
129. The learner responds too quickly and is more often wrong than not in his/her response.   _____ _____
130 The student is not reflective in his/her approach to problems.   _____ _____
131. The learner does not or cannot monitor his/her own behavior.   _____ _____
132. The student seems to rush into activities before thinking out what is required.   _____ _____

Distractibility (Attention Deficit)
133. The learner is very active and easily overstimulated. (distractible)   _____ _____
134. The learner is unable to stay in his/her seat for a reasonable period of time. (distractible) _____ _____

Perseveration and Disinhibition
135. The student has to do things one more time or repeat a previous act that is no longer
     appropriate. (perseveration)   _____ _____
136. The student is easily carried away by his/her own thoughts, giving inappropriate answers
     to questions. (disinhibition)   _____ _____
137. Other _____
     _____   _____ _____

*Cognitive-Motivational (Learned Helplessness, Attribution, Locus of Control,
and Self-Efficacy)*
138. The student does not react normally to criticism. (learned helplessness)   _____ _____
139. The learner has a low expectation for future success. (learned helplessness)   _____ _____
140. The student seems negative and just does not try. (learned helplessness)   _____ _____
141. The student feels he/she is stupid and has bad luck. (attribution)   _____ _____
142. The student gives up before trying. (attribution)   _____ _____
143. The learner blames others for his/her failure. (attribution)   _____ _____
144. The learner feels he/she cannot control his/her environment. (locus of control)   _____ _____

(continued)

	YES	NO
145. The student feels he/she is controlled by good or bad luck. (locus of control)	_____	_____
146. The learner blames the work for his/her problems, not his/her effort. (locus of control)	_____	_____
147. The student retreats from classwork and wastes a lot of time. (self-efficacy)	_____	_____
148. The learner knows what to do but says he/she cannot do it. (self-efficacy)	_____	_____
149. The student has a failure attitude. (self-efficacy)	_____	_____
150. Other _____		
_____	_____	_____

what an item may mean, refer to Chapters 1 and 2 or the glossary for an explanation of the terms. The use of these terms by the authors is based on judgment and experience. The terms are to be used as a point of reference and a point of departure. What do we see and where do we go next? The descriptors are used merely to aid the observer in the decoding of a student and to provide a framework of language to communicate observations to others participating in the diagnostic-prescriptive process.

INFORMAL ASSESSMENT

In addition to using a checklist for observation, the instructor can keep an anecdotal log of behavior as the student completes curriculum assignments and interacts with others. As areas of concern appear to cluster (e.g., memory, comprehension), the instructor can use the diagnostic information on the following pages for further study of the student. The observable behaviors in the checklists can be used to set up classroom tasks in order to confirm the types of learning problems that are occurring under instructional circumstances or testing situations. The Mann-Suiter developmental screening devices on the following pages can be used to verify previous screening data and add additional information to the diagnostic profile.

DIAGNOSTIC INFORMATION

Visual Perception (Recognition and Discrimination)

VISUAL DISCRIMINATION
Diagnosis

1. *Observable Behaviors*
   a. The students may know a word in one context but not when it is presented in a new situation.
   b. The students may have difficulty in matching shapes, geometric forms, or symbols (e.g., letters, numerals, words).
   c. The students may have difficulty in recognizing people when they change a characteristic of their physical appearance.
   d. The students cannot discriminate differences and sameness as pertains to objects and symbols.
2. *Mann-Suiter Screening*
   a. Mann-Suiter-McClung Developmental Checklists, pages 156–166.
   b. Mann-Suiter Visual Discrimination Screen, pages 181–183.

3. *Supplementary Evaluation*
   Optional or as deemed appropriate. Refer to additional tests listed on page 213.
   Prescriptive activities are found on page 389.

AUDITORY (SOUND) DISCRIMINATION
Diagnosis

1. *Observable Behaviors*
   a. Student cannot tell when sounds are the same or different.
   b. Students have difficulty with pitch, frequency, and intensity.
   c. Students have difficulty distinguishing human vs. nonhuman sounds.
   d. Students confuse similar sounding letters (e.g., d/t).
   e. Students have problems in learning phonics and in blending sounds.
2. *Mann-Suiter Screening*
   a. Mann-Suiter Auditory Discrimination Screen, page 191.
   b. Mann-Suiter-McClung Developmental Checklists, pages 156–166.
3. *Supplementary Evaluation*
   Optional or as deemed appropriate. Refer to additional tests listed on page 213.

   Prescriptive activities are found on page 390.

FIGURE-GROUND DIFFERENTIATION
Diagnosis

1. *Observable Behaviors*
   a. Students may have difficulty in attending to the task assigned.
   b. Written work may be disorganized.
   c. Students may form letters incorrectly when forced to write on a crowded page.
   d. Students may have difficulty keeping their place while they read or copy material.
   e. Students may skip sections of tests or omit parts in the workbook.
   f. Students may have difficulty in completing work presented on a crowded paper.
   g. The most frequent complaint of the teacher is that the students "never finish their work."
   h. The students may have difficulty in distinguishing an object from the irrelevant background and holding the image while scanning the total pattern.
2. *Mann-Suiter Screening*
   a. Mann-Suiter-McClung Developmental Checklists, pages 156–166.
   b. Mann-Suiter Visual Figure-Ground Screen, pages 175–181.

3. *Supplementary Evaluation*
   Optional or as deemed appropriate. Refer to additional tests listed on page 213.

   Prescriptive activities are found on page 338.

VISUAL CLOSURE—BLENDING
Diagnosis

1. *Observable Behaviors*
   a. Student may have difficulty blending letters into words visually.
   b. Students may be able to read the word *cat*, but if given the letters, they cannot put them together to form the word.
   c. The students may have difficulty in visualizing a "whole" and omit portions or details from objects or symbols.
2. *Mann-Suiter Screening*
   a. Mann-Suiter-McClung Developmental Checklists, pages 156–166.
   b. Mann-Suiter Visual Closure Screen, page 181.
3. *Supplementary Evaluation*
   Optional or as deemed appropriate. Refer to additional tests listed on page 213.

   Prescriptive activities are found on page 392.

AUDITORY CLOSURE (BLENDING)
Diagnosis

1. *Observable Behaviors*
   a. The students cannot blend sounds into syllables and words.
      Example: They can read *c-a-t* in isolation but cannot put the sounds together to make the word *cat*.
   b. Students may not be able to put sounds together to make words that they hear orally.
2. *Mann-Suiter Screening*
   a. Mann-Suiter Auditory Closure (Blending) Screen, page 191.
   b. Mann-Suiter-McClung Developmental Checklists, pages 156–166.
3. *Supplementary Evaluation*
   Optional or as deemed appropriate. Refer to additional tests listed on page 213.

   Prescriptive activities are found on page 393.

Visual Memory

Diagnosis

1. *Observable Behaviors*
   a. The students may recognize the symbol when given a model but cannot recall it.

   b. The students often experience more difficulty in spelling and writing than in reading.
   c. The students cannot "see" things or symbols in their mind's eye.
   d. The students may be able to remember all of the parts but get them in the wrong sequence (hpoe for hope). (sequencing)
   e. The students may be erratic or variable in the way they sequence words, spelling the word *the*, for example, *the, hte, or teh;* or they may have a fixed wrong image, spelling the word *the*, for example, *teh* consistently. The latter problem appears to be more difficult to ameliorate. (sequencing)
2. *Mann-Suiter Screening*
   a. Mann-Suiter-McClung Developmental Checklists, pages 156–166.
   b. Mann-Suiter Visual Memory Screen, page 189.
3. *Supplementary Evaluation*
   Optional or as deemed appropriate. Refer to additional tests listed on page 213.

   Prescriptive activities are found on page 394.

Auditory Memory-Sequencing

Diagnosis

1. *Observable Behaviors*
   a. Students may not be able to recall (a) nonverbal sounds such as bells, animal sounds, and horns and (b) verbal sounds such as letters, words, or sentences.
   b. Students may have difficulty in following a sequence of directions at home as well as in school.
   c. Students generally are able to understand and to recognize words, but they have difficulty retrieving them.
   d. The student's parents may report that the students never get correct telephone messages.
   e. Memory deficits will also probably be observed by the physical education teacher, music teacher, etc.
2. *Mann-Suiter Screening*
   a. Mann-Suiter-McClung Developmental Checklists, pages 156–166.
   b. Mann-Suiter Auditory Memory Screen, page 194.
3. *Supplementary Evaluation*
   Optional or as deemed appropriate. Refer to additional tests listed on page 213.

   Prescriptive activities are found on page 397.

Visual Language Classification

Diagnosis

1. *Observable Behaviors*
   Students with a visual language classification difficulty often cannot understand differences and sameness by category classification of objects presented visually. For example, when the students are shown a picture of a pencil and asked whether it belongs with a picture of a pen, a ship, a hat, or a cup, they cannot discern the correct classification (in this case, the pencil belongs with the pen, since both are writing tools).
2. *Mann-Suiter Screening*
   a. Mann-Suiter Visual Language Classification Screen, page 197.
   b. Mann-Suiter-McClung Developmental Checklists, pages 156–166.
3. *Supplementary Evaluation*
   Optional or as deemed appropriate. Refer to additional tests listed on page 213.

   Prescriptive activities are found on page 398.

Visual Language Association—Nonsymbolic (Object and Picture Level)

Diagnosis

1. *Observable Behavior*
   Students with this difficulty are unable to understand noncategorical relationships between objects presented to them visually. For example, when the students are shown a picture of bread and asked whether it belongs with a picture of butter, car, door, or crayon, they cannot discern the correct association. In this case, it is bread and butter.
2. *Mann-Suiter Screening*
   a. Mann-Suiter Visual Language Association Screen, page 197.
   b. Mann-Suiter-McClung Developmental Checklists, pages 156–166.
3. *Supplementary Evaluation*
   Optional or as deemed appropriate. Refer to additional tests listed on page 214.

   Prescriptive activities are found on page 400.

Visual Language Association—Symbolic (Letter, Numeral, and Word Decoding and Comprehension Skills)

Diagnosis

1. *Observable Behavior*
   a. Students may not be able to associate a word they can read with the appropriate unit of experience. These students are sometimes referred to as *word callers*. They can read, but do not understand.
   b. The students' verbal or written language and arithmetic may also be affected by this disorder in that they may not be able to associate words or numerals that they see with meaning.
2. *Mann-Suiter Screening*
   a. Mann-Suiter-McClung Developmental Checklists, pages 156–166.
   b. Mann-Suiter Alphabet-Speech Screen, page 194.
   c. Mann-Suiter Developmental Word Recognition Inventories, pages 228–240.
   d. Mann-Suiter Developmental Paragraph Reading Inventories, pages 242–270.
   e. Mann-Suiter Word Reading Screen, pages 271–276.
   f. Mann-Suiter Silent Reading and Written Language Screen, pages 285–301.
   g. Mann-Suiter Vocabulary Screen, pages 277–285.
3. *Supplementary Evaluation*
   Optional or as deemed appropriate. Refer to additional tests listed on page 214.

   Prescriptive activities are found on page 401.

Auditory Language Classification

Diagnosis

1. *Observable Behavior*
   Students with an Auditory Language Classification difficulty often cannot understand difference and sameness by category classification of objects or concepts presented orally. For example, when a student is asked whether a puppy belongs with ship, hat, door, or dog, he or she cannot discern the correct classification of puppy belonging with dog.
2. *Mann-Suiter Screening*
   a. Mann-Suiter-McClung Developmental Checklists, pages 156–166.
   b. Mann-Suiter Auditory Language Classification Screen, page 202.
   c. Mann-Suiter Developmental Reading Inventories, pages 224–301.
3. *Supplementary Evaluation*
   Optional or as deemed appropriate to additional tests listed on page 214.

   Prescriptive activities are found on page 403.

Auditory Language Association

Diagnosis

1. *Observable Behaviors*
   a. Students with this difficulty are unable to understand noncategorical relationships between words presented orally. For example, when the students are asked whether a motor belongs with a door, water, lamp, or car, they cannot discern the correct association of motor with car.
   b. Students with association problems may have difficulty in deriving meaning from words. The students can hear, but cannot associate words with meaning and, therefore, do not understand.
   c. Students may have difficulty in relating the spoken or written word with the appropriate unit of experience. (Note: Sometimes this disorder in its severe form is referred to as *childhood aphasia.)*
   d. Students may be frustrated by conversation.
   e. Difficulty may be evident with descriptors such as adjectives and adverbs.
   f. Verbal expression, or spoken language, is often affected, as are reading, writing, and arithmetic. The students may not be able to carry out a series of directions (check auditory memory).
   g. These students have difficulty with figurative language. For example, the students may not understand such statements as "he was chewed out" or "he has had it."
   h. Students may not be able to associate the *m* sound in *mother* with the *m* sound in *man,* causing difficulty in learning phonics. Students may not transfer the sound of *m* in one word to the sound of *m* in another word (check auditory memory). Ability to make this transfer is a critical skill for success in the first grade. Inability to make the transfer is an auditory-to-auditory language association problem.
   i. Students may not be able to associate the sound of *m* with the symbol *m.* This is an auditory-to-visual association problem. Ability to make this association is another one of the critical skills necessary for success in first-grade language arts.
2. *Mann-Suiter Screening*
   a. Mann-Suiter-McClung Developmental Checklists, pages 156–166.
   b. Mann-Suiter Auditory Language Association Screen, page 202.

   c. Mann-Suiter Developmental Reading Inventories, pages 224–301.
3. *Supplementary Evaluation*
   Optional or as deemed appropriate. Refer to additional tests listed on page 214.

   Prescriptive activities are found on page 404.

Visual Language Association—Graphic (Writing)

Diagnosis

1. *Observable Behaviors*
   a. Students exhibiting a disorder in this area of encoding have problems with writing in terms of using words to express concepts.
   b. Some cannot write a sentence that indicates a complete thought or write a paragraph on a theme.
   c. Others cannot write definitions of words or record in a meaningful sequence an event or real-life experience.
2. *Mann-Suiter Screening*
   a. Mann-Suiter-McClung Developmental Checklists, pages 156–166.
   b. Mann-Suiter Written Language Expression Screen, page 208.
3. *Supplementary Evaluation*
   Optional or as deemed appropriate. Refer to additional tests listed on page 213.

   Prescriptive activities are found on page 464.

Visual Motor—Gross

Diagnosis

1. *Observable Behaviors*
   a. *General Gross Motor*
      (1) Students may have large muscle difficulties that hinder them in meeting the needs of everyday life.
      (2) Students may be poor in sports and appear clumsy and uncoordinated. This condition is especially debilitating because our culture esteems physical agility and participation in sports.
      (3) Students may not be able to throw a ball and may lose their balance easily.
   b. *Balance and Coordination*
      (1) Students may be clumsy or uncoordinated and appear to have poor body control.
      (2) Students may have problems in using both sides of their bodies simultaneously, individually, or alternately.

(3) Students may use so much energy in trying to control their bodies that they do not pay attention to the more important aspects of learning or to what is happening in their environment.

c. *Eye-Foot Coordination*
Difficulty arises when students cannot get their eyes, feet, and thought processes to work together automatically or otherwise to control the movements of their bodies. Problems in this area will affect balance and coordination.

d. *Body Rhythm*
(1) Students may be continually out of step in marching activities.
(2) These are the students who the teacher says, "Just do not do well in band or rhythm activities."
(3) Students may not be able to follow a rhythm in singing.

2. *Mann-Suiter Screening*
Mann-Suiter-McClung Developmental Checklists, pages 000–000.

3. *Supplementary Evaluation*
Optional or as deemed appropriate. Refer to additional tests listed on page 000.

Prescriptive activities are found on page 000.

Visual Motor—Fine (Handwriting)

Diagnosis

1. *Observable Behaviors*
   a. Students with fine motor coordination problems (or fine motor problems) have difficulty in getting their eyes, hands, and thought processes to work together to achieve a given task.
   b. The students' handwriting is often illegible.
   c. The students may have problems in tasks requiring fine motor coordination, such as sorting, tying, bottoning, and cutting.
   d. The students may be clumsy with some tools and avoid activities requiring their use.
   e. Students may lack the finger strength necessary to carry out everyday activities.
   f. Students may not be able to hold a pencil or write using fine motor movements.
   g. Students may not be able to use eating utensils. This inability is related to difficulties with grasping. It is often observed in very young students who use the whole hand to pick something up instead of using the thumb and first two fingers as in a "three-draw chuck" (used in an electric drill).

2. *Mann-Suiter Screening*
   a. Mann-Suiter Visual Motor Screen, page 175.
   b. Mann-Suiter-McClung Developmental Checklists, pages 156–166.

3. *Supplementary Evaluation*
Optional or as deemed appropriate. Refer to additional tests listed on page 213.

Prescriptive activities are found on page 485.

Visual—Body Image

Diagnosis

1. *Observable Behaviors*
   a. The students may have difficulty in relating themselves spatially to their environment. This can also be described as a lack of inner awareness of body as the physical parts of self relate to each other and to the physical environment.
   b. The students may have difficulty in locating different parts of their bodies when asked to do so.
   c. The students may have difficulty in organizing themselves to do a physical task such as moving furniture.
   d. The students may exhibit a faulty body image as indicated by distortions in the Draw-A-Person Test or in their human figure drawings. (Note: This is often developmental in young children.)
   e. The students may exhibit inadequate control of their bodies or clumsiness.

2. *Mann-Suiter Screening*
Mann-Suiter-McClung Developmental Checklists, pages 156–166.

3. *Supplementary Evaluation*
Optional or as deemed appropriate. Refer to additional tests listed on page 213.

Prescriptive activities are found on page 481.

Visual—Spatial-Temporal

Diagnosis

1. *Observable Behaviors*
   a. The students may not be able to judge how far or how near something is in relation to themselves.
   b. The students may not have developed sidedness or laterality. Therefore, they have problems with relating themselves to objects in space.

c. The students may have problems in dressing.
d. The students may have problems with directionality or object-to-object relationships in space. These problems result in difficulty with left-to-right orientation.
e. The students may have difficulty telling time.
f. Some learners cannot organize their thinking sequentially.
g. The students may have difficulty in placing numerals in arithmetic or in numbering down the paper for a spelling test.
h. The students may have a poor sense of direction, easily getting lost and often being unable to find their way home from familiar surroundings.
i. The students may have difficulty in organizing a sequence of movements necessary to carry out a specific task. In some cases, this difficulty may affect the sequencing of letters or numerals, causing "reversals" or inversions. More often, they are a result of poor visual sequential memory.
j. Problems with words that denote space, like *before, after, left, right, in between*, and *beside*, may be evident.

2. *Mann-Suiter Screening*
Mann-Suiter-McClung Developmental Checklists, pages 156–166.

3. *Supplementary Evaluation*
Optional or as deemed appropriate. Refer to additional tests listed on page 213.

Prescriptive activities are found on page 510.

Word Retrieval

Diagnosis

1. *Observable Behaviors*
a. The students exhibit difficulty in recalling or retrieving words for use in speaking.
b. The students may not be able to express themselves in a complete sentence.
c. The students may be able to repeat immediately after they hear a letter or word but be unable to recall after longer periods of time.
d. The students may often use gestures and vocalization to make wants known.
e. Retrieving words can sometimes be achieved when seeing or feeling the concrete object.
f. The students can generally read better silently than orally.
g. The students may have nonfluent speech that includes hesitations like stuttering.

h. The students may not be able to sequence their thoughts or ideas.
i. The students may use word substitution such as *whatchamacallit, thingamajig*, or *gismo*.
j. The students may emit strange sounds for words, such as "I foga da shugum" for "I swallowed the chewing gum." Find out if they can imitate the correct pronunciation.

2. *Mann-Suiter Screening*
a. Mann-Suiter-McClung Developmental Checklists, pages 156–166.
b. Mann-Suiter Verbal Language Expression Screen, page 208.
c. Mann-Suiter Developmental Word-Recognition Inventories, pages 228–240.
d. Mann-Suiter Developmental Paragraph Reading Inventory, pages 242–270.

3. *Supplementary Evaluation*
Optional or as deemed appropriate. Refer to additional tests listed on page 214.

Prescriptive activities are found on page 407.

Syntax and Formulation

Diagnosis

1. *Observable Behaviors*
a. Students with this difficulty have problems with the smooth and natural flow of the English language. They cannot structure thoughts into grammatically correct verbal units or sentences.
b. The students may understand what you say but answer in single words or phrases with inadequate language structure.
c. Syntax may be poor—e.g., students may omit words, distort the order of words, or use poor tense.
d. The students may recognize correct sentence structure but not be able to reproduce a meaningful sequence themselves.
e. The students may use telegraphic speech (e.g., mom—dad—me—go) in attempting to formulate a sentence.
f. The students may have difficulty in expressing ideas or formulating sentences by using words.

2. *Mann-Suiter Screening*
Mann-Suiter-McClung Developmental Checklists, pages 156–166.

3. *Supplementary Evaluation*
Optional or as deemed appropriate. Refer to additional tests listed on page 214.

Prescriptive activities are found on page 407.

Nonverbal Language

Students with a nonverbal language difficulty have problems with assigning meaning to such nonverbal functions as art, religion, music, holidays, and patriotism. There is a language of art and music from which the students cannot derive meaning. Often, a nonverbal language disorder is accompanied by problems in the spatial area.

Diagnosis

1. *Observable Behaviors*
   a. The students may have difficulty judging quantity (e.g., size, time, shape, and distance), as well as the seasons of the year.
   b. The students may not be able to understand religious symbols such as a Star of David, Cross, or Crescent Moon.
   c. The students may not understand the significance of the statue of "Iwo Jima" or the "Washington Monument."
   d. Although the verbal language of the students may be good, or even superior, they appear to have difficulty in formulating good judgment about things that are symbolic.
   e. The students may also exhibit difficulty with social perception involving nonverbal relationships with people.
2. *Mann-Suiter Screening*
   a. Mann-Suiter-McClung Developmental Checklists, pages 156–166.
   b. Mann-Suiter Nonverbal Symbolic Language Screen, page 211.

Prescriptive activities are found on page 409.

Inner-Language

Diagnosis

1. *Observable Behaviors*
   a. Some types of inner-language difficulties are a result of cerebral dysfunction.
   b. Inner-language conflict may result when students have incorporated as their native language a language other than standard English and cannot or will not integrate standard English as a functional language. The other language can be sign language, a foreign language, or a dialect.
   c. The students may think or solve problems in their native language even though they can speak fluent standard English.

d. The students may have three different sounds for the same phonetic construct; for example, a student may say, "bafroom" for *bathroom,* "mover" for *mother,* and "da" for *the,* all indicating three different sounds for *th.*
   e. Some students have internalized the phonetic, or sound, system of a foreign language and have difficulty in learning the English phoneme-grapheme system.

Prescriptive activities are found on page 409.

Speech

Diagnosis

1. *Observable Behaviors*
   a. The students may exhibit poor speech patterns and be unable to say words.
   b. The students have difficulty in retrieving the motor act of speech even if they have a model or can comprehend or recall.
   c. The students may have problems with execution or articulation, exhibiting omissions (leaving out initial, medial, or final sounds), substitutions (*wabbit* for *rabbit*) distortions (lisp, sloppy *s* or a hissing sound), or additions (*sumber* for *summer*) of sounds and words.
   d. The students may use gestures and pantomime a great deal.
   e. In some cases, the tongue appears to be lost in the mouth during speech.
   f. Students will have difficulty imitating words, regardless of whom they are attempting to model.
2. *Mann-Suiter Screening*
   a. Mann-Suiter-McClung Developmental Checklists, pages 156–166.
   b. Mann-Suiter Alphabet-Speech Screen, page 194.
   c. Mann-Suiter Speech Screen, page 205.
3. *Supplementary Evaluation*
   Optional or as deemed appropriate. Refer to additional tests listed on page 214.

Prescriptive activities are found on page 410.

Motor Language Expression: Manual (Hand or Foot)

Diagnosis

1. *Observable Behaviors*
   The students are unable to express manually the function of an object even though, when asked,

they may be able to identify it from among other objects. For example, the students may be able to identify a hammer from among other objects, but not be able to show what to do with it manually.

2. *Mann-Suiter Screening*
   a. Mann-Suiter-McClung Developmental Checklists, pages 156–166.
   b. Mann-Suiter Manual Language Expression Screen, page 205.
3. *Supplementary Evaluation*
   Optional or as deemed appropriate. Refer to additional tests listed on page 214.

Prescriptive activities are found on page 440.

MANN-SUITER DEVELOPMENTAL SCREENING

The Mann-Suiter developmental screening devices are designed to do the following:

1. Supply data to support the information accumulated through the use of the developmental inventories found on pages 175–212.
2. Aid the teacher in focusing specifically on particular problem areas as they relate to language acquisition.
3. Become the basis for the selection of more specific and sophisticated standardized testing in each of the processing areas when deemed necessary.

The skill areas listed can be evaluated in total or in part as the teacher deems necessary for developing educational strategies for particular students. There is no total score. The screening devices are not designed as tests to measure the student's limit in a particular ability. Rather, they are designed to check for the minimum level of readiness abilities necessary for success in basic language tasks. It is our opinion that it is imperative that the teacher know if the student has the minimal critical skills needed for learning how to read, write, or do arithmetic. In screening of this nature, the way the student performs and the quality of his or her response is just as important as the level of achievement, or score. The examiner must try to understand the student's learning style, or patterns of learning, and determine what it is that prevents him or her from learning a particular academic task.

After an extensive review of standardized tests, a criterion of minimal functioning in eighteen areas was identified. The areas (listed in Table 6-1) were pilot tested to eliminate and modify questionable items. The normative population consisted of 436 students, ages four through twelve, with borderline intelligence or above. The population contained students from all socioeconomic levels and from different ethnic and

Table 6-1 Index for the Mann-Suiter Developmental Screening Devices in This Book

List of Screening Devices	Page	Related Activities Page
Visual:		
Visual motor	175	485
Visual figure-ground	175	388
Visual discrimination	181	389
Visual closure—Parts A and B	181	392
Visual memory	189	394
Auditory:		
Auditory discrimination	191	390
Auditory closure	191	393
Auditory memory (sentences)	194	397
Alphabet-Speech (auditory-visual association)	194	425
Language:		
Visual language classification	197	398
Visual language association	197	400
Auditory language classification	202	403
Auditory language association	202	404
Manual language expression	205	410
Speech	205	410
Verbal language expression	208	407
Written language expression	208	464
Nonverbal language	211	409

racial backgrounds. Of the 436, 291 were failing in school and 145 were making satisfactory progress, according to teacher reports.

The students were administered the appropriate subtests. The results were analyzed in relation to specific skills required for success in reading, writing, spelling, and arithmetic. For example, the majority of students who failed the visual motor screen also had difficulty in handwriting. All students who did not have difficulty in handwriting established the lower limit norms for success on the visual motor screen. Performance on the visual closure screen was compared with the student's performance in blending in reading. Visual memory was analyzed in relation to the learner's ability to remember objects, letters, or words, as well as to the learner's disabilities, such as reversals or inversions in reading, writing, spelling, and arithmetic. The same was done with all other subareas. The majority of the academically successful students met the minimum standard in all of the critical subareas, while the majority of failing students failed to meet them.

Initial content validity of the Mann-Suiter developmental screening devices was established by successive usage and review over a period of two years by over 200 teachers, counselors, and psychologists, who were requested to use the screening devices along with what they were already using to identify learning problems in children. They were requested to examine the contents carefully and, after using the devices, make suggestions regarding diagnosis, practicality, and applicability. Since 1974, when the Mann-Suiter screening devices were first published, thousands of educators have used them with students all over the United States and in foreign countries. A survey of many of these educators has indicated that developmental screening is a valuable instrument that can be used by classroom teachers, as well as support personnel, in the assessment of students with learning difficulties.

Table 6-1 is an index of all the Mann-Suiter developmental screening devices in this book.

The Mann-Suiter Developmental Screening Record Form (Form 6-3) can be utilized to summarize the data from the developmental screening devices.

MANN-SUITER VISUAL MOTOR SCREEN

Successful completion of the designs included in the Mann-Suiter Visual Motor Screen (Form 6-4) represents minimal standards for success in handwriting (Ilg & Ames, 1964).

Directions

The student is asked to copy a design exactly the way he or she sees it in each standard. The student is given three changes, but only the best effort is counted. Difficulty with these designs after age seven indicates a need for a program of comprehensive visual-motor activities to develop eye-hand readiness skills.

Normative Data (Ilg and Ames)

Design 1: ◯ A child 3 years of age should be able to make a single circle.

Design 2: ▭ A rectangular shape is normative for children after age 4.

Design 3: △ A triangle is normative for girls after age 5½ and for boys after age 6.

Design 4: ◇ The diamond is normative for children after age 6.

Scoring

Teachers must use good judgment to evaluate students' abilities on this examination. The following should be considered.

1. The lines should be fairly firm and not too erratic.
2. The angles should be good.
3. The basic shape should be easily recognizable and resemble the model.
4. Any minor imperfections should be overlooked. The following symbols should be used for correct and incorrect responses ✓ = correct, ✗ = incorrect.

Things to Look For

1. Does the student switch hands?
2. Does the student make the circle counterclockwise? A counterclockwise circle is normative for (a) right-handed girls by age 5, (b) right-handed boys by age 5½, and (c) left-handed children by age 7–9.
3. Do the reproductions get worse or better with practice?

Note: If necessary, see page 213 for more specific measuring criteria in this area.

MANN-SUITER VISUAL FIGURE-GROUND SCREEN

The Mann-Suiter Visual Figure-Ground Screen (Form 6-5) is designed to determine a student's ability to attend to a particular design (figure) while simultaneously screening out the irrelevant backgound (ground).

Directions

Using a blue, red, or green crayon, the teacher traces the standard in the upper left hand corner, saying to the student, "See how I trace this? You find all of the same thing in the big picture and trace them the way I did." The student is then handed the crayon. If the student cannot trace, he or she should color Designs 1, 3, and 4. If the student traces only one item, the teacher should say, "Can you find any more like it to trace?" If the student traces only part of each figure, the teacher should say, "Did you trace it all?" The teacher should not give any more clues. Note: Check for color blindness.

MANN-SUITER DEVELOPMENTAL SCREENING RECORD FORM

NAME _____ DATE _____

DATE OF BIRTH _____ EXAMINER _____

Screen	Minimal Requirements	Student's Response	Acceptance Yes	No	Date of Mastery
Visual Motor	○, age 3	___	___	___	_____
	☐, age 4	___	___	___	_____
	△, age 6	___	___	___	_____
	◇, age 6	___	___	___	_____
Visual Figure-Ground	10 correct responses, ages 4–5	___	___	___	_____
	12 correct responses, age 6 or older	___	___	___	_____
Visual Discrimination	2 errors, age 5 or older	___	___	___	_____
Visual Closure (Part A)	5 errors, age 4	___	___	___	_____
	3 errors, age 6	___	___	___	_____
Visual Closure (Part B) (for students reading at level one or above)	2 errors, level one	___	___	___	_____
	3 errors, other levels	___	___	___	_____
Visual Memory	3 items, any order, age 5	___	___	___	_____
	4 items, any order, age 6	___	___	___	_____
Auditory Discrimination (Part A)	4 errors, age 6	___	___	___	_____
Auditory Discrimination (Part B)	2 errors, age 7	___	___	___	_____
Auditory Closure (blending)	9 errors, age 6	___	___	___	_____
	4 errors, age 7	___	___	___	_____
Auditory Memory (sentences)	7 item errors, age 5	___	___	___	_____
	4 item errors, age 6	___	___	___	_____
Alphabet-Speech:					
Alphabet sounds (letter)	4 errors, age 7 (Part A)	___	___	___	_____
	1 error, age 8 (Part A)	___	___	___	_____
Alphabet names (letter)	4 errors, age 7 (Part A)	___	___	___	_____
	1 error, age 8 (Part A)	___	___	___	_____
Alphabet digraphs	1 error, age 6 (Part B)	___	___	___	_____

(continued)

Screen	Minimal Requirements	Student's Response	Acceptance Yes	No	Date of Mastery
Visual Language Classification	4 errors, age 4–5	_____	_____	_____	_____
	2 errors, age 6	_____	_____	_____	_____
Visual Language Association	4 errors, 4–5	_____	_____	_____	_____
	2 errors, age 6	_____	_____	_____	_____
Auditory Language Classification	4 errors, age 4–5	_____	_____	_____	_____
	2 errors, age 6	_____	_____	_____	_____
Auditory Language Association	4 errors, ages 4–5	_____	_____	_____	_____
	2 errors, age 6	_____	_____	_____	_____
Manual Language Expression	4 errors, ages 4–5	_____	_____	_____	_____
	2 errors, age 6	_____	_____	_____	_____
Speech	3 item errors, age 4–6	_____	_____	_____	_____
	2 item errors, age 7	_____	_____	_____	_____
Verbal Language Expression	4 correct responses, age 6 (at least one per item)	_____	_____	_____	_____
	6 correct responses, age 7 (at least one per item)	_____	_____	_____	_____
Written Language Expression	teacher judgment	_____	_____	_____	_____
Nonverbal Language	3 errors, age 4–6	_____	_____	_____	_____
	1 error, age 7	_____	_____	_____	_____

COMMENTS:

MANN-SUITER VISUAL MOTOR SCREEN

NAME _____ DATE _____

DATE OF BIRTH _____ HAND USED _____ EXAMINER _____

RESPONSE

1. _____

2. _____

3. _____

4. _____

MANN-SUITER VISUAL FIGURE-GROUND SCREEN

NAME _____ DATE OF BIRTH _____

DATE _____ EXAMINER _____

RESPONSES

1 _____

2. _____

(continued)

RESPONSE

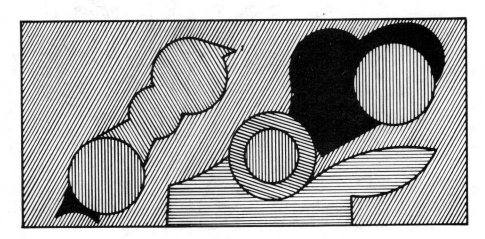

3. _____

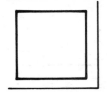

4. _____

TOTAL ACCURATE RESPONSES: _____

Scoring

1. The entire figure must be traced (or colored) to be considered correct. Count crossover in tracing or coloring (part of the tree traced or colored, for example) correct if the student keeps the basic design intact.
2. Ten or more correct responses out of a possible fourteen for children ages 4–5 indicate intact visual figure-ground perception.
   Design 1—three possible correct responses
   Design 2—three possible correct responses
   Design 3—four possible correct responses
   Design 4—four possible correct responses
3. Twelve or more correct responses for students 6 and older suggest intact visual figure-ground perception.
4. Note visual-motor control and compare with the performance in the visual-motor screen.

Things to Look For

1. Does the student become confused and fail to attend to the task?
2. How does the student perform the task? Is the student specific or does he or she just point in a random fashion?
3. Does the student go off on a tangent as a result of the stimulus picture?

Note: See page 213 for more specific evaluation in this area if necessary.

MANN-SUITER VISUAL DISCRIMINATION SCREEN

The Mann-Suiter Visual Discrimination Screen (Form 6-6) will enable the teacher to determine a student's ability to discriminate between designs or symbols that are similar in configuration.

Directions

With a practice example of five images in separate frames, the student should be asked to "Mark the one that looks the same as the first one." (To take this examination the student must understand the meaning of the word *same.*) If the practice response is incorrect, the student should be told which is the correct answer. The teacher should say, pointing, "See, this one is the same as the first one." If the response is correct, then the teacher should say, "Yes, this is the same as this," and point to the proper items. The student should be asked to do the rest by himself or herself and should be reinforced again only if necessary.

Scoring

1. Three or more errors suggest difficulty with visual discrimination for children age 5 or older.
2. The following symbols should be used ✓ = correct, ✗ = incorrect.

Things to Look For

1. Does the student go back and forth many times before making a decision?
2. Does the student have a great deal of erasures?
3. Does the student anchor a finger on the first image as he or she peruses the rest?
4. Does the student verbalize as he or she proceeds through the task?

Note: See page 213 for more specific measurement criteria in this area if necessary.

MANN-SUITER VISUAL CLOSURE SCREEN (PARTS A AND B)

Part A of the Mann-Suiter Visual Closure Screen (Form 6-7) will enable the instructor to determine the student's ability to complete designs and objects by matching and supplying missing parts. Part B tests the student's ability to take letters or letter groups that are somewhat apart from each other and put them together to make words.

Directions (Part A)

Part A of the Mann-Suiter Visual Closure Screen is appropriate for students who are at the readiness stage of development or reading below grade level 2 and exhibiting difficulties in parts-to-whole kinds of activities. Students who are having difficulty with blending in reading should be screened in this area. The instructor may find it valuable to give both Part A and Part B to students reading above grade level who are having difficulty in blending and reading in general. For items 1 through 5 the instructor should point to the standard and say to the student, "See this?" Then, indicating the three alternatives, the instructor should

MANN-SUITER VISUAL DISCRIMINATION SCREEN

NAME _____ DATE _____

DATE OF BIRTH _____ EXAMINER _____

RESPONSE

Practice:

| ○ | □ | ⬭ | △ | ○ | ____ |

1.

| M | T | M | P | O | ____ |

2.

| 3 | 2 | 3 | 5 | 8 | ____ |

3.

| H | M | N | U | H | ____ |

(continued)

RESPONSE

4.

b	D	P	b	G

_____

5.

ME	SHE	WE	HE	ME

_____

6.

SHIP	SNIP	SLIP	SHIP	SKIP

_____

7.

ARE	AIR	FIRE	ARE	ART

_____

8.

e	r	p	e	g

_____

TOTAL INCORRECT: _____

MANN-SUITER VISUAL CLOSURE SCREEN

Part A

NAME _____ DATE _____

DATE OF BIRTH _____ EXAMINER _____

RESPONSE

1. _____

2. _____

3. _____

4. _____

5. _____

(continued)

6. _____ 7. _____ 8. _____ 9. _____

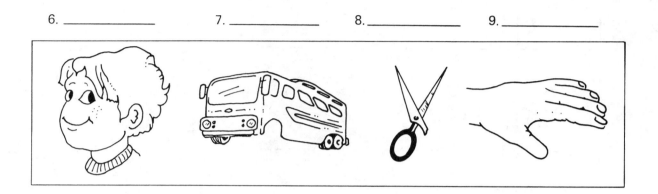

10. _____ 11. _____ 12. _____ 13. _____

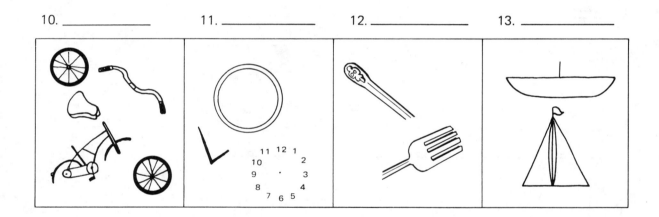

(continued)

RESPONSE

14. _____

15. _____

16. _____

17. _____

18. _____

TOTAL INCORRECT: _____

(continued)

Part B (Ages 6 And Over, Reading Above Level One)

NAME _____ DATE _____

DATE OF BIRTH _____ EXAMINER _____

LEVEL I	RESPONSE	LEVEL II	RESPONSE
c at	_____	p it	_____
n o	_____	f or	_____
r e d	_____	fu n	_____
a n d	_____	b y	_____
y ou	_____	so on	_____
th e	_____	bab y	_____
w e	_____	r i d e	_____
i t	_____	d ow n	_____
y e s	_____	he ad	_____
d og	_____	m other	_____
b i g	_____	ope n	_____
li ke	_____	ve ry	_____
h ave	_____	y e a r	_____
w as	_____	ha ppy	_____
		lett er	_____
		n ext	_____
TOTAL INCORRECT: _____		mor ning	_____
		wit h	_____

TOTAL INCORRECT: _____

(continued)

LEVEL III	RESPONSE	LEVEL IV	RESPONSE
a l o n g	_____	aw ake	_____
gr and pa	_____	gif t	_____
ri ver	_____	mi xed	_____
bl ack	_____	shir t	_____
b at h	_____	tu rn in g	_____
pa rt	_____	fa sten	_____
f ix	_____	lar ge st	_____
foo d	_____	r ained	_____
wa lk	_____	ta lks	_____
cat ch	_____	ca rry ing	_____
t ai l	_____	cof fee	_____
s low	_____	ju ice	_____
tha n	_____	s torm	_____
p uppy	_____	co r ners	_____
la ugh ing	_____	wri tes	_____
f unny	_____	doll ar	_____
fa rm	_____	hour s	_____
s tar t	_____	pe nn ies	_____

TOTAL INCORRECT: _____   TOTAL INCORRECT: _____

say, "Point to the best one that will finish the picture." For items 6 through 9, the instructor should point to each item and say, "See this? Show or tell me what is missing from this picture." Repeat the same directions for each item (picture). For items 10 through 13, the instructor should point to each item and say, "These are parts of something. When you put the parts together, what will the picture be?" The directions should be repeated for each item (picture). For items 14 through 18, the instructor should say, pointing to the model, "See this? Which two of these [pointing to the alternatives] when put together will look like this one [pointing to the first one again]?" The directions should be repeated as necessary.

Scoring (Part A)

1. Six errors or more after age 4 and four errors or more at age 6 and older suggest difficulty with visual closure.
2. Symbols to be used are ✓ = correct, ✓ = incorrect.

Directions (Part B)

Part B of the Mann-Suiter Visual Closure Screen deals with words and is appropriate for students reading below grade five but above the primer level, since word-attack skills are generally well stabilized by the time students have attained at least primer level in reading. The teacher should begin the examination at the level at which the student has experienced 100% word recognition on the Developmental Word-Recognition Reading Inventory (pages 228–240). The teacher should say to the student, "Read the words as I point to them."

Scoring (Part B)

1. Three errors at level 1 or four errors at any other level suggest difficulty with visual closure.
2. Symbols to be used are ✓ = correct, ✓ = incorrect.

Things to look for (Parts A and B)

1. Does the student exhibit guessing or trial-and-error behavior in Part A?
2. How much time does the student take to complete the task?

3. Does the student go back and forth from the standard to the choice excessively?
4. Which part of Part A does the student have difficulty with—matching, missing parts, etc.?
5. Is the student failing this screen also having difficulty dealing with spatial concepts in arithmetic?
6. Does the student know the letter sounds in Part B?
7. Can the learner read the blends in Part B?

Note: See page 213 for more specific evaluation in this area if necessary.

MANN SUITER VISUAL MEMORY SCREEN FOR OBJECTS

The Mann-Suiter Visual Memory Screen for Objects (Form 6-8) is designed to indicate a student's ability to revisualize pictures of common objects presented in groups.

Directions

The teacher says, "I am going to show you a row of little pictures. After I cover the pictures, I want you to tell me each time exactly what pictures you saw. Start at one end of the row each time and tell me all the pictures you saw. Try to tell them to me in the same order they were in a row."

Note: Number the sequence of the responses for diagnostic purposes to get an indication of the order of remembering even though this is not counted in the scoring.

Scoring

1. For children age 5, recalling three items in any order within a row suggests adequate visual memory.
2. For children age 6 and older, recalling four items in any order within a row suggests adequate visual memory.
3. Expose each row for approximately one second for each picture on it. Number one is a practice one and does not count. The order of response does not count in the scoring.
4. The exposure time for each row is as follows:
   Row 1: 2 seconds
   Row 2: 3 seconds
   Row 3: 4 seconds
   Row 4: 5 seconds
5. Use the following symbols to note responses: ✓ = correct , ✓ = incorrect.

MANN-SUITER VISUAL MEMORY SCREEN FOR OBJECTS

NAME _____ DATE _____

DATE OF BIRTH _____ EXAMINER _____

RESPONSE

Practice:

_____

_____

_____

_____

_____

LARGEST TOTAL IN ANY ROW IN ANY ORDER: _____

Things to Look For

1. Note if the student remembers the pictures from left to right or from right to left.
2. Look for perseveration; that is, repeating the same objects over again from the preceding line.

Note: See page 213 for more specific measurement in this area if necessary.

MANN-SUITER AUDITORY DISCRIMINATION SCREEN

Part A of the Mann-Suiter Auditory Discrimination Screen (Form 6-9) will enable the teacher to determine a student's ability to discriminate between words that are similar or different in the way they sound. It requires a comparison of sounds. Part B requires recall at another level of auditory discrimination.

Directions, Part A

1. The student must not see the teacher's face. The student can be turned around, or the teacher can cover his or her own face with a 3″ × 5″ card.
2. The teacher should say, "I am going to say some words and you tell me if they are the same or different." The student must understand the words *same* and *different*. If he or she does not, the teacher can call the student's name and another name for comparison. It is a good idea for the teacher to call the student's name and another name after every five responses or so to make sure the student is attending and understands what is required.
3. The teacher's voice quality must be consistent. It should not be allowed to drop on the second word.
4. On the first administration, an incorrect check mark should be put next to the wrong responses only (✔).
5. Only those responses that were wrong should be readministered immediately, marking them ✔ if wrong again or ✓ if correct.
6. If the learner corrects on the second administration, the response should be counted correct.

Scoring, Part A

Five or more uncorrected errors by children age 6 or older suggest difficulty with auditory discrimination and possible problems with learning through a phonetic approach.

Directions, Part B

Retaining instructions 1, 3, 4, and 6 from Part A, above, the teacher says the following: "The middle sound in the word *cat* is ă. What is the middle sound in the words *sad, bus, hot . . .?*"

Scoring, Part B

Three or more errors at age 7 or older suggest difficulty with auditory analysis, or going from whole to parts, and may affect blending or closure.

Note: More specific evaluation in this area can be found on page 213.

Things to Look For

1. Does the student exhibit a short attention span?
2. Is the student just guessing?
3. Does the student close his or her eyes in order to listen better?
4. Does the student have a speech (articulation) problem?
5. Does the student appear to have a hearing loss (check acuity)?

MANN-SUITER AUDITORY CLOSURE (BLENDING) SCREEN

The Mann-Suiter Auditory Closure (Blending) Screen (Form 6-10) will indicate to the teacher a student's ability to combine sounds that are presented orally to make words.

Directions

The teacher begins by saying, "I am going to make some sounds that make a word. Tell me what the word is after I finish." The teacher says each sound of the word separately with about a second's pause after each sound. If the student's response is incorrect, the teacher repeats the sounds and then says each word and asks which word the sounds were most like. Correctly identifying the word from any three words is not part of the scoring.

Scoring

1. Ten errors or more (excluding word recognition) at age 6 indicates possible difficulty with auditory closure (blending).

MANN-SUITER AUDITORY DISCRIMINATION SCREEN

NAME _____ DATE _____

DATE OF BIRTH _____ EXAMINER _____

Part A

*Discrimination of Initial and
Final Sounds (recognition)*

RESPONSE

1. shine – sign _____
2. tin – thin _____
3. pine – pine _____
4. mob – mop _____
5. mud – mug _____
6. life – like _____
7. very – fairy _____
8. ship – ship _____
9. goal – coal _____
10. moon – noon _____
11. very – berry _____
12. buff – tuff _____
13. run – run _____
14. robe – rode _____
15. bus – buzz _____
16. bill – mill _____
17. brink – drink _____
18. fling – cling _____
19. lake – lake _____
20. scream – stream _____
21. and – end _____

Part B

Discrimination of Medial Sounds (recall analysis)

RESPONSE

1. a sad _____
2. u bus _____
3. o hot _____
4. e pet _____
5. e team _____
6. i like _____
7. o boat _____
8. u mule _____
9. i bit _____
10. a cake _____

TOTAL INCORRECT: _____

*Discrimination of Medial Vowel
Sounds (recognition)*

22. mesh – mush _____
23. slid – sled _____
24. deck – dock _____
25. band – bend _____

TOTAL INCORRECT: _____

MANN-SUITER AUDITORY CLOSURE (BLENDING) SCREEN

NAME _____ DATE _____

DATE OF BIRTH _____ EXAMINER _____

RESPONSE

1. g-oat (bell, good, goat)   _____

2. sh-ip (push, shop, ship)   _____

3. m-e (be, he, me)   _____

4. t-ar (art, tar, rat)   _____

5. sp-ot (spot, pot, stop)   _____

6. dr-e-ss (grass, rage, dress)   _____

7. d-us-t (stem, dust, stair)   _____

8. br-i-ck (crib, brick, strip)   _____

9. p-ai-l (same, pail, late)   _____

10. b-a-g (gab, bag, back)   _____

11. c-a-p (tack, pack, cap)   _____

12. s-u-n (sun, mind, nuts)   _____

13. s-l-a-p (black, rap, slap)   _____

14. l-a-m-p (play, lamp, pack)   _____

15. s-t-r-ing (string, green, rip)   _____

TOTAL INCORRECT: _____

2. Five errors or more (excluding word recognition) at age 7 or older indicates possible difficulty with auditory closure (blending).
3. Symbols used for responses are ✓ = correct, ✓ = incorrect.

Things to Look For

1. Is the student able to repeat the sounds, but not the word?
2. Does the student recognize the word from among the three words?
3. Did the student reverse the whole word—that is, was the sound the student heard last the one with which he or she started the word?
4. Did the student omit one sound of the consonant blend?
5. Did the student reverse part of the word?
6. Consistent failure and difficulties with the above suggests that the student may have difficulty with instruction that emphasizes a phonics approach.

Note: See page 213 for more specific evaluation in this area.

MANN-SUITER AUDITORY MEMORY SCREEN (SENTENCES)

The Mann-Suiter Auditory Memory Screen (Sentences) (Form 6-11) is designed to determine a student's ability to repeat a sentence, a sequence of words that is characterized by a complete thought (meaning).

Directions

The teacher tells the student, "I am going to say something to you. When I finish, you say just what I said." The teacher proceeds to enunciate the sentences slowly, not repeating any. The teacher *administers all items* until the student exhibits one or more errors in eight sentences for age 5 or in five sentences for ages 6 and over.

Scoring

1. Record as errors words omitted and words added.
2. One or more errors in each of eight sentences (items) suggests difficulty with auditory memory in children age 5.

3. One or more errors in each of five sentences (items) suggests difficulty with auditory memory in students ages 6 and older.
4. Symbols for scoring are ✓ = correct, ✓ = incorrect.

Things to Look For

1. Look for associative errors, such as saying *house* for *home.*
2. Note omission of endings such as *ed, ing,* and *s.* Do not record it as wrong if this appears to be a cultural phenomenon.
3. Although the student may have given the wrong sequence, note the fact that he or she gets the gist of the meaning.

Note: See page 213 for more specific evaluation in this area if necessary.

MANN-SUITER ALPHABET-SPEECH SCREEN (AUDITORY-VISUAL ASSOCIATION)

Part A of the Mann-Suiter Alphabet-Speech Screen (Form 6-12) will indicate the student's ability to relate a symbol to its auditory referents, i.e., letter name and sound. Part B will indicate the student's ability to pronounce words containing digraphs.

Directions, Part A

1. The letters should be shown to the student in the order indicated. For children under age 6, the letters should be put on 3″ × 5″ cards.
2. The teacher should point to each letter, ask for the name of the letter, and ask for the sound the letter makes.

Scoring, Part A

1. At age 7, five or more errors on either the letter names or the sounds indicate difficulty with sound-symbol (auditory-visual) associative relationships.
2. At age 8 or older, two or more errors on either the letter names or the sounds suggest difficulty with auditory-visual associations.
3. Symbols for scoring are ✓ = correct, ✓ = incorrect.

MANN-SUITER AUDITORY MEMORY SCREEN (SENTENCES)

NAME _____ DATE _____

DATE OF BIRTH _____ EXAMINER _____

· RESPONSE

1. The boy has a big ball.   _____

2. I like to ride in the car.   _____

3. Mary is reading her new book.   _____

4. John ran fast down the wide road.   _____

5. It is time to go home from school.   _____

6. Open the door and let the dog out.   _____

7. Last Sunday we went to the beach.   _____

8. Pretty flowers come out in the spring.   _____

9. Horses like to run wild in the fields.   _____

10. The moon shone brightly in the sky at night.   _____

11. The ship blew its horn when it passed under the bridge.   _____

12. Mother put flowers on the table last night.   _____

13. The bird built its nest high up in the shady tree.   _____

14. He saw a car hit a pole on his way to school.   _____

15. I like milk and crackers after school every day.   _____

16. It was a dark and cloudy day, but Bill went swimming alone.   _____

17. The dust was so thick you could hardly find your way.   _____

18. Day after day, the dark clouds poured rain on the earth far below.   _____

19. I was keeping it for a surprise, but I will show it to you now.   _____

20. John went to Boston to see if he could pick up some good antiques.   _____

TOTAL INCORRECT: _____

MANN-SUITER ALPHABET-SPEECH SCREEN (AUDITORY-VISUAL ASSOCIATION)

NAME _____ DATE _____

DATE OF BIRTH _____ EXAMINER _____

Part A

Name	Vowels & Consonants	Sound	Name	Vowels & Consonants	Sound
____	M	____	____	T	____
____	S	____	____	H	____
____	P	____	____	G	____
____	C	____	____	E	____
____	L	____	____	K	____
____	R	____	____	Z	____
____	A	____	____	U	____
____	X	____	____	Y	____
____	F	____	____	W	____
____	O	____	____	D	____
____	B	____	____	N	____
____	Q	____	____	J	____
____	I	____	____	V	____

TOTAL INCORRECT: ____   TOTAL INCORRECT: ____

Part B

DIGRAPH SCREEN

Word	Picture	Response	Word	Picture	Response
ch		____	th		____
ch		____	th		____
sh		____	wh		____
sh		____	th		____

TOTAL INCORRECT: ____

Directions, Part B

For children below age six who cannot read, the teacher may want to know how they pronounce words containing digraphs. The teacher should show the pictures in Part B and ask the student to name the objects.

Scoring, Part B

1. Two or more errors at age 6 or older suggest difficulty with digraph speech patterns.
2. Symbols for scoring are ✓ = correct, ✓ = incorrect.

Note: See page 214 for more specific evaluation in this area if necessary.

Things to Look For

1. Does the student know more consonant than vowel sounds?
2. Does the student add a vowel sound (uh) to the consonant (buh for *b*)?
3. Is the student bilingual?
4. Does the student have a speech (articulation) problem?

MANN-SUITER VISUAL LANGUAGE CLASSIFICATION SCREEN

The Mann-Suiter Visual Language Classification Screen (Form 6-13) is designed to indicate a student's ability to classify pictures of objects by category when they are presented visually.

Directions

The teacher points to the first picture in the row (that of a cat, in the example) and says, "Look at this." Then the teacher points to each of the other pictures in that row and asks, "Which one of these is like this?" pointing to the first one again. If the student responds correctly, then the teacher says, "That's right," and continues to administer the rest of the items in the same way. If the response is incorrect, the teacher goes back and says, pointing, "See the cat. Here is another one." On completing the example, the teacher goes on to number one, repeating the directions, but giving no further help.

Scoring

1. Five errors or more for children ages 4–5 suggest difficulty with visual language classification.
2. Three errors or more for children age 6 or older suggest difficulty with visual language classification.
3. Symbols for scoring are ✓ = correct, ✓ = incorrect.

Key: (1) dog, (2) leaf, (3) cap, (4) woman, (5) truck, (6) chicken, (7) apple, (8) box, (9) knife, (10) airplane.

Things to Look For

1. How well does the student attend to the task?
2. Does the student verbalize while performing the task?
3. Does the student perseverate?
4. Does the student go off on a tangent as a result of the stimulus picture?
5. Does the student anchor by placing a finger on the first picture while he or she scans the rest?
6. Go back over some of the incorrect responses and ask the student why he or she chose the one he or she did. This may give you a clue as to how the student thinks.
7. Note any logical responses even though they may be incorrect in terms of the expected response.

Note: See page 214 for more specific evaluation in this area if necessary.

MANN-SUITER VISUAL LANGUAGE ASSOCIATION SCREEN

The Mann-Suiter Visual Language Association Screen (Form 6-14) is designed to indicate a student's ability to formulate associative relationships between pictures of objects.

Directions

1. For the practice item and items 1–6, the teacher should point to the first picture and say, "Look at this," then point to each of the other pictures and say, "Point to the one it goes with," as he or she goes back and points to the first one again. If the student's response to the sample item is correct, the teacher should say, "That is right, doll goes with carriage," and administer the rest of the items. If the answer is incorrect, the teacher should go back

MANN-SUITER VISUAL LANGUAGE CLASSIFICATION SCREEN

NAME _____ DATE _____

DATE OF BIRTH _____ EXAMINER _____

RESPONSE

Practice: _____

1. _____

2. _____

3. _____

4. _____

5. _____

(continued)

RESPONSE

6. _____

7. _____

8. _____

9. _____

10. _____

TOTAL INCORRECT: _____

MANN-SUITER VISUAL LANGUAGE ASSOCIATION SCREEN

NAME _____ DATE _____

DATE OF BIRTH _____ EXAMINER _____

RESPONSE

Practice:

_____

1.

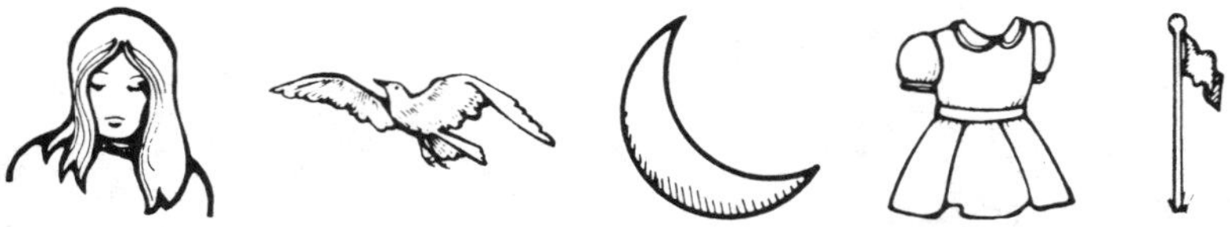

_____

2.

_____

3.

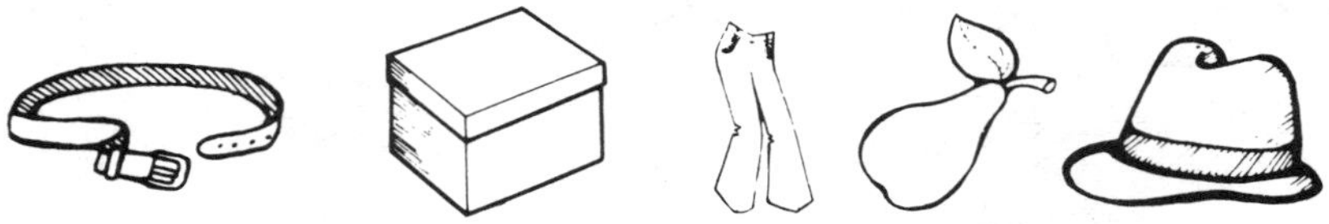

_____

4.

_____

5.

_____

(continued)

RESPONSE

6. _____

7. _____

8. _____

9. _____

10. _____

TOTAL INCORRECT: _____

and say as he or she points, "See the doll—the doll goes with the carriage," then proceed to number one, repeat the directions, but give no further help.

2. For items 7–10, the teacher should point to each picture and say, "Fish goes with fish bowl as dog goes with _____?" If the response is incorrect, or if the student does not understand, the teacher should repeat the directions and add, pointing, "Which one of these goes under the dog?" The rest of the items are administered in the same manner.

3. All items should be administered.

Scoring

1. Five errors or more for children ages 4–5 suggest difficulty with visual language association.
2. Three errors or more for children age 6 and older suggest difficulty with visual language association.
3. Symbols used for recording responses are ✓ = correct, ✗ = incorrect.

Key: (1) dress, (2) meat, (3) pants, (4) key, (5) mouse, (6) gun, (7) dog house, (8) rod and reel, (9) eye, (10) man on bed.

Things to Look For

1. Does the student attend to the task?
2. Does the student verbalize while performing the task?
3. Does the student perseverate?
4. Does the student go off on a tangent as a result of the stimulus picture?
5. Does the student anchor by placing his or her finger on the first picture while he or she scans the rest?
6. Incorrect responses should be reviewed and the student asked why he or she chose the one he or she did. This may give a clue about how he or she thinks.
7. Any logical responses should be written down even though they may be incorrect with regard to the expected response.

Note: See page 214 for more specific evaluation in this area if necessary.

MANN-SUITER AUDITORY LANGUAGE CLASSIFICATION SCREEN

The Mann-Suiter Auditory Language Classification Screen (Form 6-15) is designed to indicate a student's ability to classify objects by category when they are presented orally.

Directions

The teacher asks, "Does boy go with dress or man?" If the response is correct, the teachers says, "Yes, boy goes with man," and continues to give the rest of the items in the same way. If it is incorrect, the teacher says, "boy goes with man" and continues without any further aid.

Scoring

1. Five errors or more for children ages 4–5 suggest difficulty with auditory language classification.
2. Three errors or more for children age 6 and older suggest difficulty with auditory language classification.
3. Symbols for scoring are ✓ = correct, ✗ = incorrect.

Key: (1) radio, (2) cake, (3) tie, (4) chair, (5) water, (6) cat, (7) grapefruit, (8) notepad, (9) wool, (10) engine.

Things to Look For

1. How well does the student attend to the task?
2. Does the student perseverate?
3. Does the student go off on a tangent as a result of the stimulus picture?
4. Incorrect responses should be reviewed and the student asked why he or she chose the one he or she did. This may give a clue about how the student thinks.
5. Record any logical responses even though they may be incorrect in terms of the expected response.

Note: See page 214 for more specific evaluation in this area if necessary.

MANN-SUITER AUDITORY LANGUAGE ASSOCIATION SCREEN

The Mann-Suiter Auditory Language Association Screen (Form 6-16) is designed to indicate a student's ability to formulate associations between objects presented to him or her orally.

MANN-SUITER AUDITORY LANGUAGE CLASSIFICATION SCREEN

NAME _____ DATE _____

DATE OF BIRTH _____ EXAMINER _____

RESPONSE

Practice:	boy:	dress – man	_____
1.	television:	radio – ball	_____
2.	pie:	telephone – cake	_____
3.	shirt:	tie – bread	_____
4.	table:	pen – chair	_____
5.	milk:	water – tree	_____
6.	kitten:	cat – flower	_____
7.	orange:	lettuce – grapefruit	_____
8.	book:	glue – notepad	_____
9.	hair:	wool – smoke	_____
10.	motor:	sky – engine	_____

TOTAL INCORRECT: _____

MANN-SUITER AUDITORY LANGUAGE ASSOCIATION SCREEN

NAME _____ DATE _____

DATE OF BIRTH _____ EXAMINER _____

RESPONSE

Practice:	pencil:	wall – paper	_____
	1. look:	hand – eyes	_____
	2. belt:	pants – plate	_____
	3. bread:	ring – butter	_____
	4. paddle:	car – boat	_____
	5. rod:	reel – hat	_____
	6. apple:	jelly – glass	_____
	7. bicycle:	wheel – football	_____
	8. button:	sail – dress	_____
	9. drum:	envelope – band	_____
	10. carrot:	rabbit – bush	_____

TOTAL INCORRECT: _____

Directions

The teacher asks, "Does pencil go with wall or paper?" If the child answers correctly, the teacher says, "Yes, pencil goes with paper," and continues to give the rest of the items in the same way. If the response is incorrect, the teacher says, "Pencil goes with paper," and continues without any further aid.

Scoring

1. Five errors or more for children ages 4–5 suggest difficulty with auditory language association.
2. Three errors or more for children age 6 and older suggest difficulty with auditory language association.
3. Symbols for scoring are ✓ = correct, ✗ = incorrect.

Key: (1) eyes, (2) pants, (3) butter, (4) boat, (5) reel, (6) jelly, (7) wheel, (8) dress, (9) band, (10) rabbit

Things to Look For

1. Does the student attend to the task?
2. Does the student perseverate?
3. Does the student go off on a tangent as a result of the stimulus picture?
4. Incorrect responses should be reviewed and the student asked why he or she chose the one he or she did. This may give a clue about how the student thinks.
5. Record any logical responses even though they may be incorrect in terms of the expected response.

Note: See page 214 for more specific evaluation in this area if necessary.

MANN-SUITER MANUAL LANGUAGE EXPRESSION SCREEN

The Mann-Suiter Manual Language Expression Screen (Form 6-17) will indicate to the instructor the student's ability to express the function of an object by his or her actions without using words.

Directions

1. The teacher points to the ball and says, "Show me what you can do with this."

2. If the answer is correct, the teacher says, "Yes, now show me what you can do with this," pointing to the next picture.
3. If the student answers incorrectly, the teacher shows the student the motions of throwing and bouncing, then administers the rest of the items, giving no further aid.
4. All items should be administered.

Scoring

1. Five errors or more for children ages 4–5 suggest difficulty with manual language expression.
2. Three errors or more for children age 6 and older suggest difficulty with manual language expression.
3. Symbols for scoring are ✓ = correct, ✗ = incorrect.

Things to Look For

1. How well does the student attend to the task?
2. Does the student perseverate?
3. Does the student go off on a tangent as a result of the stimulus picture?
4. Incorrect responses should be reviewed and the student asked why he or she chose the one he or she did. This may give a clue about how the student thinks.
5. Write down any logical responses even though they may be incorrect in terms of the expected response.
6. Does the student verbalize the action as he or she performs it?

Note: See page 214 for more specific evaluation in this area if necessary.

MANN-SUITER SPEECH SCREEN

The Mann-Suiter Speech Screen (Form 6-18) is designed to indicate the presence or absence of articulation defects and other types of nonfluencies (stuttering, etc.) in children.

Directions

1. The teacher says, "I am going to say something and I want you to say it after me."
2. The teacher repeats each item as necessary.

MANN-SUITER MANUAL LANGUAGE EXPRESSION SCREEN

NAME _____ DATE _____

DATE OF BIRTH _____ EXAMINER _____

	RESPONSE		RESPONSE

Practice: _____

_____   _____

_____   _____

_____   _____

_____   _____

_____   _____

_____   _____

TOTAL INCORRECT: _____

MANN-SUITER SPEECH SCREEN

NAME _____ DATE _____

DATE OF BIRTH _____ EXAMINER _____

Speech Articulation	Adds Sounds	Distorts Sounds	Omits Sounds	Substitutes Sounds
1. The rabbit runs fast.	_____	_____	_____	_____
2. Theodore, the frog.	_____	_____	_____	_____
3. Blow the whistle.	_____	_____	_____	_____
4. She sees the ship.	_____	_____	_____	_____
5. Black bug's blood.	_____	_____	_____	_____
6. The quick brown fox.	_____	_____	_____	_____
7. Aluminum.	_____	_____	_____	_____
8. Methodist Episcopal.	_____	_____	_____	_____

TOTAL INCORRECT: _____

Check if appropriate

Hoarse voice ☐   Stuttering ☐

Nasal voice ☐   Cleft palate ☐

Loud voice (excessively) ☐   Other (explain) ☐

Soft voice (excessively) ☐

Scoring

1. Check the appropriate box for specific types of errors.
2. Consider an item incorrect if only one error is made on it.
3. For students ages 4–6, four or more incorrect items suggest difficulty with speech articulation.
4. For students age 7 and older, three or more incorrect items suggest difficulty with speech articulation.
5. Underline the letter or word that is nonfluent.

Things to Look For

1. Does the student stutter or stammer?
2. Does the student have hesitations in his or her speech?
3. Does the student's tongue appear to be lost in his or her mouth?
4. Does the student perseverate?
5. Is it difficult for the student to attend to the task?
6. Does the student exhibit cleft palate speech?

Note: See page 214 for more specific evaluation in this area if necessary.

MANN-SUITER VERBAL LANGUAGE EXPRESSION SCREEN

The Mann-Suiter Verbal Language Expression Screen (Form 6-19) is designed to indicate the student's ability to view pictures of common objects and formulate phrases or sentences that will describe or indicate a quality or function of the particular object presented.

Directions

The teacher should say, pointing to the car, "Tell me all you can about this." If the student does not understand, the teacher should say, "Tell me what it is and what it does or what you can do with it." No further aid should be given.

Scoring

1. List the number of responses in the response column. For children ages 4–6, less than four total responses (and at least one per item) suggests problems with verbal language expression. Count any logical response as correct.

2. For students age 7 and older, under six responses (and at least one per item) suggests difficulty in the area of verbal language expression.

Things to Look For

1. How well does the student attend to the task?
2. Does the student perseverate?
3. Does the student go off on a tangent as a result of the stimulus picture?
4. Does the student give one-word or short-phrase responses?
5. What is the quality of the student's verbal responses, considering the cultural and experiential background?

Note: See page 214 for more specific evaluation in this area if necessary.

MANN-SUITER WRITTEN LANGUAGE EXPRESSION SCREEN (for students age 7 and older)

The Mann-Suiter Written Language Expression Screen (Form 6-20) is designed to indicate the student's ability to take dictation.

Directions

1. For the Dictation section, the teacher says, "I want you to write some sentences exactly as I say them." The teacher repeats the sentence as necessary.
2. For the Expression section, the teacher says, "Now I want you to write your own sentence using the word *girl.*" The rest of the items are handled in the same manner.

Scoring

1. This screen is essentially for diagnostic purposes only.
2. Good teacher judgment is necessary in analyzing the responses.

Things to Look For

1. How many repetitions in presentation are necessary?
2. For 1–4, does the student reverse the order of the words?

MANN-SUITER VERBAL LANGUAGE EXPRESSION SCREEN

NAME _____ DATE _____

DATE OF BIRTH _____ EXAMINER _____

RESPONSES

_____

_____

_____

TOTAL CORRECT RESPONSES: _____

MANN-SUITER WRITTEN LANGUAGE EXPRESSION SCREEN

NAME _____ DATE _____

DATE OF BIRTH _____ EXAMINER _____

(For Students Age 7 and Over)

DICTATION (ATTACH CHILD'S DICTATION RESPONSES)

1. The cat is big.

2. Mother likes to bake cookies.

3. John went to the store yesterday.

EXPRESSION

1. Write a sentence using the word *girl.*

2. Write a sentence using the word *walking.*

3. Write a sentence using the word *he.*

4. Write a paragraph about *school.*

3. Does the student verbalize as he or she writes?
4. Does the student perseverate?
5. Does the student write things that are totally irrelevant?
6. How is the student's handwriting?

Note: See page 310 for more specific evaluation in this area if necessary.

MANN-SUITER NONVERBAL SYMBOLIC LANGUAGE SCREEN

The Mann-Suiter Nonverbal Symbolic Language Screen (Form 6-21) is designed to indicate the student's ability to associate meaning with objects or symbols that represent abstract constructs, such as art, music, and patriotism.

Directions

The teacher says, "Listen and tell me which one it is: A rabbit's foot brings you 'rain' or 'luck.'" The teacher repeats as necessary.

Scoring

1. For children ages 4–6, four or more errors suggest difficulty with nonverbal language.
2. For children age 7 and older, two or more errors suggest difficulty with nonverbal language.
3. Symbols for scoring are ✓ = correct, ✗ = incorrect.

Things to Look For

1. Does the student perseverate?
2. Does the student say things that are totally irrelevant?
3. Go back and question the incorrect responses. Look for logical answers.

Note: See page 214 for more specific evaluation in this area if necessary.

SUPPLEMENTARY EVALUATION—SCREENING

The supplementary evaluation section is designed to provide the teacher and others who are concerned with diagnosing the problems of learning-handicapped students with a list of commonly used tests related to the various areas of learning. Individuals involved with assessment may wish to reinforce their findings by using standardized tests that measure different learning characteristics in students. Professionals from other disciplines may already be using several of these instruments as a part of their basic testing battery. It is important that individuals who are responsible for defining and interpreting test data and communicating this information to teachers be able to relate this data directly to the findings attained through informal or developmental evaluation compiled by the teacher. Psychologists and special resource teachers who may be more knowledgeable and sophisticated in the area of evaluation, working together with regular classroom teachers, present a comprehensive approach to defining particular learning problems in students. The classroom teacher should become informed as to what the particular tests measure. This does not mean that expertise is required in all areas of evaluation but that the classroom teacher should at least have some basic understanding of the assessment devices presently being used in different educational settings. Each of the evaluation instruments indicated has source information listed in the References.

General Readiness

1. *The Anton Brenner Developmental Gestalt Test of School Readiness* (Brenner, 1964)
2. *Behavior Tests Used at the Gestalt Institute* (Ilg & Ames, 1964)
3. *Boehm Test of Basic Concepts* (Boehm, 1980)
4. *Brigance Diagnostic Inventory of Early Development* (Brigance, 1978)
5. *Clymer-Barrett Pre-Reading Battery* (Clymer & Barrett, 1969)
6. *Early Detection Inventory* (McGahan & McGahan, 1967)
7. *Evanston Early Identification Scale* (Landsman & Dillard, 1967)
8. *First Grade Screening Test* (Pate & Webb, 1966)
9. *Kindergarten Evaluation of Learning Potential (KELP)* (Wilson & Robeck, 1967)
10. *The Meeting Street School Screening Test* (Hainsworth & Siqueland, 1969)
11. *Metropolitan Readiness Tests* (Hildreth, Griffiths, & McGauvran, 1966)
12. Predictive Index (deHirsch, Jansky, & Langford, 1966)
13. *Preschool Attainment Record* (Doll, 1966)
14. *Pupil Rating Scale* (Myklebust, 1971)
15. *Screening Test of Academic Readiness* (Ahr, 1966)

MANN-SUITER NONVERBAL SYMBOLIC LANGUAGE SCREEN

NAME _____ DATE _____

DATE OF BIRTH _____ EXAMINER _____

RESPONSE

1. A rabbit's foot brings you: rain–luck   _____

2. A flag means your: home–country   _____

3. A pumpkin goes with: Easter–Halloween   _____

4. We get snow in the: winter–summer   _____

5. Music can make you: thirsty–happy   _____

6. When people paint pictures, they tell you how they: feel–hear   _____

7. A statue of a person means he or she was: old–famous   _____

8. A badge tells what you can: do–grow   _____

9. Our national anthem means: patriotism–mountains   _____

10. A turkey goes with: Thanksgiving–the President's birthday   _____

TOTAL INCORRECT: _____

16. *Screening Tests for Identifying Children with Specific Language Disability* (Slingerland, 1970)
17. *The Valett Developmental Survey of Basic Learning Abilities* (Valett, 1967)
18. *The Vane Kindergarten Test* (Vane, 1968)

Auditory

ACUITY
1. Audiometric Sweep Test

PERCEPTION
Discrimination
1. *Auditory Discrimination Test* (Wepman, rev. ed., 1973)
2. *Boston University Speech Sound Discrimination Picture Test* (Boston University, 1955)
3. *Goldman-Fristoe-Woodcock Test of Auditory Discrimination* (Goldman, Fristoe, & Woodcock, 1970)
4. *PERC Auditory Discrimination Test* (Drake, 1965)

Closure
1. Auditory Closure Subtest of the *Illinois Test of Psycholinguistic Abilities* (Kirk, McCarthy, & Kirk, 1968)
2. Grammatic Closure Subtest of *Illinois Test of Psycholinguistic Abilities* (Kirk, McCarthy, & Kirk, 1968)
3. *Roswell-Chall Auditory Blending Test* (Roswell & Chall, rev. ed., 1978)

IMAGERY (MEMORY-SEQUENCING)
1. *Detroit Tests of Learning Aptitude-R* (Hammill, 1985)
2. Digit Span Subtest of the *Wechsler Intelligence Scale for Children (WISC)* (Wechsler, 1955)
3. *Goldman-Fristoe-Woodcock Auditory Skills Test Battery* (Goldman, Fristoe, & Woodcock, 1975)
4. Memory Subtest of the *Illinois Test of Psycholinguistic Abilities* (Kirk, McCarthy, & Kirk, 1968)
5. Sentences Subtest of the *Wechsler Preschool and Primary Scale of Intelligence (WPSSI)* (Wechsler, 1967)
6. *Wepman Auditory Memory Span Test* (Wepman, 1973a)
7. *Wepman Auditory Sequential Memory Test* (Wepman, 1973b)

Visual

ACUITY AND OCULAR MOTOR
1. *Keystone Visual Survey Telebinocular* (Keystone View Co, 1958)
2. *Ortho-Rater* (Bausch and Lomb, 1958)
3. *Snellen Chart* (American Medical Association)
4. *Spache Binocular Vision Test* (Keystone View Co., 1961)

PERCEPTION
Discrimination
1. *Frostig Developmental Test of Visual Perception* (Frostig, 1963)
2. *Marion Monroe Visual Test #1* (Ilg & Ames, 1964)
3. *Metropolitan Readiness Test* (Hildreth, Griffiths, & McGauvran, 1966)

Closure
1. *Illinois Test of Psycholinguistic Abilities Visual Closure Subtest* (Kirk, McCarthy, & Kirk, 1968)

Figure-Ground
1. *Frostig Developmental Test of Visual Perception* (Frostig, 1963)
2. *Southern California Figure-Ground Visual Perception Test* (Ayres, 1966)
3. *Strauss and Lehtinen Figure Background Cards* (Strauss & Lehtinen, 1947)

IMAGERY (MEMORY-SEQUENCING)
1. *Benton Revised Visual Retention Test* (Benton, 1963)
2. *Detroit Tests of Learning Aptitude,* Subtests 9 and 16 (Baker & Leland, 1959)
3. *Marion Monroe Test #3* (Ilg & Ames, 1964)
4. *Memory for Designs Test* (Graham & Kendall, 1960)

VISUAL-MOTOR (GROSS AND FINE)
1. *Bender Visual-Motor Gestalt Test for Children* (Bender, 1938; Koppitz, 1964)
2. *Bruininks-Oseretsky Test of Motor Proficiency* (Bruininks, 1978)
3. *Detroit Tests of Learning Aptitude,* Subtest 5 (Baker & Leland, 1959)
4. *Developmental Test of Visual Motor Integration* (Beery & Buktenica, 1967)
5. *Draw-A-Man Test* (Goodenough, 1926)
6. *Frostig Developmental Test of Visual Perception* (Frostig, 1963)
7. *Harris Test of Lateral Dominance* (Harris, 1958)
8. *Left-Right Discrimination and Finger Localization* (Benton, 1959)
9. *Lincoln-Oseretsky Motor Development Scale* (Sloan, 1954)
10. *Minnesota Percepto-Diagnostic Test* (Fuller & Laird, 1963)
11. *Purdue Perceptual-Motor Survey* (Kephart & Roach, 1966)

12. *Slosson Drawing Coordination Test* (Slosson, 1980)
13. *Standardized Road-Map Test of Direction Sense* (Money, Alexander, & Walker, 1965)

Language

1. *Assessment of Children's Language Comprehension* (Foster, Giddan, & Stark, 1973)
2. *Basic Concept Inventory* (Engelmann, 1967)
3. *Carrow Elicited Language Inventory* (Carrow-Woolfolk, 1974)
4. *Clinical Evaluation of Language Functions* (Semel & Wiig, 1980)
5. *Developmental Sentence Analysis* (Lee, 1974)
6. *Environmental Language Inventory (ELI)* (McDonald, 1978)
7. *Houston Test for Language Development* (Crabtree, 1963)
8. *Illinois Test of Psycholinguistic Abilities* (Kirk, McCarthy, & Kirk, 1968)
9. *Let's Talk Inventory for Adolescents* (Wiig, 1982)
10. *Mecham Verbal Language Development Scale* (Mecham, 1959)
11. *Northwestern Syntax Screening Test* (Lee, 1971)
12. *Peabody Picture Vocabulary Test* (Dunn & Dunn, 1981)
13. *Picture Story Language Test* (Pronovost & Dumbleton, 1953)
14. *Slingerland Screening Tests for Specific Language Disabilities* (Slingerland, 1964)
15. *Test of Adolescent Language* (Hammill, Brown, Larsen, & Wiederholt, 1980)
16. *Test for Auditory Comprehension of Language* (Carrow, 1973)
17. *Test of Language Development* (Newcomer & Hammill, 1982)
18. *Utah Test of Language Development* (Mecham, Jex, & Jones, 1967)

SPEECH TESTS

1. *A Deep Test of Articulation* (McDonald, 1964)
2. *Goldman-Fristoe Test of Articulation* (Goldman & Fristoe, 1972)
3. *Templin-Darley Tests of Articulation* (Templin & Darley, 1960)

MEASURES OF INTELLECTUAL PERFORMANCE

1. *Kaufman Assessment Battery for Children (K-ABC)* (Kaufman & Kaufman, 1983)
2. *McCarthy Scales of Children's Abilities* (McCarthy, 1972)
3. *Stanford-Binet Intelligence Scale* (Terman & Merrill, 1973)
4. *Wechsler Intelligence Scale for Children—Revised* (Wechsler, 1974)
5. *Woodcock-Johnson Psycho-Educational Battery* (Woodcock & Johnson, 1977

MEASURES OF ADAPTIVE BEHAVIOR

1. *AAMD Adaptive Behavior Scale,* Public School Version (Lambert, Windmiller, Cole, & Figueroa, 1975)
2. *Adaptive Behavior Inventory for Children (SOMPA)* (Mercer & Lewis, 1977)
3. *Vineland Social Maturity Scale* (Doll, 1965)

CURRICULUM-BASED ASSESSMENT

The following section contains screening devices and lists of supplementary tests that can be used to assess students in spelling, reading, handwriting, written expression, mathematics, and behavior. Academic assessment in the language areas for students in grade 2 or above should start with a spelling test since spelling evaluation provides good diagnostic information in handwriting and also helps the teacher determine at which level to begin testing in reading.

SCREENING USING A SPELLING INVENTORY

A spelling inventory can be used for individual assessment or as an aid in determining the range of reading abilities and possible problem areas of a large group of students. The inventory serves two purposes:

1. The nature of the spelling errors made indicates the areas of learning that need to be further explored. Spelling inventory screening as a formal means of evaluation will either support or negate the judgments teachers make on the basis of informal observation.
2. A spelling inventory enables the teacher to determine at which point screening with reading inventories ought to begin. With this in mind, the teacher testing for reading ability should begin one level below that at which the student failed in spelling. This will reduce the degree of failure for some students and also identify quickly the more advanced learners in the class.

Christopher and colleagues (1989) found that variables predictive of high school learning disabled students were spelling, IQ, and a question from a student interview, "Do you think going into a special class/program would help you?" With the emphasis on writing at the high school level, an analysis of spelling will give the teacher additional diagnostic information.

Initial spelling measures can be used to predict reading achievement. This is based on the theory that there is a synchrony between the development stages of reading and spelling as students acquire knowledge of orthography (Bear & Barone, 1989; Ehri, 1987; Henderson & Beers, 1980; Morris & Perney, 1984). Teachers can use a spelling assessment to diagnose student's word knowledge and to organize groups for word study instruction (Henderson, 1985). Informal spelling inventories can be administered one-on-one or to small groups in short periods of time.

One of the best predictors of reading achievement is an analysis of a student's phonological awareness and letter knowledge at the beginning of kindergarten. In the primary grades, a developmental spelling assessment at the beginning of the year can be a good predictor for progress in reading and writing. If handwriting is a problem, then an individually administered oral spelling test can be given. An error analysis gives the teacher an estimate of the student's stage of development.

Diagnosis should include a developmental inventory of word knowledge to sample errors. Teachers need to analyze their students' spelling errors, identify the error features, and determine the appropriate instructional levels. This will influence the content and timing or spacing of the students' word study. In diagnosing spelling, we need to become more aware of the specific orthographic features acquired developmentally as students acquire reading vocabulary.

In classifying errors in spelling, we need to know the student's instructional level or the highest grade level at which a child spells at least half of the words correctly. Although a word may be misspelled, the attempted letters or formation of the "invented spelling" could be very diagnostic.

Developing a Spelling Inventory

Following is a simple procedure for setting up a spelling inventory.

1. Select a word sample from each basal spelling book of a given spelling series.
2. Take 15 words from the grade one speller.
3. Take 20 words from the spellers for grades 2 through 6. Note: To take a sample selection from grades 2 through 6, divide the number of words listed at the back of the spelling book by 20. If there are 300 words in the book, you would divide 300 by

20 giving you 15. Therefore, a word sample would consist of every fifteenth word in the speller. Should you decide not to develop your own inventory, you could use the Mann-Suiter Developmental Spelling Inventory (Form 6-22).

Mann-Suiter Developmental Spelling Inventory

The Mann-Suiter Developmental Spelling Inventory (Form 6-22) consists of samples of several basal and linguistic spelling lists. Table 6-2 is an analysis of the spelling skills tested for. The lists represent different spelling programs. They have been randomly selected according to level of difficulty and general orientation, and they are stratified to achieve a balance in terms of different spelling patterns, prefixes and suffixes, and configurations of words. Trial testing involved approximately 345 students, grades 1 through 8. Their performances were compared to the level of their functioning as indicated by teachers. In approximately 80 percent of the cases, there was agreement between teacher estimates of student performance and student achievement on the Mann-Suiter Developmental Spelling Inventory.

Screening Procedures

For grade 4 and below, begin testing by administering first-level spelling words. For fifth grade and above, begin testing with the third-level spelling words. Thus, for students who fail the third level there always remains a second level to which they can be dropped. In giving the test, except for the first twelve words of Level II, the teacher should (1) say the word, (2) use the word in a sentence, and (3) repeat the word again.

The first twelve words of Level II are designed to tell the teacher whether or not the learner can hear short vowel sounds in CVC (Consonant-Vowel-Consonant) pattern words and in words combining blends or digraphs. The teacher should (1) say the word, (2) sound the word out (n-o-d), and (3) say the whole word again. These words are *not* to be used in sentences. This procedure will tell whether or not the student is hearing the sounds and whether he or she is able to write the symbol that stands for the sound.

In all testing, it is important that the teacher stress to the students that even if they cannot spell a word, they should put down every sound they can hear in the word.

To screen a fourth grade class, the teacher should dictate words from Level I and Level II at the first sitting and then check the responses. At the second sitting, the teacher should test only those students

MANN-SUITER DEVELOPMENTAL SPELLING INVENTORY

Level I	Level II	Level III	Level IV
1. cat	1. nod	1. drank	1. strike
2. no	2. jug	2. swing	2. choke
3. red	3. get	3. bath	3. shook
4. see	4. sip	4. sheep	4. hobby
5. and	5. tab	5. each	5. age
6. you	6. sled	6. train	6. chopped
7. the	7. drop	7. lake	7. swimming
8. we	8. clip	8. third	8. hiding
9. it	9. ask	9. catch	9. folded
10. yes	10. shop	10. stick	10. studies
11. dog	11. thank	11. ducks	11. foolish
12. big	12. sing	12. child	12. highest
13. like	13. boat	13. jumping	13. ashes
14. have	14. home	14. shorter	14. sailor
15. was	15. doll	15. walk	15. tightly
	16. little	16. right	16. carrying
	17. father	17. puppy	17. doesn't
	18. down	18. uncle	18. through
	19. pretty	19. because	19. climb
	20. said	20. wash	20. listen

Level V	Level VI	Level VII	Level VIII
1. crime	1. scene	1. brief	1. genius
2. risky	2. hastened	2. phrase	2. ancient
3. ridge	3. trophy	3. delicious	3. variety
4. soldiers	4. whirl	4. seize	4. sphere
5. sauce	5. pierced	5. caution	5. receipt
6. ditch	6. noble	6. knowledge	6. tissue
7. address	7. ignorantly	7. museum	7. progression
8. trouble	8. rewarded	8. delaying	8. virtue
9. quietly	9. continued	9. glorious	9. noisier
10. thieves	10. enforcing	10. moisture	10. leisure
11. business	11. motoring	11. social	11. constitution
12. heroes	12. relation	12. initial	12. fiction
13. movies	13. shortage	13. request	13. angle
14. expect	14. chocolate	14. slight	14. essay
15. dismissed	15. canyon	15. citizen	15. union
16. studying	16. court	16. envy	16. schedule
17. joking	17. maples	17. banquet	17. muscles
18. reviewed	18. autograph	18. pursue	18. natural
19. ruins	19. earliest	19. league	19. technical
20. crept	20. heavens	20. average	20. cancel

Table 6-2   Analysis of Spelling Skills

LEVEL I

Words	Spelling Skill		Words	Spelling Skills
1. cat	Basic sight words		12. child	*i* followed by *ld* makes vowel long
2. no	" " "		13. jumping	*ing* ending
3. red	" " "		14. shorter	*er* ending
4. see	" " "		15. walk	Silent *l*
5. and	" " "		16. right	Silent *gh*
6. you	" " "		17. puppy	*y* as short *i*
7. the	" " "		18. uncle	Irregular spelling of *kle*
8. we	" " "		19. because	Sight word
9. it	" " "		20. wash	Sight word
10. yes	" " "			
11. dog	" " "		**LEVEL IV**	
12. big	" " "		1. strike	Vowel, consonant, plus *e*
13. like	" " "		2. choke	Vowel, consonant, plus *e*
14. have	" " "		3. shook	Short vowel sound of *oo*
15. was	" " "		4. hobby	*y* for short *i*
			5. age	*j* sound as *ge*
LEVEL II			6. chopped	Final consonant doubled and *ed*
1. nod	Short *o*		7. swimming	Final consonant doubled and *ing*
2. jug	Short *u*		8. hiding	*e* to *i* before adding *ng*
3. get	Short *e*		9. folded	Ending *ed*
4. sip	Short *i*		10. studies	*y* to *i* before adding *es*
5. tab	Short *a*		11. foolish	Root plus *ish*
6. sled	Short vowel and consonant blend *(sl)*		12. highest	Root plus *est*
7. drop	Short vowel and consonant blend *(dr)*		13. ashes	Plural, root plus *es*
8. clip	Short vowel and consonant blend *(cl)*		14. sailor	Root plus *or*
9. ask	Short vowel and consonant blend *(sk)*		15. tightly	Root plus *ly*
10. shop	Short vowel and consonant digraph *(sh)*		16. carrying	Root, final *y*, plus *ing*
11. thank	Short vowel and consonant digraph *(th)*		17. doesn't	Contraction
12. sing	Short vowel and consonant digraph *(ng)*		18. through	Sight word
13. boat	Long *o* spelled with digraph *oa*		19. climb	Silent *b*
14. home	Vowel, consonant plus *e*		20. listen	Silent *t*
15. doll	Final consonant (double)			
16. little	Ending *le*		**LEVEL V**	
17. father	Ending *er*		1. crime	Vowel, consonant, plus *e*
18. down	*ow* for *ou*		2. risky	*y* for short *i*
19. pretty	Sight word		3. ridge	*j* sound as *dge*
20. said	Sight word		4. soldiers	*j* sound as *di*
			5. sauce	*s* sound of *c*
LEVEL III			6. ditch	*tch* spelling
1. drank	Short vowel and consonant blend *(dr)*		7. address	Final consonant (double)
2. swing	Short vowel and consonant blend *(sw)*		8. trouble	The *ŭ* sound of *ou*
3. bath	Short vowel and consonant blend *(th)*		9. quietly	Root plus *ly*
4. sheep	Long *e* spelled *ee*		10. thieves	*f* changed to *v* plus *es*
5. each	Long *e* spelled *ea*		11. business	*ĭ* sound of *u*
6. train	Long *a* spelled *ai*		12. heroes	Words ending in *o* add *es* for plural
7. lake	Vowel, consonant plus *e*		13. movies	Plural, root, plus *s*
8. third	*th*, vowel, *r*		14. expect	Prefix *ex*
9. catch	*tch* spelling		15. dismissed	Prefix *dis*
10. stick	*k* sound after short vowel spelled *ck*		16. studying	Addition of *ing* following *y*
11. ducks	Plural, root plus *s*			

Table 6-2 Analysis of Spelling Skills (continued)

Words	Spelling Skill	Words	Spelling Skill
17. joking	e to i before adding ng	8. delaying	Addition of ing following y
18. reviewed	Addition of ed	9. glorious	y changes to i before adding ous
19. ruins	Vowels adjacent but not blended	10. moisture	ch spelled tu
20. crept	Short vowel and consonant blend	11. social	shul spelled cial
		12. initial	shul spelled tial
LEVEL VI		13. request	Prefix re
1. scene	Silent c	14. slight	Silent gh
2. hastened	Silent t	15. citizen	s sound spelled as c
3. trophy	ph digraph	16. envy	y says long e
4. whirl	Final l not doubled	17. banquet	kw spelled qu
5. pierced	i before e rule	18. pursue	Long u sound of ue
6. noble	Ending le	19. league	Digraph ue silent
7. ignorantly	ly ending	20. average	ij spelled age
8. rewarded	ed ending		
9. continued	e dropped for addition of ed	**LEVEL VIII**	
10. enforcing	e changes to i before adding ng	1. genius	yu spelled as iu
11. motoring	ing ending	2. ancient	sh spelled ci
12. relation	shun spelled tion	3. variety	Vowels adjacent but not blended
13. shortage	ij spelled age	4. sphere	ph digraph
14. chocolate	it spelled ate	5. receipt	i before e except after c rule
15. canyon	Sight word	6. tissue	sh spelled ss
16. court	Silent u	7. progression	shun spelled sion
17. maples	Plural, root, plus s	8. virtue	ch spelled tu
18. autograph	Addition of suffix graph	9. noisier	y changes to i and adds er
19. earliest	y to i and add est	10. leisure	zh spelled s
20. heavens	short e sound of ea	11. constitution	shun spelled tion
		12. fiction	shun spelled tion
LEVEL VII		13. angle	le ending
1. brief	i before e rule	14. essay	Double ss
2. phrase	ph digraph	15. union	y sound spelled as i
3. delicious	sh spelled ci	16. schedule	sk spelled sch
4. seize	Breaks the i before e rule	17. muscles	c has s sound
5. caution	shun spelled tion	18. natural	ch spelled tu
6. knowledge	ij spelled edge	19. technical	k spelled ch
7. museum	Vowels adjacent but not blended	20. cancel	sul spelled cel

who were able to successfully spell the words given at the first sitting, since there is no sense in testing those who have already failed the first two levels. To avoid continued frustration, a student who misses seven words at a level—which constitutes failure at that level—should not be tested any further. At the third sitting, the teacher should finish screening only those students who were successful with the previous words.

Children can usually spell only words they can read; therefore, by adding up the correct words on each paper and then placing the papers in an order from low to high, the teacher will have an immediate idea of the relative reading levels of the students. Spelling screens should occasionally be given on unlined white paper. This will give the teacher a sample of the student's handwriting, which can be analyzed for good spacing, letter production, and positioning of words on a page.

According to White,

Always have the child write the words on plain, unlined paper, as this will tell a great deal about the child's ability to organize his or her fine-motor output.

Check for evidence of good/poor teaching, and then (for visual-motor dyslexia) look for (a) poor organization of work on paper, (b) irregular shape and size of letters, (c) reversals of letters or letter-order, (d) awkward pencil grip, (e) writing of letters from bottom to top or right to left, and (f) phonetic spelling of irregular words (child lacks ability to hold the "mental picture" of a word). (1983, pp. 34–35)

Observing Spelling Behavior

Spelling ability is viewed by some teachers and school administrators equally with other academic skills. Students who are good learners but poor spellers are inordinately penalized by them for poor spelling. But deficiency in spelling does not necessarily denote that the learners have a serious learning disorder. Many students, educators, and professionals in different fields are poor spellers. Therefore, if spelling is an isolated problem, many teachers and parents do not consider the students learning disabled.

When poor spelling occurs with poor reading and arithmetic, then there is reason for concern. It appears that many of the learning skills required for good spelling are also the ones that enable students to become good readers. It is axiomatic that poor readers are generally poor spellers.

In evaluating spelling, the teacher should observe the following:

1. Has the learner isolated sound-symbol relationships (i.e., correctly associating a visual symbol with its auditory referent)?
2. Does the learner sequence visual symbols (letters) and sounds of letters (auditory)?
3. Can the learner estimate the number of letters in a word?
4. Does the learner use a logical system to arrive at the spelling of a word correctly or incorrectly?
5. What is the overall memory ability of the student?
6. Is there a great discrepancy between spelling ability and other academic skills, such as reading?
7. Is spelling automatic to the student (spells words instantly, correctly or incorrectly) or has he or she developed a unique analytical attack for each word?
8. How rapidly does the student relate the sound of the word or letters to the visual association in his or her mind? Does the visual image appear as a word or just isolated letters? Can the student verbalize what is happening in his or her mind's eye?
9. Is there a discrepancy between the student's ability to spell isolated words and his or her ability to spell phrases or sentences from dictation?
10. What does the student do with unfamiliar words that are not part of the reading program?
11. Is poor spelling disguised by illegible or unorthodox handwriting?
12. In written expression, does the student with spelling difficulties tend to substitute simple for more complex words having the same meaning?
13. Is there a great discrepancy between short-term and long-term memory of how words are spelled, requiring a great deal of intermittent reinforcement throughout the school year?
14. Does the learner have right-left scanning eye movements during the reading process that may result in two-letter reversals in spelling?
15. Is a great deal of oral spelling sequencing necessary to correct a residual spelling problem even after the student has learned to read?
16. Is the student having difficulty associating the meaning of a word with the sounds or symbols that make up the spoken word?
17. Is spelling improvement commensurate with reading improvement, or is there a residual spelling problem after reading improves?
18. Does the student appear to learn better with words of similar spelling patterns (e.g., *fat, cat, sat, mat*)?
19. Have hearing and vision been checked recently and found to be within normal limits?
20. Does the student improve with teacher-directed spelling activities? The student may need more carefully structured spelling activities. A part of the student's problem may be in the way spelling is taught and reinforced.
21. Has the student developed an emotional block to spelling due to continued failure and pressures from the home or the school?
22. What kinds of study skills does the student use for spelling in school and at home?
23. In evaluation, does the student select the spelled word from among choices (recognition) easier than he or she spells the word (recall)?
24. Is the student being confused or overloaded by the introduction of too many different phonics skills in the spelling and reading programs?
25. Does the student spell better aloud than in writing?
26. Does the student learn more words when fewer words are required to be learned in a given period of time (slower rate of input)?
27. Does the student "chunk" (use syllables or parts of words), or does he or she spell letter by letter?
28. Does the student pronounce words correctly?

Specific Spelling Errors

SPELLING ERRORS—PRIMARILY AUDITORY

The misspellings are typically nonphonetic, because the students often lack phonetic skills.

1. Substitutes *t* for *d, f* for *v, sh* for *ch*. (Auditory discrimination or cultural)
2. Does not hear subtle differences in, or discriminate between, sounds and often leaves vowels out of two-syllable words—for example, spells *plsh* for *polish*. (Auditory acuity or discrimination)
3. Discerns the beginning or ending of a word but not the middle of the word, which may be missing or spelled wrong—for example, spells *hd* for *hand*. (Auditory acuity and/or discrimination)
4. Confuses vowels—for example, spells *bit* as *bet*. (Auditory discrimination)
5. Omits the second letter in blends, spelling *fled* as *fed*. (Auditory acuity and/or discrimination)
6. Uses a synonym, such as *house* for home, in spelling. (Auditory-visual association)
7. Omits word endings such as *ed, s,* and *ing*. (Cultural or auditory discrimination)
8. Takes wild guesses with little or no relationship between the letters or words used and the spelling words dictated, such as spelling *dog* for *home* or writing *phe* for home. (Auditory-visual associative memory)

SPELLING ERRORS—PRIMARILY VISUAL

The misspellings are typically phonetic and therefore often intelligible, although incorrect.

1. Visualizes the beginning or the ending of words but omits the middle of the word—for example, spells *hapy* for *happy*. (Visual memory)
2. Gives the correct letters but in the wrong sequence. The word *the* may be written as *teh* or *hte*. (Visual-memory sequence)
3. Reverses letters or words—for example, writes *ƨ* for *s, b* for *d, on* for *no,* or was for saw.
4. Inverts letters, writing *u* for *n, m* for *w*. (Usually visual memory but could also be either visual discrimination or spatial)
5. Mixes up capitals and small letters—cAt. This error is also evident in cursive writing. (Poor transitional teaching or visual memory). Sometimes mixing of capitals and small letters is due to the student's attempt to compensate for not knowing the small letters by substituting a capital letter for the small letter he has not learned.
6. Spelling words phonetically that are nonphonetic in configuration—for example, *tuff* for *tough*. (Visual memory)

Data Collection

MANN-SUITER ANALYSIS OF ERRORS WORKSHEETS

After giving the Developmental Inventories and Screens, the teacher can indicate the errors on the Analysis of Errors Worksheet (Form 6-23). Having done this, the teacher will be better able to determine how much, and what type of, additional testing is necessary before formulating any educational strategies for a given student. Some teachers will require more information, including standardized tests, before making any decisions. The question is not how much testing is adequate but, rather, how much information is needed in order to make a decision about changing or modifying the educational program for a particular student.

Analysis of Error Patterns

Ganschow (1984) reported that error patterns reveal information about learning styles. She suggests that an examination of students' error patterns aids the teacher in finding patterns that will lead to remediation. An error analysis chart can be used for analysis. The chart, Table 6-3, should have four columns: (1) the misspelled word, (2) the word correctly spelled, (3) a space to describe types of errors, and (4) a space to propose remediation.

Supplementary Screening—Spelling

After analyzing the student's errors, the examiner may want to gain further diagnostic information from the following screening devices:

Speech   page 205
Alphabet-Speech   page 194
Auditory Discrimination   page 191
Visual Memory   page 189
Handwriting   page 306
Oral Reading   pages 224–301
Silent Reading   pages 246–270
Hearing (acuity)   page 213
Vision (acuity)   page 213

After screening the students with the developmental spelling inventory, the teacher can start testing for reading abilities. Testing for reading should begin with the students who made the lowest scores on the spelling inventory, since they are the students who will need a more accurate and comprehensive analysis of reading abilities.

MANN-SUITER ANALYSIS OF ERRORS WORKSHEET

DEVELOPMENTAL SPELLING INVENTORY

NAME _____ SCHOOL _____

DATE _____ GRADE _____ DATE OF BIRTH _____

EXAMINER _____

Auditory Errors

(A check mark indicates difficulty)

1. Makes substitutions (*t* for *d, f* for *v, sh* for *ch*) _____
2. Omits vowels (*brd* for *bird*) _____
3. Omits second consonant in blends (*rut* for *rust*) _____
4. Uses synonyms (*house* for *home*) _____
5. Makes wild guesses (*yot* for *yes*) _____
6. No response _____
7. Confuses vowel sounds (*but* for *bat*) _____
8. Omits word endings such as *ed, s, ing* _____
9. Cannot remember spelling rules _____
10. Does not discern the middle of a word (*h--d*) _____

Visual Errors

1. Writes the beginning letters only _____
2. Makes reversals of words or letters (*b* for *d,* or *on* for *no*) _____
3. Uses inversions of letters (*m* for *w*) _____
4. Mixes capital and small letters (ba*B*y) _____
5. Spells phonetically (cannot revisualize) _____
6. Spells correct letters in the wrong sequence (*teh* for *the*) _____

General Observations

1. Has the learner isolated sound-symbol relationships (i.e., correctly associating a visual symbol with its auditory referent)? _____
2. Does the learner sequence visual symbols (letters) and sounds of letters (auditory)? _____
3. Can the learner estimate the number of letters in a word? _____
4. Does the learner use a logical system to arrive at the spelling of a word correctly or incorrectly? _____
5. What is the overall memory ability of the student? _____
6. Is there a great discrepancy between spelling ability and other academic skills such as reading? _____
7. Is spelling automatic to the student (spells words instantly, correctly or incorrectly), or has the learner developed a unique analytical attack for each word? _____

(continued)

NAME _____

(A check mark indicates
difficulty)

8. How rapidly does the student relate the sound of the word or letters to the visual association in his or her mind? Does the visual image appear as a word or just isolated letters? Can the student verbalize what is happening in his or her mind's eye?   _____

9. Is there a discrepancy between the student's ability to spell isolated words and his or her ability to spell phrases or sentences from dictation?   _____

10. What does the student do with unfamiliar words that are not part of the reading program?   _____

11. Is poor spelling disguised by illegible or unorthodox handwriting?   _____

12. In written expression does the student, because of spelling difficulties, tend to substitute simple words for more complex words having the same meaning?   _____

13. Is there a great discrepancy between short-term and long-term memory of how words are spelled, requiring a great deal of intermittent reinforcement throughout the school year?   _____

14. Does the learner have right-left scanning eye movements during the reading process that may result in two-letter reversals in spelling?   _____

15. Is there a residual spelling problem even after the student has learned to read, requiring a great deal of oral spelling sequencing in training to correct this faulty learning?   _____

16. Is the student having difficulty associating the meaning of a word with the sounds or symbols that make up the spoken word?   _____

17. Is the spelling improvement commensurate with reading improvement, or is there a residual spelling problem after reading improves?   _____

18. Does the student appear to learn better with words of similar spelling patterns (e.g., *fat, cat, sat, mat*)?   _____

19. Have hearing and vision been checked recently and found to be within normal limits?   _____

20. Does the student improve with more teacher-directed spelling activities?   _____

21. Has the student developed an emotional block to spelling due to continued failure and pressures from the home or the school?   _____

22. What kinds of study skills does the student use for spelling in school and at home?   _____

23. In evaluation, does the student select the spelled word from among choices (recognition) more easily than he or she spells the word (recall)?   _____

24. Is the student being confused or overloaded by the introduction of too many different phonics skills in the spelling and reading programs?   _____

25. Does the student spell better aloud than in writing?   _____

26. Does the student learn more words when less words are required to be learned in a given period of time (slower rate of input)?   _____

27. Does the student *chunk* (use syllables or parts of words), or does he or she spell letter by letter?   _____

28. Does the student pronounce words correctly?   _____

Other Errors

Table 6-3 *Error Analysis Chart*

Misspelled Word	Correct Spelling	Types of Errors	Proposed Remediation
chop	shop	consonant digraph *sh*	compare familiar words: shell, shirt, show and church, chick, chin
wint	want	short vowel *a*	discriminate differences in the medial position: want – went – wont
wak	walk	silent *l*	use word in context
fictshun	fiction	*-shun* spelled *-tion*	review *-tion*

Supplementary Evaluation—Spelling

TEST	GRADE LEVEL	COMPONENTS	TYPE
Boder Test of Reading-Spelling Patterns	K–12	Dictated spelling	Norm-referenced
Brigance Diagnostic Comprehensive Inventory of Basic Skills (Brigance, 1982)	K–12	Dictated spelling	Criterion-referenced
The California Achievement Tests (Tiegs & Clark, 1977–1978)	1–12	Proofreading	Norm-referenced
Comprehensive Tests of Basic Skills (CBT/McGraw-Hill, 1968)	2–12	Proofreading	Norm-referenced
Diagnostic Spelling Potential Test (Arena, 1981)	2–12	Dictated spelling	Criterion-referenced
Iowa Tests of Basic Skills (Hieronymus et al., 1978)	1–9	Proofreading	Norm-referenced
Kottmeyers *Diagnostic Spelling Test (Kottmeyer, 1970)*	*2–6*	*Dictated spelling*	*Criterion-referenced*
McGraw-Hill Basic Study Skills: Spelling (Raygoz, 1970)	9–12	Proofreading	Norm-referenced
Metropolitan Achievement Tests (Durost et al., 1971)	2–4 / 2–9	Dictated word / Proofreading	Norm-referenced
Peabody Individual Achievement Test (Dunn & Markwardt, 1970)	K–12	Proofreading	Norm-referenced
Spellmaster (Cohen & Abrams, 1974)	1–8	Dictated word	Criterion-referenced
SRA Achievement Series in Arithmetic (Thorpe et al., 1974)	1–12	Proofreading	Norm-referenced
Stanford Achievement Test (Madden et al., 1973)	1–9	Proofreading	Norm-referenced
Test of Written Spelling-2 (TWS-2) (Larsen & Hammill, 1976)	1–8	Dictated word	Norm-referenced
Wide-Range Achievement Test (Jastak & Jastak, 1978)	K–12	Dictated word	Norm-referenced

It is suggested that in testing for reading with DWRI (Developmental Word Reading Inventory), the teacher begin the evaluation by dropping down to one level below the student's last successful level in spelling. If the student cannot spell at all, then the following readiness skills should be assessed:

1. Does the student know the letter names and sounds?
2. Can the student match a letter sound with its visual symbol?
3. Can the student match a letter name with its visual symbol?

READING DIAGNOSIS

In evaluating reading, educators must concern themselves with three levels of functioning:

1. Screening and differential diagnosis of the learning problems of the very young child are necessary to determine whether the child has the prerequisite skills for learning how to read. Early evaluation enables the school to make decisions that result in more appropriate approaches to initial teaching. Evaluation can be accomplished during the kindergarten year in the spring, in preparation for first grade placement in the fall. The areas to be examined would include those listed in the Mann-Suiter-McClung Developmental Checklists (Form 6-1 and 6-2) and in the estimated hierarchy of skills presented in Chapter 9. As a part of this early diagnosis of learning problems, the teacher can make decisions about specific programs and backup systems that would be appropriate for individual learners.
2. Learners who have plateaued or who have indicated a slow rate of learning will profit from an early evaluation of reading skills, because appropriate remedial programs can be instituted early by the instructor. The Mann-Suiter Developmental Reading Inventories can be utilized in this area.
3. A number of students are failing in reading because of insufficient motivation or inappropriate early teaching. These students may not indicate deficits in the learning correlates. Instead they have a history of poor motivation or behavior difficulties. In the case of the poorly taught student, a pattern of faulty learning and poorly stabilized reading skills is evident.

Students who have problems in the cognitive areas dealing with memory, perception, language, and spatial-temporal orientation will require specific analysis and a balanced program that will strengthen the weaknesses while simultaneously developing task level behaviors that educators refer to as reading skills.

Initial Testing

If a teacher is testing a student for the first time, the following procedure is suggested, regardless of the age or grade of the learner who is beyond first grade.

WHERE TO START
Turn to page 215, use the screening procedures outlined, and give the student a spelling inventory. The spelling inventory will enable the teacher to determine at which point screening with developmental reading inventories should begin. In testing for reading ability, the teacher should begin one level below that at which the student failed in spelling. Table 6-4 indicates where to start testing on the Developmental Word-Recognition Inventory.

TESTING A STUDENT BELOW THE PP3 LEVEL
The following procedure will enable the teacher to determine where to place the student in the preprimer materials. The first step is to find out how many of the words the learner can read in the PP1 series being used. The teacher puts all of the words introduced in the PP1 on 3" × 5" word cards and then shows the student all of the words, one at a time. As the student responds, the teacher places the cards into three groups: words read without hesitation, words sounded out and eventually read or read with noticeable hesitation, and words totally unknown.

The teacher will now have the following information:

1. *Group One* will be the words read without hesitation. These words are considered mastered. They have been learned and can be used by the student at the independent level.
2. *Group Two* will be the words read with difficulty. The student may have to sound them out, reads them correctly at one point and incorrectly at another, and exhibits hesitations. This category of sight words is called partial learning. These are also the "leverage" words, as they are the words that are ready to be learned and should be taught first.
3. *Group Three* words are unknown to the student. They are the words that are totally misread on repeated occasions. There is evidence of 100 percent failure and frustration.

After testing the student on his or her sight recognition of the PP1 words and placing the words into one

Table 6-4 Correlation between Spelling Inventory and Word-Recognition Reading Inventory

	Spelling Inventory	*Word-Recognition Reading Inventory*
Level I	failed*	Start at preprimer 3 level†
Level II	failed but Level I passed	Start at primer level
Level III	failed but Level II passed	Start at first-reader level
Level IV	failed but Level III passed	Start at second-reader level
Level V	failed but Level IV passed	Start at third-reader level
Level VI	failed but Level V passed	Start at fourth-reader level

*A spelling level is considered failed when a learner misses seven or more at a particular level.
†Regardless of the student's age or grade (beyond first grade), if the student fails the PP3 word-recognition and paragraph reading inventories, he or she is functioning on a beginning reading level and needs to be taught with initial teaching approaches.

of the three categories indicated above, the teacher can decide whether the student is possibly ready for the PP2 because enough of the PP1 material is known and review would suffice.

If the teacher feels that the student knows enough of the PP1 material to enable him or her to move on to PP2, the teacher uses the following method to determine where to start.

1. The teacher puts all of the words introduced in the PP2 on 3" × 5" word cards and tests the student, following the same procedure used for PP1.
2. If the student finds PP2 difficult because too many words are unknown, the teacher starts teaching at that level.
3. If the student passes the PP2 level the teacher proceeds to PP3 and tests to determine the starting point.

Most older students who fail the Mann-Suiter PP3 test have such a scattered vocabulary of known words that they find it difficult to fit into any Preprimer program. The above testing procedure will accurately place them in most reading systems.

ONGOING EVALUATION—UNDER PRIMER LEVEL

This type of ongoing evaluation is for students in established reading programs who are functioning under the primer level. When a learner completes a PP1, PP2, or PP3, he or she should be tested immediately on the words taught in that book and should not be moved on to the next book unless the words are known without hesitation. If the student has forgotten any words, they must be retaught in a different manner. All learning must be adjusted to a rate tolerable for each student, and only through ongoing testing is it possible to make sure the learner is "holding," or stabilizing, the material taught.

ONGOING EVALUATION—PRIMER LEVEL OR ABOVE

This type of ongoing evaluation is for students in an established reading program who are reading at the Primer level or above. Ongoing testing is an important part of any reading program. When a student finishes a reading book such as a primer or a 2¹ reader, the teacher needs to test to see whether the student is ready to be advanced to the next level or needs another book on the same level just completed. Some students need more than one book at each level. (At the primer and first grade level especially, some will need two or three). Use the Mann-Suiter developmental reading inventories for this testing.

An alternative would be to select two or three paragraphs from the reader the student has just completed and informally observe how he or she reads. The teacher can ask the student questions about what he or she has read. Questions in the following areas should be included: (1) main ideas, (2) inference, (3) details, and (4) vocabulary.

Observing Reading Behaviors

1. How does the student analyze problems and glean meaning?
2. Does the student have excessive body movements while reading?
3. Is the student penalized by slowness in reading?
4. Does the student prefer to read alone or in a group?
5. How does the student react to being tested? Will the student respond to an alternative type of evaluation?
6. Does the student avoid reading?
7. When the student reads, what types of material will he or she read?

8. Does the student read at home?
9. Does the student understand more after reading silently than after listening to someone read the material orally?
10. What are the student's strengths and weaknesses indicated on the Mann-Suiter-McClung Checklists (page 156)?
11. Does the student value reading?
12. Is the student's failure mechanical or is he or she deficient in comprehension?
13. Does the student substitute words that are appropriate in his or her dialect while reading?

Purposes of the Developmental Reading Inventories

The purposes of the developmental reading inventories are as follows:
1. To aid the teacher in determining the three levels of reading that have been traditionally defined as *independent, instructional,* and *frustration* levels.
2. To provide the teacher with information at the task level in the language arts area, as well as to point out possible problems that result in failure in reading.
3. To indicate the students' strengths and weaknesses by analyzing their performance at the reading task. The results of these tests can become the basis for selecting appropriate educational strategies for particular students.

Three types of reading assessment are delineated in this chapter: (1) teacher-developed inventories based on the available language arts series, (2) the Mann-Suiter Developmental Reading Inventories, and (3) the Mann-Suiter General Reading Screening.

Teacher-Developed Word Reading Inventory

To develop a word reading inventory, the teacher takes a sample of words from the back of basal reading books of each grade level. He or she selects 20 words from each level, beginning at the PP3 level (approximately every second or third word). The formula for extracting these words is similar to that described for the Mann-Suiter spelling inventory. For all grade levels, the teacher picks a sample of 20 words by dividing the number of words in the book by 20. Say there are 200 new words in the book. Two hundred divided by 20 would give 10; therefore, a sample selection would be every tenth word from the list in the back of the book. After selecting the words for each level, the teacher should go back and check that he or she has included the following:

For grade one:

1. A variety of vowel and consonant sounds in different positions.
2. Words that are similar and different in configuration (a few words may be exchanged in order to achieve this).

For grades two through six:

1. A variety of vowel and consonant sounds in different positions.
2. Words that are similar and different in configuration.
3. Words with prefixes such as *pre* and *re* and suffixes such as *ed* and *ing.*
4. Words that have abstract meanings, such as *liberty* and *justice,* as language development is also being tested.

Note: Proper nouns are not included. By convention, they are omitted.

DEVELOPING SCORING SHEETS
After having selected a word sample from the various levels and made some adjustments as recommended (using good judgment), the teacher is now ready to make up his or her own word-recognition scoring sheets. Form 6-24 illustrates a teacher's copy of word-recognition scoring sheets (Johnson & Kress, 1965). The words are typed clearly and double spaced on white paper. These sheets are to be used only by the teacher and are designed to record each student's responses.

DEVELOPING A TACHISTOSCOPE
After selecting the vocabulary and making up the score, the teacher is ready to construct a device that can be used to present the words to the student. The words should be presented in a manual tachistoscopic fashion. The instructions for making a sample word-recognition tachistoscope are presented in Figures 6-1 and 6-2 (Durrell, 1956).

Note: Primer type should be used for word list selections from PP3 through the first level.

Mann-Suiter Developmental Reading Inventories

The Mann-Suiter Developmental Reading Inventory includes a word-recognition section and a paragraph reading section. Approximately 375 students, grades 1 through 8, were administered the entire inventory, and the results were compared to their level of functioning as specified by teachers. In approximately 85 percent of the cases there was agreement between the estimates of teachers and the students' performance on the Mann-Suiter Developmental Inventories.

Form 6-24

TEACHER'S DEVELOPMENTAL WORD-RECOGNITION SCORING SHEET

NAME _____ DATE _____

√ = Correct   √^ = Incorrect   EXAMINER _____

Flash	Pre-Primer Stimulus	Untimed		Flash	Primer Stimulus	Untimed
1. _____	the	_____		1. _____	with	_____
2. _____	red	_____		2. _____	good	_____
3. _____	see	_____		3. _____	they	_____
4. _____	to	_____		4. _____	for	_____
5. _____	house	_____		5. _____	girl	_____
6. _____	said	_____		6. _____	all	_____
7. _____	little	_____		7. _____	duck	_____
8. _____	big	_____		8. _____	this	_____
9. _____	not	_____		9. _____	yellow	_____
10. _____	ball	_____		10. _____	away	_____
11. _____	get	_____		11. _____	home	_____
12. _____	in	_____		12. _____	are	_____
13. _____	went	_____		13. _____	but	_____
14. _____	and	_____		14. _____	like	_____
15. _____	dog	_____		15. _____	make	_____
16. _____	mother	_____		16. _____	come	_____
17. _____	man	_____		17. _____	my	_____
18. _____	had	_____		18. _____	one	_____
19. _____	no	_____		19. _____	want	_____
20. _____	run	_____		20. _____	what	_____
_____	Errors	_____		_____	Errors	_____
_____	Score	_____		_____	Score	_____

5 points each   5 points each

Observations:

227

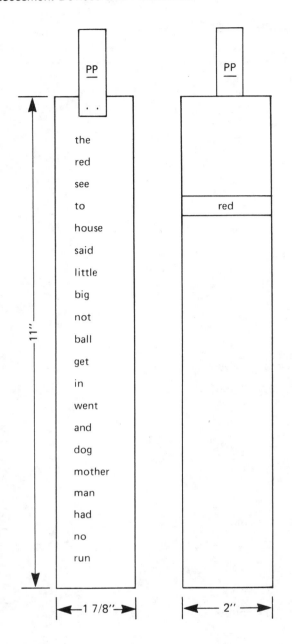

Figure 6-1 Instructions for Constructing a Tachistocope: The Screen. A tab is stapled on top of the strip for ease of handling. All words should be double spaced. Primer type should be used for PP3 through level one words. A tachistoscope can be made from oak tag or strips cut from manila folders.

DEVELOPMENTAL WORD-RECOGNITION INVENTORY

The Word-Recognition Inventory was developed by sampling different basal and linguistic word lists. These lists were representative of many different reading programs and were selected according to level of difficulty. Some stratification was accomplished in order to achieve a balance of spelling patterns, prefixes and suffixes, and different configurations of words. Two alternate sets of lists (Form A and Form B) are included. Form 6-25 is the scoring for Form A. Form 6-26 is the scoring sheet for Form B.

Administering Developmental Word-Recognition Inventory

1. During the test, the teacher should sit opposite the student at a table.
2. The first word should be centered in the window of the tachistoscope but covered with a white unlined 3" × 5" index card. (Variations of presentations to students can be used, depending on teacher preference.)
3. After asking the student to watch, the teacher should expose the whole word clearly and quickly, making sure the student initially gets only a flash presentation of the word.
4. The timing for the complete movement on the flash showing of the word should be approximately that required to say "one thousand" at a normal rate.

   Note: No more than one flash exposure should be given. This means the examiner must *be sure that the student is ready and attending.*

5. If the student responds quickly, the examiner immediately records a check, √, in the flash response column and goes on to the next word.
6. If, however, the student gives an incorrect response, the examiner records a different check, ✓, in the flash column and notes everything that is said.
7. No clues should be given, but the student should be allowed to reexamine the word and answer if he or she can. No help should be given. The answer is then recorded in the untimed column.
8. When a student does not know a word, the teacher can obtain additional information by asking if he or she knows any part of the word. The teacher can cover part of the word, ask the student if he or she knows it, and then determine if the student can blend the parts. This step is optional but helpful diagnostically.
9. The teacher must record all responses immediately and continue testing until the student misses seven of the twenty words on an untimed section for a particular grade level.

   Note: The teacher must remember to cover the teacher scoring sheet with his or her arm so that the student cannot read the words ahead of time.

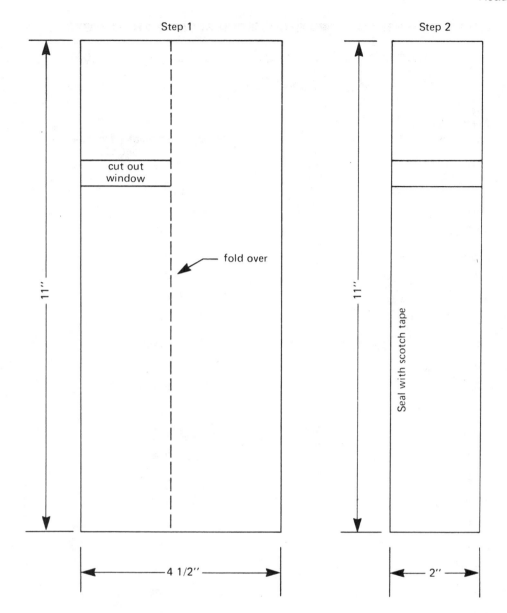

Figure 6-2 Instructions for Constructing a Tachistoscope: The Image. Material that can be used are oak tag or strips cut from a manila folder.

10. Table 6-5 is a compilation of commonly used notations that teachers can use to communicate their findings to each other.

Scoring Inventory

On the Developmental Word Reading Inventory, there is an allowance for a self-correction of errors. A response is counted accurate if

1. The student self-corrects during the timed exposure (the teacher must be sure to write down the initial response).

2. The student corrects the flash error during the untimed exposure. The error is counted only on the flash section of the test.

Note: Two scores should be obtained from each level test, one representing the student's flash vocabulary and the other his or her ability to identify words in an untimed fashion. Table 6-6 represents a score chart for flash and untimed words.

The scores on the Developmental Word-Recognition Inventory can be plotted on the Developmental Reading Summary (Form 6-27).

MANN-SUITER DEVELOPMENTAL WORD-RECOGNITION SCORING SHEET (FORM A)

NAME _____ DATE _____

√ = Correct   √ᴧ = Incorrect   EXAMINER _____

Flash	Pre-Primer Stimulus	Untimed		Flash	Primer Stimulus	Untimed
1. ____	the	____		1. ____	with	____
2. ____	red	____		2. ____	good	____
3. ____	see	____		3. ____	they	____
4. ____	to	____		4. ____	for	____
5. ____	house	____		5. ____	girl	____
6. ____	said	____		6. ____	all	____
7. ____	little	____		7. ____	duck	____
8. ____	big	____		8. ____	this	____
9. ____	not	____		9. ____	yellow	____
10. ____	ball	____		10. ____	away	____
11. ____	get	____		11. ____	home	____
12. ____	in	____		12. ____	are	____
13. ____	went	____		13. ____	but	____
14. ____	and	____		14. ____	like	____
15. ____	dog	____		15. ____	make	____
16. ____	mother	____		16. ____	come	____
17. ____	man	____		17. ____	my	____
18. ____	had	____		18. ____	one	____
19. ____	no	____		19. ____	want	____
20. ____	run	____		20. ____	what	____
____	Errors	____		____	Errors	____
____	Score	____		____	Score	____

5 points each   5 points each

Observations:

(continued)

NAME _____ DATE _____

√ = Correct   √ˆ = Incorrect   EXAMINER _____

First-Reader Level				*Second-Reader Level*		
Flash	*Stimulus*	*Untimed*		*Flash*	*Stimulus*	*Untimed*
1. ___	many	___		1. ___	head	___
2. ___	took	___		2. ___	nice	___
3. ___	feet	___		3. ___	river	___
4. ___	please	___		4. ___	string	___
5. ___	other	___		5. ___	through	___
6. ___	drop	___		6. ___	side	___
7. ___	their	___		7. ___	knew	___
8. ___	next	___		8. ___	air	___
9. ___	over	___		9. ___	grass	___
10. ___	food	___		10. ___	floor	___
11. ___	hold	___		11. ___	drink	___
12. ___	again	___		12. ___	while	___
13. ___	time	___		13. ___	anything	___
14. ___	when	___		14. ___	both	___
15. ___	flag	___		15. ___	leaves	___
16. ___	work	___		16. ___	wash	___
17. ___	thing	___		17. ___	friend	___
18. ___	going	___		18. ___	built	___
19. ___	around	___		19. ___	ghost	___
20. ___	frogs	___		20. ___	beautiful	___
___	Errors	___		___	Errors	___
___	Scores	___		___	Scores	___

5 points each   5 points each

Observations:

(continued)

NAME _____ DATE _____

√ = Correct   √ = Incorrect   EXAMINER _____

Third-Reader Level			Fourth-Reader Level		
Flash	Stimulus	Untimed	Flash	Stimulus	Untimed
1. ____	snail	____	1. ____	spy	____
2. ____	greatest	____	2. ____	fortune	____
3. ____	eight	____	3. ____	sheriff	____
4. ____	lazy	____	4. ____	silence	____
5. ____	freeze	____	5. ____	glanced	____
6. ____	gravel	____	6. ____	breathe	____
7. ____	cousin	____	7. ____	statements	____
8. ____	path	____	8. ____	design	____
9. ____	fifteen	____	9. ____	pleasantly	____
10. ____	since	____	10. ____	bacon	____
11. ____	awake	____	11. ____	courage	____
12. ____	shades	____	12. ____	islands	____
13. ____	scatter	____	13. ____	western	____
14. ____	saddle	____	14. ____	success	____
15. ____	journey	____	15. ____	trailed	____
16. ____	chief	____	16. ____	claimed	____
17. ____	tribe	____	17. ____	knowledge	____
18. ____	danger	____	18. ____	peaceful	____
19. ____	different	____	19. ____	rough	____
20. ____	stream	____	20. ____	guides	____
____	Errors	____	____	Errors	____
____	Scores	____	____	Scores	____

5 points each   5 points each

Observations:

(continued)

NAME _____ DATE _____

√ = Correct   √ˆ = Incorrect   EXAMINER _____

Fifth-Reader Level				*Sixth-Reader Level*		
Flash	*Stimulus*	*Untimed*		*Flash*	*Stimulus*	*Untimed*
1. ____	naturally	____		1. ____	fleeting	____
2. ____	products	____		2. ____	poisoned	____
3. ____	defeated	____		3. ____	membership	____
4. ____	fought	____		4. ____	detained	____
5. ____	horrible	____		5. ____	medicine	____
6. ____	article	____		6. ____	summoned	____
7. ____	regarding	____		7. ____	licensed	____
8. ____	leisure	____		8. ____	malicious	____
9. ____	invitation	____		9. ____	liquids	____
10. ____	ancient	____		10. ____	obliged	____
11. ____	haze	____		11. ____	blonde	____
12. ____	shrill	____		12. ____	abandoned	____
13. ____	acquire	____		13. ____	partial	____
14. ____	scholar	____		14. ____	imagination	____
15. ____	prevent	____		15. ____	extensive	____
16. ____	salmon	____		16. ____	politics	____
17. ____	expensive	____		17. ____	cooperation	____
18. ____	whether	____		18. ____	scenes	____
19. ____	constantly	____		19. ____	negative	____
20. ____	emperor	____		20. ____	omitted	____
____	Errors	____		____	Errors	____
____	Scores	____		____	Scores	____

5 points each   5 points each

Observations:

(continued)

NAME _____ DATE _____

√ = Correct   √̂ = Incorrect   EXAMINER _____

	Seventh-Reader Level			*Eighth-Reader Level*	
Flash	*Stimulus*	*Untimed*	*Flash*	*Stimulus*	*Untimed*
1. ____	adequately	____	1. ____	prairies	____
2. ____	sojourn	____	2. ____	evident	____
3. ____	delighted	____	3. ____	nucleus	____
4. ____	waning	____	4. ____	antiquity	____
5. ____	grasped	____	5. ____	twilight	____
6. ____	vocation	____	6. ____	memorandum	____
7. ____	prominent	____	7. ____	whimsical	____
8. ____	preposition	____	8. ____	proportional	____
9. ____	exposition	____	9. ____	intangible	____
10. ____	subscribe	____	10. ____	formulated	____
11. ____	tremor	____	11. ____	ambitious	____
12. ____	height	____	12. ____	realize	____
13. ____	scientists	____	13. ____	ultimate	____
14. ____	individual	____	14. ____	financial	____
15. ____	persuade	____	15. ____	attitude	____
16. ____	approximate	____	16. ____	obviously	____
17. ____	environment	____	17. ____	oxygen	____
18. ____	compassionate	____	18. ____	visualize	____
19. ____	crisis	____	19. ____	surgery	____
20. ____	industrious	____	20. ____	fascinated	____
____	Errors	____	____	Errors	____
____	Scores	____	____	Scores	____

5 points each   5 points each

Observations:

(continued)

MANN-SUITER DEVELOPMENTAL WORD-RECOGNITION SCORING SHEET (FORM B)

NAME _____ DATE _____

√ = Correct   √ʌ = Incorrect   EXAMINER _____

	Pre-Primer				Primer	
Flash	*Stimulus*	*Untimed*		*Flash*	*Stimulus*	*Untimed*
1. ____	look	____		1. ____	help	____
2. ____	fun	____		2. ____	why	____
3. ____	do	____		3. ____	day	____
4. ____	at	____		4. ____	that	____
5. ____	jump	____		5. ____	down	____
6. ____	up	____		6. ____	sleep	____
7. ____	can	____		7. ____	play	____
8. ____	wet	____		8. ____	walk	____
9. ____	go	____		9. ____	out	____
10. ____	bad	____		10. ____	there	____
11. ____	father	____		11. ____	must	____
12. ____	you	____		12. ____	two	____
13. ____	here	____		13. ____	baby	____
14. ____	is	____		14. ____	toy	____
15. ____	will	____		15. ____	kitten	____
16. ____	hop	____		16. ____	blue	____
17. ____	has	____		17. ____	know	____
18. ____	doll	____		18. ____	some	____
19. ____	have	____		19. ____	by	____
20. ____	too	____		20. ____	happy	____
____	Errors	____		____	Errors	____
____	Score	____		____	Score	____

5 points each   5 points each

(continued)

NAME _____ DATE _____

√ = Correct   √^ = Incorrect   EXAMINER _____

First-Reader Level				Second-Reader Level		
Flash	Stimulus	Untimed		Flash	Stimulus	Untimed
1. ____	children	____		1. ____	against	____
2. ____	name	____		2. ____	was	____
3. ____	water	____		3. ____	close	____
4. ____	old	____		4. ____	city	____
5. ____	full	____		5. ____	everyone	____
6. ____	stood	____		6. ____	build	____
7. ____	three	____		7. ____	change	____
8. ____	would	____		8. ____	farmer	____
9. ____	bring	____		9. ____	size	____
10. ____	king	____		10. ____	lunch	____
11. ____	gone	____		11. ____	because	____
12. ____	left	____		12. ____	heavy	____
13. ____	paper	____		13. ____	whole	____
14. ____	catch	____		14. ____	today	____
15. ____	came	____		15. ____	found	____
16. ____	sand	____		16. ____	read	____
17. ____	school	____		17. ____	breakfast	____
18. ____	horse	____		18. ____	town	____
19. ____	night	____		19. ____	first	____
20. ____	story	____		20. ____	gray	____
____	Errors	____		____	Errors	____
____	Scores	____		____	Scores	____

5 points each   5 points each

Observations:

(continued)

NAME _____ DATE _____

√ = Correct   √^ = Incorrect   EXAMINER _____

Third-Reader Level			Fourth-Reader Level		
Flash	Stimulus	Untimed	Flash	Stimulus	Untimed
1. _____	grounded	_____	1. _____	price	_____
2. _____	careful	_____	2. _____	future	_____
3. _____	engine	_____	3. _____	liquid	_____
4. _____	storm	_____	4. _____	interior	_____
5. _____	wonderful	_____	5. _____	region	_____
6. _____	ocean	_____	6. _____	station	_____
7. _____	clamp	_____	7. _____	anger	_____
8. _____	important	_____	8. _____	serious	_____
9. _____	wealth	_____	9. _____	concern	_____
10. _____	safely	_____	10. _____	breeze	_____
11. _____	fasten	_____	11. _____	sign	_____
12. _____	lovely	_____	12. _____	vacant	_____
13. _____	invite	_____	13. _____	freight	_____
14. _____	surface	_____	14. _____	support	_____
15. _____	grove	_____	15. _____	enough	_____
16. _____	delicious	_____	16. _____	popular	_____
17. _____	being	_____	17. _____	flakes	_____
18. _____	empty	_____	18. _____	adventure	_____
19. _____	government	_____	19. _____	cooperate	_____
20. _____	worry	_____	20. _____	possible	_____
_____	Errors	_____	_____	Errors	_____
_____	Scores	_____	_____	Scores	_____

5 points each   5 points each

Observations:

(continued)

NAME _____ DATE _____

√ = Correct   √ = Incorrect   EXAMINER _____

Fifth-Reader Level				*Sixth-Reader Level*		
Flash	*Stimulus*	*Untimed*		*Flash*	*Stimulus*	*Untimed*
1. ____	enemies	____		1. ____	athletes	____
2. ____	legend	____		2. ____	curiosity	____
3. ____	nursery	____		3. ____	automobile	____
4. ____	realize	____		4. ____	tougher	____
5. ____	weapon	____		5. ____	paragraph	____
6. ____	ambition	____		6. ____	erratic	____
7. ____	yield	____		7. ____	requires	____
8. ____	ordinary	____		8. ____	fluent	____
9. ____	terrace	____		9. ____	debris	____
10. ____	ivory	____		10. ____	thorough	____
11. ____	magnificent	____		11. ____	artificial	____
12. ____	dangerous	____		12. ____	source	____
13. ____	curtains	____		13. ____	dungeon	____
14. ____	evolved	____		14. ____	detained	____
15. ____	enormous	____		15. ____	skiing	____
16. ____	cushion	____		16. ____	rebellion	____
17. ____	source	____		17. ____	bathing	____
18. ____	bureau	____		18. ____	range	____
19. ____	solemn	____		19. ____	spectacular	____
20. ____	variations	____		20. ____	substance	____
____	Errors	____		____	Errors	____
____	Scores	____		____	Scores	____

5 points each   5 points each

Observations:

(continued)

NAME _____ DATE _____

√ = Correct   √^ = Incorrect   EXAMINER _____

Seventh-Reader Level			Eighth-Reader Level		
Flash	*Stimulus*	*Untimed*	*Flash*	*Stimulus*	*Untimed*
1. ____	stimulating	____	1. ____	grotesque	____
2. ____	challenging	____	2. ____	exuberant	____
3. ____	undoubtedly	____	3. ____	nonchalant	____
4. ____	equipment	____	4. ____	inducement	____
5. ____	malignant	____	5. ____	supplement	____
6. ____	quantity	____	6. ____	irrelevance	____
7. ____	contend	____	7. ____	contrasting	____
8. ____	commence	____	8. ____	remarkably	____
9. ____	commission	____	9. ____	deprecate	____
10. ____	precision	____	10. ____	articulate	____
11. ____	warning	____	11. ____	aspired	____
12. ____	impressive	____	12. ____	subside	____
13. ____	gorge	____	13. ____	procession	____
14. ____	pensive	____	14. ____	expedition	____
15. ____	standardize	____	15. ____	communion	____
16. ____	exhausted	____	16. ____	proposition	____
17. ____	reminiscence	____	17. ____	commerce	____
18. ____	intricate	____	18. ____	permanent	____
19. ____	contemporary	____	19. ____	content	____
20. ____	attentively	____	20. ____	grasped	____
____	Errors	____	____	Errors	____
____	Scores	____	____	Scores	____

5 points each   5 points each

Observations:

(continued)

Table 6-5   Notations for Recording Responses

Stimulus Word	Notation	Meaning
see	√	Correct response
the	√^	No response or an incorrect response
sun	s-u-n	An attempt to reproduce the word phonetically
at	it/ate	Two wrong responses
where	when √	Corrected wrong first response
that	t/h/a/t	Student named the letters he or she saw but could not say the word or any part of the word.
duck	<u>dk</u>	What the student said he or she saw

Specific Word Reading Errors

WORD READING ERRORS PRIMARILY DUE TO AUDITORY PROBLEMS.

1. The student may be able to read letters and give names of letters but be unable to identify the sounds of letters (auditory-visual associative memory and/or auditory discrimination).
2. The student may take wild guesses at words with little or no relationship between the word seen and the word called (auditory-visual associative memory).
3. The student may substitute a synonym, such as *house* for *home* (auditory-visual associative memory).
4. The student may substitute one sound for another and read *bit* for *bet* (auditory discrimination).
5. The student may know the sounds but still be unable to blend them into words (auditory closure).

WORD READING ERRORS PRIMARILY DUE TO VISUAL PROBLEMS.

1. The student may exhibit a slow rate of perception and be unable to read the word when it is flashed

Table 6-6   Score Chart for Flash and Untimed Words

Pre-Primer	Primer and Above
1 = 94%	1 = 95%
2 = 87%	2 = 90%
3 = 80%	3 = 85%
4 = 74%	4 = 80%
5 = 67%	5 = 75%
6 = 60%	6 = 70%
7 = 54%	7 = 65%
8 = 47%	8 = 60%
9 = 40%	9 = 55%
10 = 34%	10 = 50%

but be able to identify the word on the untimed presentation. Time makes the difference (rate of perception).

2. The student may discern only the beginning or the ending of a word and lose the middle (visual closure or rate of perception).
3. The student may reverse the letters in a word, for example, *was-saw, on-no* (usually visual memory, but also check visual discrimination and spatial).
4. The student may invert letters, for example, *me* for *we* (usually visual memory, but also check visual discrimination and spatial).
5. The student may fail to discriminate fine differences between letters and read *ship* for *snip* or *red* for *rod* (visual discrimination).
6. The student may add sounds to words, for example, reading *dogs* for *dog* (visual memory and/or misperception).
7. The student may try to sound words phonetically, exhibiting excessive hesitations (check visual memory). This problem can also be indicative of an oral expressive (retrieval) disorder in which the student knows the word but cannot retrieve the correct motor sequence.

In administering the Word Reading Inventory, teachers should ask themselves the following questions: (1) What do the errors on the Developmental Spelling Inventory mean diagnostically? (2) Is the student making similar errors on the Developmental Word Reading Inventory? (3) Am I observing the way he or she reads the words as well as trying to get a measure of his or her reading level?

CHECKING FOR ORAL LANGUAGE DEVELOPMENT.
Additional information can be obtained about the level of a student's word reading ability by testing the student's oral language development according to the following procedure.

1. After completing a level, the teacher can go back and select three words at random that the student has read successfully and ask him or her (a) to use the word in a sentence and (b) to tell what the word means. For example, on the PP3 list, the teacher asked a student to use the word *dog* in a *sentence*. He did it accurately and *S+* was written next to the word on the teacher scoring sheet. If the response had been wrong, the teacher would have marked *S−* next to the word. The teacher then asked the student the *meaning* of the word. The response was correct, so, *M+* was written next to the word on the teacher scoring sheet. Had the word been defined incorrectly, the teacher would have written

MANN-SUITER DEVELOPMENTAL READING SUMMARY RECORD

NAME _____ GRADE _____ AGE _____ DATE _____

EXAMINER _____

DEVELOPMENTAL WORD RECOGNITION AND READING INVENTORY

	PP3	P	1	2¹	2²	3¹	3²	4	5	6	7	8
1 % Word recognition, correct-flash												
2 % Word recognition, correct-untimed (ut)												
3 % Word recognition, accuracy– DPRI oral reading												
4 % Word recognition, average– UT and DPRI oral reading (2 and 3)*												
5 % Reading comprehension, form _____												
6 % Listening comprehension, form _____												

Average of the Untimed Word Recognition and the DPRI Oral Reading

*Difficulties noted:

Frustration Level _____

Instructional Level _____

Independent Level _____

M– next to it. Manual expressions of meaning are acceptable but should be noted.

2. Only three words should be used from each selection.

3. The Analysis of Errors worksheets (pages 302–305) contain a section on vocabulary that has been delineated into two basic *levels of conceptualization* for different grades: Concrete-Functional and Abstract. The *level of conceptualization* tells us how the student thinks. It is important for the teacher to know at what level the student is basically functioning so that the teacher can plan for an appropriate selection of materials and not overload the student with concepts that are too difficult.

    a. The Concrete-Functional level *(C-F)* includes any response that describes the quality, state of being, or function of the object to be defined. An essentially concrete-level response is that an apple is round. A response at the functional level is that an apple can be eaten.

    b. The Abstract level *(A)* includes any response that indicates a synonym, classification, or association. An abstract-level response is that an apple is a fruit.

The word meanings for any grade level can be classified according to the above-mentioned levels of conceptualization. They can be used in conjunction with the word meanings given in the Developmental Paragraph Reading Inventory (described later in this chapter), to aid the teacher in determining the student's overall level of responses. The teacher can then make the appropriate notation on the Analysis of Error Worksheets (Forms 6-40 and 6-41, pages 302–305).

OBSERVABLE BEHAVIORS. The following behaviors should be noted on the score sheet if they are present:

1. Tension or nervousness
2. Distractibility
3. Visual difficulties (ocular motor)
4. Hearing difficulties
5. Speech problems (stuttering, articulation, voice)
6. Bizarre responses

DEVELOPMENTAL PARAGRAPH READING INVENTORY

The teacher can construct a Developmental Paragraph Reading Inventory (DPRI) from any basal reading series available. The DPRI is designed to do the following:

1. Determine the learner's independent, instructional, and frustration reading levels.
2. Identify specific types of word-recognition errors.
3. Estimate comprehension ability.

Table 6-7   *Correlation between Grade Level and Length of Reading*

Level	Words (Approximate)	Questions
PP3	20–30	5
P	30–40	5
1	35–50	5
2^1	40–55	5
2^2	45–60	5
3^1	60–90	5
3^2	60–100	5
4	75–125	5
5	90–150	5
6	100–175	5

4. Determine the extent of the student's vocabulary.
5. Obtain information relative to the student's rate of performance.

Developing a Developmental Paragraph Reading Inventory

1. Select any basal reading series and take a reading selection from the back one third of each of the levels. Be sure to get a representative variety to avoid extreme variations. The following readability formulas will aid you in choosing an appropriate selection: (a) For grades one through three, use the George Spache Formula; (b) for grades four through six use the Dale-Chall Formula; and (c) for grades seven and eight use the Fry Formula. (Spache, 1953; Dale & Chall, 1948; Fry, 1968)

2. Begin at the PP3 level and proceed to as high a level as necessary for your class. Table 6-7 will help you decide upon the appropriate number of words for each reading selection.

3. Construct the teacher scoring sheet and the student's reading copy. An example of the teacher's scoring sheet of a PP3 selection is shown in Figure 6-3. The teacher's copy can be dittoed. The student's reading selection can be typed on a sheet of oak tag, on nonglossy white cardboard, on heavy white bond paper, or on pieces cut from manila folders. Use primer type for reading selections PP3 through first level.

    Note: The length of the sentences should be approximately the same length found in the appropriate grade level basal reader.

WRITING COMPREHENSION QUESTIONS FOR THE PARAGRAPH INVENTORY. Comprehension questions should be asked after every reading selection. The order of the type of questions (detail, main idea, vocabulary, or inference) should follow the sequence of the text; therefore, it will be different for each story. The ques-

MOTIVATIONAL QUESTION: Have you ever seen a red dog? Find out what kind of a dog Jane and Dick saw in this story.

Pre-Primer 3   (29 words)

THE RED DOG

"Look, look," said Jane.

"See the funny little dog.

Can you see it?

It is red."

"I see it," said Dick.

"It is a toy dog."

Errors	0	1	2	3	4	5
Percentage	100	96	93	89	86	83

Detail	1.	What did Jane see? (a funny little dog, a red dog, or a toy dog)
Vocabulary		What does the word *little* mean? (small, etc.)
Main Idea	2.	Why did Jane call the little dog funny? (it was red)
Inference	3.	Where do you think the children were? (toy store, etc.)
Detail	4.	What kind of a dog did Dick say it was? (toy)

Errors	0	1	2	3
Percentage	100	75	50	25

Figure 6-3   Mann-Suiter Developmental Paragraph Reading Inventory—Form A (Sample Teacher Scoring Sheet)

tions for each selection should be based upon that selection. Below is a list of areas the questions should cover.

1. *Vocabulary Questions:*
   Example:
   a. What does the word _____ mean?
   b. What is another meaning for the word _____ ?
   c. What is a word that can be used in place of _____ ?

   Note: Look for Concrete-Functional or Abstract Responses.

2. *Detail Questions:* Questions should be included that require the student to tell what something is or is not doing. These questions can describe a quantity, quality, state of being, or an action.
   Example:
   a. What did Jane see?
   b. What color was the dog?

3. *Main Idea Questions:* One question in each selection should reflect the essence of the story or of the main character in the story.

Example:
a. Why was Ann excited?
b. Why did Bill's mother tell him not to go swimming alone?

4. *Inference Questions:* Questions of this nature should require the student to formulate a logical deduction from several bits of available information.
   Example:
   a. What time of day was it? (The story tells about shooting stars.)
   b. How do we know that John was being teased? (The story describes the teasing of a blind boy.)

Screening Procedures for the Developmental Paragraph Reading Inventory

1. Select a level at which the student can begin with a success before he or she ultimately fails. You can also begin at the highest level at which the student had 85 to 90 percent correct on the untimed section of the Developmental Word Reading Inventory.

2. Before the student begins, tell him or her that you will ask a few questions about the story when he or she has finished. (Do not allow the student to pre-read the selection silently.)
3. Hand the student the reading selection, read the motivational question to him or her, and ask the student to read out loud to you. Be sure the student reads the title of each selection.
4. Always ask the questions as soon as the reading is completed, and permit the student to hold on to the selection so that he or she can refer to it as necessary. We do not want to penalize the student for possible difficulties with memory. However, if unusual amounts of time are used to find information, this should be noted.

   Note: If the pupil fails to respond to the questions appropriately, he or she may be asked to "explain more fully" or to "tell me more," etc. Although lack of response is considered in the total scoring, probing questions are permitted. However, use good judgment in such instances.

5. Be sure to mark the correct and incorrect responses by each question as it is answered. If there are two or three parts to the answer, give credit for the correct portion answered. For example, "What did Mary do first? Next? And last?" Each part of this question is worth one-third of the credit.

   Note: Do not forget to record unusual answers. Customarily, vocabulary questions are not counted into the comprehension score.

Scoring Procedures for the Developmental Paragraph Reading Inventory

SYMBOL NOTATION. As the student reads the selection, use the following symbols to record the types of word recognition errors made during the paragraph reading selection.

1. *Unusual Phrasing,* or Word-by-Word Reading:

   Example: A/little black dog ran/away/from home.

   (Noted but not counted as an error.)

2. *Omitted Words, Phrases, or Word Endings:*

   Example: A little black dog ran away from home. He talked and talked to her. He talk (s) to her.

   (Counted as an error.)

3. *Substitutions:*

   Example: Mary walked over the bridge.
   above

Write the substituted word above. (Counted as an error.)

4. *Additions of Words, Phrases, or Endings:*

   Example: A little black doggy ran away from home. *the*

   (Counted as an error.)

5. *Repetitions:*

   Example: A little black dog ran away from home.

   A line is drawn indicating the portion repeated. (Noted but not counted as an error.)

6. *Mispronunciation of Words:*
   Write *M* above the word.

   Example: "The big machine." The error is in placing the accent on the wrong syllable. Write out the errors. (Counted as an error.)

7. *Punctuation:*
   The student continues to read through the punctuation marks.

   Example: A little dog ran away. He ran, etc.

   (Noted but not counted as an error.)

8. *Needs Assistance:*
   If the student hesitates more than five seconds, write *P* above the word and pronounce it for the student. (Counted as an error.)

9. *Self-Correction of Errors:*

   Example: She saw a penny. *was* ✓

   Noted but not counted as an error.)

10. *Hesitations:*

    Example: A little black dog ran **haway**.

    If the student hesitates noticeably, put an *h* before the word. (Noted but not counted as an error.)

Each of the errors can be scored as indicated. Sometimes the teacher has to use his or her judgment in scoring. A good rule of thumb is to score as an error anything that changes or distorts the meaning or intent of the selection.

SUMMARY OF WORD RECOGNITION ERRORS. The student makes an error when he or she

1. Omits a word
2. Substitutes a word
3. Adds a word

4. Mispronounces a word
5. Asks the examiner to pronounce a word

Note: Proper names are not counted as errors, as they depend upon experiential factors.

SCORING OF COMPREHENSION QUESTIONS. The teacher divides 100 by the number of questions, not including vocabulary questions, to get the value of each comprehension question. For example, if the first-level reading selection has 5 questions, including 1 vocabulary question, the teacher divides 100 by 4 to get the value of each question.

After the teacher obtains the percentage correct from each of the levels tested, he or she should record the scores on the Developmental Reading Summary Record (Form 6-27), under Reading-Comprehension. Both the word-recognition and comprehension scores should be plotted to get the level of performance.

Note: It is important that the teacher listen carefully and record accurately errors made by the student. Practice will help to develop this skill. One should not expect to be an expert after the first administration.

Finding the Reading Levels
FRUSTRATION LEVEL. The student performing at the frustration level reads with symptoms such as fingerpointing, tension, or hesitant word-by-word reading. Comprehension may be extremely low. The student is completely unable to handle the reading materials presented.

INSTRUCTIONAL LEVEL. At the instructional level, the student will be able to read with at least 93 percent accuracy of word recognition and with 75 percent or better comprehension. At this point, the teacher's help is necessary; but after being given the instruction, the student should be able to handle the material independently.

INDEPENDENT LEVEL. At the independent level, the student reads with ease. It is the level to be used in selecting supplementary reading material and library books. The student has at least 97 percent word recognition and 90 percent comprehension.

SUMMARY OF SCORING.
1. *Independent Level:* 97 percent and above correct oral reading and 90 percent and above comprehension
2. *Instructional Level:* 93–96 percent oral reading and 75 percent and above comprehension
3. *Frustration Level:* Below 93 percent oral reading and below 75 percent comprehension.

Silent Reading Comprehension
Many teachers will not give a silent comprehension test because it is too time-consuming. However, for diagnostic purposes, it may be helpful to know the discrepancy between the student's oral and silent reading.

If a silent reading test is given, the teacher may want to average the scores between the oral comprehension and the silent reading comprehension in order to get a more approximate grade level. For the silent reading test, the teacher should use the Developmental Paragraph Reading Inventory—Form B (Form 6-29).

Listening Comprehension Level (Optional)
The teacher can read more difficult selections to students after they have failed one to determine whether or not they can understand higher level material and discuss what they have heard. Such selections should be beyond their instructional level. The highest level at which they can understand 75 percent of the material would determine their probable level of comprehension. Many professionals believe a student should be reading at this level of understanding. The listening comprehension scores can be recorded on the Developmental Reading Summary Record.

An alternative approach to determining the listening comprehension level would be to administer Form B of the Mann-Suiter Developmental Paragraph Reading Inventory by orally presenting the selections to the student. However, Form B should not be used for this purpose if the inventory is to be administered as a silent reading screen.

Specific Reading Errors
READING ERRORS PRIMARILY DUE TO AUDITORY PROBLEMS.
1. The student may mispronounce words, for example, read the word *chimney* as *chimley* (auditory acuity and/or discrimination).
2. The student may take wild guesses, with no relationship between the word seen and the word read (auditory-visual associative memory).
3. When stuck on a word, the student may not be able to sound it out (auditory-visual associative memory).
4. The student may be poor in blending sounds together to make words (auditory closure).
5. The student may use a synonym, for example, saying *mommy* for *mother* (auditory-visual associative memory).
6. The student may substitute words, such as *a* for *the* (auditory-visual associative memory).

READING ERRORS PRIMARILY DUE TO VISUAL DEFICITS.

1. The student may exhibit word-by-word reading or poor phrasing (rate of perception).
2. The student may be unable to keep his or her place and may skip lines or parts of lines when reading (visual figure-ground or ocular motor).
3. The student may add words that may or may not change the meaning, for example adding the word *the* when it isn't there (visual memory and/or misperception).
4. The student may repeat parts of words, phrases, and sometimes whole sentences in an attempt to get the meaning (check receptive and expressive language).
5. The student may read through punctuation, distorting the meaning of what he or she reads (check receptive and expressive language).
6. The student may reverse words or letters (visual sequential memory and/or spatial).
7. The student may invert words or letters (visual-memory and/or spatial).
8. The student may look at the beginning of a word and then say some other word that starts in the same way, for example, *surprise* for *something.* If the student self-corrects, he or she may be only looking at initial consonants and configurations (rate of perception).

OBSERVING PARAGRAPH READING BEHAVIOR. When facing unfamiliar words in a paragraph, does the student display any of the following behaviors:

1. Guesses without regard to any thought of the context read.
2. Seems unwilling to attempt to read and just waits for the teacher to say the word.
3. Seems willing to just skip the unknown word and go on.
4. Seems unable to sound out word parts and blends.
5. Tries to spell out the word he or she cannot read.
6. Makes little use of the context in attacking an unknown word.

In general, does the student behave as follows:

1. Desregards punctuation.
2. Doesn't pay attention to the story line.
3. Has a low meaning vocabulary—not adequate for the reading level under concern.
4. Makes no attempt to correct errors.
5. Exhibits frequent hesitations and makes sounds like uh. . . .
6. Drops his or her voice at the end of a sentence.
7. Reads word by word instead of in phrases or thought units.

8. Exhibits a negative and indifferent attitude. "Do I have to?"

Is there flash-untimed discrepancy or a wide range between the flash and untimed scores, with a much smaller sight vocabulary evident on the flash part of the testing? Students with this discrepancy are often slow in recognition, but able to work out the pronunciation. The untimed part of the test may be within the passing level, but the slow recognition or excessive sounding out will hinder the student in reading.

Some learners frequently substitute or add words in a paragraph, but that does not usually interfere with the overall sense and meaning. As long as it does not inferfere with the meaning or understanding of the content there is no need for undue concern.

MANN-SUITER DEVELOPMENTAL READING SUMMARY RECORD

The examiner should plot the scores for each area of reading on the Developmental Reading Summary Record (Form 6-27) to determine the student's present level of functioning. The procedure for plotting the scores is as follows:

1. Record the scores for *percentage word-recognition, correct flash,* in the appropriate boxes. These scores are used for diagnostic purposes only, giving information as to how quickly and how accurately a student perceives a word.
2. Record the scores for percentage *word-recognition, correct-untimed,* and the *percentage word-recognition, accuracy,* from the paragraph oral readings in the appropriate boxes. These two scores are averaged to give the *percentage word-recognition, average,* and are recorded in the appropriate boxes.
3. Record the *reading comprehension* and note the appropriate form. Then record the *listening comprehension* score if given.
4. Plot the final scores on the graph, indicating the level of functioning, such as PP3 or P, in the appropriate section—independent, instructional, or frustration.

EXAMPLES OF MANN-SUITER DEVELOPMENTAL PARAGRAPH READING INVENTORIES (Form A and B)

These inventories, made up of original stories, can be used to determine the reading levels of students. To administer these inventories, the teacher should follow the instructions given on page 243. Form A (Form 6-28) can be used to test oral reading comprehension. Form B (Form 6-29) can be used for retesting oral

MANN-SUITER DEVELOPMENTAL PARAGRAPH READING INVENTORY—FORM A (TEACHER SCORING SHEET)

NAME _____ DATE _____

GRADE _____ EXAMINER _____

MOTIVATIONAL QUESTION: Have you ever seen a red dog? Find out what kind of a dog Jane and Dick saw in this story.

Pre-Primer 3 (29 words)

THE RED DOG

"Look, look," said Jane.

"See the funny little dog.

Can you see it?

It is red."

"I see it," said Dick.

"It is a toy dog."

Errors	0	1	2	3	4	5
Percentage	100	97	93	89	86	83

Detail	1.	What did Jane see? (a funny little dog, a red dog, or a toy dog)
Vocabulary		What is the meaning of the word *little*? (small, etc.)
Main Idea	2.	Why did Jane call the little dog funny? (it was red)
Inference	3.	Where do you think the children were? (toy store, etc.)
Detail	4.	What kind of a dog did Dick say it was? (toy)

Errors	0	1	2	3
Percentage	100	75	50	25

(continued)

NAME _____ DATE _____

GRADE _____ EXAMINER _____

MOTIVATIONAL QUESTION: Have you seen a baby animal? This story is about a cute baby animal that a little girl named Ann saw.

Primer (40 words)

THE BABY MONKEY

One day Ann went

for a walk in the zoo.

Soon she saw something.

"A baby monkey," said Ann.

"I see a baby monkey."

Then she saw Mary and Jimmy.

"Come see the baby monkey," called Ann.

Errors	0	1	2	3	4	5	6
Percentage	100	98	95	93	90	88	85

Detail	1.	Where was Ann walking? (in the zoo)
Main Idea	2.	Why was Ann excited? (she saw a baby monkey)
Detail	3.	How many children are in the story? (three)
Vocabulary		What is the meaning of the word *zoo*? (any acceptable answer)
Inference	4.	Why do you think Ann wanted Mary and Jimmy to see the baby monkey? (any acceptable answer)

Errors	0	1	2	3
Percentage	100	75	50	25

(continued)

NAME _____ DATE _____

GRADE _____ EXAMINER _____

MOTIVATIONAL QUESTION: The family in this story went to a park. Read to find out what mother forgot to take with her.

First Reader (51 words)

FUN AT THE PARK

One hot day we went to a park to swim.

Other people were at the park, too.

"Let's get a hot dog on a bun," said Dick.

"I want ice cream," said Lisa.

"O-o-o-!" Mother cried.

"I left my money at home."

"I have some," said Dick.

Errors	0	1	2	3	4	5	6	7
Percentage	100	98	96	94	92	90	88	86

Detail	1.	What kind of a day was it? (hot)
Inference	2.	What time of day do you think it was? (afternoon, around noon, lunch time)
Main Idea	3.	What were the children planning to do at the park? (have fun, eat hot dogs, swim)
Inference	4.	How do you think Lisa felt when Mother said she forgot her money? (upset, sad, angry)
Vocabulary		What is the meaning of the words *hot dog*? (wiener, frankfurter, etc.)

Errors	0	1	2	3
Percentage	100	75	50	25

(continued)

NAME _____ DATE _____

GRADE _____ EXAMINER _____

MOTIVATIONAL QUESTION: Have you ever earned your own money? The children in this story wanted some money. Let's see how they decide to earn it.

2' Reader (55 words)

THE LEMONADE STAND

It was a hot summer day.

Bill and Ann wished they could make some money.

Ann said, "Why don't we have a lemonade stand?"

"I know where we can get some ice and lemons to make lemonade," said Bill.

"I'll ask John to help us," said Ann.

"He can get the ice."

Errors	0	1	2	3	4	5	6	7
Percentage	100	98	96	94	93	91	89	87

Vocabulary		What is the meaning of the words *lemonade stand*? (any acceptable response)
Main Idea	1.	Why did the children decide to have a lemonade stand? (to earn money)
Detail	2.	What kind of a day was it? (hot summer day)
Detail	3.	What did the children say they were going to get to make lemonade? (ice and lemons)
Inference	4.	What other things do you think they will need in order to make lemonade? (water and sugar)

Errors	0	1	2	3
Percentage	100	75	50	25

(continued)

NAME _____ DATE _____

GRADE _____ EXAMINER _____

MOTIVATIONAL QUESTION: Have you ever looked at the stars at night? What do they look like to you? This story is about a boy and girl who saw something different in the sky one night.

2^2 Reader (61 words)

A VISITOR FROM OUTER SPACE

One night Ann and Bill were looking at stars.

"Look, Ann," said Bill. "Something flashed across the sky."

"I saw it too," said Ann.

"It must have been a shooting star."

"Where do shooting stars come from?" asked Bill.

"I don't know," said Ann.

"Let's ask father."

Father said, "They are burning rocks from outer space."

Errors	0	1	2	3	4	5	6	7	8
Percentage	100	98	97	95	93	91	90	88	87

Detail	1.	What were the children doing? (looking at stars)
Inference	2.	What time of day was it? (night)
Main Idea	3.	Why is this story called, "A Visitor from Outer Space"? (the visitor is the shooting star and it's from outer space)
Detail	4.	What did father say shooting stars were? (burning rocks)
Detail	5.	Where do shooting stars come from? (outer space)
Vocabulary		What is another word for shooting star? (meteor, falling star, etc.)

Errors	0	1	2	3
Percentage	100	80	60	40

(continued)

NAME _____ DATE _____

GRADE _____ EXAMINER _____

MOTIVATIONAL QUESTION: Have you ever seen a big fire? This story tells about a very large fire and what a little girl thought would put it out.

3¹ Reader (70 words)

THE FIRE IN THE EVERGLADES

"There are many fires in the Everglades National Park," said the TV announcer.

"The fires are spreading to the Indian villages.

Smoke is clouding the sky.

The animals are being forced to leave their homes."

Ann thought, "If we only had some rain, then the animals would not have to run away.

I hope that it rains soon so the fires will be put out."

Errors	0	1	2	3	4	5	6	7	8
Percentage	100	98	97	96	95	93	92	90	89

Vocabulary		What is the meaning of the word *announcer*? (a person who announces information on the radio or TV)
Detail	1.	How did Ann find out about the fires? (TV announcer)
Detail	2.	What was clouding the sky? (Smoke)
Main Idea	3.	Why was everyone worried about the fire? (it was spreading, animals could get hurt, Indians endangered, etc.)
Detail	4.	Where was the fire? (Everglades National Park)

Errors	0	1	2	3	4
Percentage	100	80	60	40	20

Note: Everglades National Park is a proper name and therefore not counted as an error.

(continued)

NAME _____ DATE _____

GRADE _____ EXAMINER _____

MOTIVATIONAL QUESTION: Would you go swimming if you were told not to? This is a story about a boy who disobeyed his mother and found himself in trouble.

3^2 Reader (96 words)

SWIMMING ALONE

It was a dark and cloudy day, but Bill went swimming alone in the rough water.

His mother had told him not to go because it was such a poor day for swimming.

Bill disobeyed her and went anyway.

He soon swam out over his head and realized in a panic that he could not get back to the shore.

Luckily, there was a woman on the beach who heard his screams for help.

A boat soon came to his rescue.

Bill did not disobey his mother again by swimming alone in rough water.

Errors	0	1	2	3	4	5	6	7	8	9	10
Percentage	100	99	98	97	96	95	94	93	92	90	89

Vocabulary		What is the meaning of the word *disobeyed*? (to refuse, or to fail to obey)
Detail	1.	What kind of a day was it? (dark and cloudy)
Detail	2.	Who went swimming with Bill? (no one)
Main Idea	3.	Why did Bill's mother tell him not to go swimming? (because it was such a poor day, rough water, dark and cloudy day)
Detail	4.	How was he rescued? (a boat)
Inference	5.	How do you think Bill feels now about swimming alone in rough water? (any logical answer)

Errors	0	1	2	3	4
Percentage	100	80	60	40	20

(continued)

NAME _____ DATE _____

GRADE _____ EXAMINER _____

MOTIVATIONAL QUESTION: This story is about a dog who went to the movies.

4 Reader (124 words)

DUKE GOES TO THE MOVIES

Duke and his master went to the movies.

The manager said, "You can't take a dog in there.

It's against the rules."

"This is no ordinary dog," said Duke's master.

"He is well behaved and has a collar.

If he becomes noisy, we will leave."

After the show, the manager spoke to Duke's master.

He said that he was watching Duke and noticed that the dog wagged his tail

for the happy parts of the movie.

He yawned when it became dull and whined a little at the sad parts.

"What an amazing dog!" said the manager.

"Did he enjoy the movie?"

Duke's master said, "I think he may have been a little bored, since he read the book."

Errors	0	1	2	3	4	5	6	7	8	9	10	11	12
Percentage	100	99	98	98	97	96	95	94	93	92	91	91	90

Vocabulary		What is the meaning of the word *master* in this story? (his owner)
Detail	1.	Who didn't want to let Duke into the movies? (the manager)
Detail	2.	Why aren't dogs allowed in the movies? (against the rules)
Main Idea	3.	What made Duke an unusual dog? (wagged tail for happy parts, yawned when dull, whined when sad, read the book)
Inference	4.	Do you think the other people in the theatre were upset with Duke? (no—Duke made no loud noise)
Detail	5.	What did Duke do when he became bored? (yawned)

Errors	0	1	2	3	4
Percentage	100	80	60	40	20

(continued)

NAME _____ DATE _____

GRADE _____ EXAMINER _____

MOTIVATIONAL QUESTION: Have you ever dusted furniture? Some people don't want theirs dusted. See what Mr. Bradshaw's reasons are for not dusting his furniture.

5 Reader (93 words)

LEAVE THE DUST ALONE

Mr. Bradshaw had an antique shop in a small New England town.

The dust was so thick you could hardly find your way around.

He used to repair old furniture and sell it to people from the big cities who

came wandering through his little shop.

People would ask, "How much for this beat-up old chair with the dust on it?"

They thought it was old and they had a bargain.

Many liked to rummage through the dust.

"The dustier the better," he would say to his wife.

Errors	0	1	2	3	4	5	6	7	8	9	10
Percentage	100	99	98	97	96	94	93	92	91	90	89

Vocabulary		What is the meaning of the word *rummage*? (to search through things)
Detail	1.	What kind of a shop did Mr. Bradshaw own? (antique shop)
Detail	2.	Where was the shop located? (small New England town)
Main Idea	3.	Why didn't Mr. Bradshaw want to dust his furniture? (wanted it to look old)
Inference	4.	Why do you think people liked the dusty old furniture? (they thought it was old and they had a bargain)
Detail	5.	Where did people come from who bought his furniture? (big cities)

Errors	0	1	2	3	4
Percentage	100	80	60	40	20

(continued)

NAME _____ DATE _____

GRADE _____ EXAMINER _____

MOTIVATIONAL QUESTION: Have your friends ever teased you? Here's a story about someone who was teased and what he did about it.

6 Reader (138 words)

A SENSE OF HUMOR

Rosemary walked John to his classroom every day.

She was ten and he was only seven.

John was blind and when he got off the bus, he needed someone to escort

him to his room.

Rosemary was crippled, but her handicap did not prevent her from traveling

to school alone.

"What color is my blouse?" she queried one day.

"I don't know," exclaimed John.

"You can't see it," she retorted.

"It's lavender. What color is the ribbon in my hair?"

"I don't know," sighed John.

"It's crimson," she giggled,

"but you can't see it."

It was obvious that John was being teased, but he didn't lose his patience.

After thinking for a while, he said quite seriously,

"Rosemary, what color is my underwear? You don't know, do you?

That's because you can't see it."

Errors	0	1	2	3	4	5	6	7	8	9	10	11
Percentage	100	99	98	97	97	96	95	94	94	93	92	91

Detail	1.	Why did John need someone to walk him to class? (he was blind)
Detail	2.	How did John get to school? (bus)
Inference	3.	Do you think Rosemary was mean? (any rational answer)
Inference	4.	How do we know that John was being teased? (Rosemary's questions)
Main Idea	5.	What did John use to solve a situation that could have been serious? (An answer that infers humor or intelligence)
Vocabulary		What does the word *obvious* mean? (evident, apparent, clear)

Errors	0	1	2	3	4
Percentage	100	80	60	40	20

(continued)

NAME _____ DATE _____

GRADE _____ EXAMINER _____

MOTIVATIONAL QUESTION: Rats create a worldwide menace. War on rats is a continuing struggle. Read this to find out why man is having so much trouble with rats.

7 Reader (199 Words)

HUMAN'S WORST ENEMY

Except for humans, rats are the most numerous and successful mammal on earth. Like the human, the rat is a generalized animal. This means that rats are able to eat almost anything and live anywhere. They are not specialized like the anteater or tree sloth. Generalization is the key to the rats' extraordinary adaptability.

The same species that lives in a burrow in a grain field in the United States or in an attic in Europe may inhabit the crown of a coconut palm in the South Pacific. The marsh that is a good place for growing rice is also a great place for rats.

Rats love the lush American suburbs of the south, too, with their abundance of fruit and nut trees. Here they nest in the trees and have literally filled the niche of the squirrel.

The dietary habits of humans and rats are almost identical, except that we eat by day and the rats eat by night. In a world haunted by threat of famine, rats will destroy approximately a fifth of all food crops planted. Wherever humans go, it seems the rat is sure to follow, sharing the food of their table.

Errors	0	1	2	3	4	5	6	7	8	9	10	11	12
Percentage	100	99	99	98	98	97	97	96	96	95	95	94	94

Vocabulary		What is the meaning of the word *dietary* in this story? (pertaining to diet or eating)
Main Idea	1.	Why are rats so successful and numerous? (they are a generalized animal adapting to any living conditions and food)
Detail	2.	What animals are mentioned as being specialized? (anteater and tree sloth)
Inference	3.	When people talk about rodent control they are really talking about human survival. What does this statement mean? (rats are increasing and eating the food needed to feed people)
Detail	4.	Are the dietary habits of man and rat exactly the same? (no, they are almost identical except that the rat eats by night)
Detail	5.	Why do rats love the lush American suburbs of the south? (abundance of fruit and nut trees)

Errors	0	1	2	3	4	5
Percentage	100	80	60	40	20	0

(continued)

NAME _____ DATE _____

GRADE _____ EXAMINER _____

MOTIVATIONAL QUESTION: This story is about a very famous city called Pompeii that was destroyed in just a few hours. Let's read to find out what happened.

8 Reader (172 words)

POMPEII

In the brief space of a few hours a city, with a history dating back over seven centuries, disappeared. Pompeii was destroyed twice: first by an earthquake in 62 A.D., then by the eruption of Vesuvius in 79 A.D., which buried it under twelve feet of lava and ashes. The first time, it was almost entirely rebuilt. After the second disaster it was left to its fate.

The eruption of Vesuvius brought the life of that rich city of merchants and traders to an abrupt end one August morning, while the whole population was busily going about its daily business.

In a few seconds, after the first deafening roar, streams of lava, thrown up thousands of yards by the gas pressure in the volcano, were running down the slopes of Vesuvius at a giddy pace. Ashes and scalding clouds of gas, released by the burning lava, were carried by the wind onto the city, while the raging sea cut off any retreat from the coast. The fate of Pompeii was sealed.

Errors	0	1	2	3	4	5	6	7	8	9	10	11	12
Percentage	100	99	99	98	98	97	97	96	95	95	94	94	93

Vocabulary		What is the meaning of the word *raging* in this story? (extreme violence or intensity; fury)
Detail	1.	How was Pompeii destroyed the first time? (by an earthquake)
Main Idea	2.	What happened to seal Pompeii's fate? (the eruption of Vesuvius buried it under twelve feet of lava and ash)
Detail	3.	What did the winds carry onto the city? (ashes and scalding clouds of gas)
Inference	4.	Although the story doesn't say, the city of Pompeii was built very close to what kind of a mountain? (a volcano)
Detail	5.	Why couldn't the people escape in boats? (retreat was cut off by the raging sea)

Errors	0	1	2	3	4	5
Percentage	100	80	60	40	20	0

MANN-SUITER DEVELOPMENTAL PARAGRAPH READING INVENTORY—FORM B (TEACHER SCORING SHEET)

NAME _____ DATE _____

GRADE _____ EXAMINER _____

MOTIVATIONAL QUESTION: Have you ever seen a red dog? Find out what kind of a dog Dick had in this story.

Pre-Primer 3 (27 words)

MY RED DOG

"Look," said Dick.

"My dog is red."

"He is funny," said Jane.

"Can he run fast?"

"No," said Dick.

"He is a toy dog."

Errors	0	1	2	3	4
Percentage	100	97	93	89	85

Vocabulary		What is the meaning of the word *fast*? (swift, speedy)
Detail	1.	What was the boy's name? (Dick)
Detail	2.	What color was the dog? (red)
Main Idea	3.	Why did Jane call the little dog funny? (it was red)
Inference	4.	Why do you think the dog could not run fast? (toy dogs cannot run)

Errors	0	1	2	3
Percentage	100	75	50	25

(continued)

NAME _____ DATE _____

GRADE _____ EXAMINER _____

MOTIVATIONAL QUESTION: Have you ever seen a baby animal? This story is about a cute baby animal that lives in a zoo.

Primer (41 words)

JUDY

Judy is a baby monkey.

She lives with her mother.

They live at the zoo.

She likes to drink milk.

She likes to eat fruit.

She likes to play.

Judy has a little bell.

She likes to ring her bell.

Errors	0	1	2	3	4	5
Percentage	100	98	95	93	90	88

Vocabulary		What is the meaning of the word *likes*? (enjoys, cares for)
Main Idea	1.	What kind of an animal is this story about? (baby monkey)
Detail	2.	With whom does Judy live? (with her mother)
Detail	3.	What does Judy like to eat? (fruit)
Inference	4.	Why do you think Judy liked to ring the little bell? (any logical answer)

Errors	0	1	2	3	4
Percentage	100	75	50	25	0

(continued)

NAME _____ DATE _____

GRADE _____ EXAMINER _____

MOTIVATIONAL QUESTION: Have you ever seen a live cow or pig or horse? Where could a city child **see them?**

First Reader (42 words)

WHAT CITY CHILDREN MISS

Have you ever seen a cow?

Some city children have never seen one.

They have never seen a live chicken or duck.

They have never seen a live horse or pig.

Don't you think they miss a lot?

Errors	0	1	2	3	4	5
Percentage	100	98	95	93	90	88

Main Idea	1.	What does this story say city children miss? (seeing animals such as cows, chickens, ducks, horses)
Detail	2.	What are the two largest farm animals mentioned in this story? (cow, horse)
Detail	3.	What types of birds are mentioned in this story? (chicken, duck)
Inference	4.	Could some city children see more animals than country children? Explain. (zoo, etc.)
Vocabulary		What is the meaning of the word *city*? (town)

Errors	0	1	2	3
Percentage	100	75	50	25

(continued)

NAME _____ DATE _____

GRADE _____ EXAMINER _____

MOTIVATIONAL QUESTION: Have you ever earned your own money? The children in this story wanted some money and decided to sell some lemonade they had made.

2' Reader (54 words)

THREE THIRSTY CHILDREN

The afternoon was very hot.

There were not many people on the streets.

"I'm thirsty," said Ann.

"Could I have just a little bit of lemonade?"

"O.K.," said Bill.

"I'll have some too."

"So will I," said John.

By the end of the afternoon, there was no lemonade left to sell.

Errors	0	1	2	3	4	5	6
Percentage	100	98	96	94	93	90	87

Vocabulary		What is the meaning of the word *thirsty*? (feel dry and need water)
Detail	1.	What time of day was it? (afternoon)
Detail	2.	How many people were on the street? (not many)
Inference	3.	Why do you think there were not too many people on the street? (too hot)
Main Idea	4.	Why was there no lemonade left to sell? (the children drank it all)

Errors	0	1	2	3
Percentage	100	75	50	25

(continued)

NAME _____ DATE _____

GRADE _____ EXAMINER _____

MOTIVATIONAL QUESTION: Do you have a special friend? Why is he or she special? This little boy's friend was John. Let's read to find out why he was so special.

2² Reader (57 words)

I REMEMBER JOHN

Everyone has had one special friend that they will always remember.

I often think of old John.

Sometimes he held my arm when he talked to me.

I guess he was afraid I would run away.

I told him all the local news.

John couldn't get around much in his wheelchair.

He needed me.

Errors	0	1	2	3	4	5	6
Percentage	100	98	97	95	93	91	89

Vocabulary		What is the meaning of the word *special* in this story? (any response that connotes love for, or devotion to, a person)
Detail	1.	Who was the special friend in this story? (John)
Main Idea	2.	Why did John like his younger friend? (he told him all the local news)
Detail	3.	Why would he hold his arm? (so he couldn't get away)
Inference	4.	Do you think John was lonely? Explain. (any logical answer)
Detail	5.	Why couldn't John get around very well? (in a wheelchair)

Errors	0	1	2	3	4
Percentage	100	80	60	40	20

(continued)

NAME _____ DATE _____

GRADE _____ EXAMINER _____

MOTIVATIONAL QUESTION: The two boys in this story were out west digging for gold. Let's read to find out what they found.

3' Reader (60 words)

FOOL'S GOLD

"I found some!" yelled Bob.

John ran to him, and both huddled over the little rock.

It had shiny golden pieces all over it.

"It's real gold! I'm sure it's real gold!" Bob said excitedly.

"No, it's only fool's gold, or what is called iron pyrite," said John.

"It has fooled more than one man in the past."

Errors	0	1	2	3	4	5	6	7
Percentage	100	98	97	95	93	92	90	88

Detail	1.	How many people are in the story? (two)
Main Idea	2.	Why was Bob excited over the rock he found? (thought it was real gold)
Detail	3.	What color were the shiny pieces? (golden)
Inference	4.	Why is iron pyrite called fool's gold? (because it looks like real gold)
Detail	5.	Who knew it wasn't real gold? (John)
Vocabulary		What is the meaning of the word *huddled* in this story? (to crowd together)

Errors	0	1	2	3	4
Percentage	100	80	60	40	20

(continued)

NAME _____ DATE _____

GRADE _____ EXAMINER _____

MOTIVATIONAL QUESTION: What would happen if water covered all of the land in the world? This is a story about Noah and his ark. An ark is a boat, and Noah built it to keep the animals in during a bad flood.

3^2 Reader (68 words)

NOAH'S ARK

Week after week the clouds poured rain on the earth below.

Rivers and streams ran over their banks.

Pastures were covered with water.

People became afraid as whole towns were washed away.

Soon even the mountains were covered and disappeared

under the dark water.

The rain poured down, but Noah's ark remained afloat.

Inside, two of each kind of animal waited for the rain to stop.

Errors	0	1	2	3	4	5	6	7
Percentage	100	98	97	95	93	92	90	89

Vocabulary		What is the meaning of the word *ark* in this story? (a boat or ship)
Detail	1.	Who owned the ark? (Noah)
Inference	2.	How do you know this was a bad flood? (rivers and streams ran over their banks, pastures were covered with water, towns were washed away)
Detail	3.	How many of each kind of animal was in the ark? (two of each kind)
Main Idea	4.	Why were Noah and all the animals safe in the ark? (it floated)
Detail	5.	What were the animals waiting for? (the rain to stop)
Vocabulary		What is the meaning of the word *banks* in this story? (river banks)

Errors	0	1	2	3	4
Percentage	100	80	60	40	20

(continued)

NAME _____ DATE _____

GRADE _____ EXAMINER _____

MOTIVATIONAL QUESTION: Do you like surprises? In this story, grandfather has a very special surprise gift for John. Let's see what it was.

4 Reader (115 words)

GRANDFATHER'S GIFT

"All right," said grandfather, as he slowly shuffled over to the old wooden cupboard.

"I was keeping it for a surprise, but I will show it to you now."

After looking around inside for a few minutes, he drew out a bag made of coarse cloth.

Handing it to John, he said, "I have kept these for a long time.

I have had them since I was a boy.

Now they are yours."

John peered into the bag and saw a pair of gleaming silver ice skates.

He was so excited he couldn't talk.

He immediately thought about the big race next month.

He knew that grandfather had won that race long ago.

Errors	0	1	2	3	4	5	6	7	8	9	10
Percentage	100	99	98	97	97	96	95	94	93	92	91

Detail	1.	What did grandfather have hidden in the cupboard? (silver ice skates in a bag)
Inference	2.	Were the skates new? Explain. (no, grandfather had had them since he was a boy)
Inference	3.	How did grandfather feel about the race? (any logical answer)
Detail	4.	Why was the race important to grandfather? (he won it long ago)
Main Idea	5.	Why did grandfather give John the skates now? (John was old enough to race)
Vocabulary		What is the meaning of the word *gleaming* in this story? (to send out beams of light)

Errors	0	1	2	3	4	5
Percentage	100	80	60	40	20	0

(continued)

NAME _____ DATE _____

GRADE _____ EXAMINER _____

MOTIVATIONAL QUESTION: Have you ever done something that you thought was good only to find out it was wrong? Read this story to find out why Mrs. Bradshaw was crying.

5 Reader (123 words)

SURPRISE BIRTHDAY PRESENT

One Saturday, Mr. Bradshaw went to Boston to see if he could pick up some antique

bargains for resale.

He got home about 6:00 p.m.

He was surprised to see that his shop was sparkling clean.

Soon, loud talking was heard, and a small crowd gathered to see what the difficulty was.

Covered with dust, Mrs. Bradshaw was sitting and crying.

"I only did it for you as a birthday present," she sobbed.

"Why did you clean up the dust!" he was yelling.

"People like to rummage in the dust looking for bargains.

Now that you have cleaned the place up, you have reduced the profits and it will take

six months before business will be the same as usual."

Errors	0	1	2	3	4	5	6	7	8	9	10	11	12
Percentage	100	99	98	97	96	96	95	94	93	92	91	91	90

Vocabulary		What is the meaning of the word *resale* in this story? (the act of selling again)
Detail	1.	Where had Mr. Bradshaw gone? (Boston)
Inference	2.	Why wasn't he happy to see his nice clean shop? Explain. (he felt people liked to look for bargains in the dust)
Detail	3.	Why did Mrs. Bradshaw clean up the store? (birthday present)
Main Idea	4.	What was Mr. Bradshaw's reason for keeping his store dusty? (he felt people liked to rummage through dusty furniture looking for bargains)
Detail	5.	Why will it take six months before business is as usual? (it will take that long for it to get dusty again)

Errors	0	1	2	3	4
Percentage	100	80	60	40	20

(continued)

NAME _____ DATE _____

GRADE _____ EXAMINER _____

MOTIVATIONAL QUESTION: Do you know what a raft is? How would you feel if you were on a raft and a bad storm came up? This is what happened to the boy and the dog in this story.

6 Reader (173 words)

LOYAL JONATHAN

Jonathan was standing in the middle of the raft looking somewhat distressed.

As I glanced to my left, I noticed the darkness coming over the horizon.

It was evident that a storm was coming.

I quickly secured our water canteen and the little food we had available.

I tied a rope about my own waist and fastened the other end to Jonathan and

waited for the impending storm.

Soon the tempest struck in all its tropical fury.

The raft was tossed about so violently that it almost broke apart.

I started to panic, but Jonathan snuggled close, and I was given strength not to give

up by his silent courage.

He did not bark, but only whined a bit now and then.

The surging got worse, and Jonathan slipped on the wet deck of the raft, unable to

stabilize himself with his strong paws.

Finally, the wind and seas subsided.

The storm passed as swiftly as it had come, and although it left us wet and

exhausted, we were both safe.

Errors	0	1	2	3	4	5	6	7	8	9	10	11	12	13
Percentage	100	99	99	98	98	97	97	96	96	95	94	94	93	92

Vocabulary		What is the meaning of the word *distressed* in this story? (troubled or worried)
Detail	1.	What was the dog's name in the story? (Jonathan)
Main Idea	2.	How did Jonathan show his loyalty? (any logical answer)
Inference	3.	Why were the water canteen and food secured? (so they wouldn't be lost overboard)
Detail	4.	How did they feel after the storm? (wet and exhausted)
Detail	5.	How did they secure themselves to the raft? (rope tied to each other)

Errors	0	1	2	3	4
Percentage	100	80	60	40	20

(continued)

NAME _____ DATE _____

GRADE _____ EXAMINER _____

MOTIVATIONAL QUESTION: Have you ever wondered what it would be like to live in a place where the winter was nine months long? This story is about just such a place.

7 Reader (198 words)

THE LONGEST NIGHT

Since 1957, Americans have manned the world's loneliest outpost at the geographic South Pole. There, on a bleak, flat sea of ice at the bottom of the world, 22 men spend a dark lonely winter collecting scientific data in an effort to increase people's knowledge about their planet. For these men it means an almost-nine-month winter isolated from the world and the sun.

South Pole Station is at an elevation of 9,186 feet. The thickness of the ice at this location is over 9,000 feet, which means that the ground below the ice is only about 150 feet above sea level. The average temperature is 59 degrees below zero. This makes it the coldest region on the globe. Although extremely cold, the area around the pole is, by definition, a desert. The average precipitation is slightly less than half an inch, less than many desert regions of the United States.

During the 3½-month summer season, temperatures rise to nearly zero degrees Fahrenheit, while the sun shines brightly overhead 24 hours a day. Severe cases of frostbite have occurred at this time because of the difficulty in recognizing the danger of over-exposure.

Errors	0	1	2	3	4	5	6	7	8	9	10	11	12
Percentage	100	99	99	98	98	97	97	96	96	95	95	94	94

Vocabulary		What does the word *isolated* mean in this story? (to be placed alone or be in a detached situation)
Detail	1.	What is the thickness of the ice at the South Pole Station? (over 9,000 feet)
Main Idea	2.	Why is the story called The Longest Night? (refers to the 9-month period without the sun)
Detail	3.	What is the highest temperature recorded in the short summer months? (nearly 0°F)
Inference	4.	What kind of skills do you feel are necessary for the men who are sent to South Pole Station? (technical and scientific training to collect data)
Detail	5.	What is the average rainfall at South Pole Station? (less than half an inch)

Errors	0	1	2	3	4	5
Percentage	100	80	60	40	20	0

(continued)

NAME _____ DATE _____

GRADE _____ EXAMINER _____

MOTIVATIONAL QUESTION: Just about everyone has some form of a fern living near them. It might be in a pot in the house or under some trees in the yard. This story will tell you some interesting things about these very unusual plants.

8 Reader (177 words)

FERNS

Because ferns look so fragile, it is hard to realize that they are among the oldest living things on the earth and were the first plants to have roots, stems, and leaves. Around 350 million years ago, ferns and plants that looked like ferns were the principal land plants on our earth, but since then most of them have been crowded out by higher forms of vegetation better suited to the changed conditions of our earth. Today they are the highest order of flowerless plants, and some 300 different kinds live in the United States.

People have always found ferns fascinating, and as early as 3000 B.C. they were thought to have medicinal properties. It was once thought, for instance, that the beautiful maidenhair fern could stop the loss of hair and make new hair grow on a bald head. Healers used many varieties of ferns to cure such things as whooping cough, colic, and mild fevers. Today, scientists have disproved many of these strange beliefs, and ferns are popular house plants grown for their beauty.

Errors	0	1	2	3	4	5	6	7	8	9	10	11	12
Percentage	100	99	99	98	98	97	97	96	95	95	94	94	93

Vocabulary		What does the word *fragile* mean in this story? (easily damaged, delicate)
Detail	1.	What are the highest order of flowerless plants found in the United States? (ferns)
Main Idea	2.	Why have ferns slowly been crowded off the earth by other forms of vegetation? (higher forms of vegetation are better suited to the changed conditions on the earth)
Detail	3.	What types of illnesses did early healers use ferns to cure? (whooping cough, colic, fevers)
Inference	4.	From this story do you feel that ferns are on the increase or the decrease on the earth? (have slowly moved from being the dominant plant form on the earth to being a minor form)
Detail	5.	Ferns are popular today as what? (house plants)

Errors	0	1	2	3	4	5
Percentage	100	80	60	40	20	0

reading comprehension, for testing silent reading comprehension, and for testing listening comprehension.

Note: Primer type is recommended in reproducing the student copies for primer through level one selections.

General Reading Screening (Group and Individual)

Three screens were developed in response to requests by many teachers for general reading screening that could be administered to more than one student at a time. This would enable teachers to determine during the first days of school the range of language skills in their classrooms. With the Mann-Suiter general reading screens the teacher can estimate the reading, written language development, and vocabulary comprehension levels of the students. More precise individual reading evaluations can then be administered where necessary.

Knowing the estimated range of variability will enable the teacher to plan for individual needs in reading, written language expression, and vocabulary acquisition.

The three language screens are the Mann-Suiter Word Reading Screen, the Mann-Suiter Vocabulary Screen, and the Mann-Suiter Silent Reading and Written Language Screen.

MANN-SUITER WORD READING SCREEN

The Mann-Suiter Word Reading Screen has been designed to be used with individuals or groups of students in grades 2 through 8. Reading level of the selections range from preprimer through grade 8.

Rationale

The purpose of the Mann-Suiter Word Reading Screen is to give the classroom teacher an approximate beginning reading level for each student. It will estimate the wide range of ability in the classroom and serve as an aid in selecting classroom material needed for the reading program.

This screen is particularly useful for group evaluation at the beginning of the school year. The following are suggested levels for beginning screening at particular grades.

Grade 2—Preprimer, Primer, First, and Second
Grade 3—Primer, First, Second, and Third
Grade 4—First, Second, Third, and Fourth
Grade 5—Second, Third, Fourth, and Fifth
Grade 6—Third, Fourth, Fifth, and Sixth
Grade 7—Fourth, Fifth, Sixth, and Seventh
Grade 8—Fifth, Sixth, Seventh, and Eighth

Note: the teacher may have to drop down to lower levels if there is a great deal of variability within a given class of students. Good judgment should be used.

Administering the Mann-Suiter Word Reading Screen
Each student in the class will need a copy of the Student Worksheet (Form 6-30) for the level the teacher has selected to begin the screening. The lettered sections of the screen correspond to reading levels, as follows:

A. Preprimer
B. Primer
C. First
D. Second
E. Third
F. Fourth
G. Fifth
H. Sixth
I. Seventh
J. Eighth

The instructor should make sure that all the students have pencils and are ready. Detailed directions for administering the test are included on the Examiner's Copy and Answer Sheet (Form 6-31)

Scoring the Mann-Suiter Word Reading Screen
Scoring is done on the Student's Worksheet. To the right of each worksheet is a column for the teacher to check if an error has been made. The student's approximate reading level is the last word he or she knew before missing three in a row.

If a student, for example, read all of the preprimer words, but knew only two or three of the primer words, his or her testing for placement in classroom materials would begin at the primer level. If another student knew four of the primer words, but none of the first-level words, he or she would be tested for mid-primer placement or be started in an easy first-level reading book.

To aid the teacher in determining the needs of the class, a Class Score Sheet (Form 6-32) has been developed. Before entering names on the Class Score Sheet, the teacher should organize the student's papers by score, ranking them from the lowest to the highest. When entering names on the Class Score Sheet, the teacher should enter the lowest first and proceed to the highest. A copy of the Class Score Sheet can be given to the librarian, who can use the estimated scores in teaching library skills and in helping individual students to select appropriate books and other materials. Figure 6-4 is an example of a completed Class Score Sheet.

Form 6-30

MANN-SUITER WORD READING SCREEN STUDENT WORKSHEET

NAME _____ DATE _____

EXAMINER _____

Incorrect Responses

A 1. green   brown   red   purple   black   _____
    2. yellow   black   orange   brown   blue   _____
    3. big   bad   pig   dog   bed   _____
    4. no   can   hot   on   not   _____
    5. had   house   have   horse   hop   _____

B 1. the   with   went   what   want   _____
    2. sleep   like   look   help   little   _____
    3. how   know   out   now   away   _____
    4. came   some   home   one   come   _____
    5. when   walk   white   where   while   _____

C 1. around   over   again   other   also   _____
    2. many   mother   money   moon   morning   _____
    3. thing   food   their   father   took   _____
    4. children   sleep   chicken   splash   chair   _____
    5. wash   work   would   under   wish   _____

D 1. head   heavy   hide   heard   hard   _____
    2. light   through   laugh   though   right   _____
    3. front   found   flew   floor   first   _____
    4. noise   never   nothing   next   nose   _____
    5. beauty   because   both   before   bath   _____
    6. drink   bring   built   draw   burn   _____

(continued)

272

NAME _____ DATE _____

EXAMINER _____

Incorrect Responses

E
1. since   storm   safely   surface   saddle   _____
2. gravel   greatest   grounded   grove   grass   _____
3. chief   clamp   careful   clothe   clown   _____
4. danger   different   drawn   delicious   different   _____
5. eight   ocean   empty   about   except   _____
6. beach   being   bench   bounce   broke   _____

F
1. fortune   future   flakes   freight   flourish   _____
2. bacon   breeze   breathe   beetles   broad   _____
3. design   develop   distant   dainty   digest   _____
4. silence   sheriff   success   support   serious   _____
5. courage   claimed   concern   cooperate   crickets   _____
6. guide   glanced   guilty   glass   guard   _____

G
1. naturally   nursery   ninety   number   necessary   _____
2. scholar   salmon   shrill   solemn   source   _____
3. article   acquire   ancient   ambition   accurate   _____
4. evolved   enormous   expensive   emperor   explore   _____
5. legend   leisure   lower   loosely   limb   _____
6. products   prevent   prairie   presence   profitable   _____

H
1. fleeting   fluent   figure   flattery   famous   _____
2. licensed   liquids   literal   lenient   lingering   _____
3. partial   politics   poisoned   paragraph   plough   _____
4. spectacular   substance   scenes   summoned   scamper   _____
5. omitted   obliged   obvious   obsolete   obedience   _____
6. irrelevant   irregular   illicit   illusion   imitation   _____

(continued)

NAME _____ DATE _____

EXAMINER _____

Incorrect Responses

I

1. individual	industrious	impressive	intricate	induce	_____
2. prominent	preposition	persuade	pensive	precision	_____
3. exposition	environment	exhausted	equipment	evident	_____
4. adequately	approximate	attentively	administer	architect	_____
5. sojourn	subscribe	scientists	stimulating	standardize	_____
6. contend	commence	commission	contemporary	crisis	_____

J

1. prairies	proportional	procession	permanent	proposition	_____
2. financial	formulated	fascinated	furnace	fraternity	_____
3. inducement	irrelevance	intangible	inadequate	immediately	_____
4. commerce	communion	content	contrasting	circumstances	_____
5. obviously	oxygen	obligation	ordinarily	oppress	_____
6. grotesque	grasped	glistening	granting	gondola	_____

MANN-SUITER WORD READING SCREEN

Examiner's Copy and Answer Sheet
Directions

1. Say, "Find letter *[supply letter]* and put your finger on number 1."
2. Say, "One, *[supply word]*, circle the word *[supply word]*." *Note:* Check to see if all the students understand the directions.
3. Give the students approximately 15 seconds to circle their choice before moving to the next word. Keep the rate of input constant for each word.
4. After having administered the first selection, before starting the next selection, remind the students to put their finger on the next letter to the left of the page. Continue through the screens selected.

A. Preprimer
1. red
2. black
3. bad
4. on
5. horse

B. Primer
1. went
2. help
3. away
4. some
5. while

C. First
1. other
2. many
3. their
4. splash
5. wash

D. Second
1. head
2. though
3. flew
4. noise
5. both
6. draw

E. Third
1. since
2. gravel
3. clothe
4. delicious
5. except
6. being

F. Fourth
1. flourish
2. beetles
3. design
4. serious
5. courage
6. guilty

G. Fifth
1. necessary
2. salmon
3. ancient
4. emperor
5. leisure
6. prairie

H. Sixth
1. fluent
2. lenient
3. partial
4. scenes
5. obedience
6. illicit

I. Seventh
1. intricate
2. persuade
3. exposition
4. approximate
5. standardize
6. commerce

J. Eighth
1. proposition
2. fascinated
3. irrelevance
4. circumstances
5. obviously
6. grotesque

MANN-SUITER WORD READING SCREEN

Class Score Sheet

TEACHER _____ GRADE _____ DATE _____

Name	A PP	B P	C I	D II	E III	F IV	G V	H VI	I VII	J VIII
1.										
2.										
3.										
4.										
5.										
6.										
7.										
8.										
9.										
10.										
11.										
12.										
13.										
14.										
15.										
16.										
17.										
18.										
19.										
20.										
21.										
22.										
23.										
24.										
25.										
26.										
27.										
28.										
29.										
30.										
31.										
32.										
33.										

Mann-Suiter Word Reading Screen
Class Score Sheet

Grade _____   Date _____

Name	A PP	B P	C I	D II	E III	F IV	G V	H VI	I VII	J VIII
1. Mary Smith	X									
2. Becky Rubin		X								
3. Johnny Jones		X								
4. Lisa Mason		X								
5. Danny Ayres			X							

Figure 6-4   Completed Class Score Sheet

MANN-SUITER VOCABULARY SCREEN

The Mann-Suiter Vocabulary Screen is designed to be used as an individual or group oral language development assessment. Selections, ranging from first through eighth-grade level, were extrapolated from the Mann-Suiter Developmental Word-Recognition Inventory (pages 228–241). The first three words of Levels I–IV were taken from Form A of the Mann-Suiter Developmental Word-Recognition Inventory, and the second three words were taken from Form B. The first four words of Levels V–VIII were taken from Form A, and the second four words were taken from Form B.

Rationale

The purpose of the Mann-Suiter Vocabulary Screen is to indicate which students may need help in vocabulary development. By third grade, vocabulary assumes an important role in reading. Often students are thought to have a problem with inference or main-idea questions. However, the real problem in many cases is an inadequate vocabulary.

Although the vocabulary selections begin with Level I words, the Mann-Suiter Vocabulary Screen is designed primarily to be used with those reading at the second grade level and is ideally suited for readers at the third grade level or above.

Administering the Mann-Suiter Vocabulary Screen

The Mann-Suiter Vocabulary Screen should be administered to the whole class regardless of the individual reading levels of the students. An estimated oral language development level can be ascertained for each student, even those considered to be poor readers. Teachers should begin two grade levels lower than the grade of the students they are screening. To assess a third grade class at the first of the year, the teacher should begin with Level I and continue as necessary.

The screen should always be read by the instructor, who will use the Examiner's Copy (Form 6-33) and Answer Sheet (Form 6-34). Every student will need a copy of the Student's Work and Score Sheet (Form 6-35) and a pencil. The room should be quiet, and all students should indicate that they can hear the instructor.

The teacher should read the number first, asking the students to put their fingers on the number in order to keep the place. The teacher should then read the sentences clearly, just as they are written on the examiner's copy, pausing slightly between the sentence and each of the three choices. Sentences may be reread, if necessary, once more. The student circles his or her choice.

Use with Individual Students

The Mann-Suiter Vocabulary Screen can also be used for individual students. After administering the Mann-Suiter Developmental Reading Inventories, the teacher can screen the student with the Mann-Suiter Vocabulary Screen to estimate his or her level of language development. Some students read words they do not understand, and others understand words far above the level they can read. It is important to understand that performance can be erratic in some students; for example, a student may fail Level III and be borderline in Level IV. This information is diagnostic, and the student may require further assessment to find out the reason for the erratic performance.

MANN-SUITER VOCABULARY SCREEN

Examiner's Copy

Directions for administrating. Read the sentences clearly, just as they are written, pausing slightly between the sentence and each of the three choices. Sentences may be reread once more if needed.

Note: Start each sentence with the number. Have the students put their finger on the number, then read the sentence and the choices. The student circles his/her choice.

Level I

1. Again — If we say a person is going again, we mean

   another time   first time   last time

2. Next — If we say something is next to something, we mean it is

   farthest away   beside it   distant

3. Many — If we say there are many people, we mean there are

   none   two   a lot

4. night — Another word for night could be

   morning   evening   noon

5. full — If we say something is full, we mean there is

   no more room   there is room   it is empty

6. left — The opposite of left is

   over   right   under

Level II

1. built — If something was built, it was

   constructed   torn down   given away

2. through — If we say someone is through with something, we mean he is

   starting it   finished with it   getting it

3. leaves — Leaves are a part of a

   car   chair   plant

4. whole — If we say you can have the whole thing, we mean you can have

   part of it   all of it   half of it

5. change — If you change something you

   keep it the same   do nothing   make it different

6. close — If you close something, you

   open it   shut it   break it

Level III

1. gravel — Gravel is

   an insect   a mixture of sand and pebbles   a lion's roar

2. stream — A stream is a

   beach   brook   planet

3. tribe — The word tribe refers to a group of

   cars   people   mountains

4. fasten — If we fasten something, we

   secure it   unlock it   turn it on

5. surface — The surface of something is its

   interior   thickness   exterior

6. grove — A grove is a

   tunnel   small wooded area   pond

(continued)

Level IV

1. glanced — If you glanced at something, you

    looked quickly   gazed at it   didn't look

2. design — If you design something, you

    put it away   sketch an outline of it rent it

3. guide — A guide is a person who

    farms   directs   follows

4. vacant — If a building is vacant, it is

    occupied   filled   empty

5. concern — If you show concern, you are

    angry   unfriendly   interested

6. interior — Interior refers to the

    outside of something   inside of something   top of it

Level V

1. shrill — a shrill sound is

    high and piercing   soft   musical

2. prevent — If we prevent something, we

    include it   stop it   move it

3. ancient — If something is ancient, it is

    modern   fresh   very old

4. acquire — If you acquire something, you

    sell it   obtain it   give it away

5. legend — A legend is a

    myth   poem   group of soldiers

6. evolved — If something evolved, it

    died   unfolded   was changeless

7. solemn — A solemn occasion is

    serious   gay   merry

8. yield — To yield is to

    gaze   take over   surrender

Level VI

1. detained — If someone is detained, he is

    moved on   held back   promoted

2. omitted — If something is omitted, it is

    left out   added   clipped on

3. partial — If someone is partial toward something, she is

    biased   unbiased   dangerous

4. summoned — If someone is summoned, he is

    exiled   sent away   sent for

5. artificial — If something is artificial, it is

    real   not genuine   genuine

6. source — The source of something is its

    beginning   end   course

7. erratic — If a person's behavior is erratic, it is

    frugal   pleasant   eccentric

8. debris — When we speak of debris, we are discussing

    brocades   broken rubbish   paintings

(continued)

Level VII

1. tremor — If a person writes with a tremor, his writing shows

    strength   quivering   humor

2. sojourn — A sojourn refers to a

    temporary residence   permanent residence   shack

3. waning — A waning moon is

    growing   diminishing   waxing

4. compassionate — If a person is compassionate, he is

    merciful   vague   lonely

5. malignant — A malignant growth

    enhances life   sustains life   threatens life

6. pensive — If one is in a pensive mood, she is

    laughing   crying   reflecting

7. precise — If something is precise, it is

    modern   vague   clearly determined

8. intricate — An intricate pattern is

    complicated   uneasy   plain

Level VIII

1. whimsical — A whimsical idea is

    factual   realistic   capricious

2. ultimate — The ultimate truth. Ultimate here means

    challenging   fundamental   stimulating

3. obvious — If something is obvious, it is

    obscure   waning   apparent

4. ambitious — If someone is ambitious, she is

    lazy   aspiring   content

5. grotesque — If something is grotesque, it is

    oddly formed   pleasing   professional

6. articulate — If someone is articulate, he speaks with

    a brogue   an accent   distinctness

7. subside — If you are waiting for something to subside, you are waiting for it to

    go down   go up   move over

8. permanent — If something is permanent, it is

    contrasting   unchanging   changeable

MANN-SUITER VOCABULARY SCREEN ANSWER SHEET

Level I

1. another time
2. beside it
3. a lot
4. evening
5. no more room
6. right

Level II

1. constructed
2. finished with it
3. plant
4. all of it
5. make it different
6. shut it

Level III

1. mixture of sand
   and pebbles
2. brook
3. people
4. secure it
5. exterior
6. small wooded area

Level IV

1. looked quickly
2. sketched an outline
   of it
3. directs
4. empty
5. interested
6. inside of something

Level V

1. high and piercing
2. stop it
3. very old
4. obtain it
5. myth
6. unfolded
7. serious
8. surrender

Level VI

1. held back
2. left out
3. biased
4. sent for
5. not genuine
6. beginning
7. eccentric
8. broken rubbish

Level VII

1. quivering
2. temporary residence
3. diminishing
4. merciful
5. threatens life
6. reflecting
7. clearly determined
8. complicated

Level VIII

1. capricious
2. fundamental
3. apparent
4. aspiring
5. oddly formed
6. distinctness
7. go down
8. unchanging

MANN-SUITER VOCABULARY SCREEN
STUDENT'S WORK AND SCORE SHEET

NAME _____ GRADE _____ DATE _____

EXAMINER _____

Directions: Circle your choice.

Score
Right Wrong

Level I

1. another time	first time	last time
2. farthest away	beside it	distant
3. none	two	a lot
4. morning	evening	noon
5. no more room	there is room	it is empty
6. over	right	under

Right Wrong

Level II

1. constructed	torn down	given away
2. starting it	finished with it	getting it
3. car	chair	plant
4. part of it	all of it	half of it
5. keep it the same	do nothing	make it different
6. open it	shut it	break it

Right Wrong

Level III

1. an insect	a mixture of sand and pebbles	a lion's roar
2. beach	brook	planet
3. cars	people	mountains
4. secure it	unlock it	turn it on
5. interior	thickness	exterior
6. tunnel	small wooded area	pond

(continued)

NAME _____

GRADE _____ DATE _____

EXAMINER _____

Directions: Circle your choice.

Level IV

1. looked quickly	gazed at it	didn't look
2. put it away	sketch an out-line of it	rent it
3. farms	directs	follows
4. occupied	filled	empty
5. angry	unfriendly	interested
6. outside of something	inside of some-thing	top of it

Score
Right   Wrong

Level V

1. high and piercing	soft	musical
2. include it	stop it	move it
3. modern	fresh	very old
4. sell it	obtain it	give it away
5. myth	poem	group of soldiers
6. died	unfolded	was changeless
7. serious	gay	merry
8. gaze	take over	surrender

Right   Wrong

Level VI

1. moved on	held back	promoted
2. left out	added	clipped on
3. biased	unbiased	dangerous
4. exiled	sent away	sent for
5. real	not genuine	genuine
6. beginning	end	course
7. frugal	pleasant	eccentric
8. brocades	broken rubbish	paintings

Right   Wrong

(continued)

NAME _____ GRADE _____ DATE _____

EXAMINER _____

Directions: Circle your choice.

Score

Level VII

			Right	Wrong
1. strength	quivering	humor		
2. temporary residence	permanent residence	shack		
3. growing	diminishing	waxing		
4. merciful	vague	lonely		
5. enhances life	sustains life	threatens life		
6. laughing	crying	reflecting		
7. modern	vague	clearly determined		
8. complicated	easy	plain		

Level VIII

			Right	Wrong
1. factual	realistic	capricious		
2. challenging	fundamental	stimulating		
3. obscure	waning	apparent		
4. lazy	aspiring	content		
5. oddly formed	pleasing	professional		
6. a brogue	an accent	distinctness		
7. go down	go up	move over		
8. contrasting	unchanging	changeable		

Score

Right	Wrong
×	
×	
×	
	×
×	
×	

P

Figure 6-5 Example of Student's Score Sheet for Vocabulary Screen

Scoring the Mann-Suiter Vocabulary Screen

The Student's Work and Score Sheet is designed to indicate an estimate of the student's level of vocabulary development based on graded reading material.

All answers are marked either right or wrong in the score boxes to the right of the student's response.

For each level of Levels I through IV the following scoring is used:

1 error	pass
2 errors	borderline pass
3 errors	needs instruction

For each level of Levels V through VIII the following scoring is used:

1 error	pass
2 or 3 errors	borderline pass
4 errors	needs instruction

The student's score sheet would look like the example in Figure 6-5. The teacher marks P (pass), BP (borderline pass) or I (instruction) on the small line to the left of the score box.

Class Score Sheet

The Class Score Sheet (Form 6-36) can be used by the teacher in decisions about grouping students for teaching vocabulary. The chart indicates the levels of screening across the top and the students' names down the left side. The teacher can black in or mark with an X the level at which the students need instruction. (See Figure 6-6.)

Students passing at their grade level can be tested at higher levels to determine their vocabulary development.

MANN-SUITER SILENT READING AND WRITTEN LANGUAGE SCREEN

The Mann-Suiter Silent Reading and Written Language Screen (Form 6-37) is designed to be used with individuals or groups. Selections range from primer reading level through grade 8. This group screen is particularly useful for teachers who have students in remedial or special reading groups. While the special-

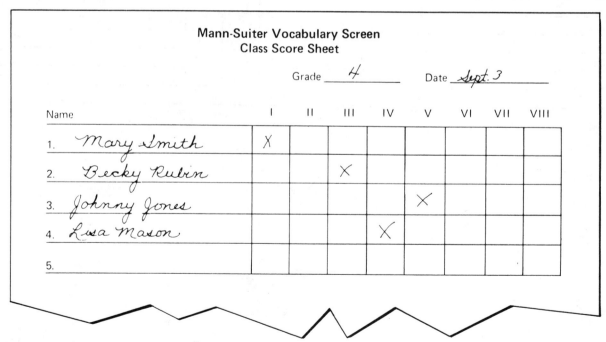

Mann-Suiter Vocabulary Screen
Class Score Sheet

Grade ___4___   Date ___Sept. 3___

Name	I	II	III	IV	V	VI	VII	VIII
1. Mary Smith	X							
2. Becky Rubin			×					
3. Johnny Jones					×			
4. Lisa Mason				×				
5.								

Figure 6-6 Example of a Class Score Sheet

MANN-SUITER VOCABULARY SCREEN
CLASS SCORE SHEET

TEACHER _____ GRADE _____ DATE _____

Name	I	II	III	IV	V	VI	VII	VIII
1.								
2.								
3.								
4.								
5.								
6.								
7.								
8.								
9.								
10.								
11.								
12.								
13.								
14.								
15.								
16.								
17.								
18.								
19.								
20.								
21.								
22.								
23.								
24.								
25.								

MANN-SUITER SILENT READING AND WRITTEN LANGUAGE SCREEN

NAME _____ DATE _____

GRADE _____ EXAMINER _____

Level Primer

Both Selections 75 words
Number Wrong _____

DAN AND PAL

Pal is a little dog.

He is white with black spots.

Pal likes to play ball.

He likes to play with Dan.

Dan is a little boy.

Pal and Dan play.

They like to play ball.

1. Pal is a little _____ .

2. He has _____ spots.

3. Dan is a little _____ .

4. Dan and Pal like to _____ .

(Continued)

(continued)

THE ZOO

Dan likes to go to the zoo.

He likes to go with Ann and Tom.

They like to look at the birds.

They like to see the monkeys.

They like to eat hot dogs.

5. Dan, _____ and _____ go to the zoo.

6. They like to see the _____ and _____ .

7. They like to eat _____ .

Scoring for optional oral reading								
Errors	0	1	2	3	4	4	6	7
Percentage	100	99	97	96	95	93	92	91

(continued)

NAME _____ DATE _____

GRADE _____ EXAMINER _____

Level I
　　　　　　　　　　　　　　　　　　　　　　　79 words
　　　　　　　　　　　　　　　　　　　　　　　Number Wrong _____

THE GIRLS

Ann and Mary are little girls. They walk to school together every day. On their way to school one day, Ann fell down. She got her dress dirty. Her pretty red hair ribbon was lost. She started to cry.

1. Ann and Mary are _____ .

2. Ann's dress got _____ .

3. Ann lost her _____ .

(Continued)

Mary tried to help Ann. She found Ann's hair ribbon and put it in her hair. It was not dirty. She helped Ann brush off her dress. Ann was not hurt, so the girls went on to school.

4. Was Ann hurt? _____

_____ .

5. What did Mary do with Ann's hair ribbon?

_____

_____ .

6. What did both girls do? _____

_____

_____ .

Scoring for optional oral reading									
Errors	0	1	2	3	4	5	6	7	8	9
Percentage	100	99	97	96	95	94	92	91	90	89

(continued)

NAME _____ DATE _____

GRADE _____ EXAMINER _____

Level II

106 words

Number Wrong _____

THE WITCH

Once upon a time there was a pretty little witch named Bell. She loved to fly through the air on her magic broom. She had a large, black cat with green eyes that always went with her. His name was Tom, and he loved to ride on her broom, too.

1. Bell loved to fly through the _____ .
2. Tom loved to ride on the _____ .
3. Tom's eyes were _____ .

Bell always wore a pointed, black hat. She always wore a long, black cape that kept her warm. Tom did not need a coat and hat, for his thick fur kept him warm. Bell and Tom loved to ride through the sky on her broom. They always went riding when the moon was full.

4. What kind of a hat did Bell have? _____
   _____ .

5. When did Bell and Tom like to go riding? _____
   _____ .

Scoring for optional oral reading										
Errors	0	1	2	3	4	5	6	7	8	9	10
Percentage	100	99	98	97	96	95	94	93	92	92	91

(continued)

NAME _____ DATE _____

GRADE _____ EXAMINER _____

Level III

127 words
Number Wrong _____

NOAH'S ARK

Do you know who Noah was? I would like to tell you a story about him. Noah lived on the earth many, many years ago. We remember him today because he built a large wooden ark. An ark is a type of boat. Noah built the ark to keep animals in during a bad flood.

1. This story is about a man named _____ .
2. Noah built a large wooden _____ .
3. An ark is a type of _____ .

Noah was told that it would rain for forty days and forty nights. It rained so hard that towns were washed away and all of the land was covered with water. Noah and the animals, however, were safe in the ark. When the rain stopped and the water went down, Noah and the animals went ashore again. They knew they were safe because they saw a rainbow in the sky.

4. How long did it rain? _____

_____ .

5. What happened to the towns in the heavy rain? _____

_____ .

Scoring for optional oral reading								
Errors	0	1	2	3	4	5	6	7	8
Percentage	100	99	97	96	95	94	92	91	90

(continued)

NAME _____ DATE _____

GRADE _____ EXAMINER _____

Level IV

99 words
Number Wrong _____

BILLY'S PET

Billy had a very unusual pet. It was what he did that made him so unusual.
Billy had a dog that could read. Unlike most dogs, Pal just loved to curl up
with a good book. He loved to read cowboy stories and, of course, anything
about dogs. He was really an unusual pet!

1. Billy had an unusual _____ .

2. His dog's name was _____ .

3. Pal loved to read stories about _____ and _____ .

Pal especially liked stories about Rin Tin Tin, a wonderful dog that did all
sorts of brave things. In one story, Rin Tin Tin saved a young child from
drowning. That was Pal's favorite dog story, and Rin Tin Tin was his hero.

4. Why was Rin Tin Tin Pal's hero? _____

_____ .

Scoring for optional oral reading									
Errors	0	1	2	3	4	5	6	7	8	9
Percentage	100	99	98	97	96	96	95	93	92	91

(continued)

NAME _____ DATE _____

GRADE _____ EXAMINER _____

Level V

122 words

Number Wrong _____

SHARKS

Everyone knows something about sharks, but not many people know how many different kinds there are. Altogether there are about 250 species. Of these, only a few are truly dangerous to man. When people speak of a man-eating shark, they are usually referring to the great white shark.

1. There are about 250 _____ of sharks.

2. Most of them are not _____.

3. The great white shark is considered _____.

Great white sharks eat a wide variety of fishes and other sea animals. They are also known to attack and kill men. They are the only sharks that have been proven to attack small boats. Luckily there are not a lot of great white sharks. However, they are found throughout the world in the warmer ocean waters. They are usually about 20 feet in length, although one specimen was recorded at 36½ feet.

4. Why are people afraid of great white sharks? _____
_____
_____.

Scoring for optional oral reading										
Errors	0	1	2	3	4	5	6	7	8	9	10
Percentage	100	99	98	98	97	96	95	94	93	93	92

(continued)

NAME _____ DATE _____

GRADE _____ EXAMINER _____

Level VI

110 words
Number Wrong _____

OUR NATIONAL EMBLEM

The dashing grace, strength, and courage of the bald eagle have impressed men for ages. However, when the bald eagle was first suggested as our national emblem back in 1776 Benjamin Franklin opposed the selection. He preferred the wild turkey because it was a thrifty bird.

1. For ages men have been impressed with the _____ .
2. In 1776 the bald eagle was first suggested as our _____
3. Benjamin Franklin preferred _____ .

Franklin believed the eagle was a coward, a bully, and a thief. He didn't feel it was fit to represent our country. What men didn't know then was that eagles mate for life, eat mostly fish, and spend more time raising their young than any other bird. About six months of the adult eagle's year is devoted to raising its young.

4. Benjamin Franklin didn't like the bald eagle, but other men of his time did. Why did they select the bald eagle to be our national emblem? _____

_____

_____

Scoring for optional oral reading										
Errors	0	1	2	3	4	5	6	7	8	9	10
Percentage	100	99	98	97	96	95	95	94	93	92	91

(continued)

NAME _____ DATE _____

GRADE _____ EXAMINER _____

Level VII

200 words
Number Wrong _____

LONDON BRIDGE IS FALLING DOWN

London Bridge is falling down,
Falling down, falling down . . .

A very old tradition holds that this incident inspired the nursery rhyme.

Norway's Olaf the Stout distinguished himself as a Viking. According to legend, sometime around the year 1010 he led a fleet up the Thames River and pulled down London Bridge.

Viking ships were open. To protect his ships, Olaf covered them with roofs built of wood and wicker. When the fleet was ready, the Vikings rowed up the river. As they neared the bridge, arrows engulfed them, and such large stones were thrown down upon them that neither their helmets nor their shields could withstand the onslaught. Many of the Viking ships were greatly damaged under the great siege.

1. Olaf the Stout was a famous _____ .

2. What did Olaf do to protect his ships? _____

_____ .

Some of the Viking ships had to retreat, but Olaf and his men rowed up under the bridge, tied ropes around the supporting posts, and then rowed their ships downstream as hard as they could. The posts were dragged along the bottom until they were loosened from the bridge. Because a large army stood on the bridge, with a great weight of stones and weapons, the bridge fell into the river when the posts were broken.

3. Why wouldn't Olaf and his Vikings be successful today? _____

_____ .

Scoring for optional oral reading											
Errors	0	1	2	3	4	5	6	7	8	9	10	11
Percentage	100	99	99	99	98	98	97	97	96	96	96	95

(continued)

NAME _____ DATE _____

GRADE _____ EXAMINER _____

Level VIII

180 words
Number Wrong _____

THE CHUCKWALLA

The chuckwalla is a strange-looking lizard almost 20 inches long that feeds exclusively on vegetation and is found in the deserts of western United States. The skin of the chuckwalla droops from its body in great folds and wrinkles; it has a sagging stomach and even a double chin. But it wears this oversize suit for a reason. Any severe fright sends it scurrying into a rock crevice where it inflates itself like a great balloon by gulping in mouthfuls of air. Wedged tightly among the rocks, the lizard is almost impossible to dislodge.

1. Where would you look for a chuckwalla? _____.

2. How do you know the chuckwalla is not a meat eater? _____

_____.

Like many desert lizards, the chuckwalla seeks shade or a burrow during the heat of day. Even though chuckwallas are cold-blooded creatures and need some sun to keep warm, they must guard against too much heat, for its effects would be lethal. Changes in the chuckwalla's skin color during the day help regulate its body temperature. In the cool morning, it turns dark to absorb more solar heat, but as the day warms it becomes progressively lighter to reflect the sun's radiation.

3. What does the author suggest is the reason for the chuckwalla's color shift?

_____

_____

_____

_____

Scoring for optional oral reading										
Errors	0	1	2	3	4	5	6	7	8	9
Percentage	100	99	99	98	98	97	97	96	96	95

ist may prefer to give an Individual Reading Inventory (page 228), the regular classroom teacher or any other trained individuals can share in the evaluation process by giving the group reading screen.

Outline of Written Questions
The reading format and the type of questions to be answered change slowly as the selections become harder.

Questions at the primer level are of the fill-in variety and only require one- or two-word written responses.

Three questions at Level I call for fill-in answers of one or two words, and three questions need sentence answers.

At Levels II and III, three questions can be answered by filling in a missing word, and two questions require a sentence answer.

At Levels IV through VI a few simple fill-in sentence responses are included, but others require more thought.

Questions at Levels VII and VIII require the drawing of conclusions.

Purpose of Written Questions
The purpose of the range of questions is to indicate to the teacher the class's wide range of abilities in the written language area.

The fill-in questions indicate whether or not the student can handle detail-type questions. The manner in which the writing is done indicates whether or not the student uses cursive or manuscript writing. It also indicates whether or not the student can copy correctly.

For the questions requiring sentence answers, the teacher needs to stress that the student write sentences if he or she can. Some students will only be able to write the phrases copied from the page. A wide range of ability may be observed.

At Levels VII and VIII the learner will have to be a little more original in his or her response. The answers should be two or three sentences long. The teacher should note how the student deals with more complex tasks.

Other Uses of the Screen
These Silent Reading Screens can also be used to evaluate oral reading. If a student has done poorly on a level he or she should have been able to complete successfully, the teacher can ask the student to read the selection orally. This may help the teacher determine what the problem may be. Just the story part of each page can be used for this purpose. The selection should be retyped on a card for the student to read. The scoring chart at the bottom of the student's

duplicator sheet should be used for scoring the oral reading. Scoring procedures are the same as those used for the Mann-Suiter Developmental Paragraph Reading Inventory (pages 228–240).

As students progress in school, more and more of their work is dependent upon reading a selection or reading instructions and responding. Usually the response required is in writing. This Mann-Suiter Silent Reading and Written Language Screen, given the first days of school, will help a teacher quickly estimate the range of needs of the students.

Administering the Mann-Suiter Silent Reading and Written Language Screen
For grades four and below, the teacher begins testing by administering selections from the primer level and Level I to all students. The students begin at the same time and then bring their work to the instructor upon completion. The teacher notes the time of completion on the back of each student's paper. The teacher will then have an idea of who works quickly and who needs extra time. After checking the completed work, the teacher continues evaluating only those who did passing work. They should be given the Level II and Level III screens at the second sitting. Those doing passing work on those screens should be given the Level IV screen, and possibly the Level V screen, at the third sitting.

It is very important that the student be encouraged to write sentences wherever requested. Sentences should be checked for punctuation and grammar.

For grades five and above, the teacher should begin evaluating with the third grade silent reading screen and follow the program outlined above.

The teacher can check answers against the Answer Sheet (Form 6-38) provided with the test.

Use for Individual Students
The Mann-Suiter Silent Reading and Written Language Screen is especially valuable to the instructor working individually with a student. After administrating the Mann-Suiter Developmental Reading Inventories and determining the student's independent reading level, the teacher can give the silent reading screen for that level for a quick evaluation of written language skills and the ability to carry out a written task. This is an area seldom assessed in testing.

The Silent Reading and Written Language Screen can also be used with students who are unable to write. They can read the test silently and answer orally.

Failure at the Independent Reading Level
When a student fails the Mann-Suiter Silent Reading and Written Language Screen at his or her inde-

MANN-SUITER SILENT READING AND WRITTEN LANGUAGE SCREEN ANSWER SHEET

Primer

Dan and Pal
1. dog
2. black
3. boy
4. play or play ball

The Zoo
5. Ann and Tom or Tom and Ann
6. birds and monkeys or monkeys and birds
7. hot dogs

Level I

The Girls
1. girls or little girls
2. dirty
3. hair ribbon or ribbon
4. No, she was not hurt.
5. She put it in her hair.
6. They went to school.

Level II

The Witch
1. air
2. broom
3. green
4. She had a pointed, black hat.
5. They went riding when the moon was full.

Level III

Noah's Ark
1. Noah
2. ark or boat
3. boat
4. It rained for forty days and forty nights.
5. The towns were washed away.

Level IV

Billy's Pet
1. pet
2. Pal
3. cowboys and dogs or dogs and cowboys
4. Rin Tin Tin did many brave things. He saved a child from drowning. (One or both of these ideas.)

Level V

Sharks
1. species
2. dangerous
3. dangerous to man or a man-eating shark
4. They are known to kill men and will attack a small boat. They are very large sharks. (Any of these ideas)

Level VI

Our National Emblem
1. bald eagle
2. national emblem
3. the turkey or wild turkey
4. The dashing grace, strength, and courage of the eagle impressed most men. (The eagle's other attributes were not known at that time.)

Level VII

London Bridge Is Falling Down
1. Viking
2. He had roofs built of wood and wicker.
3. The contrast between warfare then, with arrows and stones and boats able to pull a bridge down, and warfare today, with steel and concrete bridges and guns, should give students a chance for original writing.

Level VIII

The Chuckwalla
1. In the deserts of western United States
2. The chuckwalla feeds exclusively on vegetation.
3. The author suggests that changes in skin color during the day help regulate its body temperature.

MANN-SUITER SILENT READING AND WRITTEN LANGUAGE SCREEN SCORE SHEET

NAME _____ GRADE _____ INSTRUCTIONAL READING LEVEL _____

EXAMINER _____ DATE _____

Comprehension

☐ Silent
☐ Oral

	Pass	Border-line Pass	Needs Instruc-tion
Primer			
1 error; pass			
2 errors; borderline pass			
3 errors; needs instruction			
Level I			
1 error; pass			
2 errors; borderline pass			
3 errors; needs instruction			
Level II			
1 error; pass			
2 errors; needs instruction			
Level III			
1 error; pass			
2 errors; needs instruction			
Level IV			
1 error; borderline pass			
2 errors; needs instruction			
Level V			
1 error; borderline pass			
2 errors; needs instruction			
Level VI			
1 error; borderline pass			
2 errors; needs instruction			
Level VII			
1 error; borderline pass			
2 errors; needs instruction			
Level VIII			
1 error; borderline pass			
2 errors; needs instruction			

Written Language

	Phrases	Sen-tences	Punctu-ation Errors
Primer			
Only one word answers at this level			
Level I			
Questions 4.			
5.			
6.			
Level II			
Questions 4.			
5.			
Level III			
Questions 4.			
5.			
Level IV			
Question 4.			
Level V			
Question 4.			
Level VI			
Question 4.			
Level VII			
Questions 2.			
3.			
Level VIII			
Questions 2.			
3.			

pendent level of reading, the instructor should have the student read it aloud to determine if he or she can answer the questions orally.

If there seems to be a serious problem with written work, it may be necessary to test down one level at a time to determine at what level the student can handle written responses.

Listening Comprehension Level

These screens can also be used to determine a student's listening comprehension level. Once a student's instructional reading level has been determined through use of the Mann-Suiter Developmental Reading Inventories, the evaluator can read more difficult selections to the student to determine the highest level at which the student can understand and discuss what he or she has heard. Thus a fourth grader, for instance, reading on a second grade level may understand the content of the material presented orally on a fourth or even fifth grade level.

Scoring the Mann-Suiter Silent Reading and Written Language Screen

The Mann-Suiter Silent Reading and Written Language Screen Score Sheet (Form 6-39) is designed to indicate the student's comprehension and written language scores.

SCORING FOR THE COMPREHENSION TEST. At the top of each Mann-Suiter Silent Reading and Written Language Screen is a place for the teacher to mark the number of wrong answers to the comprehension questions.

The number of wrong answers is then plotted on the Mann-Suiter Silent Reading and Written Language Screen Score Sheet. Scoring for each reading selection is explained on the score sheet, making it easy for the teacher to mark Pass, Borderline Pass, or Needs Instruction for each level attempted.

Figure 6-7 is an example of the comprehension portion of the score sheet. The chart in Figure 6-7 indicates that the student who makes only one error is passing, and the teacher puts a check mark in the Pass column. If the student makes two errors, the check will be put in the Borderline Pass column. Borderline Pass is the lowest level of acceptable performance. If the student makes three or more errors, the check will be put in the Needs Instruction column.

Testing is discontinued when a student reaches a level where instruction is indicated.

SCORING FOR THE WRITTEN LANGUAGE TEST. This portion of the Mann-Suiter Silent Reading and Written Language Screen is designed to get a sample of the written language development of each student. All

Comprehension

Primer	☐ Silent ☐ Oral	Pass	Border-line Pass	Needs Instruc-tion
1 error; pass 2 errors; borderline pass 3 errors; needs instruction				

Figure 6-7 *Example of Comprehension Portion of Score Sheet for Silent Reading and Written Language Screen*

questions requiring sentence answers have been listed. The teacher should check whether the student answered the questions in phrases or sentences. A third column can be checked if there are punctuation or capitalization errors. (Do not be concerned about whether or not the answers are correct on this portion of the test.)

Figure 6-8 is an example of the Written Language portion of the scoring sheet.

The Mann-Suiter Silent Reading and Written Language Screen Score Sheet can be used for scoring oral comprehension by simply checking the box next to "Oral." Scoring would remain the same.

Data Collection

MANN-SUITER ANALYSIS OF ERRORS WORKSHEETS

After giving the Developmental Inventories and Screens, the teacher can indicate the errors on the Analysis of Errors Worksheets (Forms 6-40 and 6-41). Having done this, the teacher will be better able to determine how much, and what type of, additional testing is necessary before formulating any educational strategies for a given student. Some teachers will require more information, including standardized tests, before making any decisions. The questions is not how much testing is adequate but, rather, how

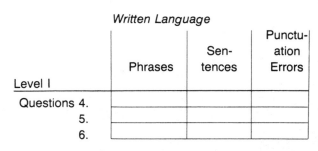

Written Language

Level I	Phrases	Sen-tences	Punctu-ation Errors
Questions 4.			
5.			
6.			

Figure 6-8 *Example of Written Language Portion of Score Sheet*

MANN-SUITER ANALYSIS OF ERRORS WORKSHEET

DEVELOPMENTAL WORD READING INVENTORY

NAME _____ SCHOOL _____

DATE _____ GRADE _____ DATE OF BIRTH _____

EXAMINER _____

(A check mark indicates
difficulty)

Auditory Errors

1. Guesses completely   _____
2. Knows letter names, but not sounds   _____
3. Makes associative error (*house* for *home*)   _____
4. Knows sounds, but cannot blend into words   _____
5. Substitutes one sound for another   _____

Visual Errors

1. Has slow rate of perception (fails flash, but gets untimed)   _____
2. Sees beginning of word only or beginning and endings only on flash   _____
3. Makes reversals (*was* for *saw*)   _____
4. Uses inversions (*me* for *we*)   _____
5. Does not discriminate fine detail (*ship* for *snip*)   _____
6. Omits sounds from words (check auditory discrimination)   _____
7. Adds sounds   _____
8. Hesitates   _____

Other Errors

MANN-SUITER ANALYSIS OF ERRORS WORKSHEET

DEVELOPMENTAL PARAGRAPH READING INVENTORY

NAME _____ SCHOOL _____

DATE _____ GRADE _____ DATE OF BIRTH _____

EXAMINER _____

(A check mark indicates difficulty)

Auditory Errors

1. Mispronounces words _____
2. Makes wild guesses _____
3. Makes associative errors (*house* for *home*) _____
4. Knows sounds but cannot blend _____
5. Needs to have words pronounced by teacher _____
6. Substitutes (*a* for *the*) _____
7. Cannot sound the word *out* _____

Visual Errors

1. Makes reversals of words (*was* for *saw*) _____
2. Transposes words and phrases (*said John* for *John said*) _____
3. Uses inversions (*me* for *we*) _____
4. Uses repetitions _____
5. Loses place and skips lines _____
6. Omits words or word endings _____
7. Makes errors of visual discrimination (reads *ship* for *snip*, or *ear* for *car*) _____
8. Reads word by word _____
9. Reads through punctuation _____
10. Exhibits hesitations _____
11. Adds words or endings _____

General Observations

Are items 1–6 true of the student when he or she is facing unfamiliar words?　　YES　　NO

1. Guesses without regard to any thought of the context read. _____ _____
2. Seems unwilling to attempt to read and just waits for the teacher to say the word. _____ _____
3. Seems willing to just skip unknown word and go on. _____ _____
4. Seems unable to sound out word parts and blends. _____ _____
5. Tries to spell out the word he or she cannot read. _____ _____
6. Makes little use of the context in attacking a word he or she does not know. _____ _____

(continued)

NAME _____

(A check mark indicates difficulty)

GENERAL ITEMS 7–31 ARE ANSWERED YES OR NO.   YES   NO

7. Disregards punctuation.   ____ ____
8. Does not pay attention to the story line.   ____ ____
9. Has a low meaning vocabulary—not adequate for the reading level under concern.   ____ ____
10. Makes no attempt to correct his or her errors.   ____ ____
11. Exhibits frequent hesitations and makes sounds like uh . . .?   ____ ____
12. Drops his or her voice at the end of a sentence.   ____ ____
13. Reads word by word instead of in phrases or thought units.   ____ ____
14. Exhibits a negative and indifferent attitude ("Do I have to?")   ____ ____
15. Cannot analyze problems and glean meaning.   ____ ____
16. Has excessive body movements while reading.   ____ ____
17. Is penalized by slowness in reading.   ____ ____
18. Prefers to read alone.   ____ ____
19. Poor reaction to being tested.   ____ ____
20. Avoids reading.   ____ ____
21. Does not read at home.   ____ ____
22. Does not understand more after reading silently than after material has been read orally to him or her.   ____ ____
23. Does not value reading.   ____ ____
24. Failure is in word recognition.   ____ ____
25. Failure is in comprehension.   ____ ____
26. Substitutes words that are appropriate in his or her dialect while reading.   ____ ____
27. Appears tense or nervous.   ____ ____
28. Is easily distracted from the task.   ____ ____
29. Has a speech problem (stuttering, articulation, voice).   ____ ____
30. Gives bizarre responses.   ____ ____
31. Does not hold the book at the appropriate length from eyes.   ____ ____

Other Errors

(continued)

NAME _____

(A check mark indicates
difficulty)

Reading Comprehension

STUDENT'S READING LEVEL ____   ____   ____   ____

1. Detail   ____   ____   ____   ____
2. Main Idea   ____   ____   ____   ____
3. Inference   ____   ____   ____   ____
4. Vocabulary   ____   ____   ____   ____
   a. Primarily
      Concrete-
      Functional
      (*C-F*)   ____   ____   ____   ____
   b. Primarily
      Abstract
      (*A*)   ____   ____   ____   ____

General Observations on Oral Reading

1. Phrasing   ____
2. Fluency   ____
3. Finger pointing   ____

General Observations on Silent Reading

1. Uses fingers   ____
2. Vocalizes   ____
3. Makes remarks   ____

Listening Comprehension

1. Grade level expectancy based on listening comprehension   ____

much information is needed in order to make a decision about changing or modifying the educational program for a particular student.

HANDWRITING ASSESSMENT

Difficulties in handwriting fall into two main categories: (1) factors that are student based and (2) factors arising from an inadequate instructional program.

1. *Student-Based Difficulties:*
   a. Lack of readiness for beginning writing may be a factor in that the student may exhibit fine motor dysfunction of the hands and fingers or poor eye-hand coordination.
   b. The student may have a visual acuity problem and need glasses.
   c. The student cannot grasp the pencil correctly or has an awkward writing position. He or she may have crippled hands or a spastic condition.

Supplementary Evaluation—Reading

TEST	GRADE LEVEL	COMPONENTS	TYPE
Botel Reading Inventory (Botel, 1978)	1–12	Phonics, word recognition	Norm-referenced
Brigance Diagnostic Inventory of Basic Skills (Brigance, 1977)	K–6	Oral reading, word recognition, comprehension	Criterion-referenced
The California Achievement Tests (Tiegs & Clark, 1977–1978)	1–12	Word meaning, comprehension	Norm-referenced
Classroom Reading Inventory (Silvaroli, 1973)	2–8	Word recognition, comprehension	Criterion-referenced
Diagnostic Reading Scales (Spache, 1981)	1–8	Word recognition, comprehension	Norm-referenced
Durrell Analysis of Reading Difficulty (Durrell & Catterson, 1980)	1–6	Word recognition, comprehension	Norm-referenced
Ekwall Reading Inventory (Ekwall, 1979)	1–8	Comprehension	Criterion-referenced
Gates-MacGinitie Reading Tests (MacGinitie, 1978)	1–12	Vocabulary, comprehension	Norm referenced
Gilmore Oral Reading Test (Gilmore & Gilmore, 1968)	1–8	Comprehension	Norm-referenced
Gray Oral Reading Test--Revised (Gray & Robinson, 1967; Weiderholt & Bryant, 1986),	1–12	Oral reading	Norm-referenced
Iowa Tests of Basic Skills (Hieronymus et al., 1982)	1–9	Word meaning, comprehension	Norm-referenced
Metropolitan Readiness Tests (Nurss & McGauvran, 1976)	K–1	Rhyming, letter recognition, visual matching, beginning consonants, etc.	Norm-referenced
Metropolitan Achievement Tests (Durost et al., 1978)	K–9	Comprehension	Norm-referenced
Peabody Individual Achievement Test (Dunn & Markwardt, 1970)	K–12	Word recognition	Norm-referenced
Stanford Achievement (Madden et al., 1973)	1–12	Word recognition, comprehension	Norm-referenced
Stanford Diagnostic Reading Test (Karisen et al., 1985)	1–13	Word recognition, comprehension	Norm-referenced
Wide-Range Achievement Test (Jastak & Jastak, 1978)	K–12	Word recognition, letter identification	Norm-referenced
Woodcock-Johnson Psychoeducational Battery (Woodcock & Johnson, 1977)	K–12	Word identification, comprehension	Norm-referenced
Woodcock Reading Mastery Tests Revised (Woodcock, 1986)	K–12	Word identification, comprehension	Norm-referenced

d. The student may not have established a dominant hand. He or she may be switching from left to right.
e. The student may have difficulty retaining visual symbols rather than having poor visual-motor coordination.
f. The student may have an emotional problem that can easily show up in deteriorating handwriting. He or she could also be physically ill.
g. The student may have no interest in writing and be unwilling to practice. He or she may exhibit indifference to established minimum standards.

2. *Program-Based Difficulties:*
a. The student may have been started in a formal writing program before he or she was ready. Possibly the student is still undecided as to which hand to use.
b. There could be insufficient interest on the part of the student due to undifferentiated group drill. The wrong positioning of paper might be a factor.
c. Not enough care taken with initial teaching may have been a factor. The student may have been allowed to practice errors. Too much practice done without supervision can cause difficulties.
d. A poorly planned transitional program from manuscript to cursive writing may be the cause of the problem in older students.

Screening for Developing a Writing Program in Primary Grades

Individual or group screening can be used to aid in determining the visual-motor and fine motor development of students.

A screening of visual-motor and fine motor skills serves the following purposes:

1. Indicates the students who lack readiness.
2. Identifies the students who have not developed a dominant hand and are still switching from left to right.
3. Indicates the students with a poor pencil grasp.
4. Identifies the students who have good visual-motor coordination and are ready for a full writing program.

Mann-Suiter Visual Motor Screen

Successful completion of the designs of the Mann-Suiter Visual Motor Screen (page 175) represents minimal standards for success in handwriting. Please note the normative data given on page 175. Give each student a copy of the screen and ask him or her to copy the designs to the left three times. This screen can also be used with groups. While the students are doing the screens, walk around the class, noting on a pad the left-handed students. Note the names of the students with a poor pencil grasp, especially the students who grasp the pencil too tightly or hold it back too far. This information can then be put on the Mann-Suiter Analysis of Errors Worksheet, page 305.

There are a number of sections in this book that will aid in the observation of fine motor skills. For younger students, administer the Mann-Suiter Visual Motor Screen on page 175. Observable Behaviors are also listed on the Mann-Suiter-McClung Developmental Checklist on page 156 and in the Visual Motor-Fine section on page 482. The Mann-Suiter-McClung Student Profile on page 336 can be used to monitor individualized programs.

Handwriting Evaluation (After Primary)

Visual-motor skills generally develop early in most students and tend to be sequential. Three primary problem areas are evident in students exhibiting handwriting difficulties:

1. Poor quality or illegible
2. Acceptable quality but below minimum standards when pressured by the requirement of speed.
3. Extremely slow rate but acceptable quality

The teacher must identify early in the school year those students whose handwriting is illegible and of poor quality under normal daily conditions. Samples of the students' "best," "fastest," and "usual" handwriting can be used for diagnostic purposes. Use materials that contain a vocabulary that is familiar to the students so they will have little difficulty with spelling or comprehension. Include sentences that contain all the letters of the alphabet. For example, "The quick brown fox jumps over the lazy dog."

1. *Usual Sample:* A sample of the student's usual work should be taken under conditions that are not fatiguing.
2. *Best Sample:* Say to the student, "Write the sample three times. Take your time and do your best. This is to be your very best effort." There should be no time limit.
3. *Fastest Sample:* Say to the student, "Now I want to see how fast you can write. I am going to give you three minutes to write the sentence as many times as you can. I will tell you when to stop."

Now you have a basis for comparing handwriting. Since reading and writing are interrelated activities, you can utilize writing to reinforce reading.

The following should be considered in evaluating handwriting:

1. Can the student copy accurately?
2. Does the student align letters properly?
3. Does the student have an unorthodox joining of letters in cursive writing?
4. Does the student use neo-graphisms or squibbles that are not really letters?
5. Is there letter fusion such as writing *brick* for *brick* ?
6. Does the student use the same hand consistently for writing?
7. Does the student write from left to right?
8. Does the student have poor spacing of letters and words?
9. Are the student's letters of irregular size?
10. Does the student's work show fatigue? For example, the last line may be noticeably poorer than the first one.
11. Does the student exhibit poor letter formation (*d* like *cl* , a like *o* , a like *u* , t like *l*)?
12. Is the student unable to recall or retrieve the motor act of writing as a form of expressive language?

Note: When evaluating an entire class, note the time it takes for each student to complete the task. (Some students can write well but take too much time.) This is important diagnostically in terms of determining the amount of written material that is required of a particular student in a given time.

Handwriting for the Older Student

Students in the second grade and higher experiencing difficulty with either manuscript or cursive writing need a slightly different approach. In addition to collecting handwriting samples of those students, ask the following questions:

1. Was handedness changed at any time?
2. How much difficulty did the older student experience with beginning writing or cursive?
3. Is the student extremely nervous or emotional? Has the handwriting become either much larger or much smaller?
4. What is the student's general physical condition? Has the student been ill or suffered a seizure?

5. What is the student's ability to draw, color, and cut?
6. Does the student have difficulty in some other basic subject, such as spelling or reading?
7. Does the student have a negative attitude toward some or all school work?

If the handwriting problem is actually rooted in reading and spelling problems, then just trying to remediate the handwriting problem by itself will not usually be successful.

As already indicated in the handwriting discussion, there are three kinds of difficulties in handwriting:

1. Handwriting that is of poor quality, or illegible.
2. Handwriting that deteriorates under pressure of speed. (By the fourth grade, speed is gradually encouraged.)
3. Handwriting that is produced at too slow a rate.

The overall objectives for good handwriting are legibility and ease of writing. The single most important factor in determining the legibility of handwriting is letter formation. Next in importance is spacing.

Additional information about handwriting can be acquired by observing the student's writing performance during class assignments. The following procedures are recommended for groups or for use with one student:

1. *Far-Point Copying:* Select a paragraph appropriate to the lowest reader's reading level and copy it on the chalkboard. The students copy at their own speed as the teacher observes and notes those who finish first to those who take the longest time.
2. *Near-Point Copying:* Same as above except the paragraph is placed within three feet of the student on small chalkboards or on an easel.
3. *A Dictation Lesson:* Pick a very easy selection that most of the students will be able to spell without difficulty and read aloud at a slow pace.
4. *A Self-Generated Paragraph:* Have students write about anything they want to for five minutes.

From these four samples listed above, check for use of space, letter formations, letter connections, accuracy, directionality, and overall quality.

Teachers cannot assume that learners who exhibit handwriting difficulties will compensate for, or automatically improve, their handwriting as they mature.

ASSESSMENT OF WRITTEN LANGUAGE EXPRESSION

The evaluation of student performance in writing, whether by formal or informal devices, should include

Supplementary Evaluation—Handwriting

TEST	GRADE LEVEL	COMPONENTS	TYPE
Basic School Skills Inventory (Hammill & Leigh, 1983)	4–0 to 6–11 (Ages)	Tasks include: grasping pencil, written sample, copying from chalk-board	Norm-referenced and criterion-referenced
Brigance Diagnostic Inventory of Basic Skills (Brigance, 1977)	Preschool-12	Handwriting sample	Criterion-referenced
Bowmar/Noble Scales (1984)	Elementary	Copying sentences	Rating scales
Slingerland Screening Tests for Identifying Children with Specific Language Disability (Slingerland, 1970)	1–6	Copying: near and far point; writing from memory	Criterion-referenced
Test of Written Language (Hammill & Larsen, 1983)	3–8	Handwriting sample	Norm-referenced
Zaner-Bloser's Evaluation Scale (1979)	1–8	Copying sentences	Rating scales

an analysis of different types of written expression, grammatic structure, and patterns of spelling that students use that can be compared to their agemates. In addition, the teacher should identify problems that are associated with:

1. How well the student uses rules of writing that are common to all situations (e.g., a sentence is comprised of a complete thought)
2. How well the student applies these rules systematically
3. Writing that is smooth, automatic, and natural as an extension of speaking and thinking
4. The student's ability to review what has been written and make appropriate changes that comply with steps 1, 2, and 3.

Another factor in writing deals with deterioration, which can be found in students who fatigue easily, become confused easily, or cannot deal with concept overload.

Several procedures can be used to evaluate student performance:

1. Informal assessment should resemble classroom writing requirements. Ask the student to produce one or more paragraphs on the following types of writing:
   a. an assigned topic
   b. a story starter to be completed
   c. a personal letter
   d. an essay answer to a question
   e. a description of an object, picture, situation
   f. a questionnaire about himself or herself

The directions could vary but should include the following:
   a. specifically what is expected: title, paragraph, story, essay, etc.
   b. amount of time allowed if warnings will be given before time is over (e.g., "You have five more minutes"). Marston and colleagues (1981), Videen, Deno, and Marston (1982), and Tindal and Parker (1989) recommend that the students put a mark or slash on their papers as certain time periods are called by the instructor.

The sample(s) should be analyzed objectively and subjectively as follows:

   a. Tindal and Parker (1989) suggest the following objective indices (p. 174):
      1. total words written
      2. correctly spelled words
      3. correct word sequence
      4. legible words
      5. mean length of correct word sequence strings
      6. percentage of correctly spelled words
      7. percentage of correct word sequences
      8. percentage of legible words
   b. A subjective rating relates more to the quality of the writing. Items to be considered are:
      1. overall quality and clarity of expression
      2. readability
      3. use of major concepts with supporting details
      4. sequence of ideas with use of appropriate terms (e.g., *first, second, finally*)

Supplementary Evaluation—Written Expression

TEST	GRADE LEVELS	COMPONENTS	TYPE
Brigance diagnostic Inventory of Basic Skills (Brigance, 1977)	K–7	Mechanical skills (punctuation and capitalization), spelling, functional writing skills	Criterion-referenced
Brigance Diagnostic Inventory of Essential Skills (Brigance, 1980)	7–12		Criterion-referenced
California Achievement Tests (Tiegs & Clark, 1970)	1.5–12	Mechanical skills, word usage, grammatical structure, spelling	Norm-referenced
Comprehensive Tests of Basic Skills (CTB/McGraw-Hill, 1968)	1–12	Mechanical skills, word usage, grammatical structure	Norm-referenced
Iowa Tests of Basic Skills (Hieronymus, Lindquist, & Hoover, 1978)	1–9	Mechanical skills, word usage, spelling	Norm-referenced
Metropolitan Achievement Tests (Durost et al., 1970)	K–9	Mechanical skills, grammatical structure, word usage, spelling	Norm-referenced
Picture Story Language Test (Grune & Stratton, 1965)	1–12	Written sample: words per sentence, total sentences, syntax, abstract-concrete score	Norm-referenced
SRA Achievement Series (Thorpe, Lefever, & Nasland, 1968)	2–9	Mechanical skills, grammatical structure	Norm-referenced
Stanford Achievement Test (Madden, Gardner, Rudman, Karisen, & Merwin, 1973)	3–9	Mechanical skills, grammatical structure	Norm-referenced
Test of Adolescent Language. Pro-Ed, Austin, Texas, 1980.	6–12	Write vocabulary words in a meaningful sentence; combine sentences into a single sentence	Norm-referenced
Test of Written Language (Hammill & Larsen, 1978)	3–8	Mechanical skills, syntax, word usage, style, spelling	Norm-referenced
Woodcock-Johnson Psycho-Educational Battery (Woodcock & Johnson, 1977)	Preschool to Adult	Spelling, proofreading of a sample for punctuation, spelling errors, usage	Norm-referenced

5. use of connecting terms (e.g., *but, then, however*)
6. quality of appropriateness of vocabulary
7. types of irrelevant statements
8. use of dialogue
9. students' attitude regarding the assignment

2. The Mann-Suiter Written Language Expression Screen found on page 208 is appropriate for younger students who may be at the sentence and short paragraph stage of writing.

3. The Mann-Suiter Silent Reading and Written Language Screen found on page 285 contains a comprehension and sentence completion format.

4. Once a baseline has been established, the instructor needs to keep dated samples of writing and anecdotal reference notes of improvement of overall writing. During the writing process, it should be noted whether the student is writing more drafts, if the quality is improved, and whether more of the specific skill areas are being transferred to content area instruction. Curriculum-based observations

should determine improvement in the quality of writing and should include an analysis of essays, reports, and text answers.

MATHEMATICS ASSESSMENT

Usually one or more formal assessments in math are given each year. Standardized assessment rarely pinpoints the learning needs of individual students. In-formal techniques, such as screening, can be used to determine generally what each student has already learned and to point out what the student still needs to learn. Informal assessments include analysis of students' daily work, observation of students at work, interviews with students, and parent-teacher conferences.

One of the most valuable ways for identifying specific errors in an algorithm is to ask the student to work

Supplementary Evaluation—Mathematics

TEST	GRADE LEVEL	COMPONENTS	TYPE
Brigance Diagnostic Inventory of Essential Skills (Brigance, 1980)	K–6	Computation; application: vocabulary, measurement, geometry, etc.	Criterion-referenced
The California Achievement Test (Tiegs & Clark, 1977–1978)	1–12	Computation; concepts; application: place value, money, time, measurement, geometry	Norm-referenced
Iowa Tests of Basic Skills (Hieronymus et al., 1978)	1–9	Computation; application of concepts: time, money, measurement, fractions	Norm-referenced
Key Math Diagnostic Arithmetic Test (Connolly et al., 1976)	K–6	Operations: whole numbers, decimals, fractions, money, word problems, measurement, time, numeration, etc.	Norm-referenced
Metropolitan Achievement Test (Durost et al., 1971)	K–9	Computation; application: problem solving, measurement, geometry, place value, etc.	Norm-referenced
Peabody Individual Achievement Test (Dunn & Markwardt, 1970)	K–12	Number recognition; problem solving: geometry and trigonometry	Norm-referenced
SRA Achievement Series in Arithmetic (Thorpe et al., 1974)	K–12	Computation; concepts; application	Norm-referenced
Stanford Achievement Test (Madden et al., 1973)	1.5–1.9	Computation: whole numbers, fractions, decimals; concepts; application of concepts	Norm-referenced
Stanford Diagnostic Arithmetic Test (SDMT) (Beatty et al., 1976)	1–12	Operations: whole numbers, decimals, fractions; number systems; numeration	Norm-referenced
The Wide-Range Achievement Test (arithmetic) (Jastak & Jastak, 1978)	K–12	Computation; counting	Norm-referenced
Woodcock-Johnson Psychoeducational Battery (Woodcock & Johnson, 1977)	K–12	Computation: whole numbers, decimals, fractions, basic algebra and trigonometry; problems: time, money, measurement, etc.	Norm-referenced

MANN-SUITER DEVELOPMENTAL ARITHMETIC INVENTORY—REVISED
(To be used for diagnostic purposes)

School _____

Teacher _____

Date _____

NAME _____ DATE OF BIRTH _____ SEX _____ BILINGUAL YES _____ NO _____

ADDRESS _____ GLASSES _____ HEARING AID _____

PERTINENT FACTS KNOWN IN PAST HISTORY _____

_____

_____

Prerequisites to Formal Arithmetic: Level 1 (Grades K–1)

Students should be tested to determine if they know their colors. Show the student cards with the following colors:

red _____   green _____   blue _____   yellow _____
purple _____   black _____   brown _____   orange _____

	YES	NO

1. Does the student know the meaning of the words *bottom, top, beside, above,* or *below?* Place a 5″ × 8″ card that has been divided into fourths and colored in the suggested order before the student and ask the following questions:

   a. What colors are on the bottom?
   b. What colors are on the top?
   c. What color is beside the blue?
   d. What color is above the yellow?
   e. What color is below the red?

blue	red
yellow	green

2. Does the student know the meaning of the words *biggest, smallest, longest, most,* or *same?* The teacher shows three cards, one at a time, and says the following:

   Card One

   a. Show me the biggest star
   b. Show me the smallest star

   Card Two

   c. Show me the longest line

   Card Three

   d. Show me the tree that has the most apples
   e. Which trees have the same number of apples?

3. Can the student count to ten pointing to each of ten objects while counting? (one-to-one correspondence)

4. Does the student know the concept of less than? The teacher asks, "Which one has less?"

(continued)

                                                                                      YES   NO

5. Does the student know the concept of more than? The teacher asks, "Which one has
   more?"   ⚃·   ⚄·⚂   ____   ____

6. Can the student reproduce the following geometric shapes with a pencil and paper?

   Normative by age 3   ○   ____   ____
   Normative by age 4   □   ____   ____
   Normative by age 6   △   ____   ____
   Normative by age 6   ◇   ____   ____

7. Can the student write numerals from 1 to 10?   ____   ____

8. Can the student count the dots in a pattern and write the corresponding numeral? (Use ditto)   ____   ____

   7____   3____   5____   9____   6____   4____

9. Can the student do simple addition and subtraction? (Use ditto)   ____   ____

   $\begin{array}{r}3\\+1\\\hline\end{array}$ $\begin{array}{r}2\\+2\\\hline\end{array}$ $\begin{array}{r}3\\+2\\\hline\end{array}$ $\begin{array}{r}2\\-1\\\hline\end{array}$ $\begin{array}{r}3\\-2\\\hline\end{array}$ $\begin{array}{r}5\\-3\\\hline\end{array}$

Basic Arithmetic Functions: Level II (Grades 1.5–3)

10. Can the student write from 1 to 100? (Use ditto)   ____   ____

11. Can the student add and subtract simple problems up to 10 in different positions? (Use ditto)

    $\begin{array}{r}7\\+2\\\hline\end{array}$ ____   ____

    $3 + 6 =$ ____   ____

    $\begin{array}{r}9\\-3\\\hline\end{array}$ ____   ____

    $8 - 3 =$ ____   ____

12. Can the student add and subtract more complex problems 11–20 in different positions?
    (Use ditto)

    $\begin{array}{r}12\\+\ 6\\\hline\end{array}$ ____   ____

    $13 + 4 =$ ____   ____

    $\begin{array}{r}11\\-\ 8\\\hline\end{array}$ ____   ____

    $12 - 4 =$ ____   ____

13. Can the student add? (Use ditto)

    a. Two place, no regrouping
       $\begin{array}{r}25\\+32\\\hline\end{array}$ ____   ____

    b. Two place, with regrouping
       $\begin{array}{r}28\\+54\\\hline\end{array}$ ____   ____

(continued)

14. **Can the student subtract? (Use ditto)**   YES   NO

    a. Two place, no regrouping

       46

      –32   ____ ____

    b. Two place, with regrouping

       37

      –29   ____ ____

15. **Can the student multiply? (Use ditto)**

    a. Multiplication of facts to 45

       4

      ×3   ____ ____

    b. Multiplication of facts to 81

       8

      ×7   ____ ____

    c. Two digit by 1 digit, no regrouping

       22

      × 4   ____ ____

    d. Two digit by 1 digit, with regrouping

       34

      × 5   ____ ____

16. **Can the student divide? (Use ditto)**

    a. Division of facts to 45

      $3\overline{)9}$ ____ ____

    b. Division of facts to 81

      $56 \div 8 =$ ____ ____

    c. Two digit by 1 digit, no remainder

      $4\overline{)88}$ ____ ____

    d. Two digit by 1 digit, with remainder

      $6\overline{)27}$ ____ ____

17. **Fractions**

    Can the student tell you

    a. What part is shaded?   ____ ____

    b. What part is not shaded?   ____ ____

    Can the student show you

    c. 1/2?   ____ ____

    d. 1/4?   ____ ____

(continued)

18. Time   YES   NO

    Can the student tell time

    a. on the hour?   6:00   _____   _____

    b. on the half hour?   3:30   _____   _____

    c. on the quarter hour?   3:15   _____   _____

    Does the student know

    d. how many days are in a week?   _____   _____

    e. how many weeks in a month?   _____   _____

    f. how many months are in a year?   _____   _____

19. Can the student solve one-operation story problems (all third level or above and presented on printed cards in order of difficulty)?

    a. Bob had 6 marbles and he found 2 more marbles. How many marbles did he have altogether? (under 10 addition) (8)   _____   _____

    b. Betty had 6 cookies, and her mother gave her 9 more cookies. How many cookies did she have altogether? (over 10 addition) (15)   _____   _____

    c. A boy had 11 pennies and he gave his brother 5 pennies. How many did he have left? (simple subtraction) (6)   _____   _____

    d. A girl spent 8 cents each for 3 candy bars. How much did she spend? (simple multiplication) (24)   _____   _____

    e. A store had 24 new shirts and sold 11 of them. How many shirts were left? (complex subtraction) (13)   _____   _____

    f. There were 16 pieces of candy to be divided among 4 boys. How many pieces of candy did each boy receive? (simple division) (4)   _____   _____

Basic Arithmetic Functions: Level III (Grades 3 and above)

20. Can the student add? (Use ditto)

    a. Three place, with regrouping?

$$\begin{array}{r} 639 \\ +249 \\ \hline \end{array}$$
                                                     _____   _____

    b. Four place, with zeros and regrouping?

$$\begin{array}{r} 4077 \\ +9540 \\ \hline \end{array}$$
                                                     _____   _____

21. Can the student subtract? (Use ditto)

    a. Three place, with regrouping?

$$\begin{array}{r} 672 \\ -386 \\ \hline \end{array}$$
                                                     _____   _____

    b. Four place, with zeros and regrouping?

$$\begin{array}{r} 1430 \\ -906 \\ \hline \end{array}$$
                                                     _____   _____

(continued)

YES   NO

22. Can the student multiply? (Use ditto)

a. Two digit by two digit?

$$\begin{array}{r} 28 \\ \times 52 \\ \hline \end{array}$$

—— ——

b. Three digit by three digit?

$$\begin{array}{r} 321 \\ \times 130 \\ \hline \end{array}$$

—— ——

23. Can the student divide? (Use ditto)

a. Three digit by 1 digit, with remainder?

$6\overline{)248}$

—— ——

b. Three digit by 2 digit, with remainder?

$35\overline{)992}$

—— ——

c. Four digit by 3 digit, with remainder?

$190\overline{)1881}$

—— ——

24. Story Problems

a. John bought 3 dozen toys at $5 a dozen. How much change should he receive from a $20 bill?   ($5)

b. If a man charged $10 for the first time he mowed your lawn and $5 a week from then on, how much would you pay him for the first four weeks?   ($25)

c. Mary has $1. How many pencils can she buy if pencils cost two for 5¢?   (40)

d. Mrs. Smith walks 2 miles a day, 3 days a week. How many miles will she walk in 3 weeks?   (18)

e. Mary has 4 boxes of cookies with 100 cookies in each box. She has given away 120 cookies so far. How many cookies does she have left?   (280)

f. Dennis bought a toy for $2.98 and a pencil for 5¢. He gave the clerk $5. How much change did he receive?   ($1.97)

g. Gloria walked 17 miles in 3 days. She walked 5 miles the first day and 6 miles the second day. How many miles did she walk the third day?   (6)

25. *Fractions:* Can the student (Use ditto)

a. show 1/2?

—— ——

b. show 2/3?

—— ——

c. show 6/8?

—— ——

d. change fractions to equivalent?

$$\frac{3}{4} = \frac{6}{8}$$

—— ——

e. reduce to lowest terms?

$$\frac{4}{8} = \frac{1}{2}$$

—— ——

(continued)

Addition: Can the student add fractions? (Use ditto)   YES   NO

a. of like denominators?

$$\frac{1}{3} + \frac{1}{3} =$$

                                                  ____ ____

b. of unlike denominators?

$$\frac{1}{3} + \frac{1}{4} =$$

                                                  ____ ____

c. mixed numbers, like denominators?

$$2\frac{1}{5} + 2\frac{1}{5} =$$

                                                  ____ ____

d. mixed numbers, unlike denominators?

$$3\frac{2}{3} + 4\frac{1}{4} =$$

                                                  ____ ____

e. renaming the sum?

$$6\frac{8}{7} = 7\frac{1}{7}$$

                                                  ____ ____

f. columns—same denominators?

$$\frac{5}{8} + \frac{3}{8} + \frac{2}{8} =$$

                                                  ____ ____

g. columns—different denominators?

$$\frac{3}{8} + \frac{2}{6} + \frac{1}{3} =$$

                                                  ____ ____

Subtraction: Can the student subtract fractions? (Use ditto)

a. of like denominators?

$$\frac{3}{4} - \frac{1}{4} =$$

                                                  ____ ____

b. of unlike denominators?

$$\frac{4}{6} - \frac{1}{3} =$$

                                                  ____ ____

c. mixed numbers, like denominators?

$$6\frac{6}{7} - 1\frac{1}{7} =$$

                                                  ____ ____

d. mixed numbers, unlike denominators?

$$3\frac{1}{2} - 2\frac{1}{6} =$$

                                                  ____ ____

e. renaming the sum?

$$8 - 5\frac{2}{3} =$$

                                                  ____ ____

f. mixed numbers with unlike denominators and renaming?

$$6\frac{1}{8} - 2\frac{1}{2} =$$

                                                  ____ ____

(continued)

Multiplication: **Can the student multiply fractions? (Use ditto)**   YES   NO

a. of like denominators?

$$\frac{1}{3} \times \frac{1}{3} =$$ ____   ____

b. of unlike denominators?

$$\frac{2}{3} \times \frac{3}{4} =$$ ____   ____

c. times whole numbers?

$$\frac{3}{4} \times 11 =$$ ____   ____

d. mixed numbers × whole numbers?

$$6\frac{2}{3} \times 7 =$$ ____   ____

e. mixed numbers × mixed numbers?

$$4\frac{1}{2} \times 3\frac{2}{3} =$$ ____   ____

f. cancelling simple fraction × mixed numbers?

$$\frac{1}{4} \times 2\frac{1}{4} =$$ ____   ____

g. changing mixed numbers to improper fraction by multiplication?

$$2\frac{3}{4} \times \frac{11}{4} =$$ ____   ____

h. change fraction to equivalent by multiplication?

$$\frac{2}{3} \times \frac{6}{9} =$$ ____   ____

Division: **Can the student divide fractions? (Use ditto)**

Understands the inversion of fractions?   ____   ____

a. divide whole number by simple fraction?

$$6 \div \frac{1}{3} =$$ ____   ____

b. divide simple fraction by simple fraction?

$$\frac{1}{2} \div \frac{1}{7} =$$ ____   ____

c. reduce to lowest terms?

$$\frac{4}{8} \div \frac{1}{2} =$$ ____   ____

d. change improper fraction to mixed or whole number?

$$\frac{12}{7} \div 1\frac{5}{7} =$$ ____   ____

e. mixed number by simple fraction?

$$3\frac{2}{3} \div \frac{1}{4} =$$ ____   ____

(continued)

	YES	NO

f. whole number by mixed number?

$6 \div 4\frac{1}{3} =$ ___ ___

g. mixed number by mixed number?

$3\frac{1}{7} \div 2\frac{1}{3} =$ ___ ___

h. simple fraction by whole number?

$\frac{3}{4} \div 6 =$ ___ ___

i. simple fraction by mixed number?

$\frac{1}{3} \div 2\frac{1}{2} =$ ___ ___

j. mixed number by whole number?

$6\frac{3}{8} \div 5 =$ ___ ___

26. Can the student? (Use ditto)
    a. add decimals? ___ ___
    b. subtract decimals? ___ ___
    c. multiply decimals? ___ ___
    d. divide decimals? ___ ___
    e. round decimals to 3 digits? ___ ___
    f. change common fraction to decimal fraction? ___ ___
    g. compute percent of whole number? ___ ___

Answers

BASIC ARITHMETIC FUNCTIONS: LEVEL II

11. Addition: 9, 11, 17, below 9
    Subtraction: 6, 1, 5, below 5
12. Addition: 18, 16, 17, below 17
    Subtraction: 3, 7, 9, below 8
13. a. 57, 69; b. 82, 74
14. a. 14, 32; b. 8, 36
15. a. 12, 35, 0; b. 56, 54, 49; c. 88, 84, 70, 99; d. 170, 252, 204, 588
16. a. 3, 5, 9, 7, 4; b. 7, 8, 6; c. 22, 15, 13; d. 4r3, 6r6, 22r3
19. a. 8; b. 15; c. 6; d. 24; e. 13; f. 4
20. a. 888, 1,160; b. 13,617, 4,902
21. a. 286, 80; b. 524, 2,085
22. a. 1,456, 3,264; b. 41,730, 67,260
23. a. 41r2, 45r3, 29r2; b. 28r12, 8r13; c. 9r171
24. a.5; b. 25; c. 40; d. 18; e. 280; f. $1.97; g. 6
25. a. $\frac{1}{2}$; b. $\frac{2}{3}$; c. $\frac{6}{8}$; d. $\frac{6}{8}$; e. $\frac{1}{2}$;

(continued)

Addition:

a. $\frac{2}{3}$; b. $\frac{7}{12}$; c. $4\frac{2}{5}$; d. $7\frac{11}{12}$; e. $7\frac{1}{7}$; f. $1\frac{1}{4}$; g. $1\frac{1}{24}$

Subtraction:

a. $\frac{1}{2}$; b. $\frac{1}{3}$; c. $5\frac{5}{7}$; d. $1\frac{1}{3}$; e. $2\frac{1}{3}$; f. $3\frac{5}{8}$

Multiplication:

a. $\frac{1}{9}$; b. $\frac{1}{2}$; c. $8\frac{1}{4}$; d. $46\frac{2}{3}$; e. $16\frac{1}{2}$; f. $\frac{9}{16}$; g. $7\frac{9}{16}$; h. $\frac{4}{9}$

Division:

a. 18; b. $3\frac{1}{2}$; c. 1; d. 1; e. $14\frac{2}{3}$; f. $1\frac{5}{13}$; g. $1\frac{17}{49}$; h. $\frac{1}{8}$; i. $\frac{2}{15}$; j. $1\frac{11}{40}$;

26. *Decimals:*

Addition: a. 2.8, 5.5   Subtraction: b. 2.0, 30.28

Multiplication: c. 6.6, 390   Division: d. 10.2, 3

Rounding to 3 digits: e. 37.9, 365, 5.55

Decimal fractions: f. .25, .10, .80, .875 or 88

Percent: g. 3; 5; 17; $10.00; 33.3; 250

DEVELOP-YOUR-OWN MATH INVENTORY KIT
(For use with Mann-Suiter Developmental Arithmetic Inventory)

ITEM	MATERIAL
1.	Use a 5″ × 8″ card divided into fourths and colored with a magic marker.
2.	Draw 3 cards. (p. 322)

	Card 1	Draw four stars of different sizes.
	Card 2	Draw three solid lines of different lengths.
	Card 3	Draw four apple trees. Two trees have three apples, one tree has two apples, and one tree has five apples.

ITEM	MATERIAL
3.	Use poker chips.
4–5.	Use dominoes.
6.	Use black line ditto (p. 323).
8–9.	Use black line ditto (p. 324).
10.	Use black line ditto (p. 325).
11–14.	Use black line ditto (p. 326).
15–16.	Use black line ditto (p. 327).
17.	Use 3″ × 4″ cards as shown on #17.
18.	Use 5″ × 8″ cards as shown on #18.
19.	Use 3″ × 4″ white cards with one story problem typewritten per card.
20–23.	Use black line ditto (p. 328).
24.	Use 3″ × 4″ white cards with one story problem typewritten per card.
25.	Use black line ditto (pp. 329–330).
26.	Use black line ditto (p. 331).

(continued)

Item 2

(continued)

Item 6

RESPONSE

1. _____

2. _____

3. _____

4. _____

(continued)

Count the dots

$$\begin{array}{cc} 3 & 2 \\ +1 & +2 \end{array}$$

$$\begin{array}{ccc} 3 & 2 & 3 & 5 \\ +2 & -1 & -2 & -3 \end{array}$$

3
+ 1

2
+ 2

3
+ 2

2
− 1

3
− 2

5
− 3

(continued)

Item 10

(continued)

Items 11–16

⑪
$$\begin{array}{r} 7 \\ +2 \\ \hline \end{array} \qquad \begin{array}{r} 6 \\ +5 \\ \hline \end{array} \qquad \begin{array}{r} 9 \\ +8 \\ \hline \end{array} \qquad \begin{array}{r} 9 \\ -3 \\ \hline \end{array} \qquad \begin{array}{r} 8 \\ -7 \\ \hline \end{array} \qquad \begin{array}{r} 6 \\ -1 \\ \hline \end{array}$$

$$3 + 6 = \underline{\hspace{1cm}} \qquad\qquad 8 - 3 = \underline{\hspace{1cm}}$$

⑫
$$\begin{array}{r} 12 \\ +6 \\ \hline \end{array} \qquad \begin{array}{r} 11 \\ +5 \\ \hline \end{array} \qquad \begin{array}{r} 15 \\ +2 \\ \hline \end{array} \qquad \begin{array}{r} 11 \\ -8 \\ \hline \end{array} \qquad \begin{array}{r} 14 \\ -7 \\ \hline \end{array} \qquad \begin{array}{r} 15 \\ -6 \\ \hline \end{array}$$

$$13 + 4 = \underline{\hspace{1cm}} \qquad\qquad 12 - 4 = \underline{\hspace{1cm}}$$

⑬ ⓐ
$$\begin{array}{r} 25 \\ +32 \\ \hline \end{array} \qquad \begin{array}{r} 42 \\ +27 \\ \hline \end{array}$$
ⓑ
$$\begin{array}{r} 28 \\ +54 \\ \hline \end{array} \qquad \begin{array}{r} 56 \\ +18 \\ \hline \end{array}$$

⑭ ⓐ
$$\begin{array}{r} 46 \\ -32 \\ \hline \end{array} \qquad \begin{array}{r} 36 \\ -4 \\ \hline \end{array}$$
ⓑ
$$\begin{array}{r} 37 \\ -29 \\ \hline \end{array} \qquad \begin{array}{r} 41 \\ -5 \\ \hline \end{array}$$

(continued)

Items 11–16 (continued)

(15) (a) $4 \times 3 =$ _____ $5 \times 7 =$ _____ $0 \times 9 =$ _____

(b) $8 \times 7 =$ _____ $9 \times 6 =$ _____ $7 \times 7 =$ _____

(c)
$$\begin{array}{r} 22 \\ \times 4 \\ \hline \end{array} \qquad \begin{array}{r} 42 \\ \times 2 \\ \hline \end{array} \qquad \begin{array}{r} 70 \\ \times 1 \\ \hline \end{array} \qquad \begin{array}{r} 33 \\ \times 3 \\ \hline \end{array}$$

(d)
$$\begin{array}{r} 34 \\ \times 5 \\ \hline \end{array} \qquad \begin{array}{r} 42 \\ \times 6 \\ \hline \end{array} \qquad \begin{array}{r} 68 \\ \times 3 \\ \hline \end{array} \qquad \begin{array}{r} 84 \\ \times 7 \\ \hline \end{array}$$

(16) (a) $3 \overline{)9} \qquad 1 \overline{)5} \qquad 5 \overline{)45} \qquad 3 \overline{)21} \qquad 4 \overline{)16}$

(b) $56 \div 8 =$ _____ $72 \div 9 =$ _____ $42 \div 7 =$ _____

(c) $4 \overline{)88} \qquad 5 \overline{)75} \qquad 7 \overline{)91}$

(d) $6 \overline{)27} \qquad 8 \overline{)54} \qquad 4 \overline{)91}$

(continued)

Items 20–23

⑳ ⓐ
$$\begin{array}{r} 639 \\ +249 \\ \hline \end{array}$$
$$\begin{array}{r} 581 \\ +579 \\ \hline \end{array}$$
ⓑ
$$\begin{array}{r} 4077 \\ +9540 \\ \hline \end{array}$$
$$\begin{array}{r} 3005 \\ +1897 \\ \hline \end{array}$$

㉑ ⓐ
$$\begin{array}{r} 672 \\ -386 \\ \hline \end{array}$$
$$\begin{array}{r} 542 \\ -462 \\ \hline \end{array}$$
ⓑ
$$\begin{array}{r} 1430 \\ -906 \\ \hline \end{array}$$
$$\begin{array}{r} 5000 \\ -2915 \\ \hline \end{array}$$

㉒ ⓐ
$$\begin{array}{r} 28 \\ \times 52 \\ \hline \end{array}$$
$$\begin{array}{r} 68 \\ \times 48 \\ \hline \end{array}$$
ⓑ
$$\begin{array}{r} 321 \\ \times 130 \\ \hline \end{array}$$
$$\begin{array}{r} 285 \\ \times 236 \\ \hline \end{array}$$

㉓ ⓐ $6\overline{)248}$ $7\overline{)318}$ $9\overline{)263}$

ⓑ $35\overline{)992}$ $76\overline{)621}$ ⓒ $190\overline{)1881}$

(continued)

Item 25

FRACTIONS: REDUCE ALL ANSWERS TO SIMPLEST TERMS

a. b. c. d. $\frac{3}{4} = \frac{}{8}$ e. $\frac{4}{8} = \frac{}{2}$

Addition

a. $\frac{1}{3} + \frac{1}{3} = \underline{\quad}$ b. $\frac{1}{3} + \frac{1}{4} = \underline{\quad}$ c. $2\frac{1}{5}$ d. $3\frac{2}{3}$
$\quad +2\frac{1}{5}$ $\quad +4\frac{1}{4}$

Rename

e. $6\frac{8}{7} =$

f. $\frac{5}{8}$
$\frac{3}{8}$
$+\frac{2}{8}$

g. $\frac{3}{8}$
$\frac{2}{6}$
$+\frac{1}{3}$

Subtraction

a. $\frac{3}{4}$ b. $\frac{4}{6}$ c. $6\frac{6}{7}$ d. $3\frac{1}{2}$ e. 8 f. $6\frac{1}{8}$
$-\frac{1}{4}$ $-\frac{1}{3}$ $-1\frac{1}{7}$ $-2\frac{1}{6}$ $-5\frac{2}{3}$ $-2\frac{1}{2}$

Multiplication

a. $\frac{1}{3} \times \frac{1}{3} =$

b. $\frac{2}{3} \times \frac{3}{4} =$

c. $\frac{3}{4} \times 11 =$

d. $6\frac{2}{3} \times 7 =$

(continued)

Item 25 *(continued)*

FRACTIONS: REDUCE ALL ANSWERS TO SIMPLEST TERMS

e. $4\frac{1}{2} \times 3\frac{2}{3} =$ f. $\frac{1}{4} \times 2\frac{1}{4} =$

g. $2\frac{3}{4} \times 1\frac{1}{4} =$ h. $\frac{2}{3} \times \frac{6}{9} =$

Division

a. $6 \div \frac{1}{3} =$ b. $\frac{1}{2} \div \frac{1}{7} =$

c. $\frac{4}{8} \div \frac{1}{2} =$ d. $\frac{12}{7} \div 1\frac{5}{7} =$

e. $3\frac{2}{3} \div \frac{1}{4} =$ f. $6 \div 4\frac{1}{3} =$

g. $3\frac{1}{7} \div 2\frac{1}{3} =$ h. $\frac{3}{4} \div 6 =$

i. $\frac{1}{3} \div 2\frac{1}{2} =$ j. $6\frac{3}{8} \div 5 =$

(continued)

Item 26

DECIMALS: REDUCE ALL ANSWERS TO SIMPLEST TERMS

a. $2.5 + 0.3 =$ $3.0 + 2.1 + .4 =$

b. $3.5 - 1.5 =$ $36 - 5.72 =$

c. $2 \times 3.3 =$ $1.3 \times 300 =$

d. $30.6 \div 3 =$ $3.6 \div 1.2 =$

<u>Rounding to 3 digits</u>

e. 37.92 ___ 365.12 ___ 5.5465 ___

<u>Write a decimal fraction equal to these common fractions</u>

f. $\frac{1}{4}$ ___ $\frac{1}{10}$ ___ $\frac{4}{5}$ ___ $\frac{7}{8}$ ___

<u>Percent</u>

g. 50% of 6 ___ 25% of 20 ___ 100% of 17 ___

5% of $\$200$ ___ 10 is what $\%$ of 30 ___ 25 is 10% of what number ___

the problem aloud. Faulty concepts will be observed almost immediately. The student must verbalize every step and the teacher takes notes.

Mann-Suiter Developmental Arithmetic Inventory and Testing Kit

The Mann-Suiter Developmental Arithmetic Inventory—Revised (Form 6–42) and the Develop-Your-Own Math Inventory Kit (Form 6–43) are designed to aid teachers in determining strengths and weaknesses in the area of arithmetic that involve computation and problem solving. Information will also be gained in the area of spatial-temporal concept formation involving the critical skills necessary for success at higher levels of performance. The inventory and kit are flexible and adaptable to examining preschool children or older students with higher mental processes.

Teachers can determine the performance skills of the students in their classes and utilize this information in preparing for the teaching of a particular arithmetical operation. Teachers will also be better able to determine the extent to which spatial-temporal problems have affected the learning of arithmetic skills.

Screening materials, including duplicated sheets, should be prepared before the school year starts. Aides or paraprofessionals can be trained to administer this inventory. As new students enter the classroom during the year, either the instructor or an assistant can easily administer this screening device.

Directions for Administration

1. For students at the kindergarten level through the first few months of grade one, start administering the inventory at the beginning with the color screening and number 1. Color blindness should be identified.
2. At the mid-grade one level, start with number 10 and continue through until the student is unsuccessful. If he or she cannot complete items 10–12, drop back and do items 7–9 to check the basic requisites of one-to-one correspondence, writing numerals, and counting 1–10.
3. Bilingual and limited English-proficient students in grade one should start at the beginning of the inventory since the earlier items assess vocabulary meaning.
4. Students in grades two and three should begin with item 10. If failure occurs quickly, then drop back and check the lower items.

5. For grades four and five, begin with item 15. The evaluator is primarily looking for a student's understanding of the concept. If accuracy is inconsistent, ask the student to do a similar problem or ask the student to explain how the problem was done.
6. The screening inventory is untimed, but the evaluator may want to note unusual slowness, carelessness, fatigue, or mannerisms that seem to interfere with correct answers.

BEHAVIORAL ASSESSMENT

Use of behavior checklists, tests, observations, and interviews with parents and teachers provides a range of important information about students who appear to have attention deficit disorders (ADD).

One of the most promising new approaches for assessment in the schools is the multigating approach (Walker, Severson, & Haring 1985). When used to screen for possible ADHD (attention deficit hyperactivity disorder) children, this system involves three assessment gates that screen for externalizing excessive behaviors. For example, in the first gate, a teacher simply ranks the children in his or her classroom from the most to the least severe for a broad set of problems. The three classroom children ranked with the most severe problems are then individually rated by the teacher with the estimated frequency of a set of specific maladaptive classroom behaviors identified by over 1,500 teachers in separate research (Walker, 1982). The most severe children are then selected from the second gate and included in the third analysis. In the third gate, the school psychologist observes the children's classroom on-task behavior as well as their positive and negative social interactions at recess. The function of each gate is to screen for the most difficult children until only the most handicapped children are finally observed in the third gate.

Use of normed-behavior checklists and structured observations of academic and social behaviors should be included. For example, screening approaches that are based on objective-behavior checklists, such as the Child Behavior Checklist and Profiles (Achenbach & Edelbrock, 1983), can be used to identify high-probability cases of ADHD (Edelbrock, 1986). Other useful approaches involve response discrepancy behavioral observations (Alessi, 1980; Deno, 1980) in which a normal peer is simultaneously observed with a referred child in a classroom across a set of objectively defined behaviors (i.e., on-task, overactivity, out-of-seat, and noncompliance). Identification of significant differences between the normal peer and the referred child can help define problem areas and serve as baselines for interventions. This approach is particularly useful when the norms for specific behaviors or child populations are not available. It allows for a direct quantitative comparison between behaviors of referred and non-referred children in various settings.

The system gives information about multiple behaviors (e.g., classroom behavior, social behavior, and on-task behavior). School psychologists should recognize that the development of valid, well-conceptualized, and reliable single measures of specific attentional processes that define this condition and suggest effective intervention is still in its infancy.

With respect to the question of maximal differentiation, the hyperkinesis index of the Conners Parent Questionnaire appears to be a predictor. The parents' observations of their children's attention span, impulsivity, and activity level, based on long-term observations in the home, seem to be powerful data for classification purposes.

The Continuous Performance Test (CPT), introduced originally by Rosvold and colleagues (1956), gives the student reaction time tasks, presented with a warning signal and preparatory interval. The CPT is a vigilance task that has been employed as a fundamental paradigm for studying sustained attention as a behavioral process (O'Dougherty, Nuechterlein, & Drew 1984).

The CPT appears to be a strong candidate for assessing aspects of attention problems in hyperactive children. A study by O'Dougherty, Neuchterlein, and Drew (1984) suggests that the CPT might be useful in discriminating between hyperactive children and other groups of children with learning problems who do not have hyperactive characteristics, such as impulsivity.

An assessment instrument, the Gordon Diagnostic System (GDS), has been developed and normed to assess attention and impulsivity in children through the use of a modified continuous performance vigilance task and a delayed task, which requires the child to delay responding to a stimulus (Gordon & Mettelman, 1987; McClure & Gordon, 1984). The tasks are presented by using a portable console that contains a microprocessor to control task presentation and analyze the results. The delay task has been described by the test authors as a measure of impulsivity (Gordon, 1979; Gordon & McClure, 1983; McClure & Gordon, 1984) or of the ability to delay responding in the presence of feedback.

Swanson, Nolan, and Pelham (SNAP) Rating Scale (Atkins, Pelham, & Licht, 1985; Pelham & Murphy, 1981) is a specific checklist that identifies individual symptoms of ADD with hyperactivity from DSM-III. Preliminary norms for the SNAP Rating Scale are available in Kirby and Grimley's text (1986, p. 36).

Child Behavior Checklist and Profiles (CBCL) for teachers and parents (Achenbach & Edelbrock, 1983) have only a few items that relate directly to attention. Nonetheless, certain subscales appear to correlate well with multifaceted diagnosis (Edelbrock, 1986); thus, T scores greater than 70 on the hyperactivity scale appear useful as a screening or selection criterion for ADHD.

NEUROLOGICAL ASSESSMENT

The general extent of brain dysfunction can be determined, and there is a broad range of neurological tests available to help identify a student's deficiencies. The results of these tests can be used to arrive at a preferred program of treatment, as well as an aid in making a prognosis.

There are tests that examine skills or abilities that comprise a large number of behaviors. Those behaviors are thought to be dysfunctional when brain injury is present. The behavior includes sensory-perceptual-motor, psychomotor, linguistic, and cognitive abilities. These skills are dependent on the integrity of the nervous system. Two aspects of assessment are generally considered when brain injury is suspected. One is the standard neurological examination, which may use high-intensity machinery; the other, which is designed to pick up minimal neurological or "soft" signs, is accomplished essentially by external assessment.

Dyslexia, for example, is a severe reading disorder with presumed neurological etiology. During the last decade, research has developed technology that has given us a much better understanding of the underlying physiology of the brain. Electrophysiological studies (EEG), postmortem studies, and computerized axial tomographic (CAT) scans give insight regarding deficient neurological structures. Magnetic resonance imaging (MRI) and positron emission tomography (PET) scanning give scientists techniques to study the mechanics of brain anatomy.

Inferring Dysfunction

Brain Electrical Activity Mapping (BEAM) is one of the promising research tools for studying the brain. By analyzing EEG recordings under various activities, including average evoked responses, researchers have been able to differentiate in many cases, for example, dyslexics from nondyslexics. Measurement of activity

Supplementary Evaluation—Cognitive-Behavioral Factors

AAMD Adaptive Behavior Scale (Nihira et al., 1974)
Barclay Classroom Climate Inventory (Barclay, 1971)
Behavior Problem Checklist (Quay & Peterson, 1967)
Behavior Rating Profile (Brown & Hammill, 1983)
Bender Visual Motor Gestalt Test for Children (Bender, 1938; Koppitz, 1963)
Blacky Pictures (Blum, 1967)
Burks' Behavior Rating Scales (Burks, 1972, 1977)
California Psychological Inventory (Gough, 1969)
California Test of Personality (Thorpe et al., 1953)
Children's Apperception-Test (CAT) (Bellak & Bellak, 1965)
Conner Rating Scales. Abbot Laboratories. Rating scales 1969
Coopersmith Self-Esteem Inventories (Coopersmith, 1981)
Devereux Adolescent Behavior Rating Scale (Spivack et al., 1967)
Devereux Child Behavior Rating Scale (Spivack & Spotts, 1966)
Devereux Elementary School Behavior Rating Scale (Spivack & Swift, 1967)
Draw-A-Person Test (Goodenough, 1926)
Draw-A-Person (Urban, 1963)
Early School Personality Questionnaire (Coan & Cattell, 1970)
Edwards Personal Preference Schedule (Edwards, 1959)
Edwards Personality Inventory (Edwards, 1966)
Eysenck Personality Inventory (Eysenck & Eysenck, 1969)
Family Relations Test (Bene & Anthony, 1957)
Hahnemann High School Behavior Rating Scale (Swift & Spivack, 1972)
Holtzman Inkblot Technique (Holtzman, 1966)
House-Tree-Person (Buck & Jolles, 1966)
House-Tree-Person (HTP) (Bieliauskas, 1963)
Human Figures Drawing Test (Koppitz, 1968)
Jr.-Sr. High School Personality Questionnaire (Cattell et al., 1969)
Kuder Personal Preference Record (Kuder, 1954)
Learning Environment Inventory (Anderson, 1973)
Minnesota Multiphasic Personality Inventory (MMPI) (Hathaway & McKinley, 1967)
Piers-Harris Children's Self-Concept Scale (Piers & Harris, 1969)
Pupil Behavior Inventory (Vinter et al., 1966)
Pupil Behavior Rating Scale (Lambert et al., 1979)
Pupil Rating Scale (Myklebust, 1981)
Rorschach Inkblot Test (Rorschach, 1966)
Scales of Independent Behavior (Woodcock-Johnson Psychoeducational Battery) (Woodcock, 1978)
School Apperception Method (Solomon & Starr, 1968)
School Interest Inventory (Cottle, 1966)
Sixteen Personality Factor Questionnaire (Cattell et al., 1970)
SRA Junior Inventory (Remmers & Bauernfeind, 1957)
Tennessee Self Concept Inventory (Fitts, 1965)
Thematic Apperception Test (TAT) (Murray, 1943)
Thematic Apperception Test (TAT) (Bellak, 1954)
Vineland Adaptive Behavior Scales (Sparrow et al., 1984)
Vineland Social Maturity Scale (Doll, 1953)
Walker Problem Behavior Identification Checklist (Walker, 1970)
Weller-Strawser Scales of Adaptive Behavior (Weller & Strawser, 1981)

in the left posterior hemisphere and in the paramedian frontal region has indicated impressive results. There is also the potential in this research for studying children who are not brain-impaired but have learning difficulties in areas of language.

Another method of inferring dysfunction is through the assessment of the students' performance on perceptual visual and motor tasks. There are tests for neurological soft signs that suggest brain dysfunction. This includes the evaluation of subtle or fine symptoms, such as difficulty with visual tracking of a moving object, mild coordination problems, fine motor problems (e.g., holding a pencil and tying shoes), or putting pegs in a board. Delayed or slow language development or problems with speech may also be present. Reading, writing, spelling, or arithmetic are the general areas affected.

The conventional neurological examination often fails to find abnormalities in patients where the main concern is the inability to learn (Lerner, 1989). Other concerns with this type of assessment is the fact that many students who are normal learners also have soft signs, and it is difficult to discern the difference between brain damage, maturational lag, poor motivation, emotional factors, or any combination of these causes of observed behavior. Hagen (1984) suggests certain areas of assessment for suspected brain injury using tests and observations of behavior. This includes the following behavior:

1. Disoriented and confused
2. Distractable and impulsive
3. Reduction in initiation of actions, cognitive flexibility, and good judgment
4. Concrete and inhibited

Cognitive assessment should include evaluation of attentional abilities, temporal ordering, memory, categorization, association, integration, analysis/synthesis, and maintenance of goal-directed behavior.

Assessment of language functions should include phonology and syntax, and formulation. Semantics testing can be both formal and informal, with an interactive examiner who explains the tasks to be accomplished. Ylvisaker (1985) notes that the test situation can affect the results because of problems with attention, memory, and motivation.

There are few formal measures of language in everyday settings. Deficits are often estimated from detailed observations compiled with selected tests of cognition.

MANN-SUITER-MCCLUNG STUDENT PROFILE

After completing the Analysis of Errors Worksheets and giving any additional tests, which tend to support or negate the findings of the Developmental Inventories, the teacher is ready to summarize the results. The student profile (Form 6-44) can be used to summarize all information gained through formal and informal evaluations. This summary will further aid the teacher in formulating educational strategies for a particular student. This concise report can also be used to describe the needs of a student to other school personnel. It should become a part of the student's cumulative record and be sent with the student when he or she transfers to another school.

Form 6-44

MANN-SUITER-McCLUNG STUDENT PROFILE

Name _____ School _____

Date _____ Grade _____ Date of Birth _____

Teacher _____ Examiner _____

SKILL		ABOVE AVERAGE	AVERAGE	BELOW AVERAGE
Auditory				
Sensory:	Hearing-Acuity	—	—	—
Perception:	Figure-Ground	—	—	—
	Closure (Blending)	—	—	—
	Discrimination	—	—	—
	Localization/Attention	—	—	—
Memory:	Short-term (Working)	—	—	—
	Semantic	—	—	—
	Sequencing	—	—	—
Visual				
Sensory	Vision-Acuity	—	—	—
Perception:	Figure-Ground	—	—	—
	Closure (Blending)	—	—	—
	Discrimination	—	—	—
Memory:	General	—	—	—
	Sequencing	—	—	—
Language				
Receptive:	Visual Language Classification	—	—	—
	Visual Language Association	—	—	—
	Auditory Language Classification	—	—	—
	Auditory Language Association	—	—	—
Expressive:	Verbal (Oral) Expression	—	—	—
(Oral)	Speech-Articulation	—	—	—
	Speech-Stuttering	—	—	—
	Speech-Voice	—	—	—
	Syntax and Formulation	—	—	—
	Word Retrieval	—	—	—
	Nonverbal-Symbolic Language	—	—	—
	Inner Language	—	—	—
	Limited English Proficiency	—	—	—
	Manual Expression	—	—	—
Handwriting:	Manuscript (legible)	—	—	—
	Cursive (legible)	—	—	—
	Speed	—	—	—
	Automatic	—	—	—
	Dictation	—	—	—
	Far-Point Copying	—	—	—

(continued)

SKILL		ABOVE AVERAGE	AVERAGE	BELOW AVERAGE
Writing: (Expression)	Plan and Organize	—	—	—
	Note Taking	—	—	—
	Syntax and Formation	—	—	—
	Edit and Proofread	—	—	—
	Revise	—	—	—
	Sequence Thoughts	—	—	—
	Uses Different styles	—	—	—
	Grammatic Structure	—	—	—
	Forming Sentences	—	—	—
	Forming Paragraphs	—	—	—
	Punctuation/Capitalization	—	—	—
	Creative	—	—	—
	Patterns of Spelling	—	—	—
	Rules of Writing	—	—	—
	Smooth/Automatic	—	—	—
	Quality/Clarity	—	—	—
	Attitude	—	—	—
	Speed/Accuracy	—	—	—
Motor:	Gross Motor	—	—	—
	Laterality (Handedness)	—	—	—
Spelling:	Rules	—	—	—
	Number of Words	—	—	—
	Phonetics	—	—	—
	Structural Analysis	—	—	—
Reading:	Word Recognition	—	—	—
	Comprehension (silent)	—	—	—
	Oral Comprehension	—	—	—
	Vocabulary (meaning)	—	—	—
	Speed/Accuracy	—	—	—
	Phonetics	—	—	—
	Smoothness	—	—	—
	Dictionary	—	—	—
	Reference	—	—	—
Arithmetic:	Computation	—	—	—
	Problem Solving	—	—	—
Behavior	Aggressive-acting out/passive	—	—	—
	Sensitive-withdrawn	—	—	—
	Immature-dependent	—	—	—
	Psychotic-neurotic	—	—	—
	Delinquent-unorthodox	—	—	—
	Social Perception	—	—	—
	Locus of Control	—	—	—
	Self-Efficacy	—	—	—
	Attribution	—	—	—

(continued)

SKILL		ABOVE AVERAGE	AVERAGE	BELOW AVERAGE
	Self-Motivated	—	—	—
	Hyperactivity	—	—	—
	Distractible	—	—	—
	Impulsive	—	—	—
	Perseveration	—	—	—
	Conduct	—	—	—
Cognition/ Strategies:	Self-Questioning			
	Self-Instruction	—	—	—
	Planning	—	—	—
	Judgment	—	—	—
	Problem Solving	—	—	—
	Organization	—	—	—
	Uses Generalization	—	—	—
	Makes Inferences	—	—	—
	Predicts/Forecasts	—	—	—
	Reasoning	—	—	—
	Sequencing Ideas	—	—	—
	Summarizes	—	—	—
	Clarifies/Verifies	—	—	—
	Uses Rehearsal	—	—	—
	Paraphrases	—	—	—
	Synthesizes	—	—	—
	Analyzes	—	—	—
	Classifies/Associates	—	—	—
	Compares/Contrasts	—	—	—
	Sees Cause/Effect Relationships	—	—	—
	Evaluates	—	—	—
	Reflective Thinking	—	—	—
Other:	_____	—	—	—
	_____	—	—	—
	_____	—	—	—
	_____	—	—	—
	_____	—	—	—

Comments

Chapter 7

Organization and Management for Instruction

CHAPTER OUTLINE

OVERVIEW

Given the pressures imposed on teachers (e.g., acquisition of competencies; local, state, and national teacher examinations; competition for merit pay based on student performance criteria; etc.), they have to begin thinking about the classroom as a mini-business. An entrepreneur starting and operating a small business and a teacher organizing a classroom have similar management concerns. It takes careful planning before the place is open for business. Although the businessperson may have more flexibility and control in running the business, certain elements are constant in both enterprises.

1. Know your product or service. It is assumed that the teacher has the experience and competencies to teach the grade level or content area. However, he or she needs to think through and be able to verbalize not only what will happen in the classroom, but how it will be unique. Is the service—in this case, delivery of effective education—refined and at a quality level ready for the consumer (stu-

dent)? What are the major goals to be achieved during the year? Can I explain my program in a clear, concise manner to parents, students, and other professionals?

2. Know your customers. Before you start designing the shop, you need to know your clientele. What kinds of students will be in the educational setting? What will be their special needs in terms of special equipment, mobility, and space allocation?

3. Selecting a location. In the business world this is a key to success. Principals and teachers also have to be concerned with accessibility and selecting the most appropriate setting for different types of educational programs. While architects may plan the location of classrooms and laboratories, the flexible use of space in a school should be considered in setting up resource rooms, team teaching, and remedial classes.

   In a school in which the educational programs for students with special needs are organized along a continuum, planning for effective classroom management must take place at three levels of procedures, as discussed in Chapter 5: general program procedures (LEVEL I), intervention procedures (LEVEL II), and special education procedures (LEVEL III). General program procedures must be planned so that those educational services for students with special needs that are at the age-appropriate group can be met as they would for any student.

4. Selecting employees. More and more classroom teachers will be working directly with and supervising ancillary personnel including aides, paraprofessionals, tutors, student tutors, volunteers, and parents. Therefore, careful consideration has to be given to interpersonal relationships and selecting people who can work well together.

5. Setting up the shop. Planning involves not only selecting what equipment and furnishings are needed, but designing a floor plan for placing everything. An attractive, well-decorated setting promotes instructor well-being and should entice the students to come to school.

6. Managing the business. Purchasing, inventory control, record-keeping, accounting, and scheduling all have to be in place before school begins. Managing all the components is a key to effective programming for students. The investment of time and resources in the development of workable programs will not pay off if this area is neglected or is allowed to get sloppy.

7. Marketing and promotion. A teacher has to constantly face the public and sell himself or herself and the product. The good teacher knows how to use all types of media to communicate with parents and students and to extend school activities into the community.

This chapter offers alternatives for organizing all of the vital components of teaching into a manageable system. It contains ideas for setting up and managing instructional programs for individuals and groups with the appropriate activities. Cooperative learning and working with other professionals are key areas. The final section includes information relevant to educator-parent communication.

ORGANIZATION OF THE CLASSROOM

A well-organized classroom allows the instructional personnel who work there the ability to complete the instructional tasks of the day with the least amount of wasted time and frustration. Since time is one of the most critical variables in classroom management, materials have to be organized to permit quick, efficient access to them by all those in the classroom

who will be using them. Teachers often lose instructional time while they search for the materials for the next lesson or hastily look for something to keep the students busy.

Before the opening of school, the teacher or teachers (if team-teaching is being used), as well as aides, paraprofessionals, and other support personnel, should plan the following major areas of the classroom: the instructional areas and the reinforcement areas.

Instructional Areas

The primary areas to draw on a floor plan first are the sections of the classroom from which the majority of teacher-directed activities will emanate. For example, in most elementary school classrooms, primary grade teachers have one area for small-group reading instruction. Because of the diversity of materials being used for students with learning problems, many teachers are using reading tables along with, or in lieu of, the more traditional reading circle of chairs. In planning such an area, the designer must consider the size and shape of the table, lighting, and noise. Teachers who are seated for a portion of the instruction time will require lines of sight to all other areas of the classroom. Teachers should sit down and see what might impede eye contact at that level. If many sections of a classroom are in use at the same time, then traffic flow and noise levels must be monitored.

Reinforcement Areas

After the major instructional areas are designated, then the remainder of the classroom space can be used by the students, individually or in groups, self-directed or instructor directed, to practice, evaluate, or review new information. Space can be allocated for the following areas:

1. Learning centers based on specific subjects with learning packets, or student-directed activities, for example, science materials and experiments.
2. Subject level areas that contain shelves, drawers, etc., with a variety of materials placed in somewhat of a developmental sequence and coded. For example, a handwriting section could have materials ranging from a piece of material A 1 (things to be squeezed to develop power in the hand) to A 40 (tracing stencils to develop cursive writing).
3. Areas that contain materials to develop language skills.

4. Interest areas such as a library center, games and recreation area, and arts and crafts area.
5. Areas for small-group or independent study (cubicles, carrels, booths).
6. Audiovisual areas for computers, listening stations, Language Masters, tape recorders, and typewriters.

The students should know where things belong, how the classroom is organized, and what the various options are for individualized learning. When material is displayed, organized, and explained to the students, there is no excuse for a disorganized, messy classroom. Materials should be returned by the students to the places where they found them.

The reinforcement areas of a classroom should not be only a place for displaying materials or keeping students busy. There should be an integration of subject areas so that the students can experience on-task activities that are enjoyable, promote success and a challenge, yet provide practice in the critical skill areas. For example, spelling games, word lists, and worksheets should be on the students' reading level and the vocabulary used can also be reinforced in handwriting lessons.

Students who work in learning centers can be more productive if the centers have a chart or poster that gives directions for using the materials, and a recordkeeping system that explains how to record material use (Charles, 1980). A clear understanding of the purpose of each assignment will promote more on-task time by the student.

Location of Materials

Regardless of what the major instructional areas are (handwriting, reading, mathematics, science), the next consideration is the location of instructional materials. The authors have found that bookcases, moveable carts, and closets in the closest proximity to the instructional area should be organized with the materials most often used by the teacher. For example, on a bookcase behind the instructional reading table, the instructor can place word cards, lesson plans, teacher's guides, workbooks, supplementary work sheets, pencils, pens, blank word cards, and phonics materials, plus a variety of other materials most often used during a directed reading session. Unless the teacher directs otherwise, the materials on these shelves are used primarily by the teacher.

The instructional team in a classroom (teacher and/or aide) need a system for storing and retrieving material. Monitoring the paper flow from students and

feedback back to them needs to be planned (i.e., in and out baskets, folders, clipboards, etc.).

File cabinets or cardboard file boxes should be organized with folders containing sufficient copies of duplicated materials for subject areas. Folders should also be prepared with copies of

1. Student progress worksheets
2. Assessment materials
3. Individualized education planning materials
4. Behavior monitoring graphs and charts
5. Student contracts
6. Letters and notices to parents
7. Happy grams or reward sheets for student progress
8. Parent/teacher conference forms
9. Holiday materials
10. General group activity sheets (puzzles, simple review, etc.) that can be used in an emergency by a substitute teacher

CODING MATERIALS

The sophistication of the system for coding materials will vary with the reading level and grade level of the students. The following types of systems are suggested.

1. A rebus or picture-clue system can be used to help very young students find materials. For example, a picture of an ear can be put over a listening area, or a picture of the type of material can be placed on a shelf (puzzles, scissors, clay, pencils, paper, etc.).
2. Photographs of students performing a task can be placed in an area.
3. Areas can be numbered, with each number representing an activity.
4. If the students know the letters, then a combination of numerals and letters can be used. For example, section A (1–15) is puzzles, Section B (1–25) contains fine motor games, etc.
5. For older students, subject level words can be used (Science Lab, Private Office, Fun and Games, etc.).
6. Materials for older students can also be marked with a code (geometric colored designs ◇, ○, ▢, Indian designs ✳, ≋, ⚞, etc.).

Codes become very helpful to peer tutors, aides, volunteers, and the student. The following techniques can be used to direct the student to the materials.

1. All of the duplicator masters can be run off and placed in folders coded with a "P4" for the fourth book in the reading series and numbered sequen-

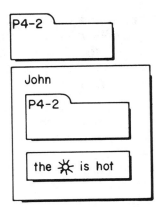

Figure 7-1

tially. Students who need reinforcement on vocabulary words can be directed to the appropriate sheet through the use of a rebus or number form (see Figure 7–1).

Other activities using additional materials can be coded on the same sheet. On the illustrated sheet, the student may be directed next to the vocabulary cards to review a phrase used on the duplicator master.

Duplicator masters completed by the instructor, paraprofessional, volunteers, or older students can be placed in a separate answer folder. The learners can self-check their answers by matching them to the model.

2. Index cards or papers in folders can also be used to direct a student to an activity. For example, a series of codes for a specified period of time can be used (9/4/91–9/20/91–A-16, B-39, G-56, etc.).

3. The materials in a classroom can also be coded into the Mann-Suiter-McClung Developmental Skills Worksheets. For example:

Item	Developmental Skills	
30 1″ multicolored blocks	Visual Discrimination-5	(page 389)
	Visual Memory Sequencing-2, 3, 4	(page 394)
	Visual Language Classification-1	(page 398)

Making Material Self-Checking

The following are examples of how material can be made self-checking:

1. Color code or draw designs on the back of puzzle pieces.
2. Laminate a duplicate of workbook or worksheet pages that have the answers written in.

3. Record answers to questions on tape that the students can listen to.
4. Write the answers on the back of flashcards.
5. For projects that require assembling or constructing of materials, place a completed model, or one at several numbered stages of development, in a container or cabinet for the learners to refer to when they have completed the task.

Students need to be able to manage themselves from the moment they enter an educational setting. When teacher-directed instruction is completed, the student needs to have methods and know strategies that will provide feedback and self-correction. Therefore, all materials have to be accessible in a well-organized scheme, coded for identification, and made self-checking where possible. This level of organization is especially important when students are coming in and out of the room during the day for resourced activities. The student should have enough alternatives available in terms of finding materials, starting to work on the correct assignment, and selecting reinforcement or recreational activities to stay on task.

Cohen, Alberto, and Troutman (1979) conclude that materials should help the learner reach a specified goal faster, more efficiently, and with a higher degree of motivation. Whether teacher-directed or student-directed, the material should provide feedback (self-checking, peer tutors, teacher or paraprofessional evaluations).

Recordkeeping

The most effective type of continuous progress evaluation for classroom purposes is an ongoing system that enables the instructor to determine at a glance whether a particular skill area, such as vocabulary, is developing at the expected rate for a particular student. A vocabulary progress chart can be used in the following manner:

1. Administer a vocabulary pretest.
2. Write the names of the learners who will be using a particular book on the vocabulary progress chart (Form 7–1). Mark the boxes under those words that the learner correctly recognized on the pretest with ⊠.
3. As new words are taught, mark the appropriate box, using the coding illustrated in Figure 7–2.
   a. On the day new words are introduced, mark the boxes with a ◳. In the chart in Figure 7–2, the word *red* was introduced to John Jones; however, he cannot read it as yet.

MANN-SUITER-McCLUNG VOCABULARY PROGRESS CHART

Instructor _____

Coding

◸ introduced word

⊠ can read word

◪ can spell word

■ can read, spell, and
write word

NEW WORDS

Name of Student																

◰ introduced word

◩ can read word

◪ can spell word (aloud or write from dictation)

■ can read, spell, and write word

Name of student	red	Flo	run	too	fun	go	play	sun	with	playing	zoo
John Jones	◰										
Lisa Mann	◩										
Becky Phillips	◪										
Chip Olinick	■										

Figure 7-2

b. When the student has learned the word and can read it without hesitation, mark the box under the word with a ◰. Lisa Mann was presented *red* and can now read the word ◩.

c. Additional information can be coded on the same box. The top half of the box can be used to indicate when the student has learned to spell the word ◪. Becky Phillips can read and spell the word *red*. She can spell the word aloud or write it from dictation.

d. To plot the mastery of a word, you may want to include information about the learner's ability to write the word (copy from a model). On the sample chart, the instructor completed the square by marking the lower half ◩ to indicate that the student can write the word. Therefore, by looking at the code, anyone reading this particular chart would understand that Chip Olinick can successfully read, spell, and write the word *red* ■. For an older student, the instructor may want to complete the box (from ◰ → ■) to indicate one of the following skills instead of just the ability to write the word: definition of the word, appropriate usage in a written or oral sentence.

4. The vocabulary progress charts can be put on clipboards or kept in your planning book for easy access.

5. By using the vocabulary charts for a designated period of time, you should gain an understanding of the learner's rate of progress. For example:
   a. The sheets could be dated to indicate a student's rate of progress for a five-day period. If all of the words introduced are not learned and the boxes show ◰ , then the progress should be carefully evaluated. The learner may require more repetitions, associative clues (pictures), or a reduction in the number of new words presented during a given period of time. If the lack of progress persists, the vocabulary, teaching techniques, and materials may require modification or substitution.
   b. Another student may know five out of seven new words at the end of the five-day period. By carefully noting the amount and rate of input, you can more accurately report student progress to parents and administrators.

6. Paraprofessionals, aides, and volunteer student helpers can use the information on the charts as a guide to the supportive activities that will reinforce the new vocabulary. For example, the sample chart indicates that John Jones needs word recognition activities, while Lisa Mann requires spelling reinforcement. In a well-organized classroom, while the teacher is working at the instructional level, supportive staff, including peer tutors, can utilize the educational materials to support the ongoing program.

Phonics Coding System

As you teach new sounds, mark the appropriate box on the phonics progress chart (Form 7–2), using coding illustrated in Figure 7–3.

1. The sound s was introduced to John Jones; however, he cannot produce the sound as yet.
2. Lisa Mann can recognize the sound.
3. Becky Phillips can recall the sound.
4. Chip Olinick can use the sound functionally in a word.

Mann-Suiter-McClung Teaching Chart

To aid the teacher, tutor, or volunteer an ongoing teaching chart is included (Form 7–3). It follows the

MANN-SUITER-McCLUNG PHONICS PROGRESS CHART

Instructor _____

Coding

☐	introduced sound
☒	can recognize sound
◤	can recall sound
■	can use sound functionally in a word

NEW SOUNDS

Name of Student																	

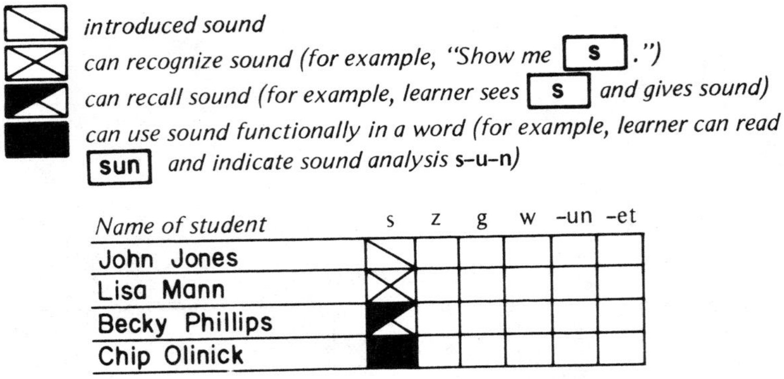

⬜ introduced sound

⊠ can recognize sound (for example, "Show me $\boxed{s}$.")

◼ can recall sound (for example, learner sees $\boxed{s}$ and gives sound)

◼ can use sound functionally in a word (for example, learner can read $\boxed{sun}$ and indicate sound analysis s–u–n)

Name of student	s	z	g	w	–un	–et
John Jones	⬜					
Lisa Mann	⊠					
Becky Phillips	◪					
Chip Olinick	◼					

Figure 7-3

Name **MARY BROWN** Date **6/9/79**

Level **6** Instructor _____

Date	Page	Taught	Reinforced	Evaluated	Retaught
6/9	3	I am m	6/10, 6/11, 6/12	6/13	ok
6/10	4	help Matt	6/11, 6/12	6/13	ok
6/11	5	Nat and Nan at an n	6/12		
6/12			page 3,4,5		
6/13				page 3,4,5	at an

Figure 7-4

unit outline presented and provides an easy way to keep a record of what has been done and the areas found to be most difficult for the pupil.

The sample chart in Figure 7–4 shows that on June 9 the pupil did page 3 in the Reader/Workbook and was taught the words *I* and *am* and the sound of the consonant letter *m*. On June 10, the pupil did page 4 in the Reader/Workbook and was taught the words *help* and *Matt*. The words *I* and *am* and the sound "m" were reinforced. On June 11, three new words (*Nat, and,* and *Nan*), the sound of *n,* and two spelling patterns were introduced, and all prior learning was reinforced. On June 12th all prior learning was reinforced. On June 13th the pupil was tested and knew the words *I, am, help,* and *Matt* and the sound of *m,* but still needed work on *at* and *an.*

An ongoing chart of this type helps the instructor to constantly reinforce the words, spelling patterns, letter names, and sounds taught. It provides an easy way to

keep track of what was taught, systematically reinforce it, evaluate the teaching, and reteach what is not known.

A student's program can be slowed down or speeded up depending upon his or her ability to retain new teachings.

In addition to using progress charts, the instructor can assess daily and weekly vocabulary and skill acquisition by writing on the cover of a file folder the words, if any, the learner recognized on a pretest (Figure 7–5).

As new words are learned, they are added to the folder and dated. At periodic intervals, the instructor can have the learner read the words on the list. The instructor can get an idea of the learner's rate of progress by noting the dates and the retention of the vocabulary.

Monday is a preferable day for evaluation. The instructor will know which words from the previous week

Form 7-3

MANN-SUITER-McCLUNG TEACHING CHART

Name _____   Date _____

Level _____   Instructor _____

Date	Page	Taught	Reinforced	Evaluated	Retaught

Figure 7-5

were learned and which ones must be reviewed. Lesson plans can be made or revised based on this information. If the learner will not give a verbal (recall) response when the card is shown, the instructor can place several cards on a desk or table and ask the child to "show" the word.

When the learner first arrives in the morning, the instructor can use word cards to go through a selected number of vocabulary words to check the learner's progress. For example, if five new words have been presented over a period of time, the instructor may wish to check these prior to introducing the next word. If the ongoing evaluation is done before the learner's scheduled reading instruction period, the instructor can provide a more successful lesson for the student.

SELECTING AND EVALUATING MATERIALS

How many and what kinds of materials are required in a regular classroom to effectively deal with the variability of students with learning and behavior problems? Before deciding what to buy or make, teachers must analyze the materials already available in a classroom or a school. For example, Figure 7–6 can be used in conducting a needs assessment for reading materials. The same general headings can also be

used for the evaluation of other subject areas (e.g., science, math, spelling, social studies).

Not all of the materials listed are required for a reading program, but a paucity or complete void in some areas may inhibit individualization of instruction. By going through such an evaluation, teachers may note the following:

1. Duplication of materials
2. Multiple use of materials
3. Which materials are the most and the least used
4. The percentage of self-checking or self-directed materials
5. Gaps in levels or skills
6. Location of materials
7. Condition and durability of equipment and materials
8. Which materials can be made by teachers, students, or volunteers

Reading Level

Considering the variability in most classrooms, many teachers would have to ascertain the availability of materials and the needs at several grade levels. It is important for the special teachers (e.g., reading, counseling, special education) and teachers from each grade level to work together to prepare a school-wide chart of materials. The reading levels can be designated in a variety of ways. In Figure 7–6 the levels reflect a range from Preprimer 1 to first grade level[2]. A wider range might have included Kindergarten readiness materials through a sixth grade level one reader (6^1). If the school is grouping on a system of levels (Level 1–20, etc.), then that designation can

Reading Level	Main Series	First Alternative	Second Alternative	A-V Feedback	Comprehension Workbooks	Phonics Workbooks	Cassettes	Specific Skill Worksheets	Games	Computers
PP^1										
PP^2										
PP^3										
PP^4										
Primer										
1^1										
1^2										

Figure 7-6   Analysis of Materials in the Classroom

be plotted. The major consideration is to use a code that administrators, teachers, aides, student teachers, or parents can pick up and instantly understand, getting a feeling for what books preceded and which ones will follow a student's placement in a series. Therefore, the concept of readability must be used in a functional manner.

Main Series

The Main Series column in Figure 7–6 is for the state-adopted, required-reading textbooks, the preferred reading series, or the program that will be used as the major reading material in a classroom or school. This of course will vary widely from school to school, but most teachers have one or two most used reading series.

As a teacher or group of teachers fill in the chart, they should place the books in piles on tables. For example, the major series can be placed on a table next to labeled levels (PP[1]-First Grade). On the chart, the teachers may wish to actually write in the number of available books ("Book Title"–56).

First and Second Alternative Series

Place on the table next to the major series, and note on the chart, the reading series that would be the first alternative, especially for students with learning problems who are experiencing failure in the main textbook series. This series is usually one that has features such as a slower rate of vocabulary acquisition, concepts that are more in keeping with the cultural or special comprehension needs of the students, or better workbooks. As a result of readability formulas or teacher feelings based on usage, the teacher tries this series first if the student cannot succeed in the major series.

It may be determined that there is no available backup series that is really appropriate for the students presently in the class; therefore, at this point, the teacher and the special teachers or curriculum specialists can begin to evaluate samples of other programs used in other schools.

Next to the samples of the first alternative series or program should be placed samples of the second, followed by all others in order of preference.

Audiovisual Feedback Equipment

The remaining columns in Figure 7–6 refer to categories of materials that supply many of the supportive, reinforcement types of activities that are more student directed. In the column for audiovisual feedback materials, such materials as the Language Master (Bell & Howell Inc.) can be listed. The teachers should list what and how many commercial or teacher-made cards are in good condition and available for use. Perhaps the school has a number of pieces of machinery in good working order, but no blank cards or many boxes of cards of the wrong lists of words, phrases, or sentences. Determining the availability of these types of machines and materials is important because they are valuable for individualized teaching of students who cannot use pencil-and-paper types of materials.

Comprehension Workbooks

Usually these materials are required after the student has acquired phonics skills or a vocabulary. Crucial factors include not only how many of various types of books are available, but also which ones are supportive to the students' ongoing major reading, writing, and spelling program. The readability level, concept load, size of print, illustrations, types of directions, and space for written response, as well as the usability by volunteers, aides, peer tutors, and, of course, the students themselves, should be noted. It may be found that a few examples of many workbooks are available, but some students with reading problems and special handicapping conditions will "fall through the cracks" and not receive much reinforcement. It is at this point that the individual needs of students will point to appropriate new acquisitions.

Phonics Workbooks

Supplementary phonics workbooks should also be evaluated with regard to size of print, illustrations, usability, etc. Their potential for modification for use with the major reading series should be considered.

Cassettes and Computers

The availability of computers, tape recorders, listening stations, and areas in the school or classroom for effective use of such equipment has to be evaluated (e.g., multiple electrical outlets and cubicles, study carrels, or other areas in which to use cassettes). Cassettes can be used for a variety of reinforcing activities (specific skills, phonics, recorded stories in readers, chapters in texts, library books, etc.).

Specific Skills Worksheets

In evaluating duplicator or printed worksheets, the instructors should consider the following:

1. Clarity and size of print
2. Appropriateness for grade level or skill being taught
3. Ease of student self-direction in use of material
4. Developmental sequence of the materials
5. Availability and organization of the material for use by teachers, aides, or students

Games

Puzzles, flash cards, card games, lotto games, etc., should provide both reinforcement and recreational value. Storage as well as durability should be noted.

The effectiveness of games has to be viewed with some caution. To reinforce or practice skills, the games have to be self-governing and practice skills previously introduced (Canney, 1978). Losing sight of the objective of the game or the reason for playing the game can be a hazard. Will the game fill time, reinforce a skill, motivate, and sustain interest? Teacher time can be lost in explaining how to play. Snyder (1981) recommends that the teacher teach two to four students to play and allow them to teach others. She also states that while games have a place in the classroom the "greatest game in town" is reading a good book.

Other Needs

After a needs assessment of all the major categories of materials, then the following can also be noted:

1. Other audiovisual material—films, filmstrips, projectors, overhead projectors, record players, records
2. Display boards—flannel boards, small chalkboards, magnetic boards, pocket charts
3. Manipulative reinforcers—moveable letters, tracing screens
4. Language development and phonics equipment—mirrors, commercial kits, puppets
5. Library books, magazines, reference books, and encyclopedias

Computers

Computers and microcomputers are becoming more prevalent in homes and accessible in the schools. A student's first exposure to the computer is often through game playing. In "user-friendly" programs that use the student's name, the immediate response to answers and praise help the learner sustain attention and maintain a high interest level. Use of the computer can be a reward for on-task performance. The computer can be used in content-area instruction for programmed learning, drill and practice, enrichment, assessment, and problem solving. Feedback is immediate. The computer is a management tool to monitor the educational process and can be used in monitoring student records and individual educational program data.

The availability of computers is determined by start-up costs for equipment, software, facilities for laboratories, personnel to monitor and maintain equipment, and training for school personnel. In planning for the utilization of computers within a school, teachers and administrators need a plan that will maximize the use of the equipment in a variety of settings. Will it be more practical to have one computer per classroom or 35 computers in one laboratory? This depends on the amount of time individual machines are not in use. A fully functioning laboratory may be more cost effective. Computers should be placed in classrooms, central laboratories, the library, and writing centers that focus on word processing and business skills. Where possible, lap-top models should be available for individual student use at school or at home. There are benefits to having enough computers for everyone in a class to be at a different terminal working on the same or different programs all at the same time. The instructor can get assessment data at the end of the day for a class profile, a three-day class average, or a student's individual profile (time on task, number of attempts, and score).

Scheduling may be a major concern. With respect to drill and practice using the computer, it is best accomplished with frequent, daily drills already learned with the idea of developing speed and automaticity. To provide follow-up and reinforcement on the computer, after direct classroom instruction requires a careful correlation of the textbook and other teaching materials with the software and on a pre-planned schedule that will coincide with the pace of the lessons.

Finding time to try out the new software before use with the students and keeping up with new software on the market requires time and recordkeeping. Joining computer clubs, attending conferences, and reading newsletters and journals provide helpful data. Preview software when you have free time and keep a prioritized list of programs that would be valuable additions to your current inventory. This will avoid costly mistakes that can occur when administrators request a quick turn-around time in purchasing materials.

Use a checklist to evaluate computer software. Look for the following features:

1. General Information
   a. title of the program
   b. publisher and author(s)
   c. copyright date
   d. cost
   e. computer brand compatibility
   f. software, hardware, and memory requirements
2. Use
   a. subject area, level, or specific skill
   b. grade level(s)
   c. time required for completion
   d. application: practice or drill, tutorial, word processing, assessment, specific skill area, instructional game, enrichment, adventure type simulation
   e. management system
3. Technical Features
   a. simple procedures for cursor movement, insertion, or deletion
   b. graphics
   c. sound and music
   d. color
   e. easy start-up with automatic boot
   f. printer requirements
   g. special features: freeze screen, student-controlled rate of usage
   h. speech synthesizer that provides feedback
   i. availability of teacher modification of the program to personalize for individual students
   j. joysticks, light pens, or paddles
4. Content
   a. clearly stated and implemented instructional objectives
   b. simple screen instructions and prompts
   c. pictures in directions
   d. prompts and screen instructions at a readability level appropriate to the learner
   e. recordkeeping or information management element for benefit of both teacher and student
   f. provision for effective involvement of student with rapid feedback
   g. a learning pace based on the diagnosed needs of the student
   h. a logical sequence and structure
   i. adequate repetition of material without being boring
   j. free of gender, race, and cultural bias
   k. correlates with textbook or curriculum materials
   l. provision of branching off to higher or lower levels of material
   m. includes rewards
   n. provides supplementary worksheets or instructional strategies

Computer-assisted instruction is further discussed under written language expression in Chapter 9. As a tool for creative writing, the writer has control of the mechanical aspects that often impede learning (e.g., speed of writing, legibility, and spelling).

MATERIALS-PROGRAM EVALUATION SYSTEM

A Materials Evaluation Paradigm (see Figure 7–7) was developed to aid in the task of identifying the materials that are relevant to the education of learning-problem students. This system will be helpful to educators who need to be more precise in determining the appropriateness and usefulness of different materials for this population of students. The system is designed to be less descriptive (what it is and what it does) and more evaluative, how it was developed and implemented and what is the proof that it works.

The system illustrates the interrelationships of three primary subareas of the classification system, which are

1. Population level (who)
2. Subject area (what)
3. Procedures (how and why)

Population Level

Part of the classification system is to delineate the population that a program is designed to serve. The following need to be addressed:

1. What level is the program designed for: primary, intermediate, or secondary?
2. Does the program specify grade levels or age levels?
3. What group of students does the program address?
4. Is the program based on skills rather than levels for a given population?
5. What level of language (reading, writing, etc.) proficiency is necessary for the student to succeed in the program?
6. How is the material to be adapted to the level of language proficiency of the student?

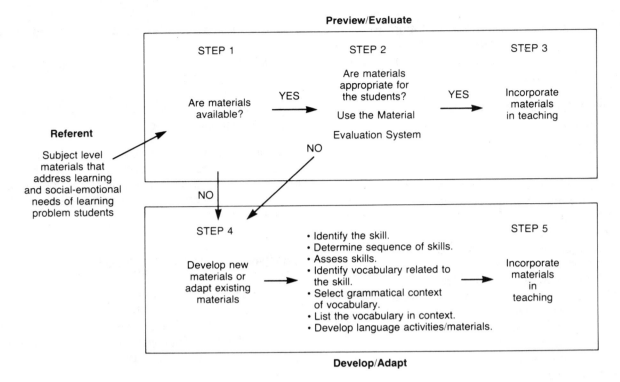

Figure 7-7 Materials Evaluation Paradigm

Subject Area

Under subject area, there are three primary subareas.

1. Curriculum (what students are required to master)
2. Instructional alternatives (how the skills are to be developed/objectives attained)
3. Assessment (how the program components and student's performance are evaluated in terms of the objectives proposed)

In all three subareas the instructor needs to understand the overall philosophy and approach regarding how the materials were designed. In the area of language or mathematics, it is important to identify the language-related activities of the program and their relationship to computation, reasoning, and problem solving. Further, it is important to know if

1. the program contains just curriculum materials without any suggested instructional approaches or materials for students to use.
2. the program just gives information about how to teach and includes some instructional materials that can be used by pupils, but really does not outline a curriculum scope and sequence.
3. there is an assessment instrument included with the program or if there is one available that can be used with the program.

Procedures

There are three aspects of procedures:

1. Development
2. Implementation
3. Validation

In each of these subareas the concern is with the human resources that were used in the development, implementation, and validation of the material. We are also concerned about the documentation available for each of these subareas. By human resources we mean who developed the program, how did they interact with each other, and were parents, students, linguists, or others involved? For documentation, we need to know if there is a report or written statement that outlines the procedures and comments on the various activities. For example, in looking at a particular program, if the concern is about the development of curriculum related to the language aspects of mathematics (e.g., story problems) for primary grade children, we may want to know something about the people (human resources) who developed the product (how and why). What documentation do they give us that suggests that this program is appropriate for students with learning disabilities? Another example would be the implementation of a particular assessment instrument used to assess the language aspects of problem solving in mathematics for secondary-age learning-problem students. As before, we are concerned with the human resources involved and the documentation of a sequence of procedures. An example of validation would be to determine the types of human resources and documentation available that indicate that a particular instructional approach to teaching the language aspects of mathematics to intermediate-level learning-disabled students produces significant results.

Materials-Program Evaluation Checklist

The Materials-Program Evaluation Checklist (Form 7–4) suggests the parameters for considering important questions. The checklist can be used by teachers and is deemed especially valuable for individuals responsible for curriculum and instructional decisions within a school or district.

The checklist can be used in several ways:

1. It can be used as a guide for making decisions about using certain materials or programs.
2. The subareas can be used individually for gathering information about a particular program.
3. The questions within certain subareas can be used as deemed appropriate by the individual(s) doing the evaluation.
4. The checklist provides a guide by which particular aspects of a program can be summarized.

INSTRUCTIONAL ALTERNATIVES

Because of the "least restrictive environment" imperative of P.L. 94–142, the most appropriate education for handicapped students is that planned within the context of their integration with nonhandicapped peers. This concept requires the use of organizational patterns and instructional alternatives that accommodate a wide range of student variability within regular classroom settings.

Comparative Instructional Approaches

DIAGNOSTIC-PRESCRIPTIVE TEACHING (DPT)
The diagnostic-prescriptive teaching approach has the following characteristics:

1. A thorough knowledge of the child's history and ecological environment is the basis for diagnosis and assessment.

2. Both enhancing and vitiating factors in the learner's history are identified. This includes habits, special problems, idiosyncrasies, aversions, and previously effective reward systems.
3. A clear definition of curriculum and objectives for both the short and long term are specified.
4. An analysis of the tasks to be mastered is accomplished. Task analysis involves the determination of specific skills, or more specifically, the prerequisite skills necessary to complete a task. This involves the variability that must be considered between good and bad performances based on extraneous factors (i.e., how the learner feels that day).
5. A comprehensive instructional plan indicates alternative strategies to be used and opportunities for both one-on-one and group activities.
6. Continued progress assessment (informal and formal) is made.
7. Periodic reevaluation with new prescriptive procedures as indicated based on the following:
   a. Has the behavior stabilized?
   b. Has the behavior increased?
   c. Has the behavior decreased?

PRECISION TEACHING (PT)
Precision teaching, as expressed by Ogdan Lindsley (1971), is a behavioral approach that utilizes the concepts inherent in the operant conditioning approach to treatment. When applied to the classroom, it involves a strong continuing management program and the following:

1. Specific behaviors or tasks are pinpointed and stated in measurable terms, such as so many words spelled in a given period of time.
2. A baseline of the frequency of a behavior is acquired and compared with the same behavior over time on a continuous basis. The behavior is charted on a daily basis. Six-cycle logarithmic paper can be used.
3. Analysis of the ongoing behavior determines if a new instructional approach should be instituted.

The main principle of this approach is that the instructor must set up a procedure for analyzing the daily changes in the students' performance.

Direct Instruction or Teaching (DI or DT)

Direct instruction is teaching behavior by a teacher, face to face with the student, that maximizes student attention to and participation in relevant academic tasks (Lewis, 1983). The importance of teacher-directed systematic instruction has gained more atten-

Form 7-4

MANN-SUITER-McCLUNG MATERIALS PROGRAM EVALUATION CHECKLIST

SUBJECT AREA _____ POPULATION LEVEL

TYPE OF MATERIAL _____ PRIMARY _____

TITLE _____ INTERMEDIATE ____

AUTHOR _____ SECONDARY _____

PUBLISHER _____ GRADE (S) _____

GROUP FOR WHICH MATERIAL IS INTENDED _____

DATE _____

RESPONDENTS AND POSITIONS:

_____

_____

_____

POPULATION DESCRIPTION	YES	NO
1. Is the population of the program delineated by		
a. age	___	___
b. grade level	___	___
c. special identity (e.g., learning disabilities, reading problems, etc.)	___	___
2. Is the rationale given as to why this program was developed for that population?	___	___

SUBJECT AREA DESCRIPTION

Curriculum

3. Is the scope of the curriculum comprehensive?	___	___
4. Is the subject matter related to student		
a. needs	___	___
b. experiences	___	___
c. learning styles	___	___
d. interests	___	___

(continued)

MANN-SUITER-McCLUNG MATERIALS PROGRAM EVALUATION CHECKLIST

	YES	NO
5. Is there an available, complete		
a. table of contents	___	___
b. glossary	___	___
c. bibliography	___	___
6. Are there evaluative materials that accompany the program?	___	___
7. Is there a scope and sequence chart that outlines the program?	___	___

Instructional Alternatives

8. Is the concept level and format of the material suitable for the instructional level of the age group?

9. Does the material teach the concept the student should know when he/she finishes the lesson?

10. Is the material appropriate for the concept area being taught?

11. Does the material have different levels of abstraction or a range of language approaches to dealing with concepts from simple concrete ideas to more complex thinking?

12. Will the material as presented permit the student to transfer a concept to other situations?

13. Will the student understand and remember the concepts on a long-term basis?

14. Are the illustrations, e.g., graphics, photographs, charts, functionally related to the content of the text?

15. Is the information presented in a logical sequence and in a sensible organization?

16. Is the format attractive, clearly typed or printed, and interesting?

17. Does the format contain variations in organization or are all the examples presented in only one structure?

18. Do the materials facilitate the use of transparencies and other visual presentations?

19. Are there teacher's manuals and other appropriate teacher aids to accompany the instructional materials?

20. Are the activities and exercises performance-related, based on objectives?

21. Are there supplementary instructional materials such as workbooks and duplicator masters available with the program?

22. Do the materials account for cultural differences?

23. Do the instructional materials incorporate activities that relate to improving basic skills?

24. Are the instructional activities related to real-life situations?

25. Is the instructional approach to teaching learning-disabled students delineated?

26. Do the materials refer to vocational and career-related goals, employability skills, and principles that enhance the work ethic?

27. Does the material incorporate instructional concepts that relate to environmental protection and the individual's role in society?

28. Is the vocabulary appropriate for the intended population (e.g., age and grade levels)?

29. Is the readability appropriate in terms of sentence length and paragraph structure?

30. Is the readability level of the material compatible with the student's independent reading level?

31. Are some of the sentences and/or passages too long?

32. Will the connectives in the sentences (e.g., *and, but, on, by, for,* etc.) confuse the student?

33. Are the directions short and clearly written?

(continued)

MANN-SUITER-McCLUNG MATERIALS PROGRAM EVALUATION CHECKLIST

Assessment	YES	NO
34. Is the assessment culture fair?	____	____
35. Is the assessment within the readability level of the population?	____	____
36. Is the assessment within the native language readability level of the population?	____	____
37. Is the assessment comprehensive?	____	____
38. Does the assessment correlate with the skills that have been taught within a given level?	____	____
39. Is the assessment easy to administer and score?	____	____

PROCEDURES

Development

40. Is there a contact person? Name, address, telephone.	____	____
41. Are the developers the ones who implemented and validated the program?	____	____
42. Does the program contain information about its development?	____	____
43. Do they indicate what types of human resources were utilized to develop the program?	____	____
44. Were the populations defined that were used to field test the material?	____	____
45. Is there any documentation of the development procedure?	____	____

Implementation

46. Is there a contact person? Name, address, telephone.	____	____
47. Are the implementers the ones who developed and validated the program?	____	____
48. Does the program contain information about how it was or is being implemented?	____	____
49. Do they indicate what types of human resources were utilized to implement the program?	____	____
50. Were the populations that were used in the implementation of the program defined?	____	____
51. Is there any documentation of the implementation procedure?	____	____

Validation

52. Is there a contact person? Name, address, telephone.	____	____
53. Are the validators the ones who developed and implemented the program?	____	____
54. Does the program contain information about its validation?	____	____
55. Do they indicate what types of human resources were utilized in the validation process?	____	____
56. Were the populations that were used to validate the program defined?	____	____
57. Is there a statistical design and report that validates the program?	____	____
58. Is there documentation of any validation procedures?	____	____

SUMMARY

tion as researchers examine effective teaching strategies. Stevens and Rosenshine (1981), Blankenship and Lilly (1981), and Baumann (1983) conclude that direct teaching by a teacher has a positive effect on student achievement. Learning disabled students need more direct instruction in order to learn. Therefore, as a part of classroom management, the instructor has to analyze how lessons will be planned and presented. Learning is enhanced when teachers have clearly formulated instructional objectives and when they are able to communicate them effectively to students.

Effective teaching requires more demonstration and modeling by the teacher during instruction. The instructor has to explain how to perform a task, then perform it, and ask the student to model the behavior. During the student performance, controlled practice is provided and the instructor prompts where necessary. Feedback is critical throughout the interaction. The student then moves to an independent practice activity that allows for feedback and later follow-up and reteaching by the instructor if necessary. This involves reviewing and checking the previous day's work and weekly and monthly reviews.

Student time on task is an important aspect of direct instruction. The instructor has to analyze how much time will be needed to accomplish a task and how effectively it will be used by the student. Academic engaged time (Berliner, 1981; Fisher et al., 1980), or time on task by the student, is critical for student achievement. During engaged time, the student is paying attention to and participating in the instructional task.

While direct instruction is better for task-related skills, the student has to be able to take the next step and generalize the instruction to other tasks and effectively use self-directed, metacognitive strategies.

Student motivation occurs within a warm, interactive environment. The instructor is concerned with successful experiences while at the same time helping the student tolerate frustration and cope with more difficult tasks.

The direct instruction approach involves several basic procedures:

1. Short-term or long-term objectives are specified.
2. The instructor devises problem-solving strategies to complement learning that requires rote memory. Students are taught to generalize information.
3. Preskills necessary to perform a particular task are specified.
4. Skills are sequenced according to the order of presentation.
5. A teaching approach is selected.

6. The format of presentation is determined (i.e., how will information be presented?)
7. Examples are selected that reflect the format that is chosen.
8. Teach until mastery is indicated. This involves review and practice.

Common Features

All of these approaches appear to have the following common features:

1. Teaching is focused on precise behaviors.
2. The learner is actively involved in the process of learning.
3. Goals and objectives are explicitly stated.
4. Mastery is foremost and practice is an essential ingredient.

Learning for Mastery

Learning for Mastery (LFM) is an adaptive program, which is group- as well as individual-oriented, and has the following features:

1. Emphasizes objectives to be achieved.
2. Requires precise identification of the tasks the student is expected to learn within a hierarchical order.
3. Depends less on how the particular children are in the classroom and more upon the material they are expected to complete.
4. Requires that planning be done before the instruction begins. Plans for mastery learning are learning packets which include a statement of subject domain, mastery tests, formative tests, correctives, extension activities, and a teaching plan.
5. Emphasizes that it is the instruction, not the child, that must be modified.
6. Involves the identification of topics within a curriculum area and the development of objectives that test learners' mastery of each of these topics.
7. Is to a large extent a group approach to teaching.

Components of Learning for Mastery are:

1. Diagnostic—Identify what the learner is to accomplish.
2. Corrective—Present the material, then check to be sure that the student has learned it. Offer more instruction if he or she has not (permits individualization).
3. Extension—Sometimes referred to as enrichment, this component is designed to provide the student

who has learned the material an opportunity to become involved in higher levels of a Taxonomy developed by Benjamin Bloom (1968), one of the foremost proponents of Mastery Learning.

Proponents of the Mastery Learning approach view this adaptive program as one that is economically practical in that resources for its implementation are, for the most part, already in place in most schools.

The majority of educators polled over many years suggests that no single conceptual framework can be applied to all situations. Rather, it is the usefulness of an approach applied to general situations that provides a framework for instruction. There are no simple answers considering the complexity of human processing systems.

Peer and Cross-Age Tutoring—Student Support System

There is evidence to suggest that tutoring improves the academic skills of the tutor as much as it does the individual being tutored (Cloward, 1967; Ehly & Larsen, 1976). Teaching as a method of learning has yet to be adequately researched, but positive results have been reported by many teachers.

Role theory implies that one becomes what one does; in this case, the tutor takes on the characteristics of the teacher. Feelings of self-confidence, importance, and authority can effect changes in behavior, attitudes, and self-perception. It is suggested that the role of friend might be a more flexible and appropriate role for the peer or cross-age tutor and would allow for more tutor development. In situations in which self-efficacy (self-esteem) may be low, tutoring might help to promote feelings of respect and trust and the working through of "problems of relationships."

Related to esteem is the idea of locus of control (Chandler, 1975). The student, within the tutoring context, may begin to feel more in control of his or her life and environment (internal locus) and less dependent on the manipulation of others (external locus). Tutoring by low-achieving students is seen as a way of taking responsibility, or "concede responsibility for one's own fate" (Chandler, 1975, p. 337). The act of tutoring may help the student (tutor) become more involved in learning and provide motivation for academic improvement.

Some behaviorists believe that students (tutors) who exhibit social inadequacy can practice and develop social skills in a fairly neutral environment through cross-aged tutorial interactions (Allen, 1976). The principles of reinforcement apply in the use of peer tutoring (Bargh & Schul, 1980), but reinforcement is considered to be only one factor in enhancing a tutor's learning.

The question of whether insights are gained through tutoring gives rise to the idea that, through tutoring, tutors have opportunities to "test and develop their own knowledge" (Lippitt & Lohman, 1965). There appears to be some importance related to the process of teaching and learning going on simultaneously. Gartner, Kohler, and Reissman state that the tutor

has the opportunity of observing another in the process of learning, perhaps leading him to reflect upon his own learning process. . . . This opportunity may increase his own awareness of the patterns of learning, for in order to teach another he may need to call upon his own experiences in learning and how he learned. (1971, p. 62)

Other factors to consider:

1. Tutors develop a respect for knowledge.
2. Continued review of knowledge promotes understanding.
3. Tutoring provides more time to study a particular subject.
4. Tutoring aids in the development of efficient "schema construction" (Bargh & Schul, 1980).
5. Tutors have an opportunity to learn or relearn what they had missed in earlier grades.

Preparation:

1. The process involves reviewing, studying, or relearning.
2. Verbalized information will more likely be remembered.
3. A review-study-rehearsal strategy seems to be effective.
4. Materials that are at the appropriate level of the tutor are most useful.
5. The director of the process must consider time on task. Time on the activity is felt to be a significant variable.

The appropriate use of peers to assist learning handicapped students is another device for promoting effective participation. Peers can serve in all instructional areas and can be a practical asset to the regular classroom teacher. This type of support is easy to implement and does not take up a lot of teacher time and energy. It releases the teacher to do other things and is useful in one-on-one interactions and in small group situations (Young, 1981; Fowler & Peterson, 1986).

In some cases it is reported that peer assistance programs are preferred to adult mediated support. Peer tutoring in the regular classroom can be accomplished in the following manner (Lloyd et al., 1988):

1. Peers, tutors, and target students can share reinforcement. In this situation, all members of a group receive the same contingency outcome (reward), including the peer tutor. The consequences of performance behavior is not placed solely on any one individual.
2. Peer assistants can manage or supervise nonacademic activities of students. In this situation, the peer tries to build higher rates of social interaction, especially with withdrawn students. It is also designed to prompt or increase appropriate behavior in the cafeteria, playground, and in other group social activities.
3. Peer tutors can also manage the academic activities of students. The peer tutor guides the learner, instructs, and gives feedback. The tutor prompts and provides consequences and feedback. Peers can play two roles simultaneously. They can share reinforcement, as in tutoring, and also act as managers. A peer manager helps the student, shares information, and gives academic support, but does not provide the consequences of behavior.
4. Peer modeling is another concept and involves demonstration of the expected responses by the peer.

In all instances, detailed instruction on procedures should be provided for the peer tutor by the teacher so that the appropriate sequence of activities is followed. Special training is required for peer assistants, including a period of supervision while learning.

Small Group Tutorials

Small group tutorial instruction can be used to teach both regular and special students in the same classroom. Learning disabled students are assigned to home rooms with nonhandicapped agemates and go to other classrooms for tutoring in reading, mathematics, or other subjects. These small tutorial groups are held in regular classrooms. When tutorials are in session, two groups of students and their respective teachers are in the same room. The period of time a student spends in these tutorials varies with need, as determined by the teacher or a "Pupil Evaluation

Team." In all cases, learning disabled students should have music, art, lunch, and recreation with nonhandicapped peers.

ACCOMMODATIONS FOR STUDENTS WITH SPECIAL NEEDS

All students will have unique problems for the tutor or volunteer to deal with; however, some students' "special needs" will require additional considerations and some modifications. The following suggestions may pertain to all students, but are especially important when the tutor works with handicapped students:

Deaf and Hard of Hearing Students

1. Use normal speech. Avoid excessive accentuation of the voice or facial distortion.
2. Face the students and avoid shadows on the face when speaking to them.
3. Use picture clues or write directions if necessary.
4. For lengthy directions or other oral material, tape record the information so that the students can then listen by amplification.
5. Be aware of similar-sounding words and use further examples.
6. Allow the students to use alternative responses to questions, such as pointing to the right answer.
7. Move student close to the front of the room.
8. Don't cover lips with a book while reading.
9. Allow another student to take duplicate notes during lectures. The student may miss valuable information when he or she looks down to write.

Paritally Sighted Students

1. Magnify the print, or retype the material by using a primary typewriter.
2. Tape record sessions with the students so that they can listen to the tape at a later time.
3. Write chalkboard directions on a separate sheet of paper.
4. Provide special magnifiers for reading. These will enlarge the print, but the reading may be slower. The student should move the magnifying glass across the entire line to get context clues.
5. Use materials from American Printing House for the Blind (1839 Frankfort Avenue, Louisville, Kentucky 40206). They include most of the basal reading series, accompanying workbooks, and

texts for science, math, social studies, history, geography, health, and occupational guidance in both large print and Braille.

6. Give more verbal descriptions of ongoing activities (Ward & McCormick, 1981).
7. Provide tactile examinations of objects (e.g., models, toys) associated with teaching to build concepts.
8. Allow the student more time to read an assignment because of the slowness of braille.
9. Use larger print on Language Master cards.
10. Closed circuit TV can be used to project an image of the page on a desk model TV monitor.
11. In reading, stories that rely on pictures may need modification.

Physically Handicapped Students

1. If the students have difficulty writing, alternatives such as typing, use of moveable letters, or writing the answers for the students may have to be used.
2. Workbooks and other materials that require writing must be completed with some consideration for the students' abilities.
3. Secure materials to the desk with a clip or tape top and bottom to prevent sliding (Glazzard, 1980).
4. Tie a pencil on a string to the desk for easier retrieval.
5. Allow another student with good note-taking skills to insert a sheet of carbon paper under his or her paper to take duplicate notes.

Students with a Slower Rate of Learning

1. Consider the students' study skills and self-direction in the completion of tasks.
2. Provide repetition and review without showing the students that they have failed.
3. Regulate the amount of work that the students complete. Insure that they have successful experiences.
4. Use pictures, models, or other visual and auditory clues to help the students learn new material.
5. Consider the attention span of the students and avoid lengthy directions that will confuse them.
6. Set up an environment where the students can work without distractions.

Emotionally Disturbed Students

Chapter 4 contains many suggestions for behavioral management.

GENERAL DISCIPLINE

Teachers can do a great deal to affect the social-emotional climate of the classroom. It is both desirable and reasonable to expect to teach in an environment that is not constantly stressful and energy depleting. An environment that is supportive of students' needs, conducive to learning because of the way it is organized, along with a basic understanding and tolerance for a modicum of disruptive behavior can become a reality. Several factors need to be considered:

1. Unproductive student behavior is often a response to boredom, failure, and/or negative peer interaction.
2. The tolerance level of the teacher is important. People differ in their willingness to put up with noise and movement.
3. Students differ in the way they respond to freedom and structure. Limitations that are established seem to be important for good classroom discipline.
4. How students complete and turn in work is important. Incoming and outgoing baskets can be used by the students when the teacher is occupied, along with daily work folders that students use independently.
5. Leaving and returning to the class are another problem. It is important to have sign-out and sign-in sheets with space for time designation, along with hall passes. Students should only be out one at a time if possible. No leaving the room during group instruction except for emergencies.
6. Create a free or a relaxation area where students can read, play games, listen to the radio, watch TV, or read magazines.
7. Allow students occasionally to start their homework in class and finish at home.
8. Establish a routine for entering and leaving the class. Stand in the doorway and greet incoming students in the morning.
9. Discipline problems seem to be proportional to the distance between the teacher and the student and the amount of time the teacher spends behind the desk. Walking around and being near the students is a good idea.
10. Discourage students from becoming judges and correction officers for those who commit minor offenses.
11. Keep a supply of rewards for appropriate behavior.
12. How the class is arranged will control a lot of behavior (e.g., adequate space between desks, clear view of chalkboard, uncluttered passage

ways, having materials available and accessible for students).

13. Use time-out procedures and locations appropriately. For example, quiet study carrels should not be used for punishment.
14. Refrain from making comparisons between students and their peers in areas involving behavior or academics.
15. Grades should not be the most important feedback that students receive regarding their work. The quality of work and improvements or gains made are also important.
16. Students should receive candid and realistic feedback and not fake praise, which causes confusion.
17. Record all important data regarding behavior. A good documenter avoids problems with denial and exaggeration.
18. Students need to know the criteria by which they are being evaluated and should have the opportunity to evaluate themselves.

Additional suggestions for specific behavior problems are found in Chapter 4.

SCHEDULING

Scheduling provides the teacher with a framework by which three aspects of teaching and learning can be planned and accounted for within the existing structure of the school.

One aspect of scheduling is learner-related activities, which accounts for students' articulation through the school day within the framework of mainstreaming. This includes subject areas as well as other related activities such as recreation, lunch, opening exercises, and closing of the school day.

Things to consider:

1. Where will the student be at any given time during the day?
2. When the student is not with me, do I know what the student will be getting or doing?
3. What period of time and when during the school day is there an opportunity for reviewing the learning outside of the main teacher's purview? How can the instruction received during the day be integrated so that the learner will go home each day with a sense of organization and with an expectation of what the new day will bring? The learner's responsibility for assignments should be clearly delineated and understood as well as where these assignments fit into the following day.

For secondary students, after a preliminary schedule of the student's daily activities is compiled, it should be discussed with the student and an opportunity provided for the learner to make choices if possible and even some modification.

The second aspect of scheduling involves the best use of teacher time. The best use of teacher time can be made by doing the following:

1. Student daily schedules should be posted and reviewed each day.
2. Daily activities should be sequenced carefully to allow enough time for coverage and to allow students enough time to transition from one activity to another. Consideration needs to be given to attention span and to opportunities for repetition, reinforcement, and review (when again in the school day will this activity, concept, or skill come up?).
3. Daily assignments should be short and able to be accomplished within the scope of the student's abilities or with the aid of a support system.
4. How will aides, assistants, and peer mediators be utilized in the daily schedule?
5. What kind of time-accounting mechanisms will be used to help the student get through the school day when posting is insufficient?
6. What are the optimal teaching times for the students, given their unique needs?
7. The overall routine of the day should be clearly delineated and available for parents upon request.
8. Plans for beginning the school day should be specified with varying activities that will be of interest to students and will provide a motivation to classroom activity.
9. Always schedule one or two alternate activities that can be implemented in emergency situations or in situations in which the activity planned is found to be inappropriate.

A third aspect of scheduling involves the knowledge of the schedule of the school. The creative, knowledgeable teacher knows who is teaching what, as well as those characteristics that provide a good match between instructor and learning handicapped student. Even cooperative teachers who are not easily disturbed by interruptions and are willing to work with handicapped children may require scheduling accommodations.

It is important to operate within the regular school schedule, but factors such as learner fatigue, low frustration tolerance, special physical needs, and special travel arrangements require careful planning and accommodations.

Team Approaches

A team teaching organization provides the flexibility necessary to cope with the various needs of learning problem students in the regular classrooms. In the elementary schools, groups of teachers assume common responsibility for several classes or a group of students. Both the teachers and the students move within a pattern of flexible grouping. At the secondary level, the teams may be within subject levels (e.g., science, social studies, English). There are several advantages to be gained by students in this organizational setting:

1. Pupils become more independent under team teaching.
2. The team concept can help the student build a sense of responsibility.
3. The team approach provides flexibility to meet the various needs of several school populations.
4. Pupils can be grouped in areas of special interest to them.
5. Student-teacher personality problems can be reduced.
6. Superior teachers are shared by all students.
7. The team approach permits greater attention to individual students.
8. Team teaching can provide for improved guidance activities.

In one school a unique example of team teaching and mainstreaming of learning disabled secondary students has resulted from two teachers, a social studies teacher and a special education teacher, working together. By combining their classes in one large room called the Learning Center, they team teach a Government class and a Practical Health/Science class. They have a common roll and grade book, and, for all practical purposes, it is one classroom with two teachers. Since all subject-level content is individualized, both regular and special students are able to progress at their own rate within a regular subject. The content is divided into instructional modules with each unit made up of four parts: (1) pretest, (2) study sheets, (3) activities—films, speakers, projects, readings, field trips, discussions, reports, lectures, and (4) post-test. A contract is signed by the student and his or her parents to agree to the class requirements. The class is an alternative to the resourcing of special education students, and, since it is individualized, it provides flexible reentry for dropout students.

While team teaching provides more opportunities for small group and individualized instruction, it also demands a more sophisticated system of classroom managment. Scheduling, recordkeeping, more accurate diagnostic teaching, student movement within classrooms, time for teacher planning, compatibility of instructional staff personalities, all require leadership and careful planning.

In this arrangement, the student with learning problems will need study skills, on-task behavior, and attention to organization and planning to complete a task.

COOPERATIVE LEARNING ARRANGEMENTS

It is unrealistic to expect students to involve themselves continually in difficult educational tasks where the motivation that consists of intrinsic (e.g., praise for self-satisfaction) or extrinsic (e.g., grades) rewards comes from the teacher alone. An innovative classroom structure is one that is designed to encourage students to work together in a cooperative learning fashion and promote peer approval. This approach can be as basic as having students discuss a common task with each other and work together to arrive at solutions to problems. Peer interaction is an essential element in cooperative learning. This approach places the teacher as the prime motivator into a different perspective.

Students who appear to learn best from cooperative learning arrangements are those who are willing to interact with others, providing explanations and being willing to argue and share with their classmates without detrimental effects (Peterson & Janicki, 1979).

The class has to be organized in a manner that requires students to cooperate and work together to achieve a common goal or objective (Johnson & Johnson, 1986; Slavin, 1983a). In this type of classroom, students are required to work together and to learn together. Students may be tested individually, but rewards are distributed on the basis of the accomplishments of the group. Cooperative learning also has the potential for attaining desirable effects in social behavior (Slavin, 1984).

Cooperative learning is a strategy for student-teacher interaction that has several basic elements (Johnson & Johnson, 1981). The first element is positive interdependence. This is where members of the group are asked to work together as a team to accomplish a specific goal. Ways to achieve positive interdependence involve achieving mutual goals (goal interdependence), dividing labor (task interdependence), and dividing materials, resources, and information among the members of the group (resource interdependence). Finally, students are given rewards (reward interdependence) for group participation.

The next element requires that students be held individually responsible and accountable for mastering the material assigned and for their contribution to the group effort. The teacher has to be "on top of the situation"; that is, he or she must be aware of students who let other students do most of the work. Such students are sometimes called "hitchhikers" or individuals who are looking for a ""free ride."

The third element entails students having to learn interpersonal skills or small-group appropriate skills so they can participate effectively in the program. Specific instruction on how to collaborate within the group is provided by the instructor. Cooperative and competitive learning has a positive effect on heterogenous or peer relationships (Johnson et al., 1984).

The teacher's role is primary as far as teaching collaborative skills so groups can function effectively. Four levels of collaborative skills are identified by Johnson and Johnson (1984, p. 174):

1. *Forming:* Management skills directed toward organizing the group and establishing minimum norms for appropriate behavior
2. *Functioning:* Management skills needed to complete the task and maintain effective working relationships among members
3. *Formulating:* Skills needed to build deeper-level understanding of the material being studied, to stimulate the use of higher-quality reasoning strategies, and to maximize mastery and retention of the assigned material
4. *Fermenting:* Skills needed to stimulate reconceptualization of the material being studied, the search for more information, and the communication of the rationale behind one's conclusions

The specific collaborative skills needed to master a specific task must be identified. Then these skills need to be communicated to the students in a simplified, understandable manner. Students with social skills deficits have problems with social integration and need to be taught social interaction in a precise manner. Collaborative skills are a subset of social skills and are necessary for all aspects of school life, especially in mainstreaming efforts (Johnson, Pittelman, & Heimlich, 1986).

WORKING WITH TEACHERS

Regular Education Initiative

The Regular Education Initiative (REI) calls for a reexamination of current categorical classification systems and special education service delivery. It calls for the integration of mildly handicapped students into the regular classrooms where they will be educated together with those served in Chapter 1 and English as a second language programs (Reynolds, Wang, & Walberg, 1987).

Reasons for such a movement include over-identification for special education services, misclassification of students, poor coordination of regular and special education programs, a lack of mainstreaming where appropriate, and the fact that there are too many procedures to follow for special education placement.

Reynolds, Wang, and Walberg (1987) suggest the following:

1. Combine the educational practices of special, compensatory, and general education—take the best of what works for each group.
2. Governmental support of pilot programs to demonstrate model integration forms of education for these groups.
3. Implement more forms of educational integration at the national level with appropriate waivers of rules and regulations. Feedback would be forthcoming and a part of the evaluation of such programs.

McKinney and Hocutt (1988b) see the proposal of REI as being exceedingly complex and representing a major change in federal policy. They caution against embracing this concept in toto before a careful and continued analysis of the merits and possible problems of such a move is made, as well as the political realities involved (local, state, and federal) and, as important, the possibility of diminished services to children.

Several questions are raised:

1. Can regular education extend the time and resources needed for even more handicapped students in their classrooms than they have to deal with under present mainstreaming programs?
2. Can special education practices be implemented in the regular classroom setting given the size of classes and the present level of regular education competence?

Many educators are concerned about the reduction of special education services that may result from this movement. The REI idea, which was conceptualized by leaders in the U.S. Department of Education (Will, 1986a), is also supported by a group of leaders in special education who see it as a means of better serving students from a programmatic as well as economic point of view. The idea is to serve as many handicapped students as possible in the regular classroom, encouraging a shared responsibility or partnership relationship between regular and special education. The groups most affected are presently labeled behaviorally disordered, learning disabled, mildly retarded, slow learners, and mildly handicapped.

The current system has been characterized as expensive and unnecessary, with a great deal of duplication of services (Stainback & Stainback, 1987). The present system sets up a competitive environment and restricts access to regular education by handicapped students (Reynolds, Wang, & Walberg, 1987).

Another criticism involves the complex scheduling that needs to be accomplished with the "pull-out" approach. Some professionals question the administrative or instructional justification for this kind of organization.

Reynolds, Wang, and Walberg (1987) suggest that three-fourths of special education students are labeled on the basis of judgment. Shepard (1987) estimates that 90 percent of special education students are mildly handicapped and cannot be distinguished in many cases from students who are low achievers. In summary, it is felt by many that special education has an abundance of overidentified categories that, in the long run, will have negative effects on handicapped students.

Those who do not support the REI contend the following:

1. Students with behavior disorders will not be appropriately served in the regular classroom.
2. Some students will be underserved.
3. Regular teachers tried to "get rid" of these students in the first place.
4. Regular teachers are not trained to serve handicapped students.
5. For the little special education services that exist, for some students it will be jeopardized.
6. The handicapped student requires a different or more comprehensive technology and cannot survive in the regular class environment even with support.
7. Special and regular educators may not work well together in this new type of organization.

There is also a serious concern being expressed over the stigma of labels attached to seriously emotionally disturbed learners, and the fact that many of these students cannot survive in the regular classes because of severe behavior problems. The point made is that not all behaviorally disordered children can be served in the regular classroom because the nature of their problems is one that requires trained staff who know how to manage very disruptive or dangerous behavior (Lloyd et al. 1988).

Several instructional models have been proposed. The direct instruction model is one that is recommended but hard to implement in regular classes. It requires highly trained teachers (Lloyd et al., 1988). Another approach, the Adaptive Learning Environment Model (ALEM), developed by Wang and colleagues, has been proposed for helping implement the REI. This approach looks promising but needs further research to substantiate its effectiveness for use in the regular classroom (Hallahan et al., 1988).

With respect to learning disabilities, regular teachers will need to learn how to individualize instruction in terms of responding to individual instructional needs of students in both the cognitive and affective domains (Bryan, Bay, & Donahue, 1988). Learning handicapped children, as a group, have difficulty with learning and remembering rules. They fail in tasks requiring verbal responses, are unable to use task-appropriate learning strategies, and, as a group, do not respond appropriately to emotional tasks that require a cognitive challenge (Ryan, Short, & Week, 1986; Palincsar & Brown, 1987). With respect to teaching, teachers dealing with heterogeneous groups of students need to (Brophy & Good, 1986; Rosenshine & Stevens, 1986):

1. Give students time to respond after asking a question.
2. Apply praise and other rewards appropriately.
3. Give all students equal opportunities to respond to questions.
4. Give students immediate feedback.
5. Work within appropriate achievement levels.
6. Give instruction that is based on small sequential increments.
7. Guarantee a moderate to high degree of success.
8. Maximize the academic learning time.

Teacher Concerns and REI

The areas of technical expertise, attitudes, skills, and philosophy are critical for success of the REI. Teachers who are intolerant or who cannot manage variability in behavior or learning will need a great deal of in-service training to deal with their insufficiencies in order to participate fully in the REI. It is reasonable to expect teachers to accommodate the learners as they develop expertise in management and discover how to overcome instructional problems. There is a point when good judgment must dictate and some students will just not fit the scheme and will require a different environment in order to stay in school (Gersten, Carnine, & Woodward, 1987). Schools are seeking high academic performance and are less flexible in terms of grades and promotions. Discipline policies are more stringent and hard-to-teach students who "act out" or who react to frustration by exhibiting misconduct are not easily tolerated. The regular educator who is asked to tighten up academic standards is caught in the conflict of meeting the needs of students and carrying out school policies. This is an administrative problem as well, and requires a very good support system.

At the secondary level, students need to adjust to what may be perceived as a hostile, humiliating environment. This is where a good homeroom counseling program is as important as the academics taught. Working within small peer group activites, peer tutoring, and having stress-reducing experiences may deal with some of these concerns. Social skills training is an important part of the REI for regular teachers, and student teachers need to learn the interventions that make a program successful. The key is good support personnel and flexibility, so when one-on-one counseling is needed a student can be pulled out for special activities.

The question of teacher receptivity to change and how much can realistically and pragmatically be accomplished needs to be dealt with initially. The regular educator absolutely needs to be part of the planning process at the beginning so that there is a "buy in" to implementing a purposeful change in school and classroom organization. Along with good planning, teachers need adequate resources and materials. If technical assistance and other types of aid are not present, the regular educator might falter because of the overload. Regular teachers need time to observe, practice, interact, and discuss concerns about modifying curriculum or using new change strategies. Teachers want their new roles clarified with a clear description of what the job entails. The culture of the school is part of the change process. This is unlike a pure definition of P.L. 94–142 in which change was mandated mainly on the existing culture of regular education. The REI requires a change both in special education and in regular education. Special education can no longer view itself as a subculture of the school (Lilly, 1988); it must now become a part of the established order (Welch, 1989). Individuals must become familiar with change strategies, systems change, and how to function as a change agent utilizing the cultural perspective of both general and special education as a basis for change.

Teacher Education

Special training is needed for those who will be working in special situations. This includes:

1. Ways to communicate with students (information acquisition and observation)
2. Assessment of behavior management strategies
3. Assessment of intervention strategies
4. Different types of assessment including their strengths and limitations
5. Assessment of parent interaction
6. Ways of evaluating preschool children
7. Evaluation of children with low incidence handicaps such as epilepsy
8. Evaluating students with limited sensory integrity (i.e., deaf, blind, etc.)
9. Clinical interview techniques

Lead teachers, who are not special education teachers yet are proficient in academic assessment and can advise in the area of curriculum modification, are needed in each school. These individuals should be a part of student intervention procedures (Levels I, one-on-one, and Level II, team approach, page 134). Parent volunteers can also be of assistance, as well as paraprofessionals who are trained and who understand how to play the appropriate role.

The whole purpose of a prereferral team concept (movement between Levels I and III, page 134) is to exhaust all possibilities prior to referral to special education. A good consultative-preventative program can reduce the need for excessive assessment.

Child intervention or study teams that can be assembled for Level II as well as Level III (page 135) type activities are sometimes called IEP Teams in the public schools. Difficulties occur when there is lack of experience and training in group process or decision-making behavior on the part of the participants. Some individuals are not accustomed to working with a mixed group of professionals or with parents in a different kind of setting (outside of the classroom). Sometimes the process itself needs to be examined periodically to see where it is flawed.

Whether team decisions are better decisions than any one member of a team can make acting alone is debatable. This is especially important in the area of student placement (West & Cannon, 1988). Teams have to be careful that they do not become "rubber stamps" and go along with the ideas of one or two members. They have to remember that they are not just a committee brought together to review an issue.

Small teams appear to be more effective than larger groups. Lines of authority need to be clearly established. The more the members vary, the more need for tighter organization (Bardon, 1983).

Problems occur around poor communication among team members. Individuals need to be flexible and open, with good interpersonal skills. Training should focus on group process (decision and dynamics) skills and interdisciplinary interactions (Fleming & Fleming, 1983).

One problem is professional vocabulary. "Don't assume anything" is a good motto to remember. Acronyms can be annoying and extremely counterproductive if half the team does not understand what is being discussed. Obtuse vocabulary should also be avoided. Professionals should communicate their own discipline-specific vocabulary in as simplified a manner as possible. A common use of vocabulary, however, is needed for all who participate in teams.

Training in Interpersonal-Communication Skills

Idol and West (1987) suggest that in-service training should include the following communication skills:

1. Team members should learn to paraphrase statements made by others.
2. Good negotiation techniques are important.
3. How to deal with resistance, anger, fear, and other types of verbal abuse is important, as well as to understand nonverbal behavior and how to deal with aggressive behavior.
4. The ability to listen and wait and not appear to be judgmental is also important.
5. The use of videotaped feedback of meetings is a good training tool.
6. Team members need to learn how to use a collaborative approach to problem identification (West & Cannon, 1988).
7. Agreement by consensus is another good technique.

Training in Group Decision Making

1. The use of structured strategy is helpful. Know the rules of the game (White, Dittrich, & Lang, 1980).
2. The Nominal Group Technique (NGT) has been found useful (Delberq, Van de Ven, & Gustafson, 1975). In this approach idea generation and idea evaluation are separated (Kaiser & Woodman, 1985).
   a. Team members each offer one idea at a time and all ideas are recorded.
   b. Each idea is discussed in open groups.
   c. The ideas are then ranked by frequency from most to least important.
   d. The rank order is discussed.
   e. A final resolution is reached.

These techniques should be used with other more familiar approaches to decision making.

Monitoring Progress by Using a Single-Subject Methodology

Summative evaluation, such as pre- and posttesting, is descriptive as well as prescriptive (Becker, 1986). Formative evaluation, which depends on continuous and frequent analysis of student progress, lends itself readily to implementation and effectively facilitates the communication of information regarding progress in the content areas between disciplines. Single-subject methodology is the best validated form of formative evaluation (Barlow & Hersen, 1984; Tawney & Gast, 1984). This method links suggested intervention with changes in student behavior. It also provides for continuous monitoring of progress and incorporates a common measurement and methodology for all the disciplines involved, leading to more effective communication concerning student progress.

Curriculum-based assessment (CBA) is a good example of this approach (Tucker, 1985). CBA is valid, reliable, and can be used to monitor continuous academic progress. CBA information lends itself very well to graphing student progress (Deno, 1985). A great deal depends on valid and reliable samples of student performance. Personal computer technology has been used successfully to manage this kind of data (Nicassio et al., 1987).

Special Educator as Consultant-Collaborator

The special educator as consultant-collaborator has been clearly established (Idol, Paolucci-Whitcomb, & Nevin, 1986). Mainstreaming mildly handicapped students depends on how well the consultation process unfolds (Will, 1986). It is essentially a decision-making process where intervention strategies are selected as appropriate for particular students (Donaldson & Christiansen, 1990). This includes:

1. Possible changes in teaching strategies
2. Ways to implement behavior management
3. New or different ways to approach the learner

A decision-making model gives the participants (teachers, specialists) a framework for deciding what the state of the situation is and how to proceed from there. Instead of just "pulling the student out," educators now ask, "How can we change or improve what is there?" This could involve some part-time assistance, new teaching ideas and materials, both part-time assistance and new materials, or even full-time assistance may be necessary in some situations.

The implementation process of this concept involves consideration of the following:

1. Where and when does the student need special assistance? Is it in reading, writing, mathematics, and at what time of the day?
2. What kind of assistance is available to help the student in the regular class at that time of the day?
3. How can this assistance be best utilized?
4. After a period has elapsed, we must determine what is working and not working even with additional assistance, new approaches, and new materials.
5. Usually a multidisciplinary team monitors the program and makes the decisions, but this is not imperative.
6. A simple but effective communication system must be established between the participating entities with a specific timeline set for process and content evaluations.

The least intrusive type of assistance is suggested for maintaining the mildly handicapped student in the regular class. An important ingredient is the pre-referral process for students beginning to have serious problems. The consultation process should result in the following:

1. Reassessment of current programming
2. A process of smooth implementation of suggested alternative actions
3. Reduction in referrals to special education
4. Verification of the regular teachers program and any new program that may be needed or that has emerged as a result of the consultation-collaborative process
5. Students should be placed out of special education services to remedial services or less
6. A great degree of reduced "pull-out" activity for special services

Essential Consultation Skills

Along with experience, good intuition, and a sense of creativity, consultation skills are viewed as necessary in five main categories (West & Cannon, 1988):

1. Interactive communication
2. Personal characteristics
3. Issues involving belief, equity, and values
4. Collaborative problem solving
5. Assessment of consultative effectiveness

Other related skills for consultative effectiveness are those skills involved with technical know-how, being able to extrapolate essential elements and formulate good judgments from observation, and having the skills necessary to train others through in-service training and in one-to-one interactions.

The technical skills deemed important (Idol-Maestas & Ritter, 1985) focus on how to use and interpret the referral system, assessment procedures, behavior management, and being able to give appropriate instructional suggestions. Other skills include establishing a good rapport with parents, exhibiting overall consulting effectiveness, and being able to locate available instructional resources as well as professional edification information. Good consultants are able to assess a student's study skills as well as academic and behavior performance rapidly and provide this information with clarity and in a manner that enables the regular teacher, team, or any other configuration of professionals to make important decisions.

The term "good engaged time" is used to describe the student-teacher interaction, but it can also be used to describe the consultant-teacher interaction in terms of process and outcomes (Idol & West, 1987).

A consultant's time can be divided into several main components that include time spent on observation, meetings, or conferences; preparation of materials and planning; demonstration or direct instruction with students; doing administrative work such as record-keeping; direct conferencing to teachers (not involving children demonstration) or parents; and doing other job-related activities.

Observation alone requires a great deal of time as far as collecting data is concerned, and that includes observing the student informally, getting baseline information, doing ongoing observations, and checking as to the reliability of the information gathered (Nelson & Stevens, 1981).

Surmounting consultative resistance can also be a major factor, as cooperation is necessary for an effective program to emerge (Piersal & Gutkin, 1983).

Written Communication

Consultants need to become adept at preparing concise reports (formal and informal), which include plans, programs, evaluation reports, summaries of meetings, and graphic illustrations. A system has to be in place so this information can be routed appropriately, with certain individuals copied when necessary. Bringing good notes along is a good way of preparing for a verbal interaction with anyone. Good documentation is very important for consultant credibility and for indicating good organizational skills. It is important to keep good records of what has transpired in order to avoid confusion in the reporting process, or when divergent opinions about specific episodes present a problem.

The Consultation Sequence

The consultation sequence is described in four steps by Tindal and Taylor-Pendergast (1989):

1. Problem identification is the first step in the process and begins when the consultant meets with someone in need of services. Discussion centers around what exists, what has been done, and what now are suggested next steps. This could include more assessment, change in instruction or behavior management, etc., and whatever else is needed to formulate a plan. The next meeting period is specified.
2. Program development is the next step. A more comprehensive process may be needed, which involves the writing of specific interventions designed to respond to the problem areas identified. This includes suggested materials necessary and further elaboration of steps to be taken to change the program, new management ideas, and ways to document the process.
3. Program implementation should begin when there is a change in the way the teacher interacts with the student, new instructional routine, a management change, changes in terms of contact with parents, and the beginning of documentation of the process.
4. Program evaluation entails collecting data on the student and the process, and determining the value of the consultative interaction. This includes quantitative as well as qualitative data and focuses on the teacher and the student. What the teacher learned from the whole interaction is an important outcome.

The key factors in the whole process are:

1. Discern critical from noncritical student problems so too much time is not spent on a minor difficulty while a student with a really serious problem becomes critical.
2. Be well organized and allow clients to do most of the data gathering.
3. Provide quick, effective demonstrations of testing, instructional, or behavior management techniques.
4. Focus on the critical problem(s), perhaps changing only one thing at a time.
5. Strive for "good engagement time" and avoid being overly judgmental. An objective demeanor is important.
6. Arrive at a consensus regarding treatment suggestions so that everyone knows clearly what the plan is designed to accomplish.
7. Follow up as soon as possible; teachers don't like to be avoided for long periods of time.
8. Document everything continuously and keep a log, if possible, similar to nurses notes.

Sometimes a plan has to be posed as an option, giving the advantages as well as the disadvantages, and let the teacher decide on its merits in order to overcome initial resistance. It is sometimes necessary to avoid strong arguments for a particular idea.

A good part of the consultation process involves establishing rapport with other teachers by being accepted as a competent professional (Heron & Kimball, 1988). This confidence and trust has to be earned over time. When it is earned, confidence in oneself will become stronger. Being viewed as an expert goes along with exhibiting good teaching skills and showing respect for others. These interpersonal and communicative skills are requisite to successful consultation. The consultant should not promise cures, but be a good listener and at the same time respond to the stated concerns of the teachers. Keep personal feelings or prejudices out of the discussions. Center the discussion around problem solving and be flexible yet systematic, showing a sincere interest. Consultants are not expected to be "expert" in all areas and should indicate a lack of knowledge or not knowing the answer instead of trying to "fake it." Success should be defined in different ways, giving credit where and when it is due. It is often better to play a behind-the-scenes role than be viewed as a star.

There is an increasing trend toward using consultative services for maintaining handicapped children in the regular classroom in keeping with the tenets of the regular education initiative (REI). The push toward increasing normalization and the continuous questioning of the efficacy of the "pull-out" model are factors that call for alternative service approaches (Graden, Casey, & Bonstrom, 1985; Polsgrove & McNeil, 1989).

Research on the effectiveness of the consultation approach has produced encouraging results (Medway & Updyke, 1985). There seems to be a clear positive effect toward modifying the behavior of all who participate in a consultant-type program. Graden, Casey, and Bonstrom (1985) suggest that a good program can significantly reduce referrals to special education.

Ecological Perspective

The ecological perspective (Heron & Kimball, 1988) views the process of providing consultation services within the environment in which it occurs. This involves staffing patterns, school disciplinary policies, curriculum goals, an analysis of the support system, as well as how the system is organized (i.e., laissez-faire, line and staff, etc.). The school's collaborative arrangements with agencies, educational and otherwise, is important to understand and provides an additional orientation by which the consultative process can be evaluated. Program effectiveness needs to be assessed on the basis of student outcomes and as an ecological service system.

The idea is to view consultation within the context of the natural environment and as a complex process, rather than only as a person-to-person interaction. The greater concept is to improve services to all children in the school within the context of the least restrictive environment.

Special educators and regular educators need a common-ground understanding of the language and procedures that are utilized in schools in order for a more effective collaboration to be developed in dealing with students with special learning needs. Effective communication begins when there is an understanding of each other's philosophical and theoretical basis for educating students. The common expression is to understand the modus operandi of each other's behavior and intentions. This understanding is vital, not only for joint responsibility for students with special needs but also for gaining each other's respect and the understanding that the students' needs come first.

School Support Teams

There is a trend toward schools providing help to all students with learning problems—even if they are not legally classified as "handicapped." Many schools are setting up "instructional support teams" for students who are determined to be having difficulty in learning. The school support teams may be made up of administrators, the students' teachers, special educators, and other support personnel. The teams meet to discuss the student's learning problems, come up with next steps, and, finally, determine with a strategy to help him or her succeed in school. If the intervention fails after a trial period, the student can always be referred to the special education system for formal evaluation.

There are many students who are not "handicapped" but who are having problems in learning and who get referred to special education because there is little informal evaluation or programming available in their schools. There is a need for earlier intervention,

without the formal and expensive evaluation procedures that are involved in special education placement. The idea is to give students instructional interventions that will help them succeed in a regular classroom. This places a greater degree of responsibility on the regular teacher. The effect of the total program is to reduce the common use of stigmatizing labels, such as educable mentally retarded or learning disabled, that are used to describe a student's handicapping condition. Instead, students could be labeled only as "eligible" for special education services, or "not eligible," but their education plans would reflect "learning goals" specific to their needs.

WORKING WITH SUPPORT PERSONNEL: AIDES, PARAPROFESSIONALS, TUTORS, AND VOLUNTEERS

The most effective program is one that is based on the premise that initially the support person and the learner must establish a friendly and helping relationship where both understand each other's role. Paraprofessionals and volunteers should be warm and responsive. If they are flexible and able to adapt to the needs of the students, a feeling of trust between the participants should emerge. The students then gain a sense of participation in the whole process and soon learn that although learning may not always be fun, there are rewards for attempting, as well as completing, the required tasks.

It is important for the support personnel to remember that the student may not have been completely successful in previous learning environments for extended periods of time. Since failure may have been a part of the student's academic life and in most cases was carried over to the home, the tutor must consciously strive for successes even if they are very small to begin with. Quick and dramatic results are rare. The learner, paraprofessional, teacher, and parents should understand this concept so that the program will not break down because of overexpectation. Neither the parents nor the support person must foster dependency by doing too much for the students. The students have to learn to cope with frustration.

Students who have failed may have experienced such negatives as threats, embarrassment, conflict, boredom, or illness, to name only a few. They may have been held in low esteem by peers, teachers, parents, and siblings; therefore, it is not unreasonable for the tutor or volunteer to face some initial resistance as the students begin to evalute themselves against a standard for success. The students may lash out verbally to try the tutor's sense of loyalty and trust. It is at this point that both the teacher and the support person focus on the students' strengths as well as work on areas that need to be improved.

The students may not be communicative with strangers at first. Through careful observation, the paraprofessional has to know the students' interests and reaction to humor, as well as when to reward and offer praise. If the support personnel consistently plan and provide successful experiences, the students' attitude should become more positive, with concomitant improvement in their acquisition of knowledge.

Concerned parents and educators are setting up, or seeking, supportive services that will respond to the need for a broader approach to reading and other programs with students. This development is in part due to the fact that teachers need additional support as they become involved in the process of trying to regulate programs in keeping with individual learners' rate and style of learning. Teachers who are concerned with truly individualizing instruction recognize that there are different types of individuals who can support them effectively with students who require more attention and more specific kinds of remedial and corrective instruction.

Teacher-directed support personnel (e.g., tutors, paraprofessionals, and volunteers) provide an additional alternative to the general classroom management of both small and large groups. They provide an opportunity for the learner to become involved in a personalized manner with an individual other than the classroom teacher who will respond, on a one-to-one basis in most situations, to individual needs. The support person who is adequately trained and motivated will invariably respond to the emotional, as well as the educational, needs of the learner.

Before designating the paraprofessionals to a specified activity, the faculty should conduct a needs assessment to accurately pinpoint critical areas where additional personnel may need to be utilized. The use of support personnel can be divided into three classifications:

1. *Simultaneous Instruction:* Support persons in this class provide simultaneous support to the ongoing general classroom instruction of the teacher and may be called a *parallel teacher.*
2. *Task Specific Instruction:* Persons in this class would have expertise to work at specified tasks such as specific skill development in reading or math.

3. *Enrichment:* Persons in this class usually have skills or talents that would enable them to work with a wider range of students within a more flexible schedule of activities.

The competencies of the paraprofessionals and volunteers, as indicated on checklists, through questionnaires, during interviews, or in letters of recommendation, should be carefully analyzed by the administrators and selected faculty. After the strengths of the volunteers or paraprofessionals have been ascertained and the school-based needs have been determined, a training program for the supportive personnel may need to be planned. The training for different types of support personnel (e.g., paraprofessionals, aides, tutors, or volunteers) should be planned within the framework of how each group can most effectively be used.

Paraprofessionals will usually have the same time restraints as the teachers and are often full-time employees. They have to be aware of the general goals and curriculum of the school. They can work within a classroom with a teacher, function as a tutor in a resource room, or provide other specific services within the school.

Tutors have more mobility within the school and flexibility in terms of when and where they can work with students. Tutors may range from classroom peers, to older students teaching younger students, to certified personnel.

Volunteers' commitment to a school may not be long term, and their services are usually free; therefore, they are usually most productive in specified jobs. A successful volunteer program requires a coordinator who monitors the training and scheduling of the volunteers to meet the ongoing needs of the school. Volunteers can be a valuable asset to enrichment programs within a school for such activities as field trips, art, drama, and library projects.

Those assisting a teacher should know what to do, when to do it, where to do it, and how it should be done. The following should be considered in orientation sessions for supportive personnel:

1. The confidentiality of student records
2. How to keep the student on task
3. How to repeat or review material in a successful, nonjudgmental manner
4. When to praise and types of appropriate reward systems
5. How to grade materials without writing negative remarks or drawing unhappy faces on papers
6. How to teach and promote good study habits
7. How to interpret directions on materials

8. How to record and monitor progress
9. How to spot-check progress daily, weekly, and monthly
10. How to interpret developmental sequences of skills or subject level sequences to know where to drop back if an activity fails
11. How to use audiovisual materials
12. How to work with students who may have special needs, disabilities, or handicaps that would require a modification of communication (e.g., for deaf or hard of hearing) or materials to be used

WORKING WITH SCHOOL PSYCHOLOGISTS

The main role of psychologists in schools is psychological-educational assessment. Their role is guaranteed by the mandates of P.L. 94–142 as part of the multidisciplinary team. The psychologist can bring other skills to the support system.

1. Provide a good background in normal child development and an understanding of the general parameters of different types of handicapping conditions.
2. Function as a guide to how the physical environment of the school and home can enhance the life of the students.
3. Bring a description of the overall impact on learning that results from specific types of deficits.
4. Give precise assessment to students in areas that go beyond the assessment used by teachers and special educators.
5. Be a consultant to teachers and staff on an ongoing basis.
6. Provide a research base for determining assessment and program effectiveness.
7. Apprise all concerned with up-to-date information based on acceptable research regarding handicapping condition and programmatic considerations.

The psychologist's role is shifting from that of a tester to that of a learning person. The role in the school is also changing from one of special or incidental testing and crisis intervention to one of a school assistance resource person and support team member.

WORKING WITH SPEECH PATHOLOGISTS

Speech pathologists work with children who have speech production types of problems such as:

Articulation Difficulties (including distortion, submission, or omission of sounds)
Substitution
Problems with Voice Quality
Primary or Secondary Stuttering

They also work with students who have language disorders in areas of expression, reception, comprehension, and inner language.

Different types of children in schools have language problems. The speech teacher may work with different numbers of children on a one-on-one basis or in small groups.

An important role for the speech therapist is one of consultant to all teachers where they can be utilized beyond their "case load" responsibilities. Teachers need to know what to look for, what to do, and what not to do. When to refer and how to work with parents are also important factors.

WORKING WITH PARENTS

Parents need to understand that few children have only a single disability. It would be simple if a learner only had a reading problem, or only was hyperactive; but learning is a complex process, and learning difficulties overlap. It is therefore difficult to answer the simple question so often asked by parents: "What is wrong with my child?"

In many situations parents of students with learning and behavior problems have become not advocates but adversaries of the school. A primary reason for this involves poor, or negative, communication between home and school and, more important, a lack of parent access to school personnel—who can assuage fears, indicate a rationale for what is being done, and include the home as part of the entire process of education. The first assumption is that all parents, regardless of socioeconomic status or cultural background, are concerned about their children. Few people will do for a child what the child's parents will do. For example, many parents want to know how to stimulate language and conceptual thinking in their children. The child-parent bond will help to support the parent's natural role as teacher and model for the child. Parents have a right to be told the truth and to be given alternatives.

Parents' Impact on Learning

Parents have a strong impact on their children's learning. Positive learning attitudes and skills that include curiosity, self-initiated behavior, persistence, and attention to and completion of tasks are a part of what the learner receives from the home and family. Therefore, any training for parents that aids them in gearing activities in the home to developing these characteristics in their children is useful.

Student learning is positively affected by

1. Behavior and statements of parents and other family members concerning the way the student feels about learning and how he or she develops learning strategies
2. Improving the family's capabilities to provide in the home the type of learning environment that develops motivation for learning and expectation for success
3. The family's concern for the student's health, nutrition, and social and psychological development
4. The parents' influence on the student in terms of motivation to attend school, to participate in school activities, and to strive for success
5. The school's responsiveness to the parents and their needs as well as to their concerns about the needs of their children

Parents play a critical role in the development of the student's cognitive or intellectual abilities as well as in providing an environment that is conducive to good physical and mental health. They help the learner to

1. Develop an interest in and a motivation for learning.
2. Use language in the process of communication and to glean meaning from words and experiences.
3. Organize the world in terms of concrete-functional and abstract relationships.
4. Gain satisfaction from achievement as well as to develop a sense of philosophical frustration.

Parents of Adolescents

Parents of the adolescent with learning problems are themselves growing older, perhaps less patient and with diminishing stamina. Some feel life is passing them by. Many have other children and are resentful of still needing to respond to every detail of one adolescent's life. Some have given up hope (e.g., he or she is just not "growing out of it," or the extra programs don't seem to be helping). Parents need a "sounding board"—someone who will listen and not commiserate with them but who will revitalize them and encourage them to "keep going."

Siegel cogently sums it up (Siegel, 1970, pp. 37, 38):

Finally, the parent and child come face to face with reality. There are no more illusions of normalcy such as "attending school" and "doing homework." Undoubtedly, the tasks which confront the grown exceptional child are more formidable than those which he faced when he was younger. To put it differently, the same exceptional child who did not fail in attending school, passing spelling tests, joining Boy Scout groups, getting promoted, etc., may nevertheless be unsuccessful in getting and holding a job, dating, marriage and military service. Seen in this light, the currently topical criterion for public education—relevancy—takes on an increased dimension here. For the younger exceptional child, his educational experiences are either relevant or irrelevant, and precisely to the degree which they have enabled him to grow up successfully within the framework of his specific diagnostic limitations.

As the adolescent grows older, he or she may become more difficult to lead or control. He or she may not so easily be forced to comply with parental wishes and may even develop facades and subterfuges where he or she is thinking one thing and behaving in another way. The problem for parents is to know when to let go, take a risk even if the consequences are less than good. Students will learn from failure, and they should be allowed to fail as long as there is someone there to stand by them.

Parents must be careful not to develop a negative mental set. They have to be continuously reminded to put the child into the context of the family and consider the totality of attributes as well as negatives. There will be surprises and great moments; these need to be emphasized during times of depression and despair. Think of it as a partnership in adjustment. Everyone is expected to do his or her own part, not just one person doing everything.

Parent-School Involvement

The first contact by school personnel with parents should begin the process of shared responsibility and the establishment of trusting relationships that will invariably benefit the student. On those occasions when parents, guardians, or members of the community are involved with school personnel to discuss the needs of the students, first impressions are often crucial to successful follow-up.

Teachers must deal with a whole set of parent-school interrelated variables. It is through the analysis of how these sets of variables impinge upon each other that educators can begin to focus on developing important priority areas. Allowing parents to participate in different aspects of programming may lead to improved communication between home and school and could result in a new commitment on both sides to the student's progress and to a clearer delineation of the goals and objectives of the program. If trust is established, and if the parents are actively involved in the educational process as informed consumers, there will be less apathy on their side. In a real sense, parents can act as buffers against poor relationships between the community and the school.

School personnel often complain that parents are inaccessible and not interested in the needs and problems of the schools. Educators have to deal with the fact that there are factors that discourage parents of exceptional children, particularly from minority populations, from becoming involved in school affairs. Those factors that include their fear of rejection, as well as the mores related to the whole concept of the handicapped in their culture, should be considered early during the year, so that school personnel can insure successful experiences at their first attempts at parent involvement. It is crucial that successful activities be planned at the beginning of the year so that parents will not become discouraged and give up.

One limiting factor for all parents is that of time to be available for school concerns. This is not uncommon in the lives of parents who work. Some parents are willing to become involved in facets of the school program, as long as they do not detract from other home and work responsibilities. Even though individuals feel that parents should make sacrifices for their children, the fact remains that more parents will become involved if the school activity does not conflict with what they perceive to be more desirable, important, and sometimes necessary activities.

Another limiting factor is that of a personal reward for involvement. When parents sense that genuine use is being made of their time and that they really are needed and important, their self-esteem is enhanced. Parents enjoy and will work in programs and attend activities where the need is clear and respect is extended to them for helping to respond to the need.

STRATEGIES FOR PROMOTING PARENT-SCHOOL INVOLVEMENT

School staff need to persist and develop a variety of strategies to involve reluctant parents or community members in school activities. Unfortunately schools have become impersonal. Students' school histories are computerized, and the once-a-year open house just isn't enough. The following suggestions are given to aid those who will be working with parents:

1. Use parents who can attract other parents. Locate the people in the community who can turn out crowds and let them invite or urge participation.
2. Ask someone to host an open house for their friends and neighbors and then take school personnel to them. Discussing school concerns face-to-face in small groups may take time, but it builds trusting relationships.
3. Use controversial issues or critical community needs to provide forums (e.g., student assessment, vandalism, dropout rate, drugs, etc.).
4. Get parents to school through their children. If the child is "on stage" at the right time and transportation is available, someone in the family may come to the school.
5. Use settings, other than the school, that are available and familiar to the community (e.g., churches, clubs, community centers).
6. Build involvement around parents' abilities. Through music, the arts, crafts, and talents (e.g., story telling, cooking, landscaping, sports, etc.), develop parent-initiated activities that will promote involvement in the schools.
7. Advertise school activities early enough to allow parents to schedule time off from jobs or to arrange for child care. Send follow-up announcements and use a variety of print and news media (e.g., letters, flyers, posters, announcements in community papers, radio, etc.).
8. Provide refreshments. Some parents must use lunch time for conferences or come to evening meetings directly from work. Coffee, sodas, juice, a sandwich, fruit, or dinners may promote larger attendance.
9. Plan parent-teacher interaction within the framework of the cultural values of the community. There may be a pattern for how things are accomplished in certain communities. Parents are not a homogeneous group and require careful study and understanding.
10. Meet specific needs by delivering well planned and executed workshops or seminars for parents. Be flexible and allow for modifications in format and delivery. Working with parents requires training and experience, especially when dealing with the kind of strategies that are needed at home to produce student growth.
11. Involve the parent in school activities when it is feasible. Match the skills of the volunteer to the job requirement. If the parent can volunteer time in

the school, provide training and experiences in the following:

   a. One-on-one or small-group tutoring

   b. Recreation, music, arts, and crafts activities

   c. Making materials that can be used in the classroom (e.g., worksheets, mounting pictures, reading material on audio tapes, games)

   d. Supervising students using audiovisual equipment in the resource center, library, or classroom

   e. Small-group activities that provide someone for a student to talk to or for story telling, etc.

   f. Clerical work—duplicating, typing

   g. Health services within the training and school board guidelines

   h. Community liaison for school projects

12. If the parents cannot come to the school, but have expressed an interest in providing assistance, send the task to them. If the materials are sent home, the parents can cut out pictures, type, telephone other parents, make bookshelves, etc.

13. Be open to innovation and creative means of parent involvement. While traditional modes of working with parents work in most cases, new approaches may be necessary wiith parents of students with special needs. Guidelines are generally designed to guarantee only a minimum level of participation.

Parent-Teacher Conferences

Parents and school personnel will have many types of interaction during the school year. Some communication is short, less formal, and involves a specific area of concern (e.g., telephone calls, notes, forms, etc.). At other times more formal and carefully planned conferences will be scheduled. These interactions require preplanning, record-keeping, and follow-up. The following general suggestions apply to all conferences. The Individual Education Plan (IEP) conferences discussed in the next section specify parents' rights and due process considerations.

BEFORE THE CONFERENCE

1. Review diagnostic data regarding the student's present level of functioning.

2. Be prepared to discuss the student's strengths as well as areas that need attention.

3. Prepare handouts to be used during the meeting.

4. Arrange a setting that will be comfortable and conducive to good interaction.

5. Be prepared for parent overreaction to an unpleasant situation or for a confrontation when students fail and have alternatives available for resolving problems.

6. Keep in mind that the student is going to worry about parent-teacher meetings. If the student isn't involved in the conference, explain why the meeting was scheduled.

7. Make a list of any pertinent data that will be needed from the parent.

8. Set up a system for recording information during the meeting and/or immediately afterward. Keep a log or anecdotal record of home visits and parent conferences. A checklist of all of the students' names, as well as date and reason for contact with parents, will provide an accurate record of which parents have and have not been contacted, will avoid misunderstandings, and will promote more effective follow-up. Develop an interview guide such as Form 7-5 and a quick self-assessment inventory of the meeting (Form 7-6).

DURING THE CONFERENCE

1. Put the parents at ease. Parents know more about their children than they are often willing to tell. Parents are not completely in the dark. They generally know when something is wrong. Information has to be elicited. Don't assume that it will be forthcoming. Information about birth history, the first few months of a child's life, as well as early school history and family relationships will provide an initial opportunity for good interaction between teacher and parents.

2. Present information in a concise manner, using a handout or other visual reference as a basis for discussion. If possible, have examples of the student's work, both good and poor. Use these examples as a basis for judgments and recommendations for further programming.

3. Do not use educational or testing jargon that is noncommunicative to parents. Parents want information in language they can understand. Define terms such as validity, correlation, and criterion-referenced assessment.

4. Function as a good and understanding listener. Permit the parents or guardian to express their fears, concerns, and goals for the student openly.

5. Most parents of adolescent children with learning problems have seen many different kinds of professionals before this meeting, and the things they were told may not check out with current findings. Discuss the types of examinations and records, if available, of visual, audiological, pediatric, gener-

MANN-SUITER-McCLUNG PARENT CONFERENCE GUIDE

STUDENT _____ DATE _____

PARENT(S)/GUARDIAN _____ TEACHER _____

Birth History:

Preschool Experiences:

Previous Grade Levels & Teachers

Notable Concerns:

Medical Concerns:

Non-School Evaluations:

_____Visual   _____Audiological   _____Pediatric/Medical
_____Neurological   _____Psychological   _____Speech and Language
_____Educational Tests

Non-School Assistance:

_____tutoring   _____counseling   _____other

Parent(s) statement of child's:

strengths _____
weaknesses _____
study habits _____
feeling about school _____

Family Information:

Comments:

MANN-SUITER-McCLUNG SELF-ANALYSIS OF PARENT-TEACHER MEETING

STUDENT _____ DATE _____

PARENT(S)/GUARDIAN _____ TEACHER _____

	Yes	No
1. Did the parent(s) leave with a sense of satisfaction?	_____	_____
2. Did I leave with a sense of satisfaction?	_____	_____
3. Was there parent-teacher agreement regarding the student's abilities and problems	_____	_____
4. Did all agree upon the course of action?	_____	_____
5. Are the differences reconcilable?	_____	_____
6. Do I need to follow-up with the parents?	_____	_____
7. Am I satisfied about what is being done for the student?	_____	_____
8. Did I learn anything new?	_____	_____

9. Is there anything that must be done immediately? _____ _____

10. Is there other follow-up that needs to be done? _____ _____

Comments:

al medical, neurological, psychological, speech and language, or educational evaluation.

6. Discuss any current supplementary tutoring, counseling, or other outside-of-school assistance the parent has gotten for the child. Parents often help and support each other through professional groups.

7. Emphasize that commitment is a critical concept in the development of individualized educational programming and is a dual responsibility. Parents in a larger sense are also accountable to their children and to the school.

8. Obtain the parents' consent for what the school is attempting to do in terms of placement and programming.

9. Know the limits of the areas within which you are competent to give advice. When parents wish advice on other matters, refer them to appropriate individuals.

10. Set up a system or line of communication that guarantees accessibility. Specify when you will be available for future conferences or informal discussion by telephone, and what types of written communication they should expect. Parents should know who to contact to get information about any aspect of the education program. When changes in programming are put into effect, parents should be notified so that they can anticipate reactions and let school personnel know about any untoward effects.

11. Promote parent advocacy through collaborative, as well as independent, action. Permit the parents to indicate the things they can and want to do. Learning disabled students need continuous reinforcement from the parents to be successful in school.

12. Involve the parents as ongoing observers of behavior at home. They can provide important information in the following areas:

    a. The learner's attitude toward school life, the teacher, and peers
    b. Study habits and attitude toward specific subjects
    c. Health information, especially if the student is receiving medical or psychological services. Report specific information regarding allergies, chronic conditions, or the use of medication
    d. Hobbies, sports, or other interests where the student has a strength or is meeting success
    e. Sibling and other family relations
    f. Recreational or other types of reading
    g. When vacations will occur

    h. When there is an unusual break in the student's schedule or daily pattern (e.g., visits by relatives, baby-sitters, for an extended period of time)

13. Always conclude a conference with a positive statement of agreement on new objectives or steps to be taken to remedy some concern of the parents.

14. Ascertain how the parents will interpret the student to neighbors, brothers and sisters, and grandparents. Clarify and summarize the main points of the student's progress.

Parents' Role in Individual Educational Programming

Many students with learning and behavior problems are in regular classrooms and may not require additional special services. Parent-teacher relationships are usually direct and only on occasion require involvement by administrators or other educators. However, the Education for All Handicapped Children Act of 1975 (P.L. 94–142), Section 504 of the Vocational Rehabilitation Act of 1973, state statutes, and judicial decisions now provide guidelines for students who will be receiving special education services through local and state agencies. These regulations directly involve the students and their parents or guardians. The students' teachers (regular teachers and specialists or resource personnel) will become involved in the development and implementation of an individualized Educational Plan (IEP) for each student receiving special help. P.L. 94–142 defines an IEP as: "...a written statement... developed in any meeting by a representative of the Local Education Agency who shall be qualified to provide, or supervise the provision of... instruction..., the teacher, the parent or guardian... and when appropriate (the) child ..."(Sec. 602 [19]).

Parents have a specific role to play in the educational programming for their child. They can act as advocates and information sources. In the assessment stages they can provide input and challenge observations by support personnel that conflict with their observations. They can secure copies of assessments and records and request outside evaluations if necessary. They can be involved in every aspect of programming for their learning disabled children, including identification, diagnosis, and the development of individual educational plans. Both regular and special education teachers need to know different ways of dealing with the emotional and intellectual needs of parents of the handicapped. They have a right to understand issues and to strive for guaranteed access, as well as to influence the planning, policies, and implementation of the educational program.

Parents are not passive receptors to the individualized educational plan. Before the initiation of the evaluation process, the parents must know why the testing is being done and what their rights will be during conferences and throughout every other phase of the development of the IEP. Parents can do the following:

1. Attend each meeting where the IEP will be planned, finalized, or reviewed.
2. Have access to their child's records and secure copies.
3. Ask for a reevaluation or seek an independent evaluation.
4. Receive a written copy of the IEP.
5. Participate and provide information during IEP conferences (medical, family relationships, study habits at home, previous educational experiences).
6. Express fears and concerns and ask questions about the language used to describe their child's level of functioning, about grading, promotion, graduation requirements, etc.
7. Request an interpreter or translator if necessary.
8. Request a due process hearing if dissatisfied with the process or the content of the IEP.

The following are specific components of the IEP and areas of parental involvement within the IEP process:

1. Statement of the Child's Present Level of Educational Performance: Parents will receive specific information on the child's demonstrated skill mastery, grade levels, and performance. At this point, clarification and definition of terms may be required by the parents.
2. Prioritized Statement of Annual and Long-Range Goals and Annual Short-Term Instructional Objectives: Parents should be sure that they fully understand the educational goals for their children and what they can do to help reach these goals. A reasonable expectation of what the student can achieve after one year in the program will be discussed. The team will also consider the child's past learning rate, observable skills, and the behavior to be demonstrated.
3. A Statement of the Specific Special Education and Related Services to Be Provided: The parents' responsibilities for at-home followup should be clearly delineated. The parents can question the expertise of those giving services and should find out who will coordinate multiple services. The par-

ent has the right to know whether one teacher will answer questions about all services or if each individual person must be consulted.

4. Statement of Extent to Which the Student Will Be Able to Participate in Least Restrictive Environment Programs, or Percent of Time in the Regular Classroom: Parents need to know whom to talk to in the school about the students' progress, what the regular or special teachers will be teaching individually, and where those subject areas or special services will show up on a periodic evaluation or report card. Detailed lesson plans are not as critical to a parent as a realistic overview of what the students will be learning, when, and why. The parents need this outline in order to be able to ask the students and the teachers about the students' progress. Parents are also vitally concerned about the pressures the students will face as they spend more time in a regular classroom with achieving peers. For this reason, the students' strengths and potential for success should be documented in order that they maintain self-confidence as well as academic progress. Parents should be given suggestions of what to do if the students have a minor setback in school (e.g., low grade on a test).
5. Specification of Projected Dates for the Initiation of Services and the Anticipated Duration of the Services: Parents should have access to good records that document the progress of the services. If it is evident that services will be either terminated or extended, the information leading to the decisions should not be a shock to the children or their parents.
6. Recommendations for Specific Procedures/Techniques/Materials: The parents are concerned about what to do at home to help the student. They are equally concerned that the curriculum for their children provide academic skills in keeping with the learner's potential.
7. Evaluation Criteria, Procedures, and Schedules: Tests, dates for testing, and methods of evaluation will be discussed.

How Parents Can Help at Home

It is difficult for most of us to imagine the degree and amount of failure perceived by many students. The academic and social world is keyed on competition and success, to the extent that many students find no arena in which they can do well. Schoolwork is beyond their capability and competition in recreational activities is too great. Other students may make fun of them or simply ignore them. Feelings of frustration and inner conflict can result from this. These feelings, in turn, detract from further performance, leading to a vicious cycle of failure and decreased efficiency. This cycle must be broken or prevented from occurring. Thus, opportunities for success and good feelings become crucial. There must be opportunity to contribute to a cause and have personal victories.

The parents must be assured that a student with learning difficulties can be helped by informed parents and teachers. In planning for the students' needs, the parents or guardians and the educators who will be involved with the students should attend to the following key areas:

1. The environment at home and at school may require more structure and some accommodation.
2. Controlling the learner may involve more consistent, yet loving, firmness. All those involved with the learner should consciously set good examples and fair standards.
3. Provision should be made at home and at school for successful experiences that will improve the learner's self-esteem. Each child is an individual and concern should be for his or her strengths as well as the weaknesses. Each student is special and has a unique way of learning.

STRUCTURING THE ENVIRONMENT

Children with learning difficulties respond to individuals in much the same way that other children do, but as a group they appear to function more effectively in more structured settings at home and in school. It appears that they often need more attention, more firmness, more clarity of instructions, more predictable outcomes, and more opportunity for success. They cannot be overloaded with too much to do at one time. Parents often fail to take these things into consideration.

Parents must become accustomed to the wide range in performance and the swings in mood that often occur. On some days the child will be alert, cooperative, and able to master the skills taught and on others he or she will be inept, sloppy, and remote, and learning unexpectedly appears to be gone. Sometimes these children are abnormally sensitive to minor changes in the environment: a visitor, the weather, or some new noise. They may also, on some days, be supersensitive to their failures and frustrations and appear to have lost all self-confidence.

Just as the school is structured, the children's home life should be structured. There should be a consistent wake-up time each morning and bedtime each night. Anxious children can be calmed if they know that things happen in a certain order. For example, bed-time is generally after bathing. If possible, meals should be served at regular times and TV, play, homework, etc., scheduled for specific times. Some students with learning problems have a very poor concept of time. They benefit from an orderly day. As they gain an appreciation of time and the progression of events during a day, they tend to become more self-directed.

ORGANIZING TIME

Organizing the children's time can be a problem. Parents run the gamut from those who act as the social directors and car-pool drivers, scheduling every minute, to those who leave the children sitting endlessly in front of a television set. Certainly, during days when school is in session, parents have to be aware of the balance between play or recreation and time for homework. For many students with learning problems, prioritizing and completing homework is a disaster. Parents and teachers must carefully monitor the amount of time required for homework and the types of assignments that the children can successfully complete at home. Teaching the students how to study and presenting new material should be a function of school and not forced on the parents. The parents' commitment should be to provide guidance, support, and review for material presented in the class.

COMPLETING TASKS

Parents should avoid asking their children to perform complex tasks at first. Responsibilities in the home should be within the capabilities of the students. Successful completion of one or two tasks for a few days or a week (e.g., placing silverware on the table and walking the dog) are more help to the parents and satisfying to the children than constant reminders of unfinished activities or chores.

Sudden decisions are often frustrating to the children. Instead of asking for immediate responses to questions (e.g., "What do you want for breakfast?") parents can help the children decide by giving them choices. It is often difficult for an impatient adult to wait for a child to make decisions.

Parents need to know that children with special needs will make greater demands on their time, energy, and understanding. Although some students need extra attention and effort, parents must be careful to budget some time for activities that do not involve the child. They need their "own time" to reduce some of the frustration and feelings of helplessness that prevail when energies are spent continually over the concern of a particular child.

Families can enjoy many pleasant recreation and learning experiences together, such as trips to the zoo or a museum. However, there will be times when the children will be left with neighbors, friends, or relatives. Such occasions should be planned and carefully explained to the children. Many learning disabled students cannot tolerate the unexpected. They find solace in overorderliness and feel secure only when situations are quite reliably predictable. Highly distractible or hyperactive children are often unable to function properly or at all when presented with a stimulating new situation, such as a field trip or a new teacher. Parents must prepare the students for new situations.

UNDERSTANDING FEELINGS

Parents as a group go through developmental stages upon learning of an abnormality that suggests an imperfect child (Solnit & Stark, 1961; Kubler-Ross, 1981; Buscaglia, 1975; Moses, 1979). Some even go through a kind of mourning for the loss of a fantasy child. It is thought that these stages act as defense mechanisms and help to reduce anxiety. Both parents may not be going through the same stages at the same time. The stages are:

1. *Denial:* First parents experience a sense of shock, then respond with denial that is manifested in a variety of feelings, such as not paying attention to symptoms or professionals and postponing attending to the problems at hand. Denial seems to encompass the concept of flight; "I'm going to see another specialist." "They are all out to make money." Some experience isolation: "No one cares about my feelings"; and guilt: "Why me?" or "What did I do wrong?"

2. *Bargaining:* After the diagnosis is accepted, thoughts turn to how the problem can be "cured." "There certainly must be a cure or a treatment if I can only find the right doctor or teacher."

3. *Anger:* After initial cooperation, the guilt and frustration sets in with resultant anger: "Why can't the school do more?" Anger leads to blame: "You make him work harder!"; or fear: "Is it retardation or a disease?" Fear and envy sometimes go together: "It's just not fair." "Some people don't know how lucky they are."

4. *Depression:* After guilt and the feeling of helplessness, the parent may become depressed. Depression often results in apathy.

5. *Acceptance:* Finally, many parents learn to cope with the problem. "There is always a possibility of change, but reality has to be recognized." "One does not give up and there are brighter moments." "So he or she has learning problems; is there anything I can do? We will just have to work it through."

Some of the children with learning disorders exhibit impulsive and other noxious behavior. In our society we have been taught to believe that a child's behavior is the result of upbringing, and when the child fails to meet society's expectations, not only the child but also the parents are to be blamed. Some parents are their own harshest critics. They blame their own child's failure on themselves. Some parents feel a vague sense of guilt about possible hereditary factors, or defective genes, and sometimes point out the same unusual behavior in a spouse or relative. This behavior is essentially pointless. Parents, for the most part, cannot take the blame for the impulsive, disruptive, aggressive, or antisocial acts of children with learning problems. Parents can, however, provide the children with the best model as well as good consistent training. At the opposite extreme are the parents who refuse to recognize their children's difficulties and feel that eventually "everything will be ok" or that they will "grow out of it."

Most frustrating to parents is the variability of behavior from one day or hour to another. This causes parents to feel "he could do better if he tried." At times, the child many be impudent, attention seeking, silly, or negativistic, behaving in any number of ways irritating and upsetting to teachers, peers, and parents. Regardless of age, overactive children are often unpopular with other children at home because of their unpleasant behavior or inability to compete. Because they are unpopular, they may continually be on the defensive. They may develop a short temper. When this is added to feelings of failure, they may develop an abrasive personality. The students may get into frequent fights at home, and other parents may exclude them from playing with their children. Instead of fighting, some children try to be the neighborhood clown. They try to win friends by giving them candy, money, or gifts that are out of proportion. Sometimes they even steal goods to give them away. It is difficult at these times to remember that the children are not willfully malicious; they are not the monsters they sometimes pretend to be. Teachers and parents must believe that sensible external controls, wisely imposed, will gradually take over and become internal controls and stay with the learners throughout life.

A learning disability does not justify lax controls and leniency. Some children feel that inconsistent discipline really means that their parents don't care enough about them to make them behave correctly. However, parents should not punish children for behavior that they cannot control, like clumsiness, excessive activity, short attention span, impatience, impulsiveness, or fear of trying something new.

The following are a few guidelines for parents:

1. Don't threaten punishment that is never carried out.
2. Make the punishment fit the act, and punish the same amount for the same act. Don't make a mountain out of a molehill.
3. Punishment should be prompt. Don't let children stew over it.
4. Avoid sermons and don't demand verbal assurance that the children will never do it again. Too much verbal behavior may overload the children and they will not attend to the specific concern.
5. Don't send children to bed as punishment. Keep this as a place of rest.
6. Stony silence or cold anger and then loving embraces should be avoided. Such actions confuse children and they may forget why they are being punished.
7. Encouraging good behavior is more beneficial than punishment.
8. Avoid belittlement, shaming, and other judgmental statements. These affect the child's self-image in a negative manner.
9. Sometimes it is prudent to avoid being led into a long explanation and defense of actions to children when what they want requires a reversal of a decision.
10. Plan to gradually increase independence and freedom much as is done at school. When children are allowed to go to play outdoors, they know that if they misbehave, they will be called back to the house. The next day, they are given the chance to try again. Start each day anew and avoid mentioning what was done, and why there was punishment, yesterday.

Working on Homework

Many parents have commented on how difficult it is to get involved in the schoolwork of their children. Some parents don't feel confident enough with the content to tutor. Parents should not be forced to be teachers if they cannot tutor effectively. This will just confuse the student. There are, however, ways to get involved that do not require tutoring. Every parent has the right to "know what's going on." The old saying, "what I don't know won't hurt me" doesn't stand up here. There is no sense waiting for the "moment of truth" in the form of a report card or a telephone call from school giving the bad news.

Getting involved can be accomplished by the following:

1. Provide a comfortable, quiet place to work and set up the time every day. Monitor the study area so no one disturbs the learner.
2. Help the child budget the homework time. Monitor to see that the child is making the best use of time.
3. Ask the student if he or she has what is needed for the assignments: pencil, pen, paper, books. If books are not needed or they were left at school, ask why!
4. Ask to see the homework assignment. Ask the child to tell you what he or she cannot do. Send a note to the teacher the next day describing what problems were encountered.
5. Praise and reward a well-completed homework or study time even if the child had problems.
6. Everyone is entitled to a "day off" or a "bad day." Allow the student to waste time or refuse to work. That's ok for today, but tomorrow we start fresh and new.
7. Read with the learner if you can for a few minutes or help him or her read assignments. Clarification is helpful, but don't be *too* helpful and do the assignment.
8. Be consistent, and once the pattern is set continue in the same way. If you change too much, you may lose the child's attention.
9. Homework is generally better accomplished before the child watches television or plays. Be flexible, if there is a special television program on, once in a while it's ok to give in.
10. Always remember to treat the student with respect. You may have to be firm, avoid confrontation. A good word, a hug, a little extra now and then goes a long way.

Many avenues of parental involvement have been discussed. Unique combinations of them will apply to any student. The overall effect of these activities and interactions should be to better organize and structure the life space of the student for more effective learning and self-actualization.

Chapter 8

Language Development

CHAPTER OUTLINE

OVERVIEW

A full range of language problems can be found in most schools. Some severe language and speech disorders will require one-on-one special training. However, most students who exhibit language disorders can benefit from general classroom activities where good modeling and effective imitation are intentionally built into the curriculum.

The language development activities in this chapter are designed for students exhibiting difficulties in language, as well as for young learners who need a comprehensive readiness curriculum. Along with the criterion behaviors, prescriptive activities are listed. Most of the subareas of language are discussed as prescriptive activities.

Other information related to the language areas can be found as follows:

· Chapter 1 discusses developmental language disorders, language components, and definitions of terms, as well as the special needs of limited English proficient students.
· Chapter 2 contains theories of language acquisition including behavioristic (environmentalist), nativistic, interactionistic, psycholinguistic, and cognitive.
· Chapter 4 provides procedures for diagnosing language disorders.
· Chapter 5 lists currently used tests of language disorders and Mann-Suiter-McClung checklists and screening devices.
· Chapter 9 includes the language activities related to reading and spelling, with emphasis on the receptive language (meaning) associated with vocabulary, and the procedures for written expression. It also discusses the relationship between listening, speaking, reading, and writing.
· Chapter 11 includes a discussion about the language aspects of mathematics.

INTRODUCTION

Language is pervasive and it is crucial for success in school. Language acquisition is a hierarchical process. We comprehend spoken language before we produce speech. Language development proceeds from listening to speaking to reading and written expression. Listening and reading are receptive processes that enable the student to comprehend speech and relate words and speech to meaning. Speaking and writing are expressive processes that produce and use words to describe, show action, or characterize a message that conveys an intended meaning.

When planning classroom activities, it is important to relate them to the major components of language: phonology, morphology, syntax, semantics, and pragmatics. *Phonology* is a study of the speech sounds of a language. Problems commonly associated with phonology include auditory discrimination, speech articulation, sound symbol relationships (e.g., /b/ to "b"), and closure or blending of sounds (e.g., /c/-/a/-/t/ is *cat*). *Morphology* is a study of morphemes or the smallest units of meaning in a language. Curricular concerns deal with appropriate use of prefixes, suffixes, verb tense forms *(ed, ing),* and plurals. *Syntax* is how words are arranged in a given order to make meaningful grammatical phrases and sentences. Students with language disorders may confuse sentence structure or speak in telegraphic speech (e.g., *me go store*). *Semantics* refers to getting meaning from words and sentences. With the meaning of vocabulary the student builds concepts. Semantics also involves figurative language and how the student understands idioms, metaphors, similes, and multiple meanings. *Pragmatics* is the use of language in social situations. Understanding the nuances of conversation and the implications of nonverbal communication can be a problem for some students.

> In order to be an efficient language user, one must have knowledge of language structure (syntax), the meanings and sounds that compose utterance (semantics and phonology), and the social conventions that guide the use of sounds and meanings (pragmatics). There is little question that language knowledge, like conceptual knowledge, is represented in different ways and at different levels. There is also little question that the different kinds of language knowledge exist along a continuum that spans the range from highly restricted language rules with limited scope to unrestricted language rules of broad scope. (Kamhi, 1988, p. 306)

Language is a system that requires learning of abstract knowledge. The object in teaching is to help the learner gain new knowledge as opposed to just acquiring a new behavior; to help learners understand what language is and the need to modify the way they conceive of their own personal language. Evidence must be provided to the learner that a change is even necessary.

> Language acquisition is a result of a dynamic interaction between cognitive processes and behavior (e.g., attention and memory) and between these processes and basic behavioral learning strategies that mediate them (e.g., discrimination, generalization, etc.). This interaction is triggered by environmental events such as the instruction of a child and his or her mother around some specific topic. (Warren, 1988, p. 293)

Warren further discusses four necessary ingredients:

1. *Cognitive Processes:* Attention, retention (short- and long-term memory), and intrinsic motivation
2. *Behavioral Learning Strategies:* Biological propensity to look for similarities and differences, detecting differences and similarities, imitation influenced by direct, delayed, and vicarious reinforcement, as well as punishment and extinction
3. *Present Knowledge Base:* Prior knowledge of language principles and readiness to learn
4. *Environmental Variables:* External environment that influences learning, modeling, manipulation by parents and teachers of settings, frequency, content, method of instruction, and overall intervention

Environmental variables that enhance or impede generalization may be classified into at least eight categories. According to Warren, these are: (1) what is taught, (2) who teaches, (3) how skills are taught, (4) what are the consequences of behavior, (5) where teaching occurs, (6) when teaching occurs, (7) how the content of training is organized, and (8) how responsible and supportive the learner's environment is to the training targets. Application of a systems perspective suggests programming of each of these dimensions.

The ability to flexibly apply existing knowledge is influenced by at least four factors: (a) the type of knowledge in question, (b) the level at which this knowledge is represented, (c) the similarity of the transfer situation to the original learning situation, and (d) performance factors, including the physical and communicative contexts in which the knowledge is applied, and the affective states and information processing demands associated with producing language forms. (Kamhi, 1988, p. 304)

Language impaired children are found to be less flexible than others in applying knowledge. This may be due to deficiencies in learning skills, which results in difficulties in acquiring knowledge and/or to problems that result from the demands of linguistic processing.

This chapter specifically addresses two important areas of oral language: listening and speaking. Oral and written language are interactive. Oral language, cognition, and reading are interrelated processes (Reid & Hresko, 1981). Too often the subjects within language arts are viewed as separate entities. However, written language proficiency evolves from previously developed oral language competence. Teachers need to be sensitive to students' speech patterns and use of oral expression. How a student talks may affect how he or she writes.

TEACHING PROCEDURES

Plan how language activities will become a part of the entire curriculum and how listening, speaking, and writing will be encouraged in all aspects of the learner's life in school. Use as many environmental settings as possible to give students opportunities to experiment with words and express themselves freely in a nonthreatening manner. Reflect on how the classroom is presently structured. Does the instructor do the majority of the speaking? What opportunities are given to the students to engage in oral language activities? For younger students, schedule show and tell times and private one-on-one conversations. Use puppets, objects, animals, games, or sports to encourage speaking. Listening can be promoted through attending to stories, records, films, videos, television programs, and guest speakers.

Older students can be given many opportunities to participate and speak in class. Reciprocal questioning, paraphrasing, roleplaying, inferring, predicting, and oral reports are part of reading and literature. Brainstorming and peer collaboration for writing, editing, and revising are integral to the writing process. Mathematics classes promote interaction by encouraging verbal discussion, oral problem solving, and reasoning. Social studies gives students a chance to engage in interviews, group projects, reports, and panel discussions, and to persuade through debates and class meetings. Science also

lends itself to speaking by having students verbalize, analyze, synthesize, problem solve, classify, explain the sequence of experiments, compare and contrast, conclude, and show evidence.

Determine the student's developmental level of speech and language. By observing communication skills and by listening to the student in a variety of settings, the teacher can establish a baseline of speech patterns, the length of utterances of sentences, the quality of language and fluency. Use a tape recorder to tape samples of individual or group language activities or conversations.

Begin at a concrete level of presentation and then move to an abstract level of conceptualization or ideation. At a lower level of conceptualization, the language involving a particular concept can be defined as essentially descriptive or functional in nature (i.e., the word used tells us what the concept is, how it looks, what it is made of, what it does, what it does not do, and what can be done with it). This level of language can be termed *concrete-functional,* or the analysis of the concepts in a concrete-functional manner. An example of this level of conceptualization would be the following: The concept of elephant can be presented using a real elephant, a picture of an elephant, the shape of an elephant, or the word *elephant.* It can also be described in concrete-functional terms such as "big," "heavy," and "it can carry people." Students who have language deficiencies should be introduced to concepts in terms of meaning by being presented with the concrete form first whenever possible. The language associated with the concept should be taught in a concrete-functional manner.

The concept elephant, to continue the example, which can be presented in different ways (concrete form, picture, shape, or word), should then be examined in an abstract sense. The appropriate sequence in teaching the concept elephant, for example, is first to teach how it is different from other things. After difference is understood, teach how it is the same as other things. For example, an elephant is different from a horse in size, shape, behavior, and so on. It is the same as a horse in that both have four legs, a mouth, and two eyes, and they are both animals. The teacher can build in the meaning of the concept elephant at different levels by teaching simple, then complex, classifications and associations. This should be accomplished first visually by using visual associative clues, such as a picture or object, and then auditorily (through communication without the use of visual associative clues).

The following is a sample language lesson dealing with the meaning of a specific concept that is within the student's range of experience:

1. *Concept:* Ball.
2. *Level of Presentation:* Object ball, picture of ball, shape of ball, or the word *ball,* depending on the presentation level best suited to the needs of the student
3. *Levels of Conceptualization:*
   a. *Concrete-Functional:* What does the ball look like and feel like? What is it made of? What can you do with it? What can you not do with it?
   b. *Abstract.* How is a ball different from a block, etc.? How is it the same as a circle, globe, etc. (classification)? What goes with ball (simple association)? Ball is to circle as block is to ____ (complex association).

During direct teaching experiences and when assisting individual students, deliberately model aspects of language. For example, have the students listen and observe as you talk aloud and demonstrate how to do a mathematics problem or a science experiment. Also demonstrate pitch and the rhythm of speech.

Some students are reluctant to speak. Elicit language by allowing them to participate at first by demonstrating or showing how to make or do something. Move to choices. Do you want a crayon or a pencil? Expand on short answers such as "pencil" by saying, "I want a pencil." For some students who do not retrieve or say words quickly, give them time to respond. Try not to look anxious or hold your breath.

Use expansion as a technique for getting students to provide more information and to enhance verbal behavior. This applies to testing as well as to teaching in terms of providing more detail and enriching verbal output related to content. Such expressions as, "Tell me more," "Give me additional information," "What else do we know about it?" "Can we express it another way?" are all helpful probes. The teacher can also restate the student's comments to include an elaboration of the original thought. For example, if the student says, "Trees have leaves," the teacher could elaborate on this concept by saying, "Yes, trees have leaves, but so do bushes and small plants."

Be sensitive to the language needs of limited English proficient students (LEP) and speakers of non-standard English. Constantly correcting a student's verbal expression often leads to the student's inhibiting any spontaneous language that may have been forthcoming. Through imitation of a good model in a variety of situations, the student's language will develop. For LEP students, a vital area of study is vocabulary development in all subject areas. Even though the student may pronounce a word, it does not follow that meanings and multiple meanings are understood.

Use the activities on the following pages in this chapter to meet the specific needs of individual students or to plan for group instruction. The readiness activities are especially appropriate for young students.

LISTENING AND VISUAL SKILLS

Hearing—Sensory

Difficulty in hearing may result from physical disorders. Auditory development is based on the integrity of the following systems.

1. *The Vibrator, or Sound Producer:* Loss of specific frequencies may prevent students from hearing certain sounds. For example, they may not hear teachers who have either low- or high-pitched voices.
2. *The Acoustic Signal, or Sound in the Air:* A clogged-up ear canal will affect the ability to hear. Some young children are continually putting things into their ears. Ears should be checked periodically by the teacher for wax buildup and foreign objects. Excessive buildup of wax may affect hearing.
3. *The Mechanical Signal, or Eardrum and/or Bones of the Middle Ear:* Damage to the eardrum itself or to the bones of the middle ear can result in mild to severe hearing loss and require the use of a hearing aid.
4. *The Hydraulic Signal, or the Inner Ear Fluid:* Inner ear infection can cause difficulty in hearing.
5. *The Electrical Signal, or the Cochlea Nerve:* Damage to the cochlea nerve may result in moderate to profound hearing loss and is quite difficult to treat.

Diagnosis

1. *Observable Behaviors*
   a. Students may cup their ears to hear.
   b. Students may be restless and exhibit poor behavior.
   c. Students may have difficulty following directions.
   d. The students may consistently ask for repetitions.
   e. Students may turn their heads unusually when trying to listen.
2. *Mann-Suiter Screening*
   Mann-Suiter-McClung Developmental Checklists, pages 156–166.
3. *Supplementary Evaluation*
   a. Audiometric Sweep Test (formal).
   b. Request that students stand in the rear of the classroom. Covering your mouth, call their

names in your usual voice. The students respond to their names by taking their seats (informal).
  c. Watch-Tick Test: From behind the student, hold a pocket watch approximately one inch from the student's ear. Place the watch to the ear intermittently, asking the student to raise a hand when he or she hears the ticking. Alternate putting the watch to the ear with putting a half dollar to the ear to see if the student is responding appropriately (informal).

Prescriptive Activities

1. Refer students for an auditory examination.
2. Change the students' seats so that they will be closer to the source of sound. Avoid seating the students near noisy air conditioners, windows, or doors.
3. Face the students when giving directions. Many teachers talk to the chalkboard.
4. Amplification would be helpful.
5. Do not speak from behind the students.
6. Watch your rate and amount of speech, or verbal input.

AUDITORY ATTENTION TO SOUND (PERCEPTION)
Diagnosis

1. *Observable Behaviors*
  a. Students with this problem may be easily distracted by competing stimuli.
  b. Students may appear to be emotionally disturbed or mentally retarded.
  c. Some students have difficulty getting meaning from sound or speech and, therefore, do not attend to auditory stimuli.

Prescriptive Activities

1. Create an awareness of sound by amplifying.
2. Attract the students' attention by using toys and musical instruments.
3. Use a clicker or some other sound signal to get the attention of the students.
4. In severe cases, you may have to turn the student's head to the source of the sound.

AUDITORY—SOUND LOCALIZATION (PERCEPTION)
Diagnosis

1. *Observable Behaviors*
  a. The learner may have difficulty finding the source of sound or the direction from which it is coming.

  b. The learner may have difficulty in assigning specific voices to specific persons.
  c. Some teachers have their desk in the back of the room and give directions from behind students. Students need to find the teacher's voice before they can attend to directions. Face the students when speaking to them.
2. *Mann-Suiter Screening*
  Mann-Suiter-McClung Developmental Checklists, pages 156–166.
3. *Supplementary Evaluation*
  To identify this problem, perform a simple "snap test." Ask the student to close his or her eyes, then snap your fingers around the student's body and have the student point to the direction of the sound. A student who cannot point to where the sound is coming from may have problems with auditory localization, and further evaluation may be indicated.

Prescriptive Activities

1. Students should practice locating sounds of bells, noise makers, and voices around the room, first with sight and then blindfolded.
2. Have the students close their eyes and point to sounds coming from different directions. Make sounds in different parts of the room, and have the students identify the sound and its location.
3. Take the students to a noisy place such as a shopping center or park and let them listen to the sounds that are present (e.g., cars, birds). Ask the students to close their eyes and tell what they hear. Have them point to the location of sounds as you name them.
4. Have blindfolded students match the classmate with the voice.
5. Hide a sound-making device, such as a small radio, for the student to find.
6. Parents or guardians can play sound-finding games at home.

AUDITORY—FIGURE-GROUND (PERCEPTION)
Diagnosis

1. *Observable Behaviors*
  a. Students may exhibit forced attention to sound, causing them to attend to extraneous noises in their environment.
  b. Students may find it difficult to attend to speech.
  c. By comparison to other students, these students may not be able to sit for long periods of time. They may appear to be distractible and hyperactive.

d. A teacher may find that students obey the commands of the teacher next door.

e. Students may not be able to focus on their own work and may tend to interfere when the teacher is working with another student.

2. *Mann-Suiter Screening*

Mann-Suiter-McClung Developmental Checklists, pages 156–166.

Developmental Skills (Criterion Reference)

The student will:

1. Identify and state the different sounds he or she hears in a room or out of doors.
2. Identify selected sounds in a room or out of doors.
3. Identify verbal sounds from among other sounds.
4. Identify from choices the picture of an object that represents a word presented amidst a background of noise.
5. Follow directions on command that are presented amidst a background of noise.
6. Identify from choices of musical themes hidden amidst a background of noise the theme that is the same as the model.

Prescriptive Activities

GENERAL ACTIVITIES

1. Select from the list of development skills the particular target skills that are to be mastered in the area of Auditory Figure-Ground. These target skills become learning or behavioral objectives. (Example Target: Auditory Figure-Ground 5—The learner will follow directions on command that are presented amidst a background of noise.)
2. If the student fails to demonstrate success in the target skills according to predetermined criteria such as failing items assessed on a standardized test or failing school tasks requiring the skills, do the following:
   a. Select from the list of developmental skills the target skill (example: Auditory Figure-Ground 5) and other related or similar skills (4, 3, 2, 1, etc.) that are deemed appropriate for developing activities that will provide success and practice for higher level functions or skills (e.g., 6). Select activities at lower levels (4, 3, 2, etc.) as necessary to insure success and provide an array of different activities that will reinforce the development of Auditory Figure-Ground skills.
   b. Develop or select from other sources additional activities related to all of the specific Auditory Figure-Ground skills listed (1–6). These activities can be coded into the system at the appropriate levels within the list of development skills.

SPECIFIC ACTIVITIES

1. Provide a place that is reasonably quiet where the students can get off by themselves for parts of the day.
2. Do not seat the students by the window, door, or noisy air conditioner.
3. Help the students select relevant from irrelevant sounds in the environment with eyes closed, then with eyes open.
4. Condition the students by introducing sound into the environment on a selective basis. Gradually add distracting noises while giving directions or telling a story. Have the students discuss what they heard.
5. Use tapes or records to help the students build in sound selectivity (ear phones can be used to screen out distraction).
6. Face the students when giving critical directions.
7. Regulate the rate of verbal input. Going slower makes a difference.
8. Drugs under *strict supervision* may help.

Vision—Sensory

Ocular-Motor Disorders can occur in the following areas:

1. *Distinguishing Light from No Light:* The individual exhibits reduced sensitivity to light, which is a prerequisite for efficient visual perception.
2. *Seeing Line Detail:* A student's disability in seeing fine detail can be determined through the Snellen Chart (American Medical Association) and a professional examination that measures visual acuity.
3. *Binocular Fusion:* The student may experience double vision resulting from uneven vision whereby the bad eye interferes with the good eye. This condition can be diagnosed through the use of the (a) Telebinocular, (b) Ortho-Rater, or (c) Massachusetts Vision Test.
4. *Convergence:* Convergence difficulties can be due to a muscular imbalance that interferes with the coordinated movement of the eyes, resulting in the inability to focus properly. Ocular-motor activities under the direction of a professional in this area should be considered.
5. *Scanning:* With scanning difficulties, the student may not be able to perform (a) natural zigzag scanning that may be required for looking at different things within the classroom; (b) visual pursuit or

tracking of a moving object; or (c) the systematic learned eye movements that are required for reading.

Diagnosis

1. *Observable Behaviors*
   a. Blinking.
   b. Crossed eyes.
   c. Clumsiness.
   d. Poor performance in physical education activities.
   e. Unusual head tilt in reading.
   f. Tearing, redness, or inflammation of eyes.
2. *Mann-Suiter Screening*
   Mann-Suiter-McClung Developmental Checklists, pages 156–166.

Prescriptive Activities

1. Students should be seated in the front of the room for chalkboard work.
2. It is the responsibility of the school to follow up with the home if corrective lenses are needed.
3. Be aware of the nature and extent of the visual problem and its possible implications for different kinds of activities. A key factor is fatigue, which may occur in students with ocular-motor difficulties.
4. Undertake specific ocular-motor activities only with the specific instruction of a qualified professional in the area of vision and with permission of the parents.

OBJECT RECOGNITION (CENTRAL BLINDNESS)
Diagnosis

1. *Observable Behaviors*
   a. The students may not be able to recognize objects but can see, describe, and reproduce objects. (This condition may be due to cerebral dysfunction.)
   b. Sometimes the students may be able to recognize objects through touch.
   c. The students may have trouble integrating a visual stimulus into a uniform whole and may concentrate on the parts.
2. *Mann-Suiter Screening*
   a. Mann-Suiter-McClung Developmental Checklists, pages 156–166.

Developmental Skills (Criterion Reference)
The student will:

1. Recognize and name familiar objects
2. Recognize and name familiar geometric forms
3. Recognize and name letters, words, and numerals that are within his or her experiential background

Prescriptive Activities

SPECIFIC ACTIVITIES

1. Give the student a choice selection verbally ("Is it a _____ , or _____ , or _____ ?").
2. Have the students associate pictures or objects with sounds.
3. Have the students associate concrete objects or pictures with words.

FIGURE-GROUND DIFFERENTIATION (PERCEPTION)
Diagnosis will be found on page 175.

Developmental Skills (Criterion Reference)
The student will:

1. Find partially hidden objects in different settings, such as classroom, playground, and home.
2. Find an object or objects hidden amongst an unrelated background.
3. View a picture of an object and find and identify the same object fully exposed or partially hidden in an unrelated background.
4. Locate and trace a design within a pattern or drawn on an unrelated background.
5. Locate and trace over a picture of a geometric form on an unrelated background.
6. Locate and name a symbol, such as a letter written on an unrelated background.
7. View a picture containing a letter, word, or numeral and locate the requested symbol that is written within an unrelated background.
8. Complete activities that require visually separating the foreground from the background, such as letters embedded in figures and color.
9. View a picture of an object and identify that object from among other objects by feeling them unseen in a bag or box.
10. Locate and identify unseen objects in a bag or box, distinguishing them from other objects by feel and revisualization.
11. Read material at his or her independent level without omitting words or lines.
12. Complete work assignments within normal time limits and without becoming confused by the material provided.

Prescriptive Activities

GENERAL ACTIVITIES

1. Select from the list of developmental skills the particular target skills that are to be mastered in the area of Visual Figure-Ground. These target skills

become learning or behavioral objectives. (Example Target: Visual Figure-Ground 8—The student will complete activities that require visually separating the foreground from the background, such as letters embedded in figures and color.)

2. If the student fails to demonstrate success in the target skills according to predetermined criteria such as failing items assessed on a standardized test or failing school tasks requiring the skills, do the following:

   a. Select from the list of developmental skills the target skill (Example: Visual Figure-Ground 8) and other related or similar skills (7, 6, etc.) that are deemed appropriate for developing activities that will provide success and practice for higher level functions or skills (9. 10, 11, etc.). Select activities at lower levels (7, 6, 5, etc.) as necessary to insure success and provide an array of different activities that will reinforce the development of Visual Figure Ground skills.

   b. Develop or select from other sources additional activities related to all of the specific Visual Figure-Ground skills listed (1–12). These activities can be coded into the system at the appropriate levels within the list of development skills.

SPECIFIC ACTIVITIES

1. Locate and describe objects for the student in the street or playground.
2. Have the learner locate and describe objects that are partially hidden in the classroom or home.
3. Students can locate hidden objects and symbols in pictures, including geometric and other forms within their experience.
4. Hold up a book and read the title, pointing to each word as it is read. Use simple titles at first to help the students differentiate the word from the space. The students do not need to be able to read the words.
5. Put the color into the materials; do not overload the walls or the chalkboard with distracting color.
6. Place pictures of geometric forms, objects, letters, and words on newspaper or other backgrounds for the students to locate and identify.
7. Block out areas in workbooks so that the students will be able to attend better to specific tasks.
8. Provide various types of maps, globes, graphs, etc. Ask the learners to find products, places, or other specific information.
9. On field trips (nature hikes, factories, symphony concerts, etc.) aid the students in locating objects, people, or printed words.

10. Have the students locate specific items in a classroom terrarium or aquarium.
11. Provide books or encyclopedia pictures depicting animals, birds, and insects that are camouflaged by protective coloring and have the students locate and discuss them.
12. Have the students find specified information in reference books, classified ads, or telephone books. Encourage the students to gradually decrease the time in locating the information.
13. Have the students locate specific items in famous paintings. For example, locate the hidden animals in Henri Rousseau's paintings.

VISUAL DISCRIMINATION (PERCEPTION)
Diagnosis will be found on page 181.

Developmental Skills (Criterion Reference)
The student will:

1. Match objects that are the same or different.
2. Match objects that are not identical but similar in characteristics.
3. Match pictures of objects that are the same or different.
4. Match pictures of objects that are not identical but similar in characteristics.
5. Match three-dimensional geometric solids.
6. Complete inserts with a square, rectangle, circle, triangle, diamond, etc.
7. Match pictures of geometric forms.
8. Match three-dimensional wooden, plastic, felt, etc., letters.
9. Match printed letters.
10. Match three-dimensional wooden, plastic, felt, etc., numerals.
11. Match printed numerals.
12. Match three-dimensional wooden, plastic, felt, etc., words.
13. Match printed words.
14. Match words that are different but have similar parts, such as ending in *ing* or *ed* or beginning with the same letter.

Prescriptive Activities

GENERAL ACTIVITIES

1. Select from the list of developmental skills the particular target skills that are to be mastered in the area of Visual Discrimination. These target skills become learning or behavioral objectives. (Example Target: Visual Discrimination 9—The learner will match printed letters.)

2. If the student fails to demonstrate success in the target skills according to predetermined criteria such as failing items assessed on a standardized test or failing school tasks requiring the skills, do the following:
   a. Select from the list of developmental skills the target skill (example: Visual Discrimination 9) and other related or similar skills (8, 7, etc.) that are deemed appropriate in terms of developing activities that will provide success and practice for higher levels functions or skills (10, 11, 12, etc.). Select activities at lower level (8, 7, 6, etc.) as necessary to insure success and provide an array of different activities that will reinforce the development of Visual Discrimination skills.
   b. Develop or select from other sources additional activities related to all of the specific Visual Discrimination skills listed (1–14). These activities can be coded into the system at the appropriate levels within the list of development skills.

SPECIFIC ACTIVITIES

1. *Concrete level.* The students should verbally describe the differences and similarities between objects. (Note: Students should be allowed to hold the objects as they describe them.)
   a. Give the learners small objects to sort into containers (e.g., nuts, bolts, buttons, seeds, shells). Ask the learners to use only the thumb, index, and middle finger in picking up the objects.
   b. Show the learners three or more objects, such as two forks, a knife, and a spoon. Ask them to indicate which objects are alike. Use familiar items in the home (toys, buttons, fruit, cereal, crayons, tools, etc.).
   c. Show the learners two objects that are similar (e.g., toy cow and toy horse; pen and pencil; radio and television; fork and spoon). Ask the learners to tell how the objects are alike and then how they are different.
   d. Have the students use colored blocks to reproduce simple designs.
   e. Have the learners put different size objects into their respective containers (e.g., cards in envelopes, food in containers, objects in boxes).
2. *Pictures*
   a. Use activity (duplicated) sheets involving finding differences and similarities in pictures, such as matching a smiling pumpkin with the one that looks different or the same. The learners should verbalize what is different or the same and how it is different or the same.
   b. Use photographs or pictures from magazines to aid the students in discriminating difference and sameness between objects and forms.

AUDITORY—SOUND DISCRIMINATION (PERCEPTION)
Diagnosis will be found on page 191.

Developmental Skills (Criterion Reference)
The student will:

1. Identify from unseen choices the object that produces a particular sound.
2. Identify from choices the picture of the object that produces a particular sound.
3. Identify from choices of closed containers pairs of objects that sound the same.
4. Identify from three or more closed containers the object that sounds different.
5. Identify from choices the object that has the same beginning sound as the model presented orally.
6. Identify from choices the rhythm that is the same as the model.
7. Identify from printed choices the letter sound that is the same as, or different from, the model presented unseen by the instructor.
8. Identify from paired words presented orally and unseen by the student the pairs that sound the same or different.
9. Identify from choices the object or picture of an object that rhymes with the model.
10. Identify from choices presented orally the word that rhymes with the model.
11. Identify from choices of pictures of words within the reading vocabulary the word that rhymes with the model presented orally.
12. Identify from choices the picture of an object that has the same beginning sound as the model presented orally.
13. Identify from choices the object that has the same ending sound as the model presented orally.
14. Identify from choices the picture of an object that has the same ending sound as the model presented orally.
15. Identify from choices the object that has the same medial sound as the model presented orally.
16. Identify from choices the picture of an object that has the same medial sound as the model presented orally.

17. Identify from choices the picture of an object that has the same beginning blend as the model presented orally.

Prescriptive Activities

GENERAL ACTIVITIES

1. Select from the list of developmental skills the particular target skills that are to be mastered in the area of Auditory (Sound) Discrimination. These target skills become learning or behavioral objectives. (Example Target: Auditory Discrimination 7—The learner will identify from printed choices the letter sound that is the same as, or different from, the model presented unseen by the instructor.)

2. If the student fails to demonstrate success in the target skills according to predetermined criteria such as failing items assessed on a standardized test or failing school tasks requiring the skills, do the following:
   a. Select from the list of developmental skills the target skill (example: Auditory Discrimination 7) and other related or similar skills (6, 5, etc.) that are deemed appropriate for developing activities that will provide success and practice for higher level functions or skills (8, 9, 10, etc.). Select activities at lower levels (6, 5, 4, etc.) as necessary to insure success and provide an array of different activities that will reinforce the development of Auditory (Sound) Discrimination skills.
   b. Develop or select from other sources additional activities related to all of the specific Auditory (Sound) Discrimination skills listed (1–17). These activities can be coded into the system at the appropriate levels within the list of development skills.

SPECIFIC ACTIVITIES

1. Begin with the recognition and discrimination of grossly different sounds in nature, such as wind, rain, fire, and thunder.
2. Teach the student to discriminate and identify social sounds within the environment (e.g., horns, bells, birds, dogs).
3. Make the student aware of the sounds of danger, such as trains, cars, and sirens.
4. Let the student listen to the subtleties of sound that are present in a quiet place such as a park or forest (wind, trees, water, birds, etc.).
5. Go on a sound hunt through the neighborhood, listening for as many different sounds as possible.

Note the things that sound similar to each other, such as types of motors, birds, car horns.
6. Identify objects in the home that make sounds (such as electrical appliances, pets, people, plumbing, radio, television) and discuss how the sounds are made.
7. Provide musical instruments, toys, or other objects (e.g., bells, squeeze toys) for the student to manipulate, recognize, and discriminate sounds.
8. Pure tones will help the student discriminate pitch, frequency, intensity, and timbre.
9. After teaching grossly different sounds, move to finer and finer discriminations, using tuning forks, musical instruments, and other sound-making devices.
10. Play a record of different musical instruments and/or voices and have the learner identify the instrument (trumpet, piano, violin, drum, etc.) or the voice (man's, woman's).
11. Have the student match different objects or pictures of objects, such as animals or musical instruments, and their concomitant sounds.
12. Fill identical (size and shape) containers, in pairs, with the same amount of contents (pennies, rice, tacks, etc.). The student rattles the containers and matches those with the same sound.
13. Ask the student to match objects on a duplicator sheet with their respective sounds as presented on record or tape.
14. Have the learner draw objects that make a particular sound.
15. Say words to the student (such as, *cat, house, hat*) and ask which two rhyme. Or say, "I'm thinking of an animal that rhymes with *hat*." Include rhyming words used in the learner's reading program.
16. Say sentences with simple rhymes for the learner to repeat (*the fat cat is on a mat*).
17. Use pictures of objects from magazines or books for matching words in rhyming activities. Words representing the pictured objects can be presented orally or on tape and matched by the learner. (Example: "Are these the same or different?")
18. Say four words and ask the student to indicate which one was different.

    go go so go
    very fairy very very
    hop hop hop hot

19. In teaching, do not teach similar sounding letters for contrast; for example, do not teach *p* and *b* or *f* and *v* together. Most important, do not overload in

teaching. Sounds should be taught one at a time. Never introduce more than one new sound in a given day.

20. Collect objects with the same beginning, ending, or middle sounds for matching activities.
21. Use pictures from magazines for purposes of matching initial, middle, and ending sounds.
22. Activities can be prepared for many of the developmental skills listed (1–17) by using the following:
    a. pictures drawn on the chalkboard
    b. acetates on the overhead projector
    c. cutting and pasting of pictures from old workbooks and magazines
    d. small objects
    e. commercial records and tapes
    f. instructor-prepared tapes
    g. movable letters, clay letters
    h. sound instruments
    i. glasses containing varied amounts of water

VISUAL CLOSURE—BLENDING (PERCEPTION)
Diagnosis will be found on page 181.

Developmental Skills (Criterion Reference)
The student will:

1. Put together pictures of up to five pieces.
2. Put together puzzles of up to fifteen pieces.
3. Assemble puzzles of over fifteen pieces.
4. Assemble three-dimensional objects such as geometric forms or models of people, animals, cars, etc.
5. Complete a partial picture of an object, thereby forming the whole object.
6. Complete a partial picture of a geometric form, thereby forming the whole object.
7. Identify the missing part from a picture of an incomplete object.
8. Identify the picture of the object with the missing part, and the part missing, from among pictures of the same object with no missing parts.
9. Locate and name the missing parts in pictures of incomplete objects.
10. Complete dot-to-dot pictures.
11. Identify, after viewing an incomplete object, the picture of the object as it would look completed.
12. Name the completed objects when shown pictures of incomplete objects.
13. Complete pictures of incomplete geometric forms by writing or by using a finger or a pointer to indicate the missing lines.

14. Complete an incomplete letter or numeral by writing.
15. Identify the complete letter or numeral that is represented by an incomplete symbol.
16. *Close,* or read a list of words with the letters spaced apart.

Prescriptive Activities

GENERAL ACTIVITIES

1. Select from the list of developmental skills the particular target skills that are to be mastered in the area of Visual Closure. These target skills become learning or behavioral objects. (Example Target: Visual Closure 13—Complete pictures of incomplete geometric forms by writing or by using a finger or a pointer to indicate the missing lines.)
2. If the student fails to demonstrate success in the target skills according to predetermined criteria such as failing items assessed on a standardized test or failing school tasks requiring the skills, do the following:
    a. Select from the list of developmental skills the target skill (example: Visual Closure 13) and other related or similar skills (12, 11, etc.) that are deemed appropriate for developing activities that will provide success and practice for higher level functions or skills (14, 15, 16, etc.). Select activities at lower levels (12, 11, 10, etc.) as necessary to insure success and provide an array of different activities that will reinforce the development of Visual Closure Skills.
    b. Develop or select from other sources additional activities related to all of the specific Visual Closure skills listed (1–16). These activities can be coded into the system at the appropriate levels within the list of development skills.

SPECIFIC ACTIVITIES

1. Activities involving the completion of simple to complex puzzles: 2 pieces, 3 pieces, 5 pieces, 9 pieces, etc., can be used.
2. Have the learner assemble objects for art, science, and social studies lessons.
3. Show pictures of simple objects with parts removed or covered, and ask the learner to identify the missing parts.
4. Ask the learner to complete incomplete pictures or geometric shapes.
5. Draw simple dot-to-dot pictures for the learner to connect.

6. Teach the blending of letters this way:

c	at

and not this way:

c	a	t

7. For additional blending activities refer to page 429.

AUDITORY CLOSURE—BLENDING (PERCEPTION)
Diagnosis will be found on page 191.

Developmental Skills (Criterion Reference)
The student will:

1. Identify from choices the object that represents the word presented by the instructor as a sequence, or spaced group, of sounds or syllables.
2. Identify from choices the picture of an object that represents the word presented by the instructor as a sequence, or spaced group, of sounds or syllables.
3. Name a word by synthesizing the sounds (letters or syllables) presented by the instructor.
4. Synthesize sounds presented by the instructor and identify from among choices the word that is represented by these sounds.

Prescriptive Activities

GENERAL ACTIVITIES

1. Select from the list of developmental skills the particular target skills that are to be mastered in the area of Auditory Closure (Blending). These target skills become learning or behavioral objectives. (Example Target: Auditory Closure 3— The learner will name a word by synthesizing the sounds (letters or syllables) presented by the instructor.)
2. If the student fails to demonstrate success in the target skills according to predetermined criteria such as failing items assessed on a standardized test or failing school tasks requiring the skills, the instructor can do the following:
   a. Select from the list of developmental skills the target skill (example: Auditory Closure 3) and other related or similar skills (2, 1, etc.) that are deemed appropriate for developing activities that will provide success and practice for higher level functions or skills (e.g., 4). Select activities at lower levels (2, 1, etc.) as necessary to insure success and provide an array of different activities that will reinforce the development of Auditory Closure (Blending) skills.
   b. Develop or select from other sources additional activities related to all of the specific Auditory Closure Blending skills listed (1–4). These activities can be coded into the system at the appropriate levels within the list of development skills.

SPECIFIC ACTIVITIES

1. The pushing together of anagrams, clay, and sandpaper letters will help the student "see" how sounds go together through physical blending.
2. Give the student a selection of toys or small objects. Slowly say the sounds of one of the objects (c-a-t). The learner will pick up the correct object.
3. Give the learner duplicator pages of pictures of objects. Slowly say the sounds of one of the pictures. The learner marks the correct picture.
4. Say the meaning of a word (an animal) and slowly blend the word *(c-a-t)*. The learner says the word *(cat)*. If the student gives an incorrect response, repeat (an animal, *c-a-t,* and then give him or her three choices. (Is it dog, cat, rat?)
5. Blend names of students in a group. The correct student raises a hand.
6. Have the learner listen to a sentence and complete the blended word. (I play with a *b-a-ll*).
7. Slowly say sounds to the student *(c-a-t)* and ask him or her to say the word. Use words within the student's daily experiences.
8. Tapes of word analysis and synthesis (e.g., *cat— c-a-t, c-at, cat*) are helpful. These can be put into games in which the student gueses the word from the sounds.
9. Say words with a sound omitted and ask the student to indicate the word. For example, "What word is this: *heli . . . ter [helicopter]*." A space is left (no sound) for the missing part.
10. Play word Bingo games by blending the words instead of calling them out.
11. Verbally indicate to the student a particular spelling pattern, such as *at, et,* and *op*. Then give the student a consonant sound, such as *c, p, f,* and ask the student to make a word. For example, say the spelling pattern *at*. "If I put a *c* [sound] in front of *at*, what word do I get—cat." Repeat the activity with the sounds *f, s, b*.
12. In teaching reading, build on spelling patterns (e.g., *at, am, an, op,* and *et*) rather than on nonsense syllables.
13. The music teacher can provide activities that will aid the student in listening to the blending of tones.

14. For additional blending activities refer to page 448.

VISUAL MEMORY
Diagnosis will be found on page 189.

Developmental Skills
The developmental skills in the area of Visual Memory are separated into two parts: (1) Visual Memory-General and (2) Visual Memory-Sequencing.

VISUAL MEMORY—GENERAL (CRITERION REFERENCE). The student will:

1. View a scene or a picture of a scene and name the things that are remembered.
2. Describe from memory the characteristics of objects that are shown and then taken away.
3. View an object and identify it from among other objects after it has been removed.
4. View objects and name these objects after they have been removed.
5. View a group of objects and identify the object that has been removed from the group sight unseen.
6. View a group of objects and identify the object that has been added to the group sight unseen.
7. Describe from memory the characteristics of pictures of objects that are shown and then taken away.
8. View a picture of an object and, after it is removed, identify the picture from among other pictures of objects.
9. View pictures of objects and name the objects after the pictures have been removed.
10. View pictures of objects and identify the picture of the object that has been removed sight unseen.
11. View pictures of objects and identify the picture of the object that has been added to the group sight unseen.
12. Reproduce an object or geometric shape utilizing pencil and paper after the object has been removed.
13. Identify a geometric figure, letter, or numeral from among choices after the model has been taken away.
14. Write or construct out of clay a letter or numeral shown and then removed.
15. Describe from memory the home, neighborhood, school, or other familiar place.

VISUAL MEMORY—SEQUENCING (CRITERION REFERENCE). The student will:

1. Imitate a series of one or more movements briefly demonstrated.
2. Reproduce from a model a pattern utilizing beads, pegboards, blocks, etc.
3. Reproduce a sequence of a pattern utilizing beads, pegboard, or blocks after the model has been shown and then removed.
4. When presented with a pattern of beads, pegs, blocks, etc., identify from choices the object that follows in order of sequence.
5. When presented with a picture of a sequence of objects, identify from choices the picture of the object that follows in sequence.
6. When presented with a picture of a sequence of objects, identify from choices the sequence that is the same.
7. Reproduce from a model comprised of symbols such as letters or words a duplicate, using movable letters or writing.
8. When presented with a group of out-of-sequence pictures, arrange the pictures in the correct order.
9. Reproduce a pattern from a model and then repeat the pattern two or more sequences, utilizing beads, pegboard, blocks, etc.
10. Reproduce a sequence of two or more letters, numbers, or words—using cards, movable symbols, or writing—after the model has been shown and then removed.
11. Reproduce a sequence of two or more geometrical shapes after the model has been shown and then removed.
12. Select from choices a sequence of letters, numbers, or words that is the same as the model that has been shown and then removed.
13. Reproduce a sequence of pictures, using cards, after a sequence of pictures has been shown and then removed.
14. Complete coded entries within a specific time period, given a sequence of samples as a model or guide: A = $\bigcirc$; B = $\square$; C = $\triangle$; etc.
15. Select from choices the correct spelling of words that are within the independent reading vocabulary.
16. Revisualize and spell words within the independent reading vocabulary, presented orally, by a written or verbal response.

Prescriptive Activities

VISUAL MEMORY—GENERAL

General Activities

1. Select from the list of developmental skills the particular target skills that are to be mastered in the

area of Visual Memory. These target skills become learning or behavioral objectives. (Example Target: Visual Memory 5—The student will view a group of objects and identify the object that has been removed from the group sight unseen.)

2. If the student fails to demonstrate success in the target skills according to predetermined criteria such as failing items assessed on a standardized test or failing school tasks requiring the skills, do the following:

   a. Select from the list of developmental skills the target skill (example: Visual Memory 5) and other related or similar skills (4, 3, etc.) that are deemed appropriate for developing activities that will provide success and practice for higher level functions or skills (6, 7, 8, etc.). Select activities at lower levels (4, 3, 2, etc.) as necessary to insure success and provide an array of different activities that will reinforce the development of Visual Memory skills.

   b. Develop or select from other sources additional activities related to all of the specific Visual Memory skills listed (1–15). These activities can be coded into the system at the appropriate levels within the list of development skills.

Specific Activities. Basic to the amelioration process for students with memory problems is the concept that recall must follow recognition. In all activities, students are first asked to match or to pick out one from among others before they are required to use their recall abilities.

1. *Reinforcing Visual Memory with Tactual-Kinesthetic Associations:*

   Students with revisualization problems can be aided in their learning through the use of the tactual-kinesthetic modality. The students should be given an opportunity to establish a visual-tactual relationship by manipulating objects with their hands. Touch and body awareness will make them aware of difference and sameness to a more concrete level. The sequence of activities in Table 8–1 will be helpful to students who have difficulties with visual perception as well as with visual memory.

2. *Visual-Tactual Associations Using Shape as a Referent:*

   a. Round and curved objects. Using spheres first, and then any round object available, do the following:

      (1) Let a learner take a suitably sized ball or sphere and cup it in his or her hands.

Table 8–1   Sequence of Activities

Sequence in Teaching	Visual–Tactual–Kinesthetic Associations
Matching and comparing	The students match a felt, wooden, plastic, clay, or sandpaper letter to another felt, wooden, plastic, clay, or sandpaper object or symbol (letter, word, or numeral).
Tracing from a model	The students trace over a felt, wooden, plastic, clay, or sandpaper object or symbol with their fingers or walk or creep over a pattern.
Reproducing from a model. (pencil, pen, clay, wet sand, finger paint, etc.)	The students copy from a felt, wooden, plastic, clay, or sandpaper model of an object or symbol (letter, word, or numeral).
Reproducing without a model (pencil, pen, clay, wet sand, finger paint, etc.)	The students reproduce the object or symbol without the model present.

(2) Draw attention to the way it looks and feels, how it fits into the palms of the student's hands.

(3) Show the student that he or she can turn it in any direction and feel its roundness.

(4) Call the student's attention to the fact that if her hands were large enough, they would fit around any ball and might even overlap.

(5) You could push a knitting needle through a ball to show that if the needle pierces the center of the ball from any point on the surface, the distance from point to center is always the same.

   b. Straight-edged objects. Starting with a cube of wood or a styrofoam shape, do the following:

      (1) Have a student take the shape into his or her hand to feel how it is unlike the sphere—it has straight edges and sharp corners that prick the palm.

      (2) Let the student feel along the straight lines and measure with his or her fingers or ruler to see that the edges are all the same length.

      (3) Use rectangular solids and have the student discover differences by looking at them and feeling them to see how they are unlike cubes.

   c. Amelioration activities should include discrimination of shape, size, sequence, position, and color.

Note: Use concrete materials first, if necessary, then pictures, geometric shapes, letters, and words. Always proceed from that which is different to that which is the same.

3. Play memory games by describing objects or pictures of objects after they have been removed. Discuss the size, color, shape, function, and classification.
4. Help the learner practice describing objects or scenes from memory. ("What does your room look like?")
5. After trips to different types of stores, rides through scenic areas, viewing of television programs, etc., discuss what the students saw. Ask the students to draw pictures and include what they remember about a particular place.
6. Objects, animals, scenes, etc., used in science and social studies lessons can be examined, then removed and discussed.

VISUAL MEMORY—SEQUENCING

General Activities

1. Select from the list of developmental skills the particular target skills that are to be mastered in the area of Visual Memory—Sequencing. These target skills become learning or behavioral objectives. (Example Target: Visual Memory—Sequencing 11—The learner will reproduce a sequence of two or more geometrical shapes after the model has been shown and then removed.)
2. If the student fails to demonstrate success in the target skills according to predetermined criteria such as failing items assessed on a standardized test or failing school tasks requiring the skills, do the following:
   a. Select from the list of developmental skills the target skill (example: Visual Memory—Sequencing 11) and other related or similar skills (10, 9, etc.) that are deemed appropriate for developing activities that will provide success and practice for higher level functions or skills (12, 13, 14, etc.). Select activities at lower levels (10, 9, 8, etc.) as necessary to insure success and provide an array of different activities that will reinforce the development of Visual Memory—Sequencing skills.
   b. Develop or select from other sources additional activities related to all of the specific Visual Memory—Sequencing skills listed (1–16). These activities can be coded into the system at the appropriate levels within the list of development skills.

Specific Activities

1. *Activities Involving Auditory-Visual Associations:*
   a. Listening and following directions. Ask the student to perform actions in certain sequences, such as the following:
      (1) Hopping, skipping, walking backwards, and walking forwards.
      (2) Going in different directions to various places, turning around, and touching objects with the left or right hand.
      (3) Tapping a sequence of sounds with the left or right foot or hand.
   b. Visual sequence and auditory associations.
      (1) Rhythm of motion related to sound can be developed by skipping, walking, running, and tapping to music.
      (2) Read sentences with rhymes, accenting the rhyming words. Ask the students to repeat in the same way as they point to the words; for example: The *cat* and the *rat sat* on a *mat.*
      (3) Say numerals in sequence, emphasizing the even or odd ones as the students point to each one, for example:

$$\underline{1}\ 2\ \underline{3}\ 4\ \underline{5}\ 6$$
$$1\ \underline{2}\ 3\ \underline{4}\ 5\ \underline{6}$$

Have the students repeat the numbers that were emphasized.

      (4) Give students practice in separating words into syllables so that they will hear and be able to repeat them in the proper order. This activity will help students with spelling, as well as with pronunciation, and will train them so that they will not be likely to make reversals or transpositions. For example, draw the syllables on the chalkboard or on paper, and have the students do the same. Have them say each syllable slowly as they do this. Start with two-syllable words and go to longer ones. This activity is called *chunking,* or *syllabication.*

      walk ing
      small er
      po si tion
      fol low ing

Chunk numbers the same way; have the students look at them, cover them, and see if they can repeat them, in groups, forwards and then backwards. This activity gives practice in sight recall.

2. Construct a simple pattern with beads, blocks, checkers, nuts, bolts, buttons, etc., for the learners to duplicate.
3. Show the learners a number of objects (begin with two or three and gradually increase the difficulty), remove them, and ask the learners to tell what they saw. Use familiar materials in the home (such as fruit, tools, cooking utensils, clothing, and toys).
4. Write a sequence of numerals, letters, or words on paper for the learners to copy, either by writing or by arranging cards.
5. Cut up simple comic strips or use sequence puzzles for the students to arrange in order.

AUDITORY MEMORY—SEQUENCING
Diagnosis will be found on page 194.

Developmental Skills (Criterion Reference)
The student will:

1. Follow one or more directions given orally.
2. Orally imitate a word or a sequence of unrelated words.
3. Imitate a sequence of related words or sentences presented orally.
4. Imitate a sequence of digits presented orally.
5. Be presented with a sequence of digits and then state the sequence in reverse order.
6. Imitate a sequence of nonsense syllables.
7. Imitate a sequence of letter names or sounds.
8. State the names of the days of the week and the months of the year.
9. Count from 1 to 100 by 1s, by 2s, by 5s, and by 10s.
10. Follow directions given orally in testing situations.

Prescriptive Activities

GENERAL ACTIVITIES

1. Select from the list of developmental skills the particular target skills that are to be mastered in the area of Auditory Memory—Sequencing. These target skills become learning or behavioral objectives. (Example Target: Auditory Memory—Sequencing 4—The learner will imitate a sequence of digits presented orally.)
2. If the student fails to demonstrate success in the target skills according to predetermined criteria such as failing items assessed on a standardized test or failing school tasks requiring the skills, do the following:
   a. Select from the list of developmental skills the target skill (example: Auditory Memory—Sequencing 4) and other related or similar skills (3, 2, etc.) that are deemed appropriate for developing activities that will provide success and practice for higher level functions or skills (5, 6, 7, etc.). Select activities at lower levels (3, 2, 1, etc.) as necessary to insure success and provide an array of different activities that will reinforce the development of Auditory Memory—Sequencing skills.
   b. Develop or select from other sources additional activities related to all of the specific Auditory Memory—Sequencing skills listed (1–10). These activities can be coded into the system at the appropriate levels within the list of developmental skills.

SPECIFIC ACTIVITIES

1. Use activities that will enable the students to better remember through associations with picture clues.
2. Slow down the verbal input and reduce the number of directions given to the students.
3. Show a student five or six objects. Call out the names of two of them and ask the student to point to the objects in the sequence called. Increase the difficulty to six as deemed appropriate.
4. Give students a series of pictures and orally indicate the order in which they should be placed. Example: cat, dog, elephant, snake. This activity can be varied to include reverse order naming. Provide the students with a sequence and have them indicate the sequence back in reverse order.
5. Use chunking exercises, for example, use telephone numbers to practice the grouping and rhythm of long sequences (e.g., 246-8392).
6. Have students listen to numerals and words and tell how many they heard.
7. Say simple phrases and then short sentences of five words (or less) for the learners to repeat (e.g., "the big, yellow ball," "the dog is black and white") in the correct sequence. Slowly expand the number of words in the sentences.
8. Present in sequence words that begin with the same letter or that have a common basis (such as fruit, parts of a house, things that are found in the bathroom) and have the students remember them and repeat them in the same sequence.
9. Have the students listen to records that ask them to perform certain actions.
10. Have the students follow commands by going through an obstacle course.
11. Perform a series of auditory acts (such as clap, stamp foot, and close door) with the students

blindfolded, and then ask , "What did I do?" "What did I do first?" "Next?" etc. When the students perform, say "What did you do?" etc.

12. Practice giving different kinds of test directions orally. Example: "Take out your pencil and paper and open your book to page 12." Begin with two or three directions (vary complexity as necessary).

13. Say a sequence of simple-to-complex directions for the learners to follow (e.g., "Open the drawer, take out two pencils, and put them on the table.") Begin with two directions and increase the number as the learners succeed.

14. Clap out rhythms with your hands or with a drum and have the learners repeat the sequence. For example, clap clap—clap clap—clap

15. Play echo games. For example, whisper a word, a phrase, or a sentence to one student, who repeats it ot the next student until it goes around the room.

16. Use sentence completion games. For example, the first student says, "On the way to school, I saw a _____ ." The next student repeats the sentence and adds one more thing.

17. Introduce the learners to simple poems. Increase the complexity of the poems, pointing out the rhyming elements.

18. Singing songs and telling jokes and riddles are helpful in developing memory.

19. Read a story to the learners. Stop on occasion and ask them questions about the plot or ask them to retell the story. If they forget details or become involved in unnecessary details, bring them back to the story by leading questions. Recall will vary depending on the selection, the student, and the time of day.

20. If the learners can write, ask them to follow simple directions by writing words, numbers, geometric shapes, etc. (e.g., "Write your name." "Draw three circles and two squares.")

21. Students should be encouraged to remember the names and/or birthdays of the members of their families and the other students in the class.

22. Encourage the students to remember their own telephone numbers and the numbers of other members of the family. They can learn these by grouping the numbers (—/—/—) or by clapping the sequence (clap clap clap/clap clap/clap clap).

23. Parents or guardians can play games such as, "What did you hear first?. . . . next?" after visiting different places or by using noises in the home or neighborhood.

24. Send students to various rooms in the house and have them bring specified items (e.g., a glass of water and a spoon). Begin with two directions and add others as the students improve.

RECEPTIVE AND EXPRESSIVE LANGUAGE

The students may be able to identify a hammer from among other objects presented visually (reception). They may be able to show what can be done with it, but be unable to talk about it in a meaningful way or describe its function (expression).

Note: Language reception must be checked first, since receptive disorders will invariably affect expression. Begin by finding out if the student understands the word (intact reception). This can be done by giving the student alternatives to choose from. ("Is this a crayon? Is this a hat? Is this chalk?") If chalk is the object and the student responds correctly, then the teacher can surmise that the student probably has an expressive language problem and not a receptive language disorder.

VISUAL LANGUAGE CLASSIFICATION
Diagnosis will be found on page 197.

Developmental Skills (Criterion Reference)
The student will:

1. Sort objects (blocks, coins, beads, nuts, bolts, etc.) by shape size, color, and position.

2. Sort objects into categories and indicate how they are alike or different.

3. Categorize pictures of objects and indicate how they are alike or different.

4. View pictures of objects and name those that can be grouped together, indicating the common characteristics or differences.

5. Place objects or pictures of objects in front of a picture or model appropriate to the classification.

6. Indicate, using pictures of objects, the single origin of several products (for example, paper, pencil, and piece of wood all come from a tree).

7. Sort pictures of objects by function and state the rationale.

8. Place pictures expressing different feelings into appropriate categories.

9. Develop written lists of objects with common characteristics.

10. Read paragraphs containing objects with common characteristics and then form written lists of objects by these specific characteristics.

11. Read paragraphs at the independent level and respond, orally or in writing, to questons dealing with classification concepts.

Prescriptive Activities

GENERAL ACTIVITIES

1. Select from the list of developmental skills the particular target skills that are to be mastered in the area of Visual Language Classification. These target skills become learning or behavioral objectives. (Example Target: Visual Language Classification 7—The learner will sort pictures of objects by function and state the rationale.)
2. If the student fails to demonstrate success in the target skills according to predetermined criteria such as failing items assessed on a standardized test or failing school tasks requiring the skills, do the following:
   a. Select from the list of developmental skills the target skill (example: Visual Language Classification 7) and other related or similar skills (6, 5, etc.) that are deemed appropriate for developing activities that will provide success and practice for higher level functions or skills (8, 9, 10, etc.). Select activities at lower levels (6, 5, 4, etc.) as necessary to insure success and provide an array of different activities that will reinforce the development of Visual Language Classification skills.
   b. Develop or select from other sources additional activities related to all of the specific Visual Language Classification skills listed (1–11). These activities can be coded into the system at the appropriate levels within the list of development skills.

SPECIFIC ACTIVITIES

1. Begin with simple activities involving concrete objects, and teach difference and sameness. Using small plastic animals or real coins (pennies, nickels, dimes, and quarters), have the students match the animals or coins appropriately. The students should verbalize the difference and then the sameness as they point to each grouping and physically manipulate the objects. Along with teaching difference and sameness, teach what an object is and what it is not. This must also be verbalized by the students. For example, ask a student to show which coin in a group of coins is not a penny and tell why.
2. Repeat the preceding activities using color discs or blocks instead of coins. Color becomes the vehicle for teaching the concept of difference and sameness.
3. Difference and sameness can also be taught using position, size, and shape as a conceptual base. For example, "this one is facing up," "this one is shorter," "this one is round," etc. Remember, the objective is to make the student understand both the concept and the language of difference and sameness.
   Note: It is important for the teacher to determine whether or not the student has a perceptual (visual discrimination, etc.) problem to overcome in addition to a language difficulty.
4. The next step is to teach symbols by matching them in terms of difference and then sameness. First use plastic or wooden letters and words, then use printed letters and word cards.
5. Help the students look for and verbalize the common elements of concrete objects, including function. For example, pencils and pens are pointed and long, and they are both used in writing.
6. Involve the students in as much motor activity as possible. Permit them to manipulate objects as they verbalize difference and sameness, in that order.

   Note: For all areas of amelioration and dysfunctions, training should follow the sequence of levels listed below. Begin at the level that is most appropriate for the individual student, using (a) concrete objects, (b) pictures, (c) geometric forms, and (d) symbols, e.g., letters, words, and numerals.

7. After the students verbalize difference and then sameness at the concrete-functional level (what the object looks like and what you can do with it), move to the abstract level, using concrete objects first, then pictures. Hold up an apple and a pear, for example, and say, "These are both round. They are both good to eat. These are both fruit." The students should do likewise. The next step would be to hold up a picture of two items and have the students give similar classifications.

   Note: Many students functioning at the concrete-functional level in language development do not do well with tasks that require more abstract language abilities. The vocabulary sections of the Mann-Suiter Developmental Inventories will give the teacher information about the student's primary level of language functioning. Language in this sense becomes the tool of thinking or conceptualization.

8. Help the learners to classifiy objects or pictures.
   a. Household objects (tools, kitchen utensils, clothes, etc.) can be sorted into categories by the learner. Discuss the common characteristics.

b. Pictures from trading stamp catalogs or magazines can be sorted into categories by the learner.

9. Show the learners a group of objects or pictures of objects and have them indicate the one that does not belong (such as apple, book, pear, peach).

10. Play a category game by naming three or four objects. The learner names the one that does not belong (bicycle, car, pencil, airplane).

VISUAL LANGUAGE ASSOCIATION—
NONSYMBOLIC (OBJECT AND PICTURE LEVEL)
Diagnosis will be found on page 197.

Developmental Skills (Criterion Reference)
The student will:

1. Point to the object or a picture of the object named by the instructor.
2. Name the object or picture of an object pointed to or otherwise indicated by the instructor.
3. Point to the size, shape, color, or position of the object or picture of an object named by the instructor.
4. Name the size, shape, color, or position of the object or picture of an object indicated by the instructor.
5. Place in the proper setting (picture or model) different objects or pictures of objects that represent the appropriate association.
6. Place the object or picture of the object related to specific job roles in the appropriate setting (picture or model).
7. View a specific object or picture of an object and state where the object belongs.
8. View an object or a picture of an object and describe the object's function.
9. Point to, or otherwise indicate from among choices, an object or picture of an object that goes with, or has a high degree of association with, the model.
10. View a model and sets of objects or pictures of sets of objects and state the association between the objects and the model.
11. View a picture of an object (model) and from among choices select the object that has the greatest degree of association with the model.
12. Select from choices of pictures of objects and connect with a line, or otherwise indicate, those pictures of objects that go together.
13. Select from choices of pictures of objects and connect with a line, or otherwise indicate, those pictures of objects that go together, stating the rationale for the association.
14. View a model or picture of a setting, identify the unrelated objects from among choices, and state the rationale.
15. View an object or a picture and complete in a logical manner an incomplete phrase or sentence stated by the instructor.
16. View a picture of an object or scene and create and express verbally a logical story.
17. View a picture of an object and select from choices the object that is the opposite of the model.
18. View a picture of a situation and select from choices the situation that is opposite of the model.
19. View a picture of an absurd circumstance or predicament and indicate verbally the absurdity.
20. View pictures of antecedents or components of a sitation and state the outcome, indicating the cause-effect relationship.
21. View pictures of analogies and select from choices the analogy that is appropriate to the model.

Prescriptive Activities

GENERAL ACTIVITIES

1. Select from the list of developmental skills the particular target skills that are to be mastered in the area of Visual Language Association at the nonsymbolic level. These target skills become learning or behavioral objectives. (Example Target: Visual Language Association-Nonsymbolic 8—View an object or a picture of an object and describe the object's function.)

2. If the student fails to demonstrate success in the target skills according to predetermined criteria such as failing items assessed on a standardized test or failing school tasks requiring the skills, do the following:
   a. Select from the list of developmental skills the target skill (example: Visual Language Association–Nonsymbolic 8) and other related or similar skills (7, 6, etc) that are deemed appropriate for developing activities that will provide success and practice for higher level functions or skills (9, 10, 11, etc). Select activities at lower levels (7, 6, 5, etc.) as necessary to insure success and provide an array of different activities that will reinforce the development of Visual Language Association skills.

b. Develop or select from other sources additional activities related to all of the specific Visual Language Association skills listed (1–21). These activities can be coded into the system at the appropriate levels within the list of development skills.

SPECIFIC ACTIVITIES

1. Build vocabulary by beginning with words within the student's experience.
2. Begin with concrete objects (for example, an apple), and have the student match the oral word with the single object first. Then ask the student to match the word with the appropriate object picked from a group of three or four objects. ("Give me an apple.")
3. Have students match oral words with pictures of objects within their experience. Begin with single words and match them to pictures, and then let the students match the word with the appropriate picture picked from a group of three or four different pictures.
4. Hold up familiar objects and have the students describe the quality and function of the objects. The students should be allowed to manipulate the objects as they describe them.
5. Hold up pictures of familiar objects and have the students describe the quality and function of the objects.
6. Try to get short-phrase or short-sentence responses from the students if they cannot give a long sentence, for example, "cotton," "soft cotton," "The cotton is soft."
7. Give the students directions by pointing or showing. For example, point to the door and motion for the student to close it.
8. Show the learners an object (shoe) and ask them to locate another object that goes with it (sock). If they cannot locate an object, provide a selection of three or more objects for the learners to select from. Discuss the associative relationships of the object.
9. Encourage the learners to use adjectives (such as soft, hard, big, little, red, fuzzy) to describe objects on a table or in a room, their clothes, etc.
10. Say sentences, leaving out a word, and have the learners supply the missing word (e.g., "The cotton feels _____ .").
11. Take the learners on trips to parks, museums, places of historical significance, etc. Discuss the qualities of the objects or scenes viewed.
12. Play games (e.g., relay races) with the learners to teach verbs—walk, run, hop, skip, jump, etc.
13. On a hike with the learners, use adverbs and discuss their meaning (e.g., walk slowly, carefully, quickly, sadly, quietly, happily, noisily, etc.).
14. As a learner moves from room to room within the house, play riddles with him or her. (e.g., "I have four legs. I am not alive.")
15. Discuss the animals in stories (e.g., pelican, pig, rat, horse). On a trip to the library, examine pictures of the animals in books and discuss their coloring, types, location, food, habitat, etc.
16. Develop simple analogies by using colored sheets of paper, blocks, or crayons. Say, "as green as." Go on a color hunt to find articles to complete the comparison.
17. Present the student with four blocks (Figure 3–1) and ask the following questions:

> What color blocks are on top?
> What color blocks are underneath?
> What color block is beneath the yellow block?
> What color block is beside the blue block?
> What color block is on top of the green block?

> (*Note:* Slow down the rate and amount of input for all activities to avoid frustration.)

VISUAL LANGUAGE ASSOCIATION—SYMBOLIC (LETTER, NUMERAL, AND WORD DECODING AND COMPREHENSION SKILLS)
Diagnosis will be found on page 224.

Developmental Skills (Criterion Reference)
The student will:

1. Select from choices the object or picture of the object that begins with the same sound as the one indicated by the instructor.
2. Select from choices the object or picture of the object that begins with the same sound as the word indicated by the instructor.
3. Identify from choices the printed letter name or numeral indicated by the instructor.
4. Identify from choices of printed letters the letter sound as indicated by the instructor.
5. Identify from choices the printed letter blend as indicated by the instructor.
6. Select from choices the object or picture of an object that ends with the same sound as the one indicated by the instructor.
7. Select from choices the object or picture of an object that ends the same as the word indicated by the instructor.

8. Select from choices the object or picture of an object that has the same middle sound as the one indicated by the instructor.

9. Select from printed words the word that has the same middle sound as the one indicated by the instructor.

10. Identify from among choices of objects or pictures of objects the one that represents the meaning of a word.

11. Connect by marking or by other means words or columns of words that have associative relationships.

12. Identify from choices the word that has the same or similar meaning as the one indicated by the instructor.

13. State a word that has the same or similar meaning as the word indicated by the instructor.

14. Identify from choices a word within the reading vocabulary.

15. Identify from choices a short phrase within the reading vocabulary.

16. Identify from choices a sentence within the reading vocabulary.

17. Identify from printed words the word that has an opposite meaning from the one indicated by the instructor.

18. State a word that has an opposite meaning from the word indicated by the instructor.

19. Select from printed words the word that completes the analogy.

20. Read a word or statement and orally complete the analogy.

21. Formulate a complete sentence indicating in concrete-functional terms what a word read represents in terms of quality, state of being, or function.

22. Read a sentence with words deleted (blank spaces) and select from choices the picture representing the word that can be inserted into the blank space.

23. Read a sentence with words deleted (blank spaces) and select from choices the printed word that can be appropriately inserted into the blank space.

24. Read a sentence with words deleted (blank spaces) and insert a word in the blank space that will appropriately complete the sentence.

25. Read grammatically incorrect sentences and restate them into grammatically correct statements.

26. Read a paragraph or story at the independent level and orally paraphrase it.

27. Read a paragraph or story at the independent level and correctly respond to questions relating to vocabulary or meaning of words.

28. Read a paragraph or story at the independent level and correctly respond to questions relating to details of the story.

29. Read a paragraph or story at the independent level and correctly respond to questions relating to the main ideas of the story.

30. Read a paragraph or story at the independent level and correctly respond to questions relating to the inferences in the story.

Prescriptive Activities

GENERAL ACTIVITIES

1. Select from the list of developmental skills the particular target skills that are to be mastered in the area of Visual Language Association—Symbolic. These target skills become learning or behavioral objectives. (Example Target: Visual Language Association—Symbolic 14—The learner will identify from choices a word within the reading vocabulary.)

2. If the student fails to demonstrate success in the target skills according to a predetermined criteria such as failing items assessed on a standardized test or failing school tasks requiring this skill, do the following:

   a. Select from the list of developmental skills the target skill (example: Visual Language Association—Symbolic 14) and other related or similar skills (13, 12, etc.) that are deemed appropriate for developing activities that will provide success and practice for higher level functions or skills (15, 16, 17, etc.). Select activities at lower levels (13, 12, 11, etc.) as necessary to insure success and provide an array of different activities that will reinforce the development of Visual Language Association—Symbolic skills.

   b. Develop or select from other sources additional activities related to all of the specific Visual Language Association skills listed (1–30). These activities can be coded into the system at the appropriate levels within the list of development skills.

SPECIFIC ACTIVITIES

1. To improve phoneme-grapheme relationships have the learner do the following:

   a. Sort objects according to the initial consonant sound.

   b. List words that begin or end with the same sound.

   c. Identify pictures or objects that have a specified medial sound (e.g., *a—cat, man*).

2. Refer to Chapter 9 for specific activities for developing sound-symbol relationships.
3. Read the definition of a word. Have the student hold up the appropriate word card.
4. Use the Cloze technique to complete sentences.

The cat _____ over the chair.

5. Have the learner rewrite figurative speech or similies in order to understand meaning.
6. Use dictionary activities to discuss the multiple meanings of words.
7. Additional Comprehension activities are located in Chapter 9.

AUDITORY LANGUAGE CLASSIFICATION
Diagnosis will be found on page 202.

Developmental Skills (Criterion Reference)
The student will:

1. Indicate the object that does not belong from among choices presented orally.
2. Name all the objects included in a particular classification, such as fruit, animals, and transportation.
3. Name the category when presented orally with a group of objects that can be classified together.
4. Name the situation when presented orally with characteristic components.
5. Indicate how objects or situations presented orally are alike or different, utilizing concrete-functional analysis as a rationale.
6. Indicate how objects or situations presented orally are alike or different, utilizing abstract reasoning as a rationale.
7. Complete sentences given orally that form analogies that involve the classification of objects or situations.

Prescriptive Activities

GENERAL ACTIVITIES

1. Select from the list of developmental skills the particular target skills that are to be mastered in the area of Auditory Language Classification. These target skills become learning or behaviorial objectives. (Example Target: Auditory Language Classification 4—The learner will name the situation when presented orally with characteristic components.)
2. If the student fails to demonstrate success in the target skills according to predetermined criteria such as failing items assessed on a standardized test or failing school tasks requiring the skills, do the following:
   a. Select from the list of developmental skills the target skill (example: Auditory Language Classification 4) and other related or similar skills (3, 2, etc.) that are deemed appropriate for developing activities that will provide success and practice for higher level functions or skills (5, 6, 7, etc.). Select activities at lower levels (3, 2, 1, etc.) as necessary to insure success and provide an array of different activities that will reinforce the development of Auditory Language Classification skills.
   b. Develop or select from other sources additional activities related to all of the specific Auditory Language Classification skills listed (1–7). These activities can be coded into the system at the appropriate levels within the list of development skills.

SPECIFIC ACTIVITIES

1. For more severely involved students or very young children, begin with simple auditory (sound) activities to teach the concept of difference and sameness. Be sure the student verbalizes what the sound is as well as what it is not. The following sequence is recommended:
   a. Gross sounds—bells, drums, dogs, etc. First teach different and same for gross sounds (between bells and drums), then for classification (all bells and all drums).
   b. Gross sound recognition. Play records of different sounds and ask the student to identify the sounds.
   c. Contrasting gross sounds. Ask the student to tell you which is loud, louder, loudest, low, lower, lowest, high, higher, highest, etc. Vary sounds in frequency, intensity, pitch, and timbre. Try to get complete sentence responses if you can. Remember to have the student verbalize what is loud as well as what is not loud.
   d. Help the student identify beginning sounds of words that are different and alike, then ending sounds that are different and alike, and, finally, medial sounds (the most difficult to discern) that are different or alike.
2. Use classification analysis games. For example, say one word, such as *ball*. The student names as many types of balls as he or she can, such as football, baseball, and handball.
3. Engage the student in category games:
   a. Which one does not belong? A cat, a dog, an umbrella.

b. What are all of these called together? A pear, a plum, a peach.

c. How many vegetables can you name?

4. Classification activities such as the following can be developed around media.

   a. Use the overhead projector for visual and auditory language classification games.

   b. Use real objects and talk about how they are the same and/or different.

   c. Draw pictures on the chalkboard for classification activities.

   d. Listen to records of different objects that can be classified together.

   e. Make duplicator masters for simple to complex activities.

   f. From old workbooks or magazines, cut out pictures that can be used for classification activities. They can be laminated, if desired.

   g. Use a pocket chart of pictures of objects for classification activities.

   h. Purchase or make tapes that contain classification activities.

   i. Have students draw objects that belong to the same classification, such as fruit, vehicles, different types of shelter.

   j. Use pictures to teach not only what an object is but also what it is not, such as, big—not big; little—not little; round—not round; live—not live. These concepts should be verbalized by the student.

AUDITORY LANGUAGE ASSOCIATION
Diagnosis will be found on page 202.

Developmental Skills (Criterion Reference)
The student will:

1. Identify from among two or more choices of objects or words the one that begins with the same sound as the one indicated by the instructor.

2. Listen to a word and its beginning sound and indicate another word that begins with the same sound.

3. Identify from among choices of objects the one that represents the meaning of the word presented orally.

4. Identify from among choices of pictures of objects the one that represents the meaning of the word presented orally.

5. Identify an object that is described in detail.

6. Identify a situation that is described in detail.

7. Describe an object indicated by the instructor in terms of function.

8. Describe a situation indicated by the instructor in terms of feelings.

9. Identify from choices the picture that represents the meaning of a sentence presented orally.

10. Identify from choices based on a paragraph or story read to him or her the correct responses to associations dealing with social or cultural relationships.

11. Identify from choices based on a paragraph or story read to him or her the correct responses to associations dealing with geographic or spatial-temporal relationships.

12. Identify from choices based on a paragraph or story read to him or her the correct responses to associations or relationships involving good judgment in life situations.

13. Verbally state an appropriate response to riddles.

14. Orally indicate a logical and rational completion to an incomplete sentence.

15. Complete analogies stated as incomplete sentences and define the rationale behind the associative relationship.

16. Appropriately and logically extend open-ended situations.

17. Orally complete in a logical manner a sentence read as an incomplete phrase by the instructor.

18. Orally complete in a logical manner paragraphs read as open sentences by the instructor.

19. Explain absurdities read in sentences, paragraphs, or stories by the instructor.

20. Explain or indicate the absurdity when presented orally with absurd situations.

21. Listen to a paragraph or story and orally paraphrase it.

22. Listen to a word and verbally state it in a complete sentence, using it in the context of concrete or functional terms.

23. Listen to a word and verbally state it in a complete sentence, using it in the context of abstract terms.

24. Restate grammatically incorrect sentences presented orally into grammatically correct statements using good syntax and formulation.

25. Respond correctly to multiple-choice or true-or-false questions related to a paragraph or story read to him or her.

26. Respond to detail questions related to a paragraph or story read to him or her.

27. Respond to main-idea questions related to a paragraph or story read to him or her.

28. Respond to inference questions related to a paragraph or story read to him or her.

29. Respond to personal questions relating to life history and environment.

30. Verbally indicate all the words that he or she can think of in a given period of time.

Prescriptive Activities

GENERAL ACTIVITIES

1. Select from the list of developmental skills the particular target skills that are to be mastered in the area of Auditory Language Association. These target skills become learning or behavioral objectives. (Example Target: Auditory Language Association 25—The student will respond correctly to multiple-choice or true-or-false questions related to a paragraph or story read to him or her.)
2. If the student fails to demonstrate success in the target skills according to predetermined criteria such as failing items assessed on a standardized test or failing school tasks requiring the skills, do the following:
   a. Select from the list of developmental skills the target skill (example: Auditory Language Association 25) and other related or similar skills (24, 23, etc.) that are deemed appropriate for developing activities that will provide success and practice for higher level functions or skills (26, 27, 28, etc.). Select activities at lower levels (24, 23, 22, etc.) as necessary to insure success and provide an array of different activities that will reinforce the development of Auditory Language Association skills.
   b. Develop or select from other sources additional activities related to all of the specific Auditory Language Association skills listed (1–30). These activities can be coded into the system at the appropriate levels within the list of development skills.

SPECIFIC ACTIVITIES

1. In severe cases or with very young children make the students aware of sound as opposed to no-sound activities. Ask the students to raise their hands when they hear the sound of machines turned on or off.
2. Begin with simple nouns within the students' experience. Use concrete objects, then use pictures of objects. Show the object or picture and discuss as follows:
   a. The quality of an object—for example, "the pencil is hard," "it has lead," "it can be made of wood." Then remove the object from sight and discuss what the students have learned immediately.
   b. The action potential or state of being of an object—for example, "the pencil is used to write with; it is not alive." After the object has been removed, the students describe from memory what they have learned.
3. Matching games like the following should be used to develop associative skills.
   a. Match environmental sounds such as horns with concrete objects and with pictures of horns.
   b. Match animal sounds with pictures of animals.
   c. Match words with concrete objects and then with pictures of objects.
   d. Match words given orally with words printed on cards.
4. Collect and use records of rhyming words and let the students hear the difference and then the sameness.
5. Use activities in which the students have to identify the source of sounds—first with their eyes open and then with their eyes shut.
6. Build vocabulary, beginning with words within the students' experience only.
7. In the beginning, ask short questions requiring short one-concept answers.
8. Say a word and tell the students to clap their hands when they hear the correct word among other words.
9. At first, build phrases by combining different action words with the same noun (for example, the boy walks, the boy runs, the boy eats).
10. Train the students to describe objects or situations from memory. ("What does an apple look like?" "What does your room look like?")
11. The intent of the following activities is for the students to verbalize associations between objects. Eventually, they should be able to do this without the object present as well as they can with the object present. Games that involve symbol or object associations will enable the students to "see" relationships more readily. For example:
    a. What-goes-with-what games, such as "What goes with shoe?"
    b. "Does bird go with feather, iron, or mountain?"
    c. What-is-the-opposite-of games: "What is the opposite of big?" "What is the opposite of high?" "What is the opposite of in?" etc.
12. Ask the student simple riddles. For example, "What is white and hard and you can write on the chalkboard with it?"
13. Ask association questions about stories read to the students and about television programs.

14. Teach cause-effect associations by asking the students such questions as the following:
    a. "When you see dark clouds in the sky, and lightning and thunder, what will happen?"
    b. "Why can't dogs fly?"
15. Use phoneme association games. For example: "Think of a word that begins like *boy* and sounds like *tag.*"
16. Build in appropriate affectional association and improve social perception by varying the emotional tone of the verbal responses to include anger, excitement, declaration, interrogation, apathy, and happiness.
    a. Use puppets and carry on a dialogue that expresses the gamut of emotions. After the dialogue, the students can select from a group of pictures the facial expressions that the puppets expressed.
    b. Play a record of verbal behavior expressing emotions. Stand behind a student, looking into a full-length mirror. As the emotions are expressed, you and the student should pattern, or pantomime, the behavior. A full-length mirror is good for developing social perception and language.
17. Discuss real-life situations with the students and alternative solutions to everyday problems. Example: "What do you do if a bigger student hits you?"
18. If the students can learn to play checkers or chess, these kinds of activities can help to develop cause-effect relationships.
19. Identify concepts in particular stories or in areas of curriculum such as science or social studies that deal with the following:
    a. Space
    b. Time
    c. Geography
    d. Social order
    e. Economy (money)
    f. Value system

    Discuss the concepts in concrete-functional terms, then discuss relationship in terms of abstract thinking.
20. Matching or comparing for associative learning for many of the developmental skills can be achieved by using the following media:
    a. Real objects
    b. Pictures of objects or situations from books and newspapers
    c. Overhead projector using acetates
    d. Chalkboard activities
    e. Duplicated sheets of paper

21. A field trip provides a good real-life experience for developing associative relationships. For example, a camel seen at the zoo is also a means of transportation in many areas of the world.
22. Discuss situations that will enable the students to take things to their natural consequences. What can happen if . . .?
23. Vocabulary building in terms of word meaning should be a part of everyday activities in all subject areas.
24. Science and social studies are good areas for developing associative learning. For example:
    a. Dual meaning of words or phrases.
    b. Cause-effect relationship in economics, war, industry, science, etc.
    c. Historical sequences and relationships.
25. Develop duplicator masters that require students to indicate things that go together.
26. Find activities in old workbooks that develop associative skills. These can be laminated for continued use.
27. Discuss how things are not related as well as how they are related.
28. Discuss concepts dealing with space-time relationships. ("How long does it take you to get home from school?" "How far is it from where you live to the shopping center?" "During what season or time of the year is your birthday?")
29. Describe funny or silly situations. ("The car flew over the bridge," or "The cat skated down the hill") Ask the learner what is funny about the statement.
30. Say a word to the students and have them give the opposite—for example, big and _____ [little]; hot and _____ [cold].
31. Present a student with several objects (for example, pencil, comb, and spoon). Have the student follow a series of directions such as the following:

    Give me the pencil and the spoon.
    Give me both the comb and the spoon.
    Give me none of the three objects.
    Give me two of the three objects.
    Give me the largest [or smallest, heaviest, roundest, smoothest, etc.] object
    Give me the ones that are not used to comb your hair.
    Give me the one you write with.

32. Ask the learners to listen to a story record, a television program, etc., and have them verbally summarize the plot or list the major events.
33. Read to the learners. As they listen to different stories, they will increase their vocabulary. En-

courage them to form visual images of the action, places, or characters in the stories.

WORD RETRIEVAL
Diagnosis will be found on page 208.

Prescriptive Activities

Note: Slow down the rate and amount of input. Wait for a response and do not rush the student. Reduce your demands for spoken language at first.

1. Give the students clues. Say, "do you mean," or give them the first letter of the word.
2. Have the students imitate single words presented verbally and associate them first with an object, then with a picture—for example, chalk (object-picture), pencil, etc. Then add qualifiers (adjectives and adverbs) in short phrases. Next, present sentences using objects then pictures of objects—for example: "Chalk is hard. I write with chalk."
3. Use cueing, such as "I write with a _____ ."
4. Use associative ideas, such as pairing: e.g., "bread and _____ ," "salt and _____ ."
5. Get the student to verbalize opposites and similarities of objects, then pictures.
6. Encourage the student to use words instead of gestures, and try to elicit short-phrase responses, then sentences.

Problems with retrieval will keep the students from quickly recalling numbers. They may recognize the correct number when they see it but be unable to say the one they want. Rapid oral drills are difficult for the students and should be avoided until the students have improved in retrieval.

The students may not be deficient in understanding quantitative relationships and may do well in computation as long as it is written and not oral.

SYNTAX AND FORMULATION
Diagnosis will be found on page 208.

Prescriptive Activities

1. Have the students verbalize their actions during meaningful play.
2. Use pictures and have the students' name the pictured objects. They should use the word in a sentence and then develop a sequence of sentences about the object.
3. Elicit a response from the student by saying a sentence, leaving out a word, and having the student supply the missing word—for example, "I have a _____ ball."

4. Scramble word cards and then build sentences using the word cards.
5. Use sequential pictures, such as comic strips or sequence puzzles, and have the student verbalize the sequence of actions.
6. Make sequence puzzles based on simple stories or themes and have the student order them.
7. Ordering, or sequence of thought, can be taught by giving students two sentences in different order and asking them to give the correct sequence. For example:
   I ate my breakfast.
   I got up in the morning.
8. A sequence of amelioration activities such as the following may be helpful.
   a. *Restructuring Verbal Responses (Imitation):* The student first repeats short sentences verbalized by the teacher indicating the correct tense. For example:
      Look at me.
      He looked at me.
      He is looking at me.
   The teacher can use the same sentences again, substituting different pronouns (e.g., *we, she*) or students' names. This activity can be reinforced by using associative clues such as pictures or filmstrips.
   b. *Understanding.* The student can indicate understanding by responding to (1) actions, (2) emotions, and (3) cause-effect relationships. For example, the student is asked questions based on pictures of actions (a boy running), emotions (a girl crying), and cause-effect relationships (a boy falling) that reflect the appropriate tense.
   Sample Activity: Understanding the verb *fall.* Show the student three pictures:
      A boy running.
      A boy tripping over a stone and falling.
      A boy on the ground.
   Say, "Show me the picture that means the boy is falling." The student repeats the sentence and indicates his or her understanding by selecting the correct response. (If the response is incorrect, repeat the sentence as necessary until it is understood.) Do the same thing with the picture of the boy on the ground. Say, "Show me the picture that means the boy has fallen."
   c. *Elicited Responses:* In this activity, the teacher provides a stimulus picture indicating (1) an action, (2) an emotion, and (3) a cause-effect relationship.

Sample Activity: In expressing the verb *eat,* for example, show the student a series of cards, one at a time, of a puppy standing over a full bowl, a puppy eating, and a puppy standing over an empty bowl. Ask, "What is the puppy doing?" for each of these pictures. The student may reply with one word, a phrase, or a sentence. With practice, one-word and phrase responses should develop into sentences. Always repeat the response in a complete sentence even though the student may answer in one word.

9. The teacher says a number of phrases or short sentences, some of which are grammatically correct, some of which are grammatically incorrect. Ask the learner to say "right" and "wrong" or "yes" and "no," or clap his or her hands whenever the correct form is used. Suggested phrases:

   a. Pour the juice up the glass.
   b. We are going.
   c. I see three dogs.
   d. I brought it with me.
   e. I see the two horse.
   f. Pour the juice in the glass.
   g. I go at home.
   h. Three cat
   i. Me go trip.
   j. I am good.
   k. Two cats
   l. Me is here.
   m. Paul's cat got away.
   n. Us is going.
   o. I be good.
   p. John cat got away.
   q. I am good.
   r. I go to class.

10. Record good and poor phrases or sentences using a cassette tape. As the learner listens, he or she can draw a happy face (or glue on a gold star) for every correct phrase on a duplicated worksheet that you have made. The student can draw a different picture (e.g., sad face) whenever he or she hears an incorrect phrase. Check the work by looking at his or her sequence of drawings and comparing it to a key of your own drawings. This is an individual or group activity.

11. Say one sentence at a time. Give the learner a selection of pictures (three). The learner points to, picks up, marks, or otherwise indicates the picture that illustrates the missing word. Do an example to illustrate the task.

12. Using pictures, write a list of analogous sentences. (Omit key word from second half of each sentence.) "Chalk is for a chalkboard, as a pencil is for _____ _____ ." The learner points to the correct picture and says the word.

13. Prepare a duplicated worksheet. Write analogous sentences with a key word omitted in the second half. The student says or reads the missing word. "I wear shoes on my feet and a tie on my _____ _____ ." "Soup is eaten with a spoon; meat is eaten with a _____ _____ ."

14. Using pictures, the teacher says a word and then the learner points to a particular item similar to it illustrated in a store catalog, in a magazine, or in a picture book. For example, say "coat"; the learner points to a jacket. The teacher and learner discuss how they are the same.

15. Have the learner search for objects in the room similar to an object displayed by the teacher. Discuss the basis of the similarity with the learner (e.g., "How are they alike?").

16. Gather a number of small objects. The learner shows and tells which ones go together (i.e., which ones are related in some way). The learner points to or otherwise identifies (naming) the items which go together. He or she could also be asked to put them together in a little group. Grouping may be done on the basis of:

    a. Descriptive characteristics of those items of the same color, size, or shape; objects made from the same materials or items found in the same place (e.g., in the kitchen)
    b. Function: how they are used together (we put butter on bread) or they all do the same thing (we garden with a hoe and a shovel)
    c. Class: they all belong to the same category (e.g., furniture)

    Do not tell the learner anything beyond asking him or her to tell you which things go together. If he or she has difficulty, give him or her an example.

17. Use loose pictures from magazines, store catalogs, old workbooks, etc. The learner sorts into groups those items that go together. Or make duplicated worksheets with pictures. The learner connects related pictures with lines made by colored crayon. Blue may connect pictures of fruit. Green may connect things that we eat.

18. What does not belong: Display objects. The learner takes out the object(s) that does not belong with others and tells why.

19. Use a catalog page: Look at a catalog and have the learner verbally identify things that go together.

20. Ask the learner why all the things found in a particular room (closet, drawer, or cupboard) go together.

21. Present the learner with worksheets on which objects from several categories are partially drawn using dotted lines. The learner finds an object in

the category which you name and completes it. (He or she may also color it in.)

22. Say a class name (e.g., fruit) to the learner. Ask him or her to draw an object (or several objects) within that class. Discuss each category asking questions. Use categories such as:

a. people
b. vegetables
c. jewelry
d. furniture
e. pets
f. plants
g. parts of the body
h. dishes
i. tools
j. musical instruments
k. weapons
l. clothing
m. toys
n. buildings
o. animals
p. drinks
q. food

NONVERBAL LANGUAGE

Diagnosis will be found on page 211. Students with a nonverbal language difficulty have problems with assigning meaning to such nonverbal functions as art, religion, music, holidays, and patriotism. There is a language of art and music from which the students cannot derive meaning. Often, a nonverbal language disorder is accompanied by problems in the spatial area.

Prescriptive Activities

1. Begin by talking about things in the students' own environment. Do they keep things that they feel will bring them luck, such as a rabbit's foot or a special toy?
2. Talk about how we remember people (include monuments, statues, tombstones, etc.).
3. Begin with a simple painting or a patriotic song and talk about how the artist or composer may have felt when painting or writing the work. For example, discuss Francis Scott Key and the *Star-Spangled Banner*.
4. With the students, make a list of pictures and objects that have symbolic significance, then have the students verbalize the relationships.
5. Ask the students to match a list of holidays with the appropriate objects and pictures.
6. Talk about the history of particular symbols in the students' environment. How did flags become symbols? Discuss other symbols for countries or people (e.g., shields, seals, crests).
7. Have the students design and name their own family crests if they can.
8. Have students collect, label, and discuss emblems and badges representing different social organiza-

tions, such as scouting, the armed forces, and local clubs.
9. See the spatial disorder section (page 510) for activities in that area.

INNER-LANGUAGE

Inner-language is the language with which one thinks. Inner-language serves to integrate experiences with a native spoken language. Inner-language can also be thought of as inner-speech. In this sense, inner-speech relates to thinking, while outer-speech provides for communication between people.

Prescriptive Activities

1. In teaching initial reading, give the learners the best model possible. Say the word correctly and elicit it correctly from the students at least one time, no matter how they wish to pronounce it later on.
2. It is important not to corrrect students' speech constantly, as they will probably incorporate standard English speech patterns when they are ready to do so.
3. The students must be told explicitly that there is a universal English phonetic system common to all English-speaking people. For communication (verbal communication as well as reading and writing), they must learn that system. Otherwise, in order to communicate, they will have to teach their own code to anyone who doesn't know it. The learners must understand, for example, that there is a voiced and unvoiced *th* that is constant regardless of how they wish to pronounce it themselves.
4. Students should be taught that there is a language of the home, of the school, and of literature. They must learn to use each one appropriately.
5. Build on words based on the students' experiences first, and give the students many opportunities to verbalize their feelings and experiences. Teachers sometimes talk too much. Remember, the sequence in learning is verbal, reading, and writing. Activities under syntax and formulation are appropriate here.
6. Remember that the sound *t* is not "tuh"; do not add a vowel to a consonant when saying the sound, as this adds to the confusion.
7. Talk about the history of language and how people learned to communicate with each other both verbally and nonverbally.
8. Develop activities that involve the students in creating their own code so that they can see more readily the function of communication.

SPEECH
Diagnosis will be found on page 205.

Prescriptive Activities

1. Make the students aware of sounds and the movements of the organs of speech by
   a. Using mirrors to illustrate positioning.
   b. Using touch to feel positioning as letters and words are formed (hands on face and throat).
2. Use additional clues, including
   a. Follow-the-leader games (i.e., look, listen, and imitate).
   b. Blowing, smiling, licking, and tongue movement activities.
   c. Peanut butter put in different places in the mouth to facilitate better tongue placement.
3. Establish a motor pattern by introducing sounds (c a t), reinforcing them with touch (feeling the organs of speech), and then by converting them into a word (verbalization) by saying the word *cat*.
4. Give the student specific verbal directions for producing the sound or word. For example, "open your mouth, purse your lips, and blow" or "place your tongue between your teeth and force air through the opening."
5. Experiment with tactual-kinesthetic associations.
   a. Use a tongue depressor or lollipop to guide placement of the tongue.
   b. Overarticulate while the student feels your face.
   c. Have the students feel their own faces and throats as they speak.
6. Repeat the word correctly at first without correcting the student each time. Intermittent correction is appropriate. Use good judgment.
7. Does the learner use a correct sound in more than one context, such as with pictures only?
8. Is the sound under concern used correctly, spontaneously in everyday situations?
9. Do the transfer situations extend beyond the therapy environment to home as well as school?

MOTOR LANGUAGE EXPRESSION: MANUAL (HAND FOOT)
Diagnosis will be found on page 205.

Prescriptive Activities

1. Begin with real objects within the student's experience:
   a. Find out if the student knows the functions and movements of parts of his or her own body. Demonstrate first on your own body. Have the student imitate and verbalize the functions. For example, "My hands can hold, give, write, hit, stroke, clap," etc. "My eyes can open, close, see, blink, wink, squint, move from side to side and up and down," etc.
   b. Use things the student is familiar with, such as a pencil, which can write, poke, erase, tickle, scratch, roll, etc.
   c. Use things the student can manipulate, such as cars, fishing poles, footballs, pans, string, bucket, paper clips, a door, or a hose.
   Note: The process in teaching is imitation (do as I do), understanding (show me the one that writes, for example, from among three objects), then elicited responses (show me what this does). Teach the object, the word, and the function simultaneously, beginning with the concrete first, then going to pictures. (Some cautionary advice: Proceed slowly! Do not "jam" or "overload" the students with too much too fast. Leave them with a success.)
2. Pantomime the motion of hammering a nail and have the students pick up the real object (a hammer) from among three or four objects.
   Note: The above activities should also develop creativity and improve the language abilities of students.

Chapter 9

Language Arts: Reading, Spelling, and Written Language Expression

CHAPTER OUTLINE

Overview
Reading
Spelling Instruction
Written Language Expression

OVERVIEW

Students who cannot read well probably cannot spell, and both of these deficiencies will affect their writing activities. Educators should consider combining the reading, writing, and spelling programs so that students are reinforcing the same vocabulary in different ways. Special education teachers and regular classroom teachers can support each other by developing language programs that build on a common vocabulary or include a supportive vocabulary program with appropriate reinforcing activities.

Instructors who require a great deal of notetaking, reading of directions, library reading, reading in testing (essay exams), oral reading, and copying from the chalkboard are presenting a problem for students who cannot read, write, or spell unless there is adequate preparation. Alternatives must be available to students such as being able to get oral directions and to take oral examinations. Students should also be able to use tape recorders and be part of some kind of buddy system. It is important that the readability of textbooks in subject level areas be analyzed and matched up with the reading levels of the students. Otherwise, the teacher may be introducing failure by using inappropriate materials.

Reading as a skill is inextricably related to a student's self-concept, and educators must keep in mind that the student is constantly in situations that result in embarrassment. Instructors should determine how to prevent unhappy language-related experiences such as being asked to write or read material that is beyond present ability levels. Avoid experiences that result in diminished self-worth, while at the same time provide opportunities for good experiences within the activity of daily school life.

Chapter 9 contains reading, spelling, and written language expression instructional activities. These teaching approaches are comprehensive and can be used with the very young child as well as the older secondary student. The testing for these areas is contained in Chapter 6, along with the special forms to be used for documentation.

READING

Stages of Reading Skill Development

The diagnostic-prescriptive approach represents a movement away from grouping students according to the traditional norm-referenced levels with resulting labels to the kind of criterion-referenced assessment and instruction that can be utilized for individualized educational programming. Assessing the achievement levels of students for norm-referenced purposes (e.g., grade level(s), quartiles, percentiles, standard grading systems) is not enough. Criterion-reference is defined as a method of determining the level and quality of an individual's performance in relation to specific instructional objectives or criteria. Students must be assessed from a developmental (criterion-referenced) point of view in terms of their skills in the critical areas of language and computation.

The following is an example of a criterion-referenced orientation to assessment and instruction. The language area of reading is delineated into three sequential criterion stages of skill development:

Stage 1: *Developmental*
The developmental stage represents the initial building blocks of reading, such as the meaning of words as a basic developmental skill necessary for comprehension.

Stage 2: Transitional
The transitional level of skill development is a further development of Stage 1 to where the basic skills are coordinated for higher level functions. These functions, once practiced and learned, become habitual and automatic responses that are vital for the next stage.

Stage 3: Academic
Stage 3 represents the academic level of criterion for success in reading. Such functions as speed and accuracy are essential for success in using the skills for academic purposes.

By understanding these interrelationships the teacher can determine the different levels of functioning within the various skill areas and then plan the student's program accordingly. This delineation of the subareas within reading is just another way of trying to understand a complex process without relying totally on the traditional grade level descriptions.

When viewed within the context of mastery of simple, intermediate, and complex skills, the teacher can discern the students' relative understanding and facility with a particular aspect of language. In any of life's tasks, whether it be for academic, recreational, or social purposes, the best example of how a skill can be manifested is the automatic nature of its performance or presentation. The good golfer or tennis player has an automatic swing. Likewise, the good reader or writer thinks more about what he or she is reading or writing than he or she does about the mechanics of the performance of the task. Knowledge gained and performed with automaticity, i.e., security, deftness,

smoothness, and confidence, is really what we are trying to accomplish.

The concept of automaticity is presented as a theme in each of the chapters dealing with language and mathematics. The same orientation, Developmental–Transitional–Academic, is presented as a basis for the understanding and discussion in each of these areas.

It is important for all who are concerned with a student's academic performance in school to understand that deficiencies in any of the areas outlined have implications for every aspect of the learner's life. Problems in perception, memory, judgment, vocabulary, etc., will affect students not only in academic areas, but also in the way they deal with everyday life situations. What students can do is just as important as what they cannot do. Emphasis must be placed on the positive by building on the students' strengths.

Teachers in the early grades need to examine students' performances and formulate some ideas about what the students will do when they are in secondary school or even when they are adults, given that their learning patterns may not alter significantly. Likewise, educators at the secondary level must consider how a particular student must have performed as a young learner failing in school; they must remember that the student, through the years, was taught by many teachers using different techniques. Students do not come to us as blank slates. Most have experienced years of failure. Trusting relationships must be established through a better understanding of what the students can do and cannot do so that the teacher will be in a better position to avoid introducing more anxiety and failure into their lives.

Reading Instruction

In examining the task of reading, we find many interrelated factors. Students, to become effective readers, must be able to do the following:

1. See a clear and unblurred image on a white field and hear the sounds of the letters and words (auditory-visual sensory input)
2. Distinguish one symbol from another and recognize the differences consistently (auditory-visual perception)
3. Remember the sounds or images of the symbols in sequence (auditory-visual memory)
4. Relate these symbols to meaning based on experience and synthesize the visual and auditory clues with the meaningful words for integrative learning (language-symbolization)

DEVELOPMENTAL SEQUENCE

The following represents a breakdown of reading skills from lower level to higher level functions. The outline will be helpful to teachers in diagnosis and in programming for students exhibiting developmental lags or irregular learning in reading.

Questions to be answered: What has to be taught first? What has to be practiced? What can be used effectively?

STAGES OF READING SKILL DEVELOPMENT

DEVELOPMENTAL	TRANSITIONAL	ACADEMIC
Word Recognition	*Word Recognition*	*Word Recognition*
Visual and auditory acuity	Expanded sight vocabulary	Speed-Rate
Visual and auditory perception	Phonic analysis	Automatic
Visual and auditory memory	Structural analysis	Accurate
Word awareness	Oral Reading	Effortless
Letter recognition	Silent Reading	Spelling
Left-to-right letter sequence		Assessment
Phonological awareness		
Sound/letter correspondences		
Initial sight word recognition		
Comprehension	*Comprehension*	*Comprehension*
Oral language development	Identifying details	Apply to all academics
Simple association	Identifying main ideas	Functional reading
Simple classification	Making inferences	Humor
Cause-effect relationships	Expanded vocabulary	Reading for pleasure
Vocabulary-meaning	Determining if information needed	Use for learning
Judgment	is there	Skimming
Acculturation	Expanded association and classification	Assessment

5. Do all of these things smoothly and with reasonable, efficient speed (input-output relationships)

Reading is a dynamic process in which perception, memory, language, and affect must function harmoniously with each other. The purpose of this section is to explore some specific patterns or techniques for teaching that can be utilized and adapted to most of the available reading series or reading programs. The primary emphasis will be on instructional approaches to reading.

We have to get students with learning problems through the requirements of the content areas and at the same time build up the students' reading skills to a level of competency that will meet life-long needs upon graduation. In order to accomplish this, certain factors should be considered:

1. The students with reading problems will need direct instruction in many aspects of reading throughout the school year (e.g., phonics, comprehension, vocabulary acquisition, study strategies).
2. Students will require motivational goals. Jobs, future careers, sports, movies, hobbies, and social life provide clues to students' preferences. The instructor's knowledge of a student's enjoyment of history and adventure, for example, may open a door to reading for pleasure.
3. Students will need assistance in organizing school subjects and in learning how to study. The instructor has to demonstrate strategies as well as promote self-instructional techniques (e.g., "These are the steps I would follow in outlining this chapter.").

Both regular and special education instructors need strategies that can be used in their classrooms. This chapter has general reading suggestions and a personalized approach to reading that has been used with older students. Additional strategies for teaching reading in the content areas are discussed along with written language expression.

AMOUNT OF INPUT

The teacher must remember that the goal is success—we do not want to leave the learner with a failure. Some teachers teach "just one more sound or word." That causes the learner to forget the other things that have been taught. The stabilization of vocabulary becomes irregular, and gaps may appear in the acquisition of skills. The learner may exhibit one or more of the following characteristics when the amount of input is not carefully controlled: anxiety, aggression, hyperactivity, lack of attention, and wild guessing when reading.

The teacher should ascertain the number of words learned within a given period of time to achieve 90 to 100 percent success. For example, if the instructor teaches two new words on Monday and the learner knows only one of them on Wednesday and seems to be losing vocabulary learned during the previous week, the amount of input may be contributing to failure. The instructor may have to introduce one new word at a session and then carefully monitor the type of repetitions required to ensure success. In the initial stages of word acquisition, the successful expansion of vocabulary is critical. it develops self-confidence in the learner and acts as a basis for building in new words and comprehension. The ability to recall words on a page will allow the learner to focus attention on comprehension and other skills.

RATE OF INPUT

The rate of input of new concepts, vocabulary, letter sounds, and directions should be monitored carefully by the teacher. How fast the teacher speaks and gives directions may determine a student's successful acquisition of information. The instructor should teach without excessive verbiage. If pronunciation or accent is a concern, a tape recorder can be utilized to present vocabulary and phonetic elements, especially in initial teaching. Any teacher-made feedback program should be as uncluttered and cleanly produced as possible. When setting goals for the learner, the teacher must make sure that speed in completing material or trying to reach levels (primer, grade level) will not interfere with realistic progress.

OPTIMAL TEACHING TIME

One concept to keep in mind is on-task learning. When is the optimal time the learner will attend to instructional input? For most students, the traditional morning language arts block of time is appropriate for reading skills. However, students with a short attention span may need shorter, more frequent teacher-directed input followed by successful reinforcement activities. Two or three concentrated five-minute instructional periods when the youngster is receptive to instruction may be more beneficial than a longer set period of time when the learner is too active or fatigued to learn.

CONTROLLED LANGUAGE INPUT

The teacher first has to determine the best possible approach to structuring and controlling the language input in terms of the learning needs of individual students. When the instructor initially presents vocabulary, concepts, and skills, directions should be simple. For some students, if may be more appropriate for the teacher to show a word card and say, *"cat,"* instead of saying, "This is *cat*" or "Look at the new word *cat*."

The type of directions given by the instructor may influence the responses by the student. Some nonverbal or reluctant students may not respond to the instructor's request for recall knowledge but will respond to a request for recognition responses. If the learner does not respond after being shown a word on a chalkboard or a card, the instructor has the option of requesting a recognition motor act from the learner rather than a recall verbal response. The instructor would say, "Give me *red*" or "Show me *red*." By getting a recognition response from the learner, the instructor at least knows that the student can select the appropriate word from among two or more choices, indicating a recognition level understanding of vocabulary. By probing for recognition responses, the instructor will have some idea about how much more repetition will be necessary to expand the vocabulary for particular students. Simultaneous with encouraging a verbal response, the instructor must develop the facility for verbal expression through a systematic approach utilizing a sequence of activities designed for this purpose.

OVERLOADING

Students with learning difficulties are often expected to learn too much material too fast, and they tend to become "overloaded," or saturated, to the extent that they cannot stabilize (learn) or retain new material. For example, students who are taught two or even three different reading programs simultaneously may stabilize few or none of the words from any of those programs. Since each book series or program essentially unfolds different words with some overlap, they tend to "wipe each other out," or displace each other, when they are taught concurrently. The students appear to be able to "hold," or retain, just so many words in a given period of time, and those words must be continually reinforced in different ways in order to be stabilized. The rate must be carefully controlled when adding new words to the student's program. Often, for each new word taught, the overloaded student may forget words previously thought to have been learned.

Controlling for Overloading

The following procedures will enable the instructor to more specifically control the rate of input and to make better decisions about how to introduce new learning to a particular student.

The teacher can order the concepts or skills to be learned, designating them as being either equivalent or hierarchical.

1. *Equivalent:* Concepts, behaviors, or skills that are of the same difficulty are equivalent. For example, for most individuals, learning the meaning of the word *house* is equivalent in difficulty to learning the meaning of the word *car*.
2. *Hierarchical:* Concepts, behaviors, or skills, that can be ordered from simple to complex, easy to hard, or prerequisite critical skills to higher-level activities are hierarchical in nature. For example, before you can learn to blend sounds together to make words, you need to learn the sounds that represent particular symbols.

TOP-DOWN/BOTTOM-UP

Reading is one of the complex skills that can be approached from different points of view. A bottom-up approach involves presenting information in a hierarchical order, beginning with the smallest of units such as letter names, sounds, and configurations, then building words and forming sentences and paragraphs. This enables the student to extract meaning or information from the text. The flow of information is external (environmental) from the text to the reader and involves the procedural building of meaning.

A top-down approach begins with the knowledge and beliefs of the reader. Students are provided clues, hints, and suggestions regarding word recognition and understanding. The expectations and thoughts of the learner are important in the top-down approach. Both bottom-up and top-down processes are important and required for effective reading instruction (Kohler, 1984; Harris & Sipay, 1985).

Although these methods have their success stories and can point to successful readers who have benefit-

ed from their instructional strategies, there are critics who feel that in some cases reading has become too segmented. They advocate a "whole-language" approach with more emphasis on bringing meaning to print. Smith (1975) and Goodman and Goodman (1977) have written books and articles stressing that reading should be more than the initial mastering of a sum of skills (e.g., decoding, phonics, or structural analysis). They advocate that comprehension enables the learner to make use of the mechanics of reading. Therefore, the instructor should provide more opportunities for verbal interaction with the student to observe how he or she attempts unknown words, describes the main ideas in material, uses oral language, and expresses grammatically appropriate material in writing (Leigh, 1980).

Comprehension has to be the outcome for all lessons—does the student understand what he or she is reading? The secondary student has to learn to deal with expository prose (textbooks). Much of the practice at all the elementary levels is done with narrative prose (stories in readers). This shift causes problems for many students. Not only must they understand facts but they have to infer and get the main ideas and related information.

Some theorists, such as Kohler (1984), suggest that students be allowed to read through a passage silently prior to reading it aloud to familiarize themselves with the meaning or semantic content. This top-down view assumes that if you know what you are reading about, you should be a better reader. The bottom-up view, on the other hand, is concerned with activities that involve identifying words to get the meaning of the passage. If words are remembered, then reading should improve. Kohler suggests that the operation of remembering letters and words is important for many cognitive processes. The processes involved in decoding mainly occur at the automatic-unconscious level.

Good readers use both phonological and visual codes, but they are likely to be good phonological coders (Perfetti & Hogaboam, 1975). They are also better and faster at spelling-to-sound translations that are governed by rules that are applied to unfamiliar material. The poor reader tends to treat a word as a single visual unit rather than as a unit comprising one or more sounds (Rozin, Poritsky, & Sotsky, 1971).

The evidence suggests that skill in phonological coding and speed of reading (time to recognize words) are main ingredients in reading ability. Good readers can switch automatically from automatic control processing (i.e., word recognition to phonic analysis).

Preschool Preparation for Learning

The likelihood that a child will succeed in first grade depends on how much he or she has learned about reading before getting there. Adams (1990) details the linguistic and literacy support that preschoolers need to become readers:

1. Daily reading to preschoolers by parents results in thousands of hours of literacy exposure. It is more than just reading the book; it also involves the enjoyment and reflection on the form and content as the parents pause and discuss passages.

2. Children need to discriminate, recognize, and name individual letters. Most children first learn the alphabet song. Then they learn the shapes that go with each of the letter names they have learned. The student has to learn the visual identities of individual letters. An important predictor of beginning reading achievement is a child's ability to recognize and name the letters of the alphabet. "Laboratory research indicates that the most critical factor beneath fluent word reading is the ability to recognize letters, spelling patterns, and whole words effortlessly, automatically, and visually. The central goal of all reading instruction—comprehension—depends critically on this ability" (Adams, 1990, p. 54).

3. Print awareness is a central goal. Preschool and kindergarten classes should be print-rich with labels. Big books or large-sized books can be effectively used to illustrate that text proceeds from top to bottom and left to right and to introduce the status of printed words. Besides books and labels, students need to see magazines, newspapers, envelopes, and so on. Print awareness can also be developed through the language experience approach where the students' spoken thoughts are written down. This refines the relationship between print and language. Children need to know that print reads left to right or that clusters of print separated by space are words.

4. Children need to understand the concept of the word. Make sure the students understand the relationship between the written and spoken word. To help develop awareness of auditory-visual correspondence, take a favorite book and point to the title. As you read the title, point to each word with a finger. (To begin with, titles with one-syllable words only should be used.) Ask the students how many words they heard. Say the title, letting the students count the words with fingers, and then ask how many words they saw. When the learners understand what you are doing; they should point to

each word as you say it. Show the students other books and see if they can tell you how many words are in the title. Whenever possible, use matching records and books so that the students can listen to someone read a short sentence or story and follow along with their fingers.

5. Early knowledge of nursery rhymes is related to development of more abstract phonological skills. Rhyming words and nursery rhymes introduce the concept of spelling-sound correspondence and phonological awareness. Children enjoy predicting words using rhymes and benefit from opportunities to think about phonology within the context of nursery rhymes.

6. Children need to know not only that letters have names but that letters can represent sounds. A second powerful predictor of reading success is phonemic awareness or a child's ability to discriminate between phonemes auditorially. "Only those prereaders who acquire awareness of phonemes (the sounds to which graphemic units map), learn to read successfully. Programs explicitly designed to develop sounding and blending skills produce better word readers than those that do not" (Adams, 1990, p. 293).

At the request of Congress, the Department of Education asked the Center for the Study of Reading to reevaluate phonics instruction. Adams's text (1990) is a comprehensive synthesis of research about beginning instruction in reading. She indicates that "proficient reading comprehension depends not just on the ability to recognize words, but the ability to recognize them relatively quickly and effortlessly. Reading achievement in the early years of school depends critically on the student's facility with the printed code. If low-achieving students can be brought up to grade level within the first three years of school, their reading performance tends not to revert but to stay at grade level" (Adams, 1990, p. 27).

The pieces of an effective reading program fit together to complement and support one another. Spelling instruction as a major component of the reading and language program enhances reading proficiency. Direct instruction in word analysis skills is critically important for low-readiness readers.

Initial Teaching

COLOR WORDS
Color words are descriptors and lend themselves to easy utilization in teaching short phrases using rebus pictures. They fit easily into any writing and spelling

program and serve as associative clues with self-checking phrase or sentence cards.

For young children, color concepts are an integral part of the total readiness program. Therefore, in introducing color words, the teacher is moving associatively from a known concept to an unknown symbol. The key in introducing color to young children is association beginning with concrete objects and then pictures. The color introduced should be as true to the actual color as possible rather than a shade of the color. Shades of a specific color should be introduced incidentally through activities so that the student will not become confused.

The teacher must be certain that the student can visually discriminate between and name colors before color words are introduced.

Color Blindness

Occasionally we find children who have difficulty in discerning differences in color due to a hereditary defect known as *color blindness*. If the teacher suspects color blindness, there are both formal and informal techniques available to identify color discrimination.

Informal: Place in front of the learner three different combinations of colors such as red, yellow, blue or green, purple, orange, etc., using crayons or pieces of paper. Give the learner a matching sample of one of the colors and ask him or her to point to the color that is the same from among the choices. Do this for all the colors. Include the color combinations of blue, purple and green, and brown, red and orange, since difficulties often show up with these combinations in color-blind students.

Formal: Evaluation of color blindness should be determined, if possible, by a visual specialist. Tests that are currently being utilized to determine color blindness include: *Dvorine Pseudo-Isochromatic Plates* (U.S.) 1944, Baltimore Waverly Press, 1953. *Each plate has an arrangement of small colored dots. The colored dots selected for the foreground form a number. These are arranged on a background of colored dots.*

Farnsworth Dichotomous Test for Color Blindness. The Psychological Corporation, 304 E. 45th St., New York, New York 10017. *An individually administered test to identify the color-blind learner. It consists of color caps that are arranged in a specified order by the evaluator.*

Instructional Sequence

To introduce color words to the learner, white 3- × 5-inch cards can be used as color flash cards. On one

side of the card the instructor prints, in front of the learner, the color word with a black felt-tip pen red . On the back of the card, the learner uses a crayon or felt-tip pen to draw the correct color. The word cards are self-checking for the learner who knows the colors before the color words are introduced. Teachers, parents, paraprofessionals, and peer tutors can use the cards for review games by saying to the student, "Give me **red**" or "Show me **red**."

Language association should be used in presenting the color. Discuss red apples and other objects that are usually red.

After the word **red** has been introduced, write the student's name on the vocabulary progress chart, and in the box next to the word place a ⬈, indicating that the word has been introduced.

After a color word is introduced on a word card, provide reinforcement through coloring of prepared materials. Most learners will stabilize the new words through the activities suggested and some repetition. However, other learners may require many more associative activities and repetitions to progress satisfactorily. The following additional activities should be used when needed.

1. Large motor tracing of words on a chalkboard prior to tracing at a desk or table.
2. Tracing the word in finger paint.
3. Tracing words that have been raised on paper. (A simple technique is to cut a piece of copper screening 8 × 10 inches and bind the edges with electrical or masking tape. Place a sheet of newsprint paper over the screen, write with a black crayon. The raised word can be easily traced with the finger.)
4. Tracing beaded, wood, felt, or raised letters.

After the lower-case word red has been mastered by the learner, the instructor should print in front of the learner a card with the capital letter Red . If the learner does not say "red," then the word must be taught as a new word and repeated through the use of reinforcement activities.

For older students with limited or no reading vocabulary who have already learned a few of the colors, it is important to transition into phrases and sentences as soon as possible. In this case, it is better not to teach the word in isolation but in conjunction with a noun.

red 🔴 red ball

Teach the word **a** by printing an **a** card for each student a . Use the card and concrete objects or little toys for the learner to read the word in context. Use 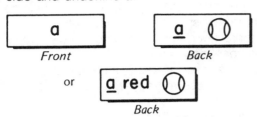 or [a] and [red] plus the real ball to form ... To make the word card self-checking, write a rebus phrase on the reverse side and underline **a**.

To introduce the word **and**, print the word on an index card in front of the learners. Say "and." Have the learners repeat the word. Place concrete objects such as a pencil and an eraser on either side of the index card.

Place the learners' hands on the objects and have them read from left to right as they press down on each object. They say "pencil and eraser." Use a variety of objects to reinforce this task. Next, use color strips to illustrate **red** and **blue**. Finally, color words within the learners' independent reading vocabulary are presented [red] [and] [blue]. The **and** card can be made self-checking by having the learners draw or paste small associative clues on the back of the card as illustrated.

Bread   *Butter*

The color word cards and the **a**, **an**, and **and** cards can be placed in a recipe box, envelope, or other container for easy access by the learner for review and the addition of new vocabulary.

1. Phrase cards can be made that are self-checking. For example:

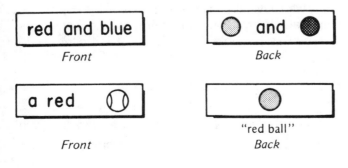

2. For older learners with legible handwriting, reinforcement through labeling, art activities, making original color books, cartoons, etc., should be encouraged.
3. Use of a typewriter is especially valuable for older students to reinforce words.

Introducing Color Concepts

Place a large colored circle, for example, red, on the wall just above the floor at eye level of the learners. On the floor place a shallow box. Introduce **red**. Ask the learners to locate in the classroom something red to go into the box. Send a piece of red paper home with the learners and ask them to bring in something the same color for the box. Name the red objects—e.g., "**red** ball." Later add the word card [red] to the circle. As other colors are added, leave the boxes in place for review.

General Color Activities

COLOR HUNTS. To teach the identification of a color as it appears in many places within the environment of the learners, take the learners on a color hunt. This activity also builds an awareness of shades and variations of a color. Give the learners an object to hold, such as a large red block. As the learners walk around, they are asked, "Show me **red**." They place the block next to the object and repeat, "**red**."

Color hunts can be used to reinforce the color and build in language. "Show me a **red** ball." "Give me a **blue** pencil."

1. Naming activities can be done: "**red** ball," "**red** crayon," etc.
2. The concept of **not** can be introduced after the color is learned—"What is **not** red?"

COLORED WATER. Colored water can be used to teach names of colors, for pouring activities, and measuring. It can be poured into labeled plastic containers after the color words are learned.

FRUIT AND VEGETABLES. Real and plastic fruit and vegetables provide many experiences to teach color.

1. All fruit and vegetables of one color can be shown, named, and eaten. For example, green grapes, green apples, and green lettuce can be used to introduce a color. Later, plastic models can be sorted into containers. The plastic fruit can be used to name color, to be placed into labeled containers, and to build simple analogies—"as **green** as grapes."

2. During snack and mealtime, colors of fruit and vegetables can be reinforced—"Today our apple is **red.**"
3. Fruit and vegetables associated with specific holidays can be emphasized to teach color concepts—orange pumpkins to be carved for Halloween; red cherries for Washington's Birthday.

ANIMALS, BIRDS, AND INSECTS. Any study of animals invites a discussion of color.

1. Library books can be used for children to locate birds and animals of a specific color.
2. Flannel board cutouts of pictures of animals can be provided for the learners to sort by color.
3. Field trips to zoos and museums should emphasize color.
4. Murals can be prepared of animals of a specific color. The pictures can be drawn, made from cutouts stenciled on colored paper, etc.
5. Colored slides of animals can be used to identify color.
6. Colored acetates of specific birds or animals provide a way to review color concepts and discuss classifications "**Red, blue, black** birds."

7. Acetates, pictures, and ditto sheets of colored animals can be labeled by the learner.

SPORTS EQUIPMENT. As young learners play on multicolored sports equipment, color can be reviewed by naming and positioning colored objects—"Mary, swing on the **yellow** swing." "Jump over the **red** jump rope." "Run around the **blue** boxes."

Color Games

SIMON SAYS
1. Give the learners colored slips of paper or small colored objects, such as pegs, beads, or buttons—"Simon says show me **red.**"
2. Using their own clothing, the learners can identify color—"Simon says show me **green.**"
3. Use color word cards—"Simon says show me **blue.**" The learner holds up | blue |

BINGO. Bingo-type games can be used to review colors and color words.

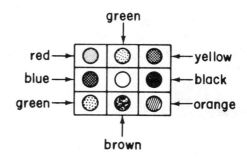

red	blue	green
green	yellow	blue
blue	blue	red

COLOR LOTTO. The instructor can use commercial lotto games to teach the matching of color.

Lotto games can be made using cardboard, colored felt-tip pens, colored stars, or other colored stickers.

Color Discrimination and Fine Motor Activities

MATCHING CARDS. Card games with matching colored designs or pictures can be used to teach color. After a pair of cards is matched, the learner must name a specified number of colors to win the game.

SORTING. A variety of colored objects can be sorted into containers by the learners. For example:

Buttons into a small basket
Beads into muffin tins
Pencils into juice cans
Pegs into a peg board
Clothespins onto a clothesline
Buttons into a pan
Small pieces of construction paper into egg cartons
Small toys, such as trucks or horses, into plastic trays
Crayons into small boxes

The containers can be labeled as the color words are introduced.

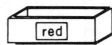

COLORED BLOCKS. Colored blocks have a variety of uses in teaching color.

1. Blocks can be sorted by color.
2. Blocks can be arranged into designs. The learner is asked to locate a specific color—"Show me **red**."

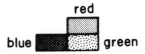

3. Blocks can be used to teach sequence—"What color comes next?"

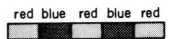

4. Blocks can be used to teach color as other concepts such as counting are reviewed—"One, two, three red blocks."

5. Colored blocks can be sorted into labeled coffee cans.

PEGBOARD

1. Colored pegs can be used for sorting activities by placing all the pegs of one color into small containers.
2. Colored pegs can be used to copy a pattern arranged by the instructor.

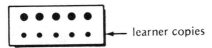

        ← learner copies

3. The learner can copy pattern cards and identify the color.

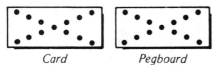

  Card   *Pegboard*

4. Next to the color word card, the learner places the correct colored peg. This can be self-checking by putting the correct color on the back of the card.

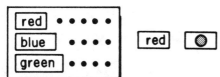

COLORED STRINGING BEADS. By stringing beads, learners can reinforce color concepts, sequencing, counting, fine motor skills, size and shape.

1. Beads can be used to introduce a color—"String all the **red** beads."
2. As other concepts are introduced, the color names can be reinforced—"String the round, **red** beads." "Count the **red** beads."
3. Beads can be used to reinforce color concepts and sequences by asking the learner to follow a pattern—"**Red, blue, red, blue.**"

FLANNEL BOARD

1. Place colored circles of yarn on a flannel board. The learner places felt pieces of the same color within the circle.

2. Color words can be used to label flannel pieces.
3. Commercial flannel materials can be used to identify the color of objects and shapes.
4. Colored magnetic pieces can be used to sort and name colors

  A B C

and colored magnetic letters can be used to label magnetic pieces.

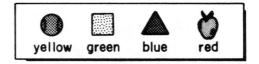

GEOMETRIC SHAPES

1. Place a large colored circle on the floor. Specific directions for group assembly can involve the circle—"Sit in the **red** circle."
2. Place many colored shapes around the room at the eye level of the students—"Find something **red**." "Find a **red** circle."
3. If the learner knows body parts, you can say, "Put your hand on something **red**."
4. Parquetry pieces, in a variety of colors and shapes, can be used for matching, naming, and sorting colors and color words—

red   blue   green

"Show me **red**." "Give me **red**." "What color is

 red?"

"Give me the piece that looks like this."
green

5. Provide the learner with small boxes or envelopes, each containing several pieces of matching shape and color, and have the learner match color words to complete a design.

6. Color Words—The learner is given several pieces of the same color and shape material and completes the design. Small boxes or envelopes can be used to contain individual pieces.

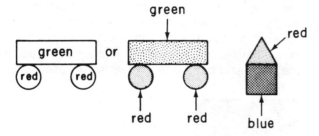

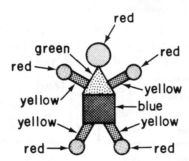

COLORED CHALK AND CRAYONS

1. Colored chalk or crayons can be used for matching activities. The learner colors circles to match those colored by the instructor.

2. Colored chalk or crayons can be used to color designs prepared by the instructor—"Color the flowers **red**."

3. After color words have been introduced, the learner can use the correct color to match the word.

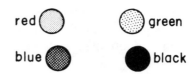

4. Colored chalk or crayons can be used to create a review activity for numerals and colors.—"Draw

"

5. Colored chalk or crayons can be used to trace color words.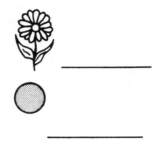

6. Colored chalk or crayons can be used to label colored pictures or geometric designs.

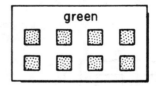

Cut-and-Paste Activities

POSTERS

1. Posters can be made by the learners by pasting cut or torn out magazine pictures of a specific color on a large sheet of paper or cardboard.

2. After a color word is learned, the learners can prepare posters and label the pictures by writing or tracing the color word.

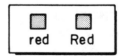 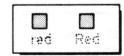

COLOR SCRAPBOOK. Learners can add pages to a color scrapbook by

Coloring ditto pages prepared by the instructor
Coloring pages from commercial coloring books
Cutting designs from colored construction paper and pasting them on paper
Cutting or tearing colored pictures from magazines, catalogues, or trading stamp books
Cutting designs from wallpaper samples

Coloring with crayon, felt-tip pen, or tempera paint pictures of objects or geometric shapes that the instructor has stenciled on pieces of newspaper

PASTING ACTIVITIES WITH CUTOUTS, STICKERS

1. The learner correctly pastes cutouts or places stickers next to the correct matching color.

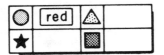

2. Next to the color word, the learner pastes cutouts of the color indicated.

red					
blue					

3. The learner will place color words next to matching color symbols.

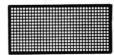

Pocket Charts

Pocket charts and small cards can be used by the learner to review color.

1. The learner will place all pictures of one color and object.

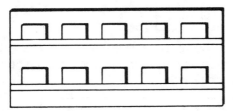

2. The learner will match the color words.

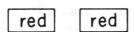

3. The learner will place a color word in the chart and place the correct pictures next to it.

4. The learner will use color words to label pictures.

Color Words Tracing Activities

1. Write the color word on a strip of cardboard. The learner traces it with a colored felt-tip pen.

red

2. Cover color words that are to be traced with a piece of acetate. The learner traces them with a grease pencil.

3. Cover color words that are to be printed on cardboard with tracing paper. The learner uses a clipboard to hold the paper and traces the word.

4. Prepare a 5- × 8-inch piece of window screening by binding the edges with tape. Over the screen place a 5- × 8-inch piece of white newsprint. If you are reviewing the word **red**, use a red crayon to print the word **red** on the newsprint. By writing over the newsprint on the screen, raised letters will appear. Remove the screen. The learner uses the index finger to trace the letters in the proper direction. After many tracings the learner will practice the word and have a red finger as an associative clue.

5. Finger paint can be used for tracing color words.
6. Ditto sheets of color words can be prepared for the learner to trace with colored pencils.

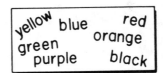
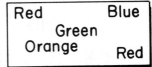

7. On clothes hangers labeled with a color word, the learner attaches the correct colored pictures with a clothespin. The correct color word is printed on the back of the picture card.

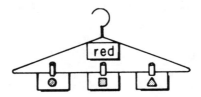

8. Prepare puzzle cards that match a color dot to a word. The student self-checks by looking for a completed colored object on the reverse side.

front   back

9. Prepare vocabulary cards with the word on one side and the color on the other.

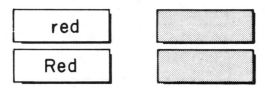

Color Word Spelling Activities

1. Movable letters of cardboard, wood, plastic, or magnetic material provide activities to review the spelling of color words. The learners can look at a color flash card $\boxed{\text{red}}$ and match the letters. They can turn the cards over, look at the $\boxed{\bigcirc}$ red circle, spell **red**, and then check their spelling.

2. Movable letters can be used to complete ditto sheets or acetates for use on an overhead projector.

3. Movable letters can be used for labeling pictures or shapes.

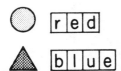

Activities for the Home

Home activities provide valuable support and can help learners to achieve success in a language arts program. It is imperative, however, that the supportive role be one of reinforcement rather than instruction. Materials should be sent home with learners for use only if they and those who work with them fully understand the nature of the task to be completed. Activities should be varied, completed in brief periods of time, and fun for the learners. The activities can be sent home on cards, on lists, in a newsletter, or presented during parent-teacher conferences, back-to-school night, or home visits.

LOCATING COLOR. Give the learner a piece of colored paper. Take the learner on a color hunt to locate and match the color to objects in the home or to colored pictures in magazines.

COLOR IN THE KITCHEN. When the learner assists in the purchase, preparation, or serving of food, emphasize color.

1. Name colors on labels of food containers.
2. Discuss the color of the food being served at snack or mealtime.
3. Decorate cupcakes or cookies with colored icing.
4. Arrange food of a particular color on a table and discuss the similarities: "as **green** as beans," "as **green** as grapes," "as **green** as lettuce," or "as **red** as an apple," "as **red** as a tomato," "as **red** as a beet."

COLOR ON TRIPS. Look for a specific color on trips to the zoo, park, supermarket, department stores, etc.

SORTING OBJECTS BY COLOR. Have the learner sort objects (buttons, small toys, crayons) into containers (egg cartons, baskets, plastic trays, coffee cans, boxes). As the color words become part of the learner's reading vocabulary, the containers can be labeled with small cards.

COLOR CHARTS. On large sheets of paper, print a color word and draw or paste a picture of the same color. The learner draws and colors or cuts pictures from magazines to paste on the poster.

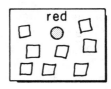

COLOR LABELS. Have the learner use color word cards or stickers ($\boxed{\text{red}}$, $\boxed{\text{blue}}$, etc.) to label blocks, geometric shapes, jars or containers of colored objects.

LABELING OF CLOTHES. Let the learner select and verbalize the color combinations of clothes he or she will be wearing for the day. Have the learner indicate the colors of different items of clothing found in drawers or closets.

ART ACTIVITIES.

1. Painting: *Sponge painting* using a soft sponge and different colored paint on paper, newsprint, etc. *Finger painting* using commercial finger painting materials. *Watercolor* in special coloring books, on newsprint, or on plain white paper.
2. Pipe Cleaners: Have the learner sculpture animals or other figures with multicolored pipe cleaners. The learner will name the colors used.
3. Color Collages: Using colored materials of different sizes, shapes, and textures (ribbons, cloth, burlap,

felt, string, paper, buttons, etc.), the student can create designs and name the colors of the materials.

4. Felt-Tip Pens: Use to color in books or to label colored objects.
5. Paper Chains: Have the student connect by pasting or stapling strips of colored paper to form a chain ⦾⦾⦾ and name the sequence of colors.
6. Vegetable Printing: Have the student dip a piece of potato or similar vegetable into tempera paint and use it to make designs on paper.

COLOR RIDDLES. Build in color association through riddles. For example:

I am a yellow fruit.
I am a favorite of monkeys.
What am I?

MEMORY GAMES

1. Give the learner first one, then more, colored objects. After the objects have been removed, the learner names the colors.
2. Show the learner objects of different colors. Cover the colored objects and remove one or more of the colors. The learner will indicate the color(s) that were removed.
3. Place colored objects in a drawer. Open the drawer for a period of one second for each object. After the drawer is closed, the learner will indicate what the object is and its color. Begin with a few objects and increase the difficulty.
4. After a trip to a store, the learner will indicate objects that he or she saw and their colors.
5. Show the learner pictures of objects of different colors in magazines. After the pictures are removed, the learner will indicate the object and its color.

SIGHT WORDS

Sight words are taught by tracing, by using cards, or by using plastic or wooden letters first as whole words and then in phrases or sentences. For example, *and* can be taught with *he* and *she*. Pin cards with the words *he, she,* and *and* on students and arrange them so that they make short phrases (Figure 9-1).

These phrases can be written on sentence strips and then cut up for the students to put back together. They can also be picture coded on the back for self-correction.

Other self-checking activities include the following:

Prepare a tachistoscope with a window and movable flap (Figure 9-2). On strips of cardboard prepare self-checking cards. The learner reads the word and

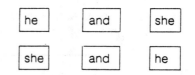

Figure 9-1   Short Phrases

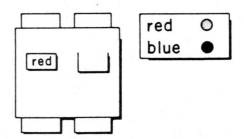

Figure 9-2   Tachistoscope

checks by lifting the flap to see the associative picture clue.

Make or purchase a spinner with words on the front and colors or pictures on the back (Figure 9-3). The student spins the dial, reads the word, places a clothespin to mark the word and self-checks on the reverse side.

Prepare vocabulary cards with the words on one side and the associative clue on the other (Figure 9-4).

Prepare a cardboard envelope with the word on top and the associative picture on a card that slides out (Figure 9-5).

VOCABULARY SELECTION

In selecting the students' beginning reading vocabulary, make sure that the words are within the students' range of experience and that they have different sounds and visual configurations. Use nouns or pronouns that can be matched to associative clues such as pictures of objects, and always make sure the students can pronounce all of the words. One of the problems encountered with some students is teaching them discrimination of short vowel sounds. Many are unable to discriminate initial- or final-sound similarities or differences. Therefore, they cannot form generalizations that apply to new words and cannot break a word into syllables or individual sounds. Although the learners may know all of the sounds of the letters, they may be unable to blend them into words. The recommended procedure, therefore, is to work from the whole to the parts.

When selecting reading materials, it is important to analyze the passages to determine if new material reinforces the word recognition lessons that were previously introduced.

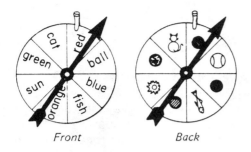

Front   Back

Figure 9–3 *Spinner*

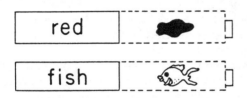

Figure 9–4 *Associative Clues*

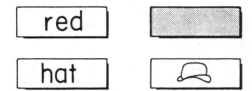

Figure 9–5 *Clue in Envelope*

PHONICS

For the learners who continue to have difficulty sounding letters, use techniques that will aid their internalization of the sounds. Remedial activities include using consonants that can be sustained, such as *m, s, sh, f, v, r,* and *l.* Ask the learners to say one sound, and then you say several sounds, including the one first given to the students. The students will hold up their hands when they hear "their" sound.

Learners with a problem in sounding letters need to concentrate on how the sound is formulated and how the lips and tongue are positioned. Mirrors can be used to help them see their mouth movements. Feathers or strips of paper can also be used to show the flow of air in the production of speech sounds.

Some students know all of the sounds but are unable to blend them. It is easier to blend syllables than single consonant and vowel sounds. It should be noted that difficulties may develop later when the students start to learn consonant blends such as *st* in *rust* and *ft* in *left.* Unless you deliberately teach the students to notice and pronounce the words correctly, they may leave out the *s* of *rust* and the *f* of *left.*

It is very important that these students hear the number of syllables in a word. Instill a consciousness of both the number and the order of sounds within the word. Always stress the rhythmic sequence of words, starting with one-syllable words, then going to two- and, finally, three-syllable words. Concrete materials for manipulation can be used effectively at this point.

Some students have difficulties with confusing letters that appear similar. They may also fail to note internal detail (misreading *log* for *leg*) and have difficulty recognizing or remembering the different configurations of such words as *ship* and *snip.* Some exhibit inversion tendencies, such as misreading *m* for *w* and *u* for *n.*

The first step in teaching consonant sounds is to print the letters on 3″ × 5″ white cards in the presence of the students, preferably next to them or from behind them so that they can see you produce it in the correct position. The letters should not be reproduced while you are facing the students, because they will be getting a reversed image. All printing should be as consistent as possible, done in heavy black ink and in lower-case letters. At this stage, teach the letter sounds only. It is usually best, initially, not to teach letter sounds in association with a key word (such as *b* for *boy*), as this may confuse the students. For example, "puh" for *p,* may be difficult for the students to learn to blend. Do not distort a consonant by adding a vowel.

The second step is to hold the card up and say to the students, "This is 'm' [sound]." The students repeat the sound with you, then they say it alone. Ask the students to think of words that begin with the sound "m." Words can be repeated by the students after you carefully pronounce them (e.g., *man, mop, monkey*). Classification games can be introduced here, for example, "I am thinking of an animal that starts with the sound "m'," or "How many things can you think of that start with 'm'?" After teaching the sounds of the two or three consonants you have selected, give a student one flash card (later the student will select the correct one from among others) and say, "Show me the *m,*" or "Give me the *m.*" This type of activity helps the learner build a strong association between the visual symbol and the auditory referent.

If a learner has difficulty making the auditory-visual association, such as sounding letters, introduce a tracing technique to form the letters. If a tracing technique is used, the learner should trace his or her fingers over the letter while saying the sound. A simple technique is to cut a piece of copper screening, 8″ × 10″, and bind the edges with electrical or masking tape. Place a sheet of newspaper over the screen, and then write on the paper with a black crayon. The student can then trace the raised letter with a finger.

In 1943, Grace Fernald said, "We find great individual differences in types of recall image" (Fernald, 1943). She then went on to explain that for some children, seeing, hearing, and speaking must be reinforced with the concrete kinesthetic experience of handling and moving individual parts. Through the sense of touch, the students establish a mental concept that is strong enough to support their memory retention.

CONSONANTS AND BLENDS

The following activities will aid teachers, paraprofessionals, and peer tutors in the reinforcement of consonant sounds:

1. Small baskets, muffin tins, juice cans, egg cartons, plastic trays, coffee cans, or boxes can be labeled with the sounds to be reinforced (Figure 9-6). The learner picks up an object or picture of an object, says the beginning sound and the word, and places the object in the correct container.

2. Place a small card with a letter on it inside a face powder compact. The learner opens the compact, looks at the letter, then, looking in the mirror, produces the sound.

3. Use alliterative phrases or sentences to practice the repetition of an initial sound. Encourage older students to write their own phrases (e.g., Susan sang silly songs).

4. Accumulate coffee cans or other containers. Paste a letter on the outside of each container and have the student place in the containers pictures from magazines or concrete objects whose initial sounds correspond to the letters. (For example, all items that begin with *m* would go into the *m* container.)

5. Make letters from cookie molds, clay, or pipe cleaners, and have the learner identify them by giving the appropriate sound. ("That's an *m.*")

6. Have learners listen to words, beginning with the same sound (for example, *hat, horse, happy*) and name other words beginning with the same sound. Vary the activity by saying three or four words that begin with the same sound and one word that does not (*man, monkey, car, marble*). The learners stop you when they hear the different word, or they name the different word after the sequence has been given.

7. Play a bingo-type game using letter sounds in place of numbers. The learner will indicate the sound while marking the letter.

8. Play "which sound does not belong" by producing three sounds (e.g., "s . . . s . . . f)." The learner will indicate the sound that does not belong.

Figure 9-6 Labeled Containers

9. Have the learner locate and identify specified sounds of letters in newspapers and magazines.

10. From magazines or catalogs have the learners cut out pictures of words on their reading list. On one side of an index card, they can paste the picture 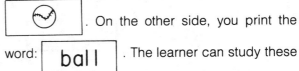. On the other side, you print the word: . The learner can study these cards alone like flash cards by looking at the picture on the front of the card, saying the word, writing the word on paper and checking themselves. The cards can be kept in a box with alphabetical dividers. Use the cards for phonics review by having the learners put all the pictures with the same beginning sound into a pile (e.g., bat, boy, bird, ball).

11. Have the learner make sound posters by pasting cut- or torn-out magazine pictures of objects beginning with a specified sound, such as *m,* on a large sheet of paper or cardboard (Figure 9-7).

12. In the boxes of a chart, the learner pastes cutouts or draws pictures of objects beginning with the specified sound (Figure 9-8).

13. Have the learner place sound cards next to the picture of the object with the corresponding beginning sound (Figure 9-9).

14. Have the learner use pocket charts and small cards to review sounds (Figure 9-10).

15. Have the learner write the beginning sound that correctly completes a word that corresponds to a given picture (Figure 9-11).

16. To review an initial consonant sound previously introduced, write words (at the learner's independent reading level) beginning with that sound on the chalkboard or on an acetate to be used on the overhead projector. The student reads the word, underlines the initial consonant,

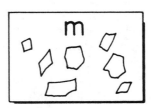

Figure 9-7 Sound Poster

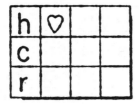

Figure 9–8   Sound Chart

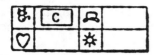

Figure 9–9   Sound Cards

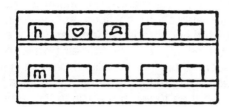

Figure 9–10   Pocket Chart

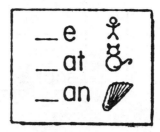

Figure 9–11   Word Completion

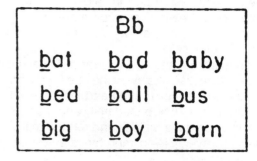

Figure 9–12   Initial Sound Review

and says the word again, emphasizing the beginning sound. (See Figure 9-12).

17. Write a blend on a fill-in chart and have the student think of words that use the blend (e.g., *sn*), listing as many words as possible under the given categories (Figure 9-13). Point out the sequence of the sounds in consonant blends as well as the form of the letters. Pronounce the words containing blends correctly.

TEACHING WORDS USING SPELLING PATTERNS

After the students have been taught their first basic sight vocabulary, word families or phonograms can be presented to them. Although many repetitions will be necessary for each new spelling pattern, that sequence of activities is necessary to help the students develop the ability to analyze and synthesize sounds. Most first-grade phonics work is done orally. Some students need the simultaneous presentation of sound and visuals such as plastic or wooden letters, and cards. When the learners have put their words into word families, immediately ask them if they see anything that is the same. They must then underline the spelling pattern that is being emphasized. Next, have the students say the words to see if they hear the identical elements (e.g., *top, hop*). The emphasis here is on the development of an awareness of consistent configurations. Exaggerate the sound you want the students to hear. The student must then exaggerate the sounds. Always use concrete materials that the students can manipulate so that they are continuously involved in doing, as well as looking and listening.

As the students start to learn the basic vocabulary, simultaneously work on improving listening skills to prevent difficulties later on with spelling. Teaching word families with concrete materials for manipulation and exaggerating the sound of letters and words you are trying to teach will help the student.

Learners should be able to see spelling patterns more readily if taught in the following manner:

1. Place the spelling patterns and words on 3″ × 5″ white cards. Show the cards to the students, while saying the words, in the following sequence:

2. Say " 'an' [showing the *an* card] as in 'man' " (also showing the *man* card). Next, show the *an* card

	Animals	Flowers	Clothes
sn	snail snake	snapdragon	sneaker

Figure 9-13 Blend Chart

and say, 'an' as in 'pan' (showing the *pan* card). The students listen and imitate.

Note: Some time may elapse before Step 2 is completed, as it takes some students longer to see these relationships.

3. When you feel that the students have mastered these two tasks, take away the cue card *an*, leaving just the whole words *man* and *pan*, and then ask the students to name the family and then the word. This may be quite difficult and require many repetitions; however, it is an important step in learning by this approach.

When success has been achieved with a few words, other word families can be introduced. Some students cannot be expected to manipulate or revisualize the letters to form word families in their minds; therefore, they must be shown how the patterns are similar. They need something concrete to manipulate in order to see exactly how the words are formed and changed. It will take much deliberate teaching, repetitions, and reinforcements before the students can be expected to see relationships between words.

Word families can be presented as members of a family living in a house together. Encourage the learners to draw a house at the top of their papers and to put the letter *e* in the doorway. Other members of the family are then printed under the house. Care should be taken to line up the family being taught. The house of *e* is shown in Figure 9-14.

Word families can also be presented with cards, raised screen letters, plastic letters, and clay. The word family can be brought to the learners' attention further by having them place the clay or plastic consonant letters in a column and then slide the single *e* down the line (as in Figure 9-15) while they say the words. Another approach to this exercise would be to have the students place three *e*'s in a row, then place the *m, h,* and *sh* in front of the *e*'s.

Prepare ditto sheets or acetates and have the learners trace or mark all of the words containing a specified spelling pattern (Figure 9-16).

Arrange charts or bulletin boards of houses (Figure 9-17). As new spelling patterns are added to the vocabulary, place word cards on the board.

If the students were learning from another series, they would learn *pan, man, a, ran, an,* and *the* before seeing the book. Remember that the goal is success, as we do not want to leave the student with a failure. Don't teach "just one more sound or word." That "jams" or "overloads" the learners, causing them to forget the other things that have been taught.

A good deal of spelling and writing is used in the sight-word approach. As soon as the learners are able, they are encouraged to transfer from their plastic or wooden letters, or cards to their own written work. When teaching families, use lined paper cut into long strips, leaving room for the student to draw a house at the top and then to list the words in the family below (Figure 9-18).

After acquiring groups of basic sight words, the students should be encouraged to write short stories using these words. They can then cut pictures out to illustrate the stories and make their own collection. This will reinforce the learning and also increase the interest level.

Throughout the process, the students should always be encouraged to look for the like elements or spelling

Figure 9-14 The House of e

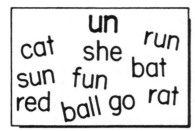

Figure 9–15   Word Building

Figure 9–16   Ditto Sheets

patterns within words. When they look at a word, they should see letter groupings that represent auditory patterns. It is important to remember that when using listening as the primary input for instruction, other areas such as visual input must be simultaneously considered during both the initial teaching period and the remedial program. Many good commercial and homemade materials are available for strengthening of problem areas.

TEACHING BLENDING

As soon as the students learn a few consonants and one vowel, they should be taught to blend those sounds into meaningful words. Nonsense syllables should not be used, and all words should be within the learners' spoken vocabulary. It is usually easiest to begin with nasal consonants and with words such as *an, man,* or *no.* As soon as the students are taught a

word, they should be asked what it means. If possible, they should demonstrate the meaning with a motor response. They should then use the word in a sentence.

In teaching blending, you can place the letters on cards. Then the cards can be physically pushed together.

The following activities could be used by the teacher.

1. The letters *a* and *n* can be presented together as a sight word or as a spelling pattern. Use cards that can be pushed together or plastic or wooden letters.
2. When the *an* pattern is understood, for example, the letter *m* can be introduced to it to form the word *man.* The student should be taught to say "an," then the *m* moved over to the *an* and say "man."

Once the first words have been taught, the learners should be allowed to mix the cards or plastic letters up and then re-form the words they have been working on. In this way, they will experience analysis and synthesis. Always have the students say the spelling pattern and then add the new letter. For instance, the learner would say "an" and then move the *p* over and say "pan." An associative clue such as a picture drawn on the back of a word card by the student will help the student remember the word better.

There is correlation between the skills involved in blending and emerging word recognition skills (Perfetti et al., 1987). "With respect to the idea that they are powerful, blending scores obtained just prior to the beginning of formal reading instruction have been shown to be strong predictors of reading achievement not only at the end of first grade but all the way through grade 4" (Chall, Roswell, & Blumenthal, 1963, in Adams, 1990, p. 76).

Blending helps the student to understand how

Figure 9–17   Bulletin Board

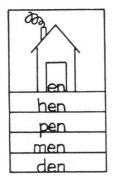

Figure 9–18 Word Family

words can be subdivided into small, meaningless sounds corresponding to phonemes. "The phonemic segmentation tasks require not only that the child have a thorough understanding that words can be completely analyzed into a series of phonemes but further that she or he be able to so analyze them, completely and on demand. The phoneme manipulation tasks require still further that the child have sufficient proficiency with the phonemic structure of words that she or he be able to add, delete, or move any designated phoneme and regenerate a word (or a nonword) from the result" (Adams, 1990, p. 80).

CONSONANT DIGRAPHS

Students need to focus on the sequences that comprise frequent consonant digraphs such as *ch, sh,* voiced and voiceless *th, wh, ph, gh,* and *ng.* Selected consonant digraphs should be taught as they are introduced in the reading series. For example, when teaching the *sh* digraph, say to the student, "When you see these two letters, they usually say /sh/; or when *s* and *h* are together, they make a special sound; or /sh/ is pronounced as it is in *she, shoe,* or *wish.*"

It is also important to point out that for some of the digraphs there are exceptions to the one sound for the two letters. For example, the digraph /ch/ has different sounds in *chef, chief,* and *chaos.*

CONSONANT BLENDS

When introducing students to two-letter consonant blends such as *bl, br, st, str, gl,* and so on, encourage the students to think of both the sequence of the sounds and form of the letters. Encourage them to think of the blends as a single unit, but keep them sounding out the letters individually until they are well established. Attention to letter groups strengthens the associations among the letters in memory.

VOWELS

Terms like *long vowel sounds* and *short vowel sounds* should not be used, as they tend to confuse some students. Some students have great difficulty learning and applying rules. Present vowel digraphs such as *oa* and *ay* with a simple explanation such as, "When you see these two letters together they usually say _____ ."

MANN-SUITER-MCCLUNG PHONICS SCREEN

The Mann-Suiter-McClung Phonics Screen (Form 9-1) can be used to keep a continuous record of a student's progress in mastering letter names, sounds, and phonic elements. Suggestions for use:

1. Prepare 3" × 4" cards with each symbol using a good felt tip pen.

   > br

2. For the consonants and vowels show the upper and lower case.

   > A   a

3. The teacher shows the student the cards in the order as shown on the form and says, "What is the name of this letter?" "What sound does it make?" Some students may know sounds but not letter names or vice versa. Only check those items that are incorrect. If the student called a letter by another name or sound, write the student's response on the line.

4. The forms can be used to monitor a student's progress on six different occasions. It is recommended that the student be checked once a month. Additional sheets can be duplicated as needed.

5. An aide or paraprofessional can easily periodically check the student and identify those areas that need additional remediation.

WORD RECOGNITION

Skilled readers are consistently faster and more accurate in the word identification of context-free words. Disabled readers need to become knowledgeable decoders with automaticity and speed as by-products of extended practice. Training in speed is useful if decoding is strengthened. When word identification is at a low level of efficiency, comprehension is at risk (Perfetti, 1986).

General sight vocabulary activities include the following:

1. Provide movable letters, and a typewriter, if available, for the learner to reproduce and reinforce the words in the reading program.

2. Encourage the learner to look for known words in books and magazines.

3. Help the learner to begin a picture dictionary using the words from the reading program.

Form 9-1

MANN-SUITER-McCLUNG PHONICS SCREEN

Name _____

Date
Tested _____

Conso-nants	Name	Sound/Name	Sound/Name	Sound	Conso-nants	Name	Sound/Name	Sound/Name	Sound
M					M				
S					S				
P					P				
C					C				
L					L				
R					R				
X					X				
F					F				
B					B				
Q					Q				
T					T				
H					H				
G					G				
K					K				
Z					Z				
Y					Y				
W					W				
D					D				
N					N				
J					J				
V					V				

Vowels					Vowels				
A					A				
E					E				
I					I				
O					O				
U					U				

Initial Blends

st- _____ _____ _____ _____ _____

sl- _____ _____ _____ _____ _____

pl- _____ _____ _____ _____ _____

cl- _____ _____ _____ _____ _____

fl- _____ _____ _____ _____ _____

gl- _____ _____ _____ _____ _____

bl- _____ _____ _____ _____ _____

dr- _____ _____ _____ _____ _____

fr- _____ _____ _____ _____ _____

tr- _____ _____ _____ _____ _____

gr- _____ _____ _____ _____ _____

cr- _____ _____ _____ _____ _____

br- _____ _____ _____ _____ _____

pr- _____ _____ _____ _____ _____

sp- _____ _____ _____ _____ _____

sn- _____ _____ _____ _____ _____

sm- _____ _____ _____ _____ _____

sw- _____ _____ _____ _____ _____

tw- _____ _____ _____ _____ _____

sc- _____ _____ _____ _____ _____

sk- _____ _____ _____ _____ _____

Digraphs

sh- _____ _____ _____ _____ _____

th- _____ _____ _____ _____ _____

wh- _____ _____ _____ _____ _____

ch- _____ _____ _____ _____ _____

tch _____ _____ _____ _____ _____

-ng _____ _____ _____ _____ _____

-nk _____ _____ _____ _____ _____

Dipthongs

ee _____ _____ _____ _____ _____

ea _____ _____ _____ _____ _____

ai _____ _____ _____ _____ _____

ay _____ _____ _____ _____ _____

oa _____ _____ _____ _____ _____

ow _____ _____ _____ _____ _____

Final Blends

-st _____ _____ _____ _____ _____

-nd _____ _____ _____ _____ _____

-nt _____ _____ _____ _____ _____

-mp _____ _____ _____ _____ _____

-ft _____ _____ _____ _____ _____

-sk _____ _____ _____ _____ _____

-lt _____ _____ _____ _____ _____

-lf _____ _____ _____ _____ _____

-lk _____ _____ _____ _____ _____

-lb _____ _____ _____ _____ _____

-ff _____ _____ _____ _____ _____

-gg _____ _____ _____ _____ _____

-ll _____ _____ _____ _____ _____

-ss _____ _____ _____ _____ _____

-tt _____ _____ _____ _____ _____

-zz _____ _____ _____ _____ _____

-ck _____ _____ _____ _____ _____

-x _____ _____ _____ _____ _____

Vowels

a _____ _____ _____ _____ _____

e _____ _____ _____ _____ _____

i _____ _____ _____ _____ _____

o _____ _____ _____ _____ _____

u _____ _____ _____ _____ _____

Vowels with 'r

ar _____ _____ _____ _____ _____

er _____ _____ _____ _____ _____

ir _____ _____ _____ _____ _____

or _____ _____ _____ _____ _____

ur _____ _____ _____ _____ _____

4. Have the learner form sentences with the word cards and read them aloud.

5. Give the learner a category and have him or her find all of the word cards for the category, or ask the learner to write the words. For example:

Toys: ball, bat
People: boy, she, he, we, mother, father, girl, baby, they
Things to do: sit, hit, shop, go, hop, fish, run
Rhyming words: cat–hat, he–she, fun–sun, boy–toy, bed–red, pet–wet

6. If the learner has a picture dictionary, encourage him or her to write lists of animals, things that go, toys, etc.

7. Have the student cut out an interesting picture from a magazine, color his or her favorite picture in a coloring book, or draw a picture. Paste the picture on a larger sheet of paper. Have the student write a few sentences about the picture. Put the completed picture on a bulletin board or wall.

8. Use word cards to review vocabulary introduced in the learner's reading program.

9. Have the student write words on a "magic" slate. Later, the words can be easily erased.

10. On heavy cardboard, trace the letters of the alphabet (lower case). Cut them out. With a paint brush, paint on glue. Before the glue dries, pour on sand. After the glue dries, shake off the excess sand. The rough, beaded letters can be used for tracing as the learner reads or spells the reading vocabulary.

11. Provide Lotto, Concentration, or Bingo word games to increase word recognition.

12. Make a list of irregular words that are high-frequency words not part of spelling patterned words. Such words include function words (*the* and *their*) and high-frequency words (*come* and *you*) (May & Eliot, 1978). The words can be selected from lists like the Mann-Suiter Everyday Word list shown in Table 9-1.

VOCABULARY DEVELOPMENT

Vocabulary knowledge and the acquisition of word meaning are critical factors in developing comprehension skills. Vocabulary is highly predictive of a student's level of reading comprehension (Sternberg, 1986). In Chapter 8 we discussed how the developing reader acquires language by listening, speaking, reading, and writing; that listening and reading are receptive language processes and speaking and writing are expressive. To glean meaning from instruction, learners require a sophisticated receptive vocabulary that can be used to comprehend meaning from text and to understand explanations and demonstrations. Semantics, a component of language, also refers to getting meaning from words and sentences.

Teachers present a vast amount of content in prescribed periods of time. They have to consider the types of preliminary activities that will enhance the acquisition of this knowledge. For example, the presentation of technical vocabulary will be a critical part of understanding science and social studies. At the secondary level there is more emphasis on reading and using vocabulary words in many contexts. Some words will need more elaboration and others will consistently need more reinforcement. To help some of the students with spelling, the instructor should write the words clearly on the chalkboard and give the pronunciation based on the context of the lesson. Dictionaries in the classroom will give the students sources in which to look up the meanings of words and will aid in the discussion of multiple meanings.

Subject-area teachers need many strategies that will make the learning of new vocabulary interesting and will aid in understanding and retention. To help students become "hooked" on words, the teacher has to have obvious as well as unpredictable ways to develop vocabulary within lessons. Presentation of vocabulary should be varied to prevent boredom for the students. The teacher has to demonstrate that words can be fascinating and should be valued as collectibles. This involves a modeling and self-monitoring of how the words are presented to students. Lectures and class presentations need to be constantly rejuvenated by an awareness by the instructor of how interesting and how clearly vocabulary is being used.

Students and the teacher initially need to discuss how important words will be to the course of study. They need to plan and organize a strategy for documenting and retrieving words for clarification, and for studying for tests. A section in a notebook should be set aside to list new words, with room for elaboration. In some cases word cards can be used (in alphabetical order) for ease of retrieval.

Before the students write the definitions of words or use them in sentences, it is important to find out what prior knowledge the students have about the terms. This semantic elaboration is very important to retention and understanding. The new learning has to be anchored by the previous repertoire of concepts. By listing the students' guesses about words first, the instructor will get a good overview of the students' general knowledge about a subject. Knowledge needs interaction and needs to be personalized. Before we can ask students to give us predictions, inferences, or unlock the meaning of new confusing information, we need to help the learners understand the message based on his or her previous experiences. To accomplish this, learners have to do more than comprehension activities. Students should be feeling that new learning, experiences, and feelings have value and applicability to the real world—present and future—and at the same time blend with the familiar things they already know. We have to increase their knowledge store and facilitate their acquisition of higher-order thinking processes.

Semantic mapping is one example of how to use visual diagrams to represent a student's prior understanding. These maps give students a chance to relate new vocabulary to prior knowledge. Used as both pre- and postreading or writing activities, the learner can identify the subcategories of superordinate concepts and the interrelationships among ideas. Chapter 12 contains a number of semantic maps that illustrate science and social studies concepts, and later in this chapter information is included about how semantic webs can be used to stimulate written expression.

Meanings of vocabulary enable students to build concepts. Chapter 8 also discusses a hierarchy for building word meaning from the concrete to functual to abstract levels. Word meanings at the concrete level lend themselves to physical representation using objects, pictures, and symbols, and are descriptive in nature. The word *boat* can be described by size, shape, color, material, and so on. At the functual level the word *boat* can be defined in terms of its use. At the abstract level the classification (transportation) and associations (what goes with it or how is it similar to a ship or a canoe) can be discussed. Similes can be practiced, such as "Boat is to water as airplane is to _____."

McKeown and Beck (1988) point out that not all words are equal. It is impossible to develop a rich understanding of all of the new words in a selected lesson. "The choice of which words to teach and what kind of attention to give them depends on a variety of factors such as importance of the words for understanding the selection, relationship to specific domains of knowledge, general utility, and relationship to other lessons and classroom events" (p. 42). An in-depth discussion of 10 to 12 new words is more valuable than a cursory pronunciation of a long list of words. A predictable presentation of pronouncing the word, discussion of a few definitions, and silent reading of the text may facilitate short-term memory for tests, but it will not give the student many opportunities to internalize the word at the abstract level. Students need to *use* words—to speak, read, and write them. They need opportunities to use multiple contexts and

strategies that will help them tie the new information to prior knowledge.

Students see many vocabulary words on a chalkboard during the year, but very few of them are really known by the end of the year. They need many uses of concepts and associations. The instructor has to select words carefully—which ones to teach now and which ones to add later. A variety of activities are needed to develop concepts and aim for spontaneous speech. Don't erase the new words. Print them in the corner of the chalkboard for a week at least or, better yet, print them on a chart. If the students use the new words at least seven times in spontaneous speech, they will more likely become personalized, internalized, or learned.

Instructional Activities
1. *Using the Dictionary:* Students need to become familiar with the parts of a dictionary and the many abbreviations that are used. Use of guide words and alphabetical order should be reviewed to help the student quickly locate words. Discussions can include diacritical markings, pronunciation, parts of speech, definitions, multiple meanings, synonyms, antonyms, and word origins (etymologies). The instructor should know before the lesson which of these needs the most emphasis. The instructor needs to monitor the types of definitions that the students are writing. If the students are merely copying synonyms or verbatim definitions out of the dictionary, they may not transfer this information to the context of the textbook. New vocabulary should be located in the textbook and in other reference sources.
2. *Locating the Words in the Textbook:* Many technical words are italicized or underlined. The student needs to locate the words in as many contexts as possible (e.g., glossary, index, titles, charts, graphs, captions, as well as in the text). Until this becomes an independent study strategy, the student should have a variety of activities in which to practice finding the words. Encourage writing of vocabulary through definitions, sentences, summaries, lecture notes, etc.
3. *Audio-Visual:* Films, filmstrips, records, videotapes, and computer software provide ways to introduce, reinforce, and review vocabulary. By stopping and replaying passages where complex terms are explained, the student may gain more understanding.
4. *Magazines, Library and Reference Materials, Newspapers:* Encourage students to find words in many sources. Plan activities where the students can use these sources for oral or written reports, posters, and term papers.

5. *Word Games:* Provide opportunities for students to play games such as Scrabble or Spill and Spell that promote word meaning.

6. *High-Frequency Words:* Make a list of the words that are more general in nature but that recur within the content of a subject area (e.g., common words, names, places).

7. *Peer and Cross-Age Tutoring:* Chapter 7 on educational management has information on how to use tutoring and cooperative learning within the classroom. Sometimes a student can learn material by explaining it to another student. The instructor should consider how to incorporate learning experiences where the student has to use new vocabulary by explaining or demonstrating what the material means.

Word Meaning

1. Ask students to pretend that they have to explain to a foreign visitor specified examples of colloquial or figurative speech (e.g., *backed out of a deal, green thumb*).

2. Give a definition of a word. The student circles the word on a page or holds up a word card.

3. If students cannot verbally express the meaning of a word, ask them to draw a picture to illustrate the meaning or multiple meanings.

4. Build the students' visual imagery by having them write what they see in their mind's eye when a word is said. Write lists of phrases to illustrate the word.

> overcast dark, dreary day
> grey clouds

5. Gipe (1978–1979) reported that relating words to be learned to familiar concepts in context is important for teaching word meanings. Gipe also suggests that vocabulary meaning should be tested prior to a lesson. Can the student define or give an example of the word?

6. Schworm (1979) increased word recognition by directing attention to the middle of words.

7. Harber (1980) found that text illustration interfered with word recognition in poor achievers and low-ability children.

Context Clues

1. On the chalkboard, a duplicator master, or the overhead projector, write incomplete sentences. Have the learner fill in the blanks with the correct words.

> run fun sun
> It is _____ to play with the dog.
> The _____ is hot.
> Can you _____ and jump?

2. Ask the learner to read the sentence and complete the missing word.

> Maria is a little g _____ .
> The f _____ was in the pond.

COMPREHENSION

Reading instruction in the last decade has shifted from skills training to meaning-based instruction. There is a renewed interest in how comprehension is taught. Short answers to teacher-directed questions have been replaced by dialogues that have more student-initiated activity. Students are learning to become more strategic and interpretative in their reading.

Reading is an active communication process. The reader brings to the reading process past experiences and prior knowledge that permit him or her to interact with the new learning and to enjoy the nuances and surprises in the new material. The reader predicts outcomes, infers cause and/or effect relationships, draws conclusions, makes judgments, and forecasts events.

For some students, learning to read is not easy or automatic. Those learners especially need to interact with print in a meaningful and successful manner. Comprehension should not be viewed as an aspect of reading that will occur after the mechanics have been mastered. These learners should begin early to attach meaning to words, phrases, and paragraphs.

Text Structure

Narrative-type stories have traditionally predominated the reading format for many elementary-level textbooks. Setting, plot, and characters are very predictable. There is often a sudden shift at the junior high school/middle school when students leave reading stories and read more expository prose from context materials. Concomitant writing problems are also noted as workbook exercises are replaced by written essays and reports (Applebee, Langer, & Mullis, 1989). Reading materials at the elementary level are now broader in scope and include not only the best examples of good literature but also news-type descriptions of events, science and social studies text structures that illustrate sequence, cause-effect, compare-contrast, and problem solving (Armbruster, Anderson, & Ostertag, 1989). Additional text-related variables are relevant to the learner and the readability level of the text.

There are a variety of strategies students can use to improve learning from textbooks. First, students can often tell the structure of a text by looking at the overall format. The titles, subheadings, and topic sentences illustrate the author's purpose in the paragraphs and act as indicators. A second method is to look at samples from content-level textbooks and discuss the most predictable types of structures usually encountered. History textbooks commonly contain problem/solution structures. A third method suggested by Armbruster, Anderson, and Ostertag (1989) is to have the students take notes in a visual representation of a structure. For example, for a problem/solution text structure, the students would write a short description of who or what is the "problem," describe the "action" of what was done to solve the problem, and, finally, write a summary of the outcome of the solution to the problem under "results." For a sequence structure, they recommend a listing of events with the students practicing using such terms as *first, second, third, next, then,* and *finally.*

Compare/contrast text structures also lend themselves to completion of frames by the students. A semantic map in Chapter 12 illustrates a social studies compare/contrast frame. In writing about comparison, students need to tell how things are similar, whereas contrast tells how two or more things are different.

Gold and Fleisher (1986) examined the deductive and inductive organization of text structure. Deductively organized paragraphs have a stated main idea with details following. Inductively structured materials often have the main idea later in the paragraph. Some readers have more difficulty with the comprehension of the latter. Too many students over-rely on the first sentence of a paragraph for main idea.

Idol (1987a) proposes the use of a critical thinking map that the student can complete during or after reading an assigned passage in a textbook. The map can be used as an outline for class discussions and later for review notes. The students need an explanation about the purpose of the activity and it should be modeled first by the instructor.

The main points to be outlined are the following:

1. *Important Events, Points, or Steps:* In social studies texts, main concepts are often presented in a compare/contrast, pro/con, or positive/negative manner. Idol suggests that within this category, the student may need to list key points under two columns.
2. *Main Idea:* The main point may be clearly stated within the passage or it may be inferred. Students very often restate the first sentence in the paragraph and fail to state adequately the author's main message.
3. *Other Viewpoints/Opinions:* In this section the student could draw a semantic map, including the points he or she knows about the subject, or write a list of questions for elaboration.

4. *Reader's Conclusions:* Using previous information from steps 1–3, the student states his conclusion about the passage.
5. *Relevance to Today:* This statement indicates how engaged the student has become with the topic, how effectively past events have been compared to present situations, and how relevant the material is to the student's background.

METACOGNITION AND READING

The student who displays metacognition rereads purposefully when meaning is unclear, skims, summarizes, predicts, paraphrases, looks for important ideas, looks for relationships, reads ahead for clarification, relates new knowledge to prior knowledge, and raises questions to clarify assignments. *Cognition* refers to intellectual functioning of the mind; *metacognition* refers to one's knowledge of this cognition. The effective reader using metacognitive strategies has the ability to monitor his or her own cognition or thinking about thinking (Babbs & Moe, 1983).

Strategy Instruction

This book has a reference to strategy instruction in almost all of the chapters. Reading is where most of the strategies are applied. Strategies are plans that a student can use as he or she encounters different situations or types of text. Some strategies are used in predicting meaning embedded in text and adjusting predictions during reading (Duffy & Roehler, 1987). Others are what Johnston (1983) calls repair strategies where the learner has to reason consciously about problems encountered while reading. Strategies are also needed for storage and retrieval of information.

Good readers use skills that are automatic and rapidly available, as well as a rich background of prior knowledge. Disabled readers can also be taught strategies and can understand when and why certain strategies should be used; however, they will need modeling of the strategy by the teacher. Practice is needed with peers and alone with guidance.

There has to be a balance between product and process. If students are fluent decoders and their prior knowledge is sufficient, then practicing strategy instruction may be beneficial. Decoders lacking in prior knowledge need background information in a particular area and vocabulary (Snider, 1989).

Paris and Lipson (1982) use a procedure to train students when to apply strategies by giving them passages that have embedded pictures of road signs. When a change of pace or rereading was called for, they used "reduce speed" for difficult parts or "yield" for unknown words.

Brown, Campione, and Day (1981) use summarization as a comprehension strategy. Students are told to delete trivial and redundant material, substitute a superordinate term for lists of items, and to select a topic sentence or invent one that summarizes the paragraph.

Brown and Palincsar (1985) use reciprocal teaching as an interactive dialogue between a teacher and all of the members of a reading group to practice comprehension. The teacher models and explains how to use self-monitoring strategies that are critical to comprehension. The teacher shows the students how to read a passage and understand what is read. He or she demonstrates by talking aloud:

1. Clarifying and understanding the purpose of reading
2. Attending to the major concepts and content
3. Self-interrogating to see if predicted goals and outcomes are being met and comprehension is occurring
4. Recovering from and dealing with distractions
5. Evaluating text for clarity
6. Drawing and testing inferences

This cooperative activity of prediction, clarification, and summarization permits the students gradually to assume the role of the teacher or discussion leader. The interaction occurs as the students alternate between being the leaders by posing good questions and giving summaries and being evaluators of what the leader has asked. The teacher becomes more of a coach.

SELF-INSTRUCTION STRATEGY
In reading, students do better when they use a self-instructional strategy, where self-statements are modeled by the teacher and rehearsed by reading aloud, then reading silently (Gagné, 1965).

Key Ideas

1. What should you say to yourself while reading a paragraph in order to better understand what it is all about?
2. What should you say to yourself while trying to answer the questions? This involves reading, modeling, and self-instructional rehearsal:
   a. The student reads the paragraph.
   b. The student models questions by the teacher.
   c. The student uses an internal dialogue that approximates the modeled passage used by the teacher (develops his or her own words and style).

Example:
   There are things I have to keep in my mind before I read a story, such as:
   (1) What is the main idea of the story, or what is it all about?
   (2) I have to pay attention to the details, such as who is doing what or where or how.
   (3) What is the sequence of what is happening? What happened first, next, etc.?
   (4) Who are the people? How do they feel and why?
   (5) I need to relax, listen to what I am saying, and ask the right questions.
   (6) If I get it wrong no one will think I am stupid, I just have to pay attention and try again.

The above is done orally and then silently and involves practice until it becomes automatic. This inner or silent speech:

1. Decreases impulsivity, reaction time, or distractibility
2. Motivates the student
3. Helps the student identify the important or salient factors
4. Aids in recall
5. Directs thinking to task-related activity
6. Helps student mediate his/her own behavior (Meichenbaum, 1977; Gagné, 1965).

LITERATURE-BASED READING INSTRUCTION
The amount and quality of the literature in reading materials has increased. Students are reading longer passages both inside and outside the framework of a basal reading series. Literature includes books, short stories, plays, poems, and informational material. A mini-library can be set up in every classroom.

The formats for instruction include cooperative study of the same passages in small group peer interaction, teacher-directed discussion, teacher-student reciprocal dialogue, or self-selection by the student in the classroom or library. A number of applications can be developed.

1. A popular children's book can be read to the class. From this, a number of creative projects can ensue (e.g., dioramas of favorite scenes, wearing of costumes, large wall size illustrations, musicals).
2. A particular genre can be selected for study (e.g., fables, mysteries, fairy tales, etc.) and the class can read a number of books by one author as well as multiple texts.
3. Book reports promote reading-writing activity.

Form 9-2 BOOK REPORT

Name _____

Title _____

Author _____

Illustrator _____

I learned these _____ facts from this book.

_____

_____

_____

_____

For third through sixth grade, use the following format:

1. My name: _____
2. Name of book: _____
3. Who wrote the book: _____
4. Who drew the pictures: _____
5. Fiction: _____ Nonfiction: _____
6. Pages: _____
7. Which person did you like best and why? _____

_____

8. Which part of the book did you like the best and why? _____

_____

9. Was the book funny? Yes _____ No _____ Tell why _____

_____

10. What did the book teach you? _____

11. Write a short summary of the book. Include the important things that happened, but not too much. Someone else may want to read the book. _____

_____

_____

_____

BOOK REPORTS

Students should be encouraged to write book reports right from the beginning. Simple formats for younger children can be used, as shown in Form 9-2.

GENERAL COMPREHENSION ACTIVITIES

The following general activities can be used to improve comprehension:

1. *Repeated Readings:* Students read and reread a passage of material aloud until they read at an established rate set by the instructor. This may increase fluency for some readers.
2. *Chart Responses:* Have the students keep a record of percentage of growth in reading comprehension. The numbers of questions answered correctly during a lesson can be plotted.
3. *Visual Imagery:* During the reading of a story or a passage, ask the student to stop and close his or her eyes and try to see a picture of the scenes and action in the material.
4. *Predict Outcomes:* Stop before the end of a story and ask the learners to guess how the story will end.
5. *Open-Ended Sentences:* Read the first part of sentences to the students and ask them to tell the ways the sentences can be finished.
6. *Paraphrase a Story:* Read a short story to the class and ask them to paraphrase it back in their own words.
7. *Sentence Combining:* Using cut-up sentences from their independent reading material, have the students arrange the words into the correct order.
8. *Self-Questioning:* Encourage the students to generate their own questions about their reading material. What did the author try to tell us in this story?
9. *Illustrations:* Suggest that the students doodle, draw cartoons, or simple figures to try to understand better the action, plot, and characters in the stories.
10. *Use Relevant Material:* Provide a variety of reading material for the students that will be interesting and relevant to their lives. Select material that they prefer to read: sports, history, fun, fantasy, animals, mysteries, comedy, science fiction.

CLOZE PROCEDURE

The cloze procedure is used to assess comprehension and as a classroom activity. Every _____ th word in a passage is omitted and the reader is asked to supply the missing words. There are a variety of ex-amples of how this procedure can be used. Blacho-wicz (1977) recommends modification of the standard cloze procedure for primary grade students. She feels that these "warm up" methods prepare the students for the predicting procedures and use of context in the types of cloze passages used in the upper grades.

1. Zip—A story is put on a wall chart or a transparency to be used on the overhead projector. Selected words are covered with tape. After the learners preview the story for context, predictions are made one at a time for the covered words. The tape is zipped or pulled off so that the feedback for the correct word can be discussed immediately.
2. Maze—In this procedure, instead of deleting words in a story or in a sentence, two words are added as distractors. For example:

The hay was stored in the   barn.
car.
pond.

Main Idea
1. Play question-and-answer games to review lessons.
2. Ask the student to write titles for short paragraphs or headlines for newspaper articles.
3. Ask the student to write a sentence or a paragraph to explain political cartoons or comic strips.
4. Have a student read a story silently. You or another student can hold up one of the following cards:

| What | When | Where | Who | Why |

The learner will tell *what* the main ideas of the story are, *when* the story occurs (time of day, etc.), *where* the events take place, *who* the characters are, and *why* the events happen. For some learners simple sheets can be used to teach main ideas. (See Figure 9-19).
5. Record short selections on a tape recorder. The learner will listen to a selection, shut off the machine, and write down the main ideas. The student can self-correct the list by listening to the instructor's summary of the main ideas.

Details
1. After the student reads a selection, ask him or her to print the subject of the selection, draw a large circle around the word, and list all the details about it that were mentioned in the passage. (See Figure 9-20).
2. Have the student underline the details in a newspaper column.

Who	_____
What	_____
Where	_____
When	_____
Why	_____

Figure 9–19   Main Ideas

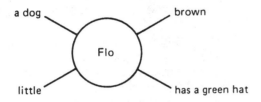

Figure 9–20   Subject and Details

Inference

1. Discuss the student's interpretation of a story in terms of truth or fantasy.
2. Let the student anticipate what will happen next in a story.
3. Use language association and classification activities. Refer to Chapter 8.
4. Have the learner list as many variations as possible for analogies.

    as green as _____
    grass
    leaves
    lettuce

5. First, discuss what kinds of questions will imply inference and list the key words usually found in those questions. Then, after a student has read a story silently, ask him or her to write questions to ask other students who have read the same material.
6. Refer to page 80 for developmental activities to help the student who has social perception problems and may be missing the emotional im-plications or humor in the story or the facial expressions in the illustrations.
7. Discuss cause-effect relationships. (What will happen if _____ ?)

Mann-Suiter-McClung Developmental Skills Worksheet

A part of the development of an Individualized Education Plan is the establishment of goals and objectives for particular students, as indicated in the previous discussion. The compilation of goals and objectives is outlined in the form of skills worksheets. These worksheets can be utilized as a frame of reference for the data accumulated on students through the diagnostic process. The information recorded on these worksheets will indicate the present level of functioning, short-term goals, and long-term goals in the developmental skills areas and in the areas related to social-emotional development. Form 9–3 lists comprehension skills.

READING AND LIMITED ENGLISH PROFICIENT STUDENTS

The following are instructional ideas that are appropriate to teaching Limited English Proficient, mildly handicapped students. Ruiz (1989) identifies six instructional principles for effective teaching of language-minority students identified as having mild disabilities.

Principle 1

Take into account students' sociocultural background and its effect on oral language, reading, writing, and second-language learning. Four areas of practice are identified by Ruiz (1989):

1. *Oral Language Development:* Children need to learn to deal with the decontextualized nature of school language. This is language that depends on precise linguistic formulations. Some children have learned to model responses to books and stories as a natural consequence of coming from homes where books and other written materials are available and deemed important. In most of these homes we find middle-class patterns of home language interaction. Decontextualized language is also facilitated by community communication networks, such as churches, recreation, and other social groups, where children learn specific patterns of language needed to obtain information or services.

    Shannon (1987) found that "Spanish speaking children's English language proficiency was positively related to their opportunities to use English in

Mann-Suiter-McClung Developmental Skills Worksheet

NAME _____   EXAMINER _____

AGE _____   DATE _____

GRADE _____

GOALS AND OBJECTIVES	Present Level	Short-Term	Long-Term

Date All Entries

COMPREHENSION SKILLS

Criterion Reference

The student will

1. determine whether a story is fact or fiction.
2. relate cause and effect relationships.
3. describe the feelings of characters.
4. be able to skim for information.
5. interpret figurative or colloquial language.
6. follow directions in given readings.
7. be able to verify information that is read.
8. distinguish between good and poor literature.
9. encapsulate an individual's point of view.
10. compare reading selections.
11. recognize elements of humor.
12. restate the main points of a news story.
13. summarize using a short sequenced approach.
14. reread purposefully when meaning is unclear.
15. predict outcomes.
16. paraphrase passages of material.
17. recognize relationships.
18. read ahead for clarification.
19. raise questions to clarify meaning.
20. use verbal rehearsal strategies effectively.

their communication networks outside the home and school" (Ruiz, 1989).

Tight family relationships with little outside experiences result in a lack of experience with precise topic centered language. This is often true of migrant families who move often or live in isolated areas. Teachers must be careful not to label these children as having language disabilities. Instead, it should be recognized that sociocultural factors are affecting these students' verbal performance. Therefore, the instructional program should include oral language activities in the curriculum. Children with language disabilities, on the other hand, tend to restrict their forms and uses of language to avoid conversation difficulties (Pearl, Donahue, & Bryan, 1981; Riel, 1983).

Language activities should include (a) peer-oriented structures that are culturally congruent with the interactive patterns of minority children (Delgado-Gaitan, 1987; Kagen, 1986); (b) a focus on problem-solving activities; and (c) precise use of language as students attempt to clarify meaning (Chaundron, 1988).

2. *Knowledge about Print:* The kinds of experience that children have with printed material prior to coming to school is important. Early experiences with books, learning the alphabet, word identification, and early attempts at writing, where children learn to print functionally, are all precursors to formal or concentrational reading. For many reasons many of these children have not had a variety of print-saturated and print-mediated experiences. The student must gain knowledge about text structures and how to interact with a variety of narrative and expository texts.

3. *Background Knowledge:* Literacy instruction should also take into account sociocultural background differences. Background knowledge of texts has a pronounced effect on students' comprehension (Anderson & Pearson, 1984). Background knowledge includes ways of using language and experience with print. Sociocultural influences of the student's background knowledge in reading, such as reading about the student's own or similar society or culture, results in faster reading and better recall of the details and gist of what is occurring in the story, as well as better summarization and retelling of stories, than those who have not had these experiences (Barnitz, 1986).

Prereading activities concerning the text are also beneficial according to Hudson (1982). Students are asked to identify the central theme of a story and relate their experiences to the theme or idea. Their accounts are recorded on the chalkboard or on tape. Then, the children read the story and later talk about the similarities or possible relationships between their own experiences and the story they have just read.

4. *Sense of Story:* A sense of story or narrative schema or sequence that relates sociocultural factors is important. A story has a setting and characters (primary and secondary), is problem(s)-oriented, with attempts to solve the problem(s). It also unfolds how the character fits into the problem, and how the situation is finally resolved. Direct instruction in story grammar and story mapping is suggested for Limited English Proficient students with learning disabilities or reading comprehension problems (Short & Ryan, 1984). An optimal learning situation would have students reading and listening to a variety of stories, many of which relate to their own experiences.

Principle 2

Take into account the students' possible learning handicaps and their effects on oral language, reading, writing, and second-language learning.

The field of learning disabilities, especially the cognitive learning models, have had an important impact on the teaching of LEP students who exhibit learning disabilities. Explicit instructions in reading and writing strategies have filtered into all aspects of the curriculum. For example, along with prereading and background knowledge activities, the teacher could demonstrate a rehearsal strategy. The concepts inherent in strategy learning are superimposed on the existing culture base curriculum.

Principle 3

Follow developmental processes in literacy acquisition. General patterns of literacy development should be followed, such as:

1. Giving students the necessary time to develop their knowledge about reading, writing, and mathematics in an interactive manner with other students and planned events

2. Accepting student errors as part of the process of learning as opposed to a bad habit. The idea is to reduce the errors and enjoy the experience (Flores, Rueda, & Porter, 1986). Focus on what the student can do and has accomplished. This is a reason to rejoice over progress.

3. Recognizing the need for a rich language activity program and building such a program into the curriculum.

Principle 4

Locate curriculum in a meaningful context where the communicative purpose is clear and authentic.

Emphasis needs to shift from drill-type activities to students communicating real messages to real audiences (Atwell, 1987; Calkins, 1986; Smith, 1985). Reading that results in meaningful oral and written communication is encouraged. Form (grammatical structure) concerns should be dealt with prior to the main reading or writing activity. Collaborative problem-solving activities are also a part of this approach.

Children are encouraged to write whole texts or stories rather than fragments. Students construct meaning from conversations and from creating written texts. The teacher exposes the learners to a rich literature of stories in magazines, whole books, and books of poems. The students have control over the topics to be selected and the audience they read to or with as they write and publish books (Atwell, 1987). They react to peer conferences with classmates on the clarity and content of their written efforts.

Principle 5
Connect curriculum with the students' personal experiences.

The students show greater progress when the language tasks give them a chance to interpret their own personal experiences (Flores, Rueda, & Porter, 1986; Willig & Swedo, 1987). The teacher needs to develop ways to connect students' personal written work with the language arts curriculum.

Principle 6
Incorporate children's literature into reading, writing, and ESL lessons.

Literature is a good way to teach reading, writing, spelling, and oral language skills concurrently. Text structure and style can be delineated through the analysis of stories and poems.

In literature, clues to meaning are more implicit than explicit. Often there is a meaning gap where interpretive skills come into play. Several language learners need to learn how to check for understanding or request clarification. These kinds of activities can lead to better English language gains (Chaundron, 1988).

Reading instruction can be brought in through literature study (Alvarez & Mangiola, 1988; Bird, 1988; Edelsky, 1988). The student selects a commercially published book that has been previewed and approved by the teacher. Children reading the same book meet to discuss their reading. They then return to reading independently and search for areas or ideas they discussed. Students keep a log on their progress and feelings about the stories. Students interact with the teacher periodically regarding their progress and

thoughts (Flores, Rueda, & Porter, 1986; Peyton, 1987; Peyton & MacKinson-Smyth, 1988).

Children who are from homes where parents are actively involved in home-based ways of teaching do better than those who only get reinforcement for doing good work in school (Leler, 1983). This is true if the parents are in a position to help the child at home. Many parents are not in the position, lacking language skills themselves. Language-minority parents can be taught to participate in a "home curriculum" program. School-home partnerships can have a literacy emphasis. Children are encouraged to read aloud at home in their native language and in English. Parents can form groups that meet to discuss stories, share books, and get ideas about how to involve their children in home activities such as illustrating stories or how to select books.

The trend in oral language development is moving toward an enriched holistic curriculum built on good literature and whole texts. The mode of this approach is that linguistic components are combined with an orientation of cultural differences and cultural uniqueness as a basis for a balanced program.

A PERSONALIZED APPROACH TO READING
A modified experience approach to reading can be used for students who are beyond the initial stages in the elementary grades, as well as for secondary and adult students. Many students have come to dislike books because of continued failure in reading over a period of years. Teachers have found that it is difficult to get older students involved in reading by using a basal series whose concepts and format are far below the students' mental age or chronological age. These books are often referred to as baby books or kid books, and secondary-age poor readers, as a group, are reluctant to use basal readers from the primer level through level 4.

Alternative approaches that have been introduced by teachers include (1) linguistic series; (2) high interest-low vocabulary books; and (3) the experience method. Most of these techniques have built-in problems for older students.

1. The vocabulary of the high interest-low vocabulary books, in most cases, is too difficult for students reading below grade level three.
2. The experience approach requires a strong visual memory. Poor visual memory prevents students from learning in a basal series. Another factor that prevents their learning is that their motivation and interest are just not high enough to compensate for their poor word attack skills. They can hold just so much before their visual memory fails.

3. The linguistic approach, like the basal reading approach, requires the student to have a good visual-memory, even though the vocabulary is presented at a slower pace. The illustrations in the linguistics and basals are often too juvenile even if the stories are not. The interest level is often not appropriate for older students.

A Linguistic-Based Experience Program

Adams (1990) comments on the work of linguists and psycholinguists and the work of Treiman (1986). She notes that a syllable can be divided into two primary parts: the *onset* and the *rime*. The rime consists of the vowel and any consonant sounds that come after it. The onset, if it is there, consists of any consonant sounds that proceed the vowel. For example, the words *I* and *itch* are rimes. In the word *cat, c-* is an onset and *-at* is a rime; in *splint*, the *spl-* is an onset and *-int* is a rime; in *spy*, the *sp-* is an onset and *-y* is a rime.

Treiman's tenet is that awareness of syllable onsets is a different and simpler challenge than awareness of individual phonemes. Onsets and rimes may provide a key to unlocking phonemic awareness. Matching rimes such as *cat, hat, fat*, and *mat* are phonograms or word families.

The following is a suggested modified experience method that incorporates a spelling pattern technique based on the linguistics approach to reading. This program is composed of four components plus a writing approach.

Component One—Students' Present Sight Vocabulary (What Do the Students Have?)

Experience has shown that students with anywhere near average intelligence acquire a sight vocabulary by merely attending school for a number of years. However, standardized testing may indicate that students have few words in their sight vocabulary, since much of their vocabulary may be composed of words that are not found on standardized tests. The first step in determining the students' actual sight vocabulary is to give them word lists, newspapers, books, etc., and have them circle or copy on paper the words they know. After the words have been checked, the students should list the words separately on 3" × 5" white cards. When they have completed this task, have them put an associative clue (such as a picture or a short phrase using the word) on the back of the card. Let the students hold the stack of cards so that they can see that they have a "reading vocabulary." Many of these students are convinced that they cannot read; therefore, they develop a poor attitude toward books

and, even more important, emotional barriers against learning to read. Therefore, it is recommended that students not receive a book until they can read it with 100 percent success. After the students have completed the stack of word cards they can read, they can put them into a small file box. The students should then be told that they are going to add many more words to their collection.

Component Two—Students' Interest (What Do the Students Like?)

Develop a vocabulary made up of words dealing with an area of interest to the students. For example, if a student is interested in cars, make up a list of words that concern cars: make, type, parts, etc. Each student and the teacher should build a list together. As the students learn the words, they write them on 3" × 5" white cards with associative clues on the back and add them to their word collection. These words will be introduced *one at a time* into the writing program.

Component Three—Spelling Patterns

Introduce the students to spelling patterns such as *at, op* and *an*. Teach these one at a time, along with the sounds of four or five consonants (such as *p, m, t*, and *g*) if the students do not already know them. The students then blend the sounds (consonants and spelling patterns) together to make words. The words are also written on 3" × 5" white cards and filed with those the students already know. The following is a list of spelling patterns and examples of combinations that can be derived therein. In teaching, the cards should be presented to the student like this:

| m | an | and not like this: | m | an |

CONSONANT VOWEL–CONSONANT ([C] VC). This pattern should be taught first. For example:

an - *m an, c an, p an, tan*
at - *c at, f at, s at, m at*
ap - *c ap, t ap, n ap, m ap*
ed - *w ed, b ed, l ed, T ed*
en - *t en, p en, h en, B en*

Following are other vowel–consonant spelling patterns:

ab, ad, ag, am
eg, em, ep, et
ib, id, ig, im, in, ip, it
ob, od, of, om, on, op, ot
ub, ud, ug, um, un, up, ut

Begin with the following consonants, as they can be sustained without distortion for longer periods of time: *f, h, l, m, n, r, s,* and *v.* Then use such sounds as *b, g, t, d,* and *p,* and add the rest of the consonants as necessary. With the above consonant–vowel sound combinations, many words can be formed. By using word cards or plastic or wooden letters that the student physically pushes together and pulls apart, you can teach analysis and synthesis of words simultaneously. The same process is used with the patterns to follow. The student can be told that this is a spelling program.

Note: Digraphs and blends are added to the pattern in the same way as the initial consonants. (Again, if word cards are used, the letters should look like this: ch at ; not like this: ch at .) For example,

at – *ch* + at = *chat*
at – *fl* + at = *flat*

Following are other digraphs and blends that can be used with spelling patterns:

ch, cl, cr
dl, dr
fl, fr
gl, gr
pl, pr
sc, sh, sn, sm, sp, st
th, tr, tw
wh, wr

CONSONANT-VOWEL CONSONANT (C V [C]). This is an alternate approach if Section 1 does not prove successful. For example:

ba - *ba d, ba t, ba g, ba m*
ca - *ca t, ca b, ca p, ca n*
da - *da d, da m, da b, Da n*
fa - *fa d, fa n, fa t, Fa b*

Other consonant–vowel spelling patterns include the following:

ma, na, pa, ra, sa, ta, va, wa
be, de, fe, ge, je, le, me, ne, pe, re, te, ve, ye
bi, di, fi, hi, ji, ki, li, mi, ni, pi, ri, si, ti, vi, wi, yi
bo, co, do, fo, go, ho, jo, lo, mo, no, po, ro, so, to
bu, cu, du, fu, gu, ju, lu, mu, nu, pu, ru, su, tu, yu

By adding the consonants *f, h, l, m, n, r, s,* and *v* as before, and then *b, g, d,* and *p,* one can form many word combinations. Other consonants are added as necessary.

CONSONANT VOWEL–CONSONANT–CONSONANT ([C] VCC). This pattern is taught next in the sequence. For example:

ash - *b ash, c ash, m ash, s ash*
ath - *b ath, m ath, p ath, r ath*
ang - *b ang, h ang, s ang, g ang*

Following are other vowel–consonant–consonant patterns:

esh, ish, ush
eth, ith, oth
ing, ong, ung
ack, eck, ick, ock, uck
aff, eff, iff, uff
all, ell, ill, oll, ull
ess, iss, oss, uss
est, ist, ost, ust
ask, esk, isk, usk
asp, isp, osp, usp

Consonant blends and digraphs can be added as necessary to build many words.

CONSONANT VOWEL–CONSONANT–VOWEL ([C] VCV). This is the next phase in teaching spelling patterns. For example:

ike - *l ike, M ike, h ike, t ike*
ake - *m ake, t ake, b ake, f ake*

Following are other vowel–consonant–vowel patterns:

age, ade, age, ame, ane, ape, ate
ede, ete
ibe, ide, ime, ine, ipe, ite
ode, ome, one, ope, ote
ube, ume, une, upe, ute

By adding the consonants mentioned previously as needed, you can add many new words to the student's list. These words can be filed on 3" × 5" white cards with associative pictures or phrases on the back. Digraphs and blends can also be added to the above vowel–consonant–consonant patterns to make words. For example:

ich	– *wh* + *ich*	= *which*
ush	– *sh* + *ush*	= *shush*
ing	– *br* + *in g*	= *bring*
	th + *in g*	= *thing*
ong	– *th* + *on g*	= *thong*

OTHER SPELLING PATTERNS. Consonant digraphs and blends can be added to the following patterns to make words:

eel	ead	oad	all
eed	eak	oak	ain
eek	eam	oan	iad
een	ean	oat	ose
eep	eal		oum
eet	eap		use

atch	athe	ange	aste
etch	ethe	enge	este
itch	ithe	inge	iste
otch	othe	onge	oste
utch	uthe	unge	uste

anch	aint	lege
ench	aize	ight
inch	aise	ount
onch	ease	
unch	east	

Component Four—Alternative Word Lists

Words from different sources can be introduced into the reading program, one at a time. They can be taken from the following areas:

1. *Everyday Word List:* An integral part of this program is the systematic introduction of words that are most common in everyday use. The Mann-Suiter Everyday Word List (Table 9-1) can be used for this purpose. As the students learn each word, they write it on 3" × 5" white cards, put an associative picture clue or phrase on the back, and put the cards in their file boxes. Introduce the words in phrases or sentences, not in isolation.
2. *Short Phrase List:* Develop cards with short phrases and sentences for inclusion in the vocabulary building program. These should have associative picture clues on the back whenever possible. Phrases can be taken from the Mann-Suiter Developmental Phrase List (Table 9-2).
3. *Subject Level Word List:* At the beginning of the semester or year, each of the subject level teachers can give the students a list of words they will need to learn (sight word and meaning) in order to succeed in that subject area. These words can be introduced into the reading program one at a time, associatively (e.g., words and phrases on word cards with pictures). This will enable the students to tie the reading program into the subject level areas.

Coordinating the Components

The components should be coordinated as in Figure 9-21. Following is a sample lesson.

Table 9–1   Mann-Suiter Everyday Word List

a	I	the
all	in	to
am	is	they
an	it	this
and	if	three
any		ten
are	jump	tell
at		two
	know	talk
be		then
been	look	that
big	like	too
blue	little	them
by	let	there
can	may	up
carry	many	
come	me	very
could	my	
	met	want
did		way
do	no	why
does	not	who
done		with
down	one	was
	once	will
eight	on	would
	of	what
for		where
four	play	when
	pretty	walk
get		went
go	run	
gone	ride	you
good	red	yes
got		your
going	see	yellow
green	some	
	so	
hop	said	
had	saw	
have	she	
he		
here		

STEP 1—THE STUDENTS LEARN A SPELLING PATTERN. Present the words as whole words first, then show how they are broken down into consonants, digraphs, or blends and patterns. The student will need to see the same spelling patterns in each of the words. The sequence of teaching is as follows:

Table 9-2   Mann-Suiter Developmental Phrases

I

it is	I hear a	I like a	a game
a big hat	did he miss	the pony is	we will walk
I see	we went to the	he rides a	her father
I took	I like my	I said	a pretty doll
in a hat	my name is	in the boat	a new book
the cat is	I live at	at school	the children
I had fun	my eyes are	I found	to the farm
I cut	he took me	a dime	a black horse
the cup	the room is	his work	a white rabbit
the bus	the kitten is	he has fun	the little boy
look at the	she is	at the farm	we will walk
I fed the	I wish I	he helped	they were
a cat is		is one	a little baby
I pet the	*II*	is pleased	a white duck
did he have		with me	a blue coat
he can	the ball is	the train	when you come
she will get	a chicken is	come in	to the tree
do you see	I took that	a ball game	you will like
he has a	my father is	he looks	a small boat
I want a	my mother is	to a game	a pretty girl
the band is	they are both	the baby	he would try
I like that	he drove a	the cat had	down the street
it was a	father drove	the cows are	a yellow hat
I saw	this is my	he was	went down
I can find	she saw the	he let	up the hill
I will	where are my	his horse	the brown horse
I play a	I put them		a big house
he sings a	here they are	*III*	a red bird
I want to	dad and I		in the garden
I kick the	the cow is	we like	into the water
she took the	the house is	after school	the little chickens
he likes to	the boy has	it snowed	my father knows
we got the	a horse is	some stories	he would go
he got a	there are	ask me	some cake
she got five	can you see	two trees	in the grass
he will ride	is there a	I am having	to the barn
I found his	I saw three	who worked	may I
can you	there were	with them	I must try
do you	one boy	would you	on the chair
I will give	two girls	your room	a baby pig
do you want	is a car	we went	some brown cows
dad got a	he knows	we can play	

First: *cat* —whole word shown on a card or with anagrams

Second: *c at* —word broken down into sound and pattern on cards or with anagrams

Third: *cat* —whole word shown on a card or with anagrams

Note: Physical manipulation of cards or letters is important for students who cannot remember the patterns.

Next, line up the letters and words as follows so that the student can see the similarities.

(a)				(b)	
at		at	at		c
cat	c	at	cat		m—at
mat	m	at	mat		p
pat	p	at	pat		f
fat	f	at	fat		

Mix up the letters and let the students build the words: *at, cat, mat, pat,* and *fat.* Have the students write the words on 3" × 5" white cards, put pictures or phrase clues on the back, and file the cards in their word boxes.

Note: The students should be tested the next day informally at their seats. Show them the word cards and ask them to identify the words. If they cannot, repeat the teaching process, letting them work for a longer period of time with the cards or plastic or wooden letters.

An alternative approach, to be used if the students do not appear to be stabilizing the words when they are introduced first as whole words, is the following:

First: *c at* —word broken down into sound and pattern on cards

Second: *cat* — whole word

Third: *c at* —word broken down again into sound and pattern (same as the first)

Fourth: *cat* —complete model

STEP II—THE STUDENTS LEARN OTHER WORDS NECESSARY FOR WRITING A SENTENCE. Now that the students have learned four words based on spelling patterns, they and the teacher can incorporate them into functional use with other words the students know, words they like, and alternative words, as follows:

1. The teacher and students select out of all the words the students know the ones they need in order to write a sentence, paragraph, or short story. For example, a student may select from his or her file cards the words *the, is, a, red, he, she, and, has, car, his, have,* and *for.*

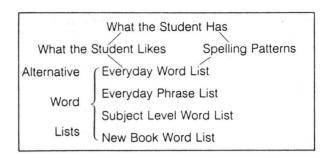

Figure 9–21 *Coordinating the Components*

2. The teacher chooses words from an alternative word list (e.g., the Mann-Suiter Everyday Word List [Table 9-1]), introducing them one at a time and teaching them in a phrase or sentence, using a write-read approach.

3. The teacher allows the students to choose words they like (e.g., hot rod) and then teaches those words, one at a time, in a phrase or sentence, using a write-read approach.

4. The teacher combines the words from the first three categories with the four words based on spelling pattern *(cat, mat, pat, fat).*

STEP III—THE STUDENTS CAN WRITE SENTENCES AND THEN PARAGRAPHS. Paragraph writing can be accomplished in three ways:

1. The teacher writes the first sentence and the student writes the next one, or vice versa. For example:
   Teacher: "Pat is a fat cat."
   Student: "The fat cat has a hot rod."

2. The student writes two sentences and the teacher writes the last one, or vice versa. For example:
   Student: "The cat is fat."
   Student: "He is with Pat in the hot rod."
   Teacher: "The red hot rod has a mat for the cat."

3. The student writes a whole paragraph based on the above vocabulary. For example:
   He has a hot rod. He is with Pat in his red car. Mat and Pat have the fat cat in the red car.

Words from each pattern should be developed into sentences, paragraphs, and then stories. In essence, the student is slowly developing a sight vocabulary. (*Note:* Only one new thing should be introduced at a time, unless the students indicate through the learning process that they can cope with more.)

STEP IV—THE STUDENTS CAN DEVELOP WORD ATTACK SKILLS THROUGH ORAL DRILL. Give the Mann-Suiter Alphabet-Speech Screen (page 194) to determine the students' sound-symbol relationship abilities (letter names and letter sounds). Note the production of the letter sounds. Are they "clean" or has there been faulty learning (e.g., "tuh" for *t*)?

Check to see if the students can blend (Mann-Suiter Visual Closure Screen [page 181] and Auditory Closure Screen [page 191]).

Using the chalkboard, present a student with a spelling pattern and a consonant, as in Figure 9-22.

Say, "If I put the 'c' [letter sound] in front of the *at* [word], what word will it make?" If the student does not respond correctly, erase the *c* and place it closer to the pattern, as in Figure 9-23. Repeat the question. If the student still cannot respond, then place the *c* next to the *at,* making the word *cat,* and say, "See. C . . . at makes cat. You say it." Follow this with further blending activities, as blending is a problem area for the student. If the student responds correctly the first time, saying "cat," then say, "What word will be made if I put a 'p' [sound] in front of the *at?*" If the response is "pat," then do the *f* sound and *m* sound. In teaching analysis and synthesis this way, *do not* use letter names, just letter sounds. (Letter names can be used in other situations). When using letter sounds, be sure that they are used cleanly. *Do not* add a vowel sound on the end of a consonant (e.g., "tuh" for "t").

The same activity can be done without using a chalkboard in the following manner. Say, "Say the spelling pattern 'op.'" The student replies. Then say, "If I put an 'm' [sound] in front of 'op,' what word will it make?" A variation would be to say "op" and then "m" and then have the student make the word *mop.* Then say "p," and so on.

You will know that the student is beginning to develop analysis and synthesis ability when you write a pattern (e.g., *ate*) and, without your asking, the student says, "Mate, date, late."

The entire approach can be introduced to the students as a spelling or writing program. If the students do begin to expand their vocabulary, their reading will improve.

STEP V—STUDENTS CAN DEVELOP NEW SIGHT VOCABULARY BY ADDING WORDS FROM A NEW-BOOK WORD LIST. The students and teacher can compare the students' baseline vocabulary (words they know) with the vocabulary of a book they would like to read. Many readers have the vocabulary at the back of the book, so it is easy to compare the lists. Otherwise, a student may have to go through a book and make a list of all the words he or she cannot read. If the list of unknown words is too long, the book is too advanced for the learner. If the list is not too long, the words can be introduced into the reading program associatively, as in the previous examples. As the students learn the words through their write-to-read program, they can begin to read the books.

The students can put the new words on cards in a word box or write or type them on a folder. They should date each new word learned, or stabilized. (See Figure 9-24) See pages 342–348 for alternative management systems for this kind of a program.

SPELLING INSTRUCTION

English orthography does not associate sounds directly to letters. Instead, English spelling has sound segments which convey meaning. Students must acquire a knowledge of how the alphabet reflects meaningful language (Gentry & Henderson, 1978). Chao (1968) states that English does not have a one-to-one correspondence like Spanish and some other languages, but a many-to-many system. "An individual phoneme (sound) can have a variety of spellings (e.g., way, weigh, wait, fate, hey, ballet, fiancee, lady). An individual grapheme (letter) can have a variety of pronunciations (e.g., one, do, dot, open, etc.)" (Barnitz, 1980). The alphabet of 26 letters can be combined into 251 different spellings for 44 sounds in English (Hull, 1976).

With the many exceptions to the rules of spelling, it would appear that English orthography is irregular. However, researchers look at its regularity. Hanna, Hodges, and Hanna (1971) studied the phoneme/grapheme relationship and structure of the English

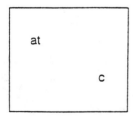

Figure 9–22   Spelling Pattern and Consonant

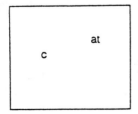

Figure 9–23   Consonant Closer to Spelling Pattern

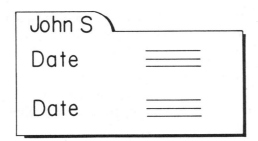

Figure 9–24

language by analyzing 17,000 words. A computer programmed with 203 rules spelled the words with 50 percent accuracy. Consonants having a single spelling were used in 80 percent of the 17,000 words. Bloomfield (1942) and Fries (1963) also examined the regularity of words by arranging them into patterns: CVC—consonant–vowel–consonant words such as *had, cat*; CVCV—consonant–vowel–consonant–vowel words such as *take*, etc. Chomsky and Halle (1968) noted the regularity of English spelling, based on the fact that the correspondence of the spelling to meaning is direct. Words such as *please* and *pleasant* are related in meaning as well as in spelling.

To help students understand how English evolved, the teacher can discuss how words have changed through the years. Some words have changed pronunciations, but the spelling has stayed the same. Many words have come from the Romance Languages with Greek and Latin contributions. Others are based on a mixture of Old English and French spelling. New words are constantly being borrowed and adapted from foreign languages.

The computer has given us a fairly accurate tally of the frequency of words used in written communication. For example, 4,500 words make up 99 percent of all words used by writers. From 2,800 to 3,000 words account for 96 percent of all the words most people will write in a lifetime (Horn, in Loomer, 1978). Graham (1983) points out that 100 words account for 50 percent of all words children use in writing, 1,000 words for 89 percent, and 3,000 for 97 percent. Graham recommends that students be taught high-frequency words in list form.

Reading and Spelling

Spelling is a skill that can be developed with the reading program. Skill in reading does not necessarily assure skill in spelling, but it is axiomatic that most poor readers are also poor spellers. Spelling differs from reading in that spelling demands complete recall of the words to be spelled.

As the student becomes more proficient in both reading and spelling, there is some diversion of emphasis. During reading the student does not have to attend to each letter since context provides understanding and the student can recognize a word using a few letters. Spelling, however, is more precise and involves an attention to all of the letters in the proper sequence. Some spellers may be good readers by using partial cues or visual clustering strategies, so reading by itself will not provide the exposure needed to attend to the letter-by-letter structure of words or the phonological component (Gill, 1989). Dulaney (1987) concluded that spelling high-frequency words from the basal reading word lists leads to an increased ability in word recognition. It is recommended that the instructor select spelling words from the learner's independent reading vocabulary. If the learner has the fine motor skill to write the words, the reading, writing, and spelling activities can be coordinated.

In order to spell fluently, students must have the following:

1. A basic spelling vocabulary learned to the automatic level so that the students do not have to stop to think
2. Ability to apply spelling generalizations to unknown words
3. Knowledge of the contextual meaning of the word to be spelled *(ate, eight)*
4. Learning new words, which includes much practice in listening to, saying, and writing words
5. Knowledge of the consistency of letter-sound relationships in the English language

The following areas of inadequacy may affect spelling:

1. Speech problems associated with articulation or faulty patterns, such as saying "gonna" for *going*
2. Auditory problems with sound discrimination or memory-sequencing
3. Visual problems with symbol discrimination or memory-sequencing
4. Visual-motor problems affecting ability to make the correct motor pattern for a particular symbol (causing reversals, inversions, and inappropriate spacing)

For a spelling program to be successful, it must emphasize good study skills, good study habits, and motivation through success and interest.

At the turn of the century, spelling was taught by rote memorization. The assumption was that each word required a separate act of learning. Today, it is felt that students should be helped to identify patterns in words, such as the *and* in *sand* and *hand*. Students should be taught to apply these spelling patterns instead of using a different strategy for each word learned. This method takes advantage of the associative processes and stabilizes the patterns of spelling in the learners' minds. Eventually, this method must be converted as much as possible into more or less reflective behavior.

Prerequisite Skills

Students should have certain basic skills before beginning a spelling program. Too often, poor spelling is the result of learning inappropriate methods. In teaching spelling, make sure the students are able to discriminate sounds and articulate English speech sounds. Note cultural or speech deviations, and be realistic in your expectation for rapid change in this area. Students should also be able to discriminate visually between letters and be able to write upper and lowercase letters of the alphabet. They need sufficient strength and control of the fine muscles of the hand and arm to control and manipulate a writing instrument if a writing-to-reading-and-spelling approach is being used.

Auditory and visual memory-sequencing and closure skills are possibly the most crucial to spelling ability. To learn to spell fluently, students must be able to remember sounds of letters in isolation as well as how to blend them into whole words. Once the students' phoneme-grapheme relationship becomes consistent, they will be able to use the following skills:

1. Auditory-analysis (to hear a word as a whole and analyze it into separate sound units)
2. Auditory-synthesis (to hear separate speech sounds and blend them into a whole word)

After the auditory analysis and synthesis have been mastered, visual memory helps the students select the *c* for spelling *cat* rather than *k*. Later, they may learn the rule that the hard *c* sound is usually spelled as a *k* only when followed by *i* or *e*, and that the word *kangaroo* does not follow the rule because it is a foreign word. Students with memory problems have difficulty in remembering spelling rules. The students need a great deal of practice using words functionally, as in writing, before they can revisualize the words. If students in a spelling program are still visually or auditorily confusing *b*, and *d*, or *m*, and *w*, they may have difficulty moving from sheer rote memory to seeing the consistent language patterns that do exist in the En-

glish language. They should eventually hear and see that the *and* in *hand* is the same *and* that is in *sand*, without having to learn each word separately. Rhyming is an important prerequisite skill in spelling.

The goal of spelling instruction is to help the students develop as automatic a motor response as possible to the words they have or visualize in their mind's eye. Developing an automatic motor response is different from taking a spelling test in that there are no external clues, such as using the word in a sentence; and the students must reauditorize the sequence of the sounds in their mind.

Recognizing a word in reading does not mean that the students have noticed it in sufficient detail to spell it correctly. Students need to develop a distant image of the word so that they can recall it at will. Great differences are found in individual recall. Some people get only very vague images, or none at all, and actually remember words in terms of audio-images, recalling a word with sound (through lip and throat movements), or even with the movement of the hand in writing the word. Other individuals, with good visual memories, remember words by actually revisualizing the letters.

One of the prerequisites to good spelling is a distinct and accurate perception of a word and the ability to describe it in detail. Students with a learning difficulty must be taught through meaningful repetition until the process becomes so automatic that they can write the word without conscious attention to the details of its spelling.

All students have their own unique ways of learning, and if they are ever to move from the realm of rote memory, or memorizing each word as a single entity, they must be aware of their own learning style, as well as the systematic order in the structure of our language. To teach the basic principles needed for transfer of knowledge of one word to another, any spelling program should consider the manner in which each student learns.

Young children have unconventional letter spellings for sound clusters. In grades 1–4, learners depend on sound strategies for spelling generally unfamiliar words. Marsh et al. (1980) and Nolen and McCartin (1984) found a strategy shift at the fifth-grade level where students switched to print strategies. There is a noticeable shift to mental visualization as a strategy. This is called "picturing in your mind's eye."

Stages of Spelling Skill Development

A criterion-referenced assessment and instructional analysis can be utilized for individualized educational programming. Assessing the spelling achievement levels of students for norm-referenced purposes (e.g., grade level(s), quartiles, percentiles, standard grading systems) is not enough. A spelling criterion-reference is defined as a method of determining the level and quality of an individual's spelling performance in relation to specific instructional objectives or criteria. Students must be assessed from a developmental (criterion-referenced) point of view in terms of their spelling skills.

The following is a spelling criterion-referenced approach to assessment and instruction. The language area of spelling is delineated into three sequential criterion stages of skill development, which are as follows:

Stage 1: Developmental
The developmental stage of spelling represents the initial building blocks of the skill area, such as learning the alphabet as a basic developmental skill necessary for getting all the letters in the right order or writing independently.

Stage 2: Transitional
The transitional level of spelling skill development is a further development of Stage 1 where the basic skills are coordinated for higher level functions. These functions, once practiced and learned, become habitual and automatic responses that are vital for the next stage, which represents the basic tools for good spelling.

Stage 3: Academic
Stage 3 represents the academic level of criterion for success in the spelling skill area. Various functions such as speed and accuracy are essential for success in using spelling skills for academic purposes.

By understanding these interrelationships the teacher can determine the different levels of functioning within the areas of spelling and then plan the student's program accordingly. This delineation of the subareas within spelling is just another way of trying to understand a complex process without relying totally on the traditional grade level descriptions.

When viewed within the context of mastery of simple, intermediate, and complex skills, the teacher can discern the students' relative understanding and facility with a particular aspect of language. In any of life's tasks, whether it be for academic, recreational, or social purposes, the best example of how a skill can be manifested is the automatic nature of its performance or presentation.

The concept of automaticity is presented as a theme in each of the chapters dealing with language and mathematics. The same orientation, Developmental–Transitional–Academic, is presented as a basis for the understanding and discussion in each of these areas.

Henderson (1985) describes five stages of word and spelling knowledge: (1) preliterate and prephonetic, (2) letter-name spelling, (3) within-word pattern spelling, (4) syllable juncture spelling, and (5) derivational constancies.

At the preliterate stage the student has not been taught spelling. He or she is learning the concept "word," spontaneously writing strings of numbers, squibbles, and letters to represent words; learning the alphabet; and is being read books and other materials. The beginning reader needs support from story and sentence context, memory, and the teacher. Stories with predictable structures and content are helpful.

During the prephonetic stage the student listens to more pattern books, as well as other books. The class produces group experience charts and the student has a chance to match words spoken to words written as he or she dictates to someone. The student is becoming aware of initial consonant sounds and is demonstrating what has been learned from oral language and exposure to the orthography. Consonant boundaries are noticed (e.g., the word *back* has /b/ and /k/).

By the letter-name spelling stage the student usually has mastered consonants, some blends and digraphs, and is beginning to work more on CVC short vowel patterns. An awareness of the phonological structure of the language is emerging. The within-word stage includes a larger sight vocabulary with more silent reading and an understanding of the rules for long vowels. Syllable-juncture spelling focuses more on the combination of syllables. In the upper grades the morphology of roots and the study of affixes is increased.

In a final phase of derivational constancies, an examination of etymology, how words from other cultures become part of the English orthography, increases the students' linguistic awareness.

Writing and Spelling

An important first step in learning to spell is the manipulation of letters and the discovery of words. Gentry and Henderson (1978) suggest that English spelling is dominated by sound segments which convey meaning and that learning to spell is acquiring knowledge of

DEVELOPMENT SEQUENCE

The following represents a breakdown of spelling based on the concept of prerequisite skills for higher level functions. The outline will be helpful to teachers in diagnosis and in programming for students exhibiting developmental lags or irregular learning in spelling.

Questions to be answered: What has to be taught? What has to be practiced? What can be used effectively?

STAGES OF SPELLING SKILL DEVELOPMENT

DEVELOPMENTAL	TRANSITIONAL	ACADEMIC
Manipulates and discovers words	Writes independently	Does creative writing
Learns how the alphabet works	Tests the orthography and internalizes the rules	Uses corrective spelling strategies
Learns letters of the alphabet	Uses more abstract strategies	Displays automaticity in spelling
Develops beginning phonetic spelling strategies	Gets all the letters, but sometimes in the wrong order	Understands that spelling represents meaning
Discriminates sounds	Uses visual images of associated meanings using spelling rules	
Develops sound/symbol relationships	Uses visual images of associated meanings using syllabication	
Sequences sounds	Shifts from sound strategies to print strategies in the intermediate grades (grade 5)	
Rhymes Words	Uses common vowel patterns	
	Uses inflectional endings	
	Has trial and error attempts to spell	
	Imitates correct models	
	Uses chunking of letters versus a letter-by-letter strategy	
	Has knowledge of spelling/meaning pattern	
	Understands basewords, prefixes, suffixes, consonant, consonant blend, digraph, vowel sound symbol association	

how the alphabet reflects meaningful language. Creative writing is a testing of the orthography and has to initially deemphasize standard spelling. The student is encouraged to use "invented spellings." Read (1975) concluded that students' invented spellings indicated the strategies they were using to determine how to spell words. Nonstandard spelling is predictable, frequent, and natural in the writing of young children.

Spelling becomes more than the number of words on a spelling test. Spelling becomes an interactive process among the child, the parents, and the teach-er. During creative writing, the teacher is monitoring attempts at spelling against a baseline of samples of writing. The student isn't graded on all attempts at writing, but is lead through to the transition to correct spelling. The parents need to know what to expect and how to encourage writing at home.

Later in this chapter is a detailed explanation of how young writers can move from a language experience approach to independent writing. Students will ask for the spelling of words when they write, and parents and teachers should write the words instead of only spelling them orally. This gives the student a model to copy.

Gentry (1981), Chomsky (1971), Di Stefano and Hagerty (1985), and Zutell (1978) promote experimentation with writing. They encourage that writing be frequent and enjoyable. Students need to practice their predictions of how they think words are spelled. Gentry (1981) supports the use of the language experience approach, creative and independent writing, and the "celebration" of mistakes in early writing as trial-and-error attempts.

Teaching Spelling

For students with learning problems to experience success in learning to spell and use spelling in content areas, the teacher has to plan a program of directed study. Students cannot study alone and learn the complexities of our language and generalize to content areas. They need a program that includes structure modeling by the teacher, opportunities for self-directed practice, and encouragement to apply spelling daily. In a heterogeneous classroom of students spelling at different levels, this obviously involves flexibility in grouping, instruction, and assessment.

Ideally, spelling should be individualized in that each student proceeds at his or her own pace at the appropriate developmental level. Using informal spelling tests and error analysis, the teacher should be able to ascertain which groups of students have similar needs on a continuum. Grouping should be flexible, based on student progress. The three traditional groups of high, medium, low will not be sufficient. Individualization does not always mean one-to-one instruction. With a combination of small groups, peer tutoring, cooperative learning, and self-monitoring by the student, a classroom teacher can provide instruction at appropriate stages.

Instruction will require more materials than only one grade-level spelling text. Word lists should come from reading programs, developmental lists, word pattern lists (such as those found on page 445), and words of interest to the student. There are important pedagogical concepts that need to be maintained throughout the planning of a spelling instructional program:

1. *Number of Words:* To keep students on a successful pace in spelling and to avoid overloading, fewer words may need to be taught each week (Bryant, Drabin, & Gettinger, 1981). Some students may start with five words, including a familiar reading pattern *(at, cat, fat, hat)* and a known sight word *(and).* The number is determined by how well the student is retaining words based on ongoing cur-

riculum-based assessment and how these words are successfully being incorporated into writing. The size of the small group or individual student's list of words will vary. Review of previously learned words has to be planned. Word lists should also include words that are not being retained and need to be reviewed. Keep them moving as fast as possible through the review words while maintaining an ongoing program with the words at the next level. Some students will go faster than others.

2. *Direct Instruction:* Supervised instruction is required for spelling. Introducing words, pretesting to check on which words are approximately at mastery, doing an error analysis, and using distributed practice require direction. For example, on Monday, students are given the word lists for the week. Since the students should already be able to read the words, a discussion of vocabulary meaning will be used to elaborate on multiple meanings and usage. Plans are made on the various ways students will use and keep track of how they will use the words in conversation, in instructional activities, and in writing. On Monday or Tuesday, a pretest is given and an error analysis is done to decide which words need attention with regard to phonics, structural analysis, or rules. The students should correct their own tests under supervision. Tuesday through Thursday are used for a large variety of activities presented in this chapter. Both teacher and students can individually review and practice self-directed study strategies, error analysis, individualized assessment. In groups, students can play games, test each other, and edit and proofread writing. Modeling by the instructor is continuous to demonstrate correct procedures. Motivation is important for spelling. Goals should be realistic in terms of improvement. Students need a challenging but not frustrating program. Students need to understand why spelling is important.

3. *Self-Directed Instruction:* Time is a critical factor in teaching. Students will not get enough classroom "group" spelling time to really learn to spell, and, while it is hoped that parents will assist at home, this is also an unrealistic expectation. Therefore, the responsibility for monitoring and promoting successful spelling has to be shared by the student. He or she has to use the self-directed strategies that will ensure learning. The student has to be given an explanation of why this is an important use of time. Among the strategies suggested in this chapter are methods to aid memory, increase meaning, and promote writing activities. To do this, the classroom needs equipment (microcomputers, language masters, tape recorders), places for stu-

dents to work in small groups or alone (study carrels), and individualized materials that promote writing and learning (games, writing center, typewriter). The student also needs the charts, graphs, and folders that will be used to monitor progress. The metacognitive strategies suggested throughout the book have to be practiced (visual imagery, word study techniques, and self-questioning strategies).

4. *Training for Transfer.* Students need to see the words they are learning to spell in many contexts and in a variety of settings. This goes beyond the use of words written on the chalkboard or seen in a spelling text. By reading and writing the words, the student is applying new knowledge in real-world situations. The artificiality of the Friday spelling test as an end product is put into proper perspective. Writing is an everyday process as a part of content area subjects and in daily journals or letters. Generalization and transfer goes beyond usage and becomes obvious when the student starts to notice how spelling generalizations occur in words. This can occur with the expansion of spelling patterns, rule application, and awareness of word meanings.

5. *Assessment:* Give weekly tests (e.g. on Fridays) and give review tests a few days later (e.g., on Mondays) to see which words the student has remembered. The Friday tests will be helpful in telling the student and the teacher whether the words selected were appropriate. Perhaps the student had too many words. Some students need a slower pace during an oral spelling test to allow for retrieval. Other students with poor handwriting may not be writing legibly during fast-paced tests. Periodic review of the words should be systematically done. Use the words the student did not retain, with a specified number of new words (the number would differ with each student), for that week's lesson. Every four weeks give a review test of words taught to see which ones are still unknown, and include those with the ongoing program. A student in this type of program would not be expected to learn a specified number of words in a given period of time and may not be expected to complete one grade's spelling book for the school year.

Besides a knowledge of how each student learns best, a teacher must have a spelling program that avoids introducing too many different vowel sounds at one time. The program should be simple, starting with letters and letter groups that most consistently represent the sounds of language.

Most commercial spelling programs are not applicable to students with learning problems because they are usually based on sets of words grouped around subjects. Little consideration is given to being consistent in the way words are presented.

Spelling programs could very easily follow the linguistic reading series presently available. By developing a language-spelling program around the reading series used, the teacher would be consistently using the same vowel sounds through writing, spelling, and reading activities. This would avoid the biggest problem most first graders face, which is "vowel cluttering." Occasionally, students are unable to develop their cognitive processing ability because too many different sounds of the same vowel are presented close together, causing vowel cluttering. (The *a* in *man* in the reading lesson becomes confused with the *a* in *Jane* on the same page and the *a* in *all* in the spelling lesson.) A combined reading-spelling program is also useful because reading should be reinforced through a motor response such as building words out of movable letters, which is also spelling.

With simple variations, most linguistic reading series follow a prescribed order of presenting words and can be an excellent outline for a spelling program. Most learners are ready for formal spelling when they have finished their first preprimers and can read simple CVC (consonant–vowel–consonant) pattern words without hesitation.

The following spelling program outline is recommended for young readers:

1. First introduce words of a simple CVC pattern (consonant–vowel–consonant). Have the students analyze them and then put them together using cards, plastic letters, or wooden letters.
2. Short vowel sounds should never be taught alone, but with a consonant (e.g., *c at*). The first spelling lesson could look like this:
   a. Select the family to be taught: *at*
   b. Select five CVC words (start with nouns if possible): *cat, pat, hat, mat, rat.*
   c. Include a simple sight word that can be used with the nouns in simple phrases: *a fat cat. Note:* The teacher should not try to teach all *at* words at one time.

The second spelling lesson would cover another short *a* family, such as *ad* with the CVC words *lad, mad, sad,* and *had,* plus the sight words *I* and *see.*

Note: Remain at each level until the students have attained absolute mastery. It is very important to overteach at this level to insure that the students have made these basic sound-symbol relationships.

In teaching lesson two, reach back into lesson one and continue to use the words in phrases. Introduce one short vowel sound at a time, including from three to five CVC words and one sight word in a lesson. After mastering the short vowels at this level, the student is ready to move on to more complex patterns. Introduce the following:

1. Words of a simple CVCC pattern, using short vowel sounds ending with a double *ff, ll, zz,* or *ss* (for example, *tiff, tell, buzz,* and *kiss*)
2. Words having two-letter blends with short vowels, such as *plan, blot, chat, bring,* and *clap*
3. Digraphs *(ch, th, sh, wh)* with short vowels, such as *chat, that, shop, shut,* and *when*
4. Three-letter blends with short vowels, as in *string, spring,* and *strap*
5. Long vowels (CVC words with an added *e,* such as *cap-cape; hat-hate; mat-mate)*
6. Long vowels with two-letter blends, as in *spade* and *stove*
7. Long vowels with digraphs, as in *shade* and *while*
8. Long vowels with three-letter blends, as in *stroke* and *strike*
9. Second sounds of *c, g,* and *s,* as in *city, garage, was*
10. *R*-controlled vowels, such as *ar, er, ir, or, ur*
11. Vowel digraphs, such as *ee* in *teen, ea* in *bread, ay* in *play*
12. Silent letters, such a *h* in *honest, t* in *listen,* and *k* in *knee*
13. Highly irregular words—impossible to decode—such as *said, the* and *was*
14. Root (base) words and affixes such as *re, de,* and *bi*
15. Words on the syntactic level of language, such as *bear-bare;* and *two-too-to*

In teaching spelling, always try to move from one known element to the new or unknown element, adding to the sound-symbol pattern already known.

Criterion Reference

Form 9-4 (Basic Phonics Analysis) and Form 9-5 (Basic Structural Analysis) can be used to monitor the skills that students have to master to be really proficient in spelling. Both of these lists can be used in the reading program.

Study Methods

Multiple strategies are recommended to avoid over-reliance on either phonics, look say, or one-study strategy. What many students need is more trials using a variety of strategies. Students with spelling problems may need the following methods:

1. Say the word, spell it, and they say it again. Next, have the student say the word and spell it. You repeat the sequence, and then have the student repeat it two or three more times before writing the word from memory.
2. Some students need a slightly different approach from method one. Say the word, spell it, and then say it again. Have the student write the word and then you correct it. The student then writes it two or three more times and finally turns the paper over and writes it again.
3. Show the student the word on a card or list and say the word. Have the student look at the word, say it, spell it, and say it again. Remove the word and have the student spell it from memory. After spelling it two or three times more, the student writes it from memory and checks the word against the stimulus card.
4. Show the word and name it. Have the student look at the word and then copy it on paper. The word is then covered and the student writes from memory and then checks it two or three more times. After spelling it two or three times more, the student writes it from memory and then checks the word against the stimulus card.
5. Show the word on a card, name the word, and spell it out orally. Have the student look at the word, spell it, and then write it on paper. Cover the word. The student then spells it orally from memory several times, writes it from memory two times, turns the paper over, writes the word from memory, and checks it with the word card. Many repetitions may be necessary.

Along with a visual-motor approach, include a great deal of practice in listening, saying words, and writing. Some of the material that can be utilized to reinforce spelling are these:

1. 3″ × 5″ white cards with associative picture clues on the back
2. Plastic, wooden, felt, or beaded letters
3. Sand trays
4. Magnetic letters
5. Typewriter
6. Computer
7. Tracing over a screen

Test–Study–Test Method

· Test—Students are given a pretest before groups of words are studied. This avoids time spent on words the students know. The students correct their own

Form 9-4

BASIC: PHONIC ANALYSIS SKILLS

The student will *read, spell* and *write* words with

1. Short Vowel a
2. Short Vowel e
3. Short Vowel i
4. Short Vowel o
5. Short Vowel u
6. Vowel Team ai
7. Vowel Team ea
8. Vowel Team ee
9. Long Vowel o
10. Vowel Team ay
11. Split Vowels a-e
12. Split Vowels i-e
13. Split Vowels o-e
14. Split Vowels u-e
15. Long Vowel i
16. Vowel Exception ea = ĕ
17. Vowel Exception ei = ā
18. Vowel Exception ie = ē
19. Consonant Digraph sh
20. Consonant Digraph ch
21. Consonant Digraph wh
22. Consonant Digraph th
23. Consonant Digraph ph
24. l Consonant Blends
25. r Consonant Blends
26. st, sp, sm, sn Consonant Blends
27. tw, sw, sc, sk Consonant Blends
28. scr Consonant Blend
29. squ Consonant Blend
30. str Consonant Blend
31. spr Consonant Blend
32. shr Consonant Blend
33. thr Consonant Blend
34. chr, sch, spl Consonant Blends
35. Silent Consonants w Before r
36. Silent Consonants k Before n
37. Silent Consonants t Before ch
38. Silent Consonants d Before ge
39. Silent Consonants l
40. Silent Consonants b
41. Silent Consonants gh
42. Silent Consonants h
43. Silent Consonants t
44. Silent Consonants n and p
45. Diphthongs ou-ow
46. Diphthongs oi-oy
47. Long o Sound of ow
48. Vowel Digraphs au-aw
49. Vowel Digraphs o͞o
50. Vowel Digraphs o͝o
51. Word Endings ck
52. Word Endings ll-ss-ff
53. Word Endings ng and nk
54. Word Endings nd and mp
55. Word Endings lp-ft-lk-ct
56. Word Endings lf-pt-lt
57. r Controllers (är)
58. r Controllers (āre)
59. r Controllers (ôr-ôre)
60. r Controllers (or-ar-er)
61. r Controllers (ir-er-ur)
62. r Controllers (ire-ere-ure)
63. Hard and Soft c
64. Hard and Soft g
65. Homonyms

The specific Phonic Skills listed have been keyed to a comprehensive remediation program in reading and spelling: "Basic Phonic Analysis Skills" by Philip H. Mann, Freida Lloyd, and Rose Marie McClung, published by Allyn and Bacon.

BASIC: STRUCTURAL ANALYSIS SKILLS

The student will

1. learn to say, spell, and write contractions that have one letter omitted and contractions that have more than one letter omitted.
2. learn to say, spell, and write verbs ending with *ing* and understand the meaning of *ing* added to a word.
3. learn to say, spell, and write verbs ending with *ed* and understand the meaning of *ed* added to a word.
4. learn to say, spell, and write words with the three sounds of *ed.*
5. learn to add *s, ed,* and *ing* to verbs ending in *y* preceded by a consonant.
6. learn to add *s, ed,* and *ing* to verbs ending in *y* preceded by a vowel.
7. learn to add *er* and *est* to adjectives and learn the meaning of these two endings.
8. learn to say, spell, and write nouns in their plural form by adding *s.*
9. learn to form the plurals of words ending in *ch, sh, s, ss,* and *x.*
10. learn to form the plurals of words ending in *y* when the *y* is preceded by a vowel or a consonant.
11. learn to form the plural of nouns ending in *f* and *fe.*
12. learn to form the plurals of words ending in *o* when the *o* comes after a vowel or a consonant.
13. learn to form the plural of words by changing the form of the word.
14. learn to say, spell, and write nouns that have the same form for singular and plural.
15. learn to say, spell, and write some nouns that have the plural form (have two parts) but mean one object; some nouns are singular in meaning but plural in form.
16. learn to say, spell, and write words using the vc/cv (vowel-consonant/consonant-vowel) pattern for syllabication.
17. learn to say, spell, and write words using the vc/cv (vowel-consonant/consonant-vowel) pattern for dividing words having unlike consonants.
18. learn to say, write, and spell the words using the v/cv (vowel/consonant-vowel) pattern of syllabication.
19. learn syllabication. He or she will say, spell, and write the words, using the vc/v (vowel-consonant/vowel) pattern.
20. learn to say, spell, and write the words using syllabication, the vc/v (vowel-consonant/vowel) pattern.
21. learn to say, spell, and write the words in syllabication: words ending in *le,* preceded by a consonant.
22. learn to say, spell, and pronounce compound words as taught in syllabication.
23. learn to say, spell, and write words using the prefix *re.*
24. learn to say, spell, and write words using the prefix *un.*
25. learn to say, spell, and write the words in the lesson on the suffix *ful.*
26. learn to say, spell, and write the words using the suffix *less.*

The basic structural analysis skills are keyed into a language remediation program; Basic Structural Analysis Skills by Philip H. Mann/Freida Lloyd/Rose Marie McClung, published by Allyn and Bacon.

papers and prepare a list of words to study. By analyzing all of the lists, the teacher can determine the words that can be deleted from the original list.

- Study—Students study the words they misspelled on the test. Group as well as individual study methods can be used. The teacher should target the high-frequency misspelled words noticed on the students' pretests. A mid-week test can be administered by a peer or the teacher.
- Test—After a posttest, the misspelled words are added to the next unit of study. The students also note on their individual lists the words that need additional practice.

Corrected Test Techniques

SELF-CORRECTION
An important aspect of the Test—Study—Test method is student correction. Fitzsimmons and Loomer (1980) have concluded that one of the most important factors in learning to spell is a student self-correcting his or her own spelling test under the direction of the teacher.

IMITATION PLUS MODELING
Another suggestion is to show a child how *not* to spell a word (negative instance of a concept), followed by showing him or her the correct spelling, rather than just correcting the poor spelling. This corrective feedback may help the student notice the ways his or her incorrect spelling differs from the correct response. Kauffman et al. (1978) compared teacher modeling (e.g., showing the student the correct way to spell a word) to imitation plus modeling (e.g., showing the student how he or she spelled the word first and then the correct way to spell the word). The imitation plus modeling technique was more successful.

Nulman and Gerber (1984) state that "Learning disabled learners require many more trials than normally achieving peers to reach criterion levels of performance" (p. 332). Therefore, the students need motivation to proofread and self-correct. General problem-solving behavior needs to be promoted, where the student looks at spelling attempts and then generates strategies that will help in later recall.

Di Stefano and Hagerty (1985) mention a technique first introduced by Horn in 1919. In it a student:

1. Pronounces the word while looking at it
2. Closes his/her eyes and tries to visualize the word and spell it correctly
3. Checks to see if his/her oral spelling of the word is correct

4. Covers the word and writes it
5. Checks his/her spelling against the model. If the student misspells the word, s/he goes back to Step 1 (p. 376)

General Spelling Activities

As the number of words known increases, the learners may be evaluated through the dictation of longer word lists and more complex sentences. To prepare the learners for the tasks of listening, spelling, and writing lists of words or sentences, use the tape recorder. Many students are under great pressure to perform on a spelling test. By listening to the instructor's voice at a slower rate of dictation and with a smaller number of words, learners can be successfully prepared for group evaluation when the rate and amount are increased. After listening to the tape and spelling the words, the learners can listen to the words being spelled aloud and correct their own paper. If the words are not spelled aloud on the tape, the students can refer to a folder containing the list to check the answer, or they can work with a peer tutor or volunteer.

OPTIONS FOR EVALUATION AND PRACTICE
The following spelling activities will provide additional reinforcement. The students build words by using spelling patterns and consonants in combination with rebus (picture) or associative clues:

1. Write a list of incomplete words of a particular pattern on the chalkboard (Figure 9-25). The learner uses the spelling pattern card ⌐at⌐, writes the letters on the blank lines, and says the words.
2. Prepare acetates for use on the overhead projector, or make duplicator masters for the learner to complete (Figure 9-26). If the learners cannot write in the missing letter, they can use movable cardboard, wood, or plastic letters.

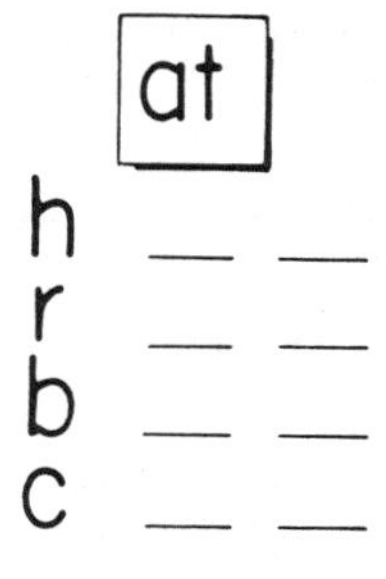

Figure 9-25

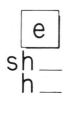

Figure 9—26

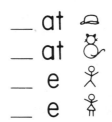

Figure 9—27

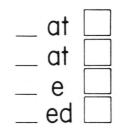

Figure 9—28

Figure 9—29

3. The learner completes words by writing or placing a movable letter on the line. The associative picture clue determines the correct response (Figure 9-27). The learner who cannot remember the correct sound to write on the line should be encouraged to use the self-checking vocabulary cards.
4. The learner recalls words using the patterns and then draws a picture of the word in the box beside the word (Figure 9-28). Nonsense words should not be encouraged. The learner who cannot recall all of the words of a pattern can use the vocabulary word cards.
5. The learner has a word family card ⌐at⌐ on the desk, but no word cards. The instructor says, "Let's write *cat.*" The learner can look at the card, if necessary as an aid in working up to total recall of the word.
6. The instructor dictates, "cat." The students are shown the initial consonant and a picture (Figure 9-29) to aid them in revisualizing the word.
7. The instructor dictates, "cat." An associative picture (Figure 9-30) aids the learner in recalling the word.
8. The instructor holds up an object (e.g., cat) and the learner writes the word on the lines.

_____ _____ _____

9. By the time short phrases, such as "a cat," are dictated, the learner has moved from completing the blanks to total recall.

Tracing and Writing in Spelling
1. Write a color word on a strip of cardboard. The learner traces it with a colored felt-tip pen (Figure 9-31).

2. Cover words that are to be traced with a piece of acetate. The learner traces them with a grease pencil.
3. Cover words that are to be traced with tracing paper. The learner uses a clipboard to hold the paper in place and traces the word with a pencil.
4. Fingerpaint can be used for tracing words.
5. Roll out thin strips of clay and form the letters of the word to be reviewed (Figure 9-32). The learner traces the word with a finger.
6. Prepare an 8″ × 10″ piece of copper window screening (Figure 9-33) by binding the edges with electrical or masking tape. (Plastic screen can be used, but it is softer, and the letters will not be as raised and as clear as they would be if copper screening were used.) Over the screen place a 5″ × 8″ piece of newsprint. (Notebook or typing paper can be used, but they are firmer, and the letters will not be as raised and as clear as they would be if newsprint were used.) Using a black crayon, write a word on the paper in plain manuscript or cursive. (The raised letters can be easily traced with the finger.) Say the word, then trace it, saying each part as you trace it, and then finish by saying the whole word. The student then says the word, traces it with a finger or fingers (saying each part of the word while tracing it), and then says the word. The student repeats this process as many times as is necessary (usually five times in the begining), or until he or she can write the word correctly without looking at the copy. The word should always be traced with the student's finger or fingers, not a pencil.

Figure 9—30

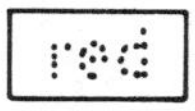

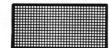

Figure 9–31

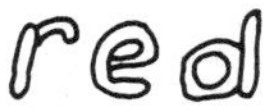

red

Figure 9–32

It is important that students trace until they can write the word without a copy. The word should always be written as a unit. In case of error, the incorrect written form must be covered or crossed out. The student then looks at the word again and traces it, if necessary, before attempting to write it again from memory.

The student then writes the word again as a whole. Never allow a student to erase the incorrect part of a word and write in the correction. To be successful, the student must write the word as a whole. The very act of erasing and correcting single letters or syllables within the word breaks it up into meaningless parts.

As students trace words, they slowly develop the ability to learn them with fewer and fewer tracings. Eventually the students reach the stage where they can look at a word, say it to themselves, and then write it.

The following can be used on acetates for use on the overhead projector or on duplicator master activity sheets:

1. The learners will copy the *at* and *un* words in the appropriate column (Figure 9-34).
2. The learners will trace the *e* pattern in red and the *at* pattern in blue (Figure 9-35).
3. The learners will illustrate the phrases in Figure 9-36.
4. The learners will label pictures (Figure 9-37).
5. The learners will complete the words in Figure 9-38.
6. The learners will translate the spelling words into a code (e.g., an original code [Figure 9-39], the International Code, Braille, the Flag Code). The learners will decode exchanged codes and lists.
7. Many of the activities listed in the reading chapter apply to spelling.

MEMORY AND SPELLING

Use tachistoscopic devices, such as turning on and off the overhead projector to flash words. The learners

Figure 9–33

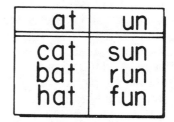

Figure 9–34

|  he | cat | bat | he | fat | rat | she | hat |

Figure 9–35

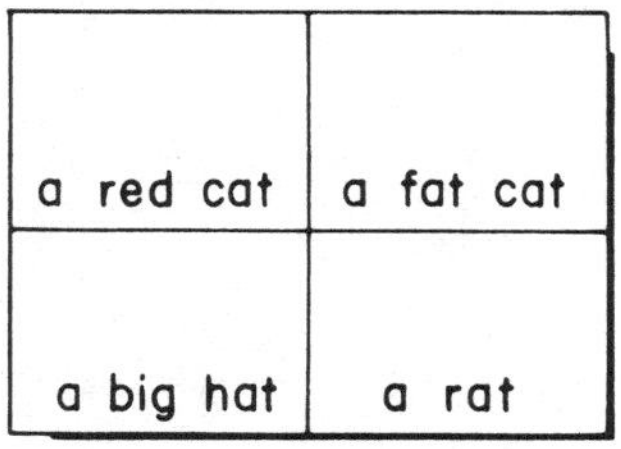

| a red cat | a fat cat |
| a big hat | a rat |

Figure 9–36

look at the word, see it in their mind's eye, and then write it down.

SELF-CHECKING SPELLING ACTIVITIES

1. The learners will cut out pictures of words on the spelling list and paste them on index cards.

 On the other side of the card,

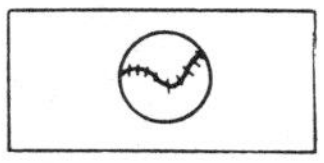

they or the instructor will print the word `ball`

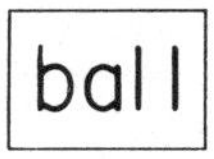

The learners can use these cards as flash cards by looking at the picture on the front of the card, saying the word, and then writing the word on paper, a

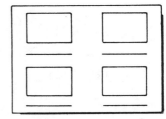

Figure 9–37

small chalkboard, or an erasable slate. By turning the card over, they can compare the words and check their own spelling.

The same cards can be kept in a recipe box containing alphabetical dividers. For a phonics review, the learners can put all the pictures beginning with the same sound behind the correct letter.

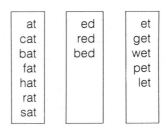

at	ed	et
cat	red	get
bat	bed	wet
fat		pet
hat		let
rat		
sat		

Figure 9–41 Reverse Side of Pattern Cards

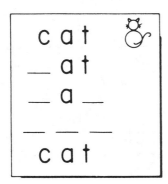

Figure 9–38

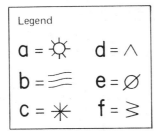

Figure 9–39

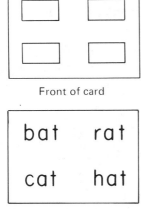

Front of card

Back of card

Figure 9–40

As the students learn the order of the alphabet, they can arrange the word cards in alphabetical order.

2. The learners or the instructor can design self-checking spelling cards to review spelling patterns (Figure 9-40). On the front of the card draw or paste pictures to illustrate the words that contain a pattern. On the reverse side, write the words. The learners can exchange picture cards and spell the words illustrated.

3. Prepare cards for spelling patterns (e.g., *at, ed, et*). On the front of each card, write one pattern, on the reserve side of the card, write the words that have been introduced that include the pattern. (See Figure 9-41). The learners write as many words as possible from memory and then turn the card over to self-check. Learners can take turns calling out the words on the reverse side of the cards, which the other students write or spell orally.

Comprehension Spelling Activities

As words from the learners' reading program are incorporated into the spelling program, the instructor should review not only the correct pronunciation of the words, but also the meanings of the words. By using only the word cards with an associative clue on the reverse side and reading the words in the context of the reading material provided, the learners may not be fully aware of the multiple meanings of the vocabulary words. Therefore, a discussion of the various meanings of words and their uses in different types of sentences should be an integral part of the spelling lesson. The following activities can be utilized to reinforce comprehension skills:

1. Riddles. Write a list of the spelling words on the chalkboard. Say, "I am thinking of an animal that lives in a cave. What is it?" The learner says the word and spells it ("bat, *b-a-t*"). The students can take turns asking other riddles.

2. Missing Words. On the chalkboard, a duplicator master, or the overhead projector write incomplete

sentences. The learner fills in the blanks with the spelling words

run fun sun

It is _____ to play with the dog.
The _____ is hot.
Can you _____ and jump?

3. Crossword Puzzles. The learner can design simple to complex crossword puzzles using the spelling words.
4. Classification. Dictate groups of spelling words. The learner will cross out the words that do not belong and will discuss the category. For example:

birds dogs   blue yellow

cats ~~was~~   ~~is~~ red

(animals)   (colors)

5. Creative Writing. The learner will cut out an interesting picture from a magazine, color a picture in a coloring book, or draw a picture and paste the illustration on a larger sheet of paper. Then the learner will write a sentence or short paragraph about the picture, using the spelling words. Creative writing should be a relaxing activity with emphasis on getting ideas on paper first and later proofing for spelling. To aid the student who cannot spell the "other" words needed to write stories, prepare with the student or the class a chart of words that the student can read and may need for a particular topic. For example: Thanksgiving—turkey, Pilgrims, Indians.
6. Dictionary. Use the dictionary to discuss definitions, multiple meanings, synonyms and antonyms, abbreviations, parts of speech, plurals, and syllabication. Provide activities where the students can practice alphabetical order using lists of words. Alphabetize words by first letters and gradually move to fifth letter order based on level of difficulty or grade level. Use fill-in sheets or the chalkboard and ask the students to write the letters that come before and after a letter (e.g., _ m _). Give all the students a dictionary. Open the dictionary to the middle or divide it into thirds. Discuss the letters located in each section. Discuss guide words and play games locating the guide words for a particular word.

PLURALS

Provide objects, pictures, and word cards for the learners to practice the concept of singular and plural. For example:

Place one toy dog and three toy dogs in groups (Figure 9-42).
By using the word cards, the students can label the groups.
If the cards have associative clues on the reverse side, they are self-checking.

Because the plural words are used in oral spelling tests or in sentence dictation, some learners may need practice in listening to the endings of words. Use a tape recorder to provide auditory experiences for the learners.

SPELLING OTHER WORD LISTS

As the learners become more proficient in spelling, they will need additional words to successfully complete reports, themes, etc. The following additional words can be used to expand the learners' spelling lists. Copies of these word lists can be placed in each student's spelling folder or spelling notebook.

1. *Subject Level Words:* Prepare word lists from Science, Math, Social Studies. Older students will gradually add these words and may need such lists of words for themes.
2. *Frequently Used Words:* Use the Mann-Suiter Everyday Word List (Table 9-1 on p. 446) and Phrase List (Table 9-2 on p. 447) for additional practice.
3. *Irregular Words:* Prepare lists of "spelling bandits" that are most often misspelled by the class.
4. *Similar Words:* As a class project, prepare lists of root words and other words that can be derived from the root (e.g., happy, happiness, unhappy).
5. *Interest Words:* Some words are personalized according to the student's individual needs, interest, and hobbies.

SELF-QUESTIONING STRATEGIES

A student has to think about what he or she is doing and verbalize the process both aloud and silently, devising a strategy for how certain words will be remembered. The training for such problems as letter confusion, lack of ending sounds, and so on should focus on the student's ability to self-regulate various procedures that utilize verbal mediation strategies such as: "What does this word look like?" "What is the way I can remember the word (mnemonic clues)?"

Figure 9–42

"What steps can I go through to practice the word?" "I know the word and the meaning. That was easy (self-reinforcement)."

COMPUTER-ASSISTED INSTRUCTION

A microcomputer can be used to give students drill, practice, and feedback in spelling (Nolen, 1980; Salisbury, 1984). Computer word-processing programs often contain a spelling-checking feature. Some of these spelling devices include a dictionary and a thesaurus feature. McLaughlin and Bialozor (1989) report improvement on six-week unit tests of spelling for mildly handicapped students when compared to traditional classroom instruction. Students entered their word lists into the software package and practiced by typing a word after a flash of the word was given on a screen. If incorrect, the word was shown again with a longer flash.

SPELLING HOMEWORK

Students can show improvement in performance in spelling if they have an effective teacher-directed program that includes individualization, feedback, modeling, and praise, and they use self-directed study strategies. Traditionally, parents and other family members also become involved in some aspect of the students' study of spelling words. This is usually done as part of homework when someone listens to the oral spelling of words. To eliminate the drudgery of this parent-child experience and to promote the continuous progress of spelling achievement, it is recommended that teachers prepare specific, written instructions for parents as to how they can assist with spelling at home.

Parents may be accustomed to seeing a spelling textbook with 20-word spelling lists that must be learned before a Friday test. Either a modification of the text or a different program is usually needed for students exhibiting spelling difficulties. Therefore, an explanation to the parents about the type of program is needed. Parents may question why some of the spelling words appear to be easier or why the student is studying fewer words each week. It will be helpful for John's parents to know that over time he will remember more of the 10 words each week he can read and use in compositions than 20 words that are often forgotten after a few days. Parents appreciate knowing how progress will be monitored and when new words will be periodically reviewed. Parents should know that John will be given a pretest on the list of words on Monday. His study efforts earlier in the week may be on a few of the words.

The parents need to have specific examples of what strategies John has learned to study words, along with how the parents should assist John in preparing for tests. It may be better for John to write the words on paper instead of only spelling them aloud. Appropriate games can be suggested, as well as samples of some of the activities mentioned in this chapter (e.g., discussion of multiple meanings, using the dictionary, etc.).

With current emphasis on "invented spellings" for younger students and the "writing process" as part of written composition, teachers are rewarding students' attempts at spelling words. Some parents may not understand why this contributes to successful acquisition of strategies in learning to spell. In writing, the teacher may be urging the student to write first and edit and proofread later. The parent needs to understand how misspelled words will be either noted or graded on other papers coming home (e.g., written compositions, reports or tests in content area subjects, etc.). Well-intentioned adults may respond to spelling errors by developing a counterproductive spelling program at home.

WRITTEN LANGUAGE EXPRESSION

For many students any form of written language expression will provoke reactions that range from fear and refusal to aggression. Essay tests, creative writing sessions, and science and social studies reports are often incomplete, of inferior quality, or ignored. The student may know the content, but be unable to express the ideas in writing. Multiple homework assignments that all require writing can cause an entire family to suffer.

Before giving subject level assignments, the teacher should first evaluate what is required for minimum success in a subject and how the student must respond to be successful. If the teacher requires note-taking, dictation, extensive copying from the chalkboard or overhead projector, essay tests, reports, and other forms of written expression, the student with learning problems is doomed to failure. This input-output discrepancy between the information received and answers returned must be considered.

Morocco and Neuman (1986) feel that students have problems with writing not only because of the usual difficulties with spelling and mechanics, but because they lack strategies to plan, compose, and edit. In the area of planning, the student becomes anxious and can't come up with anything to write about, often having difficulty generating ideas beyond a few sentences. He or she can't focus on the topic and organize the information. Composing problems arise when the student has to expand the initial text and translate thoughts to writing. Some students can tell a story or dictate sentences to others, but they have difficulty actually writing and sequencing events. The editing process requires a student to reread and prepare drafts before the final paper is submitted. At this point the learner has to deal with the reality of spelling errors and mechanical mistakes.

Students with learning problems cannot be totally excused from written assignments, therefore the teacher must accommodate to their learning needs. The following should be considered:

1. Do students have a physical disability that will preclude all writing? If so, the instructor must consider allowing the students to dictate their thoughts to a volunteer, another student, their parents, etc. A tape recorder may be used by the students or the teacher to record key information or for testing purposes.
2. Are students deficient in spelling, handwriting, and written language skills? These students are often the most negative, since their papers not only look messy, but also lack the sentence formation, punctuation, syntax, spelling, etc., that are needed for success. They usually get the most red marks on limited attempts at writing. The instructor has to be concerned about the students' feelings and gradually build up a trusting relationship before the students will begin to feel secure in writing assignments. If the students are deficient in spelling, handwriting, and reading as well as in written expression, the grading and evaluation of the written expression must be considered. If the objective for a particular lesson is to have the students express

their ideas on paper, then an alternative form of writing (e.g., typing or writing by a peer tutor) may have to be used. Bad handwriting and misspelled words may also need to be ignored in grading, with instructor comments pertaining primarily to the written expression. Sometimes the instructor has to work with the parents to prevent chastisement at home. Unless the parents realize why spelling errors were not corrected or poor writing excused, then the students run the risk of negative comments at home. During separate lessons, the instructor can begin to build up the mechanical skills of writing or spelling.

Refer to page 441 at the beginning of this chapter for an explanation of language skills in a developmental, transitional, and academic sequence.

Learning disabled students have a number of difficulties that impede their general writing ability. First, the length and quality of their compositions contain about one-third to one-half the number of sentences, total words, and ideas of nondisabled students (Myklebust, 1973; Poteet, 1978; Nodine, Barenbaum, & Newcomer, 1985). Second, LD students are more likely to view writing as an evaluative or test-taking activity instead of a process of composing for a larger audience (e.g., peers, family, etc.) (Thomas, Englert, & Gregg, 1987). Englert and colleagues (1988) point out that this causes sketchy responses. Since the student perceives that the information is being written for an adult who presumably knows the topic well, he or she does not include the elaboration that would be given if the passage was written for some-

DEVELOPMENTAL SEQUENCE

The following represents a breakdown of writing skills based on the concept of prerequisite skills for higher level functions. The outline will be helpful to teachers in diagnosis and in programming for students exhibiting developmental lags or irregular learning in writing.

Questions to be answered: What has to be taught first? What has to be practiced? What can be used effectively?

STAGES OF WRITTEN LANGUAGE SKILL DEVELOPMENT

DEVELOPMENTAL	TRANSITIONAL	ACADEMIC
Written Language	*Written Language*	*Written Language*
Oral language expression	Expanded writing	Creative writing
Basic reading vocabulary	Grammatic structure	Notetaking
Basic spelling	Syntax	Assessment
	Formulation	Homework
		Daily life

one less informed about the topic. The student often dumps or unloads everything in one statement without reflection or organization as to the message received by the reader. Third, they show deficiencies in one or more of the steps in the writing process, including organizing and planning, drafting, self-monitoring, editing, revising, and completing the final product. They spend less time on preplanning and do half as many revisions. They also include more redundancies in their writing. Writing is an end, as opposed to a means to an end. Fourth, they are less knowledgeable of text structures, the frameworks used by writers in preparing and composing different types of texts such as comparison, contrast, problem/solution, and explanation (Englert & Thomas, 1987; Thomas, Englert, & Gregg, 1987; Nodine, et al., 1985).

Beginning Writing

Language is communication. Young children's oral monologues are the beginning of "talking sentences." An important prerequisite to writing is reading to children so that they can become familiar with patterns of written language. Children like to have some stories read over and over. They can repeat phrases and are so familiar with the story that when a word is omitted they can supply the word. Wordless picture books give them an opportunity to practice telling stories that have a setting, plot, and characters.

Children encounter print from environmental labels—food labels, television, traffic signs, books, etc. They start to see that there is a way to send messages and they hypothesize about how language works. Recognition of upper- and lower-case letters in the environmental labels is a recognition of the code. Writing his or her name is often an important first visual representation. It is at this point that parents and teachers should do more printing and labeling in front of the child. The teacher should use the names of the children in a class on charts of helpers and in as many other contexts as possible.

Scribbling and drawing may come next. Vygotsky (1978) stated that children can draw speech as well as things. Freidman (1985) recommends that, after the students have drawn pictures of themselves, the teacher can draw cartoon-type balloons next to the figures. The teacher then writes what the student says in the balloons next to the figures. This application of the Learning Experience Approach involves the student watching as someone else writes down their dictation. After seeing first words or labels, the student sees the writer use space between words as sentences unfold. What he or she hears is broken down into words with pauses.

There are a number of Language Experience Approach types of activities that help the student see words move from oral language to print. The teacher, paraprofessional, or older students can write the following types of dictated material:

1. A sentence on a word card illustrating a picture
2. A sentence under a student's drawing
3. Stories about themselves
4. Retelling of stories previously read to them
5. Class poems, jokes, group stories based on a shared experience
6. Stories about pets
7. Class science experiments

As the words grow, the student can start a word bank from his or her reading program, and this will be used in writing lessons. Writing and reading improve each other, become supportive, and complement each other. Writing between the teacher and the students should increase. As the reading level of the students increases, the teacher can write more and tell less. Directions can be written on the chalkboard and comments and reactions to student work can be written. Give every student a "mail box" and encourage them to write messages to each other.

Read (1975) and Chomsky (1976) encourage parents and teachers to let children create their own spelling system at first. As they learn the sounds of speech, their "invented spelling" is a concrete way to acquire written language. Writing becomes hypothesis testing and involves risk-taking. The teacher has to refrain from letting the exactness of form take precedence over function and meaning (Wilson, 1981). The students need a sense of freedom in initial writing.

Young students often like to choose what to write about. Picture drawing or cut-out with writing about the pictures is helpful. The following sequence of pictures-to-words is suggested:

1. Obtain or draw a picture of an object: (chair)
2. Write a word for the picture: chair
3. Add describing words: big chair
4. Add other words: the big chair
5. Additional words can be written on the chalkboard: Look at the big chair in the room.

As the students move into stories and compositions, some are reluctant to write much. Kraetsch (1981) suggests that the student be told to "write as many words as you can." The reluctant writer may need a choice of stimulus pictures to write about. Verbal praise for first efforts is important. Concentration on spelling, word usage, grammar, punctuation, and capitalization can come later.

Daily writing should be done in a natural way. Students should keep all writing efforts in a folder. By dating each piece of writing, a baseline can be established to judge improvement. Periodically send home material to parents with comments on improvement of a specific skill: "Notice how John is using longer sentences" or "Mary is effectively using connective words." Explain to the parents that you want writing first and that some errors in capitalization, spelling, or punctuation may not be marked on purpose.

Criterion References

The following are criterion references for the skills necessary to achieve initial written language competency, which requires that the student will:

1. Write the letter name indicated by the instructor.
2. Write the letter corresponding to the sound indicated by the instructor.
3. Write the letter blend indicated by the instructor.
4. Circle all the words known from word lists provided by the instructor.
5. Write all the words known from word lists provided by the instructor.
6. Write a complete sentence on a theme or word provided by the instructor, using words in the reading vocabulary.
7. Write a paragraph on a theme provided by the instructor, using words in the reading vocabulary.
8. Write an appropriate definition of a word within the reading vocabulary.
9. Write a story on a theme provided by the instructor, using words in the reading vocabulary.
10. Write a logical paragraph or story based on a picture of a scene, event, or real-life experience, using words within the reading vocabulary.
11. Read a paragraph and write logical responses to questions related to the content.
12. Read a paragraph and outline the main ideas in an appropriate and logical progression.
13. Read a paragraph and write a statement summarizing the content.

Prescriptive Activities

GENERAL ACTIVITIES

1. Select from the list of developmental skills the particular target skills that are to be mastered in the area of Visual Language Association-Graphic (Writing). These target skills become learning or behavioral objectives. (Example Target: Visual Language Association-Graphic (Writing) 8—The learner will write an appropriate definition of a word within the reading vocabulary.)
2. If the student fails to demonstrate success in the target skills according to predetermined criteria such as failing items assessed on a standardized test or failing school tasks requiring the skills, do the following:
   a. Select from the list of developmental skills the target skill (example: Visual Language Association-Graphic [Writing] 8) and other related or similar skills (7, 6, etc.) that are deemed appropriate for developing activities that will provide success and practice for higher level functions or skills (9, 10, 11, etc.). Select activities at lower levels (7, 6, 5, etc.) as necessary to insure success and provide an array of different activities that will reinforce the development of Visual Language Association skills.
   b. Develop or select from other sources additional activities related to all of the specific Visual Language Association skills listed (1–13). These activities can be coded into the system at the appropriate levels within the list of development skills.
3. Many students appear to be nonreaders or limited in vocabulary acquisition. Norm-referenced, standardized tests measure only a sample of the words that can be read by the students. To gain a more accurate baseline of vocabulary (recognition), ask the students to circle all the words known from word lists (e.g., Mann-Suiter Reading and Spelling Screens, Mann-Suiter Everyday Word List) provided. Then ask the students to read the circled words. Count only the words read without hesitation. (For a more detailed description of the use of baseline information, refer to pages 153 and 444.
4. For students having difficulty writing the definitions of words, ask them to draw a picture of what a word means first and then write about the picture.
5. Refer to Chapter 8 for additional written language activities.

Specific Activities

The following writing activities can be used to incorporate the learner's reading, spelling vocabulary, and written expression into a unified language arts program.

PREPARING A CLASSROOM FOR WRITING

Three of the major areas emphasized in the 1980s were using computers in the classroom, reading comprehension, and written expression. In the decade of the 90s these areas remain important, with added emphasis on higher-order thinking skills, independence, and generalization of skills to application in content subjects and real-world activities, and whole language. Whole language emphasis is moving from isolated skills to an integration of reading, writing, speaking, and listening. The emphasis has shifted from product to process. Students in classrooms are writing more often for extended periods of time. Many schools have not only a sustained silent reading period when the conditions are optimal for everyone reading together but a writing climate that gives the students an opportunity to write long enough to generate whole passages about a topic.

Materials for writing should be available and accessible. An area of the room can be stocked with an ongoing series of materials that will promote writing. Include reference books, spelling dictionaries, a thesaurus, and a variety of books to stimulate reading and writing. Materials should include lined and unlined paper and colored pens for editing. Provide examples of good writing on laminated cards. Story starters with opening lines, unusual photographs or pictures or objects, student collections, cartoons, and slogans should be available to inspire topics for writing.

Students need a place to keep their ongoing and finished writing products. Student folders can be located in a separate box or file divider to avoid mixing written materials with other subject assignments. The folder can contain drafts of writing, spelling and reading lists, and ideas for future research or composition.

WORDS

1. Prepare duplicator masters or acetates for use on the overhead projector and have the learners trace and complete them (Figure 9-43).
2. Have the students write the singular and plural forms of words corresponding to the pictures on duplicator masters or acetates (Figure 9-44).
3. Ask the learners to use their vocabulary word cards to write pairs of rhyming words (Figure 9-45).

Salty   Salty   _____
pet   pet   _____

Figure 9-43

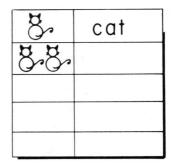

Figure 9-44

cat	hat	pet	wet
boy	toy	big	pig
day	play	go	so
shop	hop	hot	not

Figure 9-45

Things to Do	
sit	go
hit a ball	hop
shop	fish

Figure 9-46

4. Have the learners use their word cards to write all of the words they can find for a specified category (Figure 9-46).
5. Write a spelling pattern (e.g., *at*) in a house. The learner will write all the words of that pattern on the lines below. (See Figure 9-47).

SENTENCES

1. For beginning writers, use sentence completion. For example:
   a. The learner copies from a model.
      The dog is _____ big, blue
   b. The learner uses vocabulary cards or a simple dictionary to complete a sentence.
      The dog is _____ .
   c. The learner writes original sentences. The
      _____ .

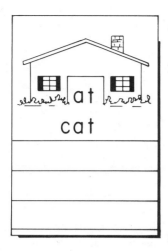

Figure 9–47

2. Use the fill-in sections of the workbook or duplicator master pages as a writing lesson. After the sentences have been corrected, the learner can write or type them.
3. Have the learner start with a short sentence and add words to make longer and longer sentences. Example:

> I saw a dog.
> I saw a brown dog.
> I saw a little, brown dog.
> I saw a little, old brown dog.
> He said, "I saw a little old, brown dog."

4. Using a reading word list, write each of the words on a separate index card. Learners or teams of learners take turns drawing cards from the shuffled deck. Each player or team tries to form phrases or sentences. When the cards are all used, the players read each other's phrases or sentences. These can be used as a writing lesson.
5. Allow the students to use pictures in sentences in place of words they cannot spell.
6. Plan activities that require writing only a few sentences, such as the following:
   a. Greeting card messages for holidays
   b. "Fortune cookie" sentence strips to exchange with secret pals.
   c. Sports cards to be illustrated with pictures from newspapers or magazines
   d. Dialogue for comic strips or cartoons
   e. Commercials or advertisement lines for products
   f. Short descriptions for travel posters
   g. Bumper stickers for desks
   h. Tongue twisters
   i. Riddles
   j. Messages on postcards
   k. Button slogans—"We are first."
   l. Captions for pictures on bulletin boards
   m. Small books about a subject, with a picture and one or two sentences on a page
   n. Labels for collections (rocks, shells, etc.)
   o. Labels for photographs
   p. Steps in an experiment
   q. Answers to "famous faces" quiz involving pictures of television personalities
7. Sentence combining. In sentence-combining practice, students are asked to combine two cue sentences into one (Mellon, 1967; Miller & Ney, 1968; O'Hare, 1973; Seidenberg, 1982). For example:
   Cue: A boy bought an apple. The apple was sweet.
   Response: A boy bought an apple that was sweet.

Sentences can be combined in clusters to make a paragraph when they are linked together to make a story.
Example:

· The day was cold. It was a windy day.
  It was a cold, windy day.
· John wanted to go swimming. Mary wanted to go to the beach.
  John and Mary wanted to go swimming at the beach.
· Swimming was not safe. They went to the movies.
  Since swimming was not safe, they decided to go to the movies.
· It was a cold, windy day. John and Mary wanted to go swimming at the beach. Since swimming was not safe, they decided to go to the movies.

Exercises can be developed around familiar ideas or themes.

STORIES

1. The learners can draw characters from a book. They can then copy sentences from the book. (See Figure 9-48.)
2. Ask the learners to cut out an interesting picture from a magazine, color their favorite pictures from a coloring book, or draw a picture. Paste the picture on a larger sheet of paper. The learner will then write a few sentences about the picture. (See Figure 9-48.)
3. Give the learners pictures. Encourage them to use their word lists for original stories. Assist with the spelling of additional words. If the students have difficulty with writing, they can dictate the story to another person or tell it into a tape recorder.
4. Have the learners prepare simple "About Me" booklets by writing sentences or drawing pictures to illustrate the following:

I wish I could
A trip to
I want to be

After school I
Games I like to play
When I was little
My one wish
Our house
Pets at home
A trip to the zoo
I like to eat

Mother
Father
What I like to do
    in school
A trip to a farm
On a bus trip I saw
Shops I like
In a barn
Toys I like
It is fun to

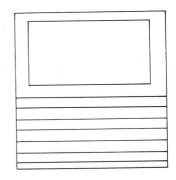

Figure 9–48

Older students can write autobiographies. (See Figure 9-48.)

5. Encourage each student to have a notebook, diary, or folder for written language materials. Contributions should include not only written assignments, but also thoughts and favorite examples of material written by others.

6. A class newspaper can give everyone an opportunity to contribute some form of writing. The student with learning problems who usually avoids writing columns or articles can provide short items such as the following:
   a. Jokes, riddles, comics
   b. Mystery word (definitions from a dictionary)
   c. Sports
   d. Mystery person (short facts about classmates and new students)
   e. Math quiz
   f. Short book reviews
   g. Dear Aunt _____ . Dear Wizard, hot-line types of columns
   h. Poems
   i. Short stories
   j. Advertisements

Written Language Expression (Academic)

CRITERION REFERENCE
The following are criterion references for the skills necessary to achieve written language expression competency for academic purposes, which requires that the student will:

1. Write a complete sentence on a theme or word provided by the instructor, using words in the reading vocabulary.
2. Write a paragraph on a theme provided by the instructor, using words in the reading vocabulary.
3. Write an appropriate definition of a word within the reading vocabulary.
4. Write a story on a theme provided by the instructor, using words in the reading vocabulary.
5. Write a logical paragraph or story based on a picture of a scene, event, or real-life experience, using words within the reading vocabulary.
6. Read a paragraph and write logical responses to questions related to the content.
7. Read a paragraph and outline the main ideas in an appropriate and logical progression.
8. Read a paragraph and write a statement summarizing the content.
9. Take dictation legibly in manuscript, within normal time limits, utilizing words at the independent reading level.
10. Take dictation legibly in cursive, within normal time limits, utilizing words at the independent reading level.
11. Take effective notes from oral presentations.
12. Take notes from readings.
13. Write good letters (personal and business).
14. Proofread with accuracy.
15. Use a correct sequence of ideas.
16. Write good explanations.
17. Use correct punctuation and indentation.
18. Write short stories and verse.
19. Edit his or her own writing.
20. Write dialogue with correct punctuation.
21. Write a comparison and contrast paragraph on a given area of study.

THE WRITING PROCESS
After the learner has progressed from writing words, sentences, and short paragraphs, he or she is ready for more sustained writing. The student therefore needs to learn how to move through a process of planning, organizing, writing, editing, and revising.

Planning and Selecting a Topic
Many students in the middle grades dread the obligatory class writing session and fear a paper with red

marks. Others find excuses to avoid filling the blank page. These students are often afraid to expose deficiencies that will prevent them from succeeding.

A place to start is to have the class write about writing. By attempting to explain why writing is difficult, the teacher will get an understanding of whether initial teaching should focus on content (thinking) or form (mechanics). Roit and McKenzie (1985) point out that older students need an integrated approach to writing, emphasizing clarity of thought and meaning of the message.

Reluctant writers need orientation activities. The instructor has to spend time motivating, stimulating, and reassuring the student that writing will not always equal a grade. The students need to learn that successful writers devote time to thinking about writing. Discuss reflective thinking prior to beginning to write. Some of the "warm-up" activities are similar to those for younger students. A basis for writing can be developed through listening activities, visual imagery, and an exposure to literature. Maya (1979) suggests the following examples:

1. Read books about characters with which the students can identify. Stop at intervals and ask questions that concern what characters look like or are doing. Discuss alternative endings to stories.
2. Practice using words to describe objects in the classroom: A crack in the wall—looks like lightning.
3. Set a mood for writing by reducing the perceived pressures. Provide help with spelling words and let the students write anonymously at times.

Diagnose a student's prior knowledge of story structure by asking them to retell stories. Stories have features, structures, content, settings, characters, and plot. Golden (1984) suggests that the student's understanding of story structure suggests how well he or she can interpret and construct stories.

Graves (1985) stresses that the prewriting, topic selection phase is very important for setting the tone for writing experiences. For students with an impoverished imagination, pair the student with a friend and let the two of them brainstorm before beginning to write. The teacher may need to work one-on-one with some students in selecting topics.

Once writing begins, the students need tips about reading and rereading their writing for clarity and the development of a personal style of expression. Dionisio (1983) recommends that students be taught organization techniques and the use of reference materials to read for additional information about topics. Stimulate writing by allowing the students to select a theme from three or more choices. Permit varieties of response to an assignment (e.g., poems, stories, interviews, etc.).

Planning involves not only understanding the purpose for writing, selecting a topic, and activating prior knowledge, but also developing an organizational plan for arranging ideas by categories and into a sequence. Many students do not have the organizational skills needed to begin writing. These students should prepare an outline before beginning to write by listing topics, main idea, and then details in outline format. The student must first outline by himself or herself and then check with the instructor before he or she begins to write.

Students should be continually reminded of writing goals so that they will have the knowledge of the desired outcomes as they become more involved in the task of writing. The communicative intent is essential in writing; otherwise, much of what is written makes sense only to the student. By questioning the student, the teacher will make him or her aware of what is intended and facilitate a clear communication of ideas. Several steps are suggested in this process (Wong et al., 1991):

1. The writing process should begin with a preteaching activity that involves a verbal expression of the desired outcome.
2. The student is asked to recall prior experiences in this type of writing activity and formulate a plan of action.
3. The actual writing process involves an interactive teaching approach in which the student makes appropriate revisions based on ongoing writing analysis.

Ideas to Stimulate Writing
1. Martin, Martin, and O'Brien (1984) developed a series of activities to use with subject-area materials to produce creative writing assignments. The acronym SPAWN stands for:

S—Special Powers—The student has the "power" to change events and to write about the consequences of their changes.

P—Problem Solving—Problems are identified (e.g., current events) and solutions are written about and discussed.

A—Alternative Viewpoints—Students assume the role of a character in history, for example, and write about their views.

W—What if—The teacher changes something in text.

N—Next—Trends, forecasts, prediction are examined and discussed.

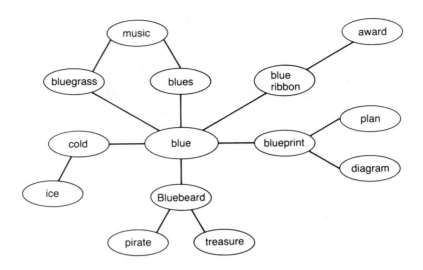

Figure 9–49

2. Use students' interests as a springboard to writing: mystery stories, heroes, sports, biographies, science fiction.

3. Rico (1978) developed a configurational stragegy that integrates right and left brain processing in the exploration of literary meaning. Use is made of word "clusters" that are developed in a free association exercise. In doing creative writing, the teacher or student selects a single word as the focal point of generating a series of free-associated words. These words are written down as a scheme representing their relationship one to the other. The configuration could be developed as a poem, an essay, or just a written assignment. The phenomenon, as Rico describes it, is an internal structure generated as associations, simultaneously using the right brain as a "structure-seeking" mechanism. The right brain in this case is activated to integrate new information into an existing conceptual framework. An example of a configuration of word associations is illustrated in Figure 9-49.

4. Everyday "life skills"-types of writing might include:
   a. Developing posters for projects and events.
   b. Writing advertisements for sales. How would you say what you wanted to say in three lines?
   c. Preparing announcements for social occasions.
   d. Writing bills of sale or agreements.
   e. Writing letters and learning to dictate letters.
   f. Writing short memos or minutes of meetings.

5. Students need to see examples of many types of formats used in writing. Reports, stories, reviews, summaries, term papers, etc. require different types of headings, titles, graphs, and charts.

6. Have students select a project idea of something they would like to do in the future and write a two-page prospectus.

7. Select a section from the newspaper or a magazine that gives the status of political, financial, or world events and write a forecast of trends. Discuss the types of vocabulary that should be used (i.e., it is projected that . . .).

8. Allow students to write freely without concern for spelling in first drafts. Use a dictionary and a thesaurus to practice selecting more difficult words, so that words that are easier to spell will not always be used.

9. Plan learning experiences in which students examine the writing styles of famous authors:
   a. Provide the students with samples of writing of three authors. Look for flair and style.
   b. Analyze a number of samples of the same author. Discuss different types of writing by the same person (e.g., short stories, magazine articles). Discuss the style and recognizable phrases.
   c. Read examples of good prose to students. Learners need many exposures to different styles of writing. Discuss how the author sets a mood, uses phrases that enhance visual imagery, introduces characters, and uses direct quotations. Note the development of the plot from problems and actions to climax and solution to problems. Analyze the endings of stories.
   d. Collins (1985) feels that students need to be-

come expressive questioners by looking at all text from the perspective of the reader and the writer. By analyzing examples of text, a guided lesson can ask such questions as: As the author, how would you express the same idea? Do you understand what the author stated in this passage?

Are the author's points clear?

How would you modify the text?

10. Encourage writing experiences that are of personal interest:
    a. Oral interviews of people regarding local history or customs.
    b. Family history of significant events.
    c. Interviews of sports or music personalities.

11. Collins (1985) suggests ways to enliven dead-end themes and dull compositions. She cites Moffett's (1968) use of the acronym AMP to teach personal writing: Autobiography, Memoir, Portrait. He encourages the students to read the three styles of writing and discusses the difference (e.g., autobiography is about the author, memoir focuses on someone in the past, and portrait is writing about a person living now). Collins advocates journal writing to help students think on paper —to see relationships, connections, and abstract ideas.

12. Students can keep a log, diary, or notebook for writing about experiences and feelings. Written expression improves with practice and should be done in some format daily. One example is, the dialogue journal. Each day the students write to the teacher about any concern or interest, and the teacher responds by commenting or asking questions. By alternating groups of students, the instructor can look at several journals a day (Gambrell, 1985).

13. Sharpen students' observational skills and use of descriptors by having them write descriptions of people, objects, and scenes (directly and from memory).

14. Magazines, such as *Child Life, Cricket, Ebony Jr., Jack and Jill, Kids, Highlights for Children,* etc., publish students' original writing. Local publications, including community newspapers, are another souce for publication. The publication guidelines for the magazines could be part of a classroom discussion.

Writing Strategies

To become independent writers, students need to be able to monitor the steps of the writing process. Raphael, Kirschner, and Englert (1986) have de-

signed a program to teach cognitive strategies in writing—Cognitive Strategy Instruction for Writing (CSIW). They have found color-coded think sheets useful in practicing the individual strategies labeled under the acronym POWER (*P*lanning, *O*rganizing, *W*riting, *E*diting, and *R*evising).

The CSIW curriculum is based on two important premises. The first premise is that teachers need support in teaching the entire writing process, which includes strategies for planning, organizing, drafting, editing, and revising. The second premise considers the student and posits that students need to understand expository text structure and require assistance to support their own efforts at writing.

Additionally, the student must recognize that the writer's sensitivity to the audience is one of the keys to successful writing. The learner is requested to place himself or herself in the place of the informant. This is accomplished through activities that involve the reading of text while keeping in mind the voice and thoughts of the reader. The learners internalize the perspective of the reader as they plan, draft, monitor, and evaluate text (Englert, 1990).

Effective instruction should include the principle of scaffolding, which is an approach that enables the learner to receive adjustable, but temporary, supports. This allows for the systematic development of new skills and abilities. Scaffolds such as using prompts or asking questions have been found useful in helping students to retrieve relevant information.

Coaching and guiding dialogue can be used to help students monitor their work. This allows the learners to think out loud and slowly gives them more responsibility for leading the dialogue. In this interaction, the teacher continues to give tips and cues while seeking independent problem solving on the part of the learner. Students need to be guided by oral or written prompts that lead them to consider using specific strategies. Some teachers use cue cards to help students with editing and revising (Tharp & Gallimore, 1988).

Harris and Graham (1985) demonstrated the efficacy of a self-control strategy training approach in improving and maintaining composition skills among learning disabled students. Students' stories, written after training, received higher-quality ratings because of the use of a number of different action words, action helpers, and describing words. Task-specific and metacognitive strategies were taught using a series of instructional steps based in part on the work done by the Kansas Institute in Research in Learning Disabilities (Schumaker et al., 1982) and from Meichenbaum's (1977) self-instructional training procedures.

The sequence included:

1. Introducing a task-specific strategy such as one composition skill (action words). The student suggests words or descriptions independently after viewing examples and their definitions on charts.
2. The student and instructor review the number of different action words used and how these action words improve a story.
3. A five-step strategy is used, which includes:
   a. Looking at pictures and writing associated action words
   b. Making up stories to use the student's own words
   c. Writing a story with action words
   d. Reading the story and self-questioning regarding quality, accuracy, and appropriateness
   e. Self-statements are made regarding helpful hints to improving the quality of work

Statements are first modeled by the instructor, such as, "I have to think clearly," "I have to think of new words," "What do I have to do to write a good story?" The student learns mainly to define action words in terms of applications (e.g., what things, people, or animals do). Similar activities are done with describing words, which are words that tell us what people, animals, places, or things look like or how they smell, feel, sound, or taste.

Editing—Proofreading—Revising
Good writing requires editing and editing requires recopying (Dudley-Marling, 1985). The word processor has made this often tedious task easier. Reluctant writers may be more willing to write longer passages and revise what they have written. Parts of text can be moved around, revised, or deleted. Students with learning problems need to proofread their writing. The typed copy from a word processor will give these students access to cleaner copy for editing. Students with slow and labored handwriting are relieved of the fear of multiple recopying of material and can quickly get their mental images on paper. The word processor also allows students to read each other's writing, add comments, and model the teacher (Smith, 1985). Some microcomputers have software for drills on spelling, capitalization, and punctuation.

As a part of editing and proofreading, students can learn to use a standard proofreading symbol system (i.e. ¶ for beginning a paragraph, ∧ for insertions, etc.). Proofreading involves a self-analysis of the quality of the writing. The learner has to go through a

strategy to check the writing for spelling, capitalization, punctuation, completion of sentences, and main ideas of the paragraph. The choice of words and variation of sentence patterns should be analyzed and rewritten if necessary.

After the student has completed writing, have him or her read the material aloud to the instructor or into a tape recorder. Discussion should involve an analysis of syntax and grammatic structure as well as style and content.

Allow students to write freely without concern for spelling in first drafts. Use a dictionary and a thesaurus to practice selecting more difficult words, so that words that are easier to spell will not always be used.

Teach a procedure for perusing material for the detection of errors. Develop a short checklist for the students to use in proofreading. For example:

_____ spelling
_____ sentence structure
_____ content
_____ grammar

During the editing process, the student is ready to conference with the teacher and peers. After rereading the materials, questions are asked regarding the clarification of ideas, missing information, the sequence of the paragraphs, and the embellishment with key phrases (e.g., *however, in other words,* etc.) or more appropriate vocabulary. A critical concept in writing is to help the students understand the concept of the first draft. During this phase, the student is told to concentrate on writing and not to stop for spelling checks or editing of grammatical errors. The author is now prepared to accept or reject the suggestions offered during editing. New material may be included from reference sources before the student proceeds to another or a final draft.

An important reinforcing concept in writing is the process of self-regulation or "self-talk" that is used by the student in directing himself or herself through different writing activities. This concept is also important for expository writers in terms of internalizing ideas and self-regulating writing performance. By talking through the writing process, the learner determines the purpose of the activity and considers the receptors or audience. The student organizes, drafts, edits, and revises to convey the intent of meaning and to achieve correct format. Research has suggested that learning disabled students, as a group, are deficient in their knowledge about writing and in their ability to self-regulate (Wong, Wong, & Blenkisop, 1989).

USING THE WORD PROCESSOR

MacArthur and Shneiderman (1986) suggest several reasons why students may benefit from using a word processor for composition. The student sees a neat and printed copy and becomes more motivated to write by avoiding tedious recopying. Spelling and handwriting problems are circumvented in the initial writing, and the student can focus on content first and later go back and edit the form. The student develops the understanding that writing is a process of repeated drafts—where the writer looks for more than spelling and mechanical errors. He or she also edits content and reviews the organization of the material. Commercial programs are available to help the learner with pre-writing skills.

Morocco and Neuman (1986) point out that when students are composing they stay highly involved and produce rich first drafts. However, they tend to become disengaged from the content during the editing of later drafts or when they are working on isolated skills. The instructor needs to become involved with the student as much as possible to motivate a high level of on-task behavior. One of the most valuable uses of the word processor in the classroom is the stimulation of collaborative writing activities between the teacher and the student or among a group of students. The accessibility of the screen gives the instructor the opportunity to observe the student's writing process. The teacher and student can work together in a manner that would be unwieldy if the teacher had to lean over and remove the pencil while the student is writing. If a student is reluctant to write and cannot think of ideas to begin the process, the instructor can write the first sentence or part of a sentence for the student to complete.

Writing in Content Areas

At the elementary level, the student may have done more creative story writing. Much of his or her reading was narrative material during language arts classes. However, in the upper grades, the writing requirements are more specific to the subject area. The material is expository material based on the language of texts. All classes will probably require some form of notetaking and outlining. These important areas of writing are discussed in Chapter 12 on study skills. This chapter also contains a section on understanding textual writing. The following types of writing and critical thinking have to be learned for success within the content areas:

Science	*Literature*	*Social Studies*	*Mathematics*
Analysis	Description	Time	Concept outline
Synthesis	Cause/effect	Sequence	Problem solution
Enumeration	prediction	Cause/effect	and proof
Problem solving	Comparison/	Comparison/	
Classification	contrast	contrast	
Generalization	Summary	Analysis	
Sequence	Conclusion	Prediction and	
Comparison and	Inference	forecast	
contrast	Narration	Interpretation	
Conclusion and	Critical evalua-		
evidence	tion of author		

The learner should practice writing up experiments for science; synopses of stories for English; Who-What-Where-When-Why answers for Social Studies questions.

Frager (1985) suggests that reading comprehension improves through writing. Writing helps the student master course content. Each class has unique writing requirements, therefore the instructor needs to provide models of the type and quality of writing expected for assignments. These can be developed with the students or they can be hand-outs (papers from previous students or papers written by the instructor). Students need to see examples of many types of formats used in writing. Reports, stories, reviews, summaries, term papers, etc., require different types of headings, titles, graphs, and charts.

The student should have a clear understanding of the format, length, style, technical requirements, and depth expected by the instructor. Frager feels that too many content teachers are locked into the pressure of covering subject material and are mainly concerned with judging the correctness or incorrectness of responses. By doing more teaching and less testing of writing, the instructor will be developing more knowledgeable students who can express themselves better. To accomplish this, the teacher has to plan learning experiences where he or she can model styles of writing. Additional activities are helpful where the student can write without penalty and profit from feedback by the teacher.

PARAPHRASING

Paraphrased summaries or abstracts of science and social studies material require the student to retain the essential content and flavor of the original. Develop with the students a list of key phrases and sentences that will enable them to break the barrier associated with thinking about how to begin writing about a subject or paraphrasing material. After the students have outlined the main ideas of the content or written opening sentences, practice using these phrases within the composition. Examples of phrases are:

It appears that _____ .
The most important thing to consider _____ .
My first impression or inclination was to _____ .
The issues involved include _____ .
Historically _____ .
It is common knowledge _____ .
The story describes _____ .
The major ideas include _____ .
It is important to _____ .
Also indicated was (or were) _____ .
Although _____ .
It seems _____ .

Discuss alternatives to using "said" in paraphrasing material. Examples are:

_____ concluded
_____ described
_____ has suggested

Based on research, _____ described
_____ indicated
_____ in his (or her) study of _____
_____ indicated
_____ and his colleagues discovered
_____ have pointed out
_____ investigated
_____ studied

Give the students samples of good, succinct writing. Have them look for:

effective sentence starters
topic sentences
transition sentences
sentences illustrating compare and contrast
conclusions

As the student reads a passage in some area of content (e.g., science), he or she can periodically stop and paraphrase the main ideas into a tape recorder. He or she can then reread the material if necessary, take notes, listen to the tape again and write a first draft summary of what has been remembered and heard. This will provide a framework for additional material and further editing.

Discuss plagarism and consequences of copying material directly from books, encyclopedias, etc. Locate copyright notices in books and explain copyright laws and procedures.

Writing activities used by some university math and science professors help make the students' thinking clearer and sharper when they apply mathematical and scientific principles. For example, math professors require students to write explanations of how they solved problems during examinations. Even if the students cannot get the correct solution, they write about areas of difficulty. Science professors ask students to record their thoughts during scientific experiments in journals. These activities are usually short, informal, and completed during class. This is in contrast to longer essays or term papers.

Students may be reluctant to "write" in content area classes that usually require little writing. Some students feel more comfortable with writing after the instructor shares samples of the process. How the process actually enhances thinking has to be demonstrated to the students. One way to encourage participation is to not grade certain tests or lessons. Ask the students to write their solutions to problems or observations in ink—no editing, erasing, or recopying. Therefore, the instructor and the students can discuss the wrong turns that may have led them to an incorrect response.

Reading-Writing-Cooperative Learning

Reading and writing reinforce each other. Cooperative learning activities that involve both areas can effectively be used to enhance literacy. Sager (1989) effectively used a joint class story-writing activity with remedial ninth graders after they read the novel *Night* (by Elie Wiesel). She wanted the students to go beyond decoding and comprehension to a deeper understanding of the events, geography, and human drama of the story. The class developed a scenario where a group of teenagers in the French Resistance interacted with the events in the novel they had read. From one paragraph to five drafts, the class became experts on hiding, rescue, geography of Europe, and events of World War II. This type of activity can also be used to advance a story. Sager feels that students need to be empowered to become involved in the emotional content and setting of text by developing compatible narrative that develops descriptive and authentic plot, mood, and character.

APPLICATIONS TO DAILY LIFE

Junior high and secondary students not only write more in the classroom; they also need to begin to develop the writing skills required for higher education and employment. They need to begin to become independent in their writing and show more confidence in handling their own correspondence. This involves less reliance on parents, teachers, and peers.

Discuss the types of writing those in various careers would do (e.g., memos, letters, scientific journals or logs). Ask the students to write descriptions of things from the point of view of the individual who does this on a day-to-day basis. For example:

1. *Police Reports:* Use the newspaper to get stories with enough basic facts. The student will write the story as a police person would write about the accident or scene of a crime. Note key phrases that might occur in this type of writing.
2. *Nurses' Notes:* Describe an incident or segment of time with a patient.
3. *Technical Reports or Results of a Test:* Write about the results of a weapons test or a car-controlled crash.
4. *Sports Report:* Write a letter to a friend about a recent sports event.
5. *Field Notes:* Write a short log after observing an event, an animal, etc.

CAPITALIZATION AND PUNCTUATION

Some students have spelling and handwriting skills as well as good imagery and can express very creative ideas in sentences. Those students, however, may require assistance in developing other kinds of skills (e.g., punctuation and grammatical structure). An integral part of developing written expression is activities that relate to the particular structural components (e.g., punctuation marks and capitalization).

TEACHING GRAMMATIC STRUCTURE

1. In oral reading activities, deliberately teach voice inflection. Read with the student and to the student to illustrate how certain forms of punctuation should be read. Use hand motions to indicate that the voice goes down at the end of sentences ending with periods and rises at the end of questions.

Refer to page 437 for additional oral reading activities.
2. Indicate to the student the key words that are often found in certain types of sentences. For example, the interrogative words—*how, when, why, where,* and *who.* Use the students' reading vocabulary to give them practice in completing and writing different types of sentences. For example:
    a. I have a _____ .
       I see a _____ .
       He has a _____ .
       What is _____ ?
       Who is _____ ?
       What has _____ ?
       What _____ ?
    b. Ask the students to use the reading or spelling words to write three sentences with a period and three with a question mark.
3. Dates can be written daily. To prevent repeated failure and copying of an incorrect response, carefully note during the first week of school the student who is making careless errors in writing the date.
4. Some form of daily practice may be required for students (even older students) who need to improve their use of capitalization and punctuation. This type of activity would be in addition to workbooks or other programmed material. For example, ask the student to write five sentences, each containing one of the following: a date, a name, a state, a quotation, or an exclamation mark. On the chalkboard write sentences without punctuation or capitalization. spend five or ten minutes a day as a class to review previously taught skills and to discuss the correct responses.
5. If a student cannot write, use moveable cardboard, magnetic, or plastic punctuation marks and word cards or sentence strips. If the materials are color coded, check to see if any of the students are color blind.

Chapter 10

Gross Motor—Body Image and Fine Motor—Handwriting

CHAPTER OUTLINE

Overview
Gross Motor
Body Image
Fine Motor
Stages of Handwriting Skill Development
Left-Handed Children
Transitional Writing

OVERVIEW

The importance of legible handwriting cannot be overstated, as it affects every aspect of academics. The gross motor and body image aspects of development are prerequisites to higher-level skills. This includes orientation to time and space, as well as to the actual process of writing. This chapter contains many suggestions regarding the integration of various activities in these areas of concern into the curriculum.

GROSS MOTOR

Criterion Reference

The following are criterion references for the skills necessary to achieve gross motor competency, which requires that the student will:

1. Crawl in an appropriate manner.
2. Creep in an appropriate manner.
3. Walk on a marked straight line without losing his or her balance.
4. Walk on a board without losing his or her balance.
5. Swing his or her arms in a coordinated manner when walking or running.
6. Run on command or by imitating a peer or adult.
7. Hop on command or by imitating a peer or adult.
8. Skip on command or by imitating a peer or adult.
9. Jump on command or by imitating a peer or adult.
10. Throw a ball on command or by imitating a peer or adult.
11. Catch a ball on command or by imitating a peer or adult.
12. Climb a ladder on command or by imitating a peer or adult.
13. Jump rope in a coordinated manner on command or by imitating a peer or adult.
14. Perform physical-motor tasks appropriate to his or her age group, in a coordinated manner.
15. Perform physical-motor tasks within normal time limits.

Prescriptive Activities

GENERAL ACTIVITIES

1. Select from the list of developmental skills the particular target skills that are to be mastered in the area of Visual Motor-Gross. These target skills become learning or behavioral objectives. (Example Target: Visual Motor-Gross 4—The student will walk on a board without losing his or her balance.)
2. If the student fails to demonstrate success in the target skills according to predetermined criteria such as failing items assessed on a standardized test or failing school tasks requiring these skills, do the following:
   a. Select from the list of developmental skills the target skill (example: Visual Motor-Gross 4) and other related or similar skills (3, 2, etc.) that are deemed appropriate for developing activities that will provide success and practice for higher level functions or skills (5, 6, 7, etc.). Select activities at lower levels (3, 2, 1, etc.) as necessary to insure success and provide an array of different activities that will reinforce the development of Visual Motor-Gross skills.
   b. Develop or select from other sources additional activities related to all of the specific Visual Motor-Gross skills listed (1–15). These activities can be coded into the system at the appropriate levels within the list of development skills.

SPECIFIC ACTIVITIES

General Gross Motor

1. Use swaying movements of the body. The learner imitates the teacher or a fellow student.
2. Games such as horse walk, leapfrog, seesaw, and pony ride are good.
3. Use rowing and climbing activities.
4. Use touch toes and Simple Simon games.
5. Use a large barrel open on both ends for the learner to crawl through. You can vary the barrel activity by turning the barrel slowly as the student crawls through.
6. Use jungle gym climbing devices.
7. A furniture dolly provides many activities for children in both the prone and seated positions.
8. Use running and jumping activities in the following ways: sideways, fast, slow, on heels, on toes, up and down steps, barefoot, squatting, and shuffling.

9. Use games such as the following:
   a. *Call Ball:* The students stand in a circle with one student in the center. The student in the center tosses the ball above his or her head while calling the name or a number assigned to a student in the circle. The student whose name or number was called tries to catch the ball. This student then takes the place of the student in the center. This game is also good for the development of eye-hand coordination.
   b. *John Over the Ocean:* The students stand in a circle with hands joined. One player, "John," stands in the center. The students walk around in a circle chanting:

      John's over the ocean.
      John's over the sea.
      John caught a ball.
      But he can't catch me.

      As they say "me," the students squat quickly. "John" tries to tag a player before he or she squats down. If John is successful, the child whom he tagged becomes "John" and the game is repeated. This game is also good for the development of awareness of space and direction.
   c. *Catch a Fish:* Have the students sit in a circle. One student, standing in the center of the circle, is the fish. A student tries to hit the fish with a large ball, saying, "I'm going to catch a fish!" When the fish in the center is hit, he or she sits in the circle. The student who has hit the fish becomes the new fish. This activity is good for the development of awareness of space and direction and for eye-hand coordination.
   d. *Stop the Ball:* Use a volleyball. The students stand astride in a circle with feet touching their neighbors' on both sides. One student is "it" and stands in the center. He or she tries to roll the ball through the feet of any student in the circle. If successful, he or she takes the place of the student, and that student becomes "it." Students use only hands to stop the ball. This game is also good for the development of awareness of space and direction and for eye-hand coordination.

Balance and Coordination

1. Use balance-beam or walking-board activities.
2. Have the students walk and balance on their toes and knees.

3. Use ladder climbing activities.
4. Twist board activities are helpful.
5. Use walking, running, and jumping activities in the following ways: sideways, fast, slow, on heels, on toes, up and down steps, barefoot, squatting, and shuffling.
6. Provide for homolateral (both arms and legs together, as in pushing), unilateral (one side of the body, as in soldiers' walk), and cross-pattern (both sides of the body simultaneously, as in walking) activities.
7. Have the students stand, jump with legs apart, then jump pulling their feet together. This activity can be varied by having the students clap their hands over their heads as they jump with legs apart.
8. Rope and pole climbing are good exercises.
9. Play games such as the following:
   a. *Walk the Tightrope:* A wide line is drawn on the ground and the students pretend that it is a tightrope and they are the circus performers walking on it. The students could then become more daring acrobats as they hop, skip, or jump the line. This activity is also good for the development of basic body movement and eye-foot coordination.
   b. *Duck, Duck, Goose:* The students form a circle. One student, the "Duck," walks around the outside of the circle, touching the other students on the head while saying "Duck." When the Duck taps a student and says "Goose" instead of "Duck," the student tapped (the "Goose") chases the Duck around the circle. The Duck must get back to the Goose's place before being tapped by the Goose. If tapped, the Duck must go into the middle of the circle. The Goose becomes the next Duck. This activity is also good for the development of awareness of space and direction.
   c. *Chicken and the Egg:* The students place their heads on their desks, with their right hands open on their desks. One student is the chicken and drops the egg (a piece of chalk) into the hand of a second student, who is seated. That student immediately gets up and tries to tag the chicken, who is safe if he or she can get back to the seat left open by the second student. This activity is also good for the development of the awareness of space and direction, eye-hand coordination, and fine muscle control.
   d. *Jack in the Box:* The teacher or a student says, "Jack is hiding down in his box until somebody opens the *lid*." The leader says the first part very quietly and slowly in order to build sus-

pense. The students squat with their hands on their heads. They are holding the lid down on the box. When the leader says the word *lid*, they all spring up and jump with their legs apart.
   e. *Camera Safari:* Ask the students if they would like to go on a camera safari to take pictures of animals in Africa. Read or tell the story while the students listen and follow through with appropriate actions. The story is read like this: "Let's go on a camera safari. . . . Get your camera. . . . Get your film. . . . Get your hat. . . . Put it on. . . . Duck your head when you leave the tent. . . . Get into the land rover with your guide. . . . Drive across the bumpy ground. . . . See the tall giraffe. . . . Get your camera ready. . . . Stop the truck. . . . Focus your camera. . . . Snap the picture. . . . Drive on. . . . Stop. . . . I see a herd of elephants. . . . Move quietly through the tall grass. . . . Tiptoe. . . . Squat down low. . . . Get your camera ready. . . . Focus. . . . Snap, etc." Give many different directions to develop movement skills.
   f. *Circle Around:* Students form a circle. The teacher and students sing:

We circle around the desks.
We circle around the room.
We circle around the toys,
On a Monday afternoon,
Whoops!

Very young students circle around to the right, hands joined. When they say, "Whoops!" they all jump up in the air and then crouch down together. Older students can circle right through the first two lines, then circle left on the last two, doing the same thing on "Whoops!" The teacher can substitute the appropriate name of the day of the week.
   g. *Do What I Do:* The teacher says or sings the following verse to the tune of "Old MacDonald Had a Farm" while doing a movement that the other players imitate:

This is what I can do.
Everybody do it too.
This is what I can do.
Now I send it on to you.

On the words, "Send it on to you," the teacher names, points to, or taps a student, who then becomes the new leader. This game can be used to further the development of body image, space and direction, balance, and large muscle control.

Eye-Foot Coordination

1. Have the students walk on masking tape: forward, backward, sideways, etc.
2. Repeat number one using a balance beam.
3. Place rope loops on the floor and have the students step into the loops.
4. Have students roll a ball with their feet to another student.
5. Have the students jump over a wriggling rope.
6. Use jump rope activities.
7. Use ladder walking activities.
8. Play games such as the following:
   a. Games such as hopscotch, kickball, and high jump are good.
   b. *Jumping the Stream:* Draw two lines to represent the banks of the stream. The students run and jump over the steam. Anyone missing the jump and landing in the stream is sent "home" to put on dry shoes and socks. The student sits and pretends to do these things, then reenters the game. This game is also good for the development of space and direction and basic body movements.
   c. *Tire Obstacle Course:* Place tires on the ground in a pattern for the students to step through. Time the students as they go through the course. Have them compete against their own best time first and then against each other.

Body Rhythm

1. Clap as the students move fast and slowly, taking small steps first and then giant steps.
2. Repeat the same activity with jumping.
3. Music activities, including marching, are helpful for body rhythm.
4. Allow students to use band instruments and lead the band after they have achieved reasonably good rhythm.
5. Play games such as the following:
   a. *Freeze:* Students move to the rhythm of music, walking, swaying, turning, etc. When the music stops, they must stop, or freeze, and hold whatever position they are in until the music starts again. This game is also good for the development of balance and basic body movement.
   b. *Mystery Music Leader:* The students stand or sit in a circle. One student is selected to be "it" and leaves the room. The teacher chooses a student in the circle to be the Mystery Music Leader. Following the beat of a metronome or rhythm stick, the leader will switch the activity from clapping to finger snapping to head nod-ding, etc. "It" will come back into the room and have three guesses to name the leader. The leader becomes "it," and a new student is selected to lead a new beat.

BODY IMAGE

Criterion Reference

The following are criterion references for the skills necessary to achieve perception of body image, which requires that the student will:

1. Locate and name parts of the body on self.
2. Locate, in pictures, body parts named by the instructor.
3. Name body parts from pictures as indicated by the instructor.
4. Draw a human figure with the body parts in proper position and in correct relationship.
5. Point to, or otherwise indicate, symmetrical body parts on self.
6. Point to the same body parts on an individual facing him or her.
7. Place body parts on models of objects.

Prescriptive Activities

GENERAL ACTIVITIES

1. Select from the list of developmental skills the particular target skills that are to be mastered in the area of Visual–Body Image. These target skills become learning or behavioral objectives. (Example Target: Visual–Body Image 5—The learner will point to, or otherwise indicate, symmetrical body parts on self.)
2. If the student fails to demonstrate success in the target skills according to predetermined criteria such as failing items assessed on a standardized test or failing school tasks requiring the skills, do the following:
   a. Select from the list of development skills the target skill (example: Visual–Body Image 5) and other related or similar skills (4, 3, etc.) that are deemed appropriate for developing activities that will provide success and practice for higher level functions or skills (6, 7, etc.). Select activities at lower levels (4, 3, 2, etc.) as necessary to insure success and provide an array of different activities that will reinforce the development of Visual–Body image skills.
   b. Develop or select from other sources additional activities related to all of the specific Visual–

Body Image skills listed (1–7). These activities can be coded into the system at the appropriate levels within the list of development skills.

SPECIFIC ACTIVITIES

1. Outline the student's body on heavy construction paper, and have the student cut it out. The student can draw facial features and clothes on the cut out figure.
2. Students can outline each other, cut out the figures, and then try to match up the outlines with the corresponding persons.
3. The students can play Simple Simon games.
4. Have the student lie down flat with eyes shut. Stroke a part on one side of the student's body and have the student move, or otherwise indicate, the corresponding part on the other side.
5. Have the students verbalize the functions of different body parts.
6. Have the students compare body parts to those of each other, to those of dolls, and finally, to those of a person in a picture.
7. Stand behind the student facing a full-length mirror and indicate body parts.
8. Pipe cleaners, clay, and wet sand are good for building figures.
9. Use activities that require the student to touch different body parts (hands, feet, etc.) to different objects in the room. For example, ask students to put their right hands on all the circles and their left hands on all the squares placed around the room.
10. Play games such as the following:
    a. *Head, Shoulders, Knees, and Toes:* The leader or teacher says the words, *head, shoulders, knees,* and *toes* in any desired sequence. A single student or a group must then touch the named parts in the order mentioned. The leader may state one order while demonstrating another order to see if the students can follow the spoken commands and not merely the actions. To vary this game, use different body parts and increase the number used as the ability of the students increases.
    b. *Relay Games:* Divide the students into two teams and place an object about twenty feet away from each team. The students must race around the objects. Give each pair of students competing against each other a direction involving body parts, such as "hop on one foot up and back," "hold your knees and walk up and back," or "put both hands on your head and skip up and back."

FINE MOTOR

Criterion Reference

The following are criterion references for the skills necessary to achieve handwriting competency, which requires that the student will:

1. Hold a pencil, pen, or crayon properly and with control.
2. Tie shoes and button buttons on command or after demonstration by peers or adults.
3. Develop handedness using one hand consistently.
4. Reproduce geometric patterns—circle, square, triangle, or diamond—upon command or after demonstration by a peer or an adult.
5. Draw a straight line from point to point on a chalkboard or paper vertically, horizontally, and on angles.
6. Draw a circle counterclockwise.
7. Color within boundaries.
8. Cut following a straight line, curved line, circle, and square.
9. Cut out pictures of objects.
10. Properly align letters.
11. Join letters properly.
12. Write from left to right.
13. Not fatigue easily.
14. Form letters properly.
15. Make proper sized letters.
16. Use good spacing.
17. Exert the normal amount of pressure.
18. Keep even margins.
19. Slant the letters correctly.
20. Write with normal speed.
21. Position the paper correctly.
22. Sit in the correct position.
23. Write letters on line.
24. Copy letters, numerals, and words in manuscript from the chalkboard or desk in an acceptable (legible) manner.
25. Copy sentences or paragraphs in manuscript from the chalkboard or desk in an acceptable (legible) manner.
26. Copy sentences in manuscript from the chalkboard or desk, within normal time limits for his or her age group, in an acceptable (legible) manner.
27. Copy letters, numerals, and words in cursive from the chalkboard or desk in an acceptable (legible) manner.
28. Copy sentences or paragraphs in cursive from the chalkboard or desk in an acceptable (legible) manner.

Table 10–1   Motor Development Equipment

1. Paper and crayons	16. Mats
2. Small chalkboards	17. Blocks
3. Walking board	18. Whiffle ball
4. Balance board	19. Balloons
5. Ladder	20. Magnets
6. Twist board	21. Pegboard
7. Clothespins	22. Puzzles
8. Small bells	23. Work bench
9. Masking tape	24. Ring toss game
10. Rope	25. Clay
11. Geometric templates	26. Beads
12. Bean bags	27. Burlap and needles
13. Playground ball	28. Sewing and lacing boards
(eight inch)	29. Finger paints
14. Ping pong ball	30. Rhythm band instruments
15. Rubber ball	31. Tape recorder
(three inch)	

29. Copy sentences in cursive from the chalkboard or desk, within normal time limits for his or her age group, in an acceptable (legible) manner.
30. Take dictation legibly in manuscript, within normal time limits, utilizing words at the independent reading level.
31. Take dictation legibly in cursive, within normal time limits, utilizing words at the independent reading level.

Prescriptive Activities

Table 10–1 lists motor development equipment that is available for the following activities.

GENERAL ACTIVITIES

1. Select from the list of developmental skills the particular target skills that are to be mastered in the area of Visual Motor–Fine. These target skills become learning or behavioral objectives. (Example Target: Visual Motor–Fine 7—The student will draw a circle counterclockwise.)
2. If the student fails to demonstrate success in the target skills according to predetermined criteria such as failing items assessed on a standardized test or failing school tasks, requiring the skills, do the following:
   a. Select from the list of developmental skills the target skill (example: Visual Motor–Fine 7) and other related or similar skills (6, 5, etc.) that are deemed appropriate for developing activities that will provide success and practice for higher level functions or skills (8, 9, 10, etc.). Select activities at lower levels (6, 5, 4, etc.) as neces-

sary to insure success and provide an array of different activities that will reinforce the development of Visual Motor–Fine skills.
   b. Develop or select from other sources additional activities related to all of the specific Visual Motor–Fine skills listed (1–18). These activities can be coded into the system at the appropriate levels within the list of development skills.

SPECIFIC ACTIVITIES

1. Provide sorting, tying, and buttoning activities.
2. Clothespin hanging is helpful.
3. Use games such as pick-up sticks and bean-bag toss.
4. Young children can scribble with a crayon or pencil (do not overdo the activity). This can be varied with music.
5. Use sewing and lacing activities.
6. Use peg boards and form boards.
7. Use tracing activities.
8. Bead-stringing activities with varied designs help to build in better discrimination.
9. Ball-bouncing and ball-throwing games are good.
10. Use a nail board with rubber bands to build designs and letters.
11. Use scissor activities with small squares of 4″ × 4″ heavy paper in the following sequence:

   a. Snipping off corners (one cut)
   b. Fringing (one cut)
   c. Fringing (two cuts without removing scissors)
   d. Cutting all the way across (no lines)
   e. Cutting following a line (straight)
   f. Cutting following a line (curved)
   g. Cutting following a circle
   h. Cutting following a square
   i. Cutting following a spiral (circular)
   j. Cutting following a spiral (square)

12. Use stencils and templates.
13. Tracing folds in paper is helpful.
14. Use dot-to-dot tracing games.
15. Have the student squeeze a ball.
16. Working with clay is a good activity. The students can roll out the thin long snakes to be used in making letters or numerals.

17. Use snapping and clapping finger games.
18. Face the student and move your finger in different directions (about two feet away) across the student's body. The student follows the finger with his eyes without moving his head. Go slowly at first.
19. Draw a line or design on the board and have the student trace and follow the finger or chalk with her eyes.
20. Establish a movement pattern with a flashlight or with a pointer and have the student verbalize while visually tracking the pattern: up, down, right, left, etc.
21. Fasten a ball to a string suspended from a stick and move it across the student's body in different patterns as the student follows it with his eyes.
22. Play games such as the following.
    a. *Bean Bag Toss:* Students toss bean bags into buckets or into any container with an opening. Place the container four to five feet from the students, increasing the distance as the children's ability increases. Numbers may be glued on the cans. Older students can keep score.
    b. *Drop the Clothespin:* From a standing position, students drop wooden clothespins into large-mouth bottles or containers. Make sure they hold the clothespin at waist height when dropping the pins.
    c. *Ring Toss:* Using rubber jar rings and coke bottles, or a commercial game, students throw the rings over the neck of the bottle. Here, again, numbers can be placed on the bottles, and older students can keep score.
    d. *Elephant and Peanut:* One student is selected to be the elephant. He sits on a chair in front of the other students, who are sitting at their desks. The elephant closes his eyes. His back is toward the other players. The elephant's peanut (an eraser or any other small article) is placed near the chair. A student selected by the teacher attempts to sneak up to the elephant and touch and pick up the peanut without being heard by the elephant. If the elephant hears someone coming, he turns to the person and says, "Roar." Then the player must return to his own seat, and another student tries. If that student picks up the peanut before the elephant hears her, she becomes the elephant, and the game is repeated. The game can be varied by adding other animal names and sounds.

STAGES OF HANDWRITING SKILL DEVELOPMENT

The following is an example of a criterion-referenced orientation to assessment and instruction. Handwriting is delineated into three sequential criterion stages of skill development:

Stage 1: Developmental
The developmental stage represents the initial building blocks of a particular skill area, such as grasp being a basic developmental skill necessary for handwriting.

Stage 2: Transitional
The transitional level of skill development is a further development of Stage 1 to where the basic skills are coordinated for higher level functions. These functions, once practiced and learned, become habitual and automatic responses that are vital for the next stage.

Stage 3: Academic
Stage 3 represents the academic level of criterion for success in handwriting and written language. Such functions as speed and accuracy are essential for success in using the skills for academic purposes.

By understanding these interrelationships the teacher can determine the different levels of functioning within the various skill areas and then plan the student's program accordingly. This delineation of the subareas within handwriting is just another way of trying to understand a complex process without relying totally on the traditional grade level descriptions.

When viewed within the context of mastery of simple, intermediate, and complex skills, the teacher can discern the student's relative understanding and facility with a particular aspect of language. In any of life's tasks, whether it be for academic, recreational, or social purposes, the best example of how a skill can be manifested is the automatic nature of its performance or presentation. The good golfer or tennis player has an automatic swing. Likewise, the good reader or writer thinks more about what he is reading or writing than he does about the mechanics of the performance of the task. Knowledge gained and performed with automaticity, i.e., security, deftness, smoothness, and confidence, is really what we are trying to accomplish.

The concept of automaticity is presented as a theme in each of the chapters dealing with language and mathematics. The same orientation, Developmental—Transitional—Academic, is presented as a basis for the understanding and discussion in each of these areas.

DEVELOPMENTAL SEQUENCE

The following represents a breakdown of writing skills based on the concept of prerequisite skills for higher level functions. The outline will be helpful to teachers in diagnosis and in programming for students exhibiting developmental lags or irregular learning in writing.

Questions to be answered: What has to be taught first? What has to be practiced? What can be used effectively?

STAGES OF HANDWRITING SKILL DEVELOPMENT

DEVELOPMENTAL	TRANSITIONAL	ACADEMIC
Handwriting	*Handwriting*	*Handwriting*
Grasp	Letters	Automatic
Power	Words	Legible
Control (Stroke ↓ | ↙○)	Numerals	Speed (rate)
Reproduce designs	Copying--near point	Use for academics
○□△◇	Copying--far point	Assessment (test-taking)
Visual memory	Manuscript	Daily life
Spatial organization	Cursive	

Readiness for Handwriting

Handwriting skills cannot be learned incidentally. For the younger students in kindergarten through first grade, training should begin with indirect preparation for writing. Fine motor dysfunction is not uncommon in these students; therefore, they need manipulative experiences designed to strengthen the muscles necessary for writing and pencil control.

TRAINING SEQUENCE

Activities that may help to develop fine motor skills necessary for writing are suggested below:

1. Cutting and manipulation of small objects such as knobs on puzzle parts, nuts and bolts, and caps on small bottles. Finger painting and clay modeling help to strengthen muscles for hand and finger control.
2. Solid, smooth, wooden geometric forms, △ ○ ▱ , help the student to concentrate on different shapes and to feel, as well as to see, the difference between a square and a triangle, for example.
3. Templates or metal insets (#1 ▢ #2 ▢) will help perfect fine motor skills—hand and finger control. These can be used as follows:
    a. The learners start with frame #1 and trace around the inside with a finger. They then trace two or three times with a soft colored pencil or plastic crayon.
    b. Then, using a different colored pencil or crayon, the students fill in the center with short strokes ⦀ ↓ always made from top to bottom.
4. Scissor Activities. The cutting exercises outlined on page 483 are helpful.
5. Material requiring coloring, cutting, and pasting can be used. Start with very-easy-to-color material that can be cut out and pasted. Slowly move into more difficult activities as the students progress.
6. Tracing sheets of interesting animals and objects makes a good individual activity. Clipboards and sheets of acetate or large plastic sheets that can be placed on a desk top can be used for tracing.
7. Duplicator master material requiring the student to connect dots to form a geometric shape or picture can be used.

GRASPING OF PENCIL

Good writing starts with proper grasping of the pencil. If the students cannot hold the pencil correctly, watch to see if they have trouble grasping other things. If they do have a problem, help them find a way to hold their pencils by using tape or a rubber band, putting the pencil through a rubber band, or using any other aid. Be sure to place a note in the students' record indicating that they have been taught an unorthodox method.

In teaching students to hold a pencil, mold their hands around their pencils. Explain what you are going to do before doing it, and then explain again afterwards. Do not speak while you are molding the students' hands around their pencils.

BEGINNING HANDWRITING

In teaching a student how to write, you must be more direct, moving from large-scale gross movements to the necessary finer movements. The teaching process starts with the following:

1. Large templates that can be used at the chalkboard or on large sheets of paper (these help the student to feel, as well as to see, the differences between different geometric shapes)
2. Small templates that can be used at the desk
3. Scribble-scrabble on the chalkboard, first with both hands and later with the dominant hand (for example, *eeee uuuu eeee*
4. Tracing over large printed letters, such as *a, b, c, d,* on a plasticized sheet using a washable crayon or grease pencil
5. Writing letters in a tray of damp sand with a finger, or writing in a tray of soft clay with a stick
6. Writing with a pencil on paper

MANUSCRIPT WRITING

Manuscript writing is based entirely upon circles and sticks, or lines. Before starting to teach, consider the maturation level in terms of the previously mentioned skills of each of the students. Successful copying of circles is normative from about age 3. By first grade, it is important not only that the students can copy a circle but also that they produce it a specific way. By age 5, most girls can make a circle from a top down in a counterclockwise direction. For most boys this form is normative at 5½ years of age. After age 6, about 90 percent of both boys and girls start their circle from the top and go down in a counterclockwise direction. The one exception to this progression is left-handed students. Lefties may be as old as 9 years before a top-to-bottom counterclockwise circle is normative. The difficult part of making a circle is the return. The use of templates helps students to develop this ability.

Left-handed students' papers should always be turned so that the top points toward the right front corner of the desk. The students should also be taught to grip their pencils farther away from the writing point than is normal for a right-handed student and to keep their hands below that which they are writing. (This prevents smearing and they can see what they have written.)

Physical comfort must always be considered, so the seating of left-handed students in the classroom is important. They should be seated at the left side of the room facing the chalkboard in order to copy material from the board more easily. Some students are slow in developing handedness. While dominant handedness is usually observable at the age of three, in some students it may not be fully developed until the age of eight.

WRITING THE ALPHABET

Many students have trouble learning to write the alphabet. The following are some suggestions for students at various stages of development.

Partial Alphabet Sheets

For students who have trouble both saying and writing the alphabet, the following method is suggested. Seven letters of the alphabet are taught at a time until they are known. (This number can be varied.) The students do *not* write the alphabet across the sheet, but down the page (Figure 10–1). This forces them to say the letters and write them in a sequence. After the students have written the alphabet down the sheet once, their work can be checked for accuracy so that they won't copy a poorly produced letter when writing down the second time. Figure 10–2 shows the actual size of the letters.

Page 104 has a good example of using prompting and fading in teaching the writing of letters. Hallahan, Kauffman, and Lloyd (1985) concluded from the work of Staats et al. (1970) that "young children learned

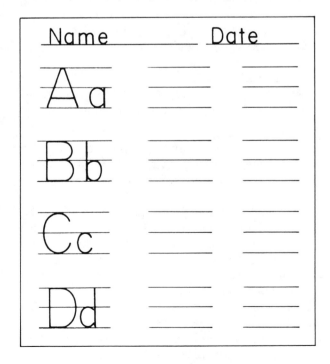

Figure 10–1   Sheet #1, Letters A–F

Figure 10–2   *Actual Size of the Letters and Lines*

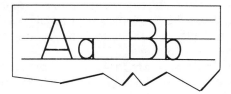

Figure 10–3

new letters in fewer attempts after they had acquired the ability to copy the first few letters. In other words, the children were able to generalize their learned behavior to new tasks" (p. 66).

Copying the Whole Alphabet
For students who have learned to write the alphabet but still need practice, the following types of activities can be used.

1. In the activity in Figure 10–3 the students see the whole alphabet just as they have been taught it, and they copy to the immediate right of each pair of letters.
2. In the activity in Figure 10–4 the students see the alphabet delineated into the capital and lowercase letters. The students copy the alphabet immediately below the written letters.
3. In the activity in Figure 10–5 the students see the alphabet written at the top of the sheet and copy it as a whole at the bottom. Activity sheets can be made with either capital or lowercase letters.
4. Students who successfully write the alphabet from memory can use activity sheets that require them to fill in missing letters.

Manuscript Versus Cursive Writing

Manuscript is taught to many beginning writers because it resembles the printed text. There are advocates of teaching cursive exclusively during the primary grades. They believe that with cursive writing there is a continuous flow of the elements giving the student experience with the total form of the word as opposed to the fragmentation of manuscript. Early (1973) feels that cursive writing has generalized

movement patterns leading to more automatic and efficient writing. Words are written in units. There is less confusion in the direction of letters and letters are difficult to reverse. The teaching emphasizes the rhythmic flow of movement.

Writing Must Have Meaning

Letters are first overlearned in isolation. Then as soon as possible, even at the readiness stage, writing should say something. Initially, students need to concentrate chiefly on learning the correct order of making the strokes. Right after this comes spacing. Whole words that have real meaning for the students and are easy to write are the best with which to start. Linguistic readers are well suited to this approach and will enable the students to begin writing that which they are already reading.

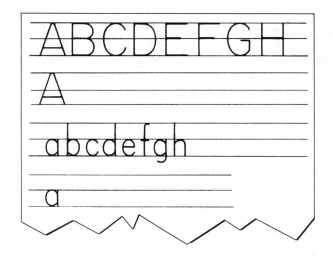

Figure 10–4

Figure 10–5

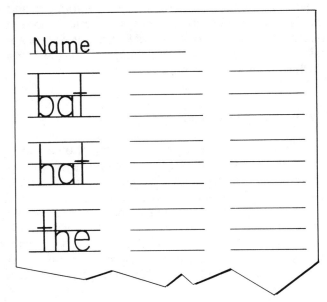

Figure 10–6

Until such time as the learners are able to write words from memory, they should have a copy or a model from which to write. The copy should be on the same kind of paper that the students use, although as the students improve they can copy phrases and sentences out of their reading books. Ten minutes at a time is usually enough writing for the younger students. Speed is never emphasized at this stage, and writing should always be supervised. Copywork from the chalkboard should be avoided in the early stages, because it forces constant refocusing of the eyes.

Word Activity Sheets

Begin with whole words that the students understand and that are easy to write. The beginning students should write from a model. The students should not just write words across the page. The words should be written one at a time down the page. (See Figure 10–6.) The words will have more meaning if the students have to stop and look at them before writing.

Cursive Writing

Many students experience difficulty learning to write in cursive. For students who are having problems, the following methods have been successful.

TRAINING FOR CURSIVE WRITING

1. *Chalkboard Activity:* The students begin with exercises at the chalkboard that can develop readiness for cursive writing. Begin with circles and figure eights (Figure 10–7), then go to */)* ,

l's, l's, and *le* combinations as fast as the students can handle them. Build in the strokes needed for the general writing program.

2. *Chalkboards Used for Desk Work:* Paint the designs shown in the preceding item on small chalkboards that the students can use at their desks. The students can then practice by tracing over these smaller models.

3. *Dittos or Teacher-Made Activity Sheets:* For starting writing, dittos and activity sheets can be used to teach the same designs as above. Encourage the student to write smaller. If writing smaller is too difficult at first, begin using first grade paper and then work toward the transitional paper and finally the third grade paper.

Students experiencing difficulty with initial attempts to make *lll* may need remedial practice with stencil forms. The following techniques are suggested.

1. *Chalkboard Activity:* Use chalk of different colors.

   Have the student make this stroke */* with one color, then take the second color and complete the *l* (i.e., *l*). At this stage do not connect the *l's*.

2. *Chalkboards Used for Desk Work:* Use a desk chalkboard with the *l* pattern painted on it. Give the students two pieces of chalk of different colors and have them make the first stroke with one color, put it down, take the second color, and complete the tracing of the *l*. A pattern of smaller connected *l's* will help them feel the rhythm of the writing.

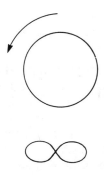

Figure 10–7

3. *Dittos or Teacher-Made Activity Sheets:* Use the same technique as in item 2, above. Colored pencils are used in place of chalk.

PROBLEMS IN CURSIVE WRITING

Any program, whether beginning or remedial, should stress good letter formation. Most errors are malformations of only a few letters.

n that looks like an *m*

a that looks like an *o*

a that looks like a *u*

a that looks like a *u*

e that looks like an *i*

i not dotted that looks like an *e*

b that looks like an *li*

d that looks like a *cl*

t uncrossed and looped like an *l*

ORDER OF PRESENTATION OF CURSIVE LETTERS

Lowercase letters should be introduced first in the following order:

l, a, d, t, u, n, m, h, k,
w, e, b, v, x, y, j, f, s,
p, r, c, i, g, o, q, and z.

The letters *b, e, f, k, r, s,* and *z* must be taught specifically. Capital letters are always practiced in usage. Always use whole words in this approach, and watch any word with an *n* in it, as this requires different spacing. Another letter that can cause confusion is *g,* as it changes with connections.

LEFT-HANDED CHILDREN

The content of most instructional material in handwriting is inappropriate for left-handed students because the left-handed student has to learn to write in the opposite direction from a right-handed child—away from the body's midline. Left-handed students need a handwriting program specifically suited to their needs.

Suggestions for Teaching Left-Handed Students

1. If possible, left-handed children should be taught by a left-handed person, who serves as a model.
2. They need to be taught to hold their pencil and paper correctly so they can see what they are writing. Pencils should be held 1 ½ inches from the point, paper slanted to the right, and bodies turned to the right when they write. This will prevent smudging. Students should be taught to write their letters either with no slant (vertically) or with a slightly backhanded slant.
3. Encourage them to write in a simple style. Elaborate flourishes or excessive loops will only slow them down as they try to acquire speed for everyday work.
4. Left-handed children need a model cursive alphabet. Each child should have one.

Seating in the Classroom

Left-handed children should be seated to the teacher's right in a classroom when he or she is facing them. Care should be taken that they are not placed so that they are forced to write notes off the board while looking over their left shoulder.

TRANSITIONAL WRITING

In teaching transitional writing begin with the easier letters; you can add the difficult letters later one at a time:

1. First, print the word in manuscript.

all

2. Then connect the letters with a dotted line, using a colored pencil

all at ant

The students then trace over the printed manuscript letter and the connecting dotted lines to form the cursive writing. Difficult letters should be written lighter than the colored dots and eventually fade out with successive tracings.

Note: Watch this problem with the letter *n:*

not pant

pan

The "n" in the middle or end of a word must have enough room in front of it for the extra hump needed in cursive.

Remediation Techniques

Remediation techniques for writing that deteriorates under pressure are as follows:

1. The students should be observed as they write to see if they are doing it correctly. For instance, *i, j,* and *t* are dotted or crossed immediately in manuscript writing but not in cursive. Many students carry this habit over into cursive, and it slows them down.
2. If the students are writing correctly but tire too easily, desk templates should be used to help them develop more strength in the muscles needed for writing.
3. Extremely slow writers should be observed. If they are slow because they can't read the material they are copying and have to copy each letter almost stroke by stroke, they may have a reading problem and not a writing problem.

The following are suggestions to help the older student practice cursive writing.

1. The students copy from material presented on the same activity sheet.
   a. Review sheets can be made for all capital letters. Students can then be given a complete review program including all of the sheets in order, or they can be given just the letters they are experiencing difficulty with.
   b. On the review sheet shown in Figure 10–8, the student first practices individual words and then copies a paragraph.
2. The students copy from a master copy to their own papers. Write a series of ten or twelve stories for the students to copy. The stories, written on regular classroom paper, are mounted on tag board. The students copy them on the same type of paper. Ditto pictures accompany each story. (See Figure 10–9.) When all of the stories of a group are completed, the pictures and stories are put together in a booklet to be taken home. The stories can be written on the approximate reading level of the students using them. The following subjects have proven popular:

For third and fourth	Animals of the Sea
	African Animals
	Endangered Animals of the World
For fourth and fifth	Early Aircraft
	Early Cars
	Monsters of the Movies
For fifth and sixth	Science Fiction Stories
	Tales of the Supernatural

Figure 10–8

3. At this level, the students copy from printed material into cursive.
   a. Many good joke and riddle books are on the market. The students copy those they like in a small (5″ × 7″) notebook in cursive.
   b. Using poetry books, have the students copy and illustrate their favorite poems. (A 5″ × 7″ notebook is best for this kind of work.)

ADDITIONAL HANDWRITING SUGGESTIONS

1. *Writing Paper:* If the colored lines on the writing paper are very light, use colored pencils to reinforce and darken the lines for the students who may have difficulty staying within the lines.
2. *Directionality:* Place a dot or an arrow → to aid the learner in left-to-right progression in writing. An arrow can be placed in the upper left-hand corner of the chalkboard.
3. *Far-Point Copying:* Some learners may require successive approximations to successful copying of material from a classroom chalkboard. The following steps are suggested as the students copy material preferably at their own reading level. The students will
   a. Copy phrases or sentences from a paper placed next to the writing paper.

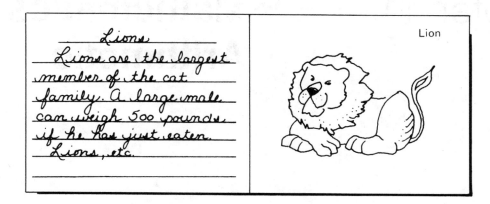

Figure 10–9

b. Copy material written on a portable chalkboard or an easel and placed directly in front of the learner.

c. Finally, copy sentences from the chalkboard. The number of sentences successfully copied in an acceptable period of time should be noted. The amount of material should be carefully monitored.

Note: Incomplete, illegible assignments may be caused by many factors. When students are completing far-point copying from a chalkboard, an acetate on an overhead projector, a television monitor, etc., the following should be considered:

1. Is the model from which the students are copying neatly written and carefully spaced?
2. Do the students view the chalkboard from an appropriate angle? Do they have to turn around to see the material?
3. Is there a glare or shadows on the board caused by improper lighting, sunlight, mobiles, etc.?
4. Is the chalkboard, and therefore the printing, placed too high on the wall?
5. Can the students read what they are copying?
6. Do the students have sufficient time to copy assignments?

4. *Practice:* Students should be encouraged to practice to a successful model. For example, if a student copies an *a*, say, "When your *a* looks like the model *a* or is your very best, stop." Some learners are required to copy to a failure when the number of times a letter is written is stressed more than the quality of the writing. Fifty *a*'s may result in too many   's. For some students, ten minutes of writing may be the limit.

5. *Size:* Wallace and Larsen (1978) suggest that, in most handwriting, the lower-case letters *i, e, u,* are ¼ space high; *t* and *p* are ½ space; capitals and *l, h, k, d,* and *b* are ¾ space high, with lower-loop letters ½ space below the line. They suggest that size can be measured by drawing baselines within a space to check measurement.

6. *Speed:* Instructors can determine the rate a student writes by dividing the total number of letters written by the number of minutes allowed. Scales of cursive letters per minute range from approximately 25 letters per minute for first-graders to over 70 letters per minute for seventh-graders (Mercer & Mercer, 1985).

7. *Spacing:* Bowmar/Noble suggests that spacing should be uniform between the letters in a word and the width of a small *H* between words.

Cat H in H a H hat.

8. *Slant:* To check slant, draw lines through the downstroke and see if the lines are parallel to each other.

9. *Vocabulary:* Teach the vocabulary associated with good handwriting (e.g, alignment, slant, etc.).

10. *Self-Monitoring:* Teach students to self-evaluate their progress in writing by comparing samples of writing to a model. Hallahan, Kauffman, and Lloyd (1985) suggest progress monitoring by giving probes (miniature tests) to assess a specific skill. After the student writes for one minute, the writing is judged on percent of letters written legibly and rate of letters written legibly. A simple chart or comment sheet can be used and dated once a week regarding progress on overall legibility, appearance, size, spacing, neatness, and speed.

Chapter 11

Mathematics and Arithmetic

CHAPTER OUTLINE

OVERVIEW

Mathematics can be envisioned as both a symbolic language and a means of indicating spatial-temporal relationships. A number sense is built early in the development of most students, as many of the concepts that deal with space, form, distance, order, and time are learned by the students through their everyday interactions with people, especially their parents, siblings, and peers. Mother helps formulate math concepts during feeding time when she says "a little bit more" or "just one more bite," etc. Problems in dealing with number concepts may result from language disorders and inability to deal with spatial-temporal relationships. Learning disabilities that affect reading, writing, and spelling tend also to affect arithmetic skills acquisition. No one basic task area can be considered in isolation in attempting to diagnose the problems of the learning-handicapped student.

PROBLEM AREAS IN ARITHMETIC

Students with learning disabilities exhibit problems in a variety of areas, which include disorders related to abstracting, generalizing, reasoning, and the various processes of memory. It is axiomatic that, in working with these students, the teacher will need to have back-up systems, materials, or programs that can provide review and reteaching opportunities. Students who have difficulty with applications are ineffective in problem solving and making decisions. Coping with the difficulties at the affective level is part of the problem.

Most arithmetic errors result from students selecting the wrong operations due in part to conceptual difficulties regarding numbers. They arrive at the use of wrong operations through the use of incorrect or inadequate strategies (Russell & Ginsburg, 1984; De Corte & Verschaffel, 1981).

Much of this is due to unfamiliarity with basic number facts (Russell & Ginsburg, 1984). These students may also have problems with retrieving number fact information. Slowness in general is debilitating, whether it be slowness in accessing facts or being slow in solving (thinking and writing) problems. Some students may have all three problems—cannot recall the facts, cannot do the work on paper, and do not know how to use the appropriate strategies.

Children with learning problems in one study exhibited poor operational efficiency (Kirby & Becker, 1988). The findings indicated that a "bottleneck" could occur if students were held back by simple operations, such as solving single-digit problems. The study also suggested that problems in arithmetic can be directly associated with very slow execution of the operations, in that learning disabled students working too slow were operationally inefficient. One explanation is that children with learning problems just do not process information as quickly as others. Another idea is that the students have not developed the automatic behavior necessary for accessing number facts or other basic operations. This may be due to a deficient working memory, which keeps them from performing more complex tasks (Torgesen, 1986).

Problems of automaticity in basic operations and reduced strategy performance have important implications for classroom instruction. The concept of overloading in instruction has a great deal of relevance in this instance. Also, teaching basic skills in context and focusing on meaning and understanding of language are important concepts.

Math Aversion

Many learning handicapped students need to overcome math anxiety before it becomes a major concern. Math anxiety or "mathophobia" is caused primarily by teachers and the process of teaching (Williams, 1988). Children entering school as a whole do not bring math anxiety with them. Tobias (1976) defines math anxiety as the "I can't" syndrome. Others talk about feelings of helplessness, paralysis, and mental disorganization associated with math problem solving (Tobias & Weissbrod, 1980).

Teacher attitudes toward math may be transmittable (Kelly & Tomhave, 1985). Many preservice elementary school majors are math-anxious (Kelly & Tomhave, 1985). Greenwood (1984) suggested that teaching methods had a lot to do with learner math anxiety. The "explain-practice-memorize-test" approach to teaching math appears to be a real source of math anxiety. This approach emphasizes memory instead of reasoning and understanding.

Teachers sometimes produce math-anxious students by saying they do not like math; making statements like, "I'm not a numbers person," or "math is not my best subject." Some reasons why people become anxious are problems associated with falling behind, being shy or lacking confidence, and not wanting to go to the board in front of the class. Teachers need to attend special workshops designed to remove the mystique and to make math fun, as well as to create new attitudes and expectations.

Math-anxious teachers need to improve their math skills, particularly with fractions and decimals. They rely primarily on textbook explanations and do-the-problems, correct the problems, and make assignments with little discussion. Many never talk about why answers are right or wrong. They appeal to the teacher's handbook rather than working out the problems for the whole class when a student challenges an answer.

To have an anxiety-free math class, the environment must be nonthreatening, and learning activities should be appropriate to the students' cognitive levels and meaningful from both the students' and teacher's perspectives. The instruction should emphasize creative and active learning strategies instead of the traditional explain-practice-memorize way of learning math. Symptoms of math anxiety include failure to hand assignments in on time, asking to be excused from the room frequently, and making negative comments about math, the math room, or the math teacher. To learn math, students must want to learn math, feel good about learning math, and be confident that they can learn it.

Reducing Math Anxiety

Three approaches to reducing anxiety are suggested (Dueball & Clowes, 1982):

1. Content area (math focus) approaches are based on the belief that the more students know about math, the less anxious they will be about math problems. Therefore, an increase in competency should result in a decrease in anxiety (Reyes, 1980).

2. Anxiety-reduction approaches, such as desensitization and support groups, focus on the anxiety itself. Counselors, psychologists, and psychiatrists play an important role in this approach.
3. A combination of content area and anxiety-reduction approaches appears to offer the best results (Tobias, 1978).

The use of manipulative aids appears to be helpful in reducing anxiety. Cooperative learning is a helper-oriented learning arrangement where peers help reduce anxiety. Math programs should directly involve students, along with an open classroom atmosphere where questions can be freely asked.

Reaction to correct and incorrect responses are important. Praise is good, but disapproval can have detrimental effects. Teachers should monitor disapproval and students' reactions. Students should always begin with math problems that result in 100 percent success if possible, then move to more difficult examples. Games that promote original thinking and that build confidence are also useful (Downie et al., 1983). The concept of celebrating mistakes applies here—no one should feel bad about making an error.

Interview the student and ask how the problem that is wrong was done (explain aloud). Just say, "How did you work that problem?" Do not comment; let the student tell what he or she did. Determine first if the student knows how to do the basic math (e.g., multiply, divide, etc.) or is having trouble with the facts. Ask open-ended questions so that the learner feels free to explain the solving of the problem.

The student needs to feel at ease with the teacher. If the student is being tested by someone other than the teacher, some explanation is in order. Just say, "I want to know how you do your arithmetic problems. I want to find out how you do them and why you are having problems so I can help you." Don't prejudge or assume you know how the student thinks. Some students use an unusual method to complete a problem that usually results in the wrong answer. Students who constantly make careless errors may lack in motivation and have diagnosed bad habits.

LANGUAGE DISORDERS IN ARITHMETIC

Difficulties in receptive and expressive language that affect reading and writing will also affect the students' performance in arithmetic. The students may not be able to understand words that are associated with word problems. They may have difficulty with words or concepts that relate to space and time. They may have problems understanding process signs and words dealing with distance and measurement. Words such as *beside, further, in between, within, upside down,* and *next to* may be difficult for the students to conceptualize. Words with a dual meaning, such as *base, times,* and *equals* are difficult in that the students may not be able to handle both meanings of these words. They may not be able to retrieve numerals or words needed for arithmetical operations, or they may be unable to express themselves in terms of mathematics in clear and sequential thought patterns.

Structure of Language of Arithmetic

Instructional issues concerning the mathematics achievement of students revolve around three basic questions. First, to what extent is language a factor in learning mathematics? Second, what are the language skills that may be related to achievement in the subject? Third, what curriculum and instructional approaches are available that take into account the language needs of the students?

There is sufficient evidence in the literature to indicate a relationship between language skills and mathematics learning. Thorndike (1912) stated that ". . . our measurement in arithmetic is a measure of two things: sheer mathematical knowledge on the one hand; and acquaintance with language on the other." Studies also indicate that there is a positive correlation between reading ability and scores on tests of problem solving in arithmetic. More recent studies indicate that there is also a positive relationship between mathematics performance and second language ability (Cossio, 1978). The relationship between language factors and mathematics achievement is not clearly understood; but it may be appropriate to assume that, in order for a student to master mathematics concepts, the language of the concepts must first be mastered.

Learning the language of the concepts involves, to a great extent, the mastery of meanings that serve a particular function in the language, as well as the words and structures that convey those meanings. This is what linguists term a language "register." Halliday (1974) refers to a "mathematics register" as the meanings that belong to the language of mathematics. This "mathematics register" is more precise than natural language, since the meaning of the terms used are very narrow in scope. This results in ". . . an almost totally nonredundant and relatively unambiguous language" (Brunner, 1973, p. 89).

It has been suggested that the "mathematics register" is composed of the following:

1. Natural language words reinterpreted in the context of mathematics. Some of these words are *set, point, field, column, sum, even* (number), *random.*
2. "Locutions" such as *right-angled triangle* and *lowest common multiple.*
3. Terms created from combinations of natural language words such as *feedback* and *output.*
4. Terms formed by combining elements of Greek and Latin words. Examples include *parabola, denominator, coefficient, assymptotic,* etc.

Vocabulary is not the only dimension of the "mathematics register" teachers need to be aware of. Styles of meaning and ways arguments are presented as part of the "language of mathematics" must also be considered. Examples of these include:

1. "a set of terms each of which stands in a constant mathematical relationship to that which precedes it"
2. "the sum of the series to *n* terms"

It is essential that the teacher be aware of the importance of attaching meaning to the symbolic code of the written and spoken language of mathematics. The world of mathematical reality for the individual learner is a function of environmental factors that interact and affect the absorption and retention of mathematical knowledge.

Many psycholinguists and researchers also emphasize that linguistic competence is multidimensional. The language functions involved in literacy are unmistakably different from the skills an individual uses to engage in an informal social conversation. The language of literacy has been described as "decontextualized" language (Cummins, 1979). This is the language that is found in textbooks or that is used in formal instruction. The kind of language used in social interaction has been described as "situated" or "context-embedded" language (Cummins, 1979), where the actual situation in which the conversation occurs provides the participant with the means to interpret the language aspects of what has taken place. Verbal and nonverbal cues such as gestures, intonation, pacing, and tone of voice offer the learner the means to interpret the language aspects of what has taken place in an actual conversation situation produced by the participants.

Language Confusion

The following are examples of how language is used to confuse the learner:

1. Sometimes the pictures or diagrams used in textbooks have nothing to do with the problem.

2. Information is sometimes given in a confusing order.
3. Multiple steps are often required, but the steps are hidden.
4. Extraneous information may be included to distract the student.
5. The problem may be impossible to solve.
6. Too many sentences may result in a readability problem.
7. The vocabulary may be misleading or too difficult.

ATTENTION DEFICIT DISORDERS IN MATHEMATICS

In the classroom inattention, impulsivity, and hyperactivity may be seen in the student's off-task behavior. The student may not complete math assignments, may appear disorganized, and may give the impression that he or she is not listening. Often careless and impulsive errors appear in mathematics computation work or on tests where the student feels the most pressure. Mathematics requires sustained attention, and children exhibiting this type of disorder, who are easily distracted, may find it difficult to participate in group lessons or activities.

COGNITIVE-MOTIVATIONAL FACTORS AND MATHEMATICS

Learned helplessness, attribution, external locus of control, and lack of a feeling of self-efficacy must be considered as contributing factors to poor performance in mathematics. Mathematics is generally perceived as a difficult subject, and students with attitudinal and motivational problems tend to become less involved in this area. High rates of the above factors in off-task behavior and poor concentration are reported in arithmetic in students exhibiting learning disabilities. This is especially true when they are presented with difficult word problems to solve. Students develop a sense of helplessness and feelings of self-doubt about the subject area. Students' low expectation—coupled with the belief that the difficulties cannot be overcome—make the work of the instructor doubly difficult.

ARITHMETIC AND READING

Good arithmetic performance depends on the quick and accurate recognition of words. It is easy to see how a student with a reading problem could have an arithmetic problem. The arithmetic problem could have nothing to do with computational skills or with how the learner thinks. It may also be related to attention, spatial temporal orientation, or poor writing (fine motor). The mathematics instructor, to some degree, will find that there is also a need to teach reading during the math lesson. Vocabulary building, paraphrasing, elaboration, and strategy instruction are typical examples of activities that apply to both reading and arithmetic.

Students need to be taught how the structure of writing for arithmetic problem solving differs from other writing (e.g., as in writing stories). Familiarity with writing patterns and structure is deemed important (Hollander, 1988). For example, in arithmetic, students have to pay attention to directions, note details, organize information, make inferences, and discern the irrelevant from the relevant.

The language of mathematics is concise. It involves a high density of information, a special vocabulary, graphic formulations, and special symbols, such as #, %, ( ), =, < >, ", @, × (Robinson, 1983). Each word is important and each statement is made once without elaboration. Students need to know how to skim, scan, and search for key words and phrases, and extrapolate the core concept(s). The sparseness of language is often frightening to learning handicapped students who may be used to descriptions and helpful clues. The student must learn how to read slowly (silently and aloud) and carefully, repeating the key phrases with voice intonation, taking care not to add words or omit words.

It has been recognized that, just because a student can read a basal reader, it does not mean that he or she can read and understand the language of mathematics with equal facility (Reutzel, 1983). Reading ability is thought not to be directly related to problem solving ability. Harvin and Gilchrist (1970) point out that good readers are not necessarily good problem solvers. Poor readers are not necessarily poor problem solvers, but poor problem solvers generally have lower reading levels. It is reported (Newman, 1977) that at least 35 percent of errors on achievement tests may be attributed to reading problems. It is reasonable to assume that, due to poor reading, the student may not be able to begin to apply the correct process in solving the problem.

Teacher-made word problems need to be easy to read. When a student is applying a previously learned concept in a word problem, he or she should not be struggling to read every word. Math material has few cues to help in decoding meaning. The independent reading level has to involve the reading of terms and vocabulary that require little help. Homework should be at an easy level of readability. In the classroom, the teacher and student can interpret directions and go over words in context as necessary. One step further is to make it a practice to determine the readability levels of all math material presented to the students.

STAGES OF ARITHMETIC SKILL DEVELOPMENT

The following is an arithmetic criterion-referenced approach to assessment and instruction. The area of arithmetic is delineated into three sequential criterion stages of skill development:

Stage 1: Developmental
The developmental stage of arithmetic represents the initial building blocks of the skill area, such as the meaning of vocabulary being a basic developmental skill necessary for understanding mathematics concepts.

Stage 2: Transitional
The transitional level of arithmetic skill development is a further development of Stage 1 to where the basic skills are coordinated for higher level functions. These functions, once practiced and learned, become habitual and automatic responses that are vital for the next stage.

Stage 3: Academic
Stage 3 represents the academic level of criterion for success in the arithmetic skill area. Such functions as speed and accuracy are essential for success in using arithmetic skills for academic purposes.

By understanding these interrelationships the teacher can determine the different levels of functioning within the area of arithmetic and then plan the student's program accordingly. This delineation of the subareas within arithmetic is just another way of trying to understand a complex process without relying totally on the traditional grade level descriptions.

When viewed within the context of mastery of simple, intermediate, and complex skills, the teacher can discern the students' relative understanding and facility with a particular aspect of language. In any of life's tasks, whether it be for academic, recreational, or social purposes, the best example of how skill can be manifested is the automatic nature of its performance or presentation. The good golfer or tennis player has an automatic swing. Likewise, the good reader or writer thinks more about what he is reading or writing than he does about the mechanics of the performance of the task. Knowledge gained and performed with automaticity, i.e., security, deftness, smoothness, and confidence, is really what we are trying to accomplish.

DEVELOPMENTAL SEQUENCE

The following represents a breakdown of arithmetic skills based on the concept of prerequisite skills for higher level functions. The outline will be helpful to teachers in diagnosis and in programming for students exhibiting developmental lags or irregular learning in arithmetic.

Questions to be answered: What has to be taught first? What has to be practiced? What can be used effectively?

STAGES OF ARITHMETIC SKILL DEVELOPMENT

DEVELOPMENTAL	TRANSITION	ACADEMIC
Visual discrimination--(matching) shape and size	Counting (oral)	Concepts applied to everyday life
Grouping or sets	Counting with meaning (one to one correspondence)	Use for problem solving
Vocabulary or spatial-temporal relationships	Auditory-visual symbol association	Use in decision making
Estimation--size, weight, shape, distance	Symbol-value association (sets)	Apply concepts to all subject level academics
Memory-sequence	Cardinal and ordinal relationships	Use concepts automatically and with ease
Directionality	Four operations	Use concepts for creative thinking and serendipity
Laterality	$+ - \times \div$	Use to organize and manage life-space
Visual-motor-fine	Fractions	
Body image	Conservation of quantity	
Short-term memory	Process signs and symbols	
Attention to task.	Measurement	
	Maps and graphs	
	Decimals/percent	
	Geometry	
	Language of mathematics --vocabulary	
	Reading to note details	
	Syntax	

The concept of automaticity is presented as a theme in each of the chapters dealing with language and mathematics. The same orientation, Developmental—Transitional—Academic, is presented as a basis for the understanding and discussion in each area.

ARITHMETIC SEQUENCE

The Mann-Suiter Grade Level Arithmetic Sequence (Form 11-1) can be used as follows:

1. The arithmetic sequence can be used to determine the skills necessary for success at a particular grade level. Items from the arithmetic inventory (pages 312–331) that measure these skills can be used by the instructor to assess these particular operations in learners. Further testing should be discontinued for the students who fail in the initial assessment. If students succeed in this initial evaluation, it indicates that they have at least the basic skills necessary for success in initial arithmetical operations at that grade level. The instruc-

tor can then continue to test to the limits of the learners' abilities with higher level items, stopping after a reasonable amount of failure. Assessment of this nature is designed to limit or reduce the amount of failure in testing. If students cannot count by ones to 10, it is unreasonable to expect them to count to 100 by fives.

2. An alternate approach in assessment would be to administer the entire inventory to all of the students and then relate the results to the particular skills that are outlined developmentally in the sequence chart. This will give the instructor a measure initially of a broader range of skills in the learners.

The suggested developmental sequence indicates the extent to which particular skills should be introduced at certain grade levels. There is room for latitude in that some students will not have mastered certain arithmetic skills for their grade level and will need to have the curriculum adjusted accordingly. The teacher must be ready to drop down and build in the prerequisite skills for individual students. The developmental sequence chart is to be used as a guide and is designed to make it easy for the teacher to determine specific skills that need to be established for a particular grade level. The teacher can add items as necessary to the arithmetic sequence.

Instructional Approaches

Three main instructional approaches are suggested for teaching mathematics:

1. Direct instruction
2. Self-instruction
3. Guided learning or mediated instruction (Goldman, 1989)

DIRECT INSTRUCTION

Direct instruction entails using the principles associated with cognitive behavior modification. Students are taught task-specific strategies with an action sequence of steps that is modeled by the instructor. The instruction is precise and can be used with individuals or groups. The instructor eventually fades out as the student takes on more responsibility for the learning.

In direct instruction:

1. Students are told what errors they are making.
2. They are requested to demonstrate the proper technique or approach modeled after the teacher.
3. They practice similar problems under the direction of the teacher.
4. They practice with diminished support from the teacher.
5. They work independently on similar problems.

SELF-INSTRUCTION

The student responds to a set of verbal prompts that guide the process. The prompts function as mediators. The instructor models the verbal prompt sequence as part of self-instructional training.

In self-instruction, a student's continuous verbal dialogue where he or she asks questions about the task has been found to be useful. The steps in self-instruction are as follows:

1. The teacher demonstrates the problem while verbally delineating the process as the student listens.
2. The teacher and the student work out a problem together as the teacher verbalizes less and the student verbalizes more.
3. The student solves a problem and the teacher observes as the student uses self-instruction (verbalization) techniques to solve the problem. The teacher corrects the errors.
4. The student solves a problem, but uses less verbalization in the process.

5. The student solves a problem and uses no verbal behavior in the process (Whitman & Johnston, 1983).

The goal is to help the student internalize the process of mathematics problem solving.

MEDIATED PERFORMANCE

The learner in this approach is guided through the experience by the instructor who models the appropriate behavior. The student is encouraged to think through the problem, ask appropriate questions, and follow the model of the teacher in this process while acting independently. The instructor uses coaching, fading, questioning, and other techniques to help the student understand the task. Self-instruction and direct instruction are more instructor dependent in terms of expertise and training.

The basis of this approach is found in how much and what kind of assistance a teacher can provide to help the student to perform correctly, as well as to stabilize a successful approach during the transfer process in teaching. A combination of modeling and coaching using hints, cues, and feedback seems to be beneficial (Ferrara, 1987b). Suggested steps include:

1. The teacher calls attention to incorrect solutions and gets the student to make another attempt.
2. The teacher verbally repeats the parts of the problem that are to be highlighted.
3. The student writes what is known about the problem.
4. The student repeats the steps of the previous problem.
5. The teacher gives hints and cues.
6. The problem is reviewed and the hints and cues are discussed.
7. The student repeats the problem on his or her own.

The nature of basic math instruction for learning handicapped and nonlearning handicapped learners is essentially the same. Math instruction does not differ in special education settings and even between categorical areas of special education (Ysseldyke et al., 1989). It also appears that there are few differences among categories regarding the quality of instruction.

More instructional time is needed to work on problem solving. Most time in arithmetic instruction in schools is allocated to computational skills (Charles & Lester, 1982). Teachers need to be explicit about how strategies should be applied to problem-solving tasks and why it is important to know how to use them (Herrmann, 1989). For example:

MANN-SUITER GRADE LEVEL ARITHMETIC SEQUENCE

A

Grade Level	One-to-One	Numerals	Sets	Ordinals
K	Matches one to one Matches shapes (discrimination) ○ □ △ ◇ Vocabulary of space and position Estimates distance, height, and quantity Order by height	Matches one to one Writes 0–5 Identifies 0–10 Identifies before and after 1–10 Counts orally 0–10	Matches equivalent sets 00 = 00 Recognizes sets 0–5 Recognizes sets with more or less	Understands first through fifth
1st		Identifies 0–50 Counts orally 0–100 Counts and writes by 10s to 100 and 5s to 50 Writes 0–50 Knows place value 0–50 Renames 1s & 10s through 50 Identifies odd and even numbers	Recognizes sets 6–10 Knows language of sets	Understands sixth through tenth
2nd		Counts and writes by 2s to 100; 3s to 36; 4s to 48; 5s to 100; 10s to 200 Writes 0–100 Knows place value 50–100 Renames 50–100 Knows odd and even numbers	Identifies equivalent subsets	Reads ordinals through twelfth
3rd		Writes in sequence 1–999 Writes from dictation 1–999 Renames 10s to 100s Knows Roman numerals I–X Knows, reads, writes 1-, 2-, and 3-place numbers	Identifies equal sets	Understands ordinals to hundredths Reads ordinals through twentieth

(continued)

A (continued)

Grade Level	One-to-One	Numerals	Sets	Ordinals
4th		Counts and writes by 6s to 72; 7s to 84; 8s to 96; 9s to 108 Knows place value to millions Knows Roman numerals XI–C Understands rounding of numbers to nearest 10	Identifies universal sets Identifies intersection of sets	Reads ordinals through thirtieth
5th		Reads and writes billions Knows Roman numerals C–M Understands rounding of whole numbers Identifies prime and composite numbers Understands common factors and Greatest Common Factors (GCF) Identifies multiples of numbers and Least Common Multiple (LCM)	Understands union of sets, disjoint sets, finite and infinite sets, empty sets	
6th		Understands integers, negative numbers, rational numbers, base numeration, place value to billions place	Understands solution sets, sets of ordered pairs	
7th		Understands primitive numbers, expanded number bases	Identifies null sets, proper and improper subsets, unequal sets	
8th		Understands scientific notation, absolute value, solving inequalities	Understands replacement set of a variable, set builder	

(continued)

B

Grade Level	Addition	Subtraction	Story Problems	Geometry
K			Solves oral problems using "one more" Solves oral problems using "one less"	Recognizes and reproduces ○ □ ▭ △ Recognizes and reproduces straight and curved lines
1st	Knows facts 1–10 Adds facts 1–10 horizontally and vertically Adds 2 digits no regrouping	Knows facts 1–10 Subtracts 2 digits no regrouping Subtracts facts 1–10 horizontally and vertically	Solves written addition and subtraction problems 0–5	Recognizes and reproduces ◇ Recognizes line segments not closed curves
2nd	Knows facts 11–20 Adds 3 digits no regrouping Completes number sentences with missing digits	Knows facts 11–20 Subtracts 3 digits no regrouping Uses number sentences with missing digits	Solves written addition and subtraction problems through 20 1-step problems	Recognizes cone, semi-circle, congruent figures, intersecting curves, labeled points
3rd	Adds 2 and 3 digits with regrouping Adds by endings	Subtracts 2 and 3 digits with regrouping Checks by addition	Solves problems using + and − × and ÷ 2-step problems	Recognizes spheres and cylinders, rays, planes, right angles, parallel lines Understands diameter and radius
4th	Knows vocabulary Adds 1 to 3 digits and 5 addends with regrouping Commutative and associative properties expanded	Knows vocabulary Subtracts 2 to 4 digits with regrouping	Solves multiple-step problems + − × ÷ Writes number sentences Solves problems with averages	Recognizes prism, pyramid, cube, triangular & rectangular prisms and tetrahedron, perpendicular and intersecting lines, planes, and line segments

(continued)

B (continued)

Grade Level	Addition	Subtraction	Story Problems	Geometry
5th	Adds 2 addends with 5 columns Adds 3 addends with 4 columns Adds 4 addends with 4 columns Adds equations Averages	Subtracts 4 and 5 digits with regrouping Understands 0	Solves multiple-step problems using fractions, decimals, ratio, measurement graphs (bar and circle)	Measures angles Understands Pythagorean Theorem Recognizes polygons Recognizes right, congruent, and similar triangles Measures triangles
6th	Adds Base 2	Subtracts Base 2	Solves problems dealing with time, work, rate, distance, and speed	Uses equations to find volume Finds perimeter and area Identifies and draws angles, isosceles and equilateral triangles
7th	Maintain concepts	Maintain concepts	Solves expanded story problems	Recognizes trapezoids, optical illusions, convex polygons, Classifies triangles Understands mean, median, and mode
8th	Maintain concepts	Maintain concepts	Solves expanded story problems	Proves triangles congruent through properties Measures exterior and interior angles Knows properties of circles, spheres, cylinders, cones, prisms, and pyramids

(continued)

C

Grade Level	Standard Measurement	Metric Measurement	Symbols of Math	Multiplication
K	Understands simple comparison in length, size, and weight			
1st	Knows days of the week Tells time on the hour, half-hour, and day Knows temperature Knows pint, quart, cup Knows inch, foot, yard Knows weight Compares inch and half-inch	Uses centimeter to find lengths	Recognizes +, −, < > =, and ≠	
2nd	Knows months of the year Relates inches to feet Knows gallon	Uses liter and milliliter	Recognizes < >, =, and ≠	Multiplies products through 25 Relates multiplication to repeated addition
3rd	Tells time in 5-minute intervals Tells time in quarter hours Converts inches, feet, yards Converts half-pint, quart Uses calendar, week, month Uses scale Measures to nearest ½ or ¼ inch Reads a digital clock Reads Celsius or Fahrenheit scale thermometer	Knows relationship of meters and centimeters, grams, and kilograms, liters and milliliters	Recognizes ×, ÷, ″, and ′	Multiplies facts through 45 Multiplies 2 digits by 1 digit, 3 digits by 1 digit, 10 digits by 1 digit
4th	Finds perimeter of shapes Understands dry measures (weight) Understands volume, area, square inch, and square mile Converts one unit of measure to another	Uses scale to read kilograms	Uses letter *n* for missing number Recognizes metric symbols: cm, m, kg, and l Recognizes ∩ intersection of sets	Knows vocabulary Multiplies facts through 81 Multiplies multiples of 100, 1,000 Multiplies with regrouping

(continued)

C (continued)

Grade Level	Standard Measurement	Metric Measurement	Symbols of Math	Multiplication
5th	Understands zones, belts, standard time Reads graphs (bar graph, line graph, pictograph) Solves time problems Finds area of squares and rectangles Uses solid measurements Reads road map Understands latitude and longitude	Shows metric comparisons Understands metric scale drawings Knows ratio of measures	Recognizes subset ⊂, super subset ⊃, union of sets ∪	Multiplies 3 digits by 3 digits Multiplies 4 digits by 3 digits Identifies prime numbers
6th	Finds approximation of area Finds area of triangle, circle Finds circumference	Understands approximation of area Knows abbreviations of metric units Converts to larger and smaller units	Recognizes %, π, c	Knows modular multiplication Knows lattice method of multiplication Knows square root Multiplies by 4 digits Multiplies with decimals and mixed fractions
7th	Finds the precision of a measurement Finds lateral and surface area Finds area of a parallelogram	Can write metric abbreviations in order: kilo, hecto, deca, deci, centi, milli Converts lengths to decimal measures	Recognizes null set ( ) Recognizes empty set ∅	Understands cubes and cube root
8th	Understands mass, conversion factors, ratio and proportion, hypotenuse and square root	Converts standard to metric measurement	Recognizes degrees n°, congruent figures ≅, absolute value |a|	Knows operations with approximate numbers Multiplies numbers written in scientific notation Multiplies negative and positive rational numbers Multiplies negative and positive integers

(continued)

D

Grade Level	Division	Fractions	Decimals/ Percent	Money
K		Divides shapes in ½ Divides sets in ½		Identifies penny, nickel, dime
1st		Divides shapes and sets in ¼		Identifies quarters Compares value of penny, nickel, dime
2nd		Divides shapes and sets in ⅓		Knows symbols $ ¢ Substitutes money values: penny, nickel, dime, quarter Identifies change after purchase
3rd	Divides facts through 45 Divides problems with remainders Divides using multiples of ten	Divides shapes and sets in ½, ¼, ⅓		Compares money value 50¢ and $1.00 Adds and subtracts money problems
4th	Knows vocabulary Divides facts through 81 Divides $3\overline{)27}$ $3\overline{)638}$ $10\overline{)181}$ Checks answers by multiplication	Adds and subtracts fractions with like denominators Adds and subtracts fractions with unlike denominators Adds and subtracts mixed numbers		Adds purchases and counts out change
5th	Divides by 2-digit divisor with quotient remainder Divides 3-digit divisor Averages	Multiplies a whole number by a fraction, A fraction by a fraction, A mixed number by a whole number, A mixed number by mixed number	Identifies place value Solves decimal- fraction and equivalence Adds, subtracts, and reads and writes decimals to tenths and hundredths Adds and subtracts 2-decimal numbers to hundredths Multiplies whole numbers by decimals	

(continued)

D (continued)

Grade Level	Division	Fractions	Decimals/ Percent	Money
6th	Divides by divisor with three or more digits Divides with fractions Divides with decimals	Divides fractions with like and unlike denominators Divides improper fractions Divides mixed numbers	Understands, reads, writes through billions Extends meaning through millionths Counts by tenths, hundredths, thousandths Adds and subtracts 2 decimals to thousandths Writes decimal equations for proper and improper fractions Multiplies decimal by decimal Divides by whole number or decimal number Computes percent of a number	
7th	Divides positive and negative integers	Simplifies expressions containing fractions Understands ratio and proportion Understands ratio and percent	Understands terminating and repeating decimals	
8th	Uses properties of division for rational numbers		Divides and multiplies decimals	

1. "Today I am going to teach you to use a strategy that will help you to find the answers to word problems found in books and on tests."
2. "Watch me and listen to me as I read the problem and talk about it as I try to figure out how to find the answer" (emphasize the words, *watch* and *listen* in voice tone) or "Watch me as I read the problem and try to get a picture in my mind of what is there and what needs to be done."
3. "In order to solve this problem I need to use a strategy. The strategy has _____ steps. Number 1 . . . 2 . . . 3 . . ." (the teacher writes them on the chalkboard as he or she speaks). "Let me repeat the steps again. Let's do another problem just like this one and we can all use the strategy."
4. "You are solving a problem. Let me help you. Let me give you a hint. Remember how I showed you how to see the problem in your mind's eye. You can close your eyes if you want to and try to see it. Tell me what you think and see."

Verbal assistance and modeling statements that make things visible to the learner are good support devices.

An overview of what is to be learned is also classified as an advance organizer (Ausubel, 1960). The overview often helps the learner identify his or her previous experiences and knowledge of the concepts or topics discussed. An outline of the key topics or headings or even a semantic map of key words or ideas can be helpful. The same techniques apply to the teaching of reading (Rakow & Gee, 1988).

With very young children, K–1 lessons should begin with simple basic objects. Use pencils, books, apples, and so on to demonstrate concepts. Once the operation of addition and subtraction is fully understood, go to written problems. With children in grades 1–2 that understand basic addition and subtraction, Sterns material or Cuisenaire rods are useful in helping students visualize operations. Cuisenaire rods are also good for teaching older students to multiply and divide and do simple fractions.

Students should not be forbidden to use their fingers at first, if this helps them to conceptualize their math problems. Numbers should be made as real as possible. As an alternative to doing just pages of addition, subtraction, and so on for homework, the student can work on one practical story problem. Problems can be written around going to the park with money, the scores of the school's baseball team, and similar events.

Computer exercises and tests are less intimidating than worksheets, since a single key can wipe out an incorrect response. Math games and puzzles are great motivators; at the same time math is learned without stress from graded studies. Students will spend hours playing math games on a computer or with one another or working math puzzles. This helps to develop a positive attitude toward math.

MODERN MATH

Modern math requires an extensive vocabulary and the understanding and correct usage of many basic and complex language skills. Vocabulary such as *sets, subsets, collection, elements, infinite sets, intersection,* and the like are difficult for some students to master. Heavy emphasis on language limits many students and results in the misunderstanding of concepts. Other pitfalls of modern math include the use of set notation in the primary grades and parents who are unable to help.

Some students do not understand the phrase "difference between" to mean subtract. Some don't understand which is larger, 34 or 33, since they are the same height. Some children find it difficult to acquire basic language concepts such as the difference between *more and less, sooner or later,* and *higher or lower.* If/then concepts are also a problem (e.g., If four cars equal 16 tires, then one car equals _____ tires).

The student with the restricted language code and a limited vocabulary usually has problems with a heavy language load. Facts can be mastered by the majority of students. Expanded notation should not be presented until the student understands place value. The use of symbols of an empty set, as well as the use of symbols for more than and less than, should be presented only after there is real understanding of the meaning of the concepts. The elimination of drill in some programs has limited some students from developing good computation skills. Use of set notation before there was a complete understanding of the concepts has resulted in confusion for a large number of LD children. An increasing number of schools are beginning to include a more traditional approach in the teaching of math in the primary grades.

Preteaching

Preteaching involves teaching a critical component or components or a task prior to introducing the entire operation. This involves:

1. Introducing and applying a new rule in arithmetic to a complex problem

2. Applying the new rule to other arithmetic problems
3. Extending the rule application to even more complex problems
4. Working the rule into complex problems with the help of the teacher
5. Working the rule into complex problems with reduced or without teacher involvement

Preteaching appears to have a positive effect on the learning of new and complex multicomponent skills in arithmetic (Kameenui & Carnine, 1986).

Mastery Learning

Students learning for mastery need to understand that they are competing only with themselves. They can work at their own pace, moving quickly through material that is easy for them and more slowly through concepts they find difficult. There are no failures, since a poor performance on a mastery test simply indicates a need for another period of study until the material is mastered and this is demonstrated. Students do not move on to a new lesson until the preceding concepts have been learned. Teacher-graded exercises and examinations often cause anxiety to the unsure and nervous learner.

Exemplary Programs

Exemplary programs are reported to have the following characteristics (Tobin & Fraser, 1989):

1. A high level of managerial efficiency is needed, where teachers maintain control-at-a-distance. Teachers move around the room and make contact with each student. Students can work by themselves or in small groups. Rules and structure are in place, but students appear to be happy and content to operate within a modicum of structure. Routines are established and followed. Students with diverse needs are encouraged to seek help and participate.
2. Good teachers use strategies that do not embarrass students. These "safety nets," such as one-on-one, private interaction to review problems instead of telling the whole class about "John's 'disaster,'" give the student a sense of security. Sarcasm is never used. Partially correct responses are accepted and rewarded.
3. Using good eye contact, calling on all students instead of just the same ones, and understanding the needs of those who do not want to risk a public

wrong response are all important for good class participation.
4. Good teachers strive for optimal student understanding of math concepts. A whole array of materials and strategies need to be employed to help students learn. Questioning, paraphrasing, clarification, and elaboration must become a part of each lesson.
5. The content knowledge of the teacher is essential to security in teaching, as well as getting away from texts, and participating in mind-expanding problem solving with students. The teacher must be able to deal with the misconceptions of students. This requires that the instructor be well-grounded in the subject matter.
6. Good teachers are said to maintain a positive learning environment. Exemplary teachers are found to be knowledgeable and "harder" as far as students perceived difficulty. They create a more favorable environment (Fraser, 1987) and are also seen as good organizers and managers.

WRITING NUMERALS

Writing numerals is different from understanding their value. Numerals must be legible to the writer and reader, and aligned so computation can be accomplished without confusion. Learning to write numerals is very much like learning to write letters and should also be part of penmanship practice.

When introducing children to a numeral form, it is helpful if the teacher analyzes the parts of the numeral aloud. Many children will learn from a "we do this first, and then we do this" approach. Others see the whole configuration at once. It is helpful to leave a completed figure on the board and draw a second model while the learners observe. Children should say the name of the numeral at the same time it is written. Children should realize that various forms of numerals (such as four) are the same numeral.

Children sometimes reverse numerals. Some children, especially left-handers, reverse consistently into second grade. Others do it only occasionally. Until the second grade, there is no need to be overly concerned. Position is not important to young children and many normal immature writers exhibit this behavior. The reasons for the reversals include a lack of concern as to how the numeral is supposed to be written or a lack of ability to remember the directions.

Occasionally a child seems to use both hands equally well. Only one hand should be used for writing. When use of either hand is equally comfortable, encourage the right hand.

For practicing numeral formation, always have the students see a model that includes all ten numerals (0–9).

Materials

1. A set of sandpaper or felt numerals
2. A set of numeral cards made from yarn or string glued on cardboard
3. Numerals cut from nubby fabric and glued onto cards
4. Numerals cut from wood or plywood (both the template and the cut-out numeral can be traced)
5. Newsprint and large felt-tip markers
6. A magic slate

For children who have trouble copying from a distance, each child should have a model of each numeral on the desk, as well as a model on the board. Children can cross out rather than erase unsatisfactory attempts so the teacher can see what they did.

Common Errors

1. Directionality Problem

$$\begin{array}{r} 38 \\ + 9 \\ \hline 137 \end{array}$$

The student added 8 and 9 correctly then added 1 to 3 and then added 9. The student became confused and went diagonally to the lower right instead of straight down. Graph paper is helpful in correcting this problem, or the teacher can give students clues by using color (magic markers) so that they will maintain proper placement in arithmetic.

2. Mirror Writing

a. $\begin{array}{r} 37 \\ -12 \\ \hline 16 \end{array}$ or b. $\begin{array}{r} 37 \\ -12 \\ \hline 1 \end{array}$

In example a, the student reversed his or her number position when writing it. In example b, mirror writing may be indicated. This can be seen in reading or writing (saw/was).

3. Visually Misperceived Signs (Rotational)

$$\begin{array}{r} 59 \\ + 3 \\ \hline 168 \end{array}$$

The student confused + sign with × sign. The teacher can circle the sign in red and call the student's attention to the process.

4. Mixed Process

$$\begin{array}{r} 29 \\ \times 3 \\ \hline 47 \end{array}$$

The first part was correct (multiplying 9 by 3 and carrying the ten to the column on the left). Instead of multiplying 2 by 3 and adding the 2, the student switched the process and added the 2 and the carried 2.

Initial Teaching Sequence

It appears that number concepts need to be developed in a sequential manner. This consideration is particularly important when teaching students who have difficulties in processing information. In arithmetic, as in other areas of skill development, the level of presentation that appears to be most successful is the concrete one. This implies that the teacher must include a great deal of manipulative activities as part of the instructional program in each of the following developmental task areas:

ENTITY IDENTIFICATION
I give you the ball; pencil; crayon; etc.
You give the ball to John.
John gives the ball to Mary.
You take the ball away from Mary.

CONCEPT OF REMOVAL (GAIN AND LOSS)
1. Show that something is there.
2. Remove and show that it is gone (nothing is there).
3. You give something and you have none or some left.
4. You get something and you have more—someone else has less.

OBJECT MEMORY (CONSTANCY)
1. Remove an object unseen from among two, three, or four and say, "What did I take away?"
2. Place an object unseen from among two, three, or four and say, "What did I put in?"

MORE AND LESS
1. Add objects to show more.
2. Remove objects to show less.
3. Show comparable quantities, and ask the child to show which has more and which less.

VISUAL DISCRIMINATION (MATCHING)
Shape

1. Begin with small geometric solids and let the students feel and describe the differences and similarities between the various forms.
2. Use form boards, including metal insets or templates, to teach discrimination.
3. Pair off objects and forms, as in a Noah's ark.
4. Pictures or dittos of objects and geometric shapes can be used for matching purposes. Have the learner look for differences as well as likenesses.

Size

1. Use insets or "nesting material"—cans that fit into cans, barrels that fit into barrels, or boxes that fit into boxes.
2. Group cylinders, blocks, etc., by size.
3. Use different-size rods or wooden dowels.
4. Montessori material that can be used here includes the Pink Tower, the Brown Staircase, and Knobless Cylinders.
5. Use pictures of geometric shapes and objects for size differentiation.
6. Use graded insets, including objects or geometric shapes. For example: · • ● ●

GROUPING OR SETS

1. Begin with hula hoops and put objects inside.
2. Use regular dominoes: [: | ::] ; then proceed to dominoes with sets: [: · | ·•·]
3. Use figure-ground activities found on page 388.
4. Use matching sets of objects and forms printed on dittos. The learner will trace around identical objects or forms with the same color crayon.
5. Use tachistoscopic activities in which the teacher exposes groups of dots for short periods. Begin with widely separated dots and gradually move the dots closer together. Blocks or coins can be used in the same manner.

VOCABULARY OF SPATIAL-TEMPORAL RELATIONSHIPS

1. Use a concrete object (such as a toy monkey) and a box or some other container to teach concepts of space such as *over, under, inside, outside, below, above, beside, next, near, alongside.*
2. The same concepts can be taught using a toy squirrel and a cardboard tree.

3. Concepts of time can be taught using stories or real experiences such as field trips that include such words as *sooner, later, late, before, after, morning, afternoon, night, past, shortly afterward, almost,* and *often.*
4. Send students on an errand and time them. How long did it take to get there? Did it take more time to get back? Was it a long or short trip?
5. Parents can do many reinforcing activities during routine, day-to-day experiences at home or when traveling.

ESTIMATION

In all of the following activities, the students will be required to make judgments about spatial relationships without physically matching at first. After making an estimation, they can check for accuracy by manipulating the material or by other physical movements, such as pacing off the distance.

Size

1. The students can estimate the size of other children in the class. Compare two students—"Who is shorter?" "Who is taller?" Then compare three or more students—"Who is the tallest?" "Who is the shortest?"
2. Ask the students to compare objects in terms of larger and smaller.
3. Place objects into various size piles and ask the students to rank them by size.
4. Use different size cards with their respective envelopes, and ask the students to estimate which card goes with which size envelope. Do not let the students physically manipulate the materials at first. Later, they can check for accuracy.
5. Give the students different size objects and different size containers, and let them estimate which object will fit into which container.
6. Have the students physically compare different size rods or dowels and rank them from smallest to largest.
7. Use ditto sheets that require the students to compare the relative size of lines and geometric forms.

Weight

1. Have the students hold and compare objects of different weights (begin with gross differences, then go to finer differences).
2. Ask the students to estimate the relative weights of objects without holding them. For example, "Which is heavier—a car or a bus?"

3. Using different piles of similar objects, the student should rank them by weight from lightest to heaviest.

Shape

1. Have the students estimate the fit of simple puzzle pieces.
2. Have the students use form boxes to make judgments about shapes.
3. Use ditto sheets that require the students to estimate shapes that interlock.

Distance

1. Ask students to estimate how many steps are required to go from one place to another (begin with short distances first).
2. Have students estimate how far they can throw a ball.
3. Have students estimate the relative distance of objects to themselves and from object to object in the classroom or outside of school. For example, "Which is closest to you—the tree or the fence?" "Which is further from the fence—the house or the telephone pole?"
4. Have students estimate the relative distance between a fixed point such as their homes or the classroom and other geographic locations that are familiar.
5. Use ditto sheets containing lines, geometric forms, or objects and have the students compare the relative distance of two or more objects from a fixed point, such as a small dot in the middle of the page, or from each other (begin with very simple comparisons).

COUNTING (ORAL)

1. Begin by teaching rote counting from one to five through songs such as "One Little, Two Little, Three Little Indians." (Later, count from one through ten.)
2. Follow the counting songs with Finger Plays. Begin with one to five and later count from one to ten.
3. Have the students do rote counting from one to ten.

COUNTING WITH MEANING (ONE-TO-ONE CORRESPONDENCE)

1. Begin by asking a student to give each student in the class a piece of paper or some other item that needs to be distributed.
2. Have the students fill a row of holes with pegs, beads, pebbles, or discs.
3. A variation of number two would be the addition of a drum beat as the learner performs each task.

4. Play Tea Time and have a student prepare settings of napkins, dishes, and utensils for a group of children who are already seated. A more advanced activity of this nature would be to prepare settings for a specific number of individuals who are not present.
5. Use paper dolls, and have the students give each one a costume.
6. Have the students match nuts and bolts and fit them together.
7. Use 2" × 2" cardboard squares, and have the students put wooden, plastic, felt, or magnetic numerals from one to five on each numbered square (later, from one to ten in each square). Begin as a matching exercise first and then go to rote memory.
8. Have the students count different groupings of students in the class.
9. Have the students count pennies, boxes, cylinders, stars in the flag, etc.
10. Have the students count things in the classroom by categories such as the number of pieces of chalk, erasers, and books on a shelf.

AUDITORY-VISUAL SYMBOL ASSOCIATION

1. Begin with wooden, plastic, felt, or magnetic numerals and have the students arrange them in order from one to five and later from one to ten. Say a numeral, hold it up, and have the students match by pointing to the correct one.
2. Have the students copy from a model as you say each numeral.
3. Have the students look in newspapers or magazines for numerals that they later can identify.
4. Use ditto sheets on which students circle all of one number while they say the number.
5. Use color-by-number games. Say a number and have the students color the area containing the number. The completed area colored by the students should form an identifiable design.

SYMBOL-VALUE ASSOCIATION (SETS)

1. Use Pop It Beads and say, "Show me one," etc.
   a. ●
   b. ● ●
   c. ● ● ●
2. Use the Maria Montessori formula as follows:
   a. Say, "This is (●) one."
      "This is (● ●) two."
      "This is (● ● ●) three."
   b. Put beads in order.
   c. Say, "Show me one." ●
      "Show me two." ● ●
      "Show me three." ● ● ●

d. Say, "Give me one." •

"Give me two." • •

"Give me three." • • •

e. Make another set the same size as item 1 above, and label as follows:

Say, "This is ⊡ ."

"This is ⊡ ."

"This is ⊡ ."

3. Use a pegboard and have the students say the correct numeral as they match the number of pegs with the symbol equivalent. See Figure 11-1, for example.

4. Use beads, buttons, blocks, or coins to correspond with numerals from one to five (later from one to ten).

5. Have the students name things that come in twos, such as feet, eyes, ears, and hands; in threes, such as tricycle wheels, or a three-legged stool; in fours, such a dog's legs, chair legs, table legs, and car's tires; in fives, such as fingers, toes, pennies to a nickel, and points on a star.

6. Have the students make impressions of groups in clay, using pennies, beans, dowels, etc.

7. Have the students find pictures in magazines or books of different numbers of items.

8. Playing cards are good for learning and identifying sets.

9. Use small cans labeled from one to ten, with a corresponding number of ice-cream sticks or counters in them, to teach symbol-value associations (sets).

CARDINAL AND ORDINAL RELATIONSHIPS

1. Begin with three or four toy cars in a line near a toy house or a garage and ask the following questions:
   a. Which one is closest?
   b. Which one is farthest away?
   c. Which car is at the beginning of the line?
   d. Which car is at the end of the line?

   Note: As the learner responds, the teacher should say, "Yes, this is the first car, or second car, etc."

Figure 11-1

e. Continue to ask questions about the third car, fourth car, etc.

2. Give the students number cards and teach the cardinal values of one to five and the values to ten later. Have the students line up in groups of five or ten. When you call the cardinal number, the student with that number holds it up.

3. Play "office building" and decide on what floors certain things will need to go.

4. Label your bookshelves first, second, third, fourth, etc.

5. After the students can read the words, begin using cardinal directions when putting assignments on the chalkboard.

6. Use ordinal numbers in everyday activities in the classroom. For example, line up the class by saying, "Row one will line up first, row five will line up second . . ."

PLACE VALUE SYSTEM

Place value allows us to use the same ten digits over and over again to express ever-enlarging numbers. In our system a digit takes on a different value as it moves to a different place.

Students need to understand that the smallest place—the one's place—is the farthest to the right, and that as you move to the left a digit takes a value 10 times greater than it had in the place before.

To teach place value, each student should have a place value frame of their own. A very simple one can be made by taking a piece of construction paper, folding it up three inches and then folding it all in thirds (see diagram). Each child should then be given 30 2-½" × ⅝" strips of a different color construction paper.

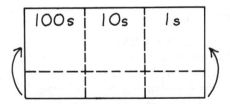

The teacher draws a place value chart on the board and asks a student to select any number of colored markers and place them in the three pockets of the frame to form a number. The teacher then duplicates the markers on the board and asks the student to come up and write the numbers the markers stand for, under the markers.

The students then take turns making new numbers. A followup activity would have them making up new numbers, showing the markers on a ditto and then writing the numbers they represent underneath.

Hundreds	Tens	Ones

304

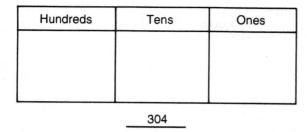

Figure 11–3

Later, this activity could be reversed and a number could be shown for a student to illustrate.

The results of behavioral intervention studies indicated that the use of manipulatives and pictures facilitated initial acquisition of place value skills. In addition, modeling, demonstration, and feedback by the teacher in problem solving was also deemed effective (Vaughn, McIntosh, & Spencer-Rowe, 1991).

SIMPLE ADDITION AND SUBTRACTION

1. Teach alignment by using "see through" color pens (see Figure 11-2).
2. Use concrete materials such as rods to represent one or entire groupings (see Figure 11-3).
3. Write basic addition and substraction number facts on small oak tag strips and place in small draw-string cloth bags. The student can reach into the bags and pull them out. Write the answers on the back of the cards to make them self-checking.
4. Using ditto sheets, teach addition and subtraction facts in all the ways shown in Figure 11-4.

SIMPLE MULTIPLICATION

1. Begin by teaching *skip counting,* for example, 2, 4, 6, 8, 10, 12, 14, 16, 18, 20, 22, 24.
   a. The students can begin with Pop It Beads or blocks and work simultaneously on small ditto sheets, on which are written the first and ending numeral (Figure 11-5). The students can count the beads and write the numerals, in that way checking their work.
   b. After the students have learned to skip count from two through ten, they can do larger ditto sheets with many different numeral combinations. Make up ditto sheets with blanks so they can be used for any numeral.

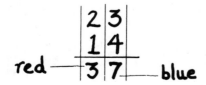

Figure 11–2

$2+3=$ $\square+3=5$ $2+\square=5$ $2+3=\square$

$$\begin{array}{r} 2 \\ +3 \\ \hline \end{array} \quad \begin{array}{r} \square \\ +3 \\ \hline 5 \end{array} \quad \begin{array}{r} 2 \\ +\square \\ \hline 5 \end{array} \quad \begin{array}{r} 3 \\ +2 \\ \hline \square \end{array}$$

$3-2=$ $\square-2=1$ $3-\square=1$ $3-2=\square$

$$\begin{array}{r} 3 \\ -2 \\ \hline \end{array} \quad \begin{array}{r} \square \\ -2 \\ \hline 1 \end{array} \quad \begin{array}{r} 3 \\ -\square \\ \hline 1 \end{array} \quad \begin{array}{r} 3 \\ -2 \\ \hline \square \end{array}$$

Figure 11–4

2. When he students have learned all of their skip counting, they can begin to use matrix sheets. The students can put the numerals across the top and down the left-hand side using different colored pencils (Figure 11-6). They can then fill in the matrix, working down or across. This will help them to see that 4 × 3, for example, is the same as 3 × 4.
3. Use ditto sheets with numerals on them. In the box at the top of the page put the multiplication fact you want the students to practice. See Figure 11-7, for example.
4. Teach multiplication in all of the ways shown in Figure 11-8.
5. Have the students do arrays, whereby the student counts the intersections. (See Figure 11-9.)
6. Use multiplication drills (See Figure 11-10.)

SIMPLE DIVISION

1. Have the students group Pop It Beads or blocks according to your directions. For example, "How many groups of 3 equal 6?"
2. Have a student distribute buttons or coins equally or with a remainder to fellow students.
3. Use a numberline to teach simple division with remainder. See Figure 11-11, for example.
4. Simple matrix sheets (Figure 11-12) can also be used to teach division.

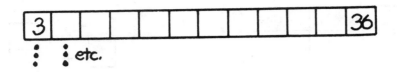

Figure 11–5

5. Teach division in all of the ways shown in Figure 11-13.
6. Use simple drills, including the one in Figure 11-14.

DECIMAL POINT

Introduce the idea that a rational number may be written in a decimal form. Through class discussion, show how each place is ten times the value of its neighbor to the right.

Thousand	Hundred	Ten	One
(10x100)	(10x10)	(10x1)	1

Note also that the place to the right is 1/10th of its neighbor to the left.

Thousand	Hundred	Ten	One
($\frac{1}{10}$ of 10,000)	($\frac{1}{10}$ of 1,000)	($\frac{1}{10}$ of 100)	($\frac{1}{10}$ of 10)

Show students that in writing money we use the decimal point to separate whole numbers from fractional parts.

1 penny equals 1/100 of a dollar.
1 penny equals .01 of a dollar or $.01.

1 dime equals 1/10 of a dollar or 10 pennies (10/100).
1 dime equals .1 of a dollar or $.10.

Later, students can be taught to read and write decimals through hundreds by using a simple place value chart. Be sure to point out that the decimal point is read as "and."

X	2	3	4	5
2				
3				
4				
5				

Figure 11–6

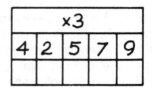

Figure 11–7

Have the students practice reading numerals as you write them on the board in this format:

73.4	seventy three and 4 tenths
80.26	eighty and 26 hundreths
1.2	one and two tenths
0.54	fifty four hundreths

Have them make up their own numerals to read to the class.

Hundreds	Tens	Ones	Tenths	Hundredths
	7	3	4	
	8	0	2	6
		1	2	
		0	5	4

SIMPLE FRACTIONS

1. Teach division of shapes and sets by using concrete objects, then repeat these on the ditto sheets. For example, see Figure 11-15.

$$3 \times 4 = \square \qquad \square \times 4 = 12 \qquad 3 \times \square = 12 \qquad 3 \times 4 = \square$$

$$\begin{array}{c} 4 \\ \times 3 \\ \hline \end{array} \qquad \begin{array}{c} 4 \\ \times \square \\ \hline 12 \end{array} \qquad \begin{array}{c} \square \\ \times 3 \\ \hline 12 \end{array} \qquad \begin{array}{c} 4 \\ \times 3 \\ \hline \square \end{array}$$

Figure 11–8

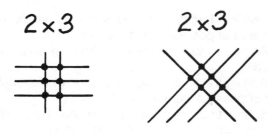

Figure 11–9

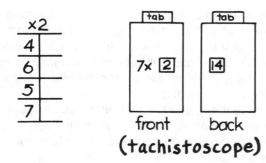

(tachistoscope)

Figure 11–10

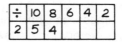

Figure 11–12

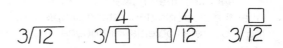

Figure 11–13

$$\div 4$$
$$8 \mid$$
$$16 \mid$$
$$36 \mid$$
$$24 \mid$$

Figure 11–14

2. Make a set of materials out of wooden dowels. Take a rod of 24-inch-long doweling and cut it into six 4-inch pieces. Leave four of the pieces whole to use for teaching division of sets and cut the other two pieces (one in half and one in fourths) to use in teaching division of shapes. The advantage of using wooden doweling is that the students can hold two or four pieces in their hands and put them together to see the whole, or they can line the four dowels up and see that ½ of 4 is 2. The dowels are also good for tracing around prior to working the problem.

3. Teach fractions 1, ½, ⅓, ⅙ using concrete material. Cut out of construction paper: (1) 1 (whole) red, (2) ½ blue, (3) ⅓ green, (6) ⅙ yellow. Let the children play with them first so they can discover what makes a whole. When the student can identify the various pieces, teach reasoning using the colored forms. Which is bigger, a third, or a sixth, etc?

Use the colored forms to teach fractional relationships.

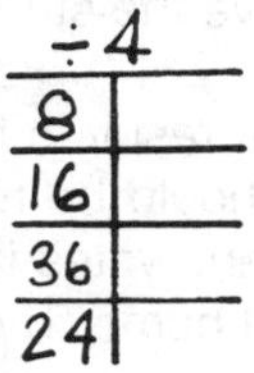

2/6 + 4/6 =   2/3 + 2/6 =
½ + ½ = 2/2 = 1   ⅓ + 2/6 =
½ + 3/6 =   ½ + ⅓ + ⅙ =
4/6 + ⅓ =

Simplifying fractiions

Simplify 6/6, use fewer than 6 pieces.

Borrowing in Subtracting fractions

Find the value of 1⅓ − ⅓. Students have to convert to work the problem.

Drill work that lets a student respond anonymously.
  a. Everybody Show Card Holder - a 5/8″ construction paper, one 8″ edge folded and stapled to make a 1″ pocket at the bottom, a set of numerals 0–9. Give addition fact, subtraction fact, or multiplication fact and a child finds the

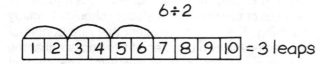

6÷2

= 3 leaps

Figure 11–11

Figure 11–15

515

numerals, places in the holder. When the teacher says "everybody show", the students hold up their holders to show the answers.
 b. Use individual chalk boards
 c. Thumbs up for right, down for wrong
 d. Bingo—teacher reads the problems and students find the answers
4. After the students understand simple fractions using concrete objects, introduce them to ditto sheets.

Use of Flash Cards
Ways to learn facts:

1. Show the flash card and answer orally.
2. Show the flash card and write the answer—watch for hesitations. Have the student write the problem three times.
3. With problems that result in hesitations or that are wrong, the work should be redone and discussed aloud as the student writes it. Parents should also test the students at home. The learner either knows the answer or doesn't and writes and says it again.
4. The student should write the entire problem and not just the answers. Having to write the problems five times is a strong motivator for learning.

TEACHING FRACTIONS TO OLDER STUDENTS

The learning disabled student in the eighth grade is likely to be working on drills in multiplication and division while his or her agemates are working on fractions, decimals, percentages, and algebra. The learning disabled student should be introduced to fractions, percentages, and decimals in a controlled manner. There is a maturity factor operating here, in that the students need to feel they are doing what the other students their own age are doing. The process involves directed, diagnostic teaching combined with using number facts that the students know reasonably well (Atkinson, 1983).

The strategy for instruction in fractions involves following a teaching sequence. Atkinson (1983, p. 403) lists the fractions teaching tasks as follows:

1. Multiplying simple fractions
2. Simplifying fractions
3. Cancelling
4. Changing mixed fractions to improper fractions and the reverse
5. Dividing simple fractions
6. Multiplying fractions, mixed numbers, and whole numbers (all possible combinations)

7. Dividing fractions, mixed numbers, whole numbers (all possible combinations)
8. Adding simple fractions, subtracting simple fractions
9. Adding fractions, mixed numbers, whole numbers (all possible combinations)
10. Subtracting fractions, mixed numbers, whole numbers (all possible combinations)

Instructional Sequence

1. Begin with multiplication of fractions; a strong feature being that both the numerator and denominator receive the same treatment in multiplication. Addition and subtraction of fractions present too many initial problems and require a more advanced understanding.
2. Provide the student with an effective stragegy that he or she can apply in a variety of ways.
3. Provide daily timed exercises in multiplication and division facts as well as fractions.
4. Practice to increase speed in doing drills.

CONSERVATION OF QUANTITY

1. Pour equal amounts of sand into two containers of the same size

 Then pour one container of sand into another long, thin container ( ).
 Finally, pour the contents of the second container into a short, wide container ( ). Ask the students to tell you which one has more sand. If they do not understand, reverse the process; then repeat it.
2. Use money to teach conservation of quantity, beginning with a nickel equals five pennies, two nickels equal a dime, or a nickel and five pennies equal a dime, etc.
3. Use rods or dowels to represent different sizes. There is also a great deal of commercial material available to teach this concept.
4. Count out twenty sticks with a student. Make four bundles of five sticks each. Take two bundles of five sticks and make one bundle of ten sticks. Tell the student that one bundle of ten sticks equals two bundles of five sticks. The student should check by counting. Then tell the student that one bundle of ten sticks and two bundles of five sticks equal the twenty sticks you started out with. The student should count to check.

5. Fill a small measuring spoon full of water. Suck up the water with an eye dropper. Count the drops as they are squeezed back into the spoon. Did the amount stay the same when it was put back in the spoon drop by drop?

MEASUREMENT

1. Begin by rechecking the estimation ability of the student.
2. Use a yardstick and have the student measure the perimeter of the room.
3. Pour two pints of liquid into a quart jar and then four quarts into a gallon container.
4. Color each foot on a yardstick a different color.
5. The students can measure their desks and other areas of the room with a ruler.
6. Use ditto sheets and rulers (first with inches and later with half inches) and have the students measure lines of different length.
7. The students should draw their own lines and tell you how long they are.
8. Obtain a scale so the students can determine the relative weights of objects in the classroom.
9. The students should use a scale in order to better understand the concepts of equivalency. For example, sixteen ounces equal a pound.

MAPS AND GRAPHS

1. Use three-dimensional or raised forms to teach maps and graphs.
2. Use clay to teach land forms such as peninsular, isthmus, island, and lake.
3. Develop a globe by covering a balloon with papier-mâché and then painting it.
4. Draw simple maps of the classroom and have the students pace off and draw it to scale.
5. The students can draw maps of their bedrooms and then of their houses.
6. Older students enjoy designing their own treasure maps. This is an effective method of teaching the concepts of land forms, map legends, etc.
7. Graphs can be constructed from strips of oak tag and colored construction paper.
8. The students can graph their own progress in arithmetic and other subject areas.
9. The students can graph baseball and football scores, as well as scores in other sports and games.

PROCESS SIGNS

1. Begin by using wooden, plastic, sandpaper, or magnetic numerals, including process signs.

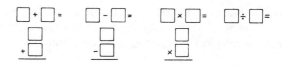

Figure 11–16

2. Blocks with numerals and process signs can also be used.
3. Use ditto sheets that include the forms shown in Figure 11-16.
4. Teach *greater than* and *less than,* using beads, blocks, or rods.
   Two is greater than one: **∶>•** One is less than two: **•<∶** The greater amount fits into the largest opening.
5. Use color-coded drawstring bags, each marked with a process sign, and in them put corresponding arithmetic problems on small oak tag strips. For example, a pink bag with a plus sign on it (🛍) will contain pink strips of oak tag with addition problems.

GEOMETRY

Learning disabled students find geometry difficult because of spatial-temporal problems. When geometry is studied from the kindergarten level up through the grades, the planar and spatial intuition of the student is enhanced (Gitter, 1976). Gitter further states that the earliest grades should include experiences in identifying geometric configurations. Young children need to learn to recognize shapes and name them. The students should have experiences examining objects and geometric forms by tracing around them with their fingers.

The geometric construct provides a source of visualization for arithmetic and algebra as well as a frame of reference by which physical space can be understood through mathematical manipulations. Gitter recommends that, to acquire such a frame of reference, children begin by

1. Visualizing various geometric configurations with and without manipulatives.
2. Constructing three-dimensional figures and then two-dimensional cut-outs in paper and cardboard.
3. Using paper folding or mirrors, etc., to examine symmetries of squares, rectangles, ellipses, circles, and solid figures like cubes, spheres, etc.
4. Using ruler and compass to compare points, lines, line segments, angles; to bisect an angle; etc.

As the student moves into the upper grades, he or she will have to learn not only more terminology, but deductive and inductive reasoning and formal proofs.

GRAPHIC LITERACY

A substantial amount of mathematical assessment involves the interpretation of graphs. Attention should be given to the development of graphic literacy by designating time for developing strategies for the interpretation of graphic information. Graphic literacy involves the ability to comprehend and draw conclusions from graphic information (Fry, 1981). It is also a valuable communication tool and one that learning disabled students would do well to master. Graphic literacy melds into the study skills segment of courses as well as having a potential for the development of creative writing. The following are useful activities:

1. Develop strategies for solving problems using graphic information.
2. Convert graphic information into mathematical statements.
3. Select and use a variety of graphic information from different math texts.
4. Use the overhead projector to explain graphic information.
5. Use newspaper articles, budget statements, and other numerical data and convert to graphic illustrations; then generate alternative analysis strategies for this information.

DEVELOPING THE CONCEPT OF TIME

Learning disabled children must develop a concept of time if they are to be successful in the study of mathematics, science, and social studies. Time has four primary components: telling time, sequence and duration, relationship between time and space, and the cyclical nature of time.

Very often the language of time is confusing because it does not represent the accuracy of the time segments used in our daily speed. For example:

"Wait just a minute." (not suggesting sixty seconds)
"I'll just be a few minutes." (how many minutes)
"This will take me ten minutes." (how many actual minutes)
"It's just about two o'clock." (how many minutes)

Language and Sense of Time

Students need to develop a vocabulary of time-related words such as *almost, before, near, after, later, now, soon, first, yesterday, last night,* etc. Examples of what moves fast and slow are useful for teaching a sense of time. Compare/contrast activities also give the student practice with time concepts (e.g., compare walking to running, early to late, cars to bicycles).

Duration, Sequence, and Cycles of Time

By seven or eight years of age, children can usually understand duration, sequence, and cycles (e.g., when something begins and ends and what occurs at about the same time each day). The student should be taught how the concept of subtraction applies to duration or intervals. A true sense of historical time does not develop until about age ten or eleven, but a sense of recent history can be taught earlier. For example, compare today to last week, month, and year. Duration can be taught by

1. Melting an ice cube (the students tell how long)
2. Burning a candle (the students determine the time elapsed)
3. Watching a turtle cross a table
4. Using a stop watch to time different activities
5. Developing a time line of events

Sequence can be taught by

1. Assembling a comic strip
2. Ordering photographs showing the growth of a plant
3. Discussing holidays on a calendar
4. Putting in order the pictures showing the highlights of a field trip

Cycles can be taught by

1. Listing what occurs when each day (once, twice, three times, etc.).
2. Examining cycles of the moon, sun, etc.

Telling Time

Generally there are three steps to telling time according to Burton and Edge (1985):

1. Understanding the concept of time (duration and sequence)
2. Using relevant nonstandard measures
3. Using nationally and universally accepted standard measures

Things to Consider for the Classroom

1. Children can learn to tell time to the hour and half hour before they gain a sense of historical time.
2. A reasonable sense of duration and sequence is necessary for using nonstandard measures, such as:
   a. Counting hand claps on the sweeps of a pendulum to see how much time has elapsed for a given event
   b. Using an egg timer to illustrate nonstandard time measurement
   c. Using a sundial

d. Showing nonstandard time by using a stop watch or a metronome
3. For standard time, do the following:
   a. Begin telling time to the hour (Hofmeister & de Fevre, 1977).
   b. With accuracy, tell time to the minute.
   c. Use counting to tell time to the minute (Reisman, 1978). The most common sequence is half hour, quarter hour, and minute.
   d. Jeffers (1979) believes in teaching the use of the digital clock as children are able to learn to use it, since it is so prevalent in our society. They can learn to use it even before they develop a concept of time.
   e. Children should watch the clock for certain specific times such as lunch.
   f. The teacher can appoint timekeepers.
   g. Make clocks from paper plates.
   h. Compare round and digital clock times.
   i. Write a daily schedule on the chalkboard.

Encourage the use of telling time throughout daily school and home routines and provide opportunities for the student to tell time by wearing a digital or regular watch.

A method of teaching time to learning disabled children, which has been found useful by many teachers, is as follows:

1. Purchase an old-fashioned Big Ben-type, large-face clock.
2. Remove the second hand and have the student
   a. Tell you when it is on the hour, just before, or just after the hour, using the hour hand only.
   b. Tell you when it is time to do certain things that involve classroom events (e.g., it is almost 12 o'clock—time for lunch).
   c. Tell you when it is about half past the hour because the hour hand is between the two numbers.
   d. Tell you when it is about a quarter after or a quarter before the hour.

The student needs to get a sense of what the hour hand really represents, after which he or she can be shown how the minute hand makes our judgment of time more precise. It is our opinion that learning disabled students have difficulty conceptualizing the concept of what an hour represents, and they neglect to stabilize the frame of reference for the hour hand. The minute hand is then introduced, and the amount of time elapsed is used in conjunction with the previously learned vocabulary. Example: It's about half past two. Looking at the hour hand it's half past two. Looking at the minute hand it's thirty minutes after two or two-thirty. Continue the sequence to the quarter hour, then to the number of minutes after and the number of minutes before the hour.

MONEY

Math sheets often fail to teach functional money skills because the illustrations of coins are often not very good. Real-type money provides more interest and the visual and tactile input that immediately transfers and generalizes to the student's reality of the environment. Real-looking coins can be purchased. Using real money sometimes causes too many problems.

The first thing the student has to understand is money organization and counting. Put all like denominations of bills or coins together and organize in diminishing value from left to right. The students should count larger values first. In transitioning the students, they need to be taught that when counting five- and one-dollar bills together, they have to shift from counting by fives to counting by ones. The same holds true for coins. Watch for perseveration from students and practice by having them count one $20, one $10, one $5, and three $1s first, before adding.

Students need to learn various bill combinations, such as:

1. $5 using 1's
2. $10 using 1's
3. $10 using 5's and 1's
4. $15 using 10's and 1's
5. $20 using 10's and 1's
6. $10 using 5's
7. $15 using 5's
8. $20 using 5's
9. $15 using 5's and 1's
10. $20 using 5's and 1's
11. $20 using 10's, 5's, and 1's
12. $20 using 10's and 5's

Introduce coin combinations in the following sequence: (1) pennies, (2) nickels, (3) nickels and pennies, (4) dimes, (5) dimes, nickels, and pennies, (6) quarters, and (7) quarters, dimes, nickels, and pennies.

Don't teach too many equivalencies at once (10¢ = 10 pennies, 10¢ = 2 nickels, 10¢ = 1 nickel and 5 pennies). Go slowly. It is recommended to teach all dimes first; then dimes with one nickel; all nickels; then quarters and nickels; followed by quarters and dimes; then quarters, dimes, and nickels; and finally, quarters, dimes, nickels, and pennies.

Making coin combinations and change should not be taught separately. Making change is done automatically at most cash registers, which show the customer the amount of money to be refunded.

CALCULATORS

Most adults use calculators at work or home for speed and accuracy in operations related to daily mathematics activities. Students should have an opportunity to use them in the classroom. Most younger students will need directions on how to operate and care for a calculator.

In the primary grades, the emphasis should be on using calculators for correction and feedback on completed pencil-and-paper tasks, for enjoyment and exploration, and in games. Sustained use may be more appropriate in the intermediate grades after the basic facts and simple operations have been mastered.

Some educators propose that calculators be permitted during achievement tests, especially for reasoning and problem-solving sections, where the steps to arriving at a solution are more informative than accuracy in the calculations.

TEACHING INTERMEDIATE AND SECONDARY STUDENTS

Theories of teaching secondary learning disabled students have focused on the development of interventions (Deshler, Schumaker, & Lenz, 1984). It is expected that these students will develop the minimum competencies in mathematics necessary to quality for high school graduation. Therefore, these students will of necessity be required to meet the same minimum competency of objectives as their agemates. Specific instructional ideas are needed which will work both to teach mathematics and to help the student to generalize math concepts to various content areas, such as science. Along with motivational deficits and learned helplessness, the learning disabled lack the strategies that enable them to succeed. The following are some suggestions that have been found to be useful in teaching mathematics. The teacher and student work together as a team.

1. The important principle is that the teacher and student agree that the skill area under study is important and needs to be learned.
2. The instructor verbalizes where the skill fits into the scheme of skills including the subskills.
3. The student reverbalizes the instructor's analysis.
4. The instructor shows the student how to practice the skill in a variety of ways.
5. The student practices the skill as the instructor observes and gives feedback.

6. The student practices the skill and self-checks. The instructor helps when needed.
7. The student extends the skill into other kinds of problems (generalization and in different settings).
8. The student takes the skill home for successful explanation and reinforcement.

Strategies for Problem Solving

Students need direct instruction in learning an awareness of strategies for problem solving. Teachers often explain "how" to solve a problem, but not how they know how to arrive at a solution. Modeling by the instructor of problem solving strategies has to occur throughout the year. Kresse (1984) recommends the following modeling sequence:

1. Visualization
2. Questioning
3. Answering
4. Giving evidence for answers
5. Reasoning or verbalizing why

Visualization is a form of "visual doodling." The student is encouraged to read a problem and draw a simple picture of the components in the problem. Visualization encourages the student to imagine or try to see the problem in his or her mind's eye.

The questioning phase involves analyzing problems on the chalkboard. The students examine a problem and decide what is extraneous information; what can be deleted and still give just enough information for working the problem.

Reasoning and verbalizing why an answer was given promotes more conscious generalization to solving similar problems in other settings. In more traditional approaches to teaching word problems, the teacher gives the students many problems with the hope that subconscious generalization will occur. In an SQ2R strategy, the student would Survey, Question, Read, and Recite and possibly check the answer. In a metacognitive approach, the student would also be asked to check his or her reasoning and to internalize an awareness of the model for the problem.

Modeling of problems and self-verbalization strategies cannot occur only at the beginning of the year. The process has to be used with each new chapter, concept, process, and skill. As a part of problem solving, students should develop the ability to classify problems according to types (Krutetskii, 1976). Travers et al. (1977) have developed a classification system that includes such categories of problems as distance-rate-time, "real life," open-search, products, and number theory. Not all word problems should be applications of the four basic operations. Day-to-day life experiences should be incorporated into problem solving activities. Cawley et al. (1979b) agree that it is possible to develop sets of problems with more than one condition and to hold some conditions constant while manipulating others.

Problem solving is different from skill practice and computation surrounded by words. A significant part of looking at problem solving is "through problems for which there are alternative ways to approach a solution" (Cawley et al., 1979b, p. 27). For the secondary and college student, solving problems is more complicated. Math-related subjects test students on their ability to apply complex concepts.

SELF-VERBALIZATION

The studies seem to suggest that children who self-verbalize and break down problems into the basic processes do better in mathematics. Lovitt and Curtiss (1968) studied the effects of having students verbalize their arithmetic problems before writing the answer. They found that verbalization improved the students' performance when compared to others who just wrote the answers. Breaking a problem into component parts, along with self-verbalization of the process, was found by Grimm et al. (1973) in a study to result in significant improvement in mathematics. Teachers also can enhance the learning process by verbalizing while doing mathematical problems with children (Smith & Lovitt, 1975).

A LANGUAGE APPROACH TO WORD PROBLEM SOLVING

There are students who do not pay attention to the various cues and features of a word problem. This could be an effect of an attention deficit. Some students may also lack appropriate solution "schemata" and have little or no frame of reference for solving a problem. They have no solution strategies that can be activated and applied to different types of word problems. With practice, the student can learn to comprehend and use math concepts and structures within the context of his or her own language.

Given the above, there are things to be considered:

1. Arithmetic language lacks redundancy; therefore, it must be translated into everyday language through verbal analysis.
2. Meanings of words differ in math context; therefore, words need to be defined and used in different contexts (normal and math usage).

3. Math language and ordinary language have syntactic differences; therefore, overt verbalization practice is necessary to differentiate among various syntactical forms. Words and phrases like *by, into, is divided by, is divided into* need to be fully understood.
4. Statements are made in which two concepts or mathematical elements are incorporated, such as "Add 10 after you multipy by 5"; therefore, verbal practice of instances of these statements is necessary so that students understand the mathematical operations and the context in which it is imbedded.

The key concept is to train the student to interpret statements with reference to his or her own language structure; then attend to the elements and organize them appropriately (plan).

Planning a Program

The following is a suggested sequence of procedures for planning a program:

1. Make a list of the skill areas to be taught. The list can be taken from the textbook, local or state scope and sequence charts, or grade level curriculum guides.
2. Within each skill area determine the hierarchy of skills to be mastered and the prerequisite critical skills for concepts that will be taught. Examples of hierarchical subskills can be found on pages 533–543.
3. Assess the present level of functioning of each student as preparation for teaching the new skills or concepts.
4. List the key vocabulary for the skill areas. The teacher should identify those terms and symbols that are essential to the understanding of the concepts that will be presented.

Planning a Word Problem Lesson

After completing steps 1–4 in planning a program, the following steps could be followed in developing a lesson. Use Form 11–2 (Form 11–3 illustrates a completed word problem lesson.)

1. State the skill, concept, or objective.
2. Write the word problem.
3. Review language.
   The language aspects of a problem need to address the following:

MATHEMATICS LESSON—WORD PROBLEMS

SKILL—CONCEPT—OBJECTIVE

WORD PROBLEM

REVIEW LANGUAGE	REVIEW ARITHMETIC
Vocabulary	*Vocabulary*
Identify Language Structures	*Identify Math Vocabulary Cues*

MATERIALS

PROBLEM SOLVING SEQUENCE

Reading the Problem—Cues—Planning—Computation

FOLLOW-UP ACTIVITIES

MATHEMATICS LESSON—WORD PROBLEMS

SKILL—CONCEPT—OBJECTIVE

Given word problems involving purchases totaling less than $50.00. The student selects the correct change, or amount left, from $50.00 or less.

WORD PROBLEM

Adam bought a bird cage for $12.00, a parakeet for $6.00, and bird seed for $2.87. How much change did he get from $50.00?

REVIEW LANGUAGE	REVIEW ARITHMETIC

REVIEW LANGUAGE

Vocabulary

bird cage   bird seed
parakeet   change

Identify Language Structures

<u>How much</u> (change . . . .)

Adam <u>*bought*</u> (a bird cage, ...)

<u>*get from*</u> ($50.00? . . . . . .)

REVIEW ARITHMETIC

Vocabulary

dollar   minus   addition
plus   equals   subtraction
cents   money

Identify Math Vocabulary Cues

bought   change

MATERIALS

Chalkboard, chalk, chart with word problems (see follow-up for example), real or play money, objects or pictures of objects mentioned in the word problem.

PROBLEM SOLVING SEQUENCE

Reading the Problem—Cues—Planning—Computation

FOLLOW-UP ACTIVITIES

a. *Vocabulary:* The vocabulary list contains words that are related to the skill being taught. These are words that the student may be unfamiliar with and needs to master in order to achieve competency in the particular skill.

b. *Language Structures:* The student must learn the meaning of certain mathematical terms and expressions that are found in this list, as well as ordinary structures used in everyday language that may be unfamiliar to the student. The teacher can also teach the skill by using colloquial expressions, phrases, and structures.

4. Review arithmetic.

The mathematics content of the lesson is discussed, and the arithmetic vocabulary to be introduced is reviewed.

a. *Vocabulary:* The vocabulary list probably contains words that have already been taught but may still need review. The student needs to exhibit an understanding of the words and how to use them in different contexts.

b. *Math Vocabulary Cues:* Since mathematics text is frequently characterized by the use of verbs in the passive voice, the meaning and use of this verb form needs to be explained (e.g., *is divided by*). The meaning of *rational terms*, such as *greater than, more than, before, after,* etc., should be included in instructional activities. There are also math cue words that help identify the key processes needed to solve the problem.

5. Determine materials.

List the materials that will be used in teaching the lesson.

6. Problem-solving sequence.

a. *Reading the problem:* Spache and Spache (1975) recommend that students be taught a general procedure in problem solving: rapid reading for general understanding, a slower reading to identify details, oral restating of a problem in the student's own words, and change intonation for key words. If the problem is written on the chalkboard, do not remove (separate) key words from the problem at this time.

b. *Cueing (Cues):* Students should know how to find the cue words. These are the keys to unlocking the problem. Different cues may result in the need for additional information or raise questions about assumptions that have to be made in order to solve a problem. What information needs to be used that is either stated in the problem or not explicit in the problem for arriving at a solution? Are there any distractors? These are words or phrases that are unnecessary to the solving of the problem.

c. *Planning:* Students need practice in reviewing the language of the problem in order to determine what information is used in order to arrive at an expected solution. What needs to be done first, next, before, after, etc.? Is there a model for this type of problem that the student can use? What are all of the alternative approaches to the solution of the problem? Students design the format (and alternatives) for the solution of problems.

d. *Computation:* Students need practice in computing the problem accurately to arrive at a solution and in examining alternative formats for doing the computation.

7. Follow-up activities.

Practice at home or in school should focus on using the same problem to solve similar problems by varying the format, numbers, sequence, social situation, items, and people (names, types).

Sample Problem-Solving Sequence

See sample lesson (Form 11–3).

1. Reading the problem

T: Read the problem silently while I read it out loud. Listen for the key words that will help you answer the questions. (problem is written on the board)

Adam bought a bird cage for $12.00, a parakeet for $6.00, and bird seed for $2.87. How much change did he get from $50.00? The teacher emphasizes the key words (intonation).

T: Now read the problem again silently and pay close attention to those words that will help you solve the problem. (students read silently)
Note: This leads into the cueing process.

T: Can someone tell me in his or her own words what the problem says? (teacher should encourage responses but not force it if students do not volunteer a response)

2. Cueing

T: What do we need to know to solve the problem? There are several cue words to help us. A cue word helps us solve the problem. Is bird cage a cue word? No. It could be anything, a fish tank or a hamster cage. What is the first cue word?

S: The first cue word is *bought.* Somebody bought something that cost a certain amount.

T: Underline the cue word. The cue word is *bought. Bought* means money was spent for something. In this problem a bird cage was *bought.*

T: What is the problem about?

S: It is about *buying* something.

T: What is the first thing that was *bought?*

S: Adam *bought* a bird cage for $12.00.

T: What else was *bought?*

S: Adam *bought* a parakeet for $6.00 and bird seed for $2.87.

T: What is the second cue word?

S: Change. (student underlines)

T: How much *change* did he get from $50.00? (cue 2 is the word *change*)

T: Did Adam give someone $50.00?

S: Yes.

T: How do we know?

S: Because he *bought* three things, and got *change.* He had to give someone money to get *change.*

T: What other information is needed to solve the problem?

S: None.

3. Planning

T: How can we solve the problem?

T: What are the cue words? *Bought* and *change* and *give,* even though the problem does not say *give*—why?
Write the cue words on the chalkboard.

Bought   Give   Change

T: What was *bought?* Under the *bought* column list each item and draw a simple illustration if desired.

S: *Bought*
Bird cage for $12.00
Parakeet for $6.00
Bird seed for $2.87

T: How much money did Adam give?

S: $50.00

T: Under *give* column write $50.00.

Give
$50.00

T: What did Adam get in return?

S: *Change.*

T: Point to the word *change.* Write a ? under the word.

T: Review:

Bought	Give	Change
Bird cage for $12.00	$50.00	?
Parakeet for $6.00		
Bird seed for $2.87		

T: How do we find how much was bought?

S: We add them up. (student goes to the board and writes the problem while verbally explaining what he or she is writing)
He or she does not do the computation.

$$\begin{array}{r} \$12.00 \\ 6.00 \\ +\quad 2.87 \\ \hline \end{array}$$

T: Do we know how much was *bought?* Point to the *bought* column on the chalkboard.

S: Yes.

T: How much money did he *give?* Point to *give* column.

S: $50.00.

T: Point to *change* column (?). Will he get any *change?*

S: Yes.

T: Set up a plan for doing the computation. (student goes to the board and writes the plan and verbally explains what he or she is writing)
Student does not do the computation.

$$\begin{array}{r} 12.00 \\ 6.00 \\ +\quad 2.87 \\ \hline ? \end{array} \qquad \begin{array}{r} \$50.00 \\ -\quad\quad ? \\ \hline \end{array}$$

4. Computation

T: Who can compute the answer? (student goes to the board and computes while verbally explaining the process)

$$\begin{array}{r} 12.00 \\ 6.00 \\ +\quad 2.87 \\ \hline \$29.87 \end{array} \qquad \begin{array}{r} \$50.00 \\ -20.87 \\ \hline \$29.13 \end{array}$$

Teacher reviews all three columns.

T: How much was *bought?* $20.87
How much did he *give?* $50.00
What is his *change?* $29.13

T: Is there another plan that can be used to help us compute the problem?

S: Yes.

$$\begin{array}{r} \$50.00 \\ -12.00 \\ \hline \$38.00 \end{array} \qquad \begin{array}{r} \$38.00 \\ -\ 6.00 \\ \hline \$32.00 \end{array} \qquad \begin{array}{r} \$32.00 \\ -\ 2.87 \\ \hline \$29.13 \end{array}$$

T: Which plan is better?

S: The first one.

T: Why?

5. Follow-up activities

Using a chart with word problems previously prepared by the instructor, he or she will have the students work each problem. The teacher will then ask the students to solve the problems on the board and verbally explain the procedure they followed to get their answer.

The practice problems should be similar to those solved as a group but should have variations in each problem. For example:

a. Problem discussed in class

Adam bought a bird cage for $12.00, a parakeet for $6.00, and bird seed for $2.87. How much change did he get from $50.00?

b. For practice problems in class or for homework

(1) Change the name of the people.

(2) Change the things bought.

(3) Change the prices paid.

(4) Change the amount of money exchanged.

(5) Change the order of the problem.

(6) Add detractors (words or facts that do not affect the computation).

Mathematics Vocabulary Development

Knowledge of word meaning is critical to performance in mathematics. Students are continually learning new terms in mathematics. Learning handicapped students need precise instructions in how to learn new terms and how to practice them in different ways. An important step in this process is to begin with prior knowledge and to determine how the concepts and the terminology already fit into their sociocultural backgrounds. Students sometimes confuse terminology, such as mixing up the words *angle* and *ankle* (Garbe, 1985).

Vocabulary instruction should be specifically built into the instructional program and taught at least 20 minutes a week (Heinrichs, 1987). Words with double meanings need to be taught specifically, such as *even, family, set, degree, scale, prime, remainder,* and so on.

Schemata can be developed around new words. (See Figure 11–17.)

Activities for Word Problems

Other activities are as follows:

1. Survey the content area material for potentially difficult words and preteach the vocabulary to the students in a simple self-defining context (Herber, 1970; Thomas & Robinson, 1977; Bender, 1975). Preteach vocabulary by preparing vocabulary cards for mathematical terms, symbols, and process signs. On one side of the card print the word or symbol. On the other side, the teacher or student illustrates the word with sample problems, sentences with the word underlined, or pictographs illustrating the concept. This procedure is very useful for words with dual meanings. The student's definition in his or her own words is preferable to material copied from a dictionary.

2. Guide the student in developing an alphabetical list of the basic mathematics words and phrases that will occur often throughout the year (see Table 11–1).

3. For bilingual students, look for mathematics terms that are exactly the same in English and in the native language. For example, in Spanish *decimal* is the same, and some words have minor changes from Spanish to English (e.g., *geometria* to *geometry*) (Pope, 1975). These types of words are known as *cognates.* Cognates can be very useful in providing students with a means with which to attach meaning to new words learned in English by transferring that meaning from their native language to English.

4. Scan the material for the function words or connectives that often influence the understanding of the solution to the problem. Such words include *but, on, to, by, for,* etc. These words can be circled and their meaning and use in solving problems explained.

Example A:

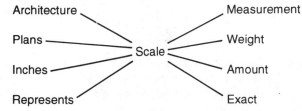

Example B:

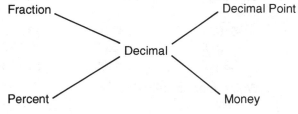

Figure 11–17

Table 11–1   Mathematics Vocabulary List

a.m.	budget	decimal point	figures
abacus	bundle	decrease	find
about	bushel	degree	finish
above	by	degree Celsius	first
acre		degree Fahrenheit	five
acreage	calculator	denominator	foot
acute angle	cancel	depth	for
add	capacity	diagonal	four
addend	cash	diameter	fourth
addition	cent	difference	fraction
after	centimeter	different	from
age	century	digit	
algebra	change	dime	gain
alike	check	dimensions	gallon
all	chord	distributive property	geometry
allowance	circle	divide	given
almost	circumference	dividend	gone
altitude	code	divisor	gram
altogether	coins	do	graph
always	collection	dollar	greater than
amount	color	double	greatest common factor
and	column	down	group
angle	common denominator	dozen	grouping property
answer	common fraction		
Arabic numbers	common multiple	each	half
are	compare	earn edge	has
area	complete	eight	have
arithmetic	compute	eighth	heavy
around	computation	eleven	height
as much as	cone	ellipse	heptagon
average	congruent	equal	hexagon
away	connect	equals	high
	container	equations	horizontal
back	convex	equilateral triangle	how many
bar graph	copy	equivalent	how much
bargain	corner	equivalent fraction	hundred
before	correct	estimate	
beginning	count	even number	if
behind	counting	every	improper
below	cube	exact	in
beneath	cubic	example	inch
beside	cue		inches
between	cup	face	incorrect
big	curved	factors	input
biggest	curvilinear triangle	false	inside
billions	cylinder	fare	integers
blanks		farthest from	intersecting lines
borrow	debt	feet	into
both	debit	few	invert
bottom	decagon	fewer	is
boxes	decade	fifth	isosceles triangle
buck	decimal	figure	

Table 11–1   (continued)

kilogram	negative numbers	pictograph	row
kilometer	never	picture	ruler
know	next	pint	
	nickel	pints	same
last	nine	place	scale
leap year	ninth	place value	scale drawing
least	no	planes	scale triangle
least common denominator	nonagon	plus	scientific notation
least common multiple	none	point	scoop
left	not	polygon	scored
length	nothing	pound	second
less than	number	prime factor	segment
light	number line	prime number	separate
line	number sentences	prism	set
line of symmetry	numeral	probability	seven
linear	numerator	problem	seventh
lines		product	several
liter	obtuse angle	proof	shape
little	o'clock	properties	share
long	octagon	protractor	short
	odd numbers	prove	side
many	of	put	sign
match	one	puzzle	since
matching	one-step	pyramid	six
means	only		sixth
measure	operation	quadrilateral	size
measurements	or	quart	smallest
median	order	quarter	solve
medium	ordered pair	quarterly	some
meter	ordinal	quatrefoil	speed
metric	other	quotient	spend
metric system	ounces		spent
middle	output		sphere
million	outside	radius	square
minuend	oval	ratio	standard numeral
minus	over	rational number	story
minutes		ray	subtract
mixed numbers	p.m.	rectangle	subtraction
mode	pair	rectangular prism	sum
money	parallel	remainder	
more	parallelogram	remainder rate	
more than	part	renames	table
most	partial	reverse	take away
much	past	rhombus	tall
multiple	pay	right	ten
multiplication	peck	right angle	tenth
multiplier	penny	right triangle	tetrahedron
multiply	pentagon	ring	than
must	per	Roman numeral	then
	percent	round	these
near	perimeter	rounded	third
negative integer	perpendicular lines	rounding	thirteen

Table 11–1 (continued)

this	true	valve	whole number
thousand	twelve	vertex	why
three	twenty	vertical	widest
through	two	volume	with
time			word
together	underline		work
ton	union	weigh	
top	unit	weight	
total	units	what	yard
trace	unlike	when	yes
trepezium	up	where	
trapezoid	upward	which	zero
triangle	use	whole	

5. Use newspapers to provide opportunities for students to locate the vocabulary used in mathematics in all sections from the advertisements to the sports pages to the financial section. Discuss the functional use of the terms and the meanings of words in context.

6. Involve students in games or group activities that will use math vocabulary. They can play games, such as developing and using codes for messages or decoding hieroglyphics. Instructional games allow the players to learn or practice a skill with deliberation toward a specific objective. Puzzles, flashcards, card and dice games, Bingo, Lotto, etc., should both provide reinforcement and have recreational value. The selection and adaptation of games should give the learner some initial success. Games, hobbies, crafts, science experiments, etc., can provide the learner with an environment that allows for questioning, decision-making, and problem solving, as opposed to the more formal teacher-led questions and solutions to problems (Horowitz, 1970). A mathematics area in the classroom for independent study may have maps, graphs, problems to be solved, and manipulative materials. Students should be encouraged not only to solve problems, but to work out their own problems and projects involving mathematical concepts.

7. It cannot be assumed that demonstrations, games, and outside activities will automatically transfer to understanding of even simple concepts in mathematics. There has to be a linkage of meaning and procedure. Students need opportunities to demonstrate their intuitive problem-solving abilities. After the demonstration of a concept, the teacher needs to elicit examples that are similar. "Can you show me ____?" "Can you think of ____?"

If the student can't think abstractly, then the teacher can go to the concrete level through the use of bottle caps, rods, blocks, models, etc. (Horowitz, 1970).

8. The way words are used often determines the difficulty of the problem even though the computation may be held constant (Cawley et al., 1979b). Example:

VERBAL PROBLEM SOLVING

A boy saw 3 cats.
Another boy saw 2 cats.
How many cats did the boys see?

A boy saw 3 cats.
Another boy saw 2 dogs.
How many animals did the boys see?

A boy saw 3 cats.
A girl saw 2 cats.
How many cats did the children see?

A boy saw 3 cats.
A girl saw 2 dogs.
How many animals did the children see?

A boy saw 3 cats.
Another boy saw 2 dogs.
Another boy saw 3 cats.
How many cats did the boys see?

A boy saw 3 cats.
Another boy saw 2 dogs.
Another boy saw 2 cars.
How many animals did the boys see?

A boy saw 3 cats.
A girl saw 2 cats.
A father saw 2 cats.
How many cats did the children see?

A boy saw 3 cats.
A girl saw 2 dogs.
A father saw 2 cars.
How many animals did the children see?

SYMBOLS

1. Discuss the implications of symbols in our lives in areas involving government relations and economics.
2. Discuss how symbols can be used to represent enormous power and to play important roles in our lives, such as:
   a. Einstein's $E = MC^2$
   b. atomic theory
   c. space shuttle
3. Discuss the history of measurement and the use of symbols in the different civilizations and how symbolic mathematics was used to unify the world and to enable us to understand the universe.

IDENTIFYING CUE WORDS IN WORD PROBLEMS

1. Initial teaching involves a substantial amount of chalkboard activity for large groups, small groups, or even one-on-one. First write the word problem on the chalkboard and then have different students underline the cue or key words. Then read the problem aloud and emphasize with accentuated voice intonation the key word. "John *bought* 2 apples."
2. Compare the order of stories in reading material with the order of the text of word problems. Reutzel (1983) notes that students are accustomed to a narrative style with a topic sentence first followed by supporting details. Arithmetic story problems are often in a reversed style of organization with important facts or cues at the beginning followed by the topic sentence. Students, therefore, must become aware that, in rereading a problem, cues can appear early in the text.
3. Cawley et al. (1979a) suggest using the cloze technique as a problem-solving activity. By inserting words in spaces, the learner's attention is directed to specified components of information in a problem.

   Mary had 20¢.
   She _____ 15¢.
   She has 5¢ left.

4. A part of identifying and writing a number sentence may include imagery and visualization. Ask the students to close their eyes and try to see what's happening in the problem. Have them draw a picture, graph, or chart to illustrate the problem. Visual doodling should be a part of the lesson (Kresse, 1984). Kresse also recommends that students not only identify key words but mentally delete unnecessary information in the problem.

PRACTICE

In preparing materials, activities, and situations where the students will engage in tasks to practice newly acquired learning, the instructor needs to differentiate between rehearsal and practice. Rehearsal is rote memorization. It focuses on one example and places the emphasis on specifics. Practice, on the other hand, is designed to develop a model from different orientations with the use of language. It is less restrictive in that it allows the student freedom in the use of language to describe functions of time and space (mathematics). The instructor needs to guide students through language activities in mathematics that will encourage the model-building aspects of practice. The following is an example:

1. Use an example to establish a model.

   $3 + 4 = 7$

2. Expand the model with the addition of language and the use of objects or visual representation (e.g., real apples or pictures of apples).

   3 apples + 4 apples = 7 apples

3. Increase the complexity of the expanded model with language.

   3 apples + 4 bananas = 7 fruits

4. Continue to expand the model with language through practice in a variety of problems.

   A boy has 3 apples. A girl has 4 bananas. How many fruits do the children have?

The following questions should be addressed when developing practice activities to determine the degree and type of practice needed in the language-related areas of mathematics:

Is there enough practice for the student to attain mastery?
Are there examples or models that the student can replicate to practice the problem?

Can the student get immediate feedback regarding his or her answers or solutions to the problems? Will answer sheets, calculators, media, or the instructor be available?

Plan the strategy for amplifying and expanding upon the text material. After diagnosing the student's learning style and strengths and weaknesses, and then scanning the material for the answers to the questions in the four steps listed above, the instructor can then plan an adaptation/development process for the areas that need modification. This may involve preteaching that includes rewriting or in some way changing the vocabulary, structure, or sequence of the existing material. Additional material may be required to provide practice and repetition. The instructor's presentation of the material may require modification (e.g., pull out vocabulary for a preparatory lesson). A variety of materials may be needed by the students to fully understand the concept. The instructor may need more than one instructional activity to present the concept (e.g., directed instruction, peer group activities, games, individualized media, student demonstration of a concept, etc.).

STORY PROBLEMS FOR PRACTICE

1. The teacher can adapt or develop problems by using materials that are easily accessible to the students. Develop a bank of problems to be solved by cutting out graphs, coupons, or sports statistics from magazines and newspapers. Develop questions that will emphasize a particular skill area.
2. Mix previously learned "models" of story problems with the current "model" (Kresse, 1984).
3. Cawley et al. (1979b) suggest that word problems can be developed around themes or situations. The same numbers and concepts can be used in a story format followed by five questions or in a display format (i.e., chart or graph) followed by five questions.
4. Having students write their own problems is recommended. This simultaneously improves writing skills and increases vocabulary (Ferguson & Fairburn, 1985).
5. Students can exchange variations on a model and use calculators to check their answers. The key isn't just checking the solution but checking the process leading to the answer.
6. Have each student develop a set of index cards with a sample word problem for each concept learned. These "model" problems can be used for review prior to tests.
7. Radebaugh (1981) suggests that teachers use literature to teach mathematics concepts. Examples are: "How Did We Find Out About Numbers?" by Isaac Asimov (Walter and Co., 1973) and "How to Count Like a Martian" by Glory St. John (Walsh, 1975).

Three kinds of arithmetic story problems can be found in texts and on tests:

1. Problems that provide the learner with just the information that is needed to solve the problem
2. Problems that have extra information not needed to solve the problem and that can confuse the learner
3. Problems that do not provide enough information and cannot be solved. Often multiple-choice sections of a test will have a choice such as: "D. not enough information provided to solve this problem."

Teachers need to review these kinds of problems with students by using different examples from books and texts, and some made up by the teacher and students. By reading the problem twice, and aloud, the student will gain a better understanding of what is wanted. Students can also estimate an answer, jot down the sequence of steps, and compare the worked-out solution with the original estimation (Wilson, 1988).

EVERYDAY MATHEMATICS SKILLS

The following skills should be built into the regular mathematics curriculum. The student should learn how to:

1. Fill out a time card and compute time differences for different periods including work, play, and leisure.
2. Keep a log of driving time, computing mileage and doing arithmetic involving the receipt of 25 cents per mile for x number of miles.
3. Go through the newspaper ads and compute costs, payments, etc., for different types of ads.
4. Measure liquids, solids, lengths and weights, and compute price per pound, ounce, quart, pint, etc.
5. Take business orders, such as for restaurants or stores.
6. Keep a checking and savings account.
7. Make out a weekly budget for all expenses.
8. Pay bills by filling out checks and keeping an organized checkbook.
9. Estimate expenses by the week, month, and year.
10. Purchase goods by going to stores and getting change and by reviewing receipts.
11. Cook by following simple recipes.
12. Use a thermometer (body and weather).

13. Develop a schedule of activities with appropriate dates and times.
14. Use a tide or fishing chart.
15. Keep a weather map—follow a hurricane path.
16. Compare coin value from various countries.
17. Locate TV and radio stations.

DEVELOPMENTAL ARITHMETIC SKILLS

The teacher should first determine the skills or operations that learners are expected to learn developmentally and that they will be expected to acquire at each particular grade level. This can be done by reviewing the state-approved scope and sequence arithmetic curriculum guides, by analyzing arithmetic text books, or by reviewing the developmental skills worksheets and the Mann-Suiter Grade Level Sequence (Form 7–2). In this way the teacher will understand the developmental sequence in arithmetic and know where to begin in terms of teaching lower level skills or prerequisite critical arithmetic skills before attempting higher level, more formal operations. A textbook should not determine what is to be taught. It is only a guide and an aid in presenting predetermined concepts and materials that learners should be able to cope with at a specific instructional level. The textbook is helpful if the learners are ready for those tasks, having mastered the prerequisite skills to the particular operations presented in the textbook. It is important that assessment be geared toward identifying specific areas of strengths (acquired skills) as well as areas of weakness or deficits at the beginning of the school year so that appropriate programs can be set up for individual learners. This will help the teacher group students more effectively, as well as providing an initial basis of comparison for future work.

Use the Mann-Suiter-McClung Developmental Skills Worksheets on the following pages (Form 11–4) to establish both short-term and long-term goals and objectives.

MANN-SUITER-McCLUNG DEVELOPMENTAL SKILLS WORKSHEET

NAME _____ EXAMINER _____

AGE _____ DATE _____

GRADE _____

	Date All Entries		
GOALS AND OBJECTIVES	Present Level	Short-Term	Long-Term

Developmental Arithmetic Skills

VISUAL DISCRIMINATION
The student will

1. complete a form board.
2. match shapes (objects) to models.
3. match pictures of shapes.
4. match pictures of numerals.
5. order objects by size.
6. order pictures of objects or shapes by size.

VOCABULARY, SPATIAL-TEMPORAL
The student will

1. understand the language of space (position), for example, *over, under, inside, behind, beside, between, below, more, less, top, bottom, in the middle of.*
2. understand the language of time, for example, *early, late, soon, now, yesterday, before, after, almost, today, tomorrow, long ago, young, old.*
3. identify objects that are close, closer, closest.

ESTIMATIONS
The student will

1. estimate size by comparing objects or pictures of objects (e.g., big/little, tall/short).
2. estimate shape by comparing objects or pictures of objects.
3. estimate distance by comparing objects or pictures of objects.
4. estimate weight by comparing objects or pictures of objects.
5. estimate conservation of space.

(continued)

NAME _____ EXAMINER _____

AGE _____ DATE _____

GRADE _____

Date All Entries

GOALS AND OBJECTIVES	Present Level	Short-Term	Long-Term

SETS

The student will

1. match one to one.
2. match equivalent sets 00–00.
3. recognize sets 0–5.
4. order sets 1–5.
5. identify sets with more or less.
6. recognize sets 6–10.
7. understand the language of sets, such as *more, fewer, equal, unequal, equivalent, nonequivalent,* and *empty set.*
8. identify universal sets.
9. identify intersection of sets.
10. understand union of sets.
11. understand disjoint sets.
12. understand finite and infinite sets.
13. understand solution sets.
14. understand sets of ordered pairs.
15. identify null sets.
16. identify proper and improper subsets.

NUMERALS

The student will

1. match one to one.
2. count orally 0–10.
3. count orally and point 0–10.
4. count orally and point 0–50.
5. count orally and point 0–100.
6. identify the numerals 0–50.
7. identify numerals before and after 1–50.
8. identify the numerals 0–100.
9. write the numerals 0–10.
10. write the numerals 0–50.
11. write the numerals 0–100.
12. write the numerals 0–999.
13. write from dictation 0–999.
14. write numerals for objects or pictures of objects in sets.
15. write numerals for words.
16. name numerals for objects or pictures of objects in sets.
17. classify numerals as odd or even.

(continued)

NAME _____   EXAMINER _____

AGE _____   DATE _____

GRADE _____

Date All Entries

GOALS AND OBJECTIVES	Present Level	Short-Term	Long-Term
18. count and write by 2s to 100; 3s to 36; 4s to 48; 5s to 100; 10s to 200; 6s to 72; 7s to 84; 8s to 96; 9s to 108.			
19. round off to nearest 10.			
20. write expanded form for numeral $(a \times 10) + 6$.			
21. give cardinal number of sets.			
22. indicate place value 0–50.			
23. indicate place value 50–100.			
24. indicate place value beyond 100.			
25. know, read, and write 1-, 2- and 3-place numbers.			
26. rename 1 through 50.			
27. rename 50 through 100.			
28. rename 100 through 500.			
29. rename over 500.			
30. indicate Roman numerals I–X.			
31. indicate Roman numerals XI–L.			
32. indicate Roman numerals C–M.			
33. read and write to millions.			
34. read and write to billions.			
35. indicate an understanding of rounding of whole numbers.			
36. classify numbers as composite, prime, or neither.			
37. understand common factors and Greatest Common Factor (GCF).			
38. identify multiples of numbers and Least Common Multiple (LCM).			
39. understand integers.			
40. understand negative numbers.			
41. understand rational numbers.			
42. understand base numeration.			
43. understand primitive numbers.			
44. understand scientific notation.			

ORDINALS

The student will

1. understand first through fifth by marking objects in ordinal positions, first to fifth.
2. understand sixth through tenth by placing pictures in specified ordinal positions to tenth.
3. place and count objects in ordinal position first through tenth.
4. label pictured events according to ordinal sequence.
5. use ordinals over tenth in functional arithmetic.
6. read ordinals out of sequence.
7. understand ordinals to hundredths.

(continued)

NAME _____   EXAMINER _____

AGE _____   DATE _____

GRADE _____

Date All Entries

GOALS AND OBJECTIVES	Present Level	Short-Term	Long-Term

ADDITION
The student will

1. understand addition facts 1–10.
2. understand addition facts 11–20.
3. add facts vertically 1–10.
4. add facts horizontally 1–10.
5. add two digits, no regrouping.
6. add three digits, no regrouping.
7. complete number sentences with missing digits.
8. add two and three digits with regrouping.
9. add one to three digits and five addends with regrouping.
10. add two addends with five columns.
11. add three addends with four columns.
12. add four addends with four columns.
13. add equations.
14. add by endings.
15. understand vocabulary of addition.
16. average a series of numerals.
17. understand commutative property.
18. understand associative property.

SUBTRACTION
The student will

1. understand subtraction facts 1–10.
2. use number sentences with missing digits.
3. understand subtraction facts 1–20.
4. understand subtraction facts 1–20 horizontally and vertically.
5. subtract two digits, no regrouping.
6. subtract three digits, no regrouping.
7. subtract two and three digits with regrouping.
8. subtract two to four digits with regrouping.
9. subtract four and five digits with regrouping.
10. check subtraction by addition.
11. understand the vocabulary of subtraction.
12. understand 0.

(continued)

NAME _____   EXAMINER _____

AGE _____   DATE _____

GRADE _____

	Present Level	Short-Term	Long-Term
GOALS AND OBJECTIVES			

Date All Entries

MULTIPLICATION

The student will

1. count and write by 10 to 100, 5 to 50, 2 to 100.
2. count and write by 3 to 36; by 4 to 48; by 5 to 60; by 6 to 72; by 7 to 84; by 8 to 96; by 9 to 108; by 10 to 120; by 11 to 132; by 12 to 144.
3. multiply facts through 45.
4. multiply facts through 81.
5. multiply facts through 144.
6. multiply two digits by one digit.
7. multiply three digits by one digit.
8. multiply ten digits by one digit.
9. multiply three digits by three digits.
10. multiply four digits by three digits.
11. multiply multiples of 100, 1000.
12. multiply with regrouping.
13. understand vocabulary of multiplication.
14. identify prime numbers.
15. know modular multiplication.
16. understand square root.
17. understand cubes and cube root.
18. multiply numbers written in scientific notation.
19. multiply positive and negative integers.

DIVISION

The student will

1. divide facts through 45.
2. divide facts through 81.
3. divide facts through 144.
4. divide problems with remainder.
5. divide using multiples of 10.
6. divide 3/27.
7. divide 6/638.
8. divide 10/181.
9. divide 325/1942.

(continued)

NAME _____ EXAMINER _____

AGE _____ DATE _____

GRADE _____

Date All Entries

GOALS AND OBJECTIVES	Present Level	Short-Term	Long-Term
10. check answers by multiplication.			
11. divide by two-digit divisor with quantity remainder.			
12. divide by three-digit divisor.			
13. understand vocabulary of division.			
14. divide with fractions.			
15. divide with decimals.			
16. divide positive and negative integers.			
STORY PROBLEMS The student will			
1. solve oral story problems involving 1 to 10 more.			
2. solve oral story problems involving 1 to 10 less.			
3. identify the process to be used in terms of key words in written story problems.			
4. solve one-operation written story problems involving addition for 1–10.			
5. solve one-operation written story problems involving addition for numbers over 10.			
6. solve one-operation written story problems involving subtraction for 1–10.			
7. solve one-operation written story problems involving subtraction for numbers over 10.			
8. solve two-operation written story problems involving addition and subtraction for 1–10.			
9. estimate the answers to written story problems.			
10. solve two-operation written story problems involving addition and subtraction for numbers over 10.			
11. solve one-operation written story problems involving multiplication for 1–10.			
12. solve one-operation written story problems involving multiplication for numbers over 10.			
13. solve one-operation written story problems involving division for numbers 1–10.			
14. solve one-operation written story problems involving division for numbers over 10.			
15. solve two-operation written story problems involving multiplication and division for 1–10.			
16. solve two-operation written story problems involving multiplication and division for numbers over 10.			
17. solve two-operation written story problems involving combination of addition, subtraction, multiplication, and division for 1–10.			
18. solve two-operation written story problems involving combination of addition, subtraction, multiplication, and division for numbers over 10.			
19. solve simple written story problems involving fractions.			
20. solve complex written story problems involving fractions.			
21. solve simple written story problems involving decimals.			
22. solve complex written story problems involving decimals.			

(continued)

NAME _____   EXAMINER _____

AGE _____   DATE _____

GRADE _____

Date All Entries

GOALS AND OBJECTIVES	Present Level	Short-Term	Long-Term
23. solve simple written story problems involving percentage.			
24. solve complex written story problems involving percentage.			
25. solve simple written story problems involving combination of fractions, decimals, and percentage.			
26. solve complex written story problems involving combination of fractions, decimals, and percentage.			
27. write number sentences and equations for story problems and match equations to story problems.			
28. solve story problems using concepts in measurement.			
29. solve story problems using graphs.			
30. solve problems dealing with time, work, rate, distance, and speed.			

MEASUREMENT

The student will

1. understand and name days of the week in order.
2. understand and name months of the year in order.
3. tell time on the hour.
4. tell time on the half hour.
5. tell time on the quarter hour.
6. tell time on 5-minute intervals.
7. read symbols of time, 6:00, and abbreviations (A.M., P.M., hr., min.) in time problems.
8. solve time problems.
9. read and understand words associated with time (*hour, half-hour, o'clock, past, after, leap year, fortnight, decade, scores, centuries, millenniums*).
10. read a digital clock.
11. determine age by computation from date of birth to present date.
12. understand temperature in degrees.
13. read Celsius or Fahrenheit scale thermometer.
14. solve temperature problems.
15. understand (convert) pint, quart, gallon (3 quarts = _____ pints)
16. use liter and milliliter.
17. understand (convert) half pint and half gallon.
18. solve problems with volume.
19. understand metric volume.
20. solve problems with metric volume.
21. understand ounce (oz.) and pound (lb.).
22. solve weight problems.
23. understand the vocabulary of weight comparisons (*full, empty, light, heavy, most, and least*).
24. know relationship of grams and kilograms.

(continued)

NAME _____   EXAMINER _____

AGE _____   DATE _____

GRADE _____

Date All Entries

GOALS AND OBJECTIVES	Present Level	Short-Term	Long-Term
25. solve metric weight problems.			
26. understand inch, foot, yard, mile.			
27. use centimeter to find lengths.			
28. measure to closest unit of measurements (inch, etc.); for example, convert inches to feet.			

28 inches

+40 inches

68 inches = 5 feet 8 inches

29. solve standard distance problems.			
30. understand metric distance.			
31. solve metric distance problems.			
32. understand standard dry measures.			
33. use the calendar.			
34. understand seasons.			
35. find the perimeter of geometric shapes or objects.			
36. find the area of shapes, rectangles, or objects.			
37. find the diameter of shapes or objects.			
38. understand time and climatic zones, belts, and standard time.			
39. understand latitude and longitude.			
40. read simple graphs (bar graph, line graph, pictograph).			
41. read complex graphs.			
42. read maps.			
43. use solid measurements.			
44. add and subtract measurements with regrouping, converting answers to simple form.			
45. find area of triangle, circle, parallelogram.			
46. find circumference.			
47. understand ratio and proportion.			

MONEY

The student will

1. identify penny, nickel, dime, quarter.			
2. identify half dollar, etc.			
3. compare value of coins (penny, nickel, dime, quarter, etc.).			
4. substitute value of coins (e.g., 2 dimes + 1 nickel = 1 quarter).			
5. know symbols $ and ¢.			
6. do simple money problems (add, subtract, multiply, divide).			
7. do complex money problems in dollar-and-cent notation.			

(continued)

NAME _____   EXAMINER _____

AGE _____   DATE _____

GRADE _____

GOALS AND OBJECTIVES	Present Level	Short-Term	Long-Term

Date All Entries

8. identify change after a purchase.
9. add purchases and count out change.

FRACTIONS
The student will

1. divide shapes (objects) in half.
2. divide sets in half.
3. divide shapes and sets in quarters and thirds.
4. divide shapes and sets beyond one third.
5. add fractions with like denominators ($\frac{1}{4} + \frac{1}{4} = $).
6. add fractions with unlike denominators ($\frac{1}{2} + \frac{1}{3} = $).
7. add mixed numbers with like denominators ($2\frac{1}{5} + 2\frac{1}{5} = $).
8. add mixed numbers with unlike denominators ($3\frac{2}{3} + 4\frac{1}{4} = $).
9. add, renaming the sum ($6\frac{8}{7} = 7\frac{1}{7}$).
10. add longer columns with same denominator ($\frac{5}{8} + \frac{3}{8} + \frac{2}{8} = $).
11. add longer columns with different denominators ($\frac{3}{8} + \frac{2}{6} + \frac{1}{3} = $).
12. subtract fractions with like denominators ($\frac{3}{4} - \frac{1}{4} = $).
13. subtract fractions with unlike denominators ($\frac{4}{6} - \frac{1}{3} = $).
14. subtract mixed numbers with like denominators ($6\frac{6}{7} - 1\frac{1}{7} = $).
15. subtract mixed numbers with unlike denominators ($3\frac{1}{2} - 2\frac{1}{6} = $).
16. subtract whole and mixed numbers with renaming ($8 - 5\frac{2}{3} = $).
17. subtract mixed numbers with unlike denominators and renaming
    ($6\frac{1}{8} - 2\frac{1}{2} = $).
18. multiply fractions with like denominators ($\frac{1}{3} \times \frac{1}{3} = $).
19. multiply fractions with unlike denominators ($\frac{2}{3} \times \frac{3}{4} = $).
20. multiply simple fraction $\times$ whole number ($\frac{3}{4} \times 11 = $).
21. multiply mixed number $\times$ whole number ($6\frac{2}{3} \times 7 = $).
22. multiply mixed number $\times$ mixed number ($4\frac{1}{2} \times 3\frac{2}{3} = $).
23. multiply cancelling simple fraction $\times$ mixed number ($\frac{1}{4} \times 2\frac{1}{4} = $).
24. change mixed number to improper fraction by multiplication ($2\frac{3}{4} = \frac{11}{4}$).
25. change fraction to equivalent by multiplication ($\frac{2}{3} = \frac{6}{9}$).
26. understand inversion of fractions.
27. divide whole number by simple fraction ($6 \div \frac{1}{3} = $).
28. divide simple fraction by simple fraction ($\frac{1}{2} \div \frac{1}{7} = $).
29. reduce to lowest terms ($\frac{4}{8} = \frac{1}{2}$).
30. change improper fraction to mixed or whole number ($\frac{12}{7} = 1\frac{5}{7}$).
31. divide mixed number by simple fraction ($3\frac{2}{3} \div \frac{1}{4} = $).
32. divide whole number by mixed number ($6 \div 4\frac{1}{3} = $).
33. divide mixed number by mixed number ($3\frac{1}{7} \div 2\frac{1}{3} = $).
34. divide simple fraction by whole number ($\frac{3}{4} \div 6 = $).

(continued)

NAME _____   EXAMINER _____

AGE _____   DATE _____

GRADE _____

Date All Entries

GOALS AND OBJECTIVES	Present Level	Short-Term	Long-Term
35. divide simple fraction by mixed number (⅓ ÷ 2½ =).			
36. divide mixed number by whole number (6⅜ ÷ 5 =).			

DECIMALS/PERCENT
The student will

1. identify place value.
2. compare decimals.
3. write decimals (_____ tens + _____ tenths =   ).
4. change decimals to fractions.
5. add and subtract decimals to tenths and hundredths.
6. add and subtract two-decimal numbers to hundredths.
7. multiply whole numbers by decimals.
8. understand, read, and write through billions.
9. extend meaning through millionths.
10. write decimal equations for proper and improper fractions.
11. multiply decimal by decimal.
12. divide by decimal number.
13. change decimal to fraction and then take percent.
14. compute fraction to percent.
15. compute percent to fraction.
16. compute percent to decimal.
17. compute percent of whole number.

GEOMETRY
The student will

1. identify and reproduce circles, squares, rectangles, triangles ○ □ ▭ △ .
2. identify and reproduce ◇ .
3. identify cone and semicircle.
4. identify sphere and cylinder.
5. identify prism, pyramid, cube.
6. identify triangular and rectangular prisms.
7. identify tetrahedron.
8. measure angles.
9. identify straight and curved lines.
10. recognize line segments.
11. recognize congruent figures.
12. recognize intersecting curves.
13. identify labeled points.
14. identify rays, planes.
15. identify right angles.

(continued)

NAME _____   EXAMINER _____

AGE _____   DATE _____

GRADE _____

	Date All Entries		
GOALS AND OBJECTIVES	*Present Level*	*Short-Term*	*Long-Term*
16. identify parallel lines.			
17. understand diameter and radius.			
18. identify perpendicular and intersecting lines, planes, and line segments.			
19. understand Pythagorean Theorem.			
20. recognize polygons.			
21. recognize right, congruent, and similar triangles.			
22. measure triangles.			
23. identify and draw angles, as well as isosceles and equilateral triangles.			
24. recognize trapezoids.			
25. identify optical illusions.			
26. understand mean, median, mode.			
27. measure exterior and interior angles.			

SYMBOLS OF ARITHMETIC
The student will

1. understand $+$ and $-$ (addition and subtraction).
2. understand $\times$ and $\div$ (multiplication and division).
3. understand $<$ and $>$ (*less than* and *greater than*).
4. understand $=$ and $\neq$ (*equal* and *not equal*).
5. understand $''$ and $'$ (inches and feet)
6. understand . and % (decimal and percent).
7. understand ____:____ (time).
8. understand set notation: $\cap$ (intersection); $\subset$ (subset); $\supset$ (super subset); $\cup$ (union); ( ) (null); $\emptyset$ (empty).
9. recognize $n°$ (degrees).

Chapter 12

Science, Social Studies, Study Skills, and Vocational Education

CHAPTER OUTLINE

OVERVIEW

This chapter contains suggestions regarding science, social studies, and vocational education and how these subject areas can be effectively taught to students exhibiting different types of learning problems. Emphasis is placed on *how* to teach, rather than on *what* to teach. The ideas can be implemented in regular as well as special instructional settings.

SCIENCE AND SOCIAL STUDIES

Before planning a science and social studies program for students exhibiting learning difficulties, the teacher should consider the learners' abilities to read, write, spell, or conceptualize ideas from the material to be covered. What areas of language are deficient to the extent that they prevent the learners from being successful in given tasks?

A student may have difficulty in basic decoding skills (reading), holding or remembering information (memory-sequencing), understanding vocabulary and integrating information (receptive language and conceptualization), or expressing ideas in a meaningful and grammatically correct manner (expressive language). The instructor has to know how the content areas (concepts, ideas, relationships) can be presented in a manner that will enable the student to conceptualize the material and integrate the information given for purposes of expanding the knowledge base in these subject areas.

A science or social studies program for students beginning in the primary grades can be based on an interest area. Dinosaurs, seasons, seeds, and plants, for instance, are good subjects because concrete materials, visual aids, and library books are usually available. Students at this level are easily involved in manipulative activities. Activities that involve developing models for social studies and science projects by collecting, sampling, cutting, and pasting are naturally motivating to the learners. Nature studies (particularly out-of-doors activities) are excellent for developing interest in science projects.

With high-interest science and social studies material, students can observe more carefully and notice necessary details. The teacher can incorporate sequential memory activities into the science or social studies program. (For instance, you may demonstrate a science experiment and ask the students what they saw first, second, and so on.) The students can be required to remember details, such as the color, shape, and size of items and the kinds of materials that were used in the experiment. The student must listen and follow a sequence of directions. Listening is a prerequisite to understanding concepts and other language activities.

Students must learn that many words have similar pronunciation but different meanings. This cannot be assumed. It must be taught explicitly and reinforced by using the concepts in many situations. Vocabulary development in science and social studies can be an integral part of the language program. Lists of words made in the science and social studies areas can be taught specifically in context through writing within the subject-level area programs. For example, the teacher responsible for the reading program can add the science, social studies, and mathematics vocabularies that are necessary for success in those areas into the reading program. The vocabulary of the subject-level areas should be tied into the material that is being covered at a given time in those areas for it to have relevance for the learner.

Other language skills that begin to develop at this level as part of the science and social studies curriculum include classification or concept development, association at the concrete-functional and abstract levels, and written expression, including simple taking of dictation, notetaking, beginning reporting (one or two sentences), and creative writing wherever appropriate.

A science or social studies program for students in the intermediate grades should emphasize the development of library and written language skills necessary for collecting information, keeping records, developing vocabulary, and writing reports on a given subject. Notetaking and reporting at this point become a major part of the students' program. Science and social studies are excellent for developing written expressive language.

Students appear to learn science better when they participate directly in experiments where they can see changes occur. It is a good idea to have some type of hands-on science activity sometime during the week. The students' interest will be aroused by the prospect of doing experiments, and they will look forward to relating information heard to actual experience with laboratory materials. Variables that have to be consid-ered with learning handicapped students are attention span and level of motivation (Scotti, 1989).

Teacher enthusiasm is another contributing factor to good science education. Teachers' opinions about their students' ability to learn may well effect how much the students actually retain (Brophy & Good, 1986). Teachers convey their feelings with more than just verbal behavior. Nonverbal behavior, which includes body language, facial expressions, gestures, and voice quality, are all important factors in teaching science (Chaiken et al., 1978).

It is helpful if the teacher has a general interest in science and enjoys teaching that subject. A science lab is very useful if the procedures for its use are consistent and understood by the students. The laboratory and that actual experimentation process needs to be perceived as nonthreatening to the students. The students need to feel that no harm will come to them.

Students should be encouraged to work in groups. The principles of cooperative learning lend themselves ideally to science activities. Organizing laboratory partners for experiments is a useful device.

Students should have something in their hands to manipulate during science experiments to understand better the concepts to be taught. The concept of an activity-centered lab where students are doing things is important for the development of both divergent and convergent thinking.

Science education can have many side benefits, such as:

1. Providing a good setting for positive social interaction
2. Providing the learner with examples of good organization and the sequencing of activities
3. Helping the learner to understand sharing, argumentation, and reflective thinking
4. Giving the learner a feeling of acceptance as well as making him or her feel comfortable in that kind of environment
5. Portraying teachers as thinkers, helpful, someone to trust, someone who can help you to think, and someone who is approving

At the secondary level, it is important for teachers to program opportunities for students to be involved in debates, discussions, meaningful writing, shared writing, and directed reading (Swicegood & Parsons, 1991). It is also important to emphasize activities that involve written language as well as remedial and functional oral exchange. In a larger sense, the instructor organizes activities that foster strategic reading, listening, writing, and verbal exchange. These behaviors are felt to be most effective within a reciprocal teaching environment where the teacher establishes a collaborative relationship with students.

Using Schema Through Concept Ladders

Using a schema approach to associative learning involves focusing on a single word or idea and identifying other words that relate to this word in terms of hierarchical schemata. A concept ladder (Gillet & Temple, 1982) can be used to delineate a schema for concepts in this fashion. Solubility is a good example. In Figure 12–1, the concept begins and ends with something observable. The concept of solubility has subsets. In Figure 12–1, the subsets listed above the concept (solubility) are associated with effects, whereas the subsets listed below the concept are basic components and characteristics.

Semantic Mapping

Another prereading strategy that activates students' schemata relative to a given topic is semantic mapping. Semantic maps are graphic representations or diagrams of a concept (Pearson & Johnson, 1978; Johnson, Pittelman, & Heimlich, 1986; Walker, 1989). When planning a science or social studies lesson, the instructor first reads the textbook assignment and reviews all classroom lecture notes and other supplementary materials. From this material, the instructor then makes a list of important words, terms, and concepts that are essential for mastery of the topic. The semantic mapping process promotes learning of vocabulary, gives the students an opportunity to relate new terms to their own experiences and prior knowledge, and enables them to see the relationships

among the words, big ideas (superordinate concepts), and secondary categories.

Provide blank maps for the students and draw a matching map on an overhead projector acetate or on the chalkboard. Another option is to start with the central core of a map, such as a circle or a square, and give the students a chance to draw the subareas on their maps as you brainstorm together. Free association of words, dialogue, and brainstorming are the key components of building a network of relationships with the students. In the center or top circle, write a subordinate concept to be discussed. The students then tell the words or concepts they know about the area. As the instructor writes these on the chalkboard, the students fill in the map for use as a postreading review. Bos and Vaughn (1988) suggest that semantic maps can also be used by the teacher to introduce technical terms found in the textbook. After words are listed on the chalkboard and the meanings are discussed, the terms can be appropriately placed on the semantic map. Figures 12–2 through 12–6 illustrate science and social studies semantic maps.

Semantic mapping (Pearson & Johnson, 1978) is best used either as a prelearning activity or as an ongoing classroom activity, as it helps students organize new material around a familiar framework.

In a social studies unit on Indians, for instance, the teacher could first assess the students' background information by using a semantic map (see Figure 12–7) that showed their concept of Indians. Usually this exercise shows that most people associate the term

Functions of Tree Parts

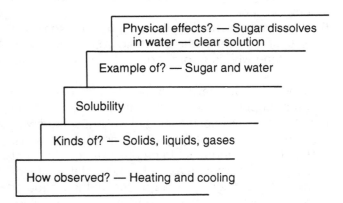

Figure 12–1   Concept Ladder

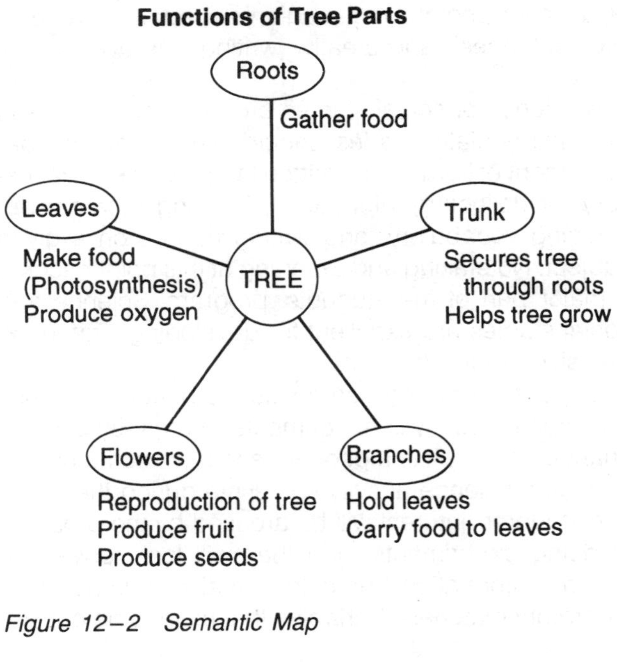

Figure 12–2   Semantic Map

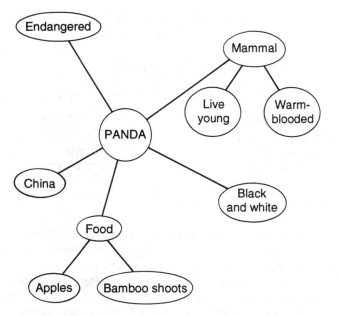

Figure 12–3   *Semantic Map*

Word Cards

Word cards are a simple way to introduce science and social studies concepts (Carr, 1985). The word is placed in the upper left corner of a 3″ × 5″ card. The student thinks of associated ideas that are written on branches. Example:

Photosynthesis

	Leaves
Food producing	
Requires light	
Requires chlorophyll	
Synthesis of organic compounds from inorganic compounds	
Synthesizing carbohydrates from CO_2 and H_2O with release of oxygen	

Indian with Plains Indians met by the pioneers as they traveled West; little is known of other Indian tribes. The stereotypical Indian lived in a tepee, hunted buffalo, rode a horse or paddled a canoe, and spent a lot of time in warfare.

As the class study proceeds and students give their assigned reports on Indian tribes, pertinent information can then be recorded on a semantic chart, as illustrated in Figure 12–8. It soon becomes apparent that the word *Indians* covers a wide variety of people and ways of living.

Semantic mapping and charting make it possible for the student to activate prior knowledge and see the relationships between new concepts and related vocabulary.

Play "Alike and Different" Games

Contrasting or determining what something is and is not enables the learner to understand scientific and social studies concepts. The object in this activity is to discuss aspects of a phenomenon or areas of study that are similar and different. Example:

How are these alike and different?
Science
Zoology—Biology
Chemistry—Physics
Mycologist—Cytologist
Algae—Fungi
Heterotrophic—Autotrophic

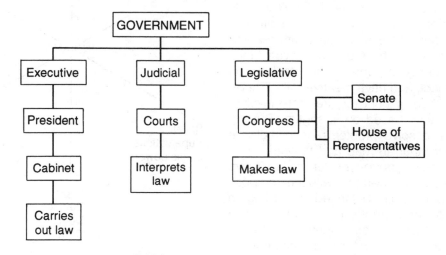

Figure 12–4   *Semantic Map*

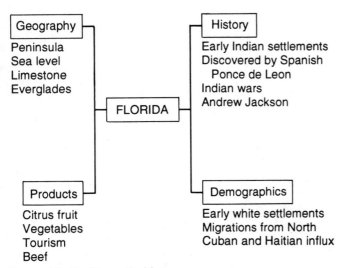

Figure 12–5 *Semantic Map*

Social Studies
Economics—Business
War—Police Action
Senate—House of Representatives
Culture—Society

Projects

A widely accepted premise suggests that science and social studies projects help develop participation. They can be extremely motivating to most students and are especially beneficial for further enhancing the language arts program in general. However, projects for the disabled reader or the student with learning problems require some modification. Projects are too often assigned or required based on reading and expressive language abilities or independent study habits. Good students who have the prerequisite skills plus some artistic or creative skills have little difficulty with such an assignment. But students with reading and writing problems may have difficulty, even if they know the science or social studies concepts, have an interest in the subject, and have creative skills. Therefore, projects for them should require more involvement and participation based on strengths. The activities should be to solve problems or to motivate thinking skills rather than to read and to write.

For some students, group-type or collaborative learning activities can be arranged, with the composition of the group carefully balanced according to selected strengths. For example, if the group is doing an experiment and report on rocks, then each student can be assigned a specific contribution based on his or her strengths. For example:

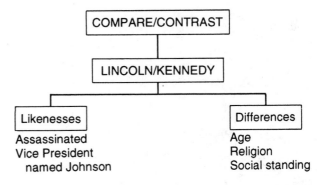

Figure 12–6 *Semantic Map*

1. The good reader reads and summarizes the textbook and other reference materials for the group.
2. The best printer or typist labels the rocks.
3. The artist prepares the charts, posters, or other visuals required in the project.
4. They all contribute to the written report (some through dictating ideas; others in writing). Everyone proofreads and checks the spelling.
5. The oral presentation and any other narrations (e.g., accompanying filmstrips or acetates for the overhead projector, introducing films) are based on strengths. There should not be undue pressure on students who stutter or are extremely shy to "participate" the first time they show an interest in a subject.

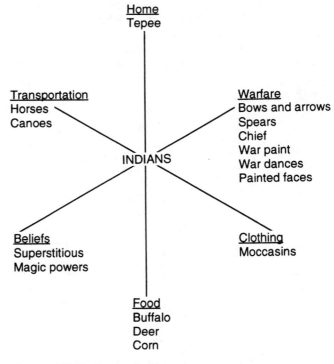

Figure 12–7 *Semantic Map*

Geographic Area	Tribe	Type of Home	Type of Transportation	Hunting	Fishing	Farming
Northeast	Iroquois	covered long house	birch bark canoes	small animals deer	yes	pumpkin corn
Southeast	Seminole	open platform thatched roof	dugout canoes	small animals deer	yes	maize
Plains Farmers	Mandan	earth lodge	horses round boats	buffalo	yes	maize, squash sunflower seeds
Plains Hunters	Sioux	tepee	horses	buffalo		maize
Plateau	Nez Perce	tepee	horses	deer, buffalo mountain sheep	salmon	
Southwest	Pueblo	adobe				corn, beans squash
Northwest	Tlingit	wooden house	dugout canoes	small animals deer	salmon	

Figure 12.8   Semantic Map

6. Rewards are presented to the group.

Gradually, the types of independent and small-group work will require students to assume more responsibility to produce quality material in their weaker areas. Prior to this, however, the students should plan how to get the assignment completed on time and with specific help if necessary. They may need a friend to help proofread the first draft but the responsibility for the finished product is their own.

Student Needs

Kurland (1983) notes that, based on his observations of how introductory science classes are taught, the problem underlying failure may not be a reading difficulty but an inability to comprehend the nature of scientific discussion. The student needs critical/analytic thinking skills for creative problem solving. He further states that physical science involves a discussion of measurement. Scientific equations are statements of the relationships of measurements rather than statements of relationships of properties. The student has to know what is to be measured, how it is to be measured, and the relationship between the measurements.

The student needs a structured way to ask and answer questions. He or she has to move from the statement of a problem through a process to evaluating evidence and drawing conclusions: Is there a meaningful question to be asked? What techniques should be used to answer it? How do you make a prediction or hypothesis? How do you move from testable questions to solution of problems? How do you use sources of reliable information: observation, experiment, books, museums, and adults? What systems can be used for classification? Which instruments can be used for measurement? How do you evaluate evidence and draw conclusions?

The student needs skills in locating material and sources of information: library, reference tools, encyclopedia, dictionary, atlas, glossary, index, using guide words, key words, alphabetical order, separating unimportant from important, seeing cause-effect relationships, putting events in order, and summarizing ideas.

Use popular science books, written by such famous scientists as Carl Sagan and Isaac Asimov, to supplement science coursework (Dole & Johnson, 1981). Fiction and nonfiction books provide reluctant readers with interesting reading material to gain concepts. Different types of books include: biographies, books of trivia questions and answers, science fiction, and easy-to-read books about careers in science or discoveries and inventions. Jobs of the future will require a higher level of basic skills that include the ability to synthesize and analyze data and the ability to make decisions from incomplete data.

STUDY SKILLS

Students with learning problems need additional learning experience in using appropriate and effective study skills. It will take more than watching how their peers, who are successful in content areas, are taking notes, organizing their time, or studying. There has to be a conscious realization by the student that he or she may need more time to study and that study skills have to be learned and practiced.

Using the Textbook

The basic difficulty for students with learning problems is that if the class is using a textbook, they can't read it. Many social studies and science textbooks are written at a higher level of readability than the grade level for which it is written. In cases like this, if there is an overdependence on the textbook, many students will have to rely only on what they hear or see in the classroom in order to understand the lesson.

For students with learning problems, once is not enough. Following are some ways to let the students who need to hear and see something over again do so.

The advent of schema theory has resulted in a closer examination of how texts are organized and what comprises their content, as well as the effects of these phenomenon on student comprehension (Meyer, 1980). One important aspect of forming schema in science education is for students to develop problem-solving skills. The way texts are constructed and assembled requires analysis by educators who desire to develop programs that focus on problem solving.

Several areas are highlighted:

1. Prereading questions are important and serve to direct the learner's attention to key points and concepts.

2. Advance organizers such as headings and subheadings in bold print also provide direction to the learner and aid in recall. Advance organizers also reduce the need for repetition of concepts (Meyer, 1980).

3. Identifying certain structures in the text is helpful, such as: "What is the problem? What is the solution? What happened before? What happened after? What happened first, second, . . . last?" Key phrases are important, such as "In conclusion," "In the following," "The author concluded," etc.

4. Students need to develop a problem-solving formula in their own words that follows accepted scientific procedures. For example:
   a. What is the problem?
   b. What will happen if (hypothesis)?
   c. What information do I have or need to get (collecting and analyzing data)?
   d. What conclusions can be drawn from the evidence?
   e. Was my hypothesis correct (hypothesis testing)?

Classroom discussion surrounding this example of a problem-solving sequence should focus on strategies for acquiring accurate information. Students also need to develop an understanding of higher-level problem-solving concepts and processes, such as:

Analysis—a breaking-down process
Synthesis—a building process
Evaluation—a testing or verification process

Material Adaptation and Modification

Many kinds of science and social studies materials may have to be modified and/or adapted so that learning handicapped students will be able to benefit from what they have to offer. Adaptation can be made in different ways:

1. Reduction in readability levels
2. Use of tape recorders
3. Written advance organizers
4. Other modifications including the mode of presentation, such as using a study guide, precision teaching, direct instruction, and using visual supports such as charts, diagrams, and printed words showing interconnections (Lovitt et al., 1986).

Introduction to a Social Studies or Science Unit

If your introduction to a science or social studies unit is based on a common textbook used by all students in the classroom and includes an overview of the project and a discussion of the pictures in the book, tape it on a cassette recorder.

In the taped introduction tell the students which page to turn to and then give a brief description of the unit you are going to study. Go through the pictures page by page, pointing out things for them to notice or asking the questions you want them to think about. Cassette lessons of this type should not be longer than 10 minutes. Leave the book and cassette recorder in an area of the room or in the media center where they can be used by all students who want to listen and look again.

Notetaking

Effective instruction occurs when the instructor is sensitive to the notetaking abilities of the learners. Teachers who write material on the chalkboard and who pace the lecture to give students more time to write down information facilitate good study habits. Instructors who stop during lectures and insert questions or verbal and nonverbal clues give the note-taker an opportunity to clarify his or her learning (Aiken, Thomas, & Shennum, 1975). Teachers can use a variety of techniques to help students learn to get the key concepts and vocabulary. During lessons that may have many new key concepts, or during a complicated sequence of events, the instructor may write an outline on the chalkboard prior to or during the class lecture. Some teachers occasionally hand out copies of their lecture notes and ask students to underline or mark the passages that were given the most emphasis.

Listening and attention are involved in taking notes. Cognitively, it entails listening to a block of information and then mentally going back quickly and pulling out the central idea, key words, the important details, and the sequence of events. It takes a great deal of practice and continuous training to determine what speakers want to emphasize. It is difficult for some students to cull out the important from the irrelevant or to isolate the main elements of a passage of text and write all of these things down so they can be retrieved for review later on. If notetaking does not highlight important information, it cannot serve the student in academic areas. Notetaking is developed along with listening and should be practiced often. Teachers should model good notetaking behavior, which includes asking appropriate questions. The student then practices how to predict, anticipate, and organize the speaker's message. Distractions and noise may interfere with the amount of material attended to by some of the students. Modifications of seating should be done if necessary.

Students need to consider the following when taking notes:

1. They have to go to class. Notes borrowed from a friend are rarely complete enough so that the information can be understood. We are becoming more aware of the importance of tying new information in with students' prior knowledge.
2. Many and complete notes are better than a few isolated phrases.
3. At the end of class, during study periods, or as part of homework, summarizing and paraphrasing the general points of the lecture will aid in retention.
4. Notes should be recopied, revised, and reviewed as soon as possible after class. Incomplete, inaccurate notes will be of little value the evening before a test.
5. Notes should be dated and kept in an orderly system of notebooks or files. It is easier to detect gaps if the notes are in the correct order.

Saski, Swicegood, and Carter (1983) recommend that students be given examples of how to record their notes and formats that will help them deal with a large amount of material. A columnar strategy has been found by a number of researchers to be effective. Students are asked to divide their notes into two to four columns. The following formats can be used:

1. Brown (1977) suggests a two-column format, with FACTS in one column and COMMENTS AND QUESTIONS in the second column.
2. Pauk (1978) and Palmatier (1973) mention a two-column format, with a wide column on the right for MAJOR INFORMATION and a narrow column on the left for CUES or key terms to aid in identification when studying.
3. Brown (1977) also recommends a three-column format, with one column for MAJOR POINTS, one for MINOR POINTS, and the last for SUPPORTING FACTS AND DETAILS.
4. Saski et al. (1983) divide the page into three columns, with a 2-inch column 1 for OLD INFORMATION, a 5-inch column 2 for NEW INFORMATION, and a 1-inch column 3 for QUESTIONS. This format can be used for lecture and textbook notes that will be used for future examinations.

Underlining

Underlining is not as efficient as notetaking unless students take time to study the material. McAndrew

(1983) has outlined the following suggestions based on research:

1. Material preunderlined by the instructor produces better recall than student-underlined passages (Smart & Bruning, 1973).
2. Students need training in underlining. Too much underlining and extraneous marking impair comprehension. The student has to be trained to underline superordinate general ideas and relevant material (Johnson & Wen, 1976). Students limited to underlining only one sentence per paragraph recalled more (Richards & August, 1975).

Time Management

Lack of on-task behavior is noted by instructors concerning learning disabled students. Part of helping students become better organized is to help them schedule short- and long-term deadlines. Students need a weekly and a monthly calendar to record due dates and the last possible moment when materials must be turned in to the teacher. The calendar can include scheduled exams and important school events as well as a projected schedule that will allow time for review, editing, typing or recopying, and other activities that will help in presenting material in final form. The teacher can write the cut-off dates on the chalkboard and give suggestions for those students who may need individual help in completing assignments (e.g., student-teacher conferences, tutorials, etc.).

Study Procedures

There are a number of study methods that have been devised to aid students in guiding themselves through the study process. At the beginning of the school year, the instructor can provide the students with a handout that lists the methods and explains when they can be used. A bulletin board can also be a method to remind the students what the various letters stand for.

PSC: (Preview-Study-Check) (Orlando, 1980)

Preview: An overview of the chapter.
Study: Read short segments, write summaries, compare summaries to text.
Check: Review notes.

SQ3R (Survey-Question-Read-Recite-Review) (Robinson, 1946)

This procedure is similar except that in the process the student stops to question and talk about the material. The SQ3R method is appropriate for prereading of content materials.

Survey: Read titles, introductory passages, headings and graphs, summaries, and end-of-chapter questions for major concepts and main ideas.
Question: State who-what-where-when-why-how questions to set a purpose for reading.
Read: Read material for content and to answer questions.
Recite: Answer questions for each major topic and subtopic.
Review: Review notes taken during reading or a lecture and determine areas for rereading or research.

Multipass (Schumaker, Deshler, et al., 1982)

In this procedure the student reads the material three times.

Survey: Read the titles, summaries, headings, cues that give an overview.
Size-up: Skim the chapter for more specific cues to answer the questions at the end of the chapter.
Sort-out: Answer the questions at the end of the chapter. For those that require additional reading, the student scans the chapter again for the sections that contain the appropriate source material.

PARS (Preview-Ask Questions-Read-Summarize) (Cheek & Cheek, 1983)

Preview: Preview the text.
Ask Questions: Formulate questions.
Read: Read.
Summarize: Cover main points and answers to questions.

OK5R (Overview-Key Idea-Read-Record-Recite-Review-Reflect) (Pauk, 1974)

This procedure is similar to SQ3R with the addition of Reflect.

ReQuest (Manzo, 1969)

ReQuest is a reciprocal questioning strategy where the students and the instructor take turns asking questions about selected paragraphs that have been read silently. The major purposes of the activity are to develop students' abilities to ask questions and to have them set purposes for reading. The teacher gives feedback and models the procedure.

TEST-TAKING SKILLS

Test performance, including the quality of responses, is vital to determining where instruction should begin. Students who do not meet preset standards of performance for a variety of purposes (grades, placement, promotion, graduation) are shifted to "special" or "remedial" kinds of programs. Student test-taking skills, emotional makeup, and motivation play an important part in overall performance. It is fair to say that for many students with learning problems there is also a deficiency in test-taking skills, resulting in performance that is not an accurate measure of their actual knowledge or ability (Scruggs, & Mastropieri, 1988).

A number of test-taking deficiencies can emerge:

1. Unfamiliarity with the examiner
2. Test anxiety and fear of the unknown
3. Attitude toward testing (hostile, anger, fear, history of failure, gives up too easily)
4. Poor knowledge of test-taking skills or lack of test awareness
5. Lack of understanding of the purpose of the test
6. Inability to use time appropriately (fixating on one problem and neglecting others)
7. Poor problem-solving behavior
8. Inability to attend to details
9. Failure to select an appropriate test strategy such as narrowing down multiple-choice questions
10. Understatement of actual knowledge
11. Confusion in transferring answers to a separate answer sheet

Many students struggle through the process of preparing for tests and then cannot cope with the anxiety of actually taking the test. Markel (1981) has divided test-taking skills into five areas: anxiety-management skills, interpersonal skills, problem-solving skills, study skills, and self-managing skills.

Anxiety-management involves helping the student reduce the tension and stress. This student may display physical signs of discomfort (e.g., shaking, stuttering, perspiration, etc.) and has trouble attending to relevant thoughts. Other students may be calm enough to sit through the exam, but they are not assertive enough to ask for help in how to take the test. These students do not ask for clarification of instructions or how much time is allotted to a test. Impulsive students may not use good problem-solving skills. They tend to rush through the material and fail to organize cognitive behavior effectively. Study skills and self-managing skills involve preparation prior to taking the test.

At the beginning of the term and several weeks before major examinations, the instructor needs to have a class discussion about effective techniques in preparing for tests. This can include procrastination and cramming, notetaking, and practice of different types of tests. The teacher can go over the formats of the types of tests that will be given in the course (e.g., true-false questions, essay, multiple-choice, etc.). Students need to know what is acceptable in order to pass the subject. Examples of exemplary answers can be reviewed. Students need to know how to pace their time during the test. Which questions to skip and come back to, how to guess, how to eliminate distracting information, and how to recognize cue words in questions should all be reviewed.

Additional Test-Taking Skills

Learning disabled students can benefit from training in the following areas:

1. When to guess and how to eliminate wrong answers
2. How to avoid absolutes such as *always, never, every,* etc.
3. Elimination of two or more similar answers
4. Elimination of obscure responses
5. Elimination of stem options (the use of contextual information in the stem of the test item)
6. Use of appropriate reasoning strategies including deductive reasoning on inferential recall items
7. How to read and follow directions
8. How to identify and follow a format
9. Reading comprehension of test items including self-monitoring

Scruggs and Mastropieri (1985) suggest a training procedure for test-taking skills, which includes:

1. Practice in stem options where the students try to understand the semantic or syntactic relationship between the stem (questions) and the response options
2. Practice in obscured options where the student eliminates the answer that just could not be correct
3. Practice in similar options (the elimination of two or more similar answers)
4. Practice in qualifiers such as *always* or *never*

A posttest lesson can focus on why students were not as successful as they anticipated, based on the amount of hours spent studying. Was the failure based on study strategies? The accuracy of notes and study materials? The content answers? The presentation of the written answer regarding spelling, handwriting, grammar, etc.? Incomplete answers? Setting up support systems may be important for some students.

They may need tutors, discussion groups, or some modification in the methods by which the material is presented. For example, some students may need to listen to the text on tape recorders. Others may need to read and review the material with a tutor before it is presented in class in order to benefit from class discussion. Instructors should talk to the students after a test and find out if they used any strategies and what types of questions were most difficult.

Academic Testing

Before taking achievement tests, students should learn to follow directions before the test, know when to guess, and how to mark answers and select the correct response. Practice is the key to success with these types of tests. Familiarity with objective tests is very important. All students should practice questions they will encounter on a test with worksheet exercises. The students need to be taught to evaluate the meaning of a question before trying to answer it and to be on guard for misleading answers. They will also need to learn how to eliminate one or two incorrect choices, thereby increasing the probability of guessing from 25 to 50 percent. Time is a critical factor. The tendency is to go slow, then speed up at the end. The student has to learn to go through the whole test and answer quickly all the items he or she knows, then go back and give the unanswered items the best educated guess possible. For essays, the student must read the question carefully and respond directly, addressing all subquestions. Main points should be listed first and embellished later on if time permits. Avoid any long, drawn-out answers that are "overkill" and move on to the next question. Even a partial answer is better than no answer at all, so the student should be encouraged to take a chance even if he or she does not have a clear response in mind and as long as one relevant point can be made.

Fatigue is another factor in writing, especially if the individual is tense and has muscle spasms. If this happens, stop and release the tension for a few seconds.

Introduce new concepts or how to take tests one at a time. Model the new response to establish or stabilize the concept and then provide worksheets for independent practice by the students. Students who practice objective tests and who practice writing responses to essay questions daily should improve their test-taking skills. Learning how to skim material is also useful and requires a great deal of practice. This must be taught with caution so that students do not omit critical information while skimming a test.

There are a number of classroom activities that the content-area teacher can do to help students become more test-wise:

1. Roleplaying, modeling, and rehearsing the types of stressful test-taking situations students commonly encounter can lead the student through the types of questions they should ask when they become confused.
2. In preparation for examinations that involve problem solving, the instructor can review with the class the many self-instructional strategies that have been mentioned throughout this book. Students have to think about the types of questions they should ask as they monitor their progress during the test-taking process.
3. Carman and Adams (1972) developed the SCORER technique, which is a mnemonic or letter-cue strategy that could be used to recall important steps in test taking:

> S = Schedule your work
> C = Clue words (e.g., *review, compare, define*)
> O = Omit difficult questions
> R = Read carefully
> E = Estimate your answers
> R = Review your work

Lee and Alley (1981) reported good results using this technique with learning disabled students.

SELF-DIRECTED ACTIVITY

Self-directed learning activities can be applied to any content area of study. The authors have chosen to discuss the essence and implications of this approach to the study of science. This approach places a great deal of responsibility on the learner, helping him or her to attend to both learning-enhancing as well as learning-impending activities (Thomas, Strage, & Curley, 1988).

The learner is encouraged to participate in as many events as possible that are regarded as imperative for effective learning, such as:

1. Listening to presentations of teachers or fellow students
2. Participation in discussion
3. Requesting clarification
4. Doing related work at home
5. Completing relevant assignments
6. Engaging in other activities designed to result in optimal learning (i.e., research, library, personal interview, readings, assignments, etc.)
7. Using self-speech or verbal mediation to get the necessary information or information omitted

A certain amount of self-regulation on the part of the learner is necessary in order to accomplish these tasks, such as:

1. Scheduling time to accomplish interim tasks
2. Designating place(s) to work
3. Organizing procedures for collecting data

Science is an excellent subject area to practice self-directed learning. The goal is to help the learner become as autonomous as possible (Thomas & Rohwer, 1986). This includes learning how to:

1. Do lab sheets in science and prepare a series of questions about what is not understood
2. Make notations regarding important concepts
3. Organize and highlight important sections
4. Review material already studied or learned
5. Make diagrams
6. Restate concepts in one's own words
7. Monitor time on task and amount covered
8. Determine what other information is needed or what is yet to be learned
9. Make learning aids such as cards or strips, drawings, etc.
10. Practice possible questions given on tests and review previous tests
11. Prepare accurate abbreviated sequential notes
12. Self-question strengths and weaknesses regarding a subject or concept
13. Follow the requirements and go beyond if possible (overlearning and extended learning)

A great deal depends on the demands presently being made on the student and how much of the above can be implemented, given the student's record of performance. Frequent and immediate feedback to the student is of prime importance. It must be constant, appropriate, and designed to reward self-regulating practices. Rewards are also part of the feedback system. The rewards should be applied to process as well as outcomes. Praise for effort is just as important as a token. Direct attributions of success to the learner and self-attribution of accomplishment by the learner of self-determined efforts are the basis for long-term changes in behavior.

Question Strategies

Learning disabled students need to learn how to formulate the kinds of questions that will allow them to extrapolate precise and essential information (Simmonds et al., 1989). Teachers can help by modeling various types of questions for students to emulate. Students need to know when to ask questions, how to ask questions, and where a question-oriented approach will be useful. Explicit training in questioning strategies is necessary and can be helpful. Questions related to academics, such as reading and arithmetic, as well as questions used for clarification of verbal information and assignments are all important for school success. Asking the right question helps the student to organize answers (Hall, 1979; Robson, 1977; Freund, 1988).

Studies have shown that comprehension skills improve in students who know appropriate questioning strategies (Raphael, 1982). Other question-related activities include text questions (Shavelson et al., 1974), prequestion activities (McNeil, 1989), completion-type questions (Rickards, 1976), and information-type questions needed to acquire specific answers (Pearson & Johnson, 1978).

Students need to learn how to ask the kinds of questions that can be used for quizzing or reviewing and for exploring and constructing meaning from what is being read. It is helpful to think out loud, exchange ideas, and bring background knowledge and information into subject-area activities.

SELF-MONITORING OF INSTRUCTION

The student has to accept personal responsibility for learning. To foster self-direction and internalization of instruction, have each student keep a record of both positive and negative classroom activities. If he or she experiences failure in a class, then the references in the log may pinpoint why.

Self-monitoring of comprehension appears to become important in silent reading. Smith and Dauer (1984) recommend that students code their responses to assigned material. For example, a code for a social studies text might be A = Agree, B = Bored, C = Confused, D = Disagree, M = Main Idea. For a science textbook, the code might be C = Clear, D = Difficulty, I = Important, S = Surprising. The students mark their responses on strips of paper that can be affixed to margins of pages of text.

This procedure should be modeled by the teacher first, using an overhead transparency of an excerpt from the textbook. The coded sections can be used as a basis for discussion with the teacher. Students can clarify confusion over concepts.

Babbs and Moe (1983) recommend the following:

1. Students remember to stop periodically to paraphrase a passage. This read-and-paraphrase plan is enhanced by writing brief answers to chapter questions.

2. Students analyze materials before reading by reading the introduction, chapter headings and subheadings, end-of-chapter questions, and summaries.
3. Each student makes a reading plan before reading a content-area textbook.

Self-Management

Self-management techniques have been applied successfully to students who exhibit sexual and conduct disorders, addictive disorders, as well as problems in academic areas (Mace & West, 1986).

Self-management techniques have been useful in helping children and adults to improve the quality of their lives. Teachers can also incorporate elements of self-management in their classrooms in areas of assessment and academic intervention. Students who learn to self-monitor enable the teacher to spend more time teaching and concentrating on academic areas of concern.

Self-reinforcement, which is a part of self-management, can be described as "the process by which an individual, usually under conditions of satisfying a performance standard, comes into contact with a stimulus that is freely available following emission of a response, which in turn increases the probability of the occurrence of the response subject to the performance standard" (Mace & West, 1986). This definition is descriptive of the process and avoids labeling (1) stimuli as reinforcers, (2) the relationship between the stimulus and target response as contingent, and (3) the spatial locus of the "reinforcer" as these are the principal points of contention among theorists (Mace & West, 1986, p. 151).

Social learning or cognitive-behavioral theory of self-reinforcement is based on the idea that individuals will learn to administer rewards to themselves if their behavior is deemed by them to meet or exceed preset performance criteria. This can include self-praise, criticism, or tangible rewards. The students are seen as controlling their own behavior by setting goals, responding to the acquisition of these goals (rewards or punishments), and maintaining established behavior. The locus of control is internal, as the reward system does not come from outside the learner. The stimulus itself becomes the reinforcer (or punisher) and the student has to meet the standard that is set. The locus of the reinforcer is mainly internal (through the student's thoughts and feelings), making the behavior essentially self-determined (Nelson et al., 1983; Malott, 1984; Jones & Evans, 1980; Hayes et al., 1985).

Implications for Teaching

1. Reinforcers such as praise or material rewards should be applied after the student has done some self-monitoring. The student's self-analysis should match the teacher's.
2. Students should set performance goals then self-evaluate and verbalize the consequences.
3. Self-management may be improved if students are explicitly reminded of the contingencies of their behavior; what will happen if . . .?
4. Teacher-controlled reinforcement programs (external rewards) may be necessary prior to installing or along with self-reinforcement approaches.
5. It is suggested that self-monitoring programs may be more successful if the student's statements are made publicly (in front of other students) rather than privately (to teachers) (Rosenfarb & Hayes, 1984).

Self-management skills have been found to be effective and can be used from preschool through high school (Workman, Helton, & Watson, 1982). An important aspect of strategy instruction involves the importance of teaching students to both ask questions and develop answering skills so that they can be more effective in their academic assignments (Reid, 1988; Knapczyk, 1991).

THE UNIT STUDY GUIDE

Students with learning problems face increasing numbers and levels of barriers as they progress through the grades. Succeeding in the content areas, especially science and social studies, is a formidable task. In this book we have tried to provide the instructor with many examples of study strategies within all areas of learning. The metacognitive strategies discussed in Chapter 2 and in the reading and spelling, written expression, mathematics and science and social studies chapters apply here as well.

The Unit Study Guide presents a method by which teachers can ensure that students with learning problems at least acquire the minimum knowledge to be successful in content area classrooms.

One concern of general educators who have students with special needs in their classrooms is how to utilize the information stated on the Individualized Educational Plan (IEP) to effectively integrate these students into an instructional program that is designed for the general population of students. There are several issues to consider:

1. Is there a discrepancy between the objectives stated in the IEP and the minimum criteria for success as established by the teacher who is offering the course? (The student may fulfill the objectives in the IEP and still fail the unit or course.)
2. The idea of equivalence (in terms of work expectancy and grading) for special needs students in regular class settings.
3. Students with special needs often come from classes in which there are small pupil-teacher ratios, and in which they received individualized instruction. These students may find it difficult to undertake the many responsibilities now placed upon them as they try to adjust to the rigors of the regular class program, even with resource teachers available to them.

Who are the support personnel, and how do they integrate the various programs? The Unit Study Guide presented here is designed as an additional support system to the student, as well as an aid to teachers and parents as they support the student in the subject level areas.

The Unit Study Guide is designed to help educators think through more precisely what it is they are teaching, how they are presenting the information, and what they need to be concerned with in terms of accommodating to individual student needs. In their day-to-day activities, effective teachers already do parts, or even all, of what is represented by the Unit Study Guide concept. Other teachers use it as a frame of reference from which to better organize what they already do in a random fashion with students. In addition, it is a valuable tool for new and less-experienced teachers and particularly student teachers in training. It enables these individuals to incorporate into their daily teaching the critical elements necessary for student success. The Guide is especially helpful in programming for secondary-age students who exhibit special needs in regular classroom settings.

Instructors should develop Unit Study Guides (USGs) for the various subject-level areas as a part of, or in conjunction with, the development of Individual Educational Plans (IEPs). This is important in cases where special-education resource teachers need to interpret the content within subject-level areas to students with special needs who will be taking these courses with regular classroom teachers. The concepts discussed are particularly applicable for students who will be mainstreamed into regular classrooms and expected to do the same work as their nonhandicapped peers in the subject-level areas. The Unit Study Guide represents the minimum or basic criteria for success in unit of study in a particular subject area and applies to *all* students in the class.

Once a Unit Study Guide is developed for a unit, for the most part it remains the same for succeeding courses, except for minor changes that are added in specific areas of content, procedures, and resources. The Guides enable students, parents, and resource teachers to have knowledge of the basic content and procedures and expected outcomes for a particular unit taught by the regular classroom teacher. With this knowledge, all work together to benefit the student.

The concept of the development of Unit Study Guides is appropriate for all academic subjects. The components listed in a USG within a particular subject area are as follows:

General student and course information
Brief description and objectives of unit of study
Basic facts and concepts
Basic skills
Basic vocabulary
Attitudes, beliefs, and values
Operations and modifications
Unit evaluation

Developing a Unit Study Guide

The following describes the components of a Unit Study Guide (See Forms 12-1, 12-2, and 12-3):

1. *Student Description*
   This section can include the following information:
   a. Brief description of the student's special needs (e.g., problems, talents, giftedness, etc.)
   b. Brief outline of basic skills (abilities and levels)
   c. Special concerns (e.g., behavior, medical, etc.)
   d. Language information (e.g., bilingual, etc.)
   e. Brief statement about the home
2. *Brief Description and Objectives of Unit of Study*
   Briefly describe the following as appropriate:
   a. Purpose or intent of the unit
   b. General outcomes stated as objectives
   c. Nature of the content
3. *Basic Facts and Concepts*
   List the minimum basic facts and concepts that all the students in the class will be required to learn. It is suggested that these be in the form of questions. Consider the following with regard to facts:
   a. The acquisition of facts depends on adequate associative memory abilities. A good memory is important if the memorization of a great deal of facts are required.

TEACHER'S MASTER COPY OF UNIT STUDY GUIDE

UNIT STUDY GUIDE (USG)

NAME OF STUDENT _____ DATE _____

STUDENT DESCRIPTION:

SUBJECT AREA (course) _____ INSTRUCTOR _____

UNIT OF STUDY _____ GRADE _____

Brief description and objectives of unit of study   Duration: _____

Basic facts and concepts

(continued)

Basic facts and concepts (continued)

Basic skills

(continued)

Basic vocabulary

Attitudes, beliefs, and values

Operations and modifications

  Reading
    Operations:
      Text:

      Supplementary reading:

      Library:

    Modifications:

(continued)

Writing
  Operations:

  Modifications:

Oral Expression
  Operations:

  Modifications:

Student Assessment
  Operations:

  Modifications:

Demonstrations and projects
  Operations:

  Modifications:

(continued)

Other operation factors

Unit Evaluation

TEACHER'S MASTER COPY OF UNIT STUDY GUIDE

SAMPLE

UNIT STUDY GUIDE (USG)

NAME OF STUDENT _____ DATE _____

STUDENT DESCRIPTION:

SUBJECT AREA (course) __Social Studies_____ INSTRUCTOR __Miss R. McClung_____

UNIT OF STUDY __Our Constitution and Government_____ GRADE ____8_____

Brief description and objectives of unit of study   Duration: __12 weeks_____

This unit of study is designed to help the student understand how government serves all of the people and that citizens have rights which include being able to choose the individuals who will run the government.

Objectives:
1. Students will gain an understanding of the role of different governmental agencies within national, state, and local areas of responsibility and how these interact with each other to serve the needs of the people.
2. Students will gain an understanding and appreciation of our Constitution and form of government through the study of basic concepts inherent in a democracy.

The content includes the study of the government and the constitution along with the history that is involved in their development.

Basic facts and concepts

1. Citizens are members of what three government groups?
2. What four things must a person prove in order to be naturalized?
3. What sets the rules of citizenship?
4. Why do we pay taxes?
5. How many colonies existed under British control in 1776? Name them.
6. What groups settled in Pennsylvania, Massachusetts, Virginia?
7. What do we celebrate on the 4th of July?
8. Why do we need a Constitution?
9. What are the Articles of Confederation?
10. What is a constitutional convention?
11. What was the Continental Congress?
12. Who were some of the important men at the "Constitutional Convention"?
13. What is the Bill of Rights?
14. What is the Declaration of Independence?

(continued)

15. Who was the first president?
16. List the executive departments of the government.
17. Who was the first Secretary of the Treasury, State?
18. What is the difference between final authority and delegated authority?
19. How does the Constitution tell the purposes of the federal government and how authority is vested?
20. What does the Constitution delegate to the states?
21. How can the Constitution be amended?
22. How many amendments have been added? List them.
23. Why do we need to change our Constitution?
24. What is the party system?
25. What authority do the federal courts have?
26. What is the Equal Rights Amendment?
27. Explain the 12th, 13th, 14th, 15th, 16th, 19th, 20th, 24th, and 26th amendments.
28. What powers are delegated to the federal government?
29. Who can vote?
30. How do you decide what candidate to vote for?
31. What are the purposes or aims of the Preamble to the Constitution?
32. What are the qualifications for the Senate (senator) and the House of Representatives (congressman)?
33. Explain the "system of checks and balances."
34. How are the number of senators and congressmen determined and for what number of years?
35. Give examples of how the Senate can "check the president."
36. Differentiate between the powers of the "House" and "Senate."
37. How is a "Bill" introduced and approved? How does it become law?
38. List three financial powers of Congress.
39. What laws cannot be passed by Congress?
40. What is a congressional committee?
41. Explain the office of the president: term, inauguration, elected by, qualifications, chief power and duty, other powers.
42. List the eleven executive (cabinet) departments.
43. Explain the purpose of the federal courts.
44. Explain the following: Supreme Court, U.S. Customs Court, U.S. District Court, Court of Claims, Court of Appeals.
45. List the branches of state government.
46. List three important executive officials of the state.
47. What are the two houses of the state legislature called?
48. Explain the general plan of state government.
49. What services do we get from local government?
50. How does the federal government work with the state government in health, education, and welfare?
51. How does the federal government work with farmers, businesspeople, wage earners, and travelers?

Basic skills

Application of facts and concepts learned in the following areas:

a. writing of compositions
b. participation in group project
c. writing performance on essay examinations
d. overall oral presentations

(continued)

Basic vocabulary

agriculture	census	delegates	misdemeanors	Senate
alien	city council	democracy	naturalized	sovereignty
allegiance	city manager	elected	nominated	speaker, the
amendment	civil	electors	oath	taxes
appointed	commerce	equality	ordinances	town
article	commission	impeach	parliament	treason
Articles of	Congress	income	patent	treaty
Confederation	Continental	incorporated	petition	union
auditor	Congress	inheritance	platform	urban
ballot	convention	judicial	Preamble	vested
bill	county	jurisdiction	property	veto
bribery	county seat	law	*pro tempore*	
budget	Declaration of	license	ratification	
cabinet	Independence	majority	register	
candidates	delegated	mayor	republic	

Attitudes, beliefs, and values

Students will indicate the following through oral statements and behavior:

a. an appreciation of freedom of choice and security within a democratic society.
b. an affirmation that opportunities are available to anyone who has the will to strive for self-fulfillment
c. a reflection of positive feelings about themselves, their parents, and society in general
d. a respect for law and property and for the individuals who are responsible for planning and carrying out legal mandates at different levels of society

Operations and modifications

Reading
Operations:
Text:
    The American Way, Nancy W. Bauer, chapter 9, "Out of Many a New Nation," pages 194–241

    The Free and the Brave, Henry F. Graff, Part 4, "Shaping a Nation" Chapter 11, "Fashioning a New Government," pages 220–245

Supplementary reading:
    Our Constitution and Government, Simplified Edition, John G. Harvey, 1973

Library:
    See class section and bibliography for this unit.

Modifications:

(continued)

Writing
Operations:

UNIT GRADE

1. Three-page essay (composition) entitled "How I View the Constitution"
   (due after 3 weeks)   15% _____
2. Note-taking in class from lectures and demonstrations
3. Essay section of unit quizzes and examinations

Modifications:

Oral Expression
Operations:

1. Oral participation in classroom discussions (desired but not mandatory or grade-dependent)

Modifications:

Student Assessment
Operations:

1. Quiz 1 (multiple-choice, fill-in, and brief essay) all
   +s (pluses) after 3 weeks   10% _____
2. Quiz 2 (multiple-choice, fill-in, and brief essay) all
   −s (minuses) after 6 weeks   10% _____
3. Quiz 3 (multiple-choice, fill-in, and brief essay) all
   0s (zeroes) after 9 weeks   10% _____
4. Unit examination—all content, 12th week   30% _____

Modifications:

Demonstrations and projects
Operations:

1. Group project presentation or committee report on
   topic to be assigned dealing with our Constitution
   and government (due after 8 weeks)   20% _____

Modifications:

(continued)

UNIT GRADE

Other operation factors

5% _____

1. Grade is based on teacher judgment in areas dealing with attitudes, beliefs, values, motivation, and overall participation.
2. Homework is assigned each class period with few exceptions and will be checked and graded periodically (written work).

Unit Evaluation

100% _____

1. Total unit grade for student
2. Brief questionnaire to resource teachers
3. Discussion with students, teachers, and parents

UNIT STUDY GUIDE (USG)

NAME OF STUDENT ___*William Smith*___ DATE ___*2/10/81*___

STUDENT DESCRIPTION: *1. Visually impaired; diagnosed as legally blind.*
2. Qualifies for Recording for the Blind Inc. services.
3. Reads material typed on a primary typewriter very slowly.
4. Writing is very difficult or impossible.
5. Reading at approximately level 7.
6. Parents very cooperative.

SUBJECT AREA (course) ___Social Studies___ INSTRUCTOR ___Miss R. McClung___

UNIT OF STUDY ___Our Constitution and Government___ GRADE ___8___

Brief description and objectives of unit of study

Duration: ___12 weeks___

This unit of study is designed to help the student to understand how government serves all of the people and that citizens have rights which include being able to choose the individuals who will run the government.

Objectives:

1. Students will gain an understanding of the role of different governmental agencies within national, state, and local areas of responsibility and how these interact with each other to serve the needs of the people.
2. Students will gain an understanding and appreciation of our Constitution and form of government through the study of basic concepts inherent in a democracy.

The content includes the study of the government and the Constitution along with the history that is involved in their development.

Basic facts and concepts

+1. Citizens are members of what three government groups?
+2. What four things must a person prove in order to be naturalized?
+3. What sets the rules of citizenship?
+4. Why do we pay taxes?
+5. How many colonies existed under British control in 1776? Name them.
+6. What groups settled in Pennsylvania, Massachusetts, Virginia?
+7. What do we celebrate on the 4th of July?
+8. Why do we need a Constitution?
+9. What are the Articles of Confederation?
+10. What is a constitutional convention?
+11. What was the Continental Congress?
+12. Who were some of the important men at the "Constitutional Convention"?
+13. What is the Bill of Rights?
+14. What is the Declaration of Independence?

(continued)

+15. Who was the first president?

+16. List the executive departments of the government.

+17. Who was the first Secretary of the Treasury, State?

+18. What is the difference between final authority and delegated authority?

+19. How does the Constitution tell the purposes of the federal government and how authority is vested?

+20. What does the Constitution delegate to the states?

+21. How can the Constitution be amended?

−22. How many amendments have been added? List them.

−23. Why do we need to change our Constitution?

−24. What is the party system?

−25. What authority do the federal courts have?

−26. What is the Equal Rights Amendment?

−27. Explain the 12th, 13th, 14th, 15th, 16th, 19th, 20th, 24th, and 26th amendments.

−28. What powers are delegated to the federal government?

−29. Who can vote?

−30. How do you decide what candidate to vote for?

−31. What are the purposes or aims of the Preamble to the Constitution?

−32. What are the qualifications for the Senate (senator) and the House of Representatives (congressman)?

−33. Explain the "system of checks and balances."

−34. How are the number of senators and congressmen determined and for what number of years?

−35. Give examples of how the Senate can "check the president."

−36. Differentiate between the powers of the "House" and "Senate."

−37. How is a "Bill" introduced and approved? How does it become law?

−38. List three financial powers of Congress.

−39. What laws cannot be passed by Congress?

−40. What is a congressional committee?

o 41. Explain the office of the president: term, inauguration, elected by, qualifications, chief power and duty, other powers.

o 42. List the eleven executive (cabinet) departments.

o 43. Explain the purpose of the federal courts.

o 44. Explain the following: Supreme Court, U.S. Customs Court, U.S. District Court, Court of Claims, Court of Appeals.

o 45. List the branches of state government.

o 46. List three important executive officials of the state.

o 47. What are the two houses of the state legislature called?

o 48. Explain the general plan of state government.

o 49. What services do we get from local government?

o 50. How does the federal government work with the state government in health, education, and welfare?

o 51. How does the federal government work with farmers, businesspeople, wage earners, and travelers?

Basic skills

Application of facts and concepts learned in the following areas:

a. writing of compositions

b. participation in group project

c. writing performance on essay examinations

d. overall oral presentations

(continued)

Basic vocabulary

agriculture	census	delegates	misdemeanors	Senate
alien	city council	democracy	naturalized	sovereignty
allegiance	city manager	elected	nominated	speaker, the
amendment	civil	electors	oath	taxes
appointed	commerce	equality	ordinances	town
article	commission	impeach	parliament	treason
Articles of	Congress	income	patent	treaty
Confederation	Continental	incorporated	petition	union
auditor	Congress	inheritance	platform	urban
ballot	convention	judicial	preamble	vested
bill	county	jurisdiction	property	veto
bribery	county seat	law	*pro tempore*	
budget	Declaration of	license	ratification	
cabinet	Independence	majority	register	
candidates	delegated	mayor	republic	

Attitudes, beliefs, and values

Students will indicate the following through oral statements and behavior:

a. an appreciation of freedom of choice and security within a democratic society.
b. an affirmation that opportunities are available to anyone who has the will to strive for self-fulfillment
c. a reflection of positive feelings about themselves, their parents, and society in general
d. a respect for law and property and for the individuals who are responsible for planning and carrying out legal mandates at different levels of society

Operations and modifications

Reading
  Operations:

Text:	*The American Way,* Nancy W. Bauer, chapter 9, "Out of Many a New Nation," pages 194–241
	The Free and the Brave, Henry F. Graff, Part 4, "Shaping a Nation" Chapter 11, "Fashioning a New Government," pages 220–245
Supplementary reading:	*Our Constitution and Government,* Simplified Edition, John G. Harvey, 1973
Library:	See class section and bibliography for this unit.

Modifications:

1. All required text book reading to be sent to Recording for the Blind, Inc. for free taping of educational books (materials)

2. Reader identified for special assignments including resource teacher.

(continued)

Writing
  Operations: **UNIT GRADE**

1. Three-page essay (composition) entitled "How I View the Constitution" (due after 3 weeks)   15% _____
2. Note-taking in class from lectures and demonstrations
3. Essay section of unit quizzes and examinations

Modifications:

1. Use of brailling in class.
2. Use of primary typewriter made available in "Learning Center."

Oral Expression
  Operations:

1. Oral participation in classroom discussions (desired but not mandatory or grade-dependent)

Modifications:

No special considerations are indicated for oral participation.

Student Assessment
  Operations:

1. Quiz 1 (multiple-choice, fill-in, and brief essay) all
   +s (pluses) after 3 weeks   10% _____
2. Quiz 2 (multiple-choice, fill-in, and brief essay) all
   −s (minuses) after 6 weeks   10% _____
3. Quiz 3 (multiple-choice, fill-in, and brief essay) all
   0s (zeroes) after 9 weeks   10% _____
4. Unit examination—all content, 12th week   30% _____

Modifications: Options:

1. Quizzes and tests retyped on Primary typewriter by resource teacher.
2. Oral quizzes and tests given when necessary.
3. Examinations given in braille and decoded by resource teacher.

Demonstrations and projects
  Operations:

1. Group project presentation or committee report on
   topic to be assigned dealing with our Constitution
   and government (due after 8 weeks)   20% _____

Modifications:

1. Participation in data collection and reporting required.
2. Excused from model building if inappropriate and
   from typing of report in Pica print.

(continued)

UNIT GRADE

Other operation factors

5% _____

1. Grade based on teacher judgment in areas dealing with attitudes, beliefs, values, motivation, and overall participation.
2. Homework is assigned each class period with few exceptions and will be checked and graded periodically (written work).

Unit Evaluation

100% _____

1. Total unit grade for student
2. Brief questionnaire to resource teachers
3. Discussion with students, teachers, and parents

b. The ability to recall facts does not necessarily require the understanding of concepts. Some students can recall names, dates, and places but cannot formulate the important concepts.

c. Students with poor memories may forget facts but learn the concepts.

d. Facts are part of the basic elements of which concepts are comprised.

e. Facts are most often stated in concrete and functional terms; e.g., what something was, was not, is, is not, does, or does not in reference to time and space.

f. Examples of basic facts:

    (1) Christopher Columbus discovered America in 1492.

    (2) Green plants need the sun's energy to carry on photosynthesis.

    (3) Red paint mixed with yellow paint does not give blue paint.

Consider the following in terms of basic concepts:

a. Concepts involve formulating generalizations, assumptions, classifications, judgments, cause-effect relationships, and inferences utilizing facts as a basis.

b. Examples of basic concepts are as follows:

    (1) Christopher Columbus represents humankind's willingness to overcome hardship and fear, to satisfy our inquisitive nature as well as our quest for power, wealth, and glory.

    (2) Photosynthesis taken to its logical conclusion suggests that the sun is critical for the existence of all life on earth.

    (3) Colors when combined interact with each other giving different colors with predictable results.

4. *Basic skills*

List the basic skills that are to be mastered for a particular unit of study. By skills we mean the following:

dexterity	application of facts and concepts
craftsmanship	to language and math such as
artistry	problem solving and creative
agility	writing
technique	virtuosity
collaboration	adaptability

5. *Basic Vocabulary*

List the important words to be understood, read, and written that are deemed essential in areas involving facts, concepts, skills, attitudes, beliefs, and values, for a particular unit of study.

6. *Attitudes, Beliefs, and Values*

List the attitudes, beliefs, and values that are deemed important to a particular unit of study. Such things as social consciousness, humanism, scientific method, logic, character, responsibility, appreciation of property, trust, truth, self-worth, and motivation are essential elements and should be listed as expected outcomes for a given unit of study. Attitudes, beliefs, and values do not always lend themselves to paper-and-pencil evaluation. Often these characteristics must be observed in the individuals.

7. *Operations and Modifications*

Specify the operations necessary for an individual student to succeed in acquiring the facts, concepts, skills, attitudes, beliefs, values, and vocabulary associated with a particular unit of study. What does a student have to do to participate effectively in the process, to acquire the content, and to indicate what he or she has learned. This includes being able to read, write, and express oneself orally (operations). Once having determined the operations that will be required, and whether or not the student in fact has the skills necessary for these operations, the teacher can then decide on what modifications will have to be made in order to accommodate to any deficiencies in the learner. Operations and modifications for academic areas include the following:

a. *Reading*

    (1) Operations: The student is required to read, at the independent level, the material assigned for a particular unit of study. The text book (pages), reference books, or other material that the student will be required to read should be listed.

    (2) Modifications: If the learner is deficient in reading, or has visual problems that affect the reading of standard print, what modification will be made so that the student can acquire the necessary information? These should be listed and could include the following:

      —peer or volunteer readers

      —recorded material on cassettes

      —material retyped using primary typewriter

      —arranging for material to be brailled

      —utilization of support services such as special education resource teachers, reading specialists, peer tutors, parents, etc., as readers

      —utilizing specialized services such as Recording for the Blind, Inc. Students certified as dyslexic by a physician may qualify for services from Recording for the Blind, Inc., 215 E. 58th Street, New York, NY 10022. (212) 751-0860.

b. *Writing*

(1) Operations: The student is required to write as a part of the requirements of the course. This could include:
—notetaking
—writing what is necessary for the preparation of projects
—writing that is required for the taking of tests

(2) Modifications: If the student has difficulty in writing due to poor fine-motor control, spatial disabilities, cerebral palsy, or visual problems, what modifications will be made to accommodate to the disability? Several modifications in the area of writing can be used, including:
—brailling to be transcribed
—use of a typewriter
—taking oral examinations
—use of demonstrations
—allowing the student more time for writing (slowness may be a factor)

c. *Oral production and expression*

(1) Operations: The student is required to participate orally in presentations as a part of course requirements. The student may have a speech problem such as stuttering, articulation difficulty, or some other type of speech impediment. This could result in a problem with understanding the learner (intelligibility). The learner may have a problem with syntax and formulation (grammatic structure) and may be unable to speak in coherent sentences. Some students may be unable to retrieve words that they want to use to express themselves or make their wants known. Some students may not even be able to verbalize their ideas.

(2) Modifications: If the student cannot or does not participate orally, consider the following:
—Reduce the stress on oral presentation.
—Allow the student to participate in activities that provide the greatest opportunity for success, such as voluntary presentations.
—Allow more time. Even though it is sometimes disconcerting, the student may need more time when presenting orally. This requires patience and understanding.
—Excuse the student. There may be situations where the student would be completely excused from oral presentations for a period of time. Opportunities to participate in presentations through demonstration and group research activities that result in the preparation of presentations should be explored.

d. *Student assessment*

(1) Operations: Students will be expected to do combinations of the following:
—take quizzes
—take tests
—be graded on oral presentation
—be graded on projects, reports, etc.
These should be listed in detail in terms of types and conditions of assessment.

(2) Modifications: What modifications will be made in the area of student assessment for students who cannot verbalize, write, or read? The following are suggested alternatives:
—oral examinations
—testing using tapes or cassettes
—using resource individuals to test the student one-on-one
—permitting the student to use a typewriter
—allowing the student to demonstrate a concept
—having tests retyped using a primary typewriter (large print)

e. *Demonstrations and projects*

(1) Operations: Students will be required to do a combination of the following:
—perform experiments
—construct models
—develop projects
—perform other physical tasks
These tasks should be specified and time lines indicated if possible.

(2) Modifications: Students who are physically unable to develop projects may be able to
—do the research
—present the project orally
—measure and collect
—guide someone else who demonstrates for them

f. *Other operation factors to consider*

(1) Can the learner utilize measurement?

(2) Can the student accomplish out-of-school assignments?

(3) Is the student organized in terms of time and space? This includes such things as homework and effective study habits. In cases of poor organization, the instructor and parents may have to coordinate their efforts to structure the life space of the learner for more effective organization and management of school-related activities.

8. *Unit Evaluation*

The instructor should list the ways in which he or she will determine how effectively the unit of study has been designed and implemented. The following can be accomplished:

a. Discuss with the students how they feel about the particular unit of study.

b. Present a simple questionnaire to the students requesting information about content, procedures, presentations, etc., and suggestions for improvement.

c. Discuss with, and/or present a simple questionnaire to, appropriate teachers and parents as to the effectiveness of the unit of study.

d. Make judgments based on the performance of nonhandicapped students in the class as well as those with special needs. If a disproportionate number of students with special needs fail the unit, it may indicate a need for a reevaluation of the procedures. It is important that the content remain constant so that there is no "watering down" of the curriculum. The instructor should, however, make any reasonable accommodation in the process to the special needs of handicapped students so that they will have every opportunity to acquire the content of the course. The Unit Study Guide is designed for this purpose.

Steps in Designing a Unit Study Guide

The following is a suggested sequence of steps to be followed in designing a USG for a subject-level area.

1. Develop a master Unit Study Guide form (see sample Form 12-2) for a particular area of study, leaving blank those areas that must be individualized for particular students, such as student's name, description of student, and modifications. *Include* the following:

a. Brief description and objectives of unit of study

b. Basic facts and concepts

c. Basic skills

d. Basic vocabulary

e. Attitudes, beliefs, and values

f. Any operations (expected work) that are required of all students; such as readings, written work, oral presentations, tests (how and when assessment will occur), and demonstrations and projects

g. How the overall unit will be evaluated

2. Make multiple copies of the master forms (as many as desired for the class).

3. The blanks can be filled in later for individual students as necessary; e.g., name of student, date, student description, and any modifications that will have to be made in terms of the particular student's needs (see sample Form 12-3).

4. Complete one of the copies for each student exhibiting special needs in the class including the modification. Then do the following:

a. Make three copies of their forms: one each for the student, resource teacher, and parent, if desired.

b. Discuss the Unit Study Guide with the individual students, resource teachers, and parents.

c. Teach the unit of study in the usual manner.

d. Upon completion of the unit of study, determine the following as part of the evaluation:

(1) benefit to the students

(2) benefit to the resource teacher

(3) benefit to the parent

(4) overall benefit as a management tool for improving communication between the individuals involved

Additional Things to Consider

1. The amount of space for the different headings in the Unit Study Guide is determined by the individual teacher who has to consider the content, procedure, and the relative importance of the particular subheadings within the USG. It is conceivable that the space designation for headings would change from unit to unit. The teacher is *not bound* by the space allotted on the sample forms. The categories are what is important. The sample forms are just examples of how a Unit Study Guide can be written. The following outline of the Unit Study Guide components can be used as a guide.

Outline of Unit-Study Guide Components

1. Name of student

2. Date

3. Student description

4. Subject area (course)
5. Instructor
6. Unit of study
7. Grade
8. Brief description and objectives of unit of study
9. Duration
10. Basic facts and concepts
11. Basic skills
12. Basic vocabulary
13. Attitudes, beliefs, and values
14. Operations and Modifications

   Reading: Operations—Modifications

   Writing: Operations—Modifications

   Oral expression: Operations—Modifications

   Student assessment: Operations—Modifications

   Demonstrations and projects: Operations—Modifications

   Other operations factors
15. Unit evaluation

2. The teacher should plan for the number of units, by specific areas of study, necessary to encompass the semester's or year's curriculum in the subject area.

3. The range of variability in terms of special needs, giftedness, etc., in the class must be determined. It is important to determine the number of students exhibiting different types of variability in learning and behavior. This includes students with special needs, giftedness, reading problems, etc., who have been assigned to the particular class or course. The area of variability could include those described as:

hearing impaired	mildly mentally
visually impaired	handicapped
physically handicapped	emotionally disturbed
learning disabled	socially maladjusted
reading disabled	mentally gifted/talented
combinations of the above	

4. The teachers concerned about a particular student should meet prior to and/or after the USGs have been developed to discuss learner strengths and weaknesses. At that time the kinds of accommodations that will need to be made for students' effective integration into least-restrictive environments (in terms of regular class participation) should be discussed, fully understood, and agreed upon. This concept goes *beyond* the IEP into the application of the areas outlined in the objectives. This is where the Unit Study Guides apply.

Grading

Cases will occur in which students with special needs, participating in regular classroom subject-level areas, are *not* expected to achieve the minimum according to the standard criteria listed in the Unit Study Guide. This must be specified at the outset as part of the Individual Educational Plan for the student. In cases where the criteria for success is set lower, the grading system must be modified. That is, the student may not be able to achieve the minimal level of success, based on the criteria established for all the students in the class. There is then a need for an optional grading system, which should be fully explained to the parents. The parents can indicate whether or not they prefer to have their child graded on the basis of the standard system or on the basis of lower-expected-performance criteria as indicated on an Individual Educational Plan. The criteria for success can then be stated for participation and for achieving several objectives, not necessarily for passing according to the regular grading system. Put another way, it can be indicated that the student can "fail" the unit (tests, projects, papers, etc., required) but succeed as far as the objectives stated in the IEP. The individual developing the IEP objectives for a given student may, for example, wish to utilize, for the first two units of study, the standard grading system as the criteria for success. If the student fails the units—even with the best support system available, including the Unit Study Guide—then alternatives should be considered, as follows:

1. Move the student to another class within the same academic subject area—one that deals with the content area in a more simplified or different manner. The criterion level for success may be within the achievement potential of the special needs student. The student may exhibit a greater aptitude to achieve with another approach in the same subject area.

2. The decision may be made to permit the student to remain in the same class, while setting the criteria for success at below the minimum level of success for the other students. This would occur when the student appears to be profiting from the experience in terms of "getting something out of the course" and for social reasons. The grade, however, for that student should carry a different connotation and should be so noted on the report card and records.

3. The student could be taught the subject by the resource teacher in a small-group setting.

Who Develops the Unit Study Guide

The Unit Study Guide can be developed by the following:

1. Regular classroom teachers who have students with special needs in their classrooms. They give the Unit Study Guide to the special education resource teacher and the student for purposes of delineating the unit of study.
2. Regular class and resource teachers as a shared responsibility, enabling both to determine collaboratively the minimum basic criteria in all the subareas as well as the operations and modifications necessary for success.
3. The special education resource teacher can develop a Unit Study Guide in anticipation of a particular course offered by the regular classroom teacher. This may be "second guessing" the regular teacher, but it is better than having none at all.

One of the most important areas of concern in this whole process is the relationship between the regular class teacher and the resource teacher. Students who receive a program based on good collaborative working relationships between the regular classroom teacher and the special education resource teacher, who use USGs as one vehicle for communication, should experience a higher probability of success than those who are not being educated within a cooperative process. In cases where students are failing within ideal situations, with every accommodation possible including the Unit Study Guides, consideration should be given to their not being able to deal with the material at that level and the program should be changed.

Summary

The Unit Study Guide is a functional management system, not intended to lock the regular classroom teacher into teaching only that which is specified on the student form. The rationale behind the USG is as follows:

1. It is designed to improve communication between the regular class teacher, the special education teacher, the student, and the parents who get copies of the USGs. The USGs enable them to understand initially what the *minimum* basic requirements are for success in a particular unit of study. This includes the allowable modifications for an individual's special needs.

2. It allows individuals other than the subject-level teacher to understand the requirements for a unit of study and hence be able to tutor the student in critical areas of concern.
3. It indicates the content of a particular subject area, enabling the concepts and vocabulary to be incorporated into a student's reading, writing, and spelling program.
4. It helps the subject-level teacher to articulate more precisely the expected student outcomes for a particular unit of study, other than merely stating objectives.
5. It serves as a means by which individuals can review a student's performance after a unit is completed to examine strengths and weaknesses. More appropriate decisions can be made in terms of working with the student or of determining if continuation in a particular course or program is advisable.
6. Students who are expected to benefit most from the USGs are those who can accomplish the minimum criteria for success in a subject-level area with the aid of a support system that includes a Unit Study Guide in combination with resource personnel.
7. It is helpful to new students coming into the class in the middle of a unit of study.
8. Its development by groups of teachers departmentally makes it easier to provide a more uniform approach to dealing with course content and procedures of particular subject areas.
9. It provides the student with special needs with a support system that should reduce the fear and anxiety that attends the unknown: e.g., What will I have to do in this course? What will I have to read or write? How will I be tested? What kind of material will I be expected to learn?

While a Unit Study Guide may appear at the outset to be a burden on the instructor, in the final analysis it will prove to be a useful device. Once developed, only minor modifications will need to be added to it, in terms of content, procedures, skills, vocabulary, operations, and modifications, etc., as new knowledge is acquired.

SCIENCE AND SOCIAL STUDIES RESOURCES

The following pages contain an array of resources that cover many content areas of the science and social studies curriculum. The free or inexpensive materials will provide the teacher with environmental education information and activities that can be incorporated into any science and social studies curriculum.

For information on a subject you are interested in, write the organizations listed and ask for their free brochures. Care should be taken to print your name and address clearly. Request all information well in advance of the time you will need it.

ACID RAIN

1. The Acid Rain Foundation, Inc., 1410 Varsity Drive, Raleigh, NC 27606
2. Public Focus, 489 College St., Suite 500, Toronto, ON, M6G 1A5 Canada

AIR POLLUTION

1. Air Waste Management Assoc., P.O. Box 2861, Pittsburgh, PA 15230
2. Zero Population Growth, 1400 16th Street, N.W., Suite 320, Washington, DC 20036
3. American Lung Assoc., 1740 Broadway, New York, NY 10019

ANIMALS—LAND

1. Michael Olaf, The Montessori Shop, 5817 College Avenue, Oakland, CA 94618
2. Pennsylvania Game Comm., P.O. Box 1567, Harrisburg, PA 17105
3. Marginal Media, P.O. Box 241, Fredonia, NY 14063
4. Consumer Information Center–K, P.O. Box 100, Pueblo, CO 81002
5. Animal Protection Institute of America, 2831 Fruitridge Road, P.O. Box 22505, Sacramento, CA 95822
6. The Humane Society of the United States, 2100 L Street, N.W., Washington, DC 20037
7. Ohio Dept. of Natural Resources, Publications Center, Fountain Square, Columbus, OH 43224
8. Agricultural Bulletin, Room 245, 30 North Murray Street, Madison, WI 53715
9. Spizzirri Publishing Co., P.O. Box 9397, Rapid City, SD 57709
10. Ampersand Press, 691 26th St., Oakland, CA 94612
11. LHS Gems, Lawrence Hall of Science, Univ. of California, Berkeley, CA 94720
12. Massachusetts Audubon Society, Public Information Office, Lincoln, MA 01773
13. Museum Products, 3175 Gold Star Highway, Mystic, CT 06355

ANIMALS—MARINE

1. Dover Publications, 31 East 2nd St., Mineola, NY 11501
2. Animal Protection Institute of America, 2831 Fruitridge Road, P.O. Box 22505, Sacramento, CA 95822
3. Center for Marine Conservation, 1725 DeSales Street, N.W., Washington, DC 20036
4. HEART, Piney Woods Wildlife Society, Box 681231, Houston, TX 77268-1231
5. American Cetacean Society, P.O. Box 2639, San Pedro, CA 90731
6. Massachusetts Audubon Society, Public Information Office, Lincoln, MA 01773
7. Ampersand Press, 691 26th St., Oakland, CA 94612
8. Bits and Pieces, 1 Puzzle Place, Ridgely, MD 21685
9. Spizzirri Pub., P.O. Box 9397, Rapid City, SD 57709
10. Animal Welfare Inst., P.O. Box 3650, Washington, DC 20007

ASTRONOMY

1. R. Woods, Consumer Info, Center–K, P.O. Box 100, Pueblo, CO 81002
2. Ampersand Press, 691 26th Street, Oakland, CA 94612
3. Michael Olaf, The Montessori Shop, 5817 College Ave., Oakland, CA 94618
4. Discovery Corner, Lawrence Hall of Science, Univ. of California, Berkeley, CA 94720

BIRDS

1. Agricultural Bulletin, Room 245, 30 North Murray St., Madison, WI 53715
2. Animal Welfare Inst., P.O. Box 3650, Washington, DC 20007
3. Educational Services, National Audubon Society, 950 Third Avenue, New York, NY 10022
4. Pennsylvania Game Comm., P.O. Box 1567, Harrisburg, PA 17105-1567
5. Distribution Center C, Cornell University, 7 Research Park, Ithaca, NY 14850
6. Dover Publications, 31 East 2d St., Mineola, NY 11501
7. Museum Products, 3175 Gold Star Highway, Mystic, CT 06355
8. The Owl's Nest, P.O. Box 5491, Fresno, CA 93755
9. Scrollcraft, 420 East Water Street, P.O. Box 38158, Urbana, OH 43078

10. Gull Lake Environmental Education Project, Kellogg Bird Sanctuary of Michigan State Univ., 12685 C Avenue, Augusta, MI 49012
11. Creative Dimensions, P.O. Box 1393, Bellingham, WA 98227

CONSERVATION OF SOIL AND WATER

1. U.S. Dept. of Agriculture, Soil Conservation Svc., P.O. Box 2890, Washington, DC 20013

DINOSAURS AND FOSSILS

1. The Carnegie Museum of Natural History, 4400 Forbes Ave., Pittsburgh, PA 15213
2. Dover Publications, 31 East 2nd St., Mineola, NY 11501
3. Museum Projects, 3175 Gold Star Highway, Mystic, CT 06355
4. Insect Lore Products, P.O. Box 1535, Shafter, CA 93263
5. Michael Olaf, The Montessori Shop, 5817 College Ave., Oakland, CA 94618
6. Spizzirri Publishing, P.O. Box 9397, Rapid City, SD 57709

ENDANGERED SPECIES

1. Animal Welfare Inst., P.O. Box 3650, Washington, DC 20007
2. The Humane Society of the U.S., 2100 L Street, N.W., Washington, DC 20037
3. Spizzirri Publishing, P.O. Box 9397, Rapid City, SD 57709
4. S. James, Consumer Information Center B, P.O. Box 100, Pueblo, CO 81002
5. The Nature Conservancy Poster, 1800 N. Kent St., Arlington, VA 22209
6. Animal Protection Inst. of America, 2831 Fruitridge Road, P.O. Box 22505, Sacramento, CA 95822

ENERGY

1. Agricultural Bulletin, Room 245, 30 N. Murray St., Madison, WI 53715
2. Educational Programs, American Gas Assoc., 1515 Wilson Blvd., Arlington, VA 22209
3. Ampersand Press, 691 26th St., Oakland, CA 94612
4. Charles Edison Fund, 101 S. Harrison St., East Orange, NJ 07108
5. NEED Project, P.O. Box 2518, Reston, VA 22090
6. Florida Solar Energy Center, 300 State Road 401, Cape Canaveral, FL 32920-4099

7. National Science Teachers' Assoc., 1742 Connecticut Ave., N.W., Washington, DC 20009

ENVIRONMENTAL ISSUES

1. Office of Public Affairs, U.S. Environmental Protection Agency, 401 M Street, S.W., Washington, DC 20460

FARMLANDS

1. Concern, Inc., 1794 Columbia Road, N.W., Washington, DC 20009
2. Museum Products, 3175 Gold Star Highway, Mystic, CT 06355
3. Scrollcraft, 420 East Water Street, P.O. Box 38158, Urbana, OH 43078
4. Soil Conservation Society of America, 7515 Northeast Ankeny Road, Ankeny, IA 50021-9764

FISH

1. Dover Publications, 31 East 2nd St., Mineola, NY 11501
2. Spizzirri Publishing, P.O. Box 9397, Rapid City, SD 57709

FLOWERS

1. Museum Products, 3175 Gold Star Highway, Mystic, CT 06355
2. Dover Publications, 31 East 2nd St., Mineola, NY 11501
3. Michael Olaf, The Montessori Shop, 5817 College Avenue, Oakland, CA 94618
4. Natural Resources Defense Council, 122 East 42nd St., New York, NY 10168

FORESTS

1. Distribution Center—MW, Cornell University, 7-8 Research Park, Ithaca, NY 14850

GARDENING

1. National Gardening Assoc., 180 Flynn Ave., Burlington, VT 05401

GEOGRAPHY

1. National Council for Geographic Education, Leonard 16A, Indiana University of Pennsylvania, Indiana, PA 15705

GLOBAL ISSUES

1. Global Tomorrow Coalition, 1325 G Street, N.W., Suite 915, Washington, DC 20005

GREENHOUSE EFFECT

1. Public Information Center, U.S. Environmental Protection Agency, 401 M Street, S.W., Washington, DC 20460
2. World Resources Institute, 1709 New York Avenue, N.W., Washington, DC 20006
3. Zero Population Growth, 1400 16th St., N.W., Suite 320, Washington, DC 20036

GROUNDWATER

1. Massachusetts Audubon Society, Publication Office, Lincoln, MA 01773
2. Agricultural Bulletin, Room 245, 30 North Murray Street, Madison, WI 53715
3. Concern, Inc., 1794 Columbia Road, N.W., Washington, DC 20009

HABITATS

1. Alley Pond Environmental Center, 228-06 Northern Boulevard, Douglaston, NY 11363
2. Defenders of Wildlife, 2244 19th St., N.W., Washington, DC 20036
3. National Institute for Urban Wildlife, 10921 Trotting Ridge Way, Columbia, MD 21044
4. The Nature Conservancy, 1800 North Kent Street, Arlington, VA 22209
5. National Audubon Society, Poster, Route 4, Box 171, Sharon, CT 06069

HAZARDOUS WASTE

1. Air & Waste Management Assoc., P.O. Box 2861, Pittsburgh, PA 15230
2. League of Women Voters of the U.S., 1730 M Street, N.W., Washington, DC 20036
3. Citizen's Clearinghouse for Hazardous Wastes, P.O. Box 926, Arlington, VA 22216
4. Public Information Center, U.S. E.P.A., 401 M Street, S.W., Washington, DC 20460

HOUSEHOLD TOXICS

1. Agricultural Bulletin, Room 245, 30 N. Murray St., Madison, WI 53715
2. S. James, Consumer Information Center–K, P.O. Box 100, Pueblo, CO 81002
3. Center for Safety in the Arts, 5 Beekman St., New York, NY 10038

INSECTS, WORMS, AND SPIDERS

1. Citizens for a Better Environment, 942 Market St., Suite 505, San Francisco, CA 94102

2. American Forestry Assoc., 1319 18th St., N.W., Washington, DC 20036
3. Museum Products, 3175 Gold Star Highway, Mystic, CT 06355
4. Michael Olaf, The Montessori Shop, 5817 College Ave., Oakland, CA 94618
5. The A.I. Root Co., P.O. Box 706, Medina, OH 44258-0706
6. LHS Gems, Lawrence Hall of Science, Univ. of California, Berkeley, CA 94720
7. Gull Lake Environmental Education Project, Kellogg Bird Sanctuary of Michigan State Univ., 12685 C Avenue, Augusta, MI 49012
8. Insect Lore Products, P.O. Box 1535, Shafter, CA 93263
9. The Butterfly Co., 51-17 Rockaway Beach Blvd., Far Rockaway, NY 11691
10. State University of New York, College of Environmental Science and Forestry, Syracuse, NY 13210
11. Massachusetts Audubon Society, Public Info. Office, Lincoln, MA 01773
12. Agricultural Bulletin, Room 245, 30 North Murray St., Madison, WI 53715
13. Alley Pond Environmental Center, 228-06 Northern Boulevard, Douglaston, NY 11363
14. Animal Town Game Co., P.O. Box 2002, Santa Barbara, CA 93120

LAKES

1. Public Focus, 489 College St., Suite 500, Toronto, Ontario, M6G 1A5
2. The University of Wisconsin, Sea Grant Institute, 1800 University Ave., Madison, WI 53705

LITTER

1. Keep America Beautiful, Inc., Mill River Plaza, 9 West Broad Street, Stamford, CT 06902
2. Troy State University/Fund for Environmental Quality, Center for Environmental Research and Service, Troy State Univ., Cowart Hall, Troy, AL 36082

MAPS AND GLOBES

1. National Council for Geographic Education, Indiana Univ. of Pennsylvania, Leonard 16A, Indiana, PA 15705

NATIONAL PARKS

1. U.S. Government Printing Office, Superintendent of Documents, Washington, DC 20402
2. The National Parks and Conservation Assoc., 1015 31st St., N.W., Washington, DC 20007

3. R. Woods, Consumer Information Center—B, P.O. Box 100, Pueblo, CO 81002
4. U.S. Dept. of the Interior, National Park Service, P.O. Box 37127, Washington, D.C. 20013-7127

NUCLEAR ENERGY

1. Publications Dept. L, Union of Concerned Scientists, 26 Church St., Cambridge, MA 02238

NUTRITION

1. S. James, Consumer Information Center—K, P.O. Box 100, Pueblo, CO 81002
2. R. Woods, Consumer Information Center—K, P.O. Box 100, Pueblo, CO 81002
3. Center for Science in the Public Interest, 1501 16th St., N.W., Washington, DC 20036

OCEANS

1. Public Information Center, U.S. EPA, 401 M Street S.W., Washington, DC 20460

PESTICIDES

1. Agricultural Bulletin, Room 245, 30 North Murray Street, Madison, WI 53715
2. Rachel Carson Council, Inc., 8940 Jones Mill Road, Chevy Chase, MD 20815
3. Concern, Inc., 1794 Columbia Road, N.W., Washington, DC 20009
4. Public Information Center, U.S. EPA, 401 M Street, S.W., Washington, DC 20460
5. Natural Resources Defense Council, 122 East 42nd Street, New York, NY 10168

PETS

1. Dover Publications, Inc., 31 East 2d Street, Mineola, NY 11501
2. The Humane Society of the U.S., 2100 L Street, N.W., Washington, DC 20037
3. Spizzirri Publishing Inc., P.O. Box 9397, Rapid City, SD 57709
4. Agricultural Bulletin, Room 245, 30 North Murray Street, Madison, WI 53715
5. Alley Pond Environmental Center, 228-06 Northern Blvd., Douglaston, NY 11363
6. Animal Protection Institute of America, 2831 Fruitridge Road, P.O. Box 22505, Sacramento, CA 95822
7. Animal Welfare Institute, P.O. Box 3650, Washington, DC 20007
8. America Humane, 9725 East Hampden Ave., Denver, CO 80231

PLANTS

1. Natural Resources Defense Council, Publications Dept., 122 East 42nd Street, New York, NY 10168
2. Michael Olaf, The Montessori Shop, 5817 College Ave., Oakland, CA 94618
3. Marginal Media, P.O. Box 241, Fredonia, NY 14063
4. Soil Conservation Society of America, 7515 Northeast Ankeny Road, Ankeny, IA 50021-9764
5. U.S. Dept. of Agriculture, Soil Conservation Service, P.O. Box 2890, Washington, DC 20013
6. Gull Lake Environmental Education Project, Kellogg Bird Sanctuary of Michigan State Univ., 12685 C Avenue, Augusta, MI 49012
7. Distribution Center C, Cornell University, 7 Research Park, Ithaca, New York 14850

POLLUTION PROBLEMS

1. Izaak Walton League, 1401 Wilson Blvd., Level B., Arlington, VA 22209

PONDS

1. Gull Lake Environmental Education Project, Kellogg Bird Sanctuary of Michigan State Univ., 12685 C Avenue, Augusta, MI 49012

POPULATION GROWTH

1. Zero Population Growth Publications, 1400 16th St., N.W., Suite 320, Washington, DC 20036

RAINFORESTS

1. National Audubon Society, Poster, Route 4, Box 171, Sharon, CT 06069

RECYCLING

1. League of Women Voters of the U.S., 1730 M Street, N.W., Washington, DC 20036
2. Glass Packaging Institute, 1133 20th St., N.W., Suite 321, Washington, DC 20036
3. Zero Population Growth, 1400 16th St., N.W., Suite 320, Washington, DC 20036

REPTILES AND AMPHIBIANS

1. Insect Lore Products, P.O. Box 1535, Shafter, CA 93263
2. Museum Products, 3175 Gold Star Highway, Mystic, CT 06355
3. Gull Lake Environmental Education Project, Kellogg Bird Sanctuary of Michigan State Univ., 12685 C Avenue, Augusta, MI 49012
4. Dover Publications, Inc., 31 East 2nd St., Mineola, NY 11501

5. Spizzirri Publishing Inc., P.O. Box 9397, Rapid City, SD 57709
6. The Carnegie Museum of Natural History, 4400 Forbes Avenue, Pittsburgh, PA 15213

ROCKS AND MINERALS

1. Michael Olaf, The Montessori Shop, 5817 College Avenue, Oakland, CA 94618

SEASHELLS

1. Dover Publications, Inc., 31 East 2nd Street, Mineola, NY 11501
2. Museum Products, 3175 Gold Star Highway, Mystic, CT 06355

SEASHORE

1. The Nature Conservancy, 1800 North Kent Street, Arlington, VA 22209
2. Gull Lake Environmental Education Project, 12685 East C Avenue, Augusta, MI 49012

STREAMS

1. Izaak Walton League, 1401 Wilson Boulevard, Level B, Arlington, VA 22209

TREES

1. State Universtiy of New York, College of Environmental Science and Forestry, Syracuse, NY 13210
2. Distribution Center C, Cornell University, 7 Research Park, Ithaca, NY 14850
3. Agricultural Bulletin, Room 245, 30 North Murray Street, Madison, WI 53715
4. Marginal Media, P.O. Box 241, Fredonia, NY 14063
5. Forest Service, U.S. Dept. of Agriculture, P.O. Box 2417, Washington, DC 20013
6. Dover Publications, Inc., 31 East 2nd St., Mineola, NY 11501

WATER

1. The Garden Club of America, 598 Madison Ave., New York, NY 10022
2. Zero Population Growth Publications, 1400 16th Street, N.W., Washington, DC 20007
3. Freshwater Foundation, 2500 Shadywood Road, Box 90, Navarre, MN 55392
4. Soil Conservation Society of America, 7515 N.E. Ankeny Road, Ankeny, IA 50021
5. Gull Lake Environmental Education Project, 12685 C Avenue, Augusta, MI 49012
6. Concern, Inc., 1794 Columbia Road, N.W., Washington, DC 20009

7. Public Information Center (PM-211B), U.S. EPA, 401 M Street, S.W., Washington, DC 20460
8. Dept. of Water Resources, Water Education Program, 1416 9th St., Room 338, P.O. Box 942836, Sacramento, CA 94236-0001

WEATHER

1. Insect Lore Products, P.O. Box 1535, Shafter, CA 93263
2. Museum Products, 3175 Gold Star Highway, Mystic, CT 06355

WETLANDS

1. National Science Teachers' Assoc., Special Publications, 1742 Connecticut Ave., N.W., Washington, DC 20009
2. Marginal Media, P.O. Box 241, Fredonia, NY 14063
3. The Izaak Walton League of America, Inc., 1401 Wilson Blvd., Level B, Arlington, VA 22209
4. Public Information Center (PM-211B), U.S. EPA, 401 M Street, S.W., Washington, DC 20460
5. National Wildlife Federation, 1412 16th Street, N.W., Washington, DC 20036

MISCELLANEOUS MATERIAL

1. Complete Environmental Education Programs
   a. "Living Lightly in the City" for Grades K–3 and 4–6
   b. "Living Lightly on the Planet" for Grades 7–9 and 10–12
      For information write: Schlitz Audubon Center, 1111 East Brown Deer Road, Milwaukee, WI 53217
2. Environmental Education Clubs for Elementary Age Children
   a. Woodsy Owl—"Give a hoot. Don't pollute."
      For information write: Forest Service, USDA, Woodsy Owl Campaign, P.O. Box 1963, Washington, DC 20013
   b. Smokey Bear—Forest Fire Prevention
      For information write: Your Local U.S. Forest Service
3. Magazines for Children
   a. *Ranger Rick*—for children 6–12 (12 issues a year)
      For information write: National Wildlife Federation, 1412 Sixteenth St., N.W., Washington, DC 20036-2266
   b. *Kind News*—for children who care about animals
      Kind News Jrs. (for grades 2–4) and *Kind News Srs.* (for Grades 5–6)

For information write: National Association for the Advancement of Humane Education, Box 362, East Haddam, CT 06423

4. Adult Environmental Education Magazines
   a. *Naturescope*—Published bi-monthly. Each issue covers a single topic (weather, birds, insects, trees, etc.) and gives complete lesson plans and reproducible work sheets for students.
   For information write: National Wildlife Federation, 1412 16th St., N.W., Washington, DC 20036
   b. *Tracks*—10 issues a year. Environmental education suggestions for the classroom teacher.
   For information write: Michigan United Conservation Clubs, P.O. Box 30235, Lansing, MI 48909
   c. *Children and Animals*—4 issues a year. Includes worksheets, posters, games, and learning centers.
   For information write: The Humane Society of the United States, 2100 L Street, N.W., Washington, DC 20037
5. Arbor Day—For information write: National Arbor Day Foundation, 100 Arbor Avenue, Nebraska City, NE 68410

VOCATIONAL EDUCATION

The major goal of schools is to facilitate the development of independent, productive citizens. Educators have to project what individuals will need in order to be independent two, three, or fours years from graduation—when the students presently in school will be expected to survive and contribute to society. Learning disabled students will require guidance and a variety of skills to participate effectively in society. They need to be viewed within the context of the various social settings that will shape their lives beyond schooling. LD adults, as a group, have problems severe enough to impair vocational and social effectiveness (Smith, 1988). Difficulties were found in some studies with daily living skills, such as handling money or organizing time (Hoffman et al., 1987). In general, reading disabilities tend to persist into adulthood (Buchanan & Wolf, 1986; Johnson & Blalock, 1987). Effects of disabilities are evident in everyday kinds of work needs, such as reading manuals, writing letters, taking notes, writing checks, completing reports, paying bills, keeping records, and paying taxes (Johnson & Blalock, 1987). Much of these difficulties are due to an inability to read, spell, or do basic mathematics.

Instruction in job-related skills and with personal skills is necessary for success in jobs for secondary LD students (Okolo, 1988). Several studies have indicated that vocational educators in general are positive about having LD students in their classes, although many lack experience in working with this population (Okolo, 1988). "The challenge is to insure that all students enjoy the employment outcomes from secondary school programs and they improve their quality of life" (Schalock, 1986, p. 39).

LD adolescents in one study (Plata & Bone, 1989) indicated a preference for skilled, semi-skilled, and unskilled occupations over managerial and professional positions. Another study of youths with handicaps found that they had higher unemployment rates and overall lower benefits (e.g., lower salaries) for their labor (Hasazi et al., 1989).

Many LD adults live at home with parents and work mainly in production-type jobs (Cobb & Crump, 1984), but some LD adults do become professionals. In one study, 47 percent of 560 adults were found to be unemployed (Chelser, 1982). Another big problem is keeping a job. Many LD adults have expressed unhappiness with their present employment (Hoffman et al., 1987).

A recent study indicated that a major problem on the job is with social relationships, such as the inability to get along with coworkers, having problems with making friends or even with making conversation, as well as a lack of self-confidence (Hoffman et al., 1987). Some LD adults have language disabilities that cause problems with using the telephone, conversation, following directions, or getting the gist or meaning from innuendo and jokes (Hasbrouck, 1983; Hoffman et al., 1987).

Career education programs for students with learning disabilities should emphasize the following elements:

1. Career counseling
2. Self-help skills development
3. Vocational training
4. Personal organization and management skills
5. Job seeking and holding skills
6. Basic academics: reading, writing, spelling, and arithmetic that are tied into vocational training, interests, and social skills development
7. Reflective thinking skills
8. Money handling and saving
9. Effective communication skills
10. Strategies for improving memory and attention

Dependence on parents and a history of failure make it difficult to "break away" and become independent. Adult learning programs and community education are currently being recommended for many LD adults. Included are adult education programs and training through trade and technical schools. Access to vocational rehabilitation programs is important, especially for those who cannot keep a job for any length of time. Personal counseling is often recommended as a concomitant to educational programs. Minskoff and associates (1987) surveyed employers and found that only half of those questioned would hire learning disabled individuals.

Adult role models can play an important part in achieving social competence. It is the social inadequacy that must be stressed in educating LD students for independent living. Parents, teachers, and the community all have an obligation to support the LD person through critical periods of vocational adjustment.

The field of learning disabilities has not as yet taken full advantage of opportunities in the area of vocational education and potential employment. The Americans with Disabilities Act (1990) strongly supports the idea that employment "is ultimately the key to mainstream functioning" (Gerber & Brown, 1991, p. 103).

The career education movement has legitimized nonacademic alternatives as viable and important components of secondary education (Halpern, 1979). The trends associated with the Vocational Rehabilitation Act of 1973 (sec. 504) and other legislation are presently showing up in greater opportunities for adolescents and young adults.

In order for students to realize these opportunities, secondary schools need to improve their resources as well as their instructional designs and methods of assessment. A balanced program must consider the following:

Academic skills
Personal-social skills
Prevocational and vocational skills
Associated work experiences

School programs need to offer better functional and academic instruction based on needs and abilities. Teachers must develop counseling skills and team teaching skills in order to meet the personal-social needs of the students. They also have to know the minimum competencies necessary for job success. This includes daily living skills as well as other necessary job-related skills.

Many learning disabled students in secondary schools are falling between the cracks, dropping out of school because they are behind in their classwork and find little in school that is satisfying. They have lost the sense of competition and, even with special assis-

tance, find school irrelevant to their everyday lives, especially if they are not college bound. They need open doors of communication. College preparation, after all, is the high priority in most high schools. Generally, articulation efforts in most schools need improvement and should be a high priority with learning-problem students. The problem often lies in areas of consistency of how things are done. Information, training, and work experience, or work-related activities that are satisfying and self-enhancing, are necessary.

Regular and special educators need in-service training in career-vocational education. Another problem is to get students through the process or program without the stigma due to labels used to describe their difficulties. All students should enter orientation sessions where they will receive information on the following for each vocational program:

Activities offered
Entrance requirements—pre-enrollment process
Related employment opportunities
Geographical location—available to student in terms of travel
Type of counseling and support services available
Other training programs within the institution
Opportunities for training outside of the institution, such as "Job Training Partnership Act" and other government-sponsored programs

Skill training should involve:

1. Work experience (general employment orientation)
2. Work study (off-campus and on-campus work situations)
3. On-the-job training (specific skill learning)
4. School-community cooperative work programs

The continuing problem of dropouts, or early leavers of educational programs, can be alleviated by early and meaningful vocational experiences. This requires key persons, procedures, and resources that will offset the conditions that the student feels are too difficult to tolerate. The principal actors need to coordinate their efforts in order to enhance the students' ability to avoid or overcome frustration in school.

Programming

Teachers of learning disabled students at the secondary level are going to have to meld the standard remedial academic program with career education for a number of students (Mori, 1980). Career education information is an important area of curriculum and vocational counseling and should be a part of all secondary programs. Learning disabled students need educational assistance in learning how to find a job, in finding out about the types of jobs that are available, and in learning about jobs that are appropriate for them. They need to understand how to deal with the whole concept of economic independence. Parents of these students have great concerns about future independence in life beyond the family (Fafard & Haubrich, 1981).

The U.S. Office of Education has designated fifteen occupational clusters:

1. Agri-business and natural resources
2. Business and office
3. Communication and media
4. Construction
5. Consumer and homemaking education
6. Environment
7. Fine arts and humanities
8. Health
9. Hospitality and recreation
10. Manufacturing
11. Marine science
12. Marketing and distribution
13. Personal services
14. Public services
15. Transportation occupations

Some require college preparation, others do not; but some form of training in each of these, from general information gathering to hands-on experience, will prove valuable to the student, regardless of whether or not the general goals include college. Career preparation in secondary school is important and should not be considered entirely as an alternative to college preparation. Units of study in each of these fifteen areas would be a good academic activity beyond the career information itself. Reading, spelling, and written expressive language could be enhanced through the study of vocational alternatives.

Special educators, regular educators, and vocational education teachers should collaboratively plan to do the following:

1. Develop or locate appropriate career material.
2. Implement and monitor a variety of experiences related to the world of work.
3. Evaluate these experiences with the students.
4. Develop follow-up accelerated procedures for those students who find that the prospect for college entrance is diminishing for a variety of reasons.
5. Counsel these students and provide an individualized program, if possible.

Assessing Student Abilities

The following scales can be useful:

1. WISC-R
2. Binet
3. California Psychological Inventory
4. Visual-Motor Integration Test
5. Bender-Gestalt
6. Bennett Hand Tool Dexterity Test
7. Purdue Pegboard
8. Stromberg Dexterity Test
9. Academic Achievement Tests
10. General Aptitude Test Battery (GATB). The GATB, which was developed and published by the federal government, uses eight pencil-paper and four apparatus tests to measure nine factors (Cronbach, 1970).
    G - General (a composite of tests titled Vocabulary, Three-Dimensional Space, and Arithmetic Reasoning)
    V - Verbal (Vocabulary)
    N - Numerical (Computation, Arithmetic Reasoning)
    S - Spatial
    P - Form Perception (Tool Matching, Form Matching)
    Q - Clerical Perception (Name Comparison)
    K - Motor Coordination (Mark Making)
    F - Finger Dexterity (Assemble, Disassemble)
    M - Manual Dexterity (Place, Turn)
11. Nonreading Aptitude Test Battery (NATB)
12. Kuder Inventories C and E
13. Strong Vocational Interest Blank

Assessment should determine:

1. What the student knows about the world of work and the requirements of specific jobs
2. The student's present work habits and areas that need improvement
3. The student's vocational interests (are they realistic?)
4. The student's strengths and weaknesses in such areas as manual dexterity, coordination, strength, physical stamina, special problems
5. Any aptitudes the student exhibits that can be improved with training and that can be matched with specific jobs
6. How much the student knows about finding a job, applying for work, and completing applications
7. If the student understands how to keep a job in terms of overall job behavior (e.g., social habits) and skill improvement

EDUCATION PLANNING

1. What changes need to be made, if any, in the curriculum (academics)?
2. What type of vocational training needs to be emphasized?
3. What kind of counseling and practical experiences are indicated?
4. Social-psychological considerations and related training should be considered.

VOCATIONAL SKILL DEVELOPMENT PLAN

1. Plan a job development skills program.
2. Develop a work adjustment program.
3. Develop general vocational skills.
4. Develop specific job skills.
5. Develop on-the-job training.
6. Develop a work-study program.

The following is a sample of Area Vocational Technical (AVT) Careers that should be included in a program of study:

Automotive (mechanic, body repair, etc.)
Clerical (bookkeeping, secretarial, etc.)
Construction (carpenter, plumber, painter, etc.)
Cosmetology (beautician, etc.)
Culinary Arts (baker, cook, etc.)
Data Processing (computer programmer)
Drafting (draftsman)
Electronics (television and radio repair)
Health (licensed practical nurse, hospital aide)
Refrigeration (air conditioner/heater repair)

HOW SUPPORTIVE SERVICES WILL BE UTILIZED

1. Local, state, and federal agencies
2. Occupational therapists, if necessary
3. Physical therapists, if necessary

The U.S. Labor Department (1975) established Criteria for School Districts that desire to participate in approved vocational training programs. The criteria are as follows:

1. School-approved students aged fourteen or fifteen can participate, given that they meet program criteria established by the school.
2. School credit must be given for in-school education and on-the-job training.
3. The school must provide classroom instruction as well as employability skill training.
4. Instructional time shall be appropriate for graduation requirements.
5. Twenty to twenty-five students are the maximum to one teacher-coordinator.
6. The teacher-coordinator shall supervise and coordinate the work and visit the work station on a regularly scheduled basis.
7. A training agreement shall be drafted that is signed by the student, the teacher-coordinator, and the employer.
8. Students can work in any occupation except mining, manufacturing, and jobs determined to be hazardous situations for minors between sixteen and eighteen years of age. Students cannot work on jobs that displace a worker already employed in the establishment of the employer.

TRANSITION FROM SCHOOL TO WORK

There is a question as to whether learning disabled students are being guided into employment opportunities appropriate for their abilities. It appears that a variety of programs do not have built-in transition to positions in business and industry. This is said to be one of the reasons for the high unemployment rate among these students (Wehman et al., 1986). Support for transitional services at the secondary level is vital to a good program. The bridge from school to work involves these types of service:

1. Time-limited employment services
2. Ongoing employment services
3. Adult employment alternatives that include general services such as personnel agencies and employment services

A good program requires parental input, a functional curriculum, and cooperation from key agencies such as rehabilitation services. An integrated (mainstreamed) program and a community-based delivery system are also critical.

FUNCTIONAL CURRICULUM

This involves preparation for local employment opportunities. The key question is, What skills are required for local jobs? Useful skills are what helps get a job. Training should be generalizable to other similar jobs and should start as early as junior high school.

INTEGRATED SCHOOL SERVICES

Handicapped students should train, learn, and work with nonhandicapped persons. This is training for the reality of work in an integrated community and works as well for those who are not handicapped.

COMMUNITY-BASED SERVICES

Students need practice and work in a variety of community-based settings. Many job training sites need to be identified. The students need the exposure to natural job environments. They need to practice in real situations.

PERSONAL JOB PLAN

Every student should have his/her transition plan outlined as follows.

Competencies to be mastered
Transition services available and to be used
List of goals and objectives
Job-seeking plans
Agencies to be contacted
Plans for managing money and travel
Who will be part of support system and how will they help
Long-term as well as short-term plans

PARENTS

Meetings should be set up to provide parents with:

1. An orientation to community agencies
2. Information regarding responsibilities of the school, agencies, and special service programs
3. Information on how to work with each of the above for maximum gain and how to go about applying for services

FOLLOW-UP

It is essential for the school to provide follow-up activities that include written communiction (questionnaires, etc.) as well as personal visits to sites. This will aid in assessing the effectiveness of the curriculum and the placement activities. Follow-up should occur at least every two to three years and a report prepared for school board perusal. The report should include student evaluations, parent reports, and reports from employees regarding the transition process. The report should also include projections for the future.

Career Exploration Activities

Students need a broad range of career exploration activities and experiences, rather than just a strict academic program. This requires integrating activities related to the world of work into existing subjects such as science, social studies, and math. Students should visit many businesses, and invited guests should speak on different occupations on a continuous basis.

This requires a close relationship with the business community. Chambers of Commerce are a good source of information about what is going on in the community and what is needed.

Cross-training with vocational educators while integrating vocational content is very useful. The teacher needs to be aware of the alternative vocational programs and services that exist in the school and community. The following are specific job-related activities:

JOB-SEEKING SKILLS

Applications

Completing an employment application accurately and legibly is crucial to securing a job. Application forms can be fragmented or complicated with high readability. Often they appear to the student to be merely a jumble of words and spaces. The following is suggested:

1. Practice with a variety of forms.
2. Have the student take it home to fill it out.
3. Practice the vocabulary of application forms.
4. Complete the forms line by line.
5. Discuss troublesome terms.
6. Use worksheets, covering vocabulary.
7. Have students correct errors.
8. Define the fifteen most used terms.
9. Stress neatness.
10. Start with easy forms and progress to the more difficult ones.

Using the Ads

This is part of how one goes about looking for a job. The following is suggested:

1. Each student is given, or brings in, the classified ads of a daily and/or Sunday newspaper.
2. Students can also use the yellow pages to make telephone contacts for interviews.
3. Ads can be pasted on worksheets and fully written out (group and individual work).
4. Be sure the student understands the information.

The Job Interviews

The job interview is the key to employment. How the student presents herself or himself is critical. The following is suggested:

1. Make a list of pre-interview ideas, such as
   a. who does the hiring
   b. how much time you have for the interview
   c. how to dress appropriately
   d. your skills and interest
   e. why you want to work for this company
   f. what else the company can do for you

2. How to begin the interview:
   a. Use last names.
   b. Shake hands, smile, and greet the person.
   c. Introduce yourself; use your full name.
   d. Tell why you are there (e.g., answered an ad, recommended, or just wanted to see if there is a need for your line of work).

DURING THE INTERVIEW
1. Listen and ask questions when necessary.
2. Don't smoke or chew gum.
3. If you are not sure, ask to have the question repeated or clarified. Speak clearly.
4. Avoid discussing personal problems.
5. Smile, be friendly, and act businesslike.
6. Maintain good eye contact.
7. Thank the person interviewing you.

Practice Speaking (role playing)
The students should practice responses to different types of questions, such as:

1. Where did you find out about the job?
2. Are you trained for the position?
3. Tell me about your education and background?
4. What was your last job and why did you leave?
5. Do you have a car, transportation?
6. What salary do you expect?
7. What is your social security number?
8. Do you get along with people?
9. Do you like to be around people or work by yourself?

LIFE SKILLS
Part of vocational education involves the study of life skills. These skills are learned either formally as modules in courses or informally through a variety of school experiences. The following are some of the essential life skills:

1. *Home Management:* What does it take to maintain a home? This includes repairs, general upkeep, and expenses and entails having a variety of skills.
2. *Money Management:* How to manage money (e.g., budget, saving, spending, etc.) is a critical skill in our society.
3. *Computer Literacy:* Computers are becoming a part of our daily lives. It is important to at least understand the rudiments of their use, or even more for job purposes.
4. *Employment Skills:* This includes specific as well as job-related skills and needs to be an integral part of the secondary curriculum.

5. *Management of Time and Movement:* It is important to understand how to organize and manage the basics of one's life, for true independence.
6. *Pursuit of Life-Long Learning:* Students need to learn how to keep up with their area of work and how to advance themselves. The process of development is continuous, and there are many resources available to those who seek them.
7. *Cultural Appreciation:* Students must acquire a taste for their own and other cultures, including literature, music, and art. So many people go through life missing the kinds of things that enhance us as human beings.

RELATED ACTIVITIES
Develop a job box of booklets that are grouped together by areas of work and job-seeking skills. The box can include forms and general information, most of which should be in an easy-to-read format. Develop a bookshelf of job-related materials from a variety of sources. Several suggested titles are:

The Newspaper You Read, by R. H. Turner. This is a 48-page student workbook, that covers such topics as how to find information in a newspaper, jobs in the printing and newspaper industries, suburban life, reckless driving, and analyzing news stories. A teacher's guide is included. It is good for reading levels 4–6. Follett Publishing Co.

Your Attitude Is Changing, by Science Research Associates, Inc. This book helps to improve the attitude of the student and prepares this person for a career. It is a guidance book written at the sixth-grade reading level and oriented to adult work.

The Jobs You Get, by R. H. Turner. This book covers such topics as job applications, how to read want ads, job interviews, letters of reference, private versus state employment agencies, and improving your speech and your handwriting. It is suitable for reading grade levels 4–6. A teacher's guide covers this six-book series. Follett Publishing Co.

How to Get a Job, by W. A. Fraenkel. This book is thirty pages long. Single copies are free. National Association for Retarded Citizens.

General Power Mechanics, by R. Worthington, M. Margules, and W. H. Crouse. This book helps the students to acquire basic understanding and skills in the repair and maintenance of common prime power sources. Technical terms are defined and explained when first introduced. The reading level is controlled at approximately grade 7. Webster/McGraw-Hill.

Your Job Interview. The kit contains two color filmstrips, two cassettes, and one teaching guide. Guidance Associates.

Pete Saves the Day, by Mafex Associates, Inc. This book is written in a story form and introduces varied employment concepts. Two prepared stories show students the basic elements in applying for employment. Mafex Associates, Inc.

Jerry Works in a Service Station, by J. M. Wade. This book is about experience in a realistic job situation. It deals with a teenage high school graduate and includes exercises on the vocational content and language-arts skills. Fearon Publishers.

Learning disabled students need exposure to career education so they can apply their interests and abilities to the world of work. This should occur early in their secondary school training. Good attitudes toward work are established early and are essential for job success and future independence. Students need to know about the current job market and what they need to do to prepare for the future. They need experiences that will help them understand the realities of the job. They need to acquire an appreciation of what work means in an individual's life.

Carl D. Perkins Vocational Education Act, 1984

One purpose of this federal legislation is to "assure that individuals who are inadequately served under vocational education programs are assured access to quality vocational education programs, especially individuals who are disadvantaged or who are handicapped." Those diagnosed as learning disabled can qualify for services under the present definition of population to be served.

"The term 'handicapped'," broadly defined, "when applied to individuals, means individuals who are mentally retarded, hard of hearing, deaf, speech impaired, visually handicapped, seriously emotionally disturbed, orthopedically impaired, or other health impaired persons, or persons with specific learning disabilities, who by reason thereof required special education and related services, and who, because of their handicapping condition, cannot succeed in the regular vocational education program without special education assistance."

Criteria for Services and Activities for the Handicapped and for the Disadvantaged

Under "SEC.204.(a) The State board shall, with respect to that portion of the allotment distributed in accordance with section 203(a) for vocational education services and activities for handicapped individuals and disadvantaged individuals, provide assurances that

(1) equal access will be provided to handicapped and disadvantaged individuals in recruitment, enrollment, and placement activities;

(2) equal access will be provided to handicapped and disadvantaged individuals to the full range of vocational programs available to nonhandicapped and nondisadvantaged individuals, including occupationally specific courses of study, cooperative education, and apprenticeship programs; and

(3) (A) vocational education programs and activities for handicapped individuals will be provided in the least restrictive environment in accordance with section 612(5)(B) of the Education of the Handicapped Act and will, whenever appropriate, be included as a component of the individualized education plan required under section 612(4) and section 614(a)(5) of such Act; and

(B) vocational education planning for handicapped individuals will be coordinated between appropriate representatives of vocational education and special education.

(b) Each local educational agency shall, with respect to that portion of the allotment distributed in accordance with section 203(a) for vocational education services and activities for handicapped individuals and disadvantaged individuals, provide information to handicapped and disadvantaged students and parents of such students concerning the opportunities available in vocational education at least one year before the students enter the grade level in which vocational education programs are first generally available in the State, but in no event later than the beginning of the ninth grade, together with the requirements for eligibility for enrollment in such vocational education programs.

(c) Each student who enrolls in vocational education programs and to whom subsection (b) applies shall receive

(1) assessment of the interests, abilities, and special needs of such student with respect to completing successfully the vocational education program;

(2) special services, including adaptation of curriculum, instruction, equipment, and facilities, designed to meet the needs described in clause (1);

(3) guidance, counseling, and career development activities conducted by professionally trained counselors who are associated with the provision of such special services; and

(4) counseling services designed to facilitate the transition from school to post-school employment and career opportunities."

The Act also makes provision for the following:

1. Programs of career guidance and counseling that encourage the elimination of sex, age, handicapping condition, and race bias and stereotyping, that provide for community outreach, that enlist the collaboration of the family, the community, business, industry, and labor, and that are accessible to all segments of the population, including women, minorities, the handicapped, and the economically disadvantaged.
2. Programs related to techniques in high technology fields that are relevant to the labor market and accessible to all segments of the population, including women, minorities, the handicapped, and the economically disadvantaged.
3. Activities and related services that insure access to, as well as a commitment to serve, all segments of the population, including women, minorities, the handicapped, and the economically disadvantaged (as demonstrated by special efforts to provide outreach information and counseling, and by the provision of remedial instruction and other assistance).
4. Research that results in effective methods for providing quality vocational education to handicapped and disadvantaged individuals as well as applied research and development on those methods.
5. Leadership development and in-service education activities for state and local vocational education instructors, counselors, and administrators.
6. A national assessment of the coordination of vocational education and post-secondary programming for handicapped and disadvantaged individuals.
7. A national center that will provide technical assistance to programs serving special populations, including the handicapped.
8. Support demonstration projects such as model programs that provide access to quality vocational education in nontraditional occupations.

The Congress, in enacting this legislation, finds that "increased economic competition requires the development of a better trained and educated workforce which our educational institutions must provide."

There are problems and deficiencies, especially in areas dealing with the handicapped, that must be rectified. This requires careful consideration of possible new directions in terms of policy and programming.

"It is the sense of the Congress that effective vocational education programs are essential to our future as a free and democratic society; that such programs are best administered by local communities, community colleges, and school boards, where the primacy of parental control can be emphasized with a minimum of Federal interference; and that as a means to strengthening vocational education and training programs, nongovernmental alternatives promoting links between public school needs and private sector sources of support should be encouraged and implemented."*

*Portions quoted directly from Carl D. Perkins Vocational Education Act, 1984.

Glossary

Abstract Level. A level of conceptualization or thinking that involves the ability to see relationships based on differences and sameness as they pertain to classification and association in all of life's experiences. An abstract response would be that an apple and an orange are both fruit.

Accommodation. Structuring the environment and the academic program to meet the needs of each learner so that the learner can be successful in every aspect of his or her school life.

Acetylcholine. Serves as a neurotransmitter at the myoneural junction and at nerve endings.

Achievement Test. An instrument that is designed to determine the degree of knowledge acquired, and/or the level of development reached, within school tasks or a particular area of learning.

Acuity. A sensory-level function that pertains to keenness of sight, hearing, or touch. Acuity is a primary-level function in terms of input where learning is concerned.

Adaptive Behavior. The adjustment of an individual to his or her environment (e.g., social-emotional behavior).

Adjudicate. A case (individual) that has been heard and settled by judicial procedure.

Advance Organizers. "Information that is presented in advance of and at a higher level of generality, inclusiveness and abstraction than the learning task itself" (Ausubel, 1960, p. 267).

Aggressive–Acting-Out Behavior. Excessive behavior manifested as disorders of conduct such as being disruptive, negative, uncooperative, destructive, and unable to control aggressive impulses.

Aggressive–Passive Behavior. Behavior that has as its basis inner conflict that results from simultaneous feelings of love and hate. It is manifested by poor academic performance.

Agraphia. The inability to express thoughts through writing due to a brain lesion in the area of the cerebral cortex.

Alexia. A form of receptive aphasia, caused by a cerebral lesion where the individual loses the ability to understand written language.

Amphetamines. Have a stimulating effect on the central and peripheral nervous systems, and depress the appetite. Abuse may result in strong dependence.

Amygdala. Part of the limbic system dealing with storage of information and emotional characteristics of stored information.

Analytical Approach. A method of learning. In reading, the learner would begin with a configuration or the whole word and then break it down into its components or sound segments.

Antisocial. A personality disorder associated with a basic lack of socialization and continuous conflict with social entities—also called psychopathic and sociopathic.

Aphasia. A disorder of language or symbolization resulting from neurological impairment that may affect areas of reception (comprehension of the spoken word) or expression. Persons with aphasia lose (partially or completely) their ability to speak, even though they know what they want to say.

Aptitude. The range or degrees of abilities necessary to function successfully in a particular system or situation.

Articulation. The execution of speech. Disorders of speech are manifested in omissions (leaving out sounds), substitutions (*teef* for *teeth*), distortions (lisping), and additions (*skippering* for *skipping*).

Associative Learning. The process of reinforcing learning by relating concepts or new learning to visual, auditory, or tactual associations. Associative learning enables the learner to stabilize (retain) that which has been taught. For example: a word is written on a card, and an associative picture clue is put on the back of the same card.

Attention. The act of focusing (attend) auditorily or visually on stimuli for a period of time without losing the context or content of that which is being presented.

Attention Deficit Disorder. This disorder is associated with problems with inattention, impulsivity, and hyperactivity, the onset of which is before age seven, having a duration of at least six months, and is not attributed to emotional disturbance or mental retardation.

Attribution. This entails the degree to which an individual attributes or associates success or failure with a given task as being within his or her perceived locus of control.

Auditory Language Association. The understanding of noncategorical relationships between words or experiences presented orally. The individual can discern that *boat* goes with *water* rather than with sky.

Auditory Language Classification. The understanding of categorical relationships between words or experiences presented orally. The individual can discern that *apple* goes with *peach* rather than with *chair.*

Auditory-to-Auditory Association. The relating of a sound to a sound (phonemes). The student with the ability to make this association can relate the sound of *t* in *time* to the sound of *t* in *touch* and transfer the association to different situations. When presented with three toys, all of which begin with different sounds, the learner will identify the toy that begins with a specific sound indicated by the instructor.

Auditory-to-Visual Association. The relating of a sound to a symbol. The student with the ability to make this association can relate the sound of *m* or its letter name to the written symbol *m* and transfer this association to different contexts, such as an *m* in words printed on the chalkboard or on a paper on a desk.

Aural Processes. Processes that essentially involve hearing.

Automaticity. The unhampered flow of information. Knowledge learned so well that it is almost subconscious, and requires little effort, such as the rapid, fluent recognition of words.

Axon. The part of a neuron by which impulses travel away from the cell body. Impulses are transmitted to other nerve cells or organs.

Balance and Coordination. The ability to use both sides of the body simultaneously, individually, or alternately.

Basal Reading Series. A program for teaching reading that incorporates a sight word vocabulary emphasizing a "look, say" approach within a system of readers, teachers, manuals, and supplementary material.

Baseline Data. Initial data that is based on the frequency of a particular bahavior that is occurring, without treatment, within a given period of time.

Behavior Management. A total process that involves dealing effectively with the needs of learners in different educational settings while anticipating, planning for, and attending to, different dimensions of their behavior within a structured environment.

Behavior Modification. A system for controlling or modifying behavior that is based on the principles of operant conditioning. The reinforcement of desired learner behavior is accomplished through the understanding of contingencies, the manipulation of the environment, and the application of appropriate reward systems.

Binocular Fusion. The process of integrating the overlapping portions of the visual fields into a single set of visual information.

Body Image. The inner awareness of self in terms of the location of the parts of the body and their relationship to each other and to the environment.

Body Rhythm. The inner awareness of rhythm in body movement such as walking, running, marching, and keeping time to music.

Brain Electrical Activity Mapping (BEAM). A procedure used to monitor brain wave activity.

Cerebral Dominance. The dominance of one hemisphere of the brain over the other hemisphere. This is generally considered a prerequisite for the establishment of a preference for using the left or right hand in children.

Cerebral Palsy. A motor disorder due to nonprogressive damage to the brain.

Checklist. A means of delineating, through observational procedures, the specific areas of learning in order to provide a basis for preliminary decisions in programming and for further evaluation.

Cholinergic. Stimulated, activated, or transmitted by choline, a neurotransmitter.

Closure. The auditory or visual formulation of a whole word from its component parts. In reading, this is called blending.

Cloze Procedure. A teaching-testing technique using the deletion of words from text and in their place inserting underlined blank spaces. The student is measured by the number of blank spaces filled.

Cocaine. Obtained from coca leaves and used as an anesthetic and a stimulant or narcotic; highly addictive ("Crack" is a crystallized form of cocaine.)

Cognitive-Behavioral Approach. The cognitive-behavioral approach attempts to apply strategies that emanate from social and developmental psychology, while adhering to the principles of experimental-clinical psychology and social science research.

Cognitive Learning. Learning that occurs as a result of the operation of the mind as we become aware of our environment through such thought processes as perceiving, thinking, and remembering.

Cognitive Modifiability. An individual's ability to adapt and use new learning strategies, at the same time breaking old and ineffective approaches to problem solving.

Cognitive-Motivational. This involves the areas of learned helplessness, attribution, locus of control, and self-efficacy as factors that affect attitude and motivation.

Cognitive-Social Skills. This entails the interpretation of the social environment and effectively dealing with social situations through the selection of socially acceptable behavior.

Cognitive Style. An individual's unique approach to dealing with new concepts or learning. It includes problem solving, adjustment to life situations, perception of parts-to-whole relationships (analysis) and whole-to-parts relationships (synthesis), and integration of the new information into the present knowledge base.

Collaborative Consultation. Professionals of diverse expertise working together to develop solutions to problems regarding student needs in a parity relationship.

Computer Assisted Instruction. Using a microcomputer to give students drill, practice, and feedback.

Contingency Management. Management of the contingencies that involve events, actions, and outcomes for purposes of improving understanding of cause-effect relationships when dealing with the behavior of learners.

Continuous Progress. The rate and amount of learning achieved over an extended period of time. Continual monitoring (observation and documentation), utilizing charting procedures, enables ongoing comparisons of a learner's progress or lack of it in the given areas of learning.

Contracting. A behavior management technique based on a written agreement between the student and the teacher where a reward is specified for a desired learner outcome. The agreement is a written document prepared by both the instructor and the learner, to adhere to a specific program or schedule of activities.

Control Factors. Factors that affect the control of learner behavior within the learning environment, a few of which are distractibility, disinhibition, and perseveration.

Convergence. The coordinated movement of the eyes that is necessary for focusing an image on the fovea.

Criterion-Referenced Measurement or Evaluation. A method of determining the level and quality of an individual's performance in relation to specific instructional objectives or criteria.

Cross-Categorical Grouping. Several different groups or categories of special needs students are clustered together for instructional purposes such as learning disabilities, mental retardation, and emotionally disturbed.

Cueing. A teaching technique used to aid learners with expressive language disorders to retrieve the correct word, e.g., "I kick with my _____ ?"

Curriculum-Based Assessment (CBA). Student assessment based on performance in areas of curriculum and materials that are appropriate for the student's own program. Continuous progress is charted and the student's program is modified accordingly.

Cylert. A trademark for preparations of methylphenidate hydrochloride—a stimulant frequently prescribed for attention deficit disorders to control attention and hyperactivity.

Declarative Memory. Memory dealing with facts such as names, dates, places; also memory of experiences, both simple (what a house looks like) and episodic (graduation from high school).

Decoding. Assigning meaning to experiences, including verbal behavior (speech, reading, and writing) and nonverbal behavior (gestures, expressions, and body movements).

Deficit Level. Level of learning at which a student is deficient in a specific ability or process. The deficiency is called a learning disability. These deficient processes keep the learner from succeeding at the skills of reading, writing, spelling, and arithmetic. A deficit in auditory discrimination may cause problems with phonics.

Delinquent-Unorthodox Behavior. Behavior, based on a "gang" psychology, that is acceptable and realistic for the peer group but unacceptable in school settings.

Dendrites. Thread-like extensions that branch into a tree-like structure of the cytoplasm of neurons, which comprise most of the receptive surface of a neuron. The branches are capable of being stimulated by the axon endings of other neurons.

Depressant. An agent that produces diminishing functional activity and reduces vital energies in general by producing muscular relaxation and diaphoresis.

Deprivation. The length of time since a reinforcer has been available to an individual.

Developmental Aphasia. A disorder of oral language related to central nervous dysfunction with onset occurring during the early stages of development.

Developmental Inventories. Tests or checklists for measuring a student's level of functioning in reading, writing, spelling, and arithmetic. They indicate the student's independent, instructional, and frustration levels.

Developmental Skills. A sequence of functional skills that incorporate the process and content necessary for language acquisition, growth, and development. It is used to operationally define learning abilities.

Dexidrine. A trademark for preparations of dextro-amphetamine sulphate—a stimulant drug frequently prescribed for attention deficit disorders to control attention and hyperactivity.

Diagnostic Teaching. Teaching that enables the instructor to gain information about the learner as a result of the teacher-learner interaction.

Direct Instruction. Concentration is focused on the academic skills or tasks to be taught, the analysis of behaviors needed to master these skills or tasks, and the instruction in sequential behavior that helps students learn the subskills that need to be mastered.

Directionality. The relationship of an object or point in space to another object or point in space. Difficulty in this developmental skill may result in left-right confusion in reading and writing.

Disassociated Behavior. Separating oneself from the task to be mastered, as in the student who exhibits a lack of attention or "gives up" when presented with an academic activity.

Discrimination. A process under the category of perception that denotes the ability of the learner to discern likenesses and differences between sounds and between symbols.

Disesteemed Learners. Students who perform poorly in school tasks but are not learning disabled, mentally handicapped, or emotionally disturbed. These students fail in school for a variety of reasons and do not ordinarily receive special education services.

Disinhibition. Inability to control one's verbal behavior. For example, learners may get carried away by their own thoughts and offer unrelated responses to that which is being discussed.

Distractibility. "Forced attention" to extraneous stimuli, resulting in poor overall attention and reduced on-task behavior.

Dysgraphia. A neurologically based writing disorder that affects the fine motor movements.

Dyslexia. A neurologically based severe reading disorder.

Electroencephalogram (EEG). The recording of the electric currents developed in the brain by means of electrodes applied to the scalp, to the surface of the brain, or within the brain itself.

Encoding. The aspect of communication that involves output through the acts of motor language expression (manual, body movement, speech and handwriting), verbal language expression (retrieval, syntax, and formulation), and written language expression.

Endocrine. Organs (glands) that secrete internally into the blood or lymph system a substance called hormone, which has an effect on other organs.

Equivalent Learning. Concepts, behaviors, or skills that are considered to be equally difficult to learn.

Executive Function. A metacognitive phenomenon, the executive function controls and coordinates the information processing system, which includes attention, perception, and memory, as well as monitoring decisions such as the strategies that need to be applied for specific learning situations.

Exemplars. Uses an instructional approach that can be extracted from to make examples and comparisons.

Expressive Language. A method of communicating by using words verbally, by writing, or by using gestures that describe or indicate a quality, a function, or a relationship.

External Locus. A form of attribution where the outcome of events is mainly due to external factors such as chance, luck, fate. Events cannot be controlled or influenced.

Extrinsic Motivation. Rewards or incentives to put forth effort or that reinforce desired behavior or least-favored learning activities; includes tokens, praise, contracting, charting, materials.

Eye-Foot Coordination. Controls of foot movements through the coordination of the eye, foot, and brain, which operate in concert with each other at the automatic level of functioning.

Fading. Showing or prompting learners to enable them to accomplish a particular task, then gradually withdrawing support after they have mastered each step or aspect.

Failure Avoidance. The opposite of success striving (a positive approach to problem solving), where the individual avoids failure as a matter of life-style.

Faulty Learning Responses. Incorrect learning habits established to meet the demands of parents, teachers, and peers to achieve specific tasks. The student may develop an unorthodox pencil grip due to early inappropriate pressure and frustration with beginning writing.

Fetal Alcohol Syndrome. A syndrome of morphogenesis and altered prenatal growth found in infants born of mothers who were chronic alcoholics during pregnancy. Symptoms include prominent forehead and mandible, microphthalmia, growth retardation, microcephaly, and mental retardation.

Figurative Language. One of the integrative functions of auditory language association. Learners with problems in this area have difficulty understanding such phrases as "He blew up," meaning he was angry.

Figure-Ground. A subcategory of perception that involves the ability to separate at will what one wishes to attend to visually or auditorily (figure) from the surrounding environment (ground).

Fine Motor (Eye-Hand) Coordination. The purposeful coordinated movements of the hand and eye operating in concert with thought patterns to achieve a specific motor task such as writing, sorting, and sewing.

Fixed-Interval Reinforcement. Reinforcement after a specific interval of time. Example: A student would be reinforced for the first response after a ten-second delay.

Fixed-Ratio Reinforcement. Reinforcement that occurs after a specific number of responses. Example: A student would be reinforced after every three responses.

Formal Tests. Tests that have been standardized and are administered under specified conditions, scored according to prescribed regulations, and interpreted in accordance with present criteria that establish reliability and validity.

Formulation. Organization of thought processes into concise patterns for smooth and natural flow of language in verbal expression and writing.

Frustration Level in Reading. The level at which the learner exhibits tension, hesitations, word-by-word reading, and low comprehension. Oral reading is below 93%, and comprehension is below 75%.

Galactosemia. A hereditary disorder of galactose metabolism due to a deficiency of the enzyme galactose, which may result in mental retardation.

Generalization. The transfer of behavior from one situation to similar situations. The greater the similarity between situations the more probable the response.

Genetic Predisposition. A latent susceptibility based on an inherited genetic factor, which may be activated under certain conditions such as stress.

Gestation. The period of development of the fetus from the time of fertilization of the ovum until birth.

Grapheme. The visual representation, or symbol, that includes letters, words, and numerals.

Gross Motor Movement. Movement that involves the balance, coordination, and large muscle activity required for efficiency in walking, running, skipping, jumping, and other physical activities.

Guided Instruction. Directing or guiding a student through a task by reviewing the steps in the process as the learner responds.

Gustatory. Related to the sense of taste.

Hallucinogen. An agent, such as LSD, that induces hallucinations.

Handedness. The consistent use of one hand over the other.

Haptic Processing. The processing of cutaneous, or tactual (touch), and kinesthetic (body movement) information.

Heroin. Diacetylmorphine used as an analgesic and narcotic; highly addictive and illegal for use in medicine.

Herpes. An inflammatory skin disease with clusters of small vesicles. Herpes simplex type II of the genitals is considered a venereal disease.

Heterogeneous. Consisting of or involving parts or elements that are dissimilar.

Hierarchical Learning. Concepts, behaviors, or skills, ordered from simple to complex and from easy to hard, that constitute a graduated system of prerequisites for learning higher level tasks.

High-Risk Students. Students who exhibit deficiencies in socialization and in the critical skills prerequisite to success in school tasks such as language arts and arithmetic. Basing their predictions on observation and other testing, examiners predict that these students will become failures in regular class settings as they are presently organized in most public schools.

Hippocampus. An important functional component of the limbic system that is critical for memory.

Homogeneous. Of a same or similar nature or kind as in intelligence.

Hormones. A chemical substance, secreted by endocrine glands, that has a regulatory effect on the activity of certain organs.

Hypoxia. (Anoxia) Reduction of oxygen to tissue below physiological level despite an adequate blood supply.

Hyperactivity. An unusual amount of movement by a learner, considering the learner's age and the physical setting in which the excessive movement is taking place.

Hyperkinesis. Excessive motor activity or mobility.

Imagery. Overall memory including the ability to remember or retain both in sequence and out of sequence that which has been seen, heard, or felt for both long and short periods of time.

Immature-Dependent Behavior. Behavior characterized by a lack of the socialization that is appropriate for the individual's particular age group.

Impulsivity. A tendency to act on impulse, without considering the consequences of the particular act.

Inattention. This disorder is observed in those who fail to complete tasks that are begun, who seem not to listen, and who appear easily distracted. The problem is associated with an Attention Deficit Disorder.

Independent Level. The level at which a student will work at ease without having to be under the constant direction of the instructor. In reading, for example, the learner will make less than four errors in one hundred consecutive words with 90% or better comprehension.

Individualized Instruction. An approach to teaching that is based on students' development, interests, abilities, and unique cognitive styles. It involves structuring the environment for each learner with respect to diagnosis, curriculum, educational management, and behavioral management.

Information Processing. A cognitive, computer-like information flow-through process that is based on a systems approach to information acquisition, processing, and related executive functions.

Inhibiting Responses. Holding back or controlling motor expression or behavior because of pressure from parents, teachers, or peers. Learners may expend a great deal of energy, suffer anxiety, and even withdraw if they do not have opportunities to "act out," or "respond motorically," within a structured environment.

Inner-Language. The language of thinking used for the integration of experiences. A native language that can be labled inner speech.

Input. Any information coming in through the auditory, visual, tactual, kinesthetic, olfactory, or gustatory modalities, the rate, amount, and sequence of which often determine success or failure in school.

Instructional Level. The point at which the teacher's aid is necessary. Following instruction, however, the learners should be able to continue with the material independently. In reading, they should be able to read with at least 93% accuracy in word recognition and 76% or better in comprehension.

Instructional Validity. The degree to which an instructional program meets its goals and objectives.

Integrated Learning. The effective utilization of mechanical-automatic skills and conceptual-thinking skills for success at academic tasks.

Integration. The assimilation and organization of information and experiences into meaningful relationships that can be used by the learner to better understand self and the relationship of self to the total environment.

Internal Locus. A form of attribution where events related to one's own behavior can be controlled by one's own efforts.

Intrinsic Motivation. A higher form of motivation emanating from within the individual who receives satisfaction from engaging in tasks and from achieving without external reward.

Invented Spelling. A first or initial unconventional attempt at writing words where the young learner has associated sounds with symbols, but has not as yet "cracked the code."

Inversion. Similar to reversal, but instead the symbol is perceived as a reversed, upside-down image (e.g., *n* for *u*, *m* for *w,* or *p* for *b*).

Ischemia. Deficiency of blood supply that may be due to an obstruction of the blood vessel(s).

Kinesthetic Sense. The awareness of, and adjustment to, one's environment in terms of body movement. The potential for using body movement has not been fully explored in teaching children.

Language. The application of meaning to words and other symbols based on one's experiences; the act of expressing oneself through a motor act or through clear, sequential verbal thought patterns.

Language Arts. The aspects of school curriculum that deal with verbal behaviors, reading, writing, and spelling.

Language Difference. Used with regard to Limited English Proficient students who have not mastered standard English, but instead use a nonstandard English that can vitiate school success.

Laterality. The establishment of sidedness and the concomitant ability to relate oneself physically to an object in space.

Learned Helplessness. A learned negative reaction to perceived failure resulting in task avoidance, lowered expectation, and lowering of performance.

Learning Strategy Instruction. Learning techniques for completing tasks and problem solving such as summarizing, using visual imagery, paraphrasing, or multipass (multiple surveys of material) activities.

Least Restrictive Environment. The placement of a student with special needs in a setting with nonhandicapped peers that is appropriate for the learner, given the nature of the handicap.

Level of Aspiration. The degree to which an individual perceives his or her potential for success in a given task.

Leverage Concepts and Skills. Concepts and skills that are partially learned and ready to be stabilized, or fully learned, with additional practice or instruction. They should be taught first in an instructional program.

Limbic System. A group of brain structures that includes the hippocampus, dentate gyrus, cingulate gyrus, septal areas, and the amygdala. It is associated with smell and aspects of emotion and behavior.

Linguistic Approach to Reading. A whole-word approach that builds vocabulary on the basis of spelling patterns rather than nonsense syllables. For example, using a consonant-vowel-consonant pattern the consonant *c* combined with the spelling pattern *at* gives *cat*. The consonants *b, p, m,* etc., added to the same pattern, will give other words.

Listening Comprehension Level. The highest level at which learners can understand 75% of the material read to them.

Localization (Auditory). Locating the source and direction of sound. The learner may have difficulty in discerning that different people have different voices or that a particular voice is specific to one particular person.

Locus of Control. This is described as having two dimensions; external, such as difficulty of task, and internal, such as affect and attitude. The perceived degree of power of each affects motivation to learn and expectancy levels.

Long-Term Memory. Recognition and recall are two aspects of long-term memory that are employed to store facts, words, and grammatic structure. Problems in this area affect all aspects of language, including the automatic responses necessary for efficient utilization.

Magnetic Resonance Imaging. A technique for viewing multiple sections of the brain through the transmission of vibration.

Mainstreaming. Providing an instructional program for handicapped students in the least restrictive environment, emphasizing normalization and placement within regular class settings whenever appropriate and possible.

Manipulatives. Materials that involve the learner in a motor act. For example, the learner may build symbols out of clay, draw symbols in wet sand, or work with blocks or beads.

Manual Language Expression. A method of communication by which one expresses the function or quality of an object by using one's hands and other parts of one's body in meaningful gestures.

Marijuana. A crude preparation of leaves and flowering tops of cannabis sativa used in cigarette form and inhaled as smoke for its euphoric effect.

Mastery Learning. A highly structured teaching-learning program that involves directed teaching using a behavioral approach and based on a sequence of instructional objectives.

Maturational Lag. Slower-than-normal development in some of the critical areas of learning. Deficits in the physical, social-emotional, and cognitive processes, if not corrected, will hamper a student in the acquisition of academic skills, even if the student has near average, average, or above average intellectual functioning.

Mechanical-Automatic Skills. Skills that deal with different levels of learning, including sensory, perception, memory, motor, and spatial-temporal orientation.

Memory (Short-term or Working). Memory that involves the ability to hold information for relatively short periods of time before it is retrieved, such as following instructions, repeating a verbal sequence, spelling words, or reproducing a pattern from memory.

Memory-Sequencing. The process of storing information for both short and long periods of time and the ability to retrieve this information when necessary and upon request. The effectiveness of this system is dependent on the integrity of the sensory and perceptual areas of learning, as well as the conceptual, integrative, and associative aspects of cognitive development.

Metabolism. The physical and chemical processes by which a living organized substance is produced, maintained, transformed to energy, and made available to the organism.

Metacognition. An individual's awareness of how he or she uses systematic and efficient strategies for learning.

Metamemory. The knowledge an individual has of information storage and retrieval, in terms of dealing with memory tasks and memory strategies within his or her own unique frame of reference.

Methadone. A synthetic narcotic with addiction liability, possessing pharmacologic actions similar to those of morphine and heroin. Used in the treatment of heroin addiction.

Minimum Competency Testing. Test criteria for grade-to-grade promotion and/or test criteria for the awarding of a high school diploma, as well as criteria for identifying students needing remedial instruction.

Mode of Learning. Avenues of input, including auditory, visual, tactual-kinesthetic, olfactory, and gustatory approaches.

Modeling-Imitation. The learning of behavior by observing others demonstrate a response. Learners are likely to imitate, or model, behavior of valued persons in their lives.

Morphology. The study of morphemes; a morpheme is the smallest meaningful linguistic unit in a language that cannot be divided into smaller meaningful part.

Motor. Involving movement or muscular activity.

Multicultural. Pertaining to the study of more than one culture.

Multiple Baseline Method. A method of determining whether or not a particular treatment is effective by examining behavior in several individuals simultaneously, establishing a continuum of baselines, and then applying a consecutive treatment program.

Multisensory Approach. The utilization of many modalities, or avenues of input, simultaneously in teaching. The student will see, hear, and touch at the same time when presented a particular task.

Myelin. A cell substance with a high proportion of lipid to protein that serves as an electrical insulator.

Negative Reinforcer. Anything unpleasant or undesirable that strengthens a desired response by terminating or decreasing when that response occurs. Negative reinforcers weaken the undesirable responses that immediately precede their onset.

Neurobiology. The biology of the nervous system.

Neuropsychology. The branch of psychology that combines neurology and psychology.

Neurotransmitter. A substance that is released from the axon terminal on excitation and travels along the synapse to either excite or inhibit the target cell.

Nonverbal Language. The assigning of meaning to gestures and expressions (body language) as well as to such cultural phenomena as art, music, holidays, and patriotism.

Norepinephrine. A principal transmitter of adrenergic neurons.

Norm-Referenced Measurement. A method of comparing an individual's performance with the average performance of the population on which a particular measuring instrument was standardized.

Object Recognition. The integration of visual stimuli into a uniform, recognizable whole. Persons with a dysfunction in this area cannot recognize objects. They tend to focus on the parts.

Ocular Motor Involving Eye Movements. Movements required for visually examining the individual details of an object, for purposes of distinguishing light from no light, seeing fine detail, binocular fusion, convergence, and scanning.

Olfactory. Related to the sense of smell.

On-Task Behavior. Learner activity that is directed specifically toward the task as specified by the teacher and not extraneous to the task. For example, when the student is assigned the task of reading, he or she is doing more than just holding the book.

Operant Conditioning. Rewarding any response that is not elicited by specific external stimuli but that occurs under a set of specific circumstances.

Optimal Teaching Time. The periods or times during the school day when the student is most receptive and responsive to participation in specific educational activities, such as reading and arithmetic.

Output. The processes involved in encoding, including motor responses (manual and body movement) as well as verbal responses (speech, syntax, and formulation).

Overcorrection. A technique designed to decrease undesirable behavior by extending the treatment beyond the correction of a simple act.

Overloading (Jamming). Giving the learner too much input too rapidly. One more spelling word or sound may result in forgetting. Students may fail at the task if they are required to "hold" too much information at a given time.

Overstimulation. Too much input for the learner to cope with, which may result in excessive motor activity, anxiety, poor attention, reduced learning, or any combination of these.

Panic-Coping. The continued attempt to deal with the frustrations imposed by the school and home in response to poor performance that results in anxiety and aggressive behavior.

Perception. A lower level of learning that can be described as more brain function in that it encompasses the subareas of discrimination, figure-ground, closure, and localization and attention as pertains to the visual and auditory processing of information.

Perinatal. Pertaining to or occurring shortly before or after birth.

Perseveration. The inability to use stop-and-go mechanisms efficiently. The learners tend to repeat an act when it is no longer appropriate. They may have difficulty in shifting from one activity to another. For example, they may repeat the previous response on tests.

Phoneme. The sound that is assigned to a symbol that may be used in different ways (e.g., the *p* in *pen* and the *p* in *spoon* are one phoneme).

Phonology. The science that deals with vocal or speech sounds of a language—phonetics.

Plateau. The level beyond which point the learner makes no significant progress in academic tasks.

Positive Reinforcer. Anything desired by the individual that tends to strengthen the response that has just occurred, making it likely that the response will recur.

Positron Emission Topography (PET). Provides a scan trace of the brain's activity as the individual performs different functions.

Postnatal. Occurring after birth with reference to the fetus.

Pragmatics. The relationship between signs or expressions and the individuals who use them, or the social aspect of language such as taking turns when speaking.

Premack Principle. The following of a low-probability behavior, such as hanging up one's clothes, with a high-probability behavior, such as watching TV or eating a favorite food.

Prenatal. Existing or occurring before birth with reference to the fetus.

Prereferral. Activities, preventive measures, or actions taken prior to referral for assessment and placement in special education.

Prescriptive Teaching. An education program for individual learners that is based on data collected through specific diagnostic procedures.

Preteaching. Instruction on the critical components of a task prior to introducing the entire concept or lesson.

Primary Reinforcers. Things such as food, drink, warmth, and sexual stimulation that satisfy biological needs, or needs that sustain life.

Procedural Memory. Memory that deals with skills such as typing, driving a car, or linguistic syntax.

Psychoanalytical Approach. An approach to dealing with problem behavior that has as its underlying assumption the idea that to effect a change in behavior the individual must undergo a restructuring of the personality.

Psychotic-Neurotic Behavior. Behavior that appears fearful, compulsive, and emotionally exhausting or bizarre and clearly not oriented in reality. The individual displaying such behavior may be self-injurious or harmful to others.

Public Law 94–142. The Education for All Handicapped Children Act passed by Congress in 1975 and reauthorized in 1986. A free and appropriate public education is guaranteed by this law.

Punishment. Verbal or physical retributive behavior designed to decrease undesirable behavior in the learner.

Rate of Input. How fast information is presented to the learner in a given period of time.

Rating Scale. A "Likert"-type scale where individuals are ranked on a variety of behaviors by peers, parents, teachers, and other appropriate persons.

Readability. A formula that can be applied to written material to determine its grade placement.

Reality Therapy. A treatment approach that entails an analysis of opportunities for learner involvement in situations where the instructor makes value judgments about specific behavior and the learners commit themselves to a plan for a sequence of actions that will modify that behavior.

Reauditorization. The retrieval of auditory images.

Receptive Language. The application of meaning to words based on experiences in terms of classification and association contingencies.

Reciprocal Teaching. An interacting way of teaching that emphasizes modeling and feedback through a dialogue between the student and the teacher (e.g., the student models the use of such techniques as self-review, clarification, questioning, and predicting in achieving a high level of comprehension [meaning] in reading).

Regular Education Initiative. It was proposed that students with special needs (disabilities) as well as low achievers be served in regular classrooms (Office of Special Education and Rehabilitation Services [OSERS]).

Reinforcer. A stimulus that results in an increase or strengthening of the behavior it follows. Praise or material rewards given to students are reinforcers if they result in desired behavior.

Reliability. Internal consistency and dependability of a test with respect to what it purports to measure.

Resource Room. A place where students go to receive special education assistance or instruction for part of the school day when they are not in the regular classroom.

Response Cost. A form of treatment in which the learner is penalized (e.g., fined) in some manner for undesirable behavior.

Retrieval. The recall of words for use in speaking and writing.

Reversals. The tendency to perceive a symbol in reverse of what it actually is, such as *was* for *saw* or *b* for *d*.

Revisualization. The recall of visual images, or the seeing of an image in the mind's eye.

Ritalin. A trademark for preparations of methylphenidate hydrochloride—a stimulant frequently prescribed for attention deficit disorders to control attention and hyperactivity.

Rubella. German measles, which is a mild viral infection. Transplacental infection in the fetus in the first trimester produced developmental abnormalities.

Satiation. The overuse of a particular reinforcer to the extent that it loses its value, becoming ineffective.

Scanning. The natural zigzag movements of the eyes when shifting from image to image. This has also been referred to as *visual tracking* and *visual pursuit*. It involves the systematic learned eye movements required for reading.

Schema Theory. A cognitive theory that focuses on how individuals acquire and organize information and how this knowledge is structured in memory as organized schemas of processes and events.

School Phobia. An unrealistic and overwhelming fear of school settings that may be accompanied by severe anxiety and physical problems.

Screening. A survey of behavior to identify learning characteristics prior to instruction and a device used for identifying those students who need further analysis or testing.

Secondary Reinforcers. Rewards like praise and tokens that are not directly related to biological needs. (Also called conditioned reinforcers.)

Self-Efficacy. One's feeling about personal worth and competency can affect outcomes of specific tasks. Self-efficacy is related to one's belief structure and how it can produce certain outcomes.

Self-Esteem. An individual's perception or feeling regarding self and self-image. Positive self-confidence and self-worth are constructive and related to success in school.

Self-Evaluation. A principle of cognitive behavior modification that refers to making judgments that affect both the quantity and quality of performance.

Self-Instruction. A principle of cognitive behavior modification where learners use language (verbal feedback) to assist them in their response to learning.

Self-Interrogation. A form of self-questioning where, for example, the student learns to question what he or she is reading.

Self-Monitoring. The student keeps some type of record of classroom activities such as notes in margins, a daily log, editing tabs attached to pages, or a code that describes material to be learned (i.e., "easy," "hard," "confusing," etc.).

Self-Questioning. A process of self-verbalization that enables the student to think out loud and silently about what he or she is doing and devising a strategy to resolve the problem at hand.

Self-Regulation. Monitoring of one's own thinking and behavior through language mediation (e.g., the learner continually makes adjustments based on problem detection such as rereading a paragraph to get the main idea).

Semantic Memory. Information that is stored in memory that is represented as meaningful such as concepts, representations, events, and the relationships that exist between these cognitive phenomenon.

Semantics. The study of the meaning of words and the rules that govern their usage, and the study of the relationships between language and significance. The vocabulary aspect of language.

Sensation (Sensory). The lowest level of learning, at which the learners receive initial input through their auditory (hearing), visual (seeing), tactual-kinesthetic (feeling), olfactory (smelling), or gustatory (taste) senses.

Sensitive-Withdrawn. The classification of behaviors that is characterized by individuals who appear frustrated in everyday life situations, shy, self-conscious, and insecure and who indicate feelings of poor self-worth.

Sequence of Input. The order of input (visual-auditory-tactual), or presentation of information and material.

Sequencing. Remembering in order that which has been heard, seen, or felt for both long and short periods of time.

Severe Discrepancy. A significant difference between a student's performance and expectation based on intellectual potential as measured by a standardized intelligence test.

Shaping. Taking the learner closer and closer to the desired behavior by rewarding successful approximations in less threatening situations.

Social Perception. The ability to interpret, or glean meaning from, gestures and expressions or understand cause-effect relationships in social situations.

Social Skills. Skills dealing with human interaction, needed to function in a society.

Soft Neurological Signs. Physiological indicators used by neurologists and others to diagnose minimum brain dysfunction.

Software. Disks containing information or a computer program used for instructional purposes.

Spacing. The introduction of similar material or concepts far enough apart to avoid confusion of the learner:

t and *d* spaced (aural)
t and *f* spaced (visual)
p and *b* spaced (aural and visual).

Spatial Orientation. The ability of an individual to relate his or her physical self to the environment in terms of distance, size, position, and direction.

Stimulant. An agent that produces stimulation to the central nervous system, such as alcohol.

Strephosymbolia. A disorder of perception where objects seem reversed, as in a mirror resulting in a tendency to reverse direction in reading (reads *saw* for *was*).

Structural Analysis. Word analysis and recognition through the analysis of subunits such as prefixes, suffixes, and stems, as well as root and compound words and syllables.

Subtype. A group within a category that shares common traits or characteristics that distinguish them as an identifiable class.

Suppression. The act of preventing an image from coming in from a less effective eye in order to avoid a double image. Suppression causes the less effective eye to become nonfunctional.

Symbolization. A synonym for language in that a symbol conveys meaning at both verbal and nonverbal levels.

Syntax. The way in which words are put together to form grammatically correct verbal units or sentences.

Synthesis (Reading). The act of blending, or the fusion of sounds into syllables and syllables into whole words.

Synthetic Approach to Reading. A part-to-whole approach beginning with letter sounds and then blending the sounds into words.

Tachistoscope. A device with which the instructor can control the presentation of visual material (words) with precise time exposures.

Tactual. Related to the sense of touch.

Target Behavior. The behavior that is to be modified and the area to which the reinforcement program is directed.

Task Analysis. Analysis of the tasks of reading, writing, spelling, arithmetic, etc., into their basic elements or processes to determine the developmental skills that are prerequisite to their mastery.

Telegraphic Speech. A deficit in verbal language expression under the subarea of syntax and formulation whereby the learner speaks as a telegram reads (e.g., hungry—give money—go eat).

Temporal Orientation. The ability to order and organize time efficiently.

Time-Out. A technique for modifying behavior by preventing its reinforcement for a given time. The learner is isolated every time he or she does something that is undesirable (target behavior).

Token Reinforcers. Objects, such as metal or colored discs, that are exchanged for tangible rewards.

Topical Markers. The location of distinguishing characteristics that identify a category or subgroup, such as in subsets of learning disabilities.

Tourette Syndrome. A syndrome of facial and social tics, with onset in childhood and progression to generalized jerking movements to any part of the body with echolalia.

Toxicity. The quality of being poisonous, such as a toxic microbe or a poison.

Toxoplasmosis. A protozoan disease characterized by lesions of the central nervous system; may lead to blindness, brain defects, and death. The only known complete hosts are cats.

Transition Writing Approach. A bridging technique that takes learners from manuscript to cursive writing by using connecting dots and tracing.

Treatment Period. The period (following the initial, or baseline, period) during which the treatment program is implemented.

Understimulated. Having insufficient input, resulting in a poor learning environment where learners exhibit little motivation or interest.

Validity. The degree to which a test measures what it purports to measure.

Variable-Interval Reinforcement. Reinforcement after different intervals of time. For example, while working, the student gets a reinforcer after 10 seconds, then after 15 seconds, and then after 5 seconds, with the intervals averaging 10 seconds.

Variable-Ratio Reinforcement. Reinforcement that occurs after a varying number of responses. For example, the student would be rewarded after 1 response, then after 5 responses, and then after 3 responses, with the number of responses between reinforcers averaging 3.

Verbal Language Expression. A subarea under receptive language that includes word retrieval, syntax, and formulation.

Visual Channel. All of the processes involved in the visual aspects of learning, including sensation, perception, imagery, and language, as well as the related areas of visual motor integration.

Visual Language Association. The cognitive ability to understand noncategorical relationships between pictures of objects or experiences. The individual can discern that a picture of a pen goes with a picture of a pencil rather than with a picture of a bucket.

Visual Language Classification. The cognitive ability to understand categorical relationships between objects or experiences presented visually. The individual can discern that a picture of an airplane goes with a picture of a car rather than with a picture of a tree.

Visual Language Graphic Association. Expression that requires the learner to use words to express ideas, events, or concepts in writing in a meaningful manner, using grammatically correct sentence structure.

Visual Language Symbol Association. The use of symbols in the process of decoding (learning and communication), including relating letters to words and associating words to ideas and concepts.

Visual-Motor Coordination. The synchronization of the eyes with the movements of the hand and the thought processes of the brain. Efficiency of these three processes operating in concert with each other is required for handwriting and other motor tasks.

Word Caller. A learner who has mastered the mechanics of reading words but cannot apply meaning to the words based on his or her experiences.

Word Processing. Using a computer-like a typewriter but with additional writing capabilities.

Zone Theory. Proposed by Vygotsky, the major concept stresses learning as a process that occurs through social interaction and interpersonal experience. The responsibility of the teacher is to pass on learning by transferring the responsibility for learning to the learner. The arena of activity for this process is known as the "zone of proximal development."

References

Achenbach, T. M., & Edelbrock, C. (1983). *Manual for the Child Behavior Checklist and Revised Child Behavior Profile*. Burlington, VT: University Associates in Psychiatry.

Ackerman, P. T., Anhalt, J. M., Dykman, R. A., & Holcomb, P. J. (1986). Effortful processing deficits in children with reading and/or attention disorders. *Brain and Cognition, 5*:22–40.

Ackerman, P. T., & Dykman, R. A. (July 1982). Automatic and effortful information-processing deficits in children with learning and attention disorders. *Topics in Learning and Learning Disabilities, 12*–22.

Ackerman, P. T., Dykman, R., & Peters, J. E. (1977). Teenage status of hyperactive and nonhyperactive learning disabled boys. *American Journal of Orthopsychiatry, 47*:577–596.

Adams, G. L. (1984). *Comprehensive Test of Adaptive Behavior*. Columbus, OH: Charles E. Merrill.

Adams, J. A. (1967): *Human Memory*. New York: McGraw-Hill.

Adams, J. A., & Dijkstra, S. (1966): Short-term memory for motor responses. *J. Exp. Psychol., 71*:314–318.

Adams, M. J. (1990). *Beginning to Read*. Cambridge, MA: MIT Press.

Adamson, G., Shrago, M., & Van Etten, G. (1972). *Basic Educational Skills Inventory: Math (Level A and Level B)*. Olathe, KS: Select-Ed.

Adelman, H. S., & Taylor, L. (1979). Enhancing the motivation and skills needed to overcome interpersonal problems. *Learning Disabilities Quarterly, 5*:438–446.

Ahr, E. (1966). *Screening Test of Academic Readiness*. Skokie, IL: Priority Innovations.

Aiken, E. G., Thomas, G. S., & Shennurn, W. A. (1975). "Memory for a lecture: Effects of notes, lecture rate, and informational density." *Journal of Educational Psychology, 67* (June):439–444.

Alberg, J. (1985). Evaluations of alternative procedures for identifying learning disabled students. Unpublished doctoral dissertation, University of North Carolina, Chapel Hill.

Alberg, J. Y. (1986). *Evaluation of alternative procedures for identifying learning disabled students in North Carolina*. Doctoral dissertation submitted to the University of North Carolina at Chapel Hill.

Alessi, G. J. (1980). Behavioral observation for the school psychologist: Responsive-discrepancy model. *School Psychology Review, 9*:31–45.

Alexander, J. E., & Heathington, B. S. (1988). *Assessing and Correcting Classroom Reading Problems*. Glenview, IL: Scott, Foresman.

Allen, V. L. (Ed.). (1976). *Children as Teachers: Theory and Research on Tutoring*. New York: Academic Press.

Alper, J. (1986). Our dual memory. *Science 86, 7*(6):44–49.

Alvarez, L. P., & Mangiola, L. (1988, February). *Literature study: A fresh approach to classroom reading for language minority students*. Presentation at the annual conference of the California Association of Bilingual Educators, San Francisco, CA.

Aman, M. G. (1978). Drugs, learning, and the psychotherapies. In J. S. Werry (Ed.), *Pediatric Psychopharmacology: The Use of Behavior Modifying Drugs in Children*. New York: Brunner/Mazel.

Aman, M. G., & Werry, J. S. (1982). Methylphenidate and diazepam in severe reading retardation. *Journal of the American Academy of Child Psychiatry, 1*:31–37.

Ambler, B., & Maples, W. (1977). Role of rehearsal in encoding and organization for free recall. *Journal of Experimental Psychology: Human Learning and Memory, 3*:295–304.

Ambert, A. (1986). Identifying language disorders in Spanish-speakers. In A. C. Willig & H. F. Greenberg (Eds.), *Bilingualism and Learning Disabilities* (pp. 15–33). New York: American Library.

American Medical Association. (1930). *Cardboard Snellen Charts for School Use*. Chicago: Author.

American Psychiatric Association (1968). *Diagnostic and Statistical Manual of Mental Disorders* (2nd ed.) (DSM II). Washington, DC: APA.

American Psychiatric Association (1980). *Diagnostic and Statistical Manual of Mental Disorders* (3rd ed.) (DSM III). Washington, DC: APA.

American Psychiatric Association. (1987). *Diagnostic and Statistical Manual of Mental Disorders: III—Revised*. Washington, DC: APA.

Americans with Disabilities Act. (1990). H. R. 2273 and S. 933.

Ames, C. (1984). Achievement attributions and self-instructions under competitive and individualistic goal structures. *Journal of Educational Psychology, 76*:478–487.

Ames, C., & Ames, R. (1984). Systems of student and teacher motivation: Toward a quality definition. *Journal of Educational Psychology, 76*:535–556.

Ammons, R. B., & Ammons, C. H. (1948). *The Full Range Picture Vocabulary Test*. New Orleans: R. B. Ammons.

Ammons, R. B., & Ammons, C. H. (1962). The Quick Test (QT): Provisional model. *Psychological Reports, 11*:111–161.

Amster, J., & Lazarus, P. (1984). Identifying problems in youthful offenders: Rationales and model. *Journal of Offender Counseling, Services and Rehabilitation, 6*:65–76.

Anders, P., Bos, C., & Filip, D. (1984). The effect of semantic feature analysis on the reading comprehension of learning disabled students. In J. Niles (Ed.), *Changing Perspectives on Research in Reading Language Processing and Instruction*. Thirty-Third Yearbook of the National Reading Conference. Rochester, NY: National Reading Conference.

Anderson, B. F. (1975). *Cognitive Psychology: The Study of Knowing, Learning, and Thinking*. New York: Academic Press.

Anderson, J. R. (1982). Acquisition of cognitive skill. *Psychological Review, 89*:369–406.

Anderson, J. R. (1983a). A spreading activation theory of memory. *Journal of Verbal Learning and Verbal Behavior, 22*:261–295.

Anderson, J. R. (1983b). *The Architecture of Cognition*. Cambridge, MA: Harvard University Press.

Anderson, J. (1985a). *Cognitive psychology and its applications* (2nd ed.). New York: W. H. Freeman.

Anderson, J. R. (1985b, December). Tutoring of mathematics skills. Paper presented at Office of Naval Research—Naval Post-Graduate School meeting on Mathematical Reasoning and Basic Mathematical Skills, San Diego, CA.

Anderson, R., Halcomb, C., & Doyle, R. (1973). The measurement of attentional deficits. *Exceptional Children, 39*:534–539.

Anderson, R. C., & Biddle, W. B. (1975). On asking people questions about what they are reading. In G. H. Bower (Ed.), *The Psychology of Learning and Motivation: Advances in Research and Theory*. (pp. 89–132). New York: Academic Press.

Anderson, R. C., & Pearson, P. D. (1984). *A Schema-Theoretic View of Basic Processes in Reading Comprehension* (Tech. Rep. No. 36). Urbana: University of Illinois, Center for the Study of Reading.

Andrews, G. R., & Debus, R. L. (1978). Persistence and the causal perception of failure: Modifying cognitive attributions. *Journal of Educational Psychology, 70*:154–166.

Applebee, A. N., Langer, J. A., & Mullis, I. V. S. (1989). *Crossroads in American Education*. Princeton, NJ: Educational Testing Service.

Arena, J. (1981). *Diagnostic Spelling Potential Test.* Novato, CA: Academic Therapy Publications.

Armbruster, B. B., Anderson, T. H., & Ostertag, J. (1989). Teaching text structure to improve reading and writing. *The Reading Teacher,* 130–137.

Atkins, M. S., Pelham, W. E., & Licht, M. H. (1985). A comparison of objective classroom measures and teacher ratings of attention deficit disorder. *Journal of Abnormal Child Psychology, 13:*155–167.

Atkinson, B. (1983). Arithmetic remediation and the learning disabled adolescent: Fractions and interest level. *Journal of Learning Disabilities, 16*(7):403–406.

Atwell, N. (1987). *In the Middle: Writing, Reading and Learning with Adolescents.* Portsmouth, NH: Heinemann.

Ausubel, D. P. (1960). The use of advance organizers in the learning and retention of meaningful verbal learning. *Journal of Educational Psychology, 51:*267–272.

Ayres, A. J. (1966). *Southern California Figure-Ground Visual Perception Test.* Los Angeles: Western Psychological Services.

Ayers, L. P. (1912). *A Scale for Measuring the Quality of Handwriting of School Children.* New York: Division of Education, Russell Sage Foundation.

Babbs, P. J., & Moe, A. J. (1983, January). Metacognition: A key for independent learning from text. *The Reading Teacher, 36* (4):422–426.

Baca, L., & Bransford, J. (1982). *An Appropriate Education for Handicapped Children of LImited English Proficiency.* Reston, VA: ERIC Clearinghouse on Handicapped and Gifted Children.

Baca, L., & Harris, K. C. (1988). Teaching migrant exceptional students. *TEACHING Exceptional Children, 20*(1):32–35.

Baddeley, A. D. (1966): Short-term memory for word sequences as a function of acoustic, semantic and formal similarity. *Quart. J. Exp. Psychol., 18:*362–365.

Baddeley, A. D. (1981). The concept of working memory: A view of its current state and probable future development. *Cognition, 10:*17–23.

Baddeley, A. D. (1986). *Working Memory.* Oxford, England: Clarendon Press.

Baddeley, A. D. (1988). But what the hell is it for? In M. M. Gruneb, P. E. Morris, & R. N. Sykes (Eds.), *Practical Aspects of Memory: Current Research and Issues* (Vol. 1). New York: Wiley.

Baddeley, A. D., & Lieberman, K. (1980). Spatial working memory. In R. Nickerson (Ed.). *Attention and Performance, VIII.* Hillsdale, NJ: Erlbaum.

Baddeley, A., Logie, R., Nimmo-Smith, T., & Brereton, N. (1985). Components of fluent reading. *Journal of Memory and Language, 24:*119–131.

Baddeley, A. D., Thomson, N., & Buchanan, M. (1975). Word length and the structure of short-term memory. *Journal of Verbal Learning and Verbal Behavior, 14*(6):575–589.

Banaji, M. R., & Crowder, R. G. (1989). The bankruptcy of everyday memory. *American Psychologist, 44*(9):1185–1193.

Bandura, A. (1977). Self-efficacy: Toward a unifying theory of behavior change. *Psychological Review, 84:*191–215.

Bandura, A. (1982). Self-efficacy mechanism in human agency. *American Psychologist, 37:*122–147.

Bandura, A. (1986). *Social Foundations of Thought and Action: A Social Cognitive Theory.* Englewood Cliffs, NJ: Prentice-Hall.

Bandura, A. (1988a). Self-regulation of motivation and action through goal systems. In V. Hamilton, G. H. Bower, & N. H. Frijda (Eds.), *Cognitive Perspectives on Emotion and Motivation* (pp. 37–61). Dordrecht, Netherlands: Kluwer Academic Publishers.

Bandura, A. (1988b). Perceived self-efficacy: Exercise of control through self-belief. In J. P. Dauwalder, M. Perrez, & V. Hobi (Eds.), *Annual Series of European Research in Behavior Therapy* (Vol. 2, pp. 27–59). Lisse, Netherlands: Swets & Zeitlinger.

Bandura, A. (1988c). Self-efficacy conception of anxiety. *Anxiety Research, 1:*77–98.

Bandura, A. (1989). Human agency in social cognitive theory. *American Psychologist, 44*(9):1175–1184.

Bandura, A., & Wood, R. E. (1989). Effect of perceived controllability and performance standards on self-regulation of complex decision-making. *Journal of Personality and Social Psychology, 56,* 805–814.

Bandura, M., & Dweck, C. (1983). Children's conceptions of intelligence in relation to achievement goals and patterns of achievement-related cognition, affect, and behavior. Unpublished manuscript, Pennsylvania State University, University Park.

Bannatyne, A. (1971). *Language, Reading and Learning Disabilities: Psychology, Neuropsychology, Diagnosis and Remediation.* Springfield, IL: Charles C. Thomas.

Bannatyne, A. (1974). Diagnosis: A note on recategorization of the WISC scaled scores. *Journal of Learning Disabilities, 7:*272–274.

Barclay, J. R. (1971). *Barclay Classroom Climate Inventory.* Lexington, KY: Educational Skills Development.

Bardon, J. (1983). Viewpoints on multidisciplinary teams in schools. *School Psychology Review, 12*(2):186–189.

Bargh, J. A., & Schul, Y. (1980). On the cognitive benefits of teaching. *Journal of Educational Psychology, 72:*593–604.

Barlow, D. H., & Hersen, M. (1984). *Single Case Experimental Designs: Strategies for Studying Behavior Change.* New York: Pergamon.

Barlow, S. M. (1982, June). Drugs in pregnancy: Effects on postnatal development and behaviour. *TIPS,* 254–256.

Barnes, T., & Forness, S. (1982). Learning characteristics of children and adolescents with various psychiatric diagnoses. In R. Rutherford (Ed.), *Severe Behavior Disorders of Children and Youth* (pp. 32–41). Reston, VA: Council for Children with Behavior Disorders.

Barnitz, J. G. (1980, January). Linguistic and cultural perspectives on spelling irregularity. *Journal of Reading:*320–326.

Barnitz, J. G. (1986). Toward understanding the effects of cross-cultural schemata and discourse structure on second language reading comprehension. *Journal of Reading Behavior, 18:*95–113.

Barr, R. B., & Knowles, G. W. (1986). *The 1984–85 School Leaver and High School Diploma Program Participant Attitude Study.* San Diego: City Schools, Planning, Research, and Evaluation Division.

Bauer, R. H. (1977). Memory processes in children with learning disabilities: Evidence for deficient rehearsal. *Journal of Experimental Child Psychology, 24:*415–430.

Bauer, R. H. (1979). Memory, acquisition, and category clustering in learning disabled children. *Journal of Experimental Child Psychology, 27:*365–387.

Bauer, R. H. (1987). Control processes as a way of understanding, diagnosing and remediating. In H. L. Swanson (Ed.), *Memory and Learning Disabilities* (pp. 41–82). Greenwich, CT: JAI Press.

Baumann, J. F. (1983, May). A generic comprehension instructional strategy. *Reading World, 22:*284–294.

Bausch and Lomb. (1958). *Ortho-Rater.* Rochester, NY.

Bayley, N., & Jones, M. (1955): Physical maturing among boys as related to behavior. In W. E. Martin & C. C. Stendler (Eds.), *Readings in Child Development.* New York: Harcourt.

Bear, D. (1987). Letter to the editor. *New England Journal of Medicine, 317:*1738–1739.

Bear, D., & Barone, D. (1989). Using children's spelling to group for word study and directed reading in the primary classroom. *Reading Psychology, 10*(3):275–292.

Beatty, L. S., Madden, R., Gardner, E. F., & Karlsen, B. (1976). *Stanford Diagnostic Arithmetic Test.* New York: Harcourt Brace Jovanovich.

Beck, S., Forehand, R., Neeper, R., & Baskin, C. (1982). A comparison of two analogue strategies for assessing children's social skills. *Journal of Consulting and Clinical Psychology, 50:*596–597.

Becker, W. C. (1986). *Applied Psychology for Teachers: A Behavioral Cognitive Approach.* Chicago: Science Research Associates.

Becker, W. C., Engelmann, S., & Thomas, D. R. (1975). *Teaching 1: Classroom Management.* Chicago: Science Research Associates.

Beery, K., & Buktenica, N. A. (1967). *Development Test of Visual Motor Integration: Administration and Scoring Manual.* Chicago: Follett Educational Corp.

Bell and Howell, Inc. "Language Master." 7100 McCormick Road, Chicago, IL 60645.

Bellak, L. (1954). *Thematic Apperception Test.* New York: C.P.S. Co.

Bellak, L., & Bellak, S. (1965). *Children's Apperception Test.* New York: C.P.S. Co.

Bellinger, D., Leviton, A., Waternaux, C., Needlemen, H., & Rabinowitz, M. (1987). Longitudinal analyses of prenatal and postnatal lead exposure and early cognitive development. *New England Journal of Medicine, 316:*1037–1043.

Belmont, J. M., & Butterfield, E. C. (1977). The instructional approach to developmental cognitive research. In R. V. Kail & J. W. Hagen, Jr. (Eds.), *Perspectives on the Development of Memory and Cognition* (pp. 437–481). Hillsdale, NJ: Erlbaum.

Belmont, J. M., & Freeseman, L. J. (1988). Journal References to Jean Piaget and Lev Vygotsky: Implications for the Acculturation of American Psychologists. Unpublished manuscript, University of Kansas Medical Center, Kansas City.

Bender, L. (1938). *A Visual Motor Gestalt Test and Its Clinical Use* (Research Monograph, No. 3). New York: American Orthopsychiatric Association.

Bender, L. (1963). Specific reading disability as a maturational lag. *Bull. Orton. Soc., 13.*

Bender, L. (1970). Use of the Visual-Motor Gestalt Test in the diagnosis of learning disabilities. *Journal of Special Education, 4:*29–39.

Bender, S. (1975). Teaching Vocabulary in High School: A Classroom Experiment. Unpublished master's thesis. University of Minnesota at Minneapolis.

Bene, E., & Anthony, J. (1957). *Family Relations Test: An Objective Technique for Exploring Emotional Attitudes in Children.* Windsor, Berkshire, England: NFER-Nelson Publishing.

Bengali, V. (1987). *Head Injury in Children and Adolescents: A Resource and Review for School and Allied Professionals.* Brandon, VT: Clinical Psychology Publishing.

Beningus, V. A., Otto, D. A., Muller, K. E., & Seiple, K. J. (1981). Effects of age and body burden of lead on CNS function in young children. *Electroencephalography and Clinical Neurophysiology, 52:*240–248.

Benton, A. (1959). *Left-Right Discrimination and Finger Localization.* New York: Hoeber-Harper.

Benton, A. (1963). *The Revised Visual Retention Test: Clinical and Experimental Application.* New York: The Psychological Corporation.

Berdine, W. H., & Blackhurst, A. E. (1985). *An Introduction to Special Education.* Boston: Little, Brown.

Berliner, D. C. (1981). Academic learning time and reading achievement. In J. T. Guthrie (Ed.), *Comprehension and Teaching Research Reviews.* Newark, DE: International Reading Association.

Berliner, D. C. (1984). The half-full glass: A review of research on teaching. In P. L. Hosford (Ed.), *Using What We Know About Teaching* (pp. 51–77). Alexandria, VA: Association for Supervision and Curriculum Development.

Berliner, D. C. (1986). In pursuit of the expert pedagogue. *Educational Researcher, 15*(7):5–13.

Berliner, D. C., & Rosenshine, B. (1977). The acquisition of knowledge in the classroom. In R. C. Anderson, R. J. Spiro, & W. E. Montague (Eds.), *Schooling and the Acquisition of Knowledge* (pp. 375–396). Hillsdale, NJ: Erlbaum.

Berman, A., & Siegal, A. W. (1976). Adaptive and learning skills in juvenile delinquents: A neuropsychological analysis. *Journal of Learning Disabilities, 9*(9):583–590.

Berry, J. M. (1987, September). A Self-Efficacy Model of Memory Performance. Paper presented at the meeting of the American Psychological Association, New York.

Berry, M. F. (1980). *Teaching Linguistically Handicapped Children.* Englewood Cliffs, NJ: Prentice-Hall.

Betz, N. E., & Hackett, G. (1986). Applications of self-efficacy theory to understanding career choice behavior. *Journal of Social and Clinical Psychology, 4:*279–289.

Biehler, R., & Snowman, J. (1986). *Psychology Applied to Teaching* (5th ed.). Boston: Houghton Mifflin.

Bieliauskas, V. (1963). *The House-Tree-Person (H-T-P) Research Review.* Los Angeles: Western Psychological Services.

Bierman, K. L., & Furman, W. (1984). The effects of social skills training and peer involvement on the social adjustment of preadolescents. *Child Development, 55:*151–162.

Bigler, E. D. (1988). *Diagnostic Clinical Neuropsychology* (rev. ed.). Austin: University of Texas Press.

Bird, L. B. (1988). Reading comprehension redefined through literature study: Creative worlds from the printed page. *The California Reader, 21*(3):9–14.

Bird, M. (1980). Reading Comprehension Strategies: A Direct Teaching Approach. Unpublished doctoral dissertation, University of Toronto.

Bishop, J. E. (1982, January 29). Gene defect linked to retarded males may solve mysteries—Does fragile-x chromosome account for many cases of hereditary condition? *Wall Street Journal, 1:* 18–19.

Blachman, B. (1983). Are assessing the linguistic factors critical in early reading? *Annals of Dyslexia, 33:*91–109.

Blachowicz, C. (1977). Cloze activities for primary readers. *The Reading Teacher, 31*(3):300–302.

Blackman, S., & Goldstein, K. M. (1982). Cognitive styles and learning disabilities. *Journal of Learning Disabilities, 15:*106–115.

Blalock, J. (1987). Intellectual levels and patterns. In D. J. Johnson & J. W. Blalock (Eds.), *Adults with Learning Disability* (pp. 47–66). New York: Grune & Stratton.

Blankenship, C., & Lilly, M. S. (1981). *Mainstreaming Students with Learning and Behavior Problems: Techniques for the Classroom Teacher.* New York: Holt, Rinehart and Winston.

Bloom, B. (1968). Learning for Mastery. *Evaluation Comment* (vol. 1, May). Center for the Study of Evaluation, University of California at Los Angeles.

Bloom, L., & Lahey, M. (1978). *Language Development and Language Disorders.* New York: Wiley.

Bloomfield, L. (1942). Linguistics and reading (Parts 1 and 2). *Elementary English, 19*(4) (April):125–130; *19*(5) (May):183–186.

Blount, R. L., Finch, A. J., Saylor, C. F., Wolfe, V. V., Pallmeyer, T. P., McIntosh, J., Griffin, J. M., & Carek, D. J. (1987). Locus of control and achievement in child psychiatric inpatients. *Journal of Abnormal Child Psychology, 15:*175–180.

Blum, G. (1967). *Blacky Pictures: A Technique for the Exploration of Personality Dynamics.* Santa Barbara, CA: Psychodynamic Instruments.

Blumenthal, A. L. (1977). *The Process of Cognition.* Englewood Cliffs, NJ: Prentice-Hall.

Boder, E. (1971). Developmental dyslexia: Prevailing diagnostic concepts and a new diagnostic approach. In H. R. Myklebust (Ed.), *Progress in Learning Disabilities: Vol 2* (pp. 293–321). New York: Grune & Stratton.

Boder, E. (1973). Developmental dyslexia: A diagnostic approach based on three atypical reading-spelling patterns. *Developmental Medicine and Child Neurology, 15:*663–687.

Boder, E., & Jarrico, S. (1982). *The Boder Test of Reading-Spelling Patterns: A Diagnostic Screening Test for Subtypes of Reading Disability.* New York: Grune and Stratton.

Boehm Test of Basic Concepts. (1980). New York: The Psychological Corporation.

Boer, G. J., Feenstra, M. G. P., Mirmiran, M., Swaab, D. F., & Van Haaren, F. (1988). *Biochemical Basis of Functional Neuroteratology: Permanent Effects of Chemicals on the Developing Brain.* Amsterdam: Elsevier.

Boersma, F. J., & Chapman, J. W. (1981). Academic self-concept, achievement expectations, and locus of control in elementary learning-disabled children. *Canadian Journal of Behavioural Science/Rev. Canad. Sci. Comp., 13:*349–358.

Bond, G. L., & Tinker, M. A. (1973). *Reading Difficulties: Their Diagnosis and Correction* (3rd ed.). New York: Appleton-Century-Crofts.

Bonnet, K. (1988). A neurological locus for Asperger syndrome and its genetics. In J. W. Swann & A. Messer (Eds.), *Disorders of the Developing Nervous System* (p. 267). New York: Alan R. Liss.

Bonnet, K. (1989). Learning disabilities: A neurobiological perspective in humans. *Remedial and Special Education, 10*(3):8–19.

Borkowski, J. G., & Cavanaugh, J. C. (1979). Maintenance and generalization of skills and strategies by the retarded. In N. Ellis (Ed.), *Handbook of Mental Deficiency* (2nd ed., pp. 569–617). Hillsdale, NJ: Erlbaum.

Borkowski, J. G., Estrada, M. T., Milstead, M., & Hale, C. A. (1989). General problem-solving skills: Relations between metacognition and strategic processing. *Learning Disability Quarterly, 12*:57–70.

Bos, C., & Vaughn, S. (1988). *Strategies for Teaching Students with Learning and Behavior Problems.* Boston: Allyn and Bacon.

Boston University Speech Sound Discrimination Picture Test. (1955). Boston: Boston University School of Education.

Botel, M. (1978). *Botel Reading Inventory.* Chicago: Follet.

Botvin, G. J., Baker, E., Botvin, E. M., Filazzola, A. D., and Millman, R. B. (1984). Prevention of alcohol misuse through the development of personal and social competence: A pilot study. *Journal of Studies on Alcohol 45*:550–552.

Bousha, D. M., & Twentyman, C. T. (1984). Mother-child interactional style in abuse, neglect, and control groups: Naturalistic observations in the home. *Journal of Abnormal Psychology, 93*:106–114.

Brainerd, C. J. (1978). *Piaget's Theory of Intelligence.* Englewood Cliffs, NJ: Prentice-Hall.

Brainerd, C. J., Kingma, J., & Howe, M. L. (1986). Long-term memory development and learning disability: Storage and retrieval loci of disabled/nondisabled differences. In S. Ceci (Ed.), *Handbook on Cognitive, Social, and Neurological Aspects of Learning Disabilities* (pp. 142–208). Hillsdale, NJ: Erlbaum.

Brandwein, H. (1973). The battered child: A definite and significant factor in mental retardation. *Mental Retardation, 11*:50–51.

Bransford, J., Delclos, V., Vye, N., Burns, M. S., & Hasselbring, T. S. (1988). *Improving the quality of assessment and instruction: Roles for dynamic assessment.* Unpublished manuscript, Vanderbilt University, John F. Kennedy Center for Research on Education and Human Development, Peabody College, Nashville, TN.

Bransford, J. D., & Johnson, M. D. (1972). Contextual prerequisites for understanding: Some investigations of comprehension and recall. *Journal of Verbal Learning and Verbal Behavior, 11*:717–726.

Brenner, A. (1964). *The Anton Brenner Developmental Gestalt Test of School Readiness.* Los Angeles: Western Psychological Services.

Brewer, W. R., & Nakamura, G. V. (1984). *The Nature and Functions of Schemas* (Tech. Rep. 325). Champaign: University of Illinois, Center for the Study of Reading.

Brier, N. (1989). The relationship between learning disability delinquency: A review and reappraisal. *Journal of Learning Disabilities, 22*(9):546–553.

Brigance, A. H. (1977). *Brigance Diagnostic Inventory of Basic Skills* (2nd ed.). North Billerica, MA: Curriculum Associates.

Brigance, A. H. (1978). *Brigance Diagnostic Inventory of Early Development.* North Billerica, MA: Curriculum Associates.

Brigance, A. H. (1980). *Brigance Diagnostic Inventory of Essential Skills.* North Billerica, MA: Curriculum Associates.

Brigance, A. H. (1982). *Brigance Diagnostic Comprehensive Inventory of Basic Skills.* North Billerica, MA: Curriculum Associates.

Brolin, D. (1976). *Vocational Preparation of Retarded Citizens.* Columbus, OH: Charles E. Merrill.

Bronfenbrenner, U. (1979). Contexts of child rearing: Problems and prospects. *American Psychologist, 34*:844–850.

Brophy, J. (1983). Classroom organization and management. *Elementary School Journal, 83,* 265–286.

Brophy, J., & Good, T. (1986). Teacher behavior and student achievement. In M. Wittrock (Ed.), *Handbook of Research on Teaching* (pp. 328–375). New York: Macmillan.

Brown, A. L. (1978). Knowing when, where, and how to remember: A problem of metacognition. In R. Glaser (Ed.), *Advances in Instructional Psychology.* Hillsdale, NJ: Erlbaum.

Brown, A. L. (1979). Metacognitive development and reading. In R. J. Spiro, B. Bruce, & W. F. Brewer (Eds.), *Theoretical Issues in Reading Comprehension.* Hillsdale, NJ: Erlbaum.

Brown, A. L. (1981). Metacognition: The development of selective attention strategies for learning from texts. In M. L. Kamil (Ed.), *Directions in Reading: Research and Instruction,* Thirtieth Yearbook of the National Reading Conference (pp. 21–43). Washington, DC: National Reading Conference.

Brown, A. L., Campione, J., & Day, J. D. (1981). Learning to learn: On training students to learn from texts. *Educational Researcher, 10*(2):14–21.

Brown, A. L., Campione, J., & Murphy, M. (1977). Maintenance and generalization of trained metamnemonic awareness of educable retarded children. *Journal of Experimental Child Psychology, 24*:191–211.

Brown, A. L., & Palincsar, A. S. (1985). *Reciprocal Teaching of Comprehension Strategies: A Natural History of One Program for Enhancing Learning* (Tech. Rep. No. 334). Urbana: University of Illinois, Center for the Study of Reading.

Brown, D. (1977) *Notemaking.* Toronto: Gage Educational Publishing.

Brown, L., Sherbenou, R. J., & Dollar, S. J. (1982). *Test of Nonverbal Intelligence.* Austin, TX: Pro-Ed.

Brown, L. L., & Hammill, D. D. (1983). *Behavior Rating Profile: Manual.* Austin, TX: Pro-Ed.

Brown, V., & McEntire, E. (1984). *Test of Mathematical Abilities.* Austin, TX: Pro-Ed.

Bruck, M., & Hebert, M. (1982). Correlates of learning disabled students' peer-interaction patterns. *Learning Disabilities Quarterly, 5*(4) (Fall):353–362.

Bruininks, R. (1978). *Bruininks-Oseretsky Test of Motor Proficiency.* Circle Pines, MN: American Guidance Services.

Bruininks, R. H., Thurlow, M. L., Lewis, D. R., & Larson, N. W. (1988). Post-school outcomes for students in special education and other students one to eight years after high school. In R. H. Bruininks, D. R. Lewis, & M. L. Thurlow (Eds.), *Assessing Outcomes, Costs and Benefits of Special Education Programs* (pp. 9–111). Minneapolis: University of Minnesota, University Affiliated Program.

Bruner, J. S. (1973). *Beyond the Information Given.* New York: W. W. Norton.

Brunner, R. B. (1973). Reading mathematical exposition. *Educational Research, 18*(3):208–213.

Bryan, T. (1974). Peer popularity of learning disabled children. *Journal of Learning Disabilities, 7*:621–625.

Bryan, T., Bay, M., & Donahue, M. (1988). Implications of the learning disabilities definition for the regular education initiative. *Journal of Learning Disabilities, 21*(1):23–28.

Bryan, T., & Bryan, J. H. (1978). *Understanding Learning Disabilities* (2nd ed.). Sherman Oaks, CA: Alfred Publishing.

Bryan, T., Werner, M., & Pearl, R. (1982). Learning disabled students' conformity responses to prosocial and antisocial situations. *Learning Disabilities Quarterly, 5*(4):344–352.

Bryant, D., Drabin, I. R., & Gettinger, M. (1981). Effects of varying unit size on spelling achievement in learning disabled children. *Journal of Learning Disabilites, 14*:200–203.

Buchanan, M., & Wolf, J. S. (1986). A comprehensive study of learning disabled adults. *Journal of Learning Disabilities, 19*:34–38.

Buck, J., & Jolles, I. (1966). *House-Tree-Person.* Los Angeles: Western Psychological Services.

Burgemeister, B. B., Blum, L. H., & Lorge, I. (1972). *Columbia Mental Maturity Scale* (3rd ed.). Cleveland: The Psychological Corporation.

Burgess, R. L., & Richardson, R. A. (1984). Coercive interpersonal contingencies as determinants of child abuse: Implications for treatment and prevention. In R. F. Dangel & R. A. Polster (Eds.), *Behavioral Parent Training: Issues in Research and Practice* (pp. 239–259). New York: Guilford.

Burks, H. (1972). *Burks' Behavior Rating Scales.* Los Angeles: Western Psychological Services.

Burks, H. (1977). *Burks' Behavior Rating Scales* (rev. ed.). Los Angeles: Western Psychological Services.

Bursuck, W., & Asher, S. (1986). The relationship between social competence and achievement in elementary school children. *Journal of Clinical Psychology, 15:*41–49.

Bursuck, W. D., & Lessen, E. (1987). A classroom-based model for assessing students with learning disabilities. *Learning Disabilities Focus, 3*(1):17–29.

Burton, G., & Edge, D. (1985). Helping children develop a concept of time. *School Science and Mathematics, 85*(2):109–120.

Buscaglia, L. (1975). *The Disabled and Their Parents: A Counseling Challenge.* Thorofare, NJ: Charles B. Slack.

Bush, K. J., Carter, D. W., Dickerson, C., Evans, G., Martin, F., Raskind, L. T., & Thomas, A. (1989). Gwinnett County: Changing its service delivery in response to population growth. *Professional School Psychology, 4*(3):189–200.

Bush, W. J., & Waugh, K. W. (1976). *Diagnosing Learning Disabilities* (2nd ed.). Columbus, OH: Charles E. Merrill.

Butterfield, E., & Belmont, J. (1977). Assessing and improving the executive cognitive functions of mentally retarded people. In I. Bialer & M. Sternlicht (Eds.), *Psychological Issues in Mental Retardation.* New York: Psychological Dimensions.

Cain, L., Levine, S., & Elzey, F. (1963). *Manual for the Cain-Levine Social Competency Scale.* Palo Alto: Consulting Psychologists Press.

Caldwell, B. (1970). *Preschool Inventory Revised Edition–1970: Handbook.* Princeton, NJ: Educational Testing Service.

California Dropouts. (1986). *A Status Report.* Sacramento: California State Department of Education.

Calkins, L. M. (1986). *The Art of Teaching Writing.* Portsmouth, NH: Heinemann.

Camp, B. W., & Dolcourt, J. L. (1977). Reading and spelling in good and poor readers. *Journal of Learning Disabilities, 10*(5):300–307.

Campbell, J. H., & Perkins, P. (1988). Transgenerational effects of drug and hormonal treatments in mammals: A review of observations and ideas. In G. J. Boer, M. G. P. Feenstra, M. Mirmiran, D. F. Swaab, & F. Van Haaren (Eds.), *Biochemical Basis of Functional Neuroteratology: Permanent Effects of Chemicals on the Developing Brain. Progress in Brain Research, Vol. 73* (pp. 535–553). Amsterdam: Elsevier.

Campione, J. C. (1989). Assisted assessment: A taxonomy of approaches and an outline of strengths and weaknesses. *Journal of Learning Disabilities, 22*(3):151–164.

Campione, J. C., & Brown, A. L. (1987). Linking dynamic assessment with school achievement. In C. S. Lidz (Ed.), *Dynamic Assessment: An Interactional Approach to Evaluation Learning Potential* (pp. 82–115). New York: Guilford Press.

Canney, G. F. (1978). Making games more relevant for reading. *The Reading Teacher, 32*(1):10–14.

Cantwell, D. P., & Satterfield, J. H. (1978). The prevalence of academic underachievement in hyperactive children. *Journal of Pediatric Psychology, 24:*161–171.

Carman, R. A., & Adams, W. R. (1972). *Study Skills: A Student's Guide for Survival.* New York: Wiley.

Carr, E. (1985). The vocabulary overview guide: A metacognitive strategy to improve vocabulary comprehension. *Journal of Reading, 28*(8):684–689.

Carrasco, R. L., Vera, A., & Cazden, C. B. (1981). Aspects of bilingual students' communicative competence in the classroom: A case study. In R. P. Duran (Ed.), *Latino Language and Communicative Behavior.* Norwood, NJ: Ablex.

Carrow, E. (1973). *Test of Auditory Comprehension of Language* (rev. ed.). Austin, TX: Learning Concepts.

Carrow, E. (1974). *Carrow Elicited Language Inventory.* Austin, TX: Learning Concepts.

Cartledge, G., & Milburn, J. (1978). The case for teaching social skills in the classroom: A review. *Review of Educational Research, 48:*133–156.

Cassel, R. (1962). *Child Behavior Rating Scale.* Los Angeles: Western Psychological Services.

Cattell, R. B., Coan, R., & Belloff, H. (1969). *Jr.-Sr. High School Personality Questionnaire.* Indianapolis: Bobbs-Merrill.

Cattell, R. B., Eber, H., & Tatsuoka, M. (1970). *Sixteen Personality Factor Questionnaire.* Champaign, IL: Institute for Personality and Ability Testing.

Catterson, J. (1979). Comprehension: The argument for a discourse analysis model. In C. Pennock (Ed.), *Reading Comprehension at Four Linguistic Levels* (pp. 2–7). Newark, DE: International Reading Association.

Cawley, J. F., Fitzmaurice, A. M., Shaw, R., Kahn, H., & Bates, H., III. (1979a). LD youth and mathematics: A review of characteristics. *Learning Disability Quarterly, 2*(1):29–44.

Cawley, J. F., Fitzmaurice, A. M., Shaw, R. A., Kahn, H., & Bates, H. (1979b). Math word problems: Suggestions for LD students. *Learning Disability Quarterly, 2*(2):25–41.

Ceci, S. J., & Baker, J. G. (1989). On learning . . . more or less: A knowledge x process x context view of learning disabilities. *Journal of Learning Disabilities, 22*(2):90–99.

Cegelka, P. T., & Prehm, H. J. (1982). *Mental Retardation: From Categories to People.* Columbus, OH: Charles E. Merrill.

Cervone, D., & Peake, P. K. (1986). Anchoring, efficacy, and action: The influence of judgmental heuristics on self-efficacy judgments and behavior. *Journal of Personality and Social Psychology, 50:*492–501.

Chaiken, A. L., Gillen, B., Derlega, V. J., Heinen, J. R., & Wilson, M. (1978). Students' reactions to teachers' physical attractiveness and nonverbal behavior: Two exemplary studies. *Psychology in the Schools, 15*(4):144–149.

Chalfant, J. C., Pysh, M., & Moultrie, R. (1979). Teacher assistance teams: A model for within-building problem solving. *Learning Disability Quarterly, 2*(3):85–96.

Chall, J. S., Roswell, F. G., & Blumenthal, S. H. (1963). Auditory blending ability: A factor in success in beginning reading. *Reading Teacher, 16:*113–118.

Chandler, T. A. (1975, July). Locus of control: A proposal for change. *Psychology in the Schools, 13:*334–339.

Chao, Y.-R. (1968). *Language and Symbolic Systems.* Cambridge, England: Cambridge University Press.

Chapman, J. W., & Boersma, F. J. (1979). Learning disabled's locus of control and mother's attitudes. *Journal of Educational Psychology, 71:*250–258.

Charles, C. M. (1980). *Individualizing Instruction* (2nd ed.). St. Louis: C. V. Mosby.

Charles, R. I., & Lester, F. K. (1982). *Problem Solving: What, Why and How.* Palo Alto, CA: Dale Seymour.

Chasnoff, I. J., Burns, K. A., Burns, W. J., & Schnoll, S. H. (1986). Prenatal drug exposure: Effects on neonatal and infant growth and development. *Neurobehavioral Toxicology and Teratology, 8:*357–362.

Chasnoff, I. J., Burns, W. J., Schnoll, S. H., & Burns, K. A. (1985). Cocaine use in pregnancy. *The New England Journal of Medicine, 313*(11):666–669.

Chasnoff, I. J., Griffith, D. R., MacGregor, S., Dirkes, K., & Burns, K. A. (1989). Temporal patterns of cocaine use in pregnancy. *Journal of the American Medical Association, 261*(12):1741–1744.

Chaundron, C. (1988). *Interactive Language Teaching.* Cambridge: Cambridge University Press.

Cheek, E. H., Jr., & Cheek, M. C. (1983). *Reading Instruction through Content Teaching.* Columbus, OH: Merrill.

Chelser, B. (1982). ACLD vocational committee completes survey on LD adult. *ACLD Newsbriefs, 5*(146):20–23.

Chinn, P. C., & Hughes, S. (1987). Representation of minority students in special education classes. *Remedial and Special Education, 8*(4):41–46.

Chomsky, C. (1971). Write first, read later. *Childhood Education, 47:*298–299.

Chomsky, C. (1976, May). *Approaching Reading through Invented Spelling.* Paper presented at the Conference on Theory and Practice of Beginning Reading Instruction, Learning Research and Development Center, University of Pittsburgh.

Chomsky, C. (1979). Approaching reading through invented spelling. In L. B. Resnick & P. A. Weaver (Eds.), *Theory and Practice of Early Reading* (Vol. 2, pp. 43–65). Hillsdale, NJ: Erlbaum.

Chomsky, N. (1965). *Aspects of the Theory of Syntax.* Cambridge, MA: MIT Press.

Chomsky, N., & Halle, M. (1968). *The Sound Pattern of English.* New York: Harper & Row.

Christopher, J. D., Giuliani, R., Holte, C. S., Beaman, A. L., & Camp, G. C. (1989). Predictor variables related to the classification of learning disabilities. *Journal of Learning Disabilities, 22*(9):588–590.

Clark, T. A. (1987). Preventing school dropouts: What can be done? *CBC Quarterly, 7*(4):1–8.

Clarren, S. K., Bowden, D. M., & Astley, S. (1985). The brain in the fetal alcohol syndrome. *Alcohol Health and Research World, 10*(1):20–23, 73.

Clarren, S. K., & Smith, D. W. (1978). The Fetal Alcohol Syndrome. *New England Journal of Medicine, 298*:1063–1067.

Clay, M. M. (1979). *Reading: The patterning of complex behavior.* Portsmouth, NH: Heinemann.

Clements, S. D., & Peters, J. E. (1962). Minimal brain dysfunctions in the school-aged child. *Archives of General Psychiatry, 6*:185–187.

Cloward, R. O. (1967). Studies in tutoring. *Journal of Experimental Education, 36*(Fall):14–25.

Clymer, T., & Barrett, T. (1969). *Clymer-Barrett Pre-Reading Battery.* Princeton, NJ: Personnel Press.

Coan, R., & Cattell, R. B. (1970). *Early School Personality Questionnaire.* Champaign, IL: Institute for Personality and Ability Testing.

Cobb, R. M., & Crump, W. D. (1984). *Post-School Status of Young Adults Identified as Learning Disabled While Enrolled in Public Schools: A Comparison of Those Enrolled and Not Enrolled in Learning Disabilities Programs* (Final rep.). Washington, DC: Office of Special Education and Rehabilitation Services, Division of Educational Services. (ERIC Document Reproduction Service No. ED 253 029).

Cohen, C. (1983). Writers' Sense of Audience: Certain Aspects of Writing by Sixth Grade Normal and Learning Disabled Children. Unpublished doctoral dissertation, Northwestern University, Evanston.

Cohen, C. R., & Abrams, R. M. (1974). *Spellmaster: Spelling, Testing and Evaluation.* Exeter, NJ: Learnco.

Cohen, S. (1983). Low birthweight. In C. C. Brown (Ed.), *Childhood Learning Disabilities and Prenatal Risk: An Interdisciplinary Data Review for Health Care Professionals and Parents* (pp. 70–78). Skillman, NJ: Johnson & Johnson.

Cohen, S. B., Alberto, P. A., & Troutman, A. (1979). Selecting and developing educational materials: An inquiry model. *Teaching Exceptional Children* (Fall):7–11.

Coie, J. D. (1985). Fitting social skills intervention to the target group. In B. H. Schneider, K. H. Rubin, & J. E. Ledingham (Eds.), *Children's Peer Relations: Issues in Assessment and Intervention* (pp. 141–156). New York: Springer-Verlag.

Coie, J. D., & Kupersmidt, J. (1983). A behavioral analysis of emerging social status in boys' groups. *Child Development, 54*:1400–1416.

Colarusso, R. P., & Hammill, D. D. (1972). *Motor-Free Visual Perception Test.* San Rafael, Ca: Academic Therapy Publications.

Coleman, M. (1976). Learning disabilities: Ten years later. *Peabody Journal of Education, 53*:180–186.

Colletti, L. F., (1979). Relationship between pregnancy and birth complications and the later development of learning disabilities. *Journal of Learning Disabilities, 12*:659–663.

Collins, C. (1985). The power of expressive writing in reading comprehension. *Language Arts, 62*(1):48–54.

Cone, T. E., & Wilson, L. R. (1981). Quantifying a severe discrepancy: A critical analysis. *Learning Disability Quarterly, 4*:359–371.

Conners, C. K. (1969). A teacher rating scale for use in drug studies with children. *American Journal of Psychiatry, 126*:885–888.

Conners, C. K. (1973). Rating scales for use in drug studies with children. *Psychopharmacology Bulletin* (Special issue, Pharmacotherapy of children), 9:24–84.

Conners, C. K., & Werry, J. S. (1979). *Pharmacotherapy.* In H. C. Quay & J. S. Werry (Eds.), *Psychopathological Disorders of Childhood.* New York: John Wiley and Sons.

Connolly, A. J. (1982). *Key Math Early Steps Program.* Circle Pines, MN: American Guidance Service.

Connolly, A. J., Nachtman, W., & Pritchett, E. M. (1976). *Key Math Diagnostic Arithmetic Test.* Circle Pines, MN: American Guidance Service.

Cooney, J. B., & Swanson, H. L. (1987). Memory and learning disabilities: An overview. In H. L. Swanson (Ed.), *Advances in Learning and Behavioral Disabilities: Memory and Learning Disabilities* (pp. 1–40). Greenwich, CT: JAI.

Coopersmith, S. (1981). *Coopersmith Self-Esteem Inventories.* Monterey, CA: Publishers Test Service.

Cosden, M. A. (1988). Microcomputer instruction and perceptions of effectiveness by special and regular education elementary school teachers. *The Journal of Special Education, 22*(2):242–253.

Cossio, M. (1978). The effects of language on mathematics placement scores in metropolitan colleges. Doctoral dissertation, Teachers College, Columbia University, New York. *Dissertation Abstracts, 38*(7-A):4002–4003.

Cotman, C., & Lynch, G. (1988). The neurobiology of learning and memory. In J. F. Kavanagh & T. J. Truss, Jr. (Eds.), *Learning Disabilities: Proceedings of the National Conference.* Parkton, MD: York Press.

Cottle, W. (1966). *School Interest Inventory.* Chicago: Riverside.

Coulter, W. A. (1980). Adaptive behavior and professional disfavor: Controversies and trends for school psychologists. *School Psychology Review, 9*:67–74.

Coulter, W. A., & Morrow, H. W. (1978). *Adaptive Behavior: Concepts and Measurements.* New York: Grune & Stratton.

Crabtree, M. (1963). *Houston Test for Language Development.* Houston: Houston Press.

Cratty, B. (1967). *Developmental Sequences of Perceptual Motor Tasks.* New York: Educational Activities.

Cronbach, L. J. (1970). *Essentials of Psychological Testing* (3rd ed.). New York: Harper & Row.

Cronbach, L. J., Gleser, G. C., Nanda, H., & Rajaratnam, N. (1972). *The Dependability of Behavioral Measurements: Theory of Generalizability for Scores and Profiles.* New York: Wiley & Sons.

Cronbach, L. J., & Snow, R. E. (1977). *Aptitude and Instructional Methods.* New York: Irvington.

CTB/McGraw-Hill (1977–1978). *California Achievement Test.* Monterey, CA: Author.

Cullum, C. M., & Bigler, E. D. (1988). Short form MMPI findings in patients with predominately lateralized cerebral dysfunction: Neuropsychological and CT-derived parameters. *Journal of Nervous and Mental Disease, 176*:332–342.

Cummins, J. (1979). Linguistic interdependence and the educational development of bilingual children. *Review of Educational Research, 49*(2) (Spring):222–251.

Cummins, J. (1984). *Bilingualism and Special Education: Issues in Assessment and Pedagogy.* Clevedon, England: Multilingual Matters. Co-published in the United States by College-Hill Press, San Diego.

Cutrona, C. E., & Troutman, B. R. (1986). Social support, infant temperament, and parenting self-efficacy: A mediational model of postpartum depression. *Child Development, 57*:1507–1518.

Dale, E., & Chall, J. (1948). *A Formula for Predicting Readability.* Columbus, OH: Bureau of Educational Research, Ohio State University.

Day, J. D. (1983). The zone of proximal development. In M. Pressley & J. R. Levin (Eds.), *Cognitive Strategy Research: Psychological Foundations.* New York: Springer-Verlag.

Day, J. D. (1986). Teaching summarization skills: Influences of student ability level and strategy difficulty. *Cognition and Instruction, 3*:193–210.

Day, J. D., & Hall, L. K. (1987). Cognitive assessment, intelligence, and instruction. In J. D. Day & J. G. Borkowski (Eds.), *Intelligence and Exceptionality* (pp. 457–480). Norwood, NJ: Ablex.

Deci, E. L., & Chandler, C. L. (1986). The importance of motivation for the future of the LD field. *Journal of Learning Disabilities, 19*:587–594.

Deci, E. L., & Ryan, R. M. (1985). The general causality orientations scale: Self-determination in personality. *Journal of Research in Personality, 19*:109–134.

Decker, S. N., & Bender, B. G. (1988). Converging evidence for multiple genetic forms of reading disability. *Brain and Language, 33*:197–215.

De Corte, E., & Verschaffel, L. (1981). Children's solution processes in elementary arithmetic problems: Analysis and improvement. *Journal of Educational Psychology, 73*:765–779.

DeFries, J., & Decker, S. (1982). Genetic aspects of reading disability: A family study. In R. Malatesha & P. Aaron (Eds.), *Reading Disorders: Varieties and Treatments* (pp. 255–279). New York: Academic Press.

DeHirsch, K. (1965). Plasticity and language disorders. In J. Helmuth (Ed.), *Learning Disorders (Vol. 1)*. Seattle: Special Child Publications.

DeHirsch, K. et al. (1966a, July): Comparisons between prematurely and maturely born children at three age levels. *Amer. J. Ortho., 36*:4.

DeHirsch, K. et al. (1966b): *Predicting Reading Failure*. New York, Harper.

DeHirsch, K. (1967, February): Differential diagnosis between aphasic and schizophrenic language in children. *J. Speech Hearing Dis., 32*(1).

DeHirsch, K., Jansky, J., & Langford, W. (1966). *Predicting Reading Failure: A Preliminary Study of Reading, Writing and Spelling Disabilities in Preschool Children*. New York: Harper & Row.

Delbecq, A. L., Van de Ven, A. H., & Gustafson, D. H. (1975). *Group Techniques for Program Planning: A Guide to Nominal Group and Delphi Processes*. Glenview, IL: Scott, Foresman.

Delgado-Gaitan, C. (1987). Traditions and transitions in the learning process of Mexican children: An ethnographic view. In G. & L. Spindler (Eds.), *Interpretive Ethnography of Education: At Home and Abroad* (pp. 173–187). Hillsdale, NJ: Erlbaum.

Deloche, G., Andreewsky, E., & Desi, M. (1982). Surface dyslexia: A case report. *Brain and Language, 15*:12–31.

Denckla, M. B. (1973). Research needs in learning disabilities: A neurologist's point of view. *Journal of Learning Disabilities, 6*:44–50.

Denckla, M. B. (1977). Minimal brain dysfunction and dyslexia: Beyond diagnosis by exclusion. In M. E. Blaw, J. Rapin, & M. Kinsbourne (Eds.), *Child Neurology*. New York: Spectrum.

Denckla, M. B. (1978a). Critical review of "Electroencephalographic and neurophysiological studies in dyslexia." In A. L. Benton & D. Pearl (Eds.), *Dyslexia: An Appraisal of Current Knowledge*. New York: Oxford University Press.

Denckla, M. B. (1978b). Minimal brain dysfunction. In J. Chall & A. Mirsky (Eds.), *Education and the Brain*. Chicago: University of Chicago Press.

Denckla, M. B., LeMay, M., & Chapman, C. A. (1985). Few CT scan abnormalities found even in neurologically impaired learning disabled children. *Journal of Learning Disabilities, 18*:132–135.

Denckla, M. B., & Rudel, R. G. (1976). Rapid "automized" naming (R.A.N.): Dyslexia differentiated from other learning disabilities. *Neuropsychologia, 14*:471–479.

Deno, S. L. (1980). Direct observation approach to measuring classroom behavior. *Exceptional Children, 46*:396–399.

Deno, S. L. (1985). Curriculum-based measurement: The emerging alternative. *Exceptional Children, 52*:219–232.

Deno, S. L. (1986). Formative evaluation of individual student programs: A new role for school psychologists. *School Psychology Review, 15*:358–382.

Deno, S. L., & Fuchs, L. S. (1987). Developing curriculum-based measurement systems for data-based special education problem solving. *Focus on Exceptional Children, 19*(8):1–16.

Deshler, D. D., & Schumaker, J. B. (1986). Learning strategies: An instructional alternative for low-achieving adolescents. *Exceptional Children, 52*(6):583–590.

Deshler, D. D., Schumaker, J. B., & Lenz, B. K. (1984). Academic and cognitive interventions for LD adolescents: Part I. *Journal of Learning Disabilities, 17*:108–117.

Dinkmeyer, D. D. (1982). *Developing Understanding of Self and Others* (rev. ed.). Circle Pines, MN: American Guidance Service.

Dionisio, M. (1983). "Write? Isn't this Reading Class?" *The Reading Teacher, 36*(8):746–750.

Di Stefano, P. P., & Hagerty, P. J. (1985, January). Teaching spelling at the elementary level: A realistic perspective. *The Reading Teacher, 38*(4):373–377.

Dodge, K. A. (1983). Behavioral antecedents of peer social status. *Child Development, 54*:1386–1399.

Dodge, K. A., Schlundt, D. C., Schocken, I., & Delugach, J. D. (1983). Social competence and children's sociometric status: The role of peer group entry strategies. *Merrill-Palmer Quarterly, 29*:309–336.

Doehring, D. G. (1983). What do we know about reading disabilities? Closing the gap between research and practice. *Annals of Dyslexia, 33*:175–183.

Doehring, D. G. (1984). Subtyping of reading disorders: Implications for remediation. *Annals of Dyslexia, 34*:205–216.

Doehring, D. G., & Hoshko, I. M. (1977). Classification of reading problems by the Q-technique of factor analysis. *Cortex, 13*:281–294.

Doehring, D. G., Hoshko, I. M., & Bryans, B. N. (1979). Statistical classification of children with reading problems. *Journal of Clinical Neuropsychology, 1*:5–16.

Dole, J. A., & Johnson, V. R. (1981). Beyond the textbook: Science literature for young people. *Journal of Reading, 24*(7):579–582.

Doll, E. A. (1953). *The Vineland Social Maturity Scale*. Circle Pines, MN: American Guidance Service.

Doll, E. A. (1965). *Vineland Social Maturity Scale: Condensed Manual of Directions* (rev. ed.). Minneapolis, MN: American Guidance Service.

Doll, E. A. (1966). *Preschool Attainment Record*. Circle Pines, MN: American Guidance Service.

Donaldson, R., & Christiansen, J. (1990). Consultation and collaboration: A decision-making model. *Teaching Exceptional Children, 22*–25.

Doss, D. A., & Sailor, P. J. (1987). *Counting Dropouts, It's Enough to Make You Want to Quit Too!* (Publication No. 86.39). Austin, TX: Austin Independent School District.

Douglas, V. I. (1972). Stop, look, and listen: The problem of sustained attention and impulse control in hyperactive and normal children. *Canadian Journal of Behavioral Science, 4*:259–282.

Douglas, V. I. (1983). Attention and cognitive problems. In M. Rutter (Ed.), *Developmental Neuropsychiatry* (pp. 280–329). London: Guilford Press.

Douglas, V. I. (1985). The response of ADD children to reinforcement: Theoretical and clinical implications. In L. M. Bloomingdale (Ed.), *Attention Deficit Disorder: Identification, Course, and Rationale* (pp. 49–66). Jamaica, NY: Spectrum.

Douglas, V. I., & Peters, K. G. (1979). Toward a clearer definition of the attentional deficit of hyperactive children. In G. Hale & M. Lewis (Eds.), *Attention and the Development of Cognitive Style* (pp. 173–247). New York: Plenum Press.

Downie, D., Slesnick, T., Stenmark, J. K., & Hall, L. (1983). We're madly in love with math! *Instructor and Teacher, 93*:70–72.

Drake, C. (1965). *PERC Auditory Discrimination Test*. Sherborn, MA: Perceptual Education and Research Center.

DSM II: *Diagnostic and Statistical Manual of Mental Disorders* (Second Edition) (1968). Washington, DC: American Psychiatric Association.

DSM III: *Diagnostic and Statistical Manual of Mental Disorders* (Third Edition) (1980). Washington, DC: American Psychiatric Association.

DSM IIIR: *Diagnostic and Statistical Manual of Mental Disorders* (Third Edition, Revised) (1987). Washington, DC: American Psychiatric Association.

Duane, D. (1988). The classroom clinician's role in finding the cause of ADD/LD. *Learning Disabilities Focus, 4*(1):6–8.

Duane, D. (1989). Commentary on dyslexia and neurodevelopmental pathology. *Journal of Learning Disabilities, 22*(4):219–229.

Dudley-Marling, C. C. (1985). Microcomputers, reading, and writing: Alternatives to drill and practice. *The Reading Teacher, 38*(4):388–391.

Dueball, K., & Clowes, D. A. (1982). The prevalence of math anxiety programs: Reality or conjecture? *Journal of Developmental and Remedial Education, 6*:6–8, 24, 32.

Duffy, F. H., Denckla, M. B., & Sandini, G. (1980). Dyslexia: Regional differences in brain electrical activity by topographic mapping. *Annals of Neurology, 7*:412–420.

Duffy, G. G., & Roehler, L. R. (1986). *Improving Classroom Reading Instruction: A Decision-Making Approach.* New York: Random House.

Duffy, G. G., & Roehler, L. R. (1987). Improving reading instruction through the use of responsive elaboration. *The Reading Teacher, 40*(6):514–521.

Duffy, G. G., Roehler, L. R., Meloth, M. S., Vavrus, L. G., Book, C., Putnam, J., & Wesselman, R. (1986). The relationship between explicit verbal explanations during reading skill instruction and student awareness and achievement: A study of reading teacher effects. *Reading Research Quarterly, 21*: 237–252.

Dulaney, K. (1987). Improving word recognition ability through spelling. *Reading Improvement, 24*(3):163–166.

Dunivant, N. (1982). *The Relationship Between Learning Disabilities and Juvenile Delinquency.* NCSCR-072. Williamsburg, VA: National Center for State Courts.

Dunn, L. M. & Dunn, L. (1981). *Peabody Picture Vocabulary Test—Revised.* Circle Pines, MN: American Guidance Service.

Dunn, L. M., & Markwardt, F. C., Jr. (1970). *Peabody Individual Achievement Test.* Circle Pines, MN: American Guidance Service.

Duran, R. P. (1988). Testing of linguistic minorities. In. R. Linn (Ed.), *Educational Measurement* (3rd ed., pp. 573–587). New York: Macmillan.

Duran, R. P. (1989). Assessment and instruction of at-risk Hispanic students. *Exceptional Children, 56*(2):154–158.

Durost, W. N., Bixler, H. H., Wrightstone, J. W., Prescott, G. A., & Balow, I. H. (1971). *Metropolitan Achievement Test.* New York: Harcourt Brace Jovanovich.

Durrell, D. (1956). *Improving Reading Instruction* (pp. 200–201). Yonkers-on-Hudson, NY: World Book Co.

Durrell, D., & Catterson, J. (1980). *Durrell Analysis of Reading Difficulty.* Cleveland, OH: The Psychological Corporation.

Dvovine, I. (1953). *Dvovine Pseudo-isochromatic Plates* (2d ed.). Baltimore: Waverly Press.

Early, G. H. (1973). The case for cursive writing. *Academic Therapy, 9*(1):105–108.

Edelbrock, C. (1983). Problems and issues in using rating scales to assess child personality and psychopathology. *School Psychology Review, 12*:293–299.

Edelbrock, C. (1984). Developmental considerations. In T. Ollendick & M. Herson (Eds.), *Child Behavioral Assessment* (pp. 20–37). New York: Pergamon.

Edelbrock, C. (1986). Behavioral ratings of children diagnosed for attention deficit disorder. *Psychiatric Annals, 16*:36–40.

Edelsky, C. (1988). Living in the author's world: Analyzing the author's craft. *The California Reader, 21*:14–17.

Edgar, E. (1987). Secondary programs in special education: Are many of them justifiable? *Exceptional Children, 53*:555–561.

Education for All Handicapped Children Act, P.L. 94–142, 89 stat. 775 (1975). Codified as amended at 20 U.S.C. §§l400–1461 (1976 and Supp. 1980).

Edwards, A. (1959). *Edwards Personal Preference Schedule.* Cleveland: The Psychological Corporation.

Edwards, A. (1966). *Edwards Personality Inventory.* Chicago: Science Research Associates.

Ehly, S. W., & Larsen, S. C. (1976). Peer tutoring to individualize instruction. *The Elementary School Journal, 76*:475–480.

Ehri, L. (1987). Does learning to spell help beginners learn to read words? *Reading Research Quarterly, 23*(1):47–65.

Ehri, L. (1989). The development of spelling knowledge and its role in reading acquisition and reading disability. *Journal of Learning Disabilities, 22*(5):356–365.

Eighth Annual Report to Congress on the Implementation of the Education of the Handicapped Act, Vol. 1. (1986). *To Assure the Free Public Education of All Handicapped Children.* Washington, DC: U.S. Department of Education.

Ekstrom, R. B., Goertz, M. E., Pollack, J. M., & Rock, D. A. (1986). Who drops out of high school and why? Findings from a national study. *Teachers College Record, 87*(3):356–373.

Ekwall, E. E. (1979). *Ekwall Reading Inventory.* Boston: Allyn and Bacon.

Elias, M. J. (1983). Improving coping skills of emotionally disturbed boys through television-based social problem solving. *American Journal of Orthopsychiatry, 53*:61–72.

Eliason, M. J., & Richman, L. C. (1988). Behavior and attention in LD children. *Learning Disability Quarterly, 11*:360–369.

Elliot, D. S., Huzinga, D., & Ageton, S. S. (1985). *Explaining Delinquency and Drug Use.* Beverly Hills: Sage.

Elliott, S. N., Gresham, F. M., & Heffer, R. W. (1987). Social-skills interventions: Research findings and training techniques. In C. A. Maher & J. E. Zins (Eds.), *Psychoeducational Interventions in the Schools* (pp. 141–159). New York: Pergamon.

Engelmann, S. (1967). *Basic Concept Inventory.* Chicago: Follett Educational Corporation.

Englert, C. S. (1990). Unraveling the mysteries of writing through strategy instruction. In T. E. Scruggs & B. Y. L. Wong (Eds.), *Intervention Research in Learning Disabilities.* New York: Springer-Verlag.

Englert, C. S., Raphael, T. E., Anderson, L. M., Anthony, H. M., Fear, K. L., & Gregg, S. L. (1988). A case for writing intervention: Strategies for writing informational text. *Learning Disabilities Focus, 3*(2):98–113.

Englert, C. S., & Thomas, C. C. (1987). Sensitivity to text structure in reading and writing: A comparison between learning disabled and non-learning disabled students. *Learning Disability Quarterly, 10*:93–105.

Enright, B. E. (1983). *Enright Diagnostic Inventory of Basic Arithmetic Skills.* North Billerica, MA: Curriculum Associates.

Erickson, M. T. (1975). The Z-score discrepancy method for identifying reading disabled children. *Journal of Learning Disabilities, 8*:308–312.

Eysenck, H., & Eysenck, S. (1969). *Eysenck Personality Inventory.* San Diego: Educational and Industrial Testing Service.

Fafard, M. B., & Haubrich, P. A. (1981). Vocational and social adjustment of learning disabled young adults: A followup study. *Learning Disability Quarterly, 4*:122–130.

Fagen, S., & McDonald, P. (1969). Behavior description in the classroom: Potential of observation for differential evaluation and program planning. *Clinical Proceedings of D.C. Children's Hospital, 25*:215–226.

Fagen, S. A., & Long, N. J. (1976). Teaching children self-control: A new responsibility for teachers. *Focus on Exceptional Children, 7*(8):1–11.

Farnsworth, D. (1947). *The Farnsworth Dichotomous Test for Color Blindness.* Cleveland, OH: The Psychological Corporation.

Farr, R. C., Prescott, G. A., Balow, I. H., & Hogan, T. P. (1978). *Metropolitan Achievement Tests: Reading Instructional Battery.* Cleveland, OH: The Psychological Corporation.

Feagans, L., & Appelbaum, M. I. (1986). Language subtypes and their validation in learning disabled children. *Journal of Educational Psychology, 78*(5):373–481.

Federal Register. (1976). *Public Law 94–142* (pp. 56966-56998). December 30, Volume 41.

Federal Register. (1977). *Procedures for Evaluating Specific Learning Disabilities.* 42(250) (December 29): Section 121a.541. Washington, DC: Department of Health, Education and Welfare, Office of Education.

Feindler, E. L., & Ecton, R. B. (1986). *Adolescent Anger Control.* New York: Pergamon.

Felton, R. H., & Wood, F. B. (1989). Cognitive deficits in reading disability and attention deficit disorder. *Journal of Learning Disabilities, 22*(1); 3–12.

Feltz, D. L., & Landers, D. M. (1983). Effects of mental practice on motor skill learning and performance: A meta-analysis. *Journal of Sport Psychology, 5*:25–57.

Ferguson, A. M., & Fairburn, J. (1985). Language experience for problem solving in mathematics. *The Reading Teacher, 38*(6):504–507.

Fernald, G. (1943). *Remedial Techniques in Basic School Subjects.* New York: McGraw-Hill.

Ferrara, R. A. (1987a, April). Dynamic Assessment of Responsiveness to Beginning Mathematics Instruction: Determinants of the Zone of Proximal Development. Poster presented at the American Educational Research Association Meeting, Washington, DC.

Ferrara, R. A. (1987b). Learning Mathematics in the Zone of Proximal Development: The Importance of Flexible Use of Knowledge. Unpublished doctoral dissertation, University of Illinois at Urbana-Champaign.

Feuerstein, R. (1980). *Instrumental Enrichment: An Intervention Program for Cognitive Modifiability.* Baltimore: University Park Press.

Feuerstein, R., Rand, Y., Hoffman, M. B., & Miller, R. (1980). *Instrumental Enrichment.* Baltimore: University Park Press.

Finch, F. (1951). *Kuhlmann-Finch Tests.* Circle Pines, MN: American Guidance Service.

Fine, M. (1986). Why urban adolescents drop into and out of public high school. *Teachers College Record, 87*(3):393–409.

Finn, J. (1982). Patterns in special education placement as revealed by OCR surveys. In K. Heller, W. Holtzman, & S. Messick (Eds.), *Placement of children in special education: A strategy for equity* (pp. 322–381). Washington, DC: National Academy Press.

Firth, I. (1972). *Components of Reading Disability.* Unpublished doctoral dissertation. University of New South Wales, Australia.

Fisher, C. W., Berliner, D. C., Filby, N. N., Marfiave, R., Cahen, L. S., & Dishaw, M. M. (1980). Teaching behaviors, academic learning time, and student achievement: An overview. In C. Denham & A. Lieberman (Eds.), *Time to Learn.* Washington, DC: National Institute of Education.

Fitts, W. (1965). *Tennessee Self Concept Inventory.* Nashville: Counselor Recordings and Tests.

Fitzsimmons, R. J., & Loomer, B. M. (1978). *Spelling: Learning and Instruction.* ERIC No. ED-138-973. Washington, DC: Government Printing Office.

Fitzsimmons, R. J., & Loomer, B. M. (1980). *Spelling: Learning and Instruction—Research and Practice.* Iowa City: The University of Iowa Press.

Flavell, J. H. (1963). *The Development Psychology of Jean Piaget.* New York: Van Nostrand.

Flavell, J. H. (1976). Metacognitive aspects of problem solving. In L. Resnick (Ed.), *The Nature of Intelligence* (pp. 231–236). Hillsdale, NJ: Erlbaum.

Flavell, J. H. (1977). *Cognitive Development.* Englewood Cliffs. NJ: Prentice-Hall.

Flavell, J. H. (1978). Cognitive Monitoring. Paper presented at the conference on Children's Oral Communication Skills, University of Wisconsin-Madison, October.

Flavell, J. H. (1979). Metacognition and cognitive monitoring: A new area of cognitive-developmental inquiry. *American Psychologist, 34*:906–911.

Flavell, J. H., Beach, D. R., & Chinsky, J. M. (1966). Spontaneous verbal rehearsal in a memory task as a function of age. *Child Development, 37*:283–299.

Flavell, J. H., & Wellman, H. M. (1976). In R. V. Kail & J. W. Hagen (Eds.), *Memory in Cognitive Development.* Hillsdale, NJ: Erlbaum.

Fleming, D. C., & Fleming, E. R. (1983). Problems in implementation of the team approach: A practitioner's perspective: *School Psychology Review, 12*(2):144–149.

Fletcher, J. M. (1989). Nonverbal learning disabilities and suicide: Classification leads to prevention. *Journal of Learning Disabilities, 22*(3):176.

Fletcher, J. M., & Copeland, D. R. (1988). Neurobehavioral effects of central nervous system prophylactic treatment of cancer in children. *Journal of Clinical and Experimental Neuropsychology, 10*:495–537.

Flicek, M., & Landau, S. (1985). Social status problems of learning disabled, hyperactive boys. *Journal of Clinical and Child Psychology, 14*:340–344.

Flores, B., Rueda, R., & Porter, B. (1986). Examining assumptions and instructional practices related to the acquisition of literacy with bilingual special education students. In A. Willig & H. Greenberg (Eds.), *Bilingualism and Learning Disabilities* (pp. 149–165). New York: American Library.

Fontana, V. J. (1971). *The Maltreated Child.* Springfield, IL: Charles C. Thomas.

Forness, S., & Kavale, K. (1988). Psychopharmological treatment: A note on classroom effects. *Journal of Learning Disabilities, 21*(3):144–147.

Forness, S. R., Sinclair, E., & Guthrie, D. (1983). Learning disability discrepancy formulas: Their use in actual practice. *Learning Disability Quarterly, 6*:107–114.

Forrest-Pressley, D. L., MacKinnon, G. E., & Waller, T. G. (Eds.). (1985). *Metacognition, Cognition, and Human Performance: Vol. 1. Theoretical Perspectives* (Vol. 1), New York: Academic Press.

Foster, R., & Gavelek, J. (1983). Development of intentional forgetting in normal and reading-delayed children. *Journal of Educational Psychology, 75*:431–440.

Foster, R., Giddan, J., & Stark, J. (1973). *Assessment of Children's Language Comprehension.* Palo Alto, CA: Consulting Psychologists Press.

Fowler, J. W., & Peterson, P. L. (1981). Increasing reading persistence and altering attributional style of learned helpless children. *Journal of Educational Psychology, 73*:251–260.

Frager, A. M. (1985). Content area writing: Are you teaching or testing? *Journal of Reading, 29*(1):58–62.

Frankenburg, W., Goldstein, A., & Camp, B. (1971). The revised Denver Developmental Screening Test: Its accuracy as a screening instrument. *Pediatrics, 79*:988–995.

Fraser, B. (1979). Child abuse in America: A de facto legislative system. *Child Abuse and Neglect, 3*:35–43.

Fraser, B. J. (1987). Psychosocial environment in classrooms of exemplary teachers. In K. Tobin & B. J. Fraser (Eds.), *Exemplary Practice in Science and Mathematics Education,* Perth: Curtin University of Technology.

Freeman, F. N. (1979). *Handwriting Measuring Scale.* Columbus, OH: Zaner-Bloser.

French, D. C. (1986). Heterogeneity of Peer Rejected Boys: Aggressive and Non-Aggressive subtypes. Paper presented at the biennial meeting of the Society for Research in Child Development, Baltimore, MD.

French, D. C., & Waas, G. A. (1985). Behavior problems of peer-neglected and peer-rejected elementary-age children: Parent and peer perspectives. *Child Development, 56*:246–252.

French, J. L. (1964). *Pictorial Test of Intelligence.* Chicago: Riverside Publishing.

Freund, L. A. (1988) Improving the questioning strategies of learning disabled children. *Learning Disabilities Research, 3*(2):78–87.

Frezza, M., di Padova, C., Pozzato, G., .Terpin, M., Baraona, E. & Lieber, C. S. (1990). High blood alcohol levels in women. *Substance Abuse Report, 21*(3):5.

Friedman, S. (1985). "If You Don't Know How to Write, You Try": Techniques that work in first grade. *The Reading Teacher, 38*(6):516–521.

Fries, C. C. (1963). *Linguistics and Reading.* New York: Holt, Rinehart and Winston.

Frostig, M. (1963). *Frostig Developmental Test of Visual Perception.* Palo Alto, CA: Consulting Psychologists Press.

Fry, E. (1968). A readability formula that saves time. *Journal of Reading, 11*(4):513–516, 575–578.

Fry, E. (1981). Graphical literacy. *Journal of Reading, 24*(5):383–390.

Frymier, J. (1988). *Manual of Instruction*. Bloomington, IN: Phi Delta Kappa Educational Foundation.

Fuchs, L. S., & Fuchs, D. (1984). Criterion-referenced assessment without measurement: How accurate for special education? *Remedial and Special Education, 5*(4):29–32.

Fuchs, L. S., & Fuchs, D. (1986). Effects of systematic formative evaluation on student achievement: A meta-analysis. *Exceptional Children, 53*:199–208.

Fuchs, L. S., & Fuchs, D. (in press). Curriculum-based assessment. In C. Reynolds & R. Kamphaus (Eds.), *Handbook of Psychological and Educational Assessment of Children (Vol. 1): Intelligence and Achievement*. New York: Guilford Press.

Fuchs, L. S., Fuchs, D., & Hamlett, C. L. (1989). Effects of instrumental use of curriculum-based measurement to enhance instructional programs. *Remedial and Special Education, 10*(2):43–52.

Fuchs, L. S., Fuchs, D., & Stecker, P. M. (1989). Effects of curriculum-based measurement on teachers' instructional planning. *Journal of Learning Disabilities, 22*(1):51–59.

Fudala, J. (1970). *Arizona Articulation Proficiency Scale*. Los Angeles: Western Psychological Services.

Fuller, G., & Laird, G. (1963, January). Minnesota Percepto-Diagnostic Test. *Journal of Clinical Psychology, 19*:3–34.

Fulmer, S. (1980). *Pre-Reading Screening Procedures and Slingerland Screening Tests for Identifying Children with Specific Language Disability, Technical Manual*. Los Angeles: Western Psychological Services.

Funk, H., & Funk, G. (1987). Applying principles of learning to spelling instruction. *Reading Improvement, 24*(3):167–170.

Gaddes, W. H. (1980). *Learning Disabilities and Brain Function*. New York: Springer-Verlag.

Gaddes, W. H. (1981). An examination of the validity of neuropsychological knowledge in educational diagnosis and remediation. In G. W. Hynd & J. E. Obrzut (Eds.), *Neuropsychological Assessment of the School-Age Child: Issues and Procedures* (pp. 27–84). New York: Grune & Stratton.

Gagné, E. D. (1985). *The Cognitive Psychology of School Learning*. Boston: Little, Brown.

Gagné, R. M. (1965). *The Conditions of Learning* (2nd ed.). New York: Holt, Rinehart and Winston.

Gagne, R. M. (1985). *The Conditions of Learning and Theory of Instruction* (4th ed.). New York: Holt.

Galaburda, A. M. (1986, November). Human Studies on the Anatomy of Dyslexia. Paper presented at the annual conference of the Orton Dyslexia Society, Philadelphia.

Galaburda, A. M. (1988a). Discussion. In J. F. Kavanagh and T. J. Truss, Jr. (Eds.), *Learning Disabilities Proceedings of the National Conference*. Parkton, MD: York Press.

Galaburda, A. M. (1988b). The pathogenesis of childhood dyslexia. In F. Plum (Ed.), *Language, Communication and the Brain*. New York: Raven Press.

Galaburda, A. M., Corsiglia, J., Rosen, G. D., & Sherman, G. F. (1987). Planum temporale asymmetry: Reappraisal since Geschwind and Levitsky. *Neuropsychologia*.

Galaburda, A. M., & Kemper, T. L. (1979). Cytoarchitectonic abnormalities in developmental dyslexia: A case study. *Annals of Neurology, 6*:94–100.

Galaburda, A. M., & Sanides, F. (1980). Cytoarchitectonic organization of the human auditory cortex. *The Journal of Comparative Neurology, 190*:597–610.

Galaburda, A. M., Sanides, F., & Geschwind, N. (1978). Human brain: Cytoarchitectonic left-right asymmetries in the temporal speech region. *Archives of Neurology, 35*:812–817.

Galaburda, A. M., Sherman, G. F., Rosen, G. D., Aboitiz, F., & Geschwind, N. (1985). Developmental dyslexia: Four consecutive patients with cortical anomalies. *Annals of Neurology, 18*:222–233.

Gallagher, J. J. (1966). Children with developmental imbalances: A psycho-educational definition. In W. M. Cruickshank (Ed.), *The Teacher of Brain-Injured Children*. Syracuse, NY: Syracuse University Press.

Gambrell, L. B. (1985). Dialogue journals: Reading-writing interaction. *The Reading Teacher, 38*(6):512–515.

Ganschow, L. (1984, December). Analyze error patterns to remediate severe spelling difficulties. *The Reading Teacher, 38*(3):288–293.

Garbarino, J. (1982). *Children and Families in the Social Environment*. New York: Aldine.

Garbe, D. C. (1985). Mathematics vocabulary and the culturally different student. *Arithmetic Teacher, 33*(2):39–42.

Gardner, E. F., Rudman, H. C., Karlsen, B., & Merwin, J. C. (1982). *Stanford Achievement Test* (7th ed.). Cleveland, OH: The Psychological Corporation.

Gardner, W. I. (1977). *Learning and Behavior Characteristics of Exceptional Children and Youth*. Boston: Allyn and Bacon.

Garofalo, J., & Lester, F. (1985). Metacognition, cognitive monitoring, and mathematical performance. *Journal for Research in Mathematics Education, 16*(3):163–176.

Gartner, A., Kohler, M. C., & Reissman, F. (1971). *Children Teach Children: Learning to Read*. New York: Harper & Row.

Gates, A. (1958). *Gates Reading Readiness Scales*. New York: Bureau of Publications, Teachers College, Columbia University.

Gelles, R. J. (1982). Child abuse and family violence: Implications for medical professionals. In E. H. Newberger (Ed.), *Child Abuse* (pp. 25–42). Boston: Little, Brown.

Gelman, R. (1979). Preschool thought. *American Psychologist, 34*:900–905.

Gentry, J. R. (1981, January). Learning to spell developmentally. *The Reading Teacher, 34*:378–381.

Gentry, J. R., & Henderson, E. H. (1978, March). Three steps to teaching beginning readers to spell. *The Reading Teacher*, 632–637.

Gerber, M. M., & Semmel, M. I. (1984). Teacher as imperfect test: Reconceptualizing the referral process. *Educational Psychologist, 19*:137–148.

Gerber, M. M., Tan, S. L., Rothman, H., & Semmel, D. S. (1986, March). *Effects of Self-Rated Competencies and Handicapped Student Behavior on Teachers' Monitoring and Use of Computers*. Technical Report No. 43, Project TEECh, University of California, Santa Barbara.

Gerber, P. J., & Brown, D. (1991). Report of the pathways to employment consensus conference on employability of persons with learning disabilities. *Learning Disabilities Research & Practice, 6*:99–103.

Gerber, P. J., & Zinkgraf, S. A. (1982). A comparative study of social-perception ability in learning disabled and nonhandicapped students. *Learning Disabilities Quarterly, 5*(Fall) (4):374–378.

Germann, G., & Tindal, G. (1985). An application of curriculum-based assessment: The use of direct and frequent measurement. *Exceptional Children, 52*:244–265.

Gersten, R., Carnine, D., & Woodward, J. (1987). Direct instruction research: The third decade. *Remedial and Special Education, 8*(6):48–56.

Geschwind, N. (1974). Anatomical foundations of language and dominance. In C. L. Ludlow & M. E. Doran-Quine (Eds.), *The Neurological Basis of Language Disorders in Children: Methods and Direction for Research* (NIH Publication No. 79–440). Bethesda, MD: U.S. Department of Health, Education and Welfare.

Geschwind, N. (1979). Anatomical foundations of language and dominance. In C. L. Ludlow & M. E. Doran-Quine (Eds.), *The Neurological Bases of Language Disorders in Children: Methods and Directions for Research* (pp. 145–153). NINCSD Monograph Series. Bethesda, MD: National Institutes of Health.

Geschwind, N. (1985). Biological foundations of reading. In F. H. Duffy & N. Geschwind (Eds.), *Dyslexia: A Neuroscientific Approach to Clinical Evaluation*. Boston: Little, Brown.

Geschwind, N., & Behan, P. (1982). Left-handedness: Association with immune disease, migraine, and developmental learning disorder. *Proceedings of the National Academy of Science, 79*:5097–5100.

Gessell, J. K. (1977). *Diagnostic Mathematics Inventory.* Monterey CA: CTB/McGraw-Hill.

Gesten, E. L., Rains, M. H., Rapkin, B. D., Weissberg, R. P., Flores de Apocada, R., Cowen, E. L., & Bowen, R. (1982). Training children in social problem-solving competencies: A first and second look. *American Journal of Community Psychology, 10:*95-115.

Gibson, E., & Rader, N. (1979). Attention: The perceiver as performer. In G. A. Hale & M. Lewis (Eds.), *Attention and Cognitive Development* (pp. 1-22). New York: Plenum.

Gill, T. (1989). The relationship between word recognition and spelling in the primary grades. *Reading Psychology, 10*(2):117-135.

Gillet, J. W., & Temple, C. (1982). *Understanding Reading Problems: Assessment and Instruction.* Boston: Little, Brown.

Gilmore, J. V., & Gilmore, E. C. (1968). *Gilmore Oral Reading Test.* Cleveland, OH: The Psychological Corporation.

Gipe, J. P. (1978-1979). Investigating techniques for teaching word meanings. *Reading Research Quarterly, 14:*624-644.

Gittelman-Klein, R. (1987). Prognosis of attention deficit disorder and its management in adolescence. *Pediatrics in Review, 8:*216-222.

Gitter, L. (1976). Basic geometric shapes and reading. *Academic Therapy, 12*(1):53-66.

William Gladden Foundation (1987). *When Children Use Drugs.*

Glaser, D., & Bentovim, A. (1979). Abuse and risk to handicapped and chronically ill children. *Child Abuse and Neglect, 3:*565-575.

Glasser, W. (1969). *Schools Without Failure.* New York: Harper & Row.

Glazzard, M. (1977). The effectiveness of three kindergarten predictors for first-grade achievement. *Journal of Learning Disabilities, 10:*95-99.

Gold, J., & Fleisher, L. S. (1986). Comprehension breakdown with inductively organized text: Differences between average and disabled readers. *Remedial and Special Education, 7*(4):26-32.

Goldberg, S. (1988). *Clinical Neuroanatomy Made Ridiculously Simple.* Miami: MedMaster, Inc.

Golden, J. M. (1984). Children's concept of story in reading and writing. *The Reading Teacher, 37*(7):578-584.

Goldman, R., Fristoe, M., & Woodcock, R. (1970). *Goldman-Fristoe-Woodcock Test of Auditory Discrimination.* Circle Pines, MN: American Guidance Service.

Goldman, R., Fristoe, M., & Woodcock, R. (1975). *Goldman-Fristoe-Woodcock Auditory Skills Test Battery.* Circle Pines MN: American Guidance Service.

Goldman, S. R. (1989). Strategy instruction in mathematics. *Learning Disability Quarterly, 12:*43-55.

Goldman, S. R., & Pellegrino, J. W. (1986). Microcomputers: Effective drill and practice. *Academic Therapy, 22:*133-140.

Goldstein, K. (1936). Modification of behavior consequent to cerebral lesion. *Psychiatric Quarterly, 10:*539-610.

Goodenough, F. (1926). *Draw-A-Person Test: The Measurement of Intelligence by Drawings.* Yonkers-on-Hudson, NY: World Book.

Goodman, K. S., & Goodman, Y. M. (1977). Learning about psycholinguistic process by analyzing oral reading. *Harvard Educational Review, 47:*317.

Gordon, M. (1979). The assessment of impulsivity and mediating behaviors in hyperactive and nonhyperactive boys. *Journal of Abnormal Child Psychology, 7:*117-126.

Gordon, M., & McClure, F. D. (1983, August). *The Objective Assessment of Attention Deficit Disorders.* Paper presented at the 91st annual convention of the American Psychological Association, Anaheim, CA.

Gordon, M., McClure, F. D., & Post, E. M. (1986). *Interpretive Guide to the Gordon Diagnostic System.* DeWitt, NY: Gordon Systems.

Gordon, M., & Mettelman, B. B. (1987). *Technical Guide to the Gordon Diagnostic System.* DeWitt, NY: Gordon Systems.

Gordon, M., & Mettelman, B. B. (in press). The assessment of attention: I. Standardization and reliability of a behavior-based measure. *Journal of Clinical Psychology.*

Gottman, J., Gonso, J., & Rasmussen, B. (1975). Social interaction, social competence, and friendship in children. *Child Development, 46:*709-718.

Gough, H. (1969). *California Psychological Inventory.* Palo Alto: Consulting Psychologists Press.

Gough, P. B., & Tunmer, W. E. (1986). Decoding, reading, and reading disability. *Remedial and Special Education, 7*(1):6-10.

Graden, J. L., Casey, A., & Bonstrom, D. (1985). Implementing a prereferral intervention system: Part II—The data. *Exceptional Children, 51*(6):487-496.

Grafman, J., Vance, S. C., Weingartner, H., Salazar, A. M., & Amin, D. (1986). The effects of lateralized frontal lesions on mood regulation. *Brain, 109:*1127-1148.

Graham, F., & Kendall, B. (1960). *Memory-for-Designs Test.* Missoula, MT: Psychological Test Specialists.

Graham, S. (1983, May). Effective spelling instruction. *The Elementary School Journal, 83:*560-596. (EJ 281 590).

Graves, D. (1978). *Balance the Basics: Let Them Write.* New York: Ford Foundation.

Graves, D. H. (1985). All children can write. *Learning Disabilities Focus, 1:*36-43.

Gray, W. S., & Robinson, H. M. (1967). *Gray Oral Reading Test.* Austin, TX: Pro-Ed.

Greenough, W. T., Larson, J. R., & Withers, G. S. (1985). Effects of unilateral and bilateral training in a reaching task on dendritic branching of neurons in the rat motor-sensory forelimb cortex. *Behavioral and Neural Biology, 44:*301-314.

Greenwood, J. (1984). My anxieties about math anxiety. *Mathematics Teacher, 77:*662-663.

Greer, J. V. (1990). The drug babies. *Exceptional Children, 56*(5):382-385.

Gresham, F. M. (1982). Misguided mainstreaming: The case for social skills training with handicapped children. *Exceptional Children, 48:*420-433.

Gresham, F. M. (1983a). Social skills assessment as a component of mainstreaming placement decisions. *Exceptional Children, 49:*331-336.

Gresham, F. M. (1983b). Social validity in the assessment of children's social skills. Establishing standards for social competency. *Journal of Psychoeducational Assessment, 1:*299-307.

Gresham, F. M. (1986a). Conceptual issues in the assessment of social competence in children. In P. Strain, M. Guralnick, & H. Walker (Eds.), *Children's Social Behavior: Development, Assessment, and Modification* (pp. 143-179). New York: Academic.

Gresham, F. M. (1986b). Conceptual and definitional issues in the assessment of children's social skills: Implications for classification and training. *Journal of Clinical Child Psychology, 15:*3-15.

Gresham, F. M. (1986c). On the malleability of intelligence: Unnecessary assumptions, reifications, and occlusion. *School Psychology Review, 15:*261-263.

Gresham, F. M. (1988). Social competence and motivational characteristics of learning disabled students. In M. Wang, M. M. Reynolds, & H. Walberg (Eds.), *Handbook of Special Education: Research and Practice* (pp. 283-302). Oxford, England: Pergamon Books.

Gresham, F. M., & Elliott, S. N. (1984). Assessment and classification of children's social skills: A review of methods and issues. *School Psychology Review, 13:*292-301.

Gresham, F. M., & Elliott, S. N. (1989). Social skills assessment technology for LD students. *Learning Disability Quarterly, 12:*141-152.

Gresham, F. M., & Reschly, D. J. (1986). Social skills deficits and low peer acceptance of mainstreamed learning disabled children. *Learning Disability Quarterly, 9:*23-32.

Gresham, F. M., & Reschly, D. J. (1987). Dimensions of social competence: Method factors in the assessment of adaptive behavior, social skills, and peer acceptance. *Journal of School Psychology, 25*(4):367-382.

Grimes, J. P., & Reschly, D. J. (1986). *Relevant Educational Assessment and Intervention Model (RE-AIM).* (Project proposal funded by the U.S. Department of Education). Des Moines, IA: Department of Education, Bureau of Special Education.

Grimm, J. A., Bijou, S. W., & Parsons, J. A. (1973). A problem-solving model for teaching remedial arithmetic to handicapped young children. *Journal of Abnormal Child Psychology, 1:*26-39.

Grise, P. J. (1986). Handicapped students and minimum competency testing. *Special Services in the School, 7*:177–185.

Gross, M. (1976). Growth of hyperkinetic children taking methylphenidate, dextroamphetamine, or imipramine/desipramine. *Pediatrics, 58*:423–425.

Grossberg, S., & Stone, G. O. (1986). Neural dynamics of word recognition and recall: Attentional priming, learning and resonance. *Psychological Reviews, 93*:46–74.

Grossman, H. J. (Ed.). (1983). *Manual on Terminology and Classification in Mental Retardation* (3rd rev. ed.). Washington, DC: American Association on Mental Deficiency.

Grossnickle, D. R. (1986). *High School Dropouts: Causes, Consequences, and Cure* (Fastback 242). Bloomington, IN: Phi Delta Kappa Educational Foundation.

Groteluschen, A. K., Borkowski, J. G., & Hale, C. (1990). Strategy instruction is often insufficient: Addressing the interdependency of executive and attributional processes. In T. E. Scruggs & B. Y. L. Wong (Eds.), *Intervention Research in Learning Disabilities*. New York: Springer-Verlag.

Guthrie, J. T. (1977, February). Research views: Story comprehension. *The Reading Teacher, 30*:574–577.

Hagen, D., (1984). *Microcomputer Resource Book for Special Education*. Reston, VA: Reston Publishing.

Hahn, A. (1987). Reaching out to America's dropouts: What to do? *Phi Delta Kappan, 69*(4):256–263.

Hainsworth, P., & Siqueland, M. (1969). *The Meeting Street School Screening Test*. Providence: Crippled Children and Adults of Rhode Island.

Hall, J., & Gallagher, J. J. (1983). Minimum competency testing and the learning disabled student. In J. McKinney & L. Feagons (Eds.), *Current Topics in Learning Disabilities*. Norwood, NJ: Ablex.

Hall, R. J. (1979). An Information-Proposing Approach to the Study of Learning Disabilities: The Effect of Cue Elaboration on the Maintenance and Generalization of Problem-Solving Strategies (Doctoral dissertation, University of California, Los Angeles, 1979). *Dissertation on Abstracts International, 40*:3948-3949A.

Hall, R. J. (1980). Information processing and cognitive training in learning disabled children: An executive level meeting. *Exceptional Education, 1*:9–16.

Hall, R. V. (1971). *Managing Behavior Part 2, Behavior Modification: Basic Principles*. Lawrence, KS: H & H Enterprises.

Hall, R. V. (1975). *Behavior Modification: Basic Principles Managing Behavior (Part 2)* (rev. ed). Lawrence, KS: H & H Enterprises.

Hallahan, D. P. (Ed.) (1983). *Exceptional Education Quarterly, 1*.

Hallahan, D. P., & Kauffman, J. M. (1976) *Introduction to Learning Disabilities: A Psycho-Behavioral Approach* (p. 1045). Englewood Cliffs, NJ: Prentice-Hall.

Hallahan, D. P., Kauffman, J. M., & Ball, D. W. (1973). Selective attention and cognitive tempo of low achieving and high achieving sixth grade males. *Perceptual and Motor Skills, 36*:579–583.

Hallahan, D. P., Kauffman, J. M., & Lloyd, J. W. (1985). *Introduction to Learning Disabilities* (2nd ed.). Englewood Cliffs, NJ: Prentice-Hall.

Hallahan, D. P., Keller, C. E., McKinney, J. D., Lloyd, J. W., & Bryan, T. (1988). Examining the research base of the regular education initiative: Efficacy studies and the adaptive learning environments model. *Journal of Learning Disabilities, 21*(1):29–35, 55.

Hallahan, D. P., Lloyd, J. W., Kauffman, J. M., & Loper, A. B. (1983). Academic problems. In R. J. Morris & T. R. Kratochwill (Eds.), *Practice of Child Therapy: A Textbook of Methods* (pp. 113–141). New York: Pergamon Press.

Hallahan, D. P., & Sapona, R. (1983). Self-monitoring of attention in learning disabled children: Past research and current issues. *Journal of Learning Disabilities, 16*:616–620.

Halliday, M. A. K. (1974). Some aspects of sociolinguistics. In E. Jacobsen (Ed.), *Interactions Between Linguistics and Mathematical Education: Final Report of the Symposium*. New York: UNESCO.

Halpern, A. (1979, April). Adolescents and young adults. *Exceptional Children*, 518–523.

Halpern, A. (1985). Transition: A look at the foundations. *Exceptional Children, 51*, 479–486.

Halpern, A., Raffeld, P., Irvin, L. K., & Link, R. (1975). *Social and Prevocational Information Battery*. Monterey, CA: CTB/McGraw-Hill.

Hamilton, L. (1989). Variables associated with child maltreatment and implications for prevention and treatment. *Early Child Development and Care, 42*:31–56.

Hamilton, S. F. (1986). Raising standards and reducing dropout rates. *Teachers College Record, 87*(3):411–429.

Hammack, F. M. (1986). Large school systems' dropout reports: An analysis of definitions, procedures and findings. *Teachers College Record, 87*(3):324–341.

Hammill, D. D. (1985). *Detroit Tests of Learning Aptitude*. Austin, TX: Pro-Ed.

Hammill, D. D., Brown, V. L., Larsen, S. G., & Wiederholt, J. L. (1980). *Test of Adolescent Language*. Austin, TX: Pro-Ed.

Hammill, D. D., & Larsen, S. S. (1978). *Test of Written Language*. Austin, TX: Pro-Ed.

Hammill, D. D., & Larsen, S. S. (1983). *Test of Written Language*. Austin, TX: Pro-Ed.

Hammill, D. D., & Leigh, J. (1983a). *Basic School Skills Inventory, Diagnostic*. Austin, TX: Pro-Ed.

Hammill, D. D., & Leigh, J. (1983b). *Basic School Skills Inventory, Screen*. Austin, TX: Pro-Ed.

Hammill, D. D., Leigh, J. E., McNutt, H., & Larsen, S. C. (1981). A new definition of learning disabilities. *Learning Disability Quarterly, 4*(4):336–342.

Hammill, D. D., Leigh, J. E., McNutt, G., & Larsen, S. C. (1988). A new definition of learning disabilities. *Learning Disability, 11*:217–223.

Hanna, P. R., Hodges, R. E., & Hanna, J. S. (1971). *Spelling: Structure and Strategies*. Boston: Houghton Mifflin.

Harber, J. R. (1980). Auditory perception and reading: Another look. *Learning Disability Quarterly, 3*(3):19–29.

Harris, A. (1958). *Harris Test of Lateral Dominance* (3d rev. ed.). New York: The Psychological Corporation.

Harris, A. (1975). *How to Increase Reading Ability* (6th ed.). New York: David McKay.

Harris, A. J., & Sipay, E. R. (1985). *How to Increase Reading Ability* (8th ed.). New York: Longman.

Harris, K. R., & Graham, S. (1985). Improving learning disabled students' composition skills: Self-control strategy training. *Learning Disability Quarterly, 8*(1):27–36.

Harris, O. (1963). *Goodenough-Harris Drawing Tests*. New York: Harcourt Brace Jovanovich.

Harris, T. L., & Hodges, R. E. (1981). *A Dictionary of Reading and Related Terms*. Newark, DE: International Reading Association.

Harrison, P. L. (1989). Adaptive behavior: Research to practice. *Journal of School Psychology, 27*(3):310–317.

Harrison, P. L., & Pottebaum, S. M. (1987). The relation between adaptive behavior and intelligence: Testing alternative explanations. *Journal of School Psychology, 25*:31–43.

Harter, S. (1978). Effectance motivation reconsidered: Toward a developmental model. *Human Development, 45*:661–669.

Harter, S. (1983). Developmental perspectives on the self-system. In E. M. Hetherington (Ed.), *Handbook of Child Psychology: Socialization, Personality, and Social Development* (Vol. 4, pp. 278–386).

Harter, S. (1985). Processes underlying the construction, maintenance, and enhancement of the self-concept in children. In J. Suls & A. Greenwald (Eds.). *Psychological Perspectives on the Self* (Vol. 3). Hillsdale, NJ: Erlbaum.

Hartup, W. W. (1974). Aggression in childhood: Developmental perspectives. *American Psychologist, 29*:336–341.

Harvey, P., Weintraub, S., & Neale, J. (1984). Distractibility in learning-disabled children: The role of measurement artifact. *Journal of Learning Disabilities, 17*:134–137.

Harvin, V. R., & Gilchrist, M. A. (1970). *Mathematics Teacher—A Reading Teacher?* Arlington, Va.: ERIC Document Reproduction Service. (ED 041 702).

Hasazi, S. B., Gordon, L. R., & Roe, C. A. (1985). Factors associated with the employment status of handicapped youth exiting high school from 1979 to 1983. *Exceptional Children, 51*(6):455–469.

Hasazi, S., Johnson, R., Hasazi, J., Gordon, L., & Hull, M. (1989). Employment of youth with and without handicaps following high school: Outcomes and correlates. *The Journal of Special Education, 23*(3):243–255.

Hasbrouck, J. M. (1983). Diagnosis of auditory perceptual disorders in previously undiagnosed adults. *Journal of Learning Disabilities, 16*:206–208

Hathaway, S., & McKinley, J. (1967). *Minnesota Multiphasic Personality Inventory*. Cleveland: The Psychological Corporation.

Hatton, D., Pizzat, F., & Pelkowski, J. (1967). *Perceptual-Motor Teaching Materials, Erie Program 1*. Boston: Teaching Resources.

Hausserman, E. (1958).*Developmental Potential of Preschool Children*. New York: Grune & Stratton.

Hayden, A. H. (1974). Perspectives of early childhood education in special education. In N. G. Haring (Ed.), *Behavior of Exceptional Children: An Introduction to Special Education*. Columbus, OH: Charles E. Merrill.

Hayes, S., Rosenfarb, I., Wulfert, E., Munt, E., Korn, Z., & Zottle, R. (1985). Self-reinforcement effects: An artifact of social standard setting? *Journal of Applied Behavior Analysis, 18*:201–214.

Haywood, H. C., & Switzky, H. N. (1986a). Intrinsic motivation and behavior effectiveness in retarded persons. In N. R. Ellis (Ed.), *International Review of Research in Mental Retardation* (Vol. 14, pp. 1–46). New York: Academic Press.

Haywood, H. C., & Switzky, H. N. (1986b). The malleability of intelligence: Cognitive processes as a function of polygenic and experiential interaction. *School Psychology Review, 15*(2):245–255.

Haywood, H. C., & Switsky, H. N. (1986c). Transactionalism and cognitive processes: Reply to Reynolds and Gresham. *School Psychology Review, 15*:264–267.

Hazel, J. S., & Schumaker, J. B. (1987, January). Social Skills and Learning Disability. Paper presented at the National Conference on Learning Disabilities, Bethesda, MD.

Heathington, B. S., & Alexander, J. E. (1978). A child-based observation checklist to assess attitudes toward reading. *The Reading Teacher, 31*:769–771.

Heckleman, R. G. (1969, Summer). A neurological impress method of remedial reading instruction. *Academic Therapy Quarterly, 4*:277–82.

Heilman, K. M., Watson, R. T., & Bowers, D. (1983). Affective disorders associated with hemispheric disease. In K. M. Heilman & P. Satz (Eds.), *Neuropsychology of Human Emotion* (pp. 45–64). New York: Guilford Press.

Heinrichs, A. S. (1987). Elementary school math instruction: Can reading specialists assist? *Reading Horizons, 28*(1): 19–25.

Heller, K., Holtzman, W., & Messick, S. (Eds.). (1982). *Placing Children in Special Education: A Strategy for Equity*. (Report of the National Research Council Panel on Selection and Placement of Students in Programs for the Mentally Retarded). Washington, DC: National Academy Press.

Henderson, E. H. (1985). *Teaching Spelling*. Boston: Houghton Mifflin.

Henderson, E. H., & Beers, J. W. (1980). *Developmental and Cognitive Aspects of Learning to Spell: A Reflection of Word Knowledge*. Newark, DE: International Reading Association.

Herber, H. (1970). *Teaching Reading in Content Areas*. Englewood Cliffs, NJ: Prentice-Hall.

Heron, T. E., & Kimball, W. H. (1988). Gaining perspective with the educational consultation research base: Ecological considerations and further recommendations. *Remedial and Special Education, 9*(6):21–28.

Herrmann, B. A. (1989). Characteristics of explicit and less explicit explanations of mathematical problem solving strategies. *Reading Research and Instruction, 28*(3):1–17.

Hess, A. G., & Lauber, D. (1985). *Dropouts from the Chicago Public Schools: An analysis of the classes of 1982, 1983, 1984*. Chicago: Chicago Panel on Public School Finances.

Hess, F. (1987). *A Comprehensive Analysis of the Dropout Phenomenon in an Urban School System*. Paper prepared for American Educational Research Association, Washington, DC.

Hiebert, B., Wong, B., & Hunter, M. (1982). Affective influences on LD adolescents. *Learning Disabilities Quarterly, 5*(Fall) (4):334–343.

Hieronymus, A. N., Lindquist, E. F., & Hoover, H. (1978). *Iowa Tests of Basic Skills*. Lombard, IL: Riverside.

Higbee, K. (1977). *Your Memory*. Englewood Cliffs, NJ: Prentice-Hall.

Higbee, K. (1979). Recent research on visual Mnemonics: Historical roots and educational fruits. *Review of Educational Research. 49*:611–629.

Hildreth, G., Griffiths, N., & McGauvran, M. (1966). *Metropolitan Readiness Tests*. New York: Harcourt Brace Jovanovich.

Hinshelwood, J. (1900). Congenital word-blindness. *Lancet, 1*:1506–1508.

Hoffman, F. J., Sheldon, K. L., Minskoff, E. H., Sautter, S. W., Steidle, E. F., Baker, D. P. Bailey, M. B., & Echols, L. D. (1987). Needs of learning disabled adults. *Journal of Learning Disabilities, 20*:43–52.

Hofmeister, A., & de Fevre, D. (1977). Time is of the essence. *Teaching Exceptional Children, 9*:82–83.

Hogan, T. P., Farr, R. C., Prescott, G. A., & Balow, I. H. (1978). *Metropolitan Achievement Tests: Mathematics Instructional Battery*. Cleveland: The Psychological Corporation.

Holahan, C. K., & Holahan, C. J. (1987a). Self-efficacy, social support, and depression in aging: A longitudinal analysis. *Journal of Gerontology. 42*:65–68.

Holahan, C. K., & Holahan, C. J. (1987b). Life stress, hassles, and self-efficacy in aging: A replication and extension. *Journal of Applied Social Psychology, 17*:574–592.

Holborow, P., & Berry, P. (1986). A multinational, cross-cultural perspective on hyperactivity. *American Journal of Orthopsychiatry, 56*:320–322.

Hollander, S. K. (1988). Teaching learning disabled students to read mathematics. *School Science and Mathematics, 88*(6):509–515.

Hollinger, J. D. (1987). Social skills for behaviorally disordered children as preparation for mainstreaming: Theory, practice, and new directions. *Remedial and Special Education, 8*(4):17–27.

Holtzman, W. (1966). *Holtzman Inkblot Technique*. Cleveland: The Psychological Corporation.

Hops, H., & Greenwood, C. (1981). Social skills deficits. In E. J. Mash & L. G. Terdal (Eds.), *Behavioral Assessment of Childhood Disorders* (pp. 347–396). New York: Guilford.

Horn, E. (1919). *Principles of Methods in Teaching Spelling as Derived from Scientific Investigation*, Part II (p. 72). Bloomington, IN: Public School Publishing Company.

Horner, R. H., McDonnel, J. J., & Bellamy, C. T. (1986). Teaching generalized skills: General case instruction in simultaneous and community settings. In R. H. Horner, L. H. Meyer, & H. D. Fredericks (Eds.), *Education of Learners with Severe Handicaps: Exemplary Service Strategies*. Baltimore: Paul H. Brookes.

Horowitz, E. C. (1981). Popularity, decentering ability, and role-taking skills in learning disabled and normal children. *Learning Disabilities Quarterly, 4*:23–38.

Horowitz, R. (1970). *Academic Therapy, 6*(1) (Fall). San Rafael, Calif.: Academic Therapy Publications.

Howell, F. M., & Freese, W. (1982). Early transition into adult roles: Some antecedents and outcomes. *American Educational Research Journal, 19*(1):51–73.

Howell, K. W., & Morehead, M. K. (1987). *Curriculum-Based Evaluation for Special and Remedial Education*. Columbus, OH: Merrill.

Howze-Brown, D. (1988). Factors predictive of child maltreatment. *Early Child Development and Care, 31*:43–54.

Hresko, W. P., & Reid, D. K. (1988). Five faces of cognition: Theoretical influences on approaches to learning disabilities. *Journal of Learning Disabilities, 11*:211–216.

Hubble, L. M., & Groff, M. (1981). Magnitude and direction of WISC-R verbal-performance IQ discrepancies among adjudicated male delinquents. *Journal of Youth and Adolescence, 10*:179–184.

Hudson, T. (1982). The effects of induced schemata on the "short circuit" in L2 reading: Nondecoding factors in L2 reading performance. *Language Learning, 32*:1–31.

Hughes, J. (1985). Evaluation of electrophysiological studies on dyslexia. In D. B. Gray, & J. F. Kavanagh, (Eds.), *Biobehavioral Measures of Dyslexia* (pp. 71–86). Parkton, MD: York Press.

Hughes, J. N. (1988). *Cognitive Behavior Therapy with Children in Schools*. New York: Pergamon.

Hughes, J. N., & Hall, R. J. (1987). Proposed model for the assessment of children's social competence. *Professional School Psychology, 2*:247–260.

Hughes, J. N., & Sullivan, K. A. (1988). Outcome assessment in social skills training with children. *Journal of School Psychology, 26*:167–183.

Hughes, J. R. (1978). Electroencephalographic and neurophysiological studies in dyslexia. In A. L. Benton, & D. Pearl (Eds.), *Dyslexia: An Appraisal of Current Knowledge* (pp. 205–240). New York: Oxford University Press.

Hull, M. (1976). *Phonics for Teachers* (2d ed.). Columbus, OH: Charles E. Merrill.

Humphreys, M. S., & Revelle, W. (1984). Personality, motivation, and performance: A theory of the relationship between individual differences and information processing. *Psychological Review. 91*:153–184.

Hunt, E., & Lansman, M. (1986). Unified model of attention and problem solving. *Psychological Review, 93*:446–461.

Hussey, H. (1988). Psychiatric disorder in young adults: A novel perspective. *American Journal of Psychiatry.*

Hynd, G. W., Cohen, M., & Obrzut, J. E. (1983). Dichotic CV testing in the diagnosis of learning disabilities in children. *Ear and Hearing, 4*:283–286.

Hynd, G. W., & Obrzut, J. E. (Eds.), *Neuropsychological Assessment of the School-Age Child: Issues and Procedures* (pp. 27–84). New York: Grune & Stratton.

Hynd, G. W., & Semrud-Clikeman, M. (1989). Dyslexia and neurodevelopmental pathology: Relationships to cognition, intelligence, and reading skill acquisition. *Journal of Learning Disabilities, 22*(4).

Iannotti, R. (1978). Effect of role-taking experiences on role taking, empathy, altruism, and aggression. *Developmental Psychology, 14*:119–124.

Idol, L. (1986). *Collaborative School Consultation: Recommendations for State Departments of Education*. Reston, VA: National Task Force on Collaborative School Consultations, Teacher Education Division, Council for Exceptional Children.

Idol, L. (1987a). A critical thinking map to improve content area comprehension of poor readers. *Remedial and Special Education, 8*(4):28–40.

Idol, L. (1987b). Group story mapping: A comprehension strategy for both skilled and unskilled readers. *Journal of Learning Disabilities, 20*(4):196–205.

Idol, L., & Croll, V. (1987). Story mapping training as a means of improving reading comprehension. *Learning Disability Quarterly, 10*(3):214–230.

Idol, L., Nevin, A., & Paolucci-Whitcomb, P. (1986). *Models of Curriculum-Based Assessment*. Austin, TX: Pro-Ed.

Idol, L., Paolucci-Whitcomb, P., & Nevin, A. (1986). *Collaborative Consultation*. Rockville, MD: Aspen Systems.

Idol, L., & West, J. F. (1987). Consultation in special education (Part II): Training and practice. *Journal of Learning Disabilities, 20*:474–497.

Idol-Maestas, L., & Ritter, S. (1985). A follow up study of resource/consulting teachers: Factors that facilitate and inhibit teacher consultation. *Teacher Education and Special Education, 8*:121–131.

Ilg, F., & Ames, L. (1964). *School Readiness: Behavior Tests Used at the Gesell Institute*. New York: Harper & Row.

Interagency Committee on Learning Disabilities. (1987). *Interagency Committee on Learning Disabilities: Report to Congress*. Washington, DC: Author.

Invernizzi, M., & Worthy, M. (1989). An orthographic-specific comparison of the spelling errors of learning disabled and normal children across four grade levels of spelling achievement. *Reading Psychology, 10*(2):173–188.

Jastak, J. E., & Jastak, S. R. (1965, 1978). *Wide-Range Achievement Test*. Wilmington, DE: Jastak Associates.

Jeffers, V. (1976). Using the digital clock to teach the telling ot time. *The Arithmetic Teacher, 26*(7):53.

Johnson, C. F., & Showers, J. (1985). Injury variables in child abuse. *Child Abuse and Neglect, 9*:207–215.

Johnson, D. (1988). Review of research on specific reading, writing, and mathematics disorders. In J. F. Kavanagh and T. J. Truss, Jr. (Eds.), *Learning Disabilities: Proceedings of the National Conference*. Parkton, MD: York Press.

Johnson, D., & Myklebust, H. (1967). *Learning Disabilities: Educational Principles and Practices*. New York: Grune & Stratton.

Johnson, D., Pittelman, D., & Heimlich, J. (1986). Semantic mapping. *The Reading Teacher, 39*:778–783.

Johnson, D., & Wen, S. (1976, October). Effects of correct and extraneous markings under time limits on reading comprehension. *Psychology in the Schools, 13*:454–456.

Johnson, D. J., & Blalock, J. W. (1987). *Adults with Learning Disabilities: Clinical Studies*. Orlando, FL: Grune & Stratton.

Johnson, D. W., & Johnson, R. (1975). *Learning Together and Alone: Cooperation, Competition, and Individualization*. Englewood Cliffs, NJ: Prentice-Hall.

Johnson, D. W., & Johnson, R. T. (1984). *Cooperation in the Classroom*. Edina, MN: Interaction Book Company.

Johnson, D. W., & Johnson, R. T. (1986). Mainstreaming and cooperative learning strategies. *Exceptional Children, 52*:553–561.

Johnson, D. W., Johnson, R. T., Holubec, E. J., & Roy, P. (1984). *Circles of Learning: Cooperation in the Classroom*. Alexandria, VA: Association for Supervision and Curriculum Development.

Johnson, D. W., Johnson, R. T., Warring, D., & Maruyama, G. (1986). Different cooperative learning procedures and cross-handicap relationships. *Exceptional Children, 53*:247–252.

Johnson, M., & Kress, R. (1965). *Informal Reading Inventories*. Reading Aids Series. Newark, DE: International Reading Association.

Johnson, R., & Johnson, D. (1980). The social integration of handicapped students into the mainstream. In M. C. Reynolds (Ed.), *Social Environment of the Schools*. Reston, VA: The Council for Exceptional Children.

Johnson, R., & Johnson, D. (1981). Building friendships between handicapped and nonhandicapped students: Effects of cooperative and individualistic instruction. *American Educational Research Journal, 18*:415–424.

Johnson, W. A., & Heinz, S. P. (1978). Flexibility and capacity demands of attention. *Journal of Experimental Psychology, 107*:420–435.

Johnston, P. (1983). *Reading Comprehension Assessment: A Cognitive Basis*. Newark, DE: International Reading Association.

Jones, R. T., & Evans, H. L. (1980). Self-reinforcement: A continuum of external cues. *Journal of Educational Psychology, 72*:625–635.

Kadushin, A., & Martin, J. (1988). *Child Welfare Services* (4th ed.). New York: Macmillan.

Kagen, S. (1986). Cooperative learning and sociocultural factors in schooling. In Bilingual Education Office, California State Department of Education (Eds.), *Beyond Language: Social & Cultural Factors in Schooling Language Minority Students* (pp. 231–298). Los Angeles: California State University, Evaluation, Dissemination and Assessment Center.

Kahneman, D. (1973). *Attention and Effort*. Englewood Cliffs, NJ: Prentice-Hall.

Kaiser, S. M., & Woodman, R. W. (1985). Multidisciplinary teams and group decision-making techniques: Possible solutions to decision-making problems. *School Psychology Review, 14*(4):457–470.

Kalfus, G. R. (1984). Peer mediated intervention: A critical review. *Child and Family Behavior Therapy, 6*:17–43.

Kameenui, E. J., & Carnine, D. W. (1986). Preteaching versus concurrent teaching of component skills of a subtraction algorithm to skill-deficient second graders: A components analysis of direct instruction. *The Exceptional Child, 33*(2):103–115.

Kameenui, E. J., Carnine, D. W., Darch, C. B., & Stein, M. (1986). Two approaches to the development phase of mathematics instruction. *The Elementary School Journal, 86*(5):1–18.

Kamhi, A. (1988). A reconceptualization of generalization and generalization problems. *Language, Speech, and Hearing Services in Schools, 19*(4):304–313.

Kamhi, A., Gentry, B., & Mauer, D. (1987). *Analogical Learning and Transfer in Language-Impaired Children.* Paper presented at the Wisconsin Symposium for Research in Child Language Disorders, Madison.

Kamphaus, R. W., & Reynolds, C. R. (1987). *Clinical and Research Applications of the K-ABC.* Circle Pines, MN: American Guidance Service.

Karlsen, B., Madden, R., & Gardner, E. F. (1978). *Stanford Diagnostic Reading Test* (1976 ed.). New York: The Psychological Corporation.

Kauffman, J. M., Hallahan, D. P., Haas, K., Brame, T., & Boren, R. (1978). Imitating children's errors to improve their spelling performance. *Journal of Learning Disabilities, 11*:217–222.

Kavale, K. A., & Forness, S. R. (1984). A meta-analysis of the validity of Wechsler Scale profiles and recategorizations: Patterns of parodies? *Learning Disability Quarterly, 7*:136–156.

Kavale, K. A., & Forness, S. R. (1985). *The Science of Learning Disabilities.* San Diego: College Hill Press.

Kavale, K. A., & Forness, S. R. (1986). School learning, time and learning disabilities: The disassociated learner. *Journal of Learning Disabilities, 19*(3):130–138.

Kavanaugh, J. F., & Truss, T. J., Jr. (Eds.). (1988). *Learning Disabilities: Proceedings of the National Conference.* Parkton, MD: York Press.

Kazdin, A. E. (1977). Assessing the clinical or applied importance of behavioral change through social validation. *Behavior Modification, 1*:427–451.

Kazdin, A. E. (1987). *Conduct Disorders in Childhood and Adolescence.* Newbury Park, CA: Sage.

Keith, T. Z., Fehrmann, P. G., Harrison, P. L., & Pottebaum, S. M. (1987). The relation between adaptive behavior and intelligence: Testing alternative explanations. *Journal of School Psychology, 25*:31–43.

Kelly, W. P., & Tomhave, W. K. (1985). A study of math anxiety/math avoidance in preservice elementary teachers. *Arithmetic Teacher, 32*(5):51–53.

Kempe, C. H., Silverman F., Steele, B., Droegemueller, W. & Silver, H. (1962). The battered child syndrome. *Journal of the American Medical Association, 181*:17–24.

Kendall, P. C. (1985). Toward a cognitive-behavioral model of child psychopathology and a critique of related interventions. *Journal of Abnormal Child Psychology, 13*:357–372.

Kendall, P. C., & Hollon, S. D. (Eds.). (1979). *Cognitive-Behavioral Interventions—Theory, Research, and Procedures.* New York: Academic Press.

Kendall, P. C., & Kane, M. (1989). Cognitive-behavioral therapy goes to school. *The Journal of School Psychology, 19*:319–323.

Kendall, P. C., & Morison, P. (1984). Integrating cognitive and behavioral procedures for the treatment of socially isolated children. In A. W. Meyers & W. E. Craighead (Eds.), *Cognitive Behavior Therapy with Children* (pp. 261–288). New York: Plenum.

Kent, G., & Gibbons, R. (1987). Self-efficacy and the control of anxious cognitions. *Journal of Behavior Therapy & Experimental Psychiatry, 18*:33–40.

Keogh, B. K. (1987). Theoretical quandaries in learning disabilities. In S. Vaughn & C. S. Bos (Eds.), *Research in Learning Disabilities.* Boston: Little, Brown.

Keogh, B. K., & Becker, L. D. (1973). Early detection of learning problems: Questions, cautions, and guidelines, *Exceptional Children, 40*:5–12.

Keogh, B. K., & Hall, R. J. (1974). WISC subtest patterns of educationally handicapped and educable mentally retarded pupils. *Psychology in the Schools, 11*:296–300.

Keogh, B. K., Major-Kingsley, S., Omori-Gordon, H., & Reid, H. P. (1982). *A system of marker variables for the field of learning disabilities.* Syracuse, NY: Syracuse University Press.

Keystone Visual Survey Telebinocular. Meadville, PA: Keystone View Co.

Kinsbourne, M. (Ed.). (1983). Brain basis of learning disabilities. *Topics of Learning and Learning Disabilities, 3*(1).

Kinsbourne, M. (1984). Beyond attention deficit: Search for the disorder in ADD. In L. M. Bloomingdale (Ed.), *Attention Deficit Disorder: Diagnostic, Cognitive, and Therapeutic Understanding* (pp. 133–145). New York: Spectrum.

Kinsbourne, M. (1986a). Models of dyslexia and its subtypes. In G. T. Pavlidis, & D. F. Fisher (Eds.), *Dyslexia: Its Neuropsychology and Treatment* (pp. 165–180). New York: Wiley.

Kinsbourne, M. (1986b). Using laterality tests to monitor disabled learners' thinking. In S. Ceci (Ed.), *Handbook of Cognitive, Social, and Neuropsychological Aspects of Learning Disabilities* (pp. 493–502). Hillsdale, NJ: Erlbaum.

Kirby, E. A., & Grimley, L. K. (1986). *Understanding and Treating Attention Deficit Disorder.* New York: Pergamon.

Kirby, J. R., & Becker, L. D. (1988). Cognitive components of learning problems in arithmetic. *Remedial and Special Education, 9*(5):7–16.

Kirk, S. A. (1967). Amelioration of mental abilities through psychodiagnostic and remedial procedures. In G. Jervis (Ed.), *Mental Retardation.* Springfield, IL: Charles C. Thomas.

Kirk, S. A., & Chalfant, J. C. (1984). *Academic and Developmental Learning Disabilities.* Denver: Love.

Kirk, S. A., & Gallagher, J. (1989). *Educating Exceptional Children.* Boston: Houghton Mifflin.

Kirk, S. A., & Kirk, W. (1971). *Psycholinguistic Learning Disabilities: Diagnosis and Remediation.* Urbana: University of Illinois Press.

Kirk, S., McCarthy, J., Kirk, W. (1968a). *Illinois Test of Psycholinguistic Abilities.* Los Angeles: Western Psychological Services.

Kirk, S., McCarthy, J., & Kirk, W. (1968b). *Illinois Test of Psycholinguistic Abilities: Rev. ed., Examiner's Manual.* Urbana: University of Illinois Press.

Kistner, J. A., & Licht, B. G. (1983). Cognitive-Motivational Factors Affecting Academic Persistence of Learning Disabled Children. Unpublished manuscript, Florida State University, Tallahassee.

Knapczyk, D. (1991). Effects of modeling in promoting generalization of student question asking and question answering. *Learning Disabilities Research & Practice, 6*:75–82.

Kneedler, R. D. (1980). The use of cognitive training to change social behaviors. *Exceptional Education Quarterly, 1*:65–73.

Knobloch, H., & Pasamanick, B. (1974). *Gesell and Amatruda's Developmental Diagnosis.* New York: Harper & Row.

Knuppel, R. (1989). Associated features of the fetal alcohol syndrome observed in 245 persons affected. As presented by K. L. Jones, National Association for Perinatal Addiction Research & Education (NAPARE) Conference.

Kohler, I. (1984). *Sensory Experience, Adaptation, and Perception.* NJ: IFA.

Kolligian, J., & Sternberg, R. J. (1987). Intelligence, information processing, and specific learning disabilities: A triarchic synthesis. *Journal of Learning Disabilities, 20*:8–17.

Koppitz, E. (1963). *The Bender Gestalt Test for Young Children.* New York: Grune & Stratton.

Koppitz, E. (1964). *The Bender Gestalt Test for Young Children.* New York: Grune & Stratton.

Koppitz, E. (1968). *Human Figures Drawing Test.* New York: Grune & Stratton.

Koppitz, E. (1975a). Bender Gestalt Test, Visual Aural Deficit Span Test and reading achievement. *Journal of Learning Disabilities, 8*:154–157.

Koppitz, E. (1975b). *The Bender Gestalt Test for Young Children: Volume II: Research and Application, 1963–1973.* New York: Grune & Stratton.

Kottmeyer, W. (1970). *Teacher's Guide for Remedial Reading.* New York: McGraw-Hill.

Kottmeyer, W., & Claus, A. (1976). *Basic Goals in Spelling* (5th ed.). New York: McGraw-Hill.

Kraetsch, G. A. (1981). The effects of oral instructions and training on the expansion of written language. *Learning Disability Quarterly, 4:*82–90.

Kraner, R. E. (1976). *Kraner Preschool Math Inventory.* Austin, TX: Learning Concepts.

Krashen, S. D. (1981). Bilingual education and second language acquisition. In *Schooling and Language Minority Students: A Theoretical Framework* (pp. 51–79). Sacramento, CA: California State Department of Education, Bilingual Education Office.

Kresse, E. C. (1984). Using reading as a thinking process to solve math story problems. *Journal of Reading, 27*(7):598–601.

Krupski, A. (1986). Attention problems in youngsters with learning handicaps. In J. K. Torgesen & B. Y. L. Wong (Eds.), *Psychological and Educational Perspectives on Learning Disabilities* (pp. 161–192). New York: Academic Press.

Krutetskii, V. A. (1976). *The Psychology of Mathematical Abilities in School Children.* (Translated from the Russian by J. Teller and edited by J. Kilpatrick & I. Wirszup). Chicago: The University of Chicago Press, p. 55.

Kubler-Ross, E. (1981). Interview, *Playboy* (May): p. 76.

Kuder, R. (1954). *Kuder Personal Preference Record.* Chicago: Science Research Associates.

Kuehne, C., Kehle, T. J., & McMahon, W. (1987). Differences between children with attention deficit disorder, children with specific learning disabilities, and normal children. *Journal of School Psychology, 25:*161–166.

Kurland, D. J. (1983, December). The nature of scientific discussion: Critical reading and the introductory science course. *Journal of Reading,* 197–201.

Kurtz, B. E., & Borkowski, J. G. (1985). Metacognition and the Development of Strategic Skills in Impulsive and Reflective Children. Paper presented at the meeting of the Society for Research on Child Development, Toronto.

Ladd, G. W., (1985). Documenting the effects of social skill training with children: Process and outcome assessment. In B. H. Schneider, K. H. Rubin, & J. E. Ledingham (Eds.), *Children's Peer Relations: Issues in Assessment and Intervention* (pp. 243–270). New York: Springer-Verlag.

LaGreca, A. M. (1981). Social behavior and social perception in learning disabled children: A review with implications for social skills training. *Journal of Pediatric Psychology, 6:*395–416.

Lahey, B. B., Stempniak, M., Robinson, E. J., & Tyroler, M. (1978). Hyperactivity and learning disabilities as independent dimensions of child behavior problems. *Journal of Abnormal Psychology, 87:*333–340.

Lambert, N. (1981). *Diagnostic and Technical Manual, AAMD Adaptive Behavior Scale—School Edition.* Monterey, CA: CTB/McGraw-Hill.

Lambert, N. M., & Sandoval, J. (1980). The prevalence of learning disabilities in a sample of children considered hyperactive, *Journal of Abnormal Child Psychology, 8:*33–50.

Lambert, N., Windmiller, M., Cole, L., & Figueroa, R. (1975). *Manual: AAMD Adaptive Behavior Scale,* Public School Version (1974 rev.). Washington, DC: American Association on Mental Deficiency.

Landsman, M., & Dillard, H. (1967). *Evanston Early Identification Scale.* Chicago: Follett Educational Corporation.

Langdon, H. W. (1983). Assessment and intervention strategies for the bilingual language disordered student. *Exceptional Children, 50:*37–46.

Langdon, H. W. (1989). Language disorder or difference? Assessing the language skills of Hispanic students. *Exceptional Children, 56*(2):160–167.

Larry P. v. *Riles,* 343 F. Supp. 1306 (N. D. Cal. 1972) (preliminary injunction), aff'd 502 F. 2d 963 (9th Cir. 1974); 495 F. Supp. 926 (N. D. Cal. 1979) (decision on merits) aff'd (9th Cir. No. 80–427 Jan. 23, 1984)

Larsen, S., & Hammill, D. (1976). *Test of Written Spelling.* Austin, TX: Pro-Ed.

Laufer, M., & Denhoff, E. (1957). Hyperkinetic behavior syndrome in children. *Journal of Pediatrics, 50,* 463–474.

Lazarus, R. S., & Folkman, S. (1984). *Stress, Appraisal, and Coping.* New York: Springer.

Leigh, J. E. (1980, Fall). Whole-language approaches: Premises and possibilities. *Learning Disability Quarterly, 3:*62–69.

Lee, L. (1971). *The Northwestern Syntax Screening Test.* Evanston, IL: Northwestern University Press.

Lee, L. (1974). *Developmental Sentence Analysis.* Evanston, IL: Northwestern University Press.

Lee, L., Koenigsknecht, R. A., & Mulhern, S. T. (1975). *Interactive Language Development Teaching.* Evanston, IL: Northwestern University Press.

Lee, P., & Alley, G. R. (1981). *Training Junior-High Students to Use a Test-Taking Strategy* (Research Rep. No. 38). Lawrence: University of Kansas, Institute for Research in Learning Disabilities.

Leler, H. (1983). Parent education and involvement in relation to the schools and to parents of school-aged children. In I. R. Haskings, & D. Adamson (Eds.), *Parent Education and Public Policy* (pp. 141–180). Norwood, NJ: Ablex.

Lenneberg, E. H. (1967). *Biological Foundations of Language.* New York: Wiley.

Lent, R. W., & Hackett, G. (1987). Career self-efficacy: Empirical status and future directions. *Journal of Vocational Behavior, 30:*347–382.

Lenz, B. K., Bulgren, J., & Hudson, P. (1990). Content enhancement: A model for promoting the acquisition of content by individuals with learning disabilities. In T. E. Scruggs & B. Y. L. Wong (Eds.), *Intervention Research in Learning Disabilities.* New York: Springer-Verlag.

Lepper, M. R., Greene, D., & Nisbett, R. E. (1973). Undermining children's intrinsic interest with extrinsic rewards: A test of the "overjustification" hypothesis. *Journal of Personality and Social Psychology, 28:*129–137.

Lerner, J. (1989). *Learning Disabilities: Theories, Diagnosis, and Teaching Strategies.* Boston: Houghton Mifflin.

Levelthal, J. M. (1987). Programs to prevent sexual abuse: What outcomes should be measured? *Child Abuse and Neglect, 11,* 169–170.

Levin, J. R. (1986). Four cognitive principles of learning strategy instruction. *Educational Psychologist, 21:*3–17.

Levine, M. (1987). *Developmental Variation and Learning Disabilities.* Cambridge, MA: Educator's Publishing Service.

Levine, M. D., Busch, B., & Aufsuser, C. (1982). The dimension of inattention among children with school problems. *Pediatrics, 70:*387–395.

Levinton, A. (1980). Otitis media and learning disorders. *Journal of Behavioral Pediatrics, 1*(2):58–63.

Lewis, R. (1983). Learning disabilities and reading: Instructional recommendations from current research. *Exceptional Children, 50*(3):230–240.

Licht, B. G. (1983). Cognitive-motivational factors that contribute to the achievement of learning-disabled children. *Journal of Learning Disabilities, 16:*483–490.

Licht, B. G., Kistner, J. A., Ozkaragoz, T., Shapiro, S., & Clausen, L. (1985). Causal attributions of learning disabled children: Individual differences and their implications for persistence. *Journal of Educational Psychology, 77:*208–216.

Lidz, C. S. (1987). *Dynamic Assessment: An Interactional Approach to Evaluating Learning Potential.* New York: Guilford.

Lieberman, L. (1982). Special educator's safety net. *Journal of Learning Disabilities, 15:*439–440.

Lilly, M. S. (1986). The relationship between general and special education: A new face on an old issue. *Counterpoint, 6*(1):10.

Lilly, M. S. (1988). The regular education initiative: A force for change in general and special education. *Education and Training in Mental Retardation, 23:*253–260.

Linares-Orama, N. (1977). Evaluation of syntax in three-year old Spanish-speaking Puerto Rican children. *Journal of Speech and Hearing Research, 20:*350–357.

Lindsley, O. R. (1971). From Skinner to precision teaching: The child knows best. In J. B. Jordan & L. S. Robbins (Eds.), *Let's Try Doing Something Else Kind of Thing*. Arlington, VA: Council for Exceptional Children.

Linn, S., Schoenbaum, S. C., Monson, R. R., Rosner, R., Stubblefield, P. C., & Ryan, K. J. (1983). The association of marijuana use with outcome of pregnancy. *American Journal of Public Health, 73*(10):1161–1164.

Lippitt, P., & Lohman, J. E. (1965, May–June). Cross-age relationships—An educational resource. *Children, 12*:113–117.

Lipsett, M. B. (1987). *Know Your Brain*. National Institute of Neurological and Communicative Disorders and Stroke, U.S. Department of Health, Education, and Welfare.

Lloyd, J. W., Crowley, E. P., Kohler, F. W., & Strain, P. S. (1988). Redefining the applied research agenda: Cooperative learning, prereferral, teacher consultation and peer-mediated interventions. *Journal of Learning Disabilities, 21*(1):43–52.

Lloyd, J. W., Keller, C. E., Kauffman, J. M., & Hallahan, D. P. (1988, January). *What Will the Regular Education Initiative Require of General Education Teachers?* Report prepared for the Office of Special Education Programs, U.S. Department of Education.

Loeber, R., & Stouthamer-Loeber, M. (1987). Prediction. In H. C. Quay (Ed.), *Handbook of Juvenile Delinquency* (pp. 325–482). New York: Wiley.

Loftus, E. F. (1979). The malleability of human memory. *American Scientist, 67*:312–320.

Loftus, G. R., & Loftus, E. F. (1976). *Human Memory: The Processing of Information*. Hillsdale, NJ: Erlbaum.

Loomer, B. M. (1978). *Educator's Guide to Spelling Research and Practice*. Des Moines: Iowa State Department of Public Instruction; Iowa City: University of Iowa Press (33 pp.). (ED 176 286).

Loper, A., Hallahan, D. P., & Ianna, S. O. (1982). Meta-attention in learning disabled and normal students. *Learning Disability Quarterly, 5*:29–36.

Lorber, R., Felton, D. K., & Reid, J. B. (1984). A social learning approach to the reduction of coercive processes in child abusive families: A molecular analysis. *Advances in Behavior Research and Therapy, 6,* 29–45.

Lou, H. C., Henriksen, L., & Bruhn, P. (1984). Focal cerebral hypoperfusion in children with dysphasia and/or attention deficit disorder. *Archives of Neurology, 42*:825–829.

Lovitt, T. C. (1989). *Introduction to Learning Disabilities* Boston: Allyn and Bacon.

Lovitt, T. C., & Curtiss, K. A. (1968). Effects of manipulating an antecedent event on mathematics response rate. *Journal of Applied Behavior Analysis, 1*:329–333.

Lovitt, T., Rudsit, J., Jenkins, J., Pious, C., & Benedetti, D. (1986). Adapting science materials for regular and learning disabled seventh graders. *Reading and Special Education, 7*(1):31–39.

Luftig, R. L. (1989). *Assessment of Learners With Special Needs*. Boston: Allyn and Bacon.

Lutey, C. (1977). *Individual Intelligence Testing*. Greeley, CO: Carol L. Lutey Publishing.

Lyon, G. R. (1983). Learning disabled readers: Identification of subgroups. In H. R. Myklebust (Ed.), *Progress in Learning Disabilities: Vol. V*. New York: Grune & Stratton.

Lyon, G. R. (1985a). Educational validation studies of learning disability subtypes. In B. Rourke (Ed.), *Learning Disabilities in Children: Advances in Subtypes Analyses*. New York: Guilford Press.

Lyon, G. R. (1985b). Identification and remediation of learning disability subtypes: Progress and pitfalls. *Learning Disability Focus, 1.*

Maag, J. W. (1989). Assessment in social skills training: Methodological and conceptual issues for research and practice. *Remedial and Special Education, 10*(4):6–17.

Maag, J. W., & Meinhold, A. C. (1985). Developing counseling skills in teachers of behaviorally disordered adolescents. In R. B. Rutherford, Jr. (Ed.), *Severe Behavior Disorders in Children and Youth* (Vol. 8, pp. 56–69). Reston, VA: Council for Children with Behavioral Disorders.

MacArthur, C. A., & Shneiderman, B. (1986). Learning disabled students' difficulties in learning to use a word processor: Implications for instruction and software evaluation. *Journal of Learning Disabilities, 19*(4):248–253.

Maccoby, E. (1966): *The Development of Sex Differences*. Stanford, CA: Stanford University Press.

MacDonald, J. D. (1978). *Environmental Languages Inventory*. Columbus, OH: Charles E. Merrill.

Mace, F. C., & West, B. J. (1986). Unresolved theoretical issues in self-management: Implications for research and practice. *Professional School Psychology, 1*(3):149–163.

MacGinitie, W. (1978). *Gates-MacGinitie Reading Tests*. Chicago: The Riverside Publishing Company.

MacMillan, D. L. (1982). *Mental Retardation in School and Society*. Boston: Little, Brown.

Madden, R., Gardner, E. F., & Collins, C. S. (1983). *Stanford Early School Achievement Test* (2d ed.). Cleveland, OH: The Psychological Corporation.

Madden, R., Gardner, E. F., Rudman, H. C. Karlsen, B., & Merwin, J. C. (1973). *Stanford Achievement Test*. New York: Harcourt Brace Jovanovich.

Magliocca, L. A., Rinaldi, R. T., Crew, J. L., & Kunzelmann, H. P. (1977). Early identification of handicapped children through a frequency sampling technique. *Exceptional Children, 43*:414–420.

Mahoney, M. J. (1974). *Cognition and Behavior Modification*. Cambridge, MA: Ballinger.

Malott, R. W. (1984). Rule-governed behavior, self-management, and the developmentally disabled: A theoretical analysis. *Analysis and Intervention in Developmental Disabilities, 4*:199–209.

Mann, J. J., Stanley, M., McBride, A., & McEwan, B. S. (1986). Increased serotonin and B-Adrenergic receptor binding in the frontal cortices of suicide victims. *Archives of General Psychiatry, 43:* 954–959.

Manzo, A. V. (1969). ReQuest procedure. *Journal of Reading, 13*:123–126.

Markel, G. (1981). Improving test-taking skills in learning disabled adolescents. *Academic Therapy, 16*(3):333–342.

Marquardt, T. P., & Saxman, J. H. (1972, June). Language comprehension and auditory discrimination in articulation deficient kindergarten children. *Journal of Speech and Hearing Research, 15*:382–389.

Marsh, G., Friedman, M., Welch, V., & Desberg, P. (1980). The development of strategies in spelling. In U. Frith (Ed.), *Cognitive Processes in Spelling* (pp. 339–353). New York: Academic Press.

Marshall et al. v. *Georgia*. U.S. District Court for the Southern District of Georgia, CV482–233, June 28, 1984; Affirmed (11th Cir. No. 80–8771, Oct. 29, 1985).

Marston, D., Lowry, L., Deno, S., & Mirkin, P. (1981). *An Analysis of Learning Trends in Simple Measures of Reading, Spelling, and Written Expression: A Longitudinal Study* (Research Report No. 49). Minneapolis: University of Minnesota Institute for Research on Learning Disabilities.

Marston, D., Tindal, G., & Deno, S. (1984). Eligibility for learning disability services: A direct and repeated measurement approach. *Exceptional Children, 50*:554–555.

Martin, C. E., Martin, M. A., & O'Brien, D. G. (1984). Spawning ideas for writing in the content areas. *Reading World, 24*(2):11–15.

Massachusetts Vision Test. (1954). Boston: Massachusetts Dept. of Public Health, Welch Allyn.

Masters, J. C., & Furman, W. (1981). Popularity, individual friendship selection, and specific peer interaction among children. *Developmental Psychology, 17*:344–350.

Mastropieri, M. A., & Scruggs, T. E. (1989). Mnemonic social studies instruction: Classroom applications. *Remedial and Special Education, 10*(3): 40–45.

Matson, J. L., Esveldt-Dawson, K., Andrasik, F., Ollendick, T. II, Petti, I., & Hersen, M. (1980). Direct, observational, and generalization effects of social skills training with emotionally disturbed children. *Behavior Therapy, 11*:522–531.

Matson, J. L., Esveldt-Dawson, K., & Kazdin, A. E. (1983). Validation of methods for assessing social skills in children. *Journal of Clinical Child Psychology, 12*:174–180.

Matson, J. L., Rotatori, A. F., & Helsel, W. J. (1983). Development of a rating scale to measure social skills in children: The Matson Evaluation of Social Skills with Youngsters (MESSY). *Behavior Research and Therapy, 21*:335–340.

Mauser, A. J. (1974). Learning disabilities and delinquent youth. *Academic Therapy, 9*(6):389–402.

May, F. B., & Eliot, S. B. (1978). A basic list of 96 irregular words for linguistic programs. *The Reading Teacher, 31*(7):794–796.

Maya, A. (1979). Write to read: Improving reading through creative writing. *The Reading Teacher, 32*(7)813–817.

Mayer, R. (1987). *Educational Psychology: A Cognitive Approach.* Boston: Little, Brown.

McAndrew, D. A. (1983). Underlining and notetaking: Some suggestions from research. *Journal of Reading, 27*(2):103–108.

McBride, M. C., & Kemper, T. L. (1982). Pathogenesis of four-layered microgyric cortex in man. *Acta Neuropathologica, 57*:93–98.

McCarthy, D. (1972). *Manual for the McCarthy Scales of Children's Abilities.* Cleveland, OH: The Psychological Corporation.

McCarthy, J. McR. (1988, July). Eligibility Criteria and Specific Learning Disabilities: Evidence from the Pre-School Population. Paper presented at the Eligibility Criteria Conference of the Association for Children and Adults with Learning Disabilities, Chicago.

McCloskey, M. L., & Quay, L. C. (1987). Effects of handicapped children's social behavior and teachers' attitudes in mainstreamed classrooms. *Elementary School Journal, 87*:425–435.

McClure, D. F., & Gordon, M. (1984). The performance of disturbed hyperactive and nonhyperactive children on an objective measure of hyperactivity. *Journal of Abnormal Child Psychology, 12*:561–572.

McDonald, E. (1964). *A Deep Test of Articulation.* Pittsburgh: Stanwix House.

McGahan, F. E., & McGahan, C. (1967). *Early Detection Inventory.* Chicago: Follett Educational Corporation.

McKeown, M. G., & Beck, I. L. (1988). Learning vocabulary: Different ways for different goals. *Remedial and Special Education, 9*(1):42–52.

McKinney, J. D. (1984). The search for subtypes of specific learning disability. *Journal of Learning Disabilities, 17*(1):43–50.

McKinney, J. D. (1987). Research on the identification of LD children: Perspectives on changes in educational policy. In S. Vaughn & C. Bos (Eds.), *Issues and Future Directions in Learning Disabilities Research* (pp. 215–237). San Diego: College-Hill Press.

McKinney, J. D. (1988). Research on conceptually and empirically derived subtypes of specific learning disabilities. In M. C. Wang, M. C. Reynolds, & H. J. Walberg (Eds.), *Handbook of Special Education: Research and Practice.* Oxford, England: Pergamon Press.

McKinney, J. D. (1989). Longitudinal research on the behavioral characteristics of children with learning disabilities. *Journal of Learning Disabilities, 22*(3):141–165.

McKinney, J. D., & Feagans, L. (March, 1982). Longitudinal Research on Learning Disabilities. Paper presented at the Association for Children and Adults with Learning Disabilities. Chicago.

McKinney, J. D., & Feagans, L. (1983). (Eds.). *Current Topics in Learning Disabilities.* (Vol. 1). Norwood, NJ: Ablex.

McKinney, J. D., & Feagans, L. (1984). Academic and behavioral characteristics: Longitudinal studies of learning disabled children and average achievers. *Learning Disability Quarterly, 7*(3):251–265.

McKinney, J. D., & Hocutt, A. M. (1988a). Policy issues in the evaluation of the regular education initiative. *Learning Disabilities Focus, 4*(1):15–23.

McKinney, J. D., & Hocutt, A. M. (1988b). The need for policy analysis in evaluating the regular education initiative. *Journal of Learning Disabilities, 21*(1):12–18.

McKinney, J. D., Short, E. J., & Feagans, L. (1985). Academic consequences of perceptual-linguistic subtypes of learning disabled children. *Learning Disabilities Research, 1.*

McKinney, J. D., & Speece, D. L. (1983). Classroom behavior and the academic progress of learning disabled students. *Journal of Applied Developmental Psychology, 4*:149–161.

McKinney, J. D., & Speece, D. L. (1986). Academic consequences and longitudinal stability of behavioral subtypes of learning disabled children. *Journal of Educational Psychology, 78*:365–372.

McLaughlin, T. F., & Bialozor, R. C. (1989). The effects of computer-assisted drill and practice on spelling performance with mildly handicapped students. *Reading Improvement, 26*(1):43–49.

McLoone, B. B., Scruggs, T. E., Mastropieri, M. A., & Zucker, S. (1986). Memory strategy instruction and training with LD adolescents. *Learning Disabilities Research. 2*:45–53.

McLoughlin, J. A., & Lewis, R. B. (1981). *Assessing Special Students: Strategies and Procedures.* Columbus, OH: Charles E. Merrill.

McNeill, D. (1970). The development of language. In P. H. Mussen (Ed.), *Carmichael's Manual of Child Psychology* (Vol. 1, 3rd ed.). New York: John Wiley & Sons.

McNeill, J. D. (1987). *Reading Comprehension: New Directions for Classroom Practice.* Glenview, IL: Scott Foresman.

NcNeill, J. D. (1989). Personal meanings versus test-driven responses to social studies texts. *Reading Psychology, 10*(4):311–319.

Meacham, J. A. (1977). Soviet investigations of memory development. In R. V. Kail & J. W. Hagen, Jr. (Eds.), *Perspectives on the Development of Memory and Cognition* (pp. 273–295). Hillsdale, NJ: Erlbaum.

Mecham, M., Jex, J. L., & Jones, J. D. (1967). *Utah Test of Language Development.* Salt Lake City, UT: Communication Research Associates.

Medway, F. J., & Updyke, J. F. (1985). Meta-analysis of consultation outcome studies. *American Journal of Community Psychology, 13*:489–505.

Meichenbaum, D. (1977). *Cognitive-Behavior Modification: An Integrative Approach.* New York: Plenum Press.

Meichenbaum, D. (1980). Teaching Thinking: A Cognitive-Behavioral Perspective. Paper presented at the NIE-LRDC Conference on Thinking and Learning Skills, Pittsburgh, October.

Meichenbaum, D. (1981). Teaching Thinking: A Cognitive Behavioral Approach. Paper presented at the meeting of the Society for Learning Disabilities and Remedial Education, New York, April.

Meichenbaum, D. (1985). *Stress Inoculation Training.* New York: Pergamon.

Meichenbaum, D., & Butler, L. (1980). Cognitive ethology: Assessing the streams of cognition and emotion. In K. Blankstein, P. Pliner, & J. Polivy (Eds.), *Assessment and Modification of Emotional Behavior* (Vol. 6, pp. 1–53). New York: Plenum.

Meichenbaum, D., & Goodman, J. (1971). Training impulsive children to talk to themselves: A means of developing self-control. *Journal of Abnormal Psychology, 77*:115–126.

Melnick, C. R., Michals, K. K., & Matalon, R. (1981). Linguistic development of children with phenylketonuria and normal intelligence. *Journal of Pediatrics, 98,* 269–272.

Mercado, A., et al. (1989). Cocaine, pregnancy, and postpartum intracerebral hemorrhage. *Obstetrics and Gynecology, 73,* 467–468.

Mercer, C. D., & Mercer, A. R. (1985). *Teaching Students With Learning Problems.* Columbus, OH: Charles E. Merrill.

Mercer, J. (1979). *System of Multicultural Pluralistic Assessment Technical Manual.* New York: Psychological Corporation.

Mercer, J., & Lewis, J. (1977). *SOMPA: Parent Interview Manual.* Cleveland, OH: The Psychological Corporation.

Mercer, J., & Lewis, J. (1978). *SOMPA: Student Assessment Manual.* Cleveland, OH: The Psychological Corporation.

Merjanian, J., Bachevalier, J., Crawford, H., & Mishkin, M. (1986). Socio-emotional disturbances in the developing rhesus monkey following neonatal limbic lesions. *Society of Neuroscience Abstracts, 12*:23.

Messerer, J., Hunt, E., Meyers, G., & Lerner, J. (1984). Feuerstein's instrumental enrichment: A new approach for activating intellectual potential in learning disabled youth. *Journal of Learning Disabilities, 17*:322–325.

Metropolitan Readiness Tests. (1950). New York: Harcourt Brace Jovanovich.

Meyer, B. (1980). Use of top-level structure in text: Key for reading comprehension of ninth grade students. *Reading Research Quarterly, 16*(1):73–101.

Meyer, B., & Freedle, R. (1984). Effects of discourse type on recall. *American Educational Research Journal, 21*(3):121–143.

Meyers, C. E., Nihira, K., & Zetlin, A. (1979). The measurement of adaptive behavior. In N. R. Ellis (Ed.), *Handbook of Mental Deficiency: Psychological Theory and Research* (2nd ed.) (pp. 215–253). Hillsdale, NJ: Erlbaum.

Michelson, L., & Mannarino, A. (1986). Social skills training with children: Research and clinical application. In P. S. Strain, M. J. Guralnick, & H. M. Walker (Eds.), *Children's Social Behavior: Development, Assessment, and Modification* (pp. 373–406). Orlando, FL: Academic Press.

Michelson, L., Sugai, D. P., Wood, R. P., & Kazdin, A. E. (1983). *Social Skills Assessment and Training with Children: An Empirically Based Approach.* New York: Plenum.

Michelson, L., & Wood, R. (1980). A group assertive training program for elementary school children. *Child Behavior Therapy, 2*:2–10.

Michigan Picture Test and Thematic Apperception Tests. (1983). Chicago: Michigan Department of Mental Health, Science Research.

Miller, G. A. (1956). The magical number seven, plus or minus two: Some limits on our capacity for processing information. *Psychol. Rev., 63*:81–97.

Miller, P., & Bigi, L. (1976). Children's Understanding of Attention; Or You Know I Can't Hear You When the Water's Running. Unpublished manuscript, University of Michigan, Ann Arbor.

Miller, P. H., & Bigi, L. (1979). The development of children's understanding of attention. *Merrill Palmer Quarterly, 25*:235–250.

Miller, T. L., & Sabatino, D. (1978). An evaluation of the teacher consultation model as an approach to mainstreaming. *Exceptional Children, 45*(2):86–91.

Minskoff, E. H., Sautter, S. W., Hoffman, F. J., & Hawks, R. (1987). Employer attitudes toward hiring the learning disabled. *Journal of Learning Disabilities, 20*:53–57.

Mishkin, M. (1972). Cortical visual areas and their interaction. In A. G. Karezmar & J. C. Eccles (Eds.), *The Brain and Human Behavior* (pp. 187–208). New York: Springer Verlag.

Mishkin, M. (1978). Memory in monkeys severely impaired by combined but not separate removal of amygdala and hippocampus. *Nature, 273*:297–298.

Mishkin, M., Malamut, B., & Bachevalier, J. (1984). Memories and habits: Two neural systems. In G. Lynch, J. L. McGaugh, & N. M. Weinberger (Eds.), *Neurobiology of Learning and Memory.* New York: Guilford Press.

Moffett, J. (1968). *A Student-Centered Language Arts Curriculum, Grades K–13: A Handbook for Teachers.* Boston: Hougton Mifflin.

Money, J., Alexander, D., & Walker, H., Jr. (1965). *A Standardized Road-Map Test of Direction Sense.* Baltimore: Johns Hopkins Press.

Moore, J., & Newell, A. (1974). How can Merlin understand? In L. W. Gregg (Ed.), *Knowledge and Cognition* (pp. 201–252). Hillsdale, NJ: Erlbaum.

Mori, A. A. (1980). Career education for the learning disabled—Where are we now? *Learning Disability Quarterly, 3*(1):91–101.

Morocco, C. C., & Neuman, S. B. (1986). Word processors and the acquisition of writing strategies. *Journal of Learning Disabilities, 19*(4):243–247.

Morris, R. D., & Perney, J. (1984). Developmental spelling as a predictor of first grade reading achievement. *Elementary School Journal, 84*:440–457.

Morrow, G. (1986). *Standardizing Practice in the Analysis of School Dropouts.* AASA Critical Issues Report. Sacramento, CA: Education News Service.

Moses, K. L. (1979). Parenting a hearing impaired child. *Volta Review, 81*:73–80.

Moss, M. (1979). *Tests of Basic Experiences: Norms and Technical Data Book.* Monterey, CA: CTB/McGraw-Hill.

Murphy, D. (1986). The prevalence of handicapping conditions among juvenile delinquents. *Remedial and Special Education, 7*(3):7–17.

Murray, C. A. (1976). *The Link Between Learning Disabilities and Juvenile Delinquency: Current Theory and Knowledge.* Washington, DC: U.S. Government Printing Office.

Murray, E. A., & Mishkin, M. (1984). Severe tactual as well as visual memory deficits follow combined removal of the amygdala and hippocampus in monkeys. *Journal of Neuroscience, 4*:2565–2580.

Murray, H. (1943). *Thematic Apperception Test.* Cambridge, MA: Harvard University Press.

Musiek, F. E., Geurkink, N. A., & Kietel, S. A. (1982). Test battery assessment of auditory perceptual dysfunction in children. *Laryngoscope, 92*:251–257.

Myklebust, H. (1954). *Auditory Disorders in Children.* New York: Grune & Stratton.

Myklebust, H. (1965). *Development and Disorders of Written Language: Vol. 1.* New York: Grune & Stratton.

Myklebust, H. (1971). *Myklebust Pupil Rating Scale.* New York: Grune & Stratton.

Myklebust, H. (1973). *Development and Disorders of Written Language: Vol 2.* New York: Grune & Stratton.

Myklebust, H. (1981). *The Pupil Rating Scale: Screening for Learning Disabilities* (rev. ed.). New York: Grune & Stratton.

Myklebust, H., Bannochie, M., & Killen, J. (1971). Learning Disabilities and cognitive processes. In H. Myklebust (Ed.), *Progress in Learning Disabilities: Vol. 2* (pp. 213–251). New York: Grune & Stratton.

Naslund, R. A., Thorpe, L. P., & Lefever, D. W. (1978). *SRA Achievement Series.* Chicago: Science Research Associates.

National Academy of Sciences. (1982). In D. J. Reschly (1988). Minority MMR overrepresentation and special education reform. *Exceptional Children, 54*(4):316–323.

National Advisory Neurological and Communicative Disorders and Stroke Council. (1988). *Decade of the Brain: Answers through Scientific Research.*

National Institute on Drug Abuse. (1987). *Youth at High Risk for Substance Abuse.* Rockville, MD: U.S. Department of Health and Human Services.

National Institute on Drug Abuse. (1989). Drug abuse and pregnancy. *NIDA Capsules, 1*–4.

National Institute of Mental Health. (1985). *Mental health, United States* (DHHS Publication No. ADM 85-1378). Washington, DC: U.S. Government Printing Office.

National Society for the Prevention of Blindness. (1961). *Vision Screening in the Schools.* New York: The Society.

Neisser, U. (1976). *Cognition and Reality: Principles and Implications of Cognitive Psychology.* San Francisco: Freeman.

Neisser, U. (1988). New vistas in the study of memory. In U. Neisser & E. Winograd (Eds.), *Remembering Reconsidered: Ecological and Traditional Approaches to the Study of Memory* (pp. 1–10). Cambridge, England: Cambridge University Press.

Nelson, C. M., & Stevens, K. B. (1981). An accountable consultation model for mainstreaming behaviorally disordered children. *Behavior Disorders, 6*:82–91.

Nelson, M., & French, J. (1974). *Henmon-Nelson Tests of Mental Ability: Primary Form I.* Chicago: Riverside Publishing.

Nelson, R. O., Hayes, S. C., Spong, R. T., Jarrett, R. B., & McKnight, D. L. (1983). Self-reinforcement: Appealing misnomer or effective mechanism? *Behavior Research and Therapy, 21*:557–566.

Nelson, W. (1959): Onset of skeletal ossification. In *Textbook of Pediatrics.* Philadelphia: Saunders.

Nelson, W. M. (1976). Cognitive-Behavioral Strategies in Modifying an Impulsive Cognitive Style. Unpublished doctoral dissertation, Virginia Commonwealth University, Richmond.

Nesbit, W. C., & Karagianis, L. D. (1982). Child abuse: Exceptionality as a risk factor. *The Alberta Journal of Educational Research, 28,* 69–76.

Newcomer, P. L., & Hammill, D. D. (1982). *Test of Language Development.* Austin, TX: Pro-Ed.

Newell, A. (1980). Reasoning problem solving and decision processes: The problem space as a fundamental category. In R. Nickerson (Ed.), *Attention and Performance VIII.* Hillsdale, NJ: Erlbaum.

Newell, A., & Rosenbloom, P. S. (1981). Mechanisms of skill acquisition and the law of practice. In J. R. Anderson (Ed.), *Cognitive Skills and Their Acquisition* (pp. 1–55). Hillsdale, NJ: Erlbaum.

Newman, M. A. (1977). An analysis of sixth-grade pupils' errors on written mathematical tasks. *Research in Mathematics Education in Australia, 1:*239–258.

Nicassio, F. J., Cristler, E. H., Miller, W. L., & Taylor, W. F. (1987). *Conceptualizing an Information System for Special Education Programming within an Intermediate Education District: Milestone One.* (ERIC Document Reproduction Services No. ED 281 565.

Nichols, P. L., & Chen, T. C. (1981). *Minimal Brain Dysfunction: A Prospective Study.* Hillsdale, NJ: Erlbaum.

Nihira, K., Foster, R., Shellhaus, M., & Leland, H. (1974). *The AAMD Adaptive Behavior Scale Manual.* Washington, DC: American Association on Mental Deficiency.

Nodine, B. F., Barenbaum, E., & Newcomer, P. (1985). Story position by learning disabled, reading disabled, and normal children. *Learning Disability Quarterly, 8:*167–181.

Nolen, P. (1980). Sound reasoning in spelling. *The Reading Teacher, 33:*538–543.

Nolen, P., & McCartin, R. (1984, November). Spelling strategies on the wide range achievement test. *The Reading Teacher, 38*(2):148–158.

Nulman, J. A., & Gerber, M. M. (1984). Improving spelling performance by imitating a child's errors. *Journal of Learning Disabilities, 17*(6):328–333.

Nurss, J. R., & McGauvran, M. E. (1976). *Metropolitan Readiness Tests, Teacher's Manual, Part II: Interpretation and Use of Test Results (Level I).* Cleveland, OH: The Psychological Corporation.

Nutrition Reviews. (1973). The growth of children given stimulant drugs. *31,* 91–92.

Ochoa, A. M., Pacheco, R., & Omark, D. R. (1988). Addressing the learning disability needs of limited-English proficient students: Beyond language and race issues. *Learning Disability Quarterly, 11:*257–264.

O'Dougherty, M., Nuechterlein, K. H., & Drew, B. (1984). Hyperactive and hypoxic children: Signal detection, sustained attention, and behavior. *Journal of Abnormal Psychology, 93:*178–191.

O'Hare, F. (1973). *Sentence-Combining: Improving Student Writing Without Formal Grammar Instruction.* Urbana, IL: National Council of Teachers of English.

Okolo, C. (1988, Spring). Instructional environments in secondary vocational education programs: Implications for LD adolescents. *Learning Disability Quarterly, 11,* 136–148.

O'Leary, K. D. (1980). Pills or skills for hyperactive children. *Journal of Applied Behavior Analysis, 13:*191–204.

Orlando, V. P. (1980). Training students to use a modified version of SQ3R: An instructional strategy; *Reading World, 20*(1):65–70.

Ortho-Rater. (1960). Rochester, NY: Bausch and Lomb.

Orr, M. T. (1987). *Keeping Students in School. A Guide to Effective Dropout Prevention Programs and Services.* San Francisco: Jossey-Bass.

Ortiz, A., & Yates, J. R. (1983). Incidence of exceptionality among Hispanics: Implications for manpower planning. *National Association of Bilingual Education Journal, 7*(3):41–53.

Orton, S. T. (1925). "Word-blindness" in school children. *Archives of Neurology and Psychiatry, 14*(5):581–615.

Orton, S. T. (1928). Specific reading disability-strephosymbolia. *Journal of the American Medical Association, 90:*1095–1099.

Orton, S. T. (1937). *Reading, Writing, and Speech Problems in Children.* New York: Norton.

Ostrom, N. N., & Jenson, W. R. (1988). Assessment of attention deficits in children. *Professional School Psychology, 3*(4):253–269.

Otis, A., & Lennon, D. (1979). *Otis-Lennon Mental Ability Test.* Cleveland, OH: The Psychological Corporation.

Paivio, A. (1971). *Imagery and Verbal Processes.* Hillsdale, NJ: Erlbaum.

Palincsar, A. S., & Brown, A. L. (1984). Reciprocal teaching of comprehension-fostering and monitoring activities. *Cognition and Instruction, 1,* 117–175.

Palincsar, A. S., & Brown, A. L. (1986). Interactive teaching to promote independent learning from text. *The Reading Teacher, 39*(8):771–777.

Palincsar, A. S., Brown, A. L., & Martin, S. M. (1987). Peer interaction in reading comprehension instruction. *Educational Psychologist, 22:*231–254.

Palincsar, A. S., & Brown, D. A. (1987). Enhanced instructional time through attention to metacognition. *Journal of Learning Disabilities, 1:*66–75.

Pallas, A. (1987). *Center for Education Statistics: School Dropouts in the United States.* Washington, DC: Office of Educational Research and Improvement, U.S. Department of Education.

Palmatier, R. (1973). A notetaking system for learning. *Journal of Reading, 17:*36–39.

Pardeck, J. T. (1988). Social treatment through an ecological approach. *Clinical Social Work Journal, 16:*92–104.

Pardeck, J. T. (1989). Child abuse and neglect: Theory, research and practice. *Early Child Development and Care, 42,* 3–10.

Paris, S., & Lipson, M. (1982). Metacognition and Reading Comprehension. Research colloquium presented at the IRA annual convention, Chicago.

Paris, S. G., & Oka, E. (1986). Self-regulated learning among exceptional children. *Exceptional Children, 53*(2):103–108.

Paris, S. G., & Oka, E. R. (1989). Strategies for comprehending text and coping with reading difficulties. *Learning Disability Quarterly, 12,* 32–42.

Parke, R. D., & Collmer, C. W. (1975). Child abuse: An interdisciplinary analysis. In E. M. Hetherington (Ed.), *Review of Child Development Research* (pp. 509–590). Chicago: University of Chicago Press.

Parker, J. G., & Asher, S. R. (1987). Peer relations and later personal adjustment: Are low-accepted children at risk? *Psychological Bulletin, 102:*357–389.

Pate, J., & Webb, W. (1966). *First Grade Screening Test.* Circle Pines, MN: American Guidance Service.

Pauk, W. (1974). *How to Study in College.* Boston: Houghton Mifflin.

Pauk, W. (1978). A notetaking format: Magical but not automatic. *Reading World, 17:*96–97.

Pearl, R., Bryan, T., & Donahue, M. (1980). Learning disabled children's attributions for success and failure. *Learning Disability Quarterly, 3*(1):3–9.

Pearl, R., & Cosden, M. (1982). Sizing up a situation: LD children's understanding of social interactions. *Learning Disabilities Quarterly, 5*(Fall) (4):371–373.

Pearl, R., Donahue, M., & Bryan, T. (1981). Learning disabled and normal children's responses to non-explicit requests for clarification. *Perceptual and Motor Skills, 53:*919–925.

Pearson, P. D., & Dole, J. A. (1987). Explicit comprehension instruction: A review of research and a new conceptualization of instruction. *The Elementary School Journal, 88*(2):151–165.

Pearson, P. D., & Johnson, D. D. (1978). *Teaching Reading Comprehension.* New York: Holt, Rinehart, & Winston.

Peck, M. L., Farberow, N. L., & Litman, R. E. (1985). *Youth suicide.* New York: Springer.

Pelham, W. E. (1981). Attention deficits in hyperactive and learning-disabled children. *Exceptional Education Quarterly, 2*(3):13–23.

Pelham, W. E., & Bender, M. E. (1984). *Behavioral assessment of psychoactive drug effects on a child's learning and behavior in an* inpatient psychiatric setting. Unpublished manuscript. Department of Psychology, Florida State University, Tallahassee.

Pelham, W. E., & Milich, R. (1984). Peer relations in children with hyperactivity/attention deficit disorder. *Journal of Learning Disabilities, 17*(9):560–566.

Pelham, W., & Murphy, H. (1981). *The SNAP Checklist: A Teacher Checklist for Identifying Children with Attention Deficit Disorders.* Unpublished manuscript, Florida State University, Tallahassee.

Perceptual Forms Test. (1956). Winter Haven, FL: Winter Haven Lions Club, Publications Committee.

Perfetti, C., (1986). Continuities in reading acquisition, reading skill, and reading disability. *Remedial and Special Education, 7*(1):11–21.

Perfetti, C., Beck, I., Bell, L., & Hughes, C. (1987). Phonemic knowledge and learning to read are reciprocal: A longitudinal study of first grade children. *Merrill-Palmer Quarterly, 33*:283–319.

Perfetti, C., & Hogaboam, T. (1975). The relationship between single word decoding and reading comprehension skill. *Journal of Educational Psychology, 67*:461–469.

Peterson, P. L., & Janicki, T. C. (1979). Individual characteristics and children's learning in large-group and small-group approaches. *Journal of Educational Psychology, 71,* 677–687.

Peyton, J. K. (1987). *Dialogue Journal Writing with Limited English Proficient Students.* Los Angeles: University of California, Center for Language Education and Research.

Peyton, J. K., & Mackinson-Smyth, J. (1988). Computer networks: A collaborative approach to literacy development. *Elementary ESOL Education News, 10*(3):5–6.

Piaget, J. (1962). Comments on Vygotsky's critical remarks concerning *The language and thought of the child,* and *Judgment and reasoning in the child* (appendix, A. Parson, Trans., E. Hanfmann & G. Vakar, Eds.). In L. S. Vygotsky, *Thought and Language* (E. Hanfmann & G. Vakar, Trans.). Cambridge, MA: MIT Press.

Piaget, J. (1970a). Piaget's theory. In I. P. Mussen (Ed.), *Carmichael's Manual of Child Psychology* (Vol. 1). New York: Wiley & Sons.

Piaget, J. (1970b). *The Science of Education and Psychology of the Child.* New York: Grossman.

Piaget, J. (1976). Piaget's theory. In B. Inhelder, H. Chipman, & C. Zwingmann (Eds.), *Piaget and His School: A Reader in Developmental Psychology.* New York: Springer-Verlag.

Piers, E., & Harris, D. (1969). *The Piers-Harris Children's Self Concept Scale.* Nashville: Counselor Recordings and Tests.

Piersal, W. C., & Gutkin, T. B. (1983). Resistance to school-based consultation: A behavioral analysis of the problem. *Psychology in the Schools, 10*:311–320.

Plata, M., & Bone, J. (1989). Perceived importance of occupations by adolescents with and without learning disabilities. *Journal of Learning Disabilities, 22*(1):64–71.

Polloway, E. A., Patton, J. R., Payne, J. S., & Payne, R. A. (1989). *Strategies for Teaching Learners With Special Needs.* Columbus, OH: Charles E. Merrill.

Polsgrove, L., & McNeil, M. (1989). The consultation process: Research and practice. *Remedial and Special Education, 10*(1):6–13.

Pope, L. (1975). *Guidelines to Teaching Remedial Reading.* Brooklyn, NY: Book-Lab.

Porter, J. E., & Rourke, B. P. (1983). Socio-emotional functioning of learning disabled children: A subtypal analysis of personality patterns. In B. P. Rourke (Ed.), *Neuropsychology of Learning Disabilities* (pp. 257–280). New York: Guilford Press.

Posner, M. I., & Boies, S. J. (1971). Components of attention. *Psychological Review, 78*:409–419.

Poteet, J. A. (1978). *Characteristics of Written Expression of Learning Disabled and Non-Learning Disabled Elementary School Students.* Muncie, IN: Ball State University. (ERIC Document Reproduction Service No. ED 1590 830).

Powers, J. L., Jaklitsch, B., & Eckenrode, J. (1989). Behavioral characteristics of maltreatment among runaway and homeless youth. *Early Child Development and Care, 42*:127–139.

Poznanski, E. (1982). The clinical phenomenology of childhood depression. *American Journal of Orthopsychiatry, 52*:308–313.

Pressley, M., Johnson, C. J., & Symons, S. (1987). Elaborating to learn and learning to elaborate. *Journal of Learning Disabilities, 20,* 76–91.

Pressley, M., Symons, S., Snyder, B. L., & Cariglia-Bull, T. (1989). Strategy instruction research comes of age. *Learning Disability Quarterly, 12,* 16–25.

Pronovost, W., & Dumbleton, C. (1953). A picture-type speech sound discrimination test. *Journal of Speech and Hearing Disorders, 18*:258–266.

Pullis, M., & Smith, D. C. (1981). Social-cognitive development of learning disabled children. In Piaget, Learning, and Learning Disabilities, edited by D. K. Reid. *Topics in Learning and Learning Disabilities, 1981. 1*:43–55.

Putnam, J. W., Rynders, J. E., Johnson, R. T., & Johnson, D. W. (1989). Collaborative skill instruction for promoting positive interactions between mentally handicapped and nonhandicapped children. *Exceptional Children, 55*(6):550–557.

Quay, H. C. (1979). Classification. In H. C. Quay & J. S. Werry (Eds.), *Psychopathological Disorders of Childhood* (2nd ed., pp. 1–42). New York: Wiley.

Quay, H. C. (1987). Intelligence. In H. C. Quay (Ed.), *Handbook of Juvenile Delinquency* (pp. 106–117). New York: Wiley.

Quay, H. C., & Peterson, D. R. (1967). *Behavior Problem Checklist.* Champaign, IL: Children's Research Center.

Quay, H. C., & Peterson, D. R. (1975). Manual for the Behavior Problem Checklist. Unpublished manuscript.

Radebaugh, R. M. (1981). Using children's literature to teach mathematics. *The Reading Teacher, 34*(8):903–906.

Rakic, P. (1988a). Defects of neuronal migration and the pathogenesis of cortical malformations. In G. J. Boer. M. G. P. Feenstra, M. Mirmiran, D. F. Swaab, & F. van Haaren (Eds.), *Biochemical Basis of Functional Neuroteratology: Permanent Effects of Chemicals on the Developing Brain. Progress in Brain Research, Vol. 73* (pp. 15–38). Amsterdam: Elsevier.

Rakic, P. (1988b). Specification of cerebral cortical areas. *Science, 24*:170–176.

Rakow, S. J., & Gee, T. C. (1988). What reading techniques do mathematics teachers find valuable? *School Science and Mathematics, 88*(3):210–217.

Rapaport, D. (1971). *Emotions and Memory.* New York: International Universities Press. (Original work published 1942)

Raphael, T. E. (1982). Question-answering strategies for children. *The Reading Teacher, 36*:186–191.

Raphael, T. E., Kirschner, B. W., & Englert, C. S. (1986). *Student's Metacognitive Knowledge about Writing* (Res. Series No. 176). East Lansing: Michigan State University, Institute for Research on Teaching.

Rapin, I., & Allen, D. A. (1988). Syndromes in developmental dysphasia and adult aphasia. In F. Plum (Ed.), *Language, Communication and the Brain.* New York: Raven Press.

Rapoport, J. L., Buchsbaum, M. S., Zahn, T. P., Weingartner, H., Ludlow, C., & Mikkelsen, E. J. (1978). Dextroamphetamine: Cognitive and behavioral effects in normal prepubertal boys. *Science, 199*:560–563.

Rappaport, M. (1981). Prevention of problems in children: The executive function of the family. *The Forum, 7*(2):11, 22.

Rappaport, S. (1983). Brain in aging and dementia. *NIH Publication,* No. 83-2625.

Rapport, M. D., Murphy, H. A., & Bailey, J. S. (1982). Ritalin vs. response cost in the control of hyperactive children: A within-subject comparison. *Journal of Applied Behavior Analysis, 15*:205–216.

Rathjen, D. P. (1984). Social skills training for children: Innovations and consumer guidelines. *School Psychology Review, 13*:302–310.

Read, C. (1975). *Children's Categorization of Speech Sounds in English.* (NCTE Research Report No. 17). Urbana, IL: National Council of Teachers of English.

Reardon, R., Hersen, M., Bellack, A., & Foley, J. (1979). Measuring social skill in grade school boys. *Journal of Behavioral Assessment, 1*:87–105.

Reid, K. (1988). *Teaching the Learning Disabled: A Cognitive Developmental Approach.* Boston: Allyn and Bacon.

Reid, D. K., & Hresko, W. P. (1981). *A Cognitive Approach to Learning Disabilities.* Austin, TX: Pro-Ed.

Reisman, F. K. (1978). *A Guide to the Diagnostic Teaching of Arithmetic* (2nd ed.). Columbus, OH: Charles E. Merrill.

Reisman, F. K. (1984). *Sequential Assessment of Mathematics Inventory.* Columbus, OH: Charles E. Merrill.

Remmers, H. H., & Bauemfeind, R. H. (1957). *SRA Junior Inventory, Form S.* Chicago: Science Research Associates.

Remmers, H. H., & Shimberg, B. (1957). *SRA Youth Inventory, Form S.* Chicago: Science Research Associates.

Reschly, D. J. (1988a). Minority MMR overrepresentation and special education reform. *Exceptional Children, 54*(4):316–323.

Reschly, D. J. (1988b). Special Education reform: School psychology revolution. *School Psychology Review, 17.*

Reschly, D. J. (1988c). Minority EMR overrepresentation: Legal issues, research findings, and reform trends. In M. C. Wang, M. C. Reynolds, & H. J. Walberg (Eds.), *The Handbook of Special Education: Research and Practice.* Oxford, England: Pergamon Press.

Reschly, D. J., & Gresham, F. M. (1988). Adaptive behavior and the mildly handicapped. In T. Kratochwill (Ed.), *Advances in School Psychology* (pp. 249–282). Hillsdale, NJ: Erlbaum.

Resnick, L. B. (1982). Syntax and semantics in learning to subtract. In T. Carpenter, J. Moser, & T. Romberg (Eds.), *Addition and Subtraction: A Cognitive Perspective* (pp. 136–158). Hillsdale, NJ: Erlbaum.

Reutzel, D. R. (1983). C⁶: A reading model for teaching arithmetic story problem solving. *The Reading Teacher, 37*(1):28–35.

Reyes, L. H. (1980). Attitudes and mathematics. In M. M. Lindquist (Ed.), *Selected Issues in Mathematics Education* (pp. 161–184). Berkeley: McCutchan.

Reynolds, C. R. (1988). Putting the individual into aptitude-treatment interaction. *Exceptional Children, 54*(4):324–331.

Reynolds, M., & Wang, M. (1983). Restructuring "special" school programs: A position paper. *Policy Studies Review, 2*(Special No. 1), 189–212.

Reynolds, M., Wang, M. C., & Walberg, H. J. (1987). The necessary restructuring of special and regular education. *Exceptional Children, 53*:391–398.

Richards, J. P., & August, G. J. (1975, December). Generative underlining strategies in prose recall. *Journal of Educational Psychology, 67*:860–865.

Rickards, J. P. (1976). Processing effects of advance organizers interspersed in text. *Reading Research Quarterly, 11*:599–622.

Rico, G. L. (1978). Reading, for non-literal meaning. In E. W. Eisner (Ed.), *Reading, the Arts, and the Creation of Meaning.* Reston, VA: National Art Education Association.

Rie, D. R., & Rie, H. E. (1977). Recall, retention and Ritalin. *Journal of Consulting and Clinical Psychology, 45*:967–972.

Riel, M. (1983). *Investigating the System of Development: The Skills and Abilities of Dysphasic Children.* La Jolla: University of California at San Diego, Center for Human Information Processing.

Roach, E., & Kephart, N. (1966). *The Purdue Perceptual-Motor Survey.* Columbus, OH: Charles E. Merrill.

Roach, E., & Kephart, N. (1978). The *Purdue Perceptual-Motor Survey.* Columbus, OH: Charles E. Merrill.

Robbins, D. A. (1982). FIRST—Letter Mnemonic Strategy: A Memorization Technique for Learning Disabled High School Students. Unpublished master's thesis. University of Kansas, Lawrence.

Robins, L. N. (1978). Sturdy childhood predictors of adult anti-social behavior: Replications from longitudinal studies. *Psychological Medicine, 8,* 611–622.

Robinson, F. P. (1946). *Effective Study.* New York: Harper and Brothers.

Robinson, H. A. (1983). *Teaching reading, writing, and study strategies: The content areas* (3rd ed.). Boston: Allyn and Bacon.

Robson, G. M. (1977). Problem-Solving Strategies in Learning Disabled and Normal Achieving Children (Doctoral dissertation, University of California, Los Angeles). *Dissertation Abstracts International, 38,* 732A.

Rogoff, B., & Gardner, W. (1984). Adult guidance of cognitive development. In B. Rogoff & J. Lave (Eds.), *Everyday Cognition: Its Development in Social Context* (pp. 95–116). Cambridge, MA: Harvard University Press.

Roit, M. L., & McKenzie, R. G. (1985). Disorders of written communication: An instructional priority for LD students. *Journal of Learning Disabilities, 18*(5):258–260.

Rootman, I. (1985). Preventing alcohol problems: A challenge for health promotion. *Health Education 24*:2–7.

Rorschach, H. (1966). *Rorschach Ink Blot Test.* New York: Grune & Stratton.

Rosenfarb, I., & Hayes, S. C. (1984). Social standard setting: The Achilles heel of informational accounts of therapeutic change. *Behavior Therapy, 15*:515–528.

Rosengarten, H., Freidman, E., & Friedhoff, A. T. (1983). Sensitive periods for the effect of haloperiodol on development of striatal dopamine receptors. *Birth Defects, 19*(4):511–513.

Rosenshine, B., & Stevens, R. (1986). Teaching functions. In M. Wittrock (Ed.), *Handbook of Research on Teaching* (3rd ed., pp. 376–391). New York: Macmillan.

Rosenthal, R. H., & Allen, T. W. (1978). An examination of attention, arousal, and learning dysfunctions of hyperkinetic children. *Psychological Bulletin, 85*:689–715.

Rosenthal, R. H., & Allen, T. W. (1980). Intratask distractability in hyperkinetic and nonhyperkinetic children. *Journal of Abnormal Child Psychology, 8*:175–187.

Rosvold, H. E., Mirsky, A. F., Sarason, I., Bransome, E. E., & Beck, L. H. (1956). A continuous performance test of brain damage. *Journal of Consulting Psychology, 20*:343–352.

Roswell, F., & Chall, J. (1978). *Roswell-Chall Auditory Blending Test* (rev. ed.). New York: The Essay Press.

Rourke, B. P. (1987). Syndrome of nonverbal learning disabilities. The final common pathway of white matter disease dysfunction? *The Clinical Neuropsychologist, 1*:209–234.

Rourke, B. P., Bakker, D. J., Fisk, J., & Strang, J. (1983). *Child Neuropsychology.* New York: Guilford Press.

Rozin, P., Poritsky, S., & Sotsky, P. (1971). American children with reading problems can easily learn to read English represented by Chinese characters. *Science, 171*:1264–1267.

Rudel, R. G. (1985). Hemispheric asymmetry and learning disabilities: Left, right or in between? In C. T. Best (Ed.), *Hemispheric Function and Collaboration in the Child.* New York: Academic Press.

Ruiz, N. T. (1989). An optimal learning environment for Rosemary. *Exceptional Children, 56*(2):130–144.

Rumberger, R. W. (1983). Dropping out of school: The influence of race, sex, and family background. *American Educational Research Journal, 20*:199–220.

Rumberger, R. W. (1987). High school dropouts: A review of issues and evidence. *Review of Educational Research, 57*:101–121.

Rumelhart, D. E. (1980). Schemata: The building blocks of cognition. In R. Spiro, B. Bruce, & W. Brewer (Eds.), *Theoretical Issues in Reading Comprehension* (pp. 33–58). Hillsdale, NJ: Erlbaum.

Rumelhart, D. E., & Norman, D. A. (1978). Accretion, tuning, and restructuring: Three modes of learning. In J. W. Cotton & R. L. Klatzky (Eds.), *Semantic Factors in Cognition* (pp. 37–54). Hillsdale, NJ: Erlbaum.

Russell, D. E. H. (1983). The incidence and prevalence of intrafamilial and extrafamilial sexual abuse of female children. *Child Abuse and Neglect, 7,* 147–153.

Russell, R. L., & Ginsburg, H. P. (1984). Cognitive analysis of children's mathematics difficulties. *Cognition and Instruction, 1*:217–244.

Rutter, M., & Giller, H. (1984). *Juvenile Delinquency.* New York: Guilford Press.

Ryan, E. B., Short, E. J., & Weed, K. A. (1986). The role of cognitive strategy training in improving the academic performance of learning disabled children. *Journal of Learning Disabilities, 19*:521–529.

Sager, M. B. (1989). Exploiting the reading-writing connection to engage students in text. *Journal of Reading,* 40–43.

Salend, S., Michael, R., & Taylor, M. (1984). Competencies necessary for instructing migrant handicapped students. *Exceptional Children, 51*:50–55.

Salisbury, D. F. (1984). How to decide when and where to use microcomputers for instruction. *Educational Technology, 24*(3):22–24.

Salvia, J., & Ysseldyke, J. E. (1985). *Assessment in Special and Remedial Education* (3rd ed.). Boston: Houghton Mifflin.

Sameroff, A. (1975). Transactional models in early social relations. *Human Development, 18*:65–79.

Saracoglu, B., Minden, H., & Wilchesky, M. (1989). The adjustment of students with learning disabilities to university and its relationship to self-esteem and self-efficacy. *Journal of Learning Disabilities, 22*(9):590–540, 560.

Sarason, I. G., & Sarason, B. R. (1981). Teaching cognitive and social skills to high school students. *Journal of Consulting and Clinical Psychology, 49*:908–918.

Saski, J., Swicegood, P., & Carter, J. (1983). Notetaking formats for learning disabled adolescents. *Learning Disability Quarterly, 6*(3):265–272.

Satterfield, J. H., Hoppe, C. M., & Schell, A. M. (1982). A prospective study of delinquency in 110 adolescent boys with attention deficit disorder and 88 normal adolescent boys. *American Journal of Psychiatry, 139*:795–798.

Saxe, G. B., Guberman, S. R., & Gearhart, M. (1987). Social processes in early number development. With Commentary by R. Gelman, and by C. M. Massey and B. Rogoff; with Reply by G. B. Saxe, S. R. Guberman, & M. Gearhart. *Monographs of the Society for Research in Child Development, 52*(2, Serial No. 216).

Scandura, J. M. (1982). Structural (cognitive task) analysis: A method for analyzing content. *Journal of Structured Learning, 7*:101–114.

Scannell, D. P. (1978). *Tests of Achievement and Proficiency.* Chicago: Riverside Publishing.

Scarr, S. (Ed.). (1979). Psychology and children: Current research and practice [Special issue]. *American Psychologist, 34*(10).

Schalock, R. (1986). Employment outcomes from secondary school programs. *Remedial and Special Education 7*(6):37–39.

Schalock, R. L., Wolzen, B., Ross, I., Elliott, B., Werbel, G., & Peterson, K. (1986). Post-secondary community placement of handicapped students: A five-year follow-up. *Learning Disability Quarterly, 9*:295–303.

Schaps, E., DiBartolo, R., Moskowitz, J., Palley, C., & Churgin, S. (1980). Primary prevention evaluation research: A review of 127 impact studies. *Journal of Drug Issues 11*:17–43.

Schechter, M. D., & Roberge, L. (1976). Sexual exploitation. In R. E. Helfer & C. H. Kempe (Eds.), *Child Abuse and Neglect: The Family and the Community.* Cambridge, MA: Ballinger.

Schiffman, G. (1965): Particulars of 240 Clinically Retarded Readers. Speech delivered at IRA Convention, Detroit.

Schmitt, B. D., & Beezley, P. (1976). The long-term management of the child and family in child abuse and neglect. *Pediatric Annals, 5*:165–176.

Schneider, W. (1986, April). Automatic and Controlled Processing. Paper presented at American Educational Research Association meeting symposium on "Automaticity and Its Implications for Instructional Design," San Francisco.

Schneider, W., & Fisk, A. D. (1984). Automatic category search and its transfer. *Journal of Experimental Psychology: Learning, Memory, and Cognition, 10:* 1–15.

Schneider, W., & Shiffrin, R. M. (1977). Controlled and automatic human information processing: I. Detection, search and attention. *Psychological Review, 84*:1–66.

School Dropouts. (1986). *Everybody's Problem.* Washington, DC: The Institute for Educational Leadership.

Schumaker, J. B., Deshler, D. D., Alley, G. R., & Denton, P. H. (1982). Multipass: A learning strategy for improving reading comprehension. *Learning Disability Quarterly, 5*(3):295–304.

Schumaker, J. B., & Ellis, E. S. (1982). Social skills training of LD adolescents: A generalization study. *Learning Disabilities Quarterly, 5*(Fall) (4):374–378.

Schumaker, J. B., & Hazel, J. S. (1984). Social skills assessment and training for the learning disabled: Who's on first and what's on second? Part II. *Journal of Learning Disabilities, 17*:492–499.

Schumaker, J. B., Hazel, J. S., Sherman, J. A., & Sheldon, J. (1982). Social skill performances of learning disabled, non-learning disabled, and delinquent adolescents. *Learning Disability Quarterly, 5*:388–397.

Schunk, D. H. (1985a). Participation in goal setting: Effects on self-efficacy and skills of learning disabled children. *The Journal of Special Education, 19*:307–317.

Schunk, D. H. (1985b). Self-efficacy and classroom learning. *Psychology in the Schools, 22*:208–223.

Schunk, D. H. (1987). Self-efficacy and motivated learning. In N. Hastings & J. Schwieso (Eds.), *New Directions in Educational Psychology: 2. Behaviour and Motivation in the Classroom* (pp. 233–251). London: The Falmer Press.

Schunk, D. H. (1989). Self-efficacy and cognitive achievement: Implications for students with learning problems. *Journal of Learning Disabilities, 22*(1):14–22.

Schunk, D. H. (in press). Self-efficacy and performance. In R. E. Ames & C. Ames (Eds.), *Research on Motivation in Education* (Vol. 3). Orlando: Academic Press.

Schunk, D. H., & Cox, P. D. (1986). Strategy training and attributional feedback with learning disabled students. *Journal of Educational Psychology, 78*:201–209.

Schunk, D. H., & Hanson, A. R. (1985). Peer models: Influence on children's self-efficacy and achievement. *Journal of Educational Psychology, 77:* 313–322.

Schunk, D. H., Hanson, A. R., & Cox, P. D. (1987). Peer model attributes and children's achievement behaviors. *Journal of Educational Psychology, 79:* 54–61.

Schunk, D. H., & Rice, J. M. (1984). Strategy self-verbalization during remedial listening comprehension instruction. *Journal of Experimental Education, 53:* 49–54.

Schworm, R. W. (1979). The effects of selective attention on the decoding skills of children with learning disabilities. *Journal of Learning Disabilities, 12*:639–644.

Scotti, W. (1989). The science lab as an example of an effective humanistic and holistic approach to teaching and learning. *Reading Improvement, 26*(2):150–155.

Scruggs, T. E., & Mastropieri, M. A. (1988). *Reconstructive Elaborations: A Model for Content Area Learning.* West Lafayette, IN: Purdue University, Department of Education.

Scruggs, T. E., & Mastropieri, M. A. (1989). Mnemonic instruction of LD students: A field-based evaluation. *Learning Disability Quarterly, 12*:119–125.

Seligman, M. E., Maier, S. F., & Geer, J. N. (1968). Alleviation of learned helplessness in the dog. *Journal of Abnormal Psychology, 73*:256–262.

Semel, E. M., & Wiig, E. H. (1975). Comprehension of syntactic structures and critical verbal elements by children with learning disabilities. *Journal of Learning Disabilities, 8*:46–51.

Semel, E. M., & Wiig, E. H. (1981). Semel auditory processing program: Training effects among children with language-learning disabilities. *Journal of Learning Disabilities, 14*:192–197.

Senf, G. M. (1986). LD research in sociological and scientific perspective. In J. K. Torgesen & B. Y. L. Wong (Eds.), *Psychological and Educational Perspectives on Learning Disabilities.* San Diego: Academic Press.

Sever, J. L. (1986). Perinatal infections and damage to the central nervous system. In M. Lewis (Ed.), *Learning Disabilities and Prenatal Risk* (pp. 194–209). University of Illinois Press, Urbana at Chicago.

Shaffer, D., & Schonfeld, I. (1984). A critical note on the value of attention deficit as a basis for a clinical syndrome. In L. M. Bloomingdale (Ed.), *Attention Deficit Disorders: Diagnostic, Cognitive, and Therapeutic Understanding* (pp. 119–131). Jamaica, NY: Spectrum.

Shannon, S. (1987). *English in el Barrio: A Sociolinguistic Study of Second Language Contact.* Unpublished doctoral dissertation, Stanford University, CA.

Shavelson, R. J., Berliner, D. C., Ravitch, M. M., & Loeding, D. (1974). Effects of position and type of question on learning from prose material: Interaction of treatments with individual differences. *Journal of Educational Psychology, 66*(1):40–48.

Shaw, H. (1971). *Spell It Right.* New York: Barnes & Noble.

Shaywitz, S. E. (1986). Prevalence of Attentional Deficits in an Epidemiologic Sample of School Children (unpublished raw data).

Shaywitz, S., & Shaywitz, B. (1988). Attention deficit disorder: Current perspectives. In J. F. Kavanagh & T. J. Truss, Jr. (Eds.), *Learning Disabilities: Proceedings of the National Conference.* Parkton, MD: York Press.

Shepard, L. (1987). The new push for excellence: Widening the schism between regular and special education. *Exceptional Children, 53*:327–329.

Sherrington, C. (1947). *The Integration Action of the Nervous System.* New Haven, CT: Yale University Press.

Shinn, M. R., Gleason, M. M., & Tindal, G. (1989). Varying the difficulty of testing materials: Implications for curriculum-based measurement. *The Journal of Special Education, 23*(2):223–233.

Shinn, M., & Marston, D. (1985). Differentiating mildly handicapped, low-achieving and regular education students: A curriculum-based approach. *Remedial and Special Education, 6*:31–45.

Shinn, M. R., Tindal, G. A., & Stein, S. (1988). Curriculum-based measurement and the identification of mildly handicapped students: A research review. *Professional School Psychology, 3*:69–86.

Short, E. J., & Ryan, E. B. (1984). Metacognitive differences between skilled and less skilled readers: Remediating deficits through story grammar and attribution training. *Journal of Educational Psychology, 76*:225–235.

Siebert, J., Carnine, D., & Stein, M. (1981). *Direct Mathematics Instruction.* Columbus, OH: Charles E. Merrill.

Siegel, E. (1970). The exceptional child grows up. *Proceedings: State Conference for Teachers of Exceptional Children.* Louisville, KY.

Silvaroli, N. J. (1973). *Classroom Reading Inventory* (2d ed.). Dubuque, IA: William C. Brown.

Silverman, R., & Zigmond, N. (1983). Self-concept in learning disabled adolescents. *Journal of Learning Disabilities, 16*:478–482.

Simmonds, E. P. M., Luchow, J. P., Kaminsky, S., & Cottone, V. (1989). Applying cognitive learning strategies in the classroom: A collaborative training institute. *Learning Disabilities Focus, 4*(2):96–105.

Sinclair, E., & Alexson, J. (1986). Learning disability discrepancy formulas: Similarities and differences among them. *Learning Disabilities Research, 1*(2):112–118.

Skinner, B. F. (1938). *The Behavior of Organisms.* New York: Appleton-Century-Crofts.

Skinner, B. F. (1959). *Verbal Behavior.* New York: Appleton-Century-Crofts.

Slate, J. R., & Charlesworth, J. R., Jr. (1989). Information processing theory: Classroom applications. *Reading Improvement, 26*(1): 2–6.

Slavin, R. E. (1983a). *Cooperative Learning.* New York: Longman.

Slavin, R. E. (1983b). When does cooperative learning increase student achievement? *Psychological Bulletin, 94*:429–445.

Slavin, R. E. (1984). Review of cooperative learning research. *Review of Educational Research, 50*, 315–342.

Slingerland, B. (1970). *Screening Tests for Identifying Children with Specific Language Disability* (rev. ed.). Cambridge, MA: Educators Publishing Service.

Sloan, W. (1954). *Lincoln-Oseretsky Motor Development Scale.* Los Angeles: Western Psychological Services.

Slosson, R. L. (1967). *Slosson Drawing Coordination Test.* East Aurora, NY: Slosson Educational Publications.

Slosson, R. L. (1971). *Slosson Intelligence Test.* East Aurora, NY: Slosson Educational Publications.

Smart, K. L., & Bruning, J. L. (1973). *An Examination of the Practical Import of the Von Restorff Effect.* ED 102 502. Arlington, VA: ERIC Document of Reproduction Service.

Smith, C. R. (1983). *Learning Disabilities: The Interaction of Learner, Task, and Setting.* Boston, Little, Brown.

Smith, D. C., Adelman, H. S., Nelson, P., Taylor, L., & Phares, V. (1987). Students' perception of control at school and problem behavior and attitudes. *Journal of School Psychology, 25,* 167–176.

Smith, D. D., & Lovitt, T. C. (1975). The use of modeling techniques to influence the acquisition of computational arithmetic skills in learning-disabled children. In E. Ramp & G. Semb (Eds.), *Behavior Analysis: Areas of Research and Application.* (pp. 283–308). Englewood Cliffs, NJ: Prentice-Hall.

Smith, F. (1975). *Comprehension and Learning: A Conceptual Framework for Teachers.* New York: Holt, Rinehart and Winston.

Smith, F. (1985). *Reading without Nonsense.* New York: Teachers College Press.

Smith, G. (1987). Effective practices for learning disabled individuals. *Learning Disabilities Focus, 3*(1):53–54.

Smith, J. E., & Deitch, K. V. (1987) Cocaine: A maternal, fetal, and neonatal risk. *Journal of Pediatric Health Care, 3,* 120–124.

Smith, J. (1988). Social and vocational problems of adults with learning disabilities: A review of the literature. *Learning Disabilities Focus, 4*(1):46–58.

Smith, J. S., & Dauer, V. L. (1984). A comprehension-monitoring strategy for reading content area materials. *Journal of Reading, 28*(2):144–147.

Smith, N. J. (1985). The word processing approach to language experience. *The Reading Teacher, 38*(6):556–559.

Smith, S. D., Kimberling, W. I., Pennington, B. F., & Lubs, M. A. (1983). Specific reading disability: Identification of an inherited form through linkage analysis. *Science, 219*:1345–1347.

Snider, V. E. (1989). Reading comprehension performance of adolescents with learning disabilities. *Learning Disability Quarterly, 12,* 87–96.

Snyder, G. V. (1981). Learner verification of reading games. *The Reading Teacher, 34*(6):686–691.

Snyder, J., & Patterson, G. R. (1987). Family interaction and delinquent behavior. In H. C. Quay (Ed.), *Handbook of Juvenile Delinquency* (pp. 216–243). New York: Wiley.

Solnit, A. J., & Stark, M. H. (1961). Mourning the birth of a defective child. *Psychoanalytic Study of the Child, 16*:523–537.

Solomon, I., & Starr, B. (1968). *School Apperception Method.* New York: Springer.

Sonnenschein, J. L. (1983). *Basic Achievement Skills Individual Screener.* Cleveland, OH: The Psychological Corporation.

Spache, G. (1953, March). A new readability formula for primary grade reading materials. *Elementary School Journal, 53*(7):410–413.

Spache, G. (1961). *Spache Binocular Vision Test.* Meadville, PA: Keystone View Co.

Spache, G. (1972). *Diagnostic Reading Scales.* Monterey, CA: CTB/McGraw-Hill.

Spache, G., & Spache, E. (1975). *Reading in the Elementary School* (3d ed.). Boston: Allyn and Bacon.

Sparrow, S., Balla, D., & Cicchetti, D. (1984). *Vineland Adaptive Scales.* Circle Pines, MN: American Guidance Service.

Special Education Today. (1985). ACALD definition of learning disabilities 2(1):1–20.

Sperry, R. W. (1968). Hemisphere deconnection and unity in conscious awareness. *American Psychologist, 23*:723–733.

Spivack, G., & Shure, M. B. (1982). The cognition of social adjustment: Interpersonal cognitive problem-solving thinking. In B. B. Lahey & A. E. Kazdin (Eds.), *Advance in Child Clinical Psychology* (Vol. 5, pp. 323–372). New York: Plenum Press.

Spivack, G., & Spotts, J. (1966). *Devereux Child Behavior Rating Scale.* Devon, PA: The Devereux Foundation Press.

Spivack, G., Spotts, J., & Haimes, P. (1967). *Devereux Adolescent Behavior Rating Scale.* Devon, PA: The Devereaux Foundation Press.

Spivack, G., & Swift, M. (1967). *Devereux Elementary School Behavior Rating Scale.* Devon, PA: The Devereux Foundation Press.

Sprague, R. L., & Sleator (1977). Methylphenidate in hyperkinetic children: Differences in dose effects on learning and social behavior. *Science, 198:*1274–1276.

Staats, A. W., Brewer, B. A., & Gross, M. C. (1970). Learning and cognitive development: Representative samples, cumulative-hierarchical learning, and experimental-longitudinal methods. *Monographs of the Society for Research in Child Development, 35*(8, Serial No. 141).

Stainback, S., & Stainback, W. (1987). Integration versus cooperation: A commentary on "Educating children with learning problems: A shared responsibility." *Exceptional Children, 54:*66–68.

Stainback, W., & Stainback, S. (1984). A rationale for the merger of special and regular education. *Exceptional Children, 51:* 102–111.

Stanford Achievement Test. (1973). New York: Harcourt Brace Jovanovich.

Stanford-Binet Intelligence Scale. (rev., 3d ed.). (1973). Boston: Houghton Mifflin.

Stankov, L. (1983). Attention and intelligence. *Journal of Educational Psychology, 75:*471–490.

Stanovich, K. E. (1986). New beginnings, old problems, In S. J. Ceci (Ed.), *Handbook of Cognitive, Social, and Neuropsychological Aspects of Learning Disabilities* (Vol. 1, pp. 229–238). Hillsdale, NJ: Erlbaum.

Starr, C., & Taggart, R. (1987). *Biology: The Unity and Diversity of Life.* Belmont, CA: Wadsworth.

Starr, R. H., Jr. (1982). A research-based approach to the prediction of child abuse. In R. H. Starr, Jr. (Ed.), *Child Abuse Prediction: Policy Implications* (pp. 105–134). Cambridge, MA: Ballinger.

Staubli, U., Fraser, D., Kessler, M., & Lynch, G. (1986). Studies on retrograde and anterograde amnesia of olfactory memory after denervation of the hippocampus by entorhinal cortex lesions. *Behavioral and Neural Biology.*

Staubi, U., Roman, F., & Lynch, G. (1985). Selective changes in synaptic responses elicited in a cortical network by behaviorally relevant electrical stimulation. *Society of Neuroscience Abstracts, 11:*837.

Steele, B. (1976). Violence within the family. In R. Helfer & G. Kempe (Eds.), *Child Abuse and Neglect: The Family and the Community.* Cambridge, MA: Ballinger.

Stengel, R. (1988). The underclass: Breaking the apple. *Time, 32*(15):41–42.

Stephens, T. (1978). *Social Skills in the Classroom.* Columbus, OH: Cedars Press.

Stephenson, R. S. (1985). *A Study of the Longitudinal Dropout Rate: 1980 Eight-Grade Cohort Followed from June, 1980 through February, 1985.* Miami, FL; Dade County Public Schools.

Sternberg, R. J. (1980). Sketch of a componential subtheory of human intelligence. *Behavioral and Brain Sciences, 3:*573–614.

Sternberg, R. J. (1981). Testing and cognitive psychology. *American Psychologist, 36:*1181–1189.

Sternberg, R. J. (1984). Toward a triarchic theory of human intelligence. *Behavioral and Brain Sciences. 7:*269–315.

Sternberg, R. J. (1986). *Intelligence Applied: Understanding and Increasing Your Intellectual Skills.* New York: Harcourt Brace Jovanovich.

Sternberg, R. M., & Wagner, R. K. (1982). Automatization failure in learning disabilities. *Topics in Learning and Learning Disabilities, 2:*1–11.

Stevens, R., & Rosenshine, B. (1981). Advances in research on teaching. *Exceptional Education Quarterly, 2*(1):1–9.

Stewart, O. & Tei, E. (1983, October). Some implications of metacognition for reading instruction. *Journal of Reading, 36*–43.

Stimbert, V. E. (1971). A technology of preschool education. *Educational Technology, 11*(2):9–13.

Stipek, D. J., & Weisz, J. R. (1981). Perceived personal control and academic achievement. *Review of Educational Research, 51:*101–137.

Strain, P. S., Kerr, M. M., & Ragland, E. U. (1981). The use of peer social initiations in the treatment of social withdrawal. In P. S.

Strain (Ed.), *The Utilization of Classroom Peers as Behavior Change Agents* (pp. 101–128). New York: Plenum Press.

Strain, P. S., & Odom, S. L. (1986). Peer social initiations: Effective intervention for social skills development of exceptional children. *Exceptional Children, 52:*543–551.

Strain, P. S., Odom, S. L., & McConnell, S. (1984). Promoting social reciprocity of exceptional children: Identification, target behavior selection, and intervention. *Remedial and Special Education, 5:*21–28.

Strain, P. S., & Shores, R. E. (1977). Social interaction development among behaviorally handicapped preschool children: Research and educational implications. *Psychology in the Schools, 14:*493–502.

Strain, P. S., & Shores, R. E. (1983). A reply to misguided mainstreaming. *Exceptional Children, 50:*271–273.

Strauss, A., & Kephart, N. C. (1955). *Psychopathology and Education of the Brain-Injured Child* (Vol. II). New York: Grune and Stratton.

Strauss, A., & Lehtinen, L. (1947). *Psychopathology and Education of the Brain-Injured Child.* (Vol. I). New York: Grune and Stratton.

Streissguth, A. P., Martin, D. C., Barr, M. M., Sandman, B. M., Kirchner, G. L., & Darby, B. L. (1984). Intrauterine alcohol and nicotine exposure: Attention and reaction time in four-year-old children. *Developmental Psychology, 20:*533–541.

Stringer, S. A., & LaGreca, A. M. (1985). Correlates of child abuse potential. *Journal of Abnormal Child Psychology, 13*(2):217–226.

Swanson, H. L. (1982). In the beginning was a strategy: Or was it a constraint? *Topics in Learning and Learning Disabilities, 2:*10–14.

Swanson, H. L. (1984a). Does theory guide teaching practice? *Remedial and Special Education, 5*(5):7–16.

Swanson, H. L. (1984b). Effects of cognitive effort and work distinctiveness and learning disabled and nondisabled readers' recall. *Journal of Educational Psychology, 76:*894–908.

Swanson, H. L. (1986). Do semantic memory deficiencies underlie disabled readers' encoding process? *Journal of Experimental Child Psychology, 41:*461–488.

Swanson, H. L. (Ed.). (1987). *Memory and Learning Disabilities: Advances in Learning and Behavioral Disabilities.* Greenwich, CT: JAI.

Swanson, H. L. (1988a). Memory subtypes in learning disabled students. *Learning Disability Quarterly, 11,* 342–356.

Swanson, H. L. (1988b). A multidirectional model for assessing learning disabled students' intelligence: An information processing framework. *Learning Disability Quarterly, 11,* 233–247.

Swanson, H. L. (1989). Phonological processes and other routes. *Journal of Learning Disabilities, 22*(8):493–497.

Swanson, H. L., Cochran, K. F., & Ewers, C. A. (1990). Can learning disabilities be determined from working memory performance? *Journal of Learning Disabilities, 23*(1):59–67.

Swanson, H. L., & Rhine, B. (1985). Strategy transformation in learning disabled children's math performance: Clues to the development of expertise. *Journal of Learning Disabilities, 18:*596–603.

Swanson, J. (1988). Discussion. In J. F. Kavanagh & T. J. Truss, Jr. (Eds.), *Learning Disabilities Proceedings of the National Conference.* Parkton, MD: York Press.

Swanson, L. (1982). Verbal short-term memory encoding of learning disabled, deaf, and normal readers. *Learning Disability Quarterly, 5*(1):21–28.

Swicegood, P. R., & Parsons, J. L. (1991). The thematic unit approach: Content and process instruction for secondary learning disabled students. *Learning Disabilities Research & Practice, 6:*112–116.

Swift, M., & Spivack, G. (1972). *Hahnemann High School Behavior Rating Scale Manual.* Philadelphia: Departmental Health Sciences, Hahnemann Medical College and Hospital.

Switsky, H. N., & Shultz, G. F. (1988). Intrinsic motivation and learning performance: Implications for individual educational programming for learners with mild handicaps. *Remedial and Special Education, 9*(4):7–14.

References

Tallal, P. (1985). Neuropsychological foundations of specific developmental disorders (language, reading, articulation). In *Psychiatry* (Vol. 3, Chap. 67, pp. 1–15). Philadelphia; Lippincott.

Tallal, P. (1988). Developmental language disorders. In J. F. Kavanagh & T. J. Truss, Jr. (Eds.). *Learning Disabilities Proceedings of the National Conference*. Parkton, MD: York Press.

Tarnowski, K. J., & Nay, S. M. (1989). Locus of control in children with learning disabilities and hyperactivity: A subgroup analysis. *Journal of Learning Disabilities, 22*(6):80–83.

Tarnowski, K. J., Prinz, R. J., & Nay, S. M. (1986). Comparative analysis of attentional deficits in hyperactive and learning disabled children. *Journal of Abnormal Psychology, 95*:341–345.

Tawney, J. W., & Gast, D. L. (1984). *Single Subject Research in Special Education*. Columbus, OH: Merrill.

Taylor, H. G., & Fletcher, J. M. (1983). Biological foundations of "specific developmental disorders": Methods, findings, and future directions. *Journal of Clinical Child Psychology, 12*:46–65.

Templin, M., & Darley, F. (1960). *The Templin-Darley Tests of Articulation*. Iowa City: University of Iowa Bureau of Research and Service.

Terman, L. M. & Merrill, M. A. (1973). *Stanford-Binet Intelligence Scale*, 1972 norms edition. Form L-M. Boston: Houghton Mifflin.

Tharp, R. G., & Gallimore, R. (1988). *Rousing Minds to Life: Teaching, Learning, and Schooling in Social Context*. New York: Cambridge University Press.

Thomas, C. C., Englert, C. S., & Gregg, S. (1987). An analysis of errors and strategies in the expository writing of learning disabled students. *Remedial and Special Education, 8*(1):21–30, 46.

Thomas, E., & Robinson, H. (1977). *Improving Reading in Every Class*. Boston: Allyn and Bacon.

Thomas, J., Strage, A., & Curley, R. (1988). Improving students' self-directed learning: issues and guidelines. *The Elementary School Journal, 88*(3):313–324.

Thomas, J. W., & Rohwer, W. D., Jr. (1986). Academic studying: Critical reading and the introductory science course. *Journal of Reading*, 197–201.

Thompson, R. F. (1986). The neurobiology of learning and memory. *Science, 233*:941–952.

Thompson, R. J. (1986). *Behavior Problems in Children with Developmental and Learning Disabilities* [Monograph No. 3]. Ann Arbor, MI: University of Michigan Press.

Thorndike, E. L. (1912). The measurement of educational products. *School Review, 5*:20.

Thorpe, L., Clark, W., & Tiegs, E. (1953). *California Test of Personality*. Monterey, CA: CTB/McGraw-Hill.

Thorpe, L. P., Lefever, D. W., & Naslund, R. A. (1968). *SRA Achievement Series*. Chicago: Science Research Associates.

Thorpe, L. P., Lefever, D. W., & Naslund, R. A. (1969, 1974). *SRA Achievement Series in Arithmetic*. Chicago: Science Research Associates.

Tiegs, E. W. & Clark, W. W. (1977–1978). *The California Achievement Tests*. Monterey, CA: CTB/McGraw-Hill.

Tindal, G., & Parker, R. (1989). Assessment of written expression for students in compensatory and special education programs. *The Journal of Special Education, 23*(2):169–175.

Tindal, G. A., & Taylor-Pendergast, S. J. (1989). A taxonomy for objectively analyzing the consultation process. *Remedial and Special Education, 10*(2):6–22.

Tobias, S. (1976). Math anxiety: Why is a smart girl like you counting on your fingers? *Ms, 92*:56–59, 92.

Tobias, S. (1978). *Overcoming Math Anxiety*. Boston: Houghton Mifflin.

Tobias, S., & Weissbrod, C. (1980). Anxiety and mathematics. An update. *Harvard Educational Review, 50*, 63–70.

Tobin, K., & Fraser, B. J. (1989). Case studies of exemplary science and mathematics teaching. *School Science and Mathematics, 89*(4), 320–334.

Torgesen, J. K. (1975). Problems and prospects in the study of learning disabilities. In E. M. Hetherington (Ed.), *Review of Child Development Research* (Vol. 5, pp. 385–440). Chicago: University of Chicago Press.

Torgesen, J. K. (1977). The role of nonspecific factors in the task performance of learning disabled children: A theoretical assessment. *Journal of Learning Disabilities, 10*:27–34.

Torgesen, J. K. (1980). Conceptual and educational implications of the use of efficient task strategies by learning disabled children. *Journal of Learning Disabilities, 13*:19–26.

Torgesen, J. K. (1981). The relationship between memory and attention in learning disabilities. *Exceptional Education Quarterly, 2*:51–61.

Torgesen, J. K. (1982). The use of rationally defined subgroups in research on learning disabilities. In J. P. Das, R. J. Mulcahy, & T. E. Wall (Eds.), *Theory and Research in Learning Disabilities* (pp. 111–131). New York: Plenum Press.

Torgesen, J. K. (1985). Memory processes in reading disabled children. *Journal of Learning Disabilities, 18*:350–357.

Torgesen, J. K. (1986). Using computers to help learning disabled children practice reading: A research based perspective. *Learning Disabilities Focus, 1*(2):72–81.

Torgesen, J. K. (1989). Cognitive and behavioral characteristics of children with learning disabilities: Concluding comments. *Journal of Learning Disabilities, 22*(3):166–168.

Torgesen, J. K., & Goldman, T. (1977). Verbal rehearsal and short-term memory in reading-disabled children. *Child Development, 48*, 56.

Torgesen, J. K., & Wong, B. Y. L. (Eds.). (1986). *Psychological and Educational Perspectives on Learning Disabilities*. Orlando, FL: Academic Press, Inc.

Travers, K. J., Pikaart, L., Suydam, M. N., & Runion, G. E. (1977). *Mathematics Teaching*. New York: Harper & Row.

Treiman, R. (1986). The division between onsets and rimes in English syllables. *Journal of Memory and Language, 25*:476–491.

Tucker, J. (Ed.). (1985). Curriculum-based assessment [Special issue]. *Exceptional Children, 52*:199–204.

Tucker, J. (1987). Curriculum-based assessment is no fad. *The Collaborative Educator, 1*(4):4, 10.

Turner, A. M., & Greenough, W. T. (1983). Synapses per neuron and synaptic dimensions in occipital cortex of rats reared on complex, social or isolation housing. *Acta Stereologica Supplement, 2*:239–244.

Turner, B. L., & Opitz, J. M. (1980). Editorial comment: x-linked mental retardation (special issue on (fra[x]). *American Journal of Medical Genetics, 7*:407–415.

Ungerleider, L. G., & Mishkin, M. (1982). Two cortical visual systems. In D. J. Ingle, R. J. W. Mansfield, & M. A. Goodale (Eds.), *Advances in the Analysis of Visual Behavior*. Cambridge, MA: MIT Press.

Urban, W. (1963). *Draw-a-Person*. Los Angeles: Western Psychological Services.

U.S. Department of Education. (1987). *What Works: Schools Without Drugs*.

U.S. Department of Education, Office of Special Education and Rehabilitative Services. (1988). *Annual Report to Congress on the Implementation of the Education for All Handicapped Children*. Washington, DC: Author.

U.S. Department of Health and Human Services. (1989). *Helping Your Students Say No to Alcohol and Other Drugs*. DHHS Publication No. ADM 89-1502.

U.S. Department of Labor (1975). Part 570—Child labor regulations, orders, and statements of interpretation. *Federal Register, 40*, No. 172, September 4.

U.S. Office of Education. (1977). Assistance to states for education of handicapped children: Procedures for evaluating specific learning disabilities. *Federal Register, 42*:65082–65085.

Vacca, R. T. (1981). *Content Area Reading*. Boston: Little, Brown.

Valett, R. (1967). *The Valett Developmental Survey of Basic Learning Abilities*. Palo Alto, CA: Consulting Psychologists Press.

Valett, R. (1968). *A Psychoeducational Inventory of Basic Learning Abilities*. Palo Alto, CA: Fearon Publishers.

Valett, R. (1969). *Modifying Children's Behavior*. Palo Alto, CA: Fearon.

Vance, H. B. & Singer, M. G. (1979). Recategorization of the WISC-R subtest scaled scores for learning disabled children. *Journal of Learning Disabilities, 12:*487–491.

Vane, J. (1968, April). The Vane Kindergarten Test. *Clinical Psychology, 24:*1–34.

Vaughn, S., & Bos, C. S. (Eds.). (1987). *Research in Learning Disabilities: Issues and Future Directions.* Boston: Little, Brown.

Vaughn, S., McIntosh, R., & Spencer-Rowe, J. (1991). Peer rejection is a stubborn thing: Increasing peer acceptance of rejected students with learning disabilities. *Learning Disabilities Research & Practice, 6:*83–88.

Vellutino, F. (1979). *Dyslexia: Theory and Research.* Cambridge, MA: MIT Press.

Videen, J., Deno, S., & Marston, D. (1982). *Correct Word Sequences: A Valid Indicator of Proficiency in Written Expression* (Research Report No. 84). University of Minnesota: Institute for Research on Learning Disabilities.

Vinter, R., Sarri, R., Vorwaller, D., & Schafer, E. (1966). *Pupil Behavior Inventory.* Ann Arbor: Campus Publishers.

Vondra, J., & Toth, S. (1989). Ecological perspectives on child maltreatment: Research and intervention. *Early Child Development and Care, 42,* 11–30.

Vygotsky, L. S. (1978). *Mind in Society: The Development of Higher Psychological Processes.* In M. Cole, V. John-Steiner, S. Scribner, & E. Souberman (Eds. and Trans.). Cambridge, MA: Harvard University Press.

Wagner, A. R. (1981). A model of automatic memory processing in animal behavior. In N. Spear & R. Ritter (Eds.), *Information Processing in Animals: Memory Mechanisms.* Hillsdale, NJ: Erlbaum.

Wagner, R. (1986). Phonological processing abilities and reading implications for disabled readers. *Journal of Learning Disabilities, 19*(10):623–629.

Wagner, R, K., & Sternberg, R. J. (1985). Practical intelligence in real-world pursuits: The role of tacit knowledge. *Journal of Personality and Social Psychology, 49:*436–458.

Walker, D. K. (1973). *Socioemotional Measures for Preschool and Kindergarten Children.* San Francisco: Jossey-Bass.

Walker, H. (1970). *Walker Problem Behavior Identification Checklist.* Los Angeles: Western Psychological Services.

Walker, H. M. (1980). *Walker Problem Behavior Identification Checklist.* Los Angeles: Western Psychological Services.

Walker, H. M. (1982). Assessment of behavior disorders in the school setting: Issues, problems, and strategies. In N. Haring & M. Noel (Eds.), *Progress or Change: Issues in Educating the Emotionally Disturbed* (Vol. 1, pp. 147–188). Seattle: University of Washington.

Walker, H. M., Severson, H., & Haring, N. (1985). Standardized Screening and Identification of Behavior Disordered Pupils in the Elementary Age Range: Rationale, Procedures, and Guidelines. Unpublished manuscript, University of Oregon, Eugene.

Walker, J. (1989). Getting them unstuck: Some strategies for the teaching of reading and science. *School Science and Mathematics, 89*(2):130–135.

Wallace, G., & Larsen, S. C. (1978). *Educational Assessment of Learning Problems: Testing for Teaching.* Boston: Allyn and Bacon.

Wang, M. C., Reynolds, M. C., & Walberg, H. J. (1988). *The Handbook of Special Education: Research and Practice.* Oxford, England: Pergamon Press.

Ward, M., & McCormick, S. (1981). Reading instruction for blind and low vision children in the regular classroom. *The Reading Teacher, 34*(4):434–444.

Warren, S. F. (1988). A behavioral approach to language generalization. *Language, Speech, and Hearing Services in Schools, 19*(4):292–303.

Warren, S. F., & Rogers-Warren, A. K. (Eds.), (1985). *Teaching Functional Language.* Austin, TX: Pro-Ed.

Wechsler, D. (1955). *Wechsler Intelligence Scale for Children: Manual.* New York: The Psychological Corporation.

Wechsler, D. (1967). *Manual for the Wechsler Preschool and Primary Scale of Intelligence.* Cleveland, OH: The Psychological Corporation.

Wechsler, D. (1974). *Manual for the Wechsler Intelligence Scale for Children–Revised.* Cleveland, OH: The Psychological Corporation.

Wechsler, D. (1981). *Manual for the Wechsler Adult Intelligence Scale–Revised.* New York: The Psychological Corporation.

Wehlage, G. G., & Rutter, R. A. (1986). Dropping out: How much do schools contribute to the problem? *Teachers College Record, 87,* 374–392.

Wehman, P. H., Kregel, J., Barcus, J. M., & Schalock, R. L. (1986). Vocational transitions for students with developmental disabilities. In W. E. Kiernan & J. A. Stark (Eds.), *Pathways to Employment for Adults with Developmental Disabilities* (pp. 113–128). Baltimore: Paul H. Brookes.

Weiner, B., Graham, S., Taylor, S. E., & Meyer W. (1983). Social cognition in the classroom. *Educational Psychologist, 18:*109–124.

Weiner, E. S. (1980). The Diagnostic Evaluation of Writing Skills (DEWS): Application of DEWS criteria to writing samples: *Learning Disability Quarterly, 3*(2):54–59.

Weintraub, S., & Mesulam, M. M. (1983). Developmental learning disabilities of the right hemisphere: Emotional, interpersonal, and cognitive components. *Archives of Neurology, 40:*463–468.

Weissberg, R. P. (1985). Designing effective social problem-solving programs for the classroom. In B. H. Schneider, K. H. Rubin, & J. E. Ledingham (Eds.), *Children's Peer Relations: Issues in Assessment and Intervention* (pp. 225–242). New York: Springer-Verlag.

Weissberg, R. P. (1988). 1980s: A change in focus of reading comprehension research: A review of reading/learning disabilities research based on an interactive model of reading. *Learning Disability Quarterly, 11,* 149–159.

Weissberg, R. P., Gesten, E. L., Carnrike, C. L., Toro, P. A., Rapkin, B. D., Davidson, E., & Cowen, E. L. (1981). Social problem-solving skills training: A competence-building intervention with second- to fourth-grade children. *American Journal of Community Psychology, 9:*411–423.

Welch, M. (1989). A cultural perspective and the second wave of educational reform. *Journal of Learning Disabilities, 22*(9):537–540, 560.

Weller, C., & Strawser, S. (1981). *Weller-Strawser Scales of Adaptive Behavior for the Learning Disabled.* Novato, CA: Academic Therapy.

Weller, C., & Strawser, S. (1987). Adaptive behavior of subtypes of learning disabled individuals. *The Journal of Special Education, 21*(1):102–115.

Weller, C., Strawser, S., & Buchanan, M. (1985). Adaptive behavior: Designator of a continuum of severity of learning disabled individuals. *Journal of Learning Disabilities, 18:*200–204.

Wepman, J. (1973a). *Wepman Auditory Discrimination Test* (rev. ed.). Chicago: Language Research Associates.

Wepman, J. (1973b). *Wepman Auditory Memory Span Test.* Los Angeles: Western Psychological Services.

Wepman, J. (1973c). *Wepman Auditory Sequential Memory Test.* Los Angeles: Western Psychological Services.

Werner, H., Strauss, A. A. (1941). Pathology of the figure-background relation in the child. *Journal of Abnormal and Social Psychology, 36:*236–248.

Werry, J. S. (1981). Drugs and learning. *Journal of Child Psychology and Psychiatry, 22*(3):283–290.

Wertsch, J. V. (1979). From social interaction to higher psychological processes: A clarification and application of Vygotsky's theory. *Human Development, 22:*1–22.

Wertsch, J. V. (Ed.). (1985a). *Culture, Communication, and Cognition: Vygotskian Perspectives.* New York: Cambridge University Press.

Wertsch, J. V. (1985b). *Vygotsky and the Social Formation of Mind.* Cambridge, MA: Harvard University Press.

West, J. F., & Cannon, G. S. (1988). Essential collaborative consultation competencies for regular and special educators. *Journal of Learning Disabilities, 21:*56–63.

Whalen, C. K., Collins, B. E., Henker, B., Alkus, S. R., Adams, D. & Stapp, S. (1978). Behavior observations of hyperactive children and methylphenidate (Ritalin) effects in systematically structured classroom environments; Now you see them, now you don't. *Journal of Pediatric Psychology, 3*:177–184.

Whalen, C. K., & Henker, B. (1980). *Hyperactive Children.* New York: Academic Press.

Whalen, C. K., Henker, B., Collins, B. E., McAulliffe, S., & Vaux, A. (1979). Peer interraction in structured communication task: Comparisons of normal and hyperactive boys and of methylphenidate (Ritalin) and placebo effects. *Child Development, 50*:388–401.

Whalen, C. K., Henker, B., & Dotemoto, S. (1981). Teacher response to the methylphenidate (Ritalin) versus placebo status of hyperactive boys in the classroom. *Child Development, 52*:1005–1014.

Whalen, C. K., Henker, B., Dotemoto, S., Vaux, A., & McAuliffe, S. (1981). Hyperactivity and methylphenidate: Peer interaction styles. In K. D. Gadow & J. Loney (Eds.), *Psychosocial Aspects of Drug Treatment for Hyperactivity* (pp. 381–415). Boulder, CO: Westview Press.

Whaley, J. F. (1981, April). Story grammars and reading instruction. *The Reading Teacher, 34*:762–771.

White, S. E., Dittrich, J. E., & Lang, J. R. (1980). The effects of group decision-making process and problem-situational complexity on implementation attempts. *Administrative Science Quarterly, 25*:428–439.

Whitman, M. B., & Johnston, M. (1983). Teaching addition and subtraction with regrouping to EMR children: A group self-instructional training program. *Behavior Therapy, 14*:127–143.

Wickens, C. D. (1980). The structure of attentional resources. In R. Nickerson (Ed.), *Attention and Performance VII* (pp. 239–257). Hillsdale, NJ: Erlbaum.

Wickens, C. D., Mountford, S. J., & Schreiner, W. S. (1981). Multiple resources, task-hemispheric integrity, and individual differences in time sharing. *Human Factors, 23*:211–219.

Wiig, E. H: (1982). *Let's Talk Inventory for Adolescents.* Columbus, OH: Merrill.

Will, M. C. (1986). Educating children with learning problems: A shared responsibility. *Exceptional Children, 52*:411–415.

Will, M. C. (1988). Educating students with learning problems and the changing role of the school psychologist. *School Psychology Review, 17*:476–478.

Williams, W. V. (1988). Answers to questions about math anxiety. *School Science and Mathematics, 88*(2):95–104.

Willig, A., & Swedo, J. (1987, April). Improving Teaching Strategies for Exceptional Hispanic Limited English Proficient Students: An Exploratory Study of Task Engagement and Teaching Strategies. Paper presented at the annual meeting of the American Educational Research Association, Washington, DC.

Wilson, G. H. (1988). Teaching reading sequence skills through mathematics. *Reading Improvement, 25*(1):46–49.

Wilson, J. A., & Robeck, M. C. (1967). *Kindergarten Evaluation of Learning Potential (KELP).* New York: McGraw-Hill.

Wilson, J. Q., & Hernnstein, R. J. (1985). *Crime and Human Nature.* New York: Simon & Schuster.

Wilson, M. J. (1981). A review of recent research on the integration of reading and writing. *The Reading Teacher 34*(8):896–901.

Witt, J. C., & Martens, B. K. (1984). Adaptive behavior: Tests and assessment issues. *School Psychology Review, 13,* 478–484.

Wolf, M. M. (1978). Social validity: The case of subjective measurement or how applied behavior analysis is finding its heart. *Journal of Applied Behavior Analysis, 11*:203–214.

Wolman, C., Bruininks, R., & Thurlow, M. L. (1989). Dropouts and dropout programs: Implications for special education. *Remedial and Special Education, 10*(5):6–20.

Wong, B. (1979a). Increasing retention of main ideas through questioning strategies. *Learning Disability Quarterly, 2*(2):42–47.

Wong, B. (1979b). The role of theory in learning disabilities. Part I: Analysis of problems. *Journal of Learning Disabilities.*

Wong, B. (1979c). The role of theory in learning disabilities. Part II: A selective review of current conceptual frameworks in learning disabilities and/or reading disability. *Journal of Learning Disabilities.*

Wong, B. Y. L., Wong, R., & Blenkisop, J. (1989). Cognitive and metacognitive aspects of learning-disabled adolescents' composing problems. *Learning Disability Quarterly, 12*:300–323.

Wong, B. Y. L., Wong, R., Darlington, D., & Jones, W. (1991). Interactive teaching: An effective way to teach revision skills to adolescents with learning disabilities. *Learning Disabilities Research & Practice, 6*:117–127.

Wood, G. (1983). *Cognitive Psychology: A Skills Approach.* Monterey, CA: Brooks/Cole.

Woodcock, R. (1973). *Woodcock Reading Mastery Tests.* Circle Pines, MN: American Guidance Service.

Woodcock, R. (1978). *Woodcock-Johnson Psychoeducational Battery.* Hingham, MA: Teaching Resources Corporation.

Woodcock, R. W., & Johnson, M. B. (1977). *Woodcock-Johnson Psychoeducational Battery.* Boston: Teaching Resources.

Woods, J. R., Plessinger, M. S., & Clark, K. E. (1987). Effect of cocaine on uterine blood flow and fetal oxygenation. *Journal of the American Medical Association, 257*(7):957–961.

Worchel, F., Nolan, B., & Wilson, V. (1987). New perspectives on child and adolescent depression. *Journal of School Psychology, 25*:411–414.

Workman, E. A., Helton, G. B., & Watson, P. J. (1982). Self-monitoring effects in a four-year old child: An ecological behavior analysis. *Journal of School Psychology, 20*:57–64.

Wright, J. D., & Vlietstra, A. G. (1975). The development of selective attention: From perceptual exploration to logical search. In H. W. Reese (Ed.), *Advances in Child Development and Behavior* (Vol. 10, pp. 196–235). New York: Academic.

Yellin, A. M., Hopwood, J. H., & Greenberg, L. M. (1982). Adults and adolescents with attention deficit disorder: Clinical and behavioral responses to psychostimulants. *Journal of Clinical Psychopharmacology, 2*:133–136.

Ylvisaker, M. (Ed.). (1985). Head injury rehabilitation: Children and adolescents. *Professional School Psychology 1*(4):307.

Young, C. C. (1981). Children as instructional agents for their handicapped peers: A review and analysis. In P. S. Strain (Ed.), *The Utilization of Classroom Peers as Behavior Change Agents* (pp. 305–326). New York & London: Plenum.

Ysseldyke, J. (1983). Current practices in making psychological decisions about learning-disabled students. In G. Senf & J. Torgesen (Eds.), *Annual Review of Learning Disabilities: Vol 1. A Journal of Learning Disabilities Reader.* Chicago: Professional Press.

Ysseldyke, J. E., O'Sullivan, P. J., Thurlow, M. L., & Christenson, S. L. (1989). Qualitative differences in reading and math instruction received by handicapped students. *Remedial and Special Education, 10*(1):14–20.

Zaner-Bloser's Evaluation Scale. (1974). Columbus, OH: Zaner-Bloser.

Zentall, S. S. (1975). Optimal stimulation as theoretical basis of hyperactivity. *American Journal of Orthopsychiatry, 45*:549–563.

Zentall, S. S., & Zentall, T. R. (1976). Activity and task performance of hyperactive children as a function of environmental stimulation. *Journal of Consulting and Clinical Psychology, 44*:693–697.

Zigler, E. (1979). Controlling child abuse in America: An effort doomed to failure. In R. Bourne & E. H. Newberger (Eds.), *Critical Perspectives on Child Abuse* (pp. 171–207). Lexington, MA: Lexington Books.

Zirpoli, T. J. (1986). Child abuse and children with handicaps. *Remedial and Special Education, 7*(2):39–48.

Zola-Morgan, S., Squire, L. R., & Amaral, D. G. (1986). Human amnesia and the medial temporal region: Enduring memory impairment following a bilateral lesion limited to field CA1 of the hippocampus. *Journal of Neuroscience, 6*:2950–2967.

Zola-Morgan, S., Squire, L. R., & Mishkin, M. (1982). The neuroanatomy of amnesia: Amygdala-hippocampus versus temporal stem. *Science, 218*:1337–1339.

Zuckerman, B., Frank, D. A., Hingson, R., Amaro, H., Levenson, S. M., Kayne, H., Parker, S., Vinci, R., Aboagye, K., Fried, L. E., Cabral, H., Timperi, R., & Bauchner, H. (1989). Effects of maternal marijuana and cocaine use on fetal growth. *The New England Journal of Medicine, 320*:762–768.

Zutell, J. (1978, October). Some psycholinguistic perspectives on children's spelling. *Language Arts, 55*:844–850.

Index